Lind's List

CAMERA PRICE GUIDE

and MASTER DATA CATALOG

1996-97

- Over 1000 Illustrations
- Full Technical Data
- Current Market Values
- More than 13,000 Collector and User Cameras

Published by Centennial Photo Service

Editor : **Barbara Lind**
Assistant Editors: **Jim McKeown**
Joan McKeown
Dieter Scheiba
Data Processing: **Terry Fisk**
Graphics: **LeeAnne Byers**

Special thanks to the many camera historians and collectors who have assisted with this project.

Special thanks also to the businesses who have chosen to advertise in this guide. These companies help to promote camera collecting, and add to the enjoyment of our hobby. By advertising here, they have also made this book less expensive for you. We hope you will consider doing business with these companies which support you and your hobby.

DISTRIBUTORS

WORLDWIDE:
Centennial Photo
11595 State Road 70
Grantsburg, WI 54840
USA
tel 1 715 689 2153
fax 1 715 689 2277

USA & CANADA:
Amphoto / Watson-Guptill
1515 Broadway
New York, NY 10036
tel 800-451-1741
fax 908-363-0338

UNITED KINGDOM:
Newpro UK Limited
Old Sawmills Road
Faringdon, Oxon
SN7 7DS England
tel (01367) 24 24 11
fax (01367) 24 11 24

AUSTRALIA:
Brighton House Publishing
Pty. Ltd.
211 Bay Street
Brighton, Victoria, 3186
tel (03) 596 8742
fax (03) 596 8743

NETHERLANDS:
Sonja Kalkman Bookimport
Postbus 3
3830 AA Leusden
tel 033 94 72 00
fax 033 95 22 51

SPAIN:
Omnicon S.A.
Hierro, 9 - 3º - 7
28045 Madrid
tel (91) 527 82 49
fax (91) 528 13 48

Lind's List Camera Price Guide 1996-97
First Printing, 1996
Printed in USA

ISBN 0-931838-26-6

INTRODUCTION

Welcome to *Lind's List Camera Price Guide*. We have designed this book to give camera collectors and users the basic specifications of over 13,000 cameras from 1839 to 1996. Current market values are based on worldwide sales data. For the English-language edition these prices are given in U.S. Dollars. For each camera, we give the model name and number, plus the following data:

Format - This is the major image size. Some cameras are adaptable for more than one image size.

Film - Plate, **Rollfilm** (including **120**, **127**, etc.), **35mm**, **Rapid** Cassette, **126** or **110** Cartridge, and sometimes only the film width (**16mm**, **21mm**).

Camera Types - Our assignments of camera types are somewhat subjective, because in many cases, a given camera fits more than one category. Likewise, some of our categories are subdivisions of others. Generally any of the subdivisions could also be described by the more general heading. In other words, various box cameras might be listed as "**Rollbox**", "**PlateBox**", "**MetalBox**", "**BakeliteBox**". Any of these could also be simply "**Box**".

The following chart lists the camera type codes we have used:

CODE	CAMERA TYPE
2-Rail	2-rail (bi-rail) view camera
3-Color	Three-color separation camera
35AF	35mm autofocus
35AF-BiF	35mm autofocus bi-focal
35AFSLR	35mm autofocus SLR
35afz	35mm autofocus zoom
35AW	weatherproof (all-weather) 35mm
35AW-AF	weatherproof autofocus 35mm
35BiFocal	35mm bi-focal compact
35C	35mm compact camera
35CAF	35mm compact autofocus
35Early	Early 35mm camera (± pre-Leica)
35El-Mot	35mm camera with electric motor transport
35Fold	Folding 35mm camera
35Half	35mm half-frame (18x24mm)
35mm	35mm camera (unspecified)
35Pan	35mm panoramic camera
35RF	35mm rangefinder camera
35SLR	35mm single-lens reflex
35SprMot	35mm camera with spring motor transport
35Ster	35mm stereo
35Strut	Strut-folding 35mm camera
35TLR	35mm twn-lens reflex
35UW	Underwater 35mm camera
35VF	35mm viewfinder camera
35ZLR	35mm Zoom Lens Reflex
110	110 (unspecified)
110AW	110 all-weather camera
110BiFoc	110 Bi-Focal (tele-wide) camera
110RF	110 rangefinder camera
110SLR	110 SLR camera
110snap	110 "snap on cartridge" or "micro"
110UW	110 underwater camera
110VF	110 viewfinder camera
126	126 (unspecified)
126RF	126 rangefinder
126SLR	126 SLR
126VF	126 viewfinder
Aerial	Aerial camera
BakeliteBox	Bakelite box camera
BakeliteRoll	Bakelite rollfilm camera
BakFoldRo	Bakelite folding rollfilm camera
Box	Box camera
Button	Button tintype
CardBox	Cardboard box camera
Dag	Daguerreian
DetectivBox	Detective box camera
Disc	Disc camera
Disguised	Disguised
Dispose	Single use (disposable) (recyclable) camera
Ferrotype	Ferrotype (Tintype) camera
Field	Field camera
Fold	Folding Camera (unspecified)
FoldBox	Folding box (ie Micromegas, Ottewill)
FoldMag	Folding magazine camera
FoldPack	Folding filmpack camera
FoldPl	Folding plate camera
FoldPress	Folding press camera (e.g. Speed Graphic)
FoldRo	Folding rollfilm camera
FoldSht	Folding sheetfilm camera (no plates)
FoldSLR	Folding Reflex
FoldSLR	Folding reflex
H&S	Hand & Stand camera

HzFold	Horizontal folding camera
HzFoldPl	Horizontal folding plate camera
HzFoldRo	Horizontal Folding rollfilm camera
Instant	Instant camera
Jumelle	Jumelle
LgSLR	Large format SLR
LgTLR	Large format TLR
MagBox	Magazine Box Camera
MedRF	Medium format rangefinder
MedSLR	Medium format SLR
MetalBox	Metal box camera
Military	Military special purpose
MiniatRo	Miniature rollfilm camera
Minicam	Minicams (½-frame 127 film plastic)
Monorail	Monorail view camera
MultiLens	Multiple lens camera
Multiply	Mulitplying camera (eg: moving back)
PackBox	Box camera for filmpacks
Panoramic	Panoramic
PlasticBox	Plastic box camera
PlasticRoll	Plastic rollfilm camera
PlateBox	Box plate camera
Press	Press (divide by rigid, folding, slr, etc)
RigidPl	Non-folding plate camera (RigidPl)
RigidRo	Non-folding rollfilm camera (RigidRo)
RollBox	Box rollfilm camera
SciMed	Scientific or Medical
SLR	SLR (unspecified)
SLR-Box	Box-form SLR
Special	Special purpose (unspecified)
SprMotRo	Rollfilm camera with spring motor
SterBox	Stereo Box
Stereo	Stereo camera (unspecified)
SterField	Stereo Field camera
SterFold	Stereo Folding
SterMagBox	Stereo Magazine Box
SterMiniat	Miniature stereo camera
SterRefl	Stereo Reflex
SterStrut	Stereo strut camera
SterTail	Stereo Tailboard
StFoldPl	Stereo Folding Plate
StFoldRo	Stereo Folding Rollfilm
StJumelle	Stereo Jumelle
Street	Street camera
StrutFold	Strut-folding camera (unspecified)
StrutPl	Strut-folding plate camera
StrutRo	Strut-folding rollfilm camera
StrutTLR	collapsible strut-fold TLR (eg: Pilot Reflex, Zecaflex)
Studio	Studio view camera
StWetPl	Stereo Wet Plate
Submin	Subminiature
Tailboard	Tailboard camera
Telesc35	Telescoping front 35mm camera
TelescPl	Telescoping front plate camera
TelescRo	Telescoping front rollfilm camera
TLR	TLR (unspecified)
TLR-Box	TLR box camera
TwinLens	Twin lens NON-REFLEX (eg: Eder Patent Camera, Liesegang Künstlerkamera)
View	View camera (unspecified)
VtFold	Vertical folding camera
VtFoldPl	Vertical folding plate camera
VtFoldRo	Vertical Folding rollfilm camera
WetPlate	Wet Plate
WideAng	Wide Angle
Yen	Yen-Kame ("No Need Darkroom")

Illustrations - References to illustrations are from standard reference works. Although we have tried to match them as closely as possible to the camera listings, they are not necessarily an exact match for shutter and lens equipment. Also, you must remember that when a camera was made for a long time period, some changes in styling or finish are normal over the years. From many available reference books, we have selected a few of the most popular, available, and authoritative ones. The *Abring* books are richly illustrated, and have been continuously available worldwide for many years. *Russian and Soviet Cameras* is complete, authoritative, and fully illustrated guide to a specialty area. *McKeown's* is the most widely used camera reference in the world, and illustrates thousands of cameras. The codes for the various reference works may be found in the following table. In some cases, the number refers to a page, where individual illustrations are not numbered. When the reference book has numbered illustrations, we have normally used the illustration number rather than a page number. The table also tells which type of numbering was used for each reference book. All of these references were made with permission from the authors. In some cases, we have agreements for sharing information, or have licensed use of information from the works of these authors. For example, Jean-Loup Princelle generously shared information from *Russian and Soviet Cameras*. This helped us to correct errors in our database without infringing on his copyrighted work.

Table of Photo References

A	Abring, Von Daguerre bis Heute	Illus. No. x
Ev	Evans, Collectors Guide to Rollei Cameras	Page x
Ex	Exakta Cameras, Aguila & Rouah	Page x
F	Francesch, Appareils Photographiques Françaises	Illus. No. x
HK	Historische Kameras, Cornwall	Illus. No. x
Hu	Hummel, Spiegelreflexkameras aus Dresden	Illus. No. x
KP	Kuribayashi-Petri Cameras, Baird	Page x
Mc	McKeown's Price Guide to Cameras (1995-1996)	Page x
OL	Histoire de L'Appareil Olympus, Francesch	Page x
Pr	Prochnow, Rollei Report	Illus. No. x
Ru	Russian & Soviet Cameras, Princelle	Page x
U	Umstätter, Verkehrs-Museum-Berlin e.V.	Illus. No. x
	Cameras illustrated in this edition of LIND'S are indicated with grey tint in the ILLUS column.	

Copyrights - All of the information in this book was compiled from **original** source material, including manufacturers' catalogs, brochures, and by examination of cameras. None of this material has been taken from other copyrighted compilations without explicit permission from the original authors. This compilation is protected by international copyright laws. We highly recommend to our readers to purchase and use books from those who do original work. We would also discourage readers from purchasing or using books which take information without permission from other copyrighted works. In our view, so-called "authors" who steal information are in the same class as "camera dealers" who steal cameras from you to sell to your friends. Unfortunately, both types of thieves exist in our midst.

Stolen Cameras - To help prevent the increasing number of camera thieves among us, Centennial Photo will maintain a list of stolen cameras on the Internet. For the first time ever, camera dealers will have the ability to give quick notice worldwide about stolen cameras. In order to protect your rights of ownership, you should immediately file a police report, then notify the world. If we all work together, the good guys can still win! For more information, or to get a current serial number list of stolen cameras, contact our web site at: http://www.camera-net.com.

Dates - We have listed dates of introduction for most camera models. These dates are approximate, and refer to the year the camera was first manufactured or marketed. They do not specifically indicate the dates that a particular shutter and lens combination was available. A new shutter or lens may have become available at a later date during the production of a camera. In some cases, we have listed the last digit of a date as "x". This indicates an approximate date in that decade. (e.g. "192x" means "1920's", or somtime between 1920 and 1930.

Lenses - Lenses listed are typical for the specified camera. Most cameras were available with various lenses fitted. For cameras with interchangeable lenses, we have usually given a common normal lens. For both fixed-lens and interchangeable-lens cameras, we sometimes show two or more lenses commonly found with the camera. When we have listed two or three lens/shutter combinations, often each of the lenses was available in each of the shutters. Therefore, with three lines of data, we can give you the possibility of 9 shutter/lens combinations. Do not be surprised to find specific combinations not listed or totally different equipment. Sometimes there are several variants of the same camera listed, such as lens, shutter, or color variants.

Used Equipent Prices - All prices are for used equipment and collectables, not new cameras. For new camera prices, please check with your favorite camera shop. Our prices for used cameras are based on worldwide sales data.

Multi-national, Multi-name Cameras - Some cameras are sold under different names on different continents. Even though the cameras are usually identical except for the name, there may be some variation in the prices listed in this guide. For example, cameras marketed in North America or Hong Kong may be lower in price than the identical models marketed under different names in Europe or Japan. Most of the used models of these cameras are found in the same marketing areas where they were sold new. For example, imagine a camera named "Euro 2000" when sold in Europe or Japan. The same camera is called "Splash 2000" in the North American market. When new, the Splash 2000 will typically have a lower "street" price in New York than the Euro 2000 will have in Berlin or Tokyo. Naturally, the used prices are influenced by the new prices. Therefore, the "Euro 2000" might have a higher used value than the "Splash 2000". Our computer is programmed to bring these used prices slightly toward each other. In reality, the name of the camera is less important than the market in which it is sold as a secondhand camera. Using our example, a used "Splash 2000" may sell for a slightly higher price in Europe than it does in North America. The "Euro 2000" would probably sell for less in the USA or in Hong Kong than it would in Europe or Japan.

Prices of Collectable Cameras - Collectable camera prices have been tracked in detail since 1970 by Jim & Joan McKeown. *Lind's List Camera Price Guide* is fortunate to have complete access to the McKeowns' database.

Leica camera prices - To achieve top prices, Leica cameras must be in truly top condition. Unfortunately, we must caution that the cameras must also be genuine. There are so many fakes and forgeries of Leica cameras, that an inexperienced buyer will be an easy target. Even experienced buyers have been misled. What the forgers lack in honesty, they make up for with expert workmanship. Normally, Leica cameras are priced "body only". In some cases, a specific lens is important to a particular camera model and the price reflects the listed lens.

Cameras with interchangeable lenses - In many cases, we have lised prices for cameras without lens and with a normal lens. These data reflect different sales at different times. Therefore, it does not necessarily follow that subtracting one from the other will give an exact value for the listed lens. Some dealers routinely separate lenses from bodies and sell each separately. Some of these same dealers might ask higher prices than others who sell the complete camera with lens. Therefore there is even the possibility that the data will reflect a lower price with lens than without, especially when the lens is of relatively low value or not in demand. This does not indicate that the lens is of no value or negative value. Rather, it might be a clue to watch for a complete camera & lens for a better value than buying "à la carte".

Condition - Prices given are for cameras in "**excellent +**" collectable and/or usable condition, normally indicated as "B" in Germany. A collectable camera in "A" condition or "**Mint**" condition can often sell for twice the normal price, while a camera in "C" or "**VG+**" condition might sell for 70-80% of the listed price. In "D" condition (anything less than VG) a camera may be difficult to sell for half of the listed price. So keep in mind that these prices are only a guide. Remember *"McKeown's Law": The price of an antique camera is entirely dependent on the moods of the buyer and seller at the time of the transaction.*

MODEL	FORMAT	FILM	TYPE	Year	LENS	Apert	FL	SHUTTER	SPEEDS	ILLUS	U.S.$
...ADAMS & CO. - London											
Aidex	2½x3½"	plate	FoldSlr	1928	Ross Xpres	3.5		focal plane	3-1000		500
Aidex	3¼x4¼"	plate	FoldSlr	1928	Ross Xpres	3.5		focal plane	3-1000		500
Challenge	4¼x6½"	plate	Tailboard	1892	Rapid Rectilinear				T,I		570
Challenge	6½x8½"	plate	Tailboard	1892	Rapid Rectilinear				T,I		570
Club	6½x8½"	plate	Field	1890	Symmetrical				T,I		350
Deluxe	3¼x4¼"	plate	MagBox	1898	Zeiss Ser. VIIa	6.3		focal plane	1/2-1000		600
Deluxe Changeable Box		plate	MagBox	1890				pneumatic	-1/1000		1000
Focal Plane Vesta	3¼x4¼"	plate	FoldPl	1912	Ross Xpres	4.5	5.5"	focal plane	3-1000	Mc51	290
Hand Camera	4x5"	plate	MagBox	1891	Rap. Symmetrical	5.5			1/2-100	Mc50	480
Hand Camera	3¼x4¼"	plate	MagBox	1891	Rap. Symmetrical	5.5			1/2-100	Mc50	440
Hat Detective Camera	3¼x4¼"	plate	Disguised	1892	Rapid Recitlinear	11			T,I	Mc50	18000
Ideal	3¼x4¼"	plate	MagBox	1892	Rapid Rectilinear	8	5.5"		1-100		120
Idento	2½x3½"	plate	StrutPl	1905	Zeiss Protar	6.3	4"		1/2-100	Mc50	290
Idento	3¼x4¼"	plate	StrutPl	1905	Zeiss Protar	6.3	5"		1/2-100	Mc50	290
Idento	4¼x6½"	plate	StrutPl	1905	Zeiss Protar	6.3	7"		1/2-100	Mc50	290
Minex	2¼x3¼"	plate	LgSLR	1910	Ross Xpres	4.5	4.75"	focal plane	1/8-1000		270
Minex	3¼x4¼"	plate	LgSLR	1910	Ross Xpres	4.5	5.5"	focal plane	1/8-1000	A555	270
Minex Stereo Reflex	3¼x6¾"	plate	SterRefl	1925	Eurynar-Anast.	4	120mm	focal plane	8-1000		2600
Minex Tropical	2¼x3¼"	plate	LgSLR	1930	Ross Xpres	4.5	4.75"	focal plane	1/8-1000	Mc50	4800
Minex Tropical	3¼x4¼"	plate	LgSLR	1930	Ross Xpres	4.5	5.5"	focal plane	1/8-1000	Mc50	5100
Minex Tropical	4x5"	plate	LgSLR	1930	Ross Xpres	4.5	6.5"	focal plane	1/8-1000	Mc50	5100
Minex Tropical	4¼x6½"	plate	LgSLR	1930	Ross Xpres	4.5	6.5"	focal plane	1/8-1000	Mc50	3900
Rollfilm Vesta	6.5x9cm	PltRo	FoldRo	1930	Ross Xpres	4.5	4.75"		1-200		200
Royal	4¼x6½"	plate	Field	1890	Rap. Symmetrical				T,I		130
Royal	6½x8½"	plate	Field	1890	Rap. Symmetrical				T,I		130
Studio Minex Reflex	4¼x6½"	plate	LgSLR					focal plane	4-64		4800
Studio Minex Reflex	6¼x7"	plate	LgSLR					focal plane	4-64	A3151	4800
Studio Minex Reflex	6½x8½"	plate	LgSLR					focal plane	4-64		4800
Vaido	3¼x4¼"	plate	H&S	1930	Ross Xpres	4.5	5.5"	focal plane	3-1000		550
Vaido	4¼x6½"	plate	H&S	1930	Ross Xpres	4.5	6.5"	focal plane	3-1000		550
Vaido Tropical	3¼x4¼"	plate	H&S	1930	Ross Xpres	4.5	5.5"	focal plane	3-1000		2000
Vaido Tropical	4¼x6½"	plate	H&S	1930	Ross Xpres	4.5	6.5"	focal plane	3-1000		2000
Verto	2¼x3¼"	plate	View	1930	Ross Combinable	5.5	4"		1-200	Mc51	170
Verto	3¼x4¼"	plate	View	1930	Ross Combinable	5.5	5.5"		1-200	Mc51	240
Vesta Mod. A	9x12cm	plate	FoldPl	1912	Ross Xpres	4.5	5.5"		1-200		150
Videx	3¼x4¼"	plate	LgSLR	1903	Ross Homocentric	6.3	5"	focal plane	1/8-1000		170
Videx	4x5"	plate	LgSLR	1903	Ross Homocentric	6.3	6"	focal plane	1/8-1000		170
Videx	4¼x6½"	plate	LgSLR	1903	Ross Homocentric	6.3	7"	focal plane	1/8-1000		170
Yale No. 1	3¼x4¼"	plate	MagBox	1895	Rapid Rectilinear	8			1/2-100		210
Yale No. 2	3¼x4¼"	plate	MagBox	1895	Cooke	6.5	5"		1/2-100		210
Yale Stereo Detect. No. 5	4x5"	plate	StMagBox	1902	Zeiss	6.3	7.5"		1/2-100		700

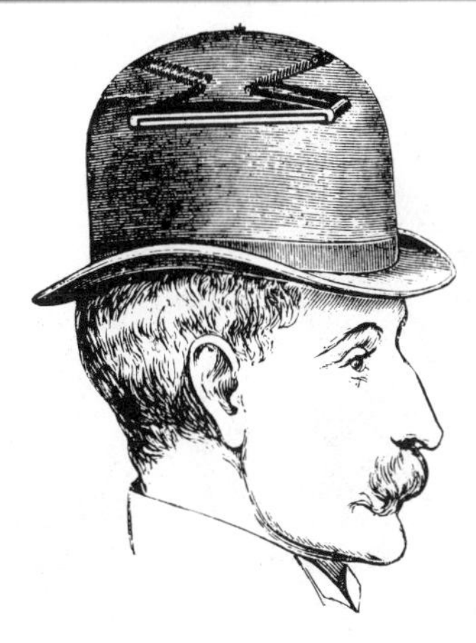

Hat Detective Camera

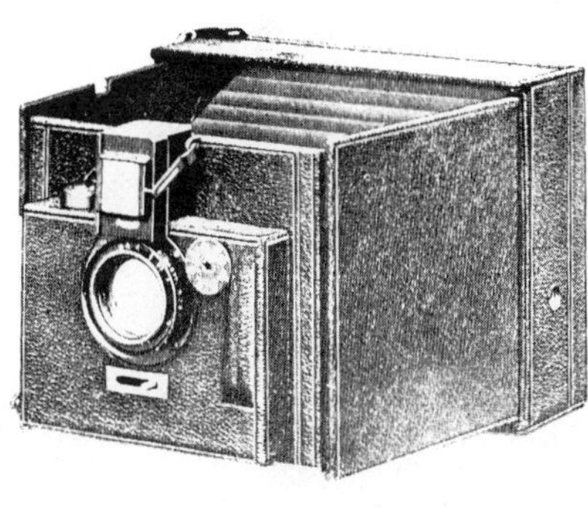

Idento

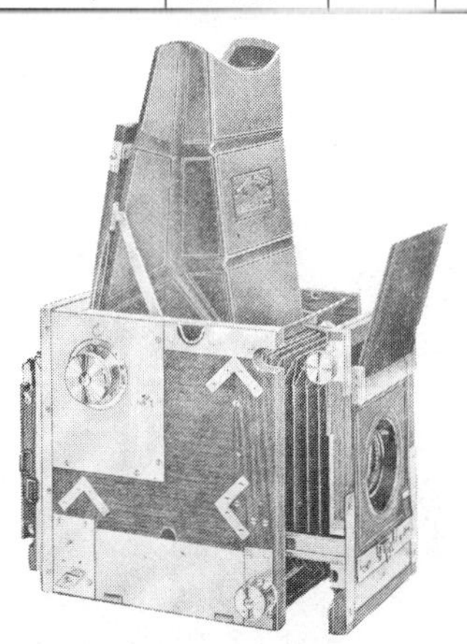

Minex Tropical

MODEL	FORMAT	FILM	TYPE	Year	LENS	Apert	FL	SHUTTER	SPEEDS	ILLUS	U.S.$
...ADOX KAMERAWERK - Wiesbaden											
Adox (I)	24x36mm	35mm	35mm	1936	Schn. Radionar	2.9	50mm	Pronto	1/25-200		40
Adox II	24x36mm	35mm	35mm	1936	Schn. Radionar	2.9	50mm	Pronto	1/25-200		40
Adox III	24x36mm	35mm	35mm	1936	Schn. Radionar	2.9	50mm	Prontor	1/25-200		40
Adox 35	24x36mm	35mm	35VF	1955	Kataplast	2.8	45mm	Prontor-S			90
Adox 66	6x6cm	120	BakeliteBox	1950	Meniscus	8			M,Z	Mc51	30
Adox 300	24x36mm	35mm	35mm	1958	Steinheil Cassar	2.8	45mm	Sync.Compur	500	A1095	200
Adox 300	24x36mm	35mm	35mm	1958	Schneider Xenar	2.8	45mm	Sync.Compur	500		210
Adrette	24x36mm	35mm	35mm	1939	Steinheil Cassar	3.5	50mm	Prontor			100
Adrette	24x36mm	35mm	35mm	1939	Schn. Radionar	2.9	50mm	Prontor II		A1098	100
Adrette	24x36mm	35mm	35mm	1939	Steinheil Cassar	2.9	50mm	Prontor			80
Adrette	24x36mm	35mm	35mm	1938	Xenon	2	50mm	Compur			100
Adrette II	24x36mm	35mm	35mm	1939	Steinheil Cassar	3.5	50mm	Prontor II			100
Adrette II	24x36mm	35mm	35mm	1939	Xenon	3.5	50mm	Compur-Rap.		HK559	100
Blitz	6x6cm	120	BakeliteBox	1950		6.3	75mm	simple			30
Golf	6x6cm	120	FoldRo	1950	Adoxar	6.3	75mm	Vario			40
Golf	6x6cm	120	FoldRo	1950	Cassar	6.3	75mm	Pronto	1-200		40
Golf IA Rapid	24x36mm	Rapid	35mm	1963	Adoxon	2.8	45mm	Prontor	B-1/125		10
Golf IIA	24x36mm	Rapid	35mm	1964	Adoxon	2.8	45mm	Pronto-Matic			20
Golf IIIA	24x36mm	35mm	35mm	1960	Radionar L	2.8	45mm	Prontor500LK			20
Golf Mess	6x6cm	120	FoldRo	1950	Cassar	4.5	75mm	Pronto	1-200		50
Juka	3x4cm	Roll	RigidRo	1950	Achromat	8	45mm	simple		Mc51	90
Luxa 66		Roll	BakeliteBox								50
Polo	24x36mm	35mm	35mm	1960	Adoxar	3.5			30-125		20
Polo IB	24x36mm	35mm	35mm								20
Polo IS	24x36mm	35mm	35mm	1962	Radionar	2.8	45mm	Pronto	30-250	A2093	20
Polomat	24x36mm	35mm	35mm	1962	Radionar L	2.8	45mm	Pronto LK	1/15-250	Mc52	20
Polomat 1	24x36mm	35mm	35mm		Radionar L	2.8	45mm	Prontor-LK	15-500		40
Polomat 2	24x36mm	35mm	35mm	1959	Radionar	2.8	45mm	Prontormat	30-300		20
Polomatic 2	24x36mm	35mm	35mm	1961	Radionar L	2.8	45mm	Prontor-Lux	30-500		20
Polomatic 3	24x36mm	35mm	35mm	1961	Radionar L	2.8	45mm	Prontor-S	30-300		20
Polomatic 3C	24x36mm	35mm	35mm	1961	Radionar L	2.8	45mm				40
Polomatic 3S	24x36mm	35mm	35mm	1961	Radionar L	2.8	45mm	Prontor-Matic	30-500	A1131	20
Rollfilm Camera	6x9cm	120	FoldRo	1950	Adoxar	4.5	105mm				30
Sport	6x9/4.5x6	120	FoldRo	1950	Steinheil Cassar	4.5	105mm	Prontor-S	1-250	A437	40
Sport	6x9/4.5x6	120	FoldRo	1950	Radionar	4.5	105mm	Prontor-S	1-250	A436	40
Sport (red)	6x9/4.5x6	120	FoldRo	1950	Radionar	4.5	105mm	Prontor-S	1-250		130
Sport 0	6x9/4.5x6	120	FoldRo	1949	Radionar	4.5	105mm	Vario	25-100		40
Sport I	6x9/4.5x6	120	FoldRo	1951	Steinheil Cassar	4.5	105mm	Prontor-S	1-250		30
Sport Ia	6x9/6x6	120	FoldRo	1950	Steinheil Cassar	4.5	105mm	Pronto	25-200		40
Sport II	6x9/4.5x6	120	FoldRo	1950	Radionar	4.5	105mm	Prontor			30
Sport IIa	6x9/6x6	120	FoldRo		Steinheil Cassar	4.5	105mm	Prontor-S	1-250		40

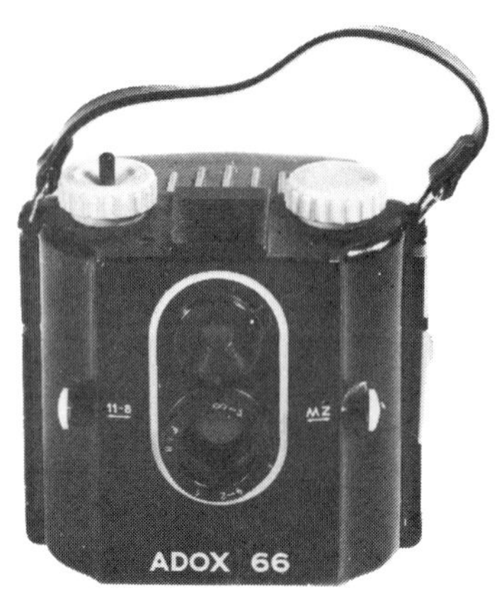

Adox 66

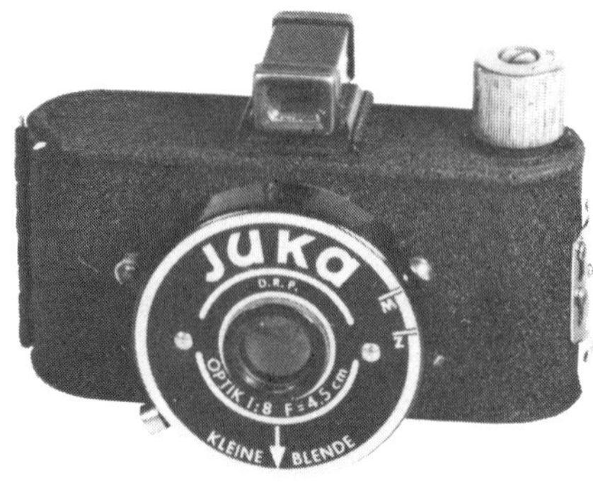

Juka

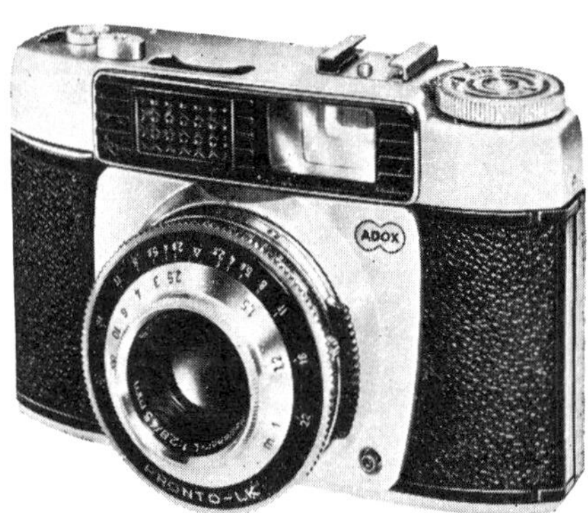

Polomat

MODEL	FORMAT	FILM	TYPE	Year	LENS	Apert	FL	SHUTTER	SPEEDS	ILLUS	U.S.$
Sport IIIa	6x9/6x6	120	FoldRo	1952	Steinheil Cassar	4.5	105mm	Prontor-SV			40
Start	6x9cm	120	FoldRo	1950	Cassar	6.3	105mm	Vario			30
Tempo	4.5x6cm	120	FoldRo	1934				Prontor			60
Trumpf	6x9/4.5x6	120	FoldRo	1932	Anastigmat	4.5	105mm	Vario			40
Trumpf II	6x9cm	120	FoldRo	1934	Anastigmat			Prontor V			30
...A.D.Y.C. - Argentina											
Koinor 4x4	4x4cm	120	RigidRo		Fixed Focus					Mc52	40
...(unknown)											
Aerial Camera KE-28B	56x72mm	70mm	Aerial	1966	Elcan	2.8	6"	focal plane	125-1000		700
...(unknown)											
Aerogard Can	13x17mm	110	Disguised	1987						Mc52	50
...AFIOM - Italy											
Kristall	24x36mm	35mm	35RF	1955	Elionar	3.5	5cm	focal plane	1/20-1000		360
Kristall II	24x36mm	35mm	35RF	1950	Trixar	3.5	50mm	focal plane	1/20-1000		500
Kristall IIa	24x36mm	35mm	35RF	1950	Vegar	3.5	50mm	focal plane	1/20-1000		440
Wega	24x36mm	35mm	35RF	1950	Trixar	3.5	50mm	focal plane	1/20-1000	A1056	330
Wega II	24x36mm	35mm	35RF	1950	Trixar	3.5	50mm	Synch FP	1/20-1000	Mc52	400
Wega IIa	24x36mm	35mm	35RF	1950	Trixar	3.5	50mm	Synch FP	1/20-1000	Mc52	370
...AGFA KAMERAWERKE - Munich											
Agfaflex I	24x36mm	35mm	35SLR	1959	Color-Apotar	2.8	50mm	Prontor-Refl.	1-300		90
Agfaflex II	24x36mm	35mm	35SLR	1959	Color-Apotar	2.8	50mm	Prontor-Refl.	1-300		90
Agfaflex III	24x36mm	35mm	35SLR	1959	Color-Solinar	2.8	50mm	Prontor-Refl.	1-300		120
Agfaflex IV	24x36mm	35mm	35SLR		Color-Solinar	2.8	50mm	Prontor-Refl.	1-300	Mc52	120
Agfaflex V	24x36mm	35mm	35SLR		Color-Solinar	2	55mm	Prontor-Refl.	1-300		140
Agfamatic I	24x36mm	35mm	35VF								50
Agfamatic Ia	24x36mm	35mm	35VF								50
Agfamatic II	24x36mm	35mm	35VF		Color-Apotar	2.8	45mm	Prontor	1-250		40
Agfamatic IIS	24x36mm	35mm	35RF								70
Agfamatic IIIS	24x36mm	35mm	35RF								50
Agfamatic 50	28x28mm	126	126VF		Colorstar	11		Parator	1/40, 1/80		10
Agfamatic 55C	28x28mm	126	126VF		Colorstar	11	40mm	Parator	1/40, 1/80		30
Agfamatic 100 Sensor	28x28mm	126	126VF	1972	Colorstar	11		Parator	1/40, 1/80		10
Agfamatic 108 Sensor	28x28mm	126	126VF	1978	Colorstar	11	42mm	Parator	1/40, 1/80		10
Agfamatic 200 Sensor	28x28mm	126	126VF	1972	Color-Agnar	8	40mm	Parator	1/40, 1/80		10
Agfamatic 208 Sensor	28x28mm	126	126VF	1978	Color-Agnar	8	40mm	Parator	1/40, 1/80		10
Agfamatic 300 Sensor	28x28mm	126	126VF	1972	Color-Agnar	8		electronic	30-1000		20
Agfamatic 500S		35mm	35RF								100
Agfamatic 508 P. Sensor	13x17mm	110	110	1978	Color-Optar	11	31mm		50, 100		20
Agfamatic 901 E Motor	13x17mm	110	110	1978	Color-Apotar	6.3	27mm		1/50-200		30
Agfamatic 901 John Player	13x17mm	110	110		Color-Apotar	6.3	27mm			A3360	110
Agfam. 901 mot (diamonds)	13x17mm	110	110	1979						A3359	100
Agfamatic 901 SE Motory	13x17mm	110	110	1980	Color-Apotar	8	27mm	electronic	30-1000	A1988	50

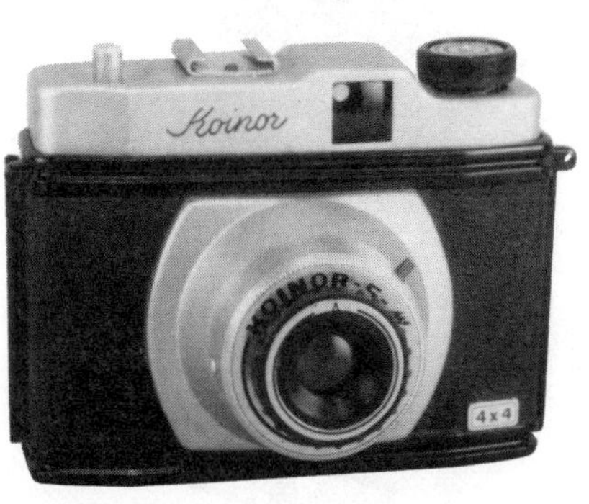

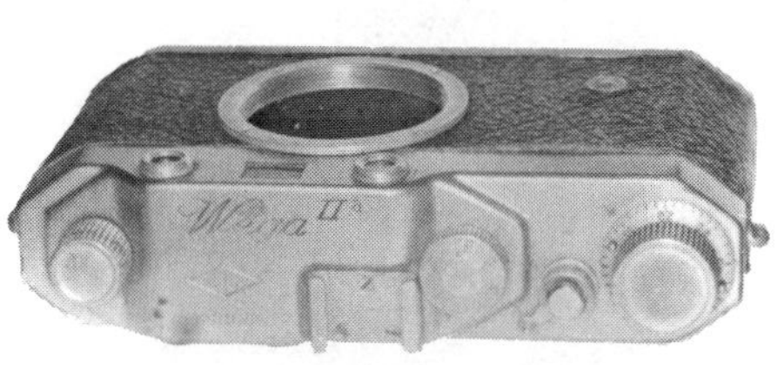

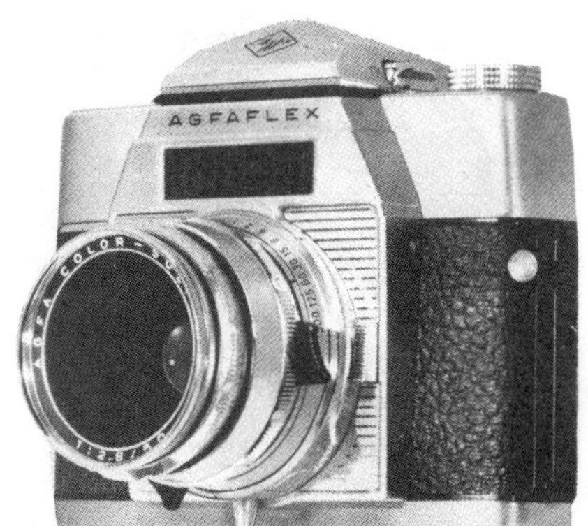

Koinor 4.4 **Wega IIa** **Agfaflex IV**

MODEL	FORMAT	FILM	TYPE	Year	LENS	Apert	FL	SHUTTER	SPEEDS	ILLUS	U.S.$
Agfamatic 1000 P. Sensor	13x17mm	110	110		Color-Agnar	9.5	26mm		50, 100		20
Agfamatic 1008 Pocket	13x17mm	110	110		Color-Apotar	9.5	27mm		50, 100		30
Agfamatic 2000 P. Sensor	13x17mm	110	110	1974	Color-Agnar	6.3	26mm		50, 100		20
Agfamatic 2008 P. Sensor	13x17mm	110	110	1976	Color-Agnar	9.5	26mm		50, 100		20
Agfamatic 2008 Tele Pocket	13x17mm	110	110	1976	Color-Agnar	11	26mm		50, 100		20
Agfamatic 3000 P. Sensor	13x17mm	110	110	1976	Color-Apotar	6.3	26mm		50, 100		20
Agfamatic 3008 P. Sensor	13x17mm	110	110	1976	Color-Apotar	6.3	26mm		50, 100		20
Agfamatic 4000 P. Sensor	13x17mm	110	110		Color-Apotar				500	A1989	20
Agfamatic 4008 Tele Pocket	13x17mm	110	110	1976	Color-Apotar	6.3	26mm	electronic	15-1/1000		30
Agfamatic 5008 Makro Poc	13x17mm	110	110	1976	Color-Solinar	2.7	26mm	electronic	15-1/1000		50
Agfamatic 6008 Makro P.	13x17mm	110	110	1976	Color-Solinar	2.7	26mm	electronic	15-1/1000		50
Ambi-Silette	24x36mm	35mm	35RF	1957	Color-Solinar	2.8	50mm	Sync.Compur	500	A1150	90
Ambiflex I	24x36mm	35mm	35SLR	1959	Color-Solinar	2.8	50mm	Prontor-Refl.	1-300		100
Ambiflex II	24x36mm	35mm	35SLR	1959	Color-Solinar	2.8	50mm	Prontor-Refl.	1-300	A1154	130
Ambiflex III	24x36mm	35mm	35SLR	1959	Color-Solinar	2.8	50mm	Prontor-Refl.	1-300		140
Automatic 66	6x6cm	120	FoldRo	1956	Color-Solinar	3.5	75mm	Pronto-SL		Mc52	700
Autostar Pocket	13x17mm	110	110	1976	Color Optar	11	31mm		50, 100		30
Autostar X-126	28x28mm	126	126VF	1976							10
Billette	6x9cm	120	FoldRo	1931	Oppar	4.5		Rim-Compur	1-300	Mc53	50
Billy	6x9cm	120	FoldRo	1928	Igetar	8.8		Automat	1/25-100		50
Billy I (post-war)	6x9cm	120	FoldRo	1950	Agnar	6.3		Vario	1/25-200	Mc53	40
Billy I (post-war)	6x9cm	120	FoldRo	1950	Agnar	6.3		Pronto	1/25-200	Mc53	30
Billy I (pre-war)	6x9cm	120	FoldRo	1931	Igestar	8.8		Automat	1/25-100	Mc53	50
Billy II	6x9cm	120	FoldRo	1931	Igestar	7.7		Billy	1/25-100	Mc53	50
Billy III	6x9cm	120	FoldRo	1932	Igestar	5.6		Pronto	1/25-125		50
Billy III	6x9cm	120	FoldRo	1932	Solinar	4.5		Rim-Compur	1-250		50
Billy Clack	6x9cm	120	StrutRo	1934	Billinar	11			B-1/25		50
Billy Clack	4.5x6cm	120	StrutRo	1934	Igenar	8.8			B-1/25	Mc53	50
Billy Compur	6x9cm	120	FoldRo	1934	Solinar	3.9		Compur	1-250		60
Billy Optima	7.5x10.5		FoldRo	1932	Solinar	4.5		Compur	1-250		120
Billy Optima	7.5x10.5		FoldRo	1932	Igestar	6.3		Pronto	1/25-125		110
Billy Record 4.5	6x9cm	120	FoldRo	1938	Apotar	4.5	105mm	Prontor II	1-150		40
Billy Record 4.5	6x9cm	120	FoldRo	1946	Apotar	4.5	105mm	Prontor-S	1-300		40
Billy Record 6.3	6x9cm	120	FoldRo	1933	Igestar	6.3	105mm	Automat	1/25-100		40
Billy Record 7.7	6x9cm	120	FoldRo	1933	Igestar	7.7	105mm	Automat	1/25-100		40
Billy Record 8.8	6x9cm	120	FoldRo	1933	Igestar	8.8	105mm	Automat	1/25-100		40
Billy Record I	6x9cm	120	FoldRo	1950	Radionar	4.5	105mm	Pronto	1/25-200		40
Billy Record I	6x9cm	120	FoldRo	1950	Agnar	4.5	105mm	Pronto	1/25-200		40
Billy Record II	6x9cm	120	FoldRo	1950	Apotar	4.5	105mm	Prontor-S	1-250		40
Billy Record II	6x9cm	120	FoldRo	1950	Solinar	4.5	105mm	Compur-Rap.	1-400		50
Billy Record III	6x9cm	120	FoldRo	1950	Solinar	4.5	105mm	Compur-Rap.	1-400		110
Billy-O	4.5x6cm	127	FoldRo	1932	Igestar	5.6	75mm	Prontor		A3035	120

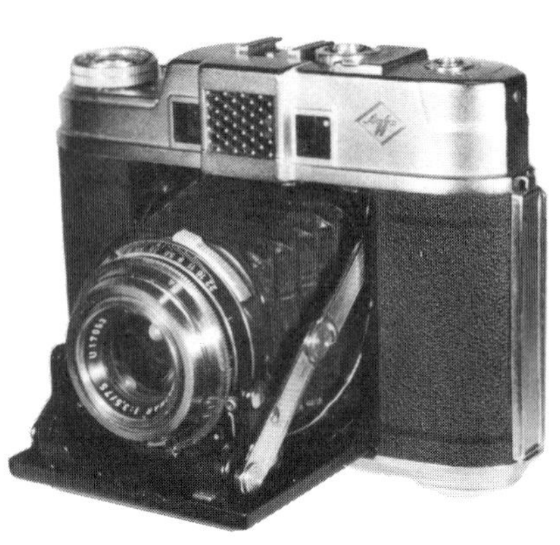

Automatic 66

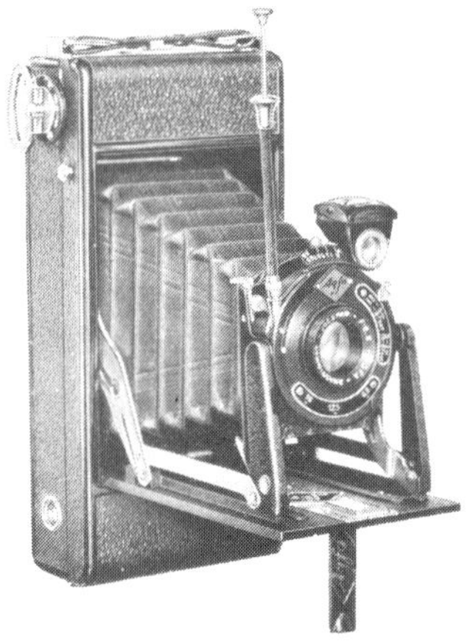

Billy I, (Pre-war)

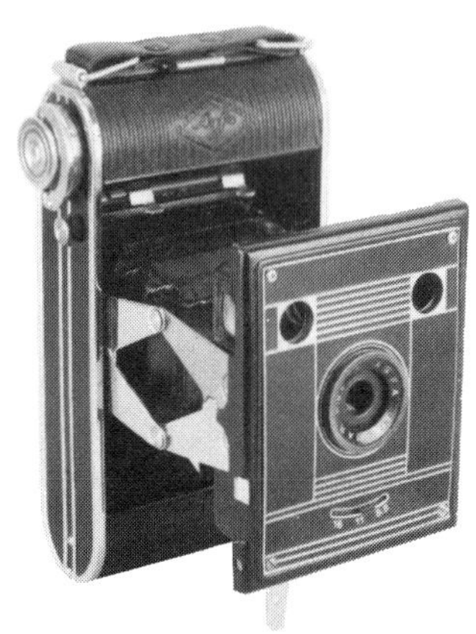

Billy Clack

MODEL	FORMAT	FILM	TYPE	Year	LENS	Apert	FL	SHUTTER	SPEEDS	ILLUS	U.S.$
Billy-O	4.5x6cm	127	FoldRo	1932	Solinar	3.9	75mm	Rim-Compur			120
Box 04	6x9/4.5x6	120	RollBox		Meniscus						60
Box 24	6x9cm	120	RollBox	1933	Meniscus		105mm	simple	M,Z		30
Box 34	6x9cm	120	RollBox	1933							40
Box 44 (black)	6x9cm	120	RollBox	1932	Meniscus		105mm	simple	M,Z		30
Box 44 (blue)	6x9cm	120	RollBox	1932	Meniscus		105mm	simple	M,Z		180
Box 45	6x9cm	120	RollBox	1930	Meniscus		105mm	simple	M,Z		10
Box 54	6x9cm	120	RollBox	1930	Meniscus		105mm	simple	M,Z	Mc54	30
Box 84	6x9cm	120	RollBox	1936	Meniscus						50
Box 94	6x9cm	120	RollBox	1937	Meniscus		105mm	simple	M,Z		20
Box B-2	6x9cm	120	RollBox	1937	Meniscus		105mm	simple	M,Z	Mc54	20
Box Spezial 64	6x9cm	120	RollBox	1930	Meniscus		105mm	simple	M,Z	Mc54	30
Clack	6x9cm	120	MetalBox	1954	Meniscus		105mm	Automat	M,Z	Mc54	20
Click I	6x6cm	120	PlasticBox	1958	Meniscus	11	105mm	Automat		F1593	10
Click II	6x6cm	120	PlasticBox	1959	Achromat	8.8		Singlo			10
Click III	6x6cm	120	PlasticBox	1960	Meniscus	11	105mm				30
Click IV	6x6cm	120	PlasticBox	1960	Achromat	8.8	105mm				30
Colorflex	24x36mm	35mm	35SLR								60
Colorflex I	24x36mm	35mm	35SLR	1959	Color-Apotar	2.8	50mm	Prontor-Refl.	1-300	A1155	80
Colorflex II	24x36mm	35mm	35SLR	1959	Color-Apotar	2.8	50mm	Prontor-Refl.	1-300		90
Compact	24x36mm	35mm	35VF	1980	Solinar	2.8	39mm	electronic	45-1250		100
Flexilette	24x36mm	35mm	35TLR	1960	Color-Apotar	2.8	4.5mm	Prontor	1-500	A1148	120
Folding plate camera	6x9cm	plate	FoldPl		Double Anast.	4.5	105mm	Compur			30
Folding plate camera	9x12cm	plate	FoldPl		Double Anast.	4.5	135mm	Compur			30
Folding rollfilm camera	6.5x11cm	116	FoldRo		Anastigmat	6.3		Agfa	1/2-1/1000		10
Heli-Clack	9x12cm	plate	FoldPl	1927	Heliar	4.5	10.5cm	Compur			360
Heli-Clack	10x13cm	plate	FoldPl	1927							360
Heli-Clack	13x18cm	plate	FoldPl	1927							360
Iso Pak	28x28mm	126	126VF		Meniscus			Parator	1/40, 1/80		10
Iso Pak C	28x28mm	126	126VF		Meniscus			Parator	1/40, 1/80		10
Iso Pak CI	28x28mm	126	126VF		Meniscus			Parator	1/40, 1/80		10
Iso Rapid I	24x36mm	Rapid	35mm	1965	Achromat	8	30mm	Parator	1/40,1/80		10
Iso Rapid I	24x24mm	Rapid	35VF		Achromat	11	41mm	Parator	1/40, 1/80		20
Iso Rapid IC	24x36mm	Rapid	35mm	1965	Achromat	8	30mm	Parator	1/40,1/80		10
Iso Rapid IF	24x36mm	Rapid	35mm	1965	Agfa Isitar	8	30mm	Parator	1/40,1/80	Mc54	10
Isola	6x6cm	120	RigidRo	1956	Agnar	6.3		Singlo			20
Isola I	6x6cm	120	RigidRo	1957	Meniscus			simple	I	Mc54	10
Isolar	6x9cm	plate	FoldPl	1927	Linear	4.5	105mm	Compur		Mc54	110
Isolar	9x12cm	plate	FoldPl	1927	Solinear	4.5	135mm	Dial-Compur	200	Mc54	140
Isolar	9x12cm	plate	FoldPl	1931	Solinar	4.5	135mm	Rim-Compur		Mc54	120
Isolar Luxus	9x12cm	plate	FoldPl	1927	Solinear	4.5	135mm	Dial-Compur	200		220
Isolette	6x6cm	120	HzFoldRo	1938	Igestar	6.3		Vario		A513	40

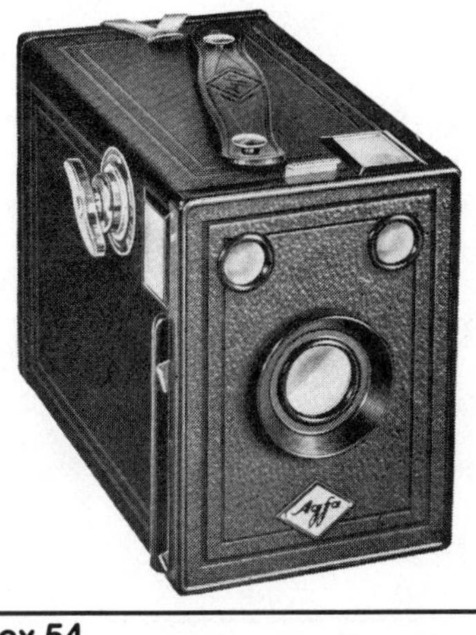

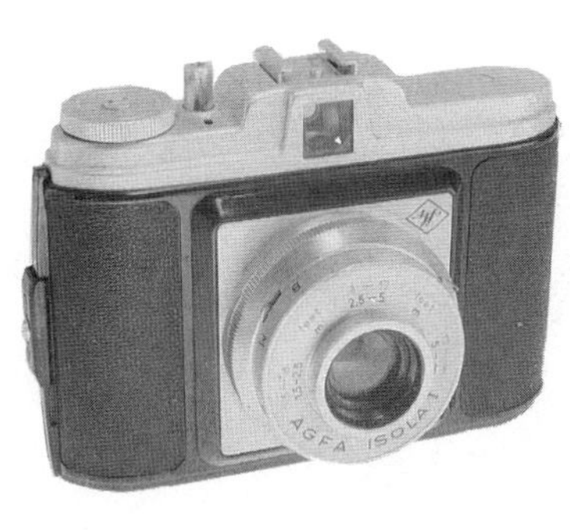

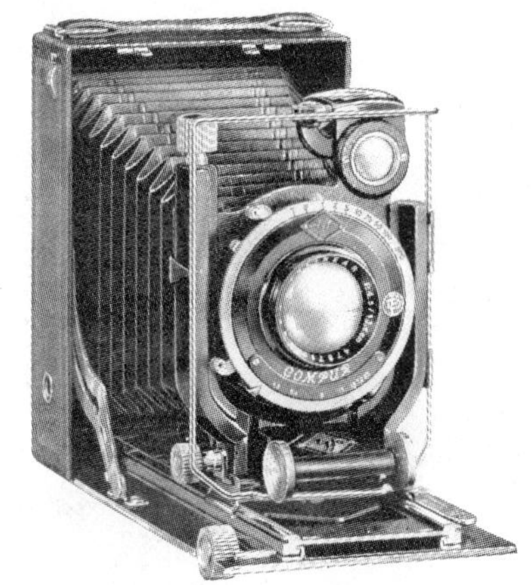

Box 54 | **Isola I** | **Isolar**

MODEL	FORMAT	FILM	TYPE	Year	LENS	Apert	FL	SHUTTER	SPEEDS	ILLUS	U.S.$
Isolette	6x6cm	120	HzFoldRo	1938	Solinar	4.5		Compur-Rap.			40
Isolette 4.5	6x6cm	120	HzFoldRo	1946	Apotar	4.5		Prontor II			20
Isolette 4.5	6x6cm	120	HzFoldRo	1946	Solinar	4.5		Compur-Rap.			20
Isolette 4.5x6cm	6x6/4.5x6	Roll	HzFoldRo	1939	Igestar	6.3		Vario			70
Isolette I	6x6cm	120	HzFoldRo	1952	Agnar	4.5	85mm	Vario			30
Isolette I	6x6cm	120	HzFoldRo	1952	Agnar	4.5	85mm	Pronto		A514	30
Isolette II	6x6cm	120	HzFoldRo	1950	Apotar	4.5		Prontor-SV		A515	30
Isolette III	6x6cm	120	HzFoldRo	1952	Solinar	4.5		Prontor-SV		Mc55	30
Isolette III	6x6cm	120	HzFoldRo	1952	Solinar	3.5		Sync.Compur		Mc55	50
Isolette L	6x6cm	120	HzFoldRo	1957	Color-Apotar	4.5	85mm	Pronto		A518	90
Isolette V	6x6cm	120	HzFoldRo	1950	Agnar	4.5	85mm	Vario			30
Isoly	4x4cm	120	RigidRo	1960	Achromat	8			30-100	F1612	10
Isoly II	4x4cm	120	RigidRo	1960	Agnar	6.3	55mm	Singlo	30-100		10
Isoly IIa	4x4cm	120	RigidRo	1960	Color-Agnar	5.6				A536	10
Isoly III	4x4cm	120	RigidRo	1960	Color-Apotar	3.9	60mm	Prontor	30-250		20
Isoly IIIa	4x4cm	120	RigidRo	1960	Color Agnar	3.5	60mm	Prontor	250		20
Isoly Junior	4x4cm	120	RigidRo	1960						Mc55	10
Isoly-Mat	4x4cm	120	RigidRo	1961	Color Agnar	5.6	55mm			A1523	20
Isomat-Rapid	24x24mm	Rapid	35VF	1965							20
Isomat-Rapid C	24x24mm	Rapid	35VF		Color Agnar	4.5	38mm	Paratic			10
Isorette	6x6cm	120	HzFoldRo	1938	Igestar	6.3	85mm	Pronto			50
Karat 2.8	24x36mm	Karat	35RF	1941	Xenar	2.8		Compur		A1048	80
Karat 2.8	24x36mm	Karat	35RF	1941	Xenar	2.8		Compur-Rap.	1-500		80
Karat 3.5	24x36mm	Karat	35VF	1938	Solinar	3.5	5.5cm	Compur		Mc55	60
Karat 3.5	24x36mm	Karat	35VF	1938	Solinar	3.5	5.5cm	Compur-Rap.	1-500	Mc55	60
Karat 4.5	24x36mm	Karat	35VF	1939	Oppar	4.5		Pronto	1/25-1/125	A1045	40
Karat 6.3	24x36mm	Karat	35VF	1937	Igestar	6.3	5cm	Automat	1/25-1/100	A1044	50
Karat IV	24x36mm	Karat	35RF	1955	Solagon	2	50mm	Prontor-SVS		A1052	120
Karat 12	24x36mm	Karat	35RF	1948	Solinar	3.5	5.5cm	Compur-Rap.	1-500		80
Karat 12	24x36mm	Karat	35RF	1948	Xenar	2.8		Compur-Rap.	1-500	A1049	80
Karat 36	24x36mm	Karat	35RF	1949	Xenar	2.8		Compur-Rap.	1-500		60
Karat 36	24x36mm	Karat	35RF	1950	Heligon	2		Sync.Compur		A1051	80
Karomat	24x36mm	Karat	35RF	1950	Xenon	2	50mm	Compur-Rap.	1-500		120
Karomat 36	24x36mm	Karat	35RF	1950	Xenar	2.8	50mm	Compur-Rap.	1-500		120
Moto-Rapid C	24x24mm	Rapid	35mm	1965	Color Isomar	8		Parator		A1970	50
Motor-Kamera	24x36mm		35mm	1962	Color Telinear	3.4	90mm			A903	130
Ninon	6.5x9cm	plate	FoldPl	1927	Helostar	6.3		Compur			200
Nitor	6.5x9cm	plate	FoldPl	1927	Helostar	6.3		Pronto			100
Nitor	6.5x9cm	plate	FoldPl	1927	Linear	4.5		Compur	250		110
Opal Luxus	4.5x6cm	plate	FoldPl	1925	Doppel Anast.		105mm	Compur			330
Opal Luxus	6.5x9cm	plate	FoldPl	1925	Solinear	4.5	105mm	Compur			290
Optima	24x36mm	35mm	35VF	1959	Color-Apotar	3.9		Compur		Mc55	50

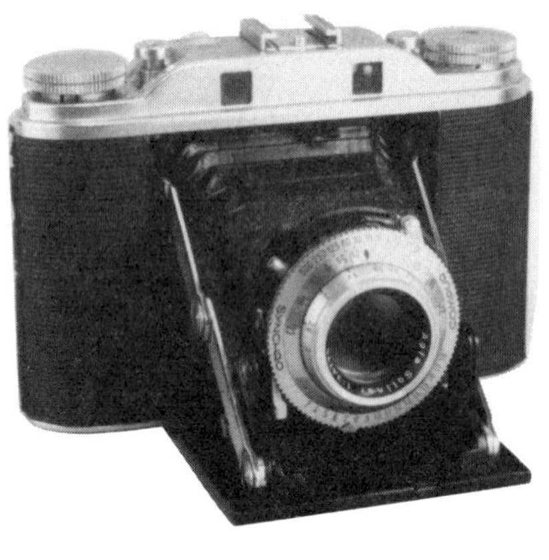

Isolette III

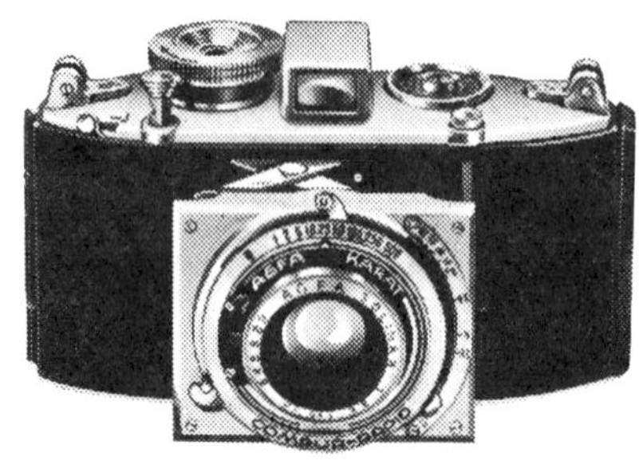

Karat 3.5

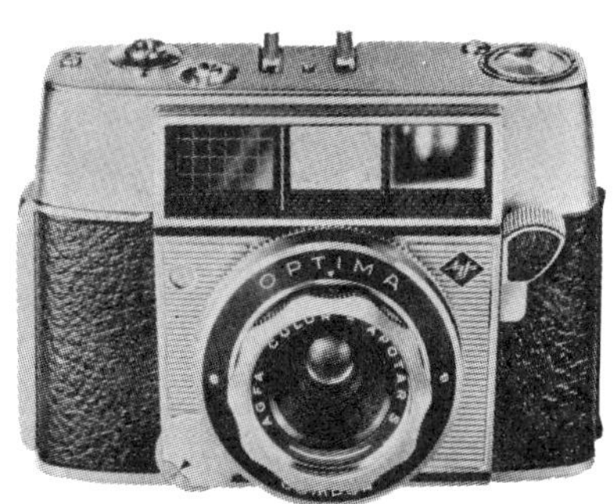

Optima

MODEL	FORMAT	FILM	TYPE	Year	LENS	Apert	FL	SHUTTER	SPEEDS	ILLUS	U.S.$
Optima I	24x36mm	35mm	35VF	1960	Color Agnar	2.8	45mm	Prontorlux		A1153	40
Optima IA	24x36mm	35mm	35VF	1962	Color Agnar	2.8	45mm	Special Auto	30-160		40
Optima II	24x36mm	35mm	35VF	1960	Color-Apotar	2.8	45mm	Prontormator	30-250		30
Optima IIS	24x36mm	35mm	35RF	1961	Color-Apotar	2.8	45mm	Prontormator	30-250		40
Optima III	24x36mm	35mm	35RF	1960	Color-Apotar	2.8	45mm	Compur Spezial	10-250		30
Optima IIIS	24x36mm	35mm	35RF	1960	Color-Apotar	2.8	45mm	Compur Spezial	10-250		70
Optima 200 Sensor	24x36mm	35mm	35VF	1969	Color-Apotar	2.8	42mm	Paratic	30-500		30
Optima 335 Sensor	24x36mm	35mm	35VF	1977	Color Agnatar	3.5	40mm	Paratronic	30-300		20
Optima 500 S	24x36mm	35mm	35VF	1963	Color-Solinar	2.8	45mm	Compur			50
Optima 500 Sensor	18x24mm	35mm	35C	1967	Color-Apotar	2.8	42mm	Paratic	30-500		30
Optima 500 SN	24x36mm	35mm	35VF	1966	Color-Solinar	2.8	45mm	Compur			30
Optima 535 Sensor	24x36mm	35mm	35VF	1977	Solitar	2.8	40mm	Paratronic	1-500		30
Optima 935 Sensor	24x36mm	35mm	35VF	1980	Solinar	2.8	39mm	electronic	30-1000	A2127	50
Optima 1035 Sensor	24x36mm	35mm	35VF		Solitar	2.8	40mm	Paratronic	1-1000		50
Optima 1535 Sensor	24x36mm	35mm	35VF		Solitar	2.8	40mm	Paratronic	30-1000		50
Optima 5000 Pocket Sensor	13x17mm	110	110VF		Color-Solinar	2.7	26mm	electronic	30-1/1000		20
Optima 5008 Makro	13x17mm	110	110VF		Color-Solinar	2.7	26mm	electronic	15-1/1000		40
Optima 6000 Pocket Sensor	13x17mm	110	110VF		Color-Solinar	2.7	26mm	electronic	30-1/1000		30
Optima Flash Sens. Elec.	24x36mm	35mm	35VF		Solitar	2.8	40mm	Paratronic	30-1/1000	A2126	70
Optima Parat	18x24mm	35mm	35Half	1964	Color-Solinar	2.8	30mm	Compur	500	A2124	70
Optima Parat	18x24mm	35mm	35Half	1964	Color Telepar	2.8	55mm	Compur	500		130
Optima Rapid 125C	24x24mm	Rapid	35VF	1966	Color-Apotar	2.8	35mm	Paratic			20
Optima Rapid 250	24x24mm	Rapid	35VF	1965	Color-Apotar	2.8	45mm	Special Auto	30-250		10
Optima Rapid 250 V	24x24mm	Rapid	35VF	1966	Color-Apotar	2.8	30mm	Special Auto	30-250		30
Optima Rapid 500 V	24x24mm	Rapid	35VF	1966	Color-Solinar	2.8	35mm	Paratic	30-500		30
Optima Reflex	24x36mm	Rapid	35TLR	1962	Color-Apotar	2.8	45mm			Mc55	160
Paramat	18x24mm	35mm	35Half	1963	Color-Apotar	2.8	30mm				50
Parat	18x24mm	35mm	35Half	1963	Color-Apotar	2.8	30mm				50
Parat I	18x24mm	35mm	35Half	1963	Color-Apotar	2.8	30mm				50
Preis-Box (black)	6x9cm	120	RollBox	1932						Mc56	40
Preis-Box (blue)	6x9cm	120	RollBox	1932						Mc56	220
Record I	6x9cm	120	FoldRo	1952	Agnar	4.5	105mm	Pronto			30
Record II	6x9cm	120	FoldRo	1952	Solinar	4.5	105mm	Sync.Compur		Mc56	40
Record III	6x9cm	120	FoldRo	1952	Apotar	4.5	105mm	Prontor-SV		Mc56	120
Record III	6x9cm	120	FoldRo	1952	Solinar	4.5	105mm	Sync.Compur		Mc56	130
Schul-Prämie Box	6x9cm	120	RollBox	1932							90
Selecta	24x36mm	35mm	35RF	1962	Color-Apotar	2.8	45mm	Pront.-MaticP			40
Selecta-Flex	24x36mm	35mm	35SLR	1963	Solinar	2.8	50mm	ProntorRefl.P	30-300	Mc56	130
Selecta-Flex	24x36mm	35mm	35SLR	1963	Solagon	2		ProntorRefl.P	30-300	Mc56	140
Selecta-Flex I	24x36mm	35mm	35SLR	1964	Color-Solinar	2.8	50mm	ProntorRefl.P	1-300		180
Selecta-Flex II	24x36mm	35mm	35SLR	1964	Color Solagon	2	55mm	Prontor	1-300		210
Selecta-M	24x36mm	35mm	35SLR	1962	Solinar	2.8	45mm	Compur	30-500	IIKG90	180

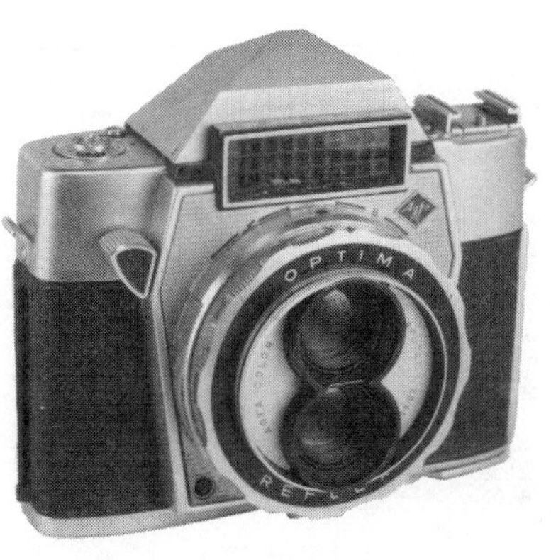

Optima Reflex

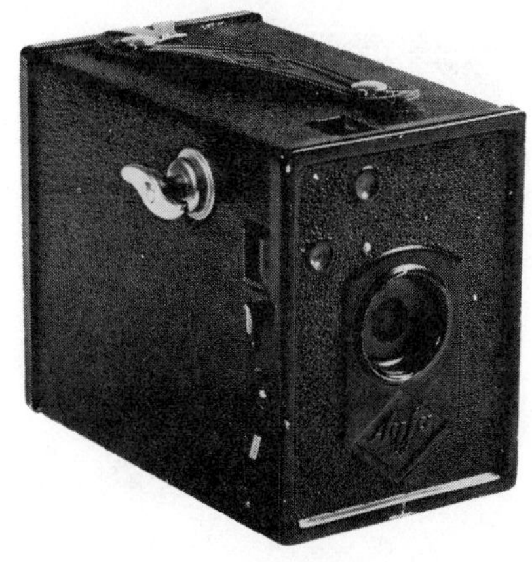

Preis-Box

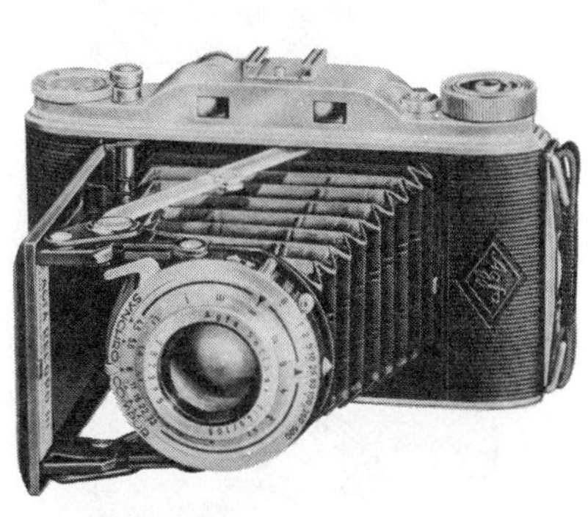

Record III

MODEL	FORMAT	FILM	TYPE	Year	LENS	Apert	FL	SHUTTER	SPEEDS	ILLUS	U.S.$
Selectronic 3	24x36mm	35mm	35SLR		Agfa Color	1.4	50mm	programmed	8-1/1000	A1706	310
Selectronic S Sensor	24x36mm	35mm	35RF	1971	Color-Solinar	2.8	45mm	Paratronic	15-500	A2125	40
Selectronic Sensor	24x36mm	35mm	35VF		Color-Apotar	2.8	45mm	Paratronic	15-500		30
Silette (I)	24x36mm	35mm	35mm	1953	Color Agnar	2.8	45mm	Prontor	30-125		30
Silette II	24x36mm	35mm	35mm								30
Silette Automatic	24x36mm	35mm	35mm	1958	Color-Solinar	28	50mm	Prontor-SLK	1-300		30
Silette F	24x36mm	35mm	35mm		Color Agnar	2.8	45mm	Prontor	30-125		30
Silette L	24x36mm	35mm	35mm		Color Agnar	2.8	45mm	Prontor	30-125		30
Silette LK	24x36mm	35mm	35mm		Color Agnar	2.8	45mm	Spezial LK	30-250		50
Silette LK Sensor	24x36mm	35mm	35mm	1969	Color Agnar	2.8	45mm	Parator	30-300		50
Silette Rapid F	24x36mm	Rapid	35mm		Color Agnar	2.8	45mm	Parator	30-250		10
Silette Rapid I	24x36mm	Rapid	35mm	1964	Color Agnar	2.8	45mm	Prontor	30-125		10
Silette Rapid L	24x36mm	Rapid	35mm		Color Agnar	2.8	45mm	Prontor	30-250		20
Silette SL	24x36mm	35mm	35VF		Color-Solinar	2.8	45mm	Prontor-SLK	1-300	A2123	40
Silette SLE	24x36mm	35mm	35mm		Color-Solinar	2.8	50mm				70
Solina	24x36mm	35mm	35VF	1960	Color-Apotar	3.5	45mm	Pronto	1/25-200		40
Solinette	24x36mm	35mm	35Fold	1952	Apotar	3.5	50mm	Prontor-SVS			50
Solinette	24x36mm	35mm	35Fold	1952	Solinar	3.5	50mm	Sync.Compur		A1021	50
Solinette II	24x36mm	35mm	35Fold	1952	Apotar	3.5	50mm	Prontor-SVS			60
Solinette II	24x36mm	35mm	35Fold	1952	Solinar	3.5	50mm	Sync.Compur			70
Speedex Clack	4.5x6cm	120	StrutRo	1934	Igenar	8.8			B-1/25		50
Speedex Clack	6x9cm	120	StrutRo	1934	Billinar	11			B-1/25		50
Speedex Compur	6x9cm	120	FoldRo	1934	Apotar	4.5	10.5cm			Mc56	50
Speedex Compur	6x9cm	120	FoldRo	1934	Solinar	3.9				Mc56	60
Speedex Compur	6x9cm	120	FoldRo	1934	Solinar	4.5				Mc56	60
Sport	13x17mm	110	110AW	1982							70
Standard (plate)	6.5x9cm	plate	FoldPl	1926	Solinar	4.5		Automat		Mc57	80
Standard (plate)	6.5x9cm	plate	FoldPl	1926	Solinar	6.3		Compur		Mc57	80
Standard (plate)	9x12cm	plate	FoldPl	1926	Solinar	6.3		Automat		Mc57	70
Standard (plate)	9x12cm	plate	FoldPl	1926	Solinar	4.5		Compur		Mc57	70
Standard (rollfilm)	6.5x11cm	116	FoldRo	1926	Solinar					Mc57	30
Standard (rollfilm)	6x9cm	120	FoldRo	1926	Solinar					Mc57	70
Standard Deluxe (plate)	6.5x9cm	plate	FoldPl	1926	Anastigmat	6.4		Automat			260
Standard Deluxe (plate)	6.5x9cm	plate	FoldPl	1926	Anastigmat	4.5		Compur			260
Standard Deluxe (roll)	6.5x11cm	116	FoldRo	1926	Anastigmat						150
Super Isolette	6x6cm	120	FoldRo	1954	Solinar	3.5	75mm	S.Comp.MXV	500		320
Super Silette	24x36mm	35mm	35RF		Solinar	3.5	45mm	Sync-Compur		A2122	60
Super Silette Automatic	24x36mm	35mm	35RF	1959	Color-Solinar	2.8	50mm	Prontor-SLK	1-300		90
Super Silette L	24x36mm	35mm	35RF	1958	Color-Solinar	2.8	50mm			Mc56	80
Super Silette LK	24x36mm	35mm	35RF		Color-Solinar						100
Super Solina	24x36mm	35mm	35RF	1960	Color-Apotar	2.8		Prontor-SVS	1-500		50
Super Solinette	24x36mm	35mm	35RF	1953	Apotar	3.5	50mm	Prontor-SVS			90

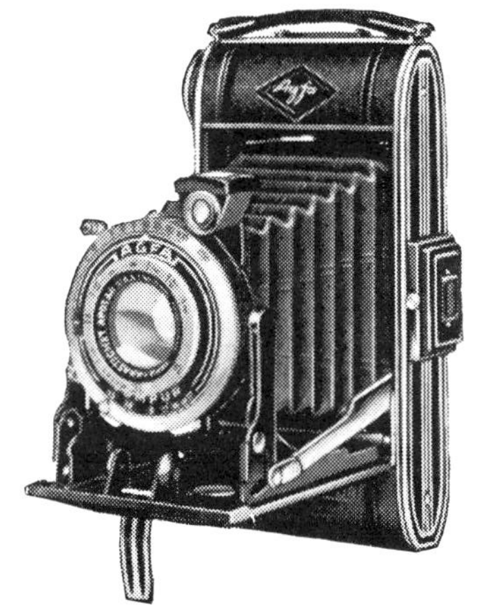

Speedex Compur

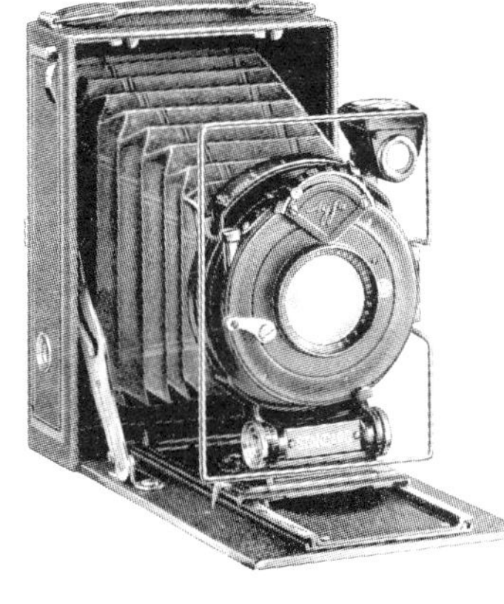

Standard

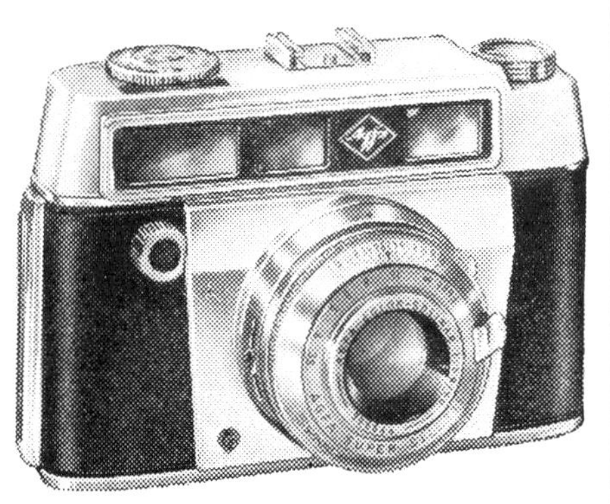

Super Silette L

MODEL	FORMAT	FILM	TYPE	Year	LENS	Apert	FL	SHUTTER	SPEEDS	ILLUS	U.S.$
Super Solinette	24x36mm	35mm	35RF	1953	Solinar	3.5	50mm	Sync-Compur		A1022	90
Superior (black)	8x14cm	125	FoldRo	1930	Solinar	4.5		Compur		Mc57	140
Superior (brown)	8x14cm	125	FoldRo	1930	Solinar	4.8		Compur		Mc57	230
Synchro-Box	6x9cm	120	MetalBox	1951	Meniscus					Mc57	10
Synchro-Box (France)	6x9cm	120	MetalBox	1952						F885	60
Tramp Pocket	13x17mm	110	110		Color-Apotar						50
Trolita	6x9cm	120	BakFoldRo	1938	Apotar	4.5	105mm	Prontor II		Mc57	210
Trolix	6x9cm	120	BakeliteBox	1936	Meniscus			Spezial	M,Z	Mc57	60
...AGFA ANSCO CORP. - Binghamton, NY, USA											
Box No. 2 (black)	6x9cm	120	RollBox	1932	Meniscus			simple		Mc57	30
Box No. 2 (colored)	6x9cm	120	RollBox	1932	Meniscus			simple		Mc57	50
Box No. 2A (black)	6.5x11cm	116	RollBox	1932	Meniscus			simple		Mc57	30
Box No. 2A (colored)	6.5x11cm	116	RollBox	1932	Meniscus			simple		Mc57	50
Cadet A-8	4x6.5cm	127	RollBox	1937	Meniscus			simple		A1339	50
Cadet A-8 Flash	4x6.5cm	127	RollBox	1937	Meniscus				M,Z		40
Cadet A-8 Special	4x6.5cm	127	RollBox	1937	Meniscus				M,Z		40
Cadet B-2	6x9cm	120	RollBox	1939	Meniscus			simple			10
Cadet B-2 Texas 100	6x9cm	120	RollBox	1936	Meniscus			simple		Mc58	310
Cadet D-6	2½x4¼"	116	RollBox	1935	Meniscus			simple			10
Captain	6x9cm	120	FoldRo		Captain				T,I	Mc58	30
Chief	6x9cm	120	MetalBox	1940	Meniscus			simple			10
Clipper PD-16	5.5x6.5cm	616	TelescRo	1938	Meniscus					Mc58	10
Clipper Special	5.5x6.5cm	616	TelescRo	1939	Anastigmat	6.3			25-100		10
Major	6x9cm	120	FoldRo								30
Memo	24x36mm	Rapid	35VF	1939	Agfa Memar	3.5		Memo	1/2-200	Mc58	80
Memo	18x24mm	Rapid	35VF	1940	Agfa Memar	3.5		Memo	1/2-200	Mc58	100
Pioneer PB-20	6x9cm	120	Box	1940	Meniscus			simple			10
Pioneer PD-16	6.5x11cm	116	Box	1940	Meniscus			simple		A3108	10
Plenax PB-20	6x9cm	120	FoldRo	1935	Antar				T,I	Mc58	10
Plenax PD-16	6.5x11cm	116	FoldRo	1935	Tripar				1/5-400	Mc58	10
Readyset Traveler	6x9cm	120	FoldRo	1931	Anastigmat					Mc58	70
Readyset Traveler	6.5x11cm	116	FoldRo	1931	Anastigmat					Mc58	70
Speedex B2	6x6cm	120	FoldRo	1940	Anastigmat	4.5			1/2-250		20
Speedex Junior	6x6cm	120	FoldRo	1940	Anastigmat	4.5			1/2-500		10
Viking	6x9cm	120	FoldRo	1940	Isomar	6.3		Synchroflash			30
Viking	6.5x11cm	116	FoldRo	1940	Isomar	7.7		Synchroflash			30
...AGILUX LTD. - Croydon, G.B.											
Agiflash	4x6.5cm	127	BakeliteRoll	1954	Meniscus	11		1-speed		Mc59	30
Agiflash 35	24x36mm	35mm	35mm			8		1-speed	I		30
Agiflash 44	4x4cm	127	PlasticRoll	1959	Meniscus	11					20
Agiflex I	6x6cm	120	MedSLR	1946	Agiflex	3.5	8cm	focal plane	25-500		120
Agiflex II	6x6cm	120	MedSLR	1949	Agiflex	3.5	30mm	focal plane	2-500	A1635	210

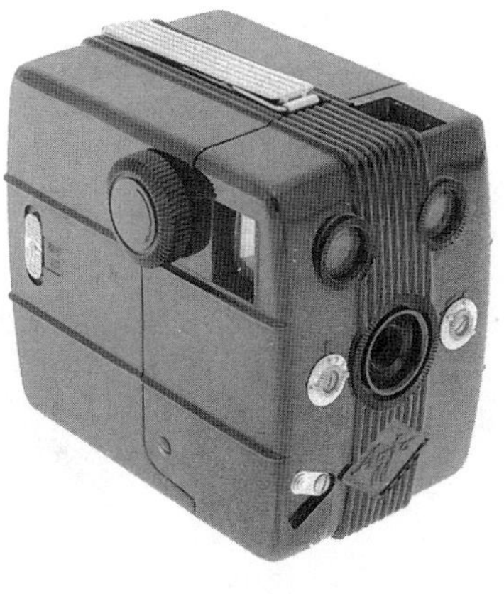

Trolix

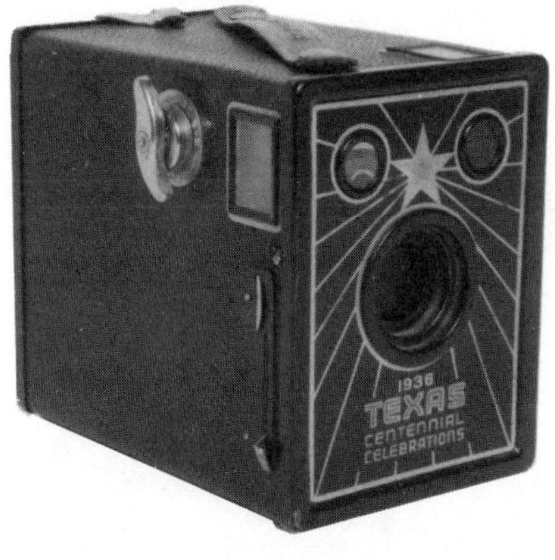

Cadet B-2 Texas 100

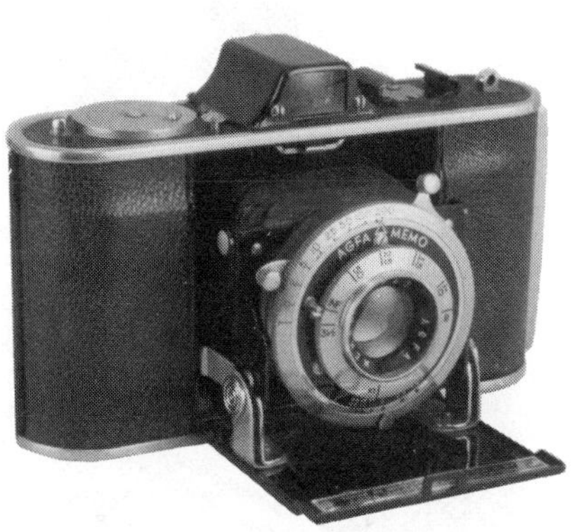

Memo

MODEL	FORMAT	FILM	TYPE	Year	LENS	Apert	FL	SHUTTER	SPEEDS	ILLUS	U.S.$
Agiflex III	6x6cm	120	MedSLR	1954	Agiflex	2.8	8cm	focal plane	2-500		290
Agifold	6x6cm	120	HzFoldRo	1955	Anastigmat	4.5	75mm			A1505	90
Agifold RF	6x6cm	120	HzFoldRo	1955	Anastigmat	4.5	75mm			Mc59	80
Agima	24x36mm	35mm	35RF	1960	Anastigmat	2.8	45mm				90
Agimatic	24x36mm	35mm	35RF	1956	Agilux	2.8	45mm	Agimatic	1-300	A2155	70
Auto Flash Super 44	4x4cm	127	PlasticRoll	1959	Fix Focus			simple	I		30
Colt 44	4x4cm	127	PlasticRoll	1961							10
...(unknown)											
Aiglon		Roll	Submin	1934	Meniscus				I	A1918	200
...AIRES CAMERA IND. CO. LTD. - Tokyo											
Aires 35-III	24x36mm	35mm	35RF	1957	Coral	1.9	45mm	Seikosha-MX		Mc59	70
Aires 35-IIIA	24x36mm	35mm	35RF	1957	Coral	1.9	45mm	Seikosha-MX	1-500		70
Aires 35-IIIC	24x36mm	35mm	35RF	1958	Coral	1.9	45mm	Seikosha-MXL	1-500	Mc59	100
Aires 35-IIIL	24x36mm	35mm	35RF	1957	Coral	1.9	45mm	Seikosha-LVX	1-500	Mc59	70
Aires 35-IIIS	24x36mm	35mm	35RF	1955	Coral	1.9	45mm	Seikosha-MXL	1-500		60
Aires 35-V	24x36mm	35mm	35RF	1959	Coral	1.5	45mm	Seikosha-MX	1-400		160
Aires Automat	6x6cm	120	TLR	1954	Zuiko	3.5	75mm	Seikosha-Rap.	1-500		130
Aires Automat	6x6cm	120	TLR	1954	Nikkor	3.5	75mm	Seikosha-Rap.	1-500		540
Airesflex	6x6cm	120	TLR	1953	Coral	3.5	75mm	Copal	1-300		90
Airesflex Z	6x6cm	120	TLR	1952	Coral	3.5	75mm	Seikosha-Rap.	1-500		90
Airesflex Z	6x6cm	120	TLR	1952	Nikkor	3.5	75mm	Seikosha-Rap.	1-500		220
Penta 35	24x36mm	35mm	35SLR	1960	Q Coral	2.8	50mm	Seikosha-SLV	1-500	Mc59	80
Penta 35 LM	24x36mm	35mm	35SLR	1961	Coral	2	50mm	Seikosha-SLV	1-500		100
Radar-Eye	24x36mm	35mm	35mm	1960	Coral	1.9	45mm	Seikosha-SLS	1-1000		50
Reflex 35	24x36mm	35mm	35SLR	1959	Coral	2.8	50mm				70
Viceroy	6x6cm	120	FoldRo		Coral	3.5	75mm	Seikosha			420
Viscount	24x36mm	35mm	35RF	1962	Coral	1.9	4.5cm	Seikosha	1-500		50
...ALBINI CO. - Milan											
Alba 63	4.5x6cm	plate	FoldPl	1914	Anastigmat	7.5			1/25-100	Mc60	190
Alba 63	4.5x6cm	plate	FoldPl	1914	Rapid Rectilinear	8			1/25-100	Mc60	190
Alba 64	6x9cm	plate	FoldPl	1914	Doppio Anast.	5.6	90mm		1/25-100		50
...ALIBERT (Charles Alibert) - Paris, France											
Photo-Sac à Main (I)	9x12cm	plate	Disguised	1895	Rapid Rectilinear					Mc60	3000
Photo-Sac à Main (II)	9x12cm	plate	Disguised	1895	Rapid Rectilinear					A3286	3000
...ALSAPHOT - France											
Ajax	6x6cm	120	TelescRo		Alsar	3.5		Alsaphot	1-300	Mc60	30
Cady	6x6cm	120	TelescRo		Anastigmat	6.3		Gitzo	25,75	Mc60	30
Cyclope	6x9cm	120	RigidRo		Saphir Anast.	3.5	105mm	Prontor-SV	1-175	Mc60	1500
Cyclope	6x9cm	120	RigidRo		Saphir Anast.	4.5	105mm	Prontor II	1-175	Mc60	1700
D'Assas	6x6cm	120	TelescRo		Alsar	3.5	75mm	Gitzo	25-200	Mc60	30
D'Assas-Lux	6x6cm	120	TelescRo		Boyer Topaz	3.5	75mm	Atos-2	1-300	Mc60	30
Dauphin	6x6cm	120	TLR		Boyer Topaz	3.5	75mm	Gitzo	25,75	Mc61	30

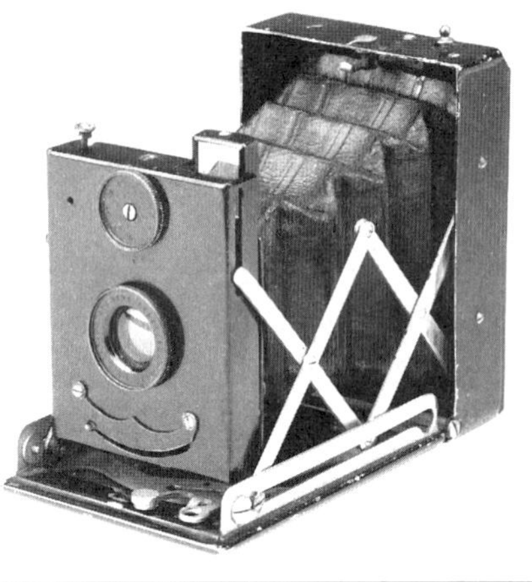
Alba 63

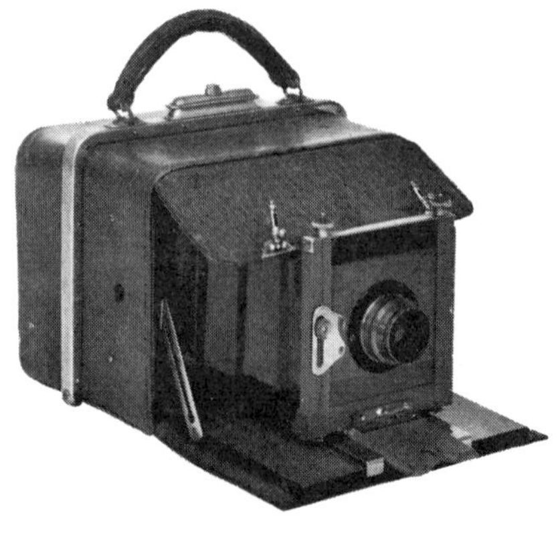
Photo-Sac à Main

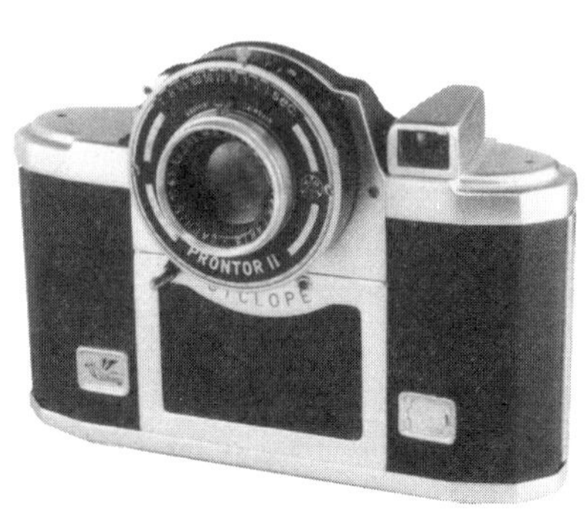

Cyclope

MODEL	FORMAT	FILM	TYPE	Year	LENS	Apert	FL	SHUTTER	SPEEDS	ILLUS	U.S.$
Maine I	24x36mm	35mm	35VF	1960	Berthiot	2.8	45mm		30-250	Mc61	30
Maine IIc	24x36mm	35mm	35VF		Berthiot	2.8	45mm			F613	30
Maine IIIa	24x36mm	35mm	35VF		Berthiot	2.8	45mm			F614	30
...AMERICAN CAMERA CO. - London											
Demon Detective Camera	2¼x2¼"	plate	RigidPl	1889	Achromat	10	30mm			Mc61	1400
...AMERICAN CAMERA MFG. CO. - Northboro, MA, USA											
Buckeye No. 2	4x5"		RollBox	1899						Mc61	70
Buckeye No. 3		Roll	RollBox	1895		8				Mc61	70
Buckeye Special		Roll	RollBox	1897						Mc61	110
Folding Buckeye No. 8	4x5"	103	FoldRo	1904							390
Folding Poco No. 15	4x5"	plate	FoldPl	1904	Rapid Rectilinear			Unicum			100
Folding Poco No. 16	4x5"	plate	FoldPl	1904	Rapid Rectilinear			Unicum			120
Tourist Buckeye No. 1	3½x3½"	101	FoldRo	1895						Mc61	180
Tourist Buckeye No. 1	3¼x4½"	Roll	FoldRo	1895						Mc61	180
Triple Bed Poco No. 19	4x5"	plate	FoldPl	1904							120
...AMERICAN OPTICAL CO. - New York, USA											
Flammang's Patent R.B.	5x7"	plate	Tailboard	1886							270
Flammang's Patent R.B.	6½x8½"	plate	Tailboard	1886							270
Henry Clay	5x7"	plate	H&S	1892				Wale		Mc62	670
Revolving Back Camera	4x5"	plate	View	1890							210
Revolving Back Camera	10x12"	plate	View	1890							210
Revolving Back Camera	20x24"	plate	View	1890							210
View camera	5x7"	plate	View	1890							220
...AMERICAN SAFETY RAZOR CORP. - New York											
ASR Fotodisc	22x24mm	Disc	Submin	1950						Mc62	650
...ANSCHÜTZ - Berlin											
Rollda	8x10.5cm	118		1900	Aplanat	7.2	135mm	Unicum	1-100		70
Rollda	9x12cm	118		1915	Aplanat	7.2	135mm	Unicum	1-100		40
...ANSCO - Binghamton, NY USA											
Admiral	2¼x2¼"	120	TLR								10
Ansco Junior	2½x4¼"	116	FoldRo	1906	Rapid Rectilinear						40
Ansco Junior No. 1	6x9cm	120	FoldRo	1924	Modico Anast.			Bionic			30
Ansco Junior No. 1A	2½x4¼"	116	FoldRo	1916	Rapid Rectilinear			Deltax			30
Ansco Junior No. 2C	2⅞x4⅞"	130	FoldRo	1917							30
Ansco Junior No. 3	8x10.5cm	118	FoldRo	1923	Rapid Rectilinear			Deltax			20
Ansco Junior No. 3A	8x14cm	122	FoldRo	1916							30
Ansco Special No. 2	6x9cm	120	RollBox	1924							40
Ansco Special No. 2A		116	RollBox	1924							40
Anscoflex	2¼x2¼"	120	TLR	1954		11				Mc63	30
Anscoflex II	2¼x2¼"	120	TLR	1954						Mc63	30
Anscomark M	24x36mm	35mm	35RF	1960	Xyton	1.9	50mm			Mc63	40
Anscomatic Cadet	28x28mm	126	126VF	1966							10

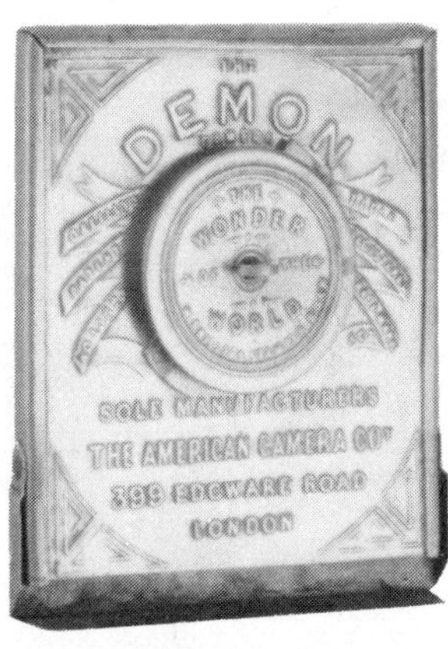

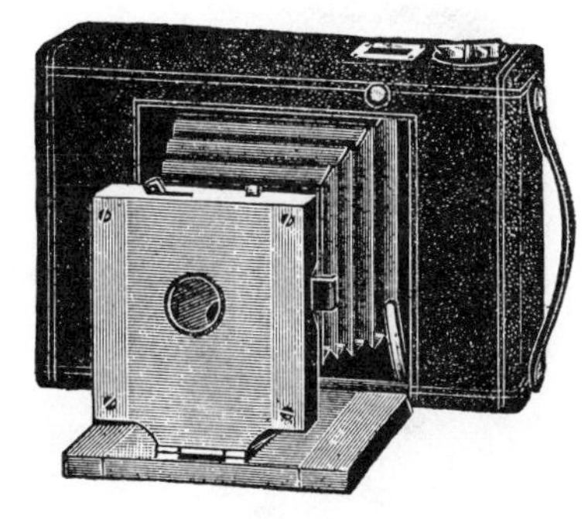

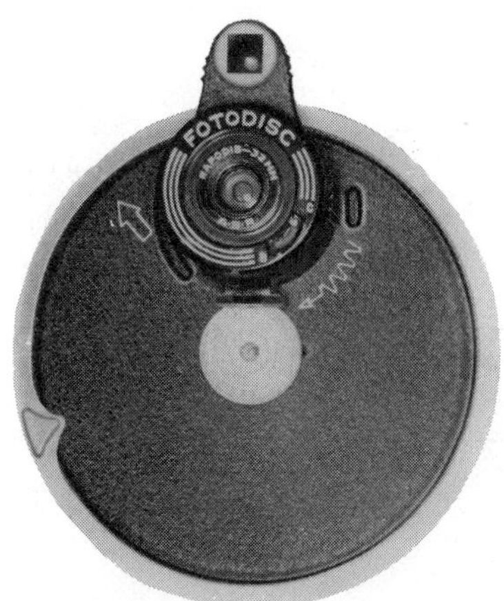

Demon Detective Camera — **Tourist Buckeye No. 1** — **ASR Fotodisc**

MODEL	FORMAT	FILM	TYPE	Year	LENS	Apert	FL	SHUTTER	SPEEDS	ILLUS	U.S.$
Anscoset	24x36mm	35mm	35RF	1960	Rokkor	2.8	45mm			Mc63	30
Arrow			RollBox	1925						Mc63	20
Automatic No. 1A	2½x4¼"	6A	FoldRo	1925	Anastigmat	6.3				Mc63	200
Automatic Reflex	2¼x2¼"	120	TLR	1947	Anastigmat	3.5	83mm		400	Mc63	180
Automatic Reflex II	2¼x2¼"	120	TLR		Anastigmat	3.5	83mm		400		200
Autoset	24x36mm	35mm	35RF	1961	Rokkor	2.8	45mm			Mc63	40
Autoset CdS	24x36mm	35mm	35RF	1964	Rokkor	2.8	45mm				50
Bingo No. 2	6x9cm	120	RollBox	1925						Mc63	20
Box camera (black)	6x9cm	120	RollBox								10
Box camera (colored)	6x9cm	120	RollBox								30
Buster Brown Junior	2½x4¼"	116	FoldRo								30
Buster Brown No. 0	4x6.5cm	127	RollBox	1923	Meniscus			simple	I,T		20
Buster Brown No. 2	6x9cm	120	RollBox	1906	Meniscus			simple	I,T		10
Buster Brown No. 2A	2½x4¼"	118	RollBox	1910	Meniscus			simple	I,T		10
Buster Brown No. 2C	2⅞x4⅞"	130	RollBox	1917	Meniscus			simple	I,T		10
Buster Brown No. 3	3¼x4¼"	124	RollBox	1906	Meniscus			simple	I,T		10
Buster Brown No. 3A	3¼x5½"	122	RollBox	1914	Meniscus			simple	I,T		20
Buster Brown Sp. No. 0	4x6.5cm	127	RollBox	1923	Meniscus			simple	I,T		30
Buster Brown Sp. No. 2	6x9cm	120	RollBox	1923	Meniscus			simple	I,T		30
Buster Brown Sp. No. 2A	2½x4¼"	118	RollBox	1923	Meniscus			simple	I,T		30
Cadet (I)	4x4cm	127	PlasticBox	1959							10
Cadet II	4x4cm	127	PlasticBox	1965						Mc64	10
Cadet III	4x4cm	127	PlasticBox		Anscar					Mc64	10
Cadet B-2	6x9cm	120	RollBox	1947				simple	I,T		10
Cadet D-6	2½x4¼"	116	RollBox	1947				simple	I,T		10
Cadet Flash	4x4cm	127	PlasticBox	1960	Anscar						10
Cadet Reflex	4x4cm	127	PlasticBox	1960	Anscar						10
Century of Progress	6x9cm	120	RollBox	1933						Mc64	90
Clipper	6x6cm	120	TelescRo	1940	Double Meniscus	14		simple	1/25,T	Mc64	10
Clipper Special	6x6cm	120	TelescRo	1940		14		simple		Mc64	10
Color Clipper	6x6cm	120	TelescRo	1940		14		simple		Mc64	20
Commander	6x9cm	120	FoldRo	1955	focusing			Vario		Mc64	30
Commercial View 1930	8x10"	plate	View	1930	various			various			390
Dollar Box	4x6.5cm	127	RollBox	1910							20
Flash Champion			TelescRo	1949						Mc64	10
Flash Clipper	6x6cm	120	TelescRo	1940				simple	I,T	Mc64	20
Fold. Bust.Brown No. 1	6x9cm	120	FoldRo	1910	achromatic			Midget	i,b,t		20
Fold. Bust.Brown No. 2	6x9cm	120	FoldRo	1914	achromatic			Actus			30
Fold. Bust.Brown No. 2A	2½x4¼"	118	FoldRo	1910	Rapid Rectilinear			Actus			30
Fold. Bust.Brown No. 3	3¼x4¼"	124	FoldRo	1914	Rapid Rectilinear			Actus			30
Fold. Bust.Brown No. 3A	3¼x5½"	122	FoldRo	1910	Rapid Rectilinear			Actus			30
Fold. Goodwin No. 1A	2½x4½"	116	FoldRo	1930							30

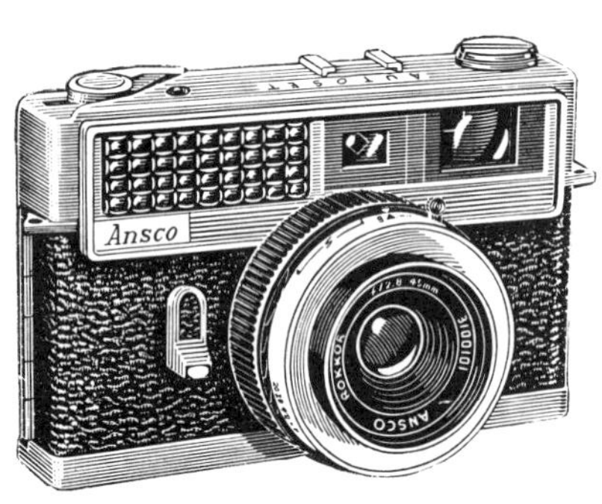

Autoset

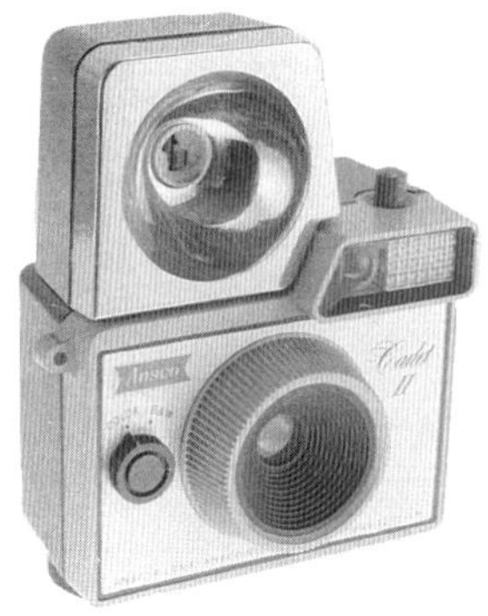

Cadet II

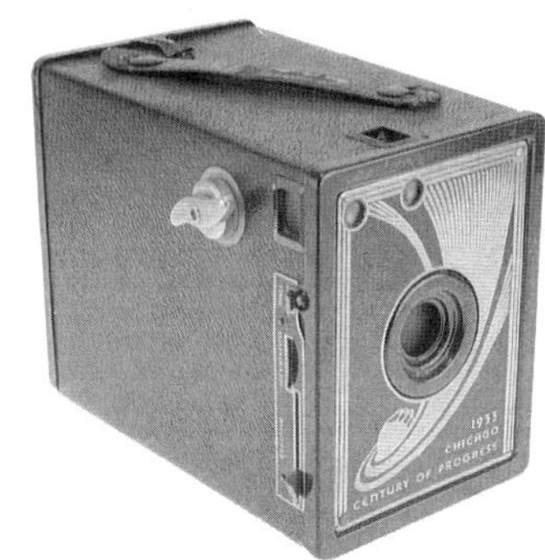

Century of Progress

MODEL	FORMAT	FILM	TYPE	Year	LENS	Apert	FL	SHUTTER	SPEEDS	ILLUS	U.S.$
Fold. Goodwin No. 3A	8x14cm	122	FoldRo		Rapid Rectilinear	US8		Ilex Autom.			30
Folding Ansco No. 1	6x9cm	120	FoldRo	1925	Anastigmat	7.5		Ilex General	1/5-100		20
Folding Ansco No. 1A	2½x4¼"	116	FoldRo	1915	Anastigmat	7.5		Ilex			20
Folding Ansco No. 3	8x10.5cm	118	FoldRo	1914							20
Folding Ansco No. 3A	8x14cm	122	FoldRo	1914	Wollensak			Ilex		Mc64	30
Folding Ansco No. 3A	8x14cm	122	FoldRo	1914	Rapid Rectilinear			Bionic		Mc64	30
Folding Ansco No. 4	8x10.5cm	118	FoldRo	1905	Wollensak			Cyko Auto			30
Folding Ansco No. 5	4x5"	123	FoldRo	1907	Wollensak			Cyko Auto			30
Folding Ansco No. 6	8x10.5cm	118	FoldRo	1907	Wollensak	4				Mc65	30
Folding Ansco No. 7	8x14cm	122	FoldRo		Wollensak						40
Folding Ansco No. 9	8x14cm	122	FoldRo	1906	Wollensak			Cyko			50
Folding Ansco No. 10	8x14cm	122	FoldRo	1907				Ansco Automatic			50
Goodwin No. 2	6x9cm	120	RollBox	1930							10
Goodwin No. 2A	2½x4¼"	116	RollBox	1930	achromatic				I,T		10
Goodwin No. 3	8x10.5cm		RollBox	1930							10
Goodwin Jr. No. 1	6x9cm	120	StrutRo	1925							30
Juniorette No. 1	6x9cm	120	FoldRo	1923	Single Achromatic	8		Deltax			20
Karomat	24x36mm	35mm	35RF	1951	Xenon	2		Compur-Rap.		Mc65	100
Kiddie Camera	4x6.5cm	127	Box	1926						Mc65	30
Lancer	4x4cm	127	RigidRo	1959		8		2-speed			20
Lancer LG	4x4cm	127	RigidRo	1962		8					30
Memar	24x36mm	35mm	35VF	1954	Apotar	3.5	45mm	Pronto		Mc65	30
Memo (leather)	18x23mm	35mm	35VF	1927	Ilex Cinemat	6.3	40mm			Mc66	110
Memo (wood)	18x23mm	35mm	35VF	1927	Wollensak	6.3		Deltax	25-100		350
Memo Automatic	18x24mm	35mm	35Half	1963							130
Memo Boy Scout Mod.	18x23mm	35mm	35VF		Wollensak	6.3		Deltax	25-100		200
Panda	6x6cm	120	TLR-Box	1939	Meniscus	14			1/25		10
Pioneer PB-20	6x9cm	120	RigidRo	1947	Meniscus	14			1/25		20
Pioneer PD-16	6.5x11cm	116	RigidRo	1947	Meniscus	14			1/25	A3108	20
Readyset No. 1	6x9cm	120	FoldRo	1920	Meniscus	14			1/25		30
Readyset No. 1A	6.5x11cm	116	FoldRo	1920	Anastigmat				I,T		30
Readyset Eagle	6x9cm	120	FoldRo	1920							30
R.S. Royal 1 (ostrich)	6x9cm	120	FoldRo	1925						A1462	60
R.S. Royal 1 (silver fox)	6x9cm	112	FoldRo	1931						Mc66	70
R.S. Royal 1A (ostrich)	6.5x11cm	116	FoldRo	1925							60
R.S. Royal 1A (silver fox)	6.5x11cm	108	FoldRo	1931						Mc66	70
R.S. Special 1 (black)	6x9cm	120	FoldRo	1940	Achromat	14			I,T		30
R.S. Special 1 (brown)	6x9cm	120	FoldRo	1940	Achromat	14			I,T		40
R.S. Special 1A (black)	6.5x11cm	116	FoldRo	1940	Achromat	14			I,T		30
R.S. Special 1A (brown)	6.5x11cm	116	FoldRo	1940	Achromat	14			I,T		40
Rediflex	6x6cm	120	TLR-Box	1950							20
Regent	24x36mm	35mm	35VF	1950	Apotar	3.5		Prontor-SV	300		30

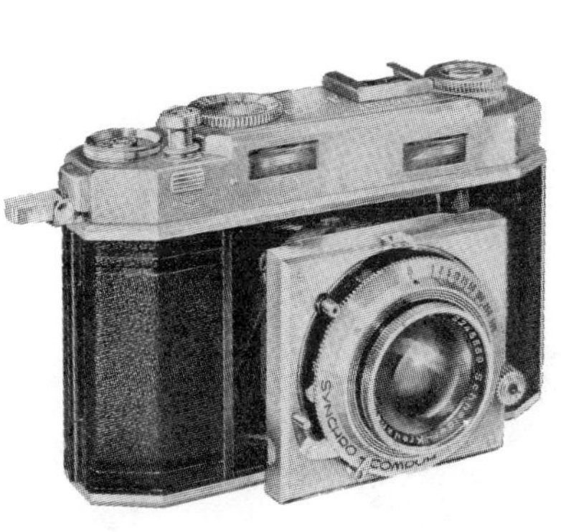

Karomat

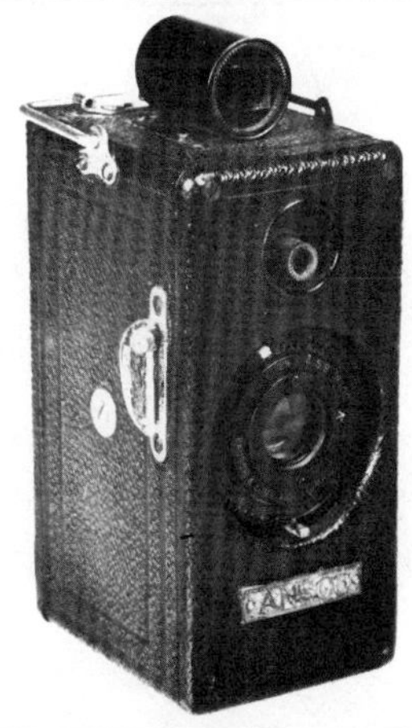

Memo (leathered)

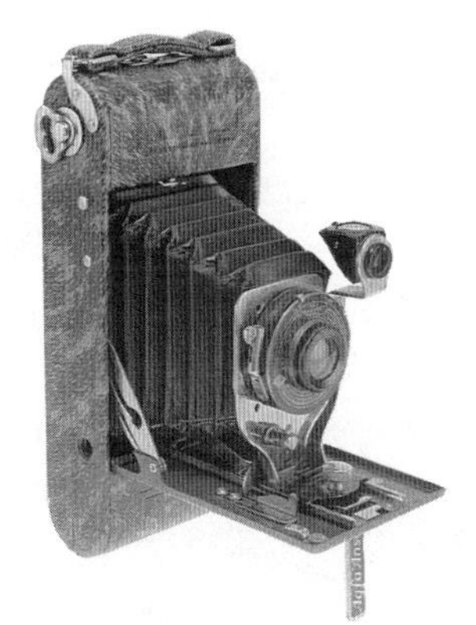

R.S. Royal 1 (silver fox)

MODEL	FORMAT	FILM	TYPE	Year	LENS	Apert	FL	SHUTTER	SPEEDS	ILLUS	U.S.$
Royal No. 1A	6.5x11cm	116	FoldRo	1925							60
Shur-Flash	6x9cm	120	RollBox	1953	Meniscus				I,T		10
Shur-Shot	6x9cm	120	RollBox	1948	Meniscus	14			1/25		10
Shur-Shot Jr.	6x9cm	120	RollBox	1948	Meniscus	14					10
Special Fold. Ansco No. 1			FoldRo	1924							20
Speedex 1A	6.5x11cm	116	HzFoldRo	1916	Anastigmat	6.3		Ilex Universal			30
Speedex 45	6x6cm	120	HzFoldRo	1946	Agnar	4.5		Vario			30
Speedex 6.3	6x6cm	120	HzFoldRo	1950	Anastigmat	6.3		Everset	1/100		20
Speedex Jr.	6x6cm	120	HzFoldRo	1945							20
Speedex Special	6x6cm	120	HzFoldRo	1946	Apotar	4.5		Prontor		Mc67	40
Speedex Special R	6x6cm	120	HzFoldRo	1953	Apotar	4.5	85mm	Prontor-SVS		Mc67	40
Studio	8x10"	plate	Studio	1947	various			various			180
Sundial		Roll	RollBox	1925							30
Super Memar	24x36mm	35mm	35RF	1956	Apotar	3.5	45mm	Prontor-SVS		Mc65	40
Super Memar LVS	24x36mm	35mm	35RF	1957	Solagon	2		S.-Comp. LVS		Mc65	50
Super Regent	24x36mm	35mm	35RF	1953	Solinar	3.5		Sync-Compur			90
Super Regent LVS	24x36mm	35mm	35RF	1955	Solinar	3.5		S.-Comp. LVS			90
Super Speedex	6x6cm	120	HzFoldRo	1953	Solinar	3.5	75mm	Synchro-Compur	1-500	Mc67	130
Titan	6x6cm	120	HzFoldRo	1949	Ansco Anastigmat	4.5	90mm		1/2-400		40
Vest Pocket No. 0	4x6.5cm	127	StrutRo	1916	Modico Anast.	7.5				Mc67	30
Vest Pocket No. 1	6x9cm	120	StrutRo	1915				Actus		Mc67	30
Vest Pocket No. 2	6x9cm	120	StrutRo	1915	Modico Anast.	7.5		Gammax		Mc67	50
Vest Pocket Junior	6x9cm	120	FoldRo	1919							30
Vest Pocket Mod. A			FoldRo		B&L Zeiss Tessar			Ansco			50
V.P. Readyset (black)	4x6.5cm	127	FoldRo	1925						Mc67	50
V.P. Readyset (colors)	4x6.5cm	127	FoldRo	1925						Mc67	70
V.P. Speedex No. 3	6x9cm	120	FoldRo	1916	Tessar	4.5		Acme Speedex		Mc68	30
V.P. Speedex No. 3	6x9cm	120	FoldRo	1916	Goerz-Celor	4.8		Acme Speedex		Mc68	30
V.P. Speedex No. 3	6x9cm	120	FoldRo	1916	Ansco Anastigmat	5		Acme Speedex		Mc68	30
V.P. Speedex No. 3	6x9cm	120	FoldRo	1916	Ansco Anastigmat	6.3		Acme Speedex		Mc68	30
V.P. Speedex No. 3	6x9cm	120	FoldRo	1916	Modico Anast.	7.5		Acme Speedex		Mc68	30
View	5x7"	plate	View		various			various			220
View	11x14"	plate	View		various			various			230
Viking (Billy Record)	6x9cm	620	FoldRo		Agnar	6.3		Pronto	200	Mc68	30
Viking (USA)	6x9cm	620	FoldRo	1946	Viking	6.3		Ansco	25-100	Mc68	30
Viking Readyset	6x9cm	120	FoldRo	1952	Isomat						30
...ANTHONY - New York											
Ascot Cycle No. 1	4x5"	plate	H&S	1899							110
Ascot Folding No. 25	4x5"	plate	H&S								110
Ascot Folding No. 29	4x5"	plate	H&S	1899							110
Ascot Folding No. 30	5x7"	plate	H&S							Mc68	110
Bijou	3¼x4¼"	plate	Tailboard	1887						Mc68	300

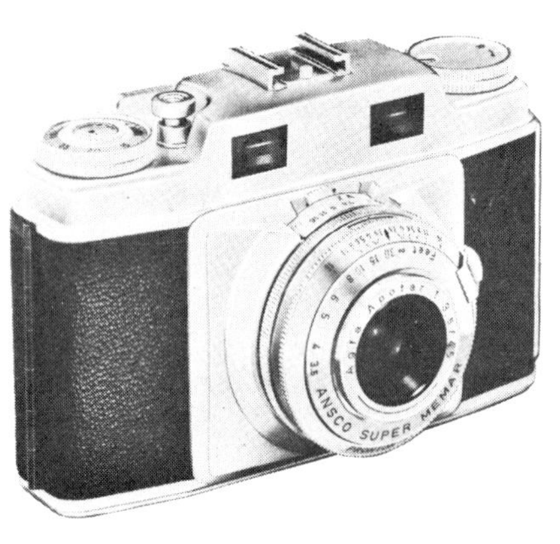

Super Memar

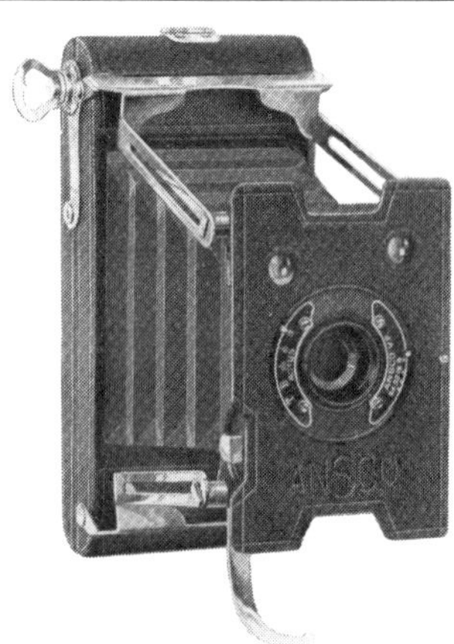

Vest Pocket No. 1

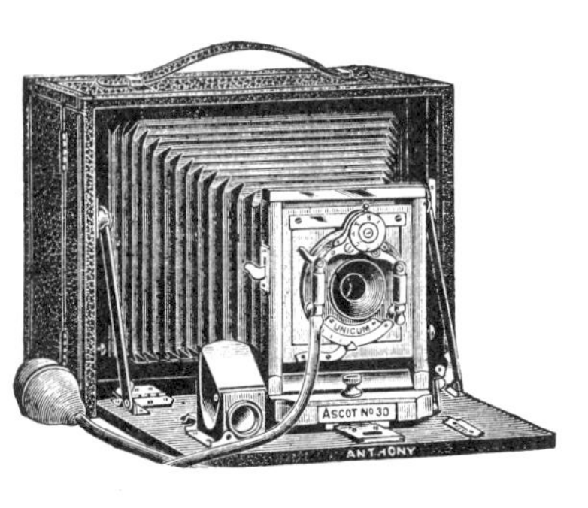

Ascot Folding No. 30

MODEL	FORMAT	FILM	TYPE	Year	LENS	Apert	FL	SHUTTER	SPEEDS	ILLUS	U.S.$
Box	3¼x4¼"	118	Box	1903							60
Box	4x5"	plate	Box	1903							60
Buckeye	3¼x4¼"	Roll	Box	1896						Mc68	70
Buckeye	4x5"	Roll	Box	1896						Mc68	70
Champion	4x5"	plate	Field	1890	Single Achromatic						280
Champion	8x10"	plate	Field	1890	Single Achromatic						280
Clifton	5x7"	plate	View	1901	various			various		Mc68	250
Clifton	8x10"	plate	View	1901	various			various		Mc68	250
Clifton	14x17"	plate	View	1901	various			various		Mc68	250
Climax Imperial	8x10"	plate	Studio	1885	various			various		Mc69	210
Climax Portrait	11x14"	plate	Studio	1888						Mc69	310
Climax Portrait	20x25"	plate	Studio	1888						Mc69	310
Climax Portrait	25x30"	plate	Studio	1888						Mc69	310
Duplex Novelette 4x5	4x5"	plate	Field	1885							370
Duplex Novelette 8x10	8x10"	plate	Field	1885							370
Duplex Novelette 11x14	11x14"	plate	Field	1885							370
Duplex Novelette Stereo	4x5"	plate	Field	1885						Mc69	510
Duplex Novelette Stereo	8x10"	plate	Field	1885						Mc69	510
Duplex Novelette Stereo	11x14"	plate	Field	1885						Mc69	510
Fairy	4x5"	plate	Field	1888	various					Mc69	290
Fairy	6½x8½"	plate	Field	1888	various					Mc69	290
Fairy	8x10"	plate	Field	1888	various					Mc69	290
Gem 4-tube CDV	8x10"	plate	MultiLens							A3223	4000
Gem Box	3¼x4¼"	plate	Box	1877							2900
Gem Box	6½x8½"	plate	Box	1877							2900
Klondike	3¼x4¼"	plate	Box	1898							90
Normandie	4x5"	plate	Field	1891	Darlot					Mc69	270
Normandie	8x10"	plate	Field	1891	Darlot					Mc69	270
Normandie	14x17"	plate	Field	1891	Darlot					Mc69	270
Novel 4x5	4x5"	plate	Field	1880				Prosch Dupl.		Mc69	270
Novel 5x7	5x7"	plate	Field	1880				Prosch Dupl.		Mc69	270
Novel 8x10	8x10"	plate	Field	1880				Prosch Dupl.		Mc69	270
Novel 11x14	11x14"	plate	Field	1880				Prosch Dupl.		Mc69	270
Novelette 4x5	4x5"	plate	Field	1885	Dallmeyer						380
Novelette 8x10	8x10"	plate	Field	1885	Achromat						380
Novelette 11x14	11x14"	plate	Field	1885							380
Novelette Stereo 4x5	4x5"	plate	Field	1885						Mc69	530
Novelette Stereo 8x10	8x10"	plate	Field	1885						Mc69	530
Novelette Stereo 11x14	11x14"	plate	Field	1885						Mc69	530
PDQ	4x5"	plate	DetectivBox	1890	Achromat				I,T	Mc69	800
Schmid's Pat. Detective	3¼x4¼"	plate	DetectivBox	1885	Rapid Rectilinear	8		rotary		Mc70	6200
Schmid's Pat. Detective	4x5"	plate	DetectivBox	1885	Rapid Rectilinear	8		rotary		Mc70	6200

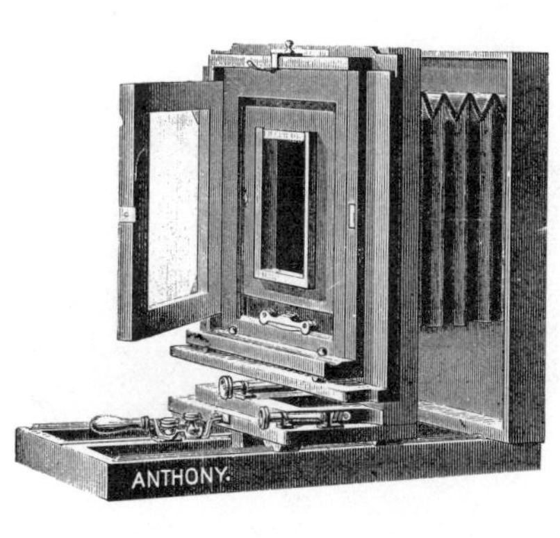

Climax Imperial

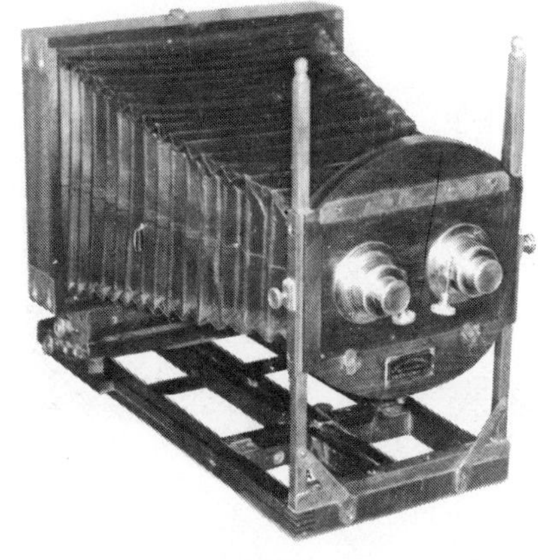

Novelette Stereo

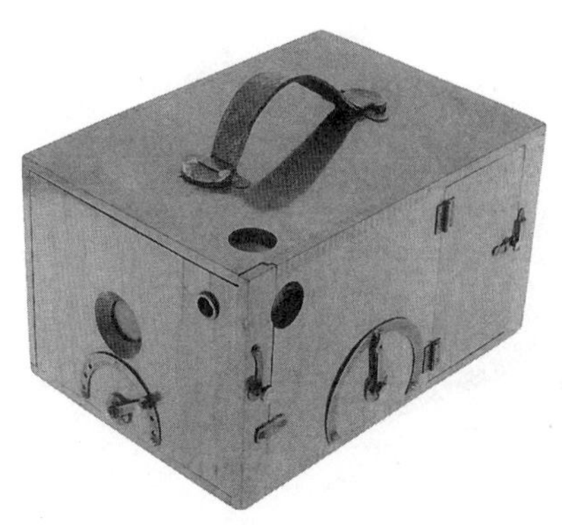

PDQ

MODEL	FORMAT	FILM	TYPE	Year	LENS	Apert	FL	SHUTTER	SPEEDS	ILLUS	U.S.$
Schmid's Pat. Detective	8x10"	plate	DetectivBox	1885	Rapid Rectilinear	8		rotary		Mc70	6200
Solograph	4x5"	plate	H&S	1901	various			various			140
Solograph	5x7"	plate	H&S	1901	various			various			140
Stereo Solograph	4¼x6½"	plate	SterFold	1901	Rapid Rectilinear			Duo		Mc70	560
Univ. Portr. & Ferrotype	3¼x4¼"	plate	MultiLens								1700
Univ. Portr. & Ferrotype	6½x8½"	plate	MultiLens								1700
Univ. Portr. & Ferrotype	8x10"	plate	MultiLens								1800
Victor	4x5"	plate	View	1891	Achromat			B&L			220
Victor	5x7"	plate	View	1891	Achromat			B&L			220
Victor	8x10"	plate	View	1891	Achromat			B&L			220
Victoria Four-Tube	5x7"	plate	Studio	1870						Mc70	1900
View	3¼x4¼"	plate	View		various			various			310
View	4¼x6½"	plate	View		various			various			310
View	6½x8½"	plate	View		various			various			310
View	18x22"	plate	View		various			various			310
...APM (Amalgamated Photographic Mfrs. Ltd.) - London											
Box	6x9cm	120	Box	1920					I		30
Box	6.5x11cm	116	Box	1920					I		30
Focal Plane Camera	9x12cm	plate	StrutPl		Kershaw Anast.	4.5	5.5"	focal plane			60
Rajar No. 6			BakFoldRo	1929						A3036	40
Reflex	6x9cm		MedSLR		Cooke Apem An.	4.5					100
Reflex	3¼x4¼"		MedSLR		Cooke Apem An.	4.5					100
...APPARATE & KAMERABAU - Friedrichshafen											
Akarelle	24x36mm	35mm	35VF	1954		2		Prontor		A2087	120
Akarelle	24x36mm	35mm	35VF	1954		3.5		Prontor			60
Akarelle Automatic S	24x36mm	35mm	35VF								70
Akarelle BW	24x36mm	35mm	35VF	1950	Wilon	2.8	50mm	Pronto			70
Akarelle V	24x36mm	35mm	35VF								30
Akarette 0	24x36mm	35mm	35VF	1949	Radionar	3.5	50mm			Mc71	100
Akarette I	24x36mm	35mm	35VF	1949	Radionar	3.5	50mm			Mc71	80
Akarette II	24x36mm	35mm	35VF	1949	Xenar	2.8	45mm			A1107	60
Akarette II	24x36mm	35mm	35VF	1949	Xenon	2	50mm				60
Akarex I	24x36mm	35mm	35RF	1953	Isco Westar	3.5	45mm	Pronto			70
Akarex III	24x36mm	35mm	35RF	1953	Xenon	2	50mm			A1108	120
Arette Ia	24x36mm	35mm	35VF	1955	Color Isconar	2.8		Prontor-SVS			40
Arette Ib	24x36mm	35mm	35VF	1955	Isconar	2.8	45mm	Prontor-SVS		A2090	40
Arette Ic	24x36mm	35mm	35RF	1957	Color Isconar	2.8		Prontor-SVS		Mc71	40
Arette Id	24x36mm	35mm	35RF	1957	Color Isconar	2.8		Prontor-SVS			40
Arette A	24x36mm	35mm	35VF	1955	Color Arettar	2.8		Pronto		A2089	40
Arette Bn	24x36mm	35mm	35VF	1958	Color Aretta	2.8		Pronto			50
Arette Bw	24x36mm	35mm	35VF	1958	Color Isconar	2.8		Prontor-SVS			50
Arette C	24x36mm	35mm	35RF	1958							40

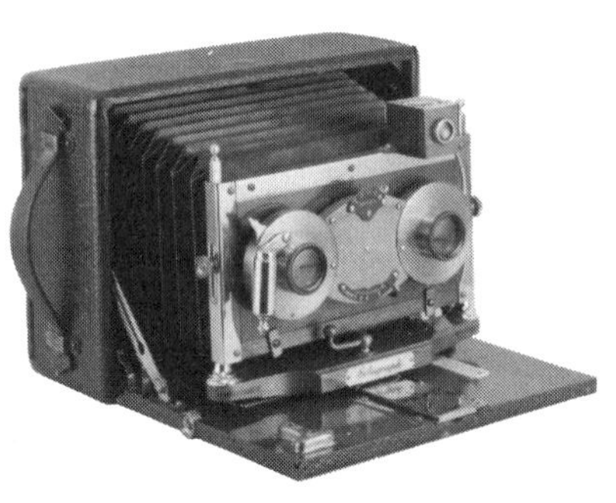

Stereo Solograph

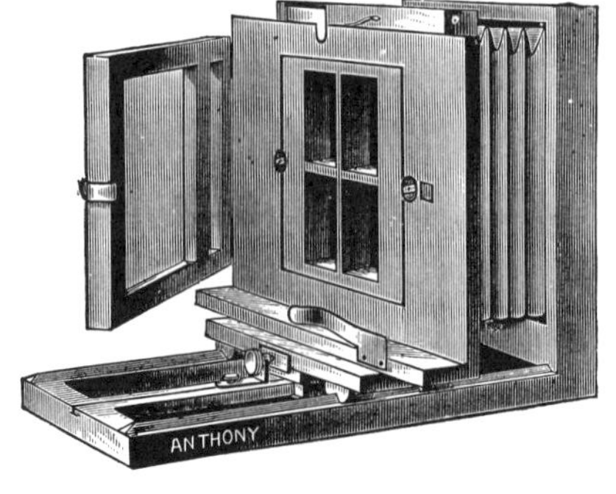

Victoria Four-Tube

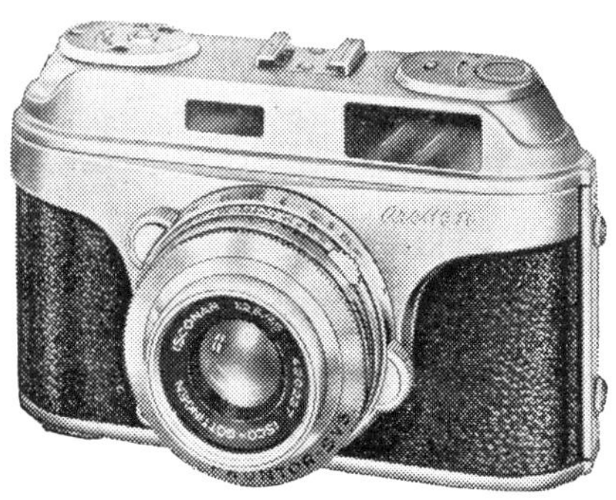

Arette Ic

MODEL	FORMAT	FILM	TYPE	Year	LENS	Apert	FL	SHUTTER	SPEEDS	ILLUS	U.S.$
Arette Dn	24x36mm	35mm	35RF	1958							40
Arette P	24x36mm	35mm	35VF	1958				Vario			40
Arette Automatic S	24x36mm	35mm	35VF	1959	Color-Westanar	2.8	45mm	Prontormat			50
Arette Automatic SE	24x36mm	35mm	35RF	1959	Color-Westanar	2.8	45mm	Prontor-SLK			50
Arette Automatic SLK	24x36mm	35mm	35VF	1959	Color-Westanar	2.8	45mm	Prontor-SLK			30
Optina IA	24x36mm	35mm	35VF	1957	Color Isconar	2.8				Mc71	70
...ARGUS INC. - Ann Arbor, Mich. & Chicago, IL USA											
A	28x28mm	126	35VF								10
A (black)	24x36mm	35mm	35VF	1936	Argus Anastigmat	4.5	50mm	Precise	25-200,B,T	Mc71	30
A (gold)	24x36mm	35mm	35VF	1936	Argus Anastigmat	4.5	50mm	Precise	25-200,B,T		140
A (gray)	24x36mm	35mm	35VF	1936	Argus Anastigmat	4.5	50mm	Precise	25-200,B,T		60
A (olive)	24x36mm	35mm	35VF	1936	Argus Anastigmat	4.5	50mm	Precise	25-200,B,T		60
A2	24x36mm	35mm	35VF	1939	Argus Anastigmat	4.5	50mm		25-200,B,T	Mc72	30
A2B	24x36mm	35mm	35VF	1939	Argus Anastigmat	4.5	50mm		25-200,B,T	Mc72	30
A2F	24x36mm	35mm	35VF	1939	Argus Anastigmat	4.5	50mm		25-200,B,T	Mc72	30
A3	24x36mm	35mm	35VF	1940	Argus Anastigmat	4	50mm		25-150,B,T	Mc72	30
A4	24x36mm	35mm	35VF	1953	Cintar	3.5	44mm				20
AA	24x36mm	35mm	35VF	1940		6.3			T,I		30
AF	24x36mm	35mm	35VF	1937	Argus Anastigmat	4.5	50mm		25-200,B,T	Mc72	30
Argoflash	24x36mm	35mm	35VF	1940		6.3			T,I		30
Argoflex 40	6x6cm	620	TLR-Box	1950						Mc72	20
Argoflex E	6x6cm	620	TLR	1940	Varex Anastigmat	4.5	75mm		200	Mc72	40
Argoflex EF	6x6cm	620	TLR	1948							40
Argoflex EM	6x6cm	620	TLR	1948							40
Argoflex Seventy-five	6x6cm	620	TLR-Box	1949							20
Argus 21	24x36mm	35mm	35VF	1947	Cintar	3.5	50mm			Mc72	40
Argus 75	6x6cm	620	TLR-Box	1958							10
Argus Seventy-five	6x6cm	620	TLR-Box	1949						A1743	20
Argus SLR	24x36mm	35mm	35SLR	1962	Mamiya-Sekor	1.7	58mm	focal plane	1-1000		70
Argus Super 75	6x6cm	620	TLR-Box	1954	Lumar	8	65mm				20
Autronic I	24x36mm	35mm	35RF	1960	Cintar	3.5	50mm		30-500	Mc72	30
Autronic 35	24x36mm	35mm	35RF	1960	Cintar	3.5	50mm		30-500	Mc72	20
Autronic C3	24x36mm	35mm	35RF	1960	Cintar	3.5	50mm		30-500	Mc72	20
B	24x36mm	35mm	35VF	1937	Argus Anastigmat	2.9	50mm	Prontor II		Mc72	50
C (black)	24x36mm	35mm	35RF	1938	Cintar	3.5	50mm	Micromatic	1/5-300	Mc72	50
C (olive)	24x36mm	35mm	35RF	1938	Cintar	3.5	50mm	Micromatic	1/5-300	Mc72	90
C2	24x36mm	35mm	35RF	1938	Cintar	3.5	50mm	Micromatic	1/5-300	Mc73	50
C3	24x36mm	35mm	35RF	1939	Cintar	3.5	50mm	Micromatic	1/5-300	Mc73	50
C3 Matchmatic	24x36mm	35mm	35RF	1958	Cintar	3.5	50mm		1/8-300	Mc73	50
C4	24x36mm	35mm	35RF	1951	Cintar	2.8	50mm			Mc73	40
C4R	24x36mm	35mm	35RF	1958	Cintar	2.8	50mm				90
C20	24x36mm	35mm	35RF	1956						Mc73	30

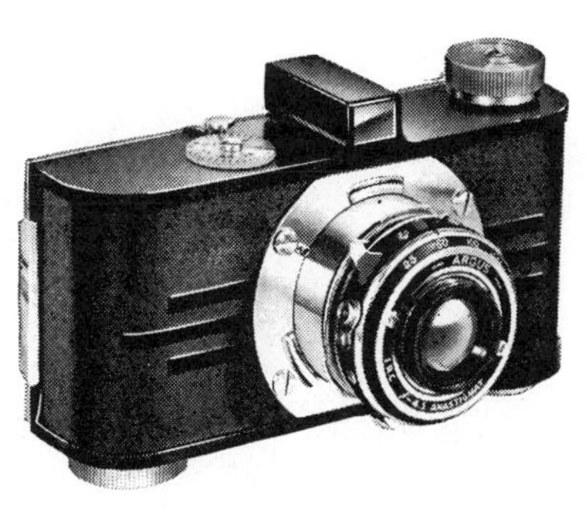

Argus A (black)

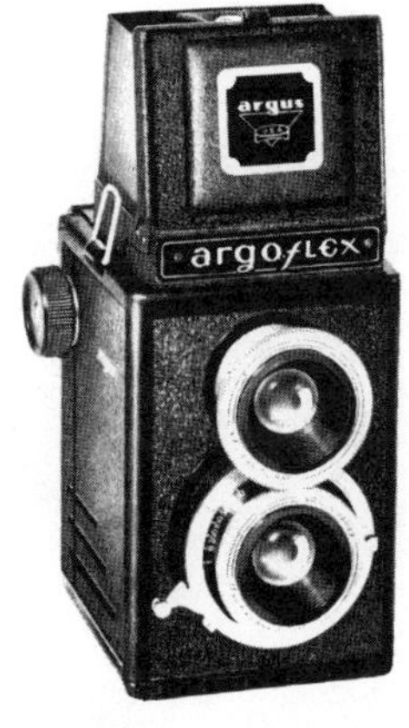

Argoflex E

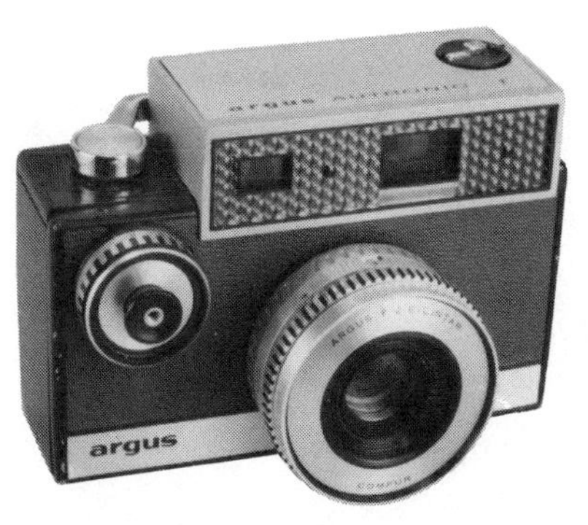

Autronic I

MODEL	FORMAT	FILM	TYPE	Year	LENS	Apert	FL	SHUTTER	SPEEDS	ILLUS	U.S.$
C33	24x36mm	35mm	35RF	1959	Cintar Bayonet	3.5	50mm		1-300		50
C44	24x36mm	35mm	35RF	1956	Cintagon	2.8	50mm			Mc73	70
C44R	24x36mm	35mm	35RF	1958	Cintagon	2.8	50mm				70
Camro 28	28x40mm	828	BakeliteRoll	1947	Lunar	9.7					30
CC (Colorcamera)	24x36mm	35mm	35VF	1941	Anastigmat	4	50mm	Self-cocking	1/25-150	Mc73	50
Delco 28	28x40mm	828	BakeliteRoll	1947	Lunar	9.7					30
FA	24x36mm	35mm	35VF	1950	Argus Anastigmat	4.5	50mm		25-150		30
Golden Shield	24x36mm	35mm	35RF	1958						Mc73	90
K	24x36mm	35mm	35VF	1939	Argus Anast.	4.5	50mm		1/200,B,T	Mc73	310
M	28x40mm	828	BakeliteRoll	1939	Anastigmat	6.3				Mc74	150
Markfinder	24x36mm	35mm	35VF	1947	Cintar	3.5	50mm			Mc72	40
Minca 28	28x40mm	828	BakeliteRoll	1947	Lunar	9.7				A1541	30
Mod. 19	24x36mm	35mm	BakeliteRoll	1947	Lunar	9.7					30
V-100	24x36mm	35mm	35RF	1958	Cintagon II	2	45mm	Sync-Compur	500,B	Mc74	30
V-100	24x36mm	35mm	35RF	1958	Cintar II	2.8	50mm	Sync-Compur	500,B	Mc74	30
...ARGUS/COSINA											
STL 1000	24x36mm	35mm	35SLR			1.8	50mm				60
...ARNOLD (Karl Arnold) - Marienberg											
Gee-Flex	4x4cm	127	TLR	1948	Victar	4.5	60mm				220
Karma-Flex 4x4 Mod. 1	4x4cm	127	MedSLR	1932	Laack Regulyt	4.5	60mm		25-100	Mc74	390
Karma-Flex 4x4 Mod. 2	4x4cm	127	TLR-Box	1932		11			M,Z	Mc74	700
Karma-Flex 6x6	6x6cm	120	TLR		Victar	3.5	75mm	focal plane	500	Mc74	800
Karma-Flex 6x6 Mod. 2	6x6cm	120	TLR		Victar	3.5	75mm	focal plane	25-500	A1572	900
Karma-Lux			TLR	1937		7.7			Z,15,50		1000
Karma-Sport	6x6cm	120	RigidRo	1935	Ludwig Victar	3.5	75mm	focal plane	25-500	Mc74	520
...ASAHI KOGAKU - Tokyo											
Asahiflex I	24x36mm	35mm	35SLR	1952	Takumar	3.5	50mm	focal plane	25-500	Mc75	370
Asahiflex Ia	24x36mm	35mm	35SLR	1953	Takumar	3.5	50mm	focal plane	25-500	Mc75	290
Asahiflex IIA	24x36mm	35mm	35SLR	1955				focal plane		Mc75	260
Asahiflex IIB (1954)	24x36mm	35mm	35SLR	1954	Takumar	2.4	58mm	focal plane	25-500	Mc75	290
Asahiflex IIB (1955)	24x36mm	35mm	35SLR	1955	Takumar	3.5	50mm	focal plane		Mc75	270
Honeyw. Pentax H1 body	24x36mm	35mm	35SLR	1960	body only	---	---		1-500		80
Honeyw. Pentax H1 + 55/2	24x36mm	35mm	35SLR	1960	Takumar	2	55mm		1-500	Mc76	100
Honeyw. Pentax H1a body	24x36mm	35mm	35SLR	1963	body only	---	---		1-500		70
Honeyw. Pentax H1a + 55/2	24x36mm	35mm	35SLR	1963	Super Takumar	2	55mm		1-500	Mc76	100
Honeyw. Pentax H2 body	24x36mm	35mm	35SLR	1959	body only	---	---		1-500		70
Honeyw. Pentax H2 + 55/2	24x36mm	35mm	35SLR	1959	Auto Takumar	2	55mm		1-500	Mc75	100
Honeyw. Pentax H3 body	24x36mm	35mm	35SLR	1960	body only	---	---		1-1000		70
Honeyw. Pentax H3 + 55/1.8	24x36mm	35mm	35SLR	1960	Auto Takumar	1.8	55mm		1-1000	Mc76	100
Pentax (original)	24x36mm	35mm	35SLR	1957	Takumar	2	55mm	focal plane		Mc75	240
Pentax 645 body	4.5x6cm		MedSLR	1984	body only	---	---				900
Pentax 645 + 75/2.8	4.5x6cm		MedSLR	1984	SMC Pentax-A	2.8	75mm			A3184	1300

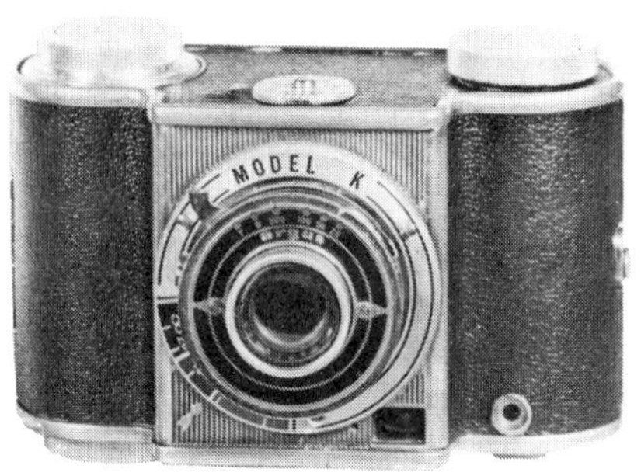

Argus K

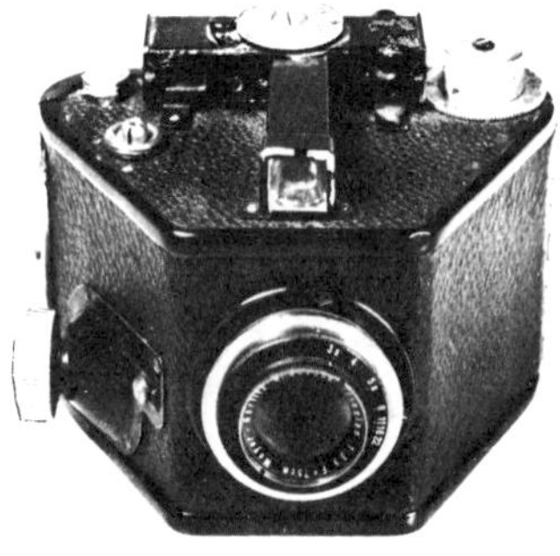
Karma-Sport

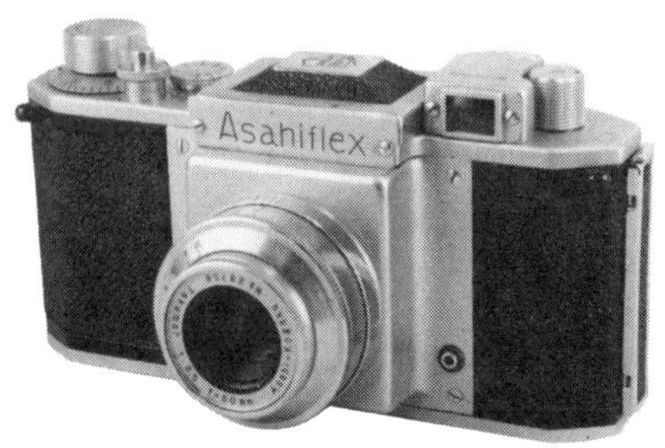

Asahiflex I

MODEL	FORMAT	FILM	TYPE	Year	LENS	Apert	FL	SHUTTER	SPEEDS	ILLUS	U.S.$
Pentax 6x7 (early) body	6x7cm	220	MedSLR	1969	body only	---	---	focal plane	1-1000		570
Pentax 6x7 (early) + 105/2.4	6x7cm	220	MedSLR	1969	SMC Takumar	2.4	105mm	focal plane	1-1000	A1631	900
Pentax 6x7 (mirror lock)	6x7cm	220	MedSLR	1976	body only	---	---	focal plane	1-1000		700
Pentax 6x7 + Prism	6x7cm	220	MedSLR	1976	body + prism	---	---	focal plane	1-1000		800
Pentax 6x7 + TTL	6x7cm	220	MedSLR	1976	body + TTL	---	---	focal plane	1-1000		1200
Pentax A3 (A3000) body	24x36mm	35mm	35SLR	1985	body only	---	---	MFC-E6			130
Pentax A3 (A3000) + 50/1.2	24x36mm	35mm	35SLR	1985	SMC Pentax-A	1.2	50mm	MFC-E6			310
Pentax Auto 110	13x17mm	110	110SLR	1979		2.8	24mm	Automatic TTL		Mc80	130
Pentax Auto 110 (clear)	13x17mm	110	110SLR	1979		2.8	24mm	Automatic TTL		Mc80	180
Pentax Auto 110 Super	13x17mm	110	110SLR	1982		2.8	24mm				190
Pentax Auto Sport	24x36mm	35mm	35AF	1988	autofocus	3.5	35mm	Program Electr.	1/30-1/250		60
Pentax ES body	24x36mm	35mm	35SLR	1971	body only	---	---	focal plane	8-1000		140
Pentax ES + 50/1.4	24x36mm	35mm	35SLR	1971	Takumar	1.4	50mm	focal plane	8-1000	Mc77	160
Pentax ESII body	24x36mm	35mm	35SLR	1973	body only	---	---	focal plane	8-1000		180
Pentax ESII + 50/1.4	24x36mm	35mm	35SLR	1973	Takumar	1.4	50mm	focal plane	8-1000	Mc77	210
Pentax Espio	24x36mm	35mm	35AFZ	1992	Power Zoom AF	4.3-8	35-70	Program Electr.	1.5-1/400		190
Pentax Espio 70	24x36mm	35mm	35AFZ	1994	Power Zoom	4.3-8	35-70	Program Electr.	1/5-1/400		140
Pentax Espio 80	24x36mm	35mm	35AFZ	1994	Power Zoom	4.1-8.7	35-80	Program Electr.	2-1/400		240
Pentax Espio 110	24x36mm	35mm	35AFZ	1994	Power Zoom AF		38-110	Program Electr.	1/5-1/400		230
Pentax Espio 115	24x36mm	35mm	35AFZ	1993	Power Zoom AF	4.0-8.5	38-115	Program Electr.	1/5-1/400		260
Pentax Espio 115 Date	24x36mm	35mm	35AFZ	1993	Power Zoom AF	4.0-8.5	38-115	Program Electr.	1/5-1/400		290
Pentax Espio 120	24x36mm	35mm	35AFZ	1994	Power Zoom AF	4.0-8.8	38-120	Program Electr.	1/5-1/400		270
Pentax Espio 140	24x36mm	35mm	35AFZ	1994	Power Zoom AF	4.1-10.	38-140	Program Electr.	2-1/400		270
Pentax Espio 928	24x36mm	35mm	35AFZ	1994	SMC Pent.-Zoom	3.5-9	28-90	Program Electr.	1/5-1/400		240
Pentax Espio Date	24x36mm	35mm	35AFZ	1992	Power Zoom AF	4.3-8	35-70	Program Electr.	1.5-1/400		210
Pentax Espio Jr.	24x36mm	35mm	35AFZ	1994	Power Zoom AF	4.3-6.7	35-60	Program Electr.	1/5-1/400		190
Pentax Espio mini	24x36mm	35mm	35CAF	1994	autofocus	3.5	32mm	Program	2-1/400		190
Pentax Espio W	24x36mm	35mm	35AFZ	1993	AF Zoom	4.5-8	28-56	Program Electr.	1/4-1/300		200
Pentax Espio W Date	24x36mm	35mm	35AFZ	1993	AF Zoom	4.5-8	28-56	Program Electr.	1/4-1/300		220
Pentax H3v body	24x36mm	35mm	35SLR	1963	body only	---	---		1-1000		100
Pentax H3v + 55/1.8	24x36mm	35mm	35SLR	1963	Super-Takumar	1.8	55mm		1-1000	Mc76	120
Pentax IQZoom	24x36mm	35mm	35AFZ	1988	AF Zoom	3.5-6.7	35-70	Program Electr.	1/40-1/250		180
Pentax IQZoom 60	24x36mm	35mm	35AFZ	1989	AF Zoom	4.5-6.7	38-60	electronic	1/30-1/250		120
Pentax IQZoom 60-X	24x36mm	35mm	35AFZ	1993	Power Zoom AF	4.5-6.7	38-60	Program Electr.	1/4-1/250		180
Pentax IQZoom 70	24x36mm	35mm	35AFZ	1988	Power Zoom AF	3.5-6.7	35-70	Program Electr.	1/5-1/250		180
Pentax IQZoom 90-WR	24x36mm	35mm	35AFZ	1992	AF Zoom	3.5-7.5	38-90	Program Electr.	1/5-1/400		230
Pentax IQZoom 90-WR D	24x36mm	35mm	35AFZ	1992	AF Zoom	3.5-7.5	38-90	Program Electr.	1/5-1/400		250
Pentax IQZoom 105 Sup.	24x36mm	35mm	35AFZ	1991	Power Zoom AF		38-105	Program Electr.	1/3-1/250		200
Pentax IQZoom 105-R	24x36mm	35mm	35AFZ	1993	Power Zoom AF		38-105	Program Electr.	1/3-1/250		300
Pentax IQZoom 110	24x36mm	35mm	35AFZ	1994	Power Zoom AF		38-110	Program Electr.	1/5-1/400		230
Pentax IQZoom 115	24x36mm	35mm	35AFZ	1993	Power Zoom AF	4.0-8.5	38-115	Program Electr.	1/5-1/400		260
Pentax IQZoom 115 Date	24x36mm	35mm	35AFZ	1993	Power Zoom AF	4.0-8.5	38-115	Program Electr.	1/5-1/400		290

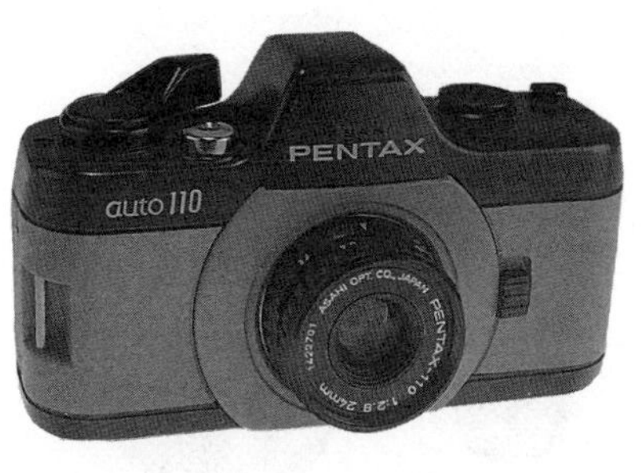

Pentax Auto 110 (brown)

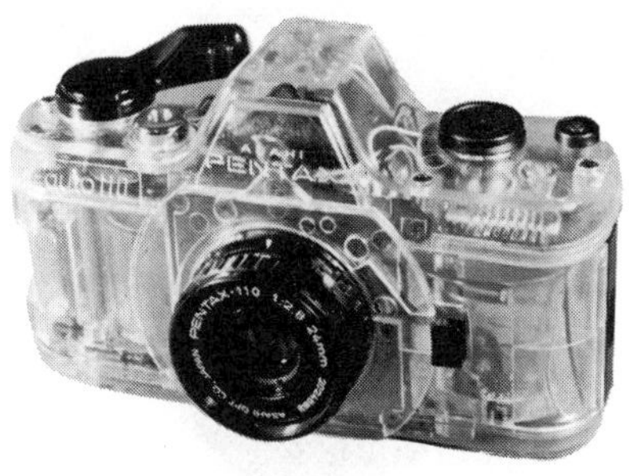
Pentax Auto 110 Super

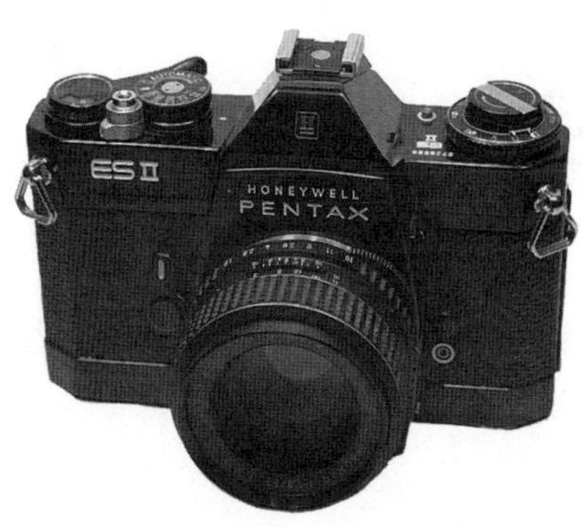

Pentax ESII

MODEL	FORMAT	FILM	TYPE	Year	LENS	Apert	FL	SHUTTER	SPEEDS	ILLUS	U.S.$
Pentax IQZoom 120	24x36mm	35mm	35AFZ	1994	Power Zoom AF	4.0-8.8	38-120	Program Electr.	1/5-1/400		270
Pentax IQZoom 140	24x36mm	35mm	35AFZ	1994	Power Zoom AF	4.1-10.	38-140	Program Electr.	2-1/400		270
Pentax IQZoom 700	24x36mm	35mm	35AFZ	1990	Zoom	3.5-6.7	35-70	Program Electr.	1/5-1/250		130
Pentax IQZoom 735	24x36mm	35mm	35AFZ	1994	Power Zoom	4.3-8	35-70	Program Electr.	1/5-1/400		140
Pentax IQZoom 835	24x36mm	35mm	35AFZ	1994	Power Zoom	4.1-8.7	35-80	Program Electr.	2-1/400		240
Pentax IQZoom 900	24x36mm	35mm	35AFZ	1990	Power Zoom AF	3.5-7.5	38-90	Program Electr.	1/5-1/250		180
Pentax IQZoom 928	24x36mm	35mm	35AFZ	1994	SMC Pent.-Zoom	3.5-9	28-90	Program Electr.	1/5-1/400		240
Pentax IQZoom Date	24x36mm	35mm	35AFZ	1988	AF Zoom	3.5-6.7	35-70	Program Electr.	1/40-1/250		360
Pentax K body	24x36mm	35mm	35SLR	1958	body only	---	---		1-1000		100
Pentax K + 55/1.8	24x36mm	35mm	35SLR	1958	Auto-Takumar	1.8	55mm		1-1000	Mc75	140
Pentax K2 body	24x36mm	35mm	35SLR	1973	body only	---	---	Titanium	8-1000		170
Pentax K2 + 50/1.4	24x36mm	35mm	35SLR	1973	SMC Pentax	1.4	50mm	Titanium	8-1000	Mc77	220
Pentax K2 DMD body	24x36mm	35mm	35SLR	1976	body only	---	---	Seiko FP	8-1000		460
Pentax K2 DMD + 50/1.2	24x36mm	35mm	35SLR	1976	SMC Pentax	1.2	50mm	Seiko FP	8-1000		560
Pentax K1000 body	24x36mm	35mm	35SLR	1977	body only	---	---	Cloth FP	1-1000		120
Pentax K1000 + 50/2	24x36mm	35mm	35SLR	1977	SMC Pentax-M	2	50mm	Cloth FP	1-1000	Mc77	160
Pentax K1000 SE body	24x36mm	35mm	35SLR	1979	body only	---	---		1-1000		120
Pentax K1000 SE + 50/2	24x36mm	35mm	35SLR	1979	SMC Pentax-M	2	50mm		1-1000	Mc77	140
Pentax KM body	24x36mm	35mm	35SLR	1973	body only	---	---		1-1000		120
Pentax KM + 50/1.4	24x36mm	35mm	35SLR	1973	SMC Pentax	1.4	50mm		1-1000	Mc77	180
Pentax KX body	24x36mm	35mm	35SLR	1973	body only	---	---		1-1000		180
Pentax KX + 50/1.4	24x36mm	35mm	35SLR	1973	SMC Pentax	1.4	50mm		1-1000	Mc77	230
Pentax LX body	24x36mm	35mm	35SLR	1980	body only	---	---	Titanium	1/75-2000		800
Pentax LX + 50/1.2	24x36mm	35mm	35SLR	1980	SMC Pentax-A	1.2	50mm	Titanium	1/75-2000	Mc78	800
Pentax ME body	24x36mm	35mm	35SLR	1976	body only	---	---	focal plane	8-1000		110
Pentax ME + 50/2	24x36mm	35mm	35SLR	1976	SMC Pentax-M	2	50mm	focal plane	8-1000		130
-- ME Super (black) body	24x36mm	35mm	35SLR	1979	body only	---	---	MFC-E2	4--2000		140
-- ME Super (black) + 50/2	24x36mm	35mm	35SLR	1979	SMC Pentax-A	2	50mm	MFC-E2	4--2000		310
-- ME Super (chrome) body	24x36mm	35mm	35SLR	1979	body only	---	---	MFC-E2	4--2000		140
-- ME Super (chrome)+ 50/2	24x36mm	35mm	35SLR	1979	SMC Pentax-A	2	50mm	MFC-E2	4--2000		270
Pentax ME-F body	24x36mm	35mm	35SLR	1977	body only	---	---	MFC-E2	4--2000		110
Pentax ME-F + 35-70	24x36mm	35mm	35SLR	1977	SMC Pentax-AF	2.8	35-70	MFC-E2	4--2000	Mc78	200
Pentax MG body	24x36mm	35mm	35SLR	1982	body only	---	---	Seiko FP	1-1000		70
Pentax MG + 50/1.4	24x36mm	35mm	35SLR	1982	SMC Pentax-M	1.4	50mm	Seiko FP	1-1000		160
Pentax Mini Sport 35	24x36mm	35mm	35VF	1988	fixed focus	3.6	35mm	Electr.	1/32-1/400		80
Pentax Mini Sport 35 II	24x36mm	35mm	35VF	1989	fixed focus	3.8	34mm	single speed	1/125		60
Pentax Mini Sport 35 AF	24x36mm	35mm	35AF	1989	autofocus	3.8	35mm	"	1/90-1/360		80
Pentax Mini Sport AFII	24x36mm	35mm	35AF	1990	autofocus	4.5	35mm	single speed	1/125		40
Pentax MV body	24x36mm	35mm	35SLR	1979	body only	---	---				100
Pentax MV + 50/1.7	24x36mm	35mm	35SLR	1979	SMC Pentax-M	1.7	50mm				120
Pentax MX body	24x36mm	35mm	35SLR	1977	body only	---	---	Cloth FP	1-1000		170
Pentax MX + 50/1.7	24x36mm	35mm	35SLR	1977	SMC Pentax-M	1.7	50mm	Cloth FP	1-1000	Mc78	200

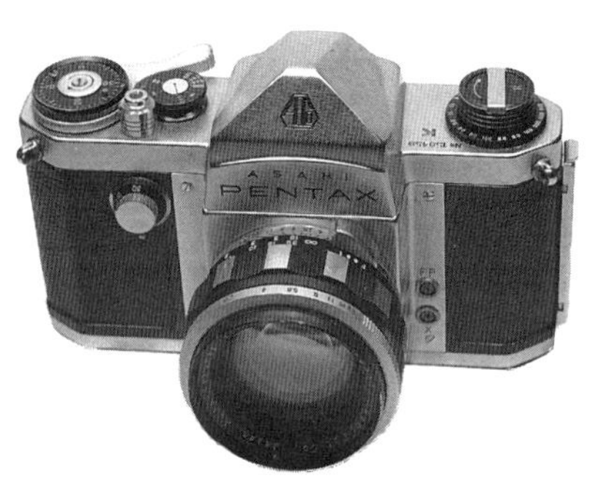

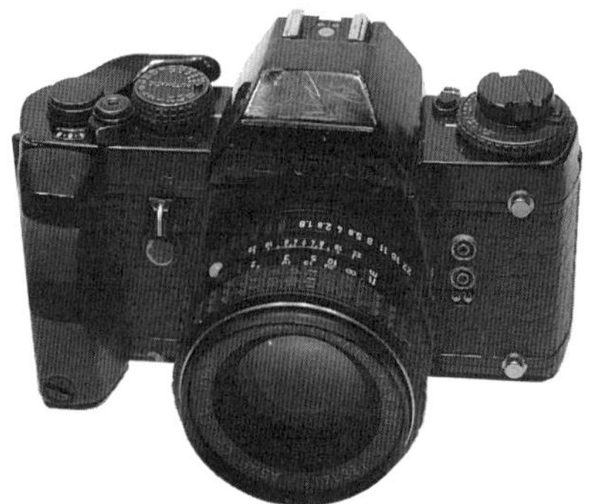

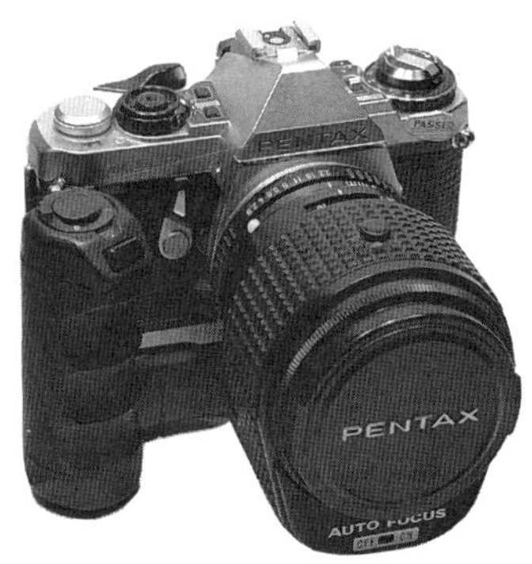

Pentax K **Pentax LX** **Pentax ME-F**

MODEL	FORMAT	FILM	TYPE	Year	LENS	Apert	FL	SHUTTER	SPEEDS	ILLUS	U.S.$
Pentax P30 (P3) body	24x36mm	35mm	35SLR	1985	body only	---	---	Seiko MFC-E7	B, 1-1000		110
Pentax P30 (P3) + 50/1.2	24x36mm	35mm	35SLR	1985	SMC Pentax-A	1.2	50mm	Seiko MFC-E7	B, 1-1000		300
Pentax P30T body	24x36mm	35mm	35SLR	1991	body only	---	---	electronic	B, 1-1000		150
Pentax P30T + 28-80	24x36mm	35mm	35SLR	1991	SMC Pentax-A	3.5-4.5	28-80	electronic	B, 1-1000		270
Pentax P50 (P5) body	24x36mm	35mm	35SLR	1987	body only	---	---	Metal FP	B, 1-1000		150
Pentax P50 (P5) + 50/1.2	24x36mm	35mm	35SLR	1987	SMC Pentax-A	1.2	50mm	Metal FP	B, 1-1000		350
Pentax PC-35 AF	24x36mm	35mm	35AF	1983	Pentax	2.8	35mm	Program Electr.	1/8-1/430		50
Pentax PC-35 AF Date	24x36mm	35mm	35AF	1983	Pentax	2.8	35mm	Program Electr.	1/8-1/430		60
Pentax PC-35 AF-M	24x36mm	35mm	35AF	1984	autofocus	2.8	35mm	Program Electr.	1/8-1/430		120
Pentax PC-35 AF-M Date	24x36mm	35mm	35AF	1984	autofocus	2.8	35mm	Program Electr.	1/8-1/430		120
Pentax PC-35R	24x36mm	35mm	35VF	1989	fixed focus	3.8	34mm	simple	1/125		40
Pentax PC-100	24x36mm	35mm	35VF	1995	fixed focus	4.5	35mm	simple	1/125		30
Pentax PC-300	24x36mm	35mm	35VF	1995	fixed focus	4.5	35mm	Program	1/45-1/250		50
Pentax PC-303	24x36mm	35mm	35AF	1990	autofocus	4.5	35mm	simple	1/125		40
Pentax PC-313	24x36mm	35mm	35AF	1992	autofocus	4.5	35mm	simple	1/125		40
Pentax PC-333	24x36mm	35mm	35AF	1988	autofocus	3.5	35mm	Program Electr.	1/30-1/250		60
Pentax PC-333 Date	24x36mm	35mm	35AF	1988	autofocus	3.5	35mm	Program Electr.	1/30-1/250		70
Pentax PC-500	24x36mm	35mm	35AF	1994	autofocus	4.5	35mm	Program	1/45-1/250		60
Pentax PC-505	24x36mm	35mm	35AF	1990	autofocus	3.8	35mm	Program Electr.	50-300		90
Pentax PC-505 Date	24x36mm	35mm	35AF	1990	autofocus	3.8	35mm	Program Electr.	50-300		100
Pentax PC-555	24x36mm	35mm	35AF	1988	autofocus	2.8	35mm	Program Electr.	1/30-1/250		140
Pentax PC-555 Date	24x36mm	35mm	35AF	1988	autofocus	2.8	35mm	Program Electr.	1/30-1/250		220
Pentax PC-606 W	24x36mm	35mm	35AW-AF	1992	autofocus	4.5	35mm	Program Electr.	1/45-1/250		70
Pentax PC-700	24x36mm	35mm	35AW-AF	1994	autofocus	4.5	35mm	Program	1/45-1/250		100
Pentax PC-700 Data	24x36mm	35mm	35AW-AF	1994	autofocus	4.5	35mm	Program	1/45-1/250		130
Pentax Pino 35	24x36mm	35mm	35VF	1984	fixed focus	3.8	38mm	simple	1/125		50
Pentax Pino 35E	24x36mm	35mm	35VF	1988	fixed focus	3.6	35mm	Electr.	1/32-1/400		80
Pentax Pino 35J	24x36mm	35mm	35VF	1989	fixed focus	3.8	34mm	simple	1/125		60
Pentax Pino AF	24x36mm	35mm	35AF	1989	autofocus	3.8	35mm	"	1/90-1/360		80
Pentax Pino J	24x36mm	35mm	35VF	1989	fixed focus	3.8	34mm	simple	1/125		40
Pentax Program A body	24x36mm	35mm	35SLR	1983	body only	---	---	MFC-E5	15-1/1000		170
Pentax Prog. A + 50/1.2	24x36mm	35mm	35SLR	1983	SMC Pentax-A	1.2	50mm	MFC-E5	15-1/1000		370
Pentax Prog. Plus body	24x36mm	35mm	35SLR	1983	body only	---	---	MFC-E5	15-1/1000		170
Pentax Prog. Plus + 50/1.2	24x36mm	35mm	35SLR	1983	SMC Pentax-A	1.2	50mm	MFC-E5	15-1/1000		370
Pentax S body	24x36mm	35mm	35SLR	1957	body only	---	---		1-500		70
Pentax S + 55/1.8	24x36mm	35mm	35SLR	1957	Takumar	1.8	55mm		1-500	Mc75	140
Pentax S1 body	24x36mm	35mm	35SLR	1960	body only	---	---		1-500		80
Pentax S1 + 55/2	24x36mm	35mm	35SLR	1960	Takumar	2	55mm		1-500	Mc76	100
Pentax S1a body	24x36mm	35mm	35SLR	1963	body only	---	---		1-500		70
Pentax S1a + 55/2	24x36mm	35mm	35SLR	1963	Super Takumar	2	55mm		1-500	Mc76	100
Pentax S2 body	24x36mm	35mm	35SLR	1959	body only	---	---		1-500		70
Pentax S2 + 55/2	24x36mm	35mm	35SLR	1959	Auto Takumar	2	55mm		1-500	Mc75	100

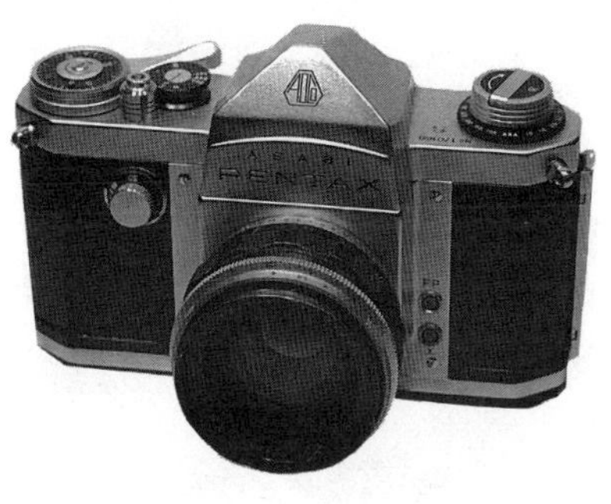

Pentax S

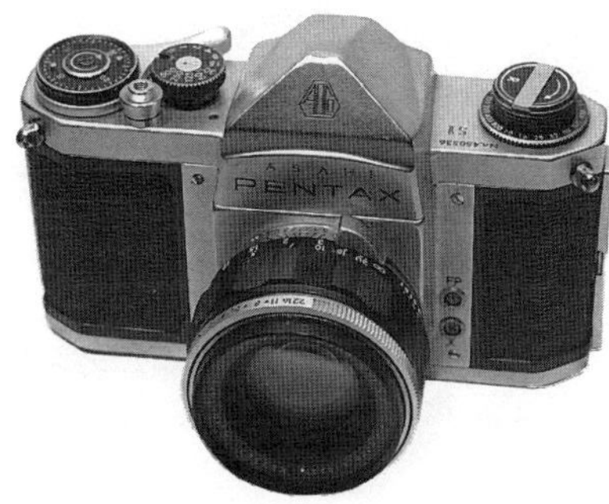

Pentax S1

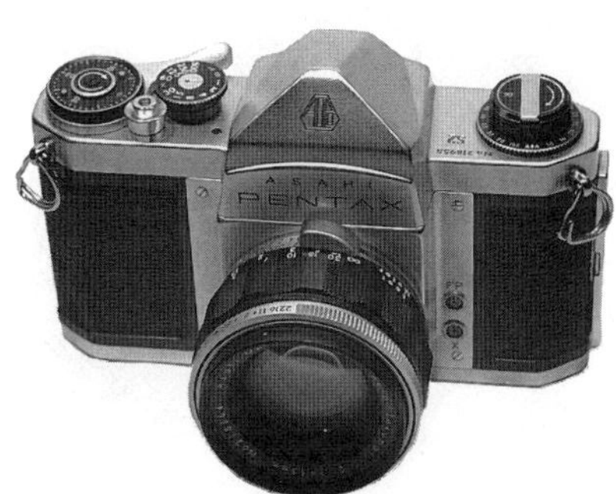

Pentax S2

MODEL	FORMAT	FILM	TYPE	Year	LENS	Apert	FL	SHUTTER	SPEEDS	ILLUS	U.S.$
Pentax S3 body	24x36mm	35mm	35SLR	1960	body only	---	---		1-1000		70
Pentax S3 + 55/2	24x36mm	35mm	35SLR	1960	Super Takumar	2	55mm		1-1000	Mc76	110
---SF7 (SF10) body	24x36mm	35mm	35AFSLR	1988	body only	---	---	electronic	B, 1-2000		170
---SF7 (SF10) + 28-80	24x36mm	35mm	35AFSLR	1988	SMC Pentax-F	3.5-4.5	28-80	electronic	B, 1-2000		270
---SFX (SF-1) body	24x36mm	35mm	35AFSLR	1988	body only	---	---	ElecFP	30-2000		240
---SFX (SF-1) + 50/1.4	24x36mm	35mm	35AFSLR	1988	Pentax-F	1.4	50mm	ElecFP	30-2000		320
---SFXN (SF1N) body	24x36mm	35mm	35AFSLR	1989	body only	---	---	electronic	B, 1-4000		200
---SFXN (SF1N) + 28-80	24x36mm	35mm	35AFSLR	1989	SMC Pentax-F	3.5-4.5	28-80	electronic	B, 1-4000		320
---Spotmatic (SP) body	24x36mm	35mm	35SLR	1964	body only	---	---	focal plane	1-1000		110
---Spotmatic (SP) + 55/1.8	24x36mm	35mm	35SLR	1964	Super Takumar	1.8	55mm	focal plane	1-1000	Mc76	150
---Spotmatic II body	24x36mm	35mm	35SLR	1971	body only	---	---	focal plane			130
---Spotmatic II + 55/1.8	24x36mm	35mm	35SLR	1971	SMC Takumar	1.8	55mm	focal plane		Mc76	170
---Spotmatic IIa body	24x36mm	35mm	35SLR	1972	body only	---	---	focal plane			110
---Spotmatic IIa + 55/1.8	24x36mm	35mm	35SLR	1972	SMC Takumar	1.8	55mm	focal plane		Mc77	140
---Spotmatic 500 body	24x36mm	35mm	35SLR	1971	body only	---	---	focal plane	1-500		100
---Spotmatic 500 + 55/1.8	24x36mm	35mm	35SLR	1971	Super Takumar	1.8	55mm	focal plane	1-500	Mc76	140
---Spotmatic 1000 body	24x36mm	35mm	35SLR	1970	body only	---	---	focal plane	1-1000		110
---Spotmatic 1000 + 55/1.8	24x36mm	35mm	35SLR	1970	Super Takumar	1.8	55mm	focal plane	1-1000	Mc77	160
---Spotmatic F body	24x36mm	35mm	35SLR	1972	body only	---	---	focal plane	1-1000		150
---Spotmatic F + 50/1.4	24x36mm	35mm	35SLR	1972	SMC Takumar	1.4	50mm	focal plane	1-1000	Mc77	210
---Spotmatic MD body	24x36mm	35mm	35SLR	1967	body only	---	---	focal plane	1-1000		310
---Spotmatic MD + 55/1.8	24x36mm	35mm	35SLR	1967	Super Takumar	1.8	55mm	focal plane	1-1000		360
Pentax Super A body	24x36mm	35mm	35SLR	1983	body only	---	---	MFC-E3	15-1/2000		200
Pentax Super A + 50/1.2	24x36mm	35mm	35SLR	1983	SMC Pentax-A	1.2	50mm	MFC-E3	15-1/2000		410
Pentax Super Prog. body	24x36mm	35mm	35SLR	1983	body only	---	---	MFC-E3	15-1/2000		200
Pentax Super Prog.+ 50/1.2	24x36mm	35mm	35SLR	1983	SMC Pentax-A	1.2	50mm	MFC-E3	15-1/2000		410
Pentax Super Sport 35	24x36mm	35mm	35AF	1984	autofocus	2.8	35mm	Program Electr.	1/8-1/430		120
Pentax SV body	24x36mm	35mm	35SLR	1963	body only	---	---		1-1000		80
Pentax SV + 55/1.8	24x36mm	35mm	35SLR	1963	Super-Takumar	1.8	55mm		1-1000	Mc76	100
Pentax Ultra Sport	24x36mm	35mm	35AF	1988	autofocus	2.8	35mm	Program Electr.	1/30-1/250		140
Pentax (P)Z-1 body	24x36mm	35mm	35AFSLR	1991	body only	---	---	electronic	B,30-8000		460
Pentax (P)Z-1 + 28-80	24x36mm	35mm	35AFSLR	1991	Pentax-FA Zoom	3.5-4.7	28-80	electronic	B,30-8000		640
Pentax (P)Z-1P body	24x36mm	35mm	35AFSLR	1995	body only	---	---	electronic	B,30-8000		630
Pentax (P)Z-1P + 50/1.4	24x36mm	35mm	35AFSLR	1995	SMC Pentax-FA	1.4	50mm	electronic	B,30-8000		680
Pentax (P)Z-10 body	24x36mm	35mm	35AFSLR	1991	body only	---	---	electronic	30-2000		220
Pentax (P)Z-10 + 28-80	24x36mm	35mm	35AFSLR	1991	Pentax-FA Zoom	3.5-4.5	28-80	electronic	30-2000		350
Pentax (P)Z-20 body	24x36mm	35mm	35AFSLR	1993	body only	---	---	electronic	30-2000		290
Pentax (P)Z-20 + 28-80	24x36mm	35mm	35AFSLR	1993	Pentax-FA Zoom	3.5-4.5	28-80	electronic	30-2000		400
Pentax Z-50P	24x36mm	35mm	35AFSLR	1993	AF	1.4	50mm	electronic	30-1/2000		420
Pentax Zoom 60	24x36mm	35mm	35AFZ	1989	AF Zoom	4.5-6.7	38-60	electronic	1/30-1/250		120
Pentax Zoom 60 Date	24x36mm	35mm	35AFZ	1989	AF Zoom	4.5-6.7	38-60	electronic	1/30-1/250		120
Pentax Zoom 60-X	24x36mm	35mm	35AFZ	1993	Power Zoom AF	4.5-6.7	38-60	Program Electr.	1/4-1/250		180

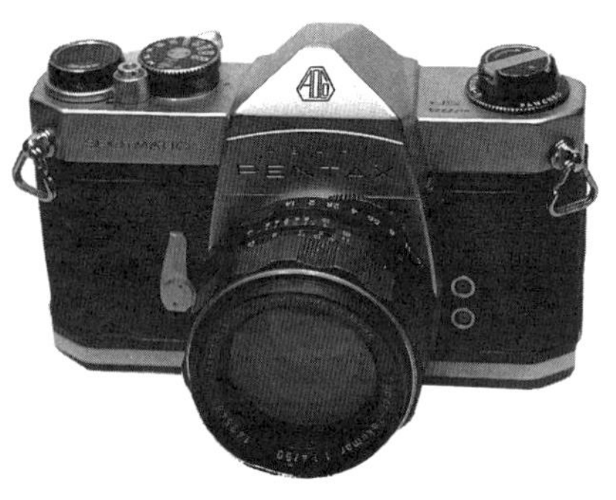

Pentax Spotmatic (SP)

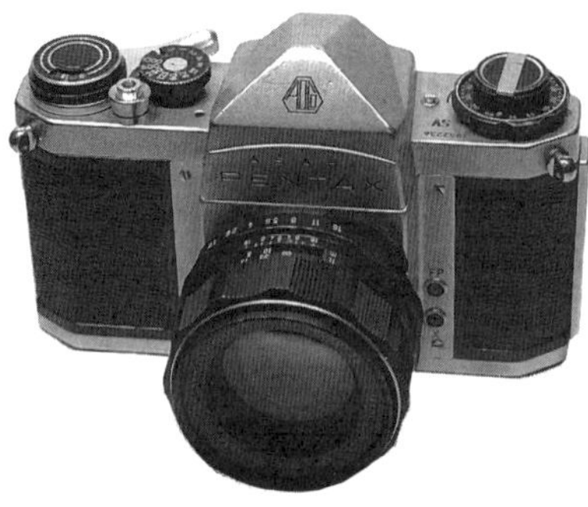

Pentax SV

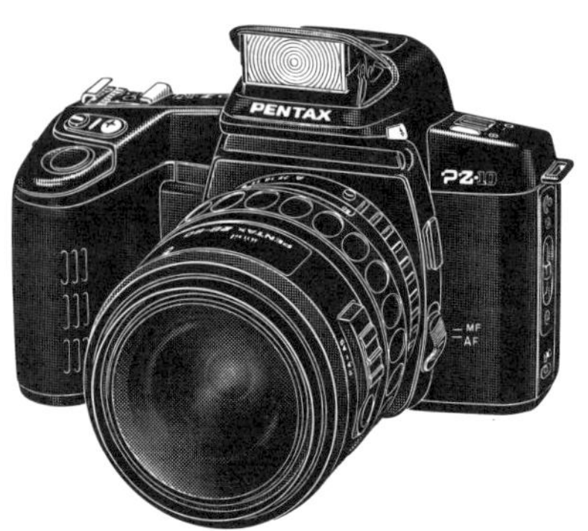

Pentax Z-10 (PZ-10)

MODEL	FORMAT	FILM	TYPE	Year	LENS	Apert	FL	SHUTTER	SPEEDS	ILLUS	U.S.$
Pentax Zoom 70	24x36mm	35mm	35AFZ	1988	AF Zoom	3.5-6.7	35-70	Program Electr.	1/40-1/250		180
Pentax Zoom 70 Date	24x36mm	35mm	35AFZ	1988	AF Zoom	3.5-6.7	35-70	Program Electr.	1/40-1/250		360
Pentax Zoom 70S	24x36mm	35mm	35AFZ	1988	Power Zoom AF	3.5-6.7	35-70	Program Electr.	1/5-1/250		180
Pentax Zoom 70S Date	24x36mm	35mm	35AFZ	1988	Power Zoom AF	3.5-6.7	35-70	Program Electr.	1/5-1/250		190
Pentax Zoom 70-X	24x36mm	35mm	35AFZ	1990	Zoom	3.5-6.7	35-70	Program Electr.	1/5-1/250		130
Pentax Zoom 90	24x36mm	35mm	35AFZ	1990	Power Zoom AF	3.5-7.5	38-90	Program Electr.	1/5-1/250		180
Pentax Zoom 90-WR	24x36mm	35mm	35AFZ	1992	AF Zoom	3.5-7.5	38-90	Program Electr.	1/5-1/400		230
Pentax Zoom 90-WR Date	24x36mm	35mm	35AFZ	1992	AF Zoom	3.5-7.5	38-90	Program Electr.	1/5-1/400		250
Pentax Zoom 105 Super	24x36mm	35mm	35AFZ	1991	Power Zoom AF		38-105	Program Electr.	1/3-1/250		200
Pentax Zoom 105-R	24x36mm	35mm	35AFZ	1993	Power Zoom AF		38-105	Program Electr.	1/3-1/250		300
Pentax Zoom 280-P	24x36mm	35mm	35AFZ	1992	AF Zoom	3.5-8	28-80	Program Electr.	1/5-1/400		220
...ASAHI OPTICAL WORKS - Japan											
Super Olympic Mod. D	24x36mm	35mm	35VF	1936	Ukas	4.5	50mm			Mc80	90
...ATAK - Czechoslovakia											
Inka	6x6cm		TLR						1/25, 1/75	Mc81	50
...BALDA-WERK - Dresden											
Balda Box	6x9cm	120	RollBox	1930	Meniscus						30
Balda C35	24x36mm	35mm	35Fold	1982						A3499	100
Balda CE35	24x36mm	35mm	35mm	1983	Baldamon	2.8	35mm	programmed			80
Balda Compact CLS	28x28mm	126	126VF	1981	Isconar	5.6	35mm			A3353	40
Balda-Kamera Nr. 1	9x12cm	plate	FoldPl	1925							50
Balda-Kamera Nr. 2	10x15cm	plate	FoldPl	1925							50
Balda-Kamera Nr. 3	9x12cm	plate	FoldPl	1925							50
Balda-Kamera Nr. 4	9x12cm	plate	FoldPl	1925							50
Baldafix	6x9cm	120	FoldRo		Enar	4.5	105mm	Prontor			50
Baldak-Box	6x9cm	120	RollBox	1938							30
Baldalette	24x36mm	35mm	35VF	1950	Schn. Radionar	2.9	50mm	Pronto			80
Baldalux	6x9cm	120	FoldRo	1952	Radionar	4.5		Prontor-SV			50
Baldamatic I	24x36mm	35mm	35RF	1959	Xenar	2.8	45mm	Sync-Compur			50
Baldamatic II	24x36mm	35mm	35RF	1960							50
Baldamatic III	24x36mm	35mm	35RF	1960							100
Baldarette	5x8cm	Roll	FoldRo	1929	Meyer Trioplan	6.8		Pronto			60
Baldax (postwar)	6x6cm	120	FoldRo	1954	Ennagon	3.5	7.5cm	Prontor-SV			40
Baldax 6x6	6x6cm	120	FoldRo	1935	Trioplan	2.9	75mm	Compur			70
Baldax 6x6	6x6cm	120	FoldRo	1935	Trioplan	2.9	75mm	Compur-Rap.			70
Baldax V.P.	4.5x6cm	120	FoldRo	1930	various	2.8					50
Baldaxette Mod. I	4.5x6cm	120	FoldRo	1936	Meyer Trioplan	2.9	75mm	Compur		A475	120
Baldaxette Mod. II	6x6cm	120	FoldRo	1936	Zeiss Tessar	2.8	80mm	Compur-Rap.			130
Baldessa	24x36mm	35mm	35VF	1957	Color Isconar	2.8	45mm	Prontor-SVS			30
Baldessa I	24x36mm	35mm	35VF	1957	Westanar	2.8	45mm	Vario			30
Baldessa Ia	24x36mm	35mm	35VF		Baldanar	2.8	45mm	Prontor-SVS			40
Baldessa Ib	24x36mm	35mm	35RF	1958	Isco	2.8	45mm			Mc83	40

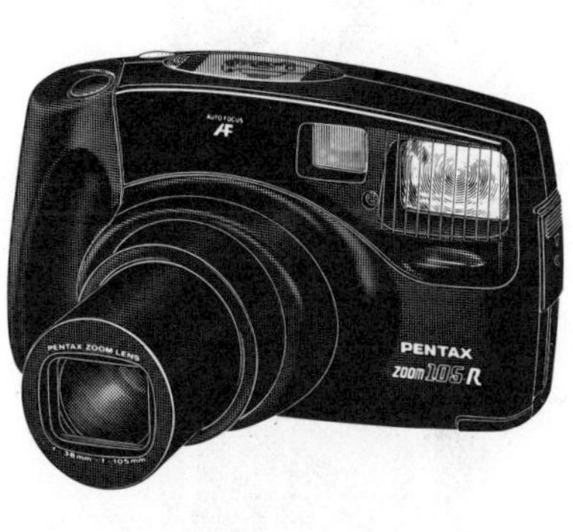

Pentax Zoom 105-R

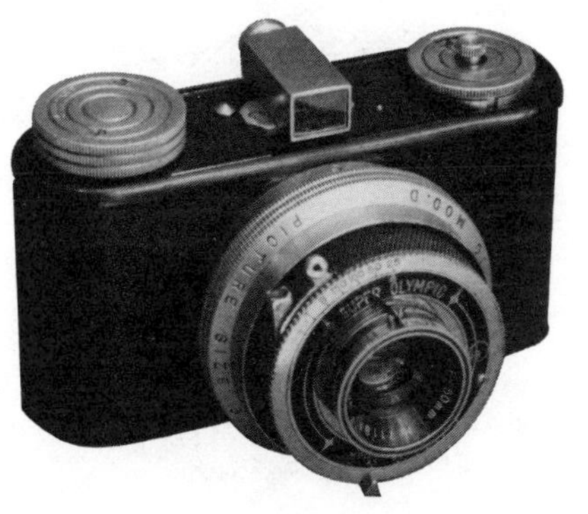

Super Olympic Mod. D

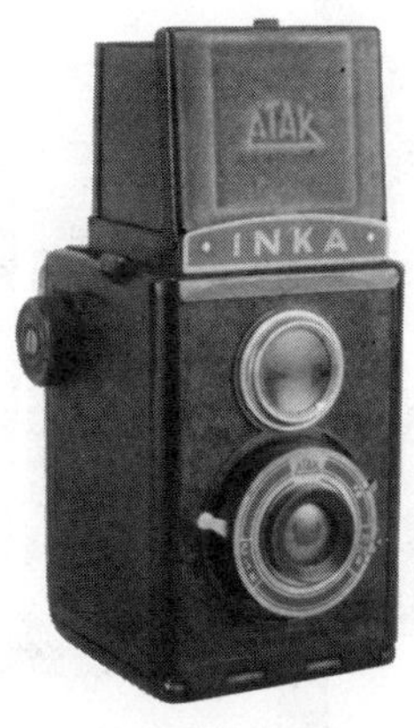

Inka

MODEL	FORMAT	FILM	TYPE	Year	LENS	Apert	FL	SHUTTER	SPEEDS	ILLUS	U.S.$
Baldessa F	24x36mm	35mm	35VF	1964							20
Baldessa LF	24x36mm	35mm	35VF	1965	Color Isconar	2.8	45mm	Prontor			30
Baldessa RF	24x36mm	35mm	35RF		Color Isconar	2.8	45mm	Prontor-SVS	1-500		30
Baldessamat	24x36mm	35mm	35VF	1960	Color Baldanar	2.8	45mm	Prontormat			30
Baldessamat F	24x36mm	35mm	35VF	1963	Baldanar	2.8	45mm	Prontor-Lux	1/30-500		30
Baldessamat RF	24x36mm	35mm	35RF	1963	Baldanar	2.8	45mm	Prontor-Lux	1/30-500		30
Baldi	3x4cm	127	FoldRo	1930	Trioplan	2.9	50mm			Mc83	60
Baldina	24x36mm	35mm	35Fold	1930	Baldanar	3.5	50mm	Prontor-S		A2052	90
Baldina (postwar)	24x36mm	35mm	35VF	1954	Xenar	2.8	50mm	Prontor-SVS			50
Baldinette	24x36mm	35mm	35Fold	1951			50mm			Mc83	60
Baldini	24x36mm	35mm	35Fold	1950							50
Baldix	6x6cm	120	FoldRo	1952	Baltar	2.9	75mm	Prontor-SV		Mc83	50
Baldixette	6x6cm	120	TelescRo	1950	Baldar	9	72mm		B,M		30
Beewee-Kamera	9x12cm	plate	FoldPl	1925	Spezial Aplanat	8		Vario			30
Central 35	24x36mm	35mm	35Fold								50
Doppel-Box	6x9cm	120	MetalBox	1933	Universal Doppel	11			Z,M	HK86	10
Dreibild-Box	6x9cm	120	RollBox	1935	Doppelobjektiv						60
Electronic 544	28x28mm	126	126	1973	Isconar	5.6	35mm		18-1/250		10
Erkania	6x9cm	120	MetalBox	1938	Juwella Anast.	6.3	105mm			Mc83	30
Fixfocus	6x9cm	120	FoldRo	1938	Trioplan	4.5	105mm	Pronto		Mc84	30
Front-Box	6x9cm	120	MetalBox	1930							30
Gloria	6x9cm	120	FoldRo	1934	Trioplan	3.8		Compur			40
Glorina	6x9cm	120	FoldRo	1936	Trioplan	3.8	105mm	Compur S	1-250		40
Hansa 35	24x36mm	35mm	35Fold	1948	Westar	3.5	50mm	Prontor-S	1-300	Mc84	50
Jubilette	24x36mm	35mm	35Fold	1938	Baltar	2.9	50mm	Compur		Mc84	60
Juventa	6x9cm	120	FoldRo	1934	Anastigmat	7.7	105mm	Singlo	25,75	HK265	50
Juwella	6x9cm	120	FoldRo	1939	Juwella Anast.	4.5	105mm	Prontor	25-125	Mc84	50
Lisette	4.5x6cm	120	FoldRo	1936	Xenar	2.8	7.5cm	Compur		Mc84	50
Mess-Baldinette	24x36mm	35mm	35Fold	1951	Baltar	2.9	5cm	Prontor-SV	1-300		40
Mess-Baldix	6x6cm	120	FoldRo	1954	Ennagon	3.5	7.5cm	Prontor-SV	1-300		70
Mess-Rigona	24x36mm	35mm	35Fold	1953	Rigonar	3.5	50mm	Pronto			120
Micky Rollbox Mod. I	4x6.5cm	127	RollBox		Meniscus			rotary	I,T	HK83	60
Micky Rollbox Mod. II	4x6.5cm	127	RollBox		Double			rotary	I,T	HK83	60
Nizza	9x12cm	plate	FoldPl	1929	Xenar	4.5		Compur	1-250	HK194	70
Piccochic	3x4cm	127	StrutRo	1932	Trioplan	2.9	50mm	Prontor		Mc84	100
Piccochic (Elmar)	3x4cm	127	StrutRo	1932	Elmar	3.5	50mm	Compur		Mc84	260
Pierrette	4x6.5cm	127	StrutRo	1934	Trioplan	3.5	75mm	Compur	1-300		210
Pinette	3x4cm	127	FoldRo	1930	Trioplan	2.9	50mm	Compur			110
Poka I	6x9cm	120	RollBox	1929	Meniscus	7.7		simple			20
Poka II	6x9cm	120	RollBox	1929	Double	11		simple			30
Poka Duplex	6x9/4.5x6	120	RollBox	1934	Double + closeup			simple			30
Pontina	6x9cm	120	FoldRo	1938	Radionar	4.5	105mm	Prontor I, II			50

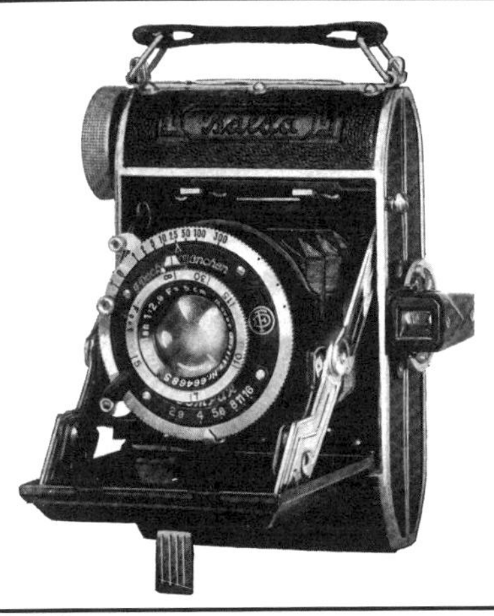

Baldi

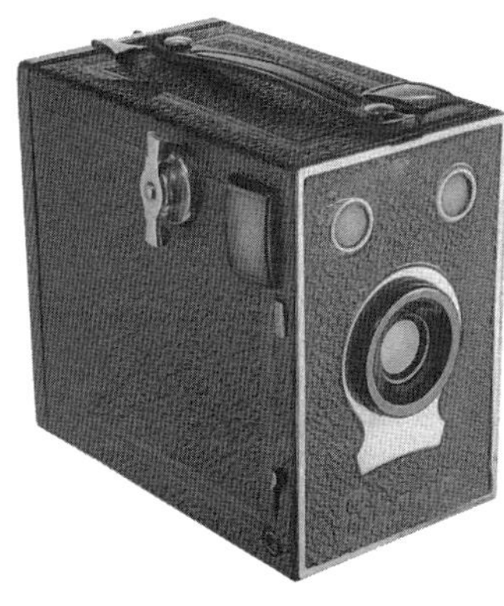

Erkania

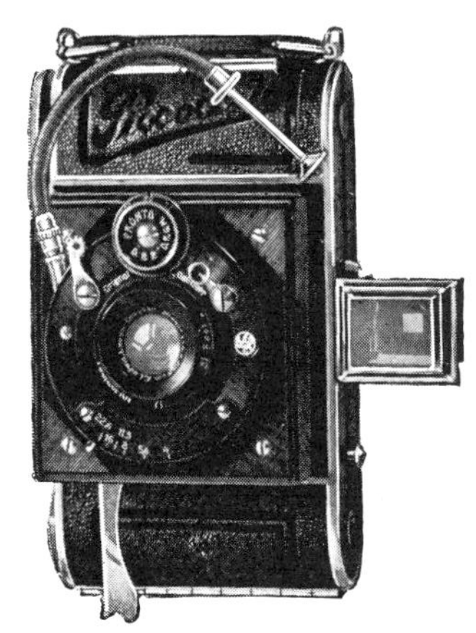

Piccochic

MODEL	FORMAT	FILM	TYPE	Year	LENS	Apert	FL	SHUTTER	SPEEDS	ILLUS	U.S.$
Prima-Box	6.5x9cm	plate	PlateBox	1929	Achromat	7.7	105mm	Merkur	M,Z	HK81	110
Primula	6x9cm	120	RollBox	1930							10
Rigona	3x4cm	127	FoldRo	1936	Trioplan	2.9	5cm	Prontor II		Mc84	70
Rollbox 120 (black)	6x9cm	120	RollBox	1934				simple		Mc85	40
Rollbox 120 (brown)	6x9cm	120	RollBox	1934				simple		Mc85	60
Rollbox 4x6.5cm	4x6.5cm	127	RollBox	1934						Mc85	20
Rollfilm-Kamera	6x9cm	120	FoldRo	1925	Spezial Aplanat	8		Vario		A415	60
Springbox	4x6.5cm	127	StrutRo	1934	Doppel-Objectiv	11					60
Super Baldamatic	24x36mm	35mm	35mm		Color Baldanar	2.8	45mm	Compur Auto		A2098	110
Super Baldamatic I	24x36mm	35mm	35mm		Xenar	2.8	50mm	Compur Auto			120
Super Baldax	6x6cm	120	FoldRo	1954	Baltar	2.9	80mm	Prontor-SVS	1-300		110
Super Baldina (folding)	24x36mm	35mm	35Fold	1937	Xenon	2	50mm	Compur-Rap.		Mc85	150
Super Baldina (telesc.)	24x36mm	35mm	35RF	1955	Xenon	2	50mm			Mc85	70
Super Baldinette	24x36mm	35mm	35RF	1951	Heligon	2	50mm	Sync-Compur		Mc85	80
Super Pontura	6x9cm	120	FoldRo	1938	Meyer Trioplan	3.8		Compur-Rap.	400	A438	390
Venus	6.5x9cm	Sheet	FoldPl	1929	Xenar	4.5	105mm	Compur	1-200		60
...BAUDRY (L. Baudry) - Angers											
Isographe Mod. 1	6x13cm	plate	SterStrut	1939	Berthiot Olor	5.7	75mm	Sector	1-200	F1264	480
Isographe Mod. 2	6x13cm	620	SterStrut	1940	Berthiot Olor	5.7	75mm	Sector	1-200	F1447	480
Isographe Mod. 3	6x13cm	620	SterStrut	1940	Boyer Saphir	4.5	75mm	Sector	1-200	F1448	480
...BAUER											
RX1	24x36mm	35mm	35SLR	1978	Neovaron	1.7	50mm				300
RX2	24x36mm	35mm	35SLR	1978	Neovaron	1.7	50mm				310
...BECK (R.J. Beck Ltd.) - London											
Beck's New Pocket Cam.	8x10.5cm	Roll	FoldRo	1905	Beck Symmetrical			Cornex			120
Cornex Mod. A	3¼x4¼"	plate	MagBox	1903	Single Achromatic	11			1/10-1/80	Mc86	60
Dai Cornex		plate	MagBox	1905	Beck Symmetrical			Unicum			220
F.O.P. Frena	3¼x4¼"	Sheet	MagBox	1900							120
Folding Frena	3¼x4¼"	Sheet	FoldMag	1905	Rapid Rectilinear	8			1/10-120		570
Folding Frena No. 8	8x10.5cm	Sheet	FoldMag	1896	Orthostigmat	8		rotary		A2966	190
Frena (original)	3¼x3¼"	Sheet	MagBox	1893	Beck Achromatic	11	4"	rotary		A2814	150
Frena No. 0	2⅝x3½"	Sheet	MagBox	1901	Rapid Rectilinear	8		rotary		Mc87	190
Frena No. 0 Presentation	2⅝x3½"	Sheet	MagBox	1901	Rapid Rectilinear	8		Frena			1400
Frena No. 2	8x10.5cm	Sheet	MagBox	1894	Rapid Rectilinear	8					160
Frena No. 2 Presentation	8x10.5cm	Sheet	MagBox	1897	Rapid Rectilinear	8				A2815	1000
Frena No. 3	4x5"	Sheet	MagBox	1896	Rapid Rectilinear	8					160
Frena No. 3 Presentation	4x5"	Sheet	MagBox	1897	Rapid Rectilinear	8					1800
Frena No. 22	8x10.5cm	Sheet	MagBox	1909	Single Achromatic	11		Frena			190
Frena No. 22 Presentation	8x10.5cm	Sheet	MagBox	1909	Single Achromatic						1800
Hill's Cloud Camera	8x10.5cm	plate	WideAng	1923							4000
Telephoto Cornex		plate	MagBox	1905	Beck Symmetrical			Unicum		HK66	290
Zambex	8x10.5cm	Sheet	FoldSht	1911	Beck Symmetrical						540

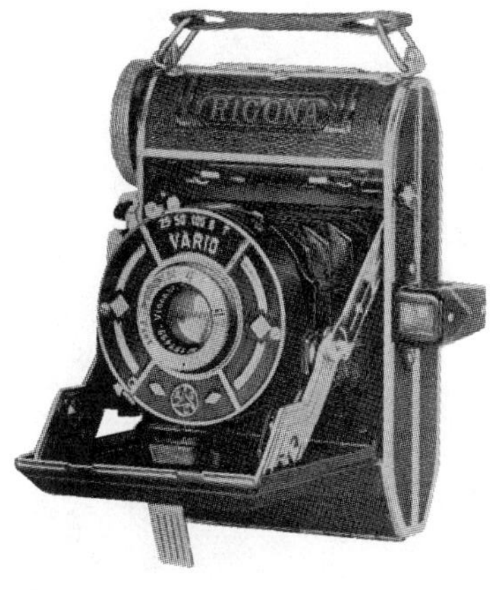

Rigona

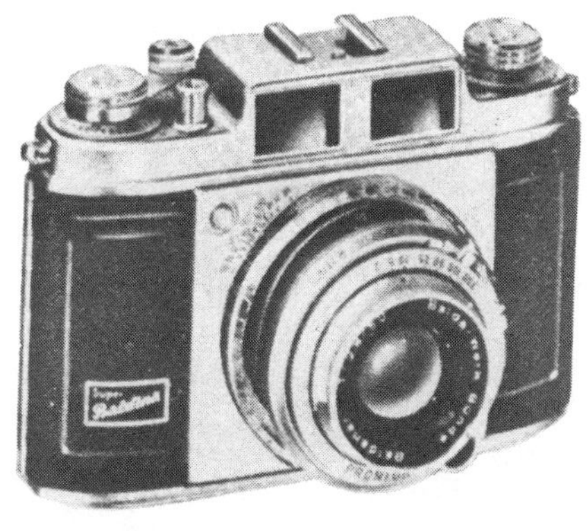

Super Baldina (telescoping)

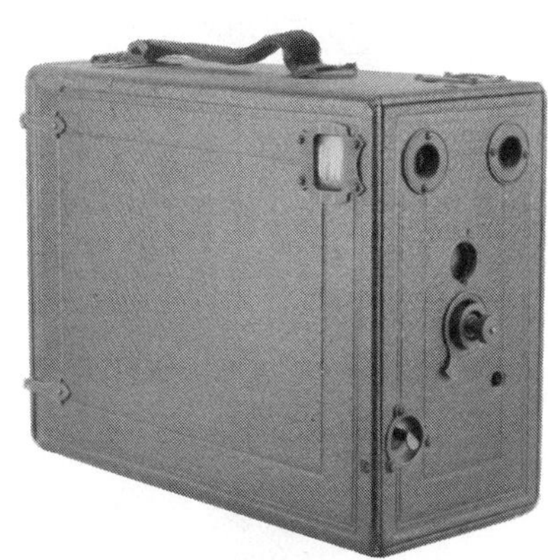

Cornex Mod. A

MODEL	FORMAT	FILM	TYPE	Year	LENS	Apert	FL	SHUTTER	SPEEDS	ILLUS	U.S.$
...BEIER (Kamera-Fabrik Woldemar Beier) - Freital, Germany											
Beier-Flex (I)	6x6cm		MedSLR	1938	Xenar	3.5	75mm	focal plane	1/25-500	Mc87	500
Beier-Flex (II)	6x6cm		MedSLR	1938	Xenar	3.5	75mm	focal plane	2-500	Mc87	380
Beiermatic	24x36mm	35mm	35VF	1961	Trioplan	3.5	45mm	Juniormatic			40
Beika	3x4cm	Roll	StrutRo	1931	Trinar	4.5	5cm	Pronto		HK231	170
Beira (folding VF)	3x4cm	Roll	StrutRo	1932	Trioplan	2.9	5cm	Compur		A1527	120
Beira (rigid VF)	3x4cm	Roll	StrutRo	1933	Trioplan	2.9	5cm	Compur		A1036	180
Beira (RF)	24x36mm	35mm	35RF	1934	Dialytar	2.7	5cm	Compur	300	Mc87	440
Beira (RF) (Elmar)	24x36mm	35mm	35RF	1934	Elmar	3.5	5cm	Compur-Rap.	500	Mc87	380
Beirax	6x9cm	120	FoldRo	1930	Ludwig Victar	4.5	105mm	Prontor		A479	30
Beirette (folding)	24x36mm	35mm	35Fold	1930	Trinar	2.9	5cm	Compur		A1038	140
Beirette (folding)	24x36mm	35mm	35Fold	1930	Trinar	3.5		Compur-Rap.			140
Beirette (rigid)	24x36mm	35mm	35VF	1971	Meritar	2.9	45mm		1/30-125	Mc87	30
Beirette Electronic	24x36mm	35mm	35VF	1966	Meritar	2.8	45mm		30-125		30
Beirette Junior (rigid)	24x36mm	35mm	35VF	1971	Trioplan	3.5	45mm		1/30-125		30
Beirette K	24x36mm	Rapid	35VF	1960	Meritar	2.9	45mm	Model II			30
Beirette K100	24x36mm	35mm	35VF	1980	Chromar	2.9	45mm				10
Beirette KS	24x36mm	Rapid	35VF	1968	Meritar	2.9	45mm	Automatic			50
Beirette KSF	24x36mm	Rapid	35VF	1968	Meritar	2.9	45mm	Automatic			30
Beirette SL100	24x36mm	35mm	35VF	1980	Meritar	2.9	45mm				10
Beirette VS	24x36mm	35mm	35VF	1968	Meritar	2.9	45mm	Automatic			20
Beirette VSN (black)	24x36mm	35mm	35VF	1960	Meritar	2.8	45mm	Priomat			30
Beirette VSN (chrome)	24x36mm	35mm	35VF	1960	Meritar	2.8	45mm	Priomat			20
Box Mod. 0	6x9cm	120	RollBox	1928	Meniscus	11	10.5cm	simple	I,T		30
Box Mod. I	6x9cm	120	RollBox	1930	Doublet	11	10.5cm	simple	I,T		30
Box Mod. II	6x9cm	120	RollBox	1933	Doublet	11	10.5cm	simple	I,T		30
Edith II 6x9	6.5x9cm	plate	FoldPl	1925	Fotar	6.3	105mm	Vario			40
Edith II 9x12	9x12cm	plate	FoldPl	1925	Fotar	6.3		Vario			40
Erika I 6x9	6.5x9cm	plate	FoldPl	1929	Anastigmat	6.3	105mm	Vario			40
Erika I 9x12	9x12cm	plate	FoldPl	1929	Anastigmat	6.3	135mm	Vario			50
Erika II 6x9	6.5x9cm	plate	FoldPl	1930	Trinar	4.5	105mm	Vario			40
Erika II 9x12	9x12cm	plate	FoldPl	1930	Trinar	4.4	135mm	Vario			50
Gloria	6x9cm	120	FoldRo	1928	Anastigmat	6.3	105mm	Automat			50
Lotte II 6x9	6.5x9cm	plate	FoldPl	1925	Anastigmat	4.5	105mm	Prontor-S		Mc88	50
Lotte II 9x12	9x12cm	plate	FoldPl	1925	Anastigmat	4.5	105mm	Prontor-S		Mc88	50
Folding camera	9x12cm	Sheet	FoldPl	1925	Trinar	4.5	105mm	Compur			50
Precisa	6x6cm	120	FoldRo	1937	Victar	4.5	75mm	Prontor			40
Precisa	6x6cm	120	FoldRo	1939	Trinar	2.9	75mm	Compur-Rap.		Mc88	40
Precisa II	6x6cm	120	FoldRo	1954	Meritar	3.5	75mm	Automat			30
Precisa II (RF)	6x6cm	120	FoldRo	1955	Xenar	2.9	75mm	Compur			60
Rifax 6x6	6x6cm	120	FoldRo		Trinar	2.9	75mm	Compur		A469	70
Rifax 6x9	6x9cm	120	FoldRo		Trinar	3.8	105mm	Prontor II	1-150		70

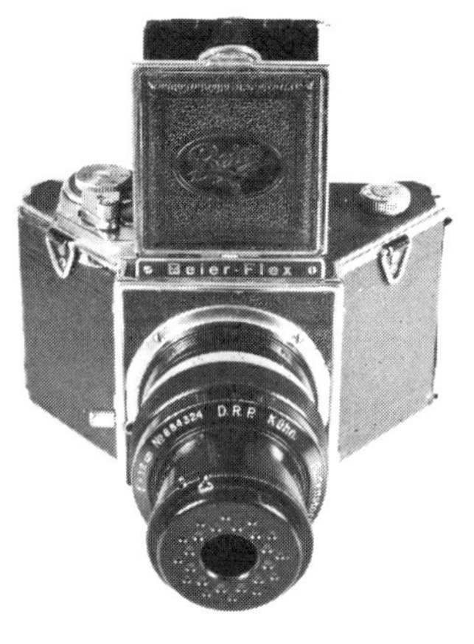

Beier-Flex

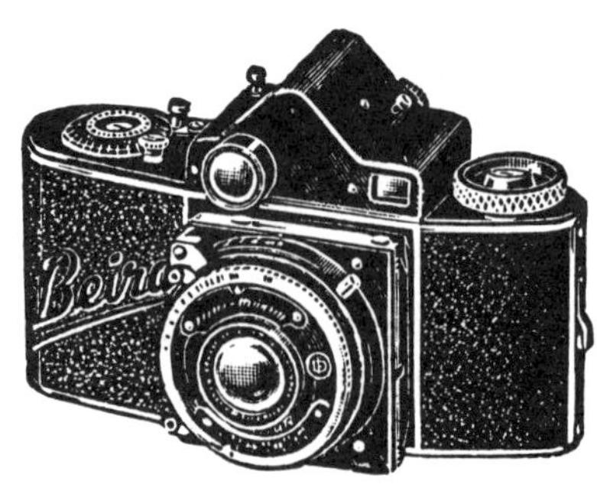

Beira (RF)

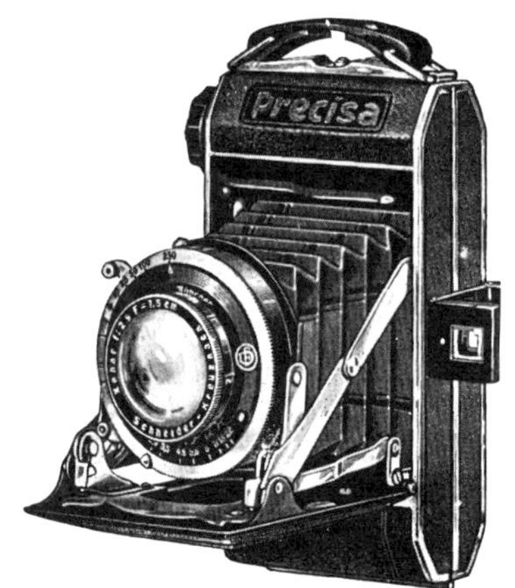

Precisa

MODEL	FORMAT	FILM	TYPE	Year	LENS	Apert	FL	SHUTTER	SPEEDS	ILLUS	U.S.$
Rifax (RF)	6x6cm	120	FoldRo	1937	Trinar	4.5	105mm	Prontor II	1-150	Mc88	110
Voran	6x9cm		FoldRo	1937	Radionar	4.5	105mm	Prontor II	1-150		50
...BELCA-WERK - Dresden											
Belfoca (I) 6x9	6x9cm	120	FoldRo	1952	Ludwig Meritar	4.5		Prontor		Mc88	30
Belfoca (I) 6x9 / 4.5x6	6x9/4.5	120	FoldRo	1952	Ludwig Meritar	4.5		Prontor		Mc88	30
Belfoca (I) 6x9 / 6x6	6x9/6x6	120	FoldRo	1952	Ludwig Meritar	4.5		Prontor		Mc88	30
Belfoca II	6x9cm	120	FoldRo	1954	Bonotar	4.5	105mm	Tempor		A1481	50
Belmira	24x36mm	35mm	35RF	1950	Trioplan	2.9		Cludor			50
Belplasca	24x30mm	35mm	35Ster	1955	Tessar	3.5	37.5mm		1-200	A793	370
Beltica	24x36mm	35mm	35Fold	1951	Zeiss Tessar	3.5	50mm	Cludor	200	A1019	40
Beltica II	24x36mm	35mm	35Fold	1952	Zeiss Tessar	2.8	50mm	Vebur	1-250		40
...(unknown)											
Bell-14		16mm	Submin	1960					simple	Mc88	40
Bell-14 (brown)		16mm	Submin	1960					simple	Mc88	40
...BELL & HOWELL - Chicago, IL USA											
Auto 35/Reflex	24x36mm	35mm	35SLR	1969	Canon EX	1.8	50mm	focal plane	1/8-500		70
Autoload 340	28x28mm	126	126	1967		3.5	40mm	programmed	1/30-250		10
Autoload 341	28x28mm	126	126	1970	Bell & Howell	3.5	40mm		1/25		10
Autoload 342	28x28mm	126	126	1970	Bell & Howell	2.8	40mm				10
Dial 35	18x24mm	35mm	35RF		Canon SE	2.8	28mm		8-250		60
Electric Eye 127	4x4cm	127	RigidRo	1958	Bell & Howell					Mc88	30
Foton	24x36mm	35mm	35RF	1948	Amotal	2.2	50mm			Mc89	800
Stereo Colorist I		35mm	35Ster	1954	Trinar	3.5		Gauthier	10-200	Mc89	250
Stereo Colorist II		35mm	35Ster	1957	Trinar	3.5		Gauthier	10-200	Mc89	300
Stereo Vivid			35Ster	1954	Steinheil Trinar	3.5	35mm	guillotine	1/10-100	Mc89	240
...BELLIENI (H. Bellieni & Fils) - Nancy, France											
Chambre Touriste	13x18cm	plate	Field	1907	Mendel R.R.					F113	270
Chambre Touriste	18x24cm	plate	Field	1907	Rectiligne Crex					F62	260
Extra Plat	9x12cm	plate	StrutPl	1911	Goerz	6.8				F188	220
Extra Plat Stereo	8x16cm	plate	SterStrut	1910	Berthiot	4.5	85mm	guillotine		F1230	1600
Jumelle 9x12	9x12cm	plate	Jumelle	1896	Goerz Doppel An.	6.8		guillotine	1/50	Mc89	310
Jumelle 9x14	9x14cm	plate	Jumelle	1896	Zeiss Protar	8	136mm	guillotine	1/50	Mc89	180
Pocket camera	9x10cm	plate	StrutPl	1902	Goerz	6.8	110mm	focal plane	1000	A303	180
Stereo Jumelle 6x13	6x13cm	plate	StJumelle	1894	Goerz	6.8		guillotine		A713	270
Stereo Jumelle 9x18	9x18cm	plate	StJumelle	1894	Zeiss	8		guillotine		A713	380
...BELOMO - Minsk, Bielorussia											
Agat-18	18x24mm	35mm	35Half	1984	Industar-104	2.8	28mm		1/60-250	Ru164	50
Agat-18K	18x24mm	35mm	35Half	1988	Industar-104	2.8	28mm		1/60-250	Ru164	50
Chaika	18x24mm	35mm	35Half	1965	Industar-69	2.8	28mm		1/30-250	Ru163	50
Chaika II	18x24mm	35mm	35Half	1967	Industar-69	2.8	28mm		1/30-250	Ru163	50
Chaika-2M	18x24mm	35mm	35Half	1972	Industar-69	2.8	28mm		1/30-250	Ru163	40
Chaika-3	18x24mm	35mm	35Half	1971	Industar-69	2.8	28mm		1/30-250	Ru163	50

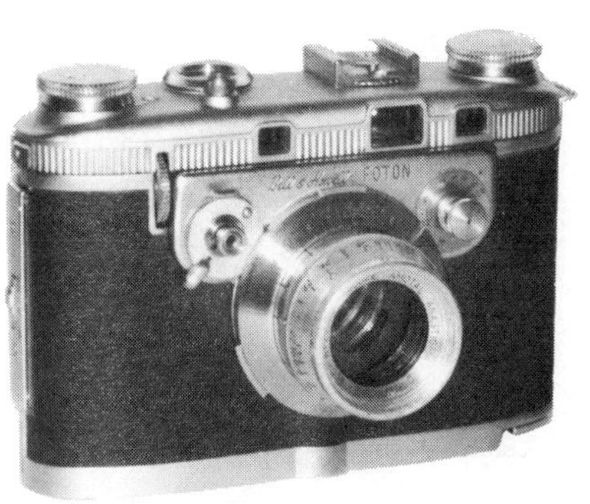

Foton

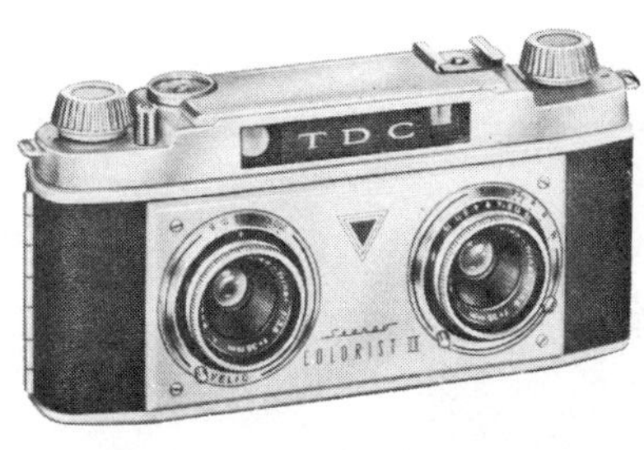

Stereo Colorist II

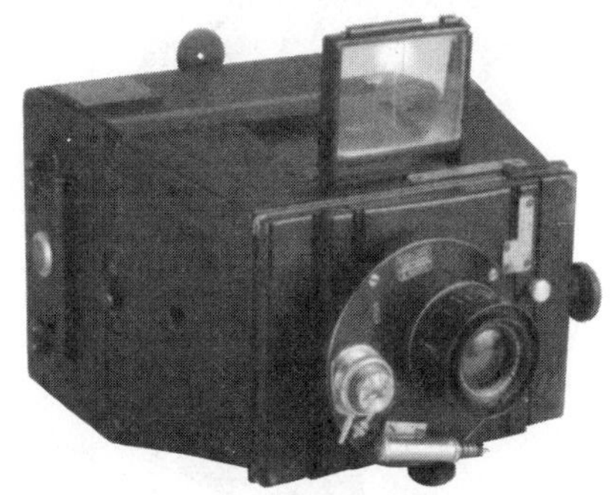
Jumelle

MODEL	FORMAT	FILM	TYPE	Year	LENS	Apert	FL	SHUTTER	SPEEDS	ILLUS	U.S.$
Siluet Rapid Auto	18x24mm	35mm	35SprMot	1970	Lira-4	2.8	28mm		1/30-250	Ru164	70
Vilia	24x36mm	35mm	35VF	1970	Triplet 69-3	4	40mm		B,30-250	Ru165	30
Vilia-Auto (Bnanr-Abto)	24x36mm	35mm	35VF	1970	Triplet 69-3	4	40mm			Mc89	30
...BENCINI - Milan											
Akrom I	3x4cm	127	RigidRo	1953					1/50	Mc89	110
Animatic 600	28x28mm	126	126	1955							10
Comet	4x4cm	127	RigidRo	1948	achromatic	11	75mm		B-1/30	HK307	20
Comet II	4x4cm	127	RigidRo	1951	achromatic	11	75mm		1/50	Mc90	20
Comet III	3x4cm	127	RigidRo	1953	achromatic	11	75mm		1/50	Mc90	70
Comet 3	3x4cm	127	RigidRo	1953	achromatic	11	75mm		1/50	Mc90	70
Comet NK 135	24x36mm	35mm	35VF		Color Bluestar	2.8	50mm			Mc90	60
Comet S	3x4cm	127	RigidRo	1950	achromatic	11	75mm		1/50		30
Cometa	4x4cm	127	RigidRo	1959	Aplanatic	8	55mm		50-100		20
Delta		120	FoldRo	1940	Aplanatic	10.4			I,B		30
Gabri	4x6cm	Roll	MetalBox	1938		11	75mm		1/30		50
Koroll	6x6cm	120	RigidRo	1951	achromatic	11	150mm		1/50	Mc90	20
Koroll II	3x4.5cm	120	RigidRo	1961		8			30-125		20
Koroll 24	3x4cm	120	RigidRo	1953	achromatic		75mm		1/50		20
Koroll 24 S	4x4cm	120	RigidRo	1953	achromatic		75mm		1/50		20
Koroll S	6x6cm	120	TelescRo	1953	achromatic	11	150mm		1/50	Mc90	20
Minicomet	2x3cm	127	RigidRo	1963	achromatic					Mc90	30
Relex	4x6cm	127	TelescRo	1949	Aplanatic	11	75mm		I		30
Rolet	3x4cm	Roll	TelescRo		Planetar	11	75mm			Mc90	30
...BENETFINK - London											
Lightning Detective	3¼x4¼"	plate	PlateBox	1895				Ilex			120
Lightning Hand Camera	3¼x4¼"	plate	MagBox	1903	achromatic			Everset	I,T	Mc90	120
Speedy Detective	3¼x4¼"	plate	MagBox		Rapid Rectilinear			Everset	I,T		120
...BENTZIN (Curt Bentzin) - Görlitz											
Astraflex II	6x6cm	120	MedSLR	1951	Tessar	3.5		focal plane	1000		180
Atelier-Reflex-Primar	9x12cm	plate	LgSLR	1940	Trioplan	3.5	21cm	focal plane			190
Atelier-Reflex-Primar	10x15cm	plate	LgSLR	1940	Tessar	3.5	25cm	focal plane			190
Flach Primar 6x9	6.5x9cm	plate	FoldPl	1925	Meyer Trioplan	4.5	105mm	Ibsor			100
Flach Primar 9x12	9x12cm	plate	FoldPl	1925	Tessar	4.5	220mm	Compur			100
Fokal-Nacht-Primar	6.5x9cm	plate	StrutPl	1925	Plasmat	1.5	9cm	focal plane	1/8-1000		1400
Fokal-Nacht-Primar	6.5x9cm	plate	StrutPl	1925	Ernostar	1.8	9cm	focal plane	1/8-1000		1300
Fokal-Primar 6x9	6.5x9cm	plate	StrutPl	1902	Tessar	4.5	105mm	focal plane	1/8-1000		120
Fokal-Primar 9x12	9x12cm	plate	StrutPl	1902	Tessar	4.5	150mm	focal plane	1/8-1000		120
Fokal-Primar 9x12	9x12cm	plate	StrutPl	1902	Tessar	2.7	165mm	focal plane	1/8-1000		160
Fokal-Primar 10x15	10x15cm	plate	StrutPl	1902	Tessar	4.5	165mm	focal plane	1/8-1000		120
Fokal-Primar 13x18	13x18cm	plate	StrutPl	1902	Tessar	4.5	210mm	focal plane	1/8-1000		120
Klapp-Reflex-Primar	6.5x9cm	plate	FoldSLR	1911	Zeiss Tessar	4.5	150mm	focal plane	1-1000	A1588	260
Klapp-Reflex-Primar	9x12cm	plate	FoldSLR	1911	Meyer Trioplan	3.5	210mm	focal plane	1-1000		190

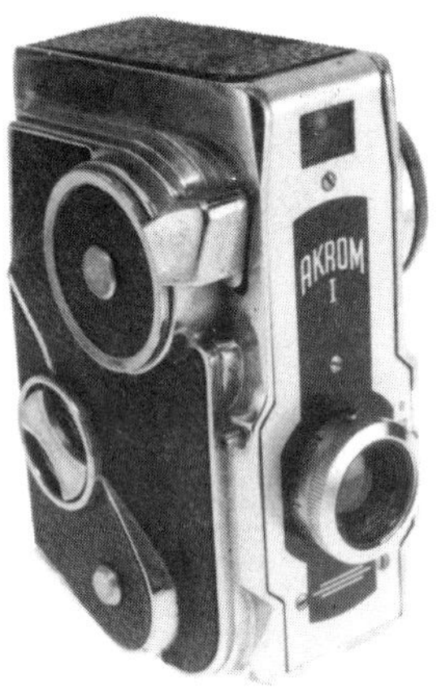

Akrom I

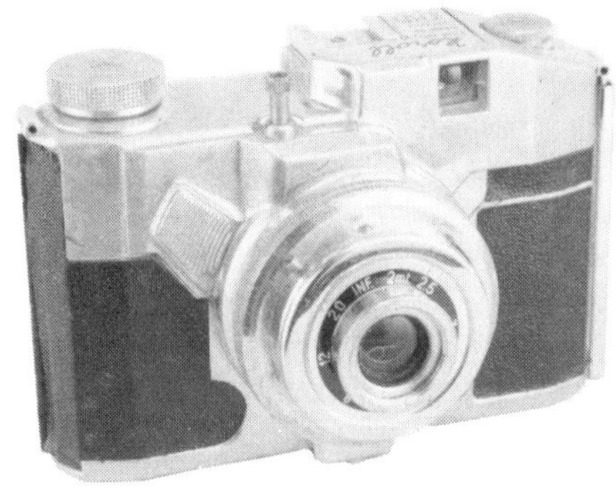

Koroll

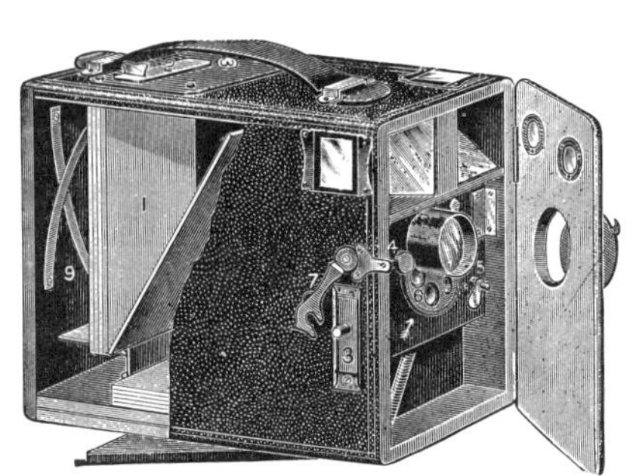

Lightning Hand Camera

MODEL	FORMAT	FILM	TYPE	Year	LENS	Apert	FL	SHUTTER	SPEEDS	ILLUS	U.S.$
Klapp-Reflex-Primar	3¼x4¼"	plate	FoldSLR	1911	Triotar	3.5	150mm	focal plane	1-1000		200
Klapp-Reflex-Primar	10x15cm	plate	FoldSLR	1911	Zeiss Tessar	4.5	210mm	focal plane	1-1000		220
Plan Primar	6.5x9cm	plate	FoldPl	1938	Meyer Trioplan	3.8		Compur		Mc91	130
Plan Primar	6.5x9cm	plate	FoldPl	1938	Zeiss Tessar	4.5		Compur		A252	130
Planovista	4x6.5cm	127	FoldRo	1930							900
Primar	9x12cm	plate	FoldPl	1921	Zeiss Tessar	4.5		Compur		Mc91	80
Primar Reflex	6x6cm	120	MedSLR	1936	Tessar	3.5	105mm	focal plane		Mc91	260
Primar Reflex 6x9	6.5x9cm	plate	LgSLR	1900	Zeiss Tessar	4.5		focal plane	1/8-1000		180
Primar Reflex 3¼x4¼	3¼x4¼"	plate	LgSLR	1900	Zeiss Tessar	4.5	180mm	focal plane	1/8-1000		210
Primar Reflex 9x12	9x12cm	plate	LgSLR	1900	Zeiss Tessar	4.5	180mm	focal plane	1/8-1000		200
Primar Reflex 10x15	10x15cm	plate	LgSLR	1900	Zeiss Tessar	3.5		focal plane	1/8-1000		200
Primar Reflex 13x18	13x18cm	plate	LgSLR	1900	Zeiss Tessar	4.5	250mm	focal plane	1/8-1000		200
Primarette	4x6.5cm	127	FoldRo	1933	Zeiss Tessar	3.5		Pronto	25-100	Mc91	1000
Primarflex	6x6cm	120	MedSLR	1936	Tessar	3.5	105mm	focal plane		Mc91	240
Primarflex II	6x6cm	120	MedSLR	1951	Tessar	3.5		focal plane	1000	Mc91	190
Rechteck Primar	9x12cm	plate	FoldPl	1912	Tessar	4.5	150mm	Compur			150
Rechteck Primar (stereo)	9x12cm	plate	StFoldPl	1912	Tessar	4.5		Stereo-Compur			520
Rechteck Primar (stereo)	10x15cm	plate	StFoldPl	1912	Tessar	4.5		Stereo-Compur			480
Reisekamera 9x12	9x12cm	plate	Field	1900	various						290
Reisekamera 10x15	10x15cm	plate	Field	1900	various						290
Reisekamera 13x18	13x18cm	plate	Field	1900	various					A1383	310
Reisekamera 18x24	18x24cm	plate	Field	1900	various						310
Roll-Primar 6x9	6x9cm	120	VtFoldRo	1935	Tessar	4.5	105mm	Compur			80
Roll-Primar 6.5x11	6.5x11cm	116	VtFoldRo	1935	Trioplan	4.5	120mm	Compur			80
Stereo-Fokal-Primar	6x13cm	plate	StrutSter	1923	Tessar	4.5	120mm			A755	370
Stereo-Reflex-Primar	6x13cm	plate	SterRefl	1918	Tessar	4.5	120mm	focal plane	1000	A1814	560
Stereo-Reisekamera	9x18cm	plate	SterField	1900	Tessar	4.5		Stereo-Compur		A1763	310
Studio camera	13x18cm	plate	Studio	1910	various					A2952	340
Studio camera	18x24cm	plate	Studio		various						440
Tropen-Reisekamera	9x12cm	plate	Field	1925	Tessar	3.5	135mm	Compur		A147	200
Universal-Quadrat-Primar	9x12cm	plate	FoldPl	1922	various			focal plane	1/3-1000	A1386	90
Universal-Quadrat-Primar	10x15cm	plate	FoldPl	1922	various			focal plane	1/3-1000		120
Universal-Quadrat-Primar	13x18cm	plate	FoldPl	1922	various			focal plane	1/3-1000		130
Zweiverschluss Primar	9x12cm	plate	FoldPl	1915	Tessar	4.5		focal plane	1000	A1386	200
...BENTZIN (Richard Bentzin) - Germany											
Atelierkamera	18x24cm	plate	Studio	1890	Goerz Doppel An.						800
Atelierkamera	24x30cm	plate	Studio	1890	Goerz Doppel An.						900
Landschaftskamera	30x40cm	plate	Tailboard	1890	Goerz Doppel An.		270mm				270
...BERMPOHL & CO. K.G. - Berlin											
Naturfarbenkamera	9x12cm	plate	3-Color		Z. Tessar	3.5	21cm	Compur		HK694	2000
Naturfarbenkamera	13x18cm	plate	3-Color		Z. Tessar	3.5	30cm	Compur		A942	2000
Naturfarbenkamera	18x24cm	plate	3-Color								1900

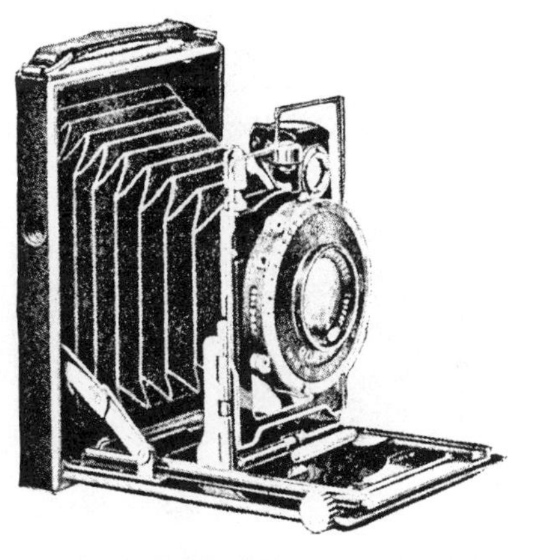

Plan Primar

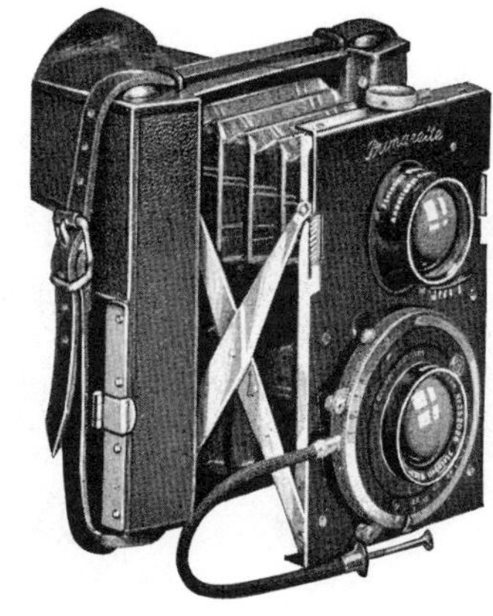

Primarette

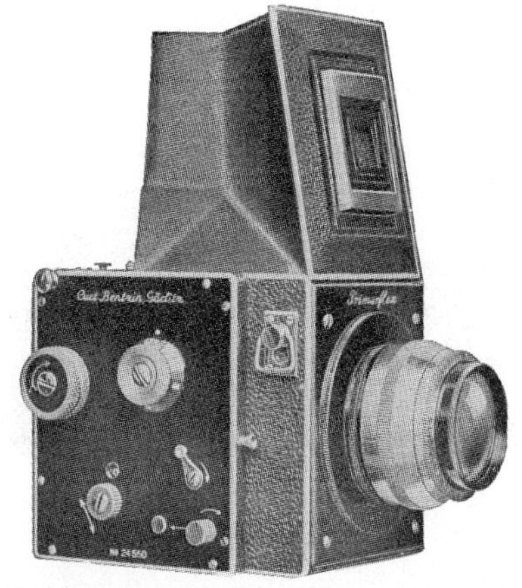

Primarflex

MODEL	FORMAT	FILM	TYPE	Year	LENS	Apert	FL	SHUTTER	SPEEDS	ILLUS	U.S.$
Bildmeister Studio Camera	3¼x4¼"	plate	Monorail	1950	various			various			510
Bildmeister Studio Camera	9x12cm	plate	Monorail	1950	various			various		A1372	540
Bildmeister Studio Camera	13x18cm	plate	Monorail	1950	various			various			700
Bildmeister Studio Camera	18x24cm	plate	Monorail	1950	various			various			700
Miethe/Bermpohl	9x12cm	plate	3-Color	1903	Dogmar	4.5	190mm			A2030	3000
...BERNER (W. Heinz) - Erfurt											
Field camera	13x18cm	plate	Field	1895	landscape						260
Field camera	18x24cm	plate	Field	1895	landscape						260
...BERNING (Otto Berning & Co.) - Düsseldorf											
Robot I	24x24mm	35mm	35SprMot	1934	Zeiss Tessar	3.5	32.5mm			Mc91	310
Robot II	24x24mm	35mm	35SprMot	1939	Schn. Xenar	2.8	37.5mm	focal plane	1-500	Mc92	180
Robot II	24x24mm	35mm	35SprMot	1939	Z. Biotar	3.8		focal plane		Mc92	180
Robot IIa	24x24mm	35mm	35SprMot	1951	Schn. Xenar	2.8		focal plane	1/2-500	Mc92	170
Robot Junior	24x24mm	35mm	35SprMot	1954	Radionar	3.5	38mm			A2072	220
Robot Luftwaffe	24x24mm	35mm	35SprMot	1940	Tele-Xenar	3.8	75mm			Mc92	480
Robot Luftwaffe	24x24mm	35mm	35SprMot	1940	Biotar	2	4cm			Mc92	480
Robot Motor-Recorder 18M	18x24mm	35mm	35El-Mot	1965				rotary	1/4-500		560
Robot Motor-Recorder 24M	24x24mm	35mm	35El-Mot	1965				rotary	1/4-500	A1170	560
Robot Motor-Recorder 36M	24x36mm	35mm	35El-Mot	1965	Xenagon	2.8	35mm	rotary	1/4-500		540
Robot Motor-Record. 36ME	24x36mm	35mm	35El-Mot	1965	Sonnar	2	50mm	rotary	1/4-500		390
Robot Recorder 24e	24x24mm	35mm	35SprMot	1959						A992	310
Robot Recorder 36	24x36mm	35mm	35SprMot	1955							200
Robot Royal III	24x24mm	35mm	35SprMot	1953	Z. Sonnar	2	50mm			A2077	510
Robot Royal 18	24x24mm	35mm	35Half	1957							2500
Robot Royal 24	24x24mm	35mm	35RF	1957	Xenon	1.9	40mm			A993	620
Robot Royal 36	24x24mm	35mm	35RF	1955	Z. Sonnar	2	50mm				550
Robot SC Electronic	16x16mm	35mm	35El-Mot	1984	Xenagon	5	30mm	automatic	4-1/500	A3496	700
Robot Star	24x24mm	35mm	35SprMot	1952	Xenon	1.9	40mm			Mc92	310
Robot Star II	24x24mm	35mm	35SprMot	1958	Xenar	2.8	38mm		1/2-500	Mc92	260
Robot Star 25	24x24mm	35mm	35SprMot	1969	Xenon	1.9	40mm		1/4-500	Mc92	400
Robot Star 50	24x24mm	35mm	35SprMot	1969	Xenon	1.9	40mm	rotary	1/2-1/500	A3491	480
Robot Star 50 D	24x24mm	35mm	35SprMot	1982	Xenon	1.9	40mm	rotary	1/2-1/500	A3493	530
Robot Star 50 DA	24x24mm	35mm	35SprMot	1982	Xenon	1.9	40mm	simple	1/500		620
...BEROFLEX A.G. - Berlin											
Beroquick Electronic	24x36mm	35mm	35VF	1980	Meritar	2.8	50mm				30
Beroquick KB 135	24x36mm	35mm	35VF	1975	Meritar	2.8	45mm		30-125		30
...BERTRAM (Ernst & Wilhelm Bertram) - Munich											
Bertram-Kamera	6x9cm		Press	1954	Xenar	3.5	105mm	Sync-Compur	1-400	Mc93	800
...BERTSCH (Adolphe Bertsch) - Paris											
Chambre Auto (cylindr.)	6x6cm	WetPl	WetPlate	1860	Achromatique					A2800	6400
Chambre Auto (rectang.)	6x6cm	WetPl	WetPlate	1860	Achromatique					A2799	7000
Chambre Auto Stereo	6.6x14cm	WetPl	StWetPl	1864	Achromatiques			Volets couplés		A2648	12000

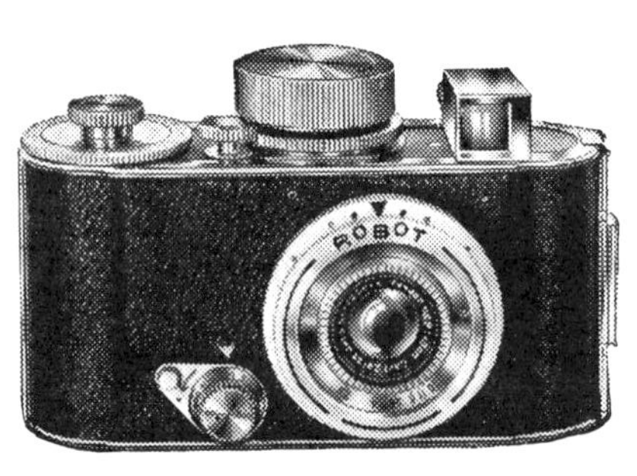

Robot I

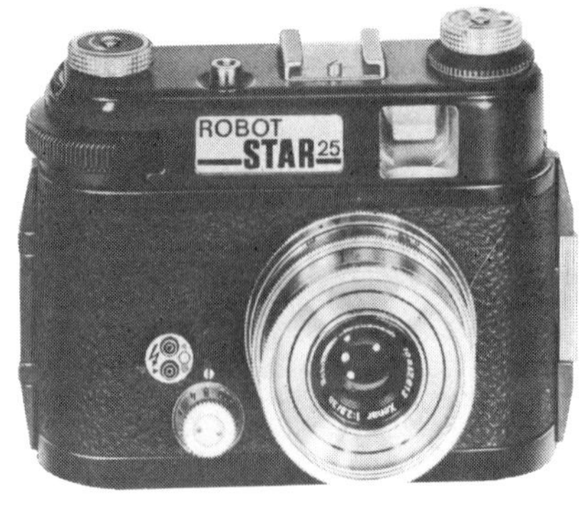

Robot Star 25

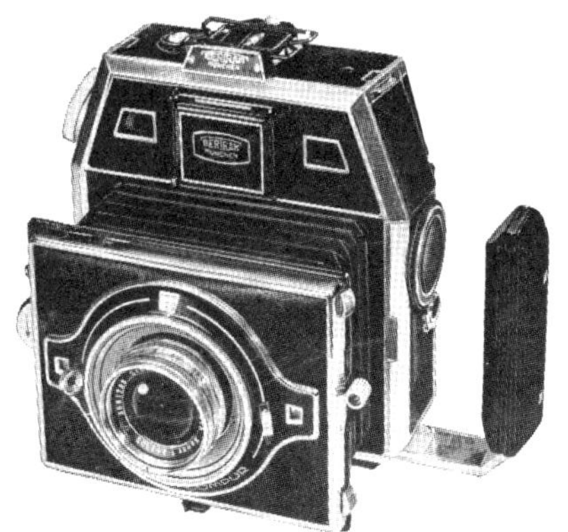

Bertram-Kamera

MODEL	FORMAT	FILM	TYPE	Year	LENS	Apert	FL	SHUTTER	SPEEDS	ILLUS	U.S.$
...BIAL & FREUND - Breslau											
Field Camera	13x18cm	plate	Field	1900							330
Magazine Camera	9x12cm	plate	MagBox	1900							140
Plate Camera	9x12cm	plate	FoldPl	1890	Anastoskop Men.	8					130
...(unknown)											
Biflex 35	11x11mm	Roll	Submin		Trioplan	2.8	20mm		10-250	Mc93	1500
...BILLCLIFF (Joshua Billcliff) - Manchester											
Field Camera		plate	Field	1890	TT&H Cooke An.	4.5					540
Royalty	4¼x6½"	plate	Field								310
Studio Camera	4¼x6½"	plate	Studio	1880						Mc93	300
Studio Camera	6½x8½"	plate	Studio	1880						Mc93	300
...BILORA (Kürbi & Niggeloh)											
Auto-Bella	24x36mm	35mm	35VF	1965	Rodenst. Trinar	2.8	45mm	Prontor-Matic		A2110	50
Auto-Bellina 4x4	4x4cm	127	RigidRo	1963	Meniscus	11		simple	M,Z	A2109	50
Bella (1954)	4x6.5cm	127	RigidRo	1954	Achromat	9	70mm	Synchro		A1557	20
Bella (1955)	4x6.5cm	127	RigidRo	1955	Achromat	8	70mm		B,50,100	A1558	30
Bella 35	24x36mm	35mm	35VF	1959	Trinar	2.8	45mm	Pronto		A2106	20
Bella 44	4x4cm	127	RigidRo	1958	Achromat	8			50-100	Mc93	30
Bella 46	4x6cm	127	RigidRo	1959	Achromat	8			50-100	A1559	30
Bella 66	6x6cm	120	RigidRo	1956						Mc93	20
Bella D	4x6.5cm	127	RigidRo	1957	Achromat	8	70mm		B,50,100		20
Bella DC	4x4cm	127	RigidRo	1960	Trinar	5.6	55mm	Vario	25-200	A1562	30
Bellaluxa 4/4	4x4cm	127	RigidRo	1962	Biloskop	8				Mc93	30
Bellina 127	4x4cm	127	TelescRo	1962	Biloxar	5.6			30-125		30
Bellina Standard	4x4cm	127	TelescRo	1962	Biloxar	5.6			30-125	A1564	30
Bilomatic C	28x28mm	126	126VF	1972	Color-Bilotar	11	40mm	simple	30, 100		30
Bilomatic CA	28x28mm	126	126VF	1972	Color Bilotar	11	40mm	simple	30, 100	A1973	50
Bilomatic F	28x28mm	126	126VF	1966	Color-Bilotar	11	40mm	simple	30, 100	A1974	50
Bilomatic X	28x28mm	126	126VF	1968	Bilotar			simple	30, 100	A1977	30
Blitz Box	6x9cm	120	MetalBox	1948	Meniscus	11		simple	M,Z	A1348	30
Blitz Box D	6x9cm	120	MetalBox	1954	Achromat			simple	M,Z	A1354	20
Bonita 66	6x6cm	120	TLR-Box	1953	Meniscus	9		Spezial	I,T	Mc93	30
Bonita Kleinkamera	24x36mm	35mm	35VF	1960	Color-Isconar	3.9	45mm	Vario	30, 125	A2108	50
Box	6x9cm	120	RollBox	1950	Meniscus	11		Bilora	I,T	Mc94	20
Boy (black)	4.5x6cm	120	BakeliteBox	1950	Anastigmat	11			I,T	Mc94	30
Boy-Luxus (brown)	4.5x6cm	120	BakeliteBox	1950	Anastigmat	11			I,T		50
Color-Box	6x9cm	120	MetalBox	1950	Rodens. Achromat	9	90mm		M,Z	A1353	30
Radix 35 B	24x24mm	Karat	35VF	1947	Anastigmat	3.5	40mm		I,T		40
Radix 35 BH	24x24mm	Karat	35VF	1947	Biloxar	3.5	38mm		1/2-1/200		50
Radix 35 S	24x24mm	Karat	35VF	1947	Radionar	3.5	38mm		I,T		50
Radix 35 SH	24x24mm	Karat	35VF	1947	Radionar	3.5	38mm		1/2-1/200		50
Radix 56 A	24x24mm	Karat	35VF	1947	Biloxar Anast.	5.6	38mm		B,I	Mc94	40

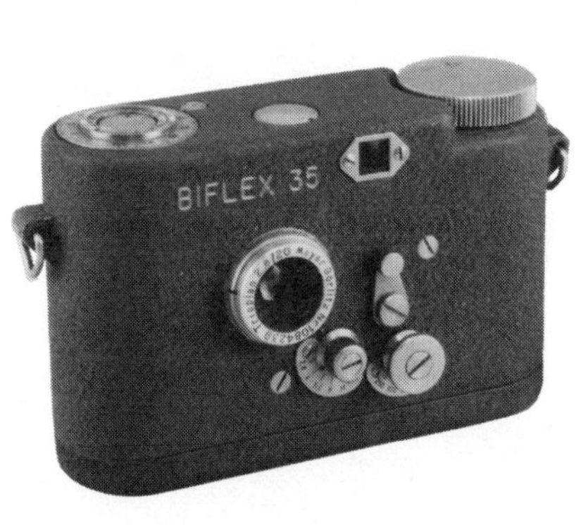

Biflex 35

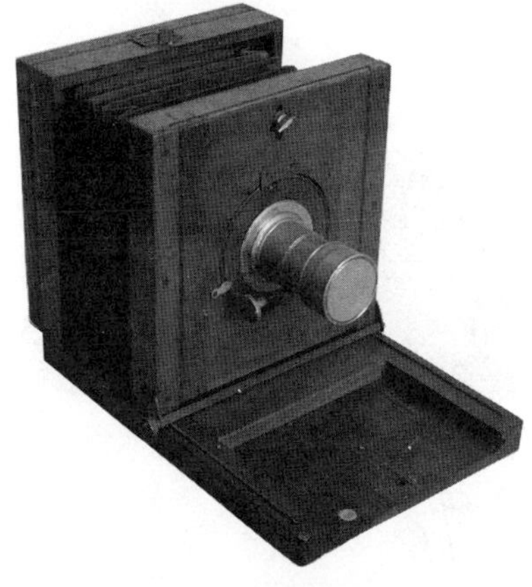
Billcliff Studio Camera

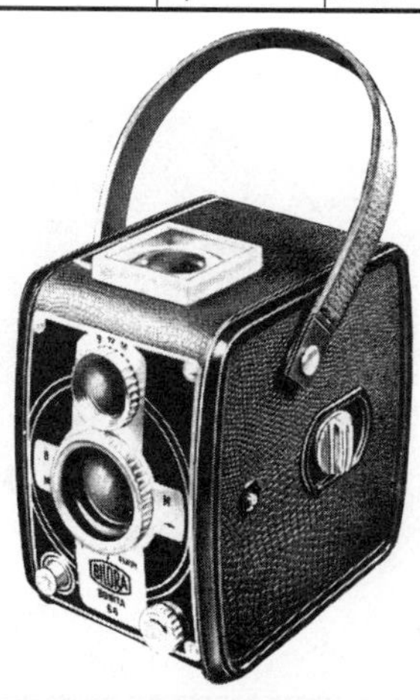

Bonita 66

MODEL	FORMAT	FILM	TYPE	Year	LENS	Apert	FL	SHUTTER	SPEEDS	ILLUS	U.S.$
Special Box	6x9cm	120	MetalBox	1952	Meniscus	11			I,T		40
Stahl Box	6x9cm	120	MetalBox	1950	Anastigmat	11			I,T		20
Standard Box	6x9cm	120	MetalBox	1950	Meniscus	11			I,T	A1352	20
...BING - Germany											
Fita	5x8cm	Roll	FoldRo	1931	Meniscus	11	105mm		M,Z		40
...BIRNBAUM - Rumburk, Czechoslovakia											
Doxa	4.5x6cm	plate	FoldPl	1928	Brilliantar	4.5	72mm				150
Doxa	9x12cm	plate	FoldPl	1909	Extra Rap. Aplan.						140
Embirflex	6x6cm	120	TLR	1939	Doxanar	4.5	75mm				190
Filmoskop	32x32mm	Roll	RollBox	1930					M,Z		450
Folding plate camera	6.5x9cm	plate	FoldPl	1925	Planostigmat	7.7	105mm				100
Perforeta	24x36mm	35mm	35VF	1935	Xenar			Doxa	25-100		100
Perforette	24x36mm	35mm	35VF	1935	Doxanar	4.5	50mm	Doxa	25-100	A3483	140
Super Embirflex	6x6cm	120	TLR	1938	Victar	2.9	75mm				180
Super Perforeta	24x36mm	35mm	35RF	1940				Compur			120
Super Perforette	24x36mm	35mm	35RF	1940				Prontor II			120
...BITTNER (L.O. Bittner) - Munich											
Roka Luxus		Roll	FoldRo	1923	Trinar	6.3	105mm	Pronto			200
...BLAIR CAMERA CO. - Connecticut, USA											
Baby Hawk-Eye	2x2½"	Roll	RollBox	1896	Rapid Rectilinear			B&L Iris	I,T		260
Century Hawk-Eye	6½x8½"	plate	FoldPl	1895	Rapid Universal			B&L Auto			420
Columbus		Roll	RollBox	1894	Rapid Rectilinear				I,T	Mc95	480
Combination Camera	4x5"		View	1882	Dallm. R.R.				I		420
Combinat. Hawk-Eye No. 3		Roll	FoldRo	1904	Rapid Rectilinear			B&L Auto			420
Detective & Combination	4x5"	plate	PlateBox	1893	Blair Rap. Rect.		6"		I,T	Mc95	310
English Compact R.B.	3¼x4¼"	plate	Field	1888	various			various		Mc95	300
English Compact R.B.	6½x8½"	plate	Field	1888	various			various		Mc95	300
English Compact R.B.	10x12"	plate	Field	1888	various			various		Mc95	300
Focus. Weno Hawk-Eye 4	4x5"	103	HzFoldRo	1902	B&L Rapid Rect.			Blair		Mc95	480
Fold. '95 Hawk-Eye	4x5"	plate	FoldPl	1895	Blair Rap. Rect.		6"		I,T		350
Fold. Hawk-Eye 5x7 Mod.1	5x7"	plate	FoldPl	1892	Rapid Rectilinear		8"	built-in	I,T	Mc95	470
Fold. Hawk-Eye 5x7 Mod.2	5x7"	plate	FoldPl	1892	B&L Rapid Rect.			B&L Iris	3-1/100	Mc95	510
Fold. Hawk-Eye No.3 Mod.3	3¼x4¼"	Roll	HzFoldRo	1905	B&L Rapid Rect.					Mc95	70
Fold. Hawk-Eye No.3 Mod.6	3¼x4¼"	Roll	HzFoldRo	1908	B&L Rapid Rect.			B&L Auto			30
Fold. Hawk-Eye 3B Mod.1	3¼x5½"	Roll	HzFoldRo	1906	B&L Rapid Rect.			B&L Iris	I,T,B		70
Fold. Hawk-Eye No.4 Mod.3	4x5"	Roll	HzFoldRo	1905	Rap. Symmetrical			Hawk-Eye	I,T,B		70
Fold. Hawk-Eye No.4 Mod.4	4x5"	Roll	HzFoldRo	1905	Rap. Symmetrical			Hawk-Eye	I,T,B		70
Fold. Weno Hawk-Eye No.4		Roll	HzFoldRo	1902	Plastigmat			B&L Automatic		Mc95	60
Hawk-Eye Camera	4x5"	plate	PlateBox	1893	Blair Rap. Rect.		6"		I	Mc95	290
Hawk-Eye (Improved)	4x5"	plate	PlateBox		Blair Rap. Rect.		6"		I,T	Mc95	310
Hawk-Eye (leather)	4x5"	plate	PlateBox	1893	Blair Rap. Rect.		6"		I	Mc95	260
Hawk-Eye Detective	4x5"	plate	PlateBox	1893	Blair Rap. Rect.		6"		I,T	Mc95	290

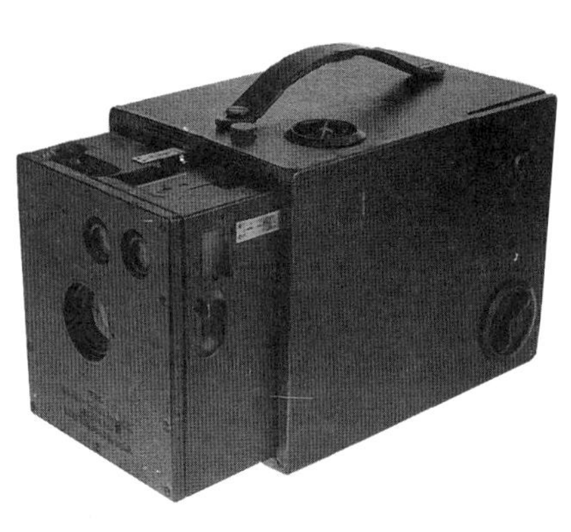

Columbus

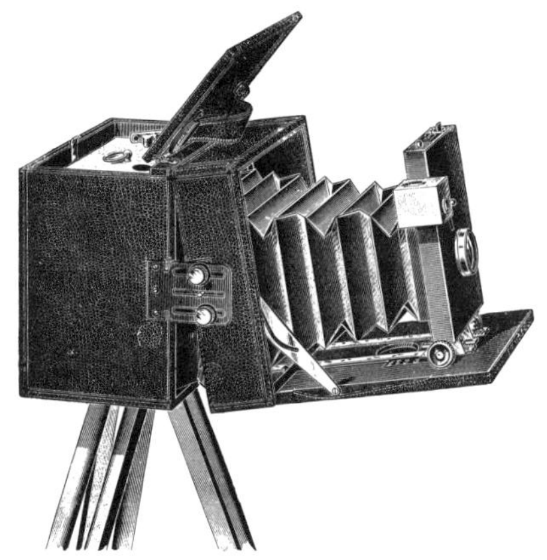

Folding Hawk-Eye 5x7

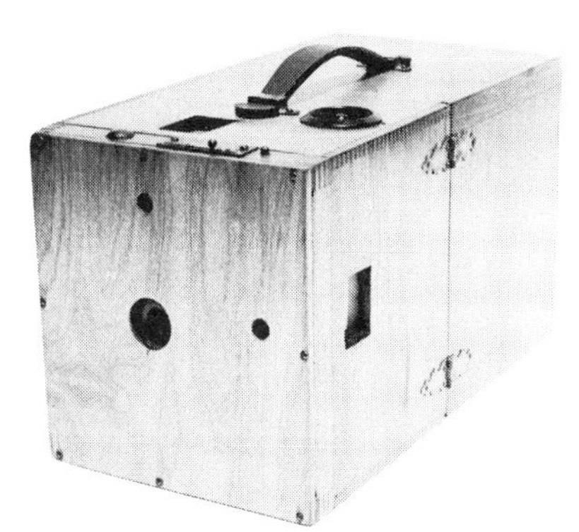

Hawk-Eye Camera (Improved)

MODEL	FORMAT	FILM	TYPE	Year	LENS	Apert	FL	SHUTTER	SPEEDS	ILLUS	U.S.$
Hawk-Eye Junior	3½x3½"	Pl+Ro	RollBox	1895	Single Achromatic					Mc96	70
Kamaret 4x5	4x5"	Roll	RollBox	1891	Blair Rap. Rect.		6"			Mc96	600
Kamaret 5x7	5x7"	Roll	RollBox	1891	Blair Rap. Rect.		8"			Mc96	900
Lucidograph No. 1	3¼x4¼"	plate	FoldPl	1885	Single Achromatic				I	Mc96	1200
Lucidograph No. 2	4¼x5½"	plate	FoldPl	1885	Blair Rap. Rect.				I	Mc96	1200
Lucidograph No. 3	5x8"	plate	FoldPl	1885	Blair Rap. Rect.				I	Mc96	1200
Petite Kamarette	3½" Ø	Roll	RollBox	1892							600
Reversible Back Camera	4x5"	plate	View	1895	Darlot						500
Reversible Back Camera	6½x8½"	plate	View	1895	Darlot						500
Reversible Back Camera	8x10"	plate	View	1895	Darlot						500
Reversible Back Improved	4x5"	plate	View	1898							290
R.B. Camera, Improved	6½x8½"	plate	View	1898							290
R.B. Camera, Improved	8x10"	plate	View	1898							290
Stereo Hawk-Eye Mod. 1	3½x7"	Roll	StFoldRo	1904	Rapid Rectilinear			B&L St. Autom.			410
Stereo Hawk-Eye Mod. 2	3½x7"	Roll	StFoldRo	1904	Rapid Rectilinear			B&L St. Autom.			410
Stereo Hawk-Eye Mod. 3	3½x7"	Roll	StFoldRo	1904	Rapid Rectilinear			B&L St. Autom.			410
Stereo Hawk-Eye Mod. 4	3½x7"	Roll	StFoldRo	1904	Rapid Rectilinear			B&L St. Autom.			410
Stereo Hawk-Eye No. 1	3½x7"	Roll	StFoldRo	1902	Rapid Rectilinear			B&L St. Autom.			440
Stereo Hawk-Eye No. 2	3½x7"	Roll	StFoldRo	1901	Rapid Rectilinear			B&L St. Autom.			460
Stereo Weno	3½x3½"	Roll	StFoldRo	1902				B&L St. Autom.		A766	240
Stereo Weno Hawk-Eye	3½x3½"	Roll	StFoldRo	1901	Rapid Rectilinear			B&L St. Autom.		A768	270
Tourist Hawk-Eye	3½x3½"	Roll	HzFoldRo	1898	Meniscus			rotary			160
Tourist Hawk-Eye	4x5"	Roll	HzFoldRo	1898	achromatic			rotary			160
Tourist Hawk-Eye Special	4x5"	Roll	HzFoldRo	1898	Rapid Rectilinear			Unicum			210
View	4x5"	plate	View								230
View	5x7"	plate	View		various			various			230
View	5x8"	plate	View		various			various			230
View	6½x8½"	plate	View		various			various			270
View	11x14"	plate	View		various			various			350
Weno Hawk-Eye No. 2	3½x3½"	101	RollBox	1904	achromatic			rotary			30
Weno Hawk-Eye No. 3	3¼x4¼"	Roll	RollBox	1904	Meniscus			rotary			30
Weno Hawk-Eye No. 4	4x5"	Roll	RollBox	1904	Meniscus			rotary	I	Mc96	30
Weno Hawk-Eye No. 6	3¼x5½"	125	RollBox	1906	achromatic			rotary			30
Weno Hawk-Eye No. 7	3¼x5½"	122	RollBox	1908	Meniscus			rotary			30
...BODENSEEWERK APPARATE UND MASCHINENBAU GmbH - Überlingen											
Boden-Stereo	24x24mm	35mm	35Ster	1954	Trinar	3.5	35mm	Velio	10-200		260
Boden-Stereo II	24x24mm	35mm	35Ster	1954	Trinar	3.5	35mm	Velio	10-200		250
...BOLSEY CORP. OF AMERICA - New York											
Bolsey 8		8mm	Submin	1956	Finon	1.8			50-600	Mc98	220
Bolsey B	24x36mm	35mm	35RF	1947	Anastigmat	3.2	44mm		200	Mc97	40
Bolsey B (red)	24x36mm	35mm	35RF	1947	Anastigmat	3.2	44mm		200		180
Bolsey B2	24x36mm	35mm	35RF	1949	Anastigmat	3.2	44mm			Mc97	40

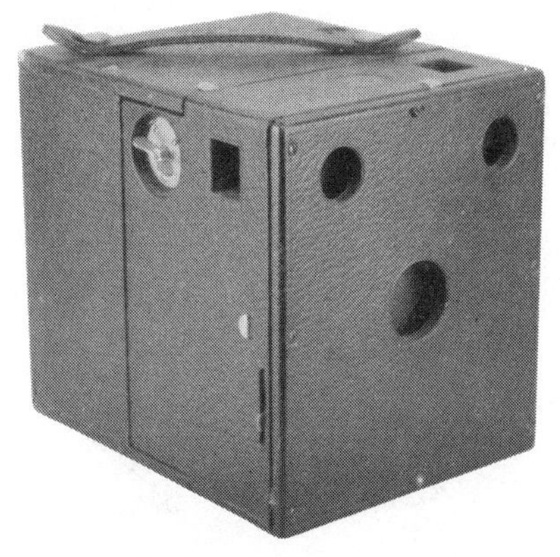

Weno Hawk-Eye No. 4

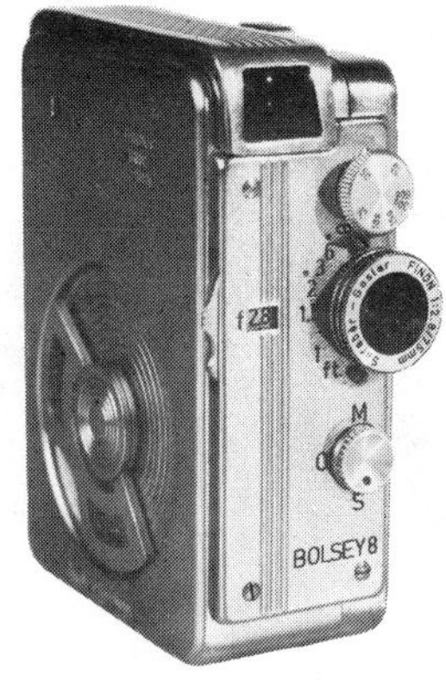

Bolsey 8

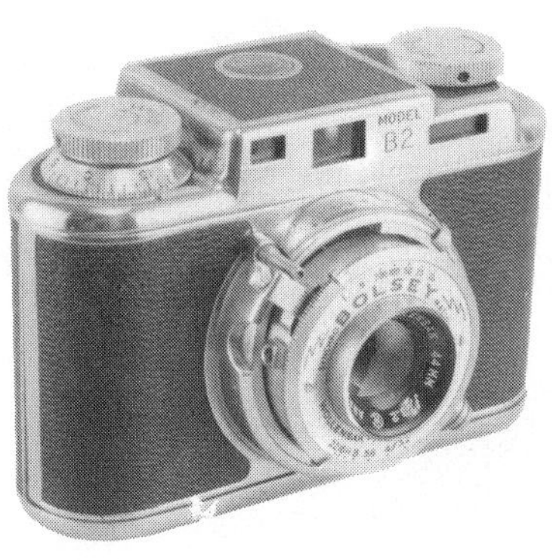

Bolsey B2

MODEL	FORMAT	FILM	TYPE	Year	LENS	Apert	FL	SHUTTER	SPEEDS	ILLUS	U.S.$
Bolsey B2 (red)	24x36mm	35mm	35RF	1949							180
Bolsey B3	24x36mm	35mm	35RF	1956	Steinheil	2.8	45mm	Gauthier	10-200	Mc97	40
Bolsey B4	24x36mm	35mm	35RF	1957	Alpha Anast.	3.5	45mm	Gauthier	10-200		40
Bolsey B22	24x36mm	35mm	35RF	1953	Wollensak Anast.	3.2	44mm			A2153	30
Bolsey BB Special	24x36mm	35mm	35mm	1954	Wollensak Anast.	3.2	44mm				30
Bolsey C	24x36mm	35mm	35TLR	1950	Wollensak Anast.	3.2	44mm	Wollensak	10-200	Mc97	100
Bolsey C22	24x36mm	35mm	35TLR	1953	Wollensak Anast.	3.2	44mm	Wollensak	10-200		110
Explorer	24x36mm	35mm	35VF	1955	Steinheil	2.8	45mm	Gauthier	25-200	Mc98	40
Jubilee	24x36mm	35mm	35RF	1955	Steinheil	2.8	45mm	Gauthier	10-200	Mc98	100
La Belle Pal	24x36mm	35mm	35VF	1952	Wollensak Anast.	4.5	44mm	Synch.-Matic		Mc98	100
Bolsey Reflex Mod. A	24x36mm	35mm	35SLR	1942	Bolca Anastigmat	2.8	50mm	focal plane	1-1000	Mc98	1100
Bolsey Reflex Mod. G	24x36mm	35mm	35SLR	1946	Angenieux	2.9	50mm	focal plane	1-1000	Mc98	290
Bolsey Reflex Mod. H	24x36mm	35mm	35SLR	1946	Angenieux	1.8	50mm	focal plane	1-1000	Mc98	370
Bolsey Uniset 8		8mm	Submin	1961	Navitar					Mc98	220
Bolsey US Air Force	24x36mm	35mm	35RF	1949	Anastgmat						160
Bolsey US Army PH324A	24x36mm	35mm	35RF	1949						Mc97	160
Bolseyflex	6x6cm	120	TLR-Box	1954		7.7	80mm			Mc97	40
...BOLTA-WERK - Nürnberg, Germany											
Boltavit	25x25mm	Roll	MiniatRo	1936	Corygon Anast.	4.5	40mm			Mc98	110
Photavit (828)		828	MiniatRo	1947	Radionar	8.8		Compur-Rap.	1-500	Mc98	120
Photavit (Bolta-size)		Roll	MiniatRo	1937	Special	7.7	40mm	Prontor II		A3303	150
Photavit 36	24x36mm	35mm	35VF	1957	Ennit	2.8	45mm	Prontor	1-300		120
Photavit 36 (meter)	24x36mm	35mm	35VF	1957	Ennit	2.8	45mm	Prontor-SVS	1-300		100
Photavit 36 Automatic	24x36mm	35mm	35VF	1957	Ennit	1.9	50mm	Prontor-SLK	1-300		100
Photavit I	24x24mm	35mm	35VF	1938	Luxar	2.9	38mm	Prontor	1-300	Mc98	150
Photavit I Deluxe	24x24mm	35mm	35VF	1938						Mc98	120
Photavit II	24x24mm	35mm	35VF	1939	Corygon	4.5	40mm			Mc98	120
Photavit III	24x24mm	35mm	35VF	1938						Mc98	140
Photavit IV	24x24mm	35mm	35VF	1938	Schneider	2.8	37.5mm	Compur	1-500	Mc98	160
Photavit V	24x24mm	35mm	35VF	1938						Mc98	100
...BONIFORTI & BALLERIO - Milano											
Perseo	24x36mm	35mm	35VF	1948	Perseo	3.5	50mm	focal plane	1/20-1000		1500
Perseo (RF)	24x36mm	35mm	35RF	1948	Perseo	3.5	50mm	focal plane	1/20-1000		2200
...BOREUX (Armand Boreux) - Basel, Switzerland											
Nanna 1	45x107	plate	StFoldPl	1909	Suter Anastigmat	6.8	62mm			HK472	370
...BOSTON CAMERA CO. - Boston, MA USA											
Hawk-Eye Detec. (leather)	4x5"	plate	DetectivBox	1888					I,T	Mc99	220
Hawk-Eye Detective (wood)	4x5"	plate	DetectivBox	1888					I,T	Mc99	310
...BOSTON CAMERA MFG. CO. - Boston, MA USA											
Bull's-Eye ("D"-window)	4x5"	Roll	RollBox	1892						Mc99	290
Bull's-Eye (round window)	4x5"	Roll	RollBox	1892						Mc99	150
Bull's-Eye "Ebonite"	4x5"	Roll	RollBox	1893						Mc99	800

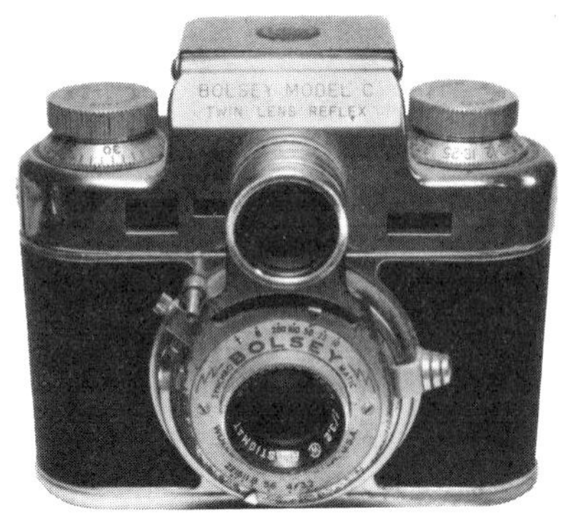

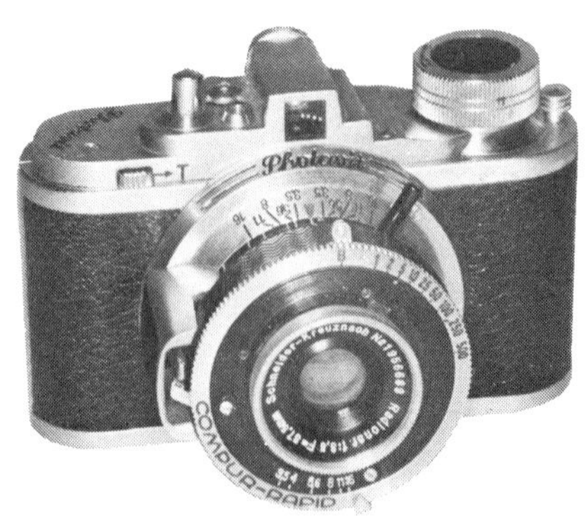

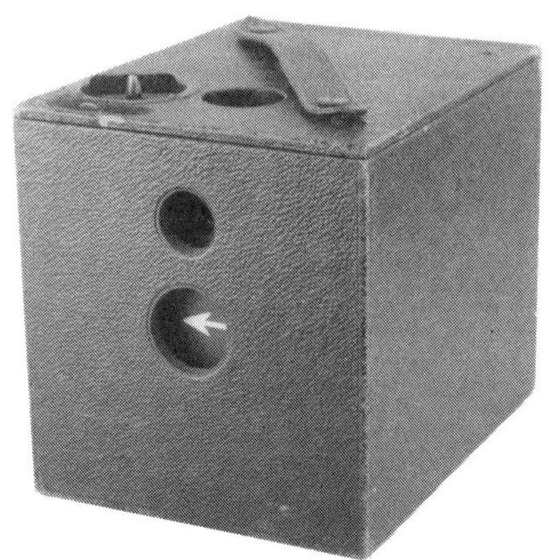

Bolsey C **Bolta Photavit (828)** **Boston Bull's-Eye**

MODEL	FORMAT	FILM	TYPE	Year	LENS	Apert	FL	SHUTTER	SPEEDS	ILLUS	U.S.$
...BOUMSELL - Paris											
Auteuil	3x4cm	127	TLRBox	1950	Topaz	3.5	50mm	Gitzo		F432	90
Azur	6x9cm	120	FoldRo	1950	Nicor Super			Azur	25-150	Mc99	30
Box Metal	6x9cm	120	MetalBox	1950						Mc99	30
Longchamp	3x4cm	127	TLR-Box	1950						Mc99	30
Photo-Magic (black)	4x6.5cm	127	RigidRo	1950	Meniscus				30	Mc99	30
Photo-Magic (wine-red)	4x6.5cm	127	RigidRo	1950	Meniscus				30	Mc99	30
...BRACK & CO. - Munich											
Field camera	13x18cm	plate	Field	1895	Blstigmat						230
Field camera	18x24cm	plate	Field								290
Linos	9x12cm	plate	FoldPl	1895	Universal Aplanat	8					160
...BRADAC (Bratri Bradácové) - Hovorcovice Czechoslovakia											
Autoflex	6x6cm	120	TLR	1937							180
Kamarad (I)	6x6cm	120	TLR	1936	Ludwig Bellar	3.9	75mm	Prontor II			130
Kamarad MII	6x6cm	120	TLR	1937	Trioplan	2.9	75mm	Compur	1-250		110
...BRANDT & WILDE NACHF. - Berlin											
Baedeker-Camera	9x12cm	plate	Disguised	1890	Weitw.-Aplanat					HK24	1300
...BRAUN (Carl Braun) - Nürnberg, Germany											
Candy	24x36mm	35mm	35mm	1988							20
Candy 2 (black)	24x36mm	35mm	35mm	1994							20
Candy 2 (red)	24x36mm	35mm	35mm	1994							20
Candy M	24x36mm	35mm	35mm	1988							20
Candy M 2 (black)	24x36mm	35mm	35mm	1994							20
Candy M 2 (red)	24x36mm	35mm	35mm	1994							20
Gloria	6x6cm	120	TelescRo	1954	Praxar	2.9	75mm	Pronto	25-200	Mc100	50
Gloria	6x6cm	120	TelescRo	1954	Praxanar	2.9	75mm	Prontor-SV	1-300	Mc100	50
Gloriette	24x36mm	35mm	35VF	1954	Steinheil Cassar	2.8	45mm	Pronto		Mc100	30
Gloriette B	24x36mm	35mm	35VF	1955	Steinheil Cassar	2.8	45mm	Prontor-SVS	1-300	A1128	50
Ideal Box S	6x6cm	120	RollBox	1953							30
Ideal Box V	6x6cm	120	RollBox	1953							30
Imperial (eye-level)	6x6cm	120	StrutRo	1953	Luxar						30
Imperial Box 6x6 Mod. S	6x6cm	120	TLR-Box	1951						Mc100	30
Imperial Box 6x6 Mod. V	6x6cm	120	TLR-Box	1951					M,Z	Mc100	30
Imperial Box 6x9 Mod. S	6x6cm	120	MetalBox	1951					M,Z	Mc100	30
Imperial Box 6x9 Mod. V	6x6cm	120	MetalBox	1951					M,Z	Mc100	30
Luxa six	6x6cm	120	StrutRo	1953	Luxar					Mc100	30
Nimco	6x6cm	120	TLR-Box	1960						Mc100	40
Norca	6x9cm	120	FoldRo	1953	Praxar	8			25,75		30
Norca I	6x9cm	120	FoldRo	1952	Praxar Achromatic	8	10.5cm		25,75		30
Norca II	6x9cm	120	FoldRo		Gotar	6.3					30
Norica II Super	6x9cm	120	FoldRo		Cassar	6.3		Vario			40
Norica III	6x9cm	120	FoldRo		Gotar	4.5		Pronto	1-250		40

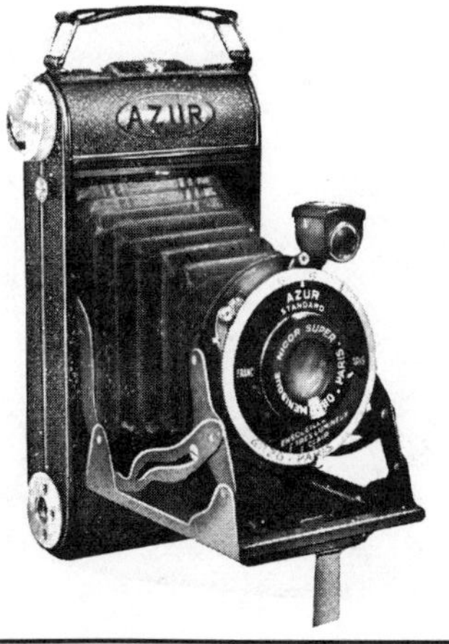

Boumsell Azur

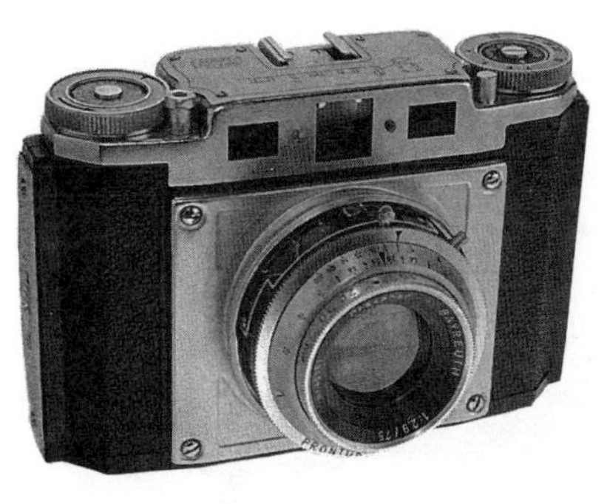

Braun Gloria

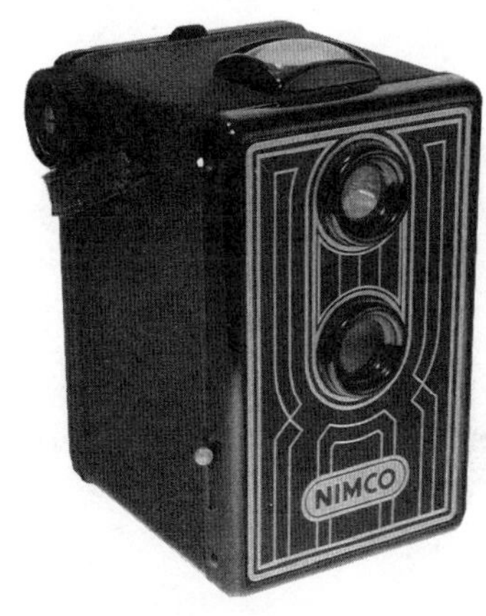

Braun Nimco

MODEL	FORMAT	FILM	TYPE	Year	LENS	Apert	FL	SHUTTER	SPEEDS	ILLUS	U.S.$
Norica IV	6x9cm	120	FoldRo		Cassar	4.5		Prontor-S			40
Pax	6x6cm	120	TelescRo	1950	Paxanar					Mc100	30
Paxette I	24x36mm	35mm	35VF	1952	Kata	2.8	45mm	SVS		A1125	50
Paxette Ia	24x36mm	35mm	35VF	1952	Kata	2.8	45mm	SVS	200		50
Paxette Ib	24x36mm	35mm	35VF	1950	Cassar	2.8	45mm	Pronto			40
Paxette IBL	24x36mm	35mm	35VF	1950	Cassar	2.8	45mm	Pronto			60
Paxette IL	24x36mm	35mm	35VF	1950	Cassar	2.8	45mm	Pronto			60
Paxette IM	24x36mm	35mm	35RF	1950	Cassar	2.8	45mm	Pronto			50
Paxette II	24x36mm	35mm	35VF	1950	Cassar	2.8	45mm	Pronto		A2100	60
Paxette IIL	24x36mm	35mm	35VF	1950	Cassar	2.8	45mm	Pronto			100
Paxette IIM	24x36mm	35mm	35RF	1953	Staeble-Kata	2.8	45mm				60
Paxette 28	28x28mm	126	126	1965	Color-Paxon	2.8	38mm	Prontor	125		50
Paxette 28 Auto	28x28mm	126	126	1965	Cassarit-L	2.8	38mm	Prontor	125		50
Paxette 28 B	28x28mm	126	126	1965	Color-Paxon	2.8	38mm	Prontor	125		40
Paxette 28 BC	28x28mm	126	126	1965	Trinar	2.8	38mm	Prontor	125		30
Paxette 28 F	28x28mm	126	126	1965	Color-Paxon	2.8	38mm	Prontor	125		30
Paxette 28 LK	28x28mm	126	126	1965	Xenar	2.8	38mm	Compur	250		30
Paxette 35	24x36mm	35mm	35VF	1965	Cassar	2.8	45mm	Prontor	125	A2101	20
Paxette 35 Auto	24x36mm	35mm	35VF	1965	Cassar	2.8	45mm	Prontormatic	125		30
Paxette 35 B	24x36mm	35mm	35VF	1965	Cassar	2.8	45mm	Prontor	125		50
Paxette 35 LK	24x36mm	35mm	35VF	1965	Cassar	2.8	45mm	Prontor	250		50
Paxette 35 SB	24x36mm	35mm	35VF	1965	Cassar	2.8	45mm	Prontor	250		50
Paxette Automatic	24x36mm	35mm	35RF	1958	Cassarit	2.8	50mm	Prontor-SLK	-300		70
Paxette Automatic I	24x36mm	35mm	35RF	1958	Cassarit	2.8	50mm	Prontor-SLK	-300		70
Paxette Automatic Super III	24x36mm	35mm	35RF	1958	Color Ultralit	2.8	50mm	Prontor-SLK	-300	Mc101	50
Paxette Electromatic I	24x36mm	35mm	35VF	1960		5.6			1/40		30
Paxette Electromatic Ia	24x36mm	35mm	35VF	1960		2.8	40mm			A1129	50
Paxette Electromatic II	24x36mm	35mm	35VF	1960		2.8			1/30-300		30
Paxette Electromatic IIs	24x36mm	35mm	35VF	1960	Katagon	5.6	40mm	Prontormat-S	1/30-300		50
Paxette Electromatic III	24x36mm	35mm	35VF	1960	Ultralit	2.8	40mm	Prontormatic	1/30-500		50
Paxette Reflex Ib	24x36mm	35mm	35SLR	1963	Reflex-Ultralit	2.8	50mm				80
Paxette Reflex Automatic	24x36mm	35mm	35SLR	1959	Reflex-Ultralit	2.8	50mm	Sync-Compur	1-500	Mc101	70
Paxette Reflex Autom. IB	24x36mm	35mm	35SLR	1961	Reflex-Ultralit	2.8	50mm	Sync-Compur	1-500		90
Paxette Reflex Autom. II	24x36mm	35mm	35SLR	1963	Reflex-Ultralit	2.8	50mm	Sync-Compur	1-500		90
Paxiflash	4x4cm	127	RigidRo	1961						Mc101	30
Paxina I	6x6cm	120	TelescRo	1952		7.7	75mm		30-100	A1526	30
Paxina II 2.9	6x6cm	120	TelescRo	1953	Steiner	2.9	75mm		25-200		20
Paxina II 3.5	6x6cm	120	TelescRo	1952	Staeble Kataplast	3.5	75mm	Vario Synch		A534	20
Paxina IIa	6x6cm	120	TelescRo	1953	Steiner	6.3	75mm	Vario			60
Paxina IIb	6x6cm	120	TelescRo	1953	Optik	8	75mm	M&B Synch			30
Paxina IIc	6x6cm	120	TelescRo	1953	Pranar		75mm	M&B Synch			30
Paxina 29	6x6cm	120	TelescRo	1953	Steinar	2.9	75mm	Pronto			40

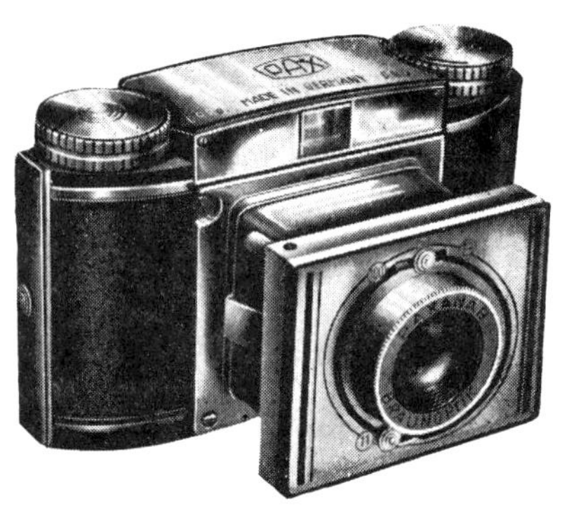

Pax

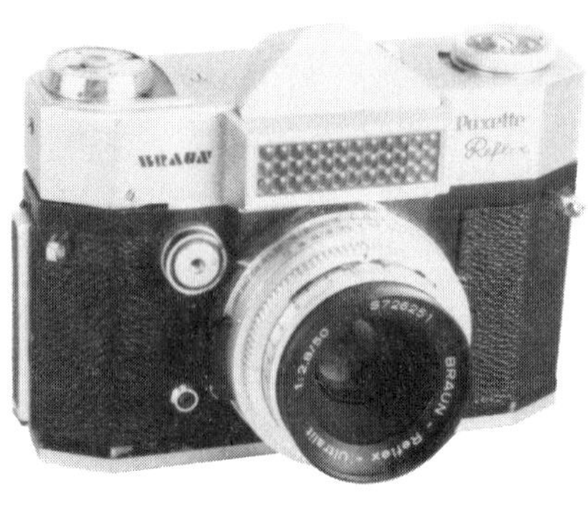

Paxette Reflex Automatic

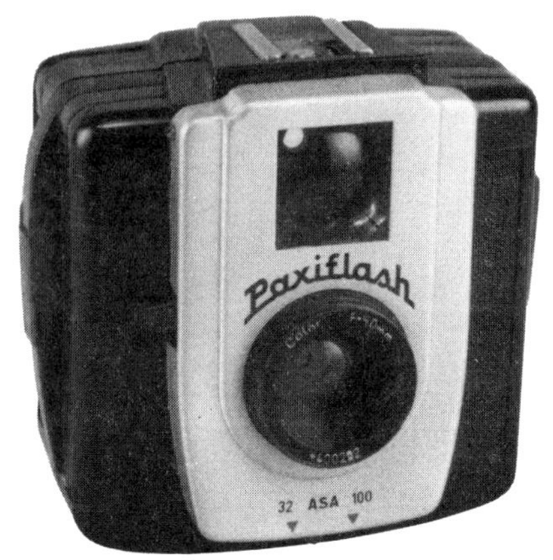

Paxiflash

MODEL	FORMAT	FILM	TYPE	Year	LENS	Apert	FL	SHUTTER	SPEEDS	ILLUS	U.S.$
Reporter	6x6cm	120	StrutRo	1953	Luxar	8	75mm	simple		Mc101	30
Super Colorette	24x36mm	35mm	35RF	1957	Cassar S	2.8		Compur			30
Super Colorette I	24x36mm	35mm	35RF	1957	Plastigon	2.8		Compur			40
Super Colorette I b	24x36mm	35mm	35RF	1957							50
Super Colorette I BL	24x36mm	35mm	35RF	1957	Cassarit	2.8	50mm	Sync-Compur	1-500		50
Super Colorette II	24x36mm	35mm	35RF	1957							70
Super Colorette II b	24x36mm	35mm	35RF	1957							90
Super Colorette II BL	24x36mm	35mm	35RF	1957	Cassarit	2.8	50mm	Sync-Compur	1-500		80
Super Paxette I	24x36mm	35mm	35RF	1957	Staeble Kata	2.8	45mm	Prontor-SVS			50
Super Paxette I b	24x36mm	35mm	35RF	1957	Kata			Pronto			50
Super Paxette I L	24x36mm	35mm	35RF	1958							70
Super Paxette II	24x36mm	35mm	35RF	1956	Cassarit	2.8	50mm	Prontor-SVS		A2099	50
Super Paxette II	24x36mm	35mm	35RF	1956	Xenar	2.8	50mm	Prontor-SVS		A2099	50
Super Paxette II B	24x36mm	35mm	35RF	1957							60
Super Paxette II BL	24x36mm	35mm	35RF	1958						A1130	90
Super Paxette II L	24x36mm	35mm	35RF	1958							50
Super Paxette 35	24x36mm	35mm	35RF	1965	Ultralit	2.8					70
Super Vier	4x4cm	127	PlasticBox	1956	Color		50mm			Mc101	30
Trend AF3	24x36mm	35mm	35AF	1993							70
Trend AF3 Date	24x36mm	35mm	35AF	1993							90
Trend Micro SM		35mm	35AF	1991		3.5	35mm		1-500		150
Trend Zoom 70	24x36mm	35mm	35AFZ	1991	Zoom Lens	3.5-6.7	35-70		¼-250		180
Trend Zoom 105	24x36mm	35mm	35AFZ	1991	Zoom Lens	4-10.9	38-105		1/3-250		270
...BRINKERT (Franz Brinkert) - Germany											
Efbe		Disc	Submin		Enna	2.8	20mm		25-100		90
...BRIZET (Andre Brizet) - Paris											
Physioscope	6x13cm	plate	StJumelle	1920	Tessar	6.3	75mm	Stereo-Compur	1-150		280
...BROOKLYN CAMERA CO. - Brooklyn, NY USA											
Brooklyn Camera	3¼x4¼"	plate	Studio	1885							260
...BRÜCKNER - Rabenau, Germany											
Field Camera	9x12cm	plate	Tailboard	1900	various			various			310
Field Camera	13x18cm	plate	Tailboard	1900	various			various			310
Field Camera	18x24cm	plate	Tailboard	1900	various			various			310
Field Camera (early)	9x12cm	plate	Field	1895	various			various			200
Field Camera (early)	10x15cm	plate	Field	1895	various			various			270
Field Camera (early)	13x18cm	plate	Field	1895	various			various			290
Field Camera (early)	18x24cm	plate	Field	1895	various			various			290
Schüler-Apparat	9x12cm	plate	Tailboard	1905	Voigtl. Collinear II	7.7		string-set			230
Union Mod. III		plate	Field	1920	Busch Rapid Apl.	7.5	260mm	roller-blind			540
...BRUNS (Christian Bruns) - Munich											
Detective camera	9x12cm	plate	DetectivBox	1893		6.3	144mm			Mc102	4500
Detective camera	12x16.5	plate	DetectivBox	1893		6.3	144mm			Mc102	4900

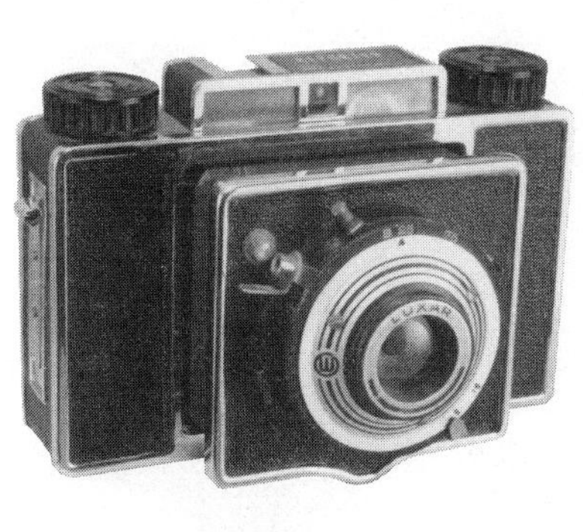

Braun Reporter

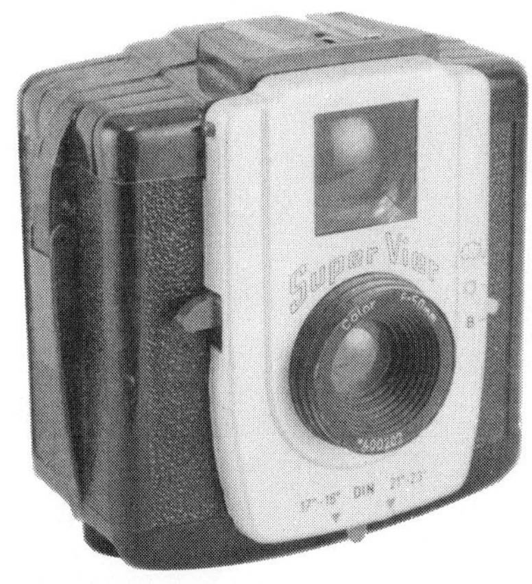

Braun Super Vier

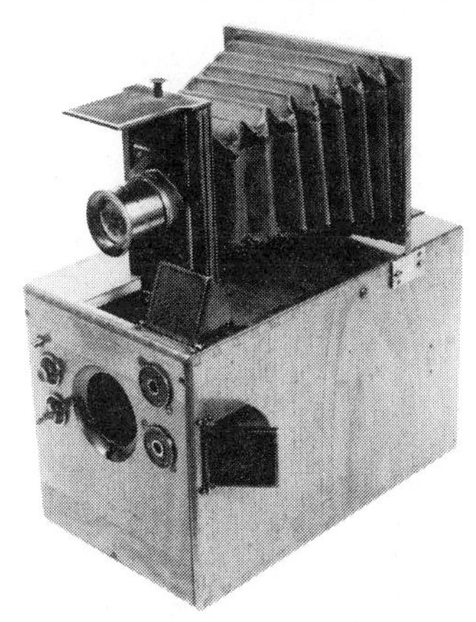

Bruns Detective Camera

MODEL	FORMAT	FILM	TYPE	Year	LENS	Apert	FL	SHUTTER	SPEEDS	ILLUS	U.S.$
...BUESS - Lausanne											
Multiprint	13x18cm	plate	Special		Corygon	3.5	105mm		1-100	Mc102	800
...BULLARD CAMERA CO. - Springfield, MA USA											
Folding Magazine Cam.	4x5"	plate	FoldMag	1898						Mc102	370
Folding camera	10x13cm	plate	FoldPl	1901	Symmetrical			Wollensak			130
Folding camera	13x18cm	plate	FoldPl	1901	Symmetrical			Wollensak			130
...BÜLTER & STAMMER - Hannover, Germany											
Baby Taschen-Kamera	6x9cm	plate	VtFoldPl	1911	Extra Rap. Aplan.	8		Vario	25-100		70
Folding camera Mod. 86	10x15cm	plate	FoldPl	1915	Euryplan			Compound			130
Zweiverschluss-Klappk.	9x12cm	plate	HzFoldPl	1911	Simplar	6.8		focal plane	1000		240
Zweiverschluss-Klappk.	10x15cm	plate	HzFoldPl	1911	Simplar	6.8		focal plane	1000		240
...BURKE & JAMES INC. - Chicago, IL											
Cub No. 2A	2½x4¼"	116	RollBox	1914	achromatic				I,T		20
Cub No. 3	3¼x4¼"	124	RollBox	1914	achromatic				I,T		10
Cub No. 3A	3¼x5½"	122	RollBox	1914	achromatic				I,T		20
Folding Ingento 3A Mod. 3	3¼x5½"	122	HzFoldRo	1915	Ilex			Ingento		Mc103	30
Folding Rexo 1A	2½x4¼"	116	VtFoldRo	1916	Anastigmat					Mc103	20
Folding Rexo 3	3¼x4¼"	124	VtFoldRo	1916	Anastigmat			Ilex			30
Folding Rexo 3	3¼x4¼"	124	VtFoldRo	1916	Rapid Rectilinear			Ilex			30
Folding Rexo 3A	3¼x5½"	122	VtFoldRo	1916							30
Grover	4x5"	plate	Monorail	1940	various			various			270
Grover	5x7"	plate	Monorail	1940	various			various			250
Grover	8x10"	plate	Monorail	1940	various			various			410
Ingento Jr. 1A	2½x4¼"	116	VtFoldRo	1915	achromatic	6.3			I,T	Mc103	30
Ingento Jr. 3A	3¼x5½"	122	VtFoldRo	1915	Ilex			Ingento	I,T	Mc103	30
Panoram 120	6x18cm	120	WideAng	1956	Ross	4	5"		1/100		220
PH-6-A	5x7"	Sheet	WideAng		Wollensak Extra	12.5		Betax No. 2			240
PH-503A/PF Fingerprint			Special	1950							110
Press	2¼x3¼"		Press		various			various			60
Press	3¼x4¼"		Press		various			various			60
Rembrandt Portrait	4x5"	plate	Studio	1950				Packard			260
Rembrandt Portrait	5x7"	plate	Studio	1950				Packard			220
Rembrandt Portrait II	4x5"	plate	Studio	1956				Packard			260
Rembrandt Portrait II	5x7"	plate	Studio	1956				Packard			220
Rexo Box	6x9cm	120	RollBox								10
Rexo Jr. 1A	2½x4¼"	116	VtFoldRo	1916	Single Achromatic			Ilex			30
Rexo Jr. 1A	2½x4¼"	116	VtFoldRo	1916	Rapid Rectilinear			Ilex			30
Rexo Jr. 2C	2⅞x2⅞"	130	VtFoldRo	1917	Rapid Rectilinear	7.5					30
Rexo Jr. 3	3¼x4¼"	124	VtFoldRo	1916	Single Achromatic			Ilex			20
Rexoette No. 2	6x9cm	120	RollBox	1910					I,T	Mc103	20
Vest Pocket Rexo			FoldRo		Wollensak Anast.	7.5		Ultex			40
View	4x5"	plate	View		various			various			280

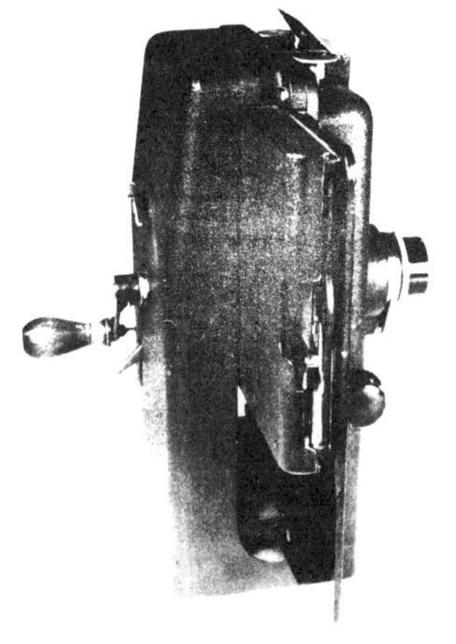

Buess Multiprint

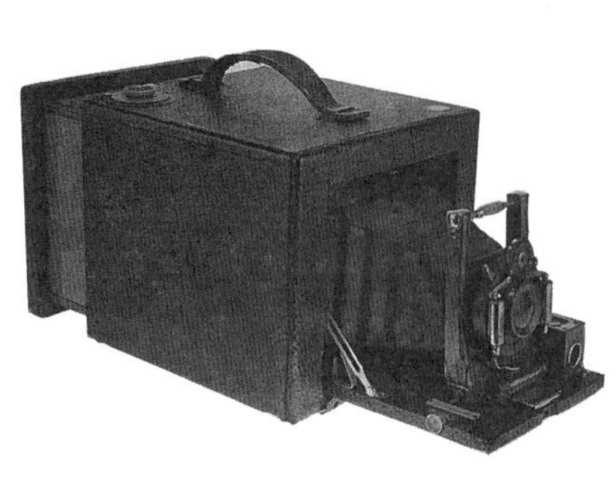

Bullard Folding Magazine Camera

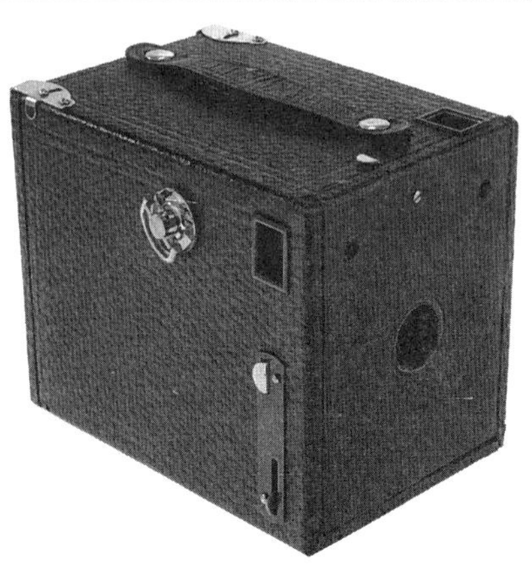

Rexoette No. 2

MODEL	FORMAT	FILM	TYPE	Year	LENS	Apert	FL	SHUTTER	SPEEDS	ILLUS	U.S.$
View	5x7"	plate	View		various			various			280
View	8x10"	plate	View		various			various			490
Watson Press	4x5"		Press		Kodak Ektar	4.7	127mm				150
Watson-Holmes Fingerprint			Special	1950							110
...BURLEIGH BROOKS INC. - Englewood, NJ											
Bee Bee Mod. A	6.5x9cm	plate	FoldPl	1938	Radionar	4.5	4.25"	Compur		Mc103	70
Bee Bee Mod. B	9x12cm	plate	FoldPl	1938	Radionar	4.5	5.25"	Compur		Mc103	70
Brooks Veriwide (f5.6)	2¼x3¼"	Roll	WideAng	1970	Super Angulon	5.6	47mm	Sync-Compur		Mc103	900
Brooks Veriwide (f8)	2¼x3¼"	Roll	WideAng	1970	Super Angulon	8	47mm	Sync-Compur		Mc103	800
...BUSCH (Emil Busch) - London, England											
Folding Plate Camera	9x12cm	plate	FoldPl	1907	Lukar	6.8	150mm	compound			70
Freewheel, Mod. B		Roll	HzFoldPl	1902	Busch	6		Woll. Regular		Mc103	140
Heda			Strut	1902	Busch Anastigmat	7.7	130mm	focal plane	1000		100
Pockam Mod. A	3¼x4¼"	Roll	HzFoldRo	1903	Busch Achromatic	6		Junior	I,T,B		70
Pockam Mod. B	9x12cm	Roll	HzFoldRo	1903	Busch Aplanat	6		Unicum	1-100	A362	70
Stereo Beecam		plate	StFoldPl		Busch Periplanet No 1			pneumatic		A778	360
...BUSCH (Emil Busch) - Rathenow, Germany											
Ageb	9x12cm	plate	FoldPl	1901	Busch Periskop	12	150mm	B&L Auto Junior		HK138	120
Ageb II	9x12cm	plate	FoldPl	1901	Busch Periskop	12	150mm	B&L Auto Junior			100
Folding Plate	9x12cm	plate	FoldPl	1914	Rapid Aplanat	7	170mm	Cronos-C			70
Folding Plate	5x7"	plate	FoldPl	1914	Tessar	4.5	165mm	Cronos-C			80
Folding Rollfilm Camera	5x7.5cm	Roll	FoldRo	1914	Corygon	4.5	90mm	Ibsor			50
Folding Rollfilm Camera	6x9cm	Roll	FoldRo	1928	Glaukar	4.5	105mm	Compur			30
Folding Rollfilm Camera	7x10cm	Roll	FoldRo		Meniscus			simple			40
Lynx	8x10.5cm	Pl+Ro	FoldRo	1910	Rapid Aplanat	8		B&L Auto Junior		HK206	180
Neostar	9x12cm	plate	FoldRo	1910	Rapid Aplanat	8		B&L Auto Junior		HK207	50
Perscheidkamera	9x12cm	plate	FoldPl	1927	Perscheid						540
Preis-Camera 9x12	9x12cm	plate	FoldPl	1901	Rapid Aplanat	6.5	150mm	Ebusch		HK141	70
Preis-Camera 10x15	10x15cm	plate	FoldPl	1901	Rapid Aplanat	7	170mm	Ebusch			200
Roia	10x15cm	plate	StrutPl	1910	Rapid Aplanat	8		focal plane		HK142	80
Stereo Reflex	6x13cm	Roll	SterRefl	1920	Roia Detective Ap.	6		focal plane	20-1000	A1814	540
Tropenkamera	6.5x9cm	plate	FoldPl	1920	Tiaranar	4.5	120mm				700
Vier-Sechs	4.5x6cm	plate	Strut	1920	Detective-Aplanat	6.8	75mm	Compound	25-100		220
...BUSCH CAMERA CORP. - Chicago											
Pressman 4x5	4x5"	plate	Press		Ektar	4.7		Rapax		Mc104	200
Pressman 6x9	6x9cm	plate	Press		Color Skopar	3.5		Compur			130
Verascope F-40	24x30cm		Ster35	1950	Berthoit	3.5	40mm	guillotine	250		540
...BUTCHER (W. Butcher & Sons) - London											
Box Carbine No. 2	2¼x3¼"	120	RollBox	1923	Aldis Uno	7.7					50
Cameo 2¼x3¼	2¼x3¼"	plate	FoldPl	1900	Ross Xpres	4.5		Compur	250	Mc104	50
Cameo 3¼x4¼	3¼x4¼"	plate	FoldPl	1900	Ross Xpres	4.5		Compur	250	Mc104	50
Cameo Stereo Mod. 0	9x18cm	plate	StFoldPl	1906	Aldis			T,B,I		Mc104	250

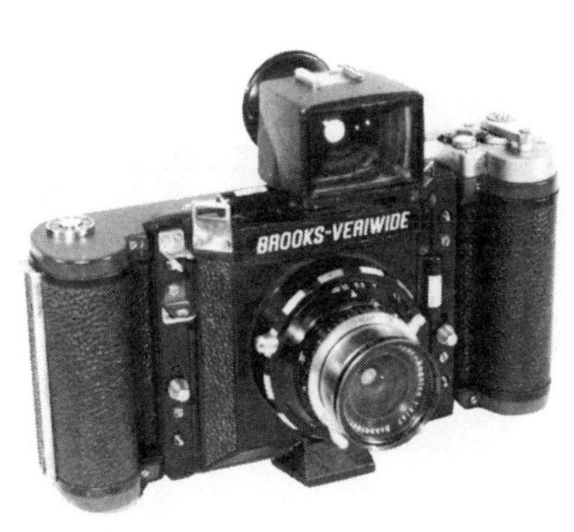

Brooks Veriwide

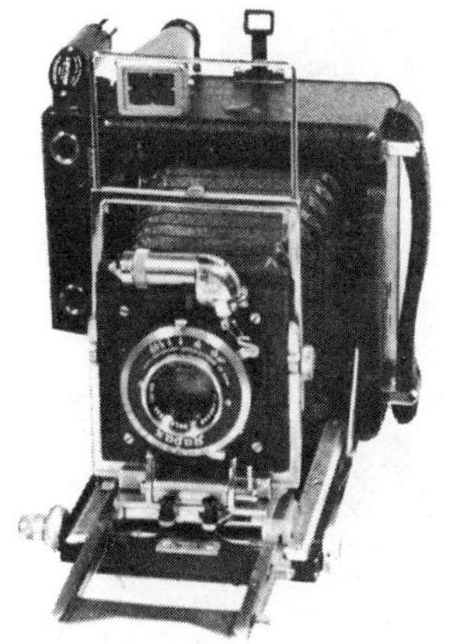
Busch Pressman 4x5

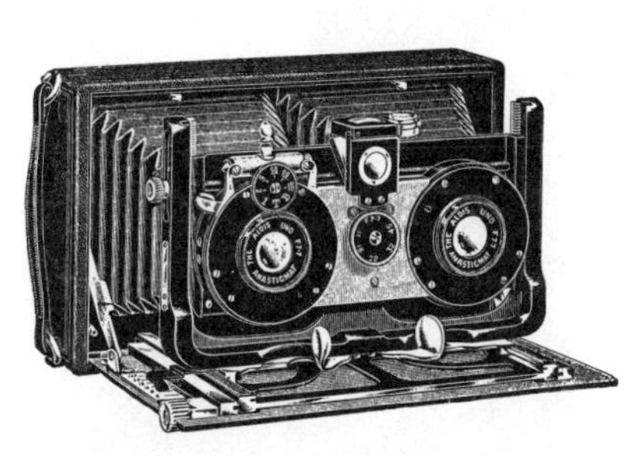
Cameo Stereo Mod. 0

MODEL	FORMAT	FILM	TYPE	Year	LENS	Apert	FL	SHUTTER	SPEEDS	ILLUS	U.S.$
Carbine 2¼x3¼	2¼x3¼"	120	FoldRo	1920	Aldis Uno	7.7				Mc104	50
Carbine 3¼x4¼	3¼x4¼	Roll	FoldRo	1920	Aldis Uno	7.7				Mc104	50
Clincher No. 1	2¼x3¼"	plate	MagBox	1913					T,I		40
Clincher No. 2	3¼x4¼"	plate	MagBox	1913					T,I		40
Clincher No. 3	3¼x4¼"	plate	MagBox	1913					T,I		40
Clincher No. 4	9x12cm	plate	MagBox	1913					T,I		40
Coronet No. 1	3¼x4¼"	plate	Field	1913	achromatic						240
Coronet No. 2	3¼x4¼"	plate	Field	1913	Primus RR						240
Dandycam Automatic	25mm	plate	Button	1913							540
Field camera	5x7"	plate	Field	1904	various			various			140
Field camera	6½x8½"	plate	Field	1904	various			various			160
Klimax Mod. I	3¼x4¼"	plate	FoldPl	1910	Aldis Uno	7.7		Lukos Sector	100	Mc104	50
Klimax Mod. II	4¼x6½"	plate	FoldPl	1910	Aldis Uno	7.7		Lukos Sector	100	Mc104	50
Little Nipper 4.5x6	4.5x6cm	plate	MagBox	1900	Meniscus				I	Mc105	170
Little Nipper 6.5x9	6.5x9cm	plate	MagBox	1900	Meniscus				I	Mc105	170
Maxim No. 1	6x6cm	120	RollBox	1903						A1336	50
Maxim No. 2	6x9cm	120	RollBox	1903							50
Maxim No. 3	6.5x11cm	Roll	RollBox	1903							50
Maxim No. 4	8x11cm	Roll	RollBox	1903							50
Midg No. 0	3¼x4¼"	plate	MagBox	1902	Rapid Rectilinear				I,T	Mc105	80
Midg No. 0 PC	3¼x5½"	plate	MagBox	1902	Rapid Rectilinear				I,T	Mc105	110
Midg No. 1	3¼x4¼"	plate	MagBox	1902	Rapid Rectilinear	11			I,T,B	Mc105	70
Midg No. 1 PC	3¼x5½"	plate	MagBox	1902	Rapid Rectilinear	11			I,T,B	Mc105	70
Midg No. 2	3¼x4¼"	plate	MagBox	1902	Rapid Rectilinear	11		simple	1/2-100	Mc105	70
Midg No. 2 PC	3¼x5½"	plate	MagBox	1902	Rapid Rectilinear	11		simple	1/2-100	Mc105	70
Midg No. 3	3¼x4¼"	plate	MagBox	1902	Rapid Rectilinear	8		Unicum	1-100	Mc105	70
Midg No. 3 PC	3¼x5½"	plate	MagBox	1902	Rapid Rectilinear	8		Unicum	1-100	Mc105	70
Midg No. 4	3¼x4¼"	plate	MagBox	1902	Rapid Rectilinear	8		B&L Automat	1-100	Mc105	70
National	4¼x6½"	plate	Field	1900	Ross Homocentric	6.3	7"	Thornton-Pickard			370
Pilot No. 2	2½x3½"	plate	MagBox	1904							50
Popular Carbine No. 1	2¼x3¼"		VtFoldRo	1920	various			various		Mc105	50
Popular Carbine No. 1A	2½x4¼"		VtFoldRo	1920	various			various		Mc105	50
Popular Carbine No. 2	2⅞x2⅞"		VtFoldRo	1920	various			various		Mc105	40
Popular Pressman	3¼x4¼"	plate	LgSLR	1909	Beck	4.5		focal plane		Mc105	230
Popular Pressman	3¼x4¼"	plate	LgSLR	1909	Dallmeyer	4.5		focal plane		Mc105	230
Popular Pressman	3¼x5½"	plate	LgSLR	1909	Ross	4.5		focal plane		Mc105	230
Primus No. 1 3¼x4¼	3¼x4¼"	plate	PlateBox	1899	Rapid Rectilinear			Thornton-Pickard			100
Primus No. 1 4x5	4x5"	plate	PlateBox	1899	Rapid Rectilinear			Thornton-Pickard			100
Primus No. 1 4¼x6½	4¼x6½"	plate	PlateBox	1899	Rapid Rectilinear			Thornton-Pickard			100
Primus No. 2 3¼x4¼	3¼x4¼"	plate	PlateBox	1899	Euryscope	6		Thornton-Pickard		Mc105	100
Primus No. 2 4x5	4x5"	plate	PlateBox	1899	Euryscope	6		Thornton-Pickard		Mc105	100
Primus No. 2 4¼x6½	4¼x6½"	plate	PlateBox	1899	Euryscope	6		Thornton-Pickard		Mc105	100

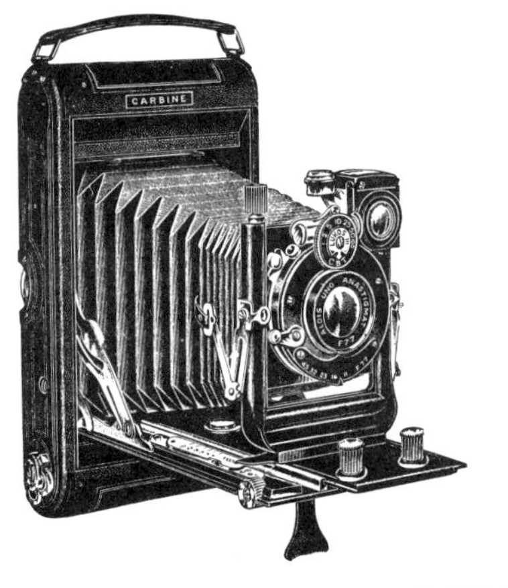

Carbine

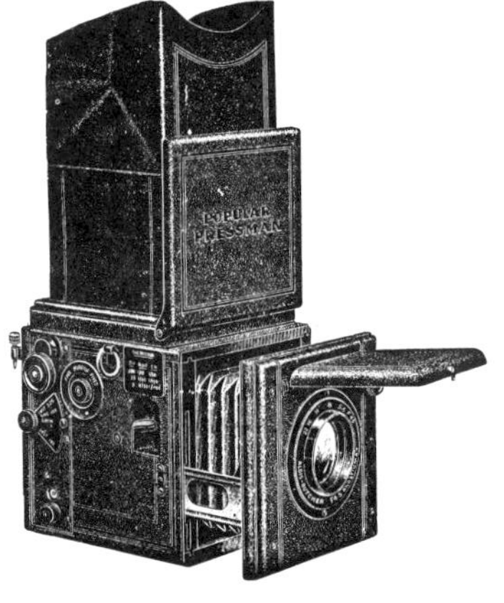

Popular Pressman

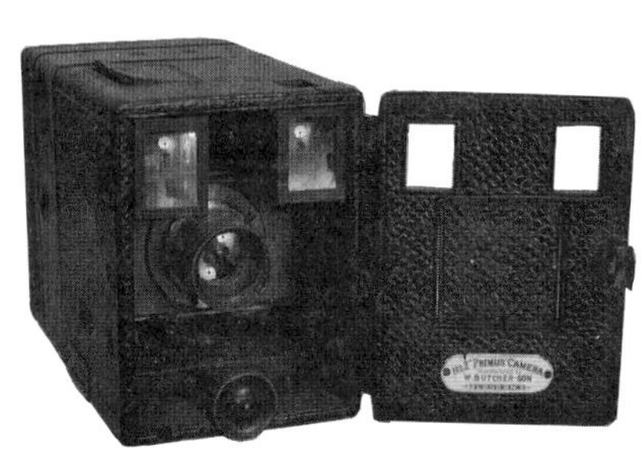

Primus No. 2

MODEL	FORMAT	FILM	TYPE	Year	LENS	Apert	FL	SHUTTER	SPEEDS	ILLUS	U.S.$
Primus No. 3 3¼x4¼	3¼x4¼"	plate	PlateBox	1899				Thornton-Pickard			180
Primus No. 3 4x5	4x5"	plate	PlateBox	1899				Thornton-Pickard			180
Primus No. 3 4¼x6½	4¼x6½"	plate	PlateBox	1899				Thornton-Pickard			180
Reflex Carbine	6x9cm	120	MedSLR	1925	Aldis Uno Anast.	7.7	4.25"		T,I	Mc105	140
Royal Mail 3-lens	3¼x4¼"	plate	MultiLens	1907							1900
Royal Mail 15-lens	3¼x4¼"	plate	MultiLens	1907						Mc105	2800
Sportie Carbine	4x6.5cm	127	RollBox	1920	Alphar	9.5					50
Stereolette	45x107	plate	StFoldPl	1910	Zeiss Tessar	4.5		Compound		Mc105	390
Stereolette	45x107	plate	StFoldPl	1910	Aldis Uno Anast.			Compound		Mc105	390
Tropical W.P. Carbine	6x6cm	120	FoldRo	1923	Aldis Uno Anast.	7.7		Lukos II			200
Tropical W.P. Carbine	6x9cm	120	FoldRo	1923	Aldis Uno Anast.	7.7		Lukos II			200
Tropical W.P. Carbine	6.5x11cm	116	FoldRo	1923	Aldis Uno Anast.	7.7		Lukos II			200
Twink	1¾x2¼"	plate	MagBox	1907	Rapid Landscape	11			I,T	A2833	240
Watch Pocket Carbine	6x6cm	120	FoldRo	1920	Aldis Uno Anast.	7.7		Lukos II		Mc106	70
Watch Pocket Carbine	6x9cm	120	FoldRo	1920	Aldis Uno Anast.	7.7		Lukos II		Mc106	70
Watch Pocket Carbine	6.5x11cm	116	FoldRo	1920	Aldis Uno Anast.	7.7		Lukos II		Mc106	70
Watch Pocket Klimax I	1¾x2¼"	plate	FoldPl	1913	Aldis Uno Anast.	7.7	3"	Lukos II			90
Watch Pocket Klimax II	1¾x2¼"	plate	FoldPl	1913	Aldis Uno Anast.	4.9	3"	Compound			90
...BUTLER BROS. - Chicago											
Pennant Camera No. 20	4x5"	plate	PlateBox							Mc106	50
Universal	2¼x3¼"	120	RollBox							Mc106	20
...CADOT (A. Cadot) - Paris											
Jumelle	9x12cm	plate	Jumelle	1905	Anastigmat			guillotine	P,I	F1084	150
Scenographe	45x107	plate	StJumelle	1900	Rapid Rectilinear	11	150mm	guillotine			240
Scenographe Panoramique	9x18cm	plate	StJumelle	1910	Anastigmat	8	110mm	guillotine		F1365	270
...CAILLON - Paris											
Biopta 45x107	45x107	pack	StJumelle	1925	Boyer Saphir	6.3		guillotine	1/20-100		290
Biopta 6x13	6x13cm	pack	StJumelle	1925	Boyer Saphir	6.3	72mm	guillotine	1/20-100		280
Bioscope 45x107	45x107		StJumelle	1915	Tessar			guillotine		Mc106	340
Bioscope 6x13	6x13cm		StJumelle	1915	Balbreck R.R.			guillotine		F1183	260
Bioscope 8x16	8x16cm		StJumelle	1915							260
Kaloscope			SterFold	1916	Hermagis	6.8	112mm				430
Megascope	6x13cm	plate	StJumelle	1915	Hermagis	6.3	85mm	guillotine	½-200		200
Scopea 45x107	45x107		StJumelle	1920	Berthoit Olor	6.8	85mm	3-speed	20-100	F1366	260
Scopea 6x13	6x13cm		StJumelle	1920	Roussel Stylor	6.3	85mm	3-speed	20-100	F1366	200
Scopea 6x9	6x9cm		StJumelle	1920	Berthoit Olor	6.8	85mm	3-speed	20-200		140
...CAMERA CORP. OF AMERICA - Chicago											
CeeAy 35	24x36mm	35mm	35rf	1949	Wollensak Anast.	4.5		Sync.Alphax	25-150	Mc107	540
CeeAy 35	24x36mm	35mm	35rf	1949	Wollensak Anast.	3.5		Sync.Alphax	10-200	Mc107	580
Perfex DeLuxe	24x36mm	35mm	35rf	1947	Wollensak	2.8				Mc107	60
Perfex Fifty-Five	24x36mm	35mm	35rf	1940	Scienar	3.5		focal plane	1-1250	Mc107	30
Perfex FortyFour	24x36mm	35mm	35rf	1939	Interchangeable	3.5	50mm	focal plane	1-1250	Mc107	70

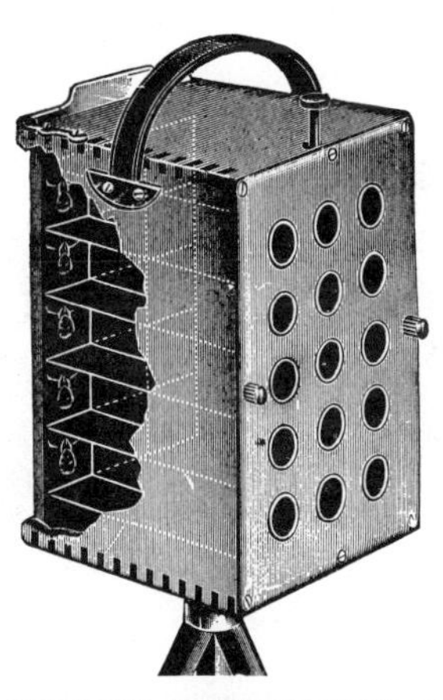

Royal Mail 15-lens

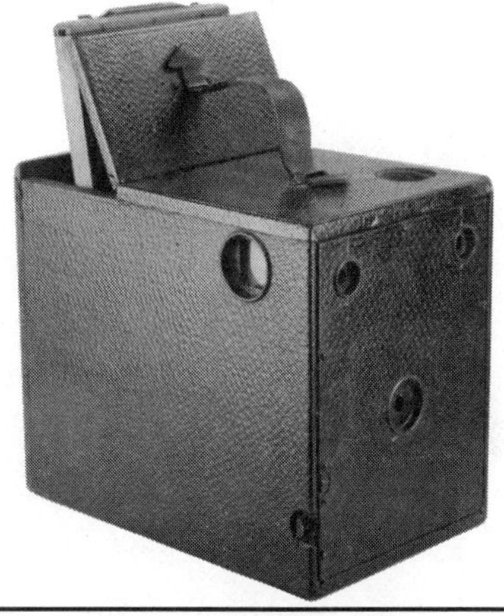

Pennant Camera No. 20

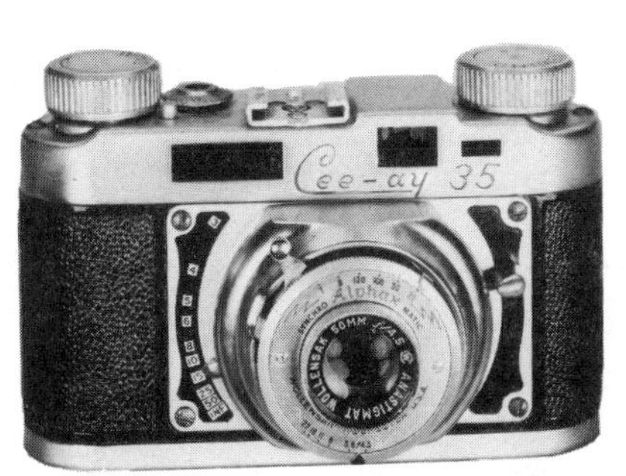

CeeAy 35

MODEL	FORMAT	FILM	TYPE	Year	LENS	Apert	FL	SHUTTER	SPEEDS	ILLUS	U.S.$
Perfex One-O-One	24x36mm	35mm	35rf	1947	Ektar	3.5		Compur-Rapid		Mc107	50
Perfex One-O-One	24x36mm	35mm	35rf	1947	Wollensak Anast.	4.5	50mm	Alphax	25-150	Mc107	50
Perfex One-O-Two	24x36mm	35mm	35rf	1948	Ektar	3.5		Compur-Rapid			50
Perfex One-O-Two	24x36mm	35mm	35rf	1948	Wollensak	3.5	50mm	Alphax			50
Perfex Speed Candid	24x36mm	35mm	35rf	1938	Graf Perfex Anast.	2.8	50mm	focal plane	25-500	Mc107	60
Perfex Thirty-Three	24x36mm	35mm	35rf	1940	Scienar Anast.	3.5	50mm	focal plane	25-500	Mc107	50
Perfex Thirty-Three	24x36mm	35mm	35rf	1940	Scienar Anast.	2.8	50mm	focal plane	25-500	Mc107	50
Perfex Twenty-Two	24x36mm	35mm	35rf	1942	Scienar Anast.	3.5		focal plane	1-1250		50
...CAMOJECT LTD - England											
Camoject	14x14mm		Submin							Mc108	120
...CANADIAN CAMERA & OPTICAL CO. - Toronto, Canada											
Gem Glencoe No. 7	5x7"	plate	FoldPl		Glencoe Convert.						130
Glencoe No. 4	4x5"	plate	FoldPl		Glencoe Convert.			Wollensak			120
...CANON - Tokyo											
Canon IIA body	24x36mm	35mm	35rf	1952	body only	---	---	focal plane	25-500		2500
Canon IIA + 50/3.5	24x36mm	35mm	35rf	1952	Serenar	3.5	50mm	focal plane	25-500		3200
Canon IIAF body	24x36mm	35mm	35rf	1953	body only	---	---	focal plane	25-500	Mc110	4200
Canon IIAF + 50/3.5	24x36mm	35mm	35rf	1953	Canon	3.5	50mm	focal plane	25-500		4800
Canon IIB body	24x36mm	35mm	35rf	1949	body only	---	---	focal plane	1-500		270
Canon IIB + 50/1.9	24x36mm	35mm	35rf	1949	Serenar	1.9	50mm	focal plane	1-500	Mc109	320
Canon IIB + 50/3.5	24x36mm	35mm	35rf	1949	Serenar	3.5	50mm	focal plane	1-500	Mc109	290
Canon IIC body	24x36mm	35mm	35rf	1950	body only	---	---	focal plane	1-500		700
Canon IIC + 50/1.9	24x36mm	35mm	35rf	1950	Serenar	1.9	50mm	focal plane	1-500		900
Canon IIC + 50/3.5	24x36mm	35mm	35rf	1950	Serenar	3.5	50mm	focal plane	1-500		800
Canon IID body	24x36mm	35mm	35rf	1952	body only	---	---	focal plane	1-500		210
Canon IID + 50/3.5	24x36mm	35mm	35rf	1952	Canon	3.5	50mm	focal plane	1-500		330
Canon IID1 body	24x36mm	35mm	35rf	1952	body only	---	---	focal plane	1-500		310
Canon IID1 + 50/3.5	24x36mm	35mm	35rf	1952	Canon	3.5		focal plane	1-500		390
Canon IID2 body	24x36mm	35mm	35rf	1955	body only	---	---	focal plane	1-500		270
Canon IID2 + 50/2.8	24x36mm	35mm	35rf	1955	Canon	2.8		focal plane	1-500		330
Canon IIF body	24x36mm	35mm	35rf	1953	body only	---	---	focal plane	1-500		220
Canon IIF + 50/3.5	24x36mm	35mm	35rf	1953	Canon	3.5	50mm	focal plane	1-500	Mc110	420
Canon IIF2 body	24x36mm	35mm	35rf	1955	body only	---	---	focal plane	1-500		290
Canon IIF2 + 50/2.8	24x36mm	35mm	35rf	1955	Canon	2.8	50mm	focal plane	1-500	Mc110	370
Canon IIS body	24x36mm	35mm	35rf	1954	body only	---	---	focal plane	1-500		270
Canon IIS + 50/1.8	24x36mm	35mm	35rf	1954	Canon	1.8	50mm	focal plane	1-500		330
Canon IIS2 body	24x36mm	35mm	35rf	1955	body only	---	---	focal plane	1-500		220
Canon IIS2 + 50/3.5	24x36mm	35mm	35rf	1955	Canon	3.5	50mm	focal plane	1-500	Mc110	290
Canon III body	24x36mm	35mm	35rf	1951	body only	---	---	focal plane	1-1000		160
Canon III + 50/1.9	24x36mm	35mm	35rf	1951	Canon Serenar	1.9	50mm	focal plane	1-1000	Mc110	310
Canon IIIA body	24x36mm	35mm	35rf	1951	body only	---	---	focal plane	1-1000		170
Canon IIIA + 50/1.9	24x36mm	35mm	35rf	1951	Canon Serenar	1.9	50mm	focal plane	1-1000		240

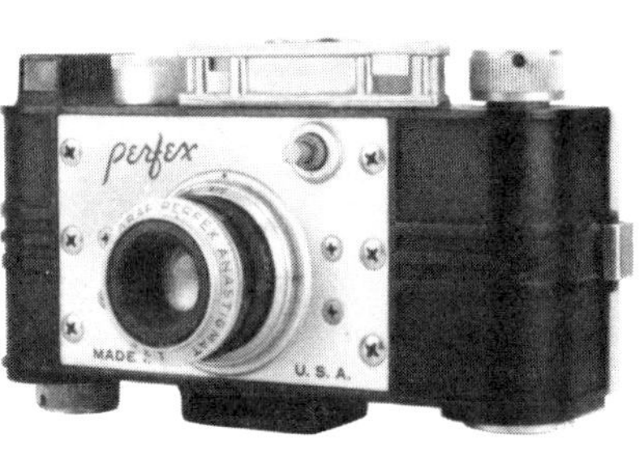

Perfex Speed Candid

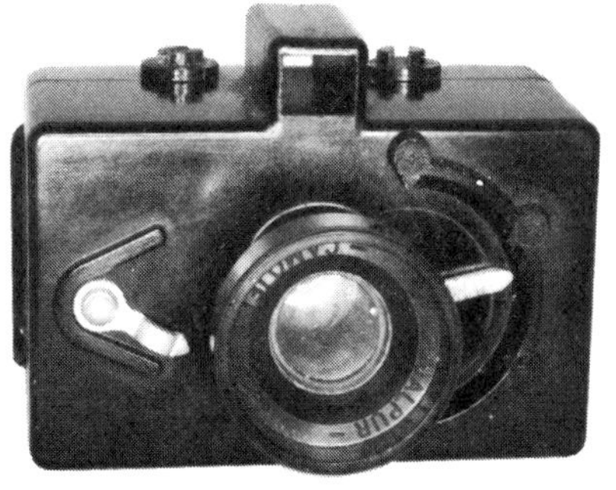

Camoject

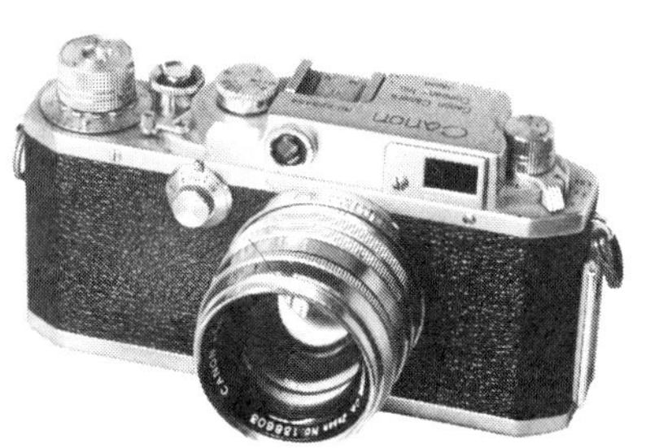

Canon IIS2

MODEL	FORMAT	FILM	TYPE	Year	LENS	Apert	FL	SHUTTER	SPEEDS	ILLUS	U.S.$
Canon IIIA Signal Corps	24x36mm	35mm	35rf	1953	Canon Serenar	1.9	50mm	focal plane	1-1000		700
Canon IV (1950)	24x36mm	35mm	35rf	1950	Serenar	1.9	50mm	focal plane	1-1000		2100
Canon IV body	24x36mm	35mm	35rf	1951	body only	---	---	focal plane	1-1000		260
Canon IV + 50/1.9	24x36mm	35mm	35rf	1951	Serenar	1.9	50mm	focal plane	1-1000		330
Canon IVF body	24x36mm	35mm	35rf	1951	body only	---	---	focal plane	1-1000	Mc110	210
Canon IVF + 50/1.8	24x36mm	35mm	35rf	1951	Serenar	1.8	50mm	focal plane	1-1000		390
Canon IVS body	24x36mm	35mm	35rf	1952	body only	---	---	focal plane	1-1000		160
Canon IVS + 50/1.8	24x36mm	35mm	35rf	1952	Serenar	1.8	50mm	focal plane	1-1000		270
Canon IVS2 body	24x36mm	35mm	35rf	1952	body only	---	---	focal plane	1-1000	Mc110	200
Canon IVS2 + 50/1.8	24x36mm	35mm	35rf	1952	Canon	1.8	50mm	focal plane	1-1000		270
Canon IVSB body	24x36mm	35mm	35rf	1952	body only	---	---	focal plane	1-1000	Mc110	310
Canon IVSB + 50/1.8	24x36mm	35mm	35rf	1952	Canon	1.8	50mm	focal plane	1-1000		430
Canon IVSB2 body	24x36mm	35mm	35rf	1954	body only	---	---	focal plane	1-1000		160
Canon IVSB2 + 50/1.8	24x36mm	35mm	35rf	1954	Canon	1.8	50mm	focal plane	1-1000	Mc110	240
Canon VL body	24x36mm	35mm	35rf	1958	body only	---	---	focal plane	1-1000		240
Canon VL + 50/1.2	24x36mm	35mm	35rf	1958	Canon	1.2	50mm	focal plane	1-1000	Mc111	390
Canon VL-2 body	24x36mm	35mm	35rf	1958	body only	---	---	focal plane	1-500		240
Canon VL-2 + 50/1.2	24x36mm	35mm	35rf	1958	Canon	1.2	50mm	focal plane	1-500		370
Canon VT body	24x36mm	35mm	35rf	1956	body only	---	---	focal plane	1-1000		270
Canon VT + 50/1.2	24x36mm	35mm	35rf	1956	Canon	1.2	50mm	focal plane	1-1000	Mc110	310
VT-Deluxe (black) body	24x36mm	35mm	35rf	1957	body only	---	---	focal plane	1-1000		1800
VT-Deluxe (black) + 50/1.2	24x36mm	35mm	35rf	1957	Canon	1.8	50mm	focal plane	1-1000		2200
VT-Deluxe (chrome) body	24x36mm	35mm	35rf	1957	body only	---	---	focal plane	1-1000		320
VT-Deluxe (chrome) + 1.2	24x36mm	35mm	35rf	1957	Canon	1.8	50mm	focal plane	1-1000	Mc111	310
VT-Deluxe-M body	24x36mm	35mm	35rf	1957	body only	---	---	focal plane	1-1000		260
VT-Deluxe-M + 50/1.8	24x36mm	35mm	35rf	1957	Canon	1.8	50mm	focal plane	1-1000		300
Canon VI-L (black) body	24x36mm	35mm	35rf	1958	body only	---	---	focal plane	1-1000		1700
Canon VI-L (black) + 50/1.2	24x36mm	35mm	35rf	1958	Canon	1.2	50mm	focal plane	1-1000		2200
Canon VI-L (chrome) body	24x36mm	35mm	35rf	1958	body only	---	---	focal plane	1-1000	Mc111	270
Canon VI-L (chrome) + 1.2	24x36mm	35mm	35rf	1958	Canon	1.2	50mm	focal plane	1-1000		350
Canon VI-T (black) body	24x36mm	35mm	35rf	1958	body only	---	---	focal plane	1-1000		1500
Canon VI-T (black) + 50/1.2	24x36mm	35mm	35rf	1958	Canon	1.2	50mm	focal plane	1-1000		1700
Canon VI-T (chrome) body	24x36mm	35mm	35rf	1958	body only	---	---	focal plane	1-1000		260
Canon VI-T (chrome) + 1.2	24x36mm	35mm	35rf	1958	Canon	1.2	50mm	focal plane	1-1000	Mc111	330
Canon 7 (black) body	24x36mm	35mm	35rf	1961	body only	---	---	focal plane	1-1000		2200
Canon 7 (black) + 50/1.2	24x36mm	35mm	35rf	1961	Canon	1.2	50mm	focal plane	1-1000		2500
Canon 7 (black) + 50/1.4	24x36mm	35mm	35rf	1961	Canon	1.4	50mm	focal plane	1-1000		2200
Canon 7 (chrome) body	24x36mm	35mm	35rf	1961	body only	---	---	focal plane	1-1000		270
Canon 7 (chrome) + 50/0.95	24x36mm	35mm	35rf	1961	Canon	.95	50mm	focal plane	1-1000	A2145	1000
Canon 7 (chrome) + 50/1.2	24x36mm	35mm	35rf	1961	Canon	1.2	50mm	focal plane	1-1000		310
Canon 7 (chrome) + 50/1.4	24x36mm	35mm	35rf	1961	Canon	1.4	50mm	focal plane	1-1000	Mc111	290
Canon 7s body	24x36mm	35mm	35rf	1964	body only	---	---	focal plane	1-1000		290

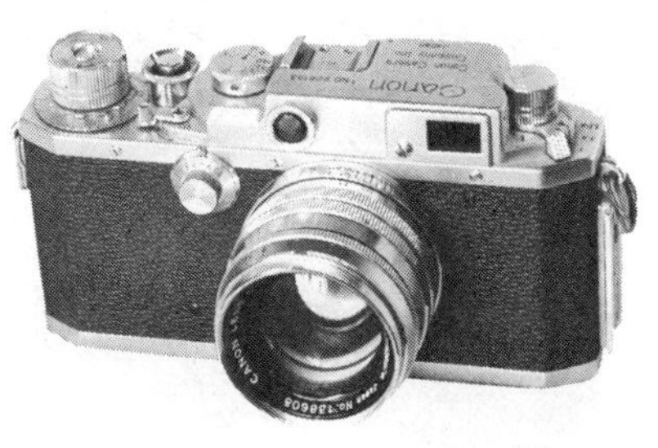

Canon IVSB2

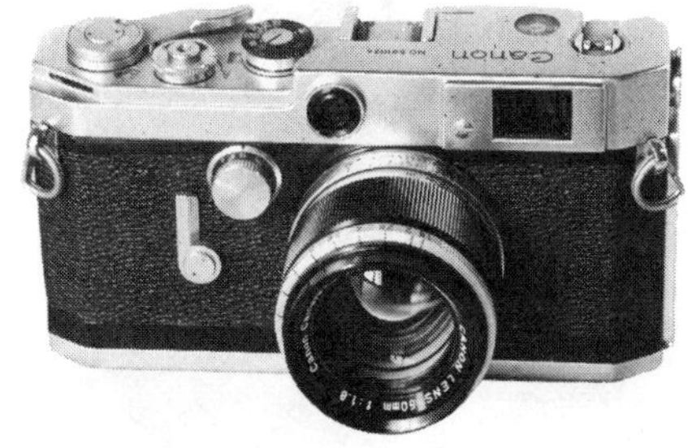

Canon VL

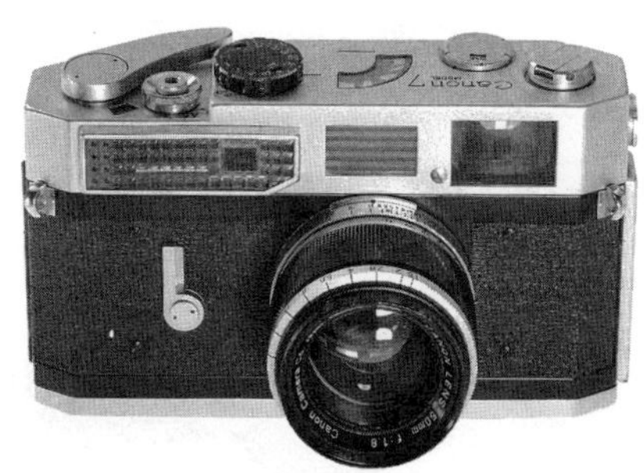

Canon 7 (chrome)

MODEL	FORMAT	FILM	TYPE	Year	LENS	Apert	FL	SHUTTER	SPEEDS	ILLUS	U.S.$
Canon 7s + 50/0.95	24x36mm	35mm	35rf	1964	Canon	.95	50mm	focal plane	1-1000	Mc111	900
Canon 7s + 50/1.2	24x36mm	35mm	35rf	1964	Canon	1.2	50mm	focal plane	1-1000	Mc111	360
Canon 7s + 50/1.4	24x36mm	35mm	35rf	1964	Canon	1.4	50mm	focal plane	1-1000	Mc111	350
Canon 7sZ body	24x36mm	35mm	35rf	1967	body only	---	---	focal plane	1-1000	Mc111	320
Canon 7sZ + 50/0.95	24x36mm	35mm	35rf	1967	Canon	.95	50mm	focal plane	1-1000	Mc111	700
Canon 7sZ + 50/1.4	24x36mm	35mm	35rf	1967	Canon	1.4	50mm	focal plane	1-1000	Mc111	370
Canon 7sZ + 50/2.0	24x36mm	35mm	35rf	1967	Canon	2	50mm	focal plane	1-1000	Mc111	350
Canon 110 E	13x17mm	110	110VF	1976	Canon	2.7	26mm	electronic	8-1/500		60
Canon 110 ED	13x17mm	110	110VF	1976	Canon	2	26mm	electronic	8-1/500		70
Canon 110 ED 20	13x17mm	110	110VF	1977	Canon	2	26mm	electronic	2-1000		70
Canon A-1 body	24x36mm	35mm	35slr	1978	body only	---	---	focal plane	30-1000		270
Canon A-1 + 50/1.4	24x36mm	35mm	35slr	1978	Canon FD	1.4	50mm	focal plane	30-1000		310
Canon A-1 + 50/1.8	24x36mm	35mm	35slr	1978	Canon FD	1.8	50mm	focal plane	30-1000		290
A35 F	24x36mm	35mm	35rf	1978	Canon	2.8	40mm	programmed	60-320		90
AE-1 (black) body	24x36mm	35mm	35slr	1976	body only	---	---	focal plane	2-1000		180
AE-1 (black) + 50/1.8	24x36mm	35mm	35slr	1976	Canon FD	1.8	50mm	focal plane	2-1000	Mc113	190
AE-1 (chrome) body	24x36mm	35mm	35slr	1976	body only	---	---	focal plane	2-1000		150
AE-1 (chrome) +50/1.8	24x36mm	35mm	35slr	1976	Canon FD	1.8	50mm	focal plane	2-1000		180
AE-1 Prog. (black) body	24x36mm	35mm	35slr	1981	body only	---	---	focal plane	2-1000		230
AE-1 Prog. (black) +50/1.8	24x36mm	35mm	35slr	1981	Canon FD	1.8	50mm	focal plane	2-1000		240
AE-1 Prog. (chrome) body	24x36mm	35mm	35slr	1981	body only	---	---	focal plane	2-1000		180
AE-1 Prog.(chrome) + 1.8	24x36mm	35mm	35slr	1981	Canon FD	1.8	50mm	focal plane	2-1000		220
Canon AF35 M	24x36mm	35mm	35AF	1983	Canon	2.8	38mm	programmed	8-500		80
Canon AF35 MII	24x36mm	35mm	35AF	1985	Canon	2.8	38mm	programmed	8-500		90
Canon AF35 MII QD	24x36mm	35mm	35AF	1985	Canon	2.8	38mm	programmed	8-500		100
Canon AF35 ML	24x36mm	35mm	35AF	1983	Canon	1.9	40mm	programmed	4-400		90
Canon AF35J	24x36mm	35mm	35AF	1987	Canon	3.5	35mm	programmed	40-250		80
Canon AF35J Quartz Date	24x36mm	35mm	35AF	1988	Canon	3.5	35mm	programmed	40-250		100
Canon AL-1 body	24x36mm	35mm	35slr	1983	body only	---	---	focal plane	2-1000		140
Canon AL-1 + 50/1.4	24x36mm	35mm	35slr	1983	Canon FD	1.4	50mm	focal plane	2-1000		190
Canon AL-1 +50/1.8	24x36mm	35mm	35slr	1983	Canon FD	1.8	50mm	focal plane	2-1000		160
Aqua Snappy	24x36mm	35mm	35uw	1986	Canon	4.5	35mm				120
Canon AS-6	24x36mm	35mm	35uw	1986	Canon	4.5	35mm				120
Canon AT-1 body	24x36mm	35mm	35slr	1977	body only	---	---	focal plane	2-1000		130
Canon AT-1 + 50/1.4	24x36mm	35mm	35slr	1977	Canon FD	1.4	50mm	focal plane	2-1000		160
Autoboy	24x36mm	35mm	35AF	1984	Canon	2.8	38mm	programmed	8-500		80
Autoboy 2	24x36mm	35mm	35AF	1985	Canon	2.8	38mm	programmed	8-500		90
Autoboy 3	24x36mm	35mm	35AF	1987	Canon	2.8	38mm	programmed	8-500		100
Autoboy 3 Quartz Date	24x36mm	35mm	35AF	1987	Canon	2.8	38mm	programmed	8-500		110
Autoboy A XL	24x36mm	35mm	35AFZ	1993	Canon	3.8-7.2	38-76	programmed			160
Autoboy D5	24x36mm	35mm	35AW-AF	1993	Canon	3.5	32mm	programmed	60-250		150
Autoboy D5 Date	24x36mm	35mm	35AW-AF	1993	Canon	3.5	32mm	programmed	60-250		150

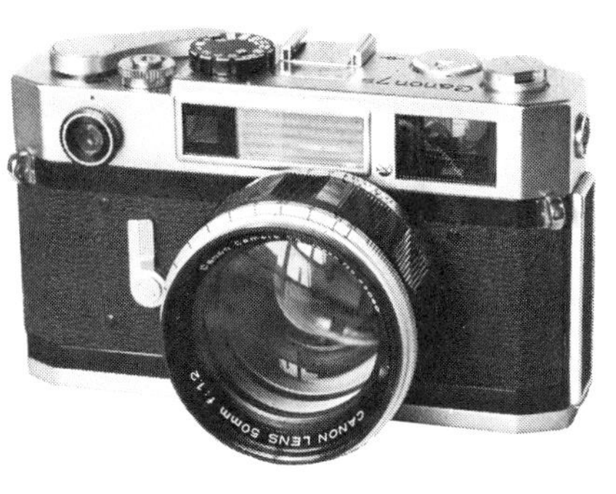

Canon 7s

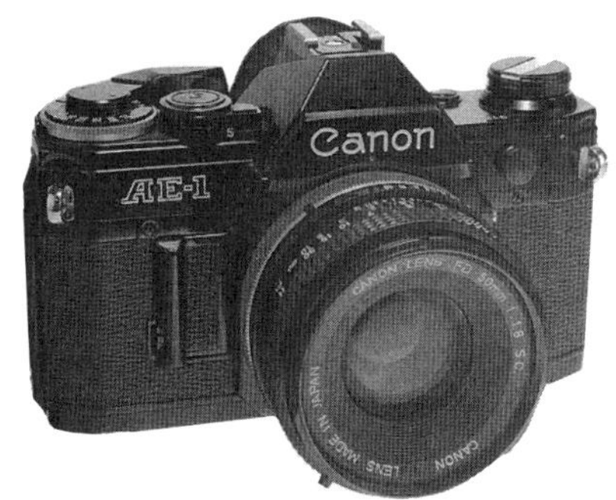

Canon AE-1

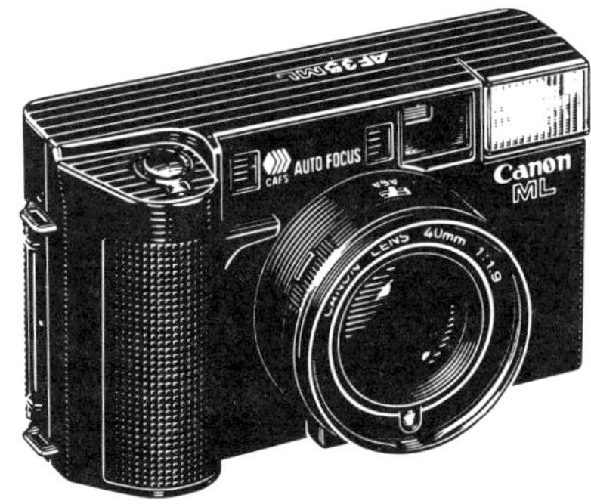

Canon AF35 ML

MODEL	FORMAT	FILM	TYPE	Year	LENS	Apert	FL	SHUTTER	SPEEDS	ILLUS	U.S.$
Autoboy F	24x36mm	35mm	35AF	1993	Canon	3.5	32mm	programmed			70
Autoboy J	24x36mm	35mm	35AFZ	1993	Canon	3.8-8	38-85	programmed			160
Autoboy J Caption	24x36mm	35mm	35AFZ	1993	Canon	3.8-8	38-85	programmed			170
Autoboy Jet	24x36mm	35mm	35AFZ	1991	Canon	2.6-6.6	35-105	programmed	100, 250		240
Autoboy Lite	24x36mm	35mm	35AF	1987	Canon	3.5	35mm	programmed	40-250		80
Autoboy Lite 2	24x36mm	35mm	35AF	1990	Canon	4.5	35mm	programmed	40-125		90
Autoboy Lite 2 Date	24x36mm	35mm	35AF	1990	Canon	4.5	35mm	programmed	40-125		90
Autoboy Lite Quartz Date	24x36mm	35mm	35AF	1988	Canon	3.5	35mm	programmed	40-250		100
Autoboy Mini	24x36mm	35mm	35AF	1992	Canon	3.5	38mm	programmed			70
Autoboy Mini Date	24x36mm	35mm	35AF	1992	Canon	3.5	38mm	programmed			70
Autoboy Mini Tele	24x36mm	35mm	35AF-BiF	1992	Canon	3.5/6	38/70	programmed	60-250		80
Autoboy Prisma	24x36mm	35mm	35AF	1989	Canon	3.5	35mm	programmed	40-125		110
Autoboy Prisma Date	24x36mm	35mm	35AF	1989	Canon	3.5	35mm	programmed	40-125		120
Autoboy S	24x36mm	35mm	35AFZ	1993	Canon	3.6-8.5	38-115	programmed	2-1/1200		210
Autoboy Super	24x36mm	35mm	35AF	1985	Canon	1.9	40mm	programmed	4-400		90
Autoboy Tele	24x36mm	35mm	35AF-BiF	1987	Canon	2.8/4.9	40/70	programmed	3-500		110
Autoboy Tele 6	24x36mm	35mm	35AF-BiF	1989	Canon	3.5/5.6	35/60	programmed	60-350		140
Autoboy Tele 6 Date	24x36mm	35mm	35AF-BiF	1989	Canon	3.5/5.6	35/60	programmed	60-350		160
Autoboy Tele Quartz Date	24x36mm	35mm	35AF-BiF	1987	Canon	2.8/4.9	40/70	programmed	3-500		120
Autoboy TW28	24x36mm	35mm	35AF	1990	Canon	4.4/6.5	28/48	programmed			90
Autoboy TW28 Date	24x36mm	35mm	35AF	1990	Canon	4.4/6.5	28/48	programmed			100
Autoboy Zoom	24x36mm	35mm	35AFZ	1989	Canon	3.5-6.7	35-70	programmed	30-250		160
Autoboy Zoom 76	24x36mm	35mm	35AFZ	1993	Canon	3.8-7.2	38-76				80
Autoboy Zoom 105	24x36mm	35mm	35AFZ	1992	Canon	3.5-8	35-105				150
Autoboy Zoom Super	24x36mm	35mm	35AFZ	1989	Canon	3.6-7.3	39-85	programmed	2-1/250		250
Canon AV-1 body	24x36mm	35mm	35slr	1979	body only	---	---	focal plane	2-1000		110
Canon AV-1 + 50/1.8	24x36mm	35mm	35slr	1979	Canon FD	1.8	50mm	focal plane	2-1000		130
Canon BF35	24x36mm	35mm	35VF	1992	Canon	4.5	35mm	programmed			50
Canon BF35 Date	24x36mm	35mm	35VF	1992	Canon	4.5	35mm	programmed			70
Canomatic C-30	28x28mm	126	126VF	1966	Canon	3.5	40mm	Programm	30-250		30
Canonet 17	24x36mm	35mm	35rf	1965	Canon	1.7	45mm	electronic	1-500		80
Canonet 19	24x36mm	35mm	35rf	1961	Canon	1.9	45mm	electronic	1-500		80
Canonet 28	24x36mm	35mm	35rf	1969	Canon	2.8	40mm	electronic	30-250	Mc114	50
Canonet G-III QL17	24x36mm	35mm	35rf	1973	Canon	1.7	40mm	electronic	1-500		130
Canonet G-III QL19	24x36mm	35mm	35rf	1973	Canon	1.9	45mm	electronic	1-500		40
Canonet QL17	24x36mm	35mm	35rf	1965	Canon SE	1.7	45mm	electronic	1-500		70
Canonet QL19	24x36mm	35mm	35rf	1965	Canon SE	1.9	45mm	electronic	1-500		100
Canonet QL25	24x36mm	35mm	35rf	1965	Canon SE	2.5	45mm	electronic	1/15-500		100
Canonex	24x36mm	35mm	35slr	1963	Canon S	2.8	48mm	focal plane	1-1000		140
Canonflex	24x36mm	35mm	35slr	1959	Sup. Canomatic R	1.8	50mm	focal plane	1-1000		150
Canonflex R2000	24x36mm	35mm	35slr	1960	Sup. Canomatic R	1.8	50mm	focal plane	1-2000		160
Canonflex RM	24x36mm	35mm	35slr	1961	Sup. Canomatic R	1.8	50mm	focal plane	1-1000		180

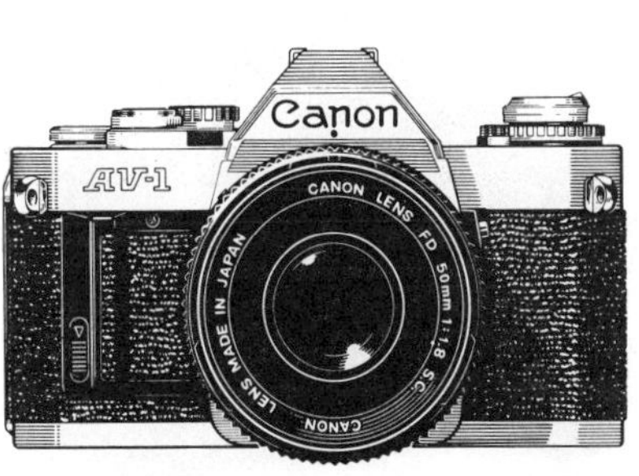

Canon AV-1

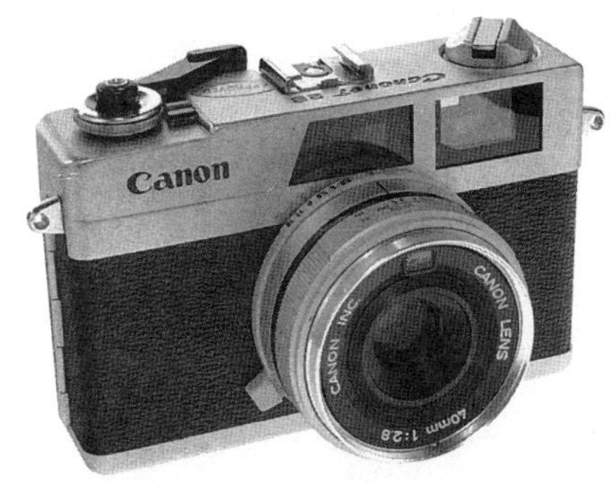

Canonet 28

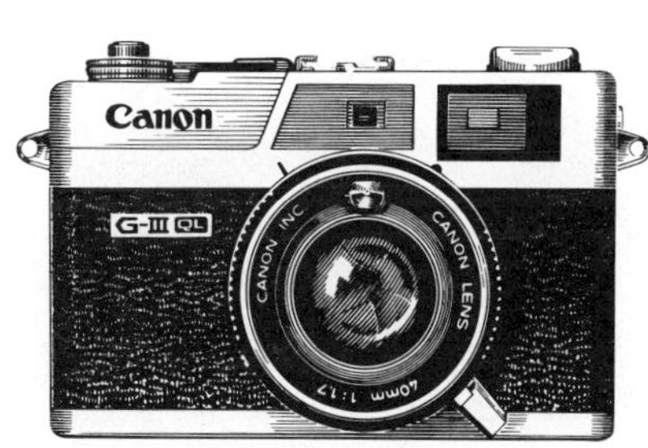

Canonet G-III QL 17

MODEL	FORMAT	FILM	TYPE	Year	LENS	Apert	FL	SHUTTER	SPEEDS	ILLUS	U.S.$
Canonflex RP	24x36mm	35mm	35slr	1960	Sup. Canomatic R	1.8	50mm	focal plane	1-1000		120
Canonmatic M70	28x28mm	126	126VF	1972	Canon	2.8	40mm	Programm	30-800		50
Canon CB35-M	24x36mm	35mm	35VF	1993	Canon	3.8	35mm		1/125		40
Canon CX-35	24x36mm	35mm	SciMed	1939	Seiki-K. Serenar	1.5	50mm				1100
Demi	18x24mm	35mm	35Half	1963	Canon	2.8	28mm	Programm	30-250		50
Demi II	18x24mm	35mm	35Half	1964	Canon			Programm			70
Demi C	18x24mm	35mm	35Half	1965	Canon						70
Demi EE17	18x24mm	35mm	35Half	1966	Canon	1.7	30mm	Programm	1/8-500		80
Demi EE28	18x24mm	35mm	35Half	1967	Canon	2.8	28mm	Programm	1/8-500		70
Demi Rapid	18x24mm	35mm	35Half	1965	Canon	2.8	50mm	Programm			50
Demi S	18x24mm	35mm	35Half	1964	Canon	1.7	30mm	Programm	1/8-500		60
Dial 35	18x24mm	35mm	35Half	1963	Canon	2.8	28mm		30-250	A901	100
Dial 35 Mod. 2	18x24mm	35mm	35Half	1968	Canon	2.8	28mm		30-250	HK693	100
Dial Rapid	18x24mm	35mm	35Half	1967	Canon	2.8	28mm				180
Canon EF body	24x36mm	35mm	35slr	1973	body only	---	---	focal plane	30-1000		220
Canon EF + 50/1.8	24x36mm	35mm	35slr	1973	Canon EF	1.8	50mm	focal plane	30-1000		240
Canon EF-M body	24x36mm	35mm	35slr	1992	body only	---	---	focal plane	2-1000		140
Canon EF-M + 50/1.8	24x36mm	35mm	35slr	1992	Canon EF	1.8	50mm	focal plane	2-1000		160
EOS 1 body	24x36mm	35mm	35afslr	1989	body only	---	---	programmed	1/8000		1000
EOS 1 + 50/1.8	24x36mm	35mm	35afslr	1989	Canon EF	1.8	50mm	programmed	1/8000		1100
EOS 1N body	24x36mm	35mm	35afslr	1994	body only	---	---	electronic	30-1/8000		1400
EOS 1N + 28-105	24x36mm	35mm	35afslr	1994	Canon EF	3.5-4.5	28-105	electronic	30-1/8000		1800
EOS 1N DP body	24x36mm	35mm	35afslr	1995	body only	---	---	electronic	30-1/8000		1500
EOS 1N DP + 50/1.8	24x36mm	35mm	35afslr	1995	Canon EF	1.8	50mm	electronic	30-1/8000		1600
EOS 1N HS body	24x36mm	35mm	35afslr	1995	body only	---	---	electronic	30-1/8000		2000
EOS 1N HS + 50/1.8	24x36mm	35mm	35afslr	1995	Canon EF	1.8	50mm	electronic	30-1/8000		2100
EOS 1N RS body	24x36mm	35mm	35afslr	1995	body only	---	---	electronic	30-1/8000		2000
EOS 1N RS + 50/1.8	24x36mm	35mm	35afslr	1995	Canon EF	1.8	50mm	electronic	30-1/8000		2200
EOS 5 body	24x36mm	35mm	35afslr	1993	body only	---	---	electronic	30-1/8000		670
EOS 5 + 28-105	24x36mm	35mm	35afslr	1993	Canon EF	3.5-4.5	28-105	electronic	30-1/8000		700
EOS 5 QD body	24x36mm	35mm	35afslr	1993	body only	---	---	electronic	30-1/8000		670
EOS 5 QD + 28-105	24x36mm	35mm	35afslr	1993	Canon EF	3.5-4.5	28-105	electronic	30-1/8000		700
EOS 10 body	24x36mm	35mm	35afslr	1990	body only	---	---	electronic	30-1/4000		390
EOS 10 + 50/1.8	24x36mm	35mm	35afslr	1990	Canon EF	1.8	50mm	electronic	30-1/4000		430
EOS 10S body	24x36mm	35mm	35afslr	1990	body only	---	---	electronic	30-1/4000		390
EOS 10S + 50/1.8	24x36mm	35mm	35afslr	1990	Canon EF	1.8	50mm	electronic	30-1/4000		430
EOS 100 body	24x36mm	35mm	35afslr	1991	body only	---	---	electronic	30-1/4000		390
EOS 100 + 28-80	24x36mm	35mm	35afslr	1991	Canon EF	3.5-5.6	28-80	electronic	30-1/4000		490
EOS 100 QD body	24x36mm	35mm	35afslr	1991	body only	---	---	electronic	30-1/4000		460
EOS 100 QD + 28-80	24x36mm	35mm	35afslr	1991	Canon EF	3.5-5.6	28-80	electronic	30-1/4000		540
EOS 500 body	24x36mm	35mm	35afslr	1993	body only	---	---	electronic	30-1/2000		290
EOS 500 + 28-80	24x36mm	35mm	35afslr	1993	Canon EF	3.5-5.6	28-80	electronic	30-1/2000		360

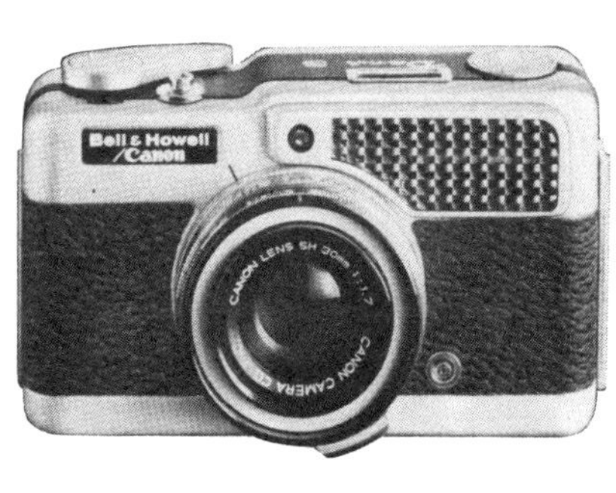

Demi S

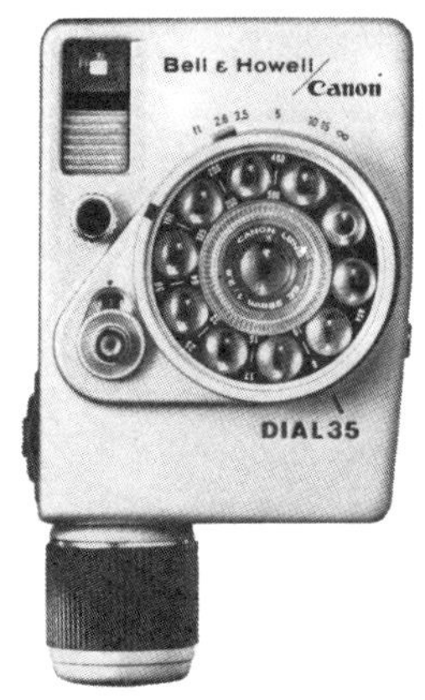

Dial 35

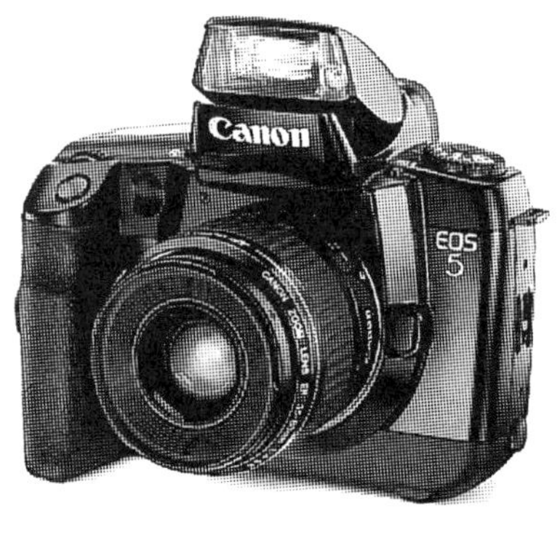

EOS 5

MODEL	FORMAT	FILM	TYPE	Year	LENS	Apert	FL	SHUTTER	SPEEDS	ILLUS	U.S.$
EOS 500 QD body	24x36mm	35mm	35afslr	1993	body only	---	---	electronic	30-1/2000		350
EOS 500 QD + 28-80	24x36mm	35mm	35afslr	1993	Canon EF	3.5-5.6	28-80	electronic	30-1/2000		440
EOS 600 body	24x36mm	35mm	35afslr	1989	body only	---	---	electronic	30-1/2000		320
EOS 600 + 50/1.8	24x36mm	35mm	35afslr	1989	Canon EF	1.8	50mm	electronic	30-1/2000		400
EOS 620 body	24x36mm	35mm	35afslr	1988	body only	---	---	electronic	30-1/4000		290
EOS 620 + 50/1.8	24x36mm	35mm	35afslr	1988	Canon EF	1.8	50mm	electronic	30-1/4000		320
EOS 630 body	24x36mm	35mm	35afslr	1989	body only	---	---	electronic	30-1/2000		320
EOS 630 + 50/1.8	24x36mm	35mm	35afslr	1989	Canon EF	1.8	50mm	electronic	30-1/2000		400
EOS 650 body	24x36mm	35mm	35afslr	1986	body only	---	---		30-1/2000		230
EOS 650 + 50/1.8	24x36mm	35mm	35afslr	1986	Canon EF	1.8	50mm		30-1/2000		240
EOS 700 body	24x36mm	35mm	35afslr	1990	body only	---	---	electronic	2-1/1000		220
EOS 700 + 35-80	24x36mm	35mm	35afslr	1990	Canon EF	4-5.6	35-80	electronic	2-1/1000		250
EOS 750 body	24x36mm	35mm	35afslr	1988	body only	---	---	electronic	2-1/1000		180
EOS 750 + 50/1.8	24x36mm	35mm	35afslr	1988	Canon EF	1.8	50mm	electronic	2-1/1000		220
EOS 750 QD body	24x36mm	35mm	35afslr	1989	body only	---	---	electronic	2-1/1000		200
EOS 750 QD + 50/1.8	24x36mm	35mm	35afslr	1989	Canon EF	1.8	50mm	electronic	2-1/1000		220
EOS 850 body	24x36mm	35mm	35afslr	1989	body only	---	---	electronic	2-1/1000		160
EOS 850 + 50/1.8	24x36mm	35mm	35afslr	1989	Canon EF	1.8	50mm	electronic	2-1/1000		180
EOS 1000 body	24x36mm	35mm	35afslr	1990	body only	---	---	electronic	30-1/1000		210
EOS 1000 + 50/1.8	24x36mm	35mm	35afslr	1990	Canon EF	1.8	50mm	electronic	30-1/1000		300
EOS 1000 F body	24x36mm	35mm	35afslr	1991	body only	---	---	electronic	30-1/1000		250
EOS 1000 F + 50/1.8	24x36mm	35mm	35afslr	1991	Canon EF	1.8	50mm	electronic	30-1/1000		330
EOS 1000 FN body	24x36mm	35mm	35afslr	1992	body only	---	---	electronic	30-1/2000		210
EOS 1000 FN + 35-80	24x36mm	35mm	35afslr	1992	Canon EF	4.0-5.6	35-80	electronic	30-1/2000		300
EOS 1000 N body	24x36mm	35mm	35afslr	1992	body only	---	---	electronic	30-1/2000		220
EOS 1000 N + 50/1.4	24x36mm	35mm	35afslr	1992	Canon EF	1.4	50mm	electronic	30-1/2000		310
EOS 1000S QD body	24x36mm	35mm	35afslr	1992	body only	---	---	electronic	30-1/2000		240
EOS 1000S QD + 50/1.4	24x36mm	35mm	35afslr	1992	Canon EF	1.4	50mm	electronic	30-1/2000		440
EOS A2 body	24x36mm	35mm	35afslr	1993	body only	---	---	electronic	30-1/8000		630
EOS A2 + 50/1.4	24x36mm	35mm	35afslr	1993	Canon EF	1.4	50mm	electronic	30-1/8000		800
EOS A2E body	24x36mm	35mm	35afslr	1993	body only	---	---	electronic	30-1/8000		540
EOS A2E + 50/1.4	24x36mm	35mm	35afslr	1993	Canon EF	1.4	50mm	electronic	30-1/8000		700
EOS Elan body	24x36mm	35mm	35afslr	1991	body only	---	---	electronic	30-1/4000		390
EOS Elan + 28-80	24x36mm	35mm	35afslr	1991	Canon EF	3.5-5.6	28-80	electronic	30-1/4000		490
EOS Kiss body	24x36mm	35mm	35afslr	1993	body only	---	---	electronic	30-1/2000		290
EOS Kiss + 28-80	24x36mm	35mm	35afslr	1993	Canon EF	3.5-5.6	28-80	electronic	30-1/2000		360
EOS Rebel body	24x36mm	35mm	35afslr	1990	body only	---	---	electronic	30-1/1000		210
EOS Rebel + 35-80	24x36mm	35mm	35afslr	1990	Canon EF	4-5.6	35-80	electronic	30-1/1000		300
EOS Rebel II body	24x36mm	35mm	35afslr	1992	body only	---	---	electronic	30-1/2000		160
EOS Rebel II + 35-80	24x36mm	35mm	35afslr	1992	Canon EF	4-5.6	35-80	electronic	30-1/2000		220
EOS Rebel S body	24x36mm	35mm	35afslr	1992	body only	---	---	electronic	30-1/2000		290
EOS Rebel S + 35-80	24x36mm	35mm	35afslr	1992	Canon EF	3.5-5.6	35-80	electronic	30-1/2000		360

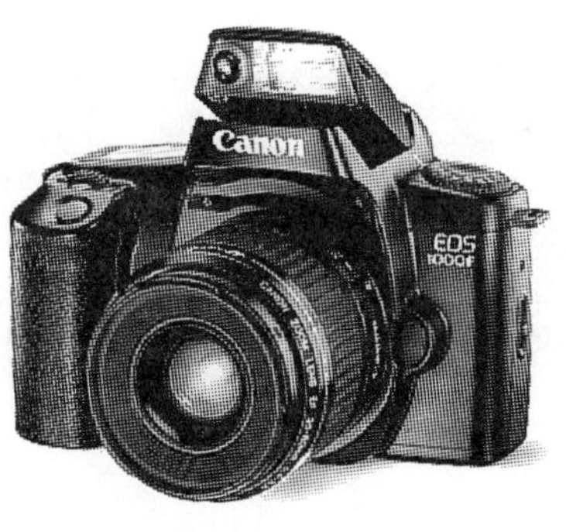

Canon EOS 1000 FN

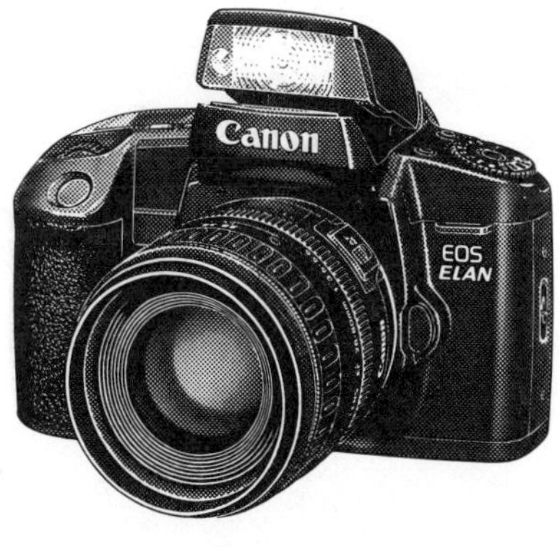

Canon EOS Elan

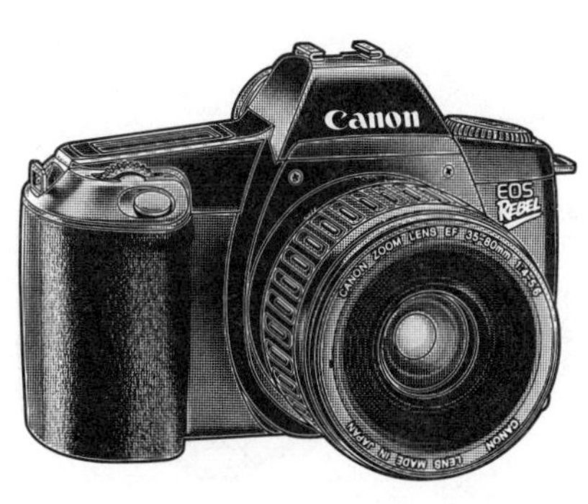

Canon EOS Rebel

MODEL	FORMAT	FILM	TYPE	Year	LENS	Apert	FL	SHUTTER	SPEEDS	ILLUS	U.S.$
EOS Rebel SII body	24x36mm	35mm	35afslr	1992	body only	---	---	electronic	30-1/2000		210
EOS Rebel SII + 35-80	24x36mm	35mm	35afslr	1992	Canon EF	4.0-5.6	35-80	electronic	30-1/2000		300
EOS Rebel XS body	24x36mm	35mm	35afslr	1993	body only	---	---	electronic	30-1/2000		270
EOS Rebel XS + 35-80	24x36mm	35mm	35afslr	1993	Canon EF	3.5-5.6	35-80	electronic	30-1/2000		300
EOS RT body	24x36mm	35mm	35afslr	1989	body only	---	---	electronic	30-1/2000		360
EOS RT + 50/1.8	24x36mm	35mm	35afslr	1989	Canon EF	1.8	50mm	electronic	30-1/2000		380
Epoca	24x36mm	35mm	35AFZ	1991	Canon	2.6-6.6	35-105	programmed	100, 250		240
Epoca 135	24x36mm	35mm	35AFZ	1992	Canon	3.2-8	38-135	programmed			240
Epoca 135 Caption	24x36mm	35mm	35AFZ	1992	Canon	3.2-8	38-135	programmed			330
Epoca Caption	24x36mm	35mm	35AFZ	1992	Canon	2.6-6.6	35-105	programmed	100, 250		240
Canon EX Auto QL	24x36mm	35mm	35slr	1969	Canon EX	1.8	50mm	focal plane	1/8-500		100
Canon EX-EE	24x36mm	35mm	35slr	1969	Canon EX	1.8	50mm	focal plane	1/8-500		130
Canon F-1 body	24x36mm	35mm	35slr	1971	body only	---	---	focal plane	1-2000		320
Canon F-1 + 50/1.4	24x36mm	35mm	35slr	1971	Canon FD	1.4	50mm	focal plane	1-2000		380
Canon F-1(N) body	24x36mm	35mm	35slr	1981	body only	---	---	focal plane	8-2000		650
Canon F-1(N) + 50/1.4	24x36mm	35mm	35slr	1981	Canon FD	1.4	50mm	focal plane	8-2000		700
Canon F-1(N) 1984 Olympic	24x36mm	35mm	35slr	1983	Canon FD	1.4	50mm	focal plane	8-2000		800
Canon F-1(N) (AE) body	24x36mm	35mm	35slr	1981	body only	---	---	focal plane	8-2000		700
Canon F-1(N) (AE) + 50/1.4	24x36mm	35mm	35slr	1981	Canon FD	1.4	50mm	focal plane	8-2000		800
Canon F-1n body	24x36mm	35mm	35slr	1976	body only	---	---	focal plane	1-2000		330
Canon F-1n + 50/1.4	24x36mm	35mm	35slr	1976	Canon FD	1.4	50mm	focal plane	1-2000		400
Canon F-1n 1980 Olympic	24x36mm	35mm	35slr	1979	Canon FD	1.4	50mm	focal plane	1-2000		520
Canon FP	24x36mm	35mm	35slr	1964	Canon FL	1.8	50mm	focal plane	1-1000		110
FT QL (black) body	24x36mm	35mm	35slr	1966	body only	---	---	focal plane	1-1000		100
FT QL (black) + 50/1.4	24x36mm	35mm	35slr	1966	Canon FL	1.4	50mm	focal plane	1-1000		180
FT QL (chrome) body	24x36mm	35mm	35slr	1966	body only	---	---	focal plane	1-1000		100
FT QL (chrome) + 50/1.4	24x36mm	35mm	35slr	1966	Canon FL	1.4	50mm	focal plane	1-1000		160
FTb QL (black) body	24x36mm	35mm	35slr	1971	body only	---	---	focal plane	1-1000		180
FTb QL (black) + 50/1.4	24x36mm	35mm	35slr	1971	Canon FD	1.4	50mm	focal plane	1-1000		240
FTb QL (black) + 50/1.8	24x36mm	35mm	35slr	1971	Canon FD	1.8	50mm	focal plane	1-1000		220
FTb QL (chrome) body	24x36mm	35mm	35slr	1971	body only	---	---	focal plane	1-1000		150
FTb QL (chrome) + 50/1.4	24x36mm	35mm	35slr	1971	Canon FD	1.4	50mm	focal plane	1-1000		200
FTb QL (chrome) + 50/1.8	24x36mm	35mm	35slr	1971	Canon FD	1.8	50mm	focal plane	1-1000		170
FTbn QL (black) body	24x36mm	35mm	35slr	1973	body only	---	---	focal plane	1-1000		190
FTbn QL (black) + 50/1.4	24x36mm	35mm	35slr	1973	Canon FD	1.4	50mm	focal plane	1-1000		230
FTbn QL (chrome) body	24x36mm	35mm	35slr	1973	body only	---	---	focal plane	1-1000		140
FTbn QL (chrome) + 50/1.4	24x36mm	35mm	35slr	1973	Canon FD	1.4	50mm	focal plane	1-1000		200
Canon FX body	24x36mm	35mm	35slr	1964	body only	---	---	focal plane	1-1000		100
Canon FX + 50/1.8	24x36mm	35mm	35slr	1964	Canon FL	1.8	50mm	focal plane	1-1000		120
Canon Hansa	24x36mm	35mm	35rf	1937	Nikkor	3.5	50mm	focal plane	20-500		4600
Canon/NK Hansa	24x36mm	35mm	35rf	1935	Nikkor	3.5	50mm	focal plane	20-500	Mc108	4600
Canon J	24x36mm	35mm	35vf	1939	Nikkor	4.5	50mm	focal plane	20-500	Mc109	7000

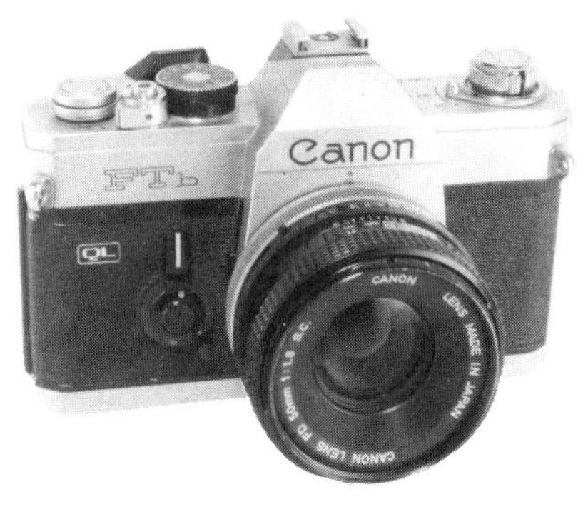

Canon FTb QL

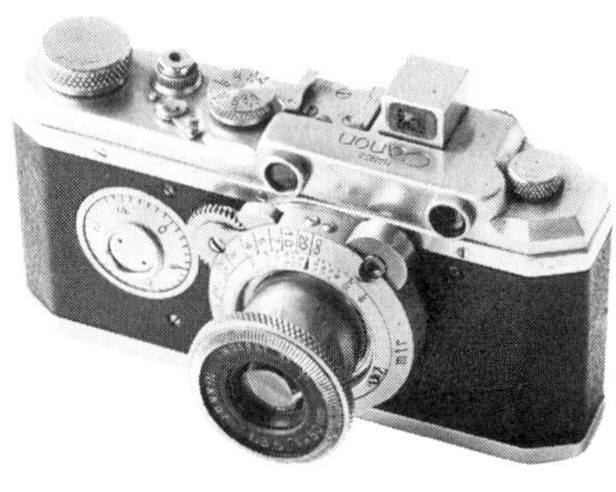
Canon/NK Hansa

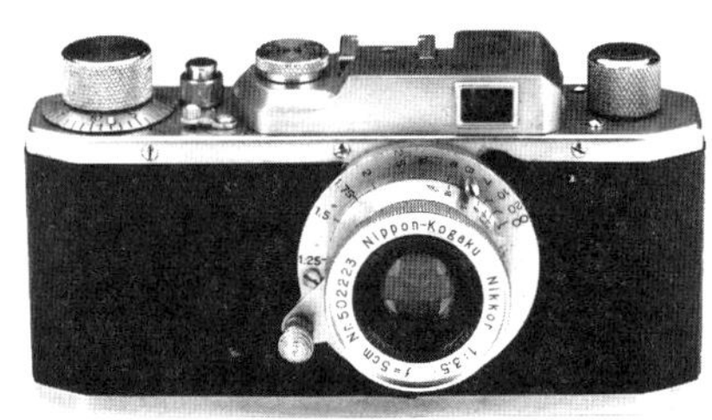

Canon J

MODEL	FORMAT	FILM	TYPE	Year	LENS	Apert	FL	SHUTTER	SPEEDS	ILLUS	U.S.$
Canon J-II	24x36mm	35mm	35vf	1945	NIkkor	3.5	50mm	focal plane	20-500	Mc109	5500
Canon JS	24x36mm	35mm	35vf	1941	Nikkor	4.5	50mm	focal plane	1-500	Mc109	6400
Jet 35	24x36mm	35mm	35AFZ	1992	Canon	3.2-8	38-135	programmed			240
Canon L-1 (black) body	24x36mm	35mm	35rf	1956	body only	---	---	focal plane	1-1000		1600
Canon L-1 (black) + 50/1.2	24x36mm	35mm	35rf	1956	Canon	1.2	50mm	focal plane	1-1000		1600
Canon L-1 (chrome) body	24x36mm	35mm	35rf	1956	body only	---	---	focal plane	1-1000		370
Canon L-1 (chrome) + 1.2	24x36mm	35mm	35rf	1956	Canon	1.2	50mm	focal plane	1-1000	Mc111	410
Canon L-2 body	24x36mm	35mm	35rf	1956	body only	---	---	focal plane	1-500		220
Canon L-2 + 50/1.2	24x36mm	35mm	35rf	1956	Canon	1.2	50mm	focal plane	1-500		380
Canon L-3 body	24x36mm	35mm	35rf	1957	body only	---	---	focal plane	1-500		290
Canon L-3 + 50/1.8	24x36mm	35mm	35rf	1957	Canon	1.8	50mm	focal plane	1-500		350
Canon LA 20	24x36mm	35mm	35VF	1995	Canon	3.8	35mm		1/125		30
Canon MC	24x36mm	35mm	35VF	1985	Canon	2.8	35mm	programmed	8-500		140
Canon MC10	24x36mm	35mm	35VF	1986	Canon	4.5	35mm	programmed	20-350		90
New Autoboy	24x36mm	35mm	35AFZ	1990	Canon	3.8-5.6	38-60	programmed			140
New Sure Shot	24x36mm	35mm	35AF	1990	Canon	4.4/6.5	28/48	programmed			90
New Sure Shot Date	24x36mm	35mm	35AF	1990	Canon	4.4/6.5	28/48	programmed			100
Canon NS	24x36mm	35mm	35rf	1940	Nikkor	4.5	50mm	focal plane	20-500	Mc109	6800
Canon P (black) body	24x36mm	35mm	35rf	1958	body only	---	---	focal plane	1-1000		1900
Canon P (black) + 50/1.2	24x36mm	35mm	35rf	1958	Canon	1.2	50mm	focal plane	1-1000		2200
Canon P (black) + 50/2.2	24x36mm	35mm	35rf	1958	Canon	2.2	50mm	focal plane	1-1000		2300
Canon P (chrome) body	24x36mm	35mm	35rf	1958	body only	---	---	focal plane	1-1000	Mc111	240
Canon P (chrome) + 50/1.2	24x36mm	35mm	35rf	1958	Canon	1.2	50mm	focal plane	1-1000		310
Canon P (chrome) + 50/2.2	24x36mm	35mm	35rf	1958	Canon	2.2	50mm	focal plane	1-1000		400
Canon Pellix	24x36mm	35mm	35slr	1965	Canon FL	1.4	50mm	focal plane	1-1000	Mc112	240
Canon Pellix QL (black)	24x36mm	35mm	35slr	1966	Canon FL	1.4	50mm	focal plane	1-1000		180
Canon Pellix QL (chrome)	24x36mm	35mm	35slr	1966	Canon FL	1.4	50mm	focal plane	1-1000		170
Photura	24x36mm	35mm	35AFZ	1991	Canon	2.6-6.6	35-105	programmed	100, 250		240
Photura 135	24x36mm	35mm	35AFZ	1992	Canon	3.2-8	38-135	programmed			240
Photura 135 Caption	24x36mm	35mm	35AFZ	1992	Canon	3.2-8	38-135	programmed			330
Photura Caption	24x36mm	35mm	35AFZ	1991	Canon	2.6-6.6	35-105	programmed	100, 250		240
Prima 4	24x36mm	35mm	35AF	1990	Canon	4.5	35mm	programmed	40-125		90
Prima 4 Date	24x36mm	35mm	35AF	1990	Canon	4.5	35mm	programmed	40-125		90
Prima 5	24x36mm	35mm	35AF	1992	Canon	3.5	38mm	programmed			70
Prima 5 Date	24x36mm	35mm	35AF	1992	Canon	3.5	38mm	programmed			70
Prima AF-7	24x36mm	35mm	35AF	1994	Canon	4.5	35mm				50
Prima AF-7 Date	24x36mm	35mm	35AF	1994	Canon	4.5	35mm				70
Prima AS-1	24x36mm	35mm	35AW-AF	1993	Canon	3.5	32mm	programmed	60-250		150
Prima AS-1 Date	24x36mm	35mm	35AW-AF	1993	Canon	3.5	32mm	programmed	60-250		150
Prima Auto Zoom	24x36mm	35mm	35AFZ	1990	Canon	3.8-5.6	38-60	programmed			140
Prima BF	24x36mm	35mm	35VF	1992	Canon	4.5	35mm	programmed			50
Prima BF Date	24x36mm	35mm	35VF	1992	Canon	4.5	35mm	programmed			70

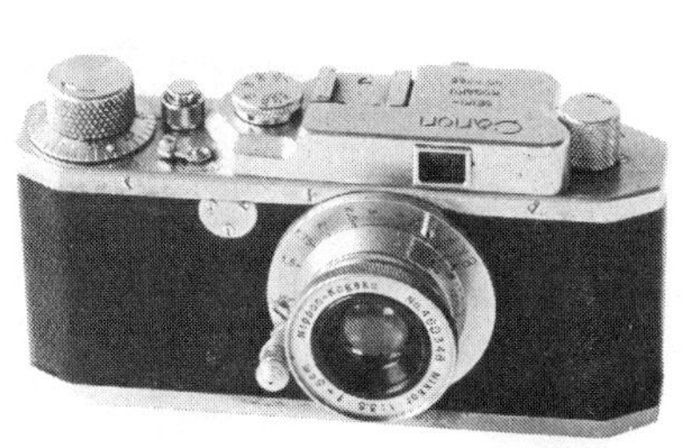

Canon J-II

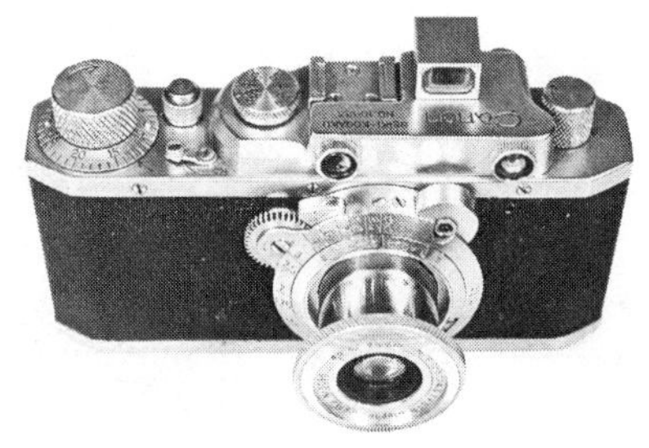

Canon NS

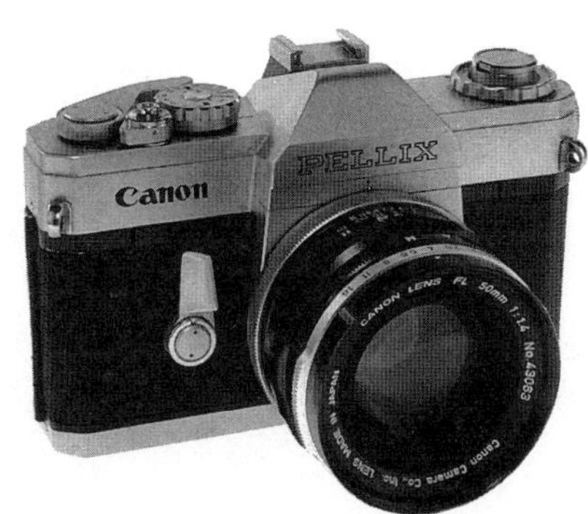

Canon Pellix

MODEL	FORMAT	FILM	TYPE	Year	LENS	Apert	FL	SHUTTER	SPEEDS	ILLUS	U.S.$
Prima Junior	24x36mm	35mm	35VF	1989	Canon	3.8	35mm		1/125		80
Prima Junior EX	24x36mm	35mm	35VF	1992	Canon	4.5	32mm				70
Prima Junior EX Date	24x36mm	35mm	35VF	1992	Canon	4.5	32mm				70
Prima Junior Hi	24x36mm	35mm	35VF	1990	Canon	4.5	35mm		60, 250		100
Prima Junior S	24x36mm	35mm	35VF	1993	Canon	3.8	35mm		1/125		40
Prima Mini	24x36mm	35mm	35AF	1993	Canon	3.5	32mm	programmed			70
Prima Shot	24x36mm	35mm	35AF	1989	Canon	3.5	35mm	programmed	40-125		110
Prima Shot Date	24x36mm	35mm	35AF	1989	Canon	3.5	35mm	programmed	40-125		120
Prima Super 85	24x36mm	35mm	35AFZ	1993	Canon	3.8-8	38-85	programmed			160
Prima Super 85 Caption	24x36mm	35mm	35AFZ	1993	Canon	3.8-8	38-85	programmed			170
Prima Super 115	24x36mm	35mm	35AFZ	1993	Canon	3.6-8.5	38-115	programmed	2-1/1200		210
Prima Tele	24x36mm	35mm	35AF-BiF	1989	Canon	3.5/5.6	35/60	programmed	60-350		140
Prima Tele Date	24x36mm	35mm	35AF-BiF	1989	Canon	3.5/5.6	35/60	programmed	60-350		160
Prima Twin	24x36mm	35mm	35AF-BiF	1990	Canon	4.4/6.5	28/48	programmed			90
Prima Twin Date	24x36mm	35mm	35AF-BiF	1990	Canon	4.4/6.5	28/48	programmed			100
Prima Twin S	24x36mm	35mm	35AF-BiF	1992	Canon	3.5/6	38/70	programmed	60-250		80
Prima Twin S Date	24x36mm	35mm	35AF-BiF	1992	Canon	3.5/6	38/70	programmed	60-250		90
Prima Zoom	24x36mm	35mm	35AFZ	1989	Canon	3.5-6.7	35-70	programmed	30-250		160
Prima Zoom 76	24x36mm	35mm	35AFZ	1993	Canon	3.8-7.2	38-76				80
Prima Zoom 76 Caption	24x36mm	35mm	35AFZ	1993	Canon	3.8-7.2	38-76				130
Prima Zoom 105	24x36mm	35mm	35AFZ	1992	Canon	3.5-8	35-105				150
Prima Zoom 105 Caption	24x36mm	35mm	35AFZ	1992	Canon	3.5-8	35-105				210
Prima Zoom F	24x36mm	35mm	35AFZ	1989	Canon	3.6-7.3	39-85	programmed	2-1/250		230
Prima Zoom F Date	24x36mm	35mm	35AFZ	1989	Canon	3.6-7.3	39-85	programmed	2-1/250		250
Prima Zoom Mini	24x36mm	35mm	35AFZ	1993	Canon	3.8-7.2	38-76	programmed			160
Prima Zoom Mini Caption	24x36mm	35mm	35AFZ	1993	Canon	3.8-7.2	38-76	programmed			180
Canon S	24x36mm	35mm	35rf	1938	Nikkor	4.5	50mm	focal plane	1-500	Mc109	7000
Canon S-II	24x36mm	35mm	35rf	1947	Canon Serenar	3.5	50mm	focal plane	1-500		440
Canon Seiki S-II	24x36mm	35mm	35rf	1946	Seiki-Kogaku	3.5	50mm	focal plane	1-500	Mc109	900
Sketchbook	24x36mm	35mm	35rf	1990	Canon	4.5	35mm		1/70		70
Snappy '84	24x36mm	35mm	35rf	1984	Canon	4.5	35mm	programmed		Mc114	70
Snappy 20	24x36mm	35mm	35VF	1984	Canon	4.5	35mm	programmed			40
Snappy 50	24x36mm	35mm	35af	1980	Canon	3.5	35mm	programmed			60
Snappy AF	24x36mm	35mm	35rf	1990	Canon	4.5	35mm	programmed	40-125		70
Snappy EL	24x36mm	35mm	35VF	1993	Canon	3.8	35mm		1/125		40
Snappy EZ	24x36mm	35mm	35VF	1989	Canon	3.8	35mm		1/125		80
Snappy LX	24x36mm	35mm	35VF	1992	Canon	4.5	35mm	programmed			50
Snappy LX Date	24x36mm	35mm	35VF	1992	Canon	4.5	35mm	programmed			70
Snappy Q	24x36mm	35mm	35rf	1990	Canon	4.5	35mm		1/70		70
Snappy S	24x36mm	35mm	35VF	1988	Canon	4.5	35mm	programmed	40-250		60
Snappy V	24x36mm	35mm	35VF	1990	Canon	4.5	35mm		60, 250		100
Sprint	24x36mm	35mm	35AF	1987	Canon	3.5	35mm	programmed	40-250		80

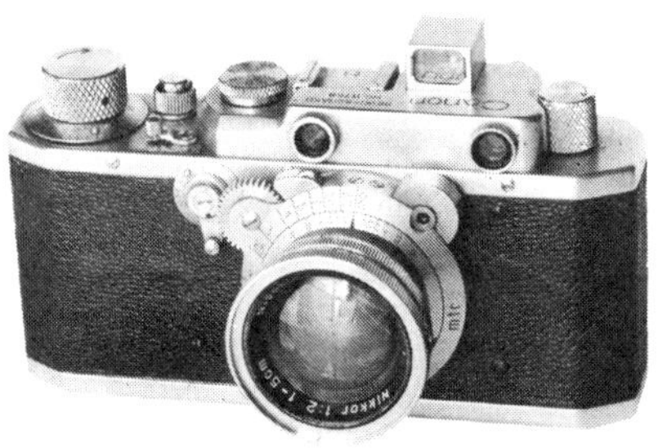

Canon S

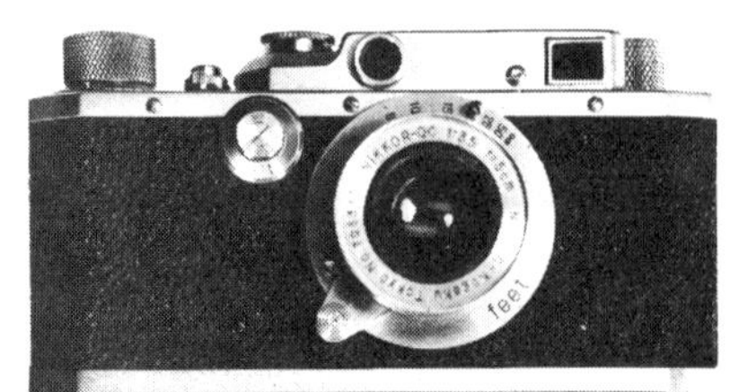

Canon Seiki S-II

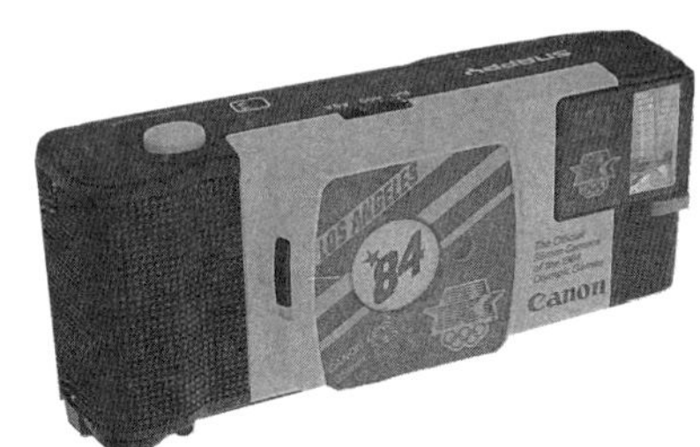

Snappy '84

MODEL	FORMAT	FILM	TYPE	Year	LENS	Apert	FL	SHUTTER	SPEEDS	ILLUS	U.S.$
Sprint Quartz Date	24x36mm	35mm	35AF	1988	Canon	3.5	35mm	programmed	40-250		100
Sure Shot	24x36mm	35mm	35AF	1985	Canon	2.8	38mm	programmed	8-500		90
Sure Shot A-1	24x36mm	35mm	35AW-AF	1993	Canon	3.5	32mm	programmed	60-250		150
Sure Shot A-1 Date	24x36mm	35mm	35AW-AF	1993	Canon	3.5	32mm	programmed	60-250		150
Sure Shot Ace	24x36mm	35mm	35AF	1989	Canon	3.5	35mm	programmed	40-125		110
Sure Shot Ace Date	24x36mm	35mm	35AF	1989	Canon	3.5	35mm	programmed	40-125		120
Sure Shot Caption Zoom	24x36mm	35mm	35AFZ	1990	Canon	3.8-5.6	38-60	programmed			140
Sure Shot EX	24x36mm	35mm	35AF	1990	Canon	4.5	35mm	programmed	40-125		90
Sure Shot EX Date	24x36mm	35mm	35AF	1990	Canon	4.5	35mm	programmed	40-125		90
Sure Shot Joy	24x36mm	35mm	35AF	1990	Canon	4.5	35mm	programmed	40-125		90
Sure Shot Joy Date	24x36mm	35mm	35AF	1990	Canon	4.5	35mm	programmed	40-125		90
Sure Shot M	24x36mm	35mm	35AF	1993	Canon	3.5	32mm	programmed			70
Sure Shot Max	24x36mm	35mm	35AF	1992	Canon	3.5	38mm	programmed			70
Sure Shot Max Date	24x36mm	35mm	35AF	1992	Canon	3.5	38mm	programmed			70
Sure Shot Mega Zoom 76	24x36mm	35mm	35AFZ	1993	Canon	3.8-7.2	38-76				80
Sure Shot M.Z. 76 Caption	24x36mm	35mm	35AFZ	1993	Canon	3.8-7.2	38-76				130
Sure Shot Mega Zoom 105	24x36mm	35mm	35AFZ	1992	Canon	3.5-8	35-105				150
Sure Shot M.Z. 105 Caption	24x36mm	35mm	35AFZ	1992	Canon	3.5-8	35-105				210
Sure Shot Multi Tele	24x36mm	35mm	35AF-BiF	1989	Canon	3.5/5.6	35/60	programmed	60-350		140
Sure Shot Multi Tele Date	24x36mm	35mm	35AF-BiF	1989	Canon	3.5/5.6	35/60	programmed	60-350		160
Sure Shot Owl	24x36mm	35mm	35AF	1994	Canon	4.5	35mm				50
Sure Shot Owl Date	24x36mm	35mm	35AF	1994	Canon	4.5	35mm				70
Sure Shot Quartz Date	24x36mm	35mm	35AF	1985	Canon	2.8	38mm	programmed	8-500		100
Sure Shot Supreme	24x36mm	35mm	35AF	1987	Canon	2.8	38mm	programmed	8-500		100
Sure Shot Supreme QD	24x36mm	35mm	35AF	1987	Canon	2.8	38mm	programmed	8-500		110
Sure Shot Tele	24x36mm	35mm	35AF-BiF	1987	Canon	2.9/4.9	40/70	programmed	3-500		110
Sure Shot Tele Max	24x36mm	35mm	35AF-BiF	1992	Canon	3.5/6	38/70	programmed	60-250		80
Sure Shot Tele QD	24x36mm	35mm	35AF-BiF	1987	Canon	2.9/4.9	40/70	programmed	3-500		120
Sure Shot Z85	24x36mm	35mm	35AFZ	1993	Canon	3.8-8	38-85	programmed			160
Sure Shot Z85 Caption	24x36mm	35mm	35AFZ	1993	Canon	3.8-8	38-85	programmed			170
Sure Shot Z115	24x36mm	35mm	35AFZ	1993	Canon	3.6-8.5	38-115	programmed	2-1/1200		210
Sure Shot Zoom	24x36mm	35mm	35AFZ	1989	Canon	3.5-6.7	35-70	programmed	30-250		160
Sure Shot Zoom Max	24x36mm	35mm	35AFZ	1993	Canon	3.8-7.2	38-76	programmed			160
Sure Shot Z. Max Caption	24x36mm	35mm	35AFZ	1993	Canon	3.8-7.2	38-76	programmed			180
Sure Shot Zoom S	24x36mm	35mm	35AFZ	1990	Canon	3.8-5.6	38-60	programmed			140
Sure Shot Zoom XL	24x36mm	35mm	35AFZ	1989	Canon	3.6-7.3	39-85	programmed	2-1/250		230
Sure Shot Zoom XL Date	24x36mm	35mm	35AFZ	1989	Canon	3.6-7.3	39-85	programmed	2-1/250		250
Canon T50 body	24x36mm	35mm	35slr	1983	body only	---	---	ElecMetFP	2-1000		120
Canon T50 + 50/1.8	24x36mm	35mm	35slr	1983	Canon FD	1.8	50mm	ElecMetFP	2-1000		140
Canon T60 body	24x36mm	35mm	35slr	1983	body only	---	---	ElecMetFP	1-1000		140
Canon T60 + 50/1.9	24x36mm	35mm	35slr	1983	Canon FD	1.9	50mm	ElecMetFP	1-1000		220
Canon T70 body	24x36mm	35mm	35slr	1984	body only	---	---	ElecMetFP	2-1000		200

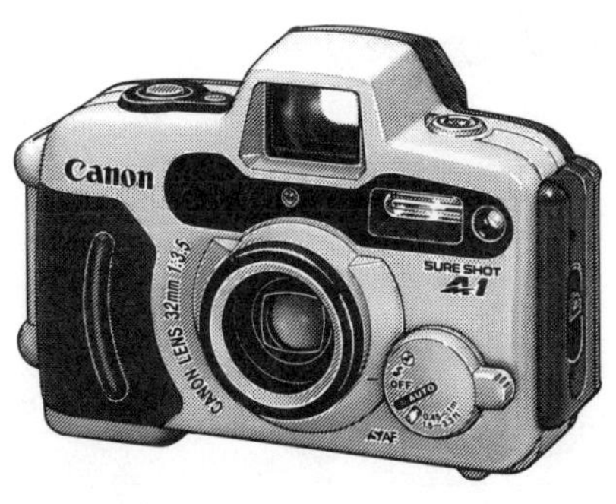

Sure Shot A-1

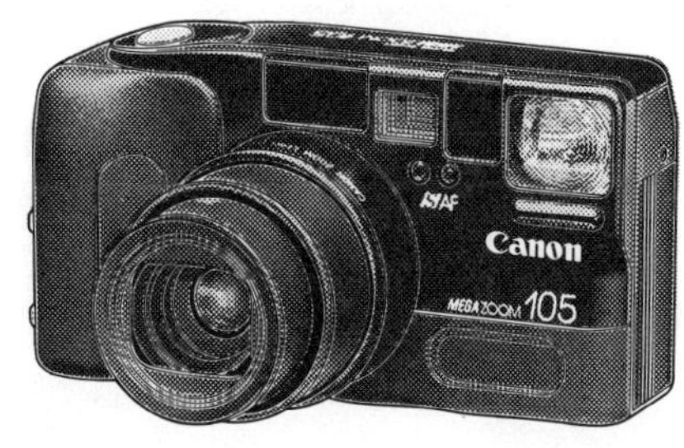

Sure Shot Mega Zoom 105

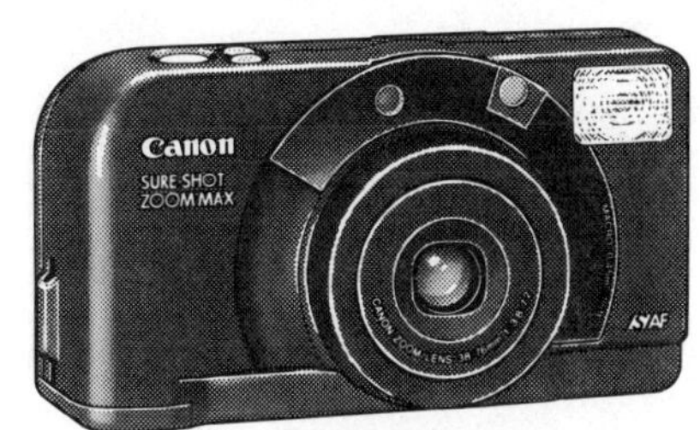

Sure Shot Zoom Max

MODEL	FORMAT	FILM	TYPE	Year	LENS	Apert	FL	SHUTTER	SPEEDS	ILLUS	U.S.$
Canon T70 + 50/1.4	24x36mm	35mm	35slr	1984	Canon FD	1.4	50mm	ElecMetFP	2-1000	A3218	250
Canon T80 body	24x36mm	35mm	35slr	1984	body only	---	---	ElecMetFP	2-1000		180
Canon T80 + 50/1.8	24x36mm	35mm	35slr	1984	Canon AC	1.8	50mm	ElecMetFP	2-1000		200
Canon T90 body	24x36mm	35mm	35slr	1985	body only	---	---	ElecMetFP	30-4000		560
Canon T90 + 50/1.4	24x36mm	35mm	35slr	1985	Canon FD	1.4	50mm	ElecMetFP	30-4000		650
Canon TL QL body	24x36mm	35mm	35slr	1968	body only	---	---	focal plane	1-500		90
Canon TL QL + 50/1.4	24x36mm	35mm	35slr	1968	Canon FL	1.4	50mm	focal plane	1-500		140
Canon TLb QL body	24x36mm	35mm	35slr	1972	body only	---	---	focal plane	1-500		90
Canon TLb QL + 50/1.8	24x36mm	35mm	35slr	1972	Canon FD	1.8	50mm	focal plane	1-500		120
Top Shot	24x36mm	35mm	35AF	1987	Canon	2.8	38mm	programmed	8-500		100
Top Shot Quartz Date	24x36mm	35mm	35AF	1987	Canon	2.8	38mm	programmed	8-500		110
Top Twin	24x36mm	35mm	35AF-BiF	1987	Canon	2.8/4.9	40/70	programmed	3-500		110
Top Twin Quartz Date	24x36mm	35mm	35AF-BiF	1987	Canon	2.8/4.9	40/70	programmed	3-500		120
Canon TX body	24x36mm	35mm	35slr	1975	body only	---	---	focal plane	1-500		80
Canon TX + 50/1.8	24x36mm	35mm	35slr	1975	Canon FD	1.8	50mm	focal plane	1-500	Mc112	120
X-Ray Canon 35	24x36mm	35mm	SciMed	1939	Nikkor	2	50mm			Mc109	1100
X-Ray Canon Seiki	24x36mm	35mm	SciMed	1939	Seiki-K. Serenar	2	50mm				1100
...(unknown)											
Capitol 120 (black)	2¼x3¼"	120	MetalBox						B,I	Mc114	30
Capitol 120 (silver)	2¼x3¼"	120	MetalBox						B,I	Mc114	30
...(unknown)											
Capta	4.5x6cm	120	BakeliteRoll	1940							30
Capta II	4.5x6cm	120	BakeliteRoll	1940						Mc250	30
Super Capta	4.5x6cm	120	BakeliteRoll	1940	Super-Capta			2-speed			30
...CARL ZEISS JENA - Jena, Germany											
Werra	24x36mm	35mm	35vf	1955	Tessar	2.8	50mm	Vebur	1-250		70
Werra I	24x36mm	35mm	35vf	1955	Tessar	2.8	50mm	Vebur	1-250	Mc114	70
Werra Ia	24x36mm	35mm	35vf	1955	Tessar	2.8	50mm	Compur	1-500		70
Werra Ib	24x36mm	35mm	35vf	1960	Tessar	2.8	50mm	Prestor	1-500		50
Werra Ic	24x36mm	35mm	35vf	1955	Tessar	2.8	50mm	Prestor	1-750		60
Werra Ie	24x36mm	35mm	35vf	1964	Tessar	2.8	50mm	Prestor	1-500		50
Werra II	24x36mm	35mm	35vf	1955	Tessar	2.8	50mm	Vebur	1-250		60
Werra IIe	24x36mm	35mm	35vf	1964	Tessar	2.8	50mm	Prestor	1-750		50
Werra III	24x36mm	35mm	35rf	1955	Tessar	2.8	50mm	Vebur	1-250		100
Werra IIIE	24x36mm	35mm	35rf	1955	Tessar	2.8	50mm	Vebur	1-250		70
Werra IV	24x36mm	35mm	35rf	1955	Tessar	2.8	50mm	Vebur	1-250		80
Werra V	24x36mm	35mm	35rf	1960	Tessar	2.8	50mm	Prestor	1-500		100
Werra Microscope Camera	24x36mm	35mm	SciMed	1960	Tessar	2.8	50mm	Pronto-Press			140
Werramat	24x36mm	35mm	35vf	1961	Tessar	2.8	50mm	Prestor	1-500		70
Werramat E	24x36mm	35mm	35vf	1964	Tessar	2.8	50mm	Prestor	1-500		70
Werramatic	24x36mm	35mm	35rf	1955	Tessar	2.8	50mm	Prestor	1-750		80
Werramatic E	24x36mm	35mm	35rf	1964	Tessar	2.8	50mm	Prestor	1-750		90

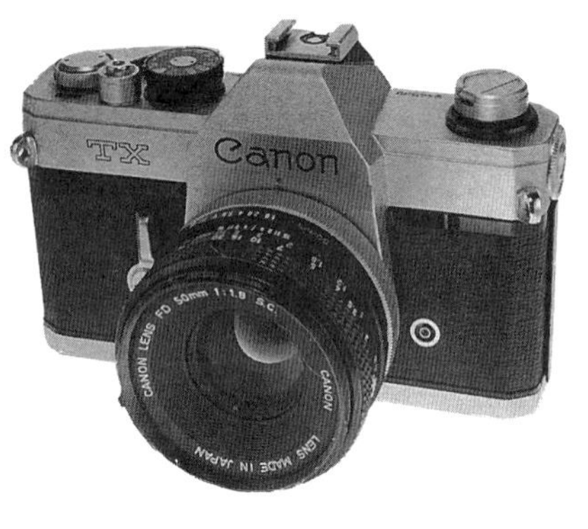

Canon TX

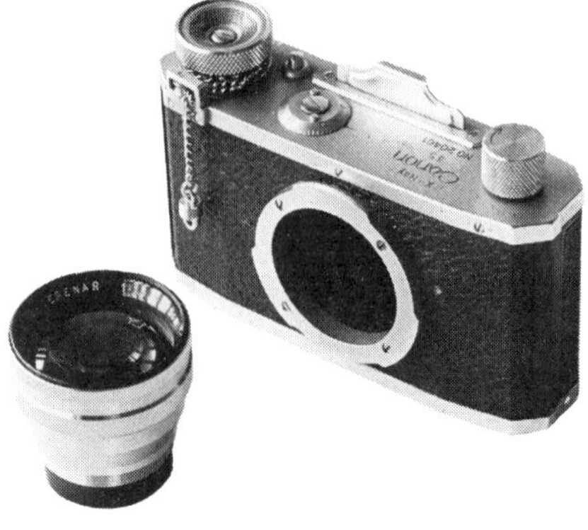

X-Ray Canon 35

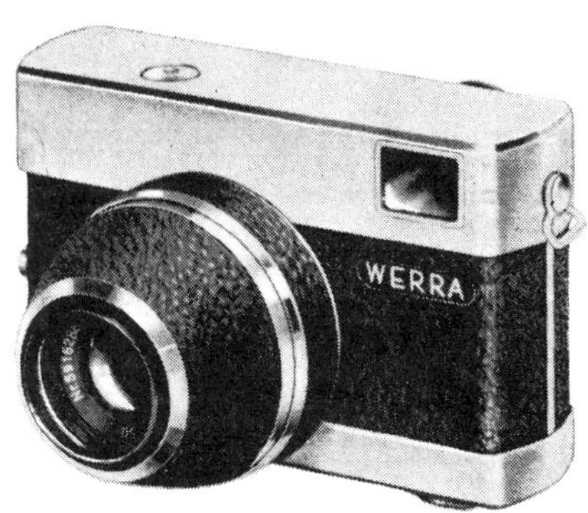

Werra I

MODEL	FORMAT	FILM	TYPE	Year	LENS	Apert	FL	SHUTTER	SPEEDS	ILLUS	U.S.$
...CARMEN S.A. - France											
Carmen	24x24mm	Roll	MiniatRo	1930	Meniscus					F1136	140
...CARPENTIER (Jules Carpentier) - Paris											
Photo Jumelle 4.5x6	4.5x6cm	plate	Jumelle	1890	Rapid Rectilinear	11		guillotine		Mc115	190
Photo Jumelle 6.5x9	6.5x9cm	plate	Jumelle	1890	Zeiss-Krauss	8	110mm	guillotine		F1105	160
Stereo Photo Jumelle	6x13cm	plate	StJumelle	1890	Rapid Rectilinear			guillotine		F1354	1400
...CENTURY CAMERA CO.											
Century Mod. 11	3¼x4¼"	plate	H&S	1902	Century R. Rect.			Automatic	I,T,B		190
Compact Mod. 10 4x5"	4x5"	plate	H&S	1902	Century R. Rect.			Automatic	I,T,B		160
Compact Mod. 10 5x7"	5x7"	plate	H&S	1902	Century R. Rect.			Automatic	I,T,B		160
Field camera 8x10"	8x10"	plate	Field	1900	Various			various			300
Field camera 11x14"	11x14"	plate	Field	1900	Various			various			260
Field camera No. 2	4¼x6½"	plate	Field	1900	Various			various			180
Folding Plate Mod. 15	5x7"	plate	H&S	1900	Rapid Convertible			Automatic	I,T,B		160
Folding Plate Mod. 40	4x5"	plate	Field	1900	Century R. Rect.			Automatic	I,T,B		160
Folding Plate Mod. 41	4x5"	plate	Field	1900	Century R. Rect.			Dbl. Pneum.	I,T,B		150
Folding Plate Mod. 42	4x5"	plate	Field	1900	Rapid Symmetr.			Automatic	I,T,B		150
Folding Plate Mod. 43	4x5"	plate	Field	1900	Rapid Symmetr.			Automatic	I,T,B		160
Fold. Plate Mod. 46 4x5"	4x5"	plate	Field	1900	Various			various			150
Fold. Plate Mod. 46 8x10"	8x10"	plate	Field	1900	Various			various			180
Folding Plate Mod. 47	5x7"	plate	Field	1900	Various			various		Mc115	110
Folding Plate Mod. 69	6½x8½"	plate	Field	1900	Various			various			190
Grand 4x5"	4x5"	plate	H&S	1901							220
Grand 4x5" Triple Conv.	4x5"	plate	H&S	1901	Triple Convertible						260
Grand 5x7"	5x7"	plate	H&S	1901							220
Grand 5x7" Triple Conv.	5x7"	plate	H&S	1901	Triple Convertible						260
Grand 6½x8½"	6½x8½"	plate	H&S	1901							220
Grand 6½x8½" Triple Conv.	6½x8½"	plate	H&S	1901	Triple Convertible						260
Grand Sr.	5x7"	plate	H&S	1903	Centar R. Rect.					Mc115	180
Grand Sr.	6½x8½"	plate	H&S	1903	Century Anast.			Century		Mc115	200
Long Focus Grand 5x7"	5x7"	plate	H&S	1902							260
Long Focus Grand 6½x8½"	6½x8½"	plate	H&S	1902							250
Petite No. 1	3¼x4¼"	plate	H&S	1904	Rapid Rectilinear			B&L Automatic	T,B,I	Mc115	140
Petite No. 2	3¼x4¼"	plate	H&S	1904	Rapid Rectilinear			B&L Automatic	T,B,I	Mc115	140
Petite No. 3	3¼x4¼"	plate	H&S	1904	Rapid Rectilinear			B&L Automatic	T,B,I	Mc115	140
Stereo	5x7"	plate	StFoldPl	1908	Tessar			Century		HK464	670
Stereo Mod. 46	5x7"	plate	StFoldPl	1900	Symmetrical		4x5"	B&L Stereo		Mc115	560
Studio camera 8x10"	8x10"	plate	Studio	1910	Various			various			350
Studio camera 11x14"	11x14"	plate	Studio	1910	Various			various			350
...CERTEX S.A. - Barcelona											
Werlisa	24x36mm	35mm	35vf	1980	achromatic	7.5	50mm				30
Werlisa Club Color	24x36mm	35mm	35vf	1982	achromatic	7.5	50mm				20

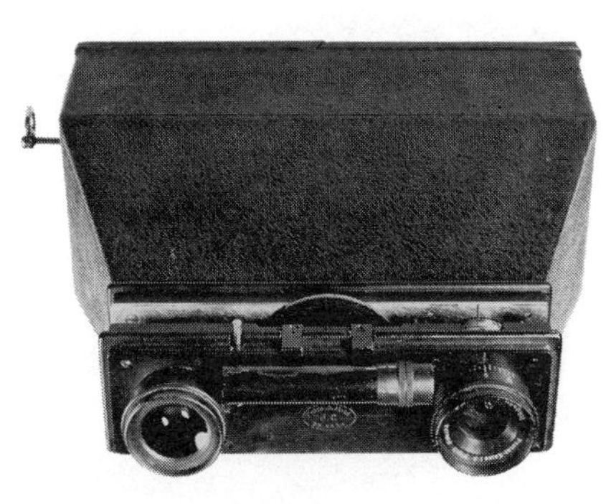

Photo Jumelle 4.5x6

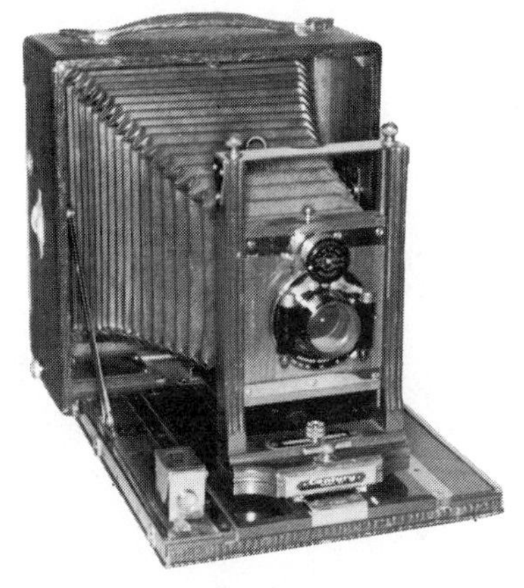

Century Stereo Mod. 47

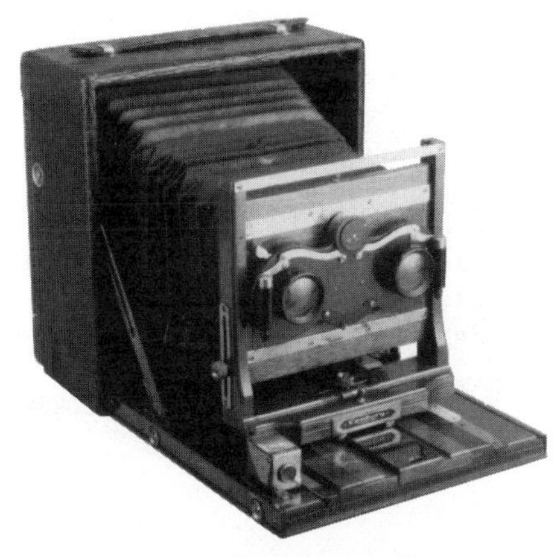

Century Stereo Mod. 46

MODEL	FORMAT	FILM	TYPE	Year	LENS	Apert	FL	SHUTTER	SPEEDS	ILLUS	U.S.$
...CERTO KAMERAWERK - Dresden											
Certi	24x36mm	35mm	35vf		Triplon	3.5	45mm	Auto			30
Certina	6x6cm	120	RigidRo	1968	achromatic	8		Spezial	1/60		20
Certix	6x9cm	120	FoldRo	1930	Certar	6.3		Vario	25-100		30
Certo 35	24x36mm	35mm	35Fold	1951	Tessar	2.8		Compur-Rapid	1-500		50
Certo Box A	6x9cm	120	RollBox	1937	Optik	11			M,Z		40
Certo Box B	6x9cm	120	RollBox	1937	Certomat	11			M,Z		30
Certo Doppel-Box	6x9/4.5x6	120	RollBox	1935	Certomat				I	HK85	70
Certo Six	6x6cm	120	VtFoldRo	1950	Tessar	2.8	80mm	Prontor-SVS			120
Certo Super 35	24x36mm	35mm	35Fold	1951	Tessar	2.8		Compur-Rapid	1-500		50
Certo-Matic	6x6cm	120	RigidRo	1960		8			1/60		30
Certo-phot	6x6cm	120	RigidRo								10
Certochrom 9x12	9x12cm	plate	VtFoldPl	1925	Xenar	4.5	135mm	Compur	1-250		40
Certochrom 10x15	10x15cm	plate	VtFoldPl	1925	Xenar	4.5	65mm	Compur	1-250		40
Certofix	6x9cm	120	VtFoldRo	1931	Radionar	6.3	105mm	Vario	25-100		30
Certokunst	9x12cm	plate	VtFoldPl	1925	Xenar	4.5	135mm	Compur	1-300		70
Certokunst	9x12cm	plate	VtFoldPl	1925	Trioplan	6.3	135mm	Vario	25-100		70
Certolob	6.5x9cm	plate	VtFoldPl	1925	Xenar	4.5	120mm	Compur	1-250		100
Certolob 0	6.5x9cm	plate	VtFoldPl	1925	Trioplan	6.3	120mm	Vario	25-100		70
Certolob XI	6.5x9cm	plate	VtFoldPl	1927	Trioplan	6.3	105mm	Vario	25-100	Mc116	90
Certolob XI/0	6.5x9cm	plate	VtFoldPl	1927	Trioplan	6.3	105mm	Vario	25-100		30
Certolux	6.5x9cm	plate	VtFoldPl	1930	Xenar	4.5	120mm				200
Certonet	6x9cm	120	VtFoldRo	1926	Radionar			Vario	25-100	Mc116	50
Certonet 0	6x9cm	120	VtFoldRo	1925	Radionar	4.5	120mm	Vario	25-100		30
Certonet XIV	6.5x11cm	116	VtFoldRo	1928	Periskop	11		Vario	25-100		50
Certonet XV	6x9cm	120	VtFoldRo	1927	Xenar	4.5	105mm	Compur			30
Certonet XV Luxus	6x9cm	120	VtFoldRo	1931	Xenar	4.5	105mm	Compur			170
Certoplat	9x12cm	plate	VtFoldPl	1929	Xenar	3.5	150mm	Compur	200		70
Certorex	9x12cm	plate	VtFoldPl	1925	Trioplan	6.3	135mm	Vario	25-100		50
Certoruf 9x12	9x12cm	plate	VtFoldPl	1929	Ennator	4.5		Compur			60
Certoruf 10x15	10x15cm	plate	VtFoldPl	1925	Unofokal	6.8	165mm	Vario	25-100		50
Certoruf 10x15	10x15cm	plate	VtFoldPl	1925	Tessar	4.5	165mm	Compur	1-300		50
Certoruhm 9x12	9x12cm	plate	FoldPl	1925	Tessar	4.5	135mm	Compur	1-300	Mc116	70
Certoruhm 10x15	10x15cm	plate	FoldPl	1925	Tessar	4.5		Compur	1-300	Mc116	70
Certosport	6.5x9cm	plate	VtFoldPl	1930	Meyer	4.5		Ibsor	1-125		50
Certosport	9x12cm	plate	VtFoldPl	1930	Xenar	4.5	4"	Compur			60
Certotix	6x9cm	120	VtFoldRo	1931	Anastigmat	4.5	4"	Vario	25-100		30
Certotrop 6.5x9	6.5x9cm	plate	VtFoldPl	1929	Triopan	2.9	6"	Compur S		Mc116	60
Certotrop 9x12	9x12cm	plate	VtFoldPl	1929	Xenar	3.5	6.5"	Compur	1-300	Mc116	70
Certotrop 10x15	10x15cm	plate	VtFoldPl	1929	Tessar	4.5		Compur	1-300	Mc116	60
Certotrop Luxus	9x12cm	plate	VtFoldPl	1930	Tessar	4.5	150mm	Compur	1-300		240
Damen-Kamera	3¼x4¼"	plate	Disguised	1900	Certomat	8	105mm	Vario	25-100	Mc116	11000

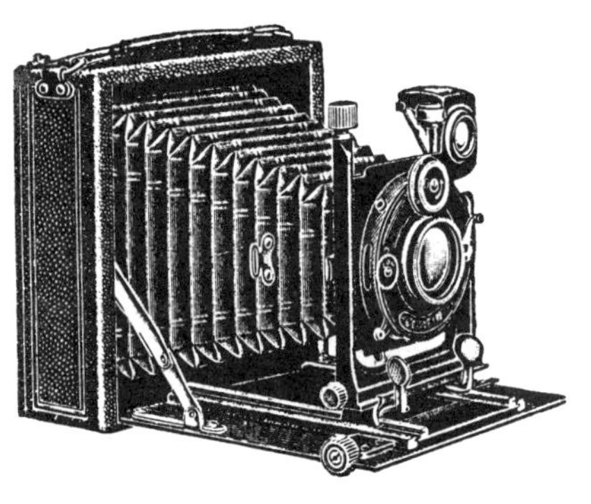

Certoruhm 10x15

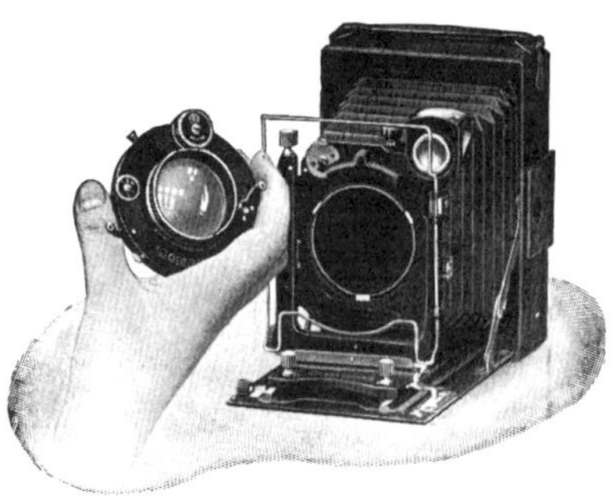

Certotrop

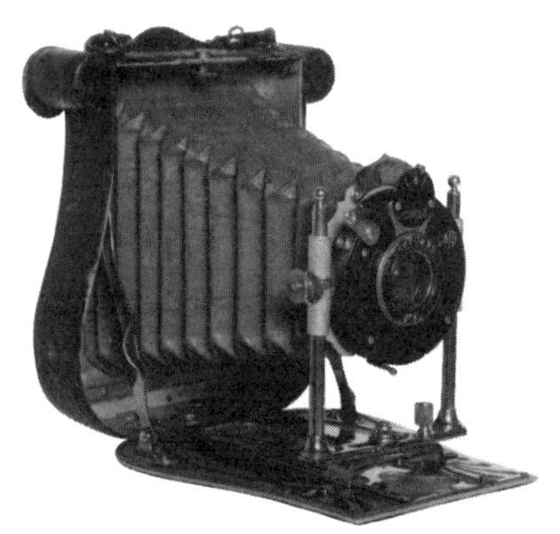

Damen-Kamera

MODEL	FORMAT	FILM	TYPE	Year	LENS	Apert	FL	SHUTTER	SPEEDS	ILLUS	U.S.$
Dollina	24x36mm	35mm	35Fold	1932	Radionar	2.9	50mm	Compur	1-300	HK552	50
Dollina "0"	24x36mm	35mm	35Fold	1937	Certar	4.5		Vario	25-100	Mc116	60
Dollina "0"	24x36mm	35mm	35Fold	1937	Cassar	2.9		Compur		Mc116	70
Dollina I (black)	24x36mm	35mm	35Fold	1936	Xenar	3.5		Compur	1-300	A1023	60
Dollina I (chrome)	24x36mm	35mm	35Fold	1936	Tessar	2.8		Compur-Rapid	1-500	A2050	60
Dollina II	24x36mm	35mm	35Fold	1936	Radionar	2.9	50mm	Compur	1-300	Mc117	120
Dollina III	24x36mm	35mm	35Fold	1938	Tessar	2.8		Compur-Rapid	1-500	Mc117	180
Dolly	3x4cm	127	StrutRo	1932	Xenar	3.5		Compur	1-300	Mc117	120
Dolly Vest Pocket A	4x6.5cm	127	VtFoldRo	1936	Radionar			Compur	1-300	Mc117	80
Dolly Vest Pocket B	4x6.5cm	127	VtFoldPl	1936	Radionar			Compur	1-300	Mc117	80
Durata	24x36mm	35mm	35Fold	1950	Trioplan	2.9	50mm	Cludor		Mc117	40
Durata II	24x36mm	35mm	35Fold	1950	Trioplan	2.9	50mm	Cludor			40
Kafota	24x36mm	35mm	35Fold	1939	Cassar	2.9		Compur			90
KN 35	24x36mm	35mm	35vf	1973	Kosmar	2.8					30
Schaja Klappkamera	9x12cm	plate	VtFoldPl	1927	Tessar	4.5	150mm				50
Super Certo II	24x36mm	35mm	35Fold	1951	Tessar	2.8		Compur-Rapid	1-500		50
Super Dollina	24x36mm	35mm	35Fold	1939	Xenon	2		Compur-Rapid	1-500	Mc117	80
Super Dollina II	24x36mm	35mm	35Fold	1951	Tessar	2.8		Compur-Rapid	1-500		140
Super-Six	6x6cm	120	HzFoldRo	1951	Tessar	2.8	80mm	Sync-Compur	1-500		140
Supersport Dolly	6x6cm	120	VtFoldRo	1935	Xenon	2		Rim-Compur		Mc117	80
Supersport Dolly	6x6cm	120	VtFoldRo	1935	Tessar	2.8		Rim-Compur		Mc117	80
Supersport Dolly Mod.C	6x6/4.5x6	120	VtFoldRo	1936	Tessar	4.5	75mm	Compur S	1-250	A1485	50
Supersport Dolly RF	6x6cm	120	VtFoldRo	1935	Xenon	2		Rim-Compur		Mc117	160
...CHADT											
Cam Watch M1 (Revue)	8x11mm	Minox	Submin	1994		4.5	14.3mm		200		100
...CHADWICK (W.I. Chadwick) - Manchester, England											
Hand Camera		plate	PlateBox	1891				Kershaw			270
Manifold	4¼x6½"	plate	SterTail	1900	Rectigraph			Thornton-Pickard			700
Stereo Camera 3¼x4¼"	3¼x4¼"	plate	SterTail	1890	Chadwick		5"	Thornton-Pickard		Mc118	570
Stereo Camera 4¼x6½"	4¼x6½"	plate	SterTail	1900	Chadwick		5"	Thornton-Pickard		Mc118	800
...(unknown)											
Champion II	24x36mm	35mm	35VF		Color-Isconar	2.8	45mm	Prontor	125	Mc118	30
Champion IV	24x36mm	35mm	35VF		Color-Isconar	2.8	45mm	Prontor	125	Mc118	30
...CHAPMAN (J.T. Chapman) - Manchester, England											
The British 3¼x4¼"	3¼x4¼"	plate	FoldPl	1903	Wray R.R.	8		roller-blind			230
The British 4¼x6½"	4¼x6½"	plate	FoldPl	1903	Wray R.R.			roller-blind			270
The British 6½x8½"	6½x8½"	plate	FoldPl	1903	Wray R.R.			roller-blind			310
The British (magazine)	3¼x4¼"	plate	MagBox	1900	Wray R.R.	8		roller-blind	15-90		220
Forward Siderigger Cam.	6½x8½"	plate	FoldPl	1880							380
Millers Patent (black)	3¼x4¼"	plate	MagBox	1900				roller-blind			200
Millers Patent (reptile)	3¼x4¼"	plate	MagBox	1900	Rapid Rectilinear	8		roller-blind			460
Stereoscopic Field Cam.	4¼x6½"	plate	StFoldPl		Wray		5x4"	Iris			540

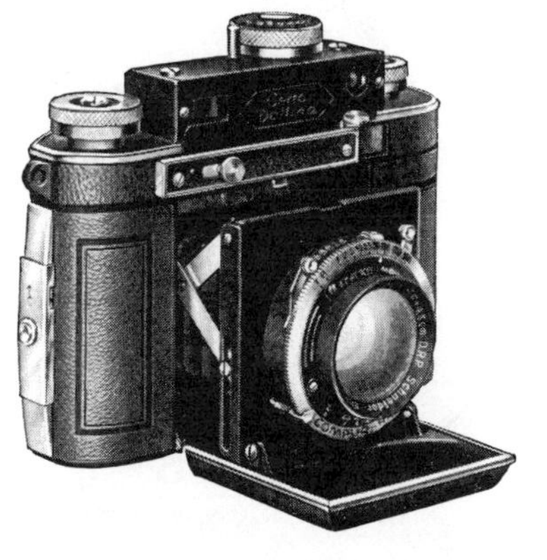

Dollina II

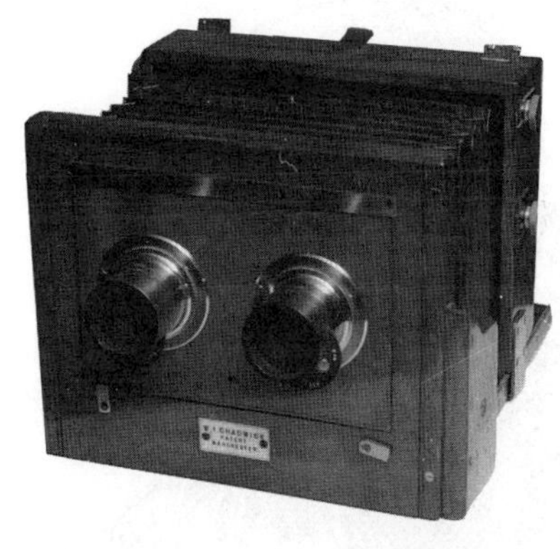

Chadwick Stereo Camera

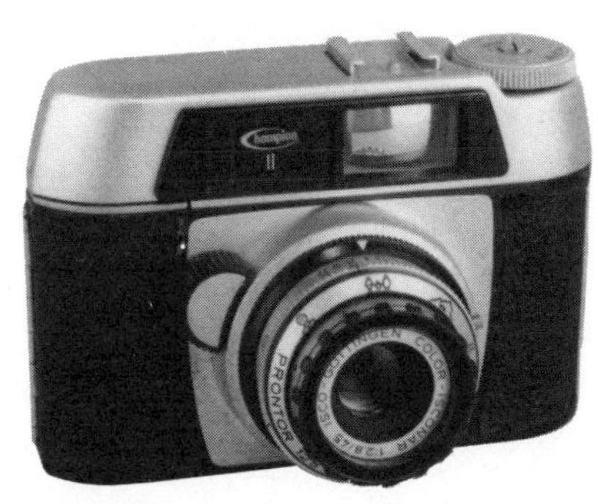

Champion II

MODEL	FORMAT	FILM	TYPE	Year	LENS	Apert	FL	SHUTTER	SPEEDS	ILLUS	U.S.$
...CHASE MAGAZINE CAMERA CO. - Newburyport, MA USA											
Chase Magazine Camera	4x5"	plate	MagBox	1899					I,T		160
...CHEVALIER (Charles Chevalier) - Paris											
Chambre à Tiroir		Dag	Dag							F77	17000
Grand Photographe	16.5x21.5	Dag	Dag							F79	9000
...CHICAGO CAMERA CO. - Chicago, USA											
Photake	2x2"	plate	RigidPl	1896	Achromat	14	120mm	guillotine		Mc118	1100
...CHICAGO FERROTYPE CO. - Chicago											
Mandel No. 2 Post Card	3½x5½"		Street	1913						Mc118	160
Mandelette	2½x3½"		Street	1929							100
Wonder Autom. Cannon	1"	Ferro	Button	1910						Mc118	1000
...CHINAGLIA DOMENICO - Belluno, Italy											
Kristall	24x36mm	35mm	35VF	1950	Krinar	3.5	50mm	focal plane	1/20-1000		390
Kristall II	24x36mm	35mm	35RF	1950	Trixar	3.5	50mm	focal plane	1/20-1000		520
Kristall IIa	24x36mm	35mm	35RF	1950	Vegar	3.5	50mm	focal plane	1/20-1000		450
Kristall IIS	24x36mm	35mm	35RF	1952	Trixar	3.5	50mm	focal plane	1/20-1000		520
Kristall III	24x36mm	35mm	35RF	1950	Trigon	2.8	50mm	focal plane	1-1000		600
Kristall IIIS	24x36mm	35mm	35RF	1952	Trigon	2.8	50mm	focal plane	1-1000		550
Kristall 53	24x36mm	35mm	35RF	1953	Berthiot	2.8	50mm	focal plane	1-1000		610
Kristall 53	24x36mm	35mm	35RF	1953	Xenon	2.0	50mm	focal plane	1-1000		610
Kristall R	24x36mm	35mm	35RF	1950	Anastigmat	3.5	50mm	focal plane	1/20-1000		700
...CHINON - Japan											
Chinon 35F	24x36mm	35mm	35VF	1982	Chinonex Color	3.8	35mm		1/125		30
Chinon 35F II	24x36mm	35mm	35VF	1984	Chinon	3.8	35mm		1/125		30
Chinon 35FA II	24x36mm	35mm	35AF	1984	Chinon	3.5	35mm	programmed			60
Chinon 35FA Super	24x36mm	35mm	35AF	1984	Chinon	2.8	35mm	programmed			70
Chinon 35FS-A	24x36mm	35mm	35AF	1984	Chinon	3.5	35mm	programmed	30-500		50
Chinon 35FS-II	24x36mm	35mm	35AF	1984	Chinon	3.5	35mm	programmed	30-500		40
Chinon Auto 1001	24x36mm	35mm	35AF	1987	Chinon	3.5	35mm	programmed	45-1000		90
Chinon Auto 2001	24x36mm	35mm	35AF	1987	Chinon	2.8	35mm	programmed	45-500		110
Chinon Auto 3001	24x36mm	35mm	35AF	1988	Chinon	2.8	35mm	programmed	45-250		120
Chinon Auto 3501	24x36mm	35mm	35AFZ	1991	Chinon	3.7-6.9	35-70	programmed	50-500		80
Chinon Auto 4001	24x36mm	35mm	35AFZ	1991	Chinon	3.6-6.9	35-70	programmed	4-500		100
Chinon Auto 5501	24x36mm	35mm	35AFZ	1993	Chinon	3.6-7.9	38-90	programmed	4-300		110
Chinon Auto 6001	24x36mm	35mm	35AFZ	1993	Chinon	3.6-7.9	38-90	programmed	4-300		110
Chinon Auto GL	24x36mm	35mm	35VF	1990	Chinon	4.5	35mm		1/125		50
Chinon Auto GL-II	24x36mm	35mm	35VF	1993	Chinon	4.5	35mm		1/125		50
Chinon Auto GL-AF	24x36mm	35mm	35AF	1990	Chinon	3.9	35mm		1/125		70
Chinon Auto GL-S	24x36mm	35mm	35VF	1990	Chinon	4.5	35mm		1/125		50
Chinon Auto GLX	24x36mm	35mm	35AF	1987	Chinon	3.9	35mm		90-410		60
Chinon Auto GLX Tele	24x36mm	35mm	35AF-BiF	1988	Chinon	4/6.4	35/60		1/90		100
Chinon Auto GX	24x36mm	35mm	35VF	1987	Chinon	4.5	35mm		1/125		40

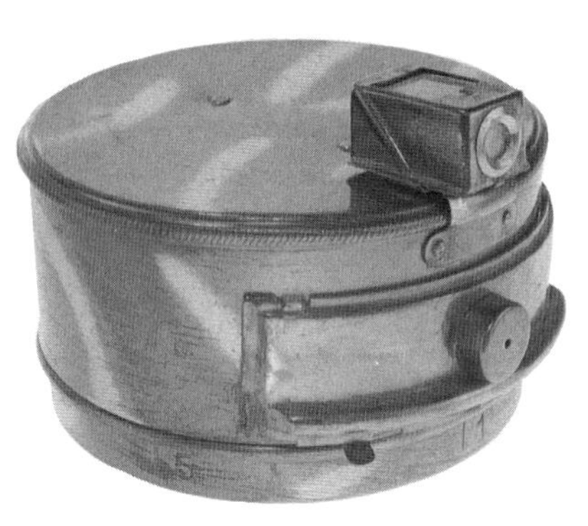
Photake

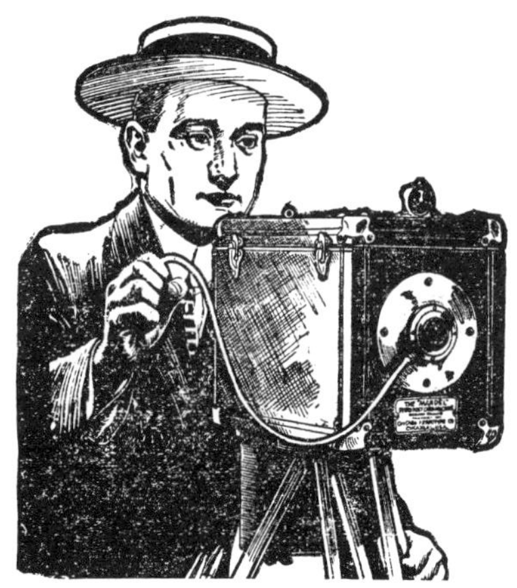
Mandel No. 2 Post Card

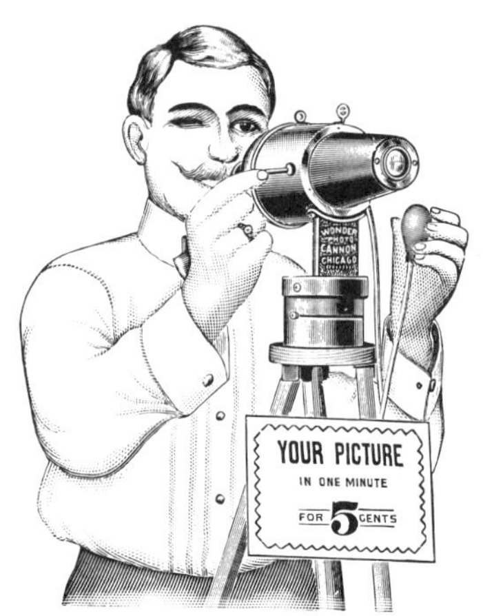

Wonder Autom. Cannon

MODEL	FORMAT	FILM	TYPE	Year	LENS	Apert	FL	SHUTTER	SPEEDS	ILLUS	U.S.$
Chinon Auto GX Tele	24x36mm	35mm	35BiFocal	1987	Chinon	4/5.6	35/55		1/100		60
Chinon Belami	24x36mm	35mm	35VF	1982	Chinon	2.8	35mm	programmed	8-1000		70
Chinon Belami AF	24x36mm	35mm	35AF	1990	Chinon	3.9	35mm		60-125		80
Chinon Bros 5501	24x36mm	35mm	35AFZ	1993	Chinon	3.6-7.9	38-90	programmed	4-300		110
Chinon Bros 6001	24x36mm	35mm	35AFZ	1993	Chinon	3.6-7.9	38-90	programmed	4-300		110
Chinon Bros-X	24x36mm	35mm	35AFZ	1991	Chinon	3.6-6.9	35-70	programmed	4-500		100
Chinon Bros-Z	24x36mm	35mm	35AFZ	1991	Chinon	3.7-6.9	35-70	programmed	50-500		80
Chinon CE-5	24x36mm	35mm	35AFSLR	1983	Auto Chinon	1.7	50mm	electronic	4-1/2000		160
Chinon CG-5	24x36mm	35mm	35AFSLR	1983	Auto Chinon	1.7	50mm	electronic	4-1/1000		180
Chinon CM-4S	24x36mm	35mm	35SLR	1982	Auto Chinon	1.4	50mm	focal plane	1-1000		110
Chinon CM-5	24x36mm	35mm	35SLR	1985	Auto Chinon	1.4	50mm	focal plane	1-1000		110
Chinon CM-7	24x36mm	35mm	35SLR	1988	Auto Chinon	1.8	50mm	focal plane	1-2000		130
Chinon CP-5	24x36mm	35mm	35SLR	1984	Auto Chinon	1.4	50mm	electronic	8 1/1000		120
CP-5S Twin Program	24x36mm	35mm	35SLR	1984	Auto Chinon	1.4	50mm	electronic	8-1/1000		180
CP-6 Twin Program	24x36mm	35mm	35SLR	1987	Auto Chinon	1.4	50mm	electronic	8-1/1000		180
Chinon CP-7m	24x36mm	35mm	35SLR	1987	Auto Chinon	1.4	50mm	electronic	8-1/2000		180
Chinon CP-9AF	24x36mm	35mm	35AFSLR	1989	Chinon AF	3.5-4.5	28-70	electronic	8-1/2000		310
Chinon CP-X Program	24x36mm	35mm	35AFSLR	1986	Chinon AF	1.4	50mm	electronic	1-1000		230
Chinon Genesis	24x36mm	35mm	35AFSLR	1989		4.1-6.4	35-80	programmed	4-300		180
Chinon Genesis II	24x36mm	35mm	35AFSLR	1990		4.1-6.4	35-80	programmed	4-300		190
Chinon Genesis III	24x36mm	35mm	35AFSLR	1991		4.4-5.6	38-110	programmed	1-1000		250
Chinon Genesis IV	24x36mm	35mm	35AFSLR	1993	Auto Chinon	4.5-5.6	38-135	focal plane	1-1200		190
Chinon GS-7 Refl. Zoom	24x36mm	35mm	35AFSLR	1989		4.1-6.4	35-80	programmed	4-300		180
Chinon GS-8	24x36mm	35mm	35AFSLR	1990		4.1-6.4	35-80	programmed	4-300		190
Chinon GS-9 Refl. Zoom	24x36mm	35mm	35AFSLR	1991		4.4-5.6	38-110	programmed	1-1000		250
Chinon GS-135	24x36mm	35mm	35AFSLR	1993	Auto Chinon	4.5-5.6	38-135	focal plane	1-1200		190
Handyzoom	24x36mm	35mm	35AFZ	1989		3.7-6.7	35-70	programmed	4-300		140
Handyzoom 5001	24x36mm	35mm	35AFZ	1991		3.7-6.7	35-70	programmed	4-300		150
Infrafocus 35F-MA	24x36mm	35mm	35AF	1982		2.8	38mm	programmed			120
Monami	24x36mm	35mm	35VF	1990	Chinon	4.5	35mm		1/125		50
Monami 35FS	24x36mm	35mm	35VF	1982	Chinon	2.8	35mm	programmed	8-500		50
Pocket Dual AF-P	24x36mm	35mm	35AF-BiF	1993	Chinon	3.9/6.3	28/52	programmed	4-180		60
Pocket Dual P	24x36mm	35mm	35BiFocal	1993	Chinon	3.9/6.3	28/52	programmed	4-180		40
Pocket Zoom	24x36mm	35mm	35AFZ	1993	Chinon	3.9-5.8	38-60	programmed	4-300		100
Pocket Zoom 70M-AF	24x36mm	35mm	35AFZ	1993	Chinon	4-6.8	38-70	programmed	4-300		100
Pocketpak 400	13x17mm	110	110VF	1983	Chinon	9-11	25mm		1/80		10
Pocketpak Flash	13x17mm	110	110VF	1983	Chinon	8	25mm		1/80		10
Splash	24x36mm	35mm	35AW	1987	Chinon	3.9	35mm	programmed	90-410		90
Splash GX	24x36mm	35mm	35AW	1988	Chinon	4.5	35mm		1/125		50
Super Genesis	24x36mm	35mm	35AFSLR	1991		4.4-5.6	38-110	programmed	1-1000		250
...CHIYODA KOGAKU SEIKO CO. LTD. - Japan											
Konan-16 Automat	10x14mm	16mm	Submin	1950	Rokkor	3.5	25mm		25-200	Mc119	270

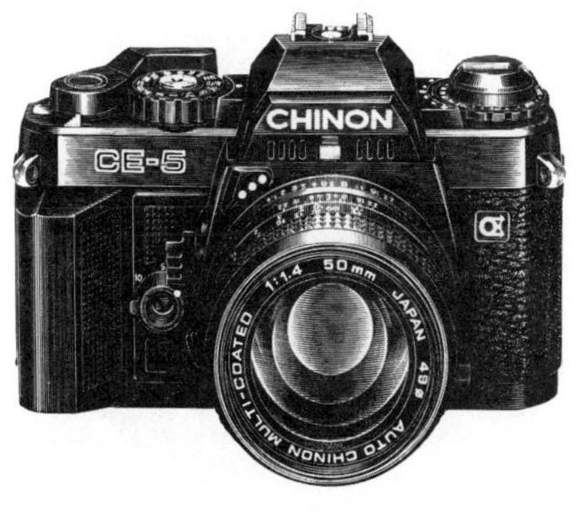

Chinon CE-5

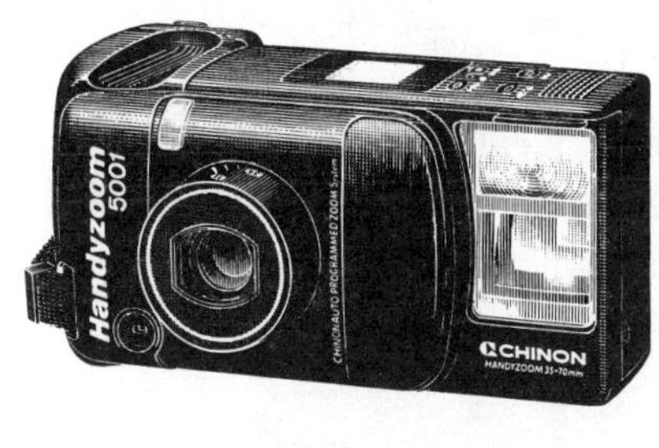

Handyzoom 5001

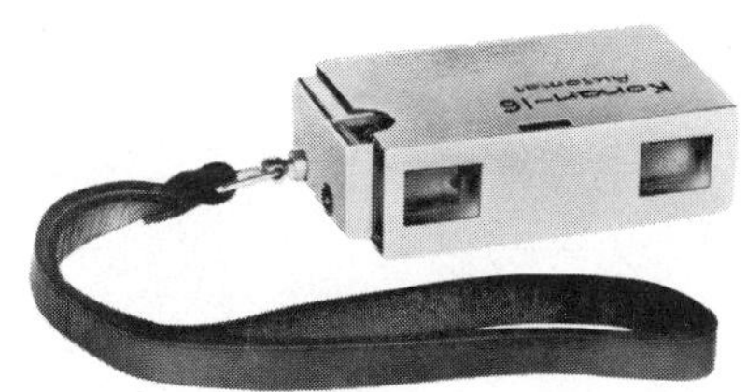

Konan-16 Automat

MODEL	FORMAT	FILM	TYPE	Year	LENS	Apert	FL	SHUTTER	SPEEDS	ILLUS	U.S.$
...CHIYODA SHOKAI - Japan											
Chiyoca 35 (I)	24x36mm	35mm	35VF	1951	Hexar	3.5	50mm	focal plane	1/20-500	Mc119	1200
Chiyoca 35-IF	24x36mm	35mm	35VF	1952	Hexar	3.5	50mm	focal plane	1/20-500		1100
Chiyoca Mod. IIF	24x36mm	35mm	35RF	1953	Lena Kogaku	3.5	50mm	focal plane	1/20-500		1100
Chiyoca Mod. IIF	24x36mm	35mm	35RF	1953	Reise Kogaku	3.5	50mm	focal plane	1/20-500		1100
Chiyoca Mod. IIIF	24x36mm	35mm	35RF	1954	Hexar	3.5	50mm	focal plane	1-500		1200
Chiyoko	6x6cm	120	TLR		Rokkor	3.5		Seikosha-MX			70
...CHRISLIN PHOTO INDUSTRY - Hicksville, NY USA											
Chrislin Insta Camera	2½x3¼"	Roll	Instant	1965						Mc119	120
...CHUO PHOTO SUPPLY - Japan											
Harmony	6x6cm	120	MetalBox	1955				3-speed			30
...(unknown)											
Cia Stereo	9x12cm	plate	SterBox	1910	Meniscus						240
...CIMA K.G. - Fürth, Germany											
Cima 44 S	4x4cm	127	RigidRo	1954	Röschlein Cymat	7.7		Cylux	25-100	Mc119	40
Luxette	4x4cm	127	RigidRo	1954	Röschlein Cymat	7.7		Cylux	25-100		40
Luxette II	4x4cm	127	RigidRo	1955	Röschlein Cymat	7.7		Cylux	25-100		30
Luxette S	4x4cm	127	RigidRo	1954	Röschlein Cymat	7.7		Sync.-Cylux			30
...CINESCOPIE (La Cinescopie) - Brussels, Belgium											
Cinescopic	24x24mm	35mm	35VF	1929	O.I.P. Labor	3.5	50mm	Ibsor	1-150	Mc119	1900
Photoscopic (fixed focus)	24x24mm	35mm	35Early	1924	O.I.P Gand Labor	3.5	45mm	Ibsor		Mc119	700
Photoscopic (focusing)	24x24mm	35mm	35Early	1924	O.I.P Gand Labor	3.5	45mm	Prontor		A877	700
...(unknown)											
Cinex (Spartus)	3x4cm	127	TLR-Box	1953					I,T	Mc391	20
Cinex Candid Camera	3x4cm	127	Minicam	1953							10
Cinex Deluxe	3x4cm	127	Minicam	1953						Mc119	10
...CIRO CAMERAS, INC. - Delaware, OH USA											
Ciro 35 Mod. R (black)	24x36mm	35mm	35RF	1949	Anastigmat	4.5	50mm	Alphax	1-150		70
Ciro 35 Mod. R (chrome)	24x36mm	35mm	35RF	1949	Anastigmat	4.5	50mm	Alphax	1-150	Mc120	60
Ciro 35 Mod. S (black)	24x36mm	35mm	35RF	1949	Anastigmat	3.5	50mm	Alphax	1-200		70
Ciro 35 Mod. S (chrome)	24x36mm	35mm	35RF	1949	Anastigmat	3.5	50mm	Alphax	1-200	Mc120	60
Ciro 35 Mod. T (black)	24x36mm	35mm	35RF	1949	Anastigmat	2.8	50mm	Rapax	1-400		70
Ciro 35 Mod. T (chrome)	24x36mm	35mm	35RF	1949	Anastigmat	2.8	50mm	Rapax	1-400	Mc120	60
Ciroflex A	2¼x2¼"	120	TLR	1940	Anastigmat	3.5	85mm	Alphax	10-200	Mc120	50
Ciroflex B	2¼x2¼"	120	TLR	1940	Velostigmat	3.5	85mm	Alphax	10-200	Mc120	50
Ciroflex C	2¼x2¼"	120	TLR	1946	Anastigmat	3.5	85mm	Rapax	1-400	Mc120	50
Ciroflex D	2¼x2¼"	120	TLR	1948	Anastigmat	3.5	85mm	Alphax	10-200	Mc120	50
Ciroflex E	2¼x2¼"	120	TLR	1948	Anastigmat	3.5	85mm	Rapax	1-400	Mc120	60
Ciroflex F	2¼x2¼"	120	TLR	1949	Raptar	3.2	83mm	Rapax	1-400	Mc120	60
...CITY SALE & EXCHANGE - London											
Ancam	3¼x4¼"	plate	MagBox	1903	Rapid Rectilinear	8			1/15-100	Mc120	110
Field camera 4¼x6½"	4¼x6½"	plate	Field		Rapid Rectilinear			Unicum			270

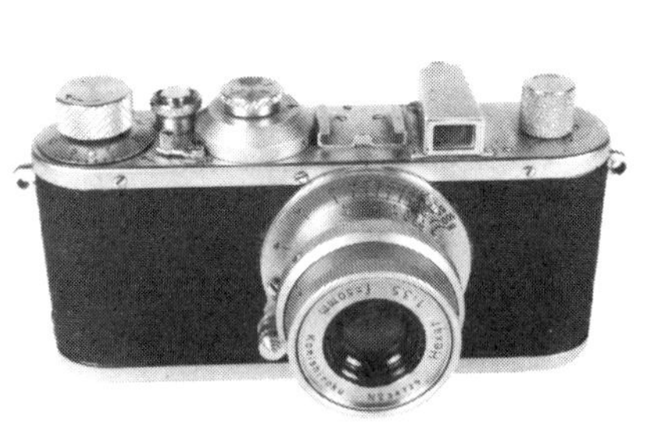

Chiyoca 35 (I)

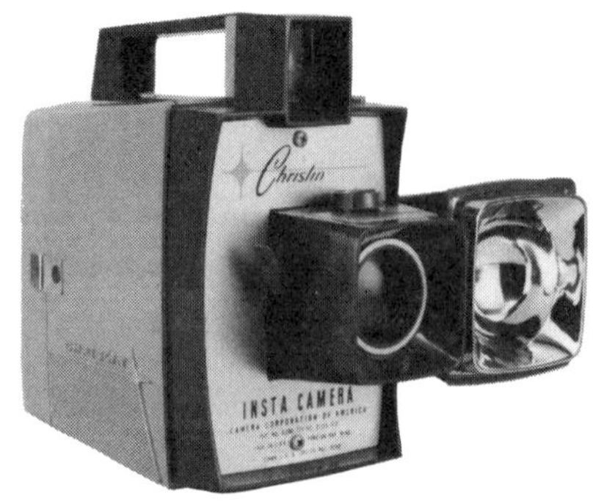

Chrislin Insta Camera

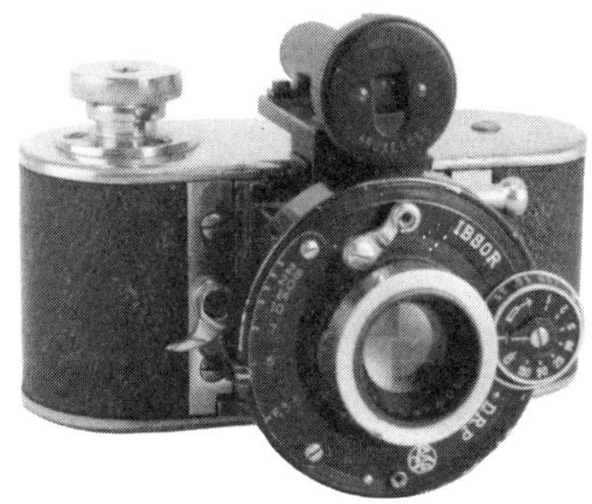

Cinescopic

MODEL	FORMAT	FILM	TYPE	Year	LENS	Apert	FL	SHUTTER	SPEEDS	ILLUS	U.S.$
Field camera 6½x8½"	6½x8½"	plate	Field		Rapid Rectilinear			Thornton-Pickard			270
Licker	2½x3½"	plate	MagBox	1902	achromatic				I,T		50
Planex 3¼x4¼"	3¼x4¼"	plate	LgSLR	1912	Various			focal plane	1/10-1000	Mc120	330
Planex 3½x2½"	3½x2½"	plate	LgSLR	1912	Various			focal plane	1/10-1000	Mc120	330
Planex 3½x5½"	3½x5½"	plate	LgSLR	1912	Various			focal plane	1/10-1000	Mc120	330
Planex 4¼x6½"	4¼x6½"	plate	LgSLR	1912	Various			focal plane	1/10-1000	Mc120	330
Planex 5x4"	5x4"	plate	LgSLR	1912	Various			focal plane	1/10-1000	Mc120	330
Salex Reflex	6.5x9cm	plate	LgSLR	1912	T.-H. Cooke	3.9	5"	focal plane	1/5-1000		120
Salex Tropical Reflex	3¼x4¼"	plate	LgSLR	1912	T.-H. Cooke	3.9		focal plane	1/5-1000		1500
Triple Diamond	4¼x6½"	plate	Field	1907	Rapid Rectilinear	8		Thornton-Pickard	15-90		280
...CLARK (Latimer Clark)											
Single-lens Stereo Camera	3½x5½"	WetPl	StWetPl	1856	Portrait					A2644	3400
...CLARUS CAMERA MFG. CO. - Minneapolis, MN USA											
MS-35	24x36mm	35mm	35RF	1946	Woll. Velostigmat	2.8	50mm	focal plane	-1000	Mc120	50
...(various)											
Classic II	24x36mm	35mm	35VF	1957							50
Classic III	24x36mm	35mm	35VF	1959						Mc120	50
Classic IV	24x36mm	35mm	35VF	1960			45mm			Mc121	50
Classic 35	24x36mm	35mm	35VF	1956	Trioplan	2.9	50mm		1-200	Mc120	50
...CLOSE & CONE - Chicago, Boston, New York USA											
Quad	3½x3½"	plate	PlateBox	1896						Mc121	150
...CLOSTER											
IIa	24x36mm	35mm	35VF	1950	Mizar	4.5	50mm	Closter	300		30
C60	24x36mm	35mm	35VF	1960	Lambron	7	50mm		I		30
Olympic	3x4cm	127	RigidRo	1959		8	56mm			Mc121	20
Princess	24x36mm	35mm	35RF	1951	Aires	3.5	50mm	leaf	1-300		50
Sport	24x36mm	35mm	35VF	1956	Closter Anast.	8	50mm				30
Sprint	24x36mm	35mm	35VF			7	50mm	Sincro-Closter	150		30
...(unknown)											
Cluny 45x107mm	45x107	plate	SterBox		Protar	9	75mm	guillotine			320
Cluny 6x13cm	6x13cm	plate	SterBox		Protar	9	110mm	guillotine			350
...(unknown)											
Colibri	13x13mm	Roll	Submin	1952							140
Colibri 2	13x13mm	Roll	Submin	1952						Mc121	140
...COLLINS (C. G. Collins) - London											
The Society	6½x8½"	plate	Field	1886							330
...COLUMBIA OPTICAL & CAMERA CO. - London											
Pecto No. 1A	4x5"	plate	FoldPl	1902				built-in			150
Pecto No. 5	9x12cm	plate	FoldPl	1897	B&L Rap. Rect.			Unicum		Mc121	200
Pecto No. 7	5x7"	plate	FoldPl	1900	Rapid Rectilinear				1-100		200
...C.O.M.I.											
Luxia (black)	18x24mm	35mm	35Half	1949	Delmak	2.9	27mm				700

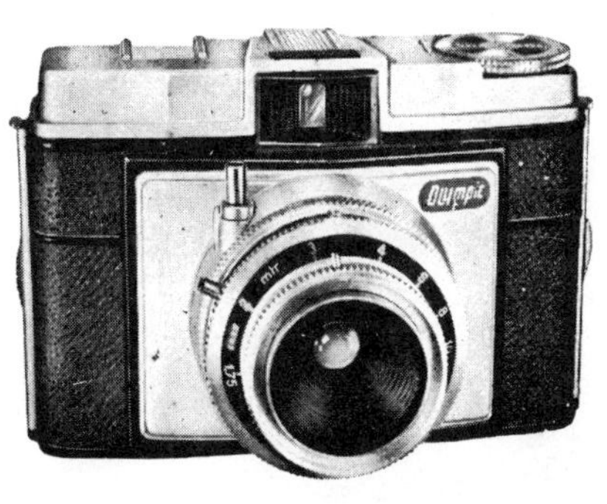

Closter Olympic

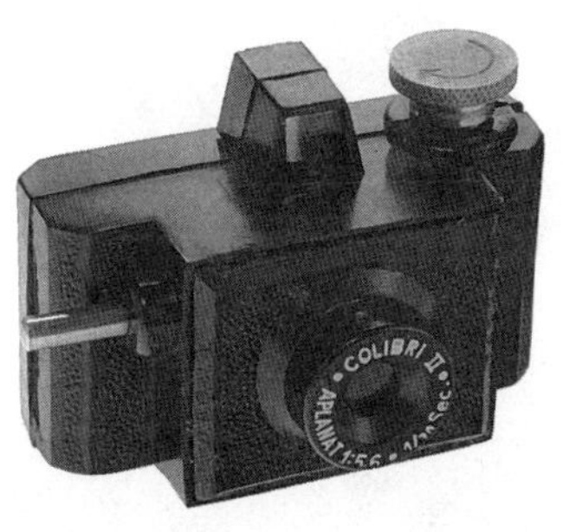

Colibri 2

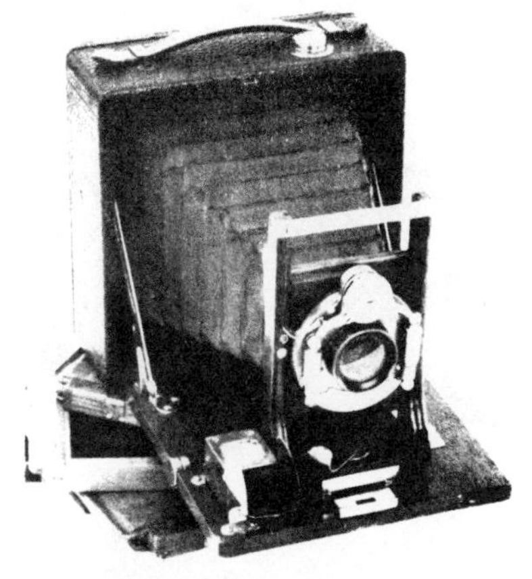

Pecto No. 5

MODEL	FORMAT	FILM	TYPE	Year	LENS	Apert	FL	SHUTTER	SPEEDS	ILLUS	U.S.$
Luxia (chrome)	18x24mm	35mm	35Half	1949	Delmak	2.9	27mm				700
Luxia (gold)	18x24mm	35mm	35Half	1949	Delmak	2.9	27mm				900
Luxia II (black)	18x24mm	35mm	35Half	1949	Delmak	2.9	27mm				560
Luxia II (chrome)	18x24mm	35mm	35Half	1949	Delmak	2.9	27mm			Mc122	590
Luxia II (gold)	18x24mm	35mm	35Half	1949	Delmak	2.9	27mm			Mc122	1300
...COMPAGNIE FRANCAISE DE PHOTOGRAPHIE											
Photosphere 8x9	8x9cm	plate	RigidPl	1888	Rapid Rectilinear			spherical		F1163	1200
Photosphere 9x12	9x12cm	plate	RigidPl	1888	Krauss	7.7	124mm	spherical		Mc122	1500
Photosphere 13x18	13x18cm	plate	RigidPl	1888	Rapid Rectilinear	8	180mm	spherical		F1165	1800
Stereo Photosphere	9x18cm	plate	Stereo	1888	Periscoptic	13	95mm	spherical		Mc122	8000
...COMPASS CAMERAS LTD. - London											
Compass	24x36mm	35mm	35RF	1938		3.5	50mm			Mc122	1300
...COMPCO											
Miraflex	6x6cm	120	TLR-Box	1950							20
Reflex	6x6cm	120	TLR-Box	1950							20
...CONCAVA S.A. - Lugano, Switzerland											
Tessina (black)	14x21mm	35mm	Submin	1960	Tessinon	2.8	25mm		2-500	Mc122	530
Tessina (chrome)	14x21mm	35mm	Submin	1960	Tessinon	2.8	25mm		2-500	Mc122	410
Tessina (gold)	14x21mm	35mm	Submin	1960	Tessinon	2.8	25mm		2-500	Mc122	700
Tessina (red)	14x21mm	35mm	Submin	1960	Tessinon	2.8	25mm		2-500	Mc122	470
Tessina L (black)	14x21mm	35mm	Submin	1969	Tessinon	2.8	25mm		2-500	Mc122	480
Tessina L (chrome)	14x21mm	35mm	Submin	1969	Tessinon	2.8	25mm		2-500	Mc122	360
Tessina L (gold)	14x21mm	35mm	Submin	1969	Tessinon	2.8	25mm		2-500	Mc122	630
Tessina L (red)	14x21mm	35mm	Submin	1969	Tessinon	2.8	25mm		2-500	Mc122	440
...CONCORD CAMERA CORP.											
Concord 801	24x36mm	35mm	35VF	1985		5.6	38mm		I		10
Concord 803	24x36mm	35mm	35VF	1985		5.6	38mm		1/60,1/100		10
Concord 808	24x36mm	35mm	35VF	1985		3.8	38mm		1/70,1/125		30
Concord 818	24x36mm	35mm	35VF	1981		5.6	38mm		1/135		10
Concord AW900	24x36mm	35mm	35VF	1987		3.5	34mm		1/135		30
...CONLEY CAMERA CO. - Rochester, MN USA											
Conley Junior No. 2	2¼x3¼"	120	VtFoldRo	1917	Rapid Rectilinear			Victo	10-100	Mc122	30
Conley Junior No. 2A	2½x4¼"	116	VtFoldRo	1917	Rapid Rectilinear			Victo	10-100		20
Folding Kewpie 2¼x3¼"	2¼x3¼"	120	VtFoldRo	1916	Single Achromatic			simple			30
Folding Kewpie 2½x4¼"	2½x4¼"	116	VtFoldRo	1916	Single Achromatic			simple			30
Folding Kewpie 3¼x4¼"	3¼x4¼"	124	VtFoldRo	1916	Single Achromatic			simple			30
Folding Kewpie 3¼x5½"	3¼x5½"	122	VtFoldRo	1916	Single Achromatic			simple			30
Folding Mod. C 3¼x4¼"	3¼x4¼"	124	VtFoldRo	1917	Vitar Anastigmat	6.3		B&L Compound			30
Folding Mod. C 3¼x5½"	3¼x5½"	122	VtFoldRo	1917	Vitar Anastigmat	6.3		B&L Compound			30
Folding Mod. E 3¼x4¼"	3¼x4¼"	124	VtFoldRo	1917	Vitar Anastigmat	6.3		B&L Compound			30
Folding Mod. E 3¼x5½"	3¼x5½"	122	VtFoldRo	1917	Vitar Anastigmat	6.3		B&L Compound			30
Folding Plate 3¼x4¼"	3¼x4¼"	plate	FoldPl	1900	Extra Rapid Conv.			Conley Safety			240

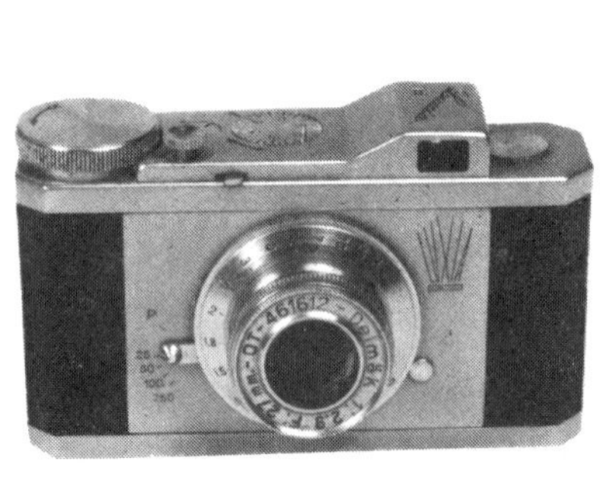

Luxia II

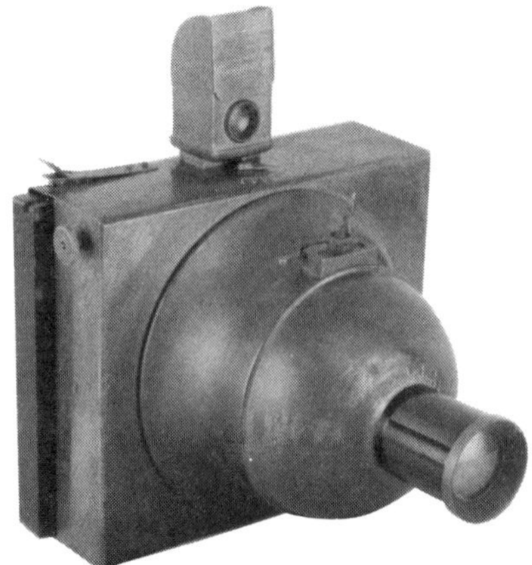

Photosphere 9x12

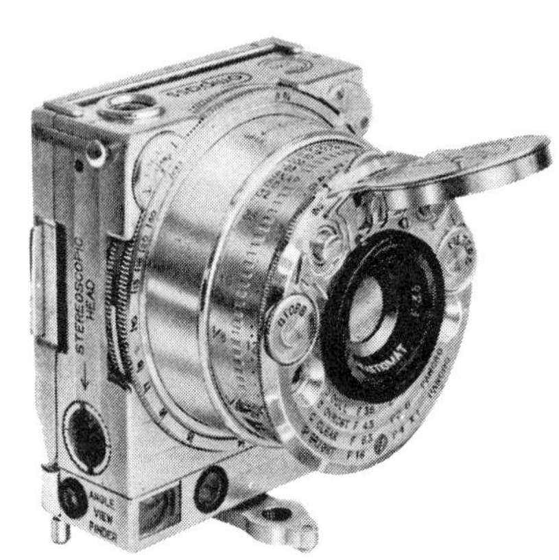

Compass

MODEL	FORMAT	FILM	TYPE	Year	LENS	Apert	FL	SHUTTER	SPEEDS	ILLUS	U.S.$
Folding Plate 3¼x5½"	3¼x5½"	plate	FoldPl	1900		8	6.5"	Conley Safety			120
Folding Plate 4x5"	4x5"	plate	FoldPl	1900	Rap. Symmetrical	8	6.5"	Conley Safety		Mc122	120
Folding Plate 5x7"	5x7"	plate	FoldPl	1908	Rapid Rectilinear	8		Conley Safety			180
Kewpie No. 2	2¼x3¼"	120	RollBox	1917	Single Achromatic			rotary	I,T		40
Kewpie No. 2A	2½x4¼"	116	RollBox	1917	Single Achromatic			rotary	I,T		40
Kewpie No. 2C	2⅞x4⅞"	130	RollBox	1917	Single Achromatic			rotary	I,T	Mc123	40
Kewpie No. 3	3¼x4¼"	124	RollBox	1917	Single Achromatic			rotary	I,T		40
Kewpie No. 3A	3¼x5½"	122	RollBox	1917	Single Achromatic			rotary	I,T		40
Long Focus R.B.Mod. XV	4x5"	plate	FoldPl	1909	Rap. Orthogrpahic			Conley Safety		Mc123	180
Long Focus R.B.Mod. XV	6½x8½"	plate	FoldPl	1909	Rap. Orthogrpahic			Conley Safety		Mc123	180
Magazine Camera	4x5"	plate	MagBox	1908						Mc123	70
Panoramic Camera	3½x12"		Panoramic	1911	Rapid Rectilinear	8		Iris	1/6-1/50		520
Shamrock Folding	4x5"	plate	VtFoldPl	1908						Mc123	70
Snap No. 2	2¼x3¼"	120	StrutRo								40
Stereo box camera	4¼x6½"	plate	SterBox	1908	Meniscus			simple	I,T		460
Stereo Magazine Camera		plate	SterMagBox	1903							430
Stereoscopic Professional	5x7"	plate	SterFoldPl	1908				Woll. Stereo		Mc123	520
Truphoto No. 2	2¼x3¼"	120	VtFoldRo		Meniscus				I,T	Mc123	50
View camera 6½x8½"	6½x8½"	plate	Field	1908	Various			various			320
View camera 8x10"	8x10"	plate	Field	1908	Various			various			340
...CONTESSA, CONTESSA-NETTEL - Stuttgart											
Adoro 6.5x9	6.5x9cm	plate	VtFoldPl	1921	Tessar	4.5	120mm	Compur			70
Adoro 9x12	9x12cm	plate	VtFoldPl	1921	Tessar	4.5	150mm	Compur			50
Adoro 10x15	10x15cm	plate	VtFoldPl	1919	Tessar	4.5	165mm	Compur			50
Alino	6.5x9cm	plate	VtFoldPl	1913	Tessar	6.3	120mm	Compur	1-250		50
Altura 6.5x9	6.5x9cm	plate	VtFoldPl	1921	Doppel Anast.	6.3	135mm	Compur			70
Altura 9x12	9x12cm	plate	VtFoldPl	1921	Citonar		165mm	Compur			70
Altura 3¼x5½"	3¼x5½"	plate	VtFoldPl	1921	Citonar		165mm	Compur			70
Altura 10x15	10x15cm	plate	VtFoldPl	1921	Citonar		165mm	Compur			70
Argus	4.5x6cm	plate	Disguised	1913	Tessar	4.5		Compur	25-100	Mc124	1300
Ballonkamera Atlanta		plate	Aerial	1914				focal plane		HK674	1200
Citoskop Stereo	45x107	plate	SterRefl	1924	Tessar	4.5	65mm	Stereo-Compur		Mc124	350
Cocarette 6x9	6x9cm	120	VtFoldRo	1920	Anastigmat	5.4	10.5cm	Compur	1-250	Mc124	30
Cocarette 6.5x11	6.5x11cm	116	VtFoldRo	1920	Rapid Rectilinear		135mm	Compur		Mc124	100
Cocarette 8x10.5	8x10.5cm	118	VtFoldRo	1920	Tessar	4.5	135mm	Compur		Mc124	50
Cocarette 8x14	8x14cm	122	VtFoldRo	1925	Tessar	4.5	150mm	Compur		Mc124	70
Cocarette Luxus 6x9	6x9cm	120	VtFoldRo	1920			105mm				180
Cocarette Luxus 6.5x11	6.5x11cm	116	VtFoldRo	1920			135mm				240
Cocarette Luxus 8x14	8x14cm	122	VtFoldRo	1925	Tessar	4.5	150mm	Compur		A3047	240
Contessa	9x12cm	plate	FoldPl	1910	Nettar Anastigmat	6.8	140mm	Compur			50
Contessa Reflex 4.5x6	4.5x6cm	plate	MedSLR	1913	Orthoscop	8					660
Contessa Reflex 6x6	6x6cm	plate	MedSLR	1913	Orthoscop	8					630

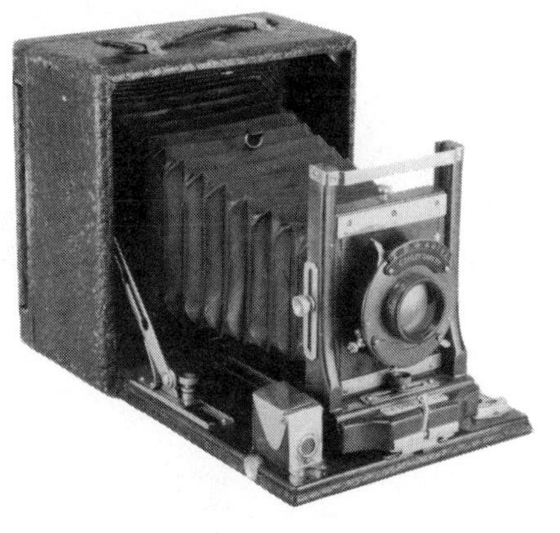

Conley Long Focus R.B.Mod.XV

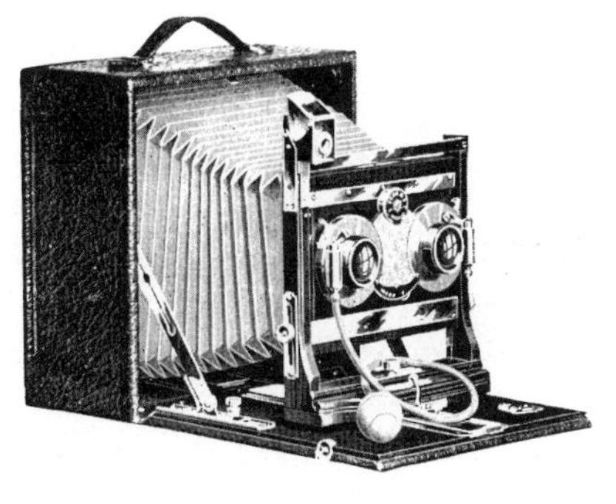

Conley Stereoscopic Professional

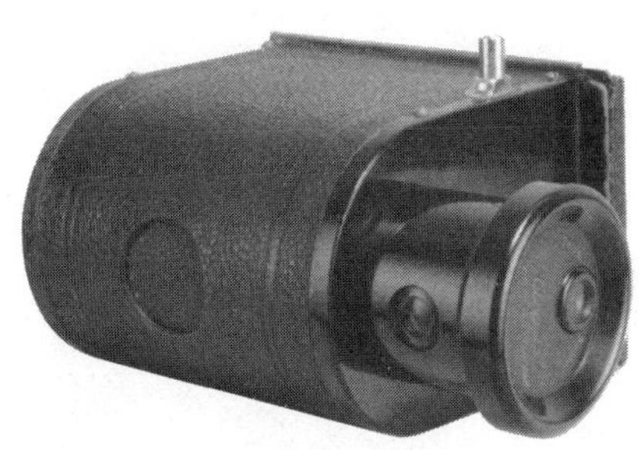

Argus

MODEL	FORMAT	FILM	TYPE	Year	LENS	Apert	FL	SHUTTER	SPEEDS	ILLUS	U.S.$
Deckrullo Tropical 6.5x9	6.5x9cm	plate	StrutPl	1919	Tessar	4.5	120mm	focal plane	2800		800
Deckrullo Tropical 9x12	9x12cm	plate	StrutPl	1919	Tessar	4.5	150mm	focal plane	2800		580
Deckrullo Tropical 10x15	10x15cm	plate	StrutPl	1919	Tessar	4.5	180mm	focal plane	2800		540
Deckrullo Tropical 13x18	13x18cm	plate	StrutPl	1919	Tessar	4.5	180mm	focal plane	2800		540
Deckrullo-Nettel 6.5x9	6.5x9cm	plate	StrutPl	1919	Tessar	4.5	120mm	focal plane	1200		180
Deckrullo-Nettel 9x12	9x12cm	plate	StrutPl	1919	Tessar	4.5	150mm	focal plane	2800		150
Deckrullo-Nettel 10x15	10x15cm	plate	StrutPl	1919	Tessar	4.5	180mm	focal plane	2800		150
Deckrullo-Nettel 13x18	13x18cm	plate	StrutPl	1919	Tessar	4.5	180mm	focal plane	2300		160
Deckr.Nettel Stereo 6x13	6x13cm	plate	SterStrut		Tessar	4.5	90mm	focal plane	2800	Mc124	360
Deckr.Nettel Stereo 10x15	10x15cm	plate	SterStrut		Tessar	4.5	120mm	focal plane	2800	Mc124	360
Deckr.Nettel Stereo Trop.	6x13cm	plate	SterStrut	1921	Tessar	4.5	65mm	focal plane	2800		1200
Deckr.Nettel Stereo Trop.	9x12cm	plate	SterStrut	1921	Tessar	2.7	65mm	focal plane	2800		1500
Deckr.Nettel Stereo Trop.	10x15cm	plate	SterStrut	1921	Tessar	4.5	120mm	focal plane	2800		1500
Donata 6.5x9	6.5x9cm	plate	VtFoldPl	1920	Tessar	6.3		Compur			70
Donata 9x12	9x12cm	plate	VtFoldPl	1920	Tessar	6.3		Compur			70
Duchessa 4.5x6	4.5x6cm	plate	StrutPl	1913	Citonar Anast.	6.3	75mm	Compur	1-100	HK139	300
Duchessa 6.5x9	6.5x9cm	plate	StrutPl	1923	Tessar	6.3	90mm	Compur	1-100	HK150	60
Duchessa Stereo	45x107	plate	StrutPl	1913	Tessar	4.5		Compur	1-250	A742	430
Duchessa Stereo (FP)	45x107	plate	StrutPl	1913	Dagor	6.8		focal plane		HK483	410
Duroll 6.5x9	6.5x9cm	plate	VtFoldRo	1913	Citonar	6.3	105mm	Derval			50
Duroll 9x12	9x12cm	plate	VtFoldRo	1913	Citonar	6.3	135mm	Compur			60
Duroll 9x14	9x14cm	plate	VtFoldRo	1913	Citonar	6.3	150mm	Compur			50
Ergo	4.5x6cm	plate	Disguised	1913	Tessar	4.5	75mm	Compur	25-100	Mc124	1100
Ergo (folding) 4.5x6	4.5x6cm	plate	StrutPl	1913	Dagor	6.8	75mm	focal plane	1000		900
Ergo (folding) 9x12	9x12cm	plate	StrutPl	1913	Dagor	6.8	150mm	focal plane	1000		100
Ergo (folding) 10x15	10x15cm	plate	StrutPl	1913	Dagor	6.8	180mm	focal plane	1000	HK147	200
Fiduca	6.5x9cm	plate	VtFoldPl	1921	Citonar	6.3	105mm	Ibso			50
Fiduca	9x12cm	plate	VtFoldPl	1921	Citonar	6.3	135mm	Ibso			50
Miroflex 6.5x9	6.5x9cm	plate	FoldSLR	1925	Tessar	4.5	105mm	focal plane	1/3-2000	A1608	390
Miroflex 9x12	9x12cm	plate	FoldSLR	1925	Tessar	4.5	150mm	focal plane	1/3-2000		310
Multum Panorama	12x16.5cm	plate	HzFoldPl	1910	Dagor	6.8		Compound	1-250		510
Multum Reflex	9x12cm	plate	LgTLR	1910	Dagor	6.8		Compound	1-250		1500
Multum Stereo	8.5x17cm	plate	SterFoldPl	1910	Dagor	6.8		Compound	1-250		510
Nettix	4.5x6cm	plate	StrutPl	1919	Citonar	6.3	75mm	Derval	25-100		220
Onito 6.5x9	6.5x9cm	plate	VtFoldPl	1919	Nettar Anastigmat	4.5		Ibsor	1-100		50
Onito 9x12	9x12cm	plate	VtFoldPl	1919	Nettar Anastigmat	4.5	135mm	Ibsor	1-100		40
Onito 10x15	10x15cm	plate	VtFoldPl	1919	Citonar	6.3	165mm	Derval	25-100		40
Piccolette	4x6.5cm	127	StrutRo	1919	Triotar	6.3	75mm	Piccar		Mc124	60
Piccolette	4x6.5cm	127	StrutRo	1919	Tessar	4.5	75mm	Dial-Compur		Mc124	70
Piccolette Luxus	4x6.5cm	127	VtFoldRo	1919	Tessar	4.5	75mm	Dial-Compur		Mc124	370
Pixie	4x6.5cm	127	StrutRo	1913	Tessar	6.3	7cm		I,T	HK208	310
Recto	4.5x6cm	plate	StrutPl	1921	Achromat	11	75mm	Acro	25-75	A337	190

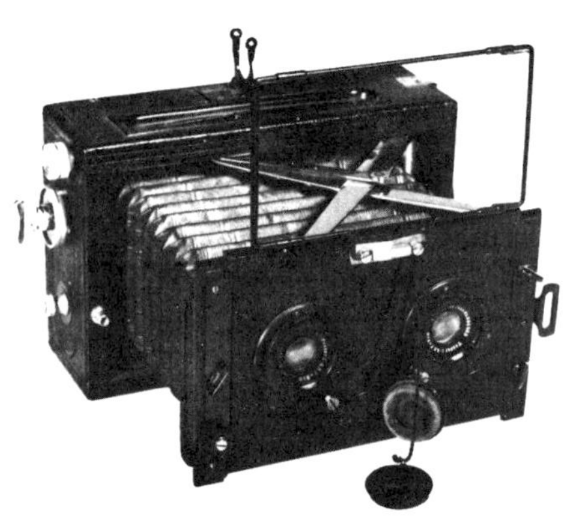

Deckrullo Nettel Stereo

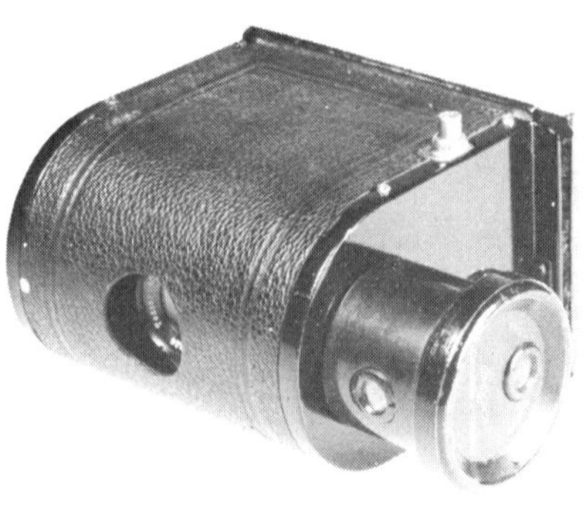

Contessa Ergo

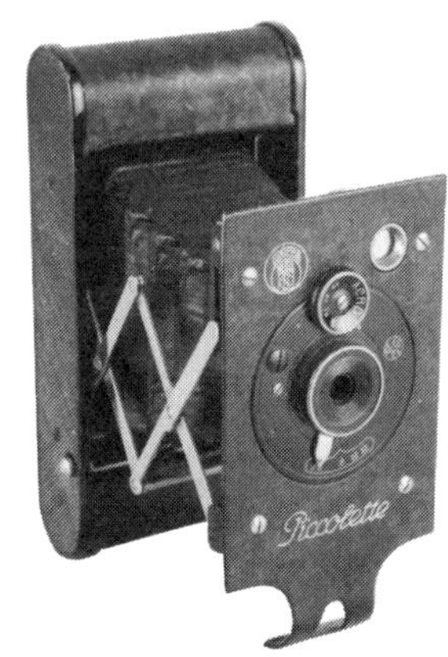

Piccolette

MODEL	FORMAT	FILM	TYPE	Year	LENS	Apert	FL	SHUTTER	SPEEDS	ILLUS	U.S.$
Sonnar 6.5x9	6.5x9cm	plate	VtFoldPl	1924	Sonnar	4.5	120mm	Compur			100
Sonnar 9x12	9x12cm	plate	VtFoldPl	1920	Sonnar	4.5	135mm	Compur			70
Sonnet	9x12cm	plate	VtFoldPl	1920	Sonnar	4.5	135mm	Compur			90
Sonnet Tropical 4.5x6	4.5x6cm	plate	VtFoldPl	1920	Zeiss	4.5	75mm	Dial-Compur	1-300	Mc125	900
Sonnet Tropical 6.5x9	6.5x9cm	plate	VtFoldPl	1920	Zeiss	4.5	120mm	Dial-Compur	1-300	Mc125	440
Sonto	13x18cm	plate	VtFoldPl	1919	Citonar	6.3	195mm	Compound	1-250		50
Stereax 45x107	45x107	plate	SterStrut	1912	Colorplaste		60mm	focal plane	1/5-1200	HK480	300
Stereax 6x13	6x13cm	plate	SterStrut	1919	Tessar	4.5	90mm	focal plane	1-1200	Mc125	300
Stereax Tropical	6x13cm	plate	SterStrut	1919	Tessar	4.5	90mm	focal plane	1-1200		900
Steroco	45x107		StJumelle	1921	Tessar	6.3	55mm	Compur	1-300	A738	240
Suevia	6.5x9cm	plate	VtFoldPl	1919	Nettar	6.3	105mm	Derval	25-100		50
Suevia	6.5x9cm	plate	VtFoldPl	1919	Extra Rap. Aplan.	7.7	105mm	Derval	25-100		60
Taxo	9x12cm	plate	VtFoldPl	1921	Extra Rap. Aplan.	8	135mm	Duvall	100		60
Tessco 6.5x9	6.5x9cm	plate	VtFoldPl	1913	Sonnar	4.5	105mm	Dial-Compur	1-200		70
Tessco 9x12	9x12cm	plate	VtFoldPl	1913	Citonar	6.3	135mm	Dial-Compur	1-200		70
Tessco 10x15	10x15cm	plate	VtFoldPl	1913	Citonar	6.3	165mm	Dial-Compur	1-200		70
Trona	9x12cm	plate	VtFoldPl	1916	Citoplast	6.3	135mm	Compur	1-200		110
Tropen (Compur)	6x9cm	plate	VtFoldPl	1920	Tessar	4.5	120mm	Compur	1-250		520
Tropen (Schlitzverschl.)	6x9cm	plate	VtFoldPl	1920	Tessar	4.5	120mm	focal plane			800
Tropen-Adoro 6.5x9	6.5x9cm	plate	VtFoldPl	1921	Tessar	4.5	120mm	Compur		Mc123	490
Tropen-Adoro 9x12	9x12cm	plate	VtFoldPl	1921	Tessar	4.5	150mm	Compur		Mc123	460
Tropen-Adoro 10x15	10x15cm	plate	VtFoldPl	1921	Tessar	4.5	165mm	Compur		Mc123	410
Volupa	10x15cm	plate	VtFoldPl	1919	Citonar	6.3	165mm	Ibso	1-100		40
Westca	4.5x6cm	plate	StrutPl	1912	Achromat		7.5cm	Iris	Z,M	HK160	180
...CORD - France											
Cord Box 6x9	6x9cm	120	CardBox	1946	Boyer Meniscus					F812	20
...CORFIELD (K.G. Corfield) - England											
Corfield 66	6x6cm	120	MedSLR	1961	Lumax	3.5	95mm	focal plane	1-500	A1629	410
Periflex (original)	24x36mm	35mm	35VF	1953	Lumax	2.8	50mm	focal plane	1000		700
Periflex (1) black	24x36mm	35mm	35VF	1954	Lumax	1.9	50mm	focal plane	1000	Mc125	230
Periflex (1) silver	24x36mm	35mm	35VF	1955	Lumar-X	2.8	50mm	focal plane	1000		200
Periflex 2	24x36mm	35mm	35VF	1958	Lumax	2.8	45mm	focal plane	500		150
Periflex 3	24x36mm	35mm	35VF	1957	Lumax	1.9	45mm	focal plane	1000		180
Periflex 3a	24x36mm	35mm	35VF	1959	Lumax	1.9	45mm	focal plane	1000		180
Periflex 3b	24x36mm	35mm	35VF	1961	Lumax	1.9	45mm	focal plane	1000		180
Periflex Gold Star	24x36mm	35mm	35VF	1961	Lumax	2.8	50mm	focal plane	1-300		140
Periflex Interplan A	24x36mm	35mm	35VF	1961	Lumax	2.8	50mm	focal plane	1000	A1079	180
Periflex Interplan B	24x36mm	35mm	35VF	1961	Lumax	1.9	50mm	focal plane	1000		180
Periflex Interplan C	24x36mm	35mm	35VF	1961	Lumax	1.9	50mm	focal plane	1000		180
...CORNU CO. - Paris											
Fama	24x36mm	35mm	35VF	1950	Flor	2.8	50mm		1-300	Mc125	90
Fama II	24x36mm	35mm	35VF	1950	Flor	2.8	50mm		1-300	F566	100

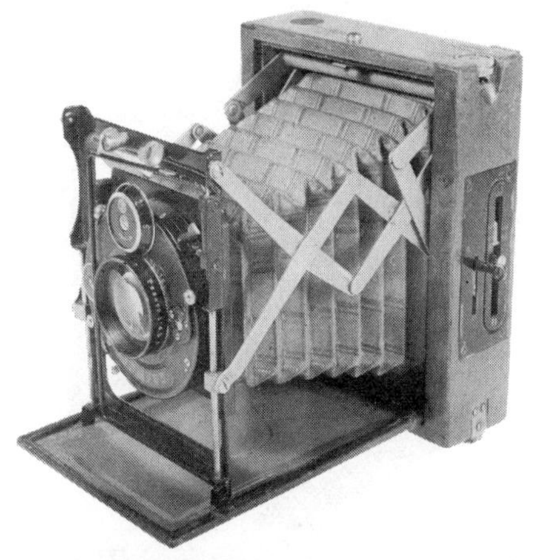

Sonnet Tropen

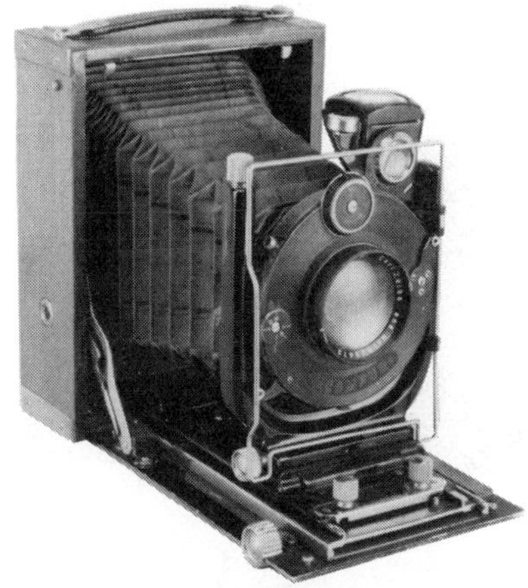

Tropen-Adoro

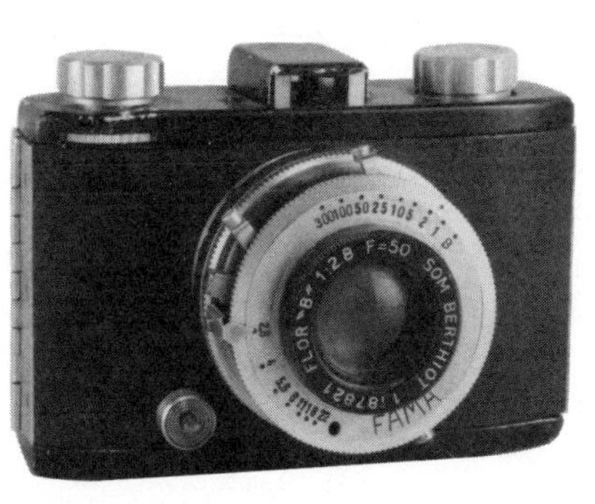

Cornu Fama

MODEL	FORMAT	FILM	TYPE	Year	LENS	Apert	FL	SHUTTER	SPEEDS	ILLUS	U.S.$
Ontobloc I	24x36mm	35mm	35VF	1946	Flor	3.5	50mm	Coronto Paris	1-300	Mc125	60
Ontobloc II	24x36mm	35mm	35VF	1948	Flor	3.5	50mm	Coronto Paris	1-300	F629	70
Ontobloc III	24x36mm	35mm	35VF	1949	Flor	3.5	50mm	Coronto Rapid	1-400	F632	70
Ontoflex Mod. A	6x9cm	120	TLR	1938	Berthiot	3.5	90mm	Compur	1-250	Mc126	370
Ontoflex Mod. B	6x9cm	120/pl	TLR	1938	Berthiot	3.5	90mm	Compur	1-250	F468	370
Ontoscope 3D	24x30mm	35mm	35Ster	1954	Flor	3.5	40mm		1-400	F1453	410
Ontoscope 45x107	45x107	plate	StJumelle	1934	Rapid Rectilinear			guillotine	P,I	F1337	220
Ontoscope 45x107	45x107	plate	StJumelle	1934	Tessar	4.5	55mm	guillotine	1/5-400	Mc126	220
Ontoscope 6x13	6x13cm	plate	StJumelle	1934	Tessar	4.5	75mm	guillotine	1/5-300	F1339	220
Ontoscope 6x13	6x13cm	plate	StJumelle	1934	Flor	4.5	85mm	guillotine	1/5-300	F1344	220
Reyna (I)	24x36mm	35mm	35VF	1940	Flor	3.5	50mm	Reyna	25-200	A1054	110
Reyna II (black)	24x36mm	35mm	35VF	1942	Flor	3.5	50mm	Reyna	25-200	Mc126	100
Reyna II (brown)	24x36mm	35mm	35VF	1942	Boyer Saphir	3.5	50mm	Compur-Rapid	1-500	F654	60
Reyna Cross II	24x36mm	35mm	35VF	1943	Berthiot	3.5	45mm	Reyna	25-200	F646	100
Reyna Cross III	24x36mm	35mm	35VF	1944	Berthiot	3.5	45mm	Micromécanic	25-200	F649	60
Reyna Cross III	24x36mm	35mm	35VF	1944	Cross	2.9	45mm	Micromécanic	25-200	F649	90
Stereo camera	6x13cm	plate	SterBox	1910	Rapid Rectilinear			guillotine		A2692	200
Week-End Bob	24x36mm	35mm	35VF							Mc126	120
...CORONET CAMERA CO. - Birmingham, England											
020 Box Camera	6x9cm	120	RollBox	1935	Meniscus	7.7			T,I	Mc126	30
3-D Stereo	4.5x5cm	127	Stereo	1953	Meniscus	11			1/50	Mc128	100
Ajax	6x9cm	120	RollBox	1935	Anastigmat	7.7			25-100	Mc126	100
Ambassador	6x9cm	120	BakeliteBox	1955						Mc126	20
Bobox	6x9cm	120	RollBox	1940	Meniscus					F811	30
Box camera	6x9cm	120	RollBox	1935	Meniscus			simple	I,T	F813	10
Box camera (colors)	6x9cm	120	RollBox	1932	Meniscus			simple	I,T		50
Cadet	6x9cm	120	BakeliteRoll		Meniscus			simple	I,T	Mc126	20
Cameo	13x18mm	Roll	Submin	1950	Meniscus			simple	I	A1926	110
Captain	6x9cm	120	BakeliteBox								30
Clipper	2¼x3¼"	120	VtFoldRo			16				Mc127	20
Commander 2	24x36mm	120	RigidRo		Achromat	8	50mm		50,100	Mc127	10
Consul	6x9cm	120	BakeliteBox							Mc127	30
Conway Popular Mod.	6x9cm	120	BakeliteBox	1930	Meniscus				I	Mc127	30
Conway Synchro Mod.	6x9cm	120	BakeliteBox	1930	Meniscus				I,T	A2890	20
Conway Super Flash	6x9cm	120	BakeliteBox							Mc127	30
Coronet	6x9cm	plate	CardBox	1929	Meniscus				I,T	Mc127	50
Coronet 44	4x4cm	127	BakeliteRoll	1950					I	A3115	20
Coronet 66	6x6cm	120	BakeliteRoll							Mc127	20
Coronet-Conway	6x9cm	plate	BakeliteBox	1950	Meniscus				I,T	A2888	20
Cub	28x40mm	828	TelescRo						I	Mc127	20
Cub Flash	28x40mm	828	TelescRo			11			I,T	Mc127	20
Dynamic 12	6x6cm	120/6	BakeliteRoll		Meniscus					Mc127	40

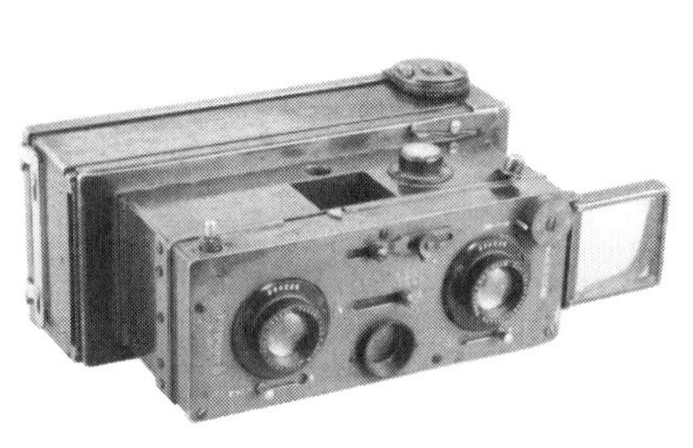

Ontoscope

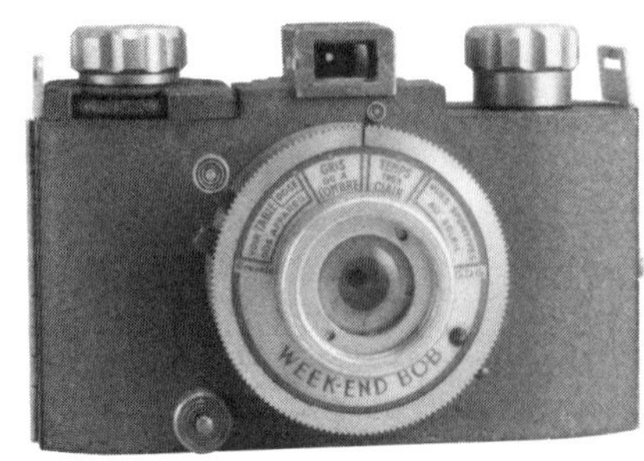

Week-End Bob

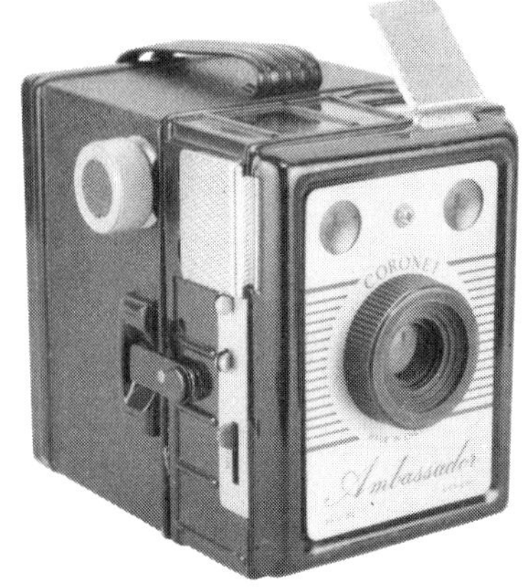

Ambassador

MODEL	FORMAT	FILM	TYPE	Year	LENS	Apert	FL	SHUTTER	SPEEDS	ILLUS	U.S.$
Eclair Box	6x9cm	120	CardBox	1950	Meniscope Tiranty					Mc127	20
Eclair Lux	6x9cm	120	MetalBox	1950	Meniscope Tiranty					Mc127	30
F-20 Coro-Flash	6x6cm	120/6	TLR-Box						I,T	Mc128	20
Fildia	6x9cm	120	CardBox	1950						F833	20
Flashmaster	6x6cm	120	BakeliteRoll		Meniscus				I	Mc128	20
Folding (black)	6x9cm	120	VtFoldRo	1935	Meniscus				I,T		10
Folding (colored)	6x9cm	120	VtFoldRo	1935	Meniscus				I,T		40
Folding (colored)	6x9cm	120	VtFoldRo	1935	Anastigmat	6.3			25-100		40
Midget (black)	13x18mm	16mm	Submin	1935	Taylor Meniscus	10			1/30	Mc128	120
Midget (blue)	13x18mm	16mm	Submin	1935	Taylor Meniscus	10			1/30	Mc128	190
Midget (brown)	13x18mm	16mm	Submin	1935	Taylor Meniscus	10			1/30	A908	130
Midget (green)	13x18mm	16mm	Submin	1935	Taylor Meniscus	10			1/30	A908	140
Midget (red)	13x18mm	16mm	Submin	1935	Taylor Meniscus	10			1/30	A908	140
Polo	6x9cm	120	MetalBox		Boyer Menisque				I	Mc128	20
Popular Twelve	6x9cm	120	BakeliteRoll	1952	Coronac					A3162	30
Rapide	6x9cm	120	VtFoldRo							Mc128	20
Rapier	6x6cm	120	BakeliteRoll							Mc128	30
Rex	6x9cm	120	CardBox	1950	Boyer Menisque					F862	20
Rex Flash	6x9cm	120	BakeliteBox							Mc128	30
Toy Camera	2½x3½"	plate	CardBox	1929	Meniscus			rotary			30
Twelve-20 (black)	6x6cm	120/6	TLR-Box	1950	Meniscus				I	A1752	20
Twelve-20 (chrome)	6x6cm	120/6	TLR-Box	1950	Meniscus				I	A1752	30
Victor	4x4cm	127	BakeliteRoll		Meniscus	11				Mc128	20
Viscount	28x40mm	828	RigidRo							Mc128	20
Vogue	28x40mm	Roll	BakFoldRo	1937	Meniscus	10			B,I	Mc129	140
...COSINA CO. - Japan											
Cosina 35 E	24x36mm	35mm	35VF								70
Cosina 35 FR	24x36mm	35mm	35VF								70
Cosina AF-35	24x36mm	35mm	35AF								100
Cosina C1	24x36mm	35mm	35SLR	1992	Cosina	2	50mm	metal FP	1-2000		210
Cosina C1s	24x36mm	35mm	35SLR	1992	Cosina	2	50mm	metal FP	1-2000		140
Cosina C2	24x36mm	35mm	35SLR		Cosina			electronic	8-1/1000		150
Cosina CT-1	24x36mm	35mm	35SLR		Cosina S	2.8	50mm		1000		100
Cosina CT-1 Super	24x36mm	35mm	35SLR	1985	Cosina	2.8-3.8	35-70	metal FP	1-2000		100
Cosina CT-1A	24x36mm	35mm	35SLR	1982	Cosinon-S	2	50mm	metal FP	1-1000		100
Cosina CT-1EX	24x36mm	35mm	35SLR	1988	Cosina	3.5-4.8	35-70	metal FP	1-2000		100
Cosina CT-1G	24x36mm	35mm	35SLR	1983	Cosinon-S	2	50mm	metal FP	1-1000		120
Cosina CT-3	24x36mm	35mm	35SLR		Cosinon-S	2	50mm	metal FP	8-1/1000		160
Cosina CT-7	24x36mm	35mm	35SLR	1982	Cosinon-S	2	50mm	metal FP	2-1/1000		180
Cosina CT-9	24x36mm	35mm	35AFSLR	1986	Cosina	3.5-4.5	35-70	metal FP	2-1/1000		120
Cosina CT-10	24x36mm	35mm	35SLR	1982	Cosinon-S	2	50mm	metal FP	4-1/1000		120
Cosina CT-90AF	24x36mm	35mm	35AFSLR	1988	Cosina	3.5-4.8	28-70	metal FP	2-1/1000		130

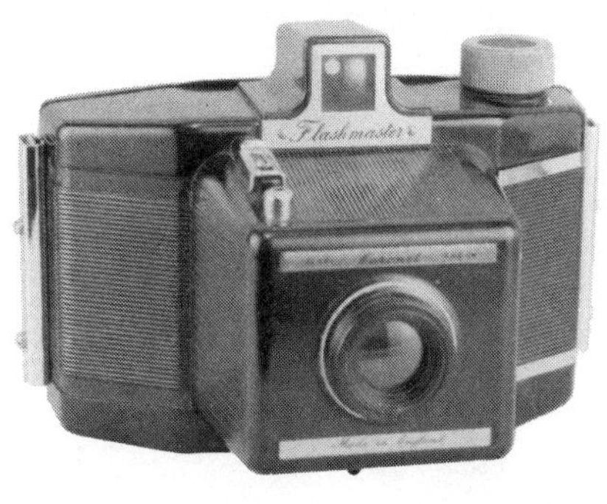

Coronet Flashmaster

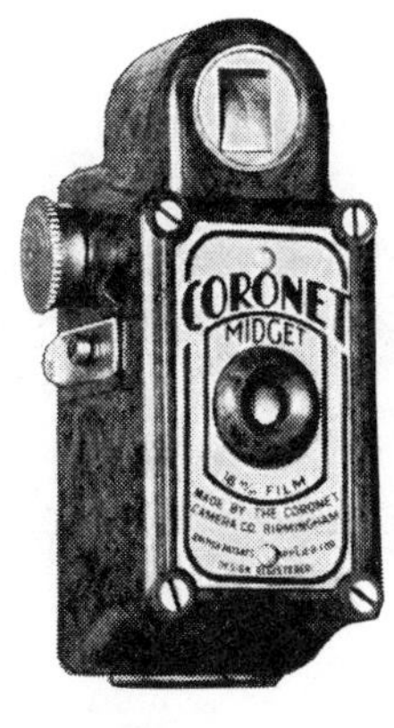

Coronet Midget

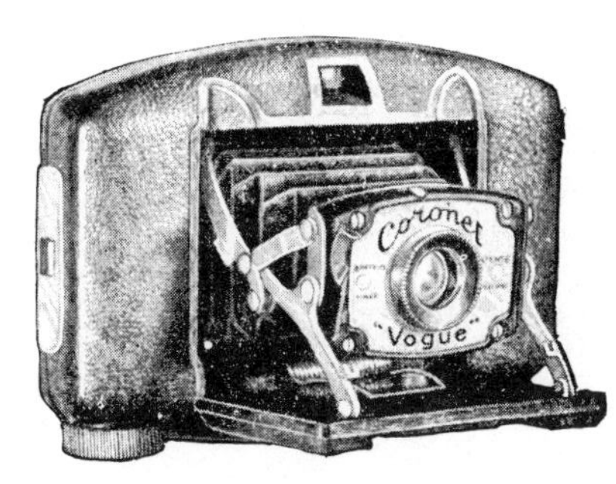

Coronet Vogue

MODEL	FORMAT	FILM	TYPE	Year	LENS	Apert	FL	SHUTTER	SPEEDS	ILLUS	U.S.$
Cosina CX-1	24x36mm	35mm	35VF	1982	Cosinon	2.8	35mm	programmed	2-1/500		70
Cosina CX-2	24x36mm	35mm	35VF	1982	Cosinon	2.8	35mm	programmed	2-1/500	A2178	80
Cosina CX-5 (black)	24x36mm	35mm	35VF	1982	Cosina	3.8	33mm	programmed			70
Cosina CX-5 (silver)	24x36mm	35mm	35VF	1982	Cosina	3.8	33mm	programmed			70
Cosina CX-5F	24x36mm	35mm	35VF	1983	Cosina	5.6	33mm		100, 250		40
Cosina CX-7	24x36mm	35mm	35AF	1983	Cosina	3.5	33mm	programmed			110
Cosina CX-70	24x36mm	35mm	35AF	1984	Cosina	3.5	33mm	programmed			120
Cosina CX-70 QD	24x36mm	35mm	35AF	1984	Cosina	3.5	33mm	programmed			140
Cosina Hi-Lite	24x36mm	35mm	35SLR	1969	Cosinon	1.4	50mm	metal FP	1-1000		60
Cosina Hi-Lite DL	24x36mm	35mm	35SLR	1970	Cosinon Auto	1.4	50mm	metal FP	1-1000		60
Cosina Hi-Lite DLR	24x36mm	35mm	35SLR	1971	Cosinon Auto	1.4	55mm	metal FP	1-1000		60
Cosina Hi-Lite EC	24x36mm	35mm	35SLR	1973	Cosinon Auto	1.4	55mm	metal FP	1-2000		70
Cosina Hi-Lite ECL	24x36mm	35mm	35SLR	1974		1.4	55mm		4-2000		70
...(unknown)											
Cosmic	24x36mm	35mm	35VF	1950		4	40mm		1/5-250	A3477	20
...COSMO CAMERA CO. - Japan											
Cosmo 35	24x36mm	35mm	35VF	1955	Cosmo	3.5	45mm				60
Micronta 35	24x36mm	35mm	35VF	1955	Micronta	3.5	45mm	Copal	10-200	Mc129	60
...CRAFTSMAN SALES CO. - Chicago, USA											
Cinex Candid Camera	1¼x1⅝"	127	Minicam						I,T	Mc129	10
...CRUISER CAMERA CO.											
Cruiser	6x9cm	120	VtFoldRo		Edinar	6.3	105mm	Vario	25-100	Mc129	20
...CRUVER-PETERS CO. INC.											
Palko	3¼x5½"	122	VtFoldRo	1918	B&L Tessar	4.5		Acme	300	Mc129	1000
...(unknown)											
Crystar (black)	14x14mm	17.5m	Submin								60
Crystar (colors)	14x14mm	17.5m	Submin								50
...CRYSTAR OPTICAL CO. - Japan											
Crystar 15	6x6/4.5x6	120	HzFoldRo	1954	C.Master Anast.	3.5	75mm		1-200	Mc130	100
Crystar 25	6x6cm	120	TLR	1954	C.Master Anast.	3.5	80mm	Fujiko	1-200		80
Crystarflex	6x6cm	120	TLR	1953	C.Master Anast.	3.5	80mm	Crystar		Mc130	70
Crystarflex II	6x6cm	120	TLR	1953	Magni	3.5	80mm	Magni		Mc130	70
...CURTIS (Thomas S. Curtis Laboratories) - Huntington Park, CA USA											
Curtis Color Master	4x5"	plate	3-Color	1948	Ilex Patagon	4.5	5.5"	Acme			480
Curtis Color Scout	2½x3"	plate	3-Color	1941	Ektar	4.5	80mm	Compur	1-200	A2040	480
One-Shot Color Camera	3¼x4¼"	plate	3-Color	1937	B&L	4.5	7.5"	Betax			500
...DACO DANGELMAIER / DACORA KAMERAWERK - Reutlingen & Munich											
Color Digna	6x6cm	120	TelescRo	1958	Achromat						30
Daci (black)	6x6cm	120	MetalBox	1948		9			I	Mc130	20
Daci (green)	6x6cm	120	MetalBox	1948		9			I	Mc130	30
Daci (grey)	6x6cm	120	MetalBox	1948		9			I	Mc130	30
Daci (red)	6x6cm	120	MetalBox	1948		9			I	Mc130	50

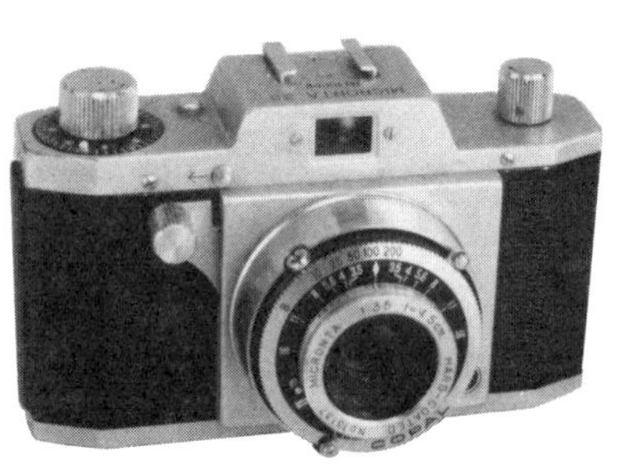

Cosmo Micronta 35

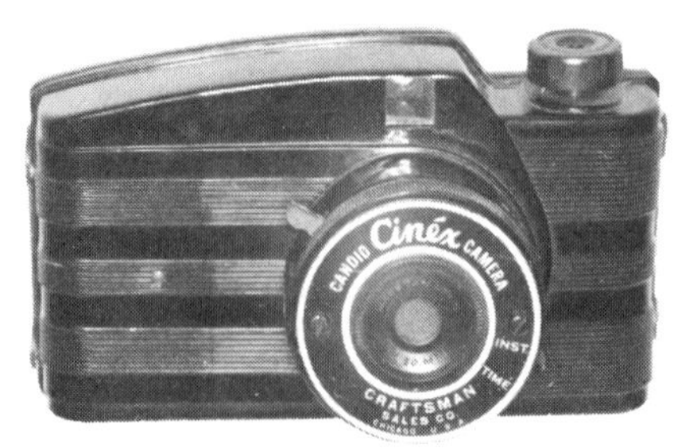

Cinex Candid Camera

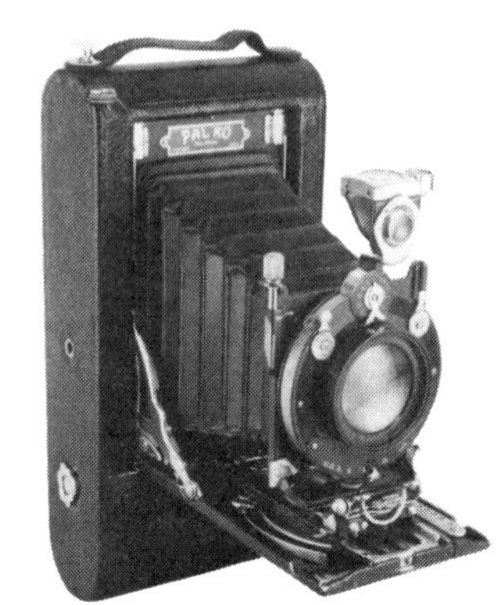

Cruver-Peters Palko

MODEL	FORMAT	FILM	TYPE	Year	LENS	Apert	FL	SHUTTER	SPEEDS	ILLUS	U.S.$
Daci Royal (black)	6x6cm	120	MetalBox	1949		9			I	Mc130	20
Daci Royal (green)	6x6cm	120	MetalBox	1950		9			I	Mc130	30
Daci Royal (grey)	6x6cm	120	MetalBox	1950		9			I	Mc130	30
Daci Royal (red)	6x6cm	120	MetalBox	1950		9			I	Mc130	50
Daco	6x6cm	120	BakeliteBox	1950	Meniscus	11			I,T	Mc130	60
Daco II	6x6cm	120	BakeliteBox	1950		8					60
Dacora I	6x6cm	120	HzFoldRo	1953	Eunar	3.5	75mm	Prontor	1-100	A1513	20
Dacora II	6x6cm	120	HzFoldRo	1954	Ennar	3.5	75mm	Pronto	25-200	Mc130	30
Dacora-Matic	24x36mm	35mm	35VF	1960	Dignar	2.8	45mm	Prontormat	300		40
Dacora-Matic 4D	24x36mm	35mm	35VF	1961	Dignar	2.8	45mm	Prontor-Lux	30-500	Mc130	40
Dacora-Matic CC	24x36mm	35mm	35VF	1961	Dignar	2.8	45mm	Prontormatic	30-500		30
Digna I	6x6cm	120	TelescRo	1954	Achromat	8		Spezial		A1550	10
Digna II	6x6cm	120	TelescRo	1958		6.3		simple	1/50	A3097	20
Dignette	24x36mm	35mm	35VF	1957	Dignar	2.8	50mm	Prontor-SVS	300	A1157	10
Dignette S-L	24x36mm	35mm	35VF	1965	Color Isconar	2.8	45mm	Prontor-S	300		20
Instacora E	28x28mm	126	126VF	1966	Color Dignar	3.5	45mm		30-125	Mc131	20
Instacora F	28x28mm	126	126VF	1966	Color Dignar	3.5	45mm		30-125		10
Instacora R	28x28mm	126	126VF	1968	Dignar Anastigmat	3.5	45mm		30-125		10
Record	6x6cm	120	HzFoldRo	1954	Dignar	4.5	75mm	Pronto			60
Royal	6x6cm	120	HzFoldRo	1955	Ennagon	3.5	75mm	Pronto			50
Subita	6x6cm	120	HzFoldRo	1953	Anastigmat	6.3	75mm	Singlo	25,75		30
Super Dignette	24x36mm	35mm	35VF	1960	Isconar	2.8	45mm	Pronto LK		Mc131	20
Super Dignette 250 LK	24x36mm	35mm	35VF	1965	Cassar	2.8	45mm	Prontor-SVS			20
Super Dignette 300 L	24x36mm	35mm	35VF	1960	Color Trinon	2.8	45mm				20
Super Dignette 500 LK	24x36mm	35mm	35VF	1965	Dignar	2.8	45mm	Vario LK		Mc131	20
Super Dignette 500 S	24x36mm	35mm	35VF	1965	Isconar	2.8	45mm	Prontor			30
Super Dignette E-B	24x36mm	35mm	35RF	1965	Cassar	2.8	45mm	Prontor-LK	1/15-500		30
Super Dignette Elec. C-R	24x36mm	35mm	35VF	1966	Trinon	2.8	45mm	Prontor	1/30-300		20
...DAIICHI KOGAKU / DAI-ICHI OPTICAL WORKS - Japan											
Ichicon 35	24x36mm	35mm	35VF	1954	Hexanon	3.5	50mm				1900
Waltax I	4.5x6cm	120	VtFoldRo	1947	Kolex Anastigmat	3.5	7cm	Dabit Super	1-500		70
Waltax Acme	4.5x6cm	120	VtFoldRo	1951	Bio-Kolex	3.5	75mm	Dabit Super	1-500		370
Waltax Jr.	4.5x6cm	120	VtFoldRo	1951	Bio-Kolex	4.5	75mm	Okako	25-150		70
Waltax Senior	4.5x6cm	120	VtFoldRo	1951	Bio-Kolex	3.5	75mm	Dabit Super	1-500	Mc131	70
Zenobia	4.5x6cm	120	VtFoldRo	1949	Hesper Anast.	3.5	75mm	D.O.C. Rapid	1-500		70
Zenobiaflex	6x6cm	120	TLR	1953	Neo-Hesper	3.5	75mm	Daiichi Rapid			100
...DAITOH OPTICAL CO. - Tokyo											
Grace	5.5x5.5cm	120	BakeliteRoll							Mc131	20
Grace Six	6x6cm	120	FoldRo	1950	Erinar Anastigmat	3.5	75mm				160
Rose Four	4x4cm	127	BakeliteRoll	1950	Alphar	4.5	55mm	Atkins Rapid	1-250		60
...DALKA INDUSTRIES PTY. LTD. - Victoria, Australia											
Dalka Candid	6x6cm	620	RigidRo	1949	Tcco		66mm	sector	T,I	Mc132	70

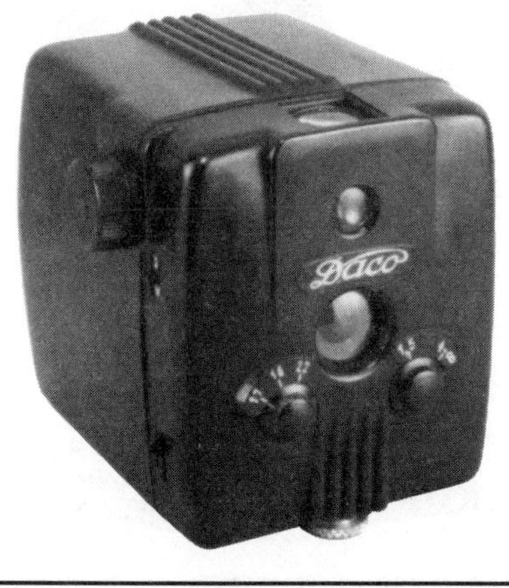

Daco

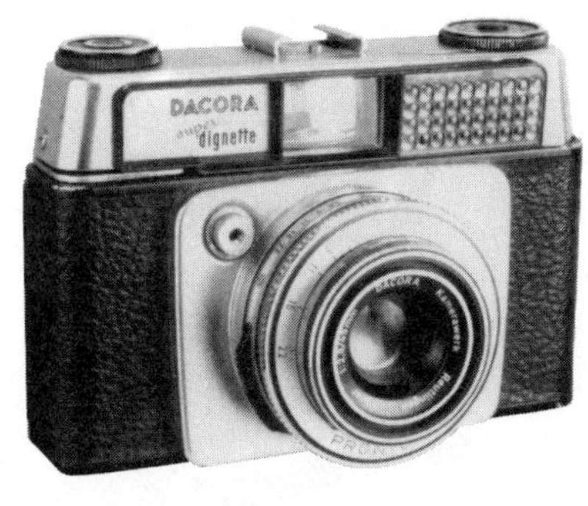

Super Dignette 500 LK

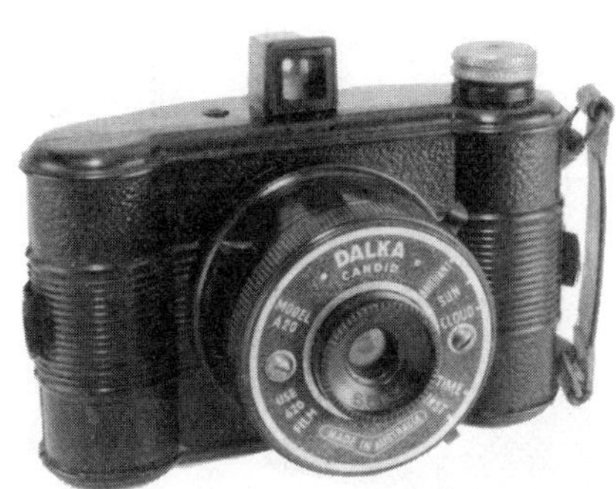

Dalka Candid

MODEL	FORMAT	FILM	TYPE	Year	LENS	Apert	FL	SHUTTER	SPEEDS	ILLUS	U.S.$
...DALLMEYER (J.H. Dallmeyer) - London											
Correspondent	4x5"	plate	H&S	1904	Stigmatic			Compound			330
Naturalist's Reflex Camera	3¼x4¼"	plate	LgSLR	1911	Grandac	4		focal plane	800		450
Naturalists Hand Camera		plate	H&S	1894							650
New Naturalists' Hand Cam.		plate	H&S	1904				Anschütz FP	1000		900
Snapshot Camera	6x9cm	pack	StrutFold	1929	Dallmeyer	6.3				A3023	60
Special Press Refl. 6.5x9	6.5x9cm	plate	LgSLR	1930	Dallmeyer			focal plane	15-1000		140
Special Press Refl. 3¼x4¼"	3¼x4¼"	plate	LgSLR	1930	Dallmeyer			focal plane	15-1000		220
Speed Camera 4.5x6	4.5x6cm	plate	FoldPress	1925	Pentac	2.9		focal plane	1/8-1000	Mc132	300
Speed Camera 6.5x9	6.5x9cm	plate	FoldPress	1925	Pentac	2.9		focal plane	1/8-1000	Mc132	200
Speed Camera 3¼x4¼"	3¼x4¼"	plate	FoldPress	1925	Pentac	2.9		focal plane	1/8-1000	Mc132	200
Studio camera 6½x8½"	6½x8½"	plate	Studio	1900	Various			various			570
Studio camera 8x10"	8x10"	plate	Studio	1900	Various			various			500
Studio camera wet / dry	4x5"	WetPl	WetPlate	1870	Various			various			1400
View camera 4x5"	4x5"	plate	Tailboard	1935	Various			various			240
View camera 8x10"	8x10"	plate	Tailboard	1935	Various			various			510
Wet plate camera	8x10"	WetPl	WetPlate	1870	Dallmeyer						700
Wet plate sliding-box		WetPl	WetPlate	1865							2300
...DAN CAMERA WORKS - Tokyo											
Dan 35 Mod. I	24x24mm	Bolta	RigidRo	1946	Dan Anastigmat	4.5	40mm	Silver-B	25-100		160
Dan 35 Mod. II	24x24mm	Bolta	RigidRo	1948	Dan Anastigmat	4.5	40mm	Silver-B	25-100	Mc132	160
Dan 35 Mod. III	24x24mm	Bolta	RigidRo	1949	Dan Anastigmat	3.5	40mm	Silver-B	25-100		160
Dan 35 IV	24x24mm	Bolta	RigidRo	1949							220
Super Dan 35	24x24mm	Bolta	RigidRo		Eria Anastigmat	3.5	45mm	Silver-C			630
...DARIER (Albert Darier) - Geneva											
Escopette	68x72mm	Roll	RollBox	1888	Steinh.Periscopic	6	90mm				10000
...DARLOT - Paris											
Rapide	8x9cm	plate	MagBox	1887						Mc132	6700
...DEARDORFF (L.F.) & SONS - Chicago, USA											
Baby Deardorff V4	4x5"	plate	Field	1936	Various			various		Mc134	900
Commercial Camera	8x10"	plate	Studio		Various			various			1100
Commercial Camera	11x14"	plate	Studio		Various			various			1900
Deardorff 4x5"	4x5"	plate	Field	1929	Various			various			600
Deardorff 5x7"	5x7"	plate	Field	1929	Various			various		Mc133	610
Deardorff 8x10"	8x10"	plate	Field	1923	Various			various		Mc133	1000
Deardorff 8x20"	8x20"	plate	Field	1949	Various			various			5300
Deardorff 10x12"	10x12"	plate	Field	1936	Various			various			3900
Deardorff 12x20"	12x20"	plate	Field	1949	Various			various			5300
Deardorff 16x20"	16x20"	plate	Field	1947	Various			various			4400
Home Portrait	5x7"	plate	Tailboard	1940	Various			various			300
Triamapro	4x5"	plate	FoldPress	1939	Various			various		Mc134	510
View	11x14"	plate	Field	1945	Various			various			1400

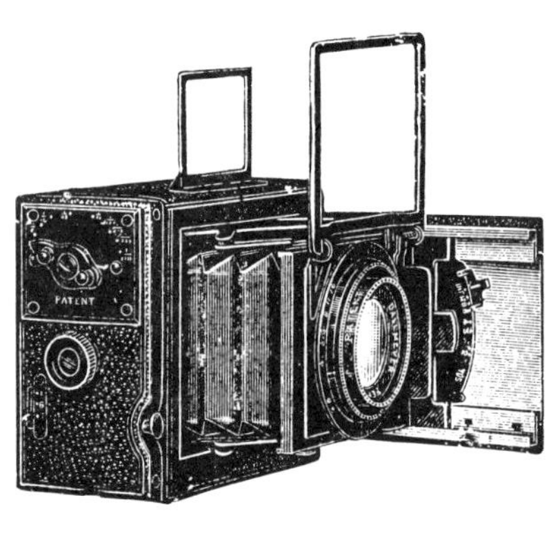

Dallmeyer Speed Camera

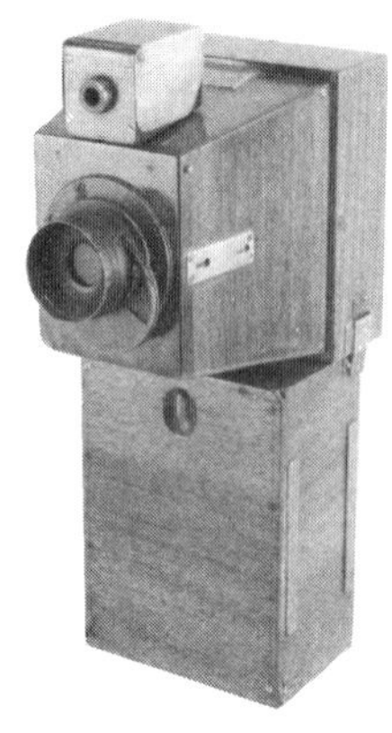

Darlot Rapide

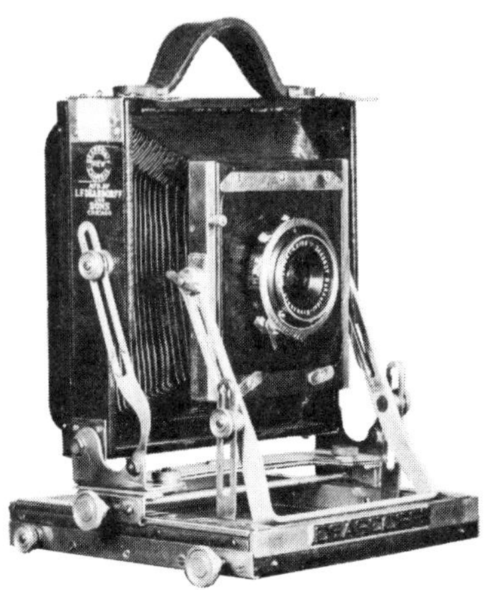

Baby Deardorff V4

MODEL	FORMAT	FILM	TYPE	Year	LENS	Apert	FL	SHUTTER	SPEEDS	ILLUS	U.S.$
...DEBRIE (Ets. Andre Debrie) - Paris											
Sept (single spring)	18x24mm	Roll	35SprMot	1923	Roussel Stylor	3.5	50mm			A1888	340
Sept (double spring)	18x24mm	Roll	35SprMot	1923	Roussel Stylor	3.5	50mm			Mc134	270
...DEFIANCE MFG. CO.											
Auto Fixt Focus	2¼x3¼"	120	VtFoldRo	1916	Goerz	4.8		Acme		Mc134	70
...DEJUR-AMSCO CORP. - New York											
DeJur D-1	24x36mm	35mm	35VF	1955	Staeble-Kata	2.8	45mm			Mc135	30
DeJur D-3	24x36mm	35mm	35RF	1957	Staeble-Kata	2.8	45mm	Prontor-S	1-300		50
DeJur DR-10	6x6cm	120	TLR	1952	DeJur Chromtar	3.5		Synchromatic	10-200	Mc135	70
DeJur DR-20	6x6cm	120	TLR	1952	DeJur Chromtar	3.5		Rapax	1-400		80
DeJur SR	24x36mm	35mm	35SLR	1960	Simlar	2.8	50mm	Seikosha-SLV	1-500		120
...DEMARIA FRERES / DEMARIA-LAPIERRE - Paris											
Caleb	9x12cm	plate	VtFoldPl	1920	Rectil. Hector					Mc135	70
Caleb Tropical	9x12cm	plate	VtFoldPl	1930	Rapid Rectilinear						520
Dehel	4.5x6cm	120	VtFoldRo			3.5	75mm	AGC		A510	40
Dehel	6x9cm	120	VtFoldRo	1950	Manar	4.5	110mm	AGC		F305	30
Field camera	24x30cm	plate	Field	1900	Extra Rap. Aplan.	8	480mm	Thornton-Pickard			350
Jumelle Caleb	6x13cm	plate	StJumelle		Tessar	8	110mm	guillotine		F1268	420
Jumelle Capsa 45x107	45x107	plate	StJumelle	1900				guillotine		A725	200
Jumelle Capsa 6x13	6x13cm	plate	StJumelle					guillotine		F1193	220
Plate camera	6.5x9cm	plate	StrutPl		Anast. Sigmar	6.3		Vario	25-100	Mc135	50
Summa	6x9cm	120	VtFoldRo		achromatic				P,I	F388	50
Telka I	6x9cm	120	VtFoldRo	1954	Anastigmat Manar	4.5		Compur	25-175	F395	40
Telka II	4.5x6cm	120	VtFoldRo	1949	Anastigmat Manar	3.5		Prontor-S	300	Mc136	70
Telka III	6x9cm	120	VtFoldRo	1948	Sagittar	3.5		AGC Prontor II		Mc136	100
Telka III A	6x9cm	120	VtFoldRo	1948	Sagittar	3.5		Prontor-SV		F398	100
Telka III B	6x9cm	120	VtFoldRo	1948	Sagittar	3.5		Prontor-SVS		F399	110
Telka Professional	6x9cm	120	VtFoldRo								170
Telka X	6x9cm	120	VtFoldRo	1950	Meniscus				P,I	F400	30
Telka XX	6x9cm	120	VtFoldRo	1950	Manar Anastigmat	4.5	110mm	Gitzo	175, 200	Mc136	40
Telka-Sport	4.5x6cm	120	VtFoldRo	1957	Sagittar	3.5	70mm	Atos	1-300	F393	200
...DEMILLY - France											
Midelly Simple	6x9cm	620	MetalBox		Meniscus			simple		Mc136	40
Midelly De Luxe	6x9cm	620	MetalBox		Boyer Topaz	4.5		Gitzo	25-200	F856	140
...DE NECK (J. De Neck) - Belgium											
Photo-Chapeau	4.5x5cm	plate	Disguised	1888	Aplanat						18000
...DETROLA CORP. - Detroit, MI USA											
Detrola 400	24x36mm	35mm	35RF	1939	Velostigmat	3.5		focal plane	1500	Mc136	500
Detrola A	3x4cm	127	35VF	1939	Meniscus			Wollensak	I,T		20
Detrola B	3x4cm	127	35VF	1939	Duomicroflex	7.9		Wollensak	I,T	Mc136	30
Detrola D	3x4cm	127	35VF	1939	Duomicroflex	4.5		Wollensak	25-200		30
Detrola E	3x4cm	127	35VF	1939	Duomicroflex	3.5		Wollensak	25-200		30

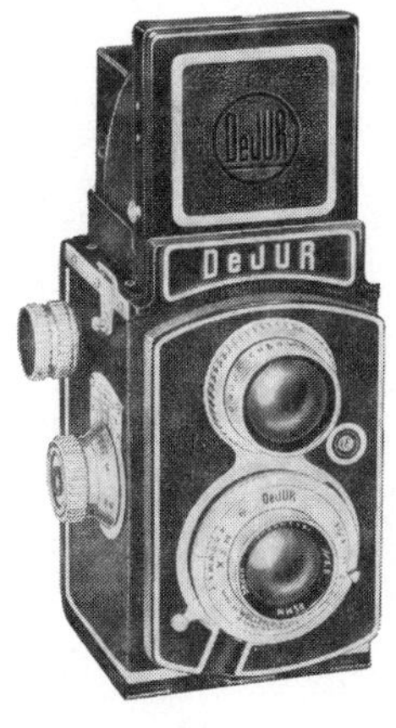

DeJur DR-10

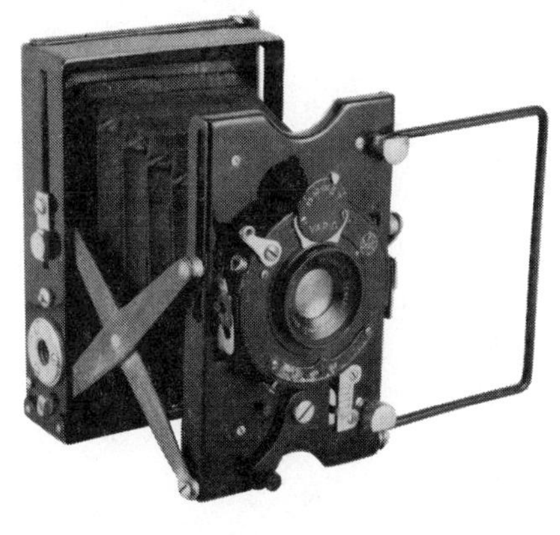

Demaria Plate Camera

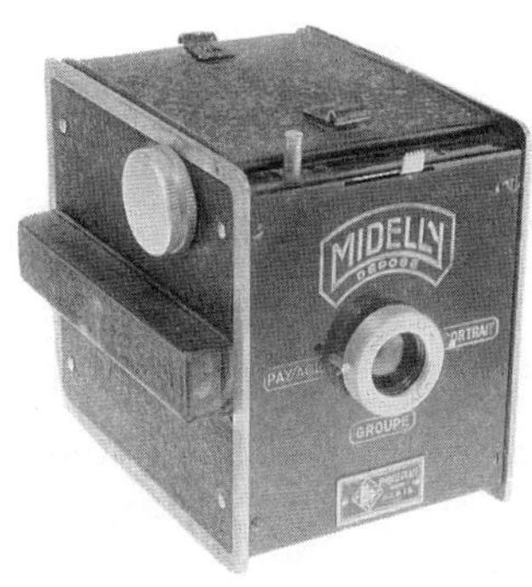

Midelly De Luxe

MODEL	FORMAT	FILM	TYPE	Year	LENS	Apert	FL	SHUTTER	SPEEDS	ILLUS	U.S.$
Detrola G	3x4cm	127	35VF	1939	Anastigmat	4.5		Wollensak	25-200	Mc136	30
Detrola GW	3x4cm	127	35VF	1939	Velostigmat	4.5		Wollensak	25-200		30
Detrola H	3x4cm	127	35VF	1939	Anastigmat	4.5		Wollensak	25-200		30
Detrola HW	3x4cm	127	35VF	1939	Velostigmat	4.5		Wollensak	25-200		30
Detrola K	3x4cm	127	35VF	1939	Anastigmat	3.5		Wollensak	25-200		20
Detrola KW	3x4cm	127	35VF	1939	Velostigmat	3.5		Wollensak	25-200		20
...DEVAUX (A. Devaux) - Paris											
le Prismac	4x4cm	102	Stereo	1905	Kenngott Anast.	8	54mm			A3276	3100
...DEVIN COLORGRAPH CO. - New York											
Tri-Color Camera 6.5x9	6.5x9cm		3-Color	1938	Goerz Dogmar	4.5	5.5"	Compound		A947	800
Tri-Color Camera 5x7"	5x7"		3-Color	1939	Apo-Tessar	9	12"	Dial-Compur			580
...DIAMANT (Société Diamant) - Paris											
Diamant	9x12cm	plate	VtFoldPl	1903	Meniscus			guillotine		A174	160
...DREXLER & NAGEL - Stuttgart											
Contessa	4.5x6cm	plate	VtFoldPl	1908	Staeble Isoplast	6.8	3"				1100
...DRUOPTA - Prague											
Corina	6x6cm	120	BakeliteRoll	1950					25-75	Mc138	30
Druoflex I	6x6cm	120	TLR	1950	Druoptar	6.3	75mm	Chrontax	1/10-200		60
Stereo camera	45x107		Stereo	1910	Rapid Rectilinear						320
Vega	24x36mm	35mm	35VF	1949	Druoptar	4.5	50mm	Etaxa	10-200		40
Vega II	24x36mm	35mm	35VF	1949	Druoptar	4.5	50mm	Etaxa	10-200	Mc138	50
Vega III	24x36mm	35mm	35VF	1957	Druoptar	3.5	50mm	Chrontax	10-200	Mc138	50
...DUBRONI (Maison Dubroni) - Paris											
Dubroni No. 1	4cm	WetPl	WetPlate	1860						F140	1900
Dubroni No. 2	5½x5½"	WetPl	WetPlate	1860						Mc138	4400
Photo-Sport	9x12cm	plate	StrutPl	1890	Darlot					A3002	1600
Photographe de Poche	5x5cm	WetPl	WetPlate	1860						F139	4500
...DUCATI (Societa Scientifica Radio Brevetti Ducati) - Milan											
Ducati Simplex	18x24mm	35mm	35RF	1950	Etar	3.5	35mm	focal plane	500	Mc138	440
Ducati Sogno	18x24mm	35mm	35RF	1950	Vitor	2.8		focal plane	500	Mc138	430
...DUFA - Czechoslovakia											
Fit	6x6/4.5x6	120	BakeliteRoll		Meniscus				25-100	Mc139	30
Fit II	6x6/4.5x6	120	BakeliteRoll		Meniscus				25-100	Mc139	30
Pionyr	6x6/4.5x6	120	BakeliteRoll		Meniscus				M,T	Mc139	50
...DURST S.A.											
Automatica	24x36mm	35mm	35VF	1956	Radionar	2.8	45mm	Prontor	1-300	Mc139	140
Duca (black)	24x36mm	Karat	35VF	1946	Ducan	11	50mm		T,I	Mc139	110
Duca (blue)	24x36mm	Karat	35VF	1946	Ducan	11	50mm		T,I	Mc139	170
Duca (brown)	24x36mm	Karat	35VF	1946	Ducan	11	50mm		T,I	Mc139	160
Duca (red)	24x36mm	Karat	35VF	1946	Ducan	11	50mm		T,I	Mc139	180
Duca (white)	24x36mm	Karat	35VF	1946	Ducan	11	50mm		T,I		200
Durst 66 (black)	6x6cm	120	RigidRo	1950	Duplor	2.2	80mm		½-200	Mc139	40

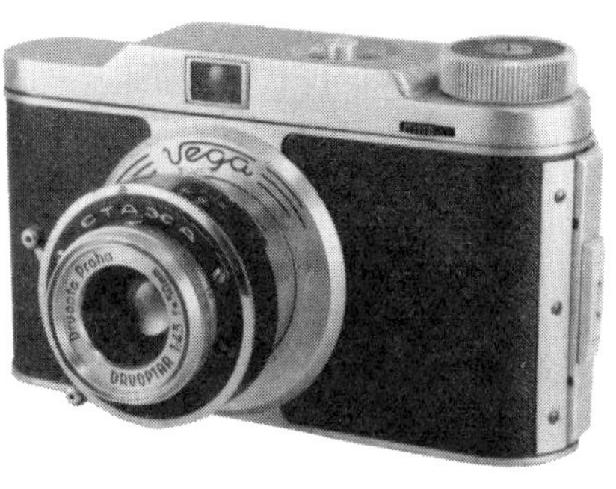

Druopta Vega II

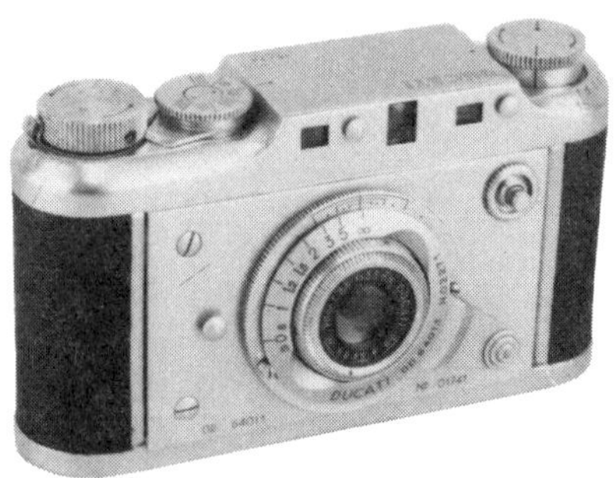

Ducati Sogno

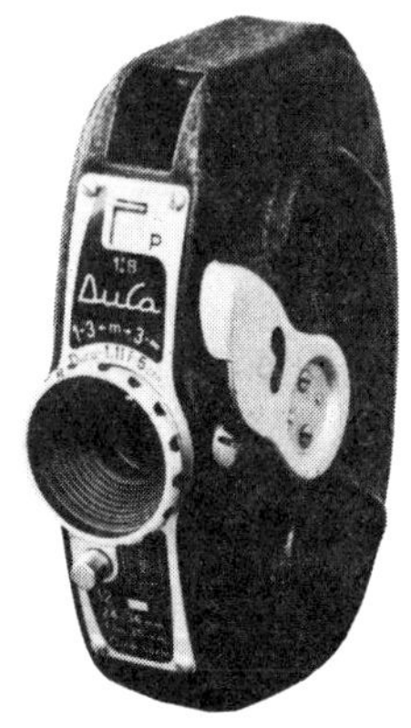

Durst Duca

MODEL	FORMAT	FILM	TYPE	Year	LENS	Apert	FL	SHUTTER	SPEEDS	ILLUS	U.S.$
Durst 66 (colors)	6x6cm	120	RigidRo	1950	Duplor	2.2	80mm		½-200	HK298	70
Gil	6x9cm	120	MetalBox	1938						Mc139	70
...EASTERN SPECIALTY MFG. CO. - Boston											
Springfield Union Camera	3½x3½"	plate	Box	1899						Mc139	500
...EASTMAN KODAK CO. - Rochester, NY USA											
Kodak A Mod. 11	6x9cm	120	FoldRo							Mc160	30
Anniversary Kodak Cam.	2¼x3¼"	120	RollBox	1930	Meniscus			rotary		Mc140	40
Auto Colorsnap 35	24x36mm	35mm	35vf	1962						Mc141	20
Autographic Kodak No. 1A	2½x4¼"	116	VtFoldRo	1914	Rapid Rectilinear		5"	Ball Bearing		Mc141	20
Autographic Kodak No. 3	3¼x4¼"	118	VtFoldRo	1914	Rapid Rectilinear			Ball Bearing		Mc141	20
Autographic Kodak No. 3A	3¼x5½"	122	VtFoldRo	1914	Rapid Rectilinear			Ball Bearing			50
Autogr. Kodak Jr. No. 1	2¼x3¼"	120	VtFoldRo	1914	Rapid Rectilinear		4.25"	Ball Bearing		Mc141	30
Autogr. Kodak Jr. No. 1A	2½x4¼"	116	VtFoldRo	1914	Rapid Rectilinear		5.25"	Ball Bearing		Mc141	20
Autogr. Kodak Jr. No. 2C	2⅞x4⅞"	130	VtFoldRo	1914	Rapid Rectilinear			Ball Bearing			50
Autogr. Kodak Jr. No. 3A	3¼x5½"	122	VtFoldRo	1914	Rapid Rectilinear			Ball Bearing		A382	10
Autogr. Kodak Spcl. No. 1	2¼x3¼"	120	VtFoldRo	1915	Kodak Anastigmat	6.3	4.25"	Optimo			40
Autogr. Kodak Spcl. No. 1A	2½x4¼"	116	VtFoldRo	1914	Kodak Anastigmat	6.3		B&L Compound			30
Autog. Kodak Spcl. 1A (RF)	2½x4¼"	116	VtFoldRo	1917	Kodak Anastigmat	6.3		Optimo			40
Autog. Kodak Spcl. No. 2C	2⅞x4⅞"	130	VtFoldRo	1923	Kodak Anastigmat	6.3	6"	Kodamatic			40
Autog. Kodak Spcl. No. 3	3¼x4¼"	118	VtFoldRo	1914	Kodak Anastigmat	6.3		Optimo		Mc141	80
Autog. Kodak Spcl. No. 3A	3¼x4¼"	118	VtFoldRo	1914	Kodak Anastigmat	6.3	6.75"	B&L Compound		Mc141	50
Autog. Kodak Spcl. 3A (RF)	3¼x5½"	122	VtFoldRo	1917	Kodak Anastigmat	6.3	6.75"	Optimo			90
Automatic 35 Camera	24x36mm	35mm	35vf	1959	Ektanar	2.8		Synchro 80		Mc141	20
Automatic 35B Camera	24x36mm	35mm	35vf	1961	Ektanar	2.8		EKC Autom.			20
Automatic 35F Camera	24x36mm	35mm	35vf	1962	Ektanar	2.8		EKC Autom.		Mc142	30
Automatic 35R4 Camera	24x36mm	35mm	35vf	1965	Ektanar	2.8		EKC Autom.		Mc142	30
Autosnap	4x4cm	127	RigidRo	1962						Mc142	10
Baby Brownie (U.K.)	1½x2½"	127	BakeliteBox								30
Baby Brownie (U.S.A.)	1½x2½"	127	BakeliteBox	1934	Meniscus			rotary		Mc144	10
Baby Brownie Special	1½x2½"	127	BakeliteBox	1939	Meniscus			rotary		Mc144	10
Baby Brownie World Fair	1½x2½"	127	BakeliteBox	1939	Meniscus			rotary		Mc144	200
Baby Hawkeye	4x6.5cm	127	Box	1936						Mc157	30
Bantam (original) f6.3	28x40mm	828	StrutRo	1935	Kodak Anastigmat	6.3	53mm	built-in		Mc142	30
Bantam (original) f12.5	28x40mm	828	StrutRo	1935	Doublet	12.5		built-in			20
Bantam Colorsnap	28x40mm	828	RigidRo		Kodak Anaston	4.5		Dakon	I	Mc142	10
Bantam Colorsnap II	28x40mm	828	RigidRo	1955	Kodak Anaston	4.5		Dakon	I		10
Bantam Colorsnap 3	28x40mm	828	RigidRo	1959	Kodak Anaston	3.9			I		10
Bantam f4.5	28x40mm	828	StrutRo	1938	Anast. Special	4.5	47mm	Bantam	20-200	Mc142	30
Bantam f5.6	28x40mm	828	StrutRo	1938	Kodak Anastigmat	5.6	50mm	built-in		Mc142	30
Bantam f6.3	28x40mm	828	StrutRo	1938	Kodak Anastigmat	6.3	53mm	built-in		Mc142	30
Bantam f8	28x40mm	828	TelescRo	1938	Kodalinear	8	40mm	built-in		Mc142	30
Bantam RF	28x40mm	828	RigidRo	1961	Ektanon	3.9	50mm	Flash 300	25-300	Mc142	30

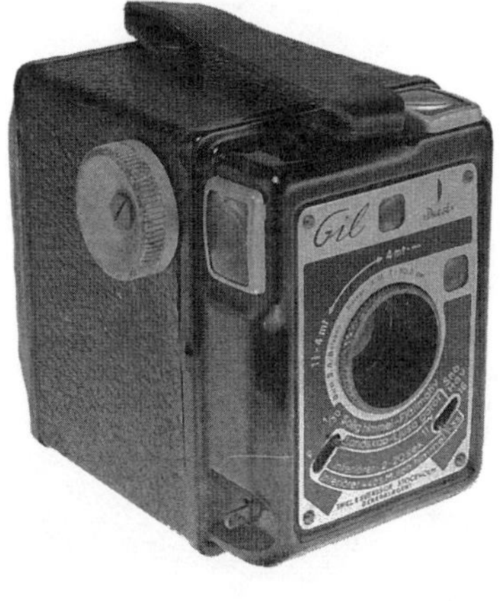

Durst Gil

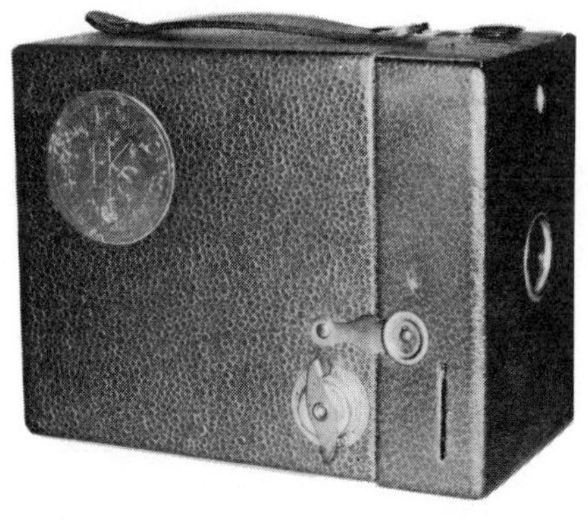

Anniversary Kodak Cam.

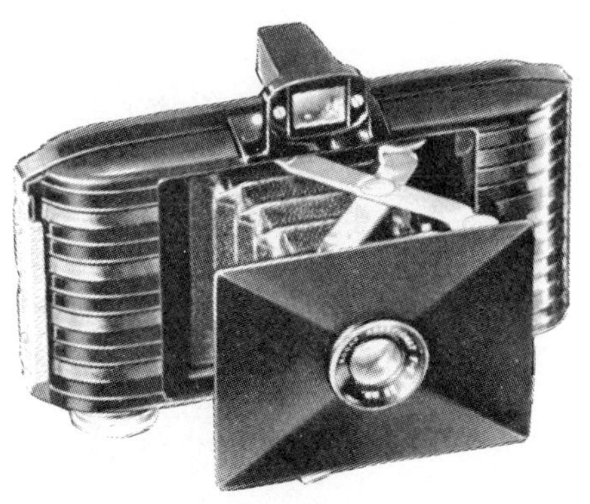

Bantam (original) f6.3

MODEL	FORMAT	FILM	TYPE	Year	LENS	Apert	FL	SHUTTER	SPEEDS	ILLUS	U.S.$
Bantam Special	28x40mm	828	FoldRo	1936	Ektar	2		Compur-Rapid	1-300	A1496	270
Bantam Special	28x40mm	828	FoldRo	1941	Ektar	2		Supermatic			290
Beau Brownie 2 (colors)	2¼x3¼"	120	RollBox	1930	Doublet			rotary			70
Beau Brownie 2 (rose)	2¼x3¼"	120	RollBox	1930	Doublet			rotary			80
Beau Brownie 2A (colors)	2½x4¼"	116	RollBox	1930	Doublet			rotary		Mc144	140
Beau Brownie 2A (rose)	2½x4¼"	116	RollBox	1930	Doublet			rotary		Mc144	110
Kodak Box 620	6x9cm	620	RollBox	1936	Periskop					A1337	10
Kodak Box 620 C	6x9cm	620	RollBox	1936	Meniscus			Kodak Spezial			70
Boy Scout Brownie	2¼x3¼"	120	Box	1932	Meniscus			rotary			260
Boy Scout Brownie Six-20	2¼x3¼"	620	Box	1933	Meniscus			rotary		Mc143	160
Boy Scout Kodak (UK)	4.5x6cm	127	FoldRo							Mc143	220
Boy Scout Kodak (USA)	4.5x6cm	127	FoldRo	1929	Meniscus			V.P. Rotary		Mc143	220
Brownie (original)	2¼x2¼"	117	Box	1900	Meniscus			rotary		Mc143	700
Brownie (1900 type)	2¼x2¼"	117	Box	1900	Meniscus			rotary		Mc143	130
Brownie (1980 type)	13x17mm	110	110	1980						Mc143	10
Brownie 44A	4x4cm	127	RigidRo	1959	Dakon				I	Mc144	10
Brownie 44B	4x4cm	127	RigidRo	1961	Dakon				I		10
Brownie 127	4x4cm	127	RigidRo	1965						Mc144	20
Brownie 127	1½x2½"	127	RigidRo	1953	Meniscus			rotary		Mc144	10
Brownie 620 (Kodak A.G.)	2¼x3¼"	620	Box	1933	Doublet	11		rotary		Mc147	20
Brownie Auto 27	4x4cm	127	RigidRo	1963	Kodar	8			40, 80	Mc144	10
Brownie Bull's-Eye (black)	2¼x3¼"	620	BakeliteBox	1954	Twindar			rotary		Mc145	20
Brownie Bull's-Eye (gold)	2¼x3¼"	620	BakeliteBox	1954	Twindar			rotary		Mc145	20
Brownie Bullet	1½x2½"	127	BakeliteBox	1957	Dakon			rotary		Mc145	10
Brownie Bullet II	1½x2½"	127	RigidRo	1961	Dakon			rotary			10
Brownie Chiquita	1½x2½"	127	BakeliteBox		Dakon			rotary			10
Brownie Cresta	2¼x2¼"	120	RigidRo	1955	Kodet					Mc145	10
Brownie Cresta II	2¼x2¼"	120	RigidRo	1956						A3095	20
Brownie Cresta III	2¼x2¼"	120	RigidRo	1960						Mc145	20
Brownie Fiesta	4x4cm	127	RigidRo	1962	Meniscus	11		built-in		Mc145	10
Brownie Fiesta R4	4x4cm	127	RigidRo	1966	Meniscus	11		built-in			10
Brownie Flash II (Australia)	2¼x3¼"	620	MetBx	1958							20
Brownie Flash II (U.K.)	2¼x3¼"	620	MetBx	1956	Kodet	14			I,T		10
Brownie Flash III	2¼x3¼"	620	MetBx	1957						Mc145	10
Brownie Flash IV	2¼x3¼"	620	MetBx	1957						Mc145	30
Brownie Flash 20	2¼x2¼"	620	RigidRo	1959		11		built-in		Mc145	10
Brownie Flash B	2¼x2¼"	620	MetBx						40,80	Mc146	30
Brownie Flash Camera	2¼x2¼"	120	BakeliteBox		Meniscus			rotary	I,T	Mc145	20
Brownie Flashmite 20	2¼x2¼"	620	RigidRo	1960		11		built-in		Mc146	10
Brownie Hawkeye	2¼x2¼"	620	BakeliteBox	1949	Meniscus			rotary		Mc147	10
Brownie Hawkeye Flash	2¼x2¼"	620	BakeliteBox	1950	Meniscus	15		rotary			10
Brownie Holiday	1½x2½"	127	BakeliteBox	1953	Kodet	15		rotary		A122	20

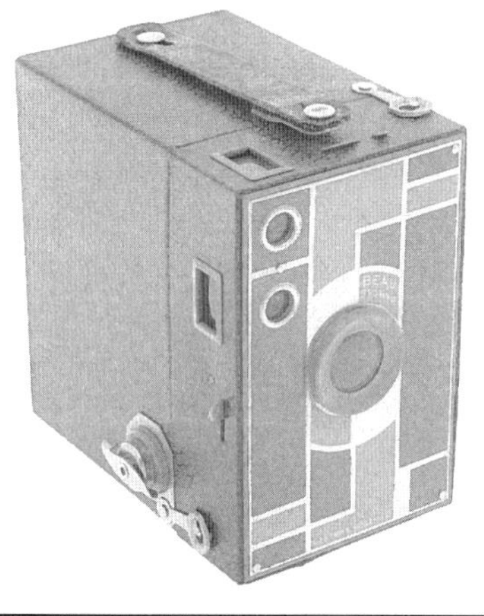

Beau Brownie 2A

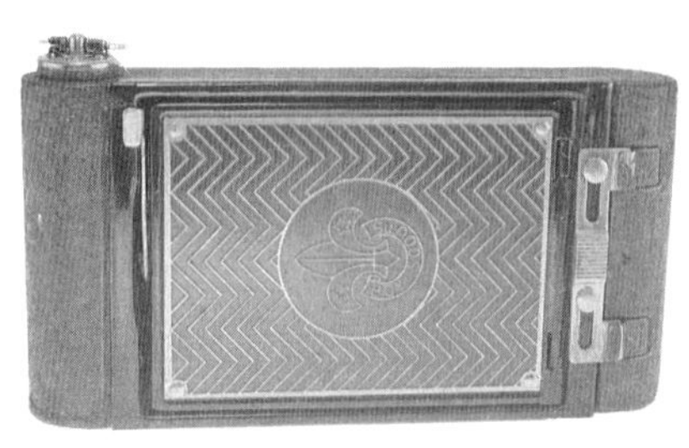

Boy Scout Kodak (UK)

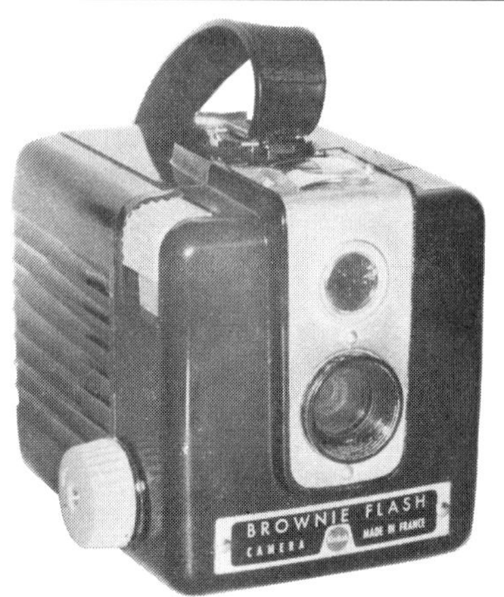

Brownie Flash Camera

MODEL	FORMAT	FILM	TYPE	Year	LENS	Apert	FL	SHUTTER	SPEEDS	ILLUS	U.S.$
Brownie Holiday Flash	1½x2½"	127	BakeliteBox	1954	Kodet	15		rotary		Mc147	10
Brownie Junior 620	2¼x3¼"	620	MetBx	1934						A2884	10
Brownie Mod. I	2¼x3¼"		MetBx	1957						Mc147	20
Brownie No. 0	1½x2½"	127	RollBox		Meniscus			rotary		Mc143	20
Brownie No. 1	2¼x2¼"	117	RollBox	1900	Meniscus			rotary		Mc143	50
Brownie No. 2	2¼x3¼"	120	RollBox	1901	Meniscus			rotary		Mc143	10
Brownie No. 2 (colors)	2¼x3¼"	120	RollBox	1929	Meniscus			rotary		Mc143	70
Brownie No. 2 (silver)	2¼x3¼"	120	RollBox	1935	Meniscus			rotary		Mc144	50
Brownie No. 2 Mod. F	2¼x3¼"	120	RollBox	1929	Meniscus			rotary			10
Br. No. 2 Mod. F (colors)	2¼x3¼"	120	RollBox	1929	Meniscus			rotary			40
Brownie No. 2A	2½x4¼"	116	RollBox	1907	Meniscus			rotary			20
Brownie No. 2A (colors)	2½x4¼"	116	RollBox	1907	Meniscus			rotary			50
Brownie No. 2C	2⅞x4⅞"	130	RollBox	1917	Meniscus Achrom.			rotary		Mc144	10
Brownie No. 3	3¼x4¼"	118	RollBox	1908	Meniscus Achrom.			rotary		Mc144	10
Brownie Pliant Six-20	2¼x3¼"	620	VtFoldRo	1939				Kodo	I,T	Mc147	30
Brownie Reflex	4x4cm	127	TLR-Box	1940	Meniscus			rotary		A651	30
Brownie Reflex 20	2¼x2¼"	620	TLR-Box	1959		11		built-in			10
Brownie Reflex Synchro	4x4cm	127	TLR-Box	1941	Meniscus			rotary		Mc147	10
Brownie Starflash (black)	1⅝x1⅝"	127	RigidRo	1957	Dakon			rotary		Mc148	10
Brownie Starflash (colors)	1⅝x1⅝"	127	RigidRo	1957	Dakon			rotary			30
Brownie Starfl. Coca-Cola	1⅝x1⅝"	127	RigidRo		Dakon			rotary		Mc148	100
Brownie Starflex	4x4cm	127	RigidRo	1957	Dakon			rotary		Mc149	10
Brownie Starlet (UK)	1½x2½"	127	RigidRo	1956	Meniscus			rotary		Mc149	10
Brownie Starlet (USA)	4x4cm	127	RigidRo	1957	Dakon			rotary		Mc149	20
Brownie Starluxe	4x4cm	127	RigidRo							Mc149	10
Brownie Starluxe 4	4x4cm	127	RigidRo	1967						Mc149	10
Brownie Starmatic	4x4cm	127	RigidRo	1959	Kodar	8		rotary		Mc149	10
Brownie Starmatic II	4x4cm	127	RigidRo	1961	Kodar	8			2 Zeiten	Mc149	10
Brownie Starmeter	4x4cm	127	RigidRo	1960	Kodar	8		rotary		Mc149	20
Brownie Starmite	4x4cm	127	RigidRo	1960	Dakon			rotary		Mc149	10
Brownie Starmite II	4x4cm	127	RigidRo	1962	Kodet	11		rotary		Mc149	10
Brownie Super 27	4x4cm	127	RigidRo	1961	Kodar	8			2 Zeiten	Mc149	10
Brownie Target Six-16	2½x4¼"	616	Box	1941	Meniscus			rotary		Mc149	10
Brownie Target Six-20	2¼x3¼"	620	Box	1941	Meniscus			rotary		Mc149	10
Brownie Twin 20	2¼x2¼"	620	RigidRo	1959		11		built-in		A3094	10
Brownie Vecta	1½x2½"	127	RigidRo	1963						Mc150	20
Buckeye Camera		plate	FoldPl	1899							140
Bull's-Eye Camera No. 2	3½x3½"	101	Box	1896	Meniscus Achrom.		4.5"	rotary		Mc150	60
Bull's-Eye Camera No. 3	3¼x4¼"	124	Box	1908	achromatic			rotary			80
Bull's-Eye Camera No. 4	4x5"	103	Box	1896	achromatic		6.25"	rotary		Mc150	70
Bull's-Eye Camera No.4/C	4x5"	103	Box	1899	achromatic		6.25"	rotary			120
Bull's-Eye Camera No.4/D	4x5"	103	Box	1900	achromatic		6.25"	rotary			120

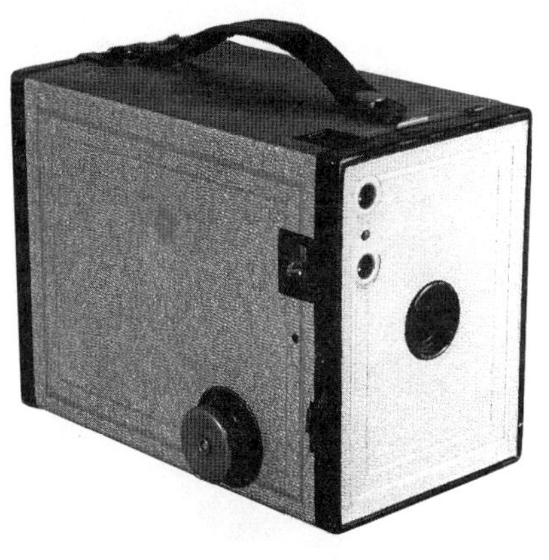

Brownie No. 2 (Silver)

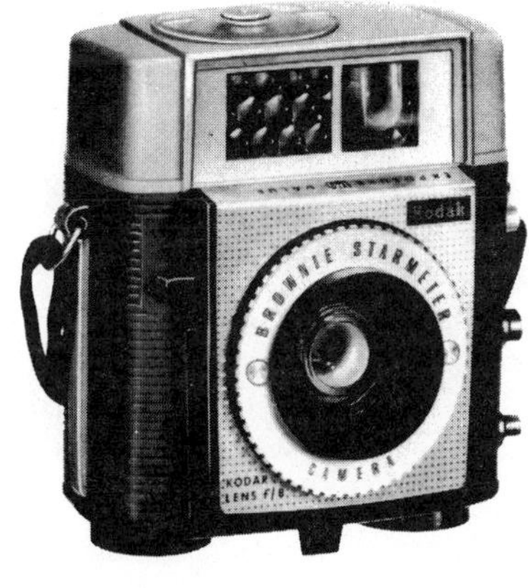

Brownie Starmeter

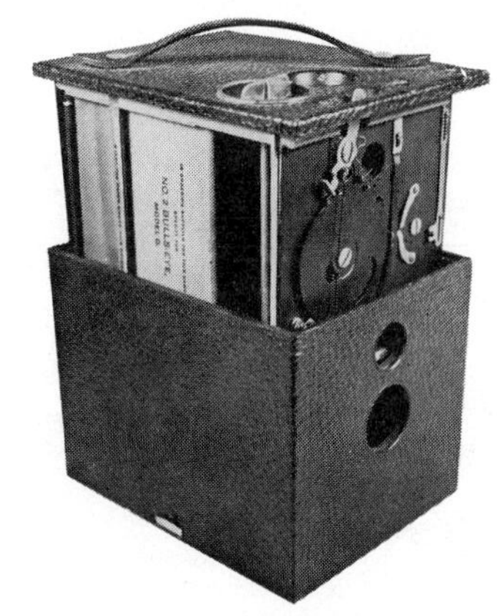

Bull's-Eye Camera No. 2

MODEL	FORMAT	FILM	TYPE	Year	LENS	Apert	FL	SHUTTER	SPEEDS	ILLUS	U.S.$
Bull's-Eye Special No. 2	3½x3½"	101	Box	1898	Rapid Rectilinear			Triple Action		A1326	80
Bull's-Eye Special No. 4	4x5"	103	Box	1898	Rapid Rectilinear			Triple Action		Mc150	100
Bullet Camera	1⅝x2½"	127	TelescRo	1936	Meniscus			rotary		Mc150	10
Bullet, N.Y. World's Fair	1⅝x2½"	127	TelescRo	1939	Meniscus			rotary			140
Bullet No. 2	3½x3½"	101	Box	1895	achromatic		4.25"	rotary		Mc150	70
Bullet No. 4	4x5"	103	Box	1896	achromatic			rotary		Mc150	110
Bullet Special No. 2	3½x3½"	101	Box	1898	Rapid Rectilinear			Triple Action		Mc150	150
Bullet Special No. 4	4x5"	103	Box	1898	Rapid Rectilinear			Triple Action			250
Cameo Focus Free	24x36mm	35mm	35VF	1993	Ektanar	4.5	35mm		1/125		30
Cameo Motor	24x36mm	35mm	35VF	1993	Ektanar	4.5	35mm				50
Cameo Motor 110	13x17mm	110	110VF	1993	Ektanar	8	28mm				20
Cameo Zoom Plus	24x36mm	35mm	35VF	1994	Ektanar	8	25mm				110
Camp Fire Girls Kodak	4.5x6cm	127	FoldRo	1931	Meniscus			V.P. Rotary		Mc151	420
Cartr.Hawk-Eye 2 Mod. A	2¼x3¼"	120	Box	1924	Meniscus			rotary		Mc157	10
Cartr.Hawk-Eye 2 Mod. B	2¼x3¼"	120	Box	1926	Meniscus			rotary		Mc157	10
Cartr.Hawk-Eye 2 Mod. C	2¼x3¼"	120	Box		Meniscus			rotary			10
Cartr.Hawk-Eye 2A Mod. A	2½x4¼"	116	Box	1924	Meniscus			rotary			10
Cartr.Hawk-Eye 2A Mod. B	2½x4¼"	116	Box	1926	Meniscus			rotary			10
Cartr. Hawkeye 2 Mod. CC	2¼x3¼"	120	Box	1927	Meniscus			rotary			10
Cartridge Kodak No. 3	4¼x3¼"	119	FoldRo	1900	Rapid Rectilinear	8		B&L Automatic		Mc151	180
Cartridge Kodak No. 4	5x4"	104	FoldRo	1897	Rapid Rectilinear	8		B&L Automatic		A358	170
Cartridge Kodak No. 5	7x5"	115	FoldRo	1898	Rapid Rectilinear	8		B&L Automatic		A357	200
Cartridge Premo No. 00	1¼x1¾"	111	RollBox	1916	Meniscus			rotary		Mc165	160
Cartridge Premo No. 2	2¼x3¼"	120	RollBox	1916	Meniscus			rotary		Mc165	10
Cartridge Premo No. 2A	2½x4¼"	116	RollBox	1916	achromatic			rotary			10
Cartridge Premo No. 2C	2⅞x4⅞"	130	RollBox	1917	achromatic			rotary			10
Century of Progress	2¼x3¼"	120	Box	1933	Doublet			rotary		Mc151	220
Century Universal	8x10"	plate	Field		Various					Mc151	390
Challenger Disc	8x10mm	Disc	Disc	1986		4.0	15mm	automatic	300		10
Champ	67x91mm	PR10	Instant	1982		12.8	100mm				10
Chevron Camera	2¼x2¼"	620	RigidRo	1953	Ektar	3.5	78mm	Synch.-Rapid	800	Mc151	240
Cirkut Camera No. 5		Roll	WideAng	1915	Triple Convertible		6.25"				900
Cirkut Camera No. 6		Roll	WideAng	1932	Triple Convertible		7"			Mc151	1300
Cirkut Camera No. 10		Roll	WideAng	1904	Triple Convertible		10.5"			A2015	3900
Cirkut Camera No. 16		Roll	WideAng	1905	Triple Convertible		15"				7000
Cirkut Outfit No. 6		Roll	WideAng	1907	Centar Series II						800
Cirkut Outfit No. 6		Roll	WideAng	1907	Triple Convertible		7.5"				900
Cirkut Outfit No. 8		Roll	WideAng	1907	Triple Convertible		10.5"			Mc151	1100
Colorburst 50	67x91mm	PR10	Instant	1979	Fixed Focus	12.8	100mm	electronic	2-1/300		10
Colorburst 100	67x91mm	PR10	Instant	1978	Focusing	11	137mm	electronic	20-300		10
Colorburst 150	67x91mm	PR10	Instant								10
Colorburst 200	67x91mm	PR10	Instant	1978	Focusing	11	137mm	electronic	20-300		10

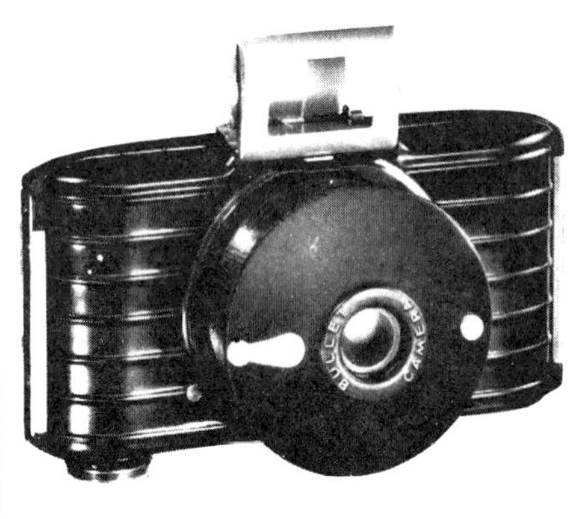

Bullet Camera

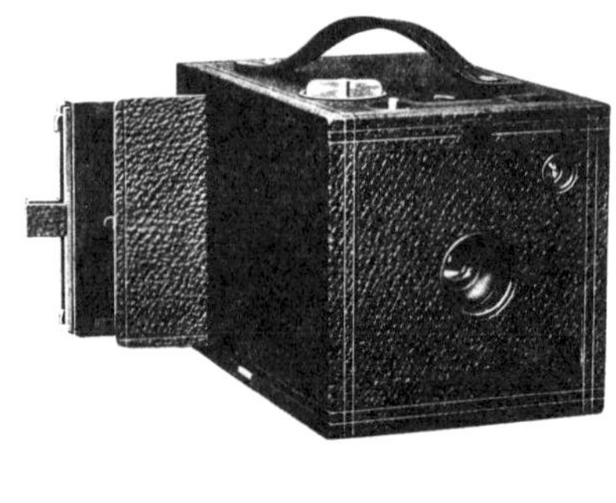

Bullet Special No. 2

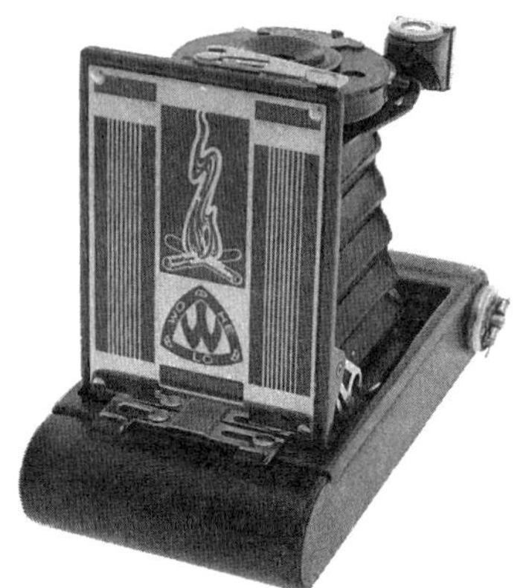

Camp Fire Girls Kodak

MODEL	FORMAT	FILM	TYPE	Year	LENS	Apert	FL	SHUTTER	SPEEDS	ILLUS	U.S.$
Colorburst 250	67x91mm	PR10	Instant	1979	Fixed Focus	12.8	100mm	electronic	2-1/300	Mc151	10
Colorburst 300	67x91mm	PR10	Instant	1978	Focusing	11	137mm	electronic	20-300		10
Colorburst 350	67x91mm	PR10	Instant	1981		2.8	100mm	electronic	2-1/300		10
Colorsnap 35	24x36mm	35mm	35vf	1959	Anaston	3.9				Mc152	20
Colorsnap 35 Mod. 2	24x36mm	35mm	35vf	1964	Anaston					Mc152	20
Daylight A	2¾x3¼"	Roll	Box	1891	achromatic		4"	sector			1500
Daylight B	3½x4"	Roll	Box	1891	achromatic		6"	sector		Mc152	700
Daylight C	4x5"	Roll	Box	1891	achromatic		7"	sector		Mc152	900
Disc 2000	8x10mm	Disc	Disc	1982		2.8	12.5mm	auto	100	A3376	10
Disc 3000	8x10mm	Disc	Disc	1983		2.8	12.5mm	auto	100		10
Disc 3100	8x10mm	Disc	Disc	1984		2.8	12.5mm	auto	100		10
Disc 3500	8x10mm	Disc	Disc	1983		2.8	12.5mm	auto	100		10
Disc 3600	8x10mm	Disc	Disc	1986		4.0	15mm	auto	300		10
Disc 4000	8x10mm	Disc	Disc	1982		2.8	12.5mm	auto	100	Mc152	20
Disc 4100	8x10mm	Disc	Disc	1984		2.8	12.5mm	auto	100		10
Disc 6000	8x10mm	Disc	Disc	1982		2.8	12.5mm	auto	100		10
Disc 6100	8x10mm	Disc	Disc	1984		2.8	12.5mm	auto	100		10
Disc 8000	8x10mm	Disc	Disc	1982		2.8	12.5mm	auto	100	A3379	30
Duaflex I (fixed focus)	2¼x2¼"	620	TLR-Box	1947	Kodet	15		simple	I,B	Mc152	10
Duaflex I (focusing)	2¼x2¼"	620	TLR-Box	1949	Kodar	8		simple	I,B	Mc152	10
Duaflex II (fixed focus)	2¼x2¼"	620	TLR-Box	1950	Kodet	15		simple	I,B	Mc152	10
Duaflex II (focusing)	2¼x2¼"	620	TLR-Box	1950	Kodar	8		simple	I,B	Mc152	10
Duaflex III (fixed focus)	2¼x2¼"	620	TLR-Box	1954	Kodet	15		simple	I,B	Mc152	10
Duaflex III (focusing)	2¼x2¼"	620	TLR-Box	1954	Kodar	8		simple	I,B	Mc152	20
Duaflex IV (fixed focus)	2¼x2¼"	620	TLR-Box	1955	Kodet	15		simple	I,B	Mc152	20
Duaflex IV (focusing)	2¼x2¼"	620	TLR-Box	1955	Kodar	8		simple	I,B	Mc152	30
Duex	4.5x6cm	620	RigidRo	1940	Doublet			simple	I,B	Mc152	10
Duo Six-20 Camera	4.5x6cm	620	HzFoldRo	1934	Kodak Anastigmat	3.5	70mm	Compur		Mc152	70
Duo Six-20 Series II	4.5x6cm	620	HzFoldRo	1937	Kodak Anastigmat	3.5	75mm	Compur-Rapid		Mc153	70
Duo Six-20 Series II (RF)	4.5x6cm	620	HzFoldRo	1939	Kodak Anastigmat	3.5	75mm	Compur-Rapid		Mc153	500
Duo Six-20 Series III	4.5x6cm	620	HzFoldRo	1939	Kodak Anastigmat	3.5	75mm	Compur-Rapid			340
Eastman Plate Cam. No. 3	3¼x4¼"	plate	H&S	1903	Rapid Rectilinear					Mc153	230
Eastman Plate Cam. No. 4	4x5"	plate	H&S	1903	Rapid Rectilinear					Mc153	290
Eastman Plate Cam. No. 5	5x7"	plate	H&S	1903	Rapid Rectilinear					Mc153	380
EK2 Instant	67x91mm	PR10	Instant	1977	Fixed Focus	12.7	100mm	electronic	15-300		10
EK4 Instant	67x91mm	PR10	Instant	1976	Focusing	11	137mm	electronic	20-300		10
EK6 Instant	67x91mm	PR10	Instant	1976	Focusing	11	137mm	electronic	20-300		10
EK8 Instant	67x91mm	PR10	Instant	1977	Focusing	11	137mm	electronic	20-300		30
EK20 Instant	67x91mm	PR10	Instant	1977	Fixed Focus	11	137mm	electronic	15-300		30
EK100 Instant	67x91mm	PR10	Instant	1978	Focusing	11		electronic	20-300		10
EK160 Instant	67x91mm	PR10	Instant	1979	Fixed Focus	12.8	100mm	electronic	2-1/300		10
EK160-EF Instant	67x91mm	PR10	Instant	1979	Fixed Focus	12.8	100mm	electronic	2-1/300		20

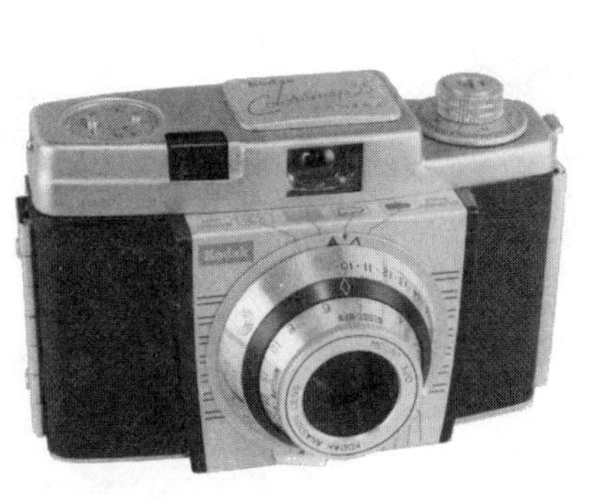

Colorsnap 35

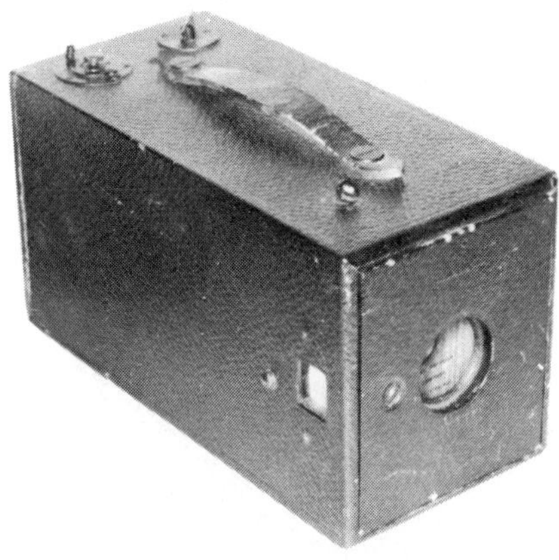

Daylight B

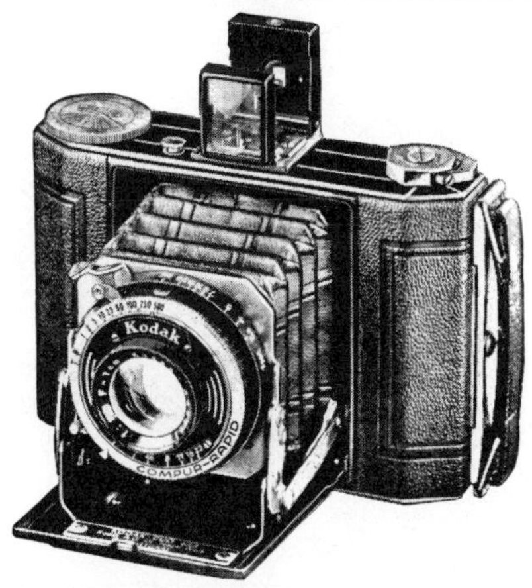

Duo Six-20 Camera

MODEL	FORMAT	FILM	TYPE	Year	LENS	Apert	FL	SHUTTER	SPEEDS	ILLUS	U.S.$
EK200 Instant	67x91mm	PR10	Instant	1978	Focusing	11	137mm	electronic	20-300		10
EK260-EF Instant	67x91mm	PR10	Instant	1981		2.8	100mm	electronic	2-1/300		20
EK300 Instant	67x91mm	PR10	Instant	1978	Focusing	11	137mm	electronic	20-300		10
Kodak Ektra	24x36mm	35mm	35rf	1941	Ektar	1.9	50mm	focal plane	1000	Mc153	580
Kodak Ektra 1	13x17mm	110	110	1978	Meniscus	11	25mm	3-speed	40-170		10
Kodak Ektra 2	13x17mm	110	110	1978	3-element	5.6	22mm	4-speed	60-500		10
Kodak Ektra 12	13x17mm	110	110	1978	Kodar	11	23mm	3-speed	40-250		10
Kodak Ektra 12-EF	13x17mm	110	110	1980	Kodar	11	23mm	3-speed	40-250		10
Kodak Ektra 22	13x17mm	110	110	1978	Kodar	9.5	25mm	3-speed	40-250		10
Kodak Ektra 22-EF	13x17mm	110	110	1978	Kodar	9.5	25mm	3-speed	40-250		20
Kodak Ektra 52	13x17mm	110	110	1978	Kodar	9.5	25mm	electronic	5-1/250		30
Kodak Ektra 100	13x17mm	110	110		Kodar	11	22mm				10
Kodak Ektra 200	13x17mm	110	110	1980	Kodar	11	22mm	3-speed	125-250	A1990	10
Kodak Ektra 250	13x17mm	110	110		Doublet	9.5	25mm	3-speed		A1990	10
Kodak Ektralite 10	13x17mm	110	110	1978		8	25mm		125-210		10
Kodak Ektralite 30	13x17mm	110	110	1979		5.6	22mm		100-500		10
Kodak Ektralite 400	13x17mm	110	110	1981	Fixed focus	6.8	24mm		60-250	A1990	10
Kodak Ektralite 450	13x17mm	110	110	1981		6.8	24mm		60-250	A1990	10
Kodak Ektralite 500	13x17mm	110	110	1980		8	22mm		125-250		10
Kodak Ektramax	13x17mm	110	110	1978	Aspheric	1.9	25mm		30-350		10
Empire State Camera	5x7"	plate	Field	1893						Mc153	170
Empire State Camera	6½x8½"	plate	Field	1893						Mc153	170
Empire State Camera	8x10"	plate	Field	1893						Mc153	170
Kodak Enlarger 16mm		616	Special	1939							30
Eureka No. 2	3½x3½"	106	Box	1898	achromatic			rotary			120
Eureka No. 2 Junior	3½x3½"	plate	Box	1898	achromatic			rotary			80
Eureka No. 4	4x5"	109	Box	1898	achromatic			rotary		Mc153	120
Falcon Camera	2x2½"	Roll	Box	1897	achromatic			rotary			110
Falcon Camera No. 2	3½x3½"	101	Box	1897	achromatic		4.5"	rotary		Mc153	100
Falcon No. 2 Improved	3½x3½"	101	Box	1899	achromatic		4.5"	rotary		Mc153	80
Fiesta Instant Camera	67x91mm	PR10	Instant	1979							10
Film Pack "Drink First Aid"	2¼x3¼"	120	Box		Meniscus			rotary			400
Film Pack Hawk-Eye No. 2	2¼x3¼"	120	Box	1922	Meniscus			rotary		A2902	20
Film Pack Hawk-Eye No. 2A	2½x4¼"	116	Box	1923	Meniscus			rotary			10
Film Premo No.1 3¼x4¼"	3¼x4¼"	pack	FoldPk	1906	B&L Rap. Rect.			Automatic		Mc165	60
Film Premo No.1 3¼x5½"	3¼x5½"	pack	FoldPk	1906	Rapid Rectilinear			Ball Bearing		Mc165	60
Film Premo No.1 4x5"	4x5"	pack	FoldPk	1906	B&L Rap. Rect.			Automatic		Mc165	60
Film Premo No.1 5x7"	5x7"	pack	FoldPk	1906	Planatograph			B&L Automatic		Mc165	60
Film Premo No.3 3¼x4¼"	3¼x4¼"	pack	FoldPk	1906	Plastigmat	6.8		B&L Automatic			40
Film Premo No.3 3¼x5½"	3¼x5½"	pack	FoldPk	1906	Tessar	6.3		Volute			40
Film Premo No.3 4x5"	4x5"	pack	FoldPk	1906	Protar	7		B&L Automatic			30
Film Premo No.3 4x5"	4x5"	pack	FoldPk	1906	Goerz	6.8		B&L Automatic			30

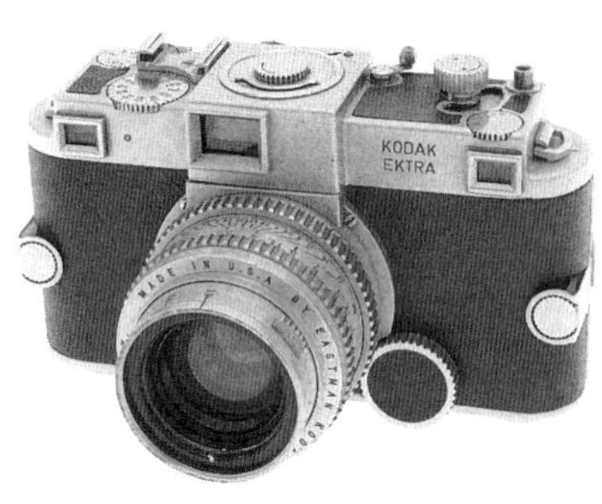

Kodak Ektra

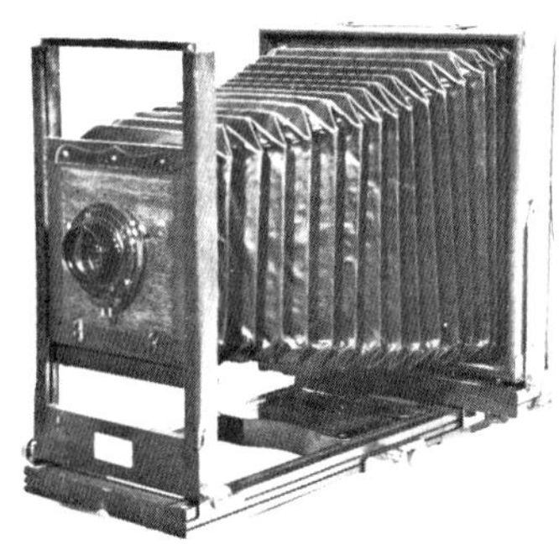

Empire State Camera

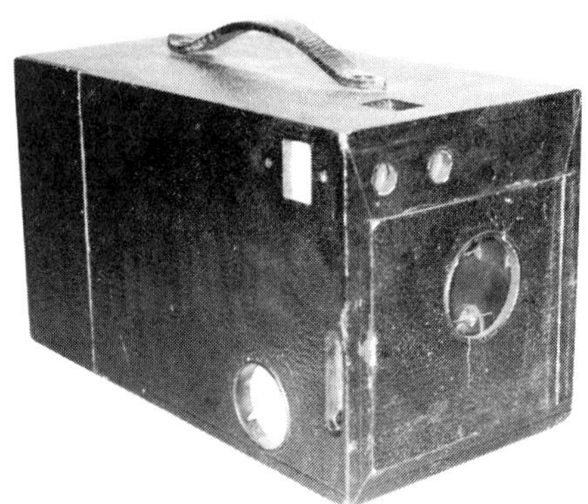

Eureka No. 4

MODEL	FORMAT	FILM	TYPE	Year	LENS	Apert	FL	SHUTTER	SPEEDS	ILLUS	U.S.$
Filmplate Premo 3¼x4¼"	3¼x4¼"	plate	FoldPl	1906	Planatograph			Automatic			70
Filmplate Premo 3¼x5½"	3¼x5½"	plate	FoldPl	1906	Tessar	6.3		Compound			70
Filmplate Premo 4x5"	4x5"	plate	FoldPl	1906	Planatograph			Automatic			70
Filmplate Premo 5x7"	5x7"	plate	FoldPl	1906	Tessar	6.3		B&L Automatic			70
Filmplate Premo Special	3¼x4¼"	plate	FoldPl	1912	Anastigmat	6.3		Compound			70
Filmplate Premo Special	3¼x5½"	plate	FoldPl	1912	Anastigmat	6.3		Compound			70
Filmplate Premo Special	4x5"	plate	FoldPl	1912	Anastigmat	6.3		Compound			70
Filmplate Premo Special	5x7"	plate	FoldPl	1912	Anastigmat	6.3		Compound			70
Fisher-Price Camera	13x17mm	110	110	1984							30
Flash Bantam	28x40mm	828	StrutRo	1947	Aanast. Special	4.5	48mm		25-200	Mc142	20
Flash Bantam	28x40mm	828	StrutRo	1948	Anastar	4.5	48mm		25-200		30
Flat Folding Kodak	4x5"	Roll	FoldRo	1894	Rapid Rectilinear			built-in		Mc154	1500
Flexo Kodak No. 2	3½x3½"	101	Box	1899	achromatic		4.5"	rotary		Mc154	60
Fling 35	24x36mm	35mm	Dispose	1988		11			1/110	Mc154	10
Fling 200	13x17mm	110	Dispose	1988		8			1/120		10
Flush Back Kodak No. 3	3¼x4¼"	118	FoldRo	1908	B&L Rap. Rect.			B&L Automatic			60
Fold. Autogr. Brownie 2	2¼x3¼"	120	VtFoldRo	1915	Rapid Rectilinear	8		Ball Bearing			10
Fold. Autogr. Brownie 2A	2½x4¼"	116	VtFoldRo	1915	Rapid Rectilinear	8		Ball Bearing		Mc146	20
Fold. Autogr. Brownie 2C	2⅞x2⅞"	130	VtFoldRo	1916	Rapid Rectilinear	8		Ball Bearing		Mc146	20
Fold. Autogr. Brownie 3A	3¼x5½"	122	VtFoldRo	1916	Rapid Rectilinear	8		Ball Bearing			10
Fold. Brownie No. 2	2¼x3¼"	120	HzFoldRo	1904	Meniscus Achrom.			Automatic		Mc146	50
Fold. Brownie No. 3	3¼x4¼"	124	HzFoldRo	1905	Meniscus Achrom.			FPK Auto		A359	50
Fold. Brownie No. 3A	3¼x5½"	122	HzFoldRo	1909	Meniscus Achrom.			FPK Auto		Mc146	40
Fold. Brownie Six-20 Mod.1	2¼x3¼"	120	VtFoldRo	1937	Meniscus				B,I	Mc146	10
Fold. Brownie Six-20 Mod.2	2¼x3¼"	120	VtFoldRo	1948						Mc146	20
Folding Bull's-Eye No. 2	3½x3½"	101	HzFoldRo	1899	Achromatic			rotary		Mc150	150
Fold. Cartr. Premo No. 2	2¼x3¼"	120	FoldRo	1916	Rapid Rectilinear			Ball Bearing			20
Fold. Cartr. Premo No. 2A	2½x4¼"	116	FoldRo	1916	Meniscus Achrom.			Ball Bearing		Mc165	20
Fold. Cartr. Premo No. 2C	2⅞x2⅞"	130	FoldRo	1917	Rapid Rectilinear			Ball Bearing			30
Fold. Cartr. Premo No. 3A	3¼x5½"	122	FoldRo	1917	Meniscus Achrom.			Ball Bearing			10
Fold. Cartr. H-E #2 (black)	2¼x3¼"	120	VtFoldRo	1926				Kodex			10
Fold. Cartr. H-E #2 (colors)	2¼x3¼"	120	VtFoldRo	1926				Kodex			30
Fold. Cartr. Hawk-Eye 2A	2½x4¼"	116	VtFoldRo	1926	Single Achromatic			Kodex			10
Fold. Cartr. Hawk-Eye 3A	3¼x5½"	122	VtFoldRo	1926	Single Achromatic			Kodak		Mc157	20
Fold. Film Pack Hawk-E. 2	2¼x3¼"	120	FoldSht	1923	Meniscus Achrom.			Hawk-Eye	I,T		20
Fold. Hawk-Eye No. 1A	2½x4¼"	116	HzFoldRo	1908	Meniscus			rotary			30
Fold. Hawk-Eye No. 3	3¼x4¼"	118	HzFoldRo	1904	Rapid Rectilinear			Automatic		Mc157	40
Fold. Hawk-Eye No. 3A	3¼x5½"	122	HzFoldRo	1908	Rapid Rectilinear			B&L Automatic			40
Fold. Hawk-Eye No. 4	4x5"	103	HzFoldRo	1904	Rapid Rectilinear			B&L Automatic			50
Fold. Hawk-Eye Special 2	2¼x3¼"	120	VtFoldRo	1928	Kodak Anastigmat	6.3					20
Fold. Hawk-Eye Special 2A	2½x4¼"	116	VtFoldRo	1928	Kodak Anastigmat	6.3				A456	20
Fold. Hawk-Eye Special 3	3¼x4¼"	118	VtFoldRo	1929	Kodak Anastigmat	6.3					20

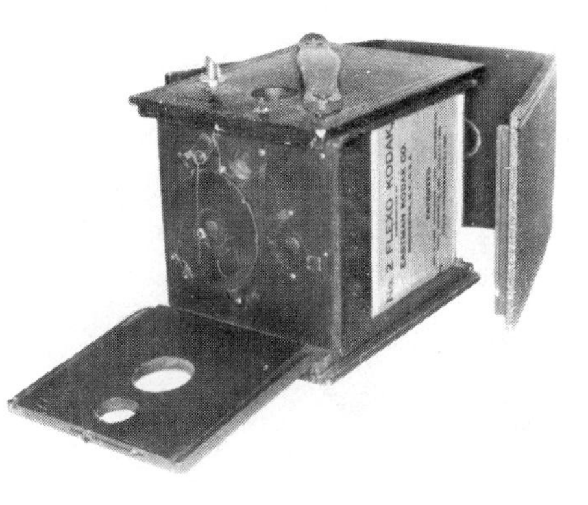

Flexo Kodak No. 2

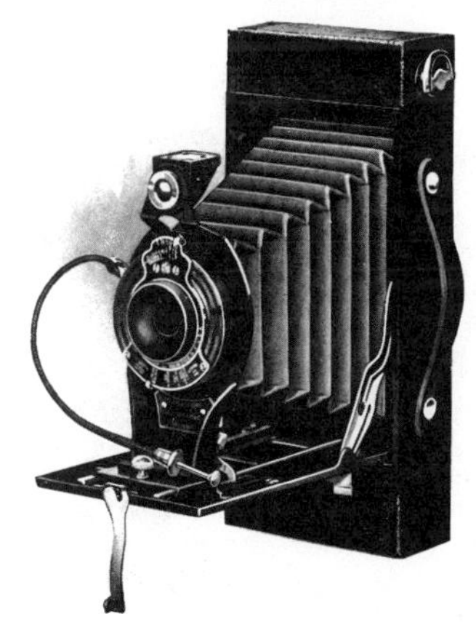

Fold. Autogr. Brownie 2C

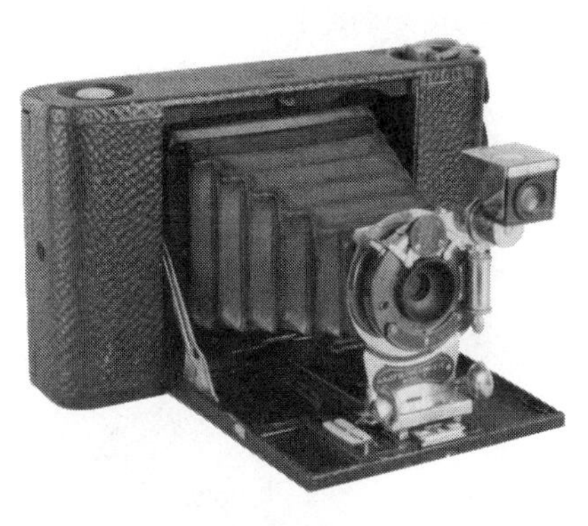

Folding Hawk-Eye No. 3

MODEL	FORMAT	FILM	TYPE	Year	LENS	Apert	FL	SHUTTER	SPEEDS	ILLUS	U.S.$
Fold. Hawk-Eye Special 3A	3¼x5½"	122	VtFoldRo	1929	Kodak Anastigmat	6.3					20
Folding Kodak No. 4	4x5"	plate	H&S	1890	B&L Universal			Sector		Mc154	630
Folding Kodak No. 4	4x5"	plate	H&S	1892	B&L Universal			Barker		Mc154	660
Folding Kodak No. 4 Impr.	4x5"	plate	H&S	1893	B&L Universal			B&L Iris		Mc154	630
Folding Kodak No. 4A	4¼x6½"	126	FoldRo	1906						Mc154	180
Folding Kodak No. 5	5x7"	plate	H&S	1890	B&L Universal			Sector		A1390	630
Folding Kodak No. 5	5x7"	plate	H&S	1892	B&L Universal			Barker			660
Fold. Kodak No. 5 Impr.	5x7"	plate	H&S	1893	B&L Universal			B&L Iris		Mc154	630
Fold. Kodak No. 5 stereo	5x7"	plate	H&S	1893	B&L Universal			B&L Iris		Mc154	800
Fold. Kodak No. 6 Impr.	6½x8½"	plate	H&S	1893	B&L Universal			B&L Iris		Mc154	900
Fold. Kodet Junior No. 4	4x5"	plate	HzFold	1894	achromatic		6"	Kodet		Mc162	670
Folding Kodet No. 3	3¼x4¼"	plate	HzFold	1894	achromatic			Kodet			700
Fold. Kodet No. 4 (early)	4x5"	plate	HzFold	1894	achromatic		6"	Kodet		Mc161	640
Folding Kodet No. 4	4x5"	plate	HzFold	1894	Rapid Rectilinear			B&L		Mc161	580
Folding Kodet No. 5	5x7"	plate	HzFold	1895	achromatic			Kodet			520
Fold. Kodet Special No. 4	4x5"	plate	HzFold	1895	Rapid Rectilinear			B&L		Mc162	490
Fold. Kodet Special No. 5	5x7"	plate	HzFold	1895	Rapid Rectilinear			B&L			580
Fold. Pocket Brownie 2	2¼x3¼"	120	HzFoldRo	1907	Meniscus Achrom.			Automatic		Mc146	70
Fold. Pocket Brownie 2A	2½x4¼"	116	HzFoldRo	1910	Meniscus Achrom.			Automatic			30
Fold.Pock.Kodak (Type 1)	2¼x3¼"	105	FoldRo	1897	Meniscus Achrom.		4"	EKC Auotm.		Mc155	180
Fold.Pock.Kodak (Type 2)	2¼x3¼"	105	FoldRo	1898	Meniscus Achrom.		4"	EKC Auotm.		Mc155	160
Fold.Pock.Kodak 0	4.5x6cm	121	FoldRo	1902	Meniscus			Automatic		Mc155	110
Fold.Pock.Kodak 1 (orig)	2¼x3¼"	105	FoldRo	1899	Meniscus Achrom.		4"	Pocket Auto		Mc155	70
Fold.Pock.Kodak 1 (2-VF)	2¼x3¼"	105	FoldRo	1905	Meniscus Achrom.		4"	Pocket Auto			50
Fold.Pock.Kodak 1 (1-VF)	2¼x3¼"	105	FoldRo	1907	Meniscus Achrom.		4"	Pocket Auto			40
Fold.Pock.Kodak 1A (orig)	2½x4¼"	116	FoldRo	1899	Meniscus Achrom.		5"	EKC Auotm.		Mc155	50
Fold.Pock.Kodak 1A (2-VF)	2½x4¼"	116	FoldRo	1905	Meniscus Achrom.		5"	EKC Auotm.		Mc155	90
Fold.Pock.Kodak 1A (1-VF)	2½x4¼"	116	FoldRo	1907	Meniscus Achrom.		5"	Pocket Auto		Mc155	60
Fold.Pock.Kodak 1A R.R.	2½x4¼"	116	FoldRo	1912	Zeiss Kodak Anast	6.3	5"	B&L Compound		Mc155	40
Fold.Pock.Kodak 2 (orig)	3½x3½"	101	FoldRo	1899	achromatic		4.5"	EKC Auotm.		Mc155	80
Fold.Pock.Kodak 2	3½x3½"	101	FoldRo	1905	Rapid Rectilinear		4.5"	FPK Auto			70
Fold.Pock.Kodak 3 (orig)	3¼x4¼"	118	FoldRo	1900	Rapid Rectilinear		5"	rotary		A373	70
Fold.Pock.Kodak 3	3¼x4¼"	118	FoldRo	1904	Zeiss Kodak Anast	6.3	5"	B&L Compound			40
Fold.Pock.Kodak 3 Deluxe	3¼x4¼"	118	FoldRo	1901	B&L Plastigmat	6.8	5"	B&L Automatic			330
Fold.Pock.Kodak 3A	3¼x5½"	122	VtFoldRo	1903	Zeiss Kodak Anast	6.3	6.5"	B&L Compound		Mc156	60
Fold.Pock.Kodak 4	4x5"	123	VtFoldRo	1907	Zeiss Kodak Anast	6.3	6.5"	B&L Compound		Mc156	80
Fold.Pock.Kodak Spcl. 1A	2½x4¼"	116	FoldRo	1908	Zeiss Kodak Anast	6.3	5"	B&L Automatic			60
Fold.Rainb.Hawk-Eye #2	2¼x3¼"	120	FoldRo	1930	Single Achromatic			Kodex			60
F.Rainb.H-E #2 (colors)	2¼x3¼"	120	FoldRo	1930	Single Achromatic			Kodex			80
F.Rainb.H-E No. 2A (black)	2½x4¼"	116	FoldRo	1930	Single Achromatic			Kodex			60
F.Rainb.H-E No. 2A (colors)	2½x4¼"	116	FoldRo	1930	Single Achromatic			Kodex			80
F.Rainb.H-E Spcl. No. 2	2¼x3¼"	120	FoldRo	1930	Anastigmat	6.3		Kodex			70

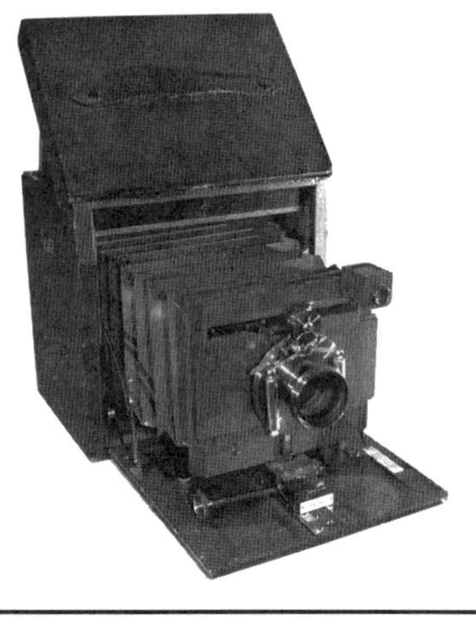

Folding Kodak No. 6 Impr.

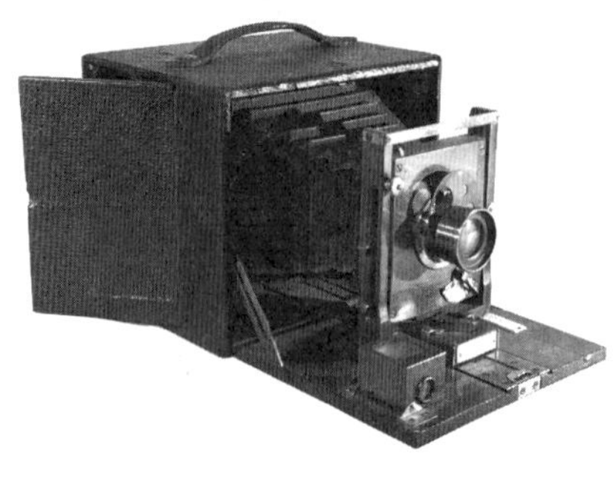

Folding Kodet No. 4

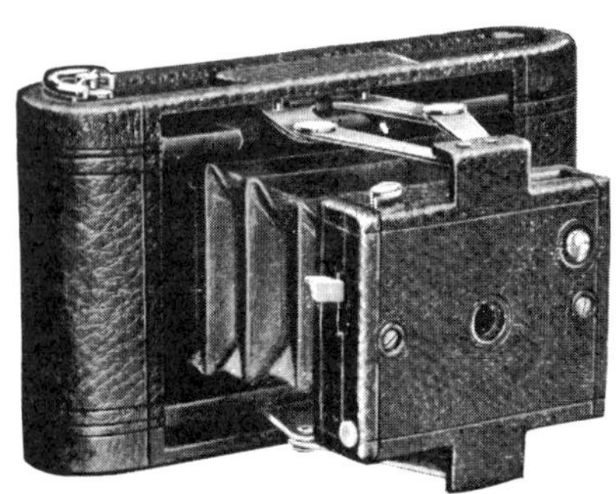

Folding Pocket Kodak No. 0

MODEL	FORMAT	FILM	TYPE	Year	LENS	Apert	FL	SHUTTER	SPEEDS	ILLUS	U.S.$
F.Rainb.H-E Spcl. No. 2A	2½x4¼"	116	FoldRo	1930	Anastigmat	6.3		Kodex			70
Fun Saver 35	24x36mm	35mm	Dispose	1990		11			1/100		10
Fun Saver 35 Flash	24x36mm	35mm	Dispose	1990		11			1/100		10
Fun Saver 35 Panoramic	24x72mm	35mm	Dispose	1990		12	25mm		1/110		10
Fun Saver 35 Vacation	24x36mm	35mm	Dispose	1994							10
Fun Saver Portrait 35	24x36mm	35mm	Dispose	1993							10
Fun Saver Telephoto 35	24x36mm	35mm	Dispose	1992		11	85mm		1/125		10
Fun Saver Wedding Pack	24x36mm	35mm	Dispose	1994		11			1/100		30
Fun Saver Weekend 35	24x36mm	35mm	Dispose	1992		11	35mm		1/150		10
Genesee	5x7"	plate	View	1886	Rapid Rectilinear						350
George Washington Box		120	Box	1932						Mc156	31000
Gift Kodak Camera No. 1A	2½x4¼"	116	FoldRo	1930	Meniscus Achrom.			Kodo		Mc156	200
Girl Guide Kodak Camera	4.5x6cm	127	FoldRo	1931	Meniscus			V.P. Rotary		Mc156	220
Girl Scout Kodak Camera	4.5x6cm	127	FoldRo	1929	Meniscus			V.P. Rotary		Mc156	180
Graffiti	13x17mm	110	110	1988	3-element	8	25mm	2-speed	125-210		10
Handle Instant Camera	67x91mm	PR10	Instant	1977		12.7	100mm	electronic	15-300	Mc156	10
Handle 2 Instant Camera	67x91mm	PR10	Instant	1979		12.7	100mm	electronic	15-300	Mc156	10
Happy Times Instant Cam.	67x91mm	PR10	Instant	1978		12.7	100mm	electronic	2-1/300	Mc156	90
Hawk-Eye No. 2	2¼x3¼"	120	Box	1913	Meniscus			rotary			10
Hawk-Eye No. 2A	2½x4¼"	116	Box	1913						Mc157	10
Hawk-Eye Special No. 2	2¼x3¼"	120	Box	1928	Meniscus			rotary			20
Hawk-Eye Special No. 2A	2½x4¼"	116	Box	1928	Meniscus			rotary			20
Hawkette Camera No. 2	2¼x3¼"	120	StrutRo	1930						Mc156	50
Hawkeye Ace	4x6.5cm	127	Box	1938					T,I	Mc157	30
Hawkeye Ace Deluxe	4x6.5cm	127	Box	1938					T,I		40
Hawkeye Disc 7000	8x10mm	Disc	Disc	1982		2.8	12.5mm	auto	100		30
Hawkeye Flashfun	4x4cm	127	RigidRo	1961	Meniscus	11		Synchro		Mc157	10
Hawkeye Flashfun II	4x4cm	127	RigidRo	1965	Meniscus	11		Synchro		Mc157	10
Hawkeye Instamatic II	28x28mm	126	126	1969	Meniscus	11			50		10
Hawkeye Instamatic A-1	28x28mm	126	126	1967	Meniscus	11			45,90	Mc158	10
Hawkeye Instamatic F	28x28mm	126	126	1963	Meniscus	11		Synchro			10
Hawkeye Instamatic R4	28x28mm	126	126	1965	Meniscus	11		Synchro			10
Hawkeye Instamatic X	28x28mm	126	126	1971	Meniscus	11					10
Hawkeye Mod. BB	2¼x3¼"	120	Box						I,T		10
Hobby	24x35mm	35mm	35C	1988	Kodak Ctd.	5.6	44mm		I		30
Instamatic 25	28x28mm	126	126VF	1966		11	43mm		40,90		10
Instamatic 26	28x28mm	126	126VF	1968		11	43mm		40,90		20
Instamatic 28	28x28mm	126	126VF	1972		11	43mm		40,90		20
Instamatic 32	28x28mm	126	126VF	1972		11	43mm		40,80		20
Instamatic 33	28x28mm	126	126VF	1963		11	43mm		40,80		20
Instamatic 36	28x28mm	126	126VF	1973		11	43mm		40,80		20
Instamatic 44	28x28mm	126	126VF	1969		11	43mm		90		10

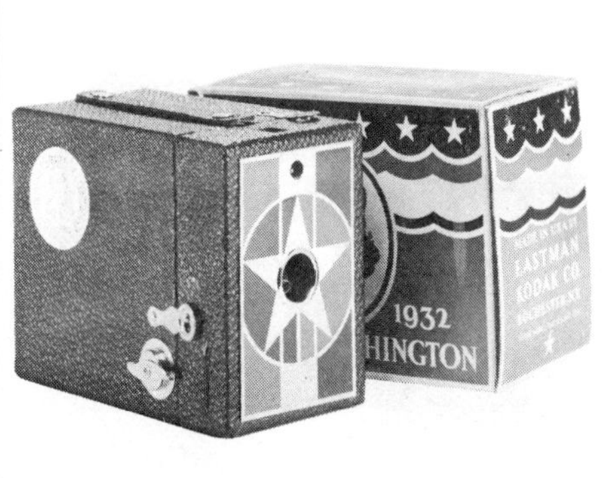

George Washington Box

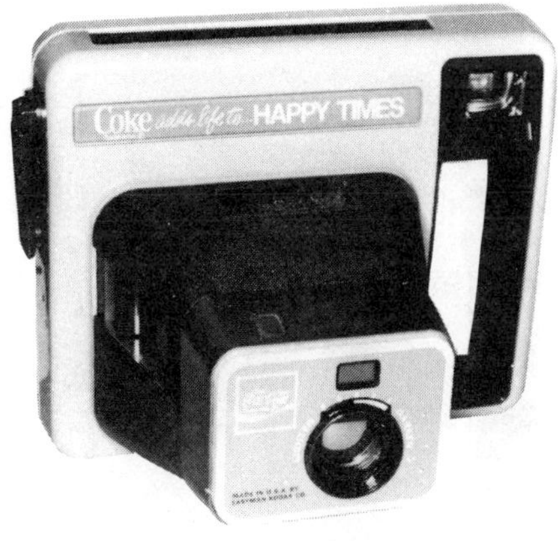

Happy Times Instant Cam.

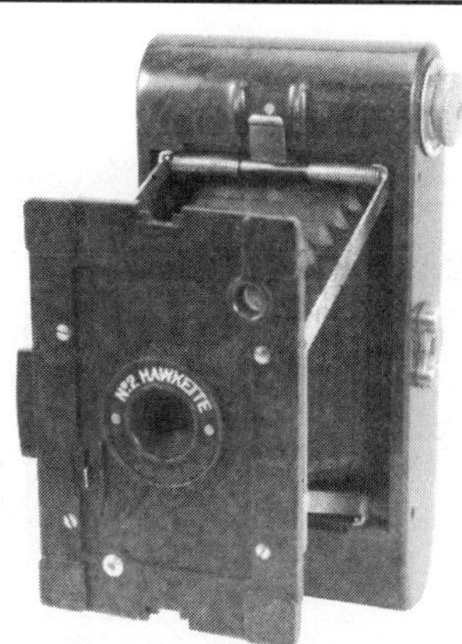

Hawkette Camera No. 2

MODEL	FORMAT	FILM	TYPE	Year	LENS	Apert	FL	SHUTTER	SPEEDS	ILLUS	U.S.$
Instamatic 50	28x28mm	126	126VF	1963		11	43mm		40,90	A1955	10
Instamatic 55-X	28x28mm	126	126VF	1971		11	43mm		60		20
Instamatic 56-X	28x28mm	126	126VF	1972		11	43mm		50		20
Instamatic 66-X	28x28mm	126	126VF	1973		11	43mm		60		20
Instamatic 76-X	28x28mm	126	126VF	1977		11	43mm		50		20
Instamatic 77-X	28x28mm	126	126VF	1977		11	43mm		50		20
Instamatic 91	13x17mm	110	126VF	1974	Triplet	11	25mm		60		10
Instamatic 92	13x17mm	110	126VF	1974	Triplet	11	25mm		60		20
Instamatic 100	28x28mm	126	126VF	1963		11	43mm		40,90	Mc159	10
Instamatic 104	28x28mm	126	126VF	1965		11	43mm		40,90		10
Instamatic 124	28x28mm	126	126VF	1967		11	43mm		40,90		10
Instamatic 130	13x17mm	110	126VF	1976	Meniscus	11	25mm		60		10
Instamatic 133	28x28mm	126	126VF	1968		11	43mm		40,80		20
Instamatic 133-X	28x28mm	126	126VF	1970		11	43mm		40,80		20
Instamatic 134	28x28mm	126	126VF	1967		11	43mm		40,90		20
Instamatic 150	28x28mm	126	126VF	1964		11	43mm		40,90		10
Instamatic 154	28x28mm	126	126VF	1965		11	43mm		40,90	Mc159	10
Instamatic 155-X	28x28mm	126	126VF	1971		11	43mm		40,80		10
Instamatic 174	28x28mm	126	126VF	1967		11	43mm		40,90		10
Instamatic 177-X	28x28mm	126	126VF	1977		11	43mm		40,80		20
Instamatic 192	13x17mm	110	126VF	1975	Triplet	11	25mm		40,80		10
Instamatic 200	28x28mm	126	126VF	1965	Kodar	7.1	41mm		40,60		10
Instamatic 204	28x28mm	126	126VF	1966	Kodar	6.6	41mm		40,60		20
Instamatic 220 (type 053)	28x28mm	126	126VF	1965		5.6	38mm		40,60		20
Instamatic 224 (type 059)	28x28mm	126	126VF	1966		5.6	38mm		40,60		10
Instamatic 230	13x17mm	110	126VF	1976		11	25mm		50100		10
Instamatic 233	28x28mm	126	126VF	1968		6.6	41mm		40,80		20
Instamatic 233-X	28x28mm	126	126VF	1970		6.6	41mm		40,80	A1959	20
Instamatic 250 (type 052)	28x28mm	126	126VF	1964		2.8			250		40
Instamatic 255-X	28x28mm	126	126VF	1971		11	41mm		40,80		20
Instamatic 277-X	28x28mm	126	126VF	1971		6.6	41mm		40,80		20
Instamatic 300	28x28mm	126	126VF	1963	Kodar	8	41mm		40,60	Mc159	20
Instamatic 304	28x28mm	126	126VF	1965	Kodar	8	41mm		40,60		10
Instamatic 314	28x28mm	126	126VF	1967	Kodar	8	41mm		45,90		10
Instamatic 324 (type 054)	28x28mm	126	126VF	1966		2.8	38mm		30125	Mc159	20
Instamatic 333 (type 066)	28x28mm	126	126VF	1968		11	43mm	electronic	10-300		30
Instamatic 333X	28x28mm	126	126VF								20
Instamatic 355-X	28x28mm	126	126VF	1971		6.7	43mm	electronic	10-300		30
Instamatic 400	28x28mm	126	126VF	1963	Kodar	8	41mm		40,60	Mc159	20
Instamatic 404	28x28mm	126	126VF	1965	Kodar	8	41mm		40,60		20
Instamatic 414	28x28mm	126	126VF	1967	Kodar	8	41mm		45,90		20
Instamatic 500 (type 048)	28x28mm	126	126VF	1963	Xenar	2.8	38mm	Compur	30-500	Mc159	50

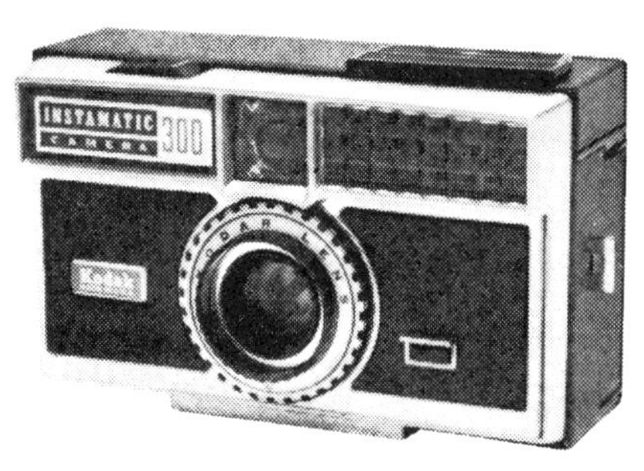

Instamatic 300

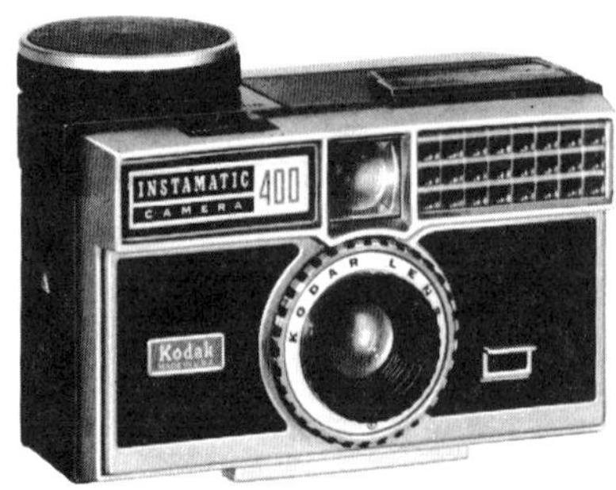

Instamatic 400

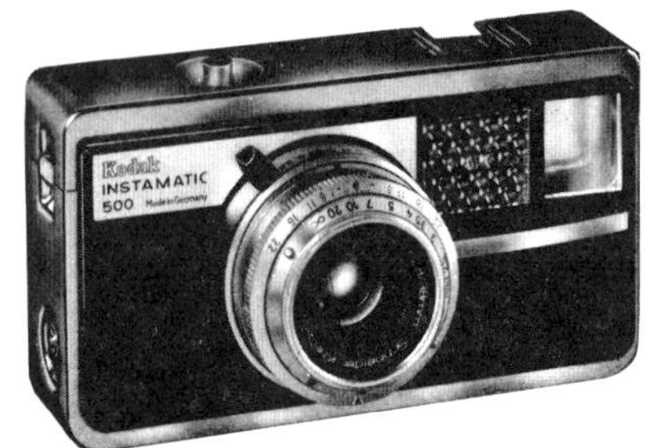

Instamatic 500 (type 048)

MODEL	FORMAT	FILM	TYPE	Year	LENS	Apert	FL	SHUTTER	SPEEDS	ILLUS	U.S.$
Instamatic 700	28x28mm	126	126VF	1963	Ektanar	2.8	38mm	Automatic	30-250	A1958	20
Instamatic 704	28x28mm	126	126VF	1965	Ektanar	2.8	38mm	Automatic	30-250		20
Instamatic 714	28x28mm	126	126VF	1968	Ektar	2.8	38mm	Automatic	30-250		30
Instamatic 800	28x28mm	126	126RF	1964	Ektanar	2.8	38mm	Automatic	30-250		30
Instamatic 804	28x28mm	126	126RF	1965	Ektanar	2.8	38mm	Automatic	30-250		40
Instamatic 814	28x28mm	126	126RF	1968	Ektar	2.8	38mm	Automatic	30-250	Mc159	20
Instamatic Reflex (black)	28x28mm	126	126slr	1969	Xenar	2.8	45mm	Compur Elec.	20-1/500		200
Instamatic Reflex (chrome)	28x28mm	126	126slr	1967	Xenar	2.8	45mm	Compur Elec.	20-1/500	Mc159	100
Instamatic S-10	28x28mm	126	126VF	1967	Kodar	11	43mm		40,125	Mc159	10
Instamatic S-20	28x28mm	126	126VF	1967	Kodar	5.6	41mm		90		10
Instamatic X-15	28x28mm	126	126VF	1970		11	43mm		45,90		10
Instamatic X-15F	28x28mm	126	126VF	1976		11	43mm		45,90		10
Instamatic X-25	28x28mm	126	126VF	1970		11	43mm		45,90		10
Instamatic X-30	28x28mm	126	126VF	1971		11	43mm	electronic	10-1/125		10
Instamatic X-30 Olympic	28x28mm	126	126VF	1972		11	43mm	electronic	10-125		20
Instamatic X-35	28x28mm	126	126VF	1970	Kodar	8	41mm		45,90		10
Instamatic X-35F	28x28mm	126	126VF	1976	Kodar	8	41mm		45,90		10
Instamatic X-45	28x28mm	126	126VF	1970	Kodar	8	41mm		45,90		20
Instamatic X-90	28x28mm	126	126RF	1970	Ektar	2.8	38mm	Automatic	30-250		30
Jiffy Kodak Six-16	2½x4¼"	616	StrutRo	1933	Twindar			built-in		Mc159	20
Jiffy Kodak Six-16 Ser. II	2½x4¼"	616	StrutRo	1937	Twindar			built-in		Mc160	30
Jiffy Kodak Six-20	2¼x3¼"	620	StrutRo	1933	Twindar			built-in		A458	10
Jiffy Kodak Six-20 Ser. II	2¼x3¼"	620	StrutRo	1937	Twindar			built-in			20
Jiffy Kodak Vest Pocket	4.5x6cm	127	StrutRo	1935	Doublet			Jiffy V.P.			20
Kodak Junior 0	6x9cm		VtFoldRo	1938	Triskop	11	105mm	Spezial	1/25		30
Kodak Junior No. 1	2¼x3¼"	120	VtFoldRo	1914	Meniscus Achrom.		4.25"	Ball Bearing		Mc160	20
Kodak Junior No. 1A	2½x4¼"	116	VtFoldRo	1914	Meniscus Achrom.		5"	Ball Bearing			30
Kodak Junior I	2¼x3¼"	620	VtFoldRo	1954				Kodette III		Mc160	10
Kodak Junior II	2¼x3¼"	620	VtFoldRo	1954	Anaston	6.3	105mm	Dakon II	25,50		20
Kodak Junior 616	2½x4¼"	616	VtFoldRo	1934	Anastigmat	6.3					40
Kodak Junior 620	2¼x3¼"	620	VtFoldRo	1936	Anastigmat	6.3				A1474	30
Kodak Jr. Six-16	2½x4¼"	616	VtFoldRo	1935	Doublet			Kodon		Mc160	20
Kodak Jr. Six-16 Ser. II	2½x4¼"	616	VtFoldRo	1937	Bimat			Kodon		Mc160	20
Kodak Jr. Six-16 Ser. III	2½x4¼"	616	VtFoldRo	1938	Kodak Anastigmat	4.5		Diomatic		Mc160	20
Kodak Jr. Six-20	2¼x3¼"	620	VtFoldRo	1935	Doublet			Kodon			20
Kodak Jr. Six-20 Ser. II	2¼x3¼"	620	VtFoldRo	1937	Bimat			Kodon		A1459	30
Kodak Jr. Six-20 Ser. III	2¼x3¼"	620	VtFoldRo	1938	Kodak Anastigmat	4.5		Diomatic			30
K-21 Aerial Camera	5x7"	Roll	Aerial	1950	Aero-Ektar	2.5	7"	focal plane	900		140
K-24 Aerial Camera	5x5"	Roll	Aerial	1950	Aero-Ektar	2.5	7"	focal plane	900		180
K-25 Aerial Camera	4x5"	Roll	Aerial	1950	Anastigmat	4.5	6.25"	focal plane			200
Kodak 35	24x36mm	35mm	35vf	1938	Kodak Anastigmat	5.6	50mm	Kodex	25-100	Mc161	30
Kodak 35	24x36mm	35mm	35vf	1938	Kodak Anaston	4.5	50mm	Fl. Diomatic		Mc161	30

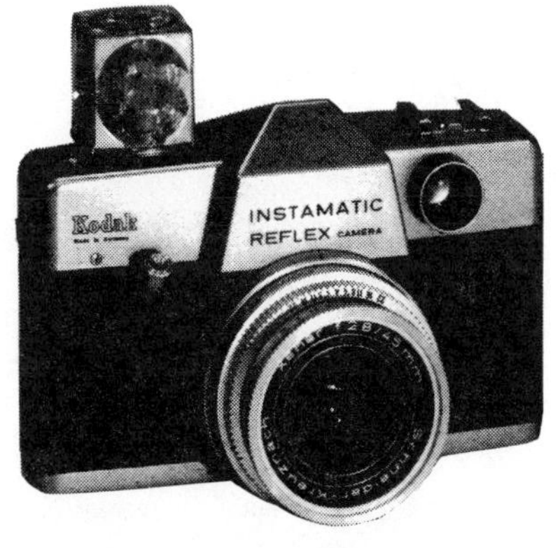

Instamatic Reflex (chrome)

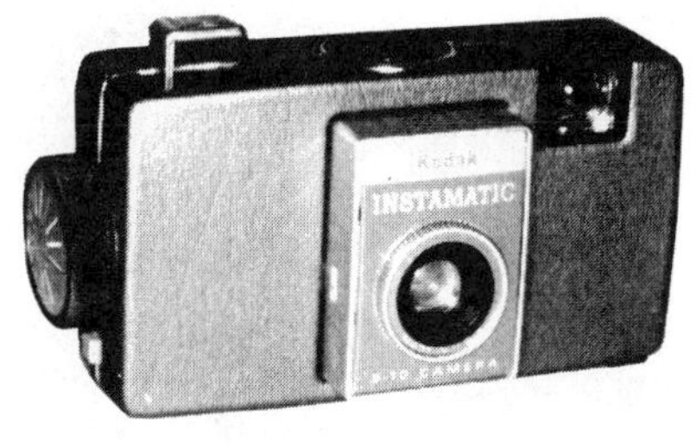

Instamatic S-10

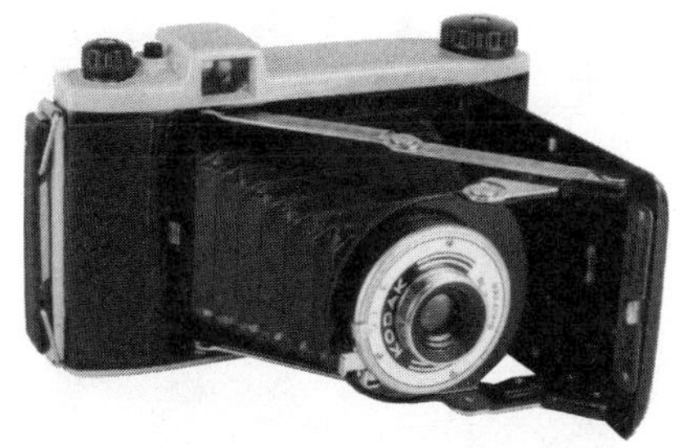

Kodak Junior I

MODEL	FORMAT	FILM	TYPE	Year	LENS	Apert	FL	SHUTTER	SPEEDS	ILLUS	U.S.$
Kodak 35 Military PH-324	24x36mm	35mm	35vf		Kodak Anastigmat	5.6	50mm	Kodex	25-100		130
Kodak 35 AF1	24x36mm	35mm	35AF	1986	Ektanar	4	35mm	Programm	1/90-300		50
Kodak 35 AF2	24x36mm	35mm	35AF	1986	Ekton	2.8	35mm	Programm	1/45-500		80
Kodak 35 EF	24x36mm	35mm	35VF	1986	Ektanar	4	35mm		1/125		40
Kodak 35 RF	24x36mm	35mm	35rf	1940	Anast. Special	3.5		Kodamatic		Mc161	40
Kodak 35 RF	24x36mm	35mm	35rf	1940	Kodak Anastar	3.5		Fl. Kodamatic			40
Kodak 66 Mod. II	6x6cm	120	HzFoldRo	1958	Anaston	6.3	75mm	Vario			30
Kodak 66 Mod. III	6x6cm	120	HzFoldRo	1958	Anaston	6.3	75mm	Vario		Mc161	30
Kodak 616	2½x4¼"	616	VtFoldRo	1934	Anastigmat	4.5		Compur S			100
Kodak 620	2¼x3¼"	620	VtFoldRo	1933	Anastigmat	6.3	100mm	Pronto S			100
Kodak 620	2¼x3¼"	620	VtFoldRo	1933	Xenar	4.5		Compur S			100
Kodak Camera (original)	2½"	Roll	RollBox	1888	Rapid Rectilinear	9	57mm	string-set		Mc140	3900
Kodak Camera (replica)			RollBox	1988							390
Kodak Camera No. 1	2½"	Roll	RollBox	1889	Rapid Rectilinear	9	57mm	sector		Mc140	1500
Kodak Camera No. 2	3½"	Roll	RollBox	1889	Rapid Rectilinear		3.25"	sector		Mc140	620
Kodak Camera No. 3	3¼x4¼"	Roll	RollBox	1890	B&L Universal		5⅝"	sector		Mc140	290
Kodak Camera No. 3 Jr.	3¼x4¼"	Roll	RollBox	1890	B&L Universal		5⅝"	sector		Mc140	530
Kodak Camera No. 4	4x5"	Roll	RollBox	1890	B&L Universal		6.5"	sector		Mc140	400
Kodak Camera No. 4 Jr.	4x5"	Roll	RollBox	1890	B&L Universal		6.5"	sector		Mc140	460
Kodak Series II No. 3A	3¼x5½"	122	VtFoldRo	1936	Kodak Anastigmat	6.3		Diodak		Mc161	40
Kodak Series III No. 1	2¼x3¼"	120	VtFoldRo	1926	Kodak Anastigmat	6.3	4.25"	Diomatic		Mc161	20
Kodak Series III No. 1A	2½x4¼"	116	VtFoldRo	1924	Kodak Anastigmat	6.3		Diomatic			20
Kodak Series III No. 2C	2⅞x2⅞"	130	VtFoldRo	1924	Kodak Anastigmat	6.3		Diomatic			20
Kodak Series III No. 3	3¼x4¼"	118	VtFoldRo	1926	Kodak Anastigmat	6.3		Diomatic		A384	30
Kodak Series III No. 3A	3¼x5½"	122	VtFoldRo	1941	Kodak Anastigmat	6.3		Diomatic		Mc161	40
Kodamatic 920	67x91mm	PR10	Instant	1982		12.8	100mm	electronic	15-400		20
Kodamatic 940	67x91mm	PR10	Instant	1983		12.8	100mm	electronic	15-250		20
Kodamatic 950	67x91mm	PR10	Instant	1983		12.8	100mm	electronic	15-300		10
Kodamatic 960	67x91mm	PR10	Instant	1982		12.8	100mm	electronic	15-250		30
Kodamatic 970L	67x91mm	PR10	Instant	1982		12.8	100mm	electronic	15-250		30
Kodamatic 980L	67x91mm	PR10	Instant	1982		11	100mm	electronic	4-150		30
Kodet No. 3	3¼x4¼"	plate	PlateBox	1894	achromatic			Kodet			1000
Kodet No. 4	4x5"	plate	PlateBox	1894	achromatic		6"	Kodet		Mc161	560
Librette No. 75	6x9cm	120	VtFoldRo	1933	Xenar	4.5	105mm	Compur S			70
Matchbox Camera	½x½"	16mm	Submin	1944		5	1"		1/50	Mc162	1500
MD35 (black)	24x36mm	35mm	35VF	1988	Ektanar	4	3.8	Programmed	145-400		50
MD35 (red)	24x36mm	35mm	35VF	1988	Ektanar	4	3.8	Programmed	145-400		50
Medalist I (620)	2¼x3¼"	620	MedRo	1941	Ektar	3.5	100mm	Supermatic	400	Mc162	200
Medalist I Disc	8x10mm	Disc	Disc	1982		2.8	12.5mm	auto	100		20
Medalist II (620)	2¼x3¼"	620	MedRo	1946	Ektar	3.5	100mm	Fl. Supermatic		Mc162	220
Medalist II Disc	8x10mm	Disc	Disc	1982		2.8	12.5mm	auto	100		20
Medalist Tele disc	8x10mm	Disc	Disc	1982		2.8	12.5mm	auto	100		20

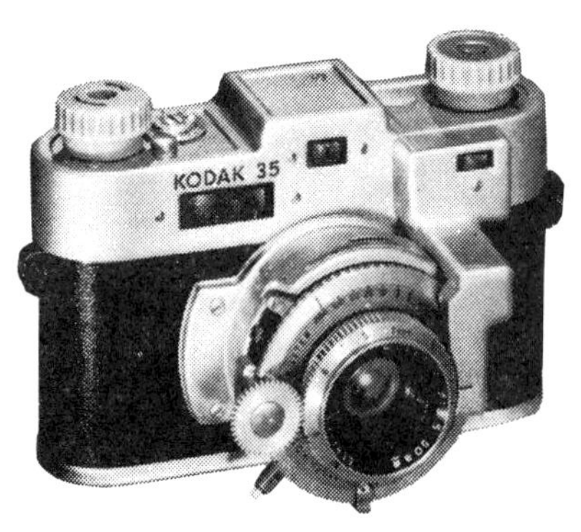

Kodak 35 RF

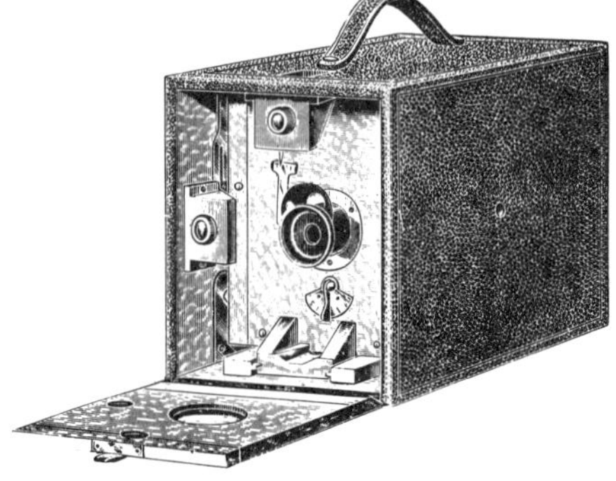

Kodet No. 4

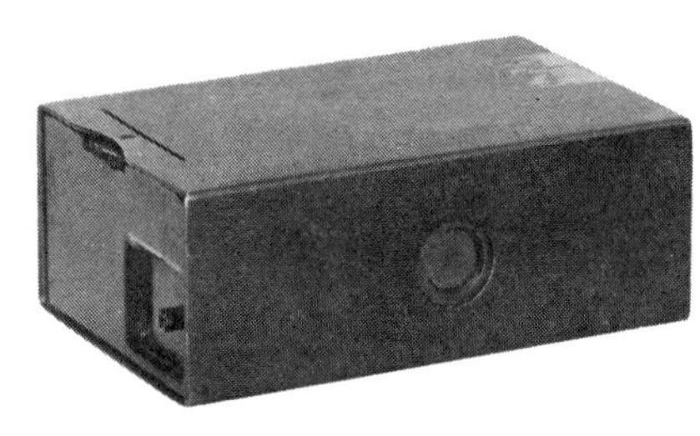

Matchbox Camera

MODEL	FORMAT	FILM	TYPE	Year	LENS	Apert	FL	SHUTTER	SPEEDS	ILLUS	U.S.$
Mickey-Matic	13x17mm	110	110	1988							50
Mini-Instamatic S30	13x17mm	110	110VF	1976		5.6	25mm		40,80		20
Mini-Instamatic S40	13x17mm	110	110VF	1976		5.6	25mm		40,80		30
Monitor Six-16	2½x4¼"	616	FoldRo	1939	Kodak Anastigmat	4.5	127mm	Kodamatic		Mc162	30
Monitor Six-16	2½x4¼"	616	FoldRo	1939	Anast. Special	4.5	127mm	Supermatic	10-400		30
Monitor Six-20	2¼x3¼"	620	FoldRo	1939	Anast. Special	4.5	127mm	Supermatic			40
Motormatic 35	24x36mm	35mm	35SprMot	1960	Ektarnar	2.8		EKC Autom.		Mc162	70
Motormatic 35F	24x36mm	35mm	35SprMot	1962	Ektarnar	2.8		EKC Autom.		A2143	30
Motormatic 35R4	24x36mm	35mm	35SprMot	1965	Ektarnar	2.8		EKC Autom.		Mc162	30
Ordinary Kodak A	2¾x3¼"	Roll	RollBox	1891	achromatic		4"	sector		Mc162	1700
Ordinary Kodak B	3½x4"	Roll	RollBox	1891	achromatic		6"	sector		Mc162	1300
Ordinary Kodak C	4x5"	Roll	RollBox	1891	achromatic		7"	sector		Mc162	1200
Ordinary Glass Plate C	4x5"	plate	PlateBox	1891	achromatic		7"	sector			1200
Panoram No. 1 Mod. A	2¼x7"	105	WideAng	1900	Rapid Rectilinear			panoramic		Mc163	370
Panoram No. 1 Mod. B	2¼x7"	105	WideAng	1901	Rapid Rectilinear			panoramic		Mc163	290
Panoram No. 1 Mod. C	2¼x7"	105	WideAng	1903	Meniscus			panoramic		Mc163	290
Panoram No. 1 Mod. D	2¼x7"	105	WideAng	1907	Meniscus			panoramic		Mc163	310
Panoram No. 3A	3¼x10⅜"	122	WideAng	1926	Meniscus			panoramic		A2018	400
Panoram No. 4 Mod. A	3½x12"	103	WideAng	1899	Rapid Rectilinear	10	5"	panoramic			290
Panoram No. 4 Mod. B	3½x12"	103	WideAng	1900	Rapid Rectilinear	10	5"	panoramic		A936	350
Panoram No. 4 Mod. C	3½x12"	103	WideAng	1903	Meniscus			panoramic		A936	230
Panoram No. 4 Mod. D	3½x12"	103	WideAng	1907	Meniscus			panoramic		A936	230
Party Star	67x91mm	PR10	Instant	1983		12.8	100mm	electronic	2-1/300		30
Party Star Trimprint	67x91mm	PR10	Instant	1984		12.8	100mm	electronic	2-1/300		30
Partyflash Instant Camera	67x91mm	PR10	Instant	1981		12.8	100mm	electronic	2-1/300		30
Partyflash II Instant Camera	67x91mm	PR10	Instant	1982		12.8	100mm	electronic	2-1/300		30
Partytime Instant Camera	67x91mm	PR10	Instant	1980		12.8	100mm	electronic	2-1/300		30
Peer 100	13x17mm	110	Disguised	1974	Triplet	11	25mm		60	A1966	390
Petite Camera	1½x2½"	127	FoldRo	1929	Meniscus			V.P. Rotary		Mc163	150
Petite "Diamond Door"	1½x2½"	127	FoldRo	1929	Meniscus			V.P. Rotary		Mc163	330
Petite "Step Pattern"	1½x2½"	127	FoldRo	1929	Meniscus			V.P. Rotary		Mc163	300
Pin-Hole Camera			RollBox		pinhole					Mc163	100
Pleaser	67x91mm	PR10	Instant	1980		12.7	100mm	electronic	15-300		10
Pleaser II	67x91mm	PR10	Instant	1982		12.8	100mm	electronic	2-300		10
Pleaser Trimprint	67x91mm	PR10	Instant	1984		12.8	100mm	electronic	2-300		10
Kodak Pliant Modèle B11	6x9cm	620	FoldRo	1950	Achromat						20
Plico	3½x3½"	101	RollBox	1904	Achromat			rotary			60
Pocket A-1	13x17mm	110	110VF	1978		11	25mm		50		10
Pocket B-1	13x17mm	110	110VF	1979		11	25mm		50	Mc163	10
Pocket Instamatic 10	13x17mm	110	110VF	1973		11	25mm		40,90	Mc163	10
Pocket Instamatic 20	13x17mm	110	110VF	1972		9.5	25mm		40,100		10
Pocket Instamatic 30	13x17mm	110	110VF	1972		9.5	25mm	electronic	5-1/160		10

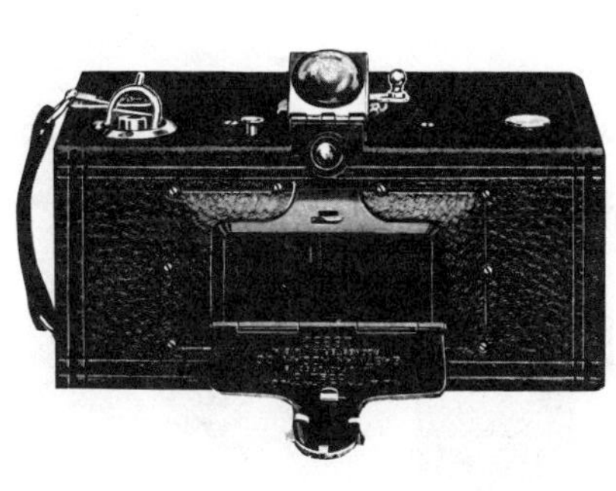

Panoram No. 1

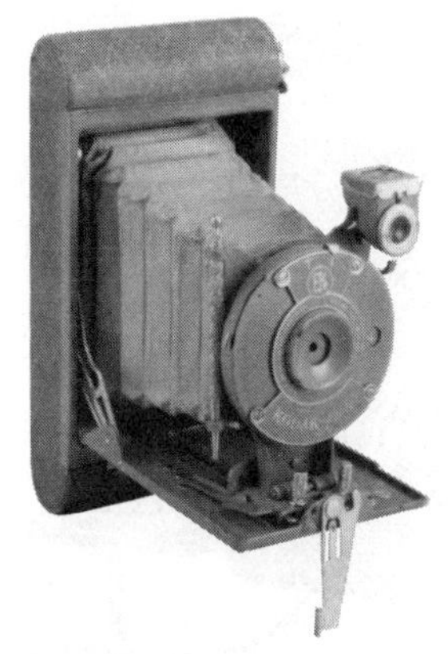

Petite Camera

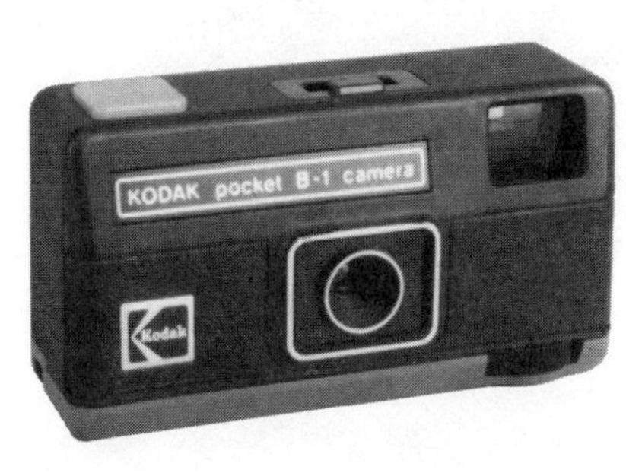

Pocket B-1

MODEL	FORMAT	FILM	TYPE	Year	LENS	Apert	FL	SHUTTER	SPEEDS	ILLUS	U.S.$
Pocket Instamatic 40	13x17mm	110	110VF	1972		8	25mm	electronic	5-1/225		10
Pocket Instamatic 50	13x17mm	110	110VF	1972	Ektar	2.7	26mm	electronic	5-1/250		30
Pocket Instamatic 60	13x17mm	110	110VF	1972	Ektar	2.7	26mm	electronic	5-1/250		30
Pocket Instamatic 100	13x17mm	110	110VF	1972		11	25mm		60	A1979	10
Pocket Instamatic 101	13x17mm	110	110VF	1974		11	25mm		60		10
Pocket Instamatic 200	13x17mm	110	110VF	1972	Triplet	11	25mm		40,80		10
Pocket Instamatic 300	13x17mm	110	110VF	1972	Triplet	5.6	25mm		40,80		10
Pocket Instamatic 400	13x17mm	110	110VF	1972	Triplet	11	25mm	electronic	20-300		10
Pocket Instamatic 500	13x17mm	110	110VF	1972	Triplet	5.6	25mm	electronic	20-300		10
Pocket Kodak (1895)	1½x2"	102	RollBox	1895	Meniscus	10	2.5"	sector		Mc163	190
Pocket Kodak (1896-1900)	1½x2"	102	RollBox	1896	Meniscus	10	2.5"	rotary		Mc163	130
Pock. Kodak Jr. No. 1	2¼x3¼"	120	FoldRo	1929	Meniscus			Kodo			10
Pock. Kodak Jr. 1 (colors)	2¼x3¼"	120	FoldRo	1929	Meniscus			Kodo			80
Pock. Kodak Jr. No. 1A	2½x4¼"	116	FoldRo	1929	Meniscus			Kodo			10
Pock. Kodak Jr. 1A (colors)	2½x4¼"	116	FoldRo	1929	Meniscus			Kodo			100
Pocket Kodak No. 1	2¼x3¼"	120	FoldRo	1926	Kodak Anastigmat	6.3		Kodex		A454	10
Pock. Kodak No. 1 (colors)	2¼x3¼"	120	FoldRo	1926	Kodar	7.9		Kodex			30
Pocket Kodak No. 1A	2½x4¼"	116	FoldRo	1926	Kodak Anastigmat	6.3		Kodex			10
Pock. Kodak 1A (colors)	2½x4¼"	116	FoldRo	1926	Kodar	7.9		Kodex			30
Pock. Kodak No. 2C	$2\frac{7}{8}$x$2\frac{7}{8}$"	130	FoldRo	1925	Kodar	7.9		Kodex			10
Pock. Kodak No. 3A	3¼x5½"	122	FoldRo	1927	Kodar	7.9		Kodex		Mc164	20
Pock. Kodak Ser. II No. 1	2¼x3¼"	120	FoldRo	1922	Meniscus Achrom.			Kodex			10
Pock. Kodak Ser. II No. 1A	2½x4¼"	116	FoldRo	1923	Kodak Anastigmat	7.7		Diomatic		Mc164	10
P. Kodak Ser. II 1A (colors)	2½x4¼"	116	FoldRo	1928	Meniscus Achrom.			Kodex		Mc164	30
Pock. Kodak Spcl. No. 1	2¼x3¼"	120	FoldRo	1926	Kodak Anastigmat	6.3		Kodamatic		Mc164	20
Pock. Kodak Spcl. No. 1	2¼x3¼"	120	FoldRo	1926	Kodak Anastigmat	4.5		Kodamatic			20
Pock. Kodak Spcl. No. 1A	2½x4¼"	116	FoldRo	1926	Kodak Anastigmat	5.6		Kodamatic			20
Pock. Kodak Spcl. No. 1A	2½x4¼"	116	FoldRo	1926	Kodak Anastigmat	4.5		Kodamatic			20
Pock. Kodak Spcl. No. 2C	$2\frac{7}{8}$x$2\frac{7}{8}$"	130	FoldRo	1928	Kodak Anastigmat	5.6		Kodamatic			20
Pock. Kodak Spcl. No. 2C	$2\frac{7}{8}$x$2\frac{7}{8}$"	130	FoldRo	1928	Kodak Anastigmat	4.5		Kodamatic			20
Pock. Kodak Spcl. No. 3	3¼x4¼"	118	FoldRo	1926	Kodak Anastigmat	6.3		Kodamatic			20
Pock. Kodak Spcl. No. 3	3¼x4¼"	118	FoldRo	1926	Kodak Anastigmat	4.5		Kodamatic			20
Pocket Premo	2¼x3¼"	pack	FoldPk	1918	Meniscus Achrom.			Ball Bearing		Mc166	50
Pocket Premo C	3¼x4¼"	plate	FoldPl	1904	Rapid Rectilinear			Gem Autom.		Mc166	50
Pocket Premo C	3¼x5½"	plate	FoldPl	1904	Rapid Rectilinear			Automatic		Mc166	50
Pony II	24x36mm	35mm	35vf	1957	Kodak Anastar	3.9	44mm		I		10
Pony IV	24x36mm	35mm	35vf	1957	Kodak Anastar	3.5	44mm	Flash 250		Mc164	10
Pony 135	24x36mm	35mm	35vf	1950	Kodak Anaston	4.5	51mm	Flash 200			10
Pony 135 "Made in France"	24x36mm	35mm	35vf	1956	Angenieux	3.5	45mm		1/25-150	Mc164	20
Pony 135 Mod. B	24x36mm	35mm	35vf	1953	Kodak Anaston	4.5	44mm	Flash 200			10
Pony 135 Mod. C	24x36mm	35mm	35vf	1955	Kodak Anaston	3.5	44mm	Flash 300			10
Pony 828	28x40mm	828	TelescRo	1949	Kodak Anaston	4.5		Flash 200		Mc164	10

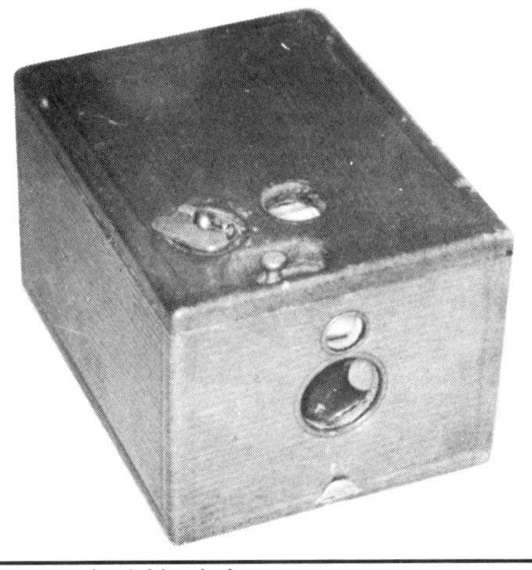

Pocket Kodak

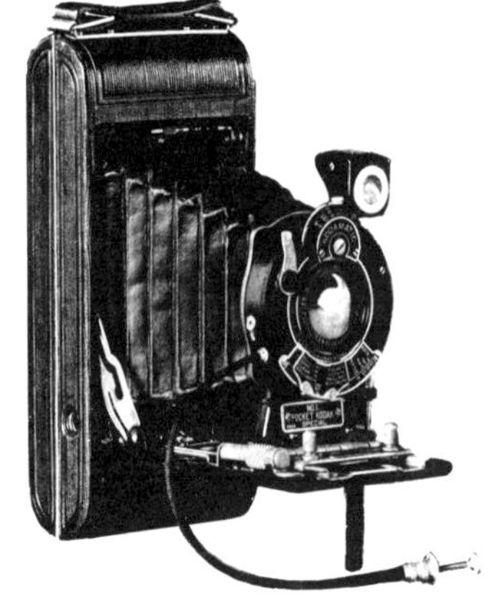

Pock. Kodak Special No. 1

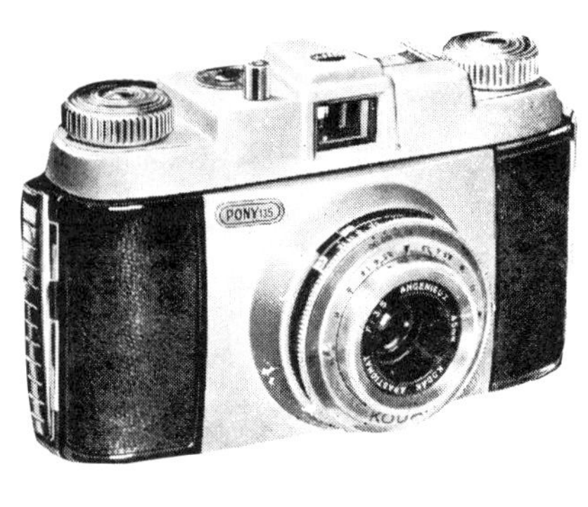

Pony 135 "Made in France"

MODEL	FORMAT	FILM	TYPE	Year	LENS	Apert	FL	SHUTTER	SPEEDS	ILLUS	U.S.$
Pony Flash	24x36mm	35mm	35vf	1956	Angenieux	3.5	45mm	Flash 200			50
Pony Microscope Camera	24x36mm	35mm	SciMed	1950							50
Pony Premo No. 1	4x5"	plate	FoldPl	1904	Rapid Rectilinear			Gem Autom.			90
Pony Premo No. 2 3¼x4¼"	3¼x4¼"	plate	FoldPl	1898	Rapid Rectilinear			Gem Autom.			90
Pony Premo No. 2 4x5"	4x5"	plate	FoldPl	1898	Rapid Rectilinear			Safety			90
Pony Premo No. 2 5x7"	5x7"	plate	FoldPl	1898	Rapid Rectilinear			Automatic			90
Pony Premo No. 3 3¼x4¼"	3¼x4¼"	plate	FoldPl	1898	Rapid Rectilinear			B&L Automatic		Mc166	80
Pony Premo No. 3 4x5"	4x5"	plate	FoldPl	1898	Rapid Rectilinear			B&L Automatic		Mc166	120
Pony Premo No. 3 5x7"	5x7"	plate	FoldPl	1898	Rapid Rectilinear			B&L Automatic		Mc166	120
Pony Premo No. 4 4x5"	4x5"	plate	FoldPl	1898	achromatic			Victor		Mc166	90
Pony Premo No. 4 5x7"	5x7"	plate	FoldPl	1898	Ross Homocentric	5.6		B&L Automatic		Mc166	110
Pony Premo No. 6 4x5"	4x5"	plate	FoldPl	1899	Victor R.R.			Victor			70
Pony Premo No. 6 5x7"	5x7"	plate	FoldPl	1899	Planatograph			B&L Automatic			140
Pony Premo No. 6 6½x8½"	6½x8½"	plate	FoldPl	1899	Victor R.R.			Victor			160
Pony Premo No. 6 8x10"	8x10"	plate	FoldPl	1899	Collinear	5.6		B&L Iris			160
Pony Premo No. 7 4x5"	4x5"	plate	FoldPl	1902	Collinear	5.6		B&L Automatic			60
Pony Premo No. 7 5x7"	5x7"	plate	FoldPl	1902	Tessar	6.3		Compound			120
Pony Premo No. 7 6½x8½"	6½x8½"	plate	FoldPl	1902	Zeiss Protar	7		Compound			160
Popular Brownie	2¼x3¼"	620	Box	1937						Mc147	20
Portr. Brownie No. 2 (black)	2¼x3¼"	120	Box	1929							10
Portr. Brownie No. 2 (color	2¼x3¼"	120	Box	1939							50
Portrait Hawkeye A-Star-A	2¼x3¼"	620	Box	1933						Mc158	50
Portrait Hawkeye No. 2	2¼x3¼"	120	Box	1930					I,T		10
Premo Box Film 3¼x4¼"	3¼x4¼"	pack	PackBox	1903	achromatic			Automatic		Mc164	20
Premo Box Film 4x5"	4x5"	pack	PackBox	1903	achromatic			Automatic		Mc164	20
Premo Junior No. 0	1¾x2¼"	pack	PackBox	1911	achromatic			rotary			30
Premo Junior No. 1	2¼x3¼"	pack	PackBox	1908	Meniscus Achrom.			rotary		Mc165	50
Premo Junior No. 1A	2½x4¼"	pack	PackBox	1909	Meniscus Achrom.			rotary		Mc165	30
Premo Junior No. 3	3¼x4¼"	pack	PackBox	1909	Meniscus Achrom.			rotary			30
Premo Junior No. 4	4x5"	pack	PackBox	1909	Meniscus Achrom.			rotary			30
Premo No. 8 3¼x5½"	3¼x5½"	plate	FoldPl	1913	Anastigmat			Ball Bearing		Mc165	50
Premo No. 8 4x5"	4x5"	plate	FoldPl	1913	Planatograph			Ball Bearing		Mc165	60
Premo No. 8 5x7"	5x7"	plate	FoldPl	1913	Planatograph			Ball Bearing		Mc165	80
Premo No. 9 3¼x5½"	3¼x5½"	plate	FoldPl	1913	Planatograph			Automatic		Mc165	50
Premo No. 9 3¼x5½"	3¼x5½"	plate	FoldPl	1913	Anastigmat	6.3		Compound		Mc165	50
Premo No. 9 4x5"	4x5"	plate	FoldPl	1913	Planatograph			Automatic		Mc165	90
Premo No. 9 4x5"	4x5"	plate	FoldPl	1913	Anastigmat	6.3		Compound		Mc165	70
Premo No. 9 5x7"	5x7"	plate	FoldPl	1913	Planatograph			Automatic		Mc165	100
Premo No. 9 5x7"	5x7"	plate	FoldPl	1913	Anastigmat	6.3		Compound		Mc165	100
Premo No. 12 2¼x3¼"	2¼x3¼"	plate	FoldPl	1916	B&L Anastigmat	6.3		Optimo		Mc165	50
Premoette	2¼x3¼"	pack	FoldPk	1906	Meniscus			Automatic		Mc166	50
Premoette Jr.	2¼x3¼"	pack	FoldPk	1911	achromatic			Special Auto			30

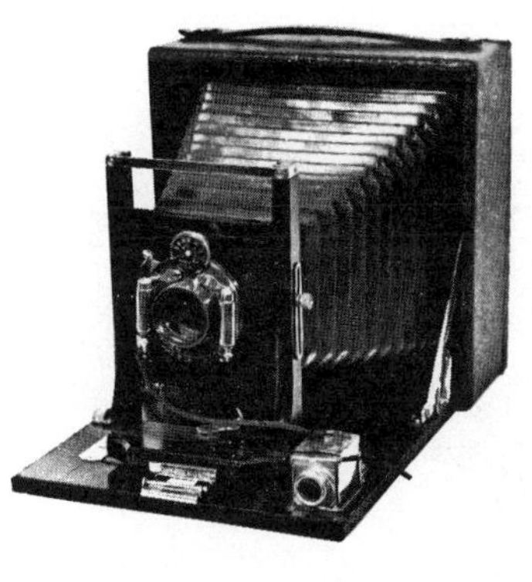

Pony Premo No. 3

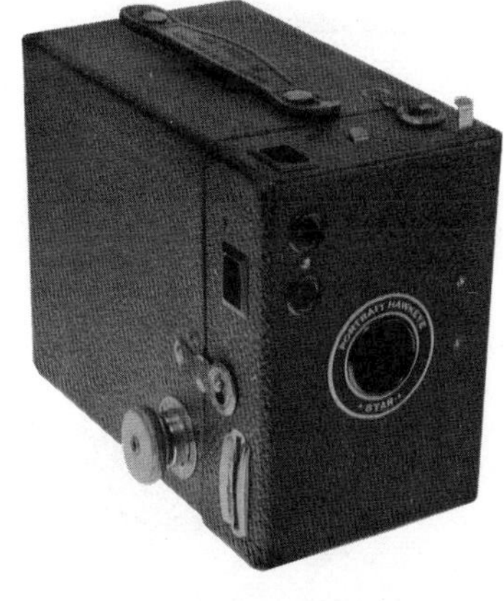

Portrait Hawkeye A-Star-A

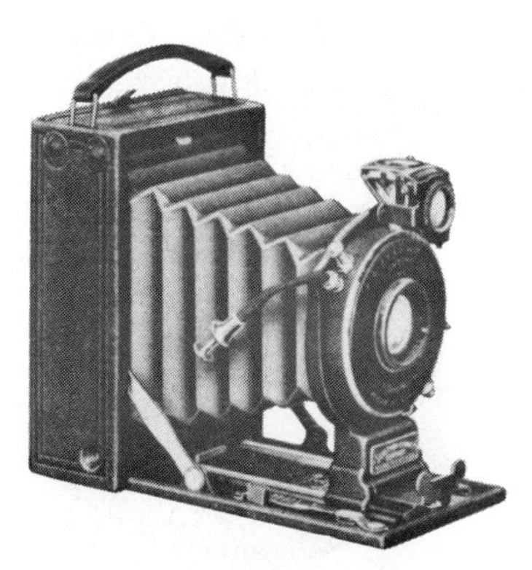

Premo No. 12

MODEL	FORMAT	FILM	TYPE	Year	LENS	Apert	FL	SHUTTER	SPEEDS	ILLUS	U.S.$
Premoette Jr. No. 1	2¼x3¼"	pack	FoldPk	1913	Planatograph			Ball Bearing		Mc166	40
Premoette Jr. No. 1 Spcl.	2¼x3¼"	pack	FoldPk	1913	Kodak Anastigmat	6.3		Ball Bearing			40
Premoette Jr. No. 1A	2½x4¼"	pack	FoldPk	1913	Meniscus Achrom.			Ball Bearing			40
Premoette Jr. No. 1A Spcl.	2½x4¼"	pack	FoldPk	1913	Kodak Anastigmat	6.3		Compound			60
Premoette No. 1	2¼x3¼"	pack	FoldPk	1906	Planatograph			Ball Bearing			50
Premoette No. 1A	2½x4¼"	pack	FoldPk	1909	Meniscus			Automatic			40
Premoette No. 1A	2½x4¼"	pack	FoldPk	1909	achromatic			Automatic			50
Premoette Senior 2½x4¼"	2½x4¼"	pack	FoldPk	1915	Kodak Anastigmat	7.7		Ball Bearing		Mc166	50
Premoette Senior 3¼x4¼"	3¼x4¼"	pack	FoldPk	1915	Rapid Rectilinear			Ball Bearing		Mc166	50
Premoette Senior 3¼x5½"	3¼x5½"	pack	FoldPk	1915	Kodak Anastigmat	7.7		Ball Bearing		Mc166	50
Premoette Special No. 1	2¼x3¼"	pack	FoldPk	1909	Rapid Rectilinear			Automatic		Mc166	50
Premoette Special No. 1A	2½x4¼"	pack	FoldPk	1909	Rapid Rectilinear			Automatic		Mc166	50
Premograph	3¼x4¼"	pack	LgSLR	1907	Single Achromatic			Premograph		Mc166	240
Premograph No. 2	3¼x4¼"	pack	LgSLR	1908	Rapid Rectilinear			Premograph		Mc167	190
Premograph No. 2	3¼x4¼"	pack	LgSLR	1908	Tessar	6.3		Compound		Mc167	190
Pupille	3x4cm	127	RigidRo	1932	Xenon	2	45mm	Compur	1-300	Mc167	290
Pupille (gold)	3x4cm	127	RigidRo		Xenon	2	45mm	Compur	1-300		1100
Quick Focus Kodak 3B	3¼x5½"	125	RollBox	1906	achromatic		6.5"	rotary		Mc167	200
Radiograph Copying Cam.	24x36mm	35mm	SciMed		Kodak Anaston	4.5	51mm	Flash 200		Mc167	30
Rainbow Hawk-Eye No. 2	2¼x3¼"	120	Box	1929	Meniscus			rotary		Mc158	10
Rainb. Hawk-Eye 2 (colors)	2¼x3¼"	120	Box	1929	Meniscus			rotary			50
Rainb. Hawk-Eye 2 Mod.B	2¼x3¼"	120	Box	1930	Meniscus			rotary			10
Rainb. Hawk-E.2 / B (colors	2¼x3¼"	120	Box	1931	Meniscus			rotary			30
Rainb. Hawk-Eye No.2A	2½x4¼"	116	Box	1931	Meniscus			rotary			10
Rainb. Hawk-Eye 2A(colors	2½x4¼"	116	Box	1931	Meniscus			rotary			100
Ranca	3x4cm	127	RigidRo	1932	Nagel Anastigmat	4.5		Pronto			230
Recomar Mod. 18	2¼x3¼"	plate	FoldPl	1932	Kodak Anaston	4.5	105mm	Compur			80
Recomar Mod. 33	3¼x4¼"	plate	FoldPl	1932	Kodak Anaston	4.5	135mm	Compur		Mc167	80
Kodak Reflex	2¼x2¼"	620	TLR	1946	Kodak	3.5		Fl. Kodamatic		Mc160	50
Kodak Reflex IA	2¼x2¼"	620	TLR	1950	Kodak	3.5		Fl. Kodamatic		Mc161	70
Kodak Reflex II	2¼x2¼"	620	TLR	1948	Kodak	3.5		Fl. Kodamatic		Mc161	60
Regent	6x9cm	620	FoldRo	1935	Xenar	3.8	105mm	Compur-Rapid		Mc167	170
Regent	6x9cm	620	FoldRo	1935	Tessar	4.5	105mm	Compur S	250	Mc167	170
Regent II	6x9cm	120	FoldRo	1939	Xenar	3.5	105mm	Compur-Rapid			1100
Retina (Type 117)	24x36mm	35mm	35Fold	1934	Xenar	3.5	50mm	Compur	300	Mc167	180
Retina (Type 118)	24x36mm	35mm	35Fold	1935	Xenar	3.5	50mm	Compur-Rapid	500	Mc168	120
Retina (Type 119)	24x36mm	35mm	35Fold	1936	Xenar	3.5	50mm	Compur-Rapid	500	Mc168	70
Retina (Type 126)	24x36mm	35mm	35Fold	1936	Ektar	3.5	50mm	Compur-Rapid	500	Mc168	70
Retina I (Type 010)	24x36mm	35mm	35Fold	1946	Xenar	3.5	50mm	Compur	300		60
Retina I (Type 013)	24x36mm	35mm	35Fold	1949	Xenar	3.5	50mm	Compur-Rapid	500		70
Retina I (Type 013/1)	24x36mm	35mm	35Fold	1950	Ektar	3.5	50mm	Compur-Rapid	500		70
Retina I (Type 141)	24x36mm	35mm	35Fold	1937	Ektar	3.5	50mm	Compur	300		80

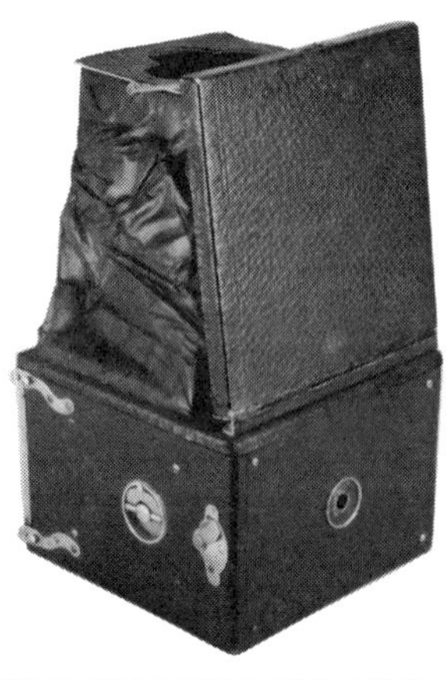
Premograph

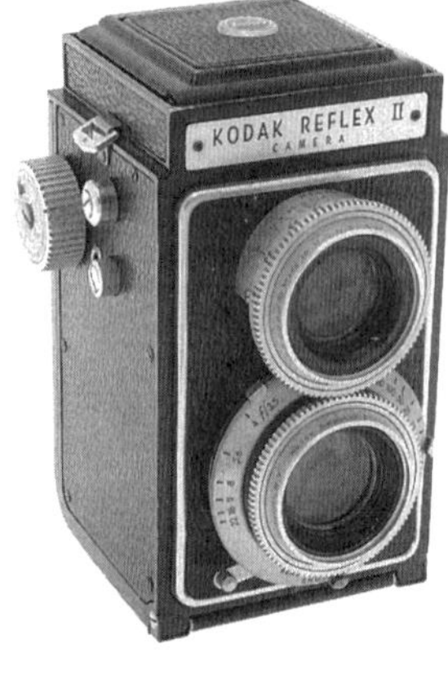

Kodak Reflex II

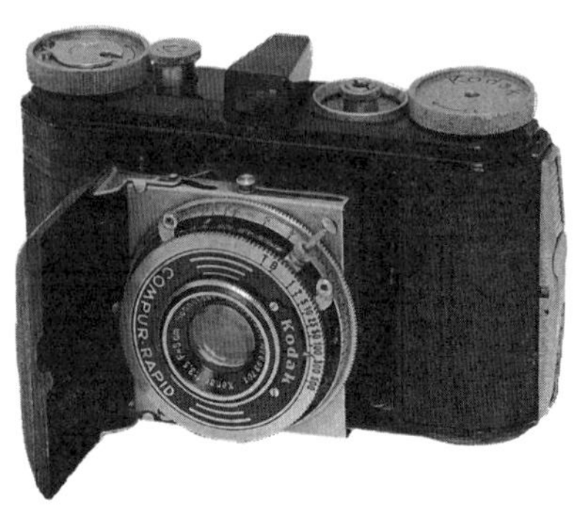

Retina (Type 117)

MODEL	FORMAT	FILM	TYPE	Year	LENS	Apert	FL	SHUTTER	SPEEDS	ILLUS	U.S.$
Retina I (Type 143)	24x36mm	35mm	35Fold	1939	Xenar	3.5	50mm	Compur	300	Mc168	90
Retina I (Type 148)	24x36mm	35mm	35Fold	1939	Xenar	3.5	50mm	Compur	300		80
Retina I (Type 148)	24x36mm	35mm	35Fold	1939	Ektar	3.5	50mm	Compur	300		100
Retina I (Type 149)	24x36mm	35mm	35Fold	1939	Xenar	3.5	50mm	Compur	300	Mc168	90
Retina I (Type 167)	24x36mm	35mm	35Fold	1941	Anastigmat	4.5	50mm	Kodak			200
Retina Ia (Type 015)	24x36mm	35mm	35Fold	1951	Xenar	3.5	50mm	Compur-Rapid	500	A1014	80
Retina Ib (Type 018)	24x36mm	35mm	35Fold	1954	Xenar	2.8	50mm	Sync-Compur		Mc169	120
Retina IB (Type 019)	24x36mm	35mm	35Fold	1957	Xenar	2.8	50mm	Sync-Compur		Mc169	90
Retina IB (Type 019/0)	24x36mm	35mm	35Fold	1957	Xenar	2.8	50mm	Sync-Compur		Mc169	160
Retina IBS (Type 040)	24x36mm	35mm	35VF	1962	Xenar	2.8	50mm	Compur			100
Retina IF (Type 046)	24x36mm	35mm	35VF	1963	Xenar	2.8	45mm	Prontor 500LK			80
Retina II (Type 011)	24x36mm	35mm	35Fold	1946	Heligon	2	50mm	Compur-Rapid	500	Mc170	100
Retina II (Type 014)	24x36mm	35mm	35Fold	1949	Xenon	2	50mm	Compur-Rapid	500	Mc170	90
Retina II (Type 122)	24x36mm	35mm	35Fold	1936	Ektar	3.5	50mm	Compur-Rapid	500		290
Retina II (Type 142)	24x36mm	35mm	35Fold	1937	Xenar	2	50mm	Compur-Rapid	500	Mc169	110
Retina IIa (Type 016)	24x36mm	35mm	35Fold	1951	Xenon	2	50mm	Compur-Rapid	500	A1015	100
Retina IIa (Type 150)	24x36mm	35mm	35Fold	1939	Xenon	2.8	50mm	Compur-Rapid	500	Mc170	140
Retina IIa (Type 150)	24x36mm	35mm	35Fold	1939	Ektar	3.5	50mm	Compur-Rapid	500	Mc170	140
Retina IIc (Type 020)	24x36mm	35mm	35Fold	1954	Xenon-C	2.8	50mm	Sync-Compur		Mc170	160
Retina IIC (Type 029)	24x36mm	35mm	35Fold	1958	Heligon-C	2.8	50mm	Sync-Compur			200
Retina IIF (Type 047)	24x36mm	35mm	35RF	1963	Xenar	2.8	45mm	Compur Spezial			90
Retina IIS (Type 024)	24x36mm	35mm	35RF	1959	Xenar	2.8	45mm	Sync-Compur		Mc171	110
Retina IIIc (Type 021)	24x36mm	35mm	35Fold	1954	Xenon-C	2	50mm	Sync-Compur		A2056	180
Retina IIIc (Type 021/1)	24x36mm	35mm	35Fold	1957	Heligon-C	2	50mm	Sync-Compur		Mc170	310
Retina IIIC (Type 028)	24x36mm	35mm	35Fold	1958	Xenon-C	2	50mm	Sync-Compur		Mc171	390
Retina IIIS (Type 027)	24x36mm	35mm	35rf	1958	Xenon	1.9	50mm	Sync-Compur		Mc171	140
Retina IIIS (Type 028/N)	24x36mm	35mm	35rf	1977	Xenon-C	2	50mm	Sync-Compur		Mc171	1000
Retina Autom. I (Type 038)	24x36mm	35mm	35vf	1960	Reomar	2.8	45mm	Prontormat-S		Mc171	50
Retina Autom. II (Type 032)	24x36mm	35mm	35vf	1960	Xenar	2.8	45mm	Compur Auto		Mc171	80
Retina Autom. III (Type 039)	24x36mm	35mm	35rf	1960	Reomar	2.8	45mm	Compur Auto		Mc171	70
Retina Reflex (Type 025)	24x36mm	35mm	35slr	1956	Xenon-C	2	50mm	Sync-Compur		A1668	100
Retina Reflex (Type 025/0)	24x36mm	35mm	35slr	1956	Heligon-C	2	50mm	Sync-Compur			440
Retina Reflex III (Type 041)	24x36mm	35mm	35slr	1960	Xenar	2.8	50mm	Sync-Compur			120
Retina Reflex IV (Type 051)	24x36mm	35mm	35slr	1964	Xenar	2.8	50mm	Sync-Compur			180
Retina Refl. IV (Type 051/N)	24x36mm	35mm	35slr	1979	Xenar	2.8	50mm	Sync-Compur			680
Retina Reflex S (Type 034)	24x36mm	35mm	35slr	1959	Xenar	2.8	50mm	Sync-Compur			110
Retina S1 (Type 060)	24x36mm	35mm	35vf	1966	Reomar	2.8	45mm	Kodak		Mc172	40
Retina S2 (Type 061)	24x36mm	35mm	35vf	1966	Reomar	2.8	45mm	Kodak		Mc172	50
Retinette (Type 012)	24x36mm	35mm	35fold	1949	Reomar	4.5	50mm	Prontor-S		Mc173	130
Retinette (Type 017)	24x36mm	35mm	35fold	1951	Reomar	4.5	50mm	Prontor-SV		Mc173	70
Retinette (Type 022)	24x36mm	35mm	35vf	1954	Reomar	3.5	45mm	Compur-Rapid	500	Mc174	40
Retinette (Type 147)	24x36mm	35mm	35fold	1939	Kodak Anastigmat	6.3	5cm	AGC 3-speed		Mc173	160

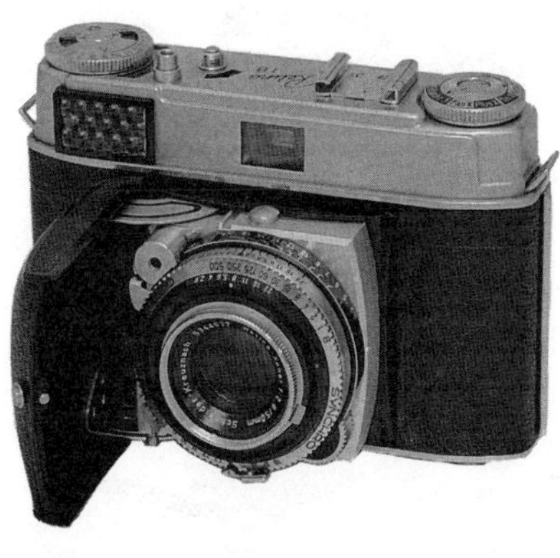

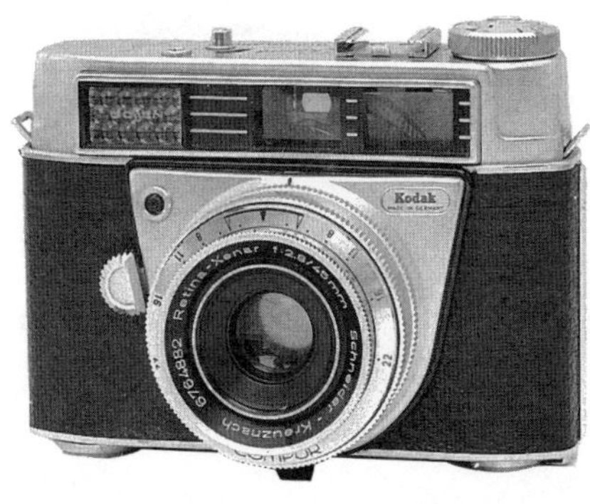

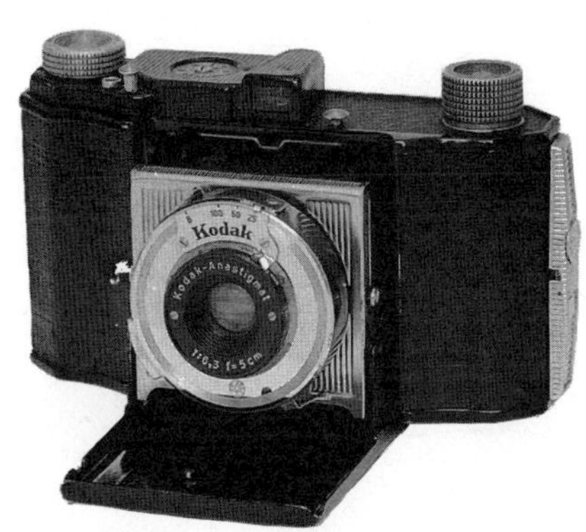

Retina IB (Typ 019/0) **Retina Automatic II (Type 032)** **Retinette (Type 147)**

MODEL	FORMAT	FILM	TYPE	Year	LENS	Apert	FL	SHUTTER	SPEEDS	ILLUS	U.S.$
Retinette f (Type 022/7)	24x36mm	35mm	35vf	1958	Angenieux	3.5	45mm	Kodak		Mc174	90
Retinette f (Type 030/7)	24x36mm	35mm	35vf	1958	Angenieux	2.8	45mm	Kodak		Mc174	50
Retinette I (Type 030)	24x36mm	35mm	35vf	1958	Reomar	3.5	45mm	Compur-Rapid	500	Mc174	40
Retinette IA (Type 035)	24x36mm	35mm	35vf	1959	Reomar	3.5	50mm	Vero		Mc174	60
Retinette IA (Type 035/7)	24x36mm	35mm	35vf	1959	Angenieux	2.8	50mm	Kodak		Mc174	50
Retinette IA (Type 042)	24x36mm	35mm	35vf	1960	Reomar	2.8	45mm	Pronto		Mc174	50
Retinette IA (Type 044)	24x36mm	35mm	35vf	1963	Reomar	2.8	45mm	Prontor 250S		Mc174	50
Retinette IB (Type 037)	24x36mm	35mm	35vf	1959	Reomar	2.8	45mm	Pronto-LK		Mc174	60
Retinette IB (Type 045)	24x36mm	35mm	35vf	1963	Reomar	2.8	45mm	Prontor 500LK		Mc175	50
Retinette II (Type 026)	24x36mm	35mm	35vf	1958	Reomar	2.8	45mm	Compur-Rapid	500	Mc175	70
Retinette II (Type 160)	24x36mm	35mm	35fold	1939	Kodak Anastigmat	3.5	5cm	Compur	300	A1011	70
Retinette IIA (Type 036)	24x36mm	35mm	35vf	1959	Reomar	2.8	45mm	Prontormat		Mc175	80
Retinette IIB (Type 031)	24x36mm	35mm	35vf	1958	Reomar	2.8	45mm	Compur-Rapid	500	Mc175	60
Kodak S100 EF	24x36mm	35mm	35VF	1987		4.5	35mm		100		30
Kodak S300 MD	24x36mm	35mm	35VF	1989	Ektanar	4.5	35mm		100		50
Kodak S350	24x36mm	35mm	35VF	1989	Ektanar	4.5	35mm		100		50
Kodak S400SL	24x36mm	35mm	35VF	1989	Ektanar	4.5	35mm		100		40
Kodak S500 AF	24x36mm	35mm	35AF	1989	Ektanar	3.5	35mm		1/80-500		90
Kodak S900 Tele	24x36mm	35mm	35AF-BiF	1988	Ektanar	5/7	34/62		100		90
Kodak S1100XL	24x36mm	35mm	35AF	1989	Ekton	2.8	35mm		45-250		120
Screen Focus Kodak No. 4	4x5"	123	FoldRo	1904	Rapid Rectilinear		6.5"	Kodak Automatic		Mc175	370
Kodak Senior Six-16	2½x4½"	616	FoldRo	1937	Kodak Anastigmat	6.3		Kodex		Mc175	20
Kodak Senior Six-20	2¼x3¼"	620	FoldRo	1937	Kodak Anastigmat	6.3		Kodex		Mc175	30
Signet 30	24x36mm	35mm	35rf	1957	Ektanar	2.8	44mm	Synchro 250		Mc175	30
Signet 35	24x36mm	35mm	35rf	1951	Ektar	3.5	44mm	Synchro 300		Mc175	20
Signet 40	24x36mm	35mm	35rf	1956	Ektanon	3.5	46mm	Synchro 400		Mc175	30
Signet 50	24x36mm	35mm	35rf	1957	Ektanar	2.8	44mm	Synchro 250		Mc176	30
Signet 80	24x36mm	35mm	35rf	1958	Ektanar	2.8				Mc176	60
Signet KE-7(1) (black)	24x36mm	35mm	35rf	1951	Ektar	3.5	44mm	Synchro 300		Mc176	160
Signet KE-7(1) (olive)	24x36mm	35mm	35rf	1951	Ektar	3.5	44mm	Synchro 300		Mc176	160
Kodak Six-16	2½x4½"	616	FoldRo	1932	Kodak Anastigmat	6.3		Diodak		Mc176	20
Kodak Six-16 (Improved)	2½x4½"	616	FoldRo	1934	Kodak Anastigmat	6.3		Diodak		Mc176	40
Six-16 Brownie (USA)	2½x4¼"	616	Box	1933	Diway			rotary			10
Six-16 Brownie Junior	2½x4¼"	616	Box	1934	Meniscus			rotary		Mc147	10
Six-16 Brownie Special	2½x4¼"	616	MetBx	1938	Meniscus			rotary		Mc147	10
Six-16 Folding Hawk-Eye	2½x4¼"	616	VtFoldRo	1933	Anastigmat	6.3		Kodex			20
Six-16 F. Hawk-Eye (brown)	2½x4¼"	616	VtFoldRo	1933	Anastigmat	6.3		Kodex			30
Kodak Six-20	2¼x3¼"	620	FoldRo	1932	Kodak Anastigmat	6.3		Diodak			30
Kodak Six-20 (Improved)	2¼x3¼"	620	FoldRo	1934	Kodak Anastigmat	4.5		Compur			50
Six-20 Brownie (UK)	2¼x3¼"	620	Box	1934							20
Six-20 Brownie (USA)	2¼x3¼"	620	Box	1933	Diway			rotary		Mc147	10
Six-20 Brownie B	2¼x3¼"	620	Box	1937							20

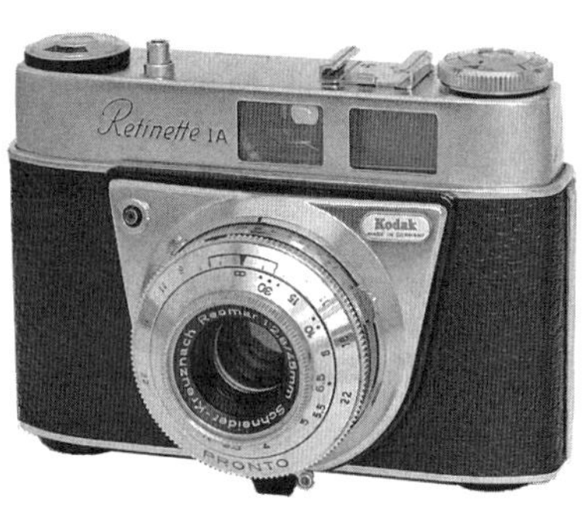

Retinette IA (Type 042)

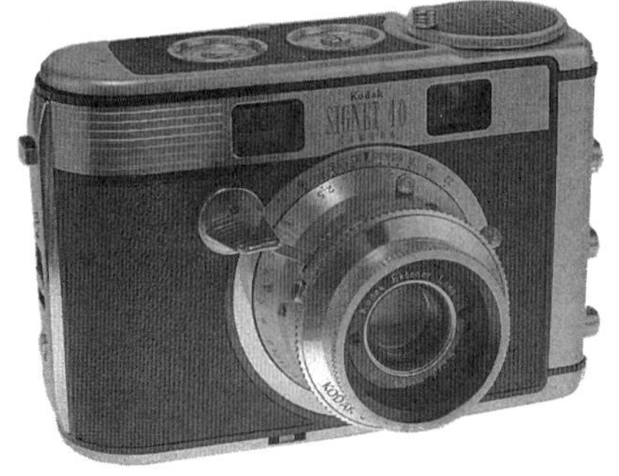

Signet 40

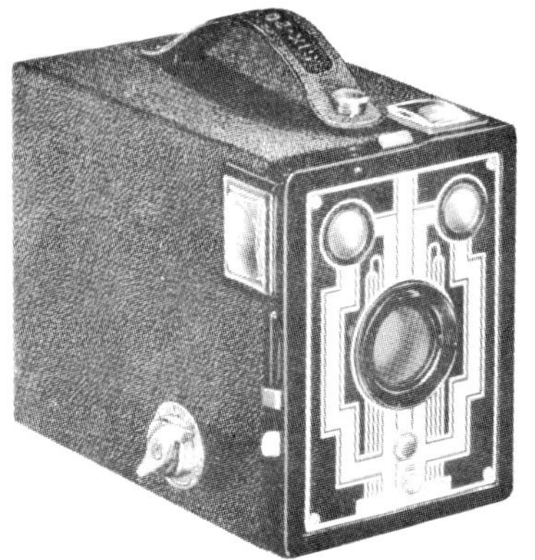

Six-20 Brownie (USA)

MODEL	FORMAT	FILM	TYPE	Year	LENS	Apert	FL	SHUTTER	SPEEDS	ILLUS	U.S.$
Six-20 Brownie C	2¼x3¼"	620	Box	1946						Mc148	20
Six-20 Brownie D	2¼x3¼"	620	Box	1946						Mc148	10
Six-20 Brownie E	2¼x3¼"	620	Box	1946						Mc148	20
Six-20 Brownie F	2¼x3¼"	620	Box	1955						Mc148	30
Six-20 Brownie Junior	2¼x3¼"	620	Box	1934	Meniscus			rotary			10
Six-20 Brownie Jr. Super	2¼x3¼"	620	MetBx	1935	Meniscus			rotary		A2895	20
Six-20 Brownie Special	2¼x3¼"	620	MetBx	1938	Meniscus			rotary			20
Six-20 Bull's-Eye Brownie	2¼x3¼"	620	BakeliteBox	1938	Meniscus				I	Mc148	10
Six-20 Flash Brownie	2¼x3¼"	620	MetBx	1940	Meniscus			rotary		Mc148	10
Six-20 Fold. Brownie Mod.2	2¼x3¼"	620	VtFoldRo	1948	Anaston	6.3	100mm	Dakon	25,50	Mc148	20
Six-20 Folding Hawk-Eye	2¼x3¼"	620	VtFoldRo	1933	Meniscus			rotary			20
Six-20 F. Hawk-Eye (brown)	2¼x3¼"	620	VtFoldRo	1933	Meniscus			rotary			30
Six-20 Kodak A	2¼x3¼"	620	FoldRo	1951	Kodak Anastar	4.5		Epsilon			20
Six-20 Kodak B	2¼x3¼"	620	FoldRo	1937	Kodak Anastigmat	6.3	105mm	Gauthier	25-100	Mc176	30
Six-20 Kodak Junior	2¼x3¼"	620	FoldRo	1933	Doublet					Mc176	30
Six-20 Portrait Brownie	2¼x3¼"	620	MetBx							Mc148	10
Six-Three Kodak No. 1A	2½x4½"	116	FoldRo	1913	Cooke Kodak	6.3		B&L Compound			40
Six-Three Kodak No. 3	3¼x4¼"	118	FoldRo	1913	Cooke Kodak	6.3		B&L Compound			40
Six-Three Kodak No. 3A	3¼x5½"	122	FoldRo	1913	Cooke Kodak	6.3		B&L Compound		Mc176	30
Special Kodak No. 1A	2¼x3¼"	120	FoldRo	1912	Tessar	6.3		B&L Compound			60
Special Kodak No. 3	3¼x4¼"	118	FoldRo	1911	Tessar	6.3		B&L Compound		Mc176	60
Special Kodak No. 3A	3¼x5½"	122	FoldRo	1910	Tessar	6.3		B&L Compound		A378	60
Kodak Special Six-16	2½x4½"	616	FoldRo	1937	Anast. Special	4.5		Compur-Rapid		Mc177	30
Kodak Special Six-20	2¼x3¼"	620	FoldRo	1937	Anast. Special	4.5		Compur-Rapid			30
Speed Kodak No. 1A	2½x4½"	116	FoldRo	1909	Cooke	5.6		focal plane	1000	Mc177	290
Speed Kodak No. 4A	4¼x6½"	126	FoldRo	1908	Dagor	6.8		focal plane	1000	Mc177	700
Kodak Sport Special	13x17mm	110	110	1987						Mc177	80
Star	13x17mm	110	110	1986	Kodar	11	22mm		125,250		10
Star 35 af	24x36mm	35mm	35af		Autofocus						50
Star 35 ef	24x36mm	35mm	35mm		Fixfocus						30
Star 35 sf	24x36mm	35mm	35mm	1990	Fixfocus				I		40
Star 235	24x36mm	35mm	35mm	1990		8	35mm		100		20
Star 275	24x36mm	35mm	35mm	1994		5.6	33mm		125		20
Star 335	24x36mm	35mm	35mm	1990	Ektanar	5.6	35mm		125		30
Star 435	24x36mm	35mm	35mm	1990	Ektanar	5.6	35mm		125		30
Star 535	24x36mm	35mm	35mm	1992	Ektanar				1/80		40
Star 575	24x36mm	35mm	35mm	1993	Ektanar	8	36mm				30
Star 635	24x36mm	35mm	35mm	1990		4.5	35mm		100		40
Star 735	24x36mm	35mm	35mm	1991							40
Star 835 AF	24x36mm	35mm	35mm	1994	Ektanar				60,250		50
Star 935	24x36mm	35mm	35mm	1991							50
Star 1035z	24x36mm	35mm	35mm	1993	Ektanar	4.3	38-60		40-500		200

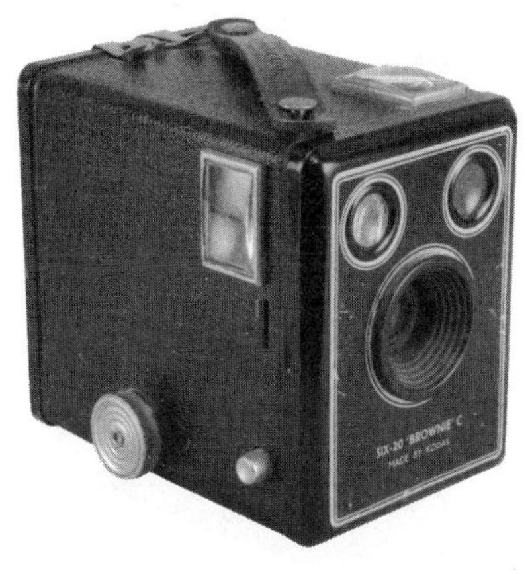

Six-20 Brownie C

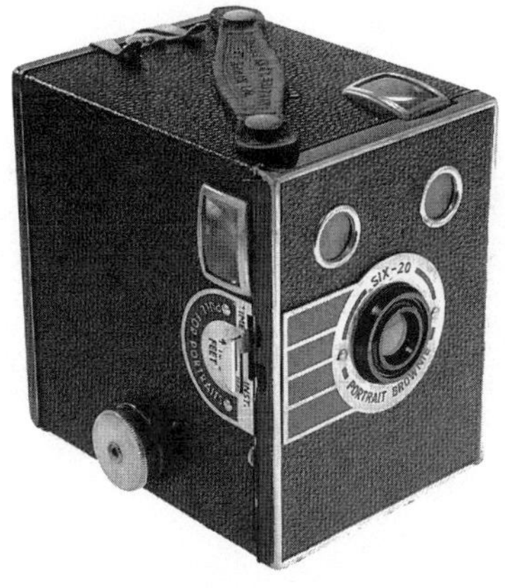

Six-20 Portrait Brownie

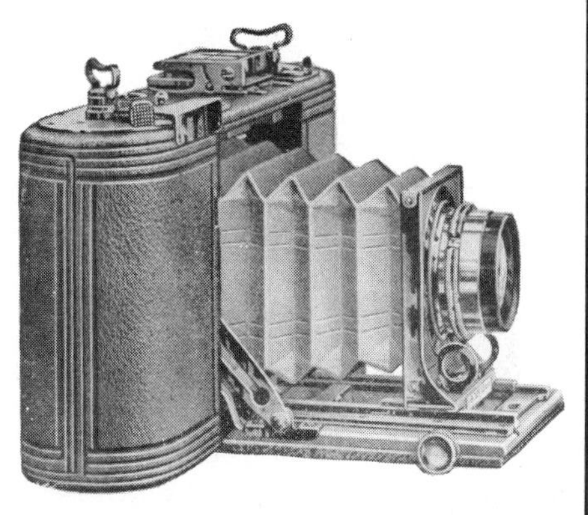
Speed Kodak No. 1A

MODEL	FORMAT	FILM	TYPE	Year	LENS	Apert	FL	SHUTTER	SPEEDS	ILLUS	U.S.$
Star 1075z	24x36mm	35mm	35mm	1993	Ektanar	4.3	38-60		40-500		130
Star Premo	3¼x4¼"	plate	FoldPl	1903	Verastigmat	6.8		B&L Automatic		Mc166	70
Star Zoom 105	24x36mm	35mm	35mm	1994					45-500		170
Startech	1⅝x1⅝"	127	SciMed	1959		27	50mm		1/40	Mc177	30
Stereo Brownie No. 2	2½x3¼"	125	StFoldRo	1905	Meniscus Achrom.			Automatic		Mc149	440
Stereo Hawk-Eye	3½x3½"	101	StFoldRo	1912	Rapid Rectilinear			B&L Stereo			460
Stereo Hawk-Eye Mod. 3	3½x3½"	101	StFoldRo	1907	Rapid Rectilinear			B&L Stereo			460
Stereo Hawk-Eye Mod. 4	3½x3½"	101	StFoldRo	1907	Rapid Rectilinear			B&L Stereo Auto			510
Kodak Stereo 35mm	24x24mm	35mm	35Ster	1954	Anaston	3.5	35mm	Flash 200	25-200	Mc177	150
Kodak Stereo Mod. 1	3¼x3¼"	101	StFoldRo	1917	Anastigmat	7.7	5.25"	Ball Bearing		Mc177	380
Kodak Stereo No. 2	3½x6"	101	SterBox	1901	Rapid Rectilinear	14	4.75"	Special		Mc177	600
Sterling II			FoldRo	1955	Anaston	4.5	105mm	Pronto	25-200	Mc177	20
Stretch 35	13x36mm	110	Dispose	1989		12	25mm		110		10
Stylelite	13x17mm	110	110	1979		8	25mm		125,210		10
Super Kodak Six-20	2¼x3¼"	620	FoldRo	1938	Aanast. Special	3.5		built-in	8 Zeiten	Mc177	1700
Suprema	2¼x2¼"	620	HzFoldRo	1938	Xenar	3.5	80mm	Compur-Rapid	1-400	Mc177	400
Target Hawk-Eye No. 2	2¼x3¼"	120	Box	1932	Meniscus			rotary			10
Target Hawk-Eye No. 2 Jr.		120	Box	1932	Meniscus			rotary			10
Target H-E No. 2 Jr. (colors)		120	Box	1932	Meniscus			rotary			40
Target H-E No. 2A (black)	2½x4½"	116	Box	1932	Meniscus			rotary			10
Target H-E No. 2A (colors)	2½x4½"	116	Box	1932	Meniscus			rotary			40
Target H-E Six-16 (black)	2½x4½"	616	Box	1932	Meniscus			rotary			10
Target H-E Six-16 (colors)	2½x4½"	616	Box	1932	Meniscus			rotary			40
Target H-E Six-20 (black)		620	Box	1932	Meniscus			rotary			10
Target H-E Six-20 (colors)		620	Box	1932	Meniscus			rotary			40
Tele Challenger Disc	8x10mm	Disc	Disc	1982		2.8	12.5mm	auto	100		10
Tele-Ektra 1	13x17mm	110	110VF	1978	2 Doublet	9.5	22mm		60-210		10
Tele-Ektra 2	13x17mm	110	110VF	1978	2 Doublet	5.6	22mm		60-500		10
Tele-Ektra 32	13x17mm	110	110	1978	Kodar	11	22mm	3-speed	40-250		20
Tele-Ektra 42	13x17mm	110	110	1978	Kodar	11	22mm	3-speed	40-250		30
Tele-Ektra 300	13x17mm	110	110	1980	3-element	8	22/44	3-speed	60-250		20
Tele-Ektra 300	13x17mm	110	110VF	1980	2 Doublet	8	22mm		60-250		20
Tele-Ektra 350	13x17mm	110	110VF	1980	2 Doublet	8	22mm		60-250	A1990	20
Tele-Ektralite 20	13x17mm	110	110VF	1979	2 Doublet	9.5	22mm		125,210		10
Tele-Ektralite 40	13x17mm	110	110VF	1979	2 Doublet	5.6	22mm		100-500		10
Tele-Ektralite 600	13x17mm	110	110VF	1980	2 Doublet	8	22mm		125,250	A1990	10
Tele-Instamatic 330	13x17mm	110	110VF	1975	Triplet	11	25mm		50-100		20
Tele-Instamatic 430	13x17mm	110	110VF	1975	Reomar	5.6	25mm		50-100		30
Tele-Instamatic 530	13x17mm	110	110VF	1976	Reomar	5.6	24/42		20-300		30
Tele-Instamatic 608	13x17mm	110	110VF	1975		11	25/43		45,125	Mc178	10
Tele-Instamatic 708	13x17mm	110	110VF	1976		5.6	25mm	electronic	30-300		30
Tele-Stylelite	13x17mm	110	110VF	1979	2 Doublet	9.5	22mm		125,250		10

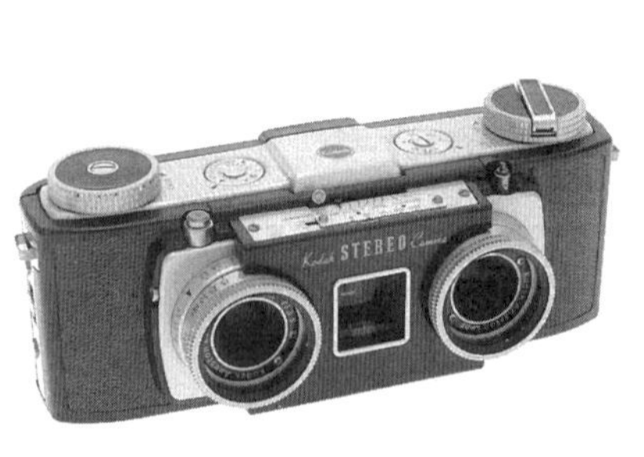

Kodak Stereo 35mm

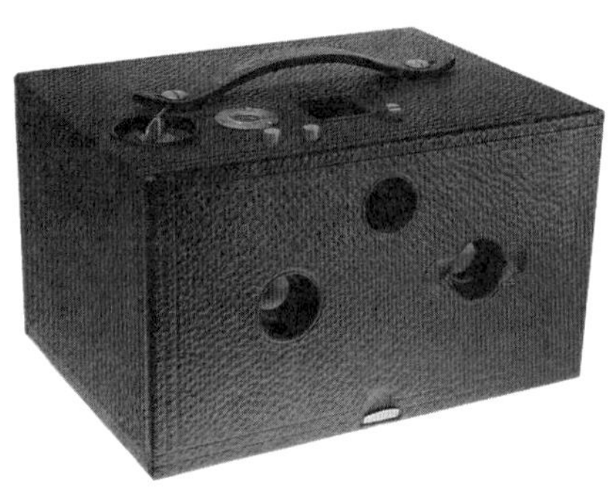

Kodak Stereo No. 2

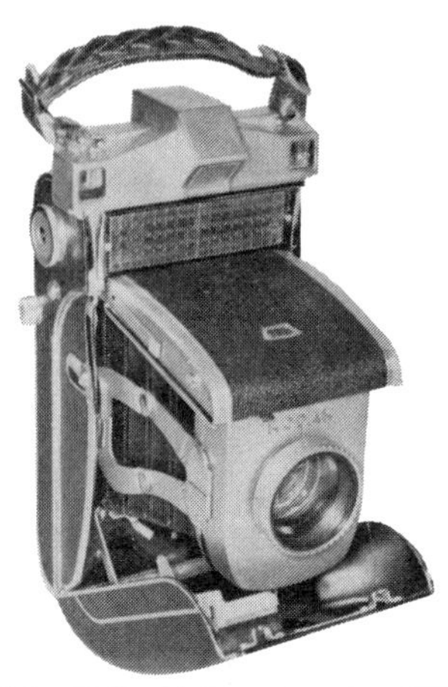

Super Kodak Six-20

MODEL	FORMAT	FILM	TYPE	Year	LENS	Apert	FL	SHUTTER	SPEEDS	ILLUS	U.S.$
Tim's Official Camera	2½x4¼"	116	Box	1930	Meniscus			rotary		Mc158	90
Tourist	2¼x3¼"	620	FoldRo	1948	Anastar	4.5		Sync.Rapid 800		Mc178	50
Tourist II	2¼x3¼"	620	FoldRo	1951	Anastar	4.5		Sync.Rapid 800		Mc178	70
Tourist II	2¼x3¼"	620	FoldRo	1951	Anaston	6.3		Fl. Diomatic		Mc178	10
Trimlite Instamatic 18	13x17mm	110	110VF	1975		11	25mm		40,90		10
Trimlite Instamatic 28	13x17mm	110	110VF	1975		9.5	25mm	electronic	30-160		20
Trimlite Instamatic 38	13x17mm	110	110VF	1975		8	25mm	electronic	5-1/225		20
Trimlite Instamatic 48	13x17mm	110	110VF	1975	Ektar	2.7	26mm	electronic	30-250		30
Trimprint 920	67x91mm	PR10	Instant	1984		12.8	100mm	electronic	15-400		30
Trimprint 940	67x91mm	PR10	Instant	1984		12.8	100mm	electronic	15-250		20
Vanity Kodak Camera	4.5x6cm	127	FoldRo	1928	Anaston	6.3	3.25"	Diomatic		Mc178	160
Vanity Kodak Ensemble	4.5x6cm	127	FoldRo	1928	Meniscus			V.P. Rotary		Mc178	700
Vest Pock. Autogr. Kodak	4.5x6cm	127	FoldRo	1915	Meniscus Achrom.			Ball Bearing		Mc178	50
Vest Pock. Autogr. Kodak	4.5x6cm	127	FoldRo	1915	Rapid Rectilinear			Ball Bearing		Mc178	40
V.P. Autogr. Kodak Special	4.5x6cm	127	FoldRo	1915	Rapid Rectilinear		3.5"	Ball Bearing		Mc178	40
V.P. Autogr. Kodak Special	4.5x6cm	127	FoldRo	1915	Anastigmat	7.7	3.5"	Ball Bearing		Mc178	50
Vest Pocket Hawk-Eye	4.5x6cm	127	FoldRo	1927	Meniscus			V.P. Rotary			30
V.P. Hawk-Eye (colors)	4.5x6cm	127	FoldRo	1927	Meniscus			V.P. Rotary			100
Vest Pocket Kodak	4.5x6cm	127	FoldRo	1912	Meniscus Achrom.			Ball Bearing		Mc178	50
Vest Pocket Kodak	4.5x6cm	127	FoldRo	1912	Anastigmat	6.9		Ball Bearing		Mc178	50
Vest Pocket Kodak	4.5x6cm	127	FoldRo	1912	Anastigmat	8		Ball Bearing		Mc178	50
Vest Pocket Kodak Mod. B	4.5x6cm	127	FoldRo	1925	Meniscus			rotary		Mc178	50
V.P. Kodak Series III	4.5x6cm	127	FoldRo	1926	Anastigmat	5.6		Diomatic			30
V.P. Kodak Series III	4.5x6cm	127	FoldRo	1926	Kodar	7.9		Kodex			30
V.P. Kodak Special (bed)	4.5x6cm	127	FoldRo	1926	Anastigmat	5.6		Diomatic		Mc179	60
V.P. Kodak Special (bed)	4.5x6cm	127	FoldRo	1926	Anastigmat	4.5		Diomatic		Mc179	60
V.P. Kodak Special (lizard)	4.5x6cm	127	FoldRo	1926	Anastigmat	4.5		Diomatic		Mc179	700
V.P. Kodak Special (struts)	4.5x6cm	127	FoldRo	1912	Anastigmat	6.9		Ball Bearing			60
V.P. Rainbow Hawk-Eye	4.5x6cm	127	FoldRo	1930	Periscope			V.P. Rotary		Mc158	30
V.P. Rainb. H-E (colors)	4.5x6cm	127	FoldRo	1930	Periscope			V.P. Rotary		Mc158	130
V.P. Rainb. H-E (rose)	4.5x6cm	127	FoldRo	1930	Periscope			V.P. Rotary		Mc158	150
View camera 5x7"	5x7"	plate	Field		Various			various		Mc179	200
View camera 6½x8½"	6½x8½"	plate	Field		Various			various		Mc179	120
View camera 8x10"	8x10"	plate	Field		Various			various		Mc179	350
Vigilant Junior Six-16	2½x4½"	616	FoldRo	1940	Kodet			Dak			20
Vigilant Junior Six-20	2¼x3¼"	620	FoldRo	1940	Bimat			Dakon		Mc179	20
Vigilant Six-16	2½x4½"	616	FoldRo	1939	Aanast. Special	4.5		Supermatic			20
Vigilant Six-20	2¼x3¼"	620	FoldRo	1939	Anastigmat	6.3		Diomatic		Mc179	20
Vollenda 620	6x6cm	620	HzFoldRo	1940	Xenar	4.5	105mm	Compur			60
Vollenda 620 (Type 107)	6x9cm	620	VtFoldRo	1934	Tessar	4.5	105mm	Compur S		Mc179	30
Vollenda 620 (Type 110)	6x9cm	620	VtFoldRo	1934	Anastigmat	6.3	120mm	Kodak		Mc179	30
Vollenda Junior 616	2½x4½"	616	VtFoldRo	1934	Anastigmat	6.3		Pronto S			50

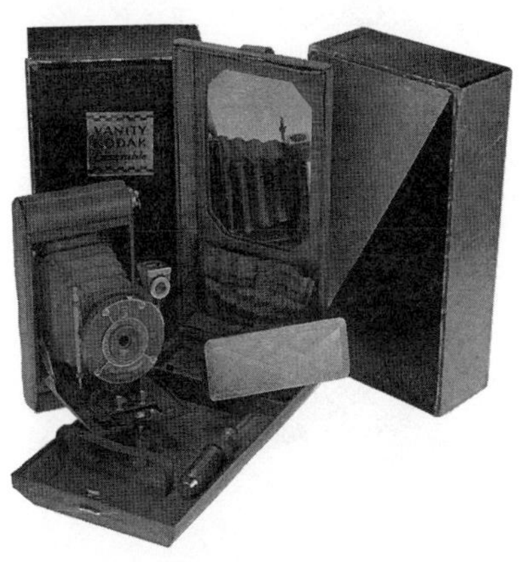

Vanity Kodak Ensemble

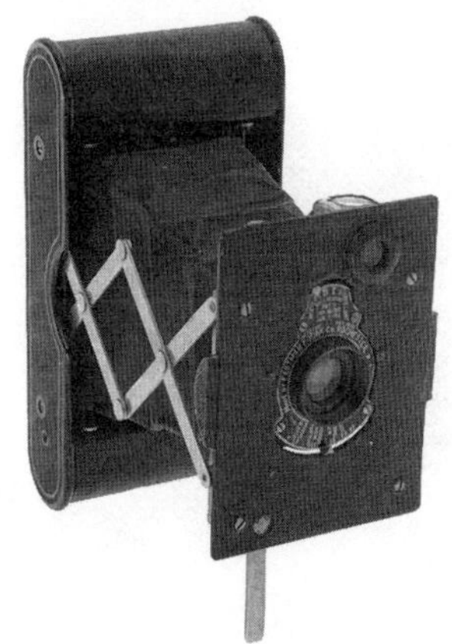

V.P. Autogr. Kodak. Spcl.

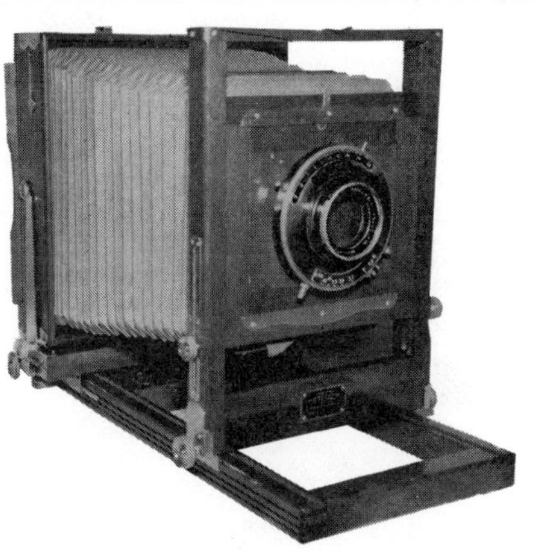

View Camera

MODEL	FORMAT	FILM	TYPE	Year	LENS	Apert	FL	SHUTTER	SPEEDS	ILLUS	U.S.$
Vollenda Junior 620	2¼x3¼"	620	VtFoldRo	1933	Anastigmat	6.3		Pronto			50
Vollenda No. 48	3x4cm	127	HzFoldRo	1932	Xenar	2.9		Compur		Mc179	90
Vollenda No. 52	4x6.5cm	127	VtFoldRo	1932	Radionar	4.5	75mm	Prontor-S			70
Vollenda No. 68 (black)	6x9cm	120	VtFoldRo	1930	Radionar	6.3	105mm	Pronto S			50
Vollenda No. 68 (brown)	6x9cm	120	VtFoldRo	1930	Radionar	6.3	105mm	Pronto S			70
Vollenda No. 70/1	6x9cm	120	VtFoldRo	1930	Anastigmat	4.5	105mm	Pronto S			70
Vollenda No. 70/2	6x9cm	120	VtFoldRo	1930	Anastigmat	4.5	105mm	Pronto S			100
Vollenda No. 72	6x9cm	120	VtFoldRo	1933	Tessar	4.5	105mm	Compur S			80
VR35 Mod. K2a	24x36mm	35mm	35VF	1986	Kodar	6.3	40mm		125		10
VR35 Mod. K4a	24x36mm	35mm	35VF	1985	Kodar	5.6	38mm		125		20
VR35 Mod. K5	24x36mm	35mm	35VF	1986		5.6	38mm		125		20
VR35 Mod. K6	24x36mm	35mm	35VF	1985		5.6	38mm		125		30
VR35 Mod. K10	24x36mm	35mm	35af	1986	Ektanar	3.5	35mm	Programmed	1/8-500		60
VR35 Mod. K12	24x36mm	35mm	35af	1986		2.8	35mm	Programmed	1/8-500		100
VR35 Mod. K14	24x36mm	35mm	35af	1986		2.8	35mm	Programmed	1/8-500		90
VR35 Mod. K40	24x36mm	35mm	35VF	1986	Ektanar	5.6	35mm	Programmed	145-400		30
VR35 Mod. K60	24x36mm	35mm	35VF	1986		4.5	35mm	Programmed	145-400		40
VR35 Mod. K80	24x36mm	35mm	35af	1987	Ektanar	3.9	35mm	Programmed	100-500		60
VR35 Mod. K300	24x36mm	35mm	35af	1986	Kodar	5.6	38mm		125		20
VR35 Mod. K400	24x36mm	35mm	35af	1986	Kodar	5.6	38mm		125		20
VR35 Mod. K500	24x36mm	35mm	35af	1986	Kodar	5.6	38mm		125		30
Weekend 35	24x36mm	35mm	Dispose	1989		11	35mm		110		10
Weno Hawk-Eye No. 2	3½x3½"	101	Box	1904	achromatic			rotary			40
Weno Hawk-Eye No. 4	4x5"	103	Box	1904	Meniscus			rotary			40
Weno Hawk-Eye No. 5	3¼x4¼"	118	Box	1904	Meniscus Achrom.			rotary			40
Weno Hawk-Eye No. 7	3¼x5½"	122	Box	1908	Meniscus			rotary			60
Winner, 1988 Olympics	13x17mm	110	110VF	1988	Meniscus	11	25mm		40,90	Mc179	10
Winner Pocket Camera	13x17mm	110	110VF	1979	Meniscus	11	25mm		40,90	Mc179	10
World's Fair Flash Camera	$1^{5}/_{8}$x$1^{5}/_{8}$"	127	RigidRo	1964	achromatic	13.5	50mm		I	Mc179	10
Zenith Kodak No. 3	3¼x4¼"	plate	PlateBox	1898	achromatic			rotary			200
Zenith Kodak No. 4	4x5"	plate	PlateBox	1898	achromatic			rotary			220
...EBNER (Albert Ebner & Co.) - Stuttgart											
Ebner 301	4.5x6cm	120	FoldRo	1934	Anastigmat	6.3	7.5cm	Vario			150
Ebner 302	4.5x6cm	120	FoldRo	1934	Trioplan	4.5	7.5cm	Vario			180
Ebner 303 (brown)	4.5x6cm	120	FoldRo	1934	Anastigmat	4.5	7.5cm	Pronto-S	25-100	Mc180	160
Ebner 303 (red)	4.5x6cm	120	FoldRo	1934	Anastigmat	4.5	7.5cm	Pronto-S	25-100	A3051	150
Ebner 304	4.5x6cm	120	FoldRo	1934	Trioplan	4.5	7.5cm	Pronto-S	25-100		180
Ebner 305	4.5x6cm	120	FoldRo	1934	Primotar	3.5	7.5cm	Pronto-S	25-100		160
Ebner 306	4.5x6cm	120	FoldRo	1934	Trioplan	4.5	7.5cm	Compur	1-300	A3050	150
Ebner 308	4.5x6cm	120	FoldRo	1934	Tessar	3.8	7.5cm	Compur	1-300		180
Ebner 331	6x9cm	120	FoldRo	1934	Trinar	6.3	105mm	Pronto	25-100	Mc180	190
Ebner 332	6x9cm	120	FoldRo	1934	Trinar	4.5	105mm	Pronto-S	25-100	HK250	190

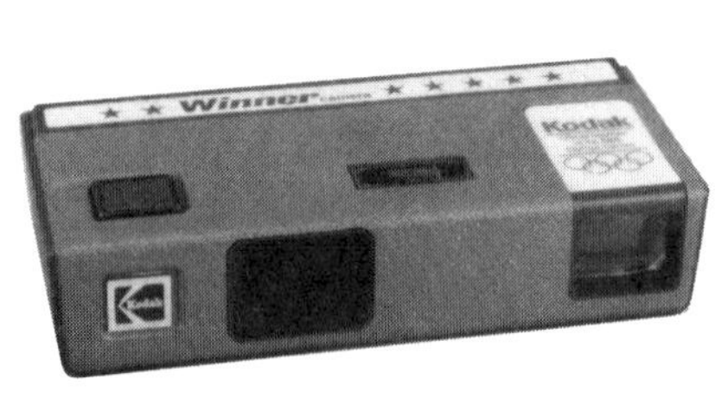

Winner, 1988 Olympics

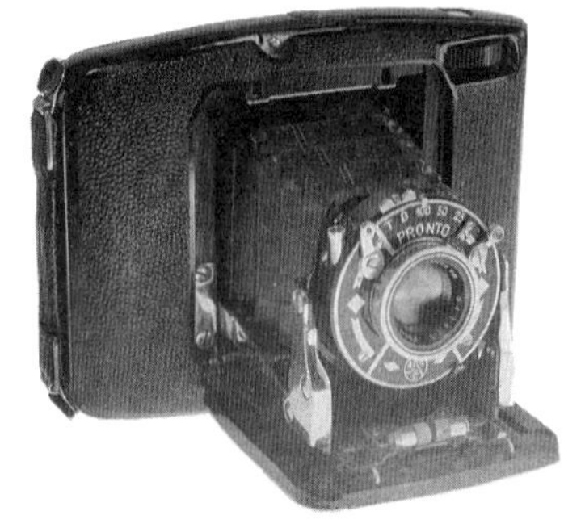

Ebner 303 (brown)

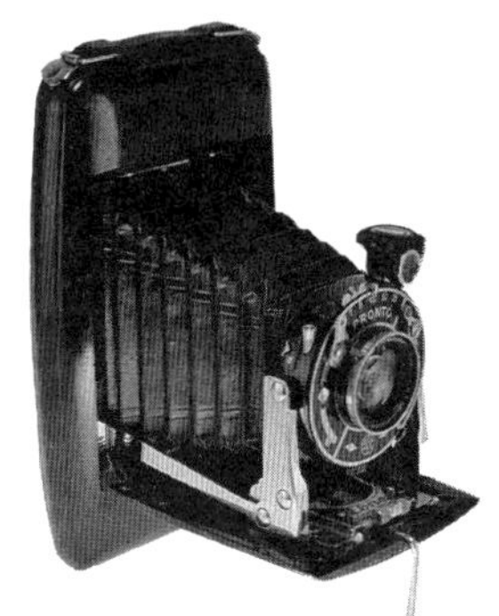

Ebner 331

MODEL	FORMAT	FILM	TYPE	Year	LENS	Apert	FL	SHUTTER	SPEEDS	ILLUS	U.S.$
Ebner 333	6x9cm	120	FoldRo	1934	Radionar	4.5	105mm	Pronto-S	25-100	A3042	190
Ebner 334	6x9cm	120	FoldRo	1934	Trinar	4.5	105mm	Compur S	1-250	HK251	170
Ebner 335	6x9cm	120	FoldRo	1934	Radionar	4.5	105mm	Compur S	1-250	HK251	180
Ebner 336	6x9cm	120	FoldRo	1934	Xenar	4.5	105mm	Compur S	1-250	HK252	180
Ebner 337	6x9cm	120	FoldRo	1934	Tessar	4.5	105mm	Compur S	1-250	HK252	170
Ebner 341	6x9cm	120	FoldRo	1934	Anastigmat	4.5	105mm	Pronto-S	1-250		180
...(unknown)											
Echoflex	6x6cm		TLR	1952	Echo	3.5		Echo	1-200		100
Echoflex	6x6cm		TLR	1955	Echor Anastigmat	3.5		Synch.-Super	1-300	Mc180	370
...EDER - Munich											
Eder Patent Camera	4.5x6cm	Roll	HzFoldRo	1933	Tessar	4.5		Compur	300	Mc180	2600
Eder Patent Camera	6x6cm	Roll	HzFoldRo	1933	Xenar	4.5		Compur	300	A780	2200
Eder Patent Camera	6x9cm	Roll	HzFoldRo	1933	Tessar	4.5		Compur	300	A1823	2200
...E.F.I.C.A. S.R.L. - Argentina											
Alas	6x9cm	120	MetBx							Mc180	30
Splendor 120	6x9cm	120	MetBx							Mc180	30
Suprema	5.5x8cm	120/6	MetBx							Mc180	30
...EHIRA K.S.K. (Ehira Camera Works) - Japan											
Astoria Super-6 IIIB	6x6cm	120	HzFoldRo	1950	Lausar	3.5	85mm		1-400		230
Ehira Chrome Six	6x6cm	120	TelescRo	1937							230
Ehira-Six	6x6cm	120	HzFoldRo	1948	Tomioka	3.5	85mm	Ehira	1-400		210
Weha Chrome Six	6x6cm	120	TelescRo	1937							230
Weha Light	6x9cm	120	FoldPl			4.5	105mm				60
...EHO-ALTISSA - Dresden											
Altiflex	6x6cm	120	TLR	1937	Ludwig Victar	4.5	75mm	Prontor		Mc181	70
Altiflex II	6x6cm	120	TLR	1939	Pololyt	2.8		Compur		Mc181	70
Altiscop	6x13cm	120	SterBox	1937	Ludwig Victar	4.5	75mm	Automat	25-100	A781	290
Altissa (eye-level finder)	6x6cm	120	Box	1930	Altissar	8				Mc181	30
Altissa (prism-shaped top)	6x6cm	120	Box	1950						Mc181	20
Altissa (pseudo-TLR)	6x6cm	120	Box	1938	Periscop	6					30
Altissa II 4.5x6	4.5x6cm	120	Box	1938	Trinar Anastigmat	3.5		Compur	1-250	Mc181	70
Altissa II 6x6	6x6cm	120	Box	1938	Trinar Anastigmat	3.5	75mm	Compur	1-250	Mc181	70
Altix (I)	24x24mm	35mm	35vf	1938	Laack	3.5	35mm			Mc181	50
Altix III	24x24mm	35mm	35vf	1947	Laack Tegonar	3.5	35mm				50
Altix IV	24x36mm	35mm	35vf	1955	Trioplan	2.9	50mm	Vebur	1-250		30
Altix V (black)	24x36mm	35mm	35vf	1957	Meritar	2.9	50mm	Tempor	1-250	Mc181	50
Altix V (colors)	24x36mm	35mm	35vf	1957	Tessar	2.8	50mm	Tempor	1-250		70
Altix-N	24x36mm	35mm	35vf	1959	Trioplan	2.9	50mm				50
Altix-NB	24x36mm	35mm	35vf	1959	Trioplan	2.9	50mm				40
Altuca	6x6cm	120	TelescRo	1952	Meritar	3.5	75mm	Prontor-SV			50
Arto (black)	6x9cm	120	RollBox	1936	Duplar	11			M,Z		50
Arto (green)	6x9cm	120	RollBox	1936	Duplar	11			M,Z		50

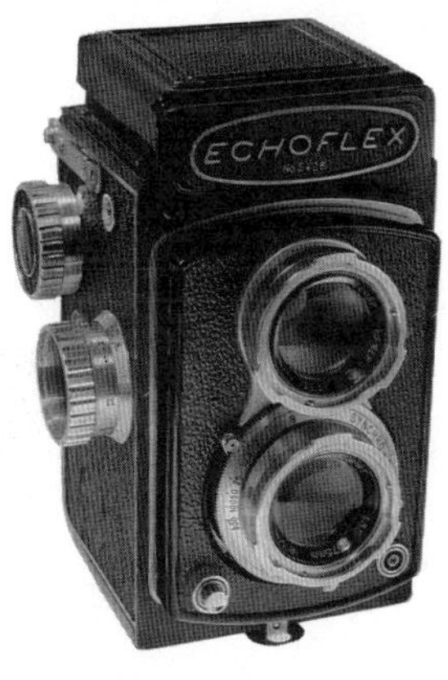

Echoflex

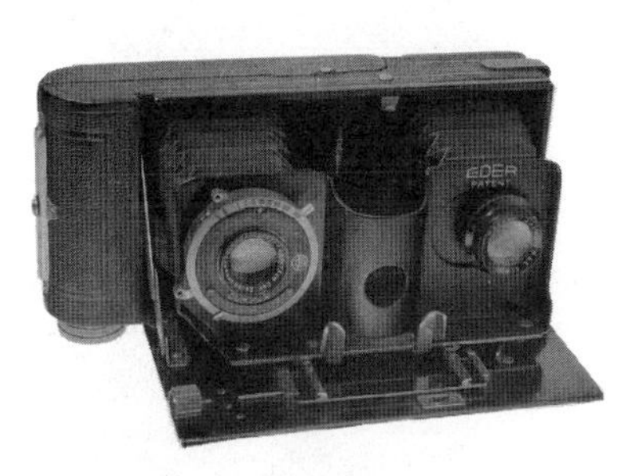

Eder Patent Camera

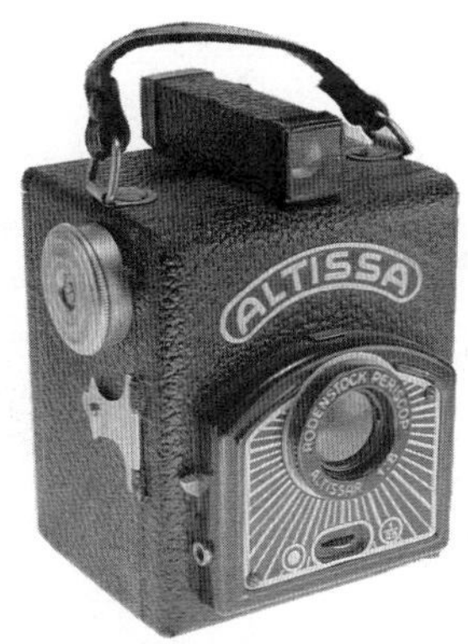

Altissa (eye-level finder)

MODEL	FORMAT	FILM	TYPE	Year	LENS	Apert	FL	SHUTTER	SPEEDS	ILLUS	U.S.$
Classic 35	24x36mm	35mm	35vf	1956	Trioplan	2.9					30
Eho box (black)	6x9cm	120	RollBox	1930	Periscop						30
Eho box (green)	6x9cm	120	RollBox	1930	Duplar	11					90
Eho box 3x4	3x4cm	127	RollBox	1932	Duplar	11	50mm		B,I	Mc181	120
Eho box 4.5x6	4.5x6cm	120	RollBox							Mc181	50
Eho Stereo Box	6x13cm	120	SterBox	1930	Duplar	11	80mm		B,I	Mc181	250
Gehaflex	6x6cm	120	TLR	1937	Trinar	2.9	75mm	Rim-Compur			100
Hafaflex	6x6cm	120	TLR	1938	Trinar	2.9	75mm	Rim-Compur			70
Juwel	6x6cm	120	RollBox								30
Mantel-Box 2	4.5x6cm		RollBox	1930	Duplar	11					140
Staufen	6x9cm	120	RollBox	1930	Eho Doppel						70
Super Altissa	6x6cm	120	RollBox	1938	Victar	4.5	75mm		1/25-100	A2847	80
...EICHAPFEL (B. Eichapfel) - Dresden											
Noviflex (I)	6x6cm	120	MedSLR	1934	Trioplan	3.5	75mm	focal plane	1/20-1000	Mc182	360
Noviflex (II)	6x6cm	120	MedSLR	1937	Ludwig Victar	3.5	75mm	focal plane	1/20-1000	Mc182	370
...ELBOW CAMERA FIRM											
Elbow flex	6x6cm	120	TLR	1954	Correct Anast.	3.5	8cm	Rectus	1-300	Mc182	80
Elbow flex II	6x6cm	120	TLR	1954	Anast. Alphar	3.5	8cm	T.S.K.	1-200		80
...ELLISON KAMRA CO. - Los Angeles, CA USA											
Ellison Kamra	24x32mm	35mm	35vf	1928		5	50mm		I,T		200
...ELOP KAMERAWERK - Glücksburg & Flensburg, Germany											
Elca	24x24mm	35mm	35vf	1948	Elocar	4.5	35mm		I	A1086	100
Elca I	24x36mm	35mm	35vf	1948	Elocar	4.5	35mm				60
Elca II	24x24mm	35mm	35vf	1948	Elocar	4.5	35mm	Prontor-S		HK571	120
Uniflex	24x36mm	35mm	35slr	1950	Elolux	1.9	50mm	focal plane	1/30-1000		460
...EMMERLING & RICHTER - Berlin											
Field camera	13x18cm	plate	Field		Various			various			160
...ENJALBERT (E. Enjalbert) - Paris											
Alpiniste	9x12cm	plate	FoldPl	1886							1000
Colis Postal			Disguised	1886							9000
Photo Revolver de Poche	16x16mm	plate	Disguised	1883						Mc183	85000
Touriste	13x18cm	plate	FoldPl	1882	Antiplanet						3900
...E.R.A.C. SELLING CO. LTD. - London											
Erac Mercury I Pistol Cam.	18x18mm	Roll	Disguised	1938	Meniscus	16			I	Mc184	380
...ERKO FOTOWERKE - Freital, Germany											
Erko	9x12cm	plate	FoldPl		Erko Spez. Anast.	8	135mm	Ibso	1-150		70
Erkofix	9x12cm	plate	FoldPl		Erko Fixar	6.8	135mm	Ibso	1-150		70
...ERNEMANN (Heinrich Ernemann Werke Aktien Gesellschaft) - Dresden											
Archimedes	9x12cm	plate	MagBox	1913	Aplanat	6.8		Automat	100	A2826	270
Archimedes Stereo	8.5x17cm	plate	Stereo	1902	Goerz						2300
Baby-Kamera	4.5x6cm	plate	StrutPl	1912	achromatic				M,Z		120
Berry 9x12	9x12cm	plate	Field	1900	Rapid Aplanat						280

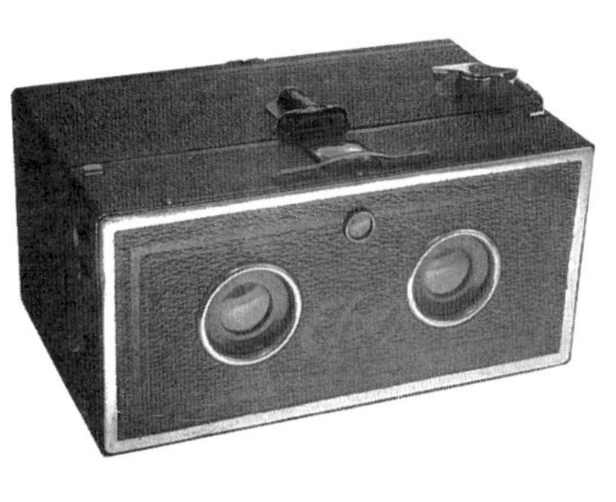

Eho Stereo Box

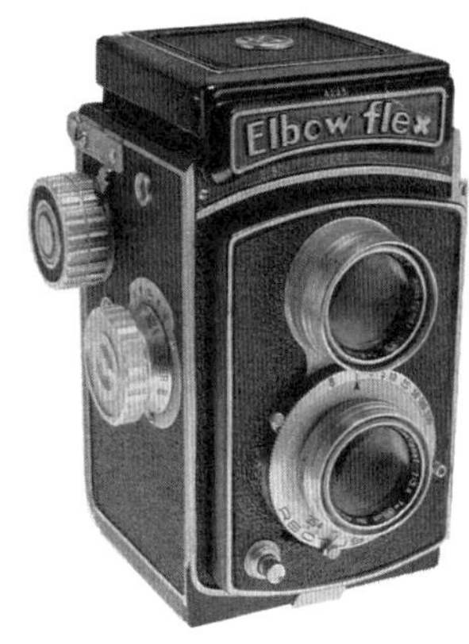

Elbow flex

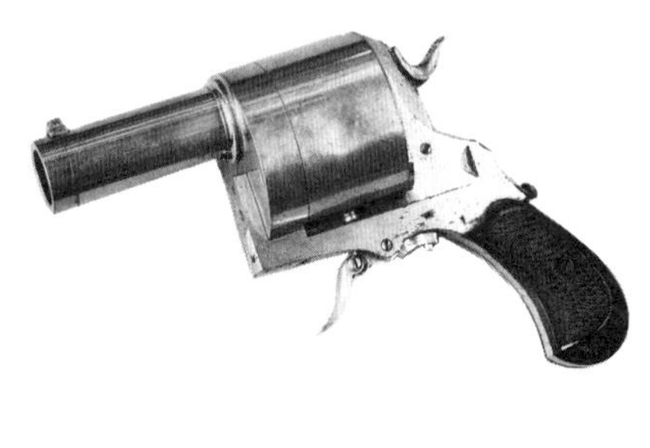

Photo Revolver de Poche

MODEL	FORMAT	FILM	TYPE	Year	LENS	Apert	FL	SHUTTER	SPEEDS	ILLUS	U.S.$
Berry 13x18	13x18cm	plate	Field	1900	Rapid Aplanat						250
Berry 18x24	18x24cm	plate	Field	1900	Rapid Aplanat						250
Bob (circular)	4.5x6cm	plate	RigidPl	1900	Meniscus					A3264	2200
Bob 0 4.5x6	4.5x6cm	120	VtFoldRo	1913	Rapid Detective			Auto		A1404	140
Bob 0 9x12	9x12cm	118	VtFoldRo	1913	Detective Aplanat			Auto		Mc184	50
Bob 0 9x14	9x14cm	122	VtFoldRo	1913	Rapid Detective			Auto		Mc184	50
Bob 00	6x9cm	120	VtFoldRo	1924	Anastigmat	6.8				Mc184	40
Bob I 4.5x6	4.5x6cm	120	VtFoldRo	1913	Aplanat	6.8		Automatic		Mc184	120
Bob I 6x9	6x9cm	120	VtFoldRo	1913	Double Anast.	6		Automatic		Mc184	50
Bob I 9x12	9x12cm	118	VtFoldRo	1913	Aplanat	6.8		Automatic		A371	50
Bob I 9x14	9x14cm	122	VtFoldRo	1913	Double Anast.	6		Automatic		Mc184	70
Bob II 9x12	9x12cm	118	VtFoldRo	1913	Tessar	6.3		Automatic		Mc184	70
Bob II 9x14	9x14cm	122	VtFoldRo	1913	Aplanat	6.8		Automatic		Mc184	70
Bob II 10x15	10x15cm	123	VtFoldRo	1913	Tessar	6.3		Automatic		Mc184	70
Bob III 6x9	6x9cm	120	VtFoldRo	1926	Ernoplast	4.5		Chronos			60
Bob III 10x15	10x15cm	123	HzFoldRo	1906	Detective Aplanat	6.8		Bob			240
Bob III 13x18	13x18cm	112	HzFoldRo	1906	Detective Aplanat	6.8		Bob			210
Bob IV 6x9	6x9cm	120	VtFoldRo	1926	Double Anast.	6.8		Chronos		Mc184	50
Bob IV Stereo 9x14	9x14cm		StFoldRo	1906	Detective Aplanat	6.8		Bob			370
Bob V 4.5x6	4x6.5cm	127	VtFoldRo	1924	Vilar	6.8		Chronos		A395	70
Bob V 6x6	6x6cm	120	VtFoldRo	1924	Tessar	4.5		Chronos			60
Bob V 6x9	6x9cm	120	VtFoldRo	1924	Vilar	6.8		Chronos		Mc185	60
Bob V 6.5x11	6.5x11cm	116	VtFoldRo	1924	Ernotar	4.5		Chronos			50
Bob V 7.25x12.5	7.25x12.5	130	VtFoldRo	1924	Tessar	4.5		Chronos			60
Bob V 8x10.5	8x10.5cm	118	VtFoldRo	1924	Ernotar	4.5		Chronos			60
Bob V Stereo	45x107	120	StFoldRo	1911	Ernos	6.8		Automatic		Mc185	350
Bob X Stereo	45x107	120	StFoldRo	1911	Anastigmat	6		Automatic			330
Bob XV 4.5x6	4x6.5cm	127	VtFoldRo	1911						Mc185	60
Bob XV 6x9	6x9cm	120	VtFoldRo	1911						Mc185	70
Bob XV 8x10.5	8x10.5cm	118	VtFoldRo	1911						Mc185	60
Bob XV Stereo	45x107	120	StFoldRo	1913	Ernon	6.8	65mm		1/100		440
Bobette I	22x33mm	Roll	StrutRo	1925	Ernoplast	4.5			25-100	Mc185	250
Bobette II	22x33mm	Roll	FoldRo	1926	Ernoplast	4.5			25-100		210
Bobette II	22x33mm	Roll	FoldRo	1926	Ernon	3.5			25-100	A394	210
Bobette II (Ernostar)	22x33mm	Roll	FoldRo	1926	Ernostar	2		Chronos			340
Boxkamera 6x6	6x6cm	120	RollBox	1910	achromatic	12				A1328	60
Boxkamera 6x9	6x9cm	120	RollBox	1910	achromatic	12				A1327	60
Boxkamera 9x12	9x12cm	plate	PlateBox	1924	achromatic					A99	100
Edison (wood body) 9x12	9x12cm	plate	Field	1900	Aplanat						1200
Edison (wood body) 10x15	10x15cm	plate	Field	1895	Doppel Anast.					A2939	310
Edison (wood body) 13x18	13x18cm	plate	Field	1900	Aplanat					HK49	310
Edison Detectiv	9x12cm	plate	MagBox	1900	Aplanat						310

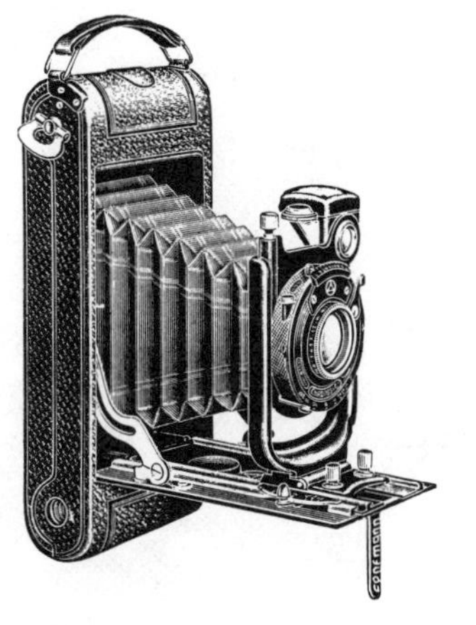

Bob V 6x9

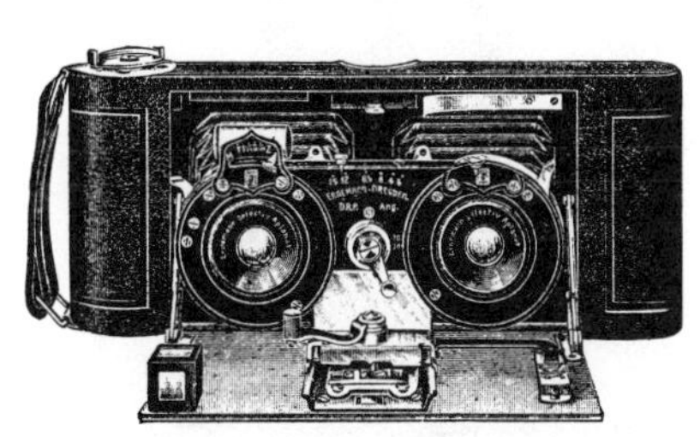

Bob V Stereo

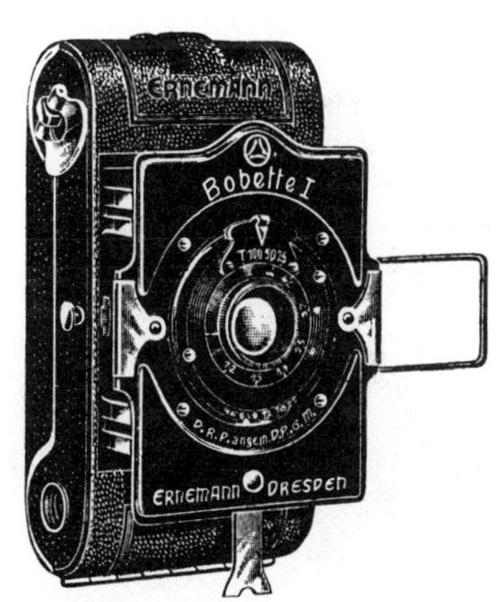

Bobette I

MODEL	FORMAT	FILM	TYPE	Year	LENS	Apert	FL	SHUTTER	SPEEDS	ILLUS	U.S.$
Edison Stereo 8x16	8x16cm	plate	SterBox	1900	Aplanat						1100
Edison Stereo 9x18	9x18cm	plate	SterBox	1900	Aplanat			2-speed		A1809	800
Er-Nox 4.5x6	4.5x6cm	plate	NFPl	1924	Ernostar	2	100mm	focal plane	20-1000	A322	1800
Ermanox 4.5x6	4.5x6cm	plate	NFPl	1924	Ernostar	2	100mm	focal plane	20-1000	Mc185	1800
Ermanox 4.5x6	4.5x6cm	plate	NFPl	1924	Ernostar	1.8	85mm	focal plane	20-1000		1800
Ermanox 6.5x9	6.5x9cm	plate	StrutPl	1925	Ernostar	1.8				Mc185	2000
Ermanox 9x12	9x12cm	plate	StrutPl	1925	Ernostar	1.8	165mm	focal plane	1/15-1500		2900
Ermanox Reflex	4.5x6cm		MedSLR	1926	Ernostar	1.8	105mm			Mc185	1300
Ernette	4.5x6cm	pack	PlateBox	1924	achromatic				T,I	Mc185	280
Erni 4.5x6	4.5x6cm	pack	PlateBox	1924	achromatic				T,I	Mc185	220
Erni 6.5x9	6.5x9cm	pack	PlateBox	1924	achromatic				T,I		280
Erni 9x12	9x12cm	pack	PlateBox	1924	achromatic				T,I		280
Erni stereo	45x107	pack	SterPl	1924	achromatic				T,I		330
Ernoflex Klapp Reflex	9x12cm	plate	FoldSLR	1914	Ernemann	6.8				Mc186	670
Ernoflex Klapp Reflex	9x12cm	plate	FoldSLR	1914	Tessar	4.5				Mc186	670
Ernoflex Klapp Refl. Mod. I	4.5x6cm	plate	FoldSLR	1924	Ernon	3.5	75mm	focal plane	1000		520
Ernoflex Klapp Refl. Mod. I	6.5x9cm	plate	FoldSLR	1924	Ernotar	4.5	135mm	focal plane	1000	Mc186	420
Ernoflex Klapp Refl. Mod. I	8x10.5cm	plate	FoldSLR	1924	Tessar	4.5				Mc186	420
Ernoflex Klapp Refl. Mod. I	9x12cm	plate	FoldSLR	1924	Ernotar	4.5	135mm	focal plane	1000	Mc186	420
Ernoflex Klapp Refl. Mod. II	8x10.5cm	plate	FoldSLR	1924						Mc186	500
Ernoflex Klapp Refl. Mod. II	9x12cm	plate	FoldSLR	1924						Mc186	500
Film K 4.5x6	4.5x6cm	120	RollBox	1917	Meniscus	12.5			T,I	Mc186	110
Film K 6x6	6x6cm	120	RollBox	1917	Meniscus	12.5			T,I	Mc186	100
Film K 6x9	6x9cm	120	RollBox	1917	Meniscus	12.5			T,I	Mc186	70
Film K 6.5x11	6.5x11cm	116	RollBox	1917	Meniscus	12.5			T,I	Mc186	80
Film K 7.25x12.5	7.25x12.5	130	RollBox	1917	Meniscus	12.5			T,I	Mc186	50
Film U	6x9cm	120	RollBox	1925	Doublet			Automatic		Mc186	220
Globus 13x18	13x18cm	plate	Field	1900				focal plane		Mc186	520
Globus 18x24	18x24cm	plate	Field	1900				focal plane		Mc186	480
Globus Salonkamera	18x24cm	plate	Studio	1910	Various			various			1700
Globus Stereo 13x18	13x18cm	plate	StFoldPl	1910	Tessar	6.3	135mm	St. Compound			700
Heag 0 6.5x9	6.5x9cm	plate	FoldPl	1918	Aplanat	6.8	105mm	Automat	25-100		50
Heag 0 9x12	9x12cm	plate	FoldPl	1918	Aplanat	6.8	135mm	Automat	25-100		50
Heag 00 6.5x9	6.5x9cm	plate	FoldPl	1914	Doppel	11		Automat	½-100	A194	60
Heag 00 9x12	9x12cm	plate	FoldPl	1914	Doppel	11		Automat	½-100	Mc186	50
Heag I 6.5x9	6.5x9cm	plate	FoldPl	1914	Detective Aplanat	6.8		Automat	½-100	Mc186	230
Heag I 9x12	9x12cm	plate	FoldPl	1914	Detective Aplanat	6.8		Automat	½-100	Mc186	230
Heag I 9x14	9x14cm	plate	FoldPl	1914	Detective Aplanat	6.8		Automat	½-100	Mc186	230
Heag I 12x16.5	12x16.5cm	plate	FoldPl	1914	Detective Aplanat	6.8		Automat	½-100	Mc186	230
Heag I stereo 9x12	9x12cm	plate	StFoldPl	1904	Detective Aplanat	6.8		Automat	½-100		350
Heag II 6.5x9	6.5x9cm	plate	FoldPl	1911	Detective Aplanat	6.8				Mc186	60
Heag II 9x12	9x12cm	plate	FoldPl	1911	Detective Aplanat	6.8				A201	60

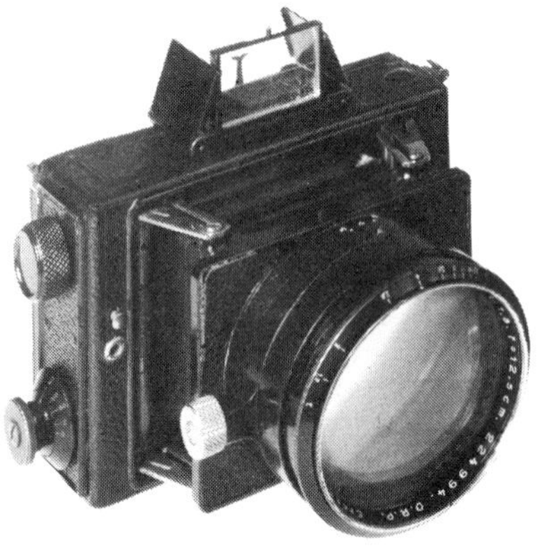

Ermanox 6.5x9

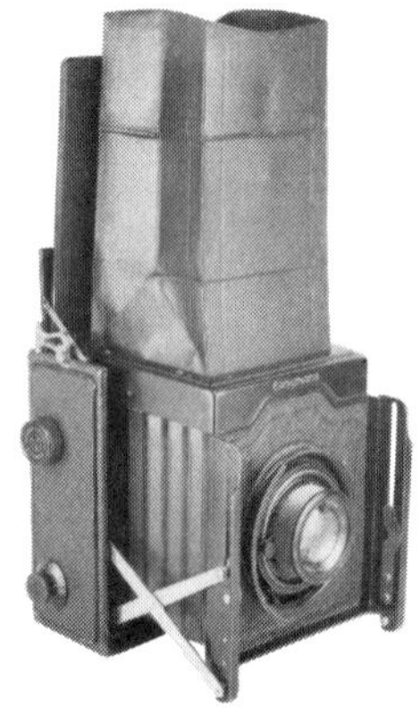

Ernoflex Klapp Refl. Mod. I

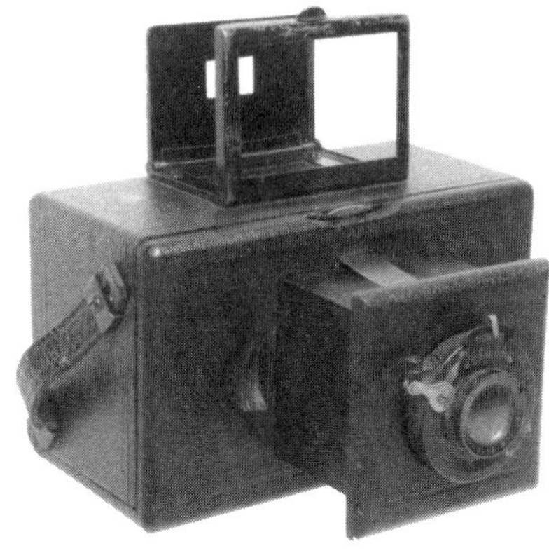

Film U

MODEL	FORMAT	FILM	TYPE	Year	LENS	Apert	FL	SHUTTER	SPEEDS	ILLUS	U.S.$
Heag II 9x14	9x14cm	plate	FoldPl	1911	Detective Aplanat	6.8				Mc186	60
Heag II 12x16.5	12x16.5cm	plate	FoldPl	1911	Detective Aplanat	6.8				Mc186	60
Heag III 6.5x9	6.5x9cm	plate	FoldPl	1926							70
Heag III 9x12	9x12cm	plate	FoldPl	1926	Anastigmat	6.8		Chronos-A			60
Heag III stereo 7x15	7x15cm	plate	StFoldPl	1910	Detective Aplanat	6.8	180mm				560
Heag III stereo 13x18	13x18cm	plate	StFoldPl	1910	Detective Aplanat	6.8	180mm				580
Heag IV 6.5x9	6.5x9cm	plate	FoldPl	1925	Detective Aplanat	6.8					70
Heag IV 9x12	9x12cm	plate	FoldPl	1925	Detective Aplanat	6.8					70
Heag IV stereo	9x18cm	plate	StFoldPl	1907	Aplanat	6.8				A1768	360
Heag V 4.5x6	4.5x6cm	plate	FoldPl	1924	Ernoplast	4.5	7.5cm	Chronos-C		A226	190
Heag V 6.5x9	6.5x9cm	plate	FoldPl	1924	Ernoplast	4.5		Chronos-C		Mc187	50
Heag V 9x12	9x12cm	plate	FoldPl	1924	Tessar	4.5		Chronos		Mc187	60
Heag VI 9x12	9x12cm	plate	FoldPl	1911	Tessar	4.5	105mm				180
Heag VI (Zwei-Verschluss)	9x12cm	plate	FoldPl	1907	Aplanat	6.8	135mm	focal plane	2000	Mc187	240
Heag VI (Zwei-Verschluss)	9x14cm	plate	FoldPl	1907	Autochromatic			focal plane	2000	Mc187	310
Heag VI stereo	9x12cm	plate	StFoldPl	1911	Tessar	4.5					460
Heag VI stereo (2-Verschl.)	9x14cm	plate	StFoldPl	1907	Ernar	6.8	135mm	focal plane	2000	Mc187	500
Heag VI stereo (2-Verschl.)	12x16.5cm	plate	StFoldPl	1907	Dagor	6.8	135mm	focal plane	2000	Mc187	510
Heag VII 6.5x9	6.5x9cm	plate	FoldPl	1924	Dogmar	6.3	10cm	Chronos-C	1/300	A198	70
Heag VII 9x12	9x12cm	plate	FoldPl	1924	Vilar	6.8		Chronos		Mc187	70
Heag IX Universal Camera	13x18cm	plate	FoldPl	1904	Anastigmat	6.8	180mm	focal plane	2500	Mc187	280
Heag XI 9x12	9x12cm	plate	FoldPl	1913	Anastigmat	6	135mm	Automat	100	Mc187	80
Heag XI 9x14	9x14cm	plate	FoldPl	1913	Anastigmat	6	135mm	Automat	100	Mc187	50
Heag XI 12x16.5	12x16.5cm	plate	FoldPl	1913	Anastigmat	6	180mm	Automat	100	Mc187	160
Heag XII 9x12	9x12cm	plate	FoldPl	1906	Aplanat	6.8	135mm	Bob	100	A2972	50
Heag XII 12x16.5	12x16.5cm	plate	FoldPl	1906				Bob		Mc187	60
Heag XII (Quer) 9x12	9x12cm	plate	FoldPl	1910	Detectiv-Aplanat	6.8	135mm		½-100	Mc187	110
Heag XII (Quer) 10x15	10x15cm	plate	FoldPl	1910	Detectiv-Aplanat	6.8	150mm		½-100	A2975	150
Heag XII Ser. III 9x12	9x12cm	plate	FoldPl	1920	Aplanat	6.3	135mm	Automat	Z,M	Mc188	100
Heag XII Ser. III 10x15	10x15cm	plate	FoldPl	1920	Aplanat	6.3	135mm	Automat	Z,M	Mc188	110
Heag XII Ser. III stereo	9x12cm	plate	StFoldPl	1925	Doppel Anast.						310
Heag XII Ser. III stereo	9x18cm	plate	StFoldPl	1925	Doppel Anast.						300
Heag XII stereo 6x13	6x13cm	plate	StFoldPl	1910	Detectiv-Aplanat	6.8	90mm		½-100		450
Heag XII stereo 9x12	9x12cm	plate	StFoldPl	1910	Vilar	6.8	105mm			Mc188	400
Heag XII stereo 9x18	9x18cm	plate	StFoldPl	1910	Ernon	6.8	135mm			Mc188	270
Heag XIV 4.5x6	4.5x6cm	plate	FoldPl	1910	Doppel Anast.	6.8		Automat			100
Heag XIV (Zwei-Verschluss)	4.5x6cm	plate	FoldPl	1910	Doppel Anast.	6	80mm	focal plane	50-2500	A3034	290
Heag XIV (Zwei-Verschluss)	9x12cm	plate	FoldPl	1910	Ernon	6.8	120mm	focal plane	50-2500	Mc188	100
Heag XV 4.5x6	4.5x6cm	plate	FoldPl	1911	Doppel Anast.	6.8	80mm	Automat		Mc188	140
Heag XV 6.5x9	6.5x9cm	plate	FoldPl	1912	Doppel Anast.	6.8		Automat	1-100		80
Heag XV 9x12	9x12cm	plate	FoldPl	1912	Detectiv-Aplanat	6.8	80mm			A2974	180
Heag XV stereo 45x107	45x107	plate	StFoldPl	1912						A757	280

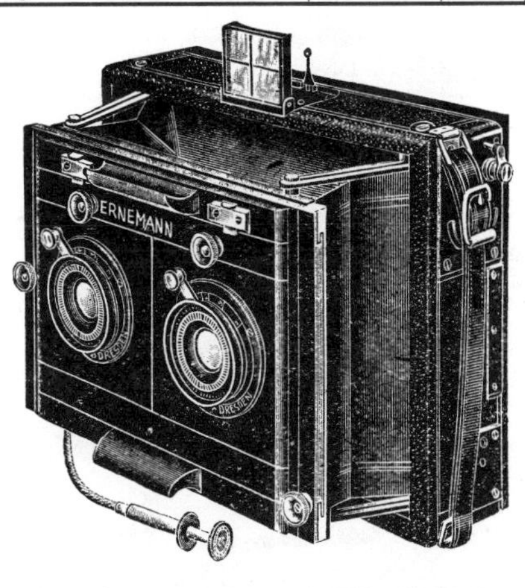

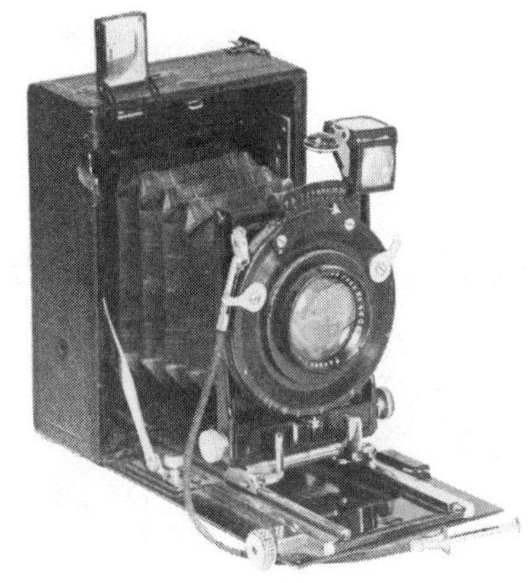

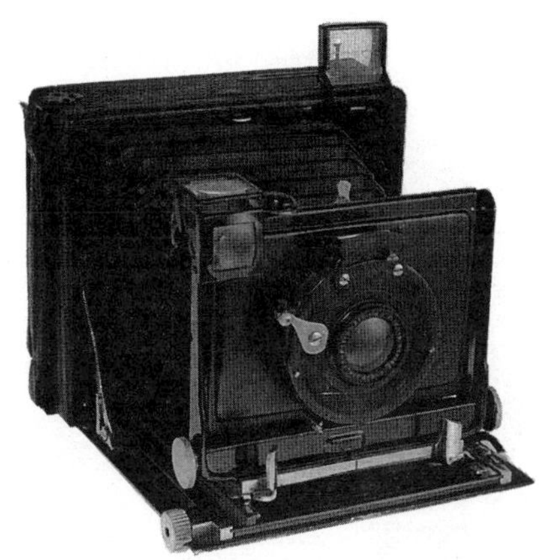

Heag IX Universal Camera **Heag XI** **Heag XII Ser. III**

MODEL	FORMAT	FILM	TYPE	Year	LENS	Apert	FL	SHUTTER	SPEEDS	ILLUS	U.S.$
Heag XV stereo 6x13	6x13cm	plate	StFoldPl	1912						A758	240
Heag XVI 9x12	9x12cm	plate	FoldPl	1913	Detectiv-Aplanat	6.8				A1447	180
Klapp 6.5x9	6.5x9cm	plate	StrutPl	1904	Tessar	4.5		focal plane	1-2500	Mc188	200
Klapp 9x12	9x12cm	plate	StrutPl	1904	Ernon	3.5	15cm	focal plane	1-2500	Mc188	180
Klapp 9x14	9x14cm	plate	StrutPl	1904	Ernostar	2.7		focal plane	1-2500	Mc188	220
Klapp 10x15	10x15cm	plate	StrutPl	1904	Ernon	3.5		focal plane	1-2500	Mc188	220
Klapp 12x16.5	12x16.5cm	plate	StrutPl	1904	Tessar	4.5		focal plane	1-2500	Mc188	230
Klapp Stereo 45x107	45x107	plate	SterStrut	1913	Doppel Anast.	6	65mm	focal plane	1-2500	A2698	1000
Klapp Stereo 9x18	9x18cm	plate	SterStrut	1904							330
Klapp Stereo-Panorama	6x13cm	plate	SterStrut	1904	Doppel Anast.	6	90mm	focal plane	1-2500	A2683	270
Liliput 4.5x6	4.5x6cm	plate	StrutPl	1914	achromatic				M,Z	Mc188	80
Liliput 6.5x9	6.5x9cm	plate	StrutPl	1914	achromatic				M,Z		100
Liliput Stereo	45x107	plate	SterStrut	1919	Meniscus			guillotine		A744	290
Luftbildkamera 13x18	13x18cm	plate	Aerial	1914							190
Mignon-Kamera	4.5x6cm	plate	StrutPl	1912	Detectiv-Aplanat	6.8			M,Z		120
Minax	4.5x6cm	plate	StrutPl	1916	Apochromat						150
Miniatur-Ernoflex	4.5x6cm	plate	FoldSLR	1925	Ernon	3.5	75mm	focal plane	1000	Mc189	1100
Miniatur-Klapp	4.5x6cm	plate	StrutPl	1925	Ernostar	2.7	75mm	focal plane	1000	A324	450
Miniatur-Klapp	4.5x6cm	plate	StrutPl	1925	Tessar	3.5		focal plane	1000		400
Miniatur-Klapp	4.5x6cm	plate	StrutPl	1925	Ernotar	4.5		focal plane	1000	Mc189	450
Minor (leathered)	9x12cm	plate	MagBox	1919	Detectiv-Aplanat	6.8	150mm				240
Minor (wood)	9x12cm	plate	MagBox		Univ.Aplanat	11	16.5cm			A2821	240
Rolf I	4x6.5cm	127	FoldRo	1924	Rapid Rectilinear	12	75mm		T,B,I	Mc189	50
Rolf II	4x6.5cm	127	FoldRo	1926	Double Anast.	6.8		Chronos			50
Rolf II	4x6.5cm	127	FoldRo	1926	Ernoplast	4.5		Chronos			50
Rundblick-Kamera	12x100cm	Roll	Panoramic	1907	Double Anast.	5.4	135mm			A2014	4800
Simplex 6.5x9	6.5x9cm	plate	FoldPl	1924		11			M,Z		80
Simplex 9x12	9x12cm	plate	FoldPl	1924		11			M,Z		60
Simplex (metal)	9x12cm	plate	FoldPl	1919		12	135mm		M,Z		110
Simplex Ernoflex 4.5x6	4.5x6cm	plate	SLR-Box	1926				focal plane	1/20-1000	A3154	700
Simplex Ernoflex 6.5x9	6.5x9cm	plate	SLR-Box	1926		4.5	10.5cm	focal plane	1/20-1000		340
Simplex Ernoflex 9x12	9x12cm	plate	SLR-Box	1926				focal plane	1/20-1000		210
Spiegel-Reflex 6.5x9	6.5x9cm	plate	LgSLR	1909	Double Anast.	6.8		focal plane	2500	Mc189	280
Spiegel-Reflex 9x9	9x9cm	plate	LgSLR	1912	Tessar	4.5	150mm	focal plane	2500	A1596	290
Spiegel-Reflex 9x12	9x12cm	plate	LgSLR	1909	Double Anast.	6.8		focal plane	2500	Mc189	280
Spiegel-Reflex 12x16.5	12x16.5cm	plate	LgSLR	1909	Tessar	4.5		focal plane	2500	Mc189	280
Stereo-Bob 9x14	9x14cm	Roll	SterRo	1905	D.An.Ernon	6.9	9cm	Stereo	1/100	A764	430
Stereo Ernoflex	45x107	plate	SterRefl	1926	Ernotar	4.5		focal plane	1/10-1000	Mc189	1400
Stereo Ernoflex	45x107	plate	SterRefl	1926	Tessar	4.5		focal plane	1/10-1000	A775	1400
Stereo Reflex 45x107	45x107	plate	SterRefl	1912	Anastigmat	6		focal plane	2500		1000
Stereo Reflex 45x107	45x107	plate	SterRefl	1912	Dagor	6.8		focal plane	2500		580
Stereo Reflex 6x13	6x13cm	plate	SterRefl	1912	Dagor	6.8		focal plane	2500		640

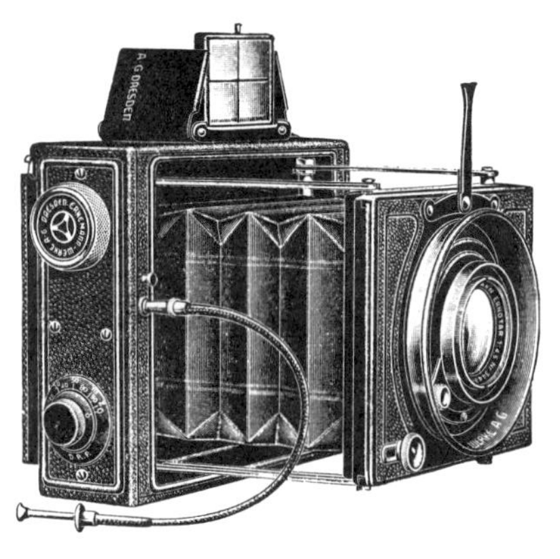

Klapp

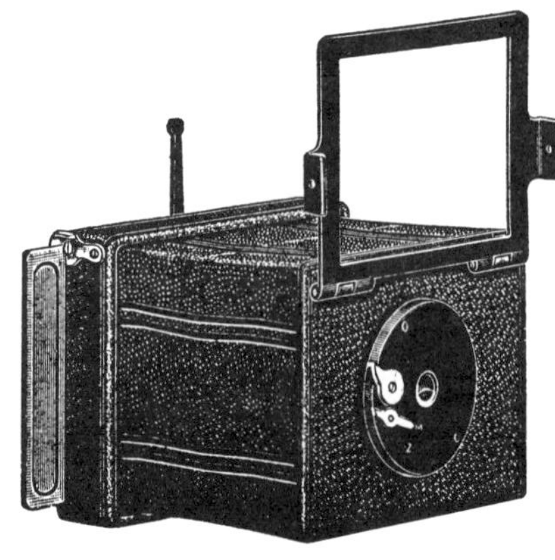

Liliput

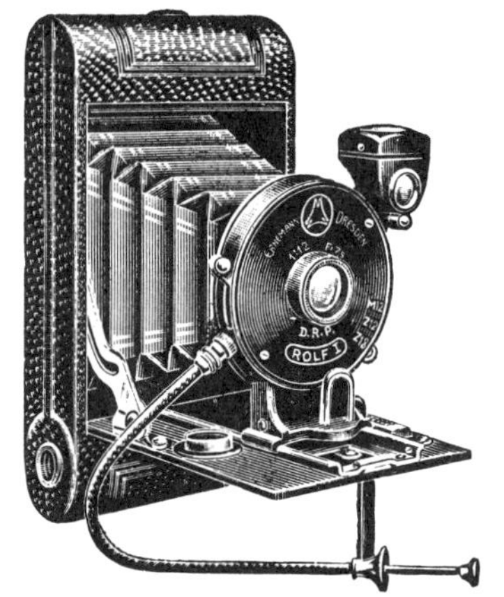

Rolf I

MODEL	FORMAT	FILM	TYPE	Year	LENS	Apert	FL	SHUTTER	SPEEDS	ILLUS	U.S.$
Stereo Reflex 6x13	6x13cm	plate	SterRefl	1912	Tessar	4.5	75mm	focal plane	2500		650
Stereo Simplex	45x107	plate	SterPl	1920	Doppel	11	60mm	guillotine	T,B,I	Mc189	180
Stereo Simplex Ernoflex	45x107	plate	SterRefl	1926	Ernon	3.5	75mm	focal plane	25-1000	Mc189	1000
Stereo Spiegel-Reflex	10x15cm	plate	SterRefl	1912	Anastigmat	6		focal plane	2500	A2697	700
Stereo Spiegel-Reflex	10x15cm	plate	SterRefl	1912	Dagor	6.8		focal plane	2500		700
Stereo Tropen-Kamera	9x12cm	plate	SterPl	1898		6.3	105mm	Stereo		A2665	460
Stereoscop-Kamera	9x18cm	plate	SterBox	1901	Meniscus				B,I	Mc189	410
Studiokamera 9x12	9x12cm	plate	Studio	1900	Various			various			390
Studiokamera 18x24	18x24cm	plate	Studio	1900	Various			various			800
Studiokamera 24x30	24x30cm	plate	Studio	1900	Various			various		A2961	1200
Tropical Heag VI (2-Versch.	9x12cm	plate	FoldPl	1914	Anastigmat	6		focal plane	2500	Mc189	1300
Tropical Heag VI (2-Versch.	9x12cm	plate	FoldPl	1914	Tessar	6.3		focal plane	2500	Mc189	1300
Tropical Heag X 9x12	9x12cm	plate	FoldPl	1920	Ernon	6.8		focal plane	2500		670
Tropical Heag X 13x18	13x18cm	plate	FoldPl	1920	Ernon	6.8		focal plane	2500		700
Tropical Heag XI 9x12	9x12cm	plate	FoldPl	1920	Vilar	6.8		Chronos		A1399	800
Tropical Heag XI 9x12	9x12cm	plate	FoldPl	1920	Ernoplast	4.5		Chronos		Mc190	800
Tropical Klapp 6.5x9	6.5x9cm	plate	StrutPl	1904	Tessar	6.3		focal plane	2500		1000
Tropical Klapp 9x12	9x12cm	plate	StrutPl	1904	Tessar	6.3		focal plane	2500	Mc190	1200
Tropical Klapp 10x15	10x15cm	plate	StrutPl	1904	Dagor	6.8		focal plane	2500	A1414	1100
Tropical Klapp 13x18	13x18cm	plate	StrutPl	1904	Tessar	6.3		focal plane	2500	Mc190	1100
Unette	22x33mm	Roll	RollBox	1924	Meniscus	12.5			T,I		180
Universal 13x18	13x18cm	plate	FoldPl	1900	Goerz Doppel An.	4.6		focal plane		A2976	550
Velo Klapp I	9x12cm	plate	StrutPl	1901	Aplanat	6.8		focal plane	1000	Mc190	180
Velo Klapp IV	9x12cm	plate	StrutPl	1904	Aplanat	6.8		focal plane	2000	Mc190	180
Velo Klapp XIV	9x12cm	plate	StrutPl	1914	Aplanat	6.8		focal plane	2500	A3019	180
...ETA Prague											
Etareta	24x36mm	35mm	35vf	1950	Etar II	3.5	50mm	Etaxa	10-200	Mc190	70
...EULITZ (Dr. Eulitz) - Harzburg											
Grisette	24x36mm	35mm	35vf	1955	Achromat		45mm			Mc190	100
...EUMIG - Austria											
Eumigetta (1)	6x6cm	120	RigidRo		Eumar	5.6	80mm			Mc190	40
Eumigetta 2	6x6cm	120	RigidRo		Eumar	4	80mm		1/25-200		50
...(unknown)											
Excella	4x4cm	127	RigidRo		Idar Optik					Mc191	30
...EXPO CAMERA CO. - New York											
Autobox	4x6.5cm	Roll	RollBox	1924	Meniscus			rotary	T,I		100
Easy-Load (black)	1⅝x2½"	Roll	RollBox	1926	Meniscus			rotary		Mc191	30
Easy-Load (colors)	1⅝x2½"	Roll	RollBox	1926	Meniscus			rotary		Mc191	50
Focal Plane Police Camera	18x28mm	Roll	Submin		achromatic			focal plane	T,I		1500
Police Camera	18x28mm	Roll	Submin	1911	achromatic			focal plane	T,I	Mc191	600
Watch Camera	16x22mm		Submin	1905						Mc191	400
Watch Camera (colors)	16x22mm		Submin	1905							2500

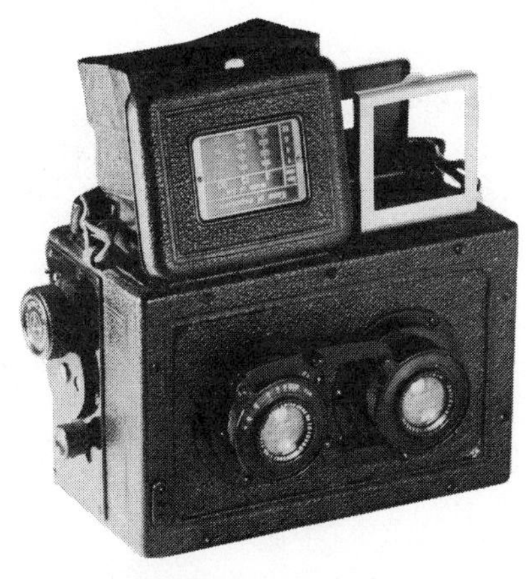
Stereo Simplex Ernoflex

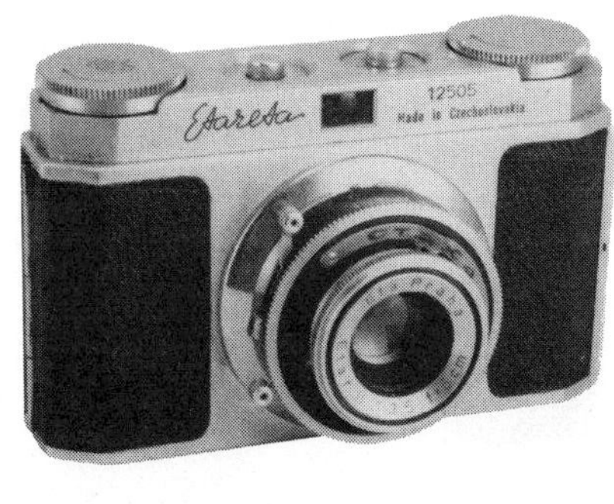

Etareta

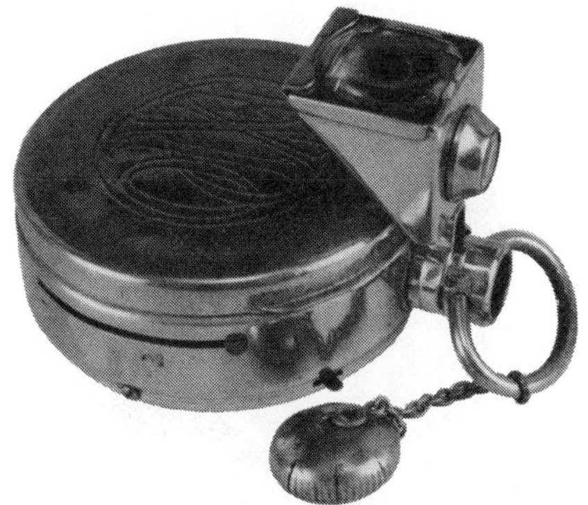
Expo Watch Camera

MODEL	FORMAT	FILM	TYPE	Year	LENS	Apert	FL	SHUTTER	SPEEDS	ILLUS	U.S.$
...FABRIK FOTOGRAFISCHE APPARATE - Lübeck											
Fotal (blue)	8x12mm	Roll	Submin	1950	Optar Anast.	2.8	20mm	Prontor II	250	Mc191	1600
Fotal (brown)	8x12mm	Roll	Submin	1950	Optar Anast.	2.8	20mm	Prontor II	250	A875	1100
Fotal (green)	8x12mm	Roll	Submin	1950	Optar Anast.	2.8	20mm	Prontor II	250	Mc191	1600
...FALCON CAMERA CO. - Chicago											
Falcon Miniature	3x4cm	127	RigidRo	1947	Wollensak		50mm		I,T	Mc191	30
Falcon Miniature Deluxe	3x4cm	127	RigidRo	1947	Graf		50mm		I,T	Mc191	30
Falcon Minicam Junior	3x4cm	127	RigidRo	1947						A3062	30
Falcon Minicam Senior	3x4cm	127	RigidRo	1947							30
Falcon Rocket	3x4cm	127	RigidRo	1947						Mc191	20
...FALLOWFIELD, JONATHAN LTD. - London											
Facile	3¼x4¼"	plate	DetectivBox	1890						Mc192	580
Falloroll	3¼x4¼"	118	FoldRo	1900	Rapid Rectilinear	8		B&L Unicum			110
Miall Hand Camera	3¼x4"	plate	DetectivBox	1893						Mc192	3200
Peritus No. 1	10x12"	plate	Field		Double Anast.	7.7	14"				260
Popular Ferrotype Camera		Ferro	Ferrotype	1911	Petzval	3.7	100mm			Mc192	1200
Prismotype	2½x3½"	Card	Street	1923	Anastigmat						1200
Studio Camera	21x27cm	plate	Studio	1860	Ross						1600
Tailboard Camera	4¼x6½"	plate	Tailboard		Brass barrel					Mc192	280
Tailboard Camera	10x12"	plate	Tailboard		Brass barrel						280
Wet plate 9-lens camera		WetPl	WetPlate	1870							4000
...FALZ & WERNER - Leipzig											
Field Camera 9x12	9x12cm	plate	Field	1900							130
Field Camera 13x18	13x18cm	plate	Field	1900	Tetrar	4.5	180mm				180
Universal Salon 18x24	18x24cm	plate	Studio	1895	Voigtländer						1800
...FAP (Société Fabrique d'Appareils Photographiques) - Suresnes											
Norca A	24x36mm	35mm	35vf	1938	Boyer Saphir	3.5	50mm	Norca	T,B,25-300	Mc192	170
Norca B	24x36mm	35mm	35vf	1945	Berthiot	3.5	50mm	Norca		F623	90
Norca Cmt	24x36mm	35mm	35vf	1945	FAP	3.5	50mm	Atos		F625	90
Norca Cmt Deluxe	24x36mm	35mm	35vf	1945	FAP	3.5	50mm	Atos		F624	110
Norca Pin-Up	24x36mm	35mm	RigidRo	1945	Anastigmat	3.5	50mm	Norca	10-300	Mc192	350
Rower	32x40mm	Roll	RigidRo	1936						Mc192	40
...FAUVEL											
Stereo 45x107	45x107	plate	SterPl	1912	Rapid Rectilinear			focal plane			450
Stereo 8x16	8x16cm	plate	SterPl	1899	various			focal plane			360
Stereo 9x14	9x14cm	plate	SterPl	1899	various			focal plane			450
Stereo 13x18	13x18cm	plate	SterPl	1899	Rapid Rectilinear			Otto Lund		F1174	460
...FED (Dzerzhinsky Commune) - Kharkov, Ukraine											
Fed-1 Type a	24x36mm	35mm	35rf	1934	FED	3.5	50mm	focal plane		Ru62	650
Fed-1 Type b	24x36mm	35mm	35rf	1935	FED	3.5	50mm	focal plane		Ru62	200
Fed-1 Type c	24x36mm	35mm	35rf	1937	FED	3.5	50mm	focal plane		Ru63	140
Fed-1 Type d	24x36mm	35mm	35rf	1939	FED	3.5	50mm	focal plane		Ru63	140

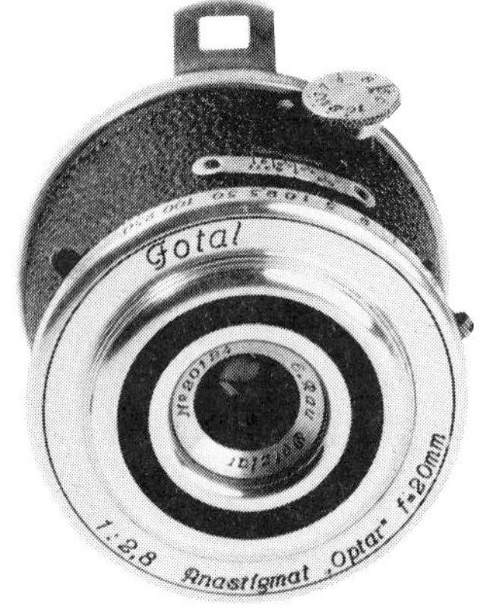

Fotal

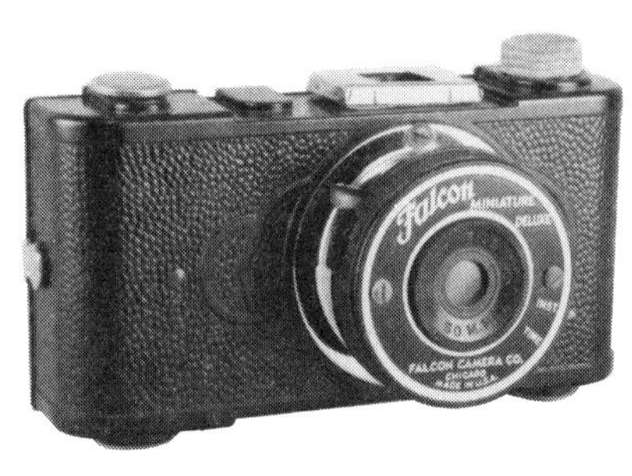

Falcon Miniature Deluxe

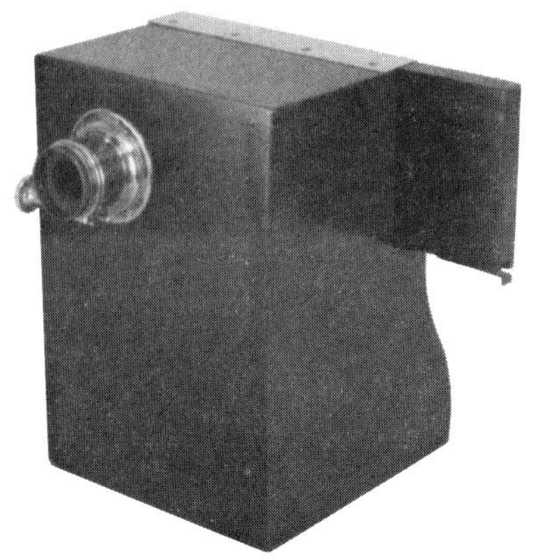

Popular Ferrotype Camera

MODEL	FORMAT	FILM	TYPE	Year	LENS	Apert	FL	SHUTTER	SPEEDS	ILLUS	U.S.$
Fed-1 Type e	24x36mm	35mm	35rf	1946	FED	3.5	50mm	focal plane		Ru64	170
Fed-1 Type f	24x36mm	35mm	35rf	1949	FED	3.5	50mm	focal plane		Ru65	130
Fed-1 Type g	24x36mm	35mm	35rf	1953	FED	3.5	50mm	focal plane		Ru65	140
Fed-2 Type a	24x36mm	35mm	35rf	1955	FED	3.5	50mm	focal plane		Ru69	90
Fed-2 Type b	24x36mm	35mm	35rf	1956	Industar-26M	2.8	5cm	focal plane		Ru69	90
Fed-2 Type c	24x36mm	35mm	35rf	1958	Industar-26M	2.8	5cm	focal plane		Ru70	80
Fed-2 Type d	24x36mm	35mm	35rf	1958	Industar-26M	2.8	5cm	focal plane		Ru70	100
Fed-2 Type e	24x36mm	35mm	35rf	1969	Industar-61	2.8	52mm	focal plane		Ru70	150
Fed-3 Type a	24x36mm	35mm	35rf	1961	Industar-26M	2.8	5cm	focal plane		Ru70	60
Fed-3 Type b	24x36mm	35mm	35rf	1963	Industar-61	2.8	52mm	focal plane		Ru70	50
Fed-4 Type a	24x36mm	35mm	35rf	1964	Industar-61	2.8	52mm	focal plane		Ru71	60
Fed-4 Type b	24x36mm	35mm	35rf	1969	Industar-61	2.8	52mm	focal plane		Ru71	50
Fed-5	24x36mm	35mm	35rf	1977	Industar-61	2.8	52mm	focal plane	1-500	Ru71	50
Fed-5 Olympic	24x36mm	35mm	35rf	1980	Industar-61	2.8	52mm	focal plane	1-500		90
Fed-5B	24x36mm	35mm	35rf	1975	Industar-61	2.8	52mm	focal plane	1-500		70
Fed-5B Olympic	24x36mm	35mm	35rf	1980	Industar-61	2.8	52mm	focal plane	1-500	Ru71	100
Fed-5C (=5S)	24x36mm	35mm	35rf	1938	Industar-61	2.8	52mm	focal plane	1-500	Ru71	50
Fed-C	24x36mm	35mm	35rf	1938	FED	2	50mm	focal plane	1000	Ru66	100
Fed Mikron	18x24mm	35mm	35Half	1968	Helios-89	1.9	30mm		1-500	Ru77	50
Fed Mikron 2	18x24mm	35mm	35Half	1977	Industar-81	2.8	38mm		30-650	Ru77	30
Fed Stereo		35mm	35Ster	1988	Industar-81	2.8	38mm			Ru79	220
Fed V	24x36mm	35mm	35rf	1938	Fed	2	50mm	focal plane		Ru66	180
Zarya (Zapa)	24x36mm	35mm	35vf	1959	Industar-26M	2.8	5cm	focal plane		Mc193	140
...FEINAK-WERKE - Munich											
Präzisionskamera	10x15cm	plate	FoldPl		Schneider Xenar	4.5	165mm	Dial-Compur			150
...FEINMECHANISCHE WERKSTÄTTEN (Ing. Karl Foitzik) - Trier											
Foinix 6x6	6x6cm	120	HzFoldRo	1951	Steinar	3.5	75mm	Prontor		Mc197	50
Foinix 35mm	24x36mm	35mm	35vf	1955	Foinar	2.8	45mm	Vario		HK595	50
Unca	6x6cm	120	HzFoldRo	1953	Steinar	3.5	75mm	Prontor-S			50
...FEINOPTISCHES WERK - Görlitz											
Astraflex-II	6x6cm	120	MedSLR	1952	Tessar	3.5	105mm	focal plane	-1000		120
...FEINWERK TECHNIK GmbH - Lahr											
Mec-16	10x14mm	16mm	Submin	1958		2.8			-1000	Mc193	100
Mec-16 (new style)	10x14mm	16mm	Submin			2.8			-1000	Mc194	80
Mec-16 SB	10x14mm	16mm	Submin	1960	Rod. Heligon	2			-1000		100
...FERRANIA - Milan											
Alfa	4x5cm	127	RigidRo	1945	Achromatic	9			I,T	Mc194	30
Box camera	6x9cm	120	RollBox	1935	Achromatic		80mm		I		40
Condor I	24x36mm	35mm	35rf	1950	Eliog	2.8	50mm	Iscus Rapid	1-500	Mc194	70
Condor Ic	24x36mm	35mm	35rf	1950	Eliog	2.8	50mm	Iscus Rapid	1-500		70
Condor II	24x36mm	35mm	35rf	1950				Iscus Rapid	1-500		120
Condor Junior	24x36mm	35mm	35vf	1950	Galileo Eliog	3.5	50mm	Iscus Rapid	1-500		80

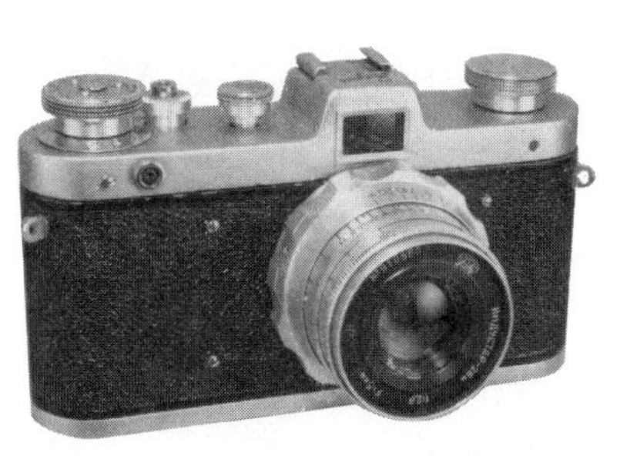

Zarya (Zapa)

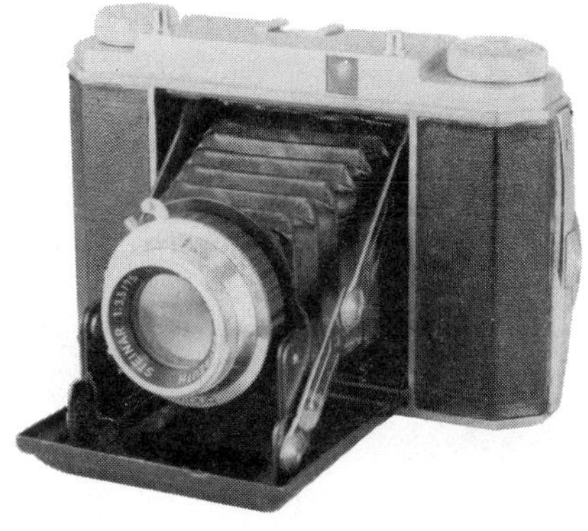

Foinix 6x6

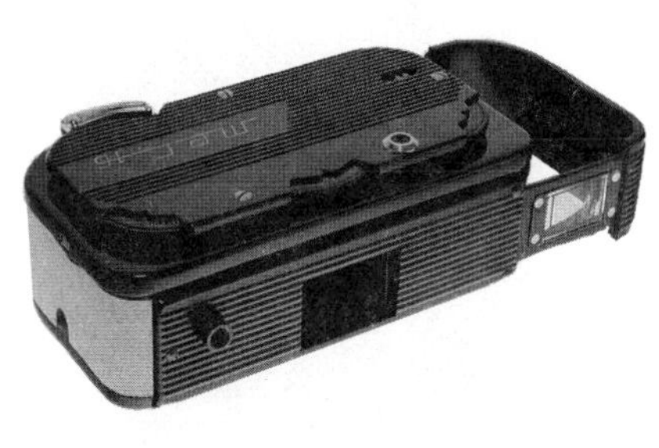

Mec-16

MODEL	FORMAT	FILM	TYPE	Year	LENS	Apert	FL	SHUTTER	SPEEDS	ILLUS	U.S.$
Condoretta	24x36mm	35mm	35vf	1951	Terog	4	4cm	Aplon B	1-300		80
Delta	4x6.5cm	127	RigidRo	1950	Biaplan	8.8	70mm				50
Elioflex		120	TLR-Box	1950	Galileo Monog	8			25-200	Mc194	60
Elioflex 2		120	TLR-Box		Anastigmat	6.3	75mm		25-200		50
Eura	6x6cm	120	RigidRo	1959	Achromatic				I,T	Mc194	10
Euralux 44	4x4cm	127	RigidRo	1961	Achromatic				I,T	Mc194	30
Ibis	4x6cm	127	RigidRo	1950	Primar	9	75mm	Simi			30
Ibis 34	3x4cm	127	RigidRo		Achromatic	7.7	58mm		50,100	Mc194	30
Ibis 44	4x4cm	127	RigidRo	1955	Achromatic	7.7	58mm		50,100		20
Ibis 6/6 (black)	6x6cm	120	RigidRo	1955	Primar	9	85mm	Simi			20
Ibis 6/6 (gray)	6x6cm	120	RigidRo	1955	Primar	9	85mm	Simi			20
Lince 2	24x36mm	35mm	35vf	1962	Cassar	2.8	45mm	Vero			30
Lince 3	24x36mm	35mm	35vf	1962	Cassar	2.8	45mm	Vero			50
Lince Rapid	24x36mm	35mm	35vf	1965	Dignar Anastigmat			3-speed			30
Lince Supermatic	24x36mm	35mm	35vf	1962	Rod. Ysarex	2.8	45mm	Prontor-Matic		Mc194	40
Rondine	4x6.5cm	127	MetBx	1948	Meniscus Linear	8.8	75mm	single speed		Mc194	40
Tanit	3x4cm	127	RigidRo	1955					I,T		30
Zeta Duplex		120	MetBx	1940	Achromat	11	80mm		P,I		30
Zeta Duplex 2	6x9cm	120	MetBx	1946	Achromat	11			P,I		30
Zeta Duplex 2 (colors)	6x9cm	120	MetBx	1946	Achromat	11			P,I		40
...FERTSCH (W.u.P. Fertsch) - Jena											
Feca	24x36mm	35mm	35vf	1955	Meritar	3.5	50mm	Junior	25-100	Mc195	90
...FETTER - France											
Photo-Eclair (5 plates)	38x38mm	plate	Disguised	1886	Rapid Rectilinear					A3263	2400
Photo-Eclair (circular plate)	38x38mm	plate	Disguised	1886	Rapid Rectilinear					F1478	2300
Strut camera 6.5x9	6.5x9cm	plate	StrutPl	1910				guillotine		Mc195	440
Strut camera 9x12	9x12cm	plate	StrutPl	1910				guillotine		Mc195	510
...FETZINGER - Vienna											
Field Camera 13x18	13x18cm	plate	Field	1900	Busch Potr. Apl.	6					220
Field Camera 16.5x21.5	16.5x21.5c	plate	Field	1900	Busch Potr. Apl.	6					170
Field Camera 18x24	18x24cm	plate	Field	1900	Busch Potr. Apl.	6	280mm				170
...FEX - Czechoslovakia											
Fex	4x6.5cm	127	RigidRo		Fexar Spec.-Optik			M,T		Mc195	40
...FEX/INDO - France											
Compa	4x6.5cm	127	RollBox	1960	Meniscus					F1140	180
Delta	6x9cm	120	TelescRo		Meniscus					Mc195	30
Elite-Fex	6x9cm	620	TelescRo	1965	2-stop			3-speed		Mc195	30
Fex 4.5	6x9cm	120	TelescRo		Color-Fexar	4.5			B,25-250	Mc195	30
Fex 5.6 Cap Nord	6x6cm	120	TelescRo		Color-Fexar	4.5			B,25-250	Mc195	30
Fex Petit	4x6.5cm	127	RigidRo	1944	Fexar Spec.-Optik				I,P		50
Impera	4x4cm	127	RigidRo	1969	Meniscus				I,T	Mc248	10
Juni-Boy 6x6	6x6cm	120	RigidRo	1948	Meniscus Supra			Synchro	I,T	Mc195	20

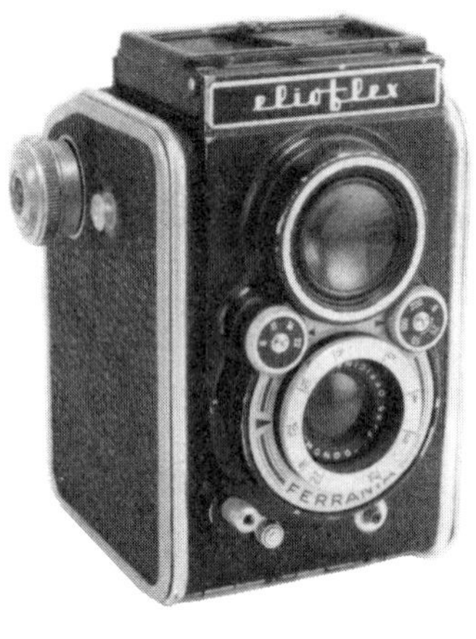

Elioflex

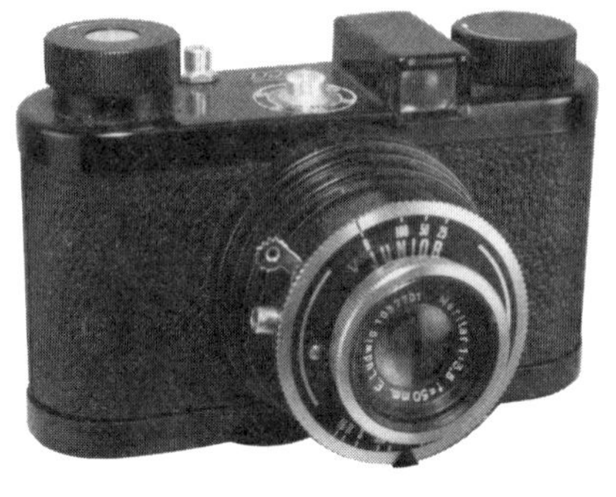
Feca

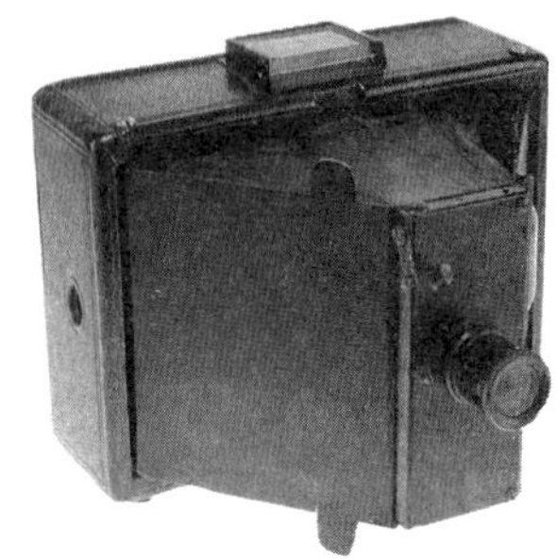
Fetter Strut Camera

MODEL	FORMAT	FILM	TYPE	Year	LENS	Apert	FL	SHUTTER	SPEEDS	ILLUS	U.S.$
Pari-Fex	4x4cm	127	RigidRo	1960	Supra			Synchro	I,T	Mc196	20
Photo Pack Matic	4x4cm	127	Dispose	1960						F1149	50
Rubi-Fex 4x4	4x4cm	127	RigidRo	1965	Meniscus			3-speed		Mc196	20
Sport-Fex	6x9cm	620	TelescRo	1966	Meniscus				I,T	F1636	30
Super-Boy (cardboard)	3x4cm	127	RollBox	1956	Meniscus				I	Mc196	70
Super-Boy (plastic)	3x4cm	127	RollBox	1956	Fexar				I	Mc196	30
Superfex	4x6.5cm	127	RigidRo	1945					P,I	Mc196	30
Superior	4.5x6cm	127	RigidRo	1940					P,I		30
Ultra-Fex	6x9cm	120	TelescRo	1946	Fexar				25-100	Mc196	30
Ultra-Reflex	6x6cm	Roll	TLR-Box	1952	Fexar meniscus				25-100	Mc196	20
Ultra-Reflex	6x9cm	Roll	TLR-Box	1952	Fexar	4.5		Atos B	25-300	Mc196	50
Uni-fex	6x9cm	120	TelescRo	1949	Meniscus				I,T	Mc196	10
Weber Fex	24x36mm	35mm	35vf	1961	Ugo Lantz Ikar	2.8	50mm	5-speed		Mc196	30
Weber Fex Junior	24x36mm	35mm	35vf	1960	Ugo Lantz Ikar	3.5	50mm	5-speed		F679	30
...FIAMMA - Florence											
Alma	13x18cm	plate	LgSLR	1920	Dallmeyer			focal plane			700
Ares 18x24	18x24cm	plate	Studio	1920	various						680
Ares 24x30	24x30mm	plate	Studio	1920	various						800
Fiamma Box	3x4cm	127	MetBx	1925	Meniscus				I,T		50
...FILMA - Milano											
Filma 4.5x6	4.5x6cm	120	MetBx	1936	Achromat	11	75mm	guillotine		Mc196	40
Filma 6x9	6x9cm	120	MetBx	1936	Achromat	11	75mm	guillotine			40
...FINETTA WERK - P.Saraber											
Ditto 99	24x36mm	35mm	35vf	1950	Finetar	2.8	45mm	focal plane	25-1000	HK686	100
Finetta	24x36mm	35mm	35vf	1950	Finetar	2.8	45mm			Mc197	50
Finetta IV D	24x36mm	35mm	35vf	1951	Finetar	2.8	45mm		25-100	A1062	50
Finetta 88	24x36mm	35mm	35vf	1954	Finetar	2.8	45mm	2-blade	25-250	Mc197	70
Finetta 99	24x36mm	35mm	35vf	1950	Finetar	2.8	45mm	focal plane	25-1000	A1064	130
Finetta 99L	24x36mm	35mm	35vf	1954	Finon-S	2.8	45mm	focal plane	1-1000		180
Finetta Super	24x36mm	35mm	35vf		Finetar	2.8	45mm	Central	25-100	A1063	60
Finette IIId	24x36mm	35mm	35vf		Achromat Finar	5.6	43mm	single speed	T,B,I	A1061	40
...FIPS MICROPHOT - W. Germany											
Fips Microphot	13x13mm	16mm	Submin			6.5	25mm				120
...FISCHER (C.F.G. Fischer) - Berlin											
Nikette	3x4cm	127	StrutRo	1932	Luxar	3.5	50mm			Mc197	240
Nikette II (black)	3x4cm	127	StrutRo	1932	Maxar	3.5	50mm			HK226	240
Nikette II (colors)	3x4cm	127	StrutRo	1932	Maxar	3.5	50mm			HK226	240
...FOLMER & SCHWING - New York City (* GRAFLEX)											
...FOTAX MINI - Sweden											
Fotax Mini	25x25mm	35mm	RigidRo	1948		8	35mm				70
Fotax Mini IIa	25x25mm	35mm	RigidRo	1948		8	35mm				100
Fotax Mini III	25x25mm	35mm	RigidRo	1950		5.6	35mm				110

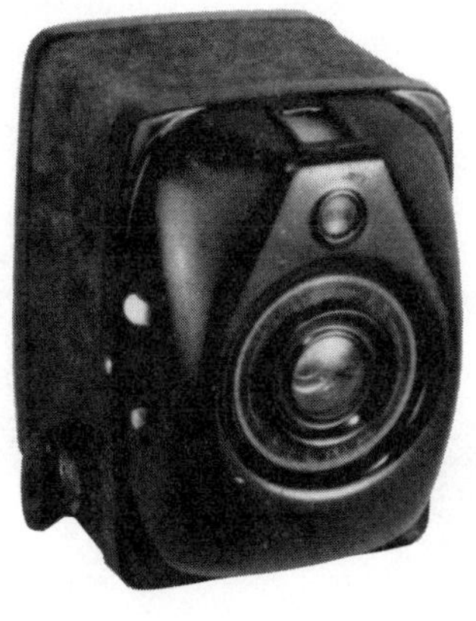

Filma

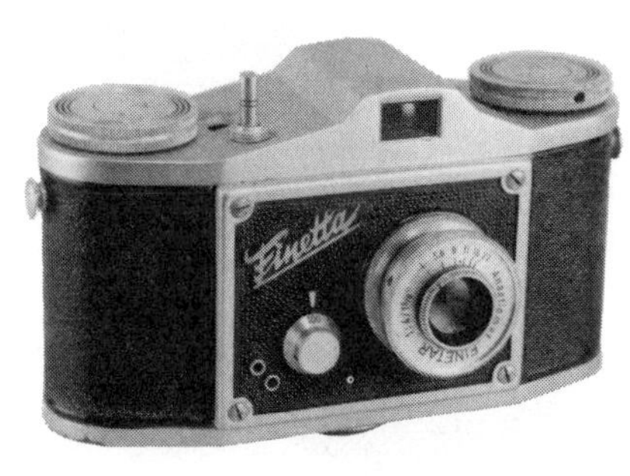

Finetta

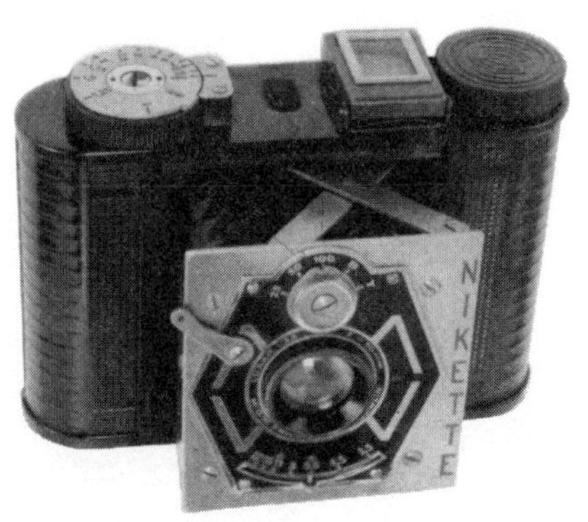

Fischer Nikette

MODEL	FORMAT	FILM	TYPE	Year	LENS	Apert	FL	SHUTTER	SPEEDS	ILLUS	U.S.$
...FOTH (C.F. Foth & CO.) - Berlin											
Derby (original)	24x36mm	127	StrutRo	1930	Foth Anastigmat	3.5	50mm	focal plane	25-500	Mc198	140
Derby (I)	3x4cm	127	StrutRo	1931	Foth Anastigmat	3.5	50mm	focal plane	25-500	Mc199	100
Derby (I)	3x4cm	127	StrutRo	1931	Foth Anastigmat	2.5	50mm	focal plane	25-500	Mc199	90
Derby II	3x4cm	127	StrutRo	1934	Foth Anastigmat	3.5	50mm	focal plane	25-500	HK232	70
Derby II (brown)	3x4cm	127	StrutRo	1934	Foth Anastigmat	3.5	50mm	focal plane	25-500		140
Derby II (French RF)	3x4cm	127	StrutRo	1937	Foth Anastigmat	3.5	50mm	focal plane	25-500		210
Derby II (USA RF)	3x4cm	127	StrutRo	1940	Foth Anastigmat	3.5	50mm	focal plane	25-500	A3052	190
Folding camera	6x9cm	120	VtFoldRo	1933	Foth Anastigmat	4.5				A417	30
Folding camera	6.5x11cm	116	VtFoldRo	1933	Foth Anastigmat	4.5					30
Folding camera, luxus	6x9cm	120	VtFoldRo	1933	Foth Anastigmat	4.5				Mc199	110
Folding camera, luxus	6.5x11cm	116	VtFoldRo	1933	Foth Anastigmat	4.5				A480	110
Foth-Flex	6x6cm	120	TLR	1934	Foth Anastigmat	3.5	75mm	Cloth FP	25-500	Mc199	180
Foth-Flex II	6x6cm	120	TLR	1935	Foth Anastigmat	3.5	75mm	Cloth FP	2-1/500	A647	140
Foth-Flex II	6x6cm	120	TLR	1935	Foth Anastigmat	2.5	75mm	Cloth FP	2-1/500	Mc199	140
...FOTO-QUELLE - Nürnberg											
Revue 3	24x36mm	35mm	35rf	1970	Industar-26M	3.5	50mm			Mc199	30
Revue 4	24x36mm	35mm	35rf	1964	Fed N-61	2.8	52mm			Mc199	40
Revue 10	24x36mm	35mm	35rf	1967	Industar 63	2.8	45mm				30
Revue 16	10x14mm	Roll	Submin	1960	Rokkor	3.5	25mm	programmed	30-250		50
Revue 16 KB	10x14mm	Roll	Submin	1964	Rokkor	2.8	20mm	programmed	30-250		50
Revue 66	6x6cm	120	MedSLR	1979	Industar	2.8	80mm	focal plane			300
Revue 100 C	24x36mm	35mm	35vf	1975	Isconar	2.8	40mm	Rectormat	30-300		30
Revue 135 Symbol	24x36mm	35mm	35vf	1975		4	40mm	programmed	15-250		30
Revue 200 C	24x36mm	35mm	35vf	1975	Isconar	2.8	40mm	Rectormat	30-300		50
Revue 300 C	24x36mm	35mm	35vf	1975	Isconar	2.8	40mm	Rectormat	30-500		70
Revue 400 C	24x36mm	35mm	35vf	1975	Isconar	2.8	40mm	Rectormat	30-500		80
Revue 700 EL	24x36mm	35mm	35rf	1978	Revuetar	2.7	38mm				100
Revue 700 SEL	24x36mm	35mm	35rf	1978	Revuetar	2.7	38mm				120
Revue Auto-Reflex	24x36mm	35mm	35SLR	1965		1.8	50mm	focal plane		A1675	100
Revue BC 2	24x36mm	35mm	35SLR	1990	Prakticar	1.8	50mm	focal plane	4-1000	Hu233	50
Revue Mini Pocket 101	13x17mm	110	110VF	1975	Revuenon						10
Revue Mini-Star	8x11mm	Minox	Submin	1965	Yashinon	2.8	18mm			Mc199	50
Revue ML	24x36mm	35mm	35SLR	1984	Revuetar	2.7	50mm	focal plane	1-1000	Hu212	50
Revue ML 50	24x36mm	35mm	35SLR	1986	Revuetar	2.7	50mm	focal plane	1-1000		50
Revue N	24x36mm	35mm	35VF	1960	Meritar	2.9	45mm				10
Revue Pocket 202	13x17mm	110	110VF	1975					40, 100		20
Revue Pocket 303	13x17mm	110	110VF	1975				electronic	10-1/500		60
Revue Pocket 350	13x17mm	110	110VF	1977	Revuenon						30
Revue Pocket 505	13x17mm	110	110VF	1975	Revuenon	2.7	24mm	electronic	15-1/500		120
Revue Pocket 606	13x17mm	110	110VF	1975	Revuenon	2.7	24mm	electronic	15-1/500		180
Revueflex	24x36mm	35mm	35slr	1972	Helios	2	58mm	focal plane	1-500	A3197	40

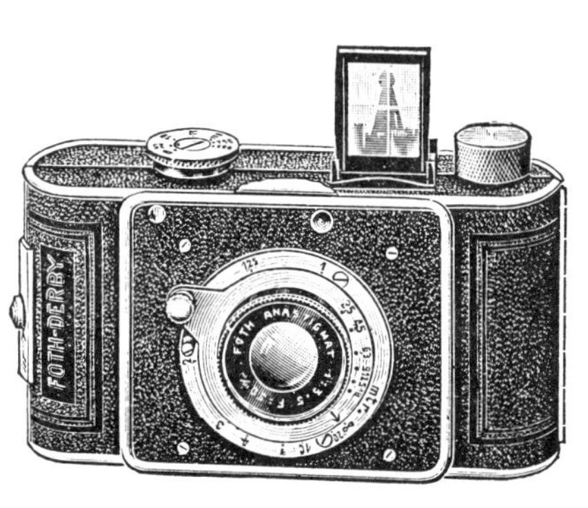

Derby (original)

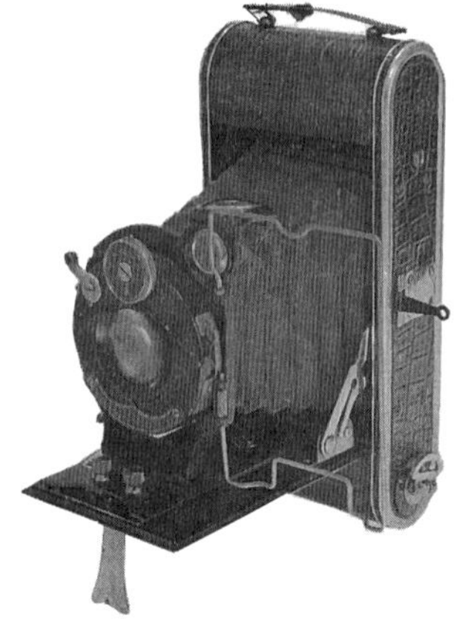

Foth Folding camera, Luxus

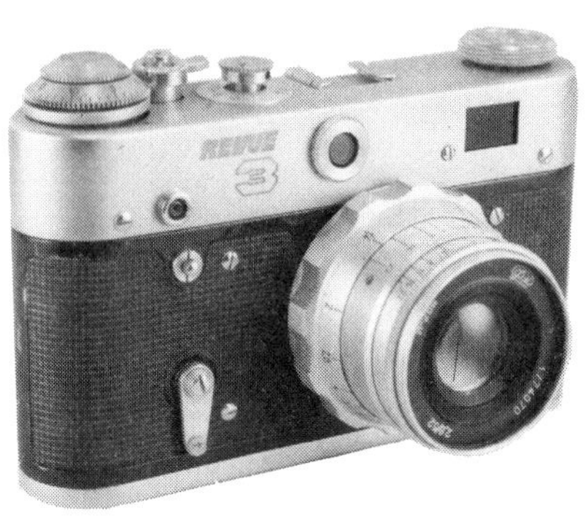

Revue 3

MODEL	FORMAT	FILM	TYPE	Year	LENS	Apert	FL	SHUTTER	SPEEDS	ILLUS	U.S.$
Revueflex 1000 S	24x36mm	35mm	35slr	1975	Revuetar	2.8	50mm	metal FP	1-1000		120
Revueflex 2000 CL	24x36mm	35mm	35slr	1975	Revuenon	1.7	55mm	metal FP	1-1000		240
Revueflex 3000 SL	24x36mm	35mm	35slr	1975	Auto Revuenon	1.4	55mm	metal FP	1-1000		280
Revueflex 3000 SL	24x36mm	35mm	35slr	1975	Auto Revuenon	1.7	55mm	metal FP	1-1000		310
Revueflex 4000 EE	24x36mm	35mm	35slr	1975	Auto Revuenon	1.7	55mm	programmed			380
Revueflex B	24x36mm	35mm	35slr	1974	Industar 63	3.5	50mm	focal plane	1-500	A3198	50
Revueflex BL	24x36mm	35mm	35slr	1975	Revuetar	2.7	45mm	focal plane	1-1000	Hu183	50
Revueflex E	24x36mm	35mm	35slr	1973	Industar-50-2	3.5	50mm	focal plane	30-500		50
Revueflex E	24x36mm	35mm	35slr	1973	Helios-44M	2	58mm	focal plane	30-500		120
Revueflex EM	24x36mm	35mm	35slr	1974	Helios-44M	2	58mm	focal plane	30-500		140
Revueflex S 200	24x36mm	35mm	35slr	1976			50mm	focal plane		Hu193	60
Revueflex SL	24x36mm	35mm	35slr	1975	Revuetar	2.7	50mm	focal plane	2-500	Hu168	50
Revueflex SL 301	24x36mm	35mm	35slr	1975	Revuetar	2.7	50mm	focal plane	2-500		50
Revueflex TL	24x36mm	35mm	35slr	1975	Revuetar	2.7	50mm	focal plane	1-1000	Hu178	50
Revueflex TL 1	24x36mm	35mm	35slr	1979	Revuetar	2.7	50mm	focal plane	1-1000	Hu201	50
Revueflex TL 25	24x36mm	35mm	35slr	1981	Revuetar	2.7	50mm	focal plane	1-1000	Hu202	50
Revueflex TL 202	24x36mm	35mm	35slr	1976			50mm	focal plane		Hu190	50
...FOTOCHROME INC. - U.S.A.											
Fotochrome Camera		Roll	RigidRo	1965						Mc200	60
...FOTOFEX-KAMERAS - Berlin											
Foto Fix	6x6cm	120	Box	1928							120
Fotofex	4.5x6cm	120	Platebox	1940	Meniscus				M,Z		160
Minifex	13x18mm	16mm	Submin	1932	Astar	2.7	25mm	Compur	300	Mc200	1800
Minifex	13x18mm	16mm	Submin	1932	Astro PanTachar	1.8	25mm	Compur	300	A886	1100
Visor-fex	6x9cm	120	FoldRo	1933						Mc200	1000
...FOTOTECNICA - Turin											
Bakina Rakina	3x4cm	127	RigidRo	1946	Clippertar	9			B,I		30
Bandi	6x6 cm	120	RollBox	1946	Aplanat		75mm		25-100		50
Eaglet	6x9cm	120	MetBx	1952							30
Filmor	6x6cm	120	MetBx	1950	Achromat			guillotine		A2872	30
Filmor II	6x9cm	120	MetBx	1950	Achromat			guillotine		A2869	30
Herman	24x36mm	35mm	35vf	1950	Tecnar Koristka				T,B,25-250	Mc200	100
Rayelle	6x9cm	120	MetBx	1954							20
Rayflex	6x9cm	120	TLR-Box	1946	Duotar Optik	9		guillotine			30
Tennar	6x9cm	620	FoldRo	1954						Mc200	30
Tennar Junior	6x9cm	620	FoldRo	1954							30
...FRANÇAIS (E. Français) - Paris											
Cosmopolite	9x12cm	plate	TLR	1892	Rapid Rectilinear					F1215	1000
Kinegraphe	8x9cm	plate	TLR	1886	Rapid Rectilinear					Mc200	2000
Photo-Magasin	6.5x8cm	plate	MagBox	1895				string-set		F473	800
...FRANKA-WERK - Beyreuth											
Bonafix	6x9cm	120	FoldRo	1950	Radionar	4.5	105mm	Vario	25-100		30

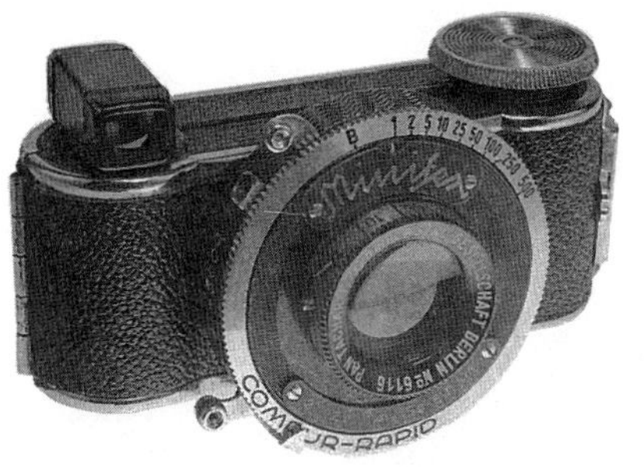

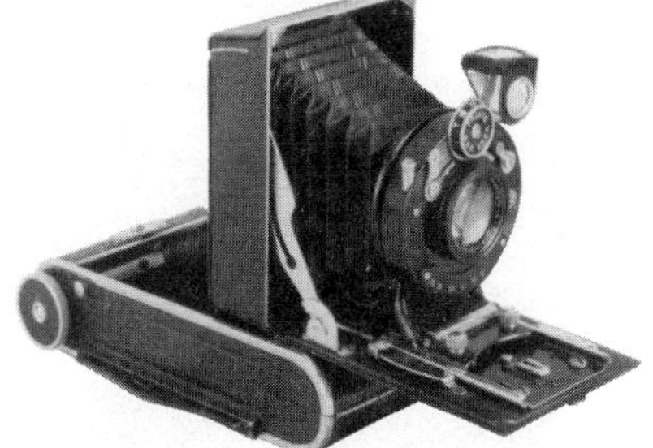

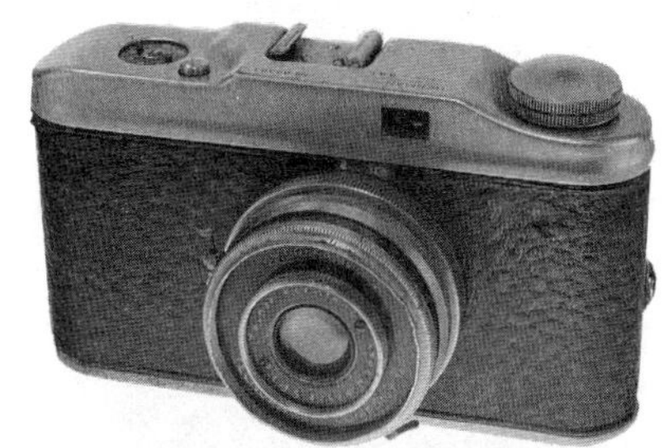

Minifex — Visor-fex — Herman

MODEL	FORMAT	FILM	TYPE	Year	LENS	Apert	FL	SHUTTER	SPEEDS	ILLUS	U.S.$
Bubi	4.5x6cm	plate	StrutPl	1914	Doppel Anast.	6.8	75mm	Compound	1-250	HK152	140
Bubi Roll 3x4	3x4cm	127	StrutRo	1932	Ludwig Victar	4.5	7.5cm	Pronto	1-200		50
Bubi Roll 4x6.5	4x6.5cm	127	StrutRo	1932	Ludwig Victar	4.5	7.5cm	Pronto	1-200	HK255	50
Champion II	24x36mm	35mm	RigidRo	1960	Color-Isconar	2.8	45mm	Prontor	125	Mc118	30
Francolor	24x36mm	35mm	35vf	1959	Frankar	2.8	45mm	Vario	25-200		20
Franka	24x36mm	35mm	35vf	1950	Radionar	2.9	50mm	Compur-Rap.	180	A1040	270
Frankarette	24x36mm	35mm	35vf	1958	Isconar	2.8	45mm	Prontor SVS	1-300		70
Frankarette E	24x36mm	35mm	35rf	1958	Isconar	2.8	45mm	Prontor SVS	1-300		50
Frankarette L	24x36mm	35mm	35vf	1958	Isconar	2.8	45mm	Prontor SVS	1-300		10
Idafix	24x36mm	35mm	FoldRo	1960	Color-Isconar	2.8	45mm	Prontor	125		20
Rolfix	6x9cm	120	FoldRo	1948	Trinar	4.5	105mm	Prontor II	1-150	Mc201	40
Rolfix Deluxe	6x9cm	120	FoldRo	1953	Radionar	4.5	105mm	Prontor SV	1-250		30
Rolfix II	6x9cm	120	FoldRo	1951	Trinar	3.5	105mm	Compur-Rap.	1-400	Mc201	60
Rolfix Jr	6x9cm	120	FoldRo	1951	Frankar	4.5	105mm	Vario	25-200	Mc201	30
Solida	4.5x6cm	120	FoldRo	1948	Radionar	2.9	7.5cm	Prontor	1-250		30
Solida I	6x6cm	120	FoldRo	1956		6.3	75mm			A1507	70
Solida II	6x6cm	120	FoldRo	1957	Anastigmat	3.5		Vario		HK295	40
Solida IIL	6x6cm	120	FoldRo	1957	Radionar	2.9	80mm	Prontor SVS			30
Solida III	6x6cm	120	FoldRo	1957	Radionar	2.9	80mm	Prontor SVS			40
Solida IIIL	6x6cm	120	FoldRo	1958	Radionar	2.9	80mm	Prontor SVS			50
Solida Jr.	6x6cm	120	HzFoldRo	1954		6.3	75mm		B,25,75		70
Solida Record B	6x6cm	120	FoldRo	1961	Spezial	8	80mm		I,T		20
Solida Record T	6x6cm	120	RigidRo	1958	Spezial	8	80mm		I,T		10
Super Frankarette	24x36mm	35mm	35vf	1958	Xenar	2.8	45mm	Prontor SVS	1-300		30
Super Frankarette E	24x36mm	35mm	35vf	1958	Xenar	2.8	45mm	Prontor SVS	1-300		40
Super Frankarette EL	24x36mm	35mm	35rf	1958	Xenar	2.8	45mm	Prontor SVS	1-300		50
Super Frankarette L	24x36mm	35mm	35vf	1958	Xenar	2.8	45mm	Prontor SVS	1-300		40
Super Frankarette SLK	24x36mm	35mm	35rf	1958	Ennit	2.8	45mm	Prontor SLK			30
...FRANKE & HEIDECKE - Braunschweig											
Heidoscop 45x107	45x107	plate	SterRefl	1921	Jena Tessar	4.5	55mm	St.Compound		Mc201	580
Heidoscop 6x13	6x13cm	plate	SterRefl	1925	Jena Tessar	4.5	75mm	St.Compound		Pr012	800
Heidoscop 6x13	6x13cm	120	SterRefl	1921	Jena Tessar	4.5	75mm	St.Compound		Pr011	1300
Ifbaflex M102	24x36mm	35mm	35SLR	1970	Ifbagon Planar	1.8	50mm	focal plane			350
Prego AF	24x36mm	35mm	35AF	1991	Rolleinar	3.5	35mm	programmed	2-500		140
Prego AF Xenar	24x36mm	35mm	35AF	1992	AF-Xenar	3.5	35mm	programmed	3-400		160
Prego AF Xenar Data	24x36mm	35mm	35AF	1993	AF-Xenar	3.5	35mm	programmed	2-500		180
Prego Zoom AF	24x36mm	35mm	35AFZ	1993	AF-Variogon	3.9-7.1	35-70	programmed	3-400		210
Prego Zoom AF Data	24x36mm	35mm	35AFZ	1994	AF-Variogon	3.9-7.1	35-70	programmed	3-400		240
Rollei-16	12x17mm	16mm	Submin	1963	Tessar	2.8	25mm			Mc201	100
Rollei-16S (black snake)	12x17mm	16mm	Submin	1966	Tessar	2.8	25mm	programmed	30-500	Mc201	150
Rollei-16S (black)	12x17mm	16mm	Submin	1966	Tessar	2.8	25mm	programmed	30-500	Mc201	120
Rollei 16S (cream)	12x17mm	16mm	Submin	1966	Tessar	2.8	25mm	programmed	30-500	Mc201	180

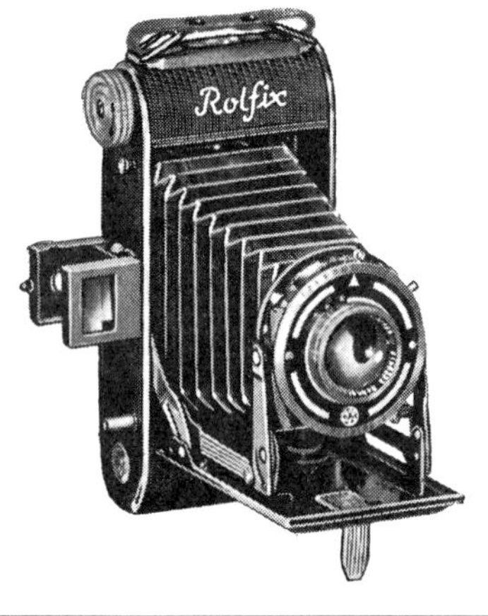

Rolfix

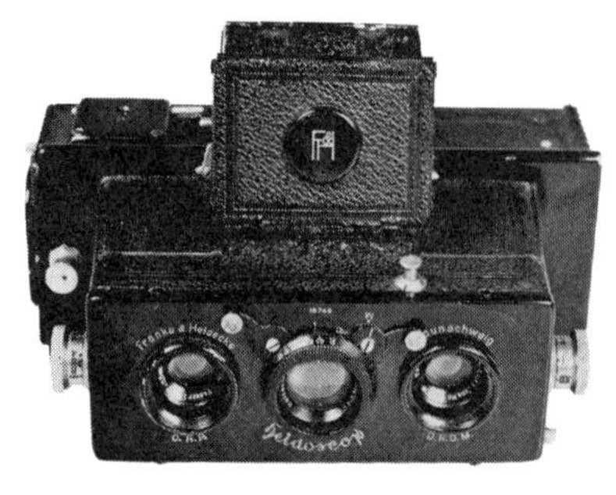

Heidoscop 45x107

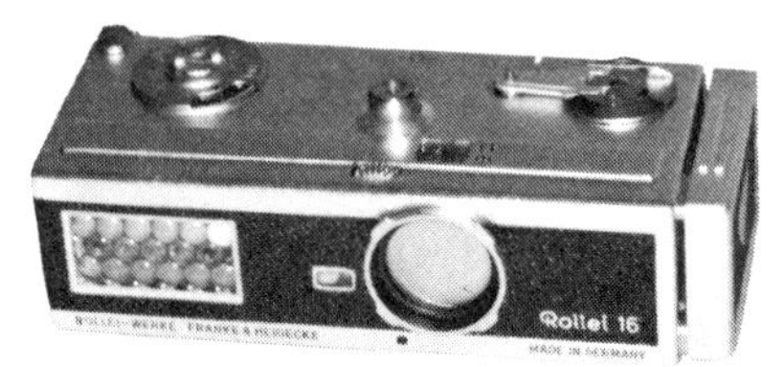

Rollei-16

MODEL	FORMAT	FILM	TYPE	Year	LENS	Apert	FL	SHUTTER	SPEEDS	ILLUS	U.S.$
Rollei-16S (green)	12x17mm	16mm	Submin	1966	Tessar	2.8	25mm	programmed	30-500	Mc201	260
Rollei-16S (red)	12x17mm	16mm	Submin	1966	Tessar	2.8	25mm	programmed	30-500	Mc201	260
Rollei 35	24x36mm	35mm	35vf	1967	Tessar	3.5	40mm	Compur	½-500	Ev195	350
Rollei 35 (gold)	24x36mm	35mm	35vf	1967	Tessar	3.5	40mm	Compur	½-500	Ev199	1100
Rollei 35 (platinum)	24x36mm	35mm	35vf	1986	Tessar	3.5	40mm	Compur	2-500		1500
Rollei 35 (Singapore)	24x36mm	35mm	35vf	1967	Tessar	3.5	40mm	Compur	½-500	Ev195	290
Rollei 35 (Singapore)	24x36mm	35mm	35vf	1967	Schneider Xenar	3.5	40mm	Compur	½-500	Ev195	350
Rollei 35 Classic (black)	24x36mm	35mm	35vf	1991	Tessar	3.5	40mm	Compur	2-500		700
Rollei 35 Classic (black)	24x36mm	35mm	35vf	1991	Sonnar	2.8	40mm	Compur	2-500		1000
Rollei 35 Classic (chrome)	24x36mm	35mm	35vf	1991	Tessar	3.5	40mm	Compur	2-500		800
Rollei 35 Classic (chrome)	24x36mm	35mm	35vf	1991	Sonnar	2.8	40mm	Compur	2-500		900
Rollei 35 Classic (gold)	24x36mm	35mm	35vf	1991	Tessar	3.5	40mm	Compur	2-500		1300
Rollei 35 Classic (titanium)	24x36mm	35mm	35vf	1991	Tessar	3.5	40mm	Compur	2-500		1100
Rollei 35B	24x36mm	35mm	35vf	1969	Zeiss Triotar	3.5	40mm	Prontor	30-500	Ev197	220
Rollei 35C (C35)	24x36mm	35mm	35vf	1969	Zeiss Triotar	3.5	40mm	Prontor	30-500	Ev198	310
Rollei 35LED	24x36mm	35mm	35vf	1978	Zeiss Triotar	3.5	40mm	Prontor	30-500	Ev206	140
Rollei 35S (black)	24x36mm	35mm	35vf	1974	HFT Sonnar	2.8	40mm	Compur	2-500	Ev200	440
Rollei 35S (chrome)	24x36mm	35mm	35vf	1974	HFT Sonnar	2.8	40mm	Compur	2-500	Ev200	360
Rollei 35S (gold)	24x36mm	35mm	35vf	1974	HFT Sonnar	2.8	40mm	Compur	2-500	Ev202	1500
Rollei 35S (silver)	24x36mm	35mm	35vf	1974	HFT Sonnar	2.8	40mm	Compur	2-500	Ev203	700
Rollei 35SE (black)	24x36mm	35mm	35vf	1980	Sonnar	2.8	40mm	Compur	2-500	Ev208	340
Rollei 35SE (chrome)	24x36mm	35mm	35vf	1980	Sonnar	2.8	40mm	Compur	2-500	Ev208	330
Rollei 35T (black)	24x36mm	35mm	35vf	1976	Tessar	3.5	40mm	Compur	2-500	Ev205	330
Rollei 35T (chrome)	24x36mm	35mm	35vf	1976	Tessar	3.5	40mm	Compur	2-500	Ev205	300
Rollei 35TE (black)	24x36mm	35mm	35vf	1980	Tessar	3.5	40mm	Compur	2-500	Ev207	330
Rollei 35TE (chrome)	24x36mm	35mm	35vf	1980	Tessar	3.5	40mm	Compur	2-500		270
Rollei A26	28x28mm	126	126vf	1973	Sonnar	3.5	40mm	programmed	30-250	Ev188	100
Rollei A110 (black)	13x17mm	110	110VF	1974	Tessar	2.8	23mm	electronic	4-400	Ev190	100
Rollei A110 (chrome)	13x17mm	110	110VF	1974	Tessar	2.8	23mm	electronic	4-400	Ev190	130
Rollei A110 (gold)	13x17mm	110	110VF	1974	Tessar	2.8	23mm	electronic	4-400		250
Rollei E110	13x17mm	110	110VF	1976	Tessar	2.8	23mm	electronic	4-250	Ev192	150
Rollei XF 35 (black)	13x17mm	110	35rf	1976	Sonnar	2.3	40mm	electronic	30-650	Ev211	120
Rollei XF 35 (chrome)	13x17mm	110	35rf	1976	Sonnar	2.3	40mm	electronic	30-650		80
Rolleicord I (leathered)	6x6cm	120	TLR	1934	Zeiss Triotar	3.8	7.5cm	Compur	1-300,B,T	Pr091	120
Rolleicord I (nickel)	6x6cm	120	TLR	1933	Zeiss Triotar	4.5	75mm	Compur	1-300,B,T	Pr090	200
Rolleicord Ia	6x6cm	120	TLR	1936	Zeiss Triotar	4.5	7.5cm	Compur	1-300,B,T	Pr092	120
Rolleicord II	6x6cm	120	TLR	1936	Zeiss Triotar	3.5	75mm	Compur	1-300,B,T	Pr096	120
Rolleicord II	6x6cm	120	TLR	1936	Zeiss Triotar	3.5	75mm	Compur-Rap.	1-500,B	Pr102	120
Rolleicord II	6x6cm	120	TLR	1936	Schneider Xenar	3.5	75mm	Compur-Rap.	1-500,B	Pr102	350
Rolleicord III	6x6cm	120	TLR	1950	Zeiss Triotar	3.5	75mm	Compur-Rap.	1-500,B	Pr212	150
Rolleicord III	6x6cm	120	TLR	1950	Schneider Xenar	3.5	75mm	Compur-Rap.	1-500,B	Pr212	200
Rolleicord IV	6x6cm	120	TLR	1953	Zeiss Triotar	3.5	75mm	Sync-Compur	1-500,B	Ev82	180

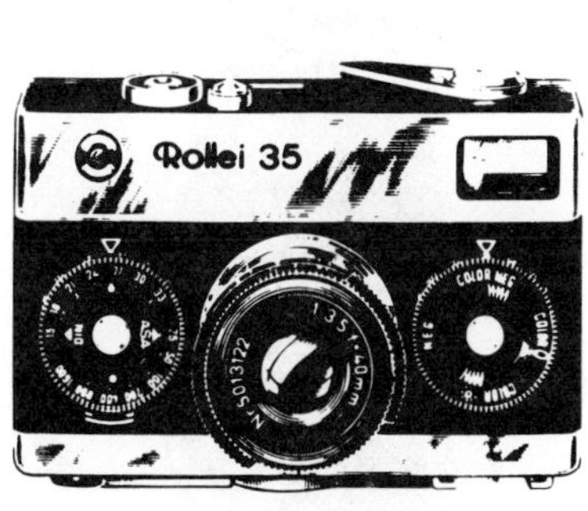

Rollei 35

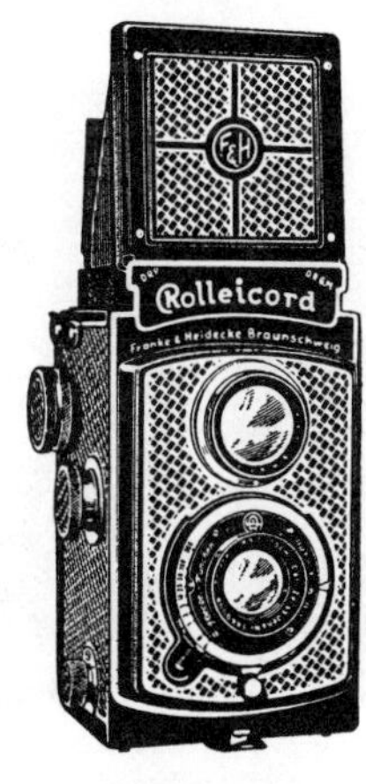

Rolleicord I (Nickel)

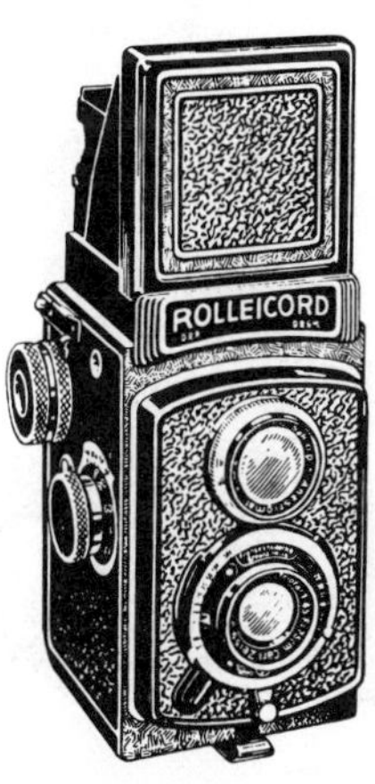

Rolleicord Ia

MODEL	FORMAT	FILM	TYPE	Year	LENS	Apert	FL	SHUTTER	SPEEDS	ILLUS	U.S.$
Rolleicord IV	6x6cm	120	TLR	1953	Schneider Xenar	3.5	75mm	Sync-Compur	1-500,B	Pr213	210
Rolleicord V	6x6cm	120	TLR	1954	Schneider Xenar	3.5	75mm	Sync-Compur	1-500,B	Pr214	200
Rolleicord Va	6x6cm	120	TLR	1957	Schneider Xenar	3.5	75mm	Sync-Compur	1-500,B	Pr215	210
Rolleicord Vb	6x6cm	120	TLR	1962	Schneider Xenar	3.5	75mm	Sync-Compur	1-500	Pr216	280
Rolleidoscop	45x107	120	SterRefl	1926	Tessar	4.5	55mm	St.Compound	1-300	Pr008	1900
Rolleidoscop	6x13cm	117	SterRefl	1926	Tessar	4.5	75mm	St.Compound	1-300	Pr015	1700
Rolleiflex I	6x6cm	117	TLR	1929	Zeiss Tessar	4.5	75mm	Rim-Compur	1-300,B,T	Pr053	200
Rolleiflex I	6x6cm	120	TLR	1929	Zeiss Tessar	3.8	75mm	Rim-Compur	1-300,B,T	Pr054	160
Rolleiflex 2.8A	6x6cm	120	TLR	1950	Zeiss Tessar	2.8	80mm	CompurRapX	1-400	Pr155	480
Rolleiflex 2.8B	6x6cm	120	TLR	1952	Zeiss Biometar	2.8	80mm	Sync-Compur	1-500	Pr157	800
Rolleiflex 2.8C	6x6cm	120	TLR	1953	Zeiss Planar	2.8	80mm	Sync-Compur	1-500	Pr158/1	470
Rolleiflex 2.8C	6x6cm	120	TLR	1953	Schn. Xenotar	2.8	80mm	Sync-Compur	1-500	Pr158/2	470
Rolleiflex 2.8D	6x6cm	120	TLR	1955	Zeiss Planar	2.8	80mm	Sync-Compur	1-500	Pr160/1	410
Rolleiflex 2.8D	6x6cm	120	TLR	1955	Schn. Xenotar	2.8	80mm	Sync-Compur	1-500	Pr160/2	410
Rolleiflex 2.8E	6x6cm	120	TLR	1955	Zeiss Planar	2.8	80mm	Sync-Compur	1-500	Pr164/1	470
Rolleiflex 2.8E	6x6cm	120	TLR	1955	Schn. Xenotar	2.8	80mm	Sync-Compur	1-500	Pr164/2	470
Rolleiflex 2.8E2	6x6cm	120	TLR	1955	Zeiss Planar	2.8	80mm	Sync-Compur	1-500	Pr172/1	460
Rolleiflex 2.8E2	6x6cm	120	TLR	1955	Schn. Xenotar	2.8	80mm	Sync-Compur	1-500	Pr172/2	460
Rolleiflex 2.8E3	6x6cm	120	TLR	1962	Zeiss Planar	2.8	80mm	S.Comp.MXV	1-500	Pr173/1	620
Rolleiflex 2.8E3	6x6cm	120	TLR	1962	Schn. Xenotar	2.8	80mm	S.Comp.MXV	1-500	Pr173/2	590
Rolleiflex 2.8F	6x6cm	120	TLR	1960	Planar	2.8	80mm	S.Comp.MXV	1-500	Pr168/1	800
Rolleiflex 2.8F	6x6cm	120	TLR	1960	Xenotar	2.8	80mm	S.Comp.MXV	1-500	Pr168/2	650
Rolleiflex 2.8F Aurum	6x6cm	120	TLR	1983	Xenotar	2.8	80mm	S.Comp.MXV	1-500	Pr190	2100
Rolleiflex 2.8F Platin	6x6cm	120	TLR	1984	Planar HFT	2.8	80mm	S.Comp.MXV	1-500	Pr191	3700
Rolleiflex 2.8GX	6x6cm	120	TLR	1986	Planar HFT	2.8	80mm	Sync-Comp	1-500		1400
Rolleiflex 2.8GX Edition	6x6cm	120	TLR	1989	Planar	2.8	80mm	Sync-Comp	1-500		1800
Rolleiflex 2.8GX Express	6x6cm	120	TLR	1994	Planar	2.8	80mm	Sync-Comp	1-500		1900
Rolleiflex 2.8GX Expr.(gold)	6x6cm	120	TLR	1994	Planar	2.8	80mm	Sync-Comp	1-500		7000
Rolleiflex 2.8GX H.Newton	6x6cm	120	TLR	1992	Planar	2.8	80mm	Sync-Comp	1-500		1800
Rolleiflex 3.5E	6x6cm	120	TLR	1959	Zeiss Planar	3.5	75mm	Sync-Compur	1-500	Pr165/	390
Rolleiflex 3.5E	6x6cm	120	TLR	1959	Schn. Xenotar	3.5	75mm	Sync-Compur	1-500	Pr165/	370
Rolleiflex 3.5E2	6x6cm	120	TLR	1959	Zeiss Planar	3.5	75mm	S.Comp.MX	1-500	Pr169/	370
Rolleiflex 3.5E2	6x6cm	120	TLR	1959	Schn. Xenotar	3.5	75mm	S.Comp.MX	1-500	Pr169/	330
Rolleiflex 3.5E3	6x6cm	120	TLR	1962	Zeiss Planar	3.5	75mm	S.Comp.MXV	1-500	Pr171/	390
Rolleiflex 3.5E3	6x6cm	120	TLR	1962	Schn. Xenotar	3.5	75mm	S.Comp.MXV	1-500	Pr171/	390
Rolleiflex 3.5F	6x6cm	120	TLR	1960	Tessar	3.5	75mm	S.Comp.MXV	1-500		590
Rolleiflex 3.5F	6x6cm	220	TLR	1960	Planar	3.5	75mm	S.Comp.MXV	1-500	Pr166/	620
Rolleiflex 3.5F	6x6cm	120	TLR	1960	Xenotar	3.5	75mm	S.Comp.MXV	1-500	Pr166/	500
Rolleiflex 4x4 (original)	4x4cm	127	TLR	1931	Zeiss Tessar	2.8	60mm	Compur	1-300,B,T	Pr079	300
Rolleiflex 4x4 (original)	4x4cm	127	TLR	1931	Zeiss Tessar	3.5	60mm	Compur-Rap.	1-500,B,T	Pr078	300
Rolleiflex 4x4 (original)	4x4cm	127	TLR	1931	Zeiss Tessar	2.8	60mm	Compur-Rap.	1-500,B,T	Pr083	290
Rolleiflex 4x4 "Sport"	4x4cm	127	TLR	1938	Zeiss Tessar	2.8	60mm	Compur-Rap.	1-500,B,T	Pr084	400

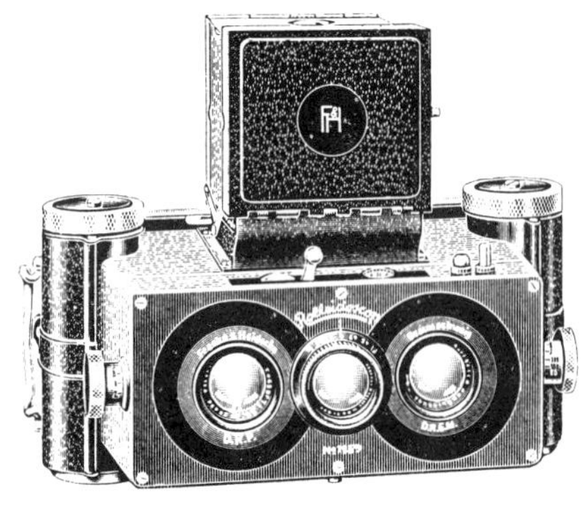

Rolleidoscop

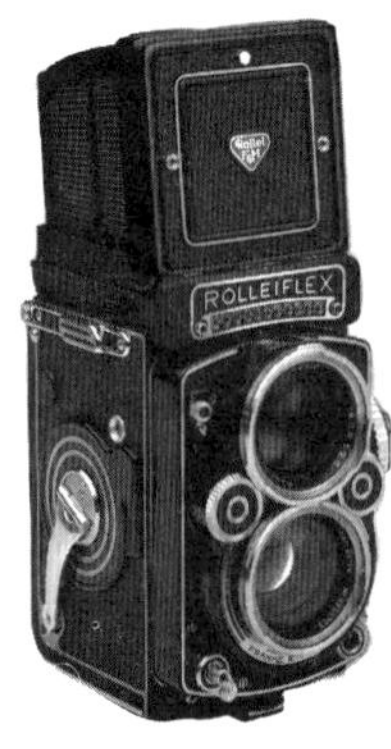

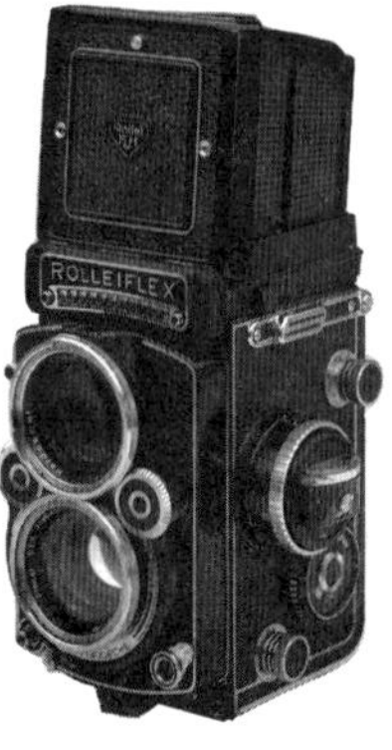

Rolleiflex 2.8F

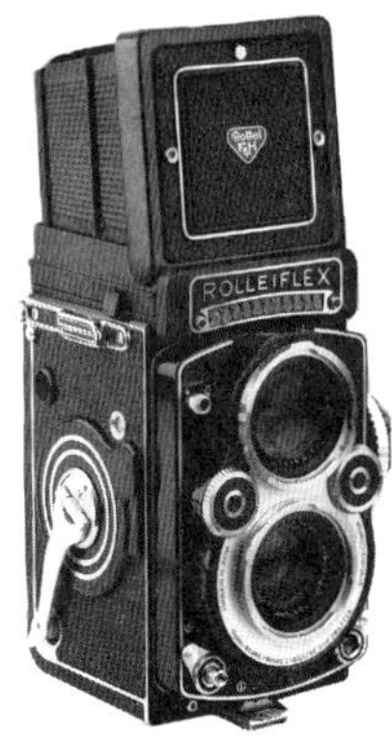

Rolleiflex 3.5F

MODEL	FORMAT	FILM	TYPE	Year	LENS	Apert	FL	SHUTTER	SPEEDS	ILLUS	U.S.$
Rolleiflex 4x4 (grey)	4x4cm	127	TLR	1957	Xenar	3.5	60mm	S.Comp.MXV	1-500	Pr196	300
Rolleiflex 4x4 (black)	4x4cm	127	TLR	1963	Xenar	3.5	60mm	S.Comp.MXV	1-500	Pr197	620
Rolleiflex 3001	24x36mm	35mm	35slr	1986	Planar	1.8	50mm	focal plane	16-1000		580
Rolleiflex 3003	24x36mm	35mm	35slr	1985	Planar	1.8	50mm	focal plane	16-1000	Ev230	1000
Rolleiflex 3003 Deluxe	24x36mm	35mm	35slr	1986	Planar	1.8	50mm	focal plane	16-1000		1100
Rolleiflex 3003 Traveller	24x36mm	35mm	35slr	1986	Planar	1.8	50mm	focal plane	16-1000		1100
Rolleiflex 6002 body	6x6cm	120	MedSLR	1986	body only	---	---	electronic	30-1/500	Ev242	900
Rolleiflex 6002 + 80/2.8	6x6cm	120	MedSLR	1986	Rolleigon	2.8	80mm	electronic	30-1/500	Ev242	1000
Rolleiflex 6003 body	6x6cm	120	MedSLR	1992	body only	---	---	electronic	20-1000		1100
Rolleiflex 6003 + 80/2.8	6x6cm	120	MedSLR	1992	Planar	2.8	80mm	electronic	20-1000		2100
Rolleiflex 6006 body	6x6cm	120	MedSLR	1984	body only	---	---		30-1/500	Ev240	1300
Rolleiflex 6006 + 80/2.8	6x6cm	120	MedSLR	1984	Planar	2.8	80mm		30-1/500	Ev240	1600
Rolleiflex 6006 gold +	6x6cm	120	MedSLR	1994	Planar	2.8	80mm	electronic	30-1/500		7000
Rolleiflex 6008 Pro. body	6x6cm	120	MedSLR	1988	body only	---	---	electronic	30-1/500		2100
Rolleiflex 6008 Pro + 80/2.8	6x6cm	120	MedSLR	1988	Planar	2.8	80mm	electronic	30-1/500		2400
Rolleiflex 6008 SRC 1000	6x6cm	120	MedSLR	1992	body only	---	---	electronic	30-1000		2200
Rolleiflex 6008 SRC 1000	6x6cm	120	MedSLR	1992	Planar	2.8	80mm	electronic	30-1000		3200
Rolleiflex Automat	6x6cm	120	TLR	1937	Zeiss Tessar	3.5	75mm	Compur-Rap.	1-500,B,T	Pr070	190
Rolleiflex Automat	6x6cm	120	TLR	1939	Zeiss Tessar	3.5	75mm	Compur-Rap.	1-500,B,T	Pr072/	190
Rolleiflex Automat	6x6cm	120	TLR	1939	Xenar	3.5	75mm	Compur-Rap.	1-500,B,T	Pr072/	140
Rolleiflex Automat II (X)	6x6cm	120	TLR	1949	Zeiss Tessar	3.5	75mm	Sync-Compur	1-500,B	Pr154/	190
Rolleiflex Automat II (X)	6x6cm	120	TLR	1949	Xenar	3.5	75mm	Sync-Compur	1-500,B	Pr154/	170
Rolleiflex Automat MX	6x6cm	120	TLR	1951	Zeiss Tessar	3.5	75mm	Sync-Compur	1-500,B	Pr156/	180
Rolleiflex Automat MX	6x6cm	120	TLR	1951	Xenar	3.5	75mm	Sync-Compur	1-500,B	Pr156/	180
Rolleiflex Automat MX-EVS	6x6cm	120	TLR	1954	Zeiss Tessar	3.5	75mm	Sync-Compur	1-500,B	Pr159/	240
Rolleiflex Automat MX-EVS	6x6cm	120	TLR	1954	Xenar	3.5	75mm	Sync-Compur	1-500,B	Pr159/	230
Rolleiflex SL2000 F	24x36mm	35mm	35slr	1981	Zeiss Planar	1.8	50mm	focal plane	16-1000	Ev229	700
Rolleiflex SL2000 F motor	24x36mm	35mm	35slr	1982	Zeiss Planar	1.8	50mm	focal plane	16-1000		550
Rolleiflex SL26	28x28mm	126	126SLR	1968	Tessar	2.8	40mm				150
SL35 (black) Singapore	24x36mm	35mm	35SLR	1972	Zeiss Planar	1.8	50mm	focal plane	1-1000	Ev220	190
SL35 (black) Singapore	24x36mm	35mm	35SLR	1972	Xenon	1.8	50mm	focal plane	1-1000	Ev220	140
SL35 (chrome) Singapore	24x36mm	35mm	35SLR	1972	Zeiss Planar	1.8	50mm	focal plane	1-1000	Ev220	180
SL35 (chrome) Singapore	24x36mm	35mm	35SLR	1972	Xenon	1.8	50mm	focal plane	1-1000	Ev220	130
SL35 (Germany)	24x36mm	35mm	35SLR	1970	Zeiss Planar	1.8	50mm	focal plane	1-1000	Ev220	220
SL35 (Germany)	24x36mm	35mm	35SLR	1970	Xenon	1.8	50mm	focal plane	1-1000	Ev220	200
Rolleiflex SL350	24x36mm	35mm	35SLR	1975	Zeiss Planar	1.8	50mm	focal plane	1-1000		330
Rolleiflex SL35E (black)	24x36mm	35mm	35SLR	1978	Zeiss Planar	1.8	50mm	focal plane	16-1000		200
Rolleiflex SL35E (black)	24x36mm	35mm	35SLR	1978	Zeiss Planar	1.4	50mm	focal plane	16-1000		250
Rolleiflex SL35E (chrome)	24x36mm	35mm	35SLR	1978	Zeiss Planar	1.8	50mm	focal plane	16-1000	Ev226	200
Rolleiflex SL35E (chrome)	24x36mm	35mm	35SLR	1978	Zeiss Planar	1.4	50mm	focal plane	16-1000	Ev226	250
Rolleiflex SL35M	24x36mm	35mm	35SLR	1976	Zeiss Planar	1.8	50mm	focal plane	1-1000	Ev223	140
Rolleiflex SL35M	24x36mm	35mm	35SLR	1976	Zeiss Planar	1.4	50mm	focal plane	1-1000	Ev223	160

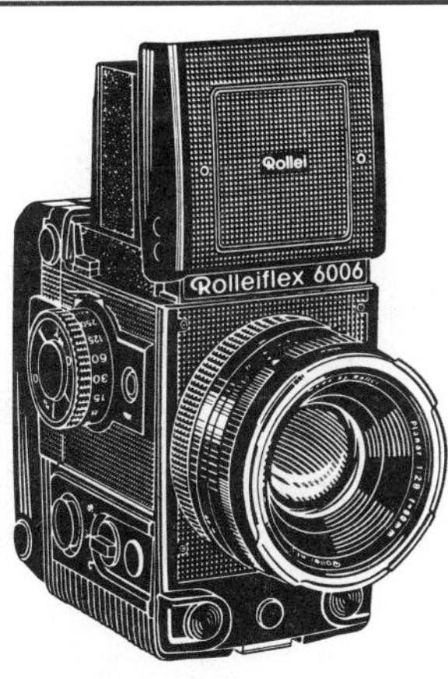

Rolleiflex 6006

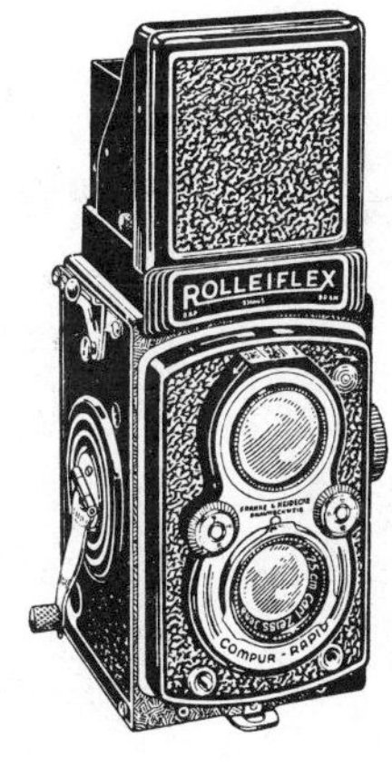

Rolleiflex Automat

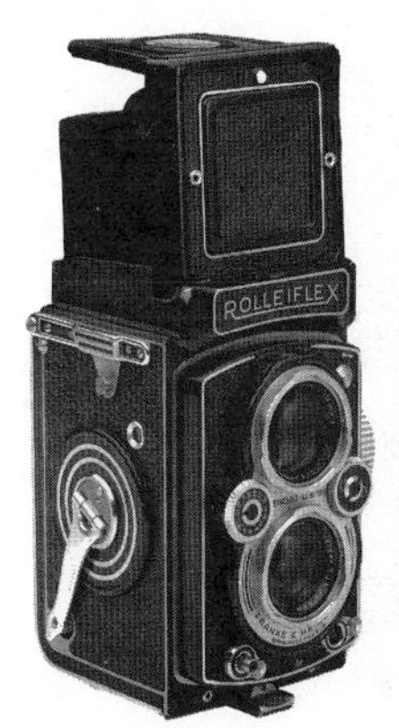

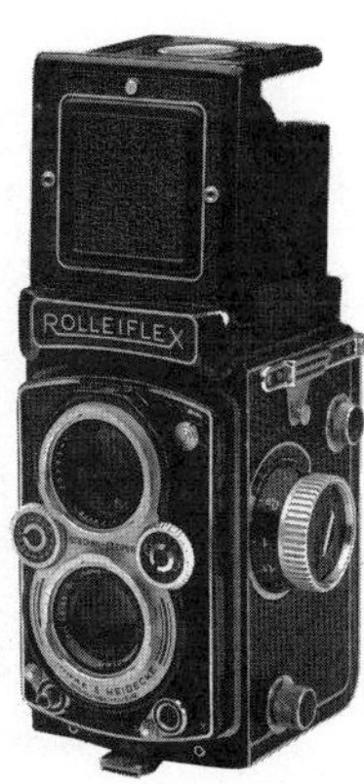

Rolleiflex Automat MX-EVS

MODEL	FORMAT	FILM	TYPE	Year	LENS	Apert	FL	SHUTTER	SPEEDS	ILLUS	U.S.$
Rolleiflex SL35ME	24x36mm	35mm	35SLR	1976	Zeiss Planar	1.8	50mm	focal plane	4-1000	Ev224	160
Rolleiflex SL35ME	24x36mm	35mm	35SLR	1976	Zeiss Planar	1.4	50mm	focal plane	4-1000	Ev224	160
Rolleiflex SL66 body	6x6cm	120	MedSLR	1966	body only	---	---	focal plane	1-1000	Pr353	530
Rolleiflex SL66 + 80/2.8	6x6cm	120	MedSLR	1966	Zeiss Planar	2.8	80mm	focal plane	1-1000	Pr366	900
Rolleiflex SL66E body	6x6cm	120	MedSLR	1982	body only	---	---	focal plane	1-1000	Pr354	1000
Rolleiflex SL66E + 80/2.8	6x6cm	120	MedSLR	1982	Zeiss Planar	2.8	80mm	focal plane	1-1000		1800
Rolleiflex SL66SE body	6x6cm	120	MedSLR	1986	body only	---	---	focal plane	1-1000	Pr356	3500
Rolleiflex SL66SE + 80/2.8	6x6cm	120	MedSLR	1986	Zeiss Planar	2.8	80mm	focal plane	1-1000		4000
Rolleiflex SL66SE Excl. Pro	6x6cm	120	MedSLR	1992	Zeiss Planar	2.8	80mm	focal plane	1-1000		5100
Rolleiflex SL66X body	6x6cm	120	MedSLR	1986	body only	---	---	focal plane	1-1000	Pr355	1400
Rolleiflex SL66X + 80/2.8	6x6cm	120	MedSLR	1986	Zeiss Planar	2.8	80mm	focal plane	1-1000	Pr366/	2000
Rolleiflex SLX body	6x6cm	120	MedSLR	1974	body only	---	---		30-1/500	Ev236	650
Rolleiflex SLX + 80/2.8	6x6cm	120	MedSLR	1974	Zeiss Planar	2.8	80mm		30-1/500	Ev236	1000
Rolleiflex Standard (old)	6x6cm	120	TLR	1932	Zeiss Tessar	4.5	75mm	Compur	1-300,B,T	Pr056	180
Rolleiflex Standard (old)	6x6cm	120	TLR	1932	Zeiss Tessar	3.8	75mm	Compur	1-300,B,T	Pr057	160
Rolleiflex Standard (old)	6x6cm	120	TLR	1932	Zeiss Tessar	3.5	75mm	Compur-Rap.	1-300,B,T	Pr058/	160
Rolleiflex Standard (new)	6x6cm	120	TLR	1939	Zeiss Tessar	3.5	75mm	Compur-Rap.	1-500,B	Pr073	290
Rolleiflex Studio	9x9cm	120	TLR	1932	Zeiss Tessar	4.5	105mm	Compur S	1-250,T,B	Ev38	10000
Rolleiflex T	6x6cm	120	TLR	1958	Zeiss Tessar	3.5	75mm	S.Comp.MXV	1-500	Pr184	360
Rolleimagic	6x6cm	120	TLR	1960	Xenar	3.5	75mm	Prontormat	30-300	Pr188	200
Rolleimagic II	6x6cm	120	TLR	1962	Xenar	3.5	75mm	Prontormat-S	30-300	Pr189	310
Rolleimat AF	24x36mm	35mm	35af	1980	Rolleinon	2.8	38mm		8-450	Ev215	90
Rolleimat AF-M	24x36mm	35mm	35af	1981	Rolleinon	2.8	38mm		8-450	Ev216	50
Rolleimat F	24x36mm	35mm	35vf	1979	Rolleinon	2.8	38mm		60-350	Ev213	60
Rolleimatic	24x36mm	35mm	35vf	1981	Rolleinar	2.8	38mm	programmed	4-500	Ev217	140
Tele Rolleiflex	6x6cm	120	TLR	1959	Zeiss Sonnar	4	135mm	S.Comp.MXV	1-500	Pr179	1200
Wide-Angle Rolleiflex	6x6cm	120	TLR	1961	Distagon	4	55mm	S.Comp.MXV	1-500	Pr180	2300
...FRIEDE (E.H. Friede) - Berlin											
Non Plus Ultra 25x30	25x30cm	plate	Field	1918	various			various			1200
Non Plus Ultra 30x40	30x40cm	plate	Field	1918	various			various		A2954	1400
Tropen-Spiegelreflexkamer	13x18cm	plate	LgTLR	1900	various			various		A1577	1200
...FUJI KOGAKU SEIKI - Japan											
Baby Balnet	3x4cm	127	FoldRo	194x	Nomular Anast.	2.9	50mm	Balnet	1-200		140
Baby Lyra	3x4cm	127	FoldRo	1941	Terionar	3.5	50mm	Picco	25-100		200
Comex	14x14mm	Roll	Submin								310
Lyra 4.5x6cm	4.5x6cm	120	FoldRo	1936	Terionar Anast.	3.5	75mm	Fujiko	1-200		130
Lyra Six	6x6cm	120	HzFoldRo	1939	Terionar	3.5	75mm	Fujiko	5-250		50
Lyraflex	6x6cm	120	TLR	1941	Terionar	3.5	75mm	Fujiko	1-200	Mc205	100
Lyraflex F	6x6cm	120	TLR	1941	Goldar	3.5	75mm	Fujiko	1-200	Mc205	100
Lyrax	4.5x6cm	120	TelescRo	1939	Terionar	3.5	75mm	Fujiko	5-250	Mc205	180
...FUJI PHOTO FILM CO - Japan											
Fujica AX-1	24x36mm	35mm	35slr	1980	Fujinon	1.9	50mm	focal plane	½-1000		140

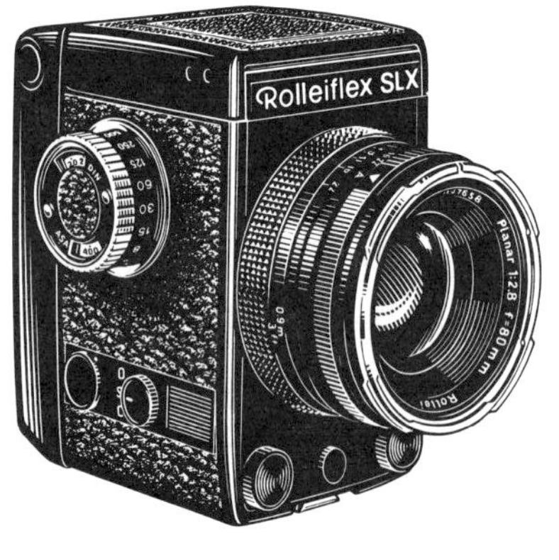

Rolleiflex SLX

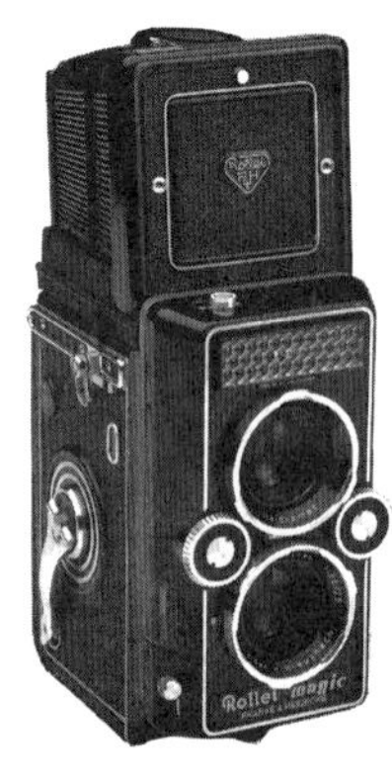

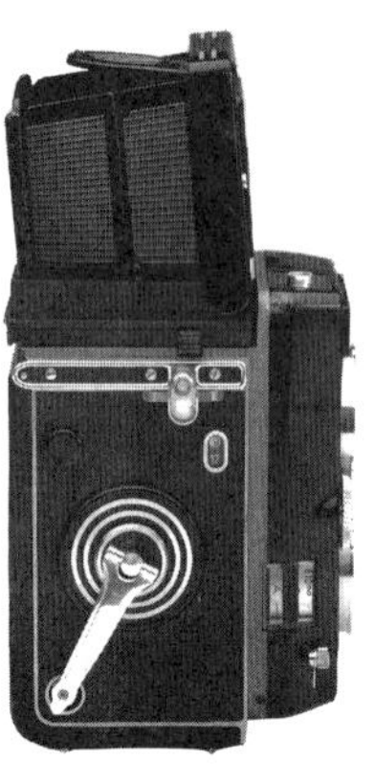

Rolleimagic

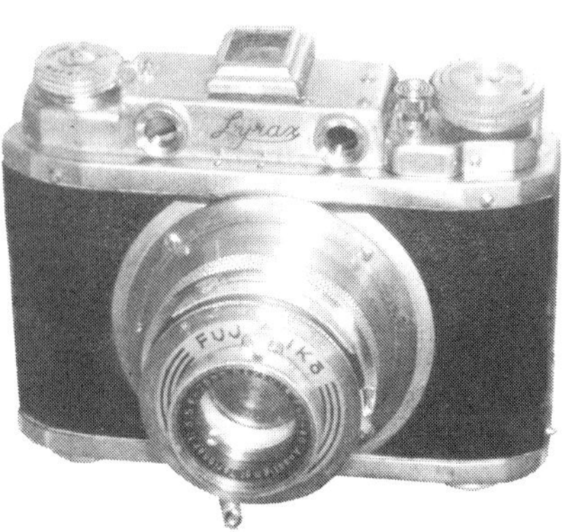

Lyrax

MODEL	FORMAT	FILM	TYPE	Year	LENS	Apert	FL	SHUTTER	SPEEDS	ILLUS	U.S.$
Fujica AX-3	24x36mm	35mm	35slr	1980	Fujinon	1.6	55mm	focal plane	½-1000		140
Fujica AX-5	24x36mm	35mm	35slr	1981	Fujinon	1.6	55mm	focal plane	½-1000		140
Fujica AZ-1	24x36mm	35mm	35slr	1977	Fujinon	3.5-4.5	43-75	focal plane	½-1000		160
Fujica Compact 35	24x36mm	35mm	35vf	1967	Fujinon	2.8	38mm		30-250		40
Fujica Compact S	24x36mm	35mm	35rf	1971	Fujinon	2.5	38mm	Seiko LA	30-250		50
Fujica Drive	24x36mm	35mm	35Half	1964	Fujinon	2.8	28mm	Seikosha-L	30-300		60
Fujica Half	24x36mm	35mm	35Half	1963	Fujinon	2.8	28mm	Seikosha-L	30-300		30
Fujica Half 1.9	24x36mm	35mm	35Half	1965	Fujinon	1.9	28mm	Seiko	1/8-500		70
Fujica HD-M	24x36mm	35mm	35uw	1984	Fujinon	2.8	38mm	electronic	8-500	A3454	180
Fujica Mini	24x36mm	35mm	35Half	1964	Fujinar-K Anast.	2.8	25mm				100
Fujica Rapid D1	18x24mm	Rapid	35Half	1966	Fujinon	2.8	28mm	Automatic	30-250	A2148	50
Fujica Rapid S	24x24mm	Rapid	35vf	1965			40mm		I		50
Fujica Rapid S2	24x24mm	Rapid	35vf	1965	Fujinar-K Anast.	2.8	28mm	Automatic	30-250	Mc205	30
Fujica V2	24x36mm	35mm	35rf	1964	Fujinon	1.8	45mm	Citizen-MLT	1-1000		30
Clear Shot	24x36mm	35mm	35vf	1994	Fujinon	8	33mm		1/100		20
Clear Shot Plus	24x36mm	35mm	35vf	1994	Fujinon	8	33mm		1/100		40
Clear Shot Super	24x36mm	35mm	35vf	1994	Fujinon	4.5	32mm		1/125		60
Discovery 80	24x36mm	35mm	35af	1992	Fujinon	5.6	35mm		1/100		60
Discovery 80 Plus	24x36mm	35mm	35af	1993	Fujinon	5.6	35mm				70
Discovery 190 Zoom	24x36mm	35mm	35afz	1993	Fujinon	6-9.3	35-55	electronic			110
Discovery 1000 Zoom QD	24x36mm	35mm	35afz	1992	Fujinon	3.8-8.2	35-80	electronic	1/9-350		150
Discovery 3000 Zoom Date	24x36mm	35mm	35afz	1992	Fujinon	4.4	38mm	electronic	1-350		230
DL-7 Plus	24x36mm	35mm	35vf	1993	Fujinon	8	35mm		1/100		20
DL-8	24x36mm	35mm	35vf	1993	Fujinon	8	35mm		1/100		20
DL-10	24x36mm	35mm	35vf	1987	Fujinon	5.6	35mm		1/125		70
DL-25 (DL-25N)	24x36mm	35mm	35vf	1992	Fujinon	5.6	35mm		1/100		30
DL-30	24x36mm	35mm	35af	1987	Fujinon	4	35mm	electronic	64-360		50
DL-50	24x36mm	35mm	35af	1985	Fujinon	4	35mm		1/125	A3504	50
DL-80	24x36mm	35mm	35af	1992	Fujinon	5.6	35mm		1/100		60
DL-90	24x36mm	35mm	35af	1993	Fujinon	5.6	35mm				70
DL-95 Super	24x36mm	35mm	35af	1994	Fujinon	4.5	34mm	electronic	140-600		70
DL-150	24x36mm	35mm	35af	1987	Fujinon	3.5	35mm	electronic	30-500		80
DL-180 Tele	24x36mm	35mm	35af	1993	Fujinon	6.5	35mm		1/100		100
DL-190 Zoom	24x36mm	35mm	35afz	1993	Fujinon	6-9.3	35-55	electronic			120
DL-200	24x36mm	35mm	35af	1985	Fujinon	2.8	32mm	electronic	40-400		80
DL-270 Zoom	24x36mm	35mm	35afz	1994	Fujinon	5	35-70	electronic			140
DL-500 Wide Date	24x36mm	35mm	35af	1991	Fujinon	3.5	28-45	electronic	2-250		110
DL-1000 Zoom	24x36mm	35mm	35afz	1992	Fujinon	3.8-8.2	35-80	electronic	1/9-350		150
DL-Super Mini	24x36mm	35mm	35af	1994	Fujinon	3.5	28mm	electronic			380
Fotojack			Dispose							Mc205	30
Fujicaflex	6x6cm	120	TLR	1954	Fujinar	2.8	83mm	Seiko.Rap.B	1-400		240
Fujicarex	24x36mm	35mm	35SLR	1962	Fujinon-S	1.9	50mm	Fuji-Synchro	1-500,B		70

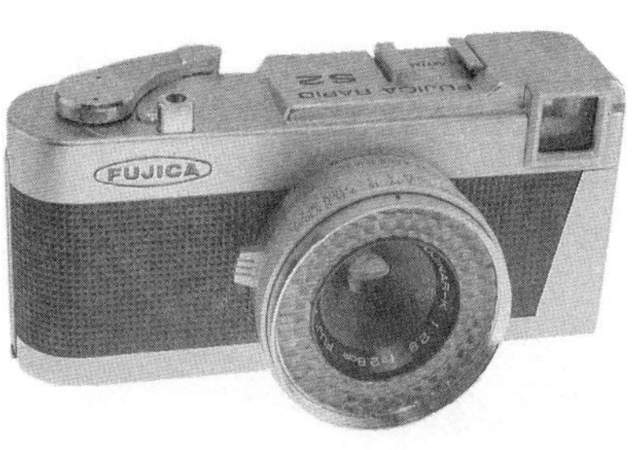

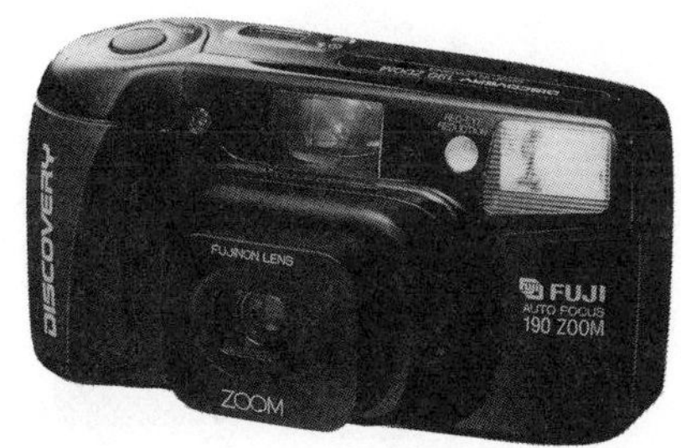

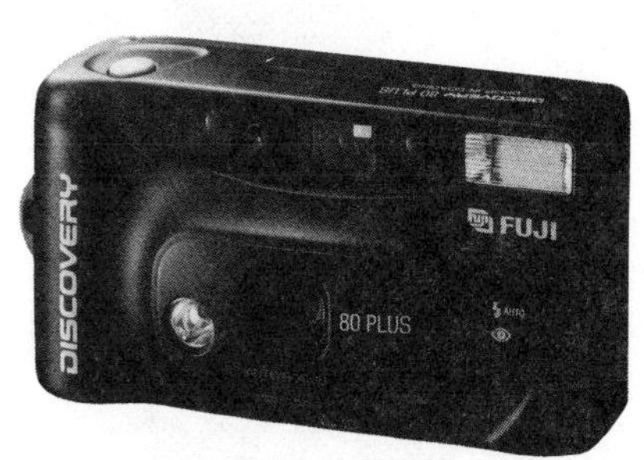

Fujica Rapid S2 | **Discovery 190 Zoom** | **Discovery 80 Plus**

MODEL	FORMAT	FILM	TYPE	Year	LENS	Apert	FL	SHUTTER	SPEEDS	ILLUS	U.S.$
Fujicarex II	24x36mm	35mm	35SLR	1963	Fujinon-S	1.9	50mm	Fuji-Synchro	1-500,B		70
Fujipet (black)	6x6cm	120	RigidRo	1959	Meniscus				I,B		30
Fujipet (green)	6x6cm	120	RigidRo	1959	Meniscus				I,B		30
Fujipet (maroon)	6x6cm	120	RigidRo	1959	Meniscus				I,B		30
Fujipet EE	6x6cm	120	RigidRo	1959	Meniscus				I,B		30
FZ-5	24x36mm	35mm	35vf	1989	Fujinon	9.5	35mm		1/100		20
FZ-6 Tele	24x36mm	35mm	35vf			9.5	35-55				40
FZ-3000 Zoom Date	24x36mm	35mm	35afz	1992	Fujinon	4.4	38mm	electronic	1-350		290
G617 Professional	6x17cm	120	WideAng	1987	Fujinon	8	105mm		1-500		2000
G690	6x9cm	120	RigidRo	1969	Fujinon	3.5	100mm		1-500		440
GS645	4.5x6cm	120	FoldRo	1983	Fujinon EBC S	3.4	75mm	Copal	1-500		630
GS645S Professional	4.5x6cm	120	RigidRo	1984	Fujinon	4	60mm	Copal	1-500	A3411	470
GS645W Professional	4.5x6cm	120	RigidRo	1985	Fujinon	5.6	45mm	Copal	1-500		550
GSW680 III Professional	6x8cm	120	RigidRo	1993	Fujinon	5.6	65mm	Copal	1-500		800
GSW690 Professional	6x9cm	120	RigidRo	1984	Fujinon	5.6	65mm	Copal	1-500		350
GSW690 II Professional	6x9cm	120	RigidRo	1986	Fujinon	5.6	65mm	Copal	1-500		540
GSW690 III Professional	6x9cm	120	RigidRo	1992	Fujinon	5.6	65mm	Copal	1-500		1000
GW670 II Professional	6x7cm	120	RigidRo	1986	Fujinon	3.5	90mm	Copal	1-500		700
GW670 III Professional	6x7cm	120	RigidRo	1992	Fujinon	3.5	90mm	Copal	1-500		1000
GW690 II Professional	6x9cm	120	RigidRo	1986	Fujinon	3.5	90mm	Copal	1-500		650
GW690 III Professional	6x9cm	120	RigidRo	1992	Fujinon	3.5	90mm	Copal	1-500		1000
GX617 Professional body	6x17cm	120	WideAng	1994	body only	---	---	Copal	1-500		1600
GX617 Professional + 90	6x17cm	120	WideAng	1994	Fujinon	5.6	90mm	Copal	1-500		3100
GX617 Professional + 105	6x17cm	120	WideAng	1994	Fujinon	8	105mm	Copal	1-500		3000
GX617 Professional + 180	6x17cm	120	WideAng	1994	Fujinon	6.7	180mm	Copal	1-500		2600
GX680 Professional body	6x8cm	120	MedSLR	1987	body only	---	---	electronic	8-400		1600
GX680 Professional + 100/4	6x8cm	120	MedSLR	1987	Fujinon	4	100mm	electronic	8-400		2300
GX680 II Professional	6x8cm	120	MedSLR	1994	Fujinon	5.6	135mm	electronic	8-400		3300
Pet 35	24x36mm	35mm	35vf	1959	Fujinar	3.5	4.5cm	Copal	25-200	Mc205	30
Pocket Fujica 200	13x17mm	110	110	1976	Fujinon	11	29mm		21916		30
Pocket Fujica 250	13x17mm	110	110	1982	Fujinon	9.5	26mm		80-320		50
Pocket Fujica 350 Flash	13x17mm	110	110	1978	Fujinon	5.6	20mm		1/125		50
Pocket Fujica 450 Flash	13x17mm	110	110	1978	Fujinon	4	20mm		1/160		50
Smart Shot	24x36mm	35mm	35vf	1994	Fujinon	8	33mm		1/100		20
Smart Shot Motor	24x36mm	35mm	35vf	1994	Fujinon	8	33mm		1/100		40
Smart Shot Super	24x36mm	35mm	35vf	1994	Fujinon	4.5	32mm		1/125		60
ST 605	24x36mm	35mm	35slr	1977	Fujinon	1.8	55mm	focal plane	½-1/700,B		100
ST 605N	24x36mm	35mm	35slr	1978	Fujinon	2.2	55mm	focal plane	½-1/700,B		100
ST 701	24x36mm	35mm	35slr	1971	Fujinon	1.8	55mm	focal plane	1-1000,B		80
ST 705	24x36mm	35mm	35slr	1977	Fujinon	1.8	55mm	focal plane	1/1500		130
ST 705W	24x36mm	35mm	35slr	1978	Fujinon	1.8	55mm	focal plane	1/1500		100
ST 801	24x36mm	35mm	35slr	1973	Fujinon	2.8	55mm	focal plane	2000		110

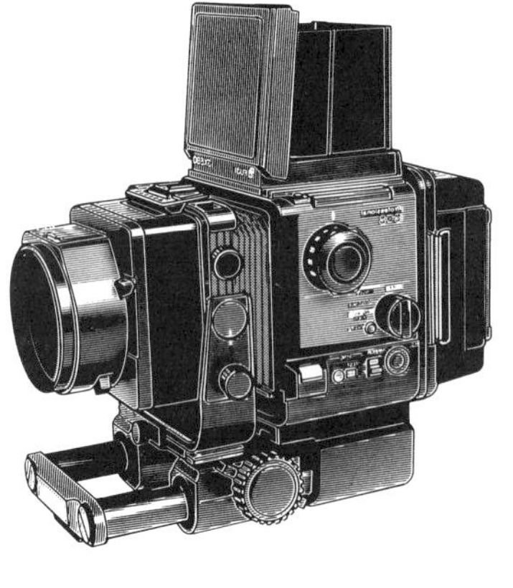

GX680 Professional

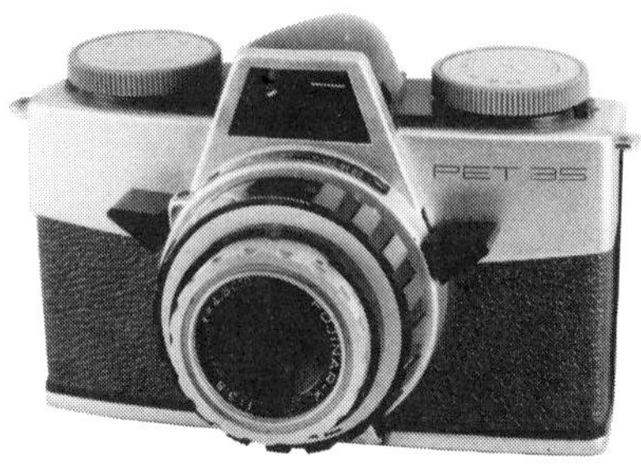

Pet 35

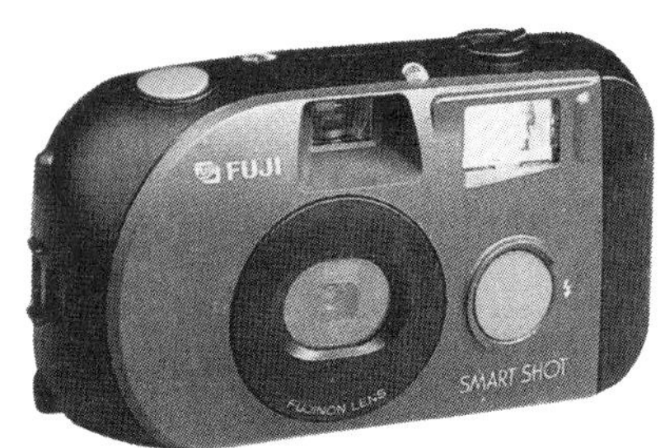

Smart Shot

MODEL	FORMAT	FILM	TYPE	Year	LENS	Apert	FL	SHUTTER	SPEEDS	ILLUS	U.S.$
ST 901	24x36mm	35mm	35slr	1974	Fujinon	3.8	55mm	focal plane	20-1/2000		120
STX-1	24x36mm	35mm	35slr	1980	Fujinon	2.2	55mm	focal plane	½-700		100
STX-1N	24x36mm	35mm	35slr	1982	Fujinon	1.9	50mm	focal plane	½-700		100
STX-2	24x36mm	35mm	35slr	1985	Fujinon	1.9	50mm	focal plane	½-1000		100
TW-3	18x24mm	35mm	35Half	1986	Fujinon	8	23/69	programmed	30-500		50
TW-300	24x36mm	35mm	35af	1986	Fujinon	3.5	38/65	programmed	6-500		120
Zoom Cardia Multi 800	24x36mm	35mm	35afz	1992	Fujinon	3.8-8.2	35-80	electronic	1/9-350		170
...FUJIMOTO MFG. CO. - Japan											
Prince Peerless	6.5x9cm	plate	FoldPl	1934	Radionar	4.5	105mm	Compur	1-250		320
Semi Prince	4.5x6cm	120	FoldRo	1935	N&H	4.5	75mm	Perfect	5-250	M206	90
Semi Prince II	4.5x6cm	120	FoldRo	1935	Radionar	4.5	75mm	Pronto	25-100		90
Semi Prince B	4.5x6cm	120	FoldRo	1935	Radionar	4.5	75mm	Pronto II	25-100	M206	90
...FUJITA OPT. IND. LTD. - Japan											
Classic 35 IV	24x36mm	35mm	35vf	1960		3.4	45mm	Fujita	B,25-300		50
Fodor 66	6x6cm	120	TLR	1962	Fujita	3.5	80mm	focal plane	5-500		120
Fujita 66SL	6x6cm	120	MedSLR	1958	Fujita	3.5	80mm	focal plane	5-500		110
Fujita 66SQ	6x6cm	120	MedSLR	1960	Fujita	2.8	80mm	focal plane	5-500		110
Fujita 66ST	6x6cm	120	MedSLR	1956	Fujita	3.5	80mm	focal plane	B,25-500		140
...FUTURA KAMERA WERK A.G. - Freiburg											
Futura	24x36mm	35mm	35rf	1951	Elor	2.8	50mm	Compur-Rap.	1-400,B,T	HK578	100
Futura-P	24x36mm	35mm	35rf	1953	Futar	3.5	45mm	Prontor-SV	1-300		70
Futura-S	24x36mm	35mm	35rf	1950	Kuhnert Frilon	1.5	50mm	Sync-Compur	1-500,B	HK584	230
Futura-SIII	24x36mm	35mm	35rf	1956	Kuhnert Frilon	1.5	50mm	Sync-Compur	1-500,B		180
...GAERTIG & THIEMANN - Görlitz											
Field camera 9x12	9x12cm	plate	Field	1895	various				I	A1366	240
Field camera 10x15	10x15cm	plate	Field	1895	various				I		270
Ideal Mod. VI	13x18cm	plate	Field	1906	Steinheil				I		240
...GALILEO OPTICAL - Milan											
Condor I	24x36mm	35mm	35rf	1947	Eliog	3.5	50mm	Iscus Rapid	B,1-500		130
Gami 16	12x17mm	16mm	Submin	1955s		1.9	25mm		2-1000	Mc207	520
...GALLUS (Usines Gallus) - Courbevoie, France											
Bakelite	6x9cm	120	FoldRo		Achromat	11			P & I	Mc207	70
Cady-Lux	6x9cm	120	FoldRo	1942	Hermos	4.5	105mm	Gallus	1-100	F294	60
Derby	3x4cm	127	StrutRo	1939	Som Berthiot Flor	3.5		focal plane		F722	70
Derby	3x4cm	127	StrutRo	1939	Saphir	3.5		focal plane		F723	70
Derby-Lux	3x4cm	127	StrutRo	1945	Boyer Saphir	3.5		focal plane	B,25-500	Mc207	180
Derlux	3x4cm	127	StrutRo	1947	Gallus Gallix	3.5	50mm	focal plane	25-500	F726	140
Derlux	3x4cm	127	StrutRo	1947	Saphir	2.8	50mm	focal plane	25-500	F727	140
Folding Rollfilm	6.5x11cm	116	FoldRo	1920	Gallus Anastigmat	6.3	120mm	Ibsor		Mc207	40
Jumelle 0	6x13cm	plate	StJumelle	1925	Anastigmat	7.5	75mm	guillotine		F1270	270
Jumelle 00	6x13cm	plate	StJumelle	1925	Achromat	7.5	75mm	guillotine			190
Jumelle Type 100	6x13cm	plate	StJumelle	1927	Roussel	4.5	75mm	guillotine	5-200	F1295	180

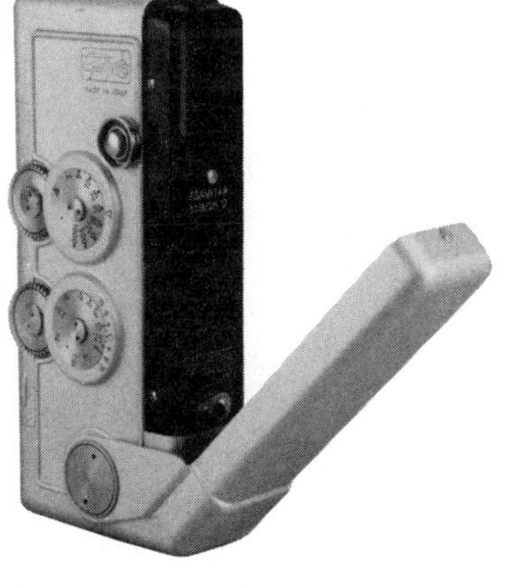

Gami 16

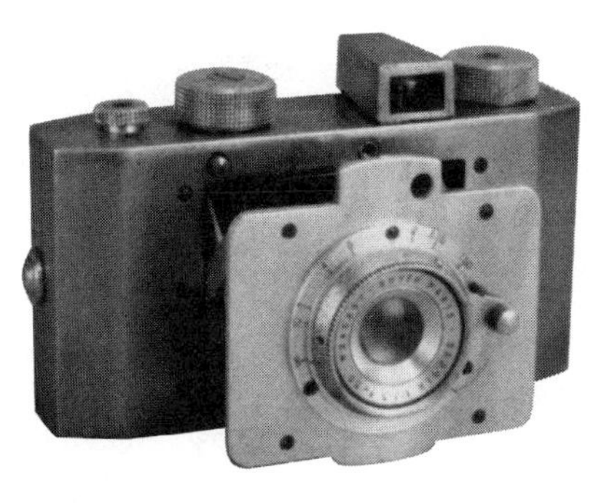

Derby-Lux

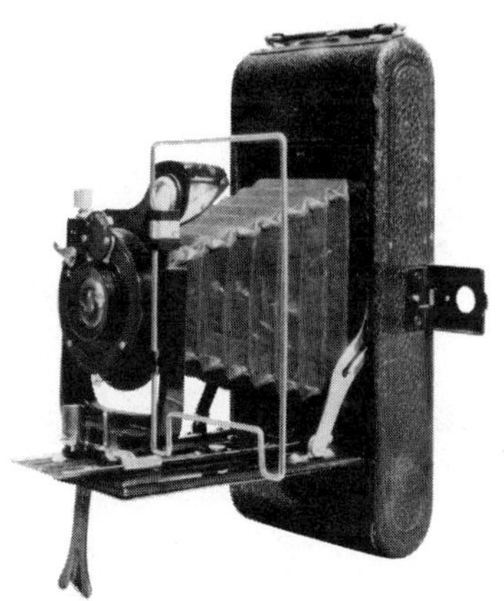

Gallus Folding Camera

MODEL	FORMAT	FILM	TYPE	Year	LENS	Apert	FL	SHUTTER	SPEEDS	ILLUS	U.S.$
Jumelle Type 100	6x13cm	plate	StJumelle	1925	Saphir	6.3	72mm	guillotine	5-200	F1294	180
Jumelle Type 150	6x13cm	plate	StJumelle	1926	Tessar	4.5	75mm	guillotine	2-1/250	F1296	200
Stereo camera 45x107	45x107	plate	StJumelle	1923	Anastigmat				1/300	Mc207	130
Stereo camera 6x9	6x9cm	plate	Stereo	1905	Gallus Anastigmat	7.5				Mc207	110
Stereo camera 6x13	6x13cm	plate	StJumelle	1923	Anastigmat				1/300	Mc207	160
...GAMMA (Societa Gamma) - Rome, Italy											
Alba	24x36mm	35mm	35vf	1956	Ennagon	2.8	45mm	Pronto	B,25-200	Mc208	50
Gamma	24x36mm	35mm	35rf	1947	Gamma	3.5		focal plane	1/20-1000	Mc208	670
Gamma IIIA	24x36mm	35mm	35rf	1955	Koriska Victor	3.5	55mm	focal plane	1-1000	HK608	800
Gamma IIIB	24x36mm	35mm	35rf	1965	Koriska Victor	3.5	55mm	focal plane	1-1000	HK608	620
Perla A	24x36mm	35mm	35rf	1951	Stigmar	3.5	50mm	Prontor-S	1-300		110
Perla AI	24x36mm	35mm	35rf	1951	Radionar	3.5	50mm	Prontor-SVS		Mc208	140
...GAMMA WORKS - Budapest											
Duflex	24x32mm	35mm	35SLR	1947				focal plane		Mc208	2000
Pajta's	6x6cm	120	RigidRo	1960	Achromat	8			T&M	Mc208	70
...GATTO (Antonio Gatto) - Pordenone, Italy											
Sonne IV	24x36mm	35mm	35rf	1948	Adlenar	3.5	50mm	focal plane	1/20-1000	Mc208	610
Sonne V	24x36mm	35mm	35rf	1950	Elionar	3.5	50mm	focal plane	1-1000		570
Sonne C	24x36mm	35mm	35rf	1950	Xenar	2.8	50mm	focal plane	1-1000		530
Sonne C4	24x36mm	35mm	35rf	1953	Elionar	3.5	50mm	focal plane	1-1000		580
...GAUMONT - Paris											
Block-Notes 4.5x6	4.5x6cm	plate	StrutPl	1904	Darlot	6.8		guillotine		Mc209	190
Block-Notes 6.5x9	6.5x9cm	plate	StrutPl	1909	Tessar	6.3		guillotine		A317	140
Block-Notes Stereo 45x107	45x107	plate	SterStrut		Tessar	6.3		guillotine		Mc209	330
Block-Notes Stereo 6x13	6x13cm	plate	SterStrut		Tessar	6.3		guillotine		Mc209	330
Elge 6.5x9	6.5x9cm	plate	MagBox	1896	Achromatic	8		guillotine	P,I	Mc209	80
Elge 9x12	9x12cm	plate	MagBox	1896				guillotine	P,I	A88	140
Folding camera 9x12	9x12cm	plate	HzFoldPl	1900	various			various		A160	330
Folding camera 12x17	12x17cm	plate	HzFoldPl	1900	various			various		A164	330
Folding camera 13x18	13x18cm	plate	HzFoldPl	1900	various			various		F42	330
Folding Spido	9x12cm	plate	StrutPl	1925	Zeiss Tessar	4.5	135mm	focal plane	-2000	A342	220
Miniature	15x20mm	Roll	Submin		Krauss Z. Tessar	2.7	2cm	single speed		Mc209	2400
Polain No.1	6x13cm	plate	StJumelle		Tessar	6.3	84mm				380
Reporter 6.5x9	6.5x9cm	plate	StrutPl	1924	Flor	3.5		focal plane	1/25-1000	A343	310
Reporter 9x12	9x12cm	plate	StrutPl	1924	Flor	3.5	135mm	focal plane	1/25-1000	F218	390
Reporter Tropical 9x12	9x12cm	plate	StrutPl	1948	Tessar	4.5	65mm	Klopcic	1-1000	F219	700
Reporter Tropical 9x14	9x14cm	plate	StrutPl								700
Spido 6.5x9	6.5x9cm	plate	Jumelle	1898	Protar	6.3	105mm	Decaux		F1124	240
Spido 9x12	9x12cm	plate	Jumelle	1898	Berthiot	6	135mm	Decaux		F1123	240
Spido 11x15	11x15cm	plate	Jumelle	1935	Berthiot	6	155mm	focal plane		F1125	560
Stereo Jumelle	8.5x17cm	plate	StJumelle	1890	Dagor			guillotine			300
Stereo Jumelle (bakelite)	6x13cm	plate	StJumelle	1931	Stereostigmat	10		guillotine			370

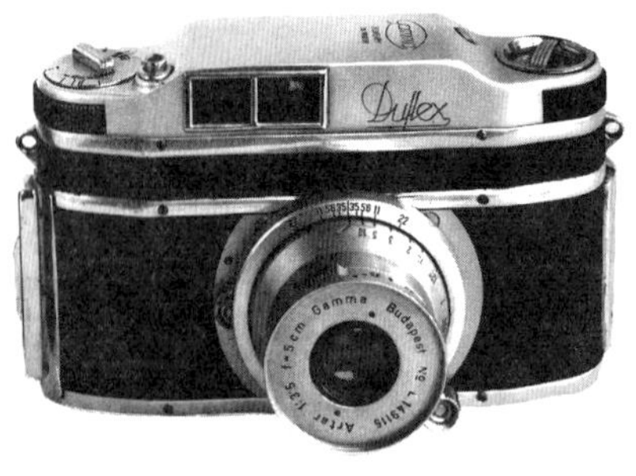

Duflex

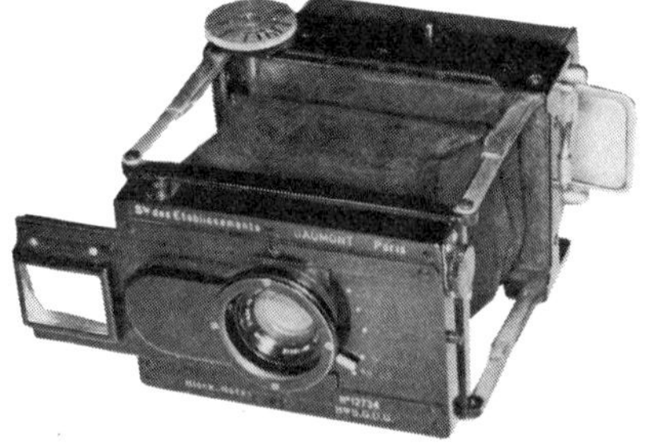

Block-Notes 4.5x6

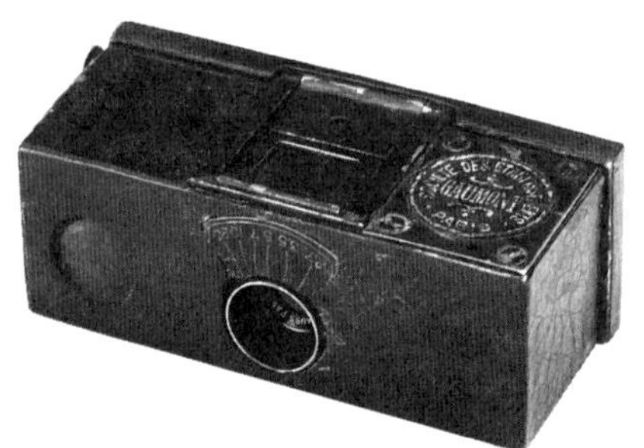

Gaumont Miniature

MODEL	FORMAT	FILM	TYPE	Year	LENS	Apert	FL	SHUTTER	SPEEDS	ILLUS	U.S.$
Stereo Spido Metallique	6x13cm	plate	StJumelle	1922	Tessar	4.5	85mm	Decaux		Mc209	340
Stereo Spido Metallique	6x13cm	120	StJumelle	1922	Tessar	4.5	85mm	Decaux			430
Stereo Spido Ordinaire	6x13cm	plate	StJumelle	1906	Protar	12.5	84mm	Decaux		F1406	250
Stereo Spido Ordinaire	8.5x17cm	plate	StJumelle	1906	Protar	12.5	183mm	Decaux		F1405	270
Strut camera	6.5x9cm	plate	StrutPl	1900	various			various		A341	140
...GENOS K.G. - Nurnberg											
Genos	25x25mm	35mm	RigidRo	1949		8			M,Z		50
Genos 6x6	6x6cm	120	BakeliteBox	1950	Genosar				M,Z		20
Genos Fix	4.5x6cm	120	BakeliteBox	1951						A2858	50
Genos Rapid	6x6cm	120	BakeliteBox	1950					M,Z	A131	30
Genos Special	6x6cm	120	BakeliteBox	1953	Achromat	8		single speed		HK112	30
Special Fix	4.5x6cm	127	BakeliteBox	1950						Mc210	30
...GERLACH - Wuppertal											
Ideal	6x6cm	120	TelescRo	1952	Color-Achromat	7	7.2mm		M,B		20
Ideal Box	6x9cm	120	MetBx	1956	Meniscus	11	110mm		M,Z		20
Ideal Color 35	24x36mm	35mm	35vf	1956	Nixon	3.5	45mm	Spezial	25-100		30
Ideal Color 35	24x36mm	35mm	35vf	1956	Nixon Anast.	3.5	45mm	Spezial	25-100	Mc210	30
Trixette	6x6cm	120	FoldRo	1955	Supra Anastigmat	5.6	75mm	Spezial	25-100		50
Trixette I	6x6cm	120	FoldRo	1956	Supra Anastigmat	5.6	75mm	Spezial	25-100		50
Trixette II	6x6cm	120	FoldRo	1958	Supra Anastigmat	5.6	75mm	Vario			50
...GERSTENDÖRFER (R. Gerstendörfer) - Wien, Austria											
Picoflex	3x4cm	127	TLR	1929	Cassar	2.9	50mm	Compur	1-300	HK387	390
Picoflex	4x4cm	127	TLR	1929	Xenar	2.9	50mm	Compur	1-300	A644	210
Wica	24x36mm	35mm	35rf	1949	Flor	2.8	50mm	focal plane	1/20-1000	A1085	1400
...GEVAERT - Lieven											
Gevabox 6x6	6x6cm	120	BakeliteBox	1950		8			I,T	A128	30
Gevabox 6x9 (single finder)	6x9cm	120	MetBx	1955		11	105mm		50100	Mc210	20
Gevabox 6x9 (two finders)	6x9cm	120	MetBx	1951		8			M,B	Mc211	30
Gevabox Special	6x9cm	120	Box	1951		11			50,100,B		30
Gevalux 144	4x4cm	127	PlasBx							Mc211	20
Gevaphot	6x9cm	620	TelescRo	1960	Meniscus				25-100	Mc211	20
Rex-Lujo	6x9cm	120	TelescRo	1944						Mc211	60
...GILLES-FALLER - Paris											
Gilfa (roll)	6x9cm	120	StrutRo	1928	various			Compur		F330	580
Gilfa (tropical)	6.5x9cm	plate	StrutPl	1927	Hermagis			Ibsor		F191	570
Studio camera	18x24cm	plate	Studio	1900	Hermagis Delor	4.5	270mm			F130	400
...GIRARD (J. Girard & Co.) - Paris											
Radieux	9x12cm	plate	MagBox	1903	Rapid Rectilinear					F1013	210
...GLUNZ - Hannover											
Camera Mod. 3	9x12cm	plate	FoldPl	1921	Trioplan	6.8	135mm	Vario			50
Camera Mod. 8	9x12cm	plate	FoldPl	1921	Helioplan	6.8	135mm	Vario	25-100		40
Camera Mod. 38	9x12cm	plate	FoldPl	1921	Steinheil Unofocal	5.4	135mm	Compur			70

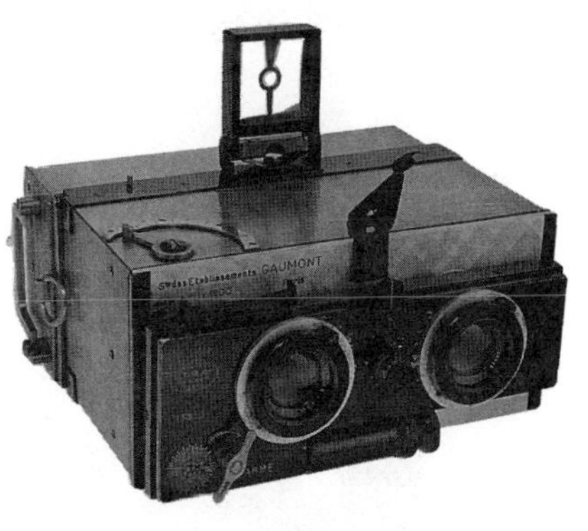

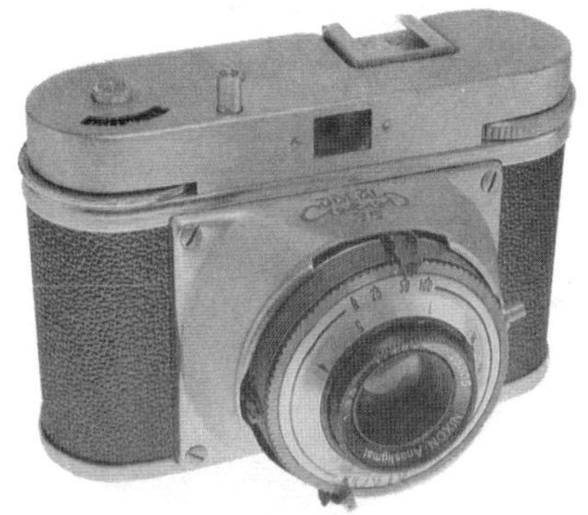

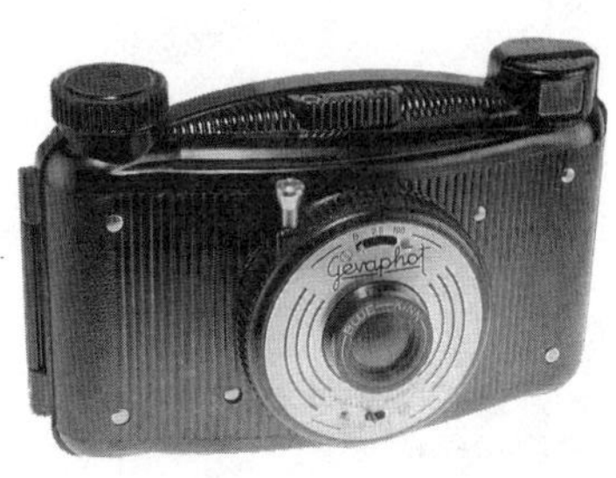

Stereo Spido Metallique | **Gerlach Ideal Color 35** | **Gevaphot**

MODEL	FORMAT	FILM	TYPE	Year	LENS	Apert	FL	SHUTTER	SPEEDS	ILLUS	U.S.$
Camera Mod. 60	9x12cm	plate	FoldPl	1921	Tessar	4.5	135mm	Compur		Mc212	40
Camera Mod. 70	10x15cm	plate	FoldPl	1921	Steinheil Unofocal	5.4	165mm	Ibso	1-100		50
Camera Mod. 400 Luxus	6.5x9cm	plate	FoldPl	1926	Tessar	4.5	12cm	Compur	250		160
Folding camera 6.5x9	6.5x9cm	plate	FoldPl	1921	Tessar	4.5	120mm	Compur	1-250		60
Folding camera 9x12	9x12cm	plate	FoldPl	1921	Zeiss Tessar	4.5	135mm	Dial-Compur			50
Folding camera 13x18	13x18cm	plate	FoldPl	1905	Hemi-Anastigmat	7.2		Unicum			120
Ingo	3x4cm	127	FoldRo	1932	Trinar	2.9	5cm	Compur	1-300	Mc212	200
Metall-Camera Mod. 400	6.5x9cm	plate	FoldPl	1921	Meyer Helioplan	6.8	120mm	Vario			70
Querformat 10x15	10x15cm	plate	FoldPl	1920	Busch Glyptar	4.5	12cm	Compur			120
Rollfilm-Camera Mod. 111	6.5x11cm	116	FoldRo	1923	Trioplan	6.3	120mm	Vario			30
Rollfilm-Camera Mod. 300	8.2x10.7	124	FoldRo	1921	Helioplan	6.8	135mm	Compur			30
Rollfilm-Camera Mod. 333	6x9cm	120	FoldRo	1923	Tessar	4.5	105mm	Compur		Mc212	30
...GOERZ (C.P. Goerz) - Berlin, Germany											
Ango 6.5x9	6.5x9cm	plate	StrutPl	1911	Dagor	6.8	90mm	focal plane			260
Ango 8x10.5	8x10.5cm	plate	StrutPl	1911	Celor	4.8	4.75"	focal plane	5-1000		150
Ango 9x12	9x12cm	plate	StrutPl	1911	Dagor	6.8		focal plane	5-1000		140
Ango 10x12.5	10x12.5cm	plate	StrutPl	1911	Dagor	6.8		focal plane	5-1000		100
Ango 10x15	10x15cm	plate	StrutPl	1911	Syntor	6.8	180mm	focal plane	5-1000	A312	90
Ango 12x16.5	12x16.5cm	plate	StrutPl	1911	Celor	4.8	180mm	focal plane	5-1000		140
Ango 13x18	13x18cm	plate	StrutPl	1911	Celor	4.8	180mm	focal plane	5-1000		140
Ango Stereo 6x13	6x13cm	plate	SterStrut	1911	Wide-Angle Apl.			focal plane	5-1000		300
Ango Stereo 9x18	9x18cm	plate	SterStrut	1911	Dagor Dop.Anast.	6.8		focal plane	5-1000	A1784	290
Anschütz 9x12	9x12cm	plate	StrutPl	1896	Doppel Anast.	6.8		focal plane	1/25-1000	Mc213	120
Anschütz 12x16.5	12x16.5cm	plate	StrutPl	1901	Pantar	6.3		focal plane	1/10-1000		130
Anschütz 13x18	13x18cm	plate	StrutPl	1903	Celor	4.5		focal plane	5-1000		120
Anschütz 18x24	18x24cm	plate	StrutPl	1903	Doppel Anast.	6.8		focal plane	5-1000	A3013	310
Anschütz (box)	9x12cm	plate	Box	1892	ExRap.Lynkeiscop			focal plane	5-1000		2200
Anschütz Tropen 9x12	9x12cm	plate	StrutPl	1911	Syntor	6.8		focal plane	5-1000		280
Anschütz Tropen 12x16.5	12x16.5cm	plate	StrutPl	1911	Dagor	6.8		focal plane	5-1000		2600
Anschütz Tropen 13x18	13x18cm	plate	StrutPl	1911	Syntor	6.8		focal plane	5-1000		2000
Anschütz-Reise-Apparat	13x18cm	plate	Tailboard	1897	Doppel Anast.		18cm	Anschütz FP	20-1000	HK46	200
Ballonkamera 9x12	9x12cm	plate	Aerial	1909	Lynkeioskop	6.3	600mm	focal plane	5-1000	A3435	520
Ballonkamera 13x18	13x18cm	plate	Aerial	1909	Lynkeioskop	6.3	600mm	focal plane	5-1000	A3440	520
Box Tengor 6x9	6x9cm	120	RollBox	1925	Frontar	11				Mc213	30
Box Tengor 6.5x11	6.5x11cm	116	RollBox	1925	Frontar	11				Mc213	50
Fliegerkamera 9x12	9x12cm	plate	Aerial	1915	Dogmar	3.5	250mm	focal plane		A3439	700
Fliegerkamera 13x18	13x18cm	plate	Aerial	1915	Dogmar	3.5	250mm	focal plane		A3437	670
Folding Reflex	4x5"	plate	FoldSLR	1910	Double					Mc213	350
Jagd-Ango 13x18	13x18cm	plate	LgSLR	1909	Lynkeioskop	6.3	600mm	focal plane	5-1000	HK667	480
Manufoc Tenax 9x12	9x12cm	plate	FoldPl	1909	Dogmar	4.5	150mm	Compur			70
Manufoc Tenax 10x15	10x15cm	plate	FoldPl	1911	Syntor	6.3	168mm	Compound	1-200		80
Manufoc Tenax 13x18	13x18cm	plate	FoldPl	1912	Celor	4.5	180mm	Compound	1-200		80

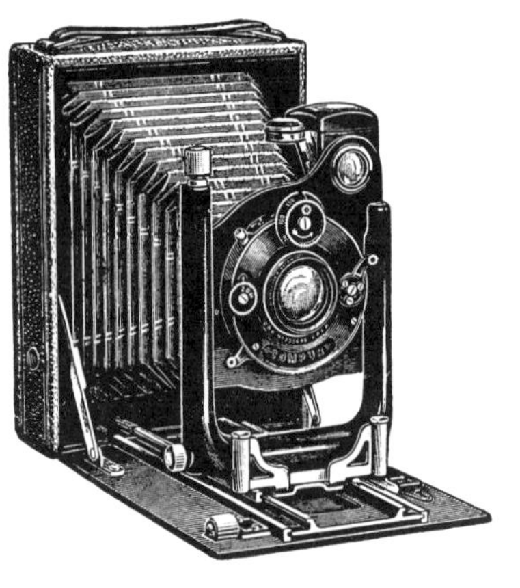

Glunz Mod. 60

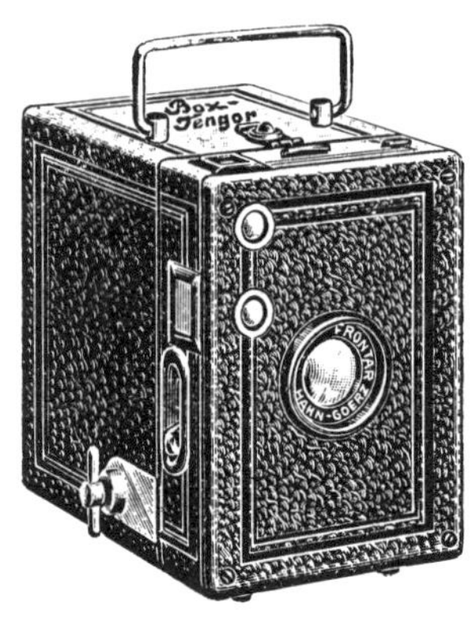

Box Tengor

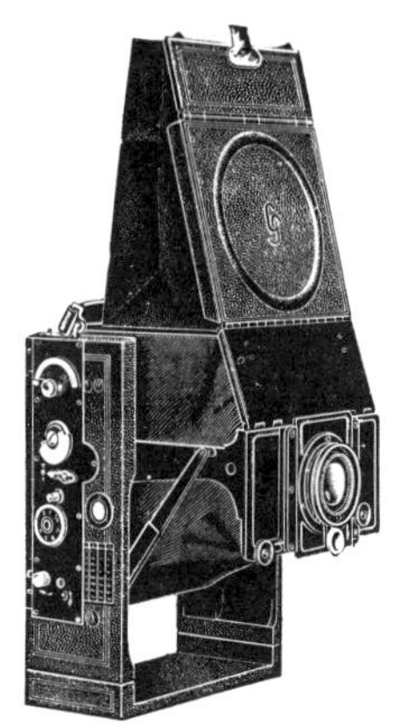

Goerz Folding Reflex

MODEL	FORMAT	FILM	TYPE	Year	LENS	Apert	FL	SHUTTER	SPEEDS	ILLUS	U.S.$
Manufoc Tenax Tropen	9x12cm	plate	FoldPl	1924	Dagor	6.8	150mm	Compur			670
Photo-Stereo-Binocle	45x50mm	plate	Disguised	1899	Dagor	6.8	75mm			Mc214	3300
Reporter	4x4.5cm	plate	Disguised	1889	Doppel Aplanat					HK13	5800
Roll Tenax 4x6.5	4x6.5cm	127	VtFoldRo	1921	Dogmar	6.3	75mm	Compur	-300	Mc214	70
Roll Tenax 6x9	6x9cm	120	VtFoldRo	1921	Tenastigmat	6.3	100mm	Compur	1-250	Mc214	70
Roll Tenax 6.5x11	6.5x11cm	115	VtFoldRo	1921	Dogmar	5	125mm	Compur		Mc214	70
Roll Tenax 8x10.5	8x10.5cm	124	VtFoldRo	1921	Tenastigmat	6.8	125mm			Mc214	70
Roll Tenax 8x14cm	3¼x5½"	122	VtFoldRo	1921	Dagor	6.8		Compur		Mc214	70
Roll Tenax Luxus (green)	4x6.5cm	127	VtFoldRo	1925	Dogmar	4.5	75mm	Compur	1-300		1100
Roll Tenax Luxus (red)	4x6.5cm	127	VtFoldRo	1925	Dogmar	4.5	75mm	Compur	1-300		1100
Roll Tengor 4x6.5	4x6.5cm	127	VtFoldRo	1925	Frontar	9	45mm	Goerz	25-100		60
Roll Tengor 6x9	6x9cm	120	VtFoldRo	1925	Tenaxiar	6.8	100mm	Goerz	25-100		40
Roll Tengor 6.5x11	6.5x11cm	116	VtFoldRo	1925	Tenaxiar	6.8	125mm	Goerz	25-100		30
Roll Tengor 8x14	8x14cm	124	VtFoldRo	1925	Tenaxiar	6.8	165mm	Pronto			50
Spiegelreflex (Night Model)	13x18cm	plate	LgSLR	1922	T.-H. Cooke	2	210mm	focal plane	1/10-1200	A1599	680
Stereo Anschütz 6x13	6x13cm	plate	SterStrut	1911	Syntor	6.8		focal plane	5-1000	Mc213	310
Stereo Anschütz 8x17	8x17cm	plate	SterStrut	1911	Dagor	6.8		focal plane	5-1000	Mc213	290
Stereo Anschütz 9x18	9x18cm	plate	SterStrut	1911	Celor	4.5		focal plane	5-1000	Mc213	310
Stereo Anschütz Tropen	8x17cm	plate	SterStrut	1890	Dagor	6.8		focal plane	5-1000		9000
Stereo Roll Tengor 6x13	6x13cm	120	SterRo	1925	Dogmar	4.5	75mm	Stereo-Compur			220
Stereo Tenax 6x13	6x13cm	plate	SterStrut	1912	Doppal Anastigma	6.8				Mc214	300
Stereo Tenax 9x18	9x18cm	plate	SterStrut	1907	Dagor	6.8	120mm	focal plane		Mc214	310
Stereo-Taschen-Tenax	45x107	plate	SterStrut	1912	Dogmar	4.5	60mm	Stereo-Compur		Mc214	260
Tandem I	9x12cm	plate	Field	1895	Lynkeioskop						270
Taro Tenax 9x12	9x12cm	plate	FoldPl	1913	Tenastigmat	6.8	135mm	Compound		A2979	70
Taro Tenax 9x12	9x12cm	plate	FoldPl	1913	Dogmar	4.5	150mm	Dial-Compur	1-150	Mc214	70
Taro Tenax 9x14	9x14cm	plate	FoldPl	1913	Dagor	6.8	165mm	Dial-Compur	1-150		90
Taro Tenax 10x15	10x15cm	plate	FoldPl	1913	Tenastigmat	6.3	168mm	Compound			60
Taro Tenax 13x18	13x18cm	plate	FoldPl	1921	Dagor	6.8	210mm	Compound			70
Taschen-Tenax 6.5x9	6.5x9cm	plate	StrutPl	1912	Dogmar	4.5	100mm	Compound	1-250,T,B	Mc214	90
Taschen-Tenax 8x10.5	8x10.5cm	plate	StrutPl	1910	Tenaxiar	6.8	120mm				90
Taschen-Tenax, Tropen	6.5x9cm	plate	StrutPl	1912	Dagor	6.8	90mm	Compound	1-250,T,B		230
Tenax, Tropen 9x12	9x12cm	plate	FoldPl	1923	Xenar	3.5	135mm	Dial-Compur	1-150		250
Tropen Ango 9x12	9x12cm	plate	StrutPl	1909	Celor	4.8	120mm	focal plane	5-1000		300
Tropen Ango 10x15	10x15cm	plate	StrutPl	1909	Dagor	6.8		focal plane	5-1000		160
Tropen Ango 13x18	13x18cm	plate	StrutPl	1911	Syntor	6.8		focal plane	5-1000		160
Vesca (black)	4.5x6cm	plate	StrutPl	1910	Celor	4.5	75mm				270
Vesca (green)	4.5x6cm	plate	StrutPl	1910	Celor	4.5	75mm				350
Westentaschen-Tenax	4.5x6cm	plate	StrutPl	1909	Celor	4.5	75mm	Compound			120
...GOERZ (Optische Anstalt C.P. Goerz) - Vienna											
Minicord	10x10mm	16mm	Submin	1951	Helgor	2	25mm	metal FP	10-400	Mc214	450
Minicord (gold)	10x10mm	16mm	Submin	1951	Helgor	2	25mm	metal FP	10-400		1800

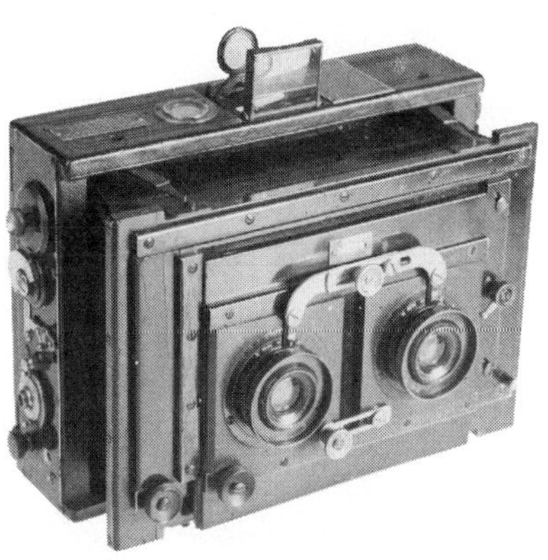

Stereo Anschütz

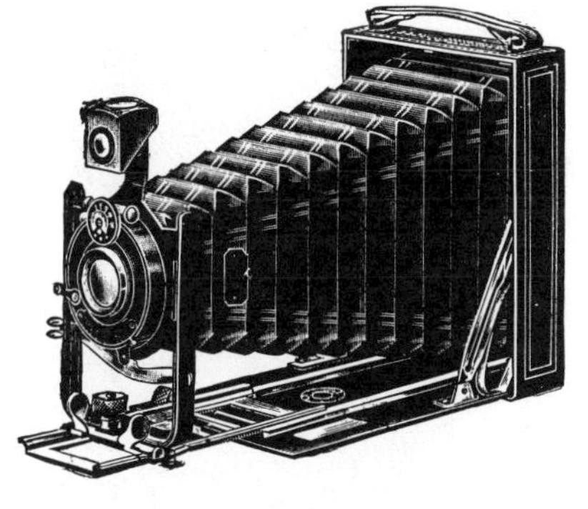

Taro Tenax

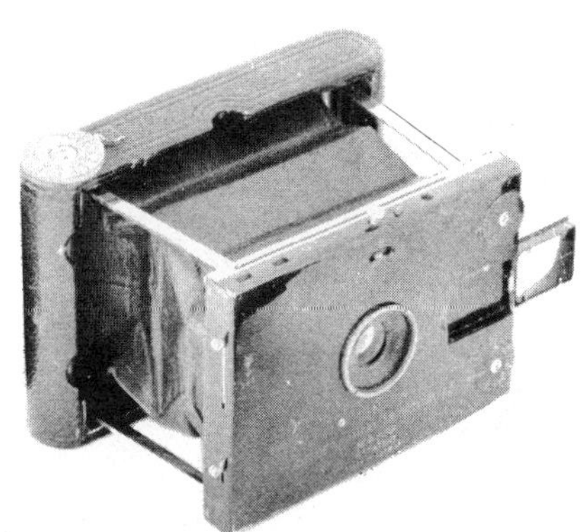

Taschen-Tenax

MODEL	FORMAT	FILM	TYPE	Year	LENS	Apert	FL	SHUTTER	SPEEDS	ILLUS	U.S.$
Minicord III	10x10mm	16mm	Submin	1958	Helgor	2	25mm	metal FP	10-400		310
...GOLDAMMER - Frankfurt											
Golda	24x36mm	35mm	35rf	1949	Radionar	2.9	50mm	Prontor-SV		A2082	90
Golda	24x36mm	35mm	35rf	1949	Trinar	3.5	45mm	Prontor II		A2081	90
Goldeck I 6x6	24x36mm	120	TelescRo	1960	Steiner Bayreuth	2.9		Prontor SVS			40
Goldeck II 6x6	24x36mm	120	TelescRo	1960	Steiner Bayreuth	2.9		Pronto	B,25-200		40
Goldeck III 6x6	24x36mm	120	TelescRo	1960	Steiner Bayreuth	3.5	75mm	Vario			40
Goldeck IV 6x6	24x36mm	120	TelescRo	1960	Steiner Bayreuth	4.5		Vario			40
Goldeck V 6x6	24x36mm	120	TelescRo	1960	Steiner Bayreuth	7.7		Acro	B,25,75		40
Goldeck VI 6x6	24x36mm	120	TelescRo	1960	Steiner Bayreuth	8		Acro			40
Goldeck 16	10x14mm	16mm	Submin	1959	Enna-Color Ennit	2.8	20mm	Prontor	9 Zeiten	A906	130
Goldix	4x4cm	127	RigidRo	195x	Goldeck	7.7	60mm	Singlo-2	30-100	Mc215	40
GuGo	6x6cm	120	TelescRo	1950	Kessar	4.5	75mm	Vario	25-200		30
...GOLDMANN - Wien											
Amateur Field Camera	9x12cm	plate	Field	1895	Doppel Anast.	4.6	150mm				200
Detective camera	9x12cm	plate	H&S	1895	Dallm. Rap. Apl.					A300	510
Field camera 13x18	13x18cm	plate	Field	1900	Aplanat						230
Field camera 18x24	18x24cm	plate	Field	1900	Aplanat					A2929	270
Press camera	9x12cm	plate	StrutPl	1900	Zeiss Tessar	6.3	135mm	focal plane	T,B,½-90	Mc215	250
Universal Detective	13x18cm	plate	H&S	1895	Steinheil						1000
Universal Spreizenkamera	9x12cm	plate	StrutPl	1900	Doppel Anast.	4.6	120mm	focal plane		A299	200
Universal Stereo 9x18	9x18cm	plate	StFoldPl	1906	Tessar	6.3	136mm	Stereo FP			1000
Universal Stereo 13x18	13x18cm	plate	StFoldPl	1906	Aplanat			Stereo FP		A2669	1100
Universal Ster.& Panorama	13x18cm	plate	StFoldPl	1890	Aplanat	7	125mm				1200
Universal Stereo Detective	9x18cm	plate	StFoldPl	1890	Tessar					HK447	2200
...GOLDSTEIN - France											
Camping	6x9cm	120	RollBox	1950	Meniscus				I,T	Mc215	20
Goldy	6x9cm	120	MetBx	1947	Meniscus				I,T	Mc215	10
Olympic	6x9cm	120	RollBox	1948	Meniscus				I,T	Mc215	30
Racing	6x9cm	120	RollBox	1947	Meniscus				I,T		10
Spring	6x9cm	120	RollBox	1947	Meniscus				I,T		10
Starmetal Goldy	6x9cm	120	MetBx	1948	Meniscus				I,T	Mc215	90
Week End (aluminum)	6x9cm	120	MetBx		Meniscus				I,T	Mc215	30
Week-End (cardboard)	6x9cm	120	RollBox	1947	Meniscus				I,T	F888	10
...GOLTZ & BREUTMANN - Berlin											
Klein-Mentor 6.5x9	6.5x9cm	plate	MedSLR	1913	Triotar	6.3	135mm	Compur	1-250		200
Klein-Mentor 9x9	9x9cm	plate	MedSLR	1913	Triotar	6.3	135mm	Compur	1-250		140
Mentor Atelier-Refl. 1928-40	6.5x9cm	plate	MedSLR	1928	Tessar	4.5		focal plane	1/8-1300		210
Mentor Atelier-Refl. 1928-40	9x12cm	plate	LgSLR	1928	Tessar	4.5		focal plane	1/8-1300	A1605	200
Mentor Atelier-Refl. 1928-40	10x15cm	plate	LgSLR	1928	Tessar	4.5		focal plane	1/8-1300		200
Mentor Atelier-Refl. 1928-40	13x18cm	plate	LgSLR	1928	Tessar	4.5		focal plane	1/8-1300		290
Mentor Atelier-Refl. 1950+	6.5x9cm	plate	MedSLR	1950	Tessar	4.5		focal plane	1/3-1000		270

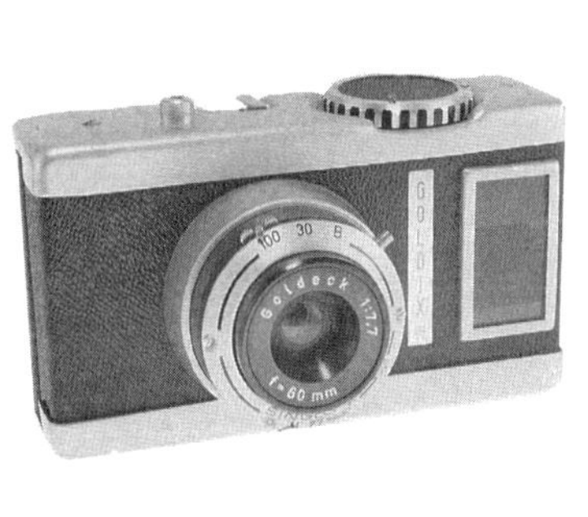

Goldammer Goldix

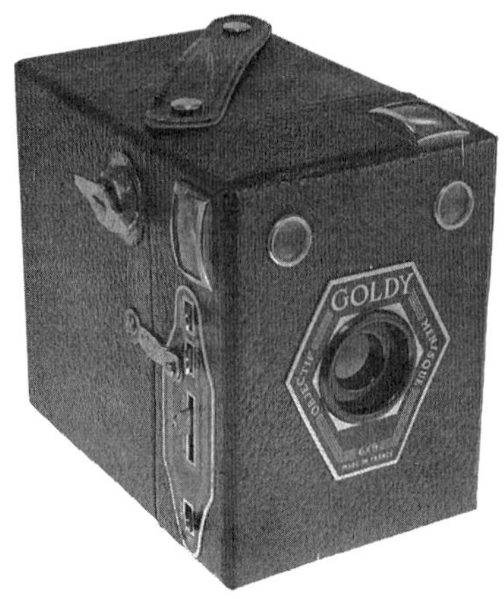

Goldstein Goldy

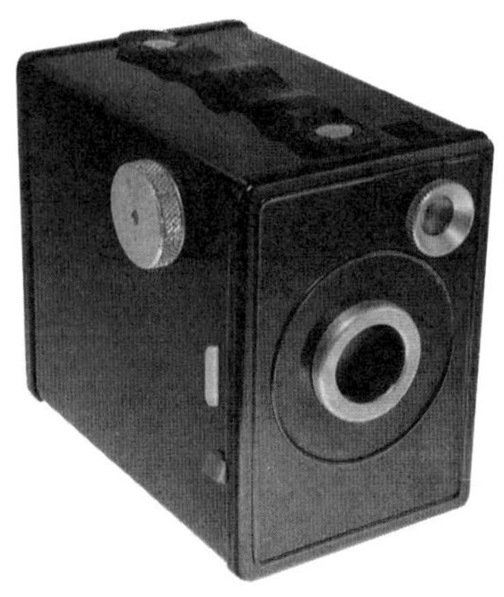

Starmetal Goldy

MODEL	FORMAT	FILM	TYPE	Year	LENS	Apert	FL	SHUTTER	SPEEDS	ILLUS	U.S.$
Mentor Atelier-Refl. 1950+	9x12cm	plate	LgSLR	1950	Tessar	4.5		focal plane	1/3-1000		250
Mentor Atelier-Refl. 1950+	10x15cm	plate	LgSLR	1950	Tessar	4.5		focal plane	1/3-1000		290
Mentor Compur Refl. 6.5x9	6.5x9cm	plate	MedSLR	1928	Zeiss Tessar	4.5	105mm	Compur	1-250	Mc215	190
Mentor Compur Refl. 9x9	9x9cm	plate	MedSLR	1928	Zeiss Tessar	2.7	120mm	Compur	1-250		190
Mentor Dreivier	3x4cm	127	RigidRo	1930	Zeiss Tessar	3.5	50mm	Compur	1-300	Mc216	1000
Mentor Klappkamera 6.5x9	6.5x9cm	plate	StrutPl	1907	Dagor	6.8	120mm	focal plane	1300		150
Mentor Klappkamera 9x12	9x12cm	plate	StrutPl	1907	Zeiss Tessar	4.5	150mm	focal plane	1300		140
Mentor II Klappka. 9x12	9x12cm	plate	StrutPl	1909	Triplan	6	125mm	focal plane			170
Mentor II Klappka. 10x15	10x15cm	plate	StrutPl	1909	Orthostigmat	6.8	150mm	focal plane			180
Mentor II Klappka. 13x18	13x18cm	plate	StrutPl	1909	Zeiss Tessar	4.5	210mm	focal plane			190
Mentor II Klappka. Stereo	6x13cm	plate	SterStrut	1914	Tessar	4.5		focal plane			370
Mentor IV Zweiverschluss	10x15cm	plate	FoldPl	1913	Aristostigmat	6.8	165mm	focal plane			150
Mentor Klapp-Reflex 6x9	6x9cm	plate	FoldSLR	1913	Zeiss Tessar	2.7		focal plane	-1000		230
Mentor Klapp-Reflex 9x12	9x12cm	plate	FoldSLR	1913	Zeiss Tessar	2.7		focal plane	-1000	Mc216	200
Mentor Klapp-Reflex 10x15	10x15cm	plate	FoldSLR	1913	Zeiss Tessar	4.5		focal plane	-1000		210
Mentor Klapp-Refl. (quadr.)	6x9cm	plate	FoldSLR	1925	Prolinear	1.9		focal plane	-1000		1000
Mentor Klapp-Refl. (quadr.)	9x9cm	plate	FoldSLR	1925	Zeiss Tessar	4.5		focal plane	-1000		180
Mentor Klapp-Refl. (quadr.)	9x12cm	plate	FoldSLR	1925	Zeiss Tessar	2.7		focal plane	-1000		210
Mentor Klapp-Refl. (quadr.)	10x15cm	plate	FoldSLR	1913	Zeiss Tessar	4.5		focal plane	-1000		210
Mentor Folding Reflex II	6x9cm	plate	FoldSLR	1924	Zeiss Tessar	4.5		focal plane	-1000		200
Mentor Fold. Refl. II 8x10.5	8x10.5cm	plate	FoldSLR	1924	Zeiss Tessar	4.5		focal plane	-1000		200
Mentor Fold. Refl. II 9x9	9x9cm	plate	FoldSLR	1924	Zeiss Tessar	2.7		focal plane	-1000		200
Mentor Fold. Refl. II 9x12	9x12cm	plate	FoldSLR	1924	Zeiss Tessar	2.7		focal plane	-1000		200
Mentor Panorama I 13x18	13x18cm	plate	View	1970	Tessar	4.5	250mm	Spezial	2-1/125		420
Mentor Panorama I 18x24	18x24cm	plate	View	1970	Apo-Tessar		210mm	Spezial	2-1/125		400
Mentor Panorama II 13x18	13x18cm	plate	View	1970	Tessar	4.5		Spezial	2-1/125		410
Mentor Reflex 6x9	6x9cm	plate	MedSLR	1898	Xenar	4.5		focal plane		A567	230
Mentor Reflex 6.5x9	6.5x9cm	plate	MedSLR	1898	Zeiss Tessar	4.5		focal plane		A566	280
Mentor Reflex 9x9	9x9cm	plate	MedSLR	1898	Heliar	4.5		focal plane		A568	220
Mentor Reflex 9x12	9x12cm	plate	LgSLR	1898	Xenar	4.5		focal plane		Mc216	220
Mentor Reflex 10x15	10x15cm	plate	LgSLR	1898	Zeiss Tessar	4.5		focal plane			230
Mentor Reflex 13x18	13x18cm	plate	LgSLR	1898	Zeiss Tessar	4.5		focal plane		A1603	230
Mentor Reflex 18x24	18x24cm	plate	LgSLR	1898	Xenar	4.5		focal plane			290
Mentor Sport Reflex 6.5x9	6.5x9cm	plate	MedSLR	1936	Tessar	4.5		focal plane	1/8-1300	HK359	220
Mentor Sport Reflex 9x12	9x12cm	plate	MedSLR	1936	Tessar	4.5	120mm	focal plane	1/8-1300	A569	260
Mentor Stereo Refl. 45x107	45x107	plate	SterSLR	1913	Tessar	4.5	75mm	focal plane	15-1000	A1818	450
Mentor Stereo Refl. 6x13	6x13cm	plate	SterSLR	1913	Tessar	4.5	90mm	focal plane	15-1000	A1817	530
Mentor Stereo Refl. 9x18	9x18cm	plate	SterSLR	1913	Tessar	4.5	135mm	focal plane	15-1000	A2693	800
Mentor Studio 13x18	13x18cm	plate	FoldPl	1960	Tessar	4.5		focal plane			310
Mentor Tropical Refl. 9x12	9x12cm	plate	LgSLR	1913	Zeiss Tessar	4.5	100mm	focal plane		A1580	1400
Mentor Universal 9x12	9x12cm	plate	FoldPl	1913	Zeiss Tessar	4.5	150mm	focal plane	1300		120
Mentorett	6x6cm	120	TLR	1936	Mentor	3.5	75mm	focal plane	1/15-1/600	A643	480

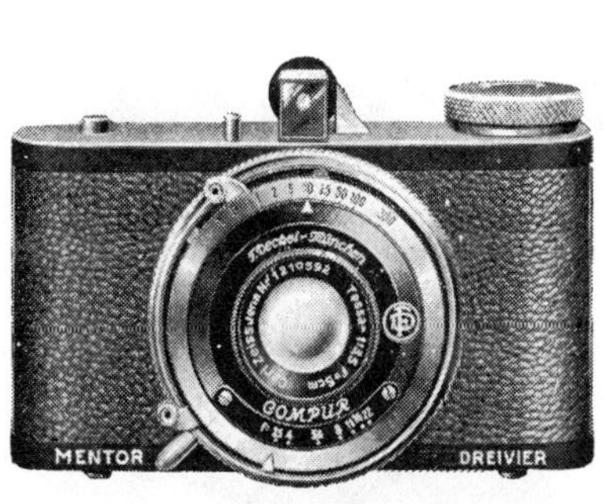

Mentor Dreivier

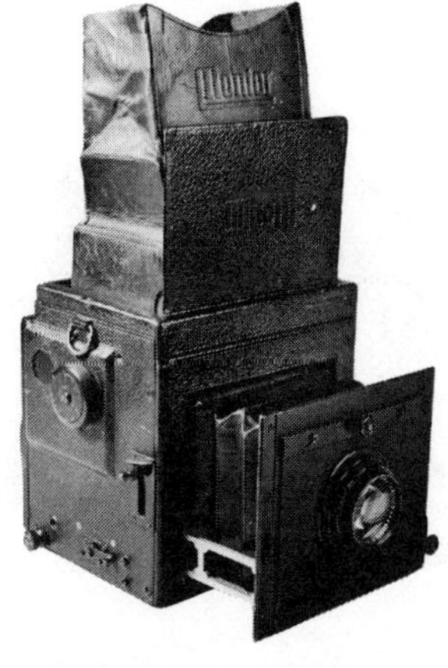

Mentor Reflex

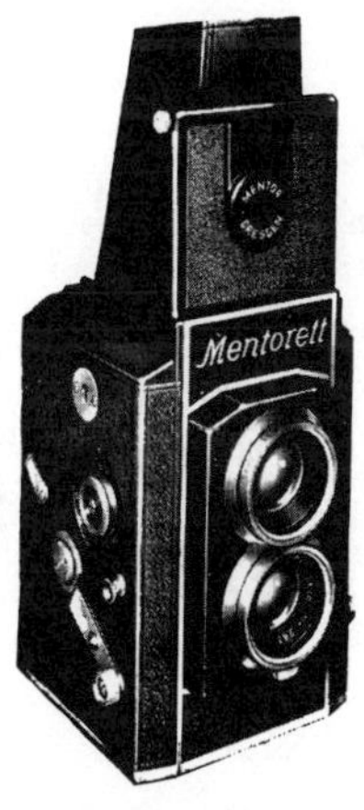

Mentorett

MODEL	FORMAT	FILM	TYPE	Year	LENS	Apert	FL	SHUTTER	SPEEDS	ILLUS	U.S.$
...GOMZ - USSR											
Almaz 102	24x36mm	35mm	35SLR	1979		1.8	50mm	focal plane	1-1000	Ru45	270
Almaz 103	24x36mm	35mm	35SLR	1982		1.8	50mm	focal plane	1-1000	Ru45	220
Fotokor	9x12cm	plate	FoldPl	1930	Gomz	4.5	135mm		25-100,K,D	Ru22	80
Junost	24x36mm	35mm	35rf	1957	T-32	3.5	45mm		B,1/8-250	Ru40	320
Komsomoletz	24x36mm	35mm	FoldPl	1936	T-22	6.3	75mm		25-100	Ru54	90
Leningrad	24x36mm	35mm	35rf	1956	Jupiter-8	2	50mm	focal plane	1-1000	Ru38	210
Lubitel	6x6cm	120	TLR-Box	1949	T-22	4.5	75mm		10-200	Ru46	40
Lubitel 2	6x6cm	120	TLR-Box	1955	T-22	4.5	75mm		10-200	Ru47	30
Lubitel 166	6x6cm	120	TLR-Box	1976	T-22	4.5	75mm		15-250	Ru47	40
Lubitel 166B	6x6cm	120	TLR-Box	1980	T-22	4.5	75mm		15-250	Ru47	50
Lubitel 166U	6x6cm	120	TLR-Box	1983	T-22	4.5	75mm		15-250	Ru47	40
Moment			Instant	1952	T-26	6.8	135mm		10-200,B	Ru50	200
Smena	24x36mm	35mm	35vf	1952		4.5	40mm		10-200,T	Ru33	40
Smena 2	24x36mm	35mm	35vf	1953		4.5	40mm		10-200,T	Ru34	50
Smena 3	24x36mm	35mm	35vf	1958						Ru34	30
Smena 4	24x36mm	35mm	35vf	1958						Ru34	30
Smena 5	24x36mm	35mm	35vf	1961						Ru34	20
Smena 6	24x36mm	35mm	35vf	1961						Ru34	30
Smena 7	24x36mm	35mm	35vf	1969						Ru34	30
Smena 8	24x36mm	35mm	35vf	1969	T-43	4	40mm		15-250	Ru35	30
Smena 8M	24x36mm	35mm	35vf	1970	T-43	4	40mm		15-250	Ru36	30
Smena Symbol	24x36mm	35mm	35vf	1971						Ru36	10
Sport	24x36mm	35mm	35slr	1936	Industar 10	3.5	50mm	focal plane	1/25-500	Ru27	580
Sputnik	6x13cm	120	SterRefl	1955		4.5	75mm		15-125	Ru48	290
Turist	6.5x9cm	plate	StrutPl	1934	Industar	3.5	105mm		1/25-1/100	Ru30	140
Voskhod	24x36mm	35mm	35rf	1964	Lomo T-48	2.8	45mm		-1/250	Ru40	120
...GRAEFE & BARDORF - Berlin											
Clarissa Nacht-Kamera	4.5x6cm	plate	RigidRo	1927	Meyer Plasmat	2	90mm	focal plane		A1433	3000
...GRAFLEX, INC. - Rochester											
Anniv. Speed Graphic	3¼x4¼"	plate	Press	1940	Kodak Anastigmat	4.5	140mm	focal plane		Mc222	100
Anniv. Speed Graphic 4x5"	4x5"	plate	Press	1940	Kodak Anastigmat	4.5		focal plane		Mc222	310
Auto Graflex 3¼x4¼"	3¼x4¼	plate	LgSLR	1906	Ross Telecentric	6.8		focal plane	1-1000	Mc218	160
Auto Graflex 4x5"	4x5"	plate	LgSLR	1906	Velostigmat	4.5		focal plane	1-1000	Mc218	180
Auto Graflex 4x5"	4x5"	plate	LgSLR	1906	Telecentric	6.8		focal plane	1-1000	A554	180
Auto Graflex 5x7"	5x7"	plate	LgSLR	1906	Ross Xpress	6.8		focal plane	1-1000	Mc218	210
Auto Graflex Jr. 2¼x3¼"	2¼x3¼"	plate	MedSLR	1914	Kodak Anastigmat			focal plane	10-1000		180
Century 35	24x36mm	35mm	35rf	1961	Prominar	3.5				Mc223	30
Century Graphic	2¼x3¼"	Sheet	Press	1949	Ektar	4.5				Mc221	290
Century Universal	8x10"	plate	View	1929							230
Ciro 35	24x36mm	35mm	35rf	1950	Anastigmat	4.5	50mm	Alphax	10-200		30
Combat Graphic	4x5"	Sheet	Press	1942	Anast. Special	4.7	127mm	focal plane	1000	Mc221	300

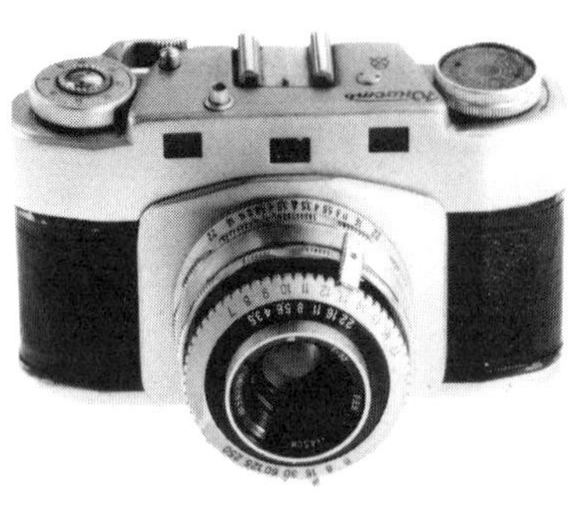

Gomz Junost

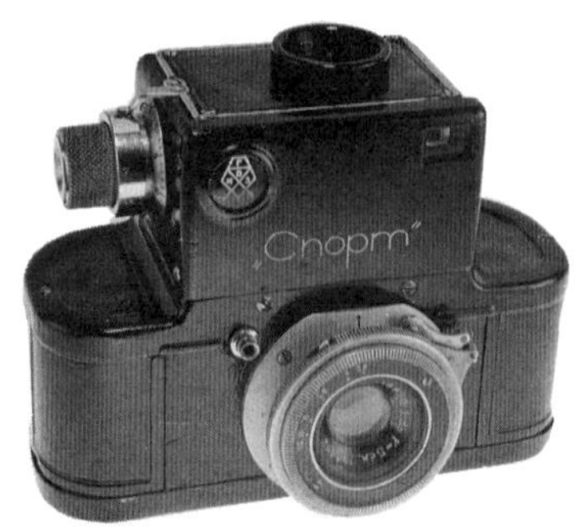

Gomz Sport

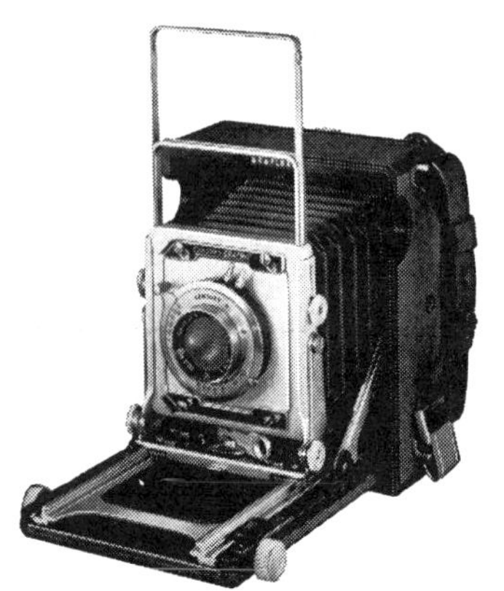

Century Graphic

MODEL	FORMAT	FILM	TYPE	Year	LENS	Apert	FL	SHUTTER	SPEEDS	ILLUS	U.S.$
Compact Graflex 3¼x5½"	3¼x5½"	plate	LgSLR	1915	Kodak Anastigmat			focal plane	10-1000	Mc219	220
Compact Graflex 5x7"	5x7"	plate	LgSLR	1916	Kodak Anastigmat			focal plane	10-1000	Mc219	270
Crown Graphic Special	4x5"	plate	Press	1958	Schneider Xenar	4.5	135mm	Sync-Compur	1-500,B		270
Crown View	4x4"	plate	View	1939							270
Deceptive Angle Graphic	3¼x4¼"	plate	Disguised	1904	Rapid Rectilinear	11	12.5cm			Mc221	3100
Finger-Print Camera	2¼x3¼"	plate	Special		Kodak Anastigmat	6.3	72mm			Mc223	110
Graflex (original) 4x5"	4x5"	plate	LgSLR	1902	interchangeable	4.5		focal plane	1200		460
Graflex (original) 5x7"	5x7"	plate	LgSLR	1902	interchangeable	6.8		focal plane	1200		460
Graflex (original) 8x10"	8x10"	plate	LgSLR	1902	interchangeable	6.8		focal plane	1200		460
Graflex 1A	2½x4¼"	116	LgSLR	1909	B&L Tessar	4.5				Mc218	180
Graflex 3A	3¼x5½"	122	LgSLR	1907	Zeiss Tessar	4.5	10"	focal plane	10-1000	Mc218	160
Graflex 22 M. 200 (black)	6x6cm	120	TLR	1950	Graftar	3.5	88mm	Synchromatic		Mc223	50
Graflex 22 M. 200 (chrome)	6x6cm	120	TLR	1950	Graftar	3.5	88mm	Synchromatic		Mc223	50
Graflex 22 M. 400 (black)	6x6cm	120	TLR	1950	Graftar	3.5	88mm	Graphex		Mc223	50
Graflex 22 M. 400 (chrome)	6x6cm	120	TLR	1950	Graftar	3.5	88mm	Graphex		Mc223	50
Graflex 22 M. 400F (black)	6x6cm	120	TLR	1950	Optar	3.5	88mm	Graphex		Mc223	50
Graflex 22 M.400F (chrome)	6x6cm	120	TLR	1950	Optar	3.5	88mm	Graphex		Mc223	50
Graflex Series B 2¼x3¼"	2¼x3¼"	plate	LgSLR	1925	Anastigmat	4.5				Mc220	220
Graflex Series B 3¼x4¼"	3¼x4¼"	plate	LgSLR	1923	Anastigmat	4.5				Mc220	100
Graflex Series B 4x5"	4x5"	plate	LgSLR	1923	Anastigmat	4.5				Mc220	160
Graflex Series B 5x7"	5x7"	plate	LgSLR	1925	Anastigmat	4.5				Mc220	200
Graphic 35	24x36mm	35mm	35rf	1955	Graflar	2.8	50mm	Prontor	1-300	Mc221	30
Graphic 35 Electric	24x36mm	35mm	35rf	1959	Quinon	1.9		Sync-Compur			100
Graphic 35 Jet	24x36mm	35mm	35rf	1961	Optar	2	50mm		1-500	Mc221	270
Graphic camera 4x5"	4x5"	plate	FoldPl	1904	Goerz Series III						200
Graphic camera 5x7"	5x7"	plate	FoldPl	1904	Goerz Series III						200
Graphic camera 8x10"	8x10"	plate	FoldPl	1904	Goerz Series III						200
Graphic No. 0	1⅝x2½"	Roll	RigidRo	1909	Zeiss Kodak Anast	6.3	72mm	focal plane	500	Mc220	290
Graphic Sr 4x5"	4x5"	plate	FoldPl	1904	B&L Convertible					Mc221	170
Graphic Sr 5x7"	5x7"	plate	FoldPl	1904	B&L Convertible					Mc221	170
Graphic View	4x5"	plate	View	1941	various			focal plane			220
Home Portrait Graflex	5x7"	plate	LgSLR	1912	Kodak Anastigmat	6.3		focal plane	½-500	Mc219	390
Inspectograph Camera	2¼x3¼"	plate	Special	1940	Kodak Anastigmat	6.3	72mm				110
KE-4(1) Combat (black)	5.5x7cm	70mm	RigidRo	1953	Ektar	2.8	4"	focal plane	1-500	A904	460
KE-4(1) Combat (olive)	5.5x7cm	70mm	RigidRo	1953	Ektar	4	8"	focal plane	1-500	Mc223	460
Miniature Speed Graphic	2¼x3¼"	plate	Press	1938	Optar	4.7	101mm	focal plane		Mc222	200
Miniature Speed Graphic	2¼x3¼"	plate	Press	1938	Ektar	3.7	107mm	focal plane		A273	200
National Graflex, Series I	2¼x2½"	120	MedSLR	1933	B&L Tessar	3.5	75mm	focal plane	-500	A584	180
National Graflex, Series II	2¼x2½"	120	MedSLR	1934	B&L Tessar	3.5	75mm	focal plane	-500	Mc219	160
Naturalists' Graflex	4x5"	plate	LgSLR	1907	Goerz Series III	6.8		focal plane	10-1000	Mc219	3300
Norita	6x6cm	120	MedSLR	1969	Noritar	2	80mm	focal plane	1-500	Mc223	370
Pacemaker Crown Graphic	2¼x3¼"	plate	Press	1947	Ektar	4.5	101mm	Supermatic	1-400	Mc221	220

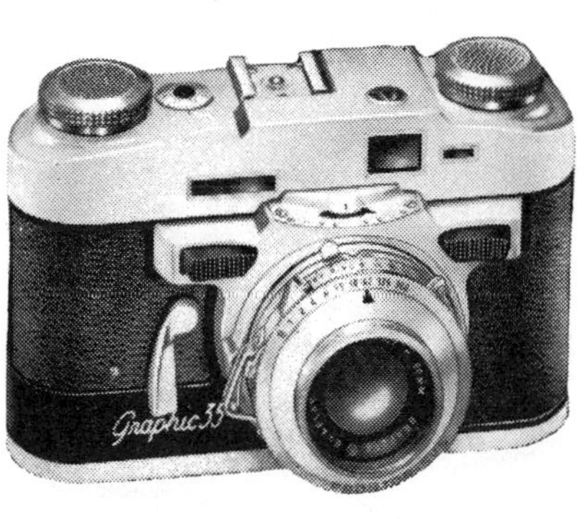

Graphic 35

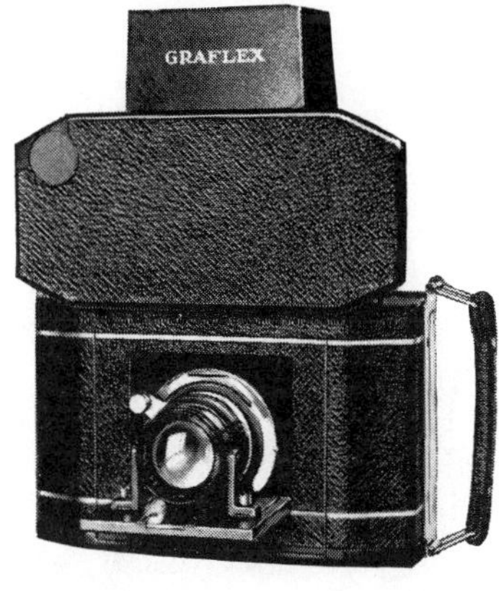

National Graflex, Series II

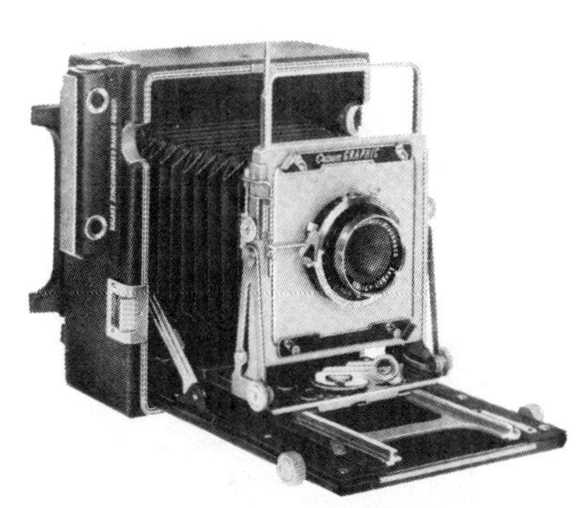

Pacemaker Crown Graphic

MODEL	FORMAT	FILM	TYPE	Year	LENS	Apert	FL	SHUTTER	SPEEDS	ILLUS	U.S.$
Pacemaker Crown Graphic	3¼x4¼"	plate	Press	1947				Supermatic	1-400	Mc221	110
Pacemaker Crown Graphic	4x5"	plate	Press	1947	Optar	4.7	135mm	Supermatic	1-400	Mc221	350
Pacemaker Milit. KE-12(1)	4x5"	plate	Press		Optar	4.5	127mm	focal plane			350
Pacemaker Speed Graphic	2¼x3¼"	plate	Press	1947	Ektar	4.5	101mm	focal plane		Mc222	220
Pacemaker Speed Graphic	3¼x4¼"	plate	Press	1947	Ektar	4.5	127mm	focal plane		Mc222	140
Pacemaker Speed Graphic	4x5"	plate	Press	1947	Ektar	4.5	127mm	focal plane		Mc222	390
Photorecord 24x36	24x36mm	35mm	Special	1934	Anastigmat	4.5	75mm				290
Photorecord 6x9	6x9cm	Sheet	Special	1934	Anastigmat	4.5	75mm			A274	100
Pre-anniv. Speed Graphic	3¼x4¼"	plate	Press	1935				focal plane		Mc222	110
Pre-anniv. Speed Graphic	4x5"	plate	Press	1928	Tessar	4.5		focal plane	10-1000	Mc222	200
Pre-anniv. Speed Graphic	5x7"	plate	Press	1932				focal plane		Mc222	240
Press Graflex 5x7"	5x7"	plate	LgSLR	1907	Plastigmat	6.8	15"	focal plane	1/5-1500	Mc219	330
Revers. Bk. Cycle Graphic	3¼x4¼"	plate	FoldPl	1900				focal plane		Mc221	150
Revers. Bk. Cycle Graphic	4x5"	plate	FoldPl	1900	Rapid Rectilinear		16"	focal plane		Mc221	150
Revers. Bk. Cycle Graphic	5x7"	plate	FoldPl	1900	Rapid Rectilinear		22"	focal plane		Mc221	200
Revers. Bk. Cycle Graphic	6½x8½"	plate	FoldPl	1900	Rapid Rectilinear		26"	focal plane		Mc221	200
Revers.Bk.Cycle Gr.Special	5x7"	plate	FoldPl	1904	Goerz Series III		23"	focal plane			220
Revers.Bk.Cycle Gr.Special	6½x8½"	plate	FoldPl	1904	Goerz Series III		27"	focal plane			220
Reversible Back Graflex	4x5"	plate	LgSLR	1902		6.8	5"	focal plane	1200	Mc219	370
Reversible Back Graflex	5x7"	plate	LgSLR	1902		6.8		focal plane	1200	Mc219	370
Revolv. Bk. Auto Graflex	3¼x4¼"	plate	LgSLR	1909	B&L Zeiss Tessar	4.5		focal plane	10-1000	Mc219	160
Revolv. Bk. Auto Graflex	4x5"	plate	LgSLR	1906	B&L Zeiss Tessar	4.5		focal plane	10-1000	Mc219	180
Revolv. Bk. Cycle Graphic	4x5"	plate	FoldPl	1907	B&L Plastigmat		17"	Volute			210
Revolv. Bk. Cycle Graphic	5x7"	plate	FoldPl	1907	B&L Plastigmat		22.5"	Volute			330
Revolv. Bk. Cycle Graphic	6½x8½"	plate	FoldPl	1907	B&L Plastigmat		26"	Volute			330
Revolv. Bk. Cycle Graphic	8x10"	plate	FoldPl	1907	B&L Plastigmat		30"	Volute			330
R.B. Graflex Junior	2¼x3¼"	plate	LgSLR	1915	B&L Zeiss Tessar	4.5				Mc219	180
R.B. Graflex Ser. B 2¼x3¼"	2¼x3¼"	plate	LgSLR	1923	Anastigmat	4.5		focal plane	10-1000	Mc220	170
R.B. Graflex Ser. B 3¼x4¼"	3¼x4¼"	plate	LgSLR	1923	Anastigmat	4.5		focal plane	10-1000	Mc220	120
R.B. Graflex Ser. B 4x5"	4x5"	plate	LgSLR	1923	Anastigmat	4.5		focal plane	10-1000	Mc220	140
R.B. Graflex Ser. C 3¼x4¼"	3¼x4¼"	plate	LgSLR	1926	Cooke Anast.	2.5	6-1/2"	focal plane	10-1000	Mc220	170
R.B. Graflex Ser. D 3¼x4¼"	3¼x4¼"	plate	LgSLR	1928				focal plane	10-1000	Mc220	100
R.B. Graflex Ser. D 4x5"	4x5"	plate	LgSLR	1928				focal plane	10-1000	Mc220	170
R.B. Super D Graflex	3¼x4¼"	plate	LgSLR	1941	Ektar	4.5	152mm	focal plane	5-1000	Mc220	180
R.B. Super D Graflex 4x5"	4x5"	plate	LgSLR	1948	Graflex Optar	5.6	190mm	focal plane		Mc220	370
R.B. Tele Graflex 3¼x4¼"	3¼x4¼"	plate	LgSLR	1915	B&L Tessar	4.5	7.5"	focal plane	1/10-1000	Mc220	110
R.B. Tele Graflex 4x5"	4x5"	plate	LgSLR	1915	Schneider	3.5	8.25"	focal plane	1/10-1000	Mc220	140
Speed Graphic (early)	3¼x4¼"	plate	Press	1915	Kodak Anastigmat	4.5		focal plane	10-1000	Mc222	110
Speed Graphic (early)	3¼x5½"	plate	Press	1912	Kodak Anastigmat			focal plane	10-1000	Mc222	160
Speed Graphic (early) 4x5"	4x5"	plate	Press	1912	Kodak Anastigmat	4.5		focal plane	10-1000	Mc222	110
Speed Graphic (early) 5x7"	5x7"	plate	Press	1912	Kodak Anastigmat			focal plane	10-1000	Mc222	180
Stereo Auto Graflex	5x7"	plate	SterSLR	1906	Tessar	6.3		focal plane	1000	Mc220	1500

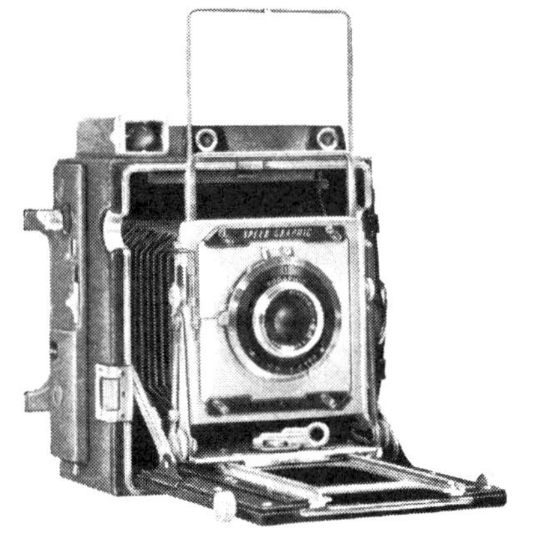

Pacemaker Speed Graphic

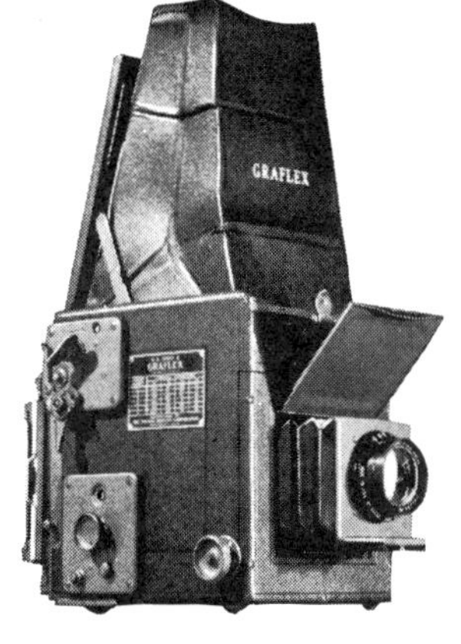

R.B. Graflex Ser. B

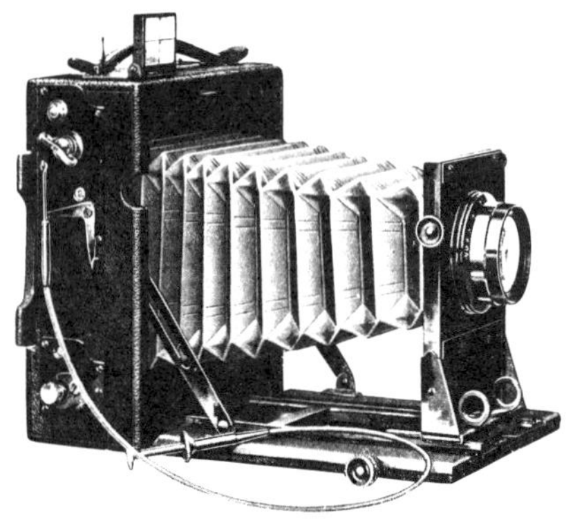

Speed Graphic (early)

MODEL	FORMAT	FILM	TYPE	Year	LENS	Apert	FL	SHUTTER	SPEEDS	ILLUS	U.S.$
Stereo Graflex	5x7"	plate	SterSLR	1904		6.3		focal plane	1000	Mc220	1900
Stereo Graphic (35mm)		35mm	Ster35	195x	Graflar	4	35mm		1/50,B	Mc222	160
Stereoscopic Graphic	5x7"	plate	StFoldPl	1902	Rapid Rectilinear	6.3		focal plane		Mc222	1800
Super Graphic	4x5"	plate	Press	1958	Schneider Xenar	4.7	135mm	focal plane		Mc222	410
Super Speed Graphic	4x5"	plate	Press	1959	Kodak Ektar	4.7	127mm	Graflex	1000		460
Tourist Graflex 4x5"	4x5"	plate	LgSLR	1902	Cooke Series III	5		focal plane	12-1200		450
Tourist Graflex 5x7"	5x7"	plate	LgSLR	1902	Cooke Series III	6.8		focal plane			450
XLRF + Planar	6x9cm	Roll	Press	1965	Planar	2.8	80mm	Sync-Compur			490
XLRF KS-98B	6x9cm	Roll	Press	1965	Tessar	3.5	100mm	Sync-Compur			670
XLS + Planar	6x9cm	Roll	Press	1965	Planar	2.8	100mm	Sync-Compur			410
XLSW + Super Angulon	6x9cm	Roll	WideAng	1965	Super Angulon	8	47mm	Sync-Compur			620
...GUÉRIN & CIE - Paris											
Le Furet	24x36mm	35mm	35vf	1923	Hermagis	4.5	40mm		I,T	F607	1200
...GUNDLACH MANHATTAN OPTICAL CO. - Rochester											
Criterion View 5x7"	5x7"	plate	Tailboard	1909	Rapid Rectilinear	8		Regno			160
Criterion View 6½x8½"	6½x8½"	plate	Tailboard	1909	Turner Reich An.	6.8		Regno			160
Criterion View 8x10"	8x10"	plate	Tailboard	1909	Rapid Rectigraph	8		Regno			160
Korona 3¼x4¼"	3¼x4¼"	plate	H&S		Convertible			Automatic			70
Korona 3¼x5½"	3¼x5½"	plate	H&S		Convertible			Automatic			70
Korona Panoramic View	5x12"	plate	WideAng	1920	Triple Convertible	6.8	10.5"	Optimo			520
Korona Panoramic View	7x17"	plate	WideAng	1920	Triple Convertible	6.8	12"	Optimo			700
Korona Panoramic View	8x20"	plate	WideAng	1920	Triple Convertible	7.5	15"	Optimo			800
Korona Panoramic View	12x20"	plate	WideAng	1920	Triple Convertible			Optimo			1200
Korona Series II-E	4x5"	plate	H&S	1900	Symmetrical			Model D			150
Korona Series IV	4x5"	plate	H&S	1902	Rapid Convertible			Woll. Auto			140
Korona Stereo 5x7"	5x7"	plate	StFoldPl	1900				stereo			460
Korona View 4x5"	4x5"	plate	Field	1900	Ilex Paragon	4.5	6.5"	Universal			170
Korona View 5x7"	5x7"	plate	Field	1900	Ilex Paragon	4.5	7.5"	Acme			170
Korona View 6½x8½"	6½x8½"	plate	Field	1900	Ilex Paragon	4.5		Acme			140
Korona View 8x10"	8x10"	plate	Field	1900	Velostigmat		12"	Autex			320
Long Focus Korona	5x7"	plate	Field	1920	Rapid Rectilinear		7.25"	Wizard Sr.			200
Milburn Korona		plate	FoldPl	1895	B&L	8		Unicum			560
...HACOFLEX - Japan											
Hacoflex	6x6cm	120	TLR	1955	Tri-Lausar	3.5	8cm		1-300	Mc225	90
...HAKING - Hong Kong											
Haco-44 (black)	4x4cm	127	TLR	1982	Hakor	3.5	60mm				110
Haco-44 (grey)	4x4cm	127	TLR	1982	Hakor	3.5	60mm			A1736	140
Halina 6-4	6x6cm	120	RigidRo		Halina Achromat	8				Mc225	30
Halina 35	24x36mm	35mm	35vf	1982	Halina Anastigmat	3.5	45mm	Automatic	25-200	Mc225	30
Halina 35X	24x36mm	35mm	35vf	1959	Halina Anastigmat	3.5	45mm	Automatic	25-200	Mc225	30
Halina A1	6x6cm	120	TLR	1952	Halina	3.5	80mm		25-100	Mc226	60
Halina Simplette EE	28x28mm	126	126	1970	Halina Achromat					A3349	30

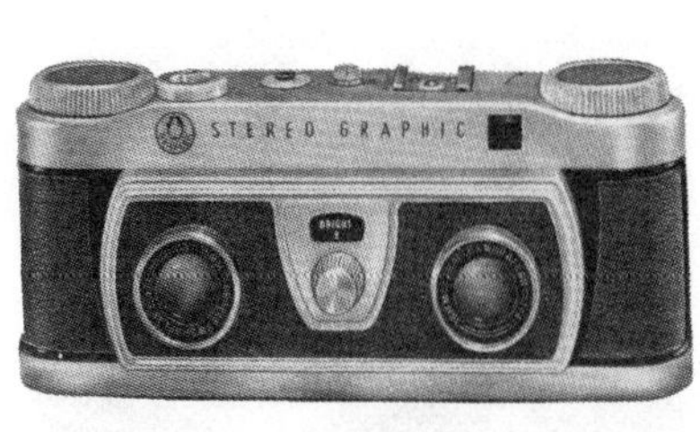

Stereo Graphic (35mm)

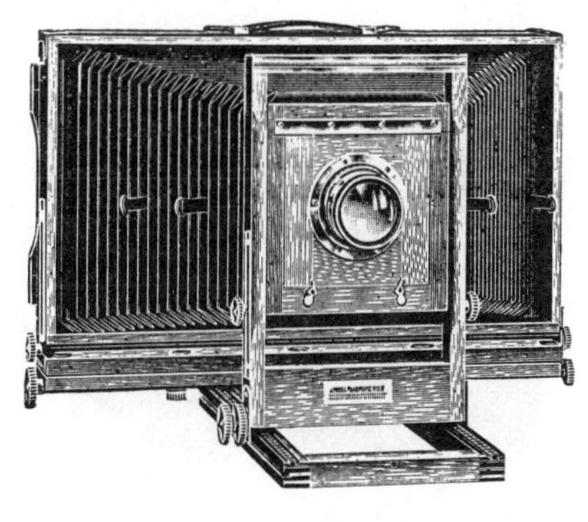

Korona Panorama View

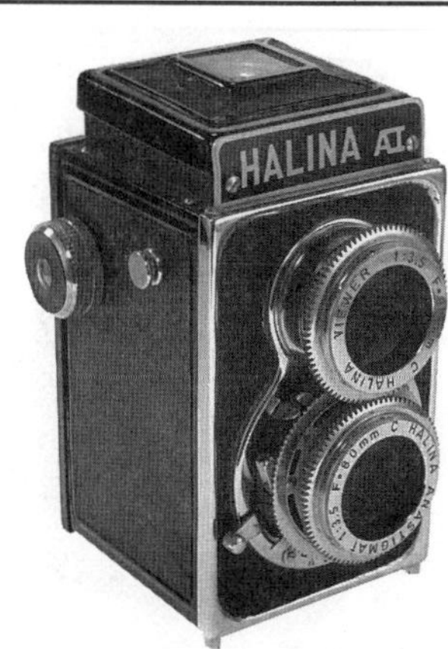

Halina A1

MODEL	FORMAT	FILM	TYPE	Year	LENS	Apert	FL	SHUTTER	SPEEDS	ILLUS	U.S.$
Halina Viceroy	6x6cm	120	TLR-Box		Dbl Meniscus	8			B&I		30
Halina-Prefect Senior	6x6cm	120	TLR-Box		Dbl Meniscus	8			B&I	Mc226	30
Kinoflex Deluxe	6x6cm	120	TLR-Box	1960	Dbl Meniscus	8			B&I		30
Micronta 35X	24x36mm	35mm	35vf	1959	Halina Anastigmat	3.5	45mm		25-200	Mc226	30
Revolution 89	24x36mm	35mm	35vf	1989						Mc226	70
Revolution 89	13x17mm	110	110	1989						Mc226	70
Roy Box	4x4cm	Roll	PlasticBox	1965	Halimar		47mm		I		10
Star-Lite Super Reflex	6x6cm	120	TLR	1958						Mc226	20
Sunscope	6x6cm	120	TLR-Box	1958	Meniscus						20
Super Mini	13x17mm	110	110	1980						A3361	70
Votar Flex	6x6cm	120	TLR-Box	1958	Dbl Meniscus	8			B&I		20
Wales Reflex	6x6cm	120	TLR-Box	1958	Dbl Meniscus	8			B&I	Mc226	20
...HAMAPHOT KG - Monheim											
Blitz-Hexi	6x6cm	120	TelescRo	1955	Synchromat	8	6.5cm			Mc227	20
Hexi-0	6x6cm	120	TelescRo	1955	Hexar	11	7.5cm				20
Hexi-I	6x6cm	120	TelescRo	1955	Synchromat	8	6.5cm				20
Hexi-Lux	6x6cm	120	TelescRo		Tricomat	8	6.5cm				50
Hamaphot Mod. P56L	6x6cm	120	TelescRo	1952	Tricomat	8	6.5cm			A1518	20
-- Mod. P56M Exportmodell	6x6cm	120	TelescRo							Mc227	20
Hamaphot Mod. P66	6x6cm	120	TelescRo	1950	Achromat	7.7	80mm		25-100	A1517	30
Moni	6x6cm	120	TelescRo	1954	Tricomat	8	6.5cm		T&M	Mc227	30
...HANAU - Paris											
le Marsouin 45x107 B	45x107	plate	StJumelle	1900	Balbreck			guillotine		F1313	370
le Marsouin 45x107 T	45x107	plate	StJumelle	1900	Tessar			guillotine		Mc227	370
le Marsouin 6x13 B	6x13cm	plate	StJumelle	1900	Balbreck			guillotine		Mc227	370
le Marsouin 6x13 T	6x13cm	plate	StJumelle	1900	Tessar			guillotine		F1312	370
Omnigraphe	9x12cm	plate	StrutPl	1890	Meniscus	11		guillotine		F206	2400
Passe-Partout 6x13cm	6x13cm	plate	RigidPl	1890	Rapid Rectilinear					Mc227	2900
Passe-Partout 8x8cm	8x8cm	plate	RigidPl	1890	Rapid Rectilinear					A3252	2900
Pocket-Focal	4.5x6cm	plate	RigidPl	1905	Krauss-Zeiss Tessar IIb		40mm	focal plane		Mc227	1000
Stereo-Pocket-Focal	45x107	plate	Stereo	1905	Tessar IIb		40mm	focal plane		F1403	2700
...HANIMEX - Sydney											
Amphibian	24x36mm	35mm	35uw	1983		2.8	35mm	programmed	60-300	A3452	120
C35	24x36mm	35mm	35rf	1959	Hanimar	2.8	45mm		B-300		30
D35	24x36mm	35mm	35rf	1959	Hanimar	2.8	45mm		B-300		30
Eaglet	6x6cm	120	MetBx	1952	achromatic		65mm		I,T	Mc228	30
Electra II	24x36mm	35mm	35vf	1962	Hanimar	2.8	45mm	automatic		Mc228	30
EX Pocket	13x17mm	110	110	1975	Tele						100
Hanimar	24x36mm	35mm	35vf	1951	Finetar	2.8	45mm	2-blade	B, 25-250	Mc228	30
Holiday	24x36mm	35mm	35rf	1958	S-Kominar	3.5	45mm	Copal	B-300		30
Holiday II	24x36mm	35mm	35rf	1958	S-Kominar	3.5	45mm	Copal	B-300		30
Holiday 35	24x36mm	35mm	35rf	1958	S-Kominar	2.8	45mm	Copal	B-300	Mc228	30

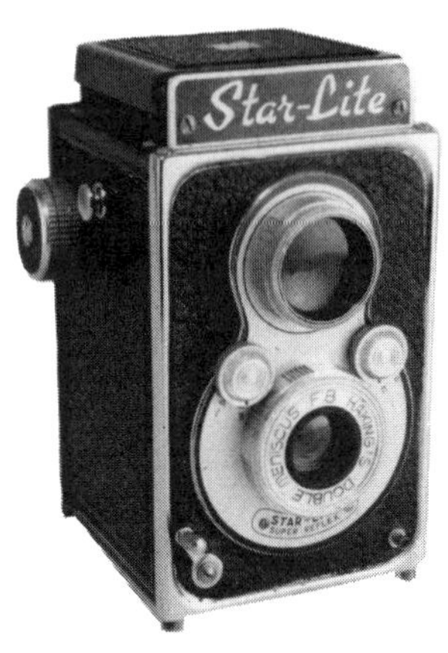

Star-Lite Super Reflex

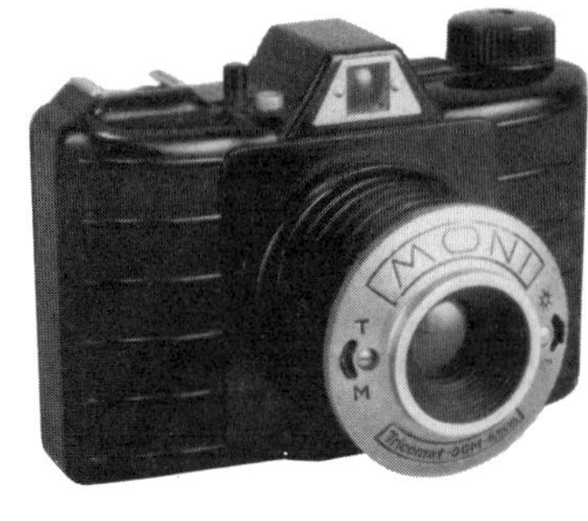

Hamaphot Moni

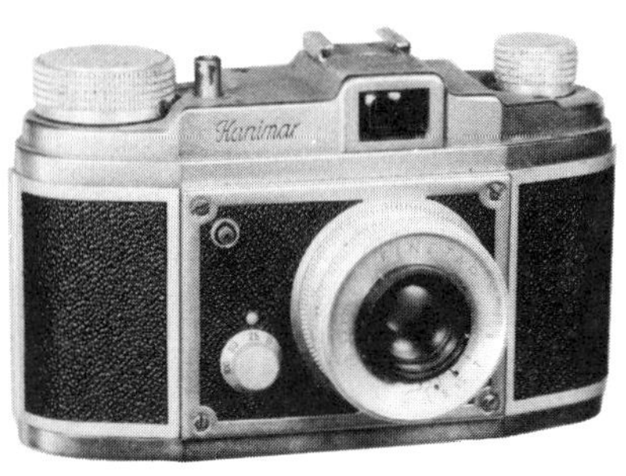

Hanimar

MODEL	FORMAT	FILM	TYPE	Year	LENS	Apert	FL	SHUTTER	SPEEDS	ILLUS	U.S.$
Mini	13x17mm	110	110	1972					I	Mc228	10
RF-35	24x36mm	35mm	35rf	1962	Hanimar	2.8	45mm		B-300	Mc228	30
Standard 120 Box	6x9cm	120	MetBx	1954						Mc228	20
VEF Zoom	13x17mm	110	110	1977							20
...HARBERS - Leipzig											
Courier Mod. IV	13x18cm	plate	Field	1892	Goerz						800
Courier Mod. V	13x18cm	plate	Field	1894	Goerz						800
Klimax	9x12cm	plate	FoldPl	1900						A149	650
Paris	13x18cm	plate	Tailboard	1900	Voigtl. Euryscop						250
Field camera 13x18	13x18cm	plate	Field	1895	Voigtl. Landschaft						220
Field camera 18x24	18x24cm	plate	Field	1905	Extra Rap. Aplan.	7.7	280mm				310
...HARUKAWA - Japan											
Septon Pen Camera	12x13mm	Roll	Submin	1953	Septon	2.8	20mm	guillotine	I,B	Mc229	900
Septon Penletto	12x13mm	Roll	Submin	1953	Septon	2.8	20mm	guillotine	I,B	Mc229	900
...HASSELBLAD - Goteborg											
201 F body	6x6cm	120	MedSLR	1994	body only	---	---	focal plane	1-1000		2400
201 F + 80/2.8	6x6cm	120	MedSLR	1994	Planar	2.8	80mm	focal plane	1-1000		3100
203 FE body	6x6cm	120	MedSLR	1994	body only	---	---	focal plane	34 min-1/2000		3200
203 FE + 80/2.8	6x6cm	120	MedSLR	1994	Planar	2.8	80mm	focal plane	34 min-1/2000		4400
205 TCC body	6x6cm	120	MedSLR	1991	body only	---	---	focal plane	16-2000		4600
205 TCC + 80/2.8	6x6cm	120	MedSLR	1991	Planar	2.8	80mm	focal plane	16-2000		6000
500 C body	6x6cm	120	MedSLR	1957	body only	---	---	Sync-Compur	1-500		410
500 C + 80/2.8	6x6cm	120	MedSLR	1957	Planar	2.8	80mm	Sync-Compur	1-500		800
500 C/M "Gold Exclusive"	6x6cm	120	MedSLR	1987	body only	---	---		1-500		2500
500 C/M "Gold Exclusive"	6x6cm	120	MedSLR	1987	Planar	2.8	80mm		1-500		3900
500 C/M "Victor Hasselblad	6x6cm	120	MedSLR	1974	Planar	2.8	80mm	Sync-Compur	1-500		2900
500 C/M (black) body	6x6cm	120	MedSLR	1970	body only	---	---	Sync-Compur	1-500		610
500 C/M (black) + 80/2.8	6x6cm	120	MedSLR	1970	Planar CF	2.8	80mm	Sync-Compur	1-500		1200
500 C/M (chrome) body	6x6cm	120	MedSLR	1970	body only	---	---	Sync-Compur	1-500		590
500 C/M (chrome) + 80/2.8	6x6cm	120	MedSLR	1970	Planar CF	2.8	80mm	Sync-Compur	1-500		1200
500 Classic body	6x6cm	120	MedSLR	1989	body only	---	---	Compur	1-500		1500
500 Classic "1941-91"	6x6cm	120	MedSLR	1991	Planar	2.8	80mm	Compur	1-500		3900
500 Classic + 80/2.8	6x6cm	120	MedSLR	1989	Planar	2.8	80mm	Compur	1-500		2100
500 EL body	6x6cm	120	MedSLR	1965	body only	---	---	Sync-Compur	1-500		480
500 EL + 80/2.8	6x6cm	120	MedSLR	1965	Planar	2.8	80mm	Sync-Compur	1-500		1000
500 EL/M (black) body	6x6cm	120	MedSLR	1972	body only	---	---	Sync-Compur	1-500		660
500 EL/M (black) + 80/2.8	6x6cm	120	MedSLR	1972	Planar	2.8	80mm	Sync-Compur	1-500		1200
500 EL/M (chrome) body	6x6cm	120	MedSLR	1972	body only	---	---	Sync-Compur	1-500		700
500 EL/M (chrome) + 80/2.8	6x6cm	120	MedSLR	1972	Planar	2.8	80mm	Sync-Compur	1-500	A1624	1300
500 EL/M "Moon" + 80/2.8	6x6cm	120	MedSLR	1979	Planar	2.8	80mm	Sync-Compur	1-500		2400
500 ELX (black) body	6x6cm	120	MedSLR	1984	body only	---	---	Sync-Compur	1-500		1000
500 ELX (black) + 80/2.8	6x6cm	120	MedSLR	1984	Planar	2.8	80mm	Sync-Compur	1-500		1800

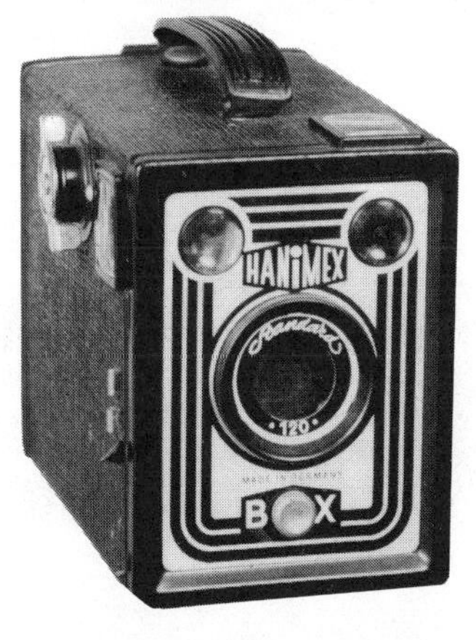

Standard 120 Box

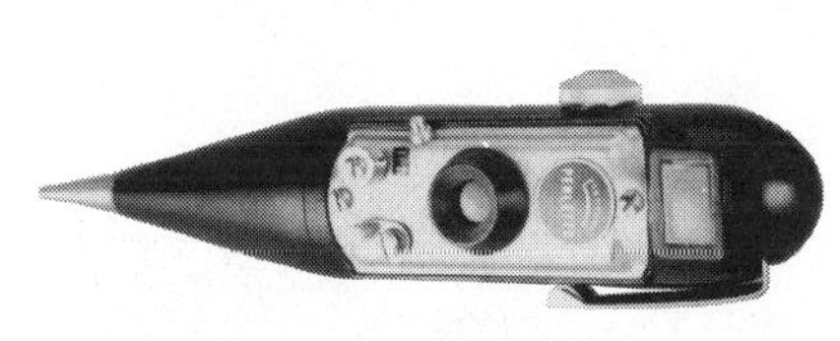

Septon Penletto

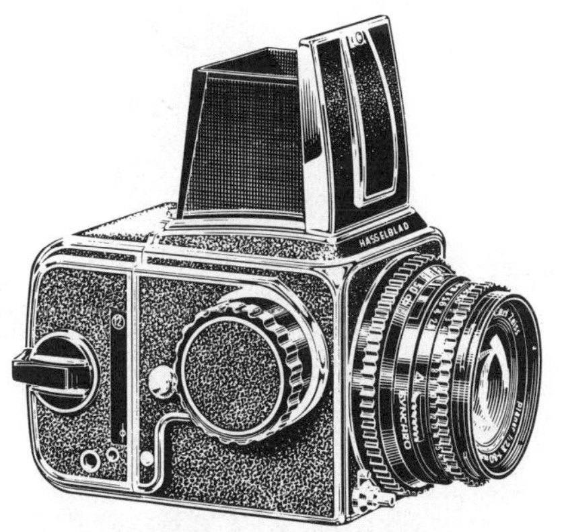

Hasselblad 500 C/M

MODEL	FORMAT	FILM	TYPE	Year	LENS	Apert	FL	SHUTTER	SPEEDS	ILLUS	U.S.$
500 ELX (chrome) body	6x6cm	120	MedSLR	1984	body only	---	---	Sync-Compur	1-500		1000
500 ELX (chrome) + 80/2.8	6x6cm	120	MedSLR	1984	Planar	2.8	80mm	Sync-Compur	1-500		1700
501 C + 80/2.8	6x6cm	120	MedSLR	1994	Planar	2.8	80mm	Sync-Compur	1-500		2100
503 CX (black) body	6x6cm	120	MedSLR	1988	body only	---	---		1-500		1200
503 CX (black) + 80/2.8	6x6cm	120	MedSLR	1988	Planar	2.8	80mm		1-500		2200
503 CX (chrome) body	6x6cm	120	MedSLR	1988	body only	---	---		1-500		1100
503 CX (chrome) + 80/2.8	6x6cm	120	MedSLR	1988	Planar	2.8	80mm		1-500		2200
503 CX (gold) + 80/2.8	6x6cm	120	MedSLR	1990	Planar	2.8	80mm		1-500		6100
553 ELX (black) body	6x6cm	120	MedSLR	1988	body only	---	---		1-500		1600
553 ELX (black) + 80/2.8	6x6cm	120	MedSLR	1988	Planar CF	2.8	80mm		1-500		2700
553 ELX (chrome) body	6x6cm	120	MedSLR	1988	body only	---	---		1-500		1600
553 ELX (chrome) + 80/2.8	6x6cm	120	MedSLR	1988	Planar CF	2.8	80mm		1-500		2500
903 SWC (black)	6x6cm	120	WideAng	1988	Biogon CF	4.5	38mm	Sync-Compur	1-500		3000
903 SWC (chrome)	6x6cm	120	WideAng	1988	Biogon CF	4.5	38mm	Sync-Compur	1-500		3000
1000 F body	6x6cm	120	MedSLR	1952	body only	---	---	focal plane	1-1000	Mc229	580
1000 F + Ektar 80/2.8	6x6cm	120	MedSLR	1952	Ektar	2.8	80mm	focal plane	1-1000	Mc229	800
1600 F body	6x6cm	120	MedSLR	1948	body only	---	---	focal plane	1-1600	Mc229	580
1600 F + Ektar 80/2.8	6x6cm	120	MedSLR	1948	Ektar	2.8	80mm	focal plane	1-1600	Mc229	1000
2000 FC body	6x6cm	120	MedSLR	1977	body only	---	---	focal plane	1-2000		560
2000 FC + 80/2.8	6x6cm	120	MedSLR	1977	Planar	2.8	80mm	focal plane	1-2000		1000
2000 FC/M body	6x6cm	120	MedSLR	1981	body only	---	---	focal plane	1-2000		900
2000 FC/M + 80/2.8	6x6cm	120	MedSLR	1981	Planar	2.8	80mm	focal plane	1-2000		1300
2000 FCW body	6x6cm	120	MedSLR	1984	body only	---	---	focal plane	1-2000		1100
2000 FCW + 80/2.8	6x6cm	120	MedSLR	1984	Planar	2.8	80mm	focal plane	1-2000	A3187	1700
2003 FCW body	6x6cm	120	MedSLR	1989	body only	---	---	focal plane	1-2000		1400
2003 FCW + 80/2.8	6x6cm	120	MedSLR	1989	Planar	2.8	80mm	focal plane	1-2000		2200
Aerial Camera HK7	7x10cm	70mm	Aerial	1941	Tele-Megor	5.5	250mm		150-400		5100
Pocket Kamera 8x11	8x11cm	plate	FoldPl	1905	Goerz Doppel An.			B&L Simplex			170
Pocket Kamera 8x11	8x11cm	plate	FoldPl	1905	Goerz Doppel An.			Unicum			170
Pocket Kamera 9x12	9x12cm	plate	FoldPl	1905	Goerz Doppel An.			B&L Simplex			170
Pocket Kamera 9x12	9x12cm	plate	FoldPl	1905	Busch Anastigmat			Unicum			170
Stereoscop	8x17cm	plate	StFoldPl	1900	Meniscus						610
Super Wide Angle (SWA)	6x6cm	120	WideAng	1954	Biogon	4.5	38mm	Sync-Compur	1-500	A1626	1600
Svenska Express 9x12	9x12cm	plate	MagBox	1893	Achromatic					Mc229	160
Svenska Express 12x16	12x16.5cm	plate	MagBox	1893	Achromatic					Mc229	200
SWC	6x6cm	120	WideAng	1959	Biogon	4.5	38mm	Sync-Compur	1-500		1500
SWC/E	6x6cm	120	WideAng	1983	Biogon	4.5	38mm	Sync-Compur	1-500		2100
SWC/M	6x6cm	120	WideAng	1979	Biogon	4.5	38mm	Sync-Compur	1-500		2100
...HENNING - Frankfurt											
Rhaco (box)	4.5x6cm	plate	Platebox	1930							60
Rhaco Folding Camera	6.5x9cm	plate	FoldPl	1930	Ennatar Anast.	4.5	105mm	Ibsor	1-125		50
Rhaco Monopol	9x12cm	plate	FoldPl	1933	Radionar	6.3	135mm	Ibso	1-100		50

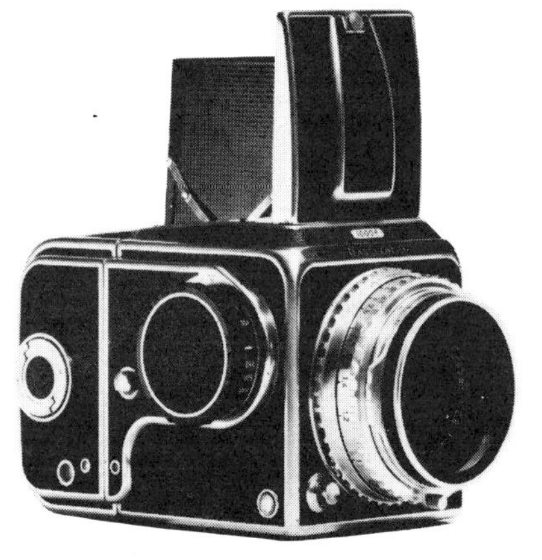

Hasselblad 1000 F

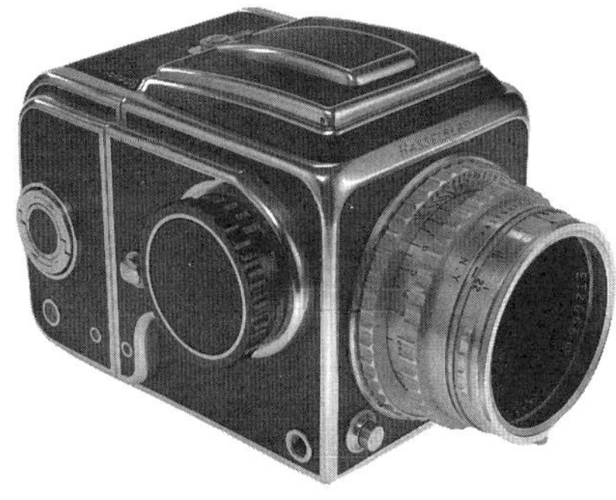

Hasselblad 1600 F

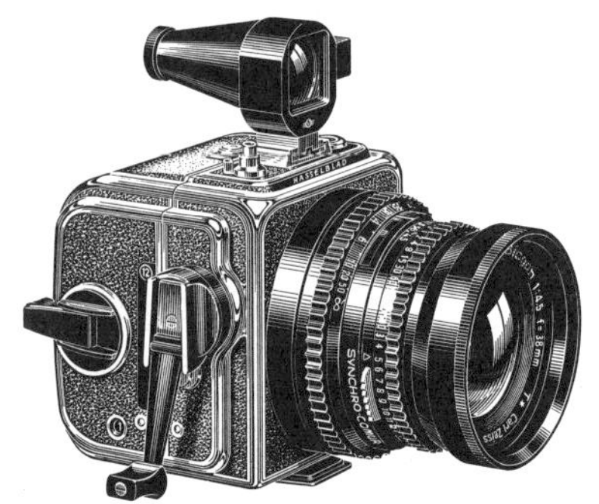

Hasselblad SWC

MODEL	FORMAT	FILM	TYPE	Year	LENS	Apert	FL	SHUTTER	SPEEDS	ILLUS	U.S.$
...HENSOLDT - Wetzlar											
Henso Reporter	24x36mm	35mm	35rf	1953	Iriar	2.8	5cm	focal plane	1-1000	HK588	1900
Henso Reporter	24x36mm	35mm	35rf	1953	Arion	1.9	50mm	focal plane	1-1000	HK588	2300
Henso Standard	24x36mm	35mm	35rf	1953	Iriar	2.8	5cm	focal plane	1-1000		1300
Henso Standard	24x36mm	35mm	35rf	1953	Arion	1.9	50mm	focal plane	1-1000		1400
...HERBERT GEORGE CO. - Chicago											
Donald Duck Camera	1⅝x1⅝"	127	RigidRo	1946	Meniscus			single speed		Mc231	30
Happi-Time	1⅝x1⅝"	127	RigidRo	1946	Meniscus			single speed			20
Herco 12	1⅝x1⅝"	127	RigidRo	1946	Meniscus			single speed			20
Herco Imperial 620	2¼x2¼"	620	PlasticBox	1948	Meniscus				I,T	Mc231	10
Herco-flex 6-20	2¼x2¼"	620	TLR-Box	1950	Meniscus				I	Mc231	10
Imperial Debonair	2¼x2¼"	620	BakeliteBox	1960	Meniscus				I,T	Mc231	10
Imperial Mark 27	2¼x2¼"	620	PlasticBox	1960	Meniscus				I,T		30
Imperial Mark XII Flash	2¼x2¼"	620	PlasticBox	1956	Meniscus				I,T		10
Imperial Reflex	2¼x2¼"	620	TLR-Box	1956	Simple				I		20
Official Boy Scout	2¼x2¼"	620	PlasticBox	1950	Meniscus				I,T		20
Official Brownie Scout	2¼x2¼"	620	PlasticBox	1950	Meniscus				I,T		20
Official Brownie Flash	2¼x2¼"	620	PlasticBox	1948	Meniscus				I,T	A2844	30
Official Camp Fire Scout	2¼x2¼"	620	PlasticBox	1948	Meniscus				I,T		0
Official Cub Scout	2¼x2¼"	620	PlasticBox	1950	Meniscus				I,T	Mc232	20
Official Girl Scout (Mk XII)	1½x1½"	127	PlasticBox	1955	Meniscus				I,T	A3103	30
Official Girl Scout 620	2¼x2¼"	620	PlasticBox	1950	Meniscus				I,T	A2846	30
Roy Rogers & Trigger	2¼x2¼"	620	PlasticBox	1948	Meniscus				I,T		30
Roy Rogers Jr	1⅝x1⅝"	127	RigidRo	1946	Meniscus			single speed			30
Royal	2¼x2¼"	620	PlasticBox	1948	Meniscus				I,T	Mc232	10
Savoy	2¼x2¼"	620	PlasticBox	1960	Meniscus				I,T	Mc232	10
Savoy Mark II			PlasticBox	1960							10
Stylex	6x9cm	620	TelescRo		Meniscus				I,T		10
...HERBST & FIRL - Görlitz											
Field camera 13x18	13x18cm	plate	FoldPl	1905	Doppel Anast.	6.8	150mm	focal plane	1-1000	A235	140
Fram-Camera Ser. II	13x18cm	plate	Tailboard	1904	Aplanat Extra Rap.	8		focal plane			450
Globus 30x40	30x40cm	plate	Field	1903	Rapid Aplanat						700
Jochim-Spezial	9x12cm	plate	HzFoldPl	1908	Dagor	6.8	240mm	Compound		A246	270
Phönix Tropical	6.5x9cm	plate	FoldPl	1924	Steinheil Unofocal						800
Salon Atelier Camera	24x30cm	plate	Studio	1900	Rapid Aplanat					A2962	1100
Studio camera	13x18cm	plate	Studio	1920	Heliar	4.5	210mm	Compound			560
Tailboard camera 13x18	13x18cm	plate	Tailboard	1900	Aplanat Extra Rap.	8					430
Tailboard camera 18x24	18x24cm	plate	Tailboard	1900	Aplanat Extra Rap.	8				A2951	370
...HERLANGO AG - Vienna											
Folding camera 7x8.5	7x8.5cm	plate	FoldPl	1928	Tessar	4.5	105mm	Compur	1-250		60
Folding camera 9x12	9x12cm	plate	FoldPl	1928	Tessar	4.5	105mm	Compur	1-250		70
Folding Plate Camera 10x1	10x15cm	plate	FoldPl								60

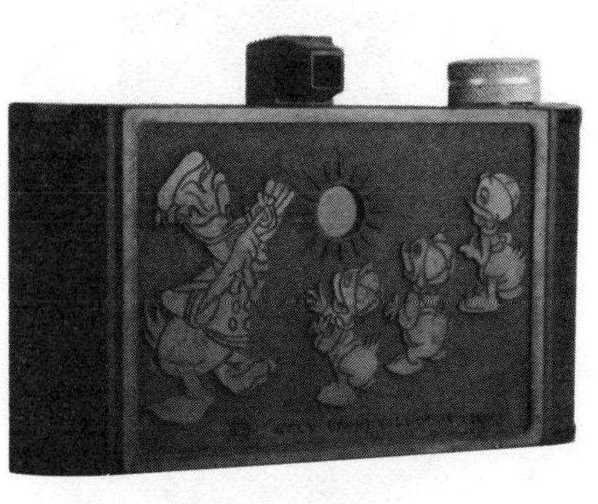

Donald Duck Camera

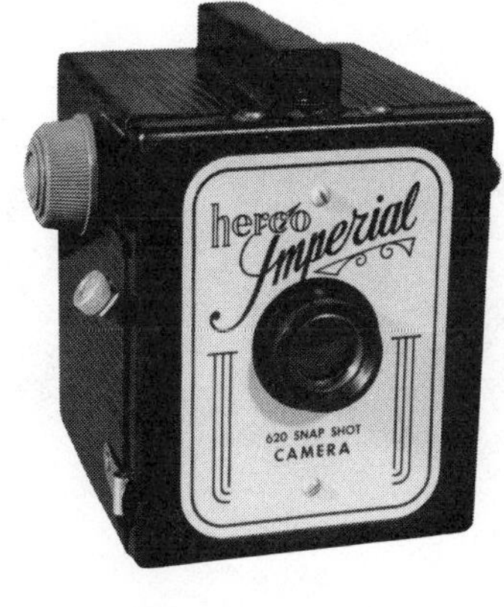

Herco Imperial 620

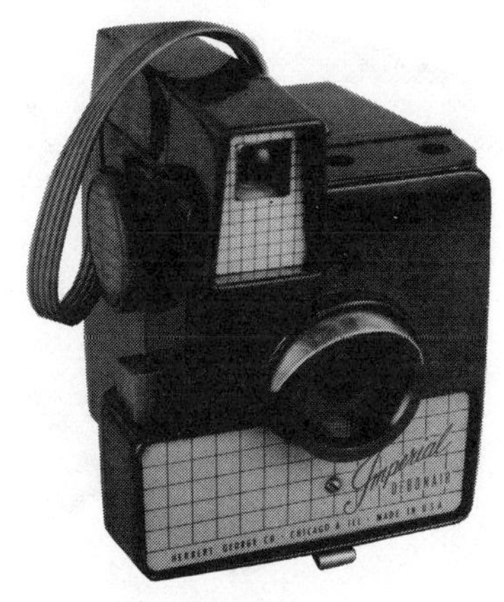

Imperial Debonair

MODEL	FORMAT	FILM	TYPE	Year	LENS	Apert	FL	SHUTTER	SPEEDS	ILLUS	U.S.$
...HERMAGIS - Paris											
Field Camera	13x18cm	plate	Field		Aplanastigmat	6.8	210mm	roller-blind			270
Hermagique	9x12cm	plate	MagBox	1898	Antivoleur	8	165mm	single speed			0
Hermo Box	6x9cm	120	MetBx	1925	Achromat			single speed		F848	70
Micromegas	3¼x4¼"	plate	FoldBox	1875	Rapid Rectilinear					Mc232	5000
Stereo Jumelle	6x13cm	plate	StJumelle	1900	Hermagis	6.8	95mm				200
Tailboard Stereo	8x16cm	plate	SterPl	1890	Aplanat	8				F1256	4200
Velocigraphe	9x12cm	plate	MagBox	1892	Rapid Rectilinear			rotary		A1308	900
Velocigraphe Stereo	8x17cm	plate	SterBox	1895	Hermagis					A2663	1700
...HEROLD MFG. CO. - Chicago											
Acro-Flash	3x4cm	127	RigidRo	1948						Mc232	20
Da-Brite	3x4cm	127	RigidRo	1948	Meniscus		50mm	rotary		Mc232	20
Flash-Master	3x4cm	127	RigidRo	1950	Meniscus			rotary		A3128	20
Herold 40	3x4cm	127	RigidRo	1950							10
Photo-Master	3x4cm	127	RigidRo	1950							10
Sparta-Fold V	6x9cm	120	FoldRo	1958					I,T	Mc232	30
Spartacord	6x6cm	620	TLR-Box	1958	Achromat	7.7	3.25"				20
Spartus 35	24x36mm	35mm	35vf	1950		4.5	50mm			A3474	20
Spartus 35F	24x36mm	35mm	35vf	1952							20
Spartus 35F Mod. 400	24x36mm	35mm	35vf	1952		7.7	5cm			Mc233	20
Spartus 120 Flash	2¼x3¼"	120	BakeliteBox	1953	Meniscus	16	120mm	rotary	1/60,T		20
Spartus Co-Flash	4x4cm	127	RigidRo	1962							20
Sunbeam 120	2¼x3¼"	120	BakeliteBox								10
Sunbeam 127 3x4	3x4cm	127	RigidRo								10
Sunbeam 127 4x4	4x4cm	127	PlasBx								10
Sunbeam Six-Twenty	2¼x2¼"	620	TLR-Box								10
...HESEKIEL - Berlin											
Original Spiegel Reflex	9x12cm	plate	LgSLR	1897	Brass barrel			focal plane		Mc233	3200
Pompadour	6.5x9cm	plate	FoldPl	1905	Certomat	8	105mm				10000
Rocktaschen-Kamera	9x12cm	plate	FoldPl	1895	Doppel Anast.			focal plane		A2944	1600
Rocktaschen-Kamera	9x12cm	plate	FoldPl	1900	Zeiss Unar	4.5	136mm	focal plane		A2944	1400
Spiegel-Magazin-Camera	9x12cm	plate	MagBox	1893	Aplanat					A2809	240
Spiegel-Magazin-Camera	12x16.5cm	plate	MagBox	1893	Doppel Anast.	6.8	180mm				270
Spiegel-Reflex-Camera	9x12cm	plate	LgSLR	1895	Doppel Anast.	6.8				HK309	3000
Spiegel-Reflex-Camera	12x16.5cm	plate	LgSLR	1893	Doppel Anast.	6.8	180mm			HK308	3400
...HESS & SATTLER - Wiesbaden, Germany											
Field camera	9x12cm	plate	Tailboard	1895	Universal Aplanat						200
Universal Duplex I		plate	FoldPl	1905	Busch Aplanat	8		Unicum			110
...HOH & HAHNE - Leipzig											
Field camera 13x18	13x18cm	plate	Field	1900	Rod. Bistigmat					U189	300
Field camera 18x24	18x24cm	plate	Field	1900	Rod. Bistigmat						200
Folding pl. (black bellows)	9x12cm	plate	FoldPl	1900	Rodenstock						50

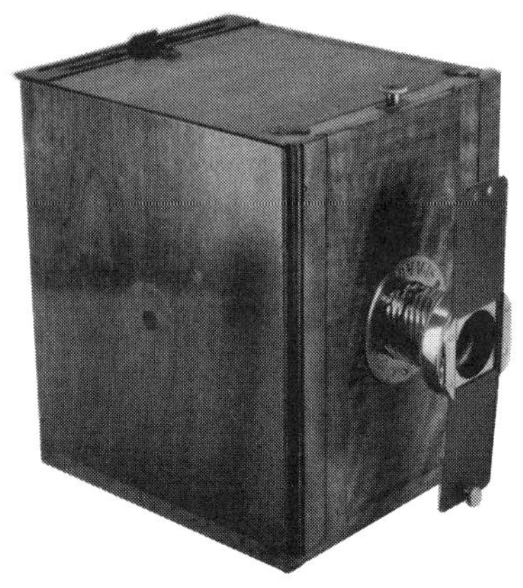

Hermagis Micromegas

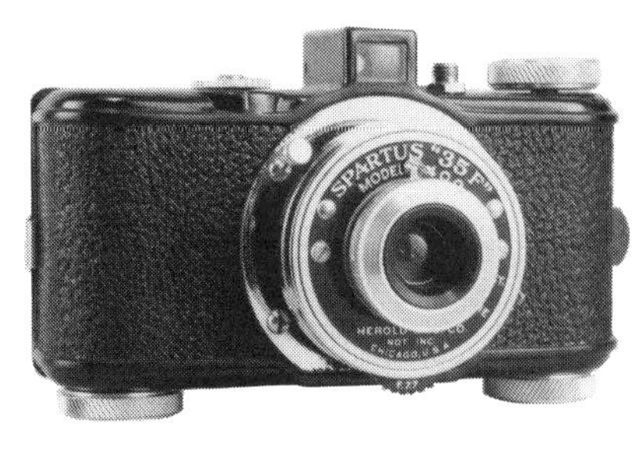

Spartus 35F Mod. 400

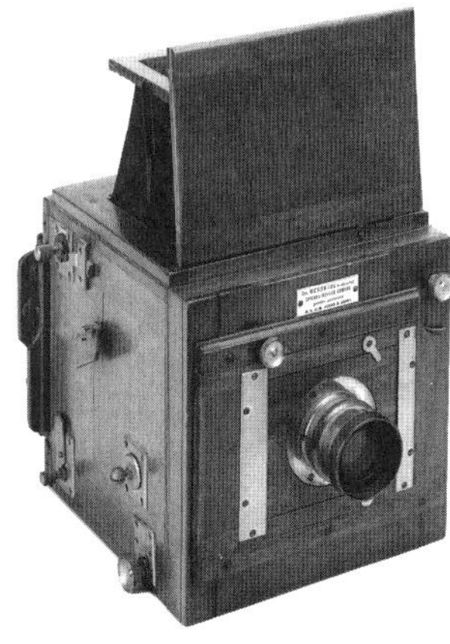

Original Spiegel Reflex

MODEL	FORMAT	FILM	TYPE	Year	LENS	Apert	FL	SHUTTER	SPEEDS	ILLUS	U.S.$
Folding plate (colored bello	9x12cm	plate	FoldPl	1900	Rodenstock						150
Folding plate camera	10x15cm	plate	FoldPl	1930	Unofokal	4.5	165mm	Compur			90
...HOUGHTON - London											
"Automatic" Magazine	3¼x4¼"	plate	MagBox	1891		8		roller-blind		Mc235	1300
All Dist.Ensign Box (black)	6x9cm	120	RollBox	1930	Meniscus					A2900	20
All Dist.Ensign Box (colors)	6x9cm	120	RollBox	1930	Meniscus					Mc235	40
All Dist.Ensign Fold.(black)	6x9cm	120	FoldRo	1930							20
All Dist.Ensign Fold.(colors	6x9cm	120	FoldRo	1930							50
All Dist.Ensign Pocket Cam	6x9cm	120	FoldRo	1930	Meniscus				TBI		20
Anastig. Ensignette No.1	1½x2¼	Roll	StrutRo	1909	Tessar Anastigmat	6.8		Simplex	25-100	Mc238	120
Anastig. Ensignette No.2	2x3"	Roll	StrutRo	1909	Cooke Anastigmat	5.8		Simplex	25-100	Mc238	110
Autorange 16-20 Ensign	4.5x6cm	120	FoldRo	1953	Ross Xpres	3.5	75mm	Epsilon	1-400,B,T		120
Autorange 220 Ensign	6x9cm	120	FoldRo	1938	Ensar	4.5		Prontor		Mc235	120
Autorange 820 Ensign	6x9cm	120	FoldRo	1957	Ross Xpres	3.8	105mm				560
Box Ensign 2¼A	2¼x2¼"	120	RollBox	1912	Meniscus				I,T		30
Box Ensign 2¼B (black)	2¼x2¼"	120	RollBox	1912	Meniscus				I,T	Mc235	20
Box Ensign 2¼B (colors)	2¼x2¼"	120	RollBox	1912	Meniscus				I,T	Mc235	40
British Ensign		Roll	FoldRo	1905	Beck Symmetrical			Unicum			100
Coronet	4¼x6½"	plate	Field		Brass-bound			roller-blind			270
Duo Ensign (black)	2¼x3¼"	120	RollBox	1929	Meniscus				I,T		20
Duo Ensign (colors)	2¼x3¼"	120	RollBox	1929	Meniscus				I,T		40
Empress 3¼x4¼"	3¼x4¼"	plate	Field	1912	Brass barrel			roller-blind			350
Empress 4¼x6½"	4¼x6½"	plate	Field	1912	Brass barrel			roller-blind			370
Empress 6½x8½"	6½x8½"	plate	Field	1912	Brass barrel			roller-blind			370
Ensign Autospeed	6x6cm	120	FoldRo	1932	Aldis	4.5	4"	focal plane	15-500		240
Ensign Cadet	1½x2½"	Roll	RollBox	1927	Achromatic			Everset	I,T	Mc236	30
Ensign Cameo 2¼x3¼"	2¼x3¼"	plate	FoldPl	1927	Aldis Uno Anast.	7.7					70
Ensign Cameo 3¼x4¼"	3¼x4¼"	plate	FoldPl	1927	Zeiss Tessar	7.7					70
Ensign Cameo 3½x5½"	3½x5½"	plate	FoldPl	1927	Aldis Uno Anast.	7.7					70
Ensign Carbine	2¼x3¼"	120	FoldRo	1922	Aldis Uno Anast.	7.7			25-100		30
Ensign Carbine No. 4	2¼x3¼"	120	FoldRo	1922	Aldis Uno Anast.	7.7			25-100		130
Ensign Carbine 4 Tropical	2¼x3¼"	120	FoldRo	1922	Aldis Uno Anast.	7.7		Compur	1-250		110
Ensign Carbine 4 Tropical	2¼x3¼"	120	FoldRo	1922	Aldis Uno Anast.	4.5		Compur	1-250		110
Ensign Carbine 7 Tropical	2¼x3¼"	120	FoldRo	1927	Tessar	4.5	120mm	Compur			150
Ensign Commando	6x6cm	120	FoldRo	1945	Ensar	3.5	75mm	Epsilon	1-300	Mc236	110
Ensign Cupid	4x6cm	120	RigidRo	1922	Meniscus Achr.	f11			I,T	Mc236	70
Ensign Deluxe Reflex 2½	2½x3½"	plate	LgSLR	1910	various			focal plane	-1000	Mc237	220
Ensign Deluxe Reflex 3¼	3¼x4¼"	plate	LgSLR	1910	various			focal plane	-1000	Mc237	220
Ensign Double-8	3x4cm	127	StrutRo	1930	Ensar Anastigmat	4.5			25-100	A3053	110
Ensign E20 (black)	2¼x3¼"	120	RollBox	1929	Meniscus				I,T	A2897	10
Ensign E20 (colors)	2¼x3¼"	120	RollBox	1929	Meniscus				I,T	Mc236	40
Ensign E26 (black)	2x3"	Roll	RollBox	1929	Meniscus				I,T		20

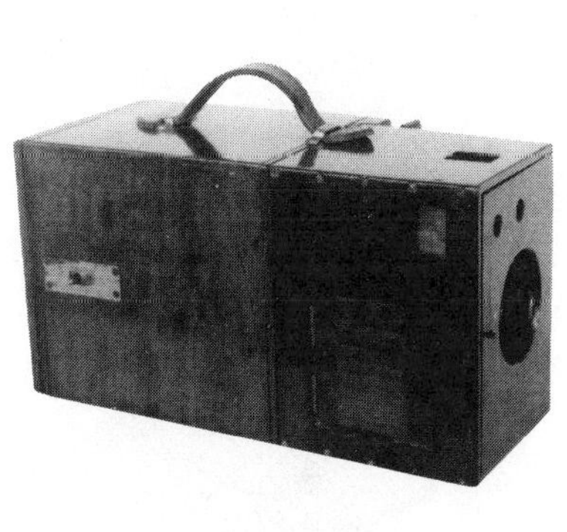

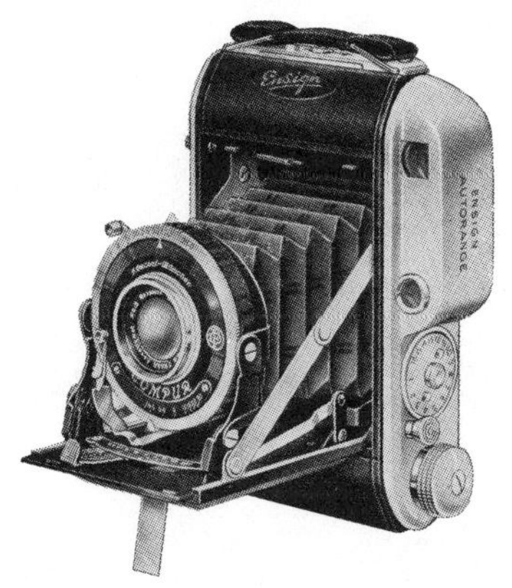

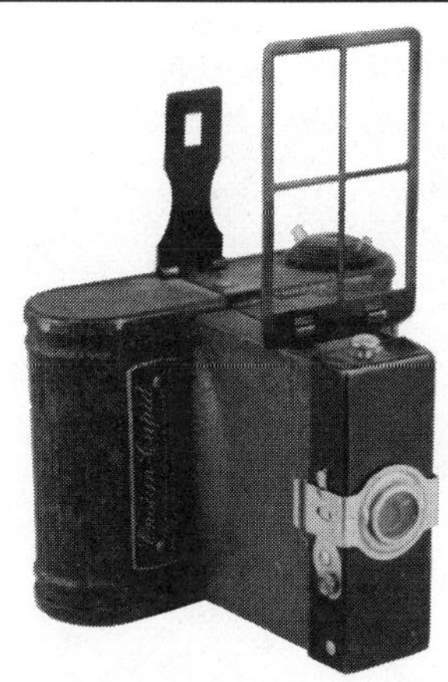

"Automatic" Magazine

Autorange 220 Ensign

Ensign Cupid

MODEL	FORMAT	FILM	TYPE	Year	LENS	Apert	FL	SHUTTER	SPEEDS	ILLUS	U.S.$
Ensign E26 (colors)	2x3"	Roll	RollBox	1929	Meniscus				I,T		40
Ensign E29 (black)	2x3"	Roll	RollBox	1929	Meniscus				I,T		20
Ensign E29 (colors)	2x3"	Roll	RollBox	1929	Meniscus				I,T		30
Ensign Folding Reflex 2¼	2¼x3¼"	plate	FoldSLR	1912	Tessar	4.5	135mm	focal plane	1-1000	A572	190
Ensign Folding Reflex 3¼	3¼x4¼"	plate	FoldSLR	1912	Tessar	4.5	150mm	focal plane	1-1000		200
Ensign Ful-Vue (black)	6x6cm	120	TLR-Box	1939	Simple				I,T	Mc236	50
Ensign Ful-Vue (blue)	6x6cm	120	TLR-Box	1945	Simple				I,T		80
Ensign Ful-Vue (grey)	6x6cm	120	TLR-Box	1945	Simple				I,T		70
Ensign Ful-Vue (red)	6x6cm	120	TLR-Box	1945	Simple				I,T		80
Ensign Ful-Vue Super	6x6cm	120	TLR-Box	1938	Achromat	11		2-speed		A1751	30
Ensign Greyhound	6x9cm	120	FoldRo	1950	Meniscus					Mc236	40
Ensign Mascot A3	3¼x4¼"	plate	MagBox	1910				Everset	I,T		60
Ensign Mascot D3	3¼x4¼"	plate	MagBox	1910	Rapid Rectilinear	11					60
Ensign Mickey Mouse	1¼x1⅝"	Roll	RollBox	1935					I,T	Mc236	100
Ensign Midget Mod. 22	1¼x1½"	E-10	FoldRo	1934	Meniscus				I,T	Mc236	80
Ensign Midget Mod. 33	1¼x1½"	E-10	FoldRo	1934	Meniscus				25-100		80
Ensign Midget Mod. 55	1¼x1½"	E-10	FoldRo	1934	Ensar Anastigmat	6.3			25-100	Mc237	80
Ensign Midget S/33	1¼x1½"	E-10	FoldRo	1935	fixed focus				25-100	Mc237	120
Ensign Midget S/55	1¼x1½"	E-10	FoldRo	1935	Ensar Anastigmat	6.3			25-100		120
Ensign Multex	1¼x1½"	127	RigidRo	1936	Ross Xpres	2.9		focal plane	T,1-1000	Mc237	220
Ensign Pocket E-20	2¼x3¼"	120	FoldRo	1938	fixed focus				I,T	Mc237	30
Ensign Popular Reflex 2½	2½x3½"	plate	LgSLR	1910	various			focal plane	-1000	Mc237	220
Ensign Popular Reflex 3¼	3¼x4¼"	plate	LgSLR	1910	various			focal plane	-1000	Mc237	200
Ensign Pressman Reflex	3¼x4¼"	plate	LgSLR	1929	Tessar	4.5	165mm		15-1000		200
Ensign Ranger	2¼x3¼"	120	FoldRo	1953						Mc237	40
Ensign Ranger II	2¼x3¼"	120	FoldRo	1953	Ensar	6.3	105mm				50
Ensign Ranger Special	2¼x3¼"	120	FoldRo	1953							40
Ensign Reflex 2½x3½"	2½x3½"	plate	LgSLR	1910	various			focal plane	-1000	A561	220
Ensign Reflex 3¼x4¼"	3¼x4¼"	plate	LgSLR	1910	various			focal plane	-1000	Mc237	220
Ensign Reflex Box	2¼x3¼"	120	SLR-Box	1938	Achromat	11			2-spd	A3158	120
Ensign Reflex Tropical	2¼x3¼"	plate	LgSLR	1925	various			focal plane	-1000		560
Ensign Roll Film Reflex	6x9cm	120	MedSLR	1927	Aldis Uno	6.3			I,T	Mc237	130
Ensign Roll Film Reflex	6x9cm	120	MedSLR	1927	Cooke Luxor	6.3			I,T	Mc237	140
Ensign Roll Film Refl. Trop.	6x9cm	120	MedSLR	1925	Aldis Uno			focal plane	25-500	A577	620
Ensign Roll Film Refl. Trop.	6x9cm	120	MedSLR	1925	Anastigmat			focal plane	25-500		620
Ensign Selfix 12-20	6x6cm	120	FoldRo	1952	Ross Xpres	3.5	75mm	Epsilon	1/400		50
Ensign Selfix 12-20 Special	2¼x2¼"	120	FoldRo	1952	Ross Xpres	3.5					100
Ensign Selfix 16-20	4.5x6cm	120	FoldRo	1952	Ross Xpress	3.8					100
Ensign Selfix 20	2¼x3¼"	120	FoldRo	1933	Ensar	4.5	105mm	Epsilon	1-150		30
Ensign Selfix 220	2¼x2¼"	120	FoldRo	1938	Ensar	6.3	75mm	Ensign			60
Ensign Selfix 320	2¼x2¼"	120	FoldRo	1938	Ensar	4.5		Prontor II			50
Ensign Selfix 420	2¼x3¼"	120	FoldRo		Ensar Anastigmat	4.5	105mm	Prontor II		Mc237	40

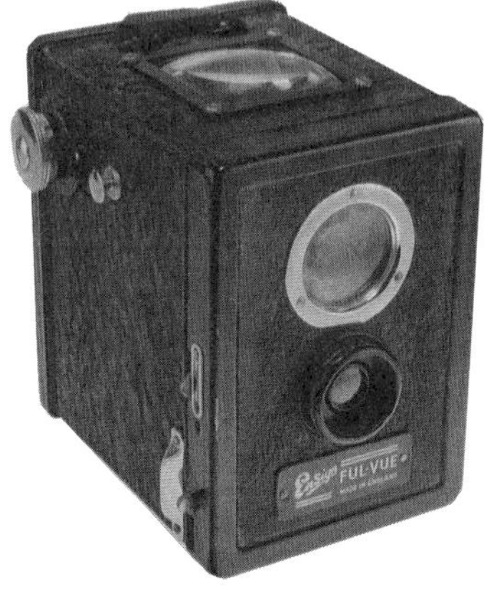

Ensign Ful-Vue

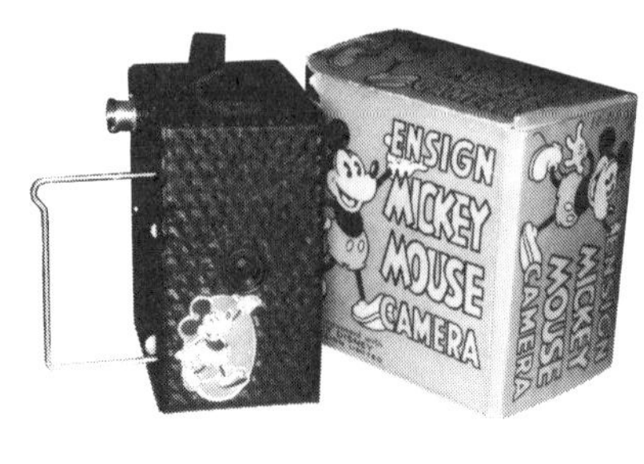

Ensign Mickey Mouse

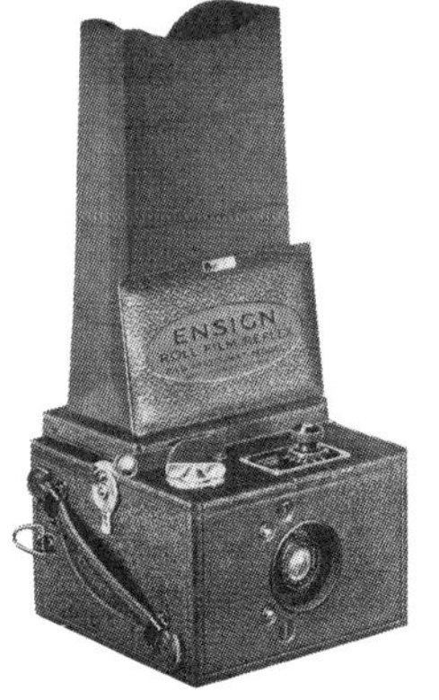

Ensign Roll Film Reflex

MODEL	FORMAT	FILM	TYPE	Year	LENS	Apert	FL	SHUTTER	SPEEDS	ILLUS	U.S.$
Ensign Selfix 820	2¼x3¼"	120	FoldRo	1952	Ross Xpres	3.8	105mm	Epsilon	1-250		90
Ensign Selfix 820 Special	2¼x3¼"	120	FoldRo	1953	Xpres	3.8	105mm				190
Ensign Special Reflex 2¼	2¼x3¼"	plate	LgSLR	193x	Ross Xpress	4.5	6"	focal plane	15-1000		240
Ensign Special Reflex 3¼	3¼x4¼"	plate	LgSLR	193x	Ross Xpress	4.5	6"	focal plane	15-1000		240
Ensign Special Reflex Trop.	2¼x3¼"	plate	LgSLR	193x	Ross Xpress	4.5	5"	focal plane	15-1000		570
Ensign Special Reflex Trop.	3¼x4¼"	plate	LgSLR	193x	Ross Xpress	4.5	6"	focal plane	15-1000		570
Ensign Speed Film Reflex	6x9cm	120	SLR-Box	1925	Ensar Anastigmat	4.5		focal plane	25-500,T	A581	170
Ensign Speed Trop. Refl.	6x9cm	120	SLR-Box	1925	Aldis Anastigmat	7.7	108mm	focal plane	25-500		630
Ensign S.S. Cameo (black)	2½x3½"	plate	FoldPl	1932	Dallmeyer Dalmac	3.5		Compur			50
Ensign S.S. Cameo (brown)	2½x3½"	plate	FoldPl	1932	Dallmeyer Dalmac	3.5		Compur			120
Ensignette Deluxe No.1	1½x2¼	Roll	StrutRo	1909	Cooke Anastigmat	5.8		Simplex	25-100	Mc238	120
Ensignette Deluxe No.2	2x3"	Roll	StrutRo	1909	Tessar Anastigmat	6.8		Simplex	25-100	Mc238	120
Ensignette Junior No.2	2¼x3¼"	Roll	StrutRo	1909	Meniscus			single speed			80
Ensignette No.1	1½x2¼	Roll	StrutRo	1909	Meniscus			single speed		Mc238	90
Ensignette No.2	2x3"	Roll	StrutRo	1909	Meniscus			single speed		A385	80
Folding Klito (early)	3¼x4¼"	plate	FoldPl	1900	ExRapid Rectimat			Ensign Jr.		Mc238	60
Folding Klito (later)	3¼x4¼"	Sheet	FoldPl	1912	Rapid Achromatic			Ensign Jr.		Mc238	70
Holborn Magazine Camera	3¼x4¼"	plate	MagBox	1900							220
Holborn Stamp Camera	3¼x4¼"	plate	MultiLens	1901							410
Junior Box Ensign	6x9cm	120	RollBox	1932	Meniscus			2-speed	I,T		30
Junior Box Ensign Mod. E	6x9cm	120	RollBox	1927	Meniscus			2-speed	I,T		30
Klito No. 0 2¼x3¼"	2¼x3¼"	plate	MagBox	1905	Rapid Rectlinear			rotary		Mc238	150
Klito No. 0 3¼x4¼"	3¼x4¼"	plate	MagBox	1905	Rapid Rectlinear			rotary		Mc238	70
Klito No. 1	3¼x4¼"	plate	MagBox	1905	Rapid Rectlinear			guillotine			50
Klito No. 3	3¼x4¼"	plate	MagBox	1905	Beck Symmetrical	8		guillotine			180
Mascot No.1	6.5x9cm	plate	MagBox		Fixed Focus	11			I,T	Mc238	40
Pocket Ensign 2¼B	2¼x3¼"	120	StrutRo	1912					I,T	Mc237	20
Royal Mail Stereolette	45x107	plate	SterBox					guillotine			1000
Shuttle	3¼x4¼"	plate	MagBox	1892				internal			640
Studio camera	12x15"	plate	Tailboard	1914	Brass Dallmeyer		5"				520
Ticka	16x22mm		Submin	1905	Meniscus	11	30mm		I,T	Mc238	350
Ticka, (silver)	16x22mm		Submin	1905	Meniscus	11	30mm		I,T		3800
Ticka, Focal plane	16x22mm		Submin	1905	Meniscus	11	30mm	focal plane		Mc238	1900
Ticka, Watch-Face	16x22mm		Submin	1912	Meniscus	11	30mm		I,T	Mc239	1900
Triple Victo 4¾x6½"	4¾x6½"	plate	Field	190x	Taylor H. Cooke			Thornton-Pickard		A146	350
Triple Victo 12x15"	12x15"	plate	Field	190x	Taylor H. Cooke			Thornton-Pickard			350
Triple Victo Tropical	4¾x6½"	plate	Field	1908	Taylor H. Cooke			Thornton-Pickard		Mc239	410
Tudor	3¼x4¼"	plate	Field	1906	Aldis Anastigmat			Automat			90
Vest Pocket Ensign	1⅝x2½"	127	StrutRo	1926	Achromatic	11		3-speed			70
Victo 3¼x4¼"	3¼x4¼"	plate	Field	1900	Rapid Rectilinear			Thornton-Pickard			310
Victo 5x7"	5x7"	plate	Field	1900	Rapid Rectilinear			Automatic			330
Victo 10x12"	10x12"	plate	Field	1900	Rapid Rectilinear			Automatic			310

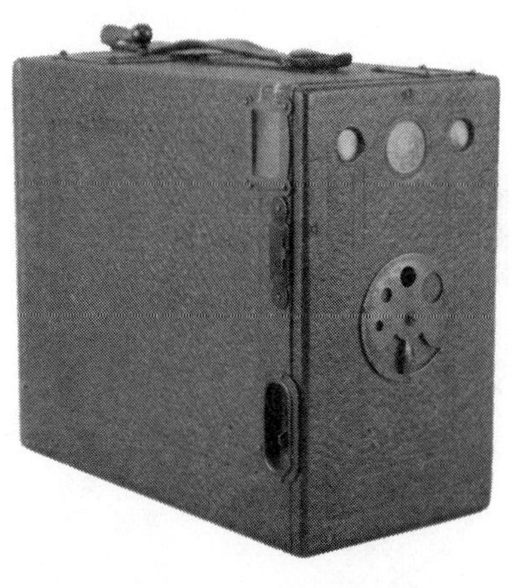

Mascot No. 1

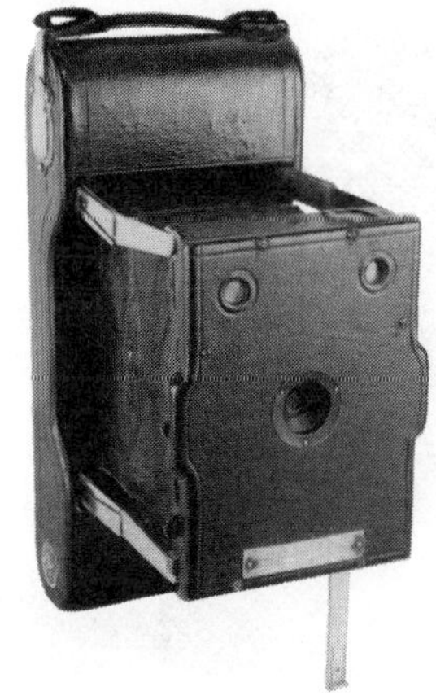

Pocket Ensign 2¼B

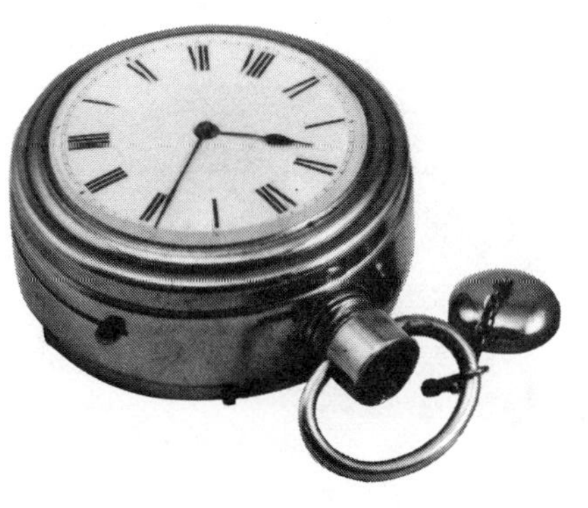

Ticka, Watch-Face

MODEL	FORMAT	FILM	TYPE	Year	LENS	Apert	FL	SHUTTER	SPEEDS	ILLUS	U.S.$
Victo Stereo	5x7"	plate	StField	1900	Rapid Rectilinear			Automatic			800
Victo-Superbe 4¾x6½"	4¾x6½"	plate	Field	1912	Taylor H. Cooke			roller-blind			470
Victo-Superbe 12x15"	12x15"	plate	Field	1912	Taylor H. Cooke			Ensign Sector			470
...HUNTER (R.F. Hunter, Ltd) - London											
Gilbert	2¼x3¼"	120	MetBx								100
Hunter 35	24x36mm	35mm	35vf		Steiner	3.5	45mm		25-100		30
Purma Plus	1¼x1¼"	127	RigidRo	1951	Purma Anastigmat	6.3	55mm	focal plane	1-500	Mc239	40
Purma Special	1¼x1¼"	127	RigidRo	1934	Beck Anastigmat	6.3	2.25"			Mc239	40
...HUTH BROS. - Dresden											
Field camera	13x18cm	plate	Tailboard	1895	Univ.Rap.Aplanat	8		roller-blind			230
Folding plate camera 9x12	9x12cm	plate	VtFoldPl	1902	Symmetrical	8		Junior	1-100		190
Folding plate camera 13x18	13x18cm	plate	VtFoldPl	1902	Symmetrical	8		Wollensak	1-100		190
...HÜTTIG - Dresden											
Afpi	9x12cm	plate	FoldPl	1900	Periscop	9	135mm			A1389	120
Atom 50	4.5x6cm	plate	VtFoldPl	1908	Dagor	6.8	90mm	Compound	1-250	A2987	250
Atom 53	4.5x6cm	plate	HzFoldPl	1908	Helios	8	90mm	Compound	1-250		290
Cameo Stereo	9x18cm	plate	StFoldPl	1908	Symmetrical	8					130
Cupido 9x12	9x12cm	plate	VtFoldPl	1908	Extra Rap. Aplan.	8	125mm	Hüttig	B,T,1-100	A185	50
Cupido 9x12	9x12cm	plate	VtFoldPl	1908	Extra Rap. Aplan.	8	125mm	Compound		Mc239	50
Cupido 10x15	10x15cm	plate	VtFoldPl	1908	Anastigmat	6.8	165mm	Compound			50
Detective Magazine camera	6.5x9cm	plate	MagBox	1895	Achromat					A1303	240
Detective Magazine camera	9x12cm	plate	MagBox	1895	Achromat					A53,54	240
Excelsior	9x12cm	plate	FoldPl	1892	Rapid Aplanat	8	160mm	3-speed		A2985	800
Fichtner's Excelsior Detect.	9x12cm	plate	MagBox	1892	Goerz Lynkeioskop		125mm	3-speed		A2812	1300
Folding plate camera	9x12cm	plate	H&S	1906	Periscop	11		pneumatic		Mc240	100
Folding plate camera	9x12cm	plate	H&S	1905	Periscop	9	135mm			Mc240	90
Furror Geheim-Camera	9x12cm	plate	MagBox	1893	Rapid Aplanat	8	160mm	3-speed		A2808	700
Gnom (metal) 4.5x6	4.5x6cm	plate	MagBox	1900	Meniscus			rotary		Mc240	270
Gnom (metal) 6x9	6x9cm	plate	MagBox	1900	Meniscus			rotary		Mc240	270
Gnom (metal) 6.5x9	6.5x9cm	plate	MagBox	1900	Meniscus			rotary		Mc240	270
Gnom (metal) 9x12	9x12cm	plate	MagBox	1900	Meniscus			rotary	M,Z	Mc240	270
Gnom (wood) 4.5x6	4.5x6cm	plate	MagBox	1905					M,Z	Mc240	110
Hekla	9x12cm	plate	FoldPl	1906	Extra Rap. Aplan.	8	130mm	focal plane			120
Helios	9x12cm	plate	StrutPl	1907	Anastigmat	4.5	185mm	focal plane	6-1000	Mc240	140
Helios Stereo	9x18cm	plate	StStrut	1907	Extra Rap. Aplan.	8	130mm	focal plane		HK458	270
Ideal 6.5x9	6.5x9cm	plate	VtFoldPl	1908	Helios	8	105mm	Automat	25-100,B,T		80
Ideal 9x12	9x12cm	plate	VtFoldPl	1908	Lloyd	8	125mm	Automat	25-100,B,T	Mc240	70
Ideal 13x18	13x18cm	plate	VtFoldPl	1908	Helios	8	190mm	Automat	25-100,B,T		70
Ideal Stereo 6x13	6x13cm	plate	StFoldPl	1907	Extra Rap. Aplan.	8	105mm	Ster. Automat	1-100,T,B	Mc240	220
Ideal Stereo 9x13	9x13cm	plate	StFoldPl	1907	Extra Rap. Aplan.	8	125mm	Ster. Automat	1-100,T,B		160
Ideal Stereo 9x18	9x18cm	plate	StFoldPl	1907	Lloyd	6.8	120mm	Sector	1-250		260
Juwel	13x18cm	plate	FoldPl	1905	Extra Rap. Anast.	8	130mm	Lloyd	1-100,B,T,	Mc240	270

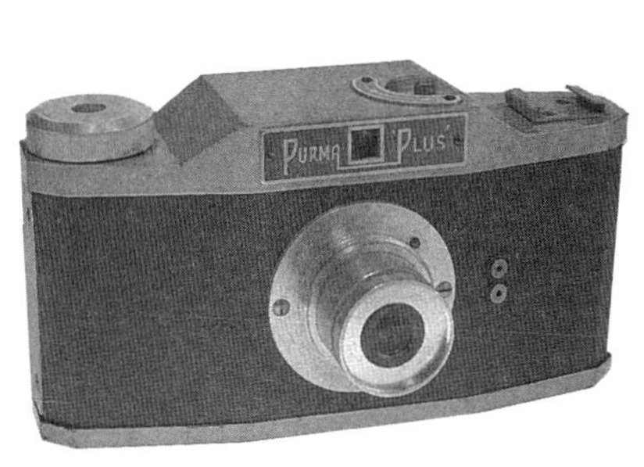

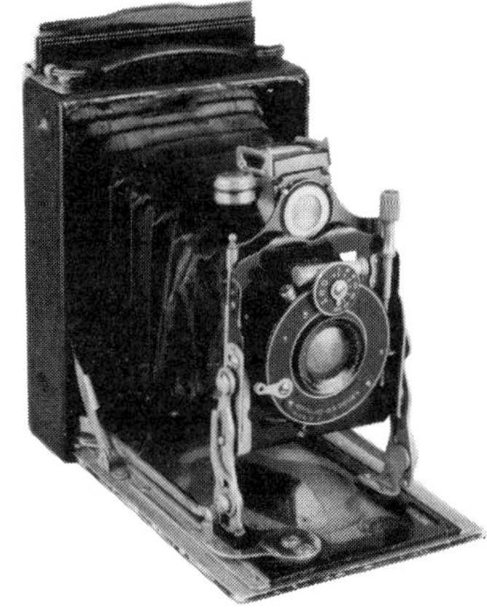

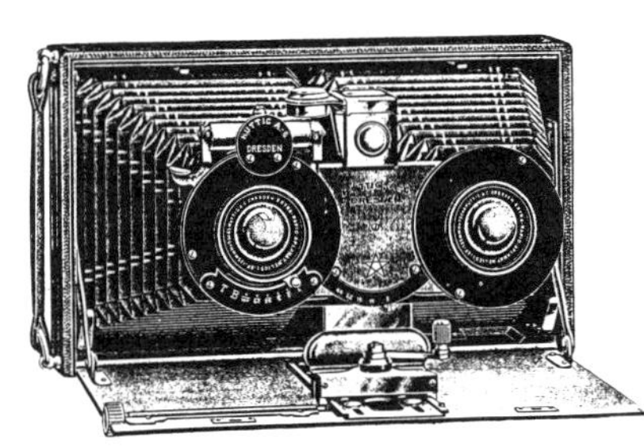

Purma Plus — **Hüttig Cupido** — **Hüttig Ideal Stereo**

MODEL	FORMAT	FILM	TYPE	Year	LENS	Apert	FL	SHUTTER	SPEEDS	ILLUS	U.S.$
Künstler-Camera 6.5x9	6.5x9cm	plate	LgSLR	1906	Tessar	4.5		focal plane	1-1000		200
Künstler-Camera 9x12	9x12cm	plate	LgSLR	1906	Lloyd	6.8	180mm	focal plane	1-1000	A1591	230
Künstler-Camera 13x18	13x18cm	plate	LgSLR	1906	Novar	6	180mm	focal plane	1-1000		230
Lloyd 8x10.5	8x10.5cm	124/pl	FoldRo	1905	Goerz Doppel An.	4.8	120mm	Compound	1-250	A370	100
Lloyd 8x14	8x14cm	122	FoldRo	1905	Helios	8	150mm	Compound	1-250		100
Lloyd 9x12	9x12cm	124/pl	FoldRo	1905	Universal Aplanat	8	130mm	Compound	1-250	A182	120
Lloyd 9x12	9x12cm	plate	FoldRo	1905	Goerz Dagor	6.8	135mm	Compound	1-250		90
Lloyd 13x18	13x18cm	plate	FoldRo	1905	Extra Rap. Aplan.	8		focal plane			220
Magazine camera 6.5x9	6.5x9cm	plate	MagBox	1900	Focusing Aplanat			single speed			70
Magazine camera 9x12	9x12cm	plate	MagBox	1900	Focusing Aplanat			single speed			70
Merkur No. 11 6x9	6x9cm	plate	MagBox	1905	Achromat	11			M,Z		90
Merkur No. 12 6.5x9	6.5x9cm	plate	MagBox	1905	Achromat	11			M,Z		90
Merkur No. 13 6x9	6x9cm	plate	MagBox	1905	Achromat	11			M,Z	A1322	90
Merkur No. 14 6.5x9	6.5x9cm	plate	MagBox	1905	Achromat	11			M,Z	HK60	90
Merkur No. 15 9x12	9x12cm	plate	MagBox	1906	Achromat	11			M,Z		80
Merkur No. 16 9x12	9x12cm	plate	MagBox	1906	Achromat	11			M,Z	Mc240	80
Monopol No. 20 12x16.5	12x16.5cm	plate	MagBox	1900	Zeiss Anast						270
Monopol No. 21 13x18	13x18cm	plate	MagBox	1900	D.A.Goerz						200
Monopol No. 27 6x9	6x9cm	plate	MagBox	1905	Achromat						70
Monopol No. 28 6.5x9	6.5x9cm	plate	MagBox	1905	Achromat					Mc240	70
Monopol No. 29 9x12	9x12cm	plate	MagBox	1905	Achromat						100
Nelson No. 113C 9x12	9x12cm	plate	FoldPl	1907	Hüttig Aplanat	8	125mm	pneumatic	1-100,B,T		70
Nelson No. 113F 9x12	9x12cm	plate	FoldPl	1907	D.A.Lloyd	6.8	135mm	Compound	1-250		70
Novitas 9x12	9x12cm	plate	MagBox	1900	Universal Aplanat	16					80
Record Stereo 9x12	9x12cm	plate	StStrut	1908	Aristostigmat	6.8	120mm	focal plane		Mc240	410
Record Stereo 9x18	9x18cm	plate	StStrut	1908	Aristostigmat	6.8	120mm	focal plane			330
Reicka 685 10x15	10x15cm	plate	StFoldPl	1908	Hekla	6.8	120mm			A2984	900
Reicka 9x12	9x12cm	plate	FoldPl	1908	Tessar	6.3	150mm			A2984	100
Spiegel-Reflex I No. 55	9x12cm	plate	LgSLR	1898	Universal Aplanat	16				HK316	360
Spiegel-Reflex I No. 56	12x16.5cm	plate	LgSLR	1898	Universal Aplanat	16					360
Spiegel-Reflex I No. 57	13x18cm	plate	LgSLR	1898	Universal Aplanat	16					370
Spiegel-Reflex II No. 59	9x12cm	plate	LgSLR	1900	Universal Aplanat	16				HK314	360
Spiegel-Reflex II No. 60	12x16.5cm	plate	LgSLR	1900	Universal Aplanat	16					360
Spiegel-Reflex II No. 61	13x18cm	plate	LgSLR	1900	Universal Aplanat	16					370
Stereo Detective	9x18cm	plate	SterBox	1900					M,Z		630
Stereo Lloyd 9x18	9x18cm	plate	StFoldPl	1905	Rapid Aplanat	8	125mm	Compound	1-250	A779	240
Stereo Lloyd 9x18	9x18cm	plate	StFoldPl	1905	Novar	6	125mm	Compound	1-250	HK454	240
Stereolette	45x107	plate	StFoldPl	1909	Helios	8	65mm	I,B,T			260
Toska	9x12cm	plate	FoldPl	1907	Univ.Rap.Aplanat	7	130mm				60
Trilby No. 30	9x12cm	plate	MagBox	1905	Achromat			Automat	M,Z,1-100	Mc241	110
Trilby No. 33	9x12cm	plate	MagBox	1905	Helios	8		Automat	M,Z	A1321	110
Tropical plate camera	6x9cm	plate	FoldPl		Steinheil Triplan	4.5	135mm	Compound	1-150		630

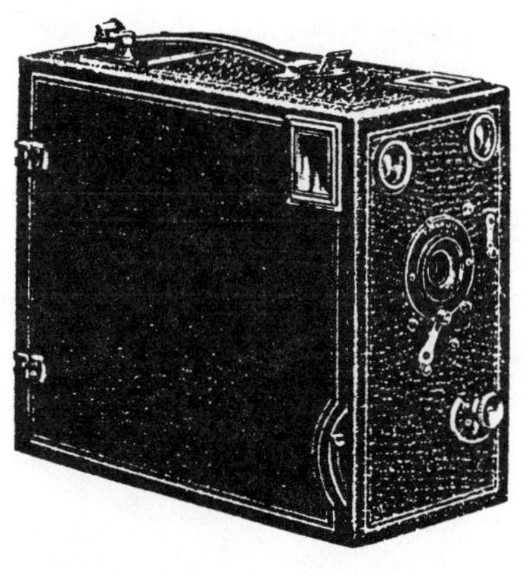

Monopol No. 28

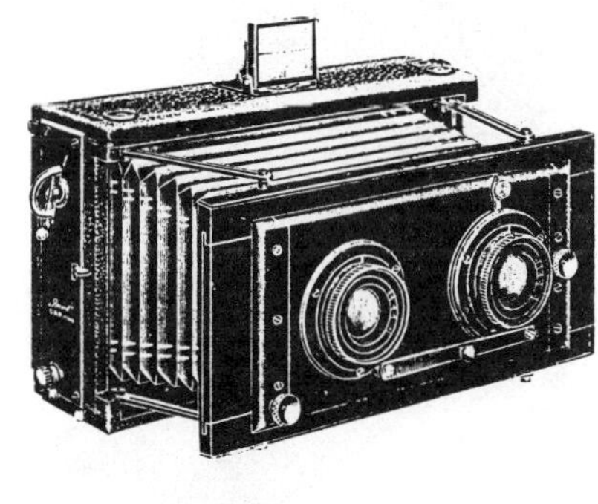

Record Stereo

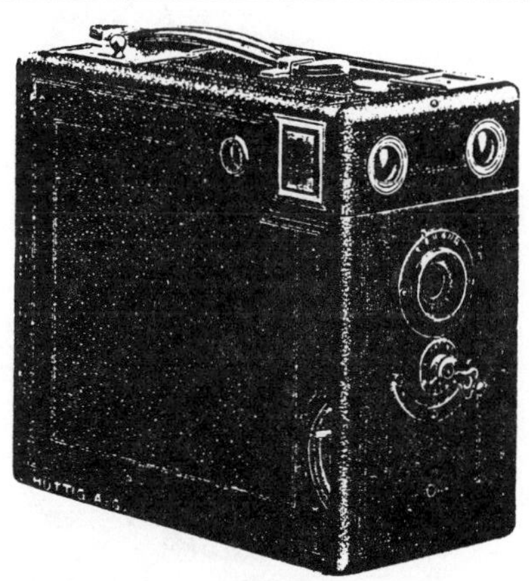

Triby No. 30

MODEL	FORMAT	FILM	TYPE	Year	LENS	Apert	FL	SHUTTER	SPEEDS	ILLUS	U.S.$
Unicum (leather)	6.5x9cm	plate	Platebox	1910	Aplanat				M,Z	A97	100
Unicum (wood) No. 101	6x9cm	plate	Platebox	1900	Aplanat				M,Z		180
Unicum (wood) No. 102	9x12cm	plate	Platebox	1900	Aplanat				M,Z		180
Zeus Mod. I (No. 6)	9x12cm	plate	LgSLR	1896	Periscop			focal plane		HK312	700
Zeus Mod. II No. 54 6.5x9	6.5x9cm	plate	LgSLR	1897	Aplanat			focal plane			580
Zeus Mod. II No. 54 9x12	9x12cm	plate	LgSLR	1897	Aplanat			focal plane			500
...ICA A.G. - Dresden											
Alpha 175	9x12cm	plate	FoldPl	1914	Helios	8	130mm	Compound	1-250		70
Alpha 490	6x6cm	plate	HzFoldRo	1919	Periskop	12.5	75mm		1/40	Mc241	80
Alpha 492	6x6cm	plate	HzFoldRo	1919	Novar	6.8	75mm		1/40		80
Atom 50 (vertical)	4.5x6cm	plate	FoldPl	1909	Rapid Rectilinear	8			IBT	Mc241	220
Atom 51 (vertical)	4.5x6cm	plate	FoldPl	1909	Hekla	6.8	65mm	Compound	1-300		220
Atom 53 R (horizontal)	4.5x6cm	plate	FoldPl	1909	Hekla	6.8	65mm	Compound	1-300		290
Atom 53 U (horizontal)	4.5x6cm	plate	FoldPl	1909	Tessar	4.5	65mm	Compound	1-300	Mc241	290
Aviso 1	4.5x6cm	plate	MagBox	1914	Landschaft		70mm	single speed	M,Z	A1334	150
Aviso 4	4.5x6cm	plate	Platebox	1919	Landschaft		70mm	single speed	M,Z	A1333	160
Bébé 40	4.5x6cm	plate	StrutPl	1911	Novar	6.8	75mm	Compound	1-250		210
Bébé 41 E	6.5x9cm	plate	StrutPl	1911	Novar	6.8	120mm	Dial-Compur		A315	180
Bébé 41 U	6.5x9cm	plate	StrutPl	1911	Tessar	4.5	120mm	Dial-Compur		HK155	180
Bosco 2 (Serie J)	6x9cm	120	RollBox	1925							160
Briefmarken Camera	9x12cm	plate	MultiLens	1910	15-lenses						4400
Cameo Stereo	9x18cm	plate	StFoldPl	1913	Helios	8	130mm				200
Corrida 151	9x12cm	plate	VtFoldPl	1910	Helios	8	130mm	Automat	1-100		60
Corrida 155	9x12cm	plate	VtFoldPl	1912	Novar	6.8	135mm	Automat	1-100		60
Corrida 156	9x12cm	plate	VtFoldPl	1914	Tessar	6.3	135mm	Automat	1-100		60
Cupido 75	6.5x9cm	plate	VtFoldPl	1914	Lloyd	6.8	115mm	Dial-Compur		Mc241	70
Cupido 75 H	6.5x9cm	plate	VtFoldPl	1914	Maximar	6.8	115mm	Dial-Compur		Mc241	70
Cupido 75 U	6.5x9cm	plate	VtFoldPl	1914	Tessar	4.5	12cm	Dial-Compur		Mc241	70
Cupido 77	9x12cm	plate	VtFoldPl	1914	Litonar	4.5	12cm	Compound			50
Cupido 80	9x12cm	plate	VtFoldPl	1914	Dagor	6.8	135mm	Compound		Mc241	50
Delta	9x12cm	plate	FoldPl	1912	Hekla	6.8	135mm	Compound			60
Elegant	13x18cm	plate	Tailboard	1910							210
Excelsior	24x30mm	plate	Field	1916	Trinar	6.3	300mm				1000
Favorit 265	9x12cm	plate	FoldPl	1925	Hekla	6.8	135mm	Compur		Mc241	70
Favorit 266 (tropical)	9x12cm	plate	FoldPl	1925	Tessar	4.5	150mm	Compur			410
Favorit 335	10x15cm	plate	FoldPl	1925	Dominar	4.5	165mm	Compur			110
Favorit 425	13x18cm	plate	FoldPl	1925	Icar	6.3	210mm	Dial-Compur	1-150		220
Halloh 505	8x10.5cm	124	FoldRo	1914	Litonar	6.8	135mm	Dial-Compur	1-250,B,T		60
Halloh 506	8x10.5cm	124	FoldRo	1914	Tessar	4.5	12cm	Dial-Compur	1-250,B,T	Mc241	60
Halloh 510	8x10.5cm	124	FoldRo	1914	Hekla	6.8	135mm	Automat	25-100		70
Halloh 511	8x10.5cm	124	FoldRo	1914	Tessar	4.5	12cm	Dial-Compur	1-250,B,T		70
Halloh 570	8x14cm	122	FoldRo	1914	Helios	8	150mm	Dial-Compur	1-250,B,T		100

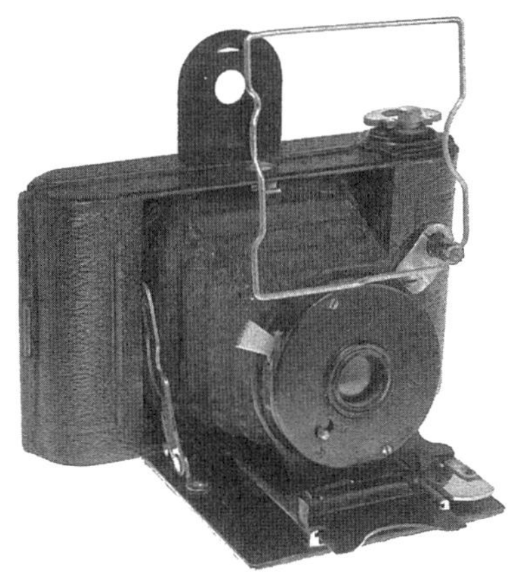

Ica Alpha

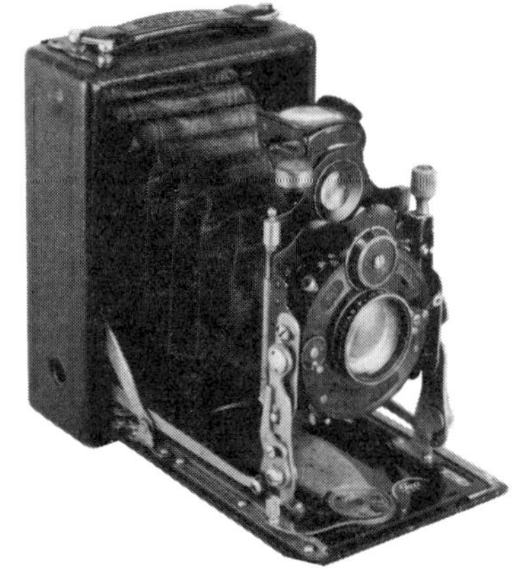

Ica Cupido 75 H

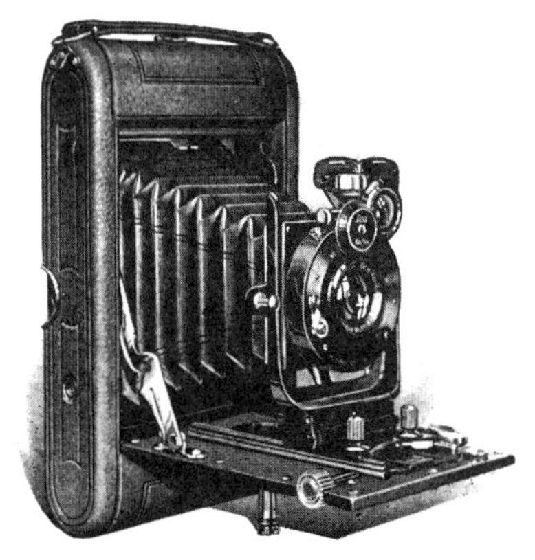

Ica Halloh 506

MODEL	FORMAT	FILM	TYPE	Year	LENS	Apert	FL	SHUTTER	SPEEDS	ILLUS	U.S.$
Hekla 168	9x12cm	plate	FoldPl	1912	Hekla Anastigmat	6.8	135mm	Automat	25-100		50
Hochtourist 820	13x18cm	plate	Field	1914	Tessar	4.5	210mm				360
Hochtourist 821	18x24cm	plate	Field	1914	Tessar	4.5	210mm				570
Hochtourist 823	13x18cm	plate	Field	1914	Trinar	6.3					360
Hochtourist 824	18x24cm	plate	Field	1914	Helioplan	4.5	210mm				570
Icar 180	9x12cm	plate	FoldPl	1913	Dominar	4.5	135mm	Dial-Compur	1-200,T,B		50
Icarette I 495	6x6cm	120	HzFoldRo	1921	Helios	8	75mm	Automat	25-100	A398	80
Icarette I 495 Z	6x6cm	120	HzFoldRo	1921	Icar	6.3	75mm	Automat	25-100	Mc242	80
Icarette I 496 Z	6x6cm	120/pl	HzFoldRo	1921	Icar	6.3	75mm	Automat	25-100	Mc242	110
Icarette II 500	6x9cm	120	VtFoldRo	1922	Tessar	6.3	120mm	Compur	1-250		70
Icarette III 501	6.5x11cm	116	VtFoldRo	1919	Hekla	6.8	12cm	Compur			70
Icarette III 502	6.5x11cm	116	VtFoldRo	1919	Novar	6.8	135mm	Derval			70
Icarette IIIA 503	6.5x11cm	116	VtFoldRo	1924	Helios	8	135mm	Automat	25-100		70
Ideal 111	6.5x9cm	plate	VtFoldPl	1915	Tessar	6.3	90mm	Dial-Compur		A265	70
Ideal 205	9x12cm	plate	VtFoldPl	1915	Hekla	6.8	135mm	Dial-Compur			70
Ideal 225	9x12cm	plate	VtFoldPl	1915	Tessar	4.5	150mm	Dial-Compur			90
Ideal 246	9x12cm	plate	VtFoldPl	1915	Helios	8	130mm	Dial-Compur		Mc242	70
Ideal 325	10x15cm	plate	VtFoldPl	1915	Hekla	6.8	165mm	Dial-Compur			140
Ideal 385	13x18cm	plate	VtFoldPl	1915	Tessar	4.5	210mm	Dial-Compur			110
Ingo 395 E	13x18cm	plate	HzFoldPl	1914	Novar Anastigmat	6.8	180mm	Automat	25-100		110
Ingo 395 R	13x18cm	plate	HzFoldPl	1914	Hekla	6.8	180mm	Automat	25-100		110
Ingo 395 U	13x18cm	plate	HzFoldPl	1914	Tessar	4.5	180mm	Automat	25-100		110
Jul 400	13x18cm	plate	HzFoldPl	1910	Helios	8	190mm	Automat	1-100		140
Jul 400 E	13x18cm	plate	HzFoldPl	1910	Novar	6.8	180mm	Automat	1-100		140
Jul 400 U	13x18cm	plate	HzFoldPl	1910	Tessar	4.5	180mm	Compur	1-250		140
Juwel 270 R	9x12cm	plate	FoldPl	1909	Double Anast.	6.8	135mm	Compound			240
Juwel 270 Z	9x12cm	plate	FoldPl	1909	Icar	6.3	135mm	Automat	1-100		240
Juwel 440 H	13x18cm	plate	FoldPl	1910	Double Anast.	6.8	18cm	Compound			300
Juwel 440 U	13x18cm	plate	FoldPl	1910	Tessar	4.5	21cm	Compound			300
Künstler Reflex 748 H	6x9cm	plate	LgSLR	1910	Maximar	6.8	135mm	focal plane	-1000	Mc243	220
Künstler Reflex 748 U	6x9cm	plate	LgSLR	1910	Tessar	4.5	135mm	focal plane	-1000	Mc243	220
Künstler Reflex 750 H	9x12cm	plate	LgSLR	1910	Maximar	6.8	165mm	focal plane	15-1000		210
Künstler Reflex 750 S	9x12cm	plate	LgSLR	1910	Amatar	6.8	180mm	focal plane	15-1000		210
Künstler Reflex 750 U	9x12cm	plate	LgSLR	1910	Tessar	4.5	150mm	focal plane	15-1000	A1592	210
Klapp-Palmos 255 U	9x12cm	plate	HzFoldPl	1910	Tessar	4.5	150mm	focal plane	15-1000	A244	160
Klapp-Palmos 255 V	9x12cm	plate	HzFoldPl	1910	Protar	6.3	13cm	focal plane	15-1000		160
Klapp-Stereo-Palmos 695S	9x12cm	plate	StFoldPl	1910	Dopp.-Amatar	6.8	13.5cm	focal plane	1/30-1000		480
Klapp-Stereo-Palmos 695T	9x12cm	plate	StFoldPl	1910	Tessar	6.3	15cm	focal plane	1/30-1000		560
Klapp-Stereo-Palmos 695U	9x12cm	plate	StFoldPl	1910	Tessar	4.5	15cm	focal plane	1/30-1000		480
Klappreflex 6.5x9 K	6.5x9cm	plate	FoldSLR	1925	Dominar	4.5		focal plane			270
Klappreflex 6.5x9 U	6.5x9cm	plate	FoldSLR	1925	Tessar	4.5		focal plane		A1589	270
Klappreflex 755K	9x12cm	plate	FoldSLR	1924	Dominar	4.5	150mm	focal plane			270

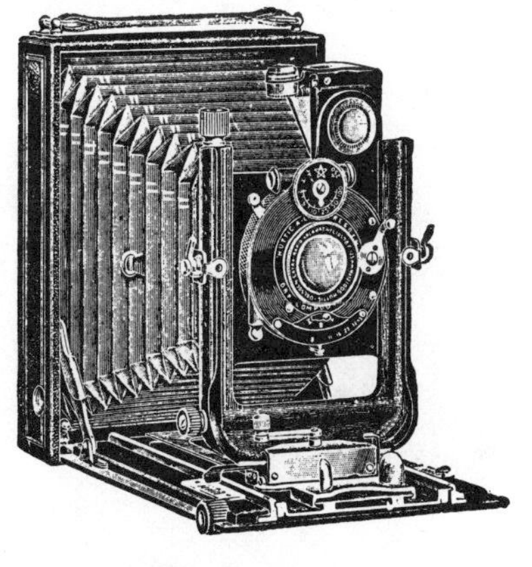

Ica Ideal 246

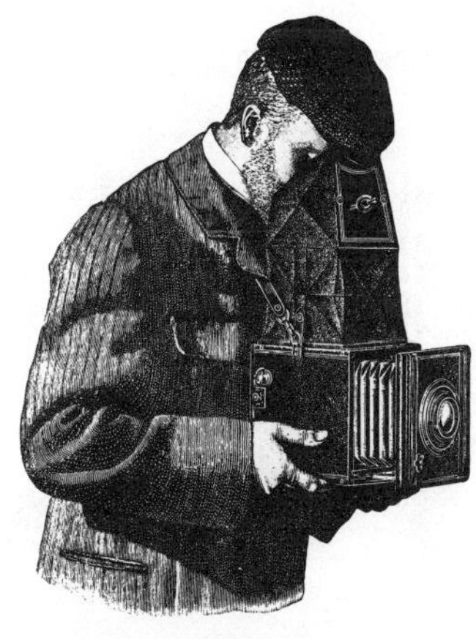

Ica Künstler Reflex 748 H

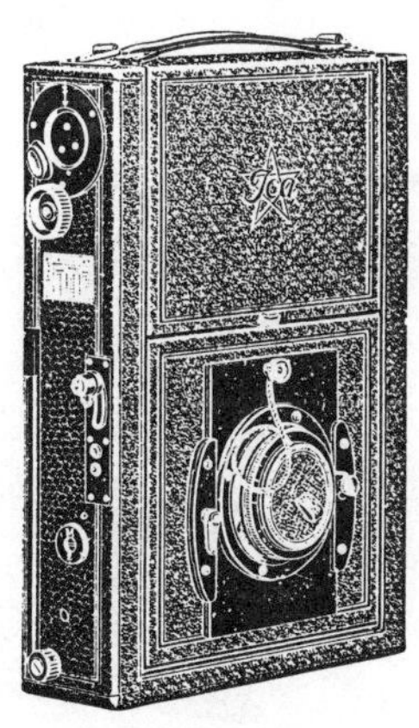

Ica Klappreflex 755K

MODEL	FORMAT	FILM	TYPE	Year	LENS	Apert	FL	SHUTTER	SPEEDS	ILLUS	U.S.$
Klappreflex 755U	9x12cm	plate	FoldSLR	1924	Tessar	4.5	150mm	focal plane		A1590	270
Lloyd 510E	8x10.5cm	124	FoldRo	1922	Novar	6.8	135mm	Compur	1-200		70
Lloyd 510T	8x10.5cm	124	FoldRo	1922	Tessar	6.3	135mm	Compur	1-200		70
Lloyd 535E	8x10.5cm	124	FoldRo	1910	Novar	6.8	135mm	Automat	25-100		60
Lloyd 535K	8x10.5cm	124	FoldRo	1910	Dominar	4.5	135mm	Compur	1-200		60
Lloyd 575E	8x14cm	122	FoldRo	1912	Novar	6.8	150mm	Automat	25-100		100
Lloyd 575T	8x14cm	122	FoldRo	1912	Tessar	6.3	150mm	Compur	1-200		100
Lloyd 575Z	8x14cm	122	FoldRo	1912	Icar	6.3	150mm	Compur	1-200		100
Lloyd Stereo 660C	9x18cm	Roll/pl	StFoldRo	1910	Double Anast.	6.8	120mm	Compur	1-150		320
Lloyd Stereo 660R	9x18cm	Roll/pl	StFoldRo	1910	Double Anast.	6.8	120mm	St.Compound	1-100		320
Lloyd Stereo 660T	9x18cm	Roll/pl	StFoldRo	1910	Tessar	6.3	120mm	Compur	1-150		320
Lloyd Stereo 660T	9x18cm	Roll/pl	StFoldRo	1910	Tessar	6.3	120mm	St.Compound	1-100		320
Lloyd-Cupido 540R	8x10.5cm	124	VtFoldRo	1910	Hekla	6.8	135mm	Compound			150
Lloyd-Cupido 540T	8x10.5cm	124	VtFoldRo	1910	Tessar	6.3	135mm	Compound		A368	150
Lloyd-Cupido 560R	8x10.5cm	124	HzFoldRo	1922	Hekla	6.8	100mm	Compound		A1446	150
Lloyd-Cupido 560T	8x10.5cm	124	HzFoldRo	1922	Tessar	6.3	135mm	Compound			150
Lola 135	9x12cm	plate	VtFoldPl	1912	Periskop Alpha	11		Automatic	25-100		50
Lola 136	9x12cm	plate	VtFoldPl	1914	Periskop Alpha	11		Automatic	25-100		50
Lola 511E	8x10.5cm	124	VtFoldRo	1922	Novar	6.8		Automatic	25-100		70
Lola 511T	8x10.5cm	124	VtFoldRo	1922	Tessar	6.3		Compur			70
Lola 511Z	8x10.5cm	124	VtFoldRo	1922	Icar	6.3		Automatic	25-100		70
Maximar 107K	6.5x9cm	plate	VtFoldPl	1924	Dominar	4.5	105mm	Compur			90
Maximar 107Q	6.5x9cm	plate	VtFoldPl	1924	Litonar	4.5	105mm	Compur			90
Maximar 207C	9x12cm	plate	VtFoldPl	1914	Litonar	4.5	135mm	Compur			70
Maximar 207E	9x12cm	plate	VtFoldPl	1914	Novar	4.5	135mm	Compound			70
Maximar 207H	9x12cm	plate	VtFoldPl	1914	Maximar	6.8	135mm	Compur			70
Maximar 207R	9x12cm	plate	VtFoldPl	1914	Hekla	6.8	135mm	Compound		A263	70
Maximar 207S	9x12cm	plate	VtFoldPl	1914	Amatar	6.8	135mm	Compound			70
Maximar 207T	9x12cm	plate	VtFoldPl	1914	Tessar	6.3	135mm	Compur			70
Minimal 235	9x12cm	Sheet	VtFoldPl	1912	Goerz Dagor	6.8	120mm	Compound		Mc242	70
Minimal 235R	9x12cm	Sheet	VtFoldPl	1912	Hekla	6.8	135mm	Automatic		Mc242	70
Minimum Palmos 450P	4.5x6cm	plate	StrutPl	1925	Zeiss Tessar	2.7	80mm	focal plane	50-1000		440
Minimum Palmos 450T	4.5x6cm	plate	StrutPl	1925	Zeiss Tessar	4.5	80mm	focal plane	50-1000		380
Minimum Palmos 454T	6x9cm	plate	StrutPl	1909	Zeiss Tessar	4.5	120mm	focal plane	50-1000	A306	190
Minimum Palmos 454U	6.5x9cm	plate	StrutPl	1909	Zeiss Tessar	6.3	120mm	focal plane	50-1000	Mc242	190
Minimum Palmos 455T	3¼x4¼"	plate	StrutPl	1909	Zeiss Tessar	6.3	15cm	focal plane	50-1000	Mc242	180
Minimum Palmos 455U	3¼x4¼"	plate	StrutPl	1909	Zeiss Tessar	4.5	15cm	focal plane	50-1000	Mc242	180
Minimum Palmos 456T	9x12cm	plate	StrutPl	1909	Zeiss Tessar	6.3	120mm	focal plane	50-1000	Mc242	160
Minimum Palmos 456U	9x12cm	plate	StrutPl	1909	Zeiss Tessar	4.5	120mm	focal plane	50-1000	Mc242	160
Minimum Palmos 457T	10x15cm	plate	StrutPl	1909	Zeiss Tessar	6.3	165mm	focal plane	50-1000		240
Minimum Palmos 457U	10x15cm	plate	StrutPl	1909	Zeiss Tessar	4.5	165mm	focal plane	50-1000		240
Nelson 225	9x12cm	plate	VtFoldPl	1912	Tessar	4.5	135mm	Compound	T,B,1-150		70

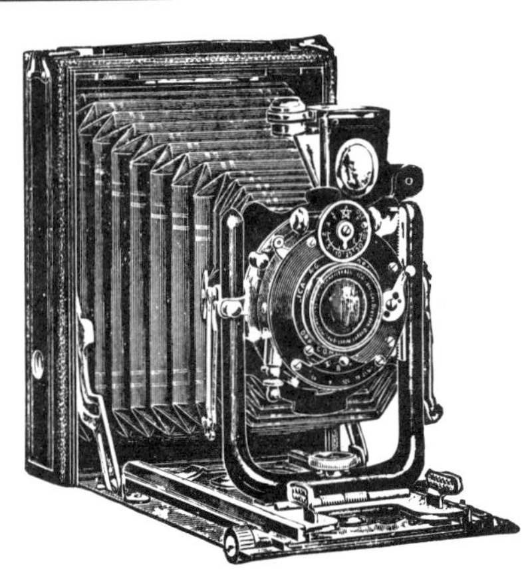

Ica Minimal 235

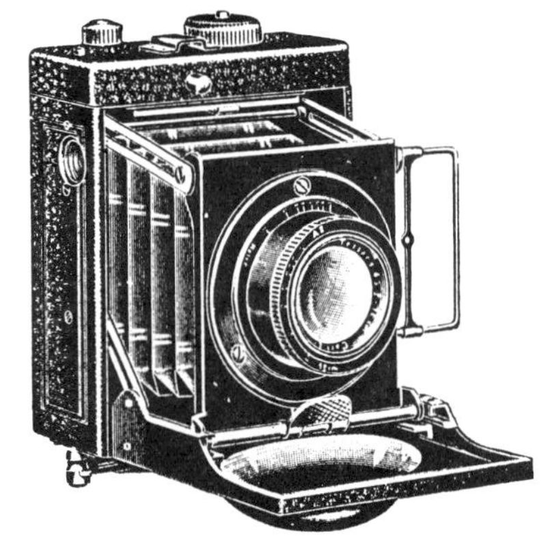

Ica Minimum Palmos 450

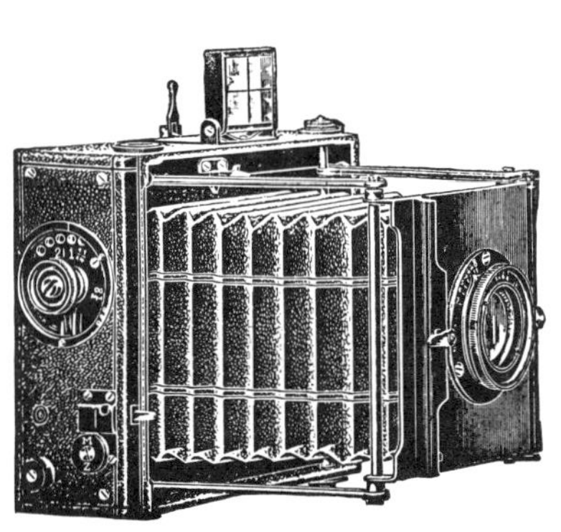

Ica Minimum Palmos 455

MODEL	FORMAT	FILM	TYPE	Year	LENS	Apert	FL	SHUTTER	SPEEDS	ILLUS	U.S.$
Nelson 226	9x12cm	plate	VtFoldPl	1912	Tessar	4.5	135mm	Compound	T,B,1-150		70
Nero 9x12	9x12cm	plate	MagBox	1905				guillotine	I,T	Mc242	80
Niklas 109E	6.5x9cm	plate	VtFoldPl	192x	Novar	4.5	10.5cm	Compur		Mc243	90
Niklas 109U	6.5x9cm	plate	VtFoldPl	192x	Tessar	4.5	120mm	Compur		Mc243	90
Niklas 205G	9x12cm	plate	VtFoldPl	1924	Dominar	4.5	135mm	Compur	1-200		100
Niklas 205S	9x12cm	plate	VtFoldPl	1924	Amatar	6.8	135mm	Compur	1-200		100
Niklas 205U	9x12cm	plate	VtFoldPl	1924	Tessar	4.5	135mm	Compur	1-200		100
Niklas 365C	13x18cm	plate	VtFoldPl	1922	Litonar	6.8	18cm	Compur	1-200		170
Niklas 365UU	13x18cm	plate	VtFoldPl	1922	Tessar	4.5	21cm	Compur	1-200		170
Nixe 555D	9x12cm	plate	VtFoldRo	1909	Helios	8	130mm	Compound	T,B,1-150	Mc243	110
Nixe 555D	9x12cm	plate	VtFoldRo	1909	Helios	8	130mm	Automat	1-100	Mc243	110
Nixe 555U	9x12cm	plate	VtFoldRo	1909	Tessar	4.5	135mm	Compur	1-200	Mc243	110
Nixe 555Z	9x12cm	plate	VtFoldRo	1909	Icar	6.3	135mm	Compur	1-200	Mc243	110
Nixe 595D	9x14cm	122	VtFoldRo	1909	Helios	8	150mm	Automat	1-100		80
Nixe 595T	9x14cm	122	VtFoldRo	1909	Tessar	6.3	150mm	Compur	1-200		80
Nixe 595Z	9x14cm	122	VtFoldRo	1909	Icar	6.3	165mm	Compur	1-200		80
Nixe 595Z	9x14cm	122	VtFoldRo	1909	Icar	6.3	165mm	Automat	1-100		80
Onix 37 (Onix II)	6x9cm	120	RollBox	1924	Achromat	12.5	12cm				100
Onix 38	6.5x11cm	116	RollBox	1925	Achromat	12.5	14cm				160
Orix 209/O	9x12cm	plate	VtFoldPl	1924	Litonar	4.5	135mm	Compur	1-200		50
Orix 209/U	9x12cm	plate	VtFoldPl	1924	Tessar	4.5	135mm	Compur	1-200		50
Orix 308C	10x15cm	plate	VtFoldPl	1914	Litonar	6.8	16.5cm	Compur	1-200		70
Orix 308J	10x15cm	plate	VtFoldPl	1914	Maximar	5.4	15cm	Compur	1-200		70
Perfekt 13x18	13x18cm	plate	Field	1910	Trinar	6.3					210
Perfekt 18x24	18x24cm	plate	Field	1910	Trinar	6.3					270
Perfekt 24x30	24x30cm	plate	Field	1910	Trinar	6.3	300mm				500
Periscop 9x12	9x12cm	plate	FoldPl	1909	Alpha	9.5	115mm				60
Plaskop 602	6x13cm	plate	StJumelle	1924	Novar Anastigmat	6.8	7.5cm	guillotine	M,Z	HK499	200
Plaskop 603	45x107	plate	StJumelle	1922	Achromat	12.5	65mm	guillotine	M,Z	Mc243	140
Plaskop 603/2	45x107	plate	StJumelle	1922	Novar Anastigmat	6.8	65mm	guillotine	M,Z	Mc243	140
Polyscop 603	45x107	plate	StJumelle	1911	Achromat		65mm		M,Z	A730	200
Polyscop 603/1	45x107	plate	StJumelle	1911	Achromat		65mm		M,Z		200
Polyscop 605	45x107	plate	StJumelle	1911	Hekla	6.8	65mm		3-150		200
Polyscop 605/1E	45x107	plate	StJumelle	1911	Novar	6.8	65mm		3-150	A736	200
Polyscop 605/1U	45x107	plate	StJumelle	1911	Tessar	4.5	65mm	Compur	1-250	A732	200
Polyscop 606	45x107	plate	StJumelle	1911	Tessar	6.3	65mm	Compur	1-250		210
Polyscop 606/1	45x107	plate	StJumelle	1911	Hekla	6.8	65mm	Compur	3-150		220
Polyscop 607	45x107	plate	StJumelle	1911	Novar	6.8	65mm		3-150		230
Polyscop 607/1	45x107	plate	StJumelle	1911	Tessar	6.3	65mm	Compur	1-250		240
Polyscop 608	45x107	plate	StStrut	1911	Hekla	6.8	65mm	Compur	3-250		290
Polyscop 608/1	45x107	plate	StStrut	1911	Tessar	6.3	65mm	Compur	3-250	A737	290
Polyscop 608/2R	45x107	plate	StStrut	1911	Hekla	6.8	65mm	Compur	3-250		290

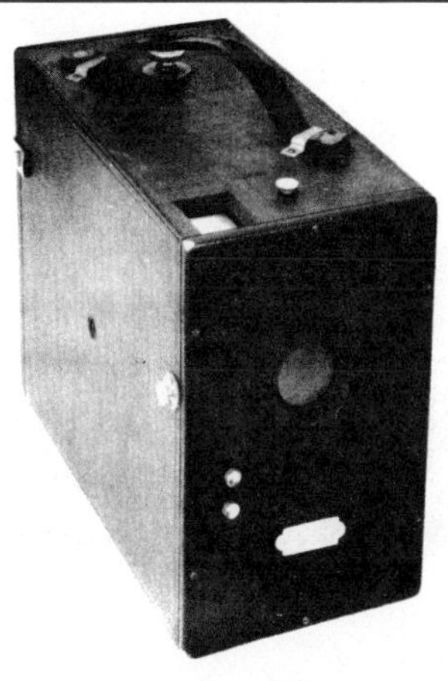

Ica Nero

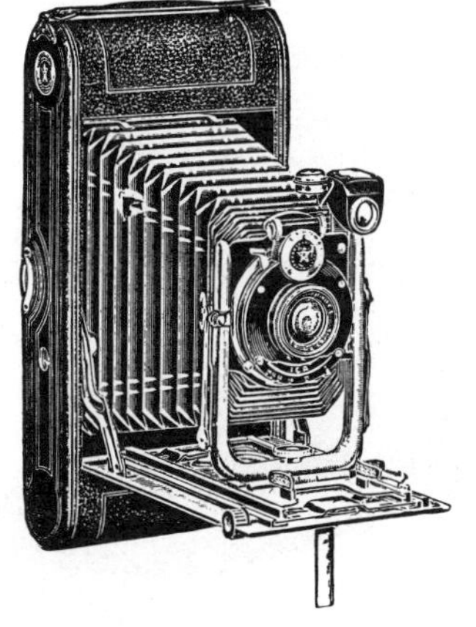

Ica Nixe 555

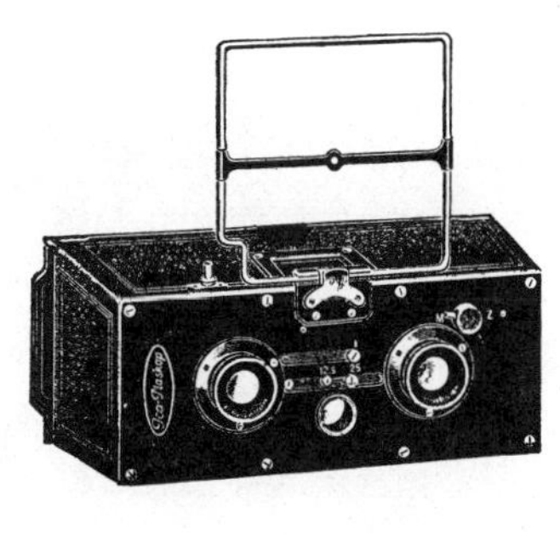

Ica Plaskop

MODEL	FORMAT	FILM	TYPE	Year	LENS	Apert	FL	SHUTTER	SPEEDS	ILLUS	U.S.$
Polyscop 608/2U	45x107	plate	StStrut	1911	Tessar	6.3	65mm	Compur	3-250		290
Polyscop 608/3R	45x107	plate	StStrut	1911	Hekla	6.8	65mm	Compur	3-250		200
Polyscop 608/3U	45x107	plate	StStrut	1911	Tessar	4.5	65mm	Compur	3-250		200
Polyscop 609R	6x13cm	plate	StJumelle	1911	Hekla	6.8	90mm		1-150		220
Polyscop 609U	6x13cm	plate	StJumelle	1911	Tessar	6.3	90mm	Compur	1-250		220
Polyscop 609/1R	6x13cm	plate	StJumelle	1911	Hekla	6.8	90mm		1-150	Mc243	220
Polyscop 609/1U	6x13cm	plate	StJumelle	1911	Tessar	4.5	90mm	Compur	1-250	A735	220
Reicka 155	9x12cm	plate	FoldPl	1910	Lloyd	6.8	150mm	Automat	1-100		70
Reicka 155H	9x12cm	plate	FoldPl	1910	Maximar	6.8	165mm	Compound	T,B,1-150		70
Reicka 305D	10x15cm	plate	FoldPl	1910	Helios	8	165mm	Automat	1-100		90
Reicka 305E	10x15cm	plate	FoldPl	1910	Novar	6.8	165mm	Automat	1-100		90
Reicka 311	10x15cm	plate	FoldPl	1910	Baldour	8	165mm	Compound	T,B,1-150		90
Reicka 311L	10x15cm	plate	FoldPl	1910	Lloyd	6.8	165mm	Lloyd XI			90
Rekord 460T	9x12cm	plate	StrutPl	1910	Tessar	6.3	135mm	focal plane	15-1000	A301	130
Rekord 460U	9x12cm	plate	StrutPl	1910	Tessar	4.5	150mm	focal plane	15-1000		130
Rekord 465T	13x18cm	plate	StrutPl	1910	Tessar	6.3	180mm	focal plane	15-1000		140
Rekord 465U	13x18cm	plate	StrutPl	1910	Tessar	4.5	180mm	focal plane	15-1000		140
Sirene 105	6x9cm	plate	StrutPl	1914	Eurynar	6.8	10.5cm	Ibso			50
Sirene 105B	6x9cm	plate	StrutPl	1914	Periskop	11	12cm	Ibso			50
Sirene 135	9x12cm	plate	StrutPl	1914	Eurynar	6.8	13.5cm	Automat			50
Sirene 135B	9x12cm	plate	StrutPl	1914	Periskop	11	14.5cm	Automat			50
Stereo Atom	45x107	plate	StFoldPl	1909	Maximar	5.4	65mm	Compound	1-250	A1771	310
Stereo Ideal 650	9x18cm	plate	StFoldPl	1914	Lloyd	6.8	12cm	Automat	1-100		330
Stereo Ideal 650R	9x18cm	plate	StFoldPl	1914	Hekla	6.8	12cm	Automat	1-100		330
Stereo Ideal 650T	9x18cm	plate	StFoldPl	1914	Tessar	6.3	12cm	Compound	1-250	A1773	330
Stereo Ideal 651R	6x13cm	plate	StFoldPl	1910	Double Anast.	6.8	90mm	St.Compound		Mc243	310
Stereo Ideal 651T	6x13cm	plate	StFoldPl	1910	Tessar	6.3	90mm	St.Compound		Mc243	310
Stereo Ideal 651U	6x13cm	plate	StFoldPl	1910	Tessar	4.5	90mm	St.Compound		A765	310
Ster.Minimum Palmos 693U	6x13cm	plate	StStrut	1924	Tessar	4.5	7.5cm	focal plane	1/30-1000	A1776	540
Ster.Minimum Palmos 696	9x18cm	plate	StStrut	1924	Tessar	4.5	135mm	focal plane	1/30-1000	A751	480
Ster.Minimum Palmos 696H	9x18cm	plate	StStrut	1912	Maximar	6.8	135mm	focal plane	7-1000		480
Ster.Panorama Rekord 705	9x18cm	plate	StStrut	1912	Hekla	6.8	135mm	focal plane			330
Ster.Panorama Rekord 705	9x18cm	plate	StStrut	1912	Tessar	6.3	135mm	focal plane			330
Ster.Panorama Rekord 705	9x18cm	plate	StStrut	1912	Tessar	4.5	135mm	focal plane			330
Ster.Panorama Rekord 710	9x18cm	plate	StStrut	1914	Maximar	6.8	135mm	focal plane		A2680	460
Ster.Panorama Rekord 710	9x18cm	plate	StStrut	1914	Hekla	6.8	135mm	focal plane		A2680	460
Stereo Reicka 680	10x15cm	plate	StFoldPl	1910	Maximar	6.8	13.5cm	St.Compound		Mc243	620
Stereo Toska 680	10x15cm	plate	StFoldPl	1922	Hekla	6.8	135mm	Compound	1-250		390
Stereo-Panorama-Lloyd 67	9x18cm	Roll	StFoldRo	1910	Tessar	6.3	135mm	Automat XI	1-100	Mc242	320
Stereo-Panorama-Lloyd 67	8x14cm	122	StFoldRo	1910	Double Anast.	6.8	135mm	St.Compound	1-100	Mc242	320
Stereofix 604	45x107	plate	StJumelle	1914	Tessar	4.5	65mm	Compur	1-250	A741	220
Stereofix 604/1	45x107	plate	StJumelle	1914	Maximar	6.8	60mm	Automat	25-100		220

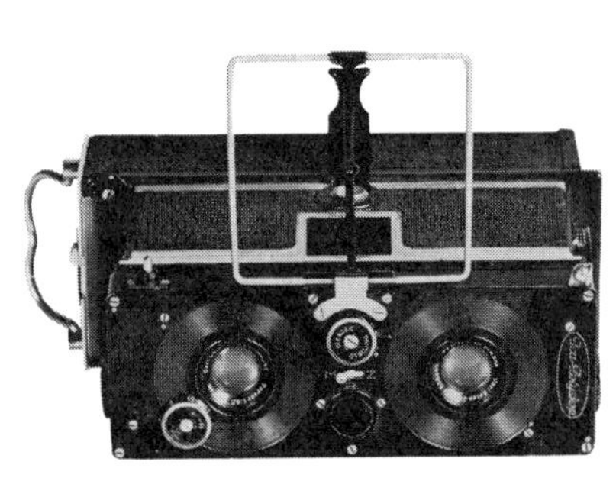

Ica Polyscop 609/1R

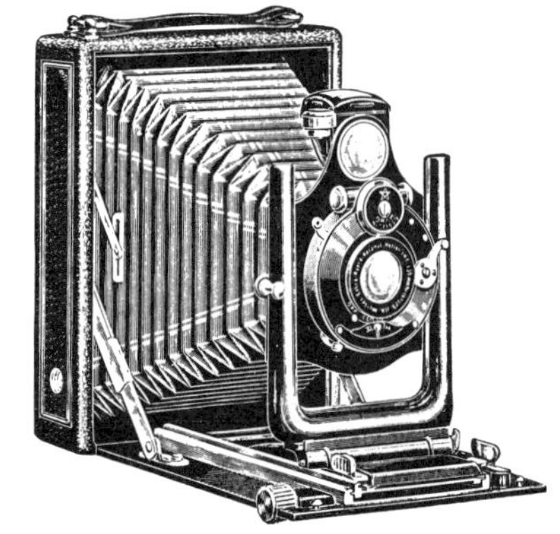

Ica Reicka 311

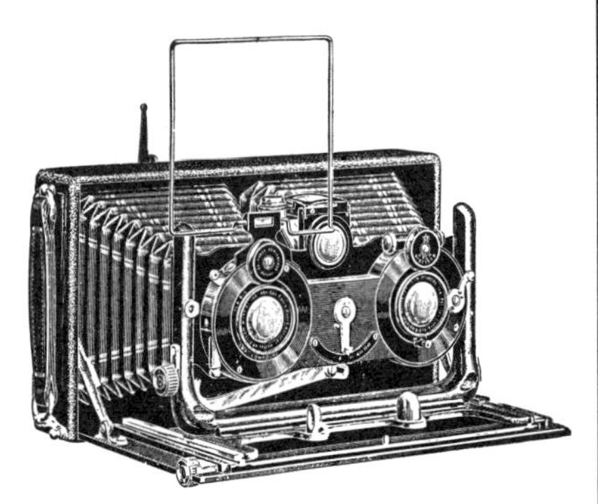

Ica Stereo Ideal 651

MODEL	FORMAT	FILM	TYPE	Year	LENS	Apert	FL	SHUTTER	SPEEDS	ILLUS	U.S.$
Stereolette 610	45x107	plate	StFoldPl	1912	Hekla	6.8	60mm	Compound	1-250		240
Stereolette 610	45x107	plate	StFoldPl	1912	Helios	8	65mm	Compound	1-250	Mc243	240
Stereolette 611	45x107	plate	StFoldPl	1919	Novar	6.8	65mm	Compur	1-250	A767	230
Stereolette Cupido 620	45x107	plate	StFoldPl	1912	Tessar	6.3	90mm	Compur	1-250	A762	280
Teddy 146	9x12cm	plate	FoldPl	1914	Helios	8	130mm	Automat	25-100		70
Toska 160	9x12cm	plate	FoldPl	1914	Doppel Amatar	6.8	135mm	Automat	25-100		60
Toska 180	9x12cm	plate	FoldPl	1914	Rap.Aplan. Helios	8	130mm	Automat	25-100		60
Toska 210	9x12cm	plate	FoldPl	1914	Doppel Amatar	6.8	135mm	Compound			60
Toska 215	9x12cm	plate	FoldPl	1914	Rap.Aplan. Helios	8	130mm	Compound		A186	60
Toska 330	10x15cm	plate	FoldPl	1914	Novar	6.8	165mm	Compur	1-200		380
Toska 400	13x18cm	plate	FoldPl	1920	Protar	6.3	20.5cm	Compur	1-200		380
Toska 402 (Stereo)	13x18cm	plate	StFoldPl	1920	Tessar	6.3	13.5cm	Compur	1-200		410
Trilby 5	6x9cm	plate	MagBox	1912	Landschafts				I,T	HK72	80
Trilby 11	6x9cm	plate	MagBox	1912	Achromat		120mm		I,T		80
Trilby 12	6.5x9cm	plate	MagBox	1912	Achromat		120mm	guillotine	I,T		80
Trilby 13	6x9cm	plate	MagBox	1912	Achromat		120mm	guillotine	I,T		90
Trilby 14	6.5x9cm	plate	MagBox	1912	Achromat		120mm	guillotine	I,T		90
Trilby 15	6.5x9cm	plate	MagBox	1912	Achromat		120mm	guillotine	I,T		90
Trilby 17	9x12cm	plate	MagBox	1912	Landschafts			guillotine	I,T	HK73	110
Trilby 18	9x12cm	plate	MagBox	1912	Achromat	12.5	140mm	guillotine	I,T		160
Trilby 20	9x12cm	plate	MagBox	1912	Achromat	11	140mm	guillotine	I,T	A87	170
Trilby 29	9x12cm	plate	MagBox	1912	Achromat	12.5	140mm	Automat	1-100		100
Trilby 31	9x12cm	plate	MagBox	1912	Achromat		135mm	Automat	1-100	HK74	100
Trilby 33	9x12cm	plate	MagBox	1912	Alpha	11	145mm	Automat	25-100	HK75	100
Trilby 33	9x12cm	plate	MagBox	1912	Helios	8	130mm	Automat	25-100	HK75	100
Triplex 410	13x18cm	plate	FoldPl	1912	Dagor	6.8	180mm	Compound			270
Trix 185	9x12cm	plate	FoldPl	1912	Hekla	6.8	135mm	Compound			60
Trix 220	9x12cm	plate	FoldPl	1912	Helios	8	125mm	Compound			70
Trix 311	10x15cm	plate	FoldPl	1912	Hekla	6.8	165mm	Compur	1-200		60
Trix 365	13x18cm	plate	FoldPl	1912	Icar	6.3	210mm	Automat	25-100		110
Trona	4.5x6cm	plate	FoldPl	1912	Tessar	4.5	75mm	Compur			100
Trona 110	6x9cm	plate	FoldPl	1912	Tessar	4.5	105mm	Compur			80
Trona 110	6.5x9cm	plate	FoldPl	1912	Litonar	4.5	105mm	Compur			80
Trona 210E	9x12cm	plate	FoldPl	1912	Novar	6.8	135mm	Automat	25-100		80
Trona 210U	9x12cm	plate	FoldPl	1912	Tessar	4.5	135mm	Compur			80
Trona 212	3¼x4¼"	plate	FoldPl	1912	Tessar	4.5	135mm	Compur			80
Trona 515	8x10.5cm	plate	FoldRo	1912	Baldour	8		Compound			80
Tropica 285D	9x12cm	plate	FoldPl	1912	Helios	8	130mm	Automat	25-100		580
Tropica 285R	9x12cm	plate	FoldPl	1912	Hekla	6.8	135mm	Compound			580
Tropica 285T	9x12cm	plate	FoldPl	1912	Tessar	6.3	135mm	Compound			580
Tropica 345H	10x15cm	plate	FoldPl	1914	Maximar	6.8	16.5cm	Automat	1-100		700
Tropica 345T	10x15cm	plate	FoldPl	1914	Tessar	6.3	16.5cm	Compur			700

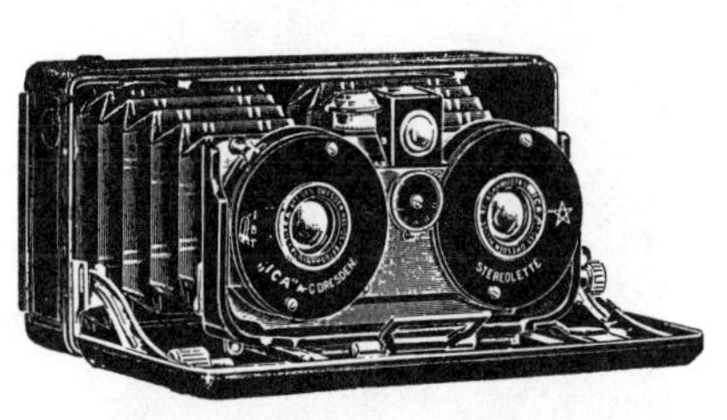

Ica Stereolette 610

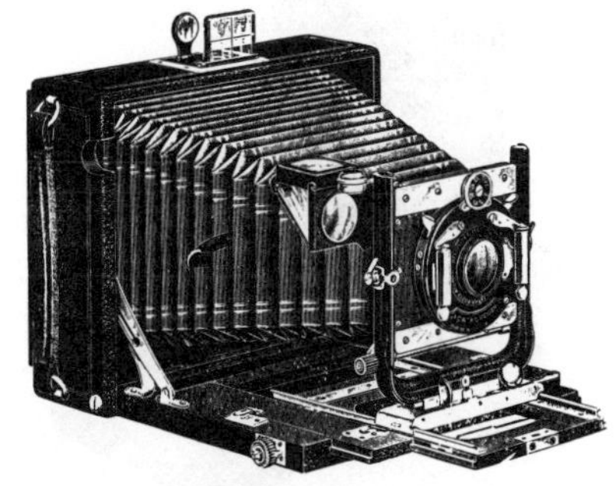

Ica Triplex 410

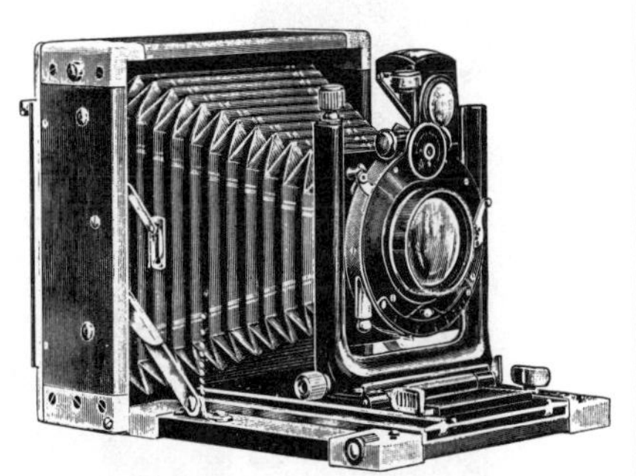

Ica Tropica 285

MODEL	FORMAT	FILM	TYPE	Year	LENS	Apert	FL	SHUTTER	SPEEDS	ILLUS	U.S.$
Tropica 345V	10x15cm	plate	FoldPl	1914	Protar	6.3	170mm	Compur			700
Tropica 345Z	10x15cm	plate	FoldPl	1914	Icar	6.3	16.5cm	Automat	1-100		700
Tropica 435E	13x18cm	plate	FoldPl	1912	Novar	6.8	180mm	Automat	1-100		900
Tropica 435T	13x18cm	plate	FoldPl	1912	Tessar	6.3	210mm	Compur			900
Tropica 435U	13x18cm	plate	FoldPl	1912	Tessar	4.5	16.5cm	Compur			900
Tudor Reflex 748 F	6.5x9cm	plate	LgSLR	1918	Orix	4.5	16.5cm	focal plane	1-1000		210
Tudor Reflex 748 U	6.5x9cm	plate	LgSLR	1918	Tessar	4.5	150mm	focal plane	1-1000		210
Tudor Reflex 749 T	9x9cm	plate	LgSLR	1918	Tessar	6.3	150mm	focal plane	1-1000		220
Tudor Reflex 749 U	9x9cm	plate	LgSLR	1918	Tessar	4.5	150mm	focal plane	1-1000		220
Tudor Reflex 756 G	9x12cm	plate	LgSLR	1918	Dominar	4.5	150mm	focal plane			190
Tudor Reflex 756 U	9x12cm	plate	LgSLR	1918	Tessar	4.5	150mm	focal plane		A1593	190
Tudor Reflex 756/1 F	9x12cm	plate	LgSLR	1918	Orix	4.5	165mm	focal plane			190
Tudor Reflex 756/1 U	9x12cm	plate	LgSLR	1918	Tessar	4.5	150mm	focal plane			190
Tudor Reflex 758 F	9x12cm	plate	LgSLR	1918	Orix	4.5	210mm	focal plane			190
Tudor Reflex 758 U	9x12cm	plate	LgSLR	1918	Tessar	4.5	180mm	focal plane			190
Tudor Reflex 758/1 F	9x12cm	plate	LgSLR	1918	Orix	4.5	210mm	focal plane			190
Tudor Reflex 758/1 U	9x12cm	plate	LgSLR	1918	Tessar	4.5	180mm	focal plane			190
Universal Juwel 275G	9x12cm	plate	FoldPl	1924	Dominar	4.5	135mm	Compound			300
Universal Juwel 275T	9x12cm	plate	FoldPl	1924	Tessar	6.3	15cm	Compound			300
Universal Juwel 440R	13x18cm	plate	FoldPl	1924	Double Anast.	6.8	18cm	Compound			300
Universal Juwel 440U	13x18cm	plate	FoldPl	1924	Tessar	4.5	21cm	Compound			300
Universal-Palmos 275S	9x12cm	plate	FoldPl	1910	Doppel-Amatar	6.8	150mm	Compound			220
Universal-Palmos 275U	9x12cm	plate	FoldPl	1910	Tessar	4.5	150mm	Compur			220
Universal-Palmos 275V	9x12cm	plate	FoldPl	1910	Protar	7	140mm	Compound			220
Victrix K	4.5x6cm	plate	FoldPl	1912	Ica Dominar	4.5	75mm	Automat	25-100	Mc244	120
Victrix R	4.5x6cm	plate	FoldPl	1912	Hekla	6.8	75mm	Compur		Mc244	120
Volta 105B	6.5x9cm	plate	FoldPl	1910	Periskop	11	120mm	Automat	25-100		50
Volta 105E	6.5x9cm	plate	FoldPl	1910	Novar	6.8	10.5cm	Automat	25-100		50
Volta 106B	6.5x9cm	plate	FoldPl	1924	Periskop	11	120mm	Automat	25-100		50
Volta 106E	6.5x9cm	plate	FoldPl	1924	Novar	6.8	10.5cm	Automat	25-100		50
Volta 125B	9x12cm	plate	FoldPl	1912	Periskop	11	145mm	Automat	25-100	Mc244	50
Volta 125E	9x12cm	plate	FoldPl	1912	Novar Anastigmat	6.8	135mm	Automat	25-100	Mc244	50
Volta 146A	9x12cm	plate	FoldPl	1914	Achromat	12	145mm	Automat	1-100		50
Volta 146E	9x12cm	plate	FoldPl	1914	Novar Anastigmat	6.8	135mm	Automat	25-100		50
Volta 295D	10x15cm	plate	FoldPl	1912	Helios	8	150mm	Automat	1-100		60
Volta 295R	10x15cm	plate	FoldPl	1912	Hekla	6.8	165mm	Automat	1-100		60
Volta 295U	10x15cm	plate	FoldPl	1912	Tessar	4.5	165mm	Compur			60
Volta 355D	13x18cm	plate	FoldPl	1912	Helios	8	190mm	Automat	1-100		60
Volta 355E	13x18cm	plate	FoldPl	1912	Novar	6.8	180mm	Compur			60
Volta 355R	13x18cm	plate	FoldPl	1912	Hekla	6.8	180mm	Automat	1-100		60
...IDAM - Colombes											
Belco	36x36mm	127	RigidRo	1951	Bilux	4.5					70

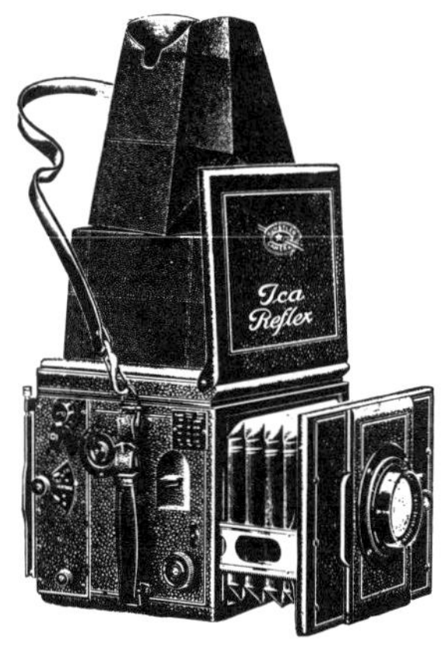

Ica Tudor Reflex 756

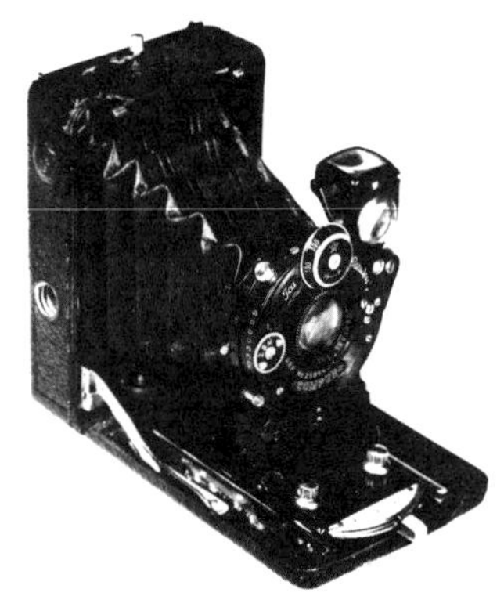

Ica Victrix

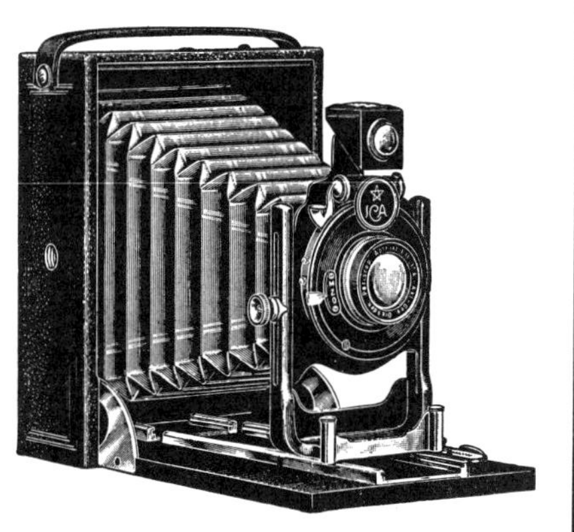

Ica Volta 125 B

MODEL	FORMAT	FILM	TYPE	Year	LENS	Apert	FL	SHUTTER	SPEEDS	ILLUS	U.S.$
Clic	3x3cm	828	RigidRo	1953	Bilux	8		single speed		F1139	70
Roc	4x4cm	127	RigidRo	1951	Bilux	4.5	40mm			F1157	90
...IHAGEE KAMERAWERK - Dresden											
Ama 420	9x12cm	plate	VtFoldPl	1925	Anastigmat	6.8	135mm	Vario	25-100		70
Ama 420	9x12cm	plate	VtFoldPl	1925	Anastigmat	6.3	135mm	Vario	25-100		70
Auto-Ultrix	6x9cm	120	FoldRo	1931	Radionar	4.5	105mm	Compur	1-300	Mc246	80
Derby 310	6.5x9cm	plate	FoldPl	1924	Periscop	11	105mm	Vario	25-100		80
Derby 320	9x12cm	plate	FoldPl	1924	Periscop	11	135mm	Vario	25-100		50
Duplex ☛ "Luxus-Duplex", "Patent-Duplex", "Zweiverschluß-Duplex".											0
Elbaflex 175	24x36mm	35mm	35SLR	1969	Domiplan	2.9	50mm	sector	30-175	Hu056	70
Elbaflex VX500	24x36mm	35mm	35SLR	1969	Tessar	2.8	50mm	focal plane	12-1000	Ex88	110
Elbaflex VX1000	24x36mm	35mm	35SLR	1969	Domiplan	2.8	50mm	focal plane	12-1000	Ex87	120
Exa "System" Rheinmetall	24x36mm	35mm	35SLR	1954	Trioplan	3.5	50mm	sector	25-150	A1652	340
Exa "Varex"	24x36mm	35mm	35SLR	1950	Domiplan	2.9	50mm	sector	25-250	Hu038	150
Exa (F,X)	24x36mm	35mm	35SLR	1957	Meritar	2.8	50mm	sector	25-150	Ex104	70
Exa (M,X)	24x36mm	35mm	35SLR	1952	Domiplan	2.9	50mm	sector	25-150	Ex100	120
Exa (V,E)	24x36mm	35mm	35SLR	1951	Meritar	2.8	50mm	sector	25-150	Hu041	80
Exa I	24x36mm	35mm	35SLR	1963	Domiplan	2.9	50mm	sector	30-175	Ex106	80
Exa Ia	24x36mm	35mm	35SLR	1964	Domiplan	2.9	50mm	sector	30-175	Ex108	60
Exa Ib (all black)	24x36mm	35mm	35SLR	1984	Domiplan	2.9	50mm	sector	30-175	Hu061	80
Exa Ib (black front)	24x36mm	35mm	35SLR	1983	Meritar	2.8	50mm	sector	30-175	Hu060	70
Exa Ib (chrome)	24x36mm	35mm	35SLR	1977	Domiplan	2.9	50mm	sector	30-175	Ex109	50
Exa Ic	24x36mm	35mm	35SLR	1985	Meritar	2.8	50mm	sector	30-175	Hu062	70
Exa II	24x36mm	35mm	35SLR	1960	Domiplan	2.9	50mm	focal plane	½-250	Ex110	70
Exa IIa (no lugs)	24x36mm	35mm	35SLR	1963	Meritar	2.8	50mm	focal plane	½-250	Ex111	70
Exa IIa (strap lugs)	24x36mm	35mm	35SLR	1963	Domiplan	2.9	50mm	focal plane	½-250	Ex112	60
Exa IIb	24x36mm	35mm	35SLR	1964	Domiplan	2.9	50mm	focal plane	½-250	Ex113	70
Exa 500	24x36mm	35mm	35SLR	1966	Meritar	2.8	50mm	focal plane	½-250	Ex114	70
Exakta II	24x36mm	35mm	35SLR	1949	Tessar	2.8	50mm	focal plane	12-1/1000	Ex55	160
Exakta 66 (post-war)	6x6cm	120	MedSLR	1954	Zeiss Tessar	2.8	80mm	MX-Sync	12-1/1000	Ex182	540
Exakta 66 (pre-war)	6x6cm	120	MedSLR	1938	Tessar	2.8	80mm	focal plane	12-1/1000	Ex178	1200
Exakta 66 (pre-war)	6x6cm	120	MedSLR	1938	Biotar	2	80mm	focal plane	12-1/1000		1900
Exakta 66 (pre-war)	6x6cm	120	MedSLR	1938	Primoplan	1.9	80mm	focal plane	12-1/1000		1900
Exakta 66 (West Germany 1	6x6cm	120	MedSLR	1984	Xenotar	2.8	80mm	focal plane	1-1000	A3186	630
Exakta 66 Mod. 2	6x6cm	120	MedSLR	1993	Xenotar	2.8	80mm	focal plane	1-1000		700
Exakta 100	24x36mm	35mm	35SLR	1969	Domiplan	2.9	50mm	sector	30-175	Hu057	70
Exakta 500	24x36mm	35mm	35SLR	1969	Tessar	2.8	50mm	focal plane	2-500	Hu070	90
Exakta A (original)	4x6.5cm	127	MedSLR	1933	Exaktar	3.5	70mm	focal plane	25-1000	Ex12	260
Exakta A (1933)	4x6.5cm	127	MedSLR	1933	Exaktar	3.5	75mm	focal plane	25-1000	Ex15	260
Exakta A (1934)	4x6.5cm	127	MedSLR	1934	Exaktar	3.5	75mm	focal plane	25-1000	Ex16	250
Exakta A (1935)	4x6.5cm	127	MedSLR	1935	Xenar	3.5	75mm	focal plane	25-1000		330
Exakta A (1938)	4x6.5cm	127	MedSLR	1938	Xenar	3.5	75mm	focal plane	25-1000		250

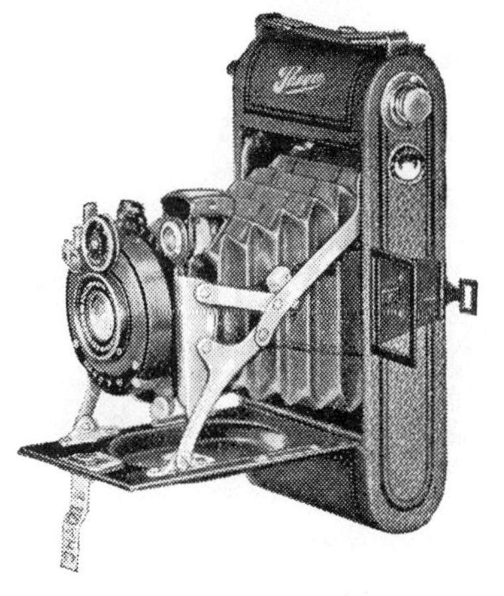

Auto-Ultrix

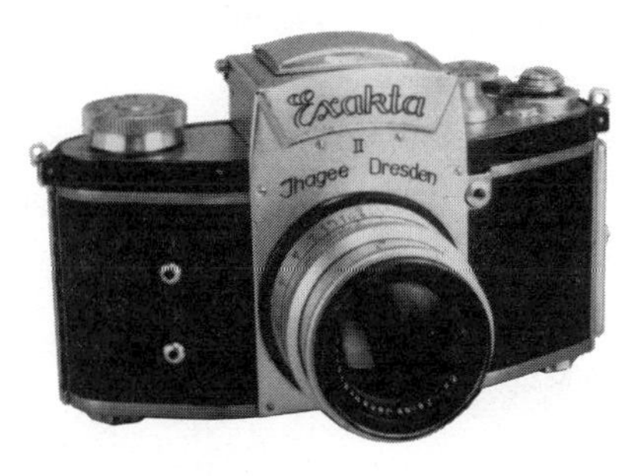

Exakta II

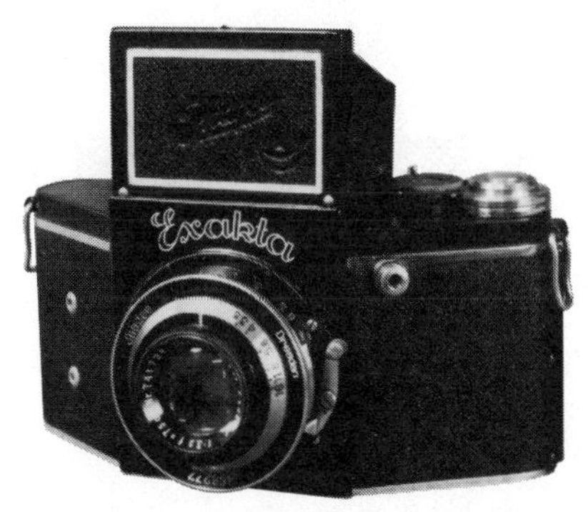

Exakta A (original)

MODEL	FORMAT	FILM	TYPE	Year	LENS	Apert	FL	SHUTTER	SPEEDS	ILLUS	U.S.$
Exakta B (1934)	4x6.5cm	127	MedSLR	1934	Tessar	3.5	75mm	focal plane	12-1/1000	Ex18	250
Exakta B (1935)	4x6.5cm	127	MedSLR	1935	Tessar	2.8	75mm	focal plane	12-1/1000	Ex21	200
Exakta B (1936)	4x6.5cm	127	MedSLR	1936	Tessar	2.8	75mm	focal plane	12-1/1000	Ex22	200
Exakta B (1938)	4x6.5cm	127	MedSLR	1938	Tessar	2.8	75mm	focal plane	12-1/1000	Ex23	200
Exakta C	4x6.5cm	127	MedSLR	1935	Xenar	3.5	75mm	focal plane	12-1/1000	Ex28	270
Exakta EDX 3	24x36mm	35mm	35SLR	1978	Exaktar	1.7	55mm	Copal Square	1-1000,B		90
Exakta FE 2000	24x36mm	35mm	35SLR	1977	Exaktar	1.7	55mm	focal plane	1-1000	Ex99	90
Exakta HS-1	24x36mm	35mm	35SLR	1983	Exakta	1.8	50mm	Copal Square	1-1000,B		60
Exakta HS-10	24x36mm	35mm	35SLR	1988	Exakta	1.8	50mm	Copal Square	1-2000		60
Exakta HS-40	24x36mm	35mm	35SLR	1988	Exakta	1.8	50mm	Copal Square	8-1000		70
Exakta Jr. (1936)	4x6.5cm	127	MedSLR	1934	Anastigmat	4.5	75mm	focal plane	25-500	Ex32	290
Exakta Jr. (1937)	4x6.5cm	127	MedSLR	1935	Anastigmat	4.5	75mm	focal plane	25-500	Ex33	290
Exakta Jr. (1938)	4x6.5cm	127	MedSLR	1936	Anastigmat	4.5	75mm	focal plane	25-500		290
Exakta Real	24x36mm	35mm	35SLR	1967	Curtagon	2.8	35mm	focal plane	2-1/1000	Ex92	630
Exakta RTL 1000	24x36mm	35mm	35SLR	1970	Oreston	1.8	50mm	focal plane	8-1000	Ex90	80
Exakta TL 500	24x36mm	35mm	35SLR	1976	Exaktar	1.8	50mm	Copal Square	1-500,B	Ex98	80
Exakta TL 1000	24x36mm	35mm	35SLR	1977	Exaktar	1.8	50mm	Copal Square	1-1000,B		80
Exakta Twin TL	24x36mm	35mm	35SLR	1973	Exaktar	1.4	55mm	Copal Square	1-1000,B	Ex97	140
Exakta V (=Varex)	24x36mm	35mm	35SLR	1950	Tessar	2.8	50mm	focal plane	12-1/1000	Ex59	140
Exakta Varex	24x36mm	35mm	35SLR	1950	Xenon	2	50mm	focal plane	12-1/1000	Ex57	140
Exakta Varex IIA (early)	24x36mm	35mm	35SLR	1957	Pancolar	2	50mm	focal plane	12-1/1000	Ex69	130
Exakta Varex IIA (later)	24x36mm	35mm	35SLR	1961	Pancolar	2	50mm	focal plane	12-1/1000	Ex75	110
Exakta Varex IIB	24x36mm	35mm	35SLR	1963	Pancolar	2	50mm	focal plane	12-1/1000	Ex81	130
Exakta Varex VX	24x36mm	35mm	35SLR	1951	Tessar	2.8	50mm	focal plane	12-1/1000	Ex62	110
Exakta Varex VX (1954)	24x36mm	35mm	35SLR	1954	Tessar	2.8	50mm	focal plane	12-1/1000	Ex63	130
Exakta Varex VX (1955)	24x36mm	35mm	35SLR	1955	Xenon	2	50mm	focal plane	12-1/1000	Ex66	110
Exakta Varex VX (1956)	24x36mm	35mm	35SLR	1956	Xenon	2	50mm	focal plane	12-1/1000	Ex67	160
Exakta VX	24x36mm	35mm	35SLR	1951	Xenon	2	50mm	focal plane	12-1/1000	Ex61	110
Exakta VX (1954)	24x36mm	35mm	35SLR	1954	Xenon	2	50mm	focal plane	12-1/1000		110
Exakta VX (1955)	24x36mm	35mm	35SLR	1955	Xenon	2	50mm	focal plane	12-1/1000		110
Exakta VX (1956)	24x36mm	35mm	35SLR	1956	Tessar	2.8	50mm	focal plane	12-1/1000		120
Exakta VX IIA (early)	24x36mm	35mm	35SLR	1957	Tessar	2.8	50mm	focal plane	12-1/1000		130
Exakta VX IIA (later)	24x36mm	35mm	35SLR	1961	Tessar	2.8	50mm	focal plane	12-1/1000		110
Exakta VX IIB	24x36mm	35mm	35SLR	1963	Tessar	2.8	50mm	focal plane	12-1/1000		120
Exakta VX 500	24x36mm	35mm	35SLR	1969	Pancolar	2	50mm	focal plane	30-500	Ex88	140
Exakta VX 1000	24x36mm	35mm	35SLR	1967	Tessar	2.8	50mm	focal plane	12-1/1000	Ex84	150
Folding plate camera 6x9	6x9cm	plate	FoldPl	1920	Tessar	4.5	105mm	Compur			90
Folding plate cam. 9x12	9x12cm	plate	FoldPl	1920	Tessar	4.5	135mm	Compur		Mc246	90
Folding rollfilm cam. 4.5x6	4.5x6cm	120	FoldRo	1930	Anastigmat	4.5	70mm	Compur			130
Folding rollfilm cam. 6x9	6x9cm	120	FoldRo	1930	Anastigmat	4.5	105mm	Prontor			60
Kine Exacta I ("c")	24x36mm	35mm	35SLR	1937	Exaktar	3.5	50mm	focal plane	12-1/1000	Ex50	630
Kine Exakta I (original)	24x36mm	35mm	35SLR	1936	Tessar	2.8	50mm	focal plane	12-1/1000	Ex46	1100

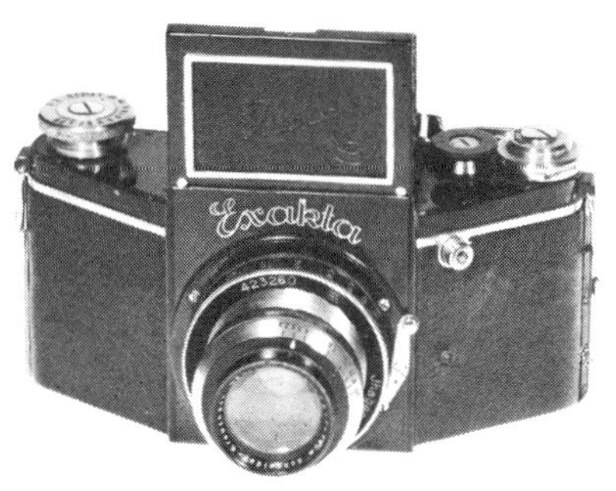

Exakta B (1934)

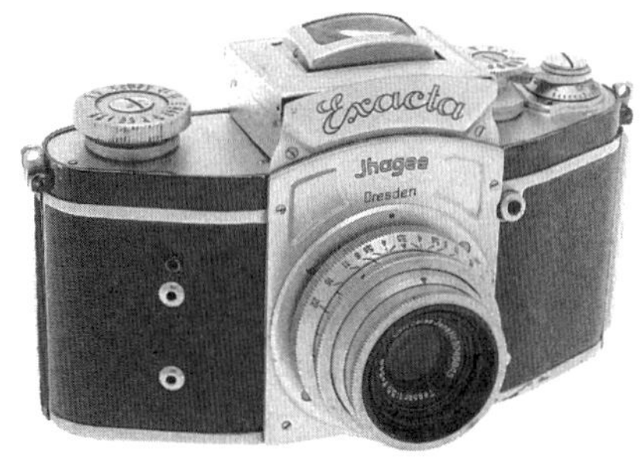

Kine Exacta I ("c")

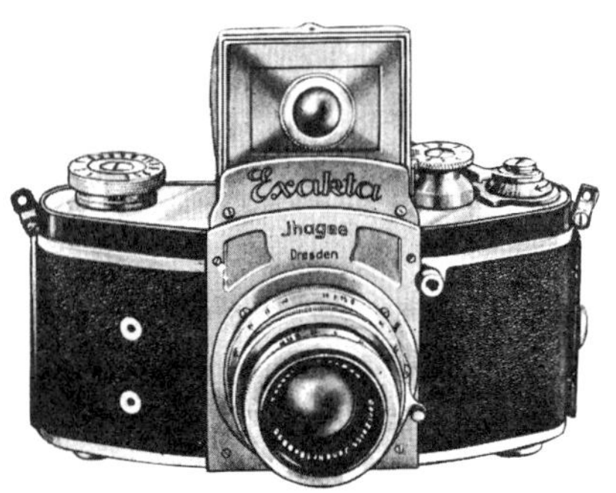

Kine Exakta I (original)

MODEL	FORMAT	FILM	TYPE	Year	LENS	Apert	FL	SHUTTER	SPEEDS	ILLUS	U.S.$
Kine Exakta I (rect. magnif.)	24x36mm	35mm	35SLR	1937	Primotar	3.5	50mm	focal plane	12-1/1000	Ex49	140
Kleinbild-Ultrix 3x4	3x4cm	127	TelescRo	1931	Anastigmat	6.3	70mm	Compur	1-300		120
Kleinbild-Ultrix 4x6.5	4x6.5cm	127	TelescRo	1931	Anastigmat	4.5	70mm	Compur	1-300		100
Luxus-Duplex 810	6.5x9cm	plate	VtFoldPl	1925	Veraplan	4.5	10.5cm	Compur	1-300		70
Luxus-Duplex 820	9x12cm	plate	VtFoldPl	1925	Trioplan	3.5	135mm	Compur	1-300		70
Mikrobie 500HV	4.5x6cm	plate	FoldPl	1922	Anastigmat	6.3	85mm	Prontor	25-100		140
Mikrobie 500TC	4.5x6cm	plate	FoldPl	1922	Veraplan	4.5	85mm	Compur	1-300		140
Mikrobie 595SR	6.5x9cm	plate	FoldPl	1922	Triplax	6.8	105mm	Prontor	25-100		70
Mikrobie 595TC	6.5x9cm	plate	FoldPl	1922	Veraplan	4.5	105mm	Compur	1-300		70
Nachtkamera 4.5x6	4.5x6cm	plate	Platebox	1929	Plasmat	1.5	90mm	focal plane	15-1000	HK181	2900
Nachtkamera 4.5x6	4.5x6cm	plate	Platebox	1929	Plasmat	2	90mm	focal plane	15-1000		2900
Nachtkamera 6.5x9	6.5x9cm	plate	Platebox	1929	Plasmat	2	125mm	focal plane	15-1000	HK179	2400
Nachtreflex 4.5x6	4.5x6cm	plate	SLR-Box	1930	Plasmat	1.5	90mm	focal plane	15-1000	A1612	3100
Nachtreflex 4.5x6	4.5x6cm	plate	SLR-Box	1930	Plasmat	2	90mm	focal plane	15-1000		3100
Nachtreflex 6.5x9	6.5x9cm	plate	SLR-Box	1930	Plasmat	2	125mm	focal plane	15-1000	HK347	2500
Night Exakta (Typ A)	4x6.5cm	127	MedSLR	1936	Biotar	2	80mm	focal plane	25-1000		510
Night Exakta (Typ A)	4x6.5cm	127	MedSLR	1936	Primoplan	1.9	80mm	focal plane	25-1000		510
Night Exakta (Typ B)	4x6.5cm	127	MedSLR	1936	Xenon	2	80mm	focal plane	12-1/1000	Mc245	460
Night Exakta (Typ B)	4x6.5cm	127	MedSLR	1936	Dallmeyer	1.9	3"	focal plane	12-1/1000	Ex27	460
Parvola 1350	4x6.5cm	127	TelescRo	1933	Tessar	3.5	50mm	Compur	1-200		90
Parvola 1450	3x4cm	127	TelescRo	1933	Tessar	2.8		Compur			130
Patent Klapp Reflex 6.5x9	6.5x9cm	plate	FoldSLR	1925	Veraplan	4.5	12cm	focal plane	-1000	A573	330
Patent Klapp Reflex 9x9	9x9cm	plate	FoldSLR	1929	Xenar	4.5	150mm	focal plane	-1000		330
Patent Klapp Reflex 9x12	9x12cm	plate	FoldSLR	1927	Dogmar	4.5	150mm	focal plane	-1000	Mc246	330
Patent Klapp Reflex 10x15	10x15cm	plate	FoldSLR	1927	Tessar	4.5	165mm	focal plane	-1000		330
Patent-Duplex 710	6.5x9cm	plate	VtFoldPl	1924	Steinheil	3.5	105mm	Compur			70
Patent-Duplex 720	9x12cm	plate	VtFoldPl	1924	Trioplan	3.5	135mm	Compur			80
Photoknips 100	4.5x6cm	plate	StrutPl	1924	Achromatic				25-100	HK177	240
Photoknips 200	4.5x6cm	plate	StrutPl	1924	Anastigmat	6.3			25-100	HK178	220
Photoknips No. 2	6.5x9cm	plate	StrutPl	1915	Achromatic				25-100		240
Plan-Paff-Reflex 4.5x6	4.5x6cm	plate	SLR-Box	1921	Trioplan	4.5	80mm		M,Z		180
Plan-Paff-Reflex 6x9	6.5x9cm	plate	SLR-Box	1921	Trioplan	6.8	105mm		M,Z		160
Roll-Paff-Reflex 20	6x6cm	120	SLR-Box	1921	Trioplan	6.8	90mm		M,Z	Mc246	100
Roll-Paff-Reflex Luxus	6x6cm	120	SLR-Box	1927	Doppel Anast.	6.3	90mm		M,Z		130
RTL 1000 (no "Exakta")	24x36mm	35mm	35SLR	1969	Oreston	1.8	50mm	focal plane	8-1000	Ex91	90
Serien-Reflex 2110PP	6.5x9cm	plate	SLR-Box	1928	Trioplan	3.5	120mm	focal plane	15-1000	HK334	240
Serien-Reflex 2110T	6.5x9cm	plate	SLR-Box	1928	Veraplan	4.5	120mm	focal plane	15-1000	HK334	240
Serien-Reflex 2113M	9x9cm	plate	SLR-Box	1929	Anastigmat	4.5	150mm	focal plane	15-1000	HK334	240
Serien-Reflex 2113Y	9x9cm	plate	SLR-Box	1929	Plasmat	4.5	125mm	focal plane	15-1000	HK334	240
Serien-Reflex 2120PP	9x12cm	plate	SLR-Box	1928	Trioplan	3.5	150mm	focal plane	15-1000	HK334	250
Serien-Reflex 2120Z	9x12cm	plate	SLR-Box	1928	Tessar	4.5	150mm	focal plane	15-1000	HK334	250
Sportkamera 1810	6.5x9cm	plate	StrutPl	1928	Anastigmat	4.5	105mm	focal plane	15-1000		380

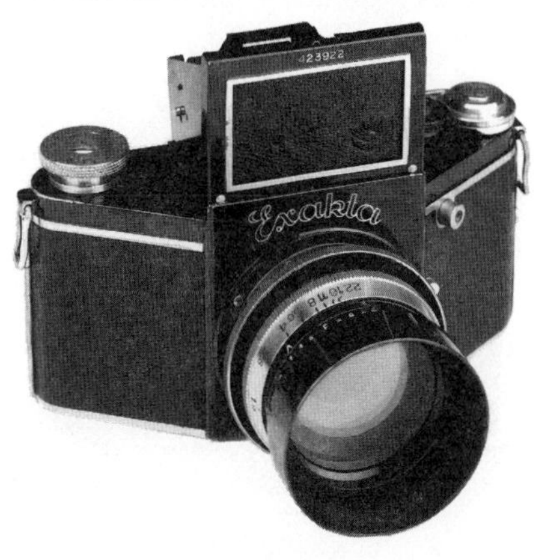

Night Exakta (Type B)

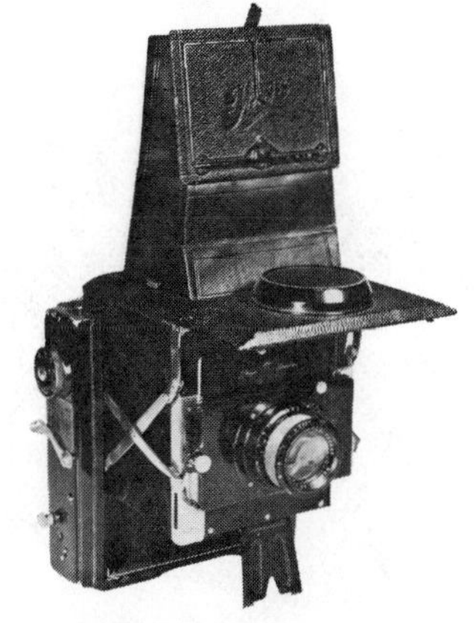

Ihagee Patent Klapp-Reflex

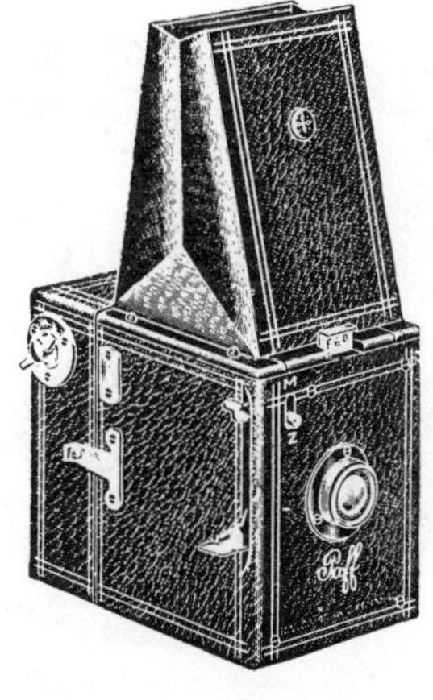

Roll-Paff-Reflex 20

MODEL	FORMAT	FILM	TYPE	Year	LENS	Apert	FL	SHUTTER	SPEEDS	ILLUS	U.S.$
Sportkamera 1820	9x12cm	plate	StrutPl	1928	Tessar	3.5	135mm	focal plane	15-1000		270
Sportkamera 1830	10x15cm	plate	StrutPl	1928	Plasmat	4.5	16.5cm	focal plane	15-1000		270
Stereo Automat	6x13cm	plate	StFoldPl	1912	Trioplan	6.3	80mm	Prontor	25-100		280
Tropen-Neugold 910	6.5x9cm	plate	FoldPl	1927	Tessar	5.6	105mm	Compur			900
Tropen-Neugold 920	9x12cm	plate	FoldPl	1927	Dagor	6.8	135mm	Compur		A1400	1000
Tropen-Neugold 930	10x15cm	plate	FoldPl	1927	Tessar	4.5	16.5cm	Compur			1200
Ultrix 1460 ZC	6x9cm	120	FoldRo	1925	Tessar	4.5	105mm	Compur	1-300		70
Ultrix 2960 HC	6x9cm	120	FoldRo	1931	Anastigmat	6.8	105mm	Compur	1-300		70
Ultrix Simplex (brown)	6x9cm	120	FoldRo	1928	Luxar		105mm	Vario	25-100		110
Ultrix Simplex 1360	6x9cm	120	FoldRo	1924	Trioplan	6.8	105mm	Compur	1-300		60
Ultrix Stereo HV	7x13cm	Roll	StFoldRo	1924	Trioplan	6.3	80mm	Pronto		A759	270
Ultrix Stereo TC	7x13cm	Roll	StFoldRo	1924	Anastigmat	4.5	80mm	Compur	1-300	HK502	270
Venus 610 PV	6.5x9cm	plate	HzFoldPl	1925	Trioplan	6.3	105mm	Vario	25-100		100
Venus 610 TC	6.5x9cm	plate	HzFoldPl	1925	Veraplan	6.8	105mm	Compur	1-300		100
Victor 510 HC	6.5x9cm	plate	VtFoldPl	1923	Trioplan	6.3	105mm	Compur	1-300		60
Victor 510 RV	6.5x9cm	plate	VtFoldPl	1923	Veraplan	6.8	105mm	Prontor	25-100		60
Victor 520 HC	9x12cm	plate	VtFoldPl	1923	Trioplan	6.3	105mm	Compur	1-300		50
Victor 520 MC	9x12cm	plate	VtFoldPl	1923	Ihagee Anast.	4.5	105mm	Compur	1-300		50
Victor 530 HC	10x15cm	plate	VtFoldPl	1923	Trioplan	6.3	165mm	Compur	1-300		50
Victor 530 RC	10x15cm	plate	VtFoldPl	1923	Veraplan	6.8	165mm	Compur	1-300		50
Victor 540 RC	13x18cm	plate	VtFoldPl	1923	Veraplan	6.8	18cm	Compur	1-300		90
Victor 540 WC	13x18cm	plate	VtFoldPl	1923	Tessar	6.3	18cm	Compur	1-300		90
Volks-Auto-Ultrix	6x9cm	120	FoldRo	1936	Anastigmat	4.5	105mm	Prontor II		A1465	80
VX 100 (no "Exakta")	24x36mm	35mm	35SLR	1964	Domiplan	2.9	50mm	focal plane	30-175	Ex109	70
VX 200 (no "Exakta")	24x36mm	35mm	35SLR	1966	Meritar	2.8	50mm	focal plane	2-250	Hu200	80
VX 500 (no "Exakta")	24x36mm	35mm	35SLR	1969	Tessar	2.8	50mm	focal plane	30-500	Ex89	140
VX 1000 (no "Exakta")	24x36mm	35mm	35SLR	1969	Tessar	2.8	50mm	focal plane	12-1/1000	Ex87	130
Westent.-Auto-Ultrix 2850	4.5x6cm	120	FoldRo	1930	Anastigmat	3.5	70mm	Prontor	25-100		80
Westent.-Auto-Ultrix 4850	4.5x6cm	120	FoldRo	1930	Tessar	3.5	105mm	Compur	1-300		100
Zweiverschl.-Duplex 1010	6.5x9cm	plate	FoldPl	1928	Tessar	3.5	105mm	focal plane	15-1000		180
Zweiverschl.-Duplex 1020	9x12cm	plate	FoldPl	1927	Xenar	4.5	135mm	focal plane	15-1000		200
Zweiverschl.-Duplex 1030	10x15cm	plate	FoldPl	1928	Xenar	3.5	165mm	focal plane	15-1000		180
Zweiverschl.-Duplex 2320	9x12cm	plate	FoldPl	1929	Trioplan	3.5	135mm	Compur	1-300		70
...ILFORD LTD - England											
Advocate I	24x36mm	35mm	35vf	1953	Dallmeyer Anast.	4.5	35mm		25-200		110
Advocate II	24x36mm	35mm	35vf	1953	Dallmeyer Anast.	3.5	35mm		25-200		120
Advocate III	24x36mm	35mm	35vf	1953	Wray Lustar	3.5	35mm		25-200		110
Advocate IV	24x36mm	35mm	35vf	1953	Ross	3.5	35mm		25-200		110
Craftsman	2¼x2¼"	120	TLR-Box	1948		9			25-75	Mc247	40
Envoy	2¼x2¼"	120	BakeliteBox	1953	Optimax				I	Mc247	30
Sporti 4	1½x1½"	127	RigidRo	1953	Subitar					Mc247	30
Sportsman	24x36mm	35mm	35vf	1960	Dacora Dignar	2.8		Pronto LK	15-500	Mc247	20

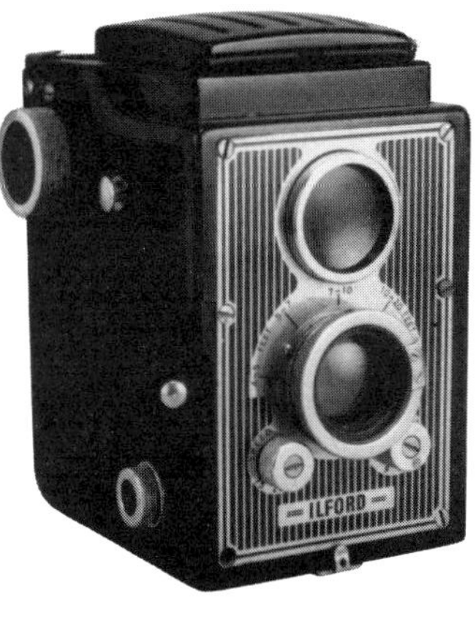

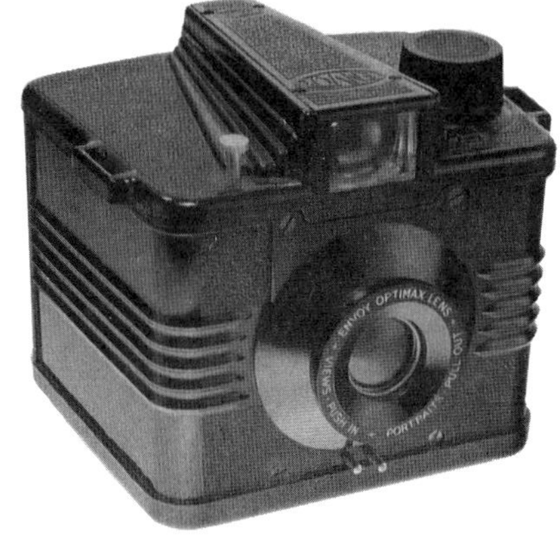

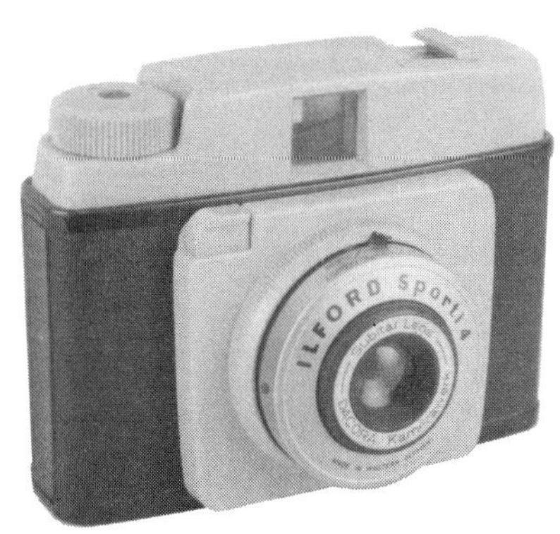

Craftsman **Envoy** **Sporti 4**

MODEL	FORMAT	FILM	TYPE	Year	LENS	Apert	FL	SHUTTER	SPEEDS	ILLUS	U.S.$
Sportsmaster	24x36mm	35mm	35vf	1960	Dacora Dignar	2.8		Prontor-Lux	30-500		50
Sprite	4x4cm	127	RigidRo		Kaligar	8	60mm				10
Sprite 35	24x36mm	35mm	35vf	1951	fixed focus	8			I	Mc247	20
Witness	24x36mm	35mm	35rf	1951	Daron	2.9	50mm	focal plane	1-1000	Mc247	1400
...IMPERIAL CAMERA CORP. - Chicago											
Adventurer (black)	6x6cm	620	PlasBx	1956							20
Adventurer (colors)	6x6cm	620	PlasBx	1956							30
Boy Scouts Official Camera	4x4cm	127	PlasBx	1964	Meniscus					Mc247	30
Cinex (black)	4x4cm	127	PlasBx	1964							10
Cinex (colors)	4x4cm	127	PlasBx	1964	Meniscus						20
Cubex IV (black)	4x4cm	127	PlasBx	1964	Meniscus				I,B		10
Cubex IV (colors)	4x4cm	127	PlasBx	1964	Meniscus						20
Delta (black)	4x4cm	127	PlasBx	1964	Meniscus				I,B		10
Delta (colors)	4x4cm	127	PlasBx	1964	Meniscus						20
Deltex (black)	4x4cm	127	PlasBx	1964	Meniscus				I,B		10
Deluxe Six-Twenty TLR	6x6cm	620	TLR-Box	1960						Mc247	10
Girl Scouts Official Camera	4x4cm	127	PlasBx	1964	Meniscus					Mc247	20
Lark	4x4cm	127	PlasBx	1964	Meniscus				1/40		10
Mark XII Flash	6x6cm	620	PlasBx	1956					I,T		10
Mark 27	4x4cm	127	PlasBx	1964	Meniscus				I,B	Mc247	10
Matey 127 Flash (black)	4x4cm	127	PlasBx	1964	Meniscus						10
Matey 127 Flash (colors)	4x4cm	127	PlasBx	1964	Meniscus						20
Mercury Satellite (black)	4x4cm	127	PlasBx	1964	Meniscus						10
Mercury Satellite (colors)	4x4cm	127	PlasBx	1964	Meniscus						20
Nor-Flash 127 (black)	4x4cm	127	PlasBx	1964	Meniscus						10
Nor-Flash 127 (colors)	4x4cm	127	PlasBx	1964	Meniscus						20
Rambler Flash	4x4cm	127	PlasBx	1964	Meniscus						20
Reflex	6x6cm	620	PlasBx	1956	Duo						10
Roy (black)	4x4cm	127	PlasBx	1964	Meniscus				1/40		10
Roy (colors)	4x4cm	127	PlasBx	1964	Meniscus						20
Satellite II (black)	4x4cm	127	PlasBx	1964	Meniscus						10
Satellite II (colors)	4x4cm	127	PlasBx	1964	Meniscus						20
Savoy (black)	6x6cm	620	PlasBx	1956							10
Savoy (colors)	6x6cm	620	PlasBx	1956							20
Six-twenty (black)	6x6cm	620	PlasBx	1956							10
Six-twenty (colors)	6x6cm	620	PlasBx	1956							20
Six-Twenty Reflex (black)	6x6cm	620	TLR-Box	1956							10
Six-Twenty Reflex (colors)	6x6cm	620	TLR-Box	1956							20
...INDO - Lyon & Paris											
Comodor 127	4x4cm	127	PlasBx	1978						Mc248	20
Compact 126 XR	28x28mm	126	126	1978	Ugo-Lantz		45mm			Mc248	20
Safari X	28x28mm	126	126	1978	Sup.Synchrotonic					Mc248	10

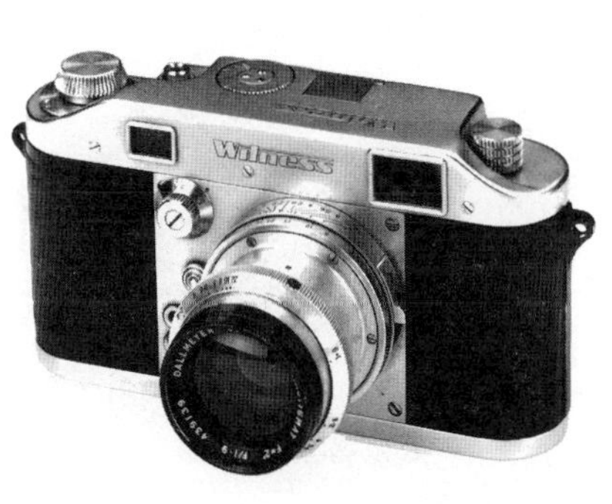

Ilford Witness

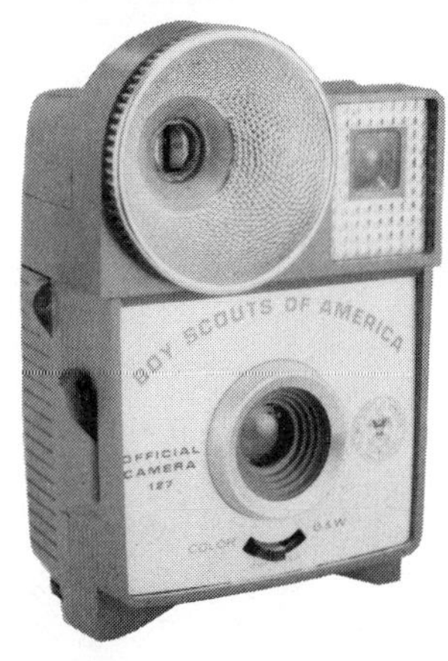

Imperial Boy Scouts Camera

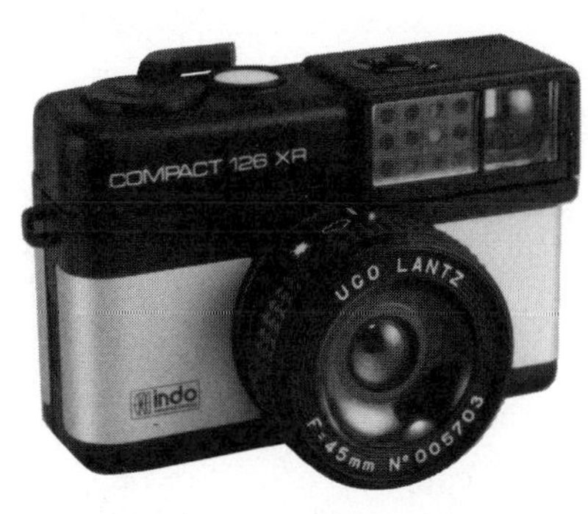

Indo Compact 126 XR

MODEL	FORMAT	FILM	TYPE	Year	LENS	Apert	FL	SHUTTER	SPEEDS	ILLUS	U.S.$
...INDRA CAMERA - Frankfurt											
Indra-Lux	4x4cm	127	RigidRo	1949	Wetzlar	7.7	60mm		M,Z	Mc248	220
...ISING - Bergneustadt											
Isis	6x6cm	120	TelescRo	1954	Steiner	4.5	75mm	Pronto	25-200	Mc249	50
Isoflex I	6x6cm	120	TLR-Box	1952	focusing						30
Puck	3x4cm	127	TelescRo	1948	Cassar	2.8	50mm	Prontor II		Mc249	90
Pucky	6x6cm	120	TLR-Box	1949		9	8cm		M,Z	Mc249	30
Pucky I	6x6cm	120	TLR-Box	1950		7.7	8cm	Synchro	M,Z	A126	30
Pucky Ia	6x6cm	120	TLR-Box	1950	Achromat	7.7	8cm	Synchro	M,Z		30
Pucky II	6x6cm	120	TLR-Box	1950	Achromat	6.3	80mm		M,Z		30
...ISO - Milan											
Bilux	24x36mm	35mm	35rf	1950	Iriar	3.5	50mm	focal plane	1-1000	Mc249	1200
Duplex 120	24x24mm	120	Stereo	1950	Iperang	6.3		3-speed			220
Duplex Super 120	24x24mm	120	Stereo	1950	Iriar	3.5			P,10-200	Mc249	370
Junior	24x36mm	35mm	35rf	1952	Trixar	3.5	50mm	focal plane			1000
Lux	24x36mm	35mm	35rf	1947	Trixar	3.5	50mm	focal plane			1200
Reporter	24x36mm	35mm	35rf	1954	Iriar	2.8	50mm	focal plane			1100
Standard	24x36mm	35mm	35rf	1953	Iriar	2.8	50mm	focal plane			800
...ISOKAWA KOKI - Japan											
Isocaflex	6x6cm	120	TLR	1952	Isunar	3.5	75mm		1-200,B		100
...ISOPLAST GmbH - Germany											
Baby-Blitz	32x40mm	Juka	RigidRo	1954	Meniscus	11	50mm		1/50		100
Filius-Kamera	32x40mm	Juka	RigidRo	1954	Meniscus	11	50mm		1/50		100
Fips Microphot	13x13mm	16mm	Submin	1954	Achromat	6.5	25mm		1/50		120
...JANSEN (Emil Jansen) - Barmen											
Ejot	4.5x6cm	120	FoldRo	1933	Ejotar Anastigmat	4.5	75mm	Vario		Mc249	80
...JAPY & CIE - France											
le Pascal	40x55mm	Roll	RollBox	1898	Meniscus			2-speed,B		Mc249	460
...JEANNERET & CIE. - Paris											
Monobloc	6x13cm	plate	StJumelle	1915	Boyer	4.5	85mm	pneumatic		Mc249	290
Monobloc	6x13cm	plate	StJumelle	1915	Roussel Stylor	6.3	85mm	pneumatic		Mc249	290
...JEM (J. E. Mergott Co.) - Newark											
Jem Jr. 120	2¼x3¼"	120	MetBx	194x	Meniscus			simple		Mc250	10
Jem Jr. 120, Girl Scout	2¼x3¼"	120	MetBx	194x	Meniscus			simple			50
...JONTE (F. Jonte) - Paris											
Automatique	9x12cm	plate	MagBox	1890	Aplanat			sector		F898	700
Field camera	5x7"	plate	Field	1895	various			various		F26	270
...JOS-PE GmbH - Hamburg & Munich											
Tri-color Camera 4.5x6	4.5x6cm	plate	3-Color	1925	Quintar	2.5	105mm	Compound		A950	2000
Tri-color Camera 9x12	9x12cm	plate	3-Color	1925	Cassar	3	180mm	Compound	1/50	Mc250	1800
...JOTA - Germany											
Jota Box	6x9cm	plate	MetBx	1949	Meniscus			simple			70

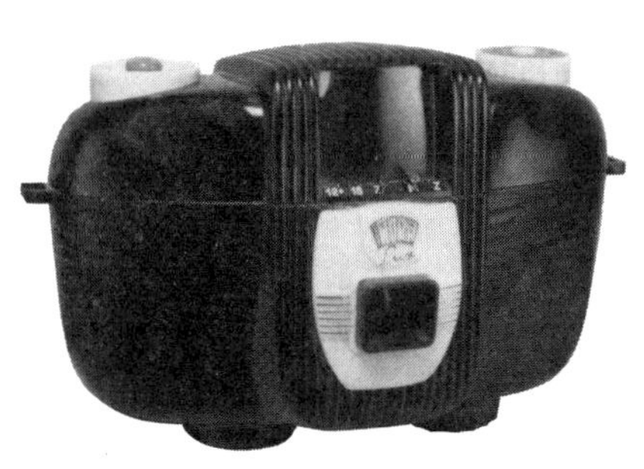

Indra-Lux

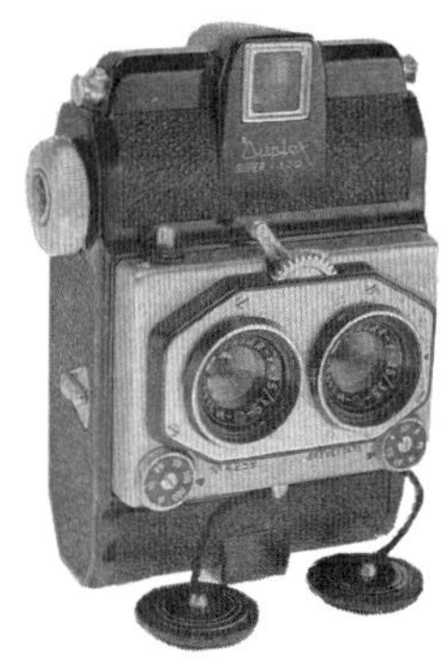

Duplex Super 120

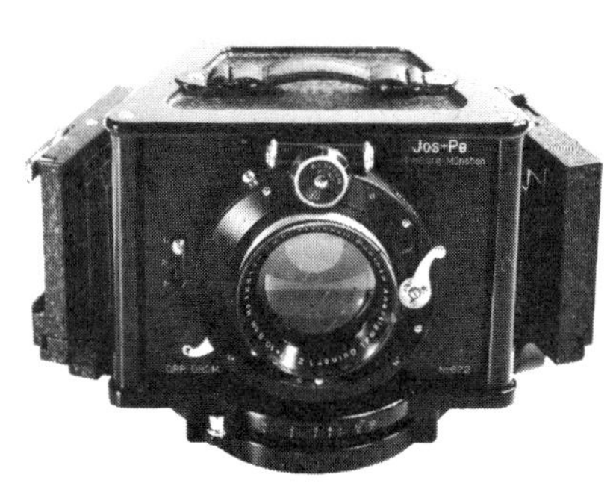

Jos-Pe Tri-color Camera

MODEL	FORMAT	FILM	TYPE	Year	LENS	Apert	FL	SHUTTER	SPEEDS	ILLUS	U.S.$
...JOUGLA (J. Jougla) - Paris											
Sinnox	9x12cm	plate	MagBox	1901	Rapid Rectilinear			Woll. pneum.		F1026	230
...JOUX (L.Joux & Cie) - Paris											
Alethoscope 45x107	45x107	plate	StPlate	1905	Rectil. Balbreck			guillotine		F1168	230
Alethoscope 6x9	6x9cm	plate	StPlate	1905	Rectil. Balbreck			guillotine			230
Ortho Jumelle Duplex	6.5x9cm	plate	StJumelle	1895	Z Krauss Anast.	8	110mm	guillotine		F1091	230
Steno-Jumelle 6.5x9	6.5x9cm	plate	Jumelle	1895	Z Krauss Anast.	8	110mm	guillotine		Mc250	240
Steno-Jumelle 9x12	9x12cm	plate	Jumelle	1895	Z Krauss Anast.	8	110mm	guillotine		F1127	240
Steno-Jumelle Stereo	8x16cm	plate	StJumelle	1898	Z Krauss Anast.	8	110mm	guillotine		F1377	480
Stereo Pochette	6x13cm	plate	StFoldPl	1898	Rectilinear			guillotine		F1384	460
...JUMEAU & JANNIN - France											
Le Cristallos 6x9	6x9cm	Roll	FoldRo	1890							320
Le Cristallos 9x12	9x12cm	Roll	FoldRo	1890							320
...JUNKA-WERKE - Zirndorf b/Nürnberg											
Exhibit	3x4cm	Roll	RigidRo	1937	Achromat	8	45mm	simple		Mc250	100
Junka	3x4cm	Roll	RigidRo	1937	Achromat	8	45mm	simple		Mc251	60
...KAFTANSKI (Fritz Kaftanski) - Paris											
Banco 4.5	2¼x3¼"	120	TelescRo	1948	Transpar-Tiranty	4.5	80mm		B,25-150	Mc251	30
Banco Perfect	2¼x3¼"	120	TelescRo	1948	focusing					Mc251	20
Kaftax	2¼x3¼"	120	RigidRo	1948	fixed focus					Mc251	20
...KALART CO. - New York City											
Kalart Press camera	3¼x4¼"	plate	Press	1948	Wollensak Raptar	4.5	127mm	Rapax	1-400	Mc251	240
...KALIMAR - Japan											
Colt 44	4x4cm	127	RigidRo	1960	Kaligar	8	60mm	simple			20
Kali-flex	6x6cm	120	TLR-Box	1966	Kalimar	8					10
Kalimar 44	4x4cm	127	RigidRo	1960	Kaligar	8	60mm	simple			20
Kalimar A	24x36mm	35mm	35vf	1955	Terionon	3.5	45mm	synchro	-1/200	Mc251	30
Kalimar Reflex	6x6cm	120	MedSLR	1956	Kaligar	3.5	80mm	focal plane	1-500	Mc251	100
Kalimar Six Sixty	6x6cm	120	MedSLR	1963	Kaligar	2.8		cloth FP	1/5-500	Mc251	140
TLR 100	6x6cm	120	TLR		Lomo T-22	4.5	75mm		B,15-250	Mc252	20
...KALOS CAMERABAU GmbH - Karlsruhe											
Kalos	9x12mm	16mm	Submin	1950	Mikro-Anastigmat	4.5	20mm		30,50,100	HK624	400
Kalos Spezial	9x12mm	16mm	Submin	1950	Staeble-Werk Kata	2.8	25mm		30,50,100	Mc252	400
...KAMERA & APPARATEBAU - Vienna											
Sport-Box 2	3x4cm	127	BakeliteBox	1950		8	50mm		M,T		50
Sport-Box 3	3x4cm	127	BakeliteBox	1950		8	50mm		M,T		50
...KAMERAWERKE THARANDT - Germany											
Vitaflex	6x6cm	120	TLR-Box	1949	Brillantar	3.5	75mm				70
Vitaflex F	6x6cm	120	TLR-Box	1949	Flabonar	4.5	75mm				70
Vitaflex R	6x6cm	120	TLR-Box	1949	Pololyt	3.5	75mm				70
...KENNGOTT - W. Kenngott, Stuttgart											
Folding plate camera 6.5x9	6.5x9cm	plate	FoldPl	1920	Leltmeyr Sytar	4.8	105mm	Ibsor	1-125		50

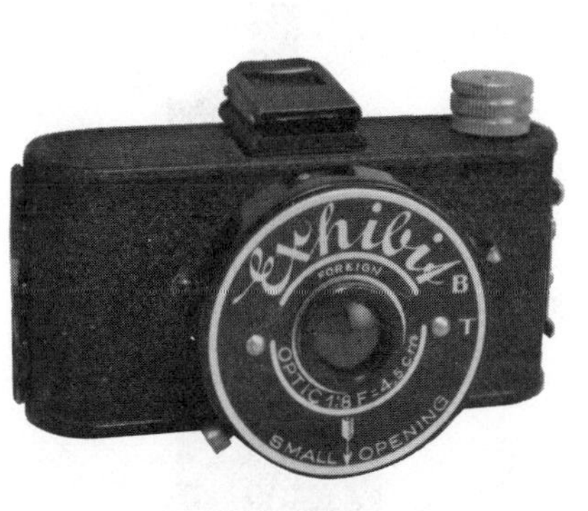

Junka-Werke Exhibit

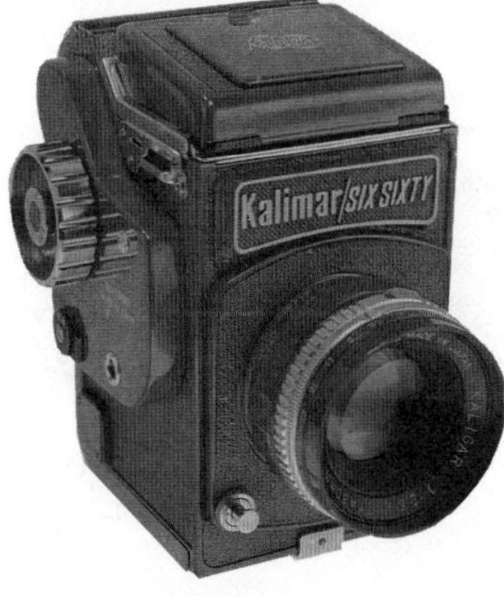

Kalimar Six Sixty

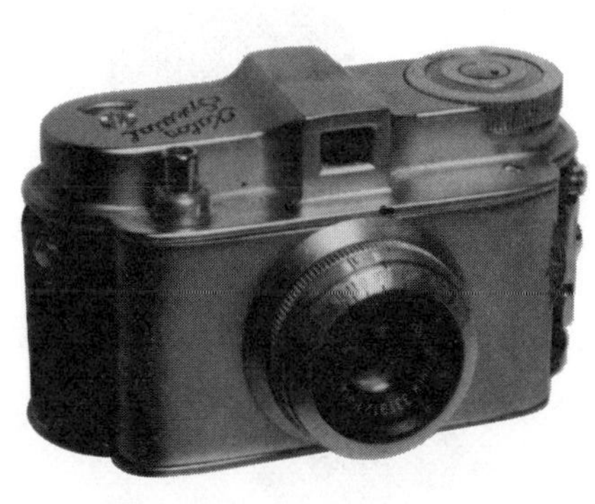
Kalos Spezial

MODEL	FORMAT	FILM	TYPE	Year	LENS	Apert	FL	SHUTTER	SPEEDS	ILLUS	U.S.$
Folding plate camera 9x12	9x12cm	plate	FoldPl	1920	Dialytar	4.5	150mm	Compur			50
Folding plate camera 10x15	10x15cm	plate	FoldPl	1920	Kenngott D.Anast.	6.8	180mm	Koilos	1-300		70
Folding plate camera, Trop.	10x15cm	plate	FoldPl	1920	Steinheil Unifocal	4.5	150mm	Koilos	1-100,T,B		800
Iris	6x9cm	120	FoldRo	1930	Anastigmat	4.5	105mm	Pronto			40
Klappkamera	6.5x9cm	plate	StrutPl	1929	Regulit	6.3	105mm				50
Matador	6.5x9cm	plate	FoldPl	1930	Spezial Aplanat	8	105mm	Vario		HK183	70
Parfait (306)	6.5x9cm	plate	MagBox	1929	Steinheil Anast.						40
Phoenix 6.5x9	6.5x9cm	plate	FoldPl	1924	Lumar Anastigmat	4.5		Compur	1-300		530
Phoenix 9x12	9x12cm	plate	FoldPl	1924	Tessar	4.5	135mm	Dial-Compur	1-300		530
Phoenix 9x14	9x14cm	plate	FoldPl	1924	Tessar	6.8	165mm	Compound	1-100		530
Supra No. 2	6.5x9cm	plate	FoldPl	1930	Xenar	4.5	105mm	Compur	1-250		40
Touriste	9x12cm	plate	Field	1905	Universal Aplanat						210
...KERN - Aarau, Switzerland											
Bijou 6.5x9	6.5x9cm	plate	H&S	1925	Kern Anastigmat	4.5		Compur	1-200		480
Bijou 9x12	9x12cm	plate	H&S	1925	Kern Anastigmat	4.5		Compur	1-200		480
Präzisionskamera	9x12cm	plate	FoldPl	1928	Kern Anastigmat	6.5	150mm				450
Stereo Kern	20x20mm	35mm	Ster35	1930	Kern Anastigmat	3.5	35mm	guillotine	25-300		1000
Stereo Kern SS	20x20mm	35mm	Ster35	1920	Kernon	3.5	35mm	guillotine	25-300	Mc253	1300
Stereo Kern SS	20x20mm	35mm	Ster35	1930	Kern Anastigmat	3.5	35mm	guillotine	25-300	Mc253	1300
...KERSHAW - A. Kershaw & Sons, Ltd.											
Curlew I	6x9cm	120	FoldRo	1948							140
Curlew II	6x9cm	120	FoldRo	1948							110
Curlew III	6x9cm	120	FoldRo	1948							140
Eight-20 King Penguin	2¼x3¼"	Roll	FoldRo	1953					B,I	Mc253	20
Eight-20 Penguin	6x9cm	Roll	FoldRo	1953						Mc253	20
Kershaw 110	6x6cm	120	FoldRo			11			B,I	Mc253	20
Kershaw 450	6x6cm	120	FoldRo		Anastigmat	4.5		Velio		Mc253	30
Kershaw Patent Reflex	6x9cm	plate	LgSLR	1905						Mc254	230
Peregrine I	6x6cm	120	FoldRo		T.-H. Adotal	3.5	80mm	Talykron	1-400		140
Peregrine II	6x6cm	120	FoldRo		T.-H. Adotal	3.5	80mm	Talykron	1-400		180
Peregrine III	6x6cm	120	FoldRo		T.-H. Adotal	2.8	80mm	Talykron	1-400		370
Raven	6x9cm	Roll	FoldRo	1930	Kershaw Anast.	4.4	4"		25-100	Mc254	30
...KIEV ARSENAL - Kiev, Ukraine											
John Player Special	10x14mm	16mm	Disguised	1981	Industar	3.5	23mm	guillotine	30-200	Mc254	520
Kiev	24x36mm	35mm	35rf	1947	Jupiter-8	2	50mm	focal plane		Ru145	120
Kiev "No-Name"	24x36mm	35mm	35rf	1963	Sonnar	2	50mm	focal plane	½-1250,B	Ru147	480
Kiev-2	24x36mm	35mm	35rf	1950	Jupiter-8	2	50mm	focal plane	½-1250,B	Ru146	120
Kiev-2A	24x36mm	35mm	35rf	1955	Jupiter-8	2	50mm	focal plane	½-1250,B	Ru146	90
Kiev-3	24x36mm	35mm	35rf	1952	Jupiter-8	2	50mm	focal plane	½-1250,B	Ru146	140
Kiev-3A	24x36mm	35mm	35rf	1955	Jupiter-8	2	50mm	focal plane	½-1250,B	Ru146	100
Kiev-4	24x36mm	35mm	35rf	1957	Jupiter-8	2	50mm	focal plane	½-1250,B	Ru147	110
Kiev-4A	24x36mm	35mm	35rf	1958	Jupiter-8	2	50mm	focal plane	½-1250,B	Ru147	110

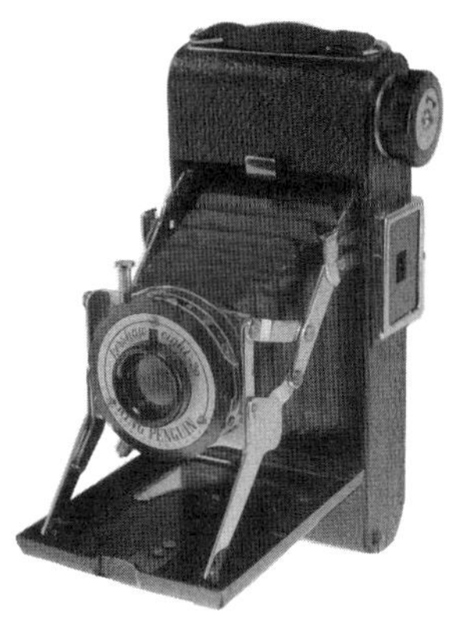

Eight-20 King Penguin

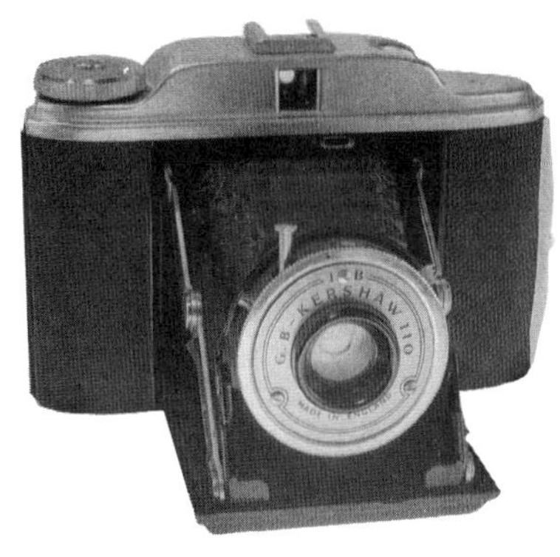

Kershaw 110

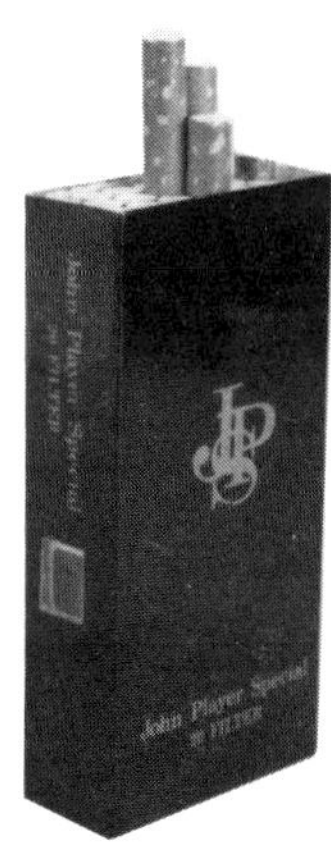

Kiev John Player Special

MODEL	FORMAT	FILM	TYPE	Year	LENS	Apert	FL	SHUTTER	SPEEDS	ILLUS	U.S.$
Kiev-4AM	24x36mm	35mm	35rf	1980	Jupiter-8M	2	50mm	focal plane	½-1250,B	Ru147	100
Kiev-5	24x36mm	35mm	35rf	1967	Jupiter-8M	2	50mm	focal plane	½-1000	Ru149	290
Kiev-6C	6x6cm	120	MedSLR	1971	Vega-12	2.8	90mm	focal plane	½-1000	Ru157	210
Kiev-6C TTL	6x6cm	120	MedSLR	1980	Vega-12	2.8	90mm	focal plane	½-1000	Ru157	220
Kiev-10 Automat	24x36mm	35mm	35slr	1965	Helios-81	2	50mm	focal plane	½-1000	Ru152	170
Kiev-15 TEE	24x36mm	35mm	35slr	1974	Helios-81	2	50mm	focal plane	½-1000	Ru153	110
Kiev-15 TTL	24x36mm	35mm	35slr	1980	Helios-81	2	50mm	focal plane	½-1000	Ru153	200
Kiev-17	24x36mm	35mm	35slr	1977	Helios-81	2	53mm	focal plane	1-1000	Ru154	140
Kiev-19	24x36mm	35mm	35slr	1985	Helios-81	2	50mm	focal plane	½-500	Ru154	110
Kiev 30	13x17mm	16mm	Submin	1974	Industar-M	3.5	23mm	guillotine	30-200	Ru159	50
Kiev 30M	13x17mm	16mm	Submin	1987	Industar-M	3.5	23mm	guillotine	30-200	Ru159	50
Kiev 35A	24x36mm	35mm	35Fold	1985	Kopcap	2.8	35mm	focal plane	30-500	Ru155	70
Kiev 35AM	24x36mm	35mm	35Fold	1990	Kopcap	2.8	35mm	focal plane	30-500	Ru155	90
Kiev-60 TTL	6x6cm	120	MedSLR	1984	Volna-3	2.8	80mm	focal plane	½-1000	Ru157	180
Kiev-80	6x6cm	120	MedSLR	1975	Vega-12B	2.8	90mm	focal plane	½-1000	Ru156	250
Kiev-88	6x6cm	120	MedSLR	1980	Volna-3	2.8	80mm	focal plane	½-1000	Ru156	350
Kiev-88 TTL	6x6cm	120	MedSLR	1980	Volna-3	2.8	80mm	focal plane	½-1000	Ru156	310
Kiev 303 (black)	13x17mm	16mm	Submin	1990	Industar-M	3.5	23mm	guillotine	30-250	Ru159	50
Kiev 303 (red)	13x17mm	16mm	Submin	1990	Industar-M	3.5	23mm	guillotine	30-250	Ru159	50
Kiev 303 (white)	13x17mm	16mm	Submin	1990	Industar-M	3.5	23mm	guillotine	30-250	Ru159	50
Kiev 1949-1989	13x17mm	16mm	Submin	1989	Industar-M	3.5	23mm	guillotine	30-200	Mc255	100
Kiev-Vega	10x14mm	16mm	Submin	1960	Industar-M	3.5	23mm	guillotine	30-200	Ru159	80
Kiev-Vega 2	10x14mm	16mm	Submin	1961	Industar-M	3.5	23mm	guillotine	30-200	Ru159	80
Salyut	6x6cm	120	MedSLR	1957	Industar	2.8	80mm	focal plane	½-1500	Ru156	210
Salyut-S	6x6cm	120	MedSLR	1972	Vega-12B	2.8	90mm	focal plane	½-1000	Ru156	260
Zenit 80	6x6cm	120	MedSLR	1975	Industar	2.8	80mm	focal plane	½-1000	Ru156	280
...KILFITT (Heinz Kilfitt) - Munich											
Mecaflex	24x24mm	35mm	35SLR	1953	Kilar	3.5	40mm	Prontor-Refl.		A544	1000
Mecaflex	24x24mm	35mm	35SLR	1953	Kilar	2.8	40mm	Prontor-Refl.		Mc256	1000
...KING KG - Bad Liebenzell											
Azore V	24x36mm	35mm	35rf	1955		3.5	50mm		1/300		30
Azore V	24x36mm	35mm	35rf	1955	Cassarit	2.8	50mm	Prontor-SVS			30
Dominant	24x36mm	35mm	35vf		Cassar	2.8	45mm	Prontor500LK			20
Mastra V35	24x36mm	35mm	35vf	1958	Cassar	2.8	45mm	Vero		Mc256	20
Regula IP	24x36mm	35mm	35vf	1951	Cassar	2.8	45mm	Prontor-S		A1164	50
Regula IPa	24x36mm	35mm	35vf	1954	Cassar	3.5	45mm	Pronto		A1165	50
Regula IPa	24x36mm	35mm	35vf	1954	Cassar	2.8	45mm	Prontor-SV	1-300		50
Regula IIId	24x36mm	35mm	35rf	1957	Ennit	2.8	50mm	Prontor-SVS		A1165a	90
Regula IIId	24x36mm	35mm	35rf	1957	Color Westagon	1.9	50mm	Prontor-SVS		A1165a	90
Regula 118	13x17mm	110	110	1978	fixed focus	9.5	32mm		60		20
Regula 218 L	13x17mm	110	110	1978	fixed focus	9.5	32mm		50-125		30
Regula 218 LE	13x17mm	110	110	1978	fixed focus	9.5	32mm		50-125		20

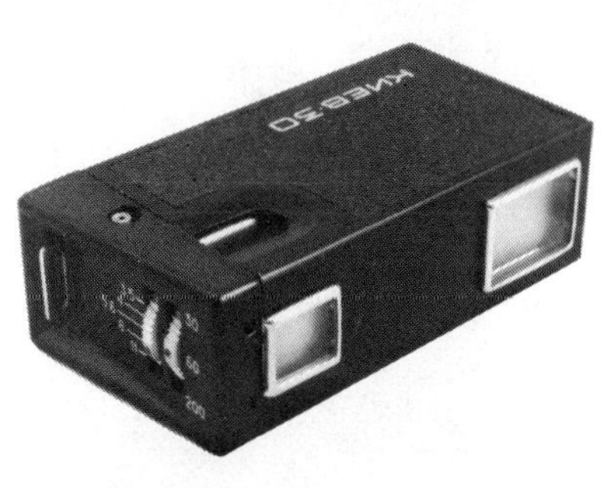

Kiev 30

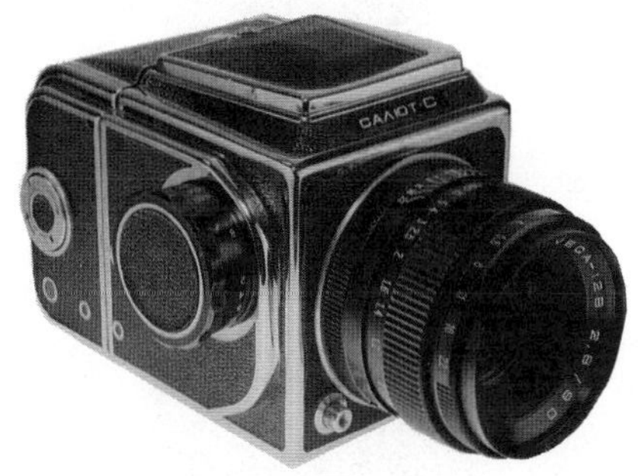

Kiev Salyut-S

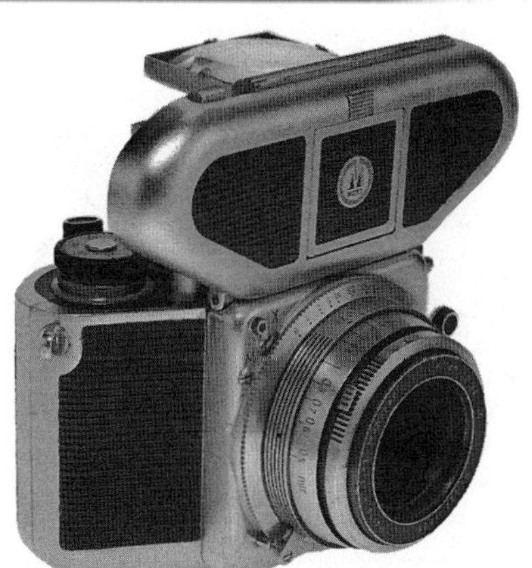

Kilfitt Mecaflex

MODEL	FORMAT	FILM	TYPE	Year	LENS	Apert	FL	SHUTTER	SPEEDS	ILLUS	U.S.$
Regula 410	13x17mm	110	110	1978	fixed focus	9.5	30mm		100		30
Regula 430	13x17mm	110	110	1978	fixed focus	5.6	27mm		100		30
Regula 460 EL	13x17mm	110	110	1978	fixed focus	5.6	25mm	electronic	10-1/500		30
Regula 510	13x17mm	110	110	1978	fixed focus	9.5	32mm		100-250		30
Regula 510 Tele	13x17mm	110	110	1978	fixed focus	9.5	32/42		100-250		30
Regula 530	13x17mm	110	110	1978	fixed focus	5.6	27mm		100-250		30
Regula Cita	24x36mm	35mm	35vf	1957	Cassar	3.5	45mm	Prontor-SVS			60
Regula Cita	24x36mm	35mm	35vf	1957	Cassar	2.8	45mm	Prontor-SVS			60
Regula Cita III	24x36mm	35mm	35rf	1957	Cassar	2.8	45mm	Prontor-SVS			70
Regula Cita III	24x36mm	35mm	35rf	1957	Tessar	2.8	50mm	Prontor-SVS			70
Regula Citalux 300	24x36mm	35mm	35rf	1957	Cassar S	2.8	45mm			Mc256	320
Regula Disc 2001	8x10mm	Disc	Disc	1983	fixed focus	5.6	12.5mm		1/200		40
Regula Disc 3001	8x10mm	Disc	Disc	1983	fixed focus	2.8	12.5mm		1/200		50
Regula Disc 4001	8x10mm	Disc	Disc	1983	fixed focus	2.8	12.5mm		1/200	A3381	70
Regula Oga	24x36mm	35mm	35VF	1960	Color Gotar	2.8	45mm				20
Reg. Refl.2000CTL(black)	24x36mm	35mm	35SLR	1969	Isco Westomat	1.9	50mm	focal plane	1-2000	A3196	260
Reg. Refl.2000CTL(chrome)	24x36mm	35mm	35SLR	1969	Isco Westomat	1.9	50mm	focal plane	1-2000		230
Regula Reflex CTL	24x36mm	35mm	35SLR	1966	Isco Westomat	1.9	50mm	focal plane	1-2000,B		130
Regula Reflex K650	24x36mm	35mm	35SLR	1972	Westomat	1.9	50mm	focal plane			300
Kalimar/Regula Refl. K650	24x36mm	35mm	35SLR	1972	Westomat	1.9	50mm	focal plane			300
Regula Reflex SL	24x36mm	35mm	35SLR	1966	Isco Westomat	1.9	50mm	focal plane	1-2000,B		120
Regula Sprinty	24x36mm	35mm	35vf	1963	Color Gotar	2.8	45mm	Rectamat	30-250		30
Regula Sprinty B	24x36mm	35mm	35vf	1956	Color Gotar	2.8	45mm	Rectamat	30-250		30
Regula Sprinty BC300	24x36mm	35mm	35vf	1970	Color Gotar	2.8	45mm	Rectamat	30-300		30
Regula Sprinty C300	24x36mm	35mm	35vf	1970	Color Gotar	2.8	45mm	Rectamat	30-300		20
Regula Sprinty CC300	24x36mm	35mm	35vf	1970	Color Isconar	2.8	45mm	Rectamat	30-300		30
Regulette	24x36mm	35mm	35vf	1960	Cassar	2.8	45mm	Vero	30-250		30
Regulette	24x36mm	35mm	35vf	1960	Cassar	2.8	45mm	Pronto	30-250		30
Regulette 300 SB	24x36mm	35mm	35vf	1965	Cassar	2.8	45mm	Prontor-S	30-300		40
Ringfoto Reflex	24x36mm	35mm	35SLR	1976	Cassaron	2.8	50mm	focal plane	1-2000	A1676	110
...KINN - France											
Kinaflex	6x6cm	120	TLR	1951	Berhtiot Flor	3.5	75mm	Atos-2		Mc257	70
Kinax (I)	6x9cm	120	FoldRo	1949	Berthiot	4.5	105mm			F336	30
Kinax II	6x9cm	120	FoldRo	1950	Som Berthiot	4.5	105mm	Kinax		F338	30
Kinax II	6x9cm	120	FoldRo	1950	Major Kinn	4.5	105mm	Kinax		F338	30
Kinax Alsace (black)	6x9cm	620	FoldRo	1952	Berthiot	6.3	100mm	Kinax	25-100		30
Kinax Alsace (burgundy)	6x9cm	620	FoldRo	1952	Berthiot	6.3	100mm	Kinax	25-100		50
Kinax Baby	6x9cm	120	FoldRo	1950	Meniscus					Mc257	30
Kinax Cadet	6x9cm	120	FoldRo	1950	Cadet	6.3	105mm	Kinax	1-100		30
Kinax Junior	6x9cm	Roll	FoldRo	1950	Kior Anastigmat	6.3	100mm		25-150	F333	40
Kinax Major	6x9cm	120	FoldRo	1950							30
Super Kinax	6x9cm	620	FoldRo	1950	Bellor	3.5	100mm			F335	50

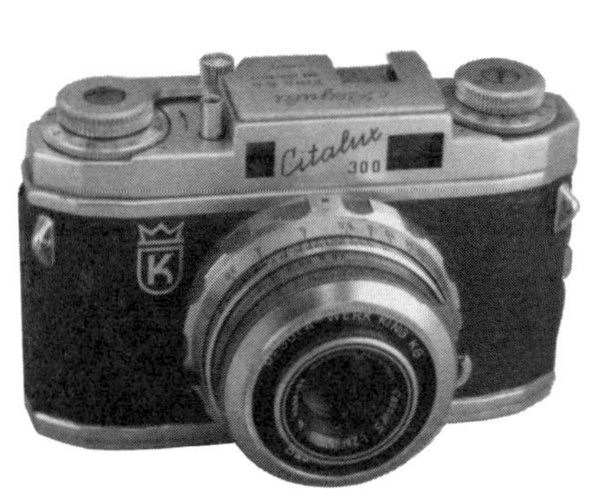

Regula Citalux 300

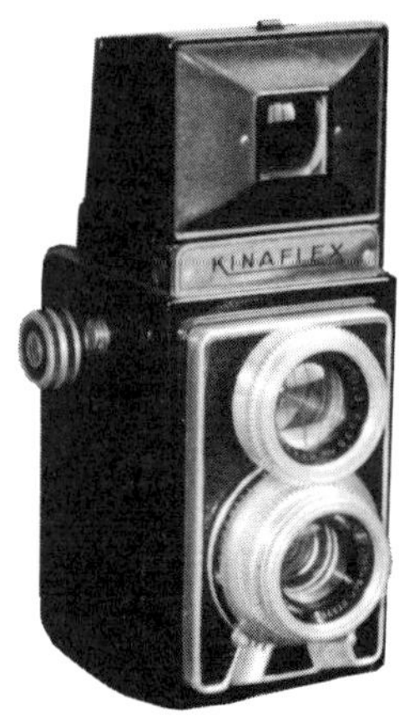

Kinaflex

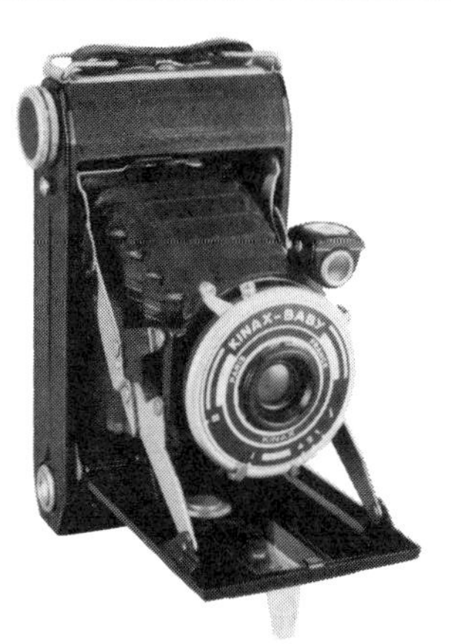

Kinax Baby

MODEL	FORMAT	FILM	TYPE	Year	LENS	Apert	FL	SHUTTER	SPEEDS	ILLUS	U.S.$
...KLEFFEL (L.G. Kleffel & Sohn) - Berlin											
Field cam. (brown bellows)	13x18cm	plate	Field	1890	various						270
Field cam. (green bellows)	13x18cm	plate	Field	1890	various						280
Stereo Wet-plate	30x30cm	WetPl	StWetPl	1890	Steinheil						2000
...KNOLL - Leipzig											
Field camera	13x18cm	plate	Field	1905	Doppel-Rigonar	6.3	240mm				290
...KOCHMANN (Franz Kochmann) - Dresden											
Enolde	6x9cm	plate	FoldRo	1931	Enolde Anast.	4.5			3 Zeiten	Mc258	260
Enolde	6x9cm	plate	FoldRo	1931	Zeiss Tessar	4.5		Compur		A482	260
Enolde I	6.5x9cm	plate	FoldPl	1930	Enolde	4.5	105mm				50
Enolde II	6.5x9cm	plate	FoldPl	1930	Enolde	4.5	105mm				50
Enolde III	6.5x9cm	plate	FoldPl	1930	Enolde	4.5	105mm				50
Enolde Spiegel-Reflex	9x12cm	plate	SLR-Box	1925	Polynar	6.8	120mm		M,Z	A1598	280
Korelle 3x4	3x4cm	127	StrutRo	1933	E. Ludwig Vidar	4.5	50mm	Vario		Mc258	80
Korelle 4x6.5	4x6.5cm	127	StrutRo	1930	Schn. Radionar	3.5	75mm	Prontor-II		Mc258	140
Korelle 4x6.5	4x6.5cm	127	StrutRo	1930	Xenar	2.8	75mm	Compur		A1494	140
Korelle 4x6.5	4x6.5cm	127	StrutRo	1930	Schn. Radionar	3.5	75mm	Compur-Rapid		HK280	140
Korelle 6x6	6x6cm	120	StrutRo	1937	Xenar	3.5	75mm	Prontor	25-125		170
Korelle 6x6	6x6cm	120	StrutRo	1937	Xenar	3.5	75mm	Prontor-II	1-150	HK283	170
Korelle 6x6 + Tessar	6x6cm	120	StrutRo	1937	Tessar	2.8	75mm	Compur-Rapid			210
Korelle 6x9	6x9cm	120	VtFoldRo	1934	Radionar	4.5	105mm	Prontor		A1468	50
Korelle 6x9	6x9cm	120	VtFoldRo	1934	Radionar	4.5	105mm	Compur			50
Korelle 6x9	6x9cm	120	VtFoldRo	1934	Xenar	3.5	105mm	Compur			50
Korelle K (black)	18x24mm	35mm	RigidRo	1933	Tessar	3.5	35mm	Compur	1-300		390
Korelle K (black) + Elmar	18x24mm	35mm	RigidRo	1933	Elmar	3.5	35mm	Compur	1-300		800
Korelle K (brown)	18x24mm	35mm	RigidRo	1933	Tessar	3.5	35mm	Compur	1-300		700
Korelle K (brown)	18x24mm	35mm	RigidRo	1933	Trioplan	2.8	35mm	Compur	1-300		700
Korelle K (brown) + Elmar	18x24mm	35mm	RigidRo	1933	Elmar	3.5	35mm	Compur	1-300		1000
Korelle P	4x6.5cm	plate	StrutPl	1933	Tessar	2.8	75mm	Compur	1-250	Mc258	430
Korelle P	4x6.5cm	plate	StrutPl	1933	Xenar	2.9	75mm	Compur	1-250	A345	430
Reflex-Korelle (I)	6x6cm	120	MedSLR	1935	Victar	2.9	75mm	focal plane	1/10-1000	Mc258	110
Reflex-Korelle (I)	6x6cm	120	MedSLR	1935	Radionar	2.9	75mm	focal plane	1/10-1000	HK354	110
Reflex-Korelle (Ia)	6x6cm	120	MedSLR	1936	Radionar	2.9	75mm	focal plane	25-500	HK355	120
Reflex-Korelle (Ia)	6x6cm	120	MedSLR	1936	Tessar	2.8	75mm	focal plane	25-500	A597	120
Reflex-Korelle II	6x6cm	120	MedSLR	1940	Radionar	2.9	75mm	focal plane	2-1/500	HK355	120
Reflex-Korelle II	6x6cm	120	MedSLR	1940	Tessar	2.8	75mm	focal plane	2-1/500	HK355	120
Reflex-Korelle III (black)	6x6cm	120	MedSLR	1940	Tessar	2.8	80mm	focal plane	2-1/1000		140
Reflex-Korelle III (chrome)	6x6cm	120	MedSLR	1940	Xenar	3.5	80mm	focal plane	2-1/1000	HK356	140
Sport Korelle 66	6x6cm	120	StrutRo	1939	Xenar	3.5	80mm	focal plane	1-1000	HK296	360
Sport Korelle 66	6x6cm	120	StrutRo	1939	Tessar	2.8	80mm	focal plane	1-1000		360
...KÖHNLEIN (Konrad Köhnlein) - Nürnberg											
Wiko Standard	13x17mm	16mm	Submin	1936	Laack Poloyt	4.5	30mm	focal plane	20-200	Mc258	1500

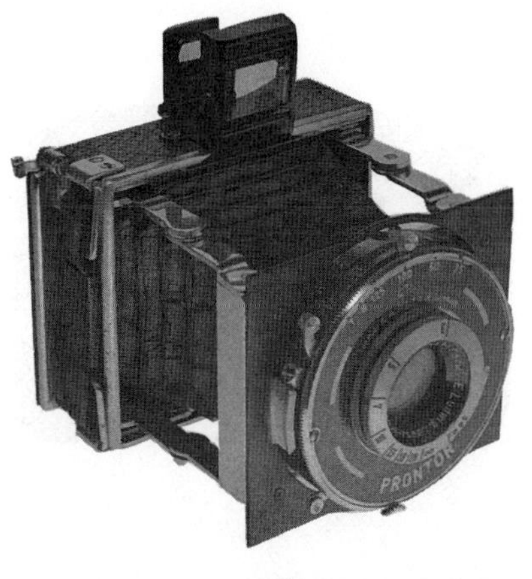

Korelle P

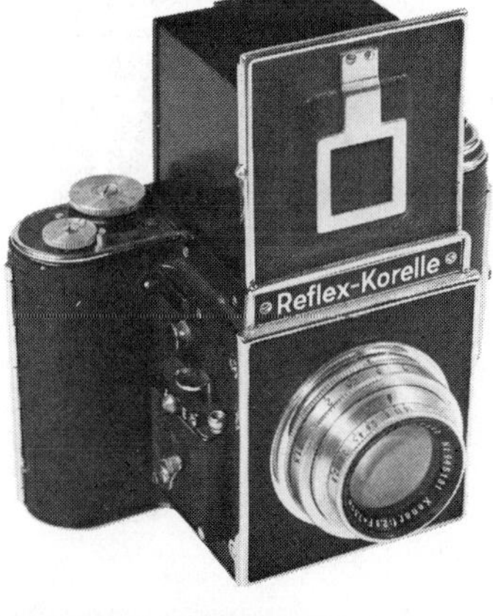

Reflex-Korelle (I)

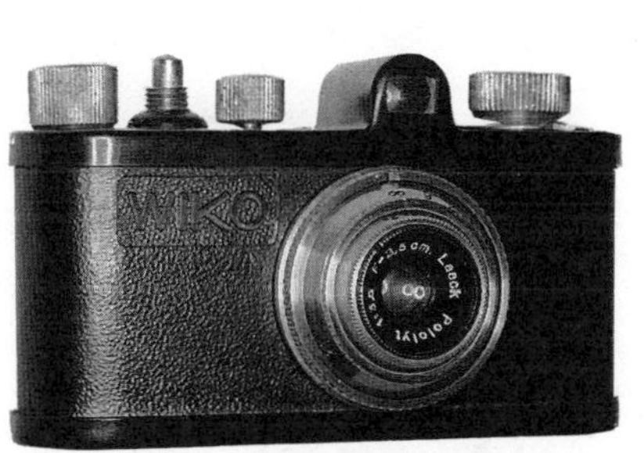

Wiko Standard

MODEL	FORMAT	FILM	TYPE	Year	LENS	Apert	FL	SHUTTER	SPEEDS	ILLUS	U.S.$
...KÓLAR (Václav Kólar) - Modrany & Prague											
Box Kolex	4.5x6cm	plate	MetBx	1932	Rekolar	6.3	75mm	Pronto			200
Box Kolex	4.5x6cm	plate	MetBx	1932	Rekolar	6.3	75mm	Vario			200
Kola 24x36	24x36mm	35mm	RigidRo	1932	Kolyt	3.5	50mm	Compur		A1528	220
Kola 3x4	3x4cm	127	RigidRo	1932	Dialytar	4.5	50mm	Compur		A1528	220
Kola 4x4	4x4cm	127	RigidRo	1932	Primotar	4.5	50mm	Compur		A1528	220
Kola A 24x36	24x36mm	35mm	RigidRo	1932	Tessar	2.8	60mm	Compur		A1528	220
Kola A 3x4	3x4cm	127	RigidRo	1932	Trioplan	3.5	50mm	Compur		A1528	220
Kola A 4x4	4x4cm	127	RigidRo	1932	Xenar	3.5	50mm	Compur		A1528	220
Kola (folding rollfilm)	4.5x6cm	120	FoldRo	1934	Rekolat	6.3	75mm	Vario	25-100		50
Kola Diar	32x32mm	Roll	RigidRo	1933	Achromat	11	50mm	Siko			200
Kolar	6.5x7.5cm	111	TelescRo	193x	Rekolar	6.3	75mm	Vario			70
Kolarex 555	4x6.5cm	127	FoldRo	1932	Rekolar	6.3		Vario			110
Kolarex 556	4x6.5cm	127	FoldRo	1932	Kolyt	3.5		Compur			110
Kolarex 558	4x6.5cm	127	FoldRo	1932	Dialytar	4.5		Compur			110
Kolarex 560	4x6.5cm	127	FoldRo	1932	Primotar	4.5		Compur			110
Kolarex 563	4x6.5cm	127	FoldRo	1932	Trioplan	3.5		Prontor-S			110
Kolarex 595	4x6.5cm	127	FoldRo	1932	Crexar	3.5		Prontor-S			110
Kolex 504	4.5x6cm	plate	VtFoldPl	1932	Rekolar	4.5	75mm	Vario		Mc259	190
Kolex 505	4.5x6cm	plate	VtFoldPl	1932	Rekolar	6.3	75mm	Vario		Mc259	190
Kolex 506	4.5x6cm	plate	VtFoldPl	1932	Kolyt	3.5	75mm	Compur		Mc259	190
Kolex 510	4.5x6cm	plate	VtFoldPl	1932	Primotar	4.5	75mm	Compur		Mc259	190
Kolex 511	4.5x6cm	plate	VtFoldPl	1932	Trioplan	3.5	75mm	Compur		Mc259	190
Kolex 512	4.5x6cm	plate	VtFoldPl	1932	Rekolar	3.5	75mm	Pronto		Mc259	190
Turist	4x6cm	Roll	FoldRo	1937	Rekolar	4.5	75mm	Vario			140
Turist 589	4x6cm	Roll	FoldRo	1937	Primotar	4.5	75mm	Vario			140
...KOLBE & SCHULZE - Freital b/Dresden											
Autix	6x9cm	120	FoldRo	1932	Akor	6.3	105mm	Vario			50
Autix	6x9cm	120	FoldRo	1932	Vidar	6.3	105mm	Ibsor			50
Tixette	6.5x9cm	plate	VtFoldPl	1930	Vidar	6.3	105mm	Pronto			140
Tixette	6.5x9cm	plate	VtFoldPl	1930	Xenar	4.5	105mm	Compur			140
...KOMAMURA - Japan											
Horseman 450	4x5"	plate	Monorail	1978	various			various		A1439	900
Horseman 570	5x7"	plate	Monorail	1982	various			various			1100
Horseman VH	6x9cm	120	Press	1983	various			Seiko	1-500		1100
Horseman VH-R	6x9cm	120	Press	1981	various			Seiko	1-500	A1409	1300
...KONISHIROKU KOGAKU / KONICA CORP. - Japan											
Acom-1	24x36mm	35mm	35slr	1977	Hexanon AR	1.7	50mm	focal plane	8-1000		110
Aiborg	24x36mm	35mm	35afz	1993		3.5-8.5	35-105	programmed	6.4-1/500		180
Autoreflex	24x36mm	35mm	35slr	1967	Hexanon	1.4	57mm	focal plane	1-1000	Mc260	130
Autoreflex A	24x36mm	35mm	35slr	1969	Hexanon	1.8	52mm	Automatic TTL	1-1000		120
Autoreflex A3	24x36mm	35mm	35slr	1974	Hexanon	1.8	52mm	focal plane	1-1000		90

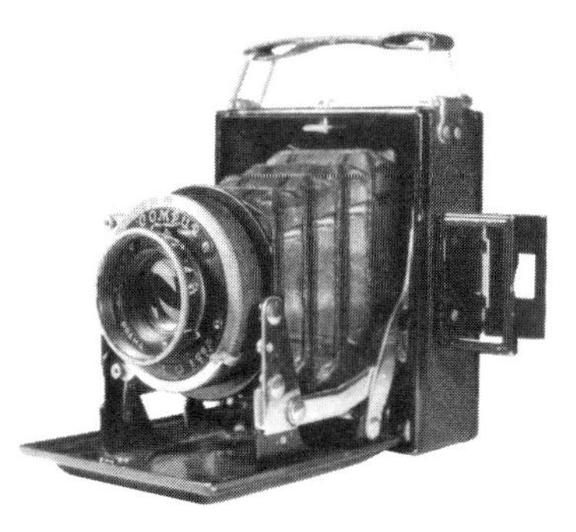

Kolar Kolex 505

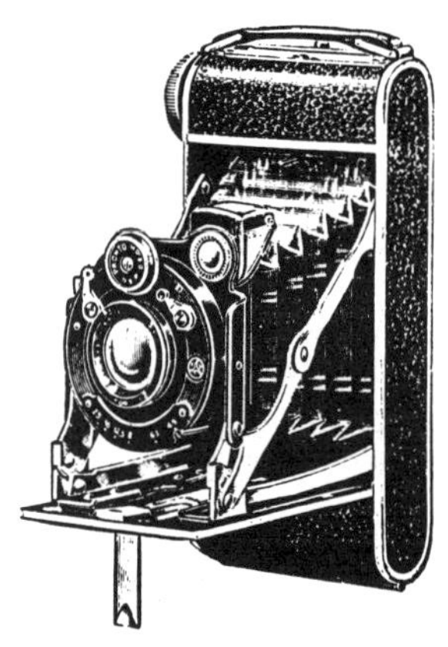

Kolbe & Schulze Autix

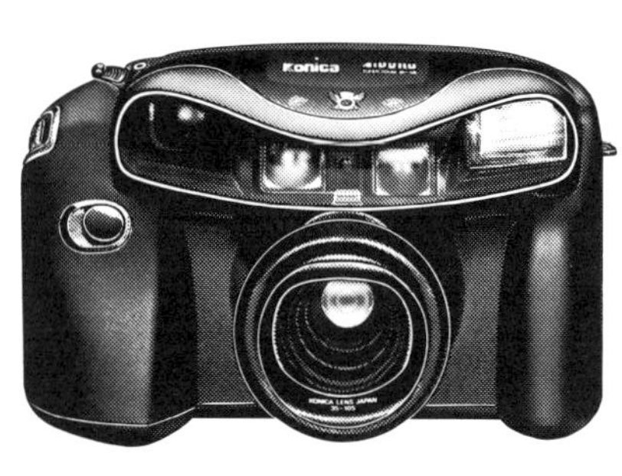

Konishiroku Aiborg

MODEL	FORMAT	FILM	TYPE	Year	LENS	Apert	FL	SHUTTER	SPEEDS	ILLUS	U.S.$
Autoreflex T	24x36mm	35mm	35slr	1968	Hexanon	1.7	50mm	Automatic TTL	1-1000		100
Autoreflex T2	24x36mm	35mm	35slr	1971	Hexanon	1.8	52mm	focal plane	1-1000		130
Autoreflex T3	24x36mm	35mm	35slr	1973	Hexanon	1.4	57mm	focal plane	1-1000		130
Autoreflex T3N	24x36mm	35mm	35slr	1976	Hexanon	1.4	57mm	focal plane	1-1000		150
Autoreflex T4	24x36mm	35mm	35slr	1978	Hexanon AR	1.7	50mm	focal plane	1-1000		150
Autoreflex TC	24x36mm	35mm	35slr	1977	Hexanon AR	1.7	50mm	focal plane	8-1000	A1700	110
Baby Pearl	3x4cm	127	FoldRo	1934	Hexar	4.5	50mm	Rox	B,25,100	Mc259	160
Baby Pearl	3x4cm	127	FoldRo	1934	Optar	4.5	50mm	Rox	B,25,100	Mc259	140
Big Mini BM-201 (black)	24x36mm	35mm	35caf	1990	Konica	3.5	35mm	programmed	3.6-1/500		100
Big Mini BM-201 (gold)	24x36mm	35mm	35caf	1990	Konica	3.5	35mm	programmed	3.6-1/500		100
Big Mini BM-201 D (black)	24x36mm	35mm	35caf	1990	Konica	3.5	35mm	programmed	3.6-1/500		100
Big Mini BM-201 D (gold)	24x36mm	35mm	35caf	1990	Konica	3.5	35mm	programmed	3.6-1/500		100
Big Mini BM-300	24x36mm	35mm	35af	1995		3.5	35mm	programmed	7.5-1/360		120
Big Mini BM-301 (black)	24x36mm	35mm	35af	1992		3.5	35mm	programmed	7.5-1/360		120
Big Mini BM-301 (chrome)	24x36mm	35mm	35af	1992		3.5	35mm	programmed	7.5-1/360		120
Big Mini BM-302	24x36mm	35mm	35af	1993	Konica	3.5	35mm	programmed	7.5-1/360		120
Big Mini BM-302 Date	24x36mm	35mm	35af	1993	Konica	3.5	35mm	programmed	7.5-1/360		120
Big Mini BM-310Z	24x36mm	35mm	35afz	1991		3.6-6.8	35-70	programmed	3.3-1/360		120
Big Mini BM-311Z	24x36mm	35mm	35afz	1991		3.6-6.8	35-70	programmed	3.3-1/360		120
Big Mini HG	24x36mm	35mm	35af	1995		3.5	35mm	programmed	7.5-1/360		120
Big Mini Jr BM-20 (black)	24x36mm	35mm	35vf	1995		4.5	34mm		80-250		60
Big Mini Jr BM-20 (red)	24x36mm	35mm	35vf	1995		4.5	34mm		80-250		70
Big Mini SR BM-100	24x36mm	35mm	35af	1995		4.3	34mm		4-250		70
Big Mini Zoom BM-410Z	24x36mm	35mm	35afz	1993		3.6-6.8	35-70	programmed	3.3-1/360		140
Big Mini Zoom BM-410Z D	24x36mm	35mm	35afz	1993		3.6-6.8	35-70	programmed	3.3-1/360		160
Big Mini Zoom BM-510Z	24x36mm	35mm	35afz	1994	Konica	3.9-7.4	35-70	programmed	4.5-1/360		170
Big Mini Zoom BM-510Z D	24x36mm	35mm	35afz	1994	Konica	3.9-7.4	35-70	programmed	4.5-1/360		180
Dr. Finder EFP-30 (black)	24x36mm	35mm	35vf	1993	Konica	4.5	35mm		1/125		30
Dr. Finder EFP-30 (red)	24x36mm	35mm	35vf	1993	Konica	4.5	35mm		1/125		30
Dr. Finder Jr. EPJ-10	24x36mm	35mm	35vf	1993	Konica	9.5	35mm				30
Electron	24x36mm	35mm	35rf	1969	Hexanon	1.8	45mm	Copal			60
Genbakantoku 28	24x36mm	35mm	35af	1991	Konica	3.5	28mm	programmed	4-280		110
Hexar	24x36mm	35mm	35af	1993	Hexar	2	35mm	programmed	30-1/250		560
Hexar Classic	24x36mm	35mm	35af	1993	Hexar	2	35mm	programmed	30-1/250		630
Hexar Gold	24x36mm	35mm	35af	1993	Hexar	2	35mm	programmed	30-1/250		1300
Hexar Rhodium	24x36mm	35mm	35af	1994	Hexar	2	35mm	programmed	30-1/250		1300
Idea 4x5"	4x5"	plate	FoldPl	1909	Tessar	6.3	16.5cm	Compur	1-200		410
Idea 13x18	13x18cm	plate	FoldPl	1909	Wollensak	6.8		Optimo	1-300		440
Idea A	8x10.5cm	plate	FoldPl	1922	Prontor-S	8			T,B,I		120
Idea A	8x10.5cm	plate	FoldPl	1922	Anastigmat	7.5			10-100		120
Idea Hand Camera 6.5x9	6.5x9cm	plate	FoldPl	1930	Trinar Anastigmat	6.3	10.5cm	Ibsor	1-125		70
Idea Hand Camera 8x10.5	8x10.5cm	plate	FoldPl	1930	Trinar Anastigmat	6.3	135mm	Koilos	25 100		70

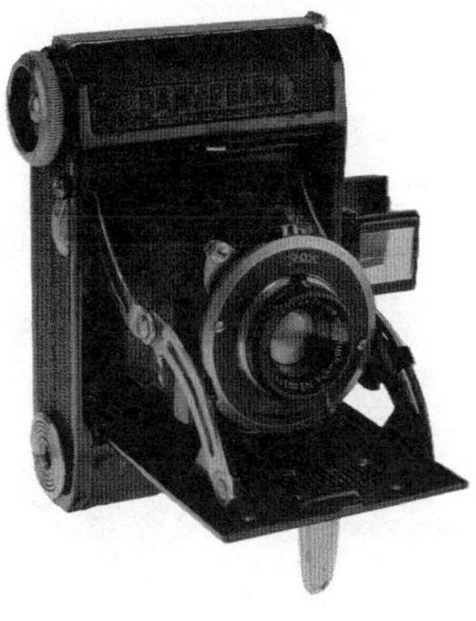

Baby Pearl

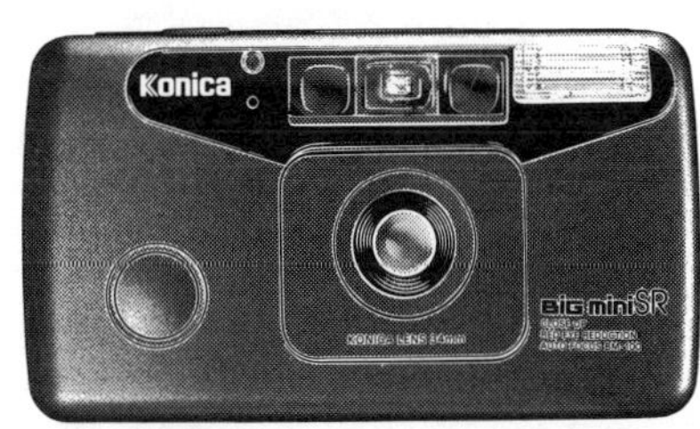

Big Mini SR BM-100

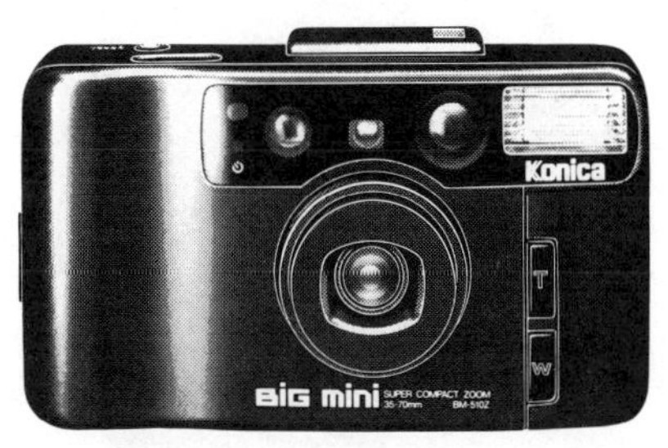

Big Mini Zoom BM-510Z

MODEL	FORMAT	FILM	TYPE	Year	LENS	Apert	FL	SHUTTER	SPEEDS	ILLUS	U.S.$
Instant Press	73x95mm	INST	Instant	1987		4.5	110mm	Copal	1-500		250
Jump	24x36mm	35mm	35aw	1988	Konica	4	35mm		1/125		60
Jump Auto (green / violet)	24x36mm	35mm	35aw	1991	Konica	4.5	34mm		1/125		70
Jump Auto (violet / gray)	24x36mm	35mm	35aw	1991	Konica	4.5	34mm		1/125		70
Jump Auto II	24x36mm	35mm	35aw	1991	Konica	4.5	34mm		1/125		50
Jump Auto III	24x36mm	35mm	35aw	1991	Konica	4.5	34mm		1/125		50
Jump Auto-date	24x36mm	35mm	35aw	1988	Konica	4	35mm		1/125		60
Jump Shot	24x36mm	35mm	35aw	1993		4.5	34mm		50, 125		100
Kanpai	24x36mm	35mm	35vf	1990	Konica	5.6	34mm	programmed	1-200		100
Kanpai Date	24x36mm	35mm	35vf	1991	Konica	5.6	34mm	programmed	1-200		110
Koni-Omega Rapid	6x7cm	Roll	Press	1965	Hexanon	3.5	90mm			Mc259	160
Koni-Omega Rapid M	6x7cm	Roll	Press	1967	Hexanon	3.5	90mm				390
Koni-Omegaflex M	6x7cm	Roll	Press	1969	Hexanon	4.5	180mm			Mc259	290
Konica (I) Occupied Japan	24x36mm	35mm	35rf	1948	Hexanon	2.8	50mm	Konirapid	1-500	A2140	100
Konica I	24x36mm	35mm	35rf	1950	Hexar	3.5	50mm	Konirapid-S	1-500	Mc259	100
Konica I (Signal Corps)	24x36mm	35mm	35rf	1953	Hexanon	2.8	50mm	Konirapid-S	1-500	A2141	150
Konica II	24x36mm	35mm	35rf	1951	Hexanon	2.8	50mm	Konirap.-MFX	1-500	Mc259	90
Konica III	24x36mm	35mm	35rf	1956	Hexanon	2	48mm	Konirap.-MFX	1-500	Mc259	160
Konica IIIA	24x36mm	35mm	35rf	1958	Hexanon	2	48mm	Konirap.-MFX	1-500	Mc260	80
Konica IIIM	24x36mm	35mm	35rf	1959	Hexanon	1.8	50mm	Seikosha-SLV	1-500	Mc260	130
Konica A4 (black)	24x36mm	35mm	35caf	1990	Konica	3.5	35mm	programmed	3-500		100
Konica A4 (silver)	24x36mm	35mm	35caf	1990	Konica	3.5	35mm	programmed	3-500		100
Konica A4 Date (black)	24x36mm	35mm	35caf	1990	Konica	3.5	35mm	programmed	3-500		160
Konica A4 Date (silver)	24x36mm	35mm	35caf	1990	Konica	3.5	35mm	programmed	3-500		160
Konica AA-35 (black)	18x24mm	35mm	35Half	1983	Hexanon	4	24mm	programmed	60-250		60
Konica AA-35 (gold)	18x24mm	35mm	35Half	1983	Hexanon	4	24mm	programmed	60-250		60
Konica AA-35 (red)	18x24mm	35mm	35Half	1984	Hexanon	4	24mm	programmed	60-250		60
Konica AF3 (black)	24x36mm	35mm	35af	1983	Konica	2.8	35mm	programmed	60-500		60
Konica AF3 (blue)	24x36mm	35mm	35af	1983	Konica	2.8	35mm	programmed	60-500		60
Konica AF3 (red)	24x36mm	35mm	35af	1983	Konica	2.8	35mm	programmed	60-500		60
Konica AF3 (silver)	24x36mm	35mm	35af	1983	Konica	2.8	35mm	programmed	60-500		60
Konica AF3 (wine)	24x36mm	35mm	35af	1983	Konica	2.8	35mm	programmed	60-500		60
Konica AF3 (yellow)	24x36mm	35mm	35af	1983	Konica	2.8	35mm	programmed	60-500		60
Konica AF3D (black)	24x36mm	35mm	35af	1983	Konica	2.8	35mm	programmed	60-500		60
Konica AF3D (red)	24x36mm	35mm	35af	1983	Konica	2.8	35mm	programmed	60-500		60
Konica AQ-110	13x17mm	110	110UW	1988	Konica	4.5	25.5mm		1/125		60
Konica Auto S	24x36mm	35mm	35rf	1960	Hexanon	1.9	47mm	Copal	1-500	Mc260	70
Konica Auto S1.6	24x36mm	35mm	35rf	1968	Hexanon	1.6	45mm		1-500		50
Konica C35	24x36mm	35mm	35rf	1969	Hexanon	2.8	38mm	programmed	30-650		50
Konica C35 AF	24x36mm	35mm	35af	1977	Hexanon	2.8	38mm	programmed	60-250		90
Konica C35 AF2	24x36mm	35mm	35af	1981	Hexanon	2.8	38mm	programmed	60-250		50
Konica C35 AF2D	24x36mm	35mm	35af	1982	Hexanon	2.8	38mm	programmed	60-250		50

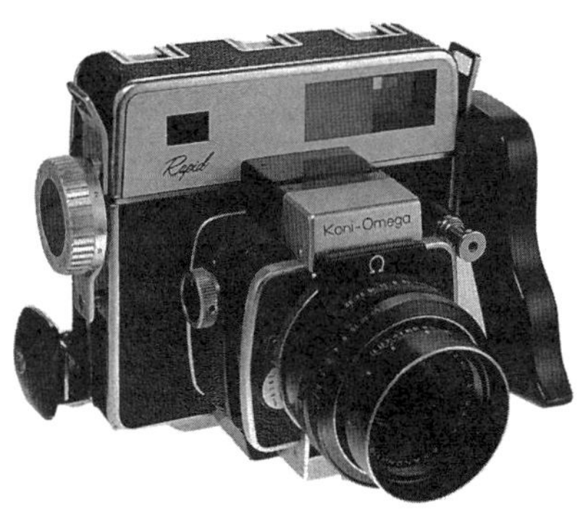

Koni-Omega Rapid

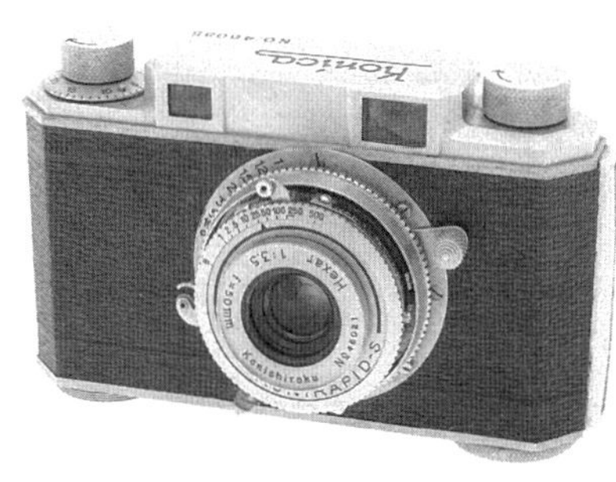

Konica I

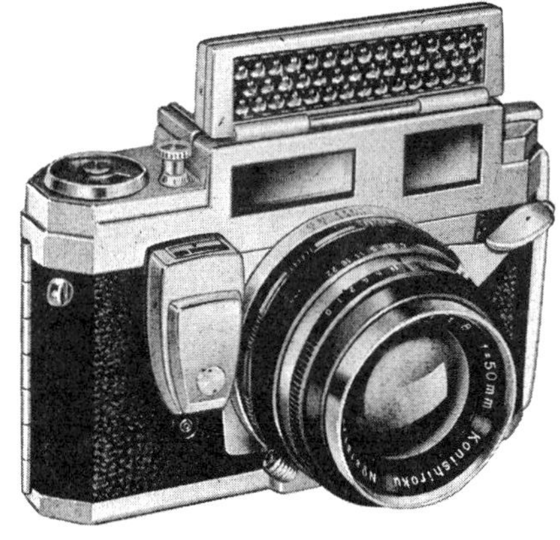

Konica IIIM

MODEL	FORMAT	FILM	TYPE	Year	LENS	Apert	FL	SHUTTER	SPEEDS	ILLUS	U.S.$
Konica C35 EF	24x36mm	35mm	35rf	1975	Hexanon	2.8	35mm	programmed	60-250		50
Konica C35 EF3 (black)	24x36mm	35mm	35vf	1980	Hexanon	2.8	35mm	programmed	60-500		50
Konica C35 EF3 (blue)	24x36mm	35mm	35vf	1980	Hexanon	2.8	35mm	programmed	60-500		50
Konica C35 EF3 (gold)	24x36mm	35mm	35vf	1980	Hexanon	2.8	35mm	programmed	60-500		60
Konica C35 EF3 (red)	24x36mm	35mm	35vf	1980	Hexanon	2.8	35mm	programmed	60-500		50
Konica C35 EF3 (white)	24x36mm	35mm	35vf	1980	Hexanon	2.8	35mm	programmed	60-500		50
Konica C35 EF3D (black)	24x36mm	35mm	35vf	1981	Hexanon	2.8	35mm	programmed	60-500		60
Konica C35 EF3D (red)	24x36mm	35mm	35vf	1981	Hexanon	2.8	35mm	programmed	60-500		60
Konica C35 EFD	24x36mm	35mm	35rf	1978	Hexanon	2.8	35mm	programmed	60-250		50
Konica C35 EF-P	24x36mm	35mm	35vf	1977	Hexanon	4	38mm		1/125		50
Konica C35 MF	24x36mm	35mm	35af	1981	Hexanon	2.8	38mm	programmed	60-250		70
Konica C35 MFD	24x36mm	35mm	35af	1982	Hexanon	2.8	38mm	programmed	60-250		70
---EFJ AutoD.(black)	24x36mm	35mm	35vf	1982		4	36mm				50
Konica EFJ AutoDate(blue)	24x36mm	35mm	35vf	1982		4	36mm				50
Konica EFJ AutoDate(red)	24x36mm	35mm	35vf	1982		4	36mm				50
Konica EFJ AutoD.(yellow)	24x36mm	35mm	35vf	1982		4	36mm				50
Konica EFP-2	24x36mm	35mm	35vf	1985	Hexanon	5.6	38mm				20
Konica EFP-3 (black)	24x36mm	35mm	35vf	1988	Konica	4.2	36mm		1/125		50
Konica EFP-3 (red)	24x36mm	35mm	35vf	1988	Konica	4.2	36mm		1/125		50
Konica EFP-10	24x36mm	35mm	35vf	1990	Konica	5.6	38mm		1/100		30
Konica EFP-20 (black)	24x36mm	35mm	35vf	1991	Konica	4.2	36mm		1/125		30
Konica EFP-20 (red)	24x36mm	35mm	35vf	1991	Konica	4.2	36mm		1/125		30
Konica EFP-J	24x36mm	35mm	35vf	1991	Konica	8	33mm		1/125		10
Konica EU mini (black)	24x36mm	35mm	35vf	1994		6.7	28mm	programmed	1/60, 180		50
Konica EU mini (blue)	24x36mm	35mm	35vf	1994		6.7	28mm	programmed	1/60, 180		50
Konica EU mini (red)	24x36mm	35mm	35vf	1994		6.7	28mm	programmed	1/60, 180		50
Konica Eye	18x24mm	35mm	35Half	1966	Hexanon	1.9	30mm	Copal B			50
Konica Eye 2	18x24mm	35mm	35Half	1967	Hexanon	1.8	32mm	Copal B			50
Konica F	24x36mm	35mm	35slr	1960				Vertical metal	-2000		500
Konica FC-1	24x36mm	35mm	35slr	1983	Hexanon AR	1.8	50mm	focal plane	2-1/1000		160
Konica FM	24x36mm	35mm	35slr	1965	Hexanon	1.4	50mm	focal plane	1-1000,B		100
Konica FP	24x36mm	35mm	35slr	1963	Hexanon	1.4	50mm	focal plane	1-1000,B		100
Konica FP-1	24x36mm	35mm	35slr	1983	Hexanon AR	1.8	50mm	focal plane	30-1000		160
Konica FS	24x36mm	35mm	35slr	1961	Hexanon	2	50mm	focal plane	1-1000,B		120
Konica FS-1	24x36mm	35mm	35slr	1983	Hexanon AR	1.8	50mm	focal plane	2-1/1000		220
Konica FT-1 Motor (black)	24x36mm	35mm	35SLR	1985	Hexanon AR	1.8	50mm	focal plane	2-1/1000		160
Konica FT-1 Mot. (chrome)	24x36mm	35mm	35SLR	1985	Hexanon AR	1.2	57mm	focal plane	2-1/1000		160
Konica FTA	24x36mm	35mm	35SLR	1968	Hexanon	1.4	57mm	focal plane	1-1000		100
Konica FTA (new)	24x36mm	35mm	35SLR	1970	Hexanon	1.4	57mm	focal plane	1-1000		130
Konica Gsk-99	6x6cm	120	Aerial	1939	Simlar	2.5	7.5cm		1/100-400		800
Konica MG	24x36mm	35mm	35af	1985		3.5	35mm	programmed	50-500		70
Konica MG/D	24x36mm	35mm	35af	1985		3.5	35mm	programmed	50-500		70

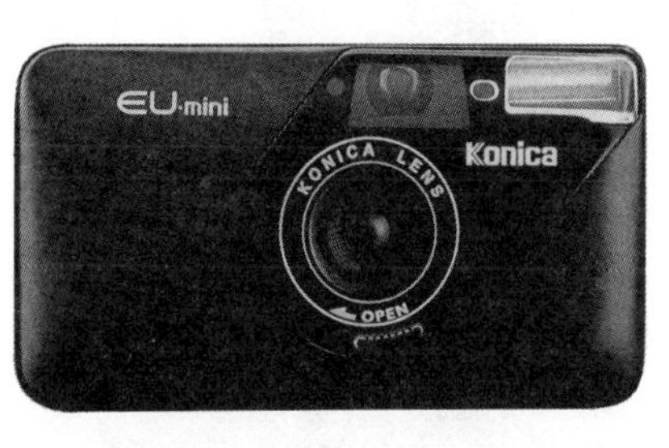

Konica EU mini

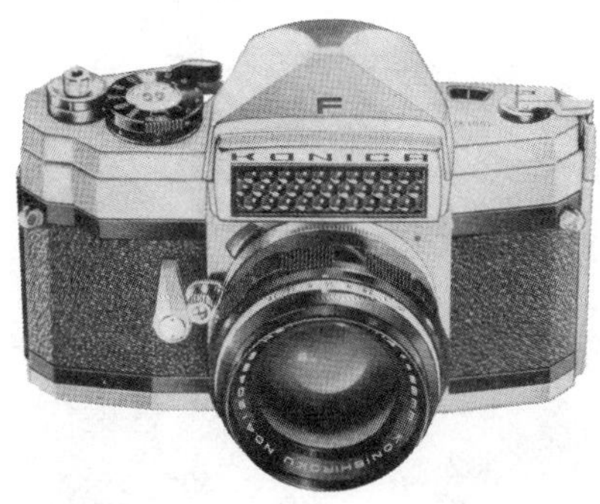

Konica F

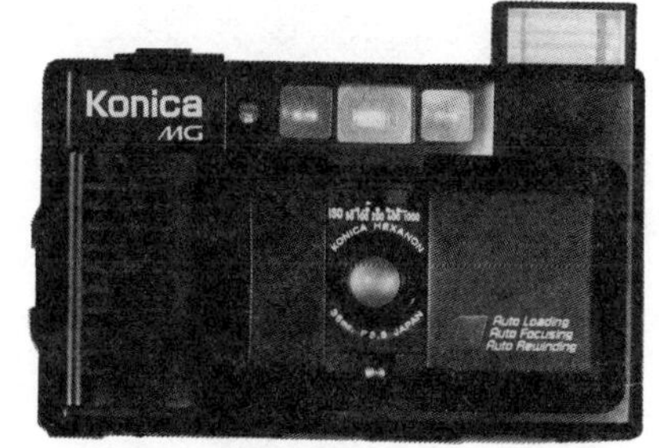

Konica MG

MODEL	FORMAT	FILM	TYPE	Year	LENS	Apert	FL	SHUTTER	SPEEDS	ILLUS	U.S.$
Konica MR.70	24x36mm	35mm	35AF-BiF	1985	Hexanon	3.2,5.8	38/70	programmed	25-250		90
Konica MR.70 Auto-Date	24x36mm	35mm	35AF-BiF	1985	Hexanon	3.2,5.8	38/70	programmed	25-250		120
Konica MR.70LX	24x36mm	35mm	35AF-BiF	1988	Konica	3.2,5.8	38/70	programmed	8-250		70
Konica MR.70LX Auto-Date	24x36mm	35mm	35AF-BiF	1988	Konica	3.2,5.8	38/70	programmed	8-250		80
Konica MR.640	24x36mm	35mm	35aw	1990	Konica	3.5,5.2	40/60	programmed	5-500		110
Konica MR.640 Auto-date	24x36mm	35mm	35aw	1990	Konica	3.5,5.2	40/60	programmed	5-500		160
Konica MS-40	24x36mm	35mm	35af	1989		3.5	40mm	programmed	5-500		120
Konica MT-7	24x36mm	35mm	35vf	1987	Konica	4	36mm		1/125		60
Konica MT-9	24x36mm	35mm	35af	1988	Konica	3.5	35mm	programmed	10-500		90
Konica MT-9 Date	24x36mm	35mm	35af	1988	Konica	3.5	35mm	programmed	10-500		100
Konica MT-10	24x36mm	35mm	35af	1990	Konica	4.5	35mm	programmed	1/35, 180		70
Konica MT-10D	24x36mm	35mm	35af	1990	Konica	4.5	35mm	programmed	1/35, 180		90
Konica MT-11	24x36mm	35mm	35af	1985	Konica	2.8	35mm	programmed	4-500		80
Konica MT-11 Date	24x36mm	35mm	35af	1985	Konica	2.8	35mm	programmed	4-500		100
Konica MT-100	24x36mm	35mm	35af	1991		4.5	34mm	programmed	2-1/500		70
Konica MT-100 Date	24x36mm	35mm	35af	1991		4.5	34mm	programmed	2-1/500		70
Konica S	24x36mm	35mm	35rf	1960	Hexanon	1.8	50mm	focal plane	1-500		50
Konica SII	24x36mm	35mm	35rf	1962	Hexanon	2	48mm	focal plane	1-500		50
Konica TC-X	24x36mm	35mm	35SLR	1985	Hexanon AR	1.8	50mm	focal plane	1-1000		120
Koniflex	6x6cm	120	TLR	1952	Hexanon	3.5	85mm		1-400		80
Koniflex II Tele	6x6cm	120	TLR	1955	Tele Hexanon	4.5	135mm		1-400	A1726	130
Konilette	28x36mm	Cass	BkltFold	1953	Konitar	4.5	50mm	Copal	25-200		90
Konilette 35	24x36mm	35mm	35vf	1959	Konitar	3.5	45mm		25-200	Mc260	50
Lily Hand Camera	6.5x9cm	plate	VtFoldPl	1930	Tessar	4.5		Compur			70
Lily No. 1	8x10.5cm	plate	FoldPl	1909	Wollensak	6.3		Optimo			70
Lily No. 2	8x10.5cm	plate	HzFoldPl	1916	Tessar	6.3		Compound			70
Machine-gun Type 89	18x24mm	35mm	Military	1930	Hexar	4.5	75mm			Mc261	680
Manbow	24x36mm	35mm	35aw	1988	Konica	4	35mm		1/125		60
Mermaid (pink)	24x36mm	35mm	35uw	1994	Konica	3.5	35mm	programmed	7.5-1/360		200
Mermaid (yellow)	24x36mm	35mm	35uw	1994	Konica	3.5	35mm	programmed	7.5-1/360		200
Off-road 28	24x36mm	35mm	35af	1991	Konica	3.5	28mm	programmed	4-280		110
Off-road 28 Date	24x36mm	35mm	35af	1991	Konica	3.5	28mm	programmed	4-280		120
Panorama Zoom	24x36mm	35mm	35afz	1991	Konica	3.5-5.6	28-56	programmed	4-280		60
Pearl (Showa 8)	6x9cm	120	VtFoldRo	1933	Prontor-S				25-100,T,B		70
Pearl (Special Pearl)	8x10.5cm	124	VtFoldRo	1913	Anastigmat	6.3					160
Pearl I	4.5x6cm	120	FoldRo	1949	Hexar	4.5	75mm	Durax	T,B,1-100		120
Pearl II	8x10.5cm	124	VtFoldRo	1909	doublet	8				Mc260	160
Pearl III	8x10.5cm	124	VtFoldRo	1909	Prontor-S	8					180
Pearl IV	4.5x6cm	120	VtFoldRo	1958	Hexar	3.5	75mm	Seikosha-MXL	B,1-500		180
Pearl No.2	6x9cm	120	VtFoldRo	1923	Prontor-S				25-100,T,B		70
Pearlette	4x6.5cm	127	StrutRo	1925	Rokuohsha Optar	6.3	75mm	Echo	25-100	Mc260	200
Photo Pie	24x36mm	35mm	35vf	1991	Konica	8	33mm		1/125		10

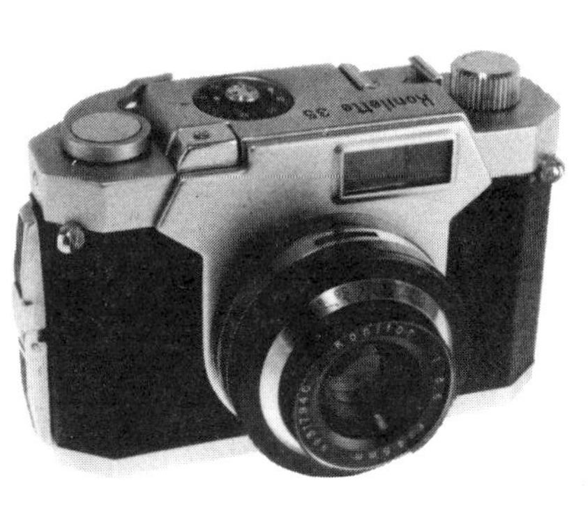

Konilette 35

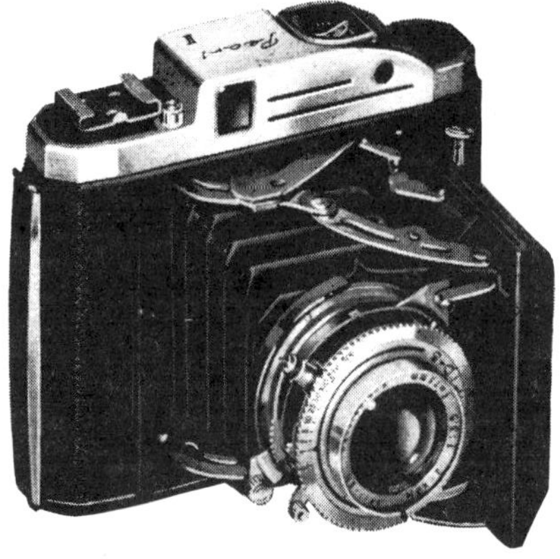

Konishiroku Pearl II

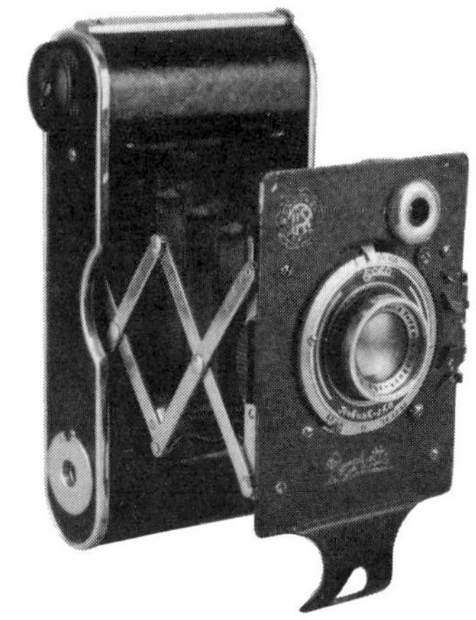

Konishiroku Pearlette

MODEL	FORMAT	FILM	TYPE	Year	LENS	Apert	FL	SHUTTER	SPEEDS	ILLUS	U.S.$
Pop (blue)	24x36mm	35mm	35vf	1983	Konica	4	36mm		1/125		30
Pop (pink)	24x36mm	35mm	35vf	1983	Konica	4	36mm		1/125		30
Pop (red)	24x36mm	35mm	35vf	1983	Konica	4	36mm		1/125		30
Pop (silver)	24x36mm	35mm	35vf	1983	Konica	4	36mm		1/125		30
Pop-10	24x36mm	35mm	35vf	1985	Konica	4	35mm		1/125		40
Pop AF-30	24x36mm	35mm	35af	1993		4.5	35mm		1/125		60
Pop Auto-date	24x36mm	35mm	35vf	1983	Konica	4	36mm		1/125		40
Pop EF-20	24x36mm	35mm	35vf	1993	Konica	4.5	35mm		1/125		20
Pop EF-80	24x36mm	35mm	35vf	1994		4.3	34mm		60-250		40
Pop Super	24x36mm	35mm	35vf	1989		4.5	34mm		1/125		40
Pop Super Date	24x36mm	35mm	35vf	1990		4.5	34mm		1/125		50
Rapid Omega 100	6x9cm	120/2	Press	1975	Hexanon	3.5	90mm			Mc260	190
Rapid Omega 200	6x9cm	120/2	Press	1975	Hexanon	3.5	90mm				290
Sakura	4x5cm	127	BakeliteRoll	1931	Rokuoh-Sha				B,I		120
Sakura Pocket Prano	9x12cm	plate	VtFoldPl	1907	Prontor-S	8			T,B,I		480
Semi-Pearl	4.5x6cm	120	FoldRo	1938	Hexar	4.5	75mm		-1/100		60
Snappy	14x14mm	Roll	Submin	1949	Optar	3.5	25mm	guillotine	25-100	A3310	180
Snappy	14x14mm	Roll	Submin	1949	Cherry Tele	5.6	40mm	guillotine	25-100	Mc261	210
Snappy Camera Set	14x14mm	Roll	Submin	1949	Cherry Tele	5.6	40mm	guillotine	25-100	Mc261	310
Tomato	24x36mm	35mm	35vf	1987	Konica	4	35mm		1/125		30
Top's	24x36mm	35mm	35vf	1993	Konica	4.5	35mm		1/125		40
Top's AF-300	24x36mm	35mm	35af	1993	Konica	4.5	35mm		1/2, 160		60
Top's AF-300 SP	24x36mm	35mm	35af	1994		4.5	34mm	programmed			90
Top's EF-200 SP	24x36mm	35mm	35vf	1994		4.5	34mm		1/50, 125		60
Z-up 28W	24x36mm	35mm	35afz	1991	Konica	3.5-6.6	28-56	programmed	4-280		120
Z-up 28W Date	24x36mm	35mm	35afz	1991	Konica	3.5-6.6	28-56	programmed	4-280		140
Z-up 80	24x36mm	35mm	35afz	1989	Konica	3.8-7.3	40-80	programmed	1-500		160
Z-up 80RC	24x36mm	35mm	35afz	1991	Konica	3.8-7.2	40-80	programmed	1-500		140
...KORSTEN - Paris											
Litote 45x107	4.5x10.7	plate	StJumelle	1902	Aplanat			guillotine	3 Zeiten	A1804	170
Litote 45x107	4.5x10.7	plate	StJumelle	1902	Krauss			guillotine	3 Zeiten	F1309	170
Litote 6x13	6x13cm	plate	StJumelle	1902	Krauss			guillotine	3 Zeiten	F1309	150
...KOSSATZ (Konstantin) - Berlin											
Spiegel-Reflex	13x18cm	plate	LgSLR	189x	Goerz Dogmar	4.5	240mm	focal plane			460
...KOWA OPTICAL - Japan											
Kallo W	24x36mm	35mm	35rf	1955	Prominar	2.8		Seikosha	B,1-500		40
Kallo WF	24x36mm	35mm	35rf	1955	Prominar	2.8		Seikosha	B,1-500		50
Kalloflex	6x6cm	120	TLR	1954	Prominar	3.5	75mm	Seikosha	1-500	Mc261	100
Komaflex-S	4x4cm	127	MedSLR	1960	Prominar	2.8	65mm	Seikosha-SLV	B,1-500	Mc261	170
Kowa E	24x36mm	35mm	35slr	1962	Prominar	2	50mm	Seikosha-SLV	B,1-500	Mc261	50
Kowa H	24x36mm	35mm	35slr	1963	Fixed Kowa	2.8	48mm	Seikosha	30-300	Mc261	50
Kowa SE	24x36mm	35mm	35slr	1964	Fixed Kowa	1.9	50mm	Seikosha-SLV	1-500	Mc261	60

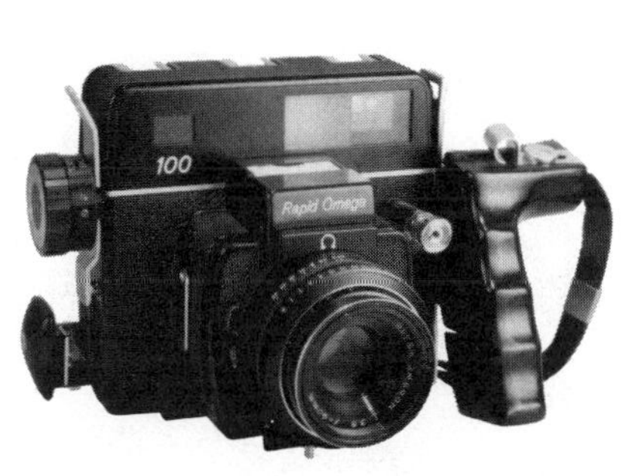

Rapid Omega 100

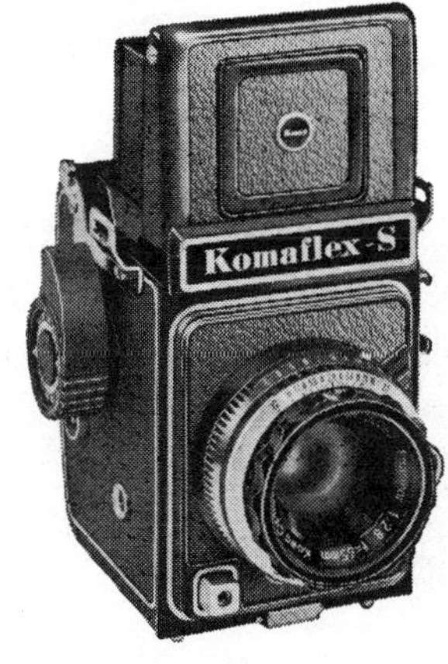

Komaflex-S

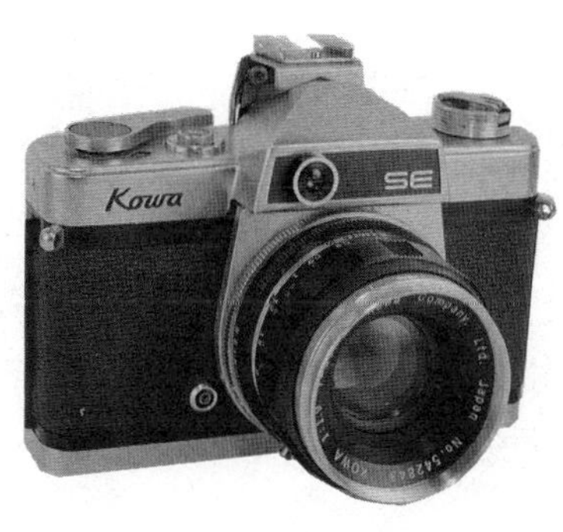

Kowa SE

MODEL	FORMAT	FILM	TYPE	Year	LENS	Apert	FL	SHUTTER	SPEEDS	ILLUS	U.S.$
Kowa SER	24x36mm	35mm	35slr	1964	Kowa	2.8	48mm	Seikosha-SLV	1-500		70
Kowa SET	24x36mm	35mm	35slr	1967	Fixed Kowa	1.8	50mm	Seikosha-SLV	1-500	Mc261	50
Kowa SETR	24x36mm	35mm	35slr	1968	Kowa	1.9	50mm	Seikosha-SLV	1-500		50
Kowa SETR2	24x36mm	35mm	35slr	1970	Kowa	1.8	50mm	Seikosha-SLV	1-500		50
Kowa Six	6x6cm	120/2	MedSLR	1968	Kowa	2.8	85mm	focal plane			420
Kowa Six MM	6x6cm	120/2	MedSLR	1971	Kowa	2.8	85mm	focal plane			350
Kowa Super 66	6x6cm	120/2	MedSLR	1974	Kowa	2.8	85mm				440
Kowa SW	24x36mm	35mm	35vf	1964	Fixed Kowa	3.2	28mm	Seikosha-SLV	B,1-500	Mc262	300
Kowa UW190	24x36mm	35mm	35vf	1972	Non-changeable	4	19mm				330
Kowaflex E	24x36mm	35mm	35slr	1962	Prominar	2	50mm	Seikosha-SLV	B,1-500		50
Kowaflex SE	24x36mm	35mm	35slr	1964	Kowa	1.9	50mm	Seikosha-SLV	B,1-500		50
Ramera (black)	10x14mm	16mm	Disguised	1959	Prominar	3.5	23mm		B,50-200	Mc262	150
Ramera (blue)	10x14mm	16mm	Disguised	1959	Prominar	3.5	23mm		B,50-200	A3320	150
Ramera (red)	10x14mm	16mm	Disguised	1959	Prominar	3.5	23mm		B,50-200	Mc262	150
Ramera (white)	10x14mm	16mm	Disguised	1959	Prominar	3.5	23mm		B,50-200		150
Super Lark Zen-99	4x6/4x4	127	RigidRo	1960	Prominar	11	70mm		I,T		20
Zen-99	4x6.5/4x4	127	RigidRo	1960	Prominar	11	70mm		I,T		20
...KOZY CAMERA CO.											
Pocket Kozy	3½x3½"	Roll	FoldRo	1895	Meniscus	2	5"	simple	T		1600
Pocket Kozy, Improved	3½x3½"	Roll	FoldRo	1898	Meniscus	2	5"	simple	T	Mc262	1000
...KRASNOGORSKII MECHANICHESKII ZAVOD "KMZ" - Kranogorsk											
Drug (Dpyr)	24x36mm	35mm	35rf	1960	Jupiter-8	2	50mm	focal plane	B,½-1000	Mc262	120
F-21 (automatic)	18x24mm	21mm	Submin	197x		2.9	28mm				700
F-21 (black)	18x24mm	21mm	Submin	1960		2	28mm			Ru139	700
F-21 (grey)	18x24mm	21mm	Submin	1960		2.8	28mm			Mc262	490
F-21 Button-camera	18x24mm	21mm	Disguised	197x		2.9	28mm			Mc262	1300
FT-2	24x110	35mm	Panoramic	1958	Industar	5	50mm		100-400	Mc263	400
Global-H	24x58mm	35mm	Panoramic	1967		2.8	28mm		30-125	Ru130	400
Horizont	24x58mm	35mm	Panoramic	1967		2.8	28mm		30-125	Mc263	400
Horizont Revue	24x58mm	35mm	Panoramic	1971		2.8	28mm		30-125		400
Iskra	6x6cm	120	HzFoldRo	1960	Industar-58	3.5	75mm		T,1-1/500	Ru134	160
Iskra-2	6x6cm	120	HzFoldRo	1961	Industar-58	3.5	75mm		T,1-1/500	Ru134	130
Mir	24x36mm	35mm	35rf	1959	Jupiter-8	2	50mm	focal plane	30-500	Mc263	90
Mir	24x36mm	35mm	35rf	1959	Industar-58	3.5	50mm	focal plane	30-500	Ru91	90
Moscow (1)	6x9cm	120	FoldRo	1946	Industar	3.5	105mm	Moment	1-250	Ru132	110
Moscow (1)	6x9cm	120	FoldRo	1946	Industar	4.5	11cm	Moment	1-250	Ru132	110
Moscow-2	6x9cm	120	FoldRo	1947	Industar	4.5	11cm	Moment	1-250	Mc263	160
Moscow-3	6x9cm	plate	FoldRo	1950	Industar	4.5	11cm	Moment	1-250	Ru132	70
Moscow-4	6x9cm	120	FoldRo	1956	Industar	4.5	11cm	Moment	1-250	Ru134	70
Moscow-5	6x9cm	120	FoldRo	1956	Industar	3.5	105mm	Moment	1-250	Ru134	100
Narciss (black)	14x21mm	16mm	Submin	1961	Vega-M-1	2.8	35mm		2-500	Mc263	340
Narciss (white)	14x21mm	16mm	Submin	1961	Industar-60	2.8	35mm		2-500	Ru137	340

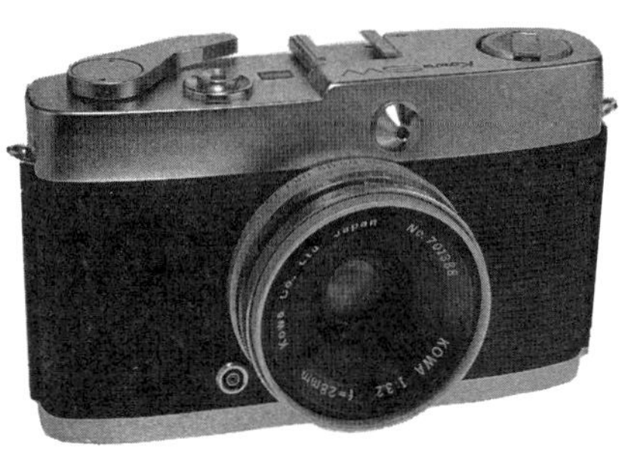

Kowa SW

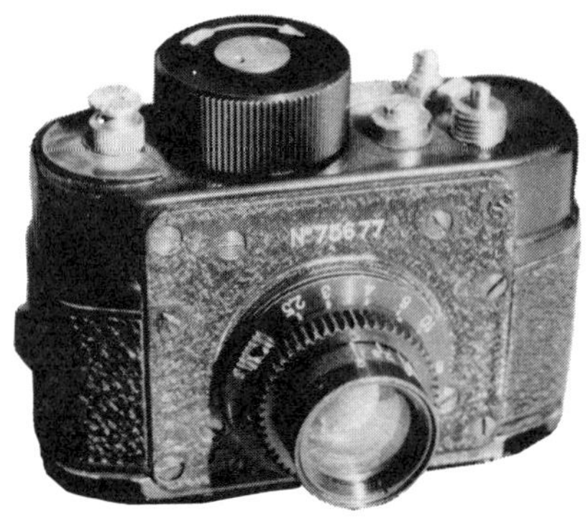
Krasnogorskii F-21

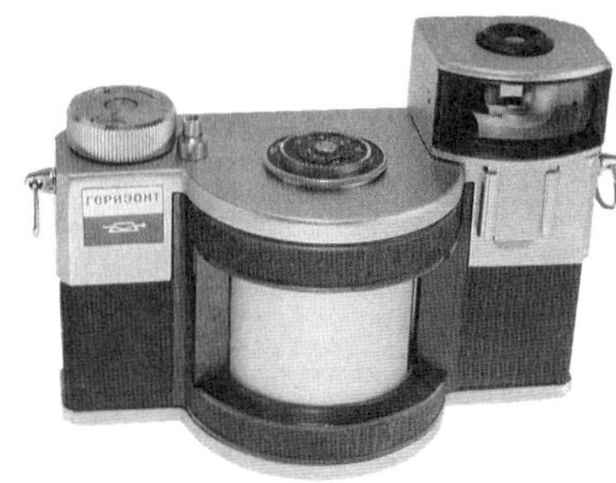
Krasnogorskii Horizont

MODEL	FORMAT	FILM	TYPE	Year	LENS	Apert	FL	SHUTTER	SPEEDS	ILLUS	U.S.$
Start (Cmapm)	24x36mm	35mm	35slr	1958	Helios	2	58mm	focal plane		Mc263	240
Zenit	24x36mm	35mm	35slr	1952	Industar	3.5	50mm	focal plane	25-500	Ru105	60
Zenit 3	24x36mm	35mm	35slr	1960	Industar-50	3.5	50mm	focal plane	30-500	Ru106	30
Zenit 3M	24x36mm	35mm	35slr	1962	Industar-50	3.5	50mm	focal plane	30-500	Ru107	30
Zenit 4	24x36mm	35mm	35slr	1964	Vega	2.8	50mm	focal plane	1-500	Ru108	140
Zenit 5	24x36mm	35mm	35slr	1964	Vega	2.8	50mm	focal plane	1-500	Ru108	330
Zenit 6	24x36mm	35mm	35slr	1964	Rubin	2.8	37-80	focal plane	1-500	Ru109	200
Zenit 7	24x36mm	35mm	35slr	1969	Rubin	2.8	37-80	focal plane	1-500	Ru112	170
Zenit 10	24x36mm	35mm	35slr	1981	Industar-50	3.5	50mm	focal plane	30-500	Ru116	70
Zenit 11	24x36mm	35mm	35slr	1981	Helios-44M	2	58mm	focal plane	30-500	Ru116	70
Zenit 12	24x36mm	35mm	35slr	1983	Helios-44M	2	58mm	focal plane	30-500	Ru117	90
Zenit 12 sd	24x36mm	35mm	35slr	1983	Helios-44M	2	58mm	focal plane	30-500	Ru117	70
Zenit 12 XP	24x36mm	35mm	35slr	1983	Helios-44M	2	58mm	focal plane	30-500	Ru117	50
Zenit 14	24x36mm	35mm	35slr	1987	Helios-44	2	58mm	focal plane	1-1000	Ru118	70
Zenit 19	24x36mm	35mm	35slr	1979	Zenitar-M	1.7	50mm	focal plane	1-1000	Ru116	50
Zenit 20	24x36mm	35mm	35slr	1982	Zenitar-M	1.7	50mm	focal plane	15-1000	Ru117	70
Zenit 22	24x36mm	35mm	35slr	1982						Ru117	70
Zenit 122	24x36mm	35mm	35slr	1990	Helios-44M	2	58mm	focal plane	1-1000	Ru118	80
Zenit Automat	24x36mm	35mm	35slr	1984	Helios	2	58mm	focal plane	1-1000	Ru118	100
Zenit B	24x36mm	35mm	35slr	1968	Industar-50	3.5	50mm	focal plane	30-500	Mc264	50
Zenit B	24x36mm	35mm	35slr	1968	Helios-44	2	58mm	focal plane	30-500	Ru111	50
Zenit-C (S)	24x36mm	35mm	35slr	1955	Industar	3.5	50mm	focal plane	25-500	Mc263	60
Zenit E (black)	24x36mm	35mm	35slr	1965	Helios-44	2	58mm	focal plane	30-500	Ru110	50
Zenit E (chrome)	24x36mm	35mm	35slr	1965	Industar-50	3.5	50mm	focal plane	30-500	Mc264	50
Zenit EM	24x36mm	35mm	35slr	1972	Helios-44	2	58mm	focal plane	30-500	Mc264	50
Zenit ET	24x36mm	35mm	35slr	1981	Industar-50	3.5	50mm	focal plane	30-500	Ru116	60
Zenit ET	24x36mm	35mm	35slr	1981	Helios-44	2	58mm	focal plane	30-500	Ru116	70
Zenit Photo Sniper	24x36mm	35mm	35slr	1968	Tair-3	4.5	300mm	focal plane	30-500	Ru124	200
Zenit S	24x36mm	35mm	35slr	1955	Industar-22	3.5	50mm	focal plane	25-500	Ru105	50
Zenit TTL	24x36mm	35mm	35slr	1977	Helios-44M	2	58mm	focal plane	30-500	Mc264	70
Zenum 3M	24x36mm	35mm	35slr	1962	Industar-50	3.5	50mm	focal plane	30-500	Ru107	50
Zorki 1a	24x36mm	35mm	35rf	1949	Industar-22	3.5	50mm	focal plane		Ru89	70
Zorki 1b	24x36mm	35mm	35rf	1950	Industar-22	3.5	50mm	focal plane		Ru89	120
Zorki 1c	24x36mm	35mm	35rf	1951	Industar-22	3.5	50mm	focal plane		Ru89	60
Zorki 1d	24x36mm	35mm	35rf	1953	Industar-22	3.5	50mm	focal plane			70
Zorki 1e	24x36mm	35mm	35rf	1954	Industar-22	3.5	50mm	focal plane	25-500	Ru89	60
Zorki 2	24x36mm	35mm	35rf	1952	Industar-22	3.5	50mm	focal plane		Ru90	120
Zorki 2C (S)	24x36mm	35mm	35rf	1956	Industar-50	3.5	50mm	focal plane	25-500	Ru90	60
Zorki 3	24x36mm	35mm	35rf	1951	Jupiter-8	2	52mm	focal plane	25-1000	Ru90	110
Zorki 3C (S)	24x36mm	35mm	35rf	1955	Jupiter-8	2	52mm	focal plane	1-1000	Ru91	60
Zorki 3M	24x36mm	35mm	35rf	1954	Jupiter-8	2	52mm	focal plane		Ru90	80
Zorki 4	24x36mm	35mm	35rf	1956	Industar-50	3.5	50mm	focal plane	1-1000	Mc264	70

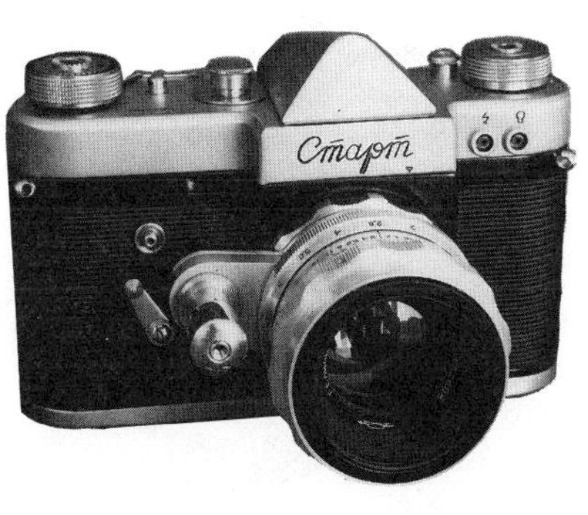

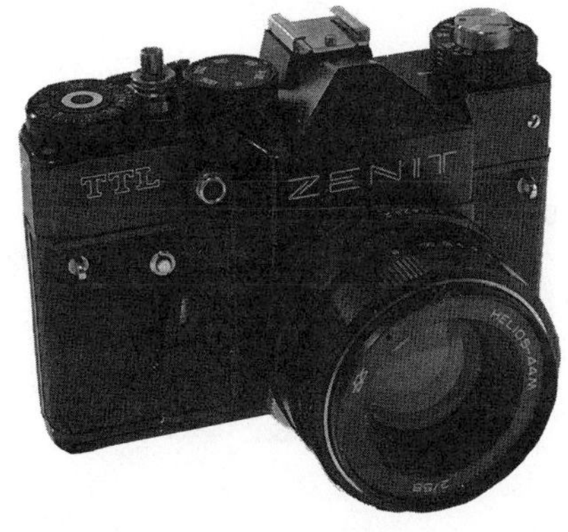

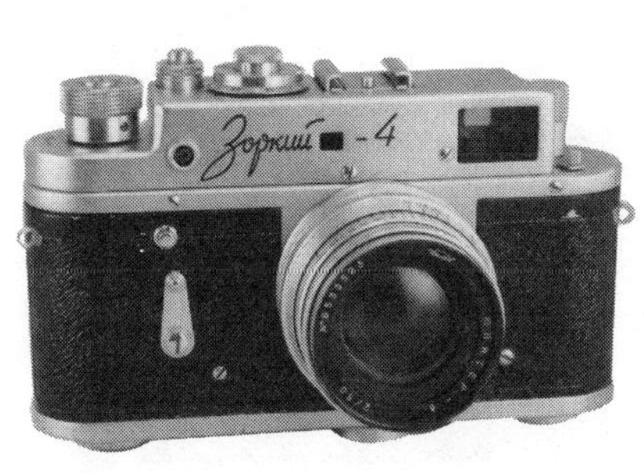

Krasnogorskii Start (Cmapm) **Zenit TTL** **Zorki 4**

MODEL	FORMAT	FILM	TYPE	Year	LENS	Apert	FL	SHUTTER	SPEEDS	ILLUS	U.S.$
Zorki 4 (Anniversary)	24x36mm	35mm	35rf	1967	Jupiter-8	2	50mm	focal plane	1-1000	Ru91	120
Zorki 4K	24x36mm	35mm	35rf	1973	Jupiter-8	2	50mm	focal plane	1-1000	Ru92	80
Zorki 5 (type 1)	24x36mm	35mm	35rf	1958	Industar-50	3.5	50mm	focal plane	25-500	Ru92	70
Zorki 5 (type 2)	24x36mm	35mm	35rf	1959	Jupiter-8	2	50mm	focal plane	25-500	Ru92	100
Zorki 6	24x36mm	35mm	35rf	1959	Industar-50	3.5	50mm	focal plane	30-500	Ru92	100
Zorki 6	24x36mm	35mm	35rf	1959	Jupiter-8	2	50mm	focal plane	30-500	Ru92	100
Zorki 10	24x36mm	35mm	35rf	1964	Industar-63	2.8	45mm	leaf	30-500	Mc264	50
Zorki 11	24x36mm	35mm	35vf	1964	Industar-63	2.8	45mm	leaf	30-500	Ru97	50
Zorki 12	18x24mm	35mm	35vf	1967	Helios-98	2.8	28mm	leaf	30-500	Ru97	70
Zorki C (S)	24x36mm	35mm	35rf	1956	Industar-22	3.5	50mm	focal plane	25-500	Ru90	90
...KRAUSS (E. Krauss) - Paris											
Actis 9x12	9x12cm	plate	VtFoldPl	1913	Zeiss Tessar	6.3	136mm	Compound		R1-21	100
Actis 10x15	10x15cm	plate	VtFoldPl	1913	Zeiss Tessar	6.3	163mm	Compound		R1-21	120
Eka	30x44mm	Specl	35vf	1924	Zeiss Tessar	3.5	50mm	Compur	1-300	Mc265	1000
Liliput	4x6.5cm	plate	StrutPl	1920	Zeiss Tessar	4.5	75mm	Compur			160
le Mondain 4.5x6	4.5x6cm	plate	StrutPl	1906	Tessar	6.3				F204	410
le Mondain 6.5x9	6.5x9cm	plate	StrutPl	1906	Tessar	6.3					210
le Mondain 9x12	9x12cm	plate	StrutPl	1906	Tessar	6.3					210
le Mondain (stereo) 45x107	45x107	plate	SterStrut	1906	Tessar	6.3					410
le Mondain (stereo) 6x13	6x13cm	plate	SterStrut	1906	Tessar	6.3					410
Photo-Revolver	18x35mm	plate	Submin	1920	Tessar	4	40mm	3-speed	T,25-100	Mc265	2600
Photo-Revolver	18x35mm	Roll	Submin	1920	Tessar	4	40mm	3-speed	T,25-100	A829	3600
Polyscop	45x107	plate	StJumelle	1909	Tessar	6.3					270
Polyscop	45x107	plate	StJumelle	1909	Tessar	4.5					270
Takyr	9x12cm	plate	StrutPl	1906	Tessar	6.3	136mm	focal plane		Mc265	220
Tykta III (horizontal)	9x12cm	plate	HzFoldRo	1905	Tessar	6.3	136mm	sector		A3026	110
Tykta III (vertical)	9x12cm	plate	VtFoldRo	1905	Kalloptat	7.7	136mm	E.K.		R1-8	110
Tykta X	6.5x9cm	plate	StrutPl	1905	Unar	6.3	112mm	focal plane			110
Tykta XI	9x12cm	plate	StrutPl	1905	Unar	4.7	136mm	focal plane			90
...KRAUSS (G.A. Krauss) - Stuttgart											
Knirps	4x6.5cm	plate	StrutPl	1920	Zeiss Tessar	6.3	75mm	Compur		R24-5	200
Knirps	4x6.5cm	plate	StrutPl	1920	Zeiss Tessar	4.5	75mm	Compur		HK170	200
Nanos	4.5x6cm	plate	StrutPl	1920	Tessar	4.5	75mm			A335	140
Peggy I	24x36mm	35mm	35Strut	1931	Tessar	3.5	50mm	Compur	1-300	Mc265	490
Peggy II	24x36mm	35mm	35Strut	1934	Xenon	2	50mm	Compur	1-300	Mc265	420
Rollette	5x8cm	Roll	VtFoldRo	192x	Rollar	6.3	90mm	Pronto	25-100	Mc265	50
Rollette Luxus	5x8cm	Roll	VtFoldRo	1928	Rollar	6.3	90mm	Pronto	25-100	R24-1	140
Stereoplast	45x107	plate	StJumelle	1921	Krauss	4.5	55mm		-1/300	R24-6	340
...KREMP - Wetzlar											
Kreca	24x36mm	35mm	35Strut	1930	Kreca	2.9	50mm	Rim-Compur	-1/300	Mc265	500
...KROHNKE (Emil Krohnke) - Dresden											
Photo-Oda	18x18mm	Roll	Submin	1902	Meniscus			simple		Mc265	11000

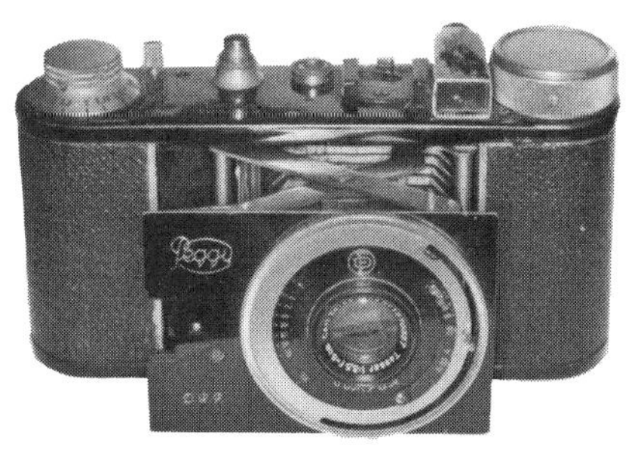

Krauss, G.A. Peggy I

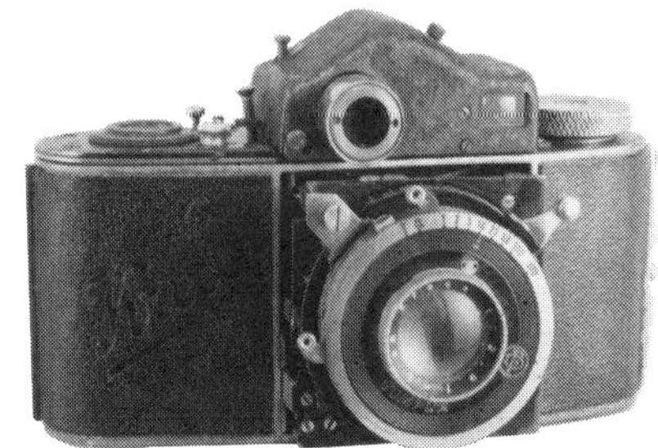

Kremp Kreca

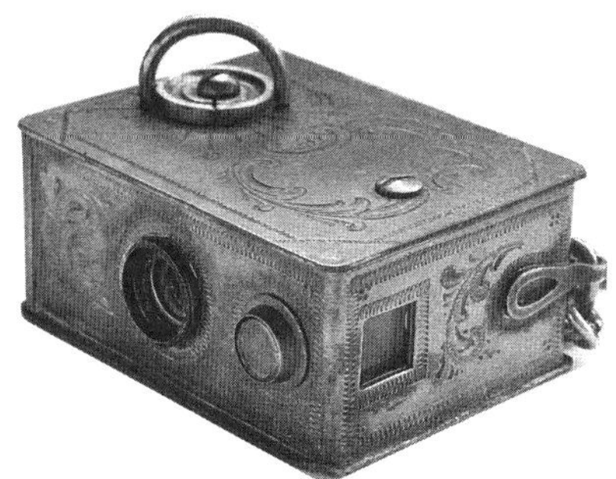

Krohnke Photo-Oda

MODEL	FORMAT	FILM	TYPE	Year	LENS	Apert	FL	SHUTTER	SPEEDS	ILLUS	U.S.$
...KRÜGENER (Dr. Rudolf Krügener) - Bockheim/Frankfurt											
Alpha	9x12cm	plate	MagBox	1901	Aplanat			guillotine		A2828	270
Alpha	9x12cm	plate	MagBox	1901	Periscop			guillotine		U163	270
Delta (plate & rollfilm) 9x9	9x9cm	pl//ro	HzFoldPl	1905	Extra Rap. Aplan.	9		Delta	25-100		370
Delta (plate & rollfilm) 9x12	9x12cm	pl//ro	HzFoldPl	1900	Extra Rap. Aplan.	9	150mm	built-in		A356	270
Delta (plate & rollfilm) 9x12	9x12cm	pl//ro	HzFoldPl	1905	Extra Rap. Aplan.	9	150mm	Unicum			180
Delta (plate) 9x12	9x12cm	plate	VtFoldPl	1905	Dagor	6.8	120mm	Delta	25-100	Mc265	160
Delta (plate) 9x12	9x12cm	plate	HzFoldPl	1900	Euryscop Anast.	6.8	120mm	Delta	25-100	A154	160
Delta (plate) 10x15	10x15cm	plate	HzFoldPl	1900	Extra Rap. Aplan.	9		Delta	25-100		150
Delta (rollfilm) 6x9	6x9cm	120	HzFoldRo	1900	Achromat			built-in	M,Z		160
Delta (rollfilm) 8x10.5	8x10.5cm	Roll	HzFoldRo	1903	Tessar	6.3	136mm			A1442	200
Delta Detective 6x8	6x8cm	plate	MagBox	1890	Aplanat			guillotine		A1304	670
Delta Detective 11x16.5	11x16.5	plate	MagBox	1898	Achromat						670
Delta Detective 13x18	13x18cm	plate	MagBox	1892	Achromat						900
Delta Klapp	8x10.5cm	Roll	FoldRo	1899	Achromat				25-100	A1442	140
Delta Magazine (leather)	9x12cm	plate	MagBox	1895	Achromat			simple		A57	290
Delta Mag. (vertical, leather	9x12cm	plate	MagBox	1895	Achromat			simple		A89	290
Delta Magazine (wood)	9x12cm	plate	MagBox	1892	Achromat			simple		Mc266	900
Delta Magazine (wood)	9x12cm	plate	MagBox	1892	Aplanat			simple		A56	900
Delta Patronen-Flach-Kam.	6x9cm	Roll	HzFoldRo	1900	Anastigmat	6			25-100		130
Delta Patronen-Flach-Kam.	8x10.5cm	Roll	HzFoldRo	1900	Anastigmat	6			25-100		130
Delta Patronen-Flach-Kam.	9x12cm	Roll	HzFoldRo	1900						U782	130
Delta Periskop	9x12cm	plate	FoldPl	1900	Rapid Periscop	12		Delta	25-100	Mc266	160
Delta Stereo	9x18cm	plate	StFoldPl	1898	Periplanat					A760	350
Delta Stereo	9x18cm	pl//ro	StFoldRo	1898	Extra Rap. Aplan.						350
Delta-Teddy	9x12cm	plate	VtFoldPl	1898	Delta Achromat			3-speed		A168	160
Electus	6x8cm	plate	MagBox	1889	Steinheil			Instant			1400
Halloh	9x14cm	plate	FoldRo	1909	Syntor	6.8	150mm				220
Helvetia	9x12cm	plate	FoldPl	1905	Rapid Aplanat						90
Jumelle	6x10.7cm	plate	Jumelle	1895	Periscop						300
Million	9x18cm	Roll	SterBox	1903	Periscop			guillotine			250
Minimum Delta	9x12cm	plate	FoldPl	1909	Extra Rap. Aplan.			pneumatic	25-100	A179	90
Normal Simplex	9x12cm	plate	MagBox	1892	Antiplanat						1700
Plaskop	45x107	plate	SterStrut	1907	Simplex	7.7	60mm		2-100	Mc266	390
Plaskop	45x107	plate	SterStrut	1907	Delta	6	60mm		2-100	Mc266	390
Plastoscop	45x107	plate	SterStrut	1907	Simplex	7.7	60mm		2-100	Mc266	370
Ronda	9x12cm	plate	VtFoldPl	1907	Dagor	8.8	150mm				100
Simplex Folien Kamera	9x12cm	Sheet	MagBox	1893	Aplanat			guillotine		HK36	900
Simplex Magazine	6x8cm	plate	MagBox	1898	Steinheil	10	100mm	sector	I	Mc266	1600
Simplex Magazine	6x8cm	plate	MagBox	1898	Periscop	10	100mm	sector	I	Mc266	1600
Stereo	6x13cm	plate	StFoldPl	1906	Extra Rap. Aplan.	6.8	90mm	Stereo Auto	1-100	A1769	220
Taschenbuch-Camera	40x40mm	plate	Disguised	1889	achromatic	12	65mm	guillotine	T,I	Mc266	3700

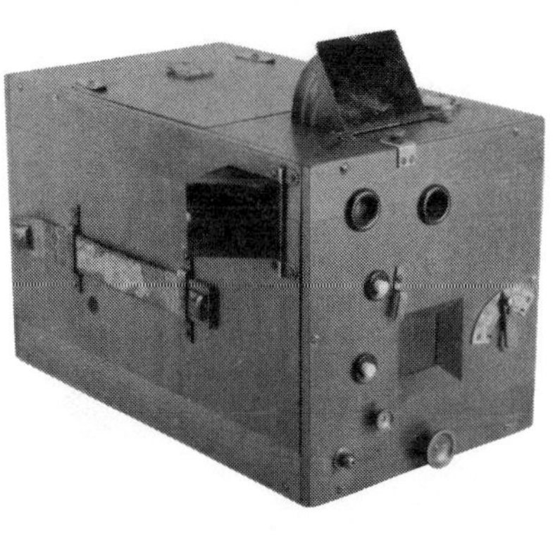

Delta Magazine

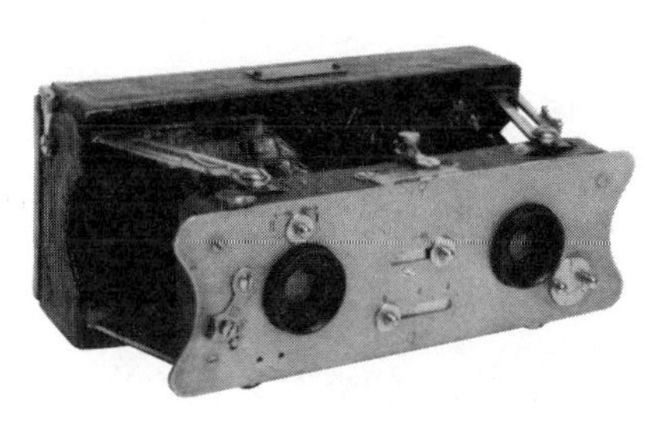

Plastoscop

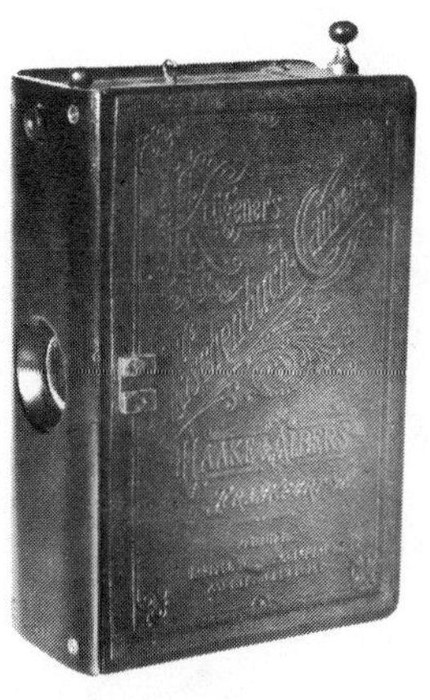

Taschenbuch-Camera

MODEL	FORMAT	FILM	TYPE	Year	LENS	Apert	FL	SHUTTER	SPEEDS	ILLUS	U.S.$
...KRÜGENER (W. Krügener) - Eltville											
Kronos	4.5x6cm	plate	StrutPl	1920	Anticomar	4.2	75mm	Compur	1-250	HK166	200
Kronos Stereo	45x107	plate	SterStrut	1920	Anticomar	3.5	75mm	Compur	1-250	HK491	340
Nestor	6x6cm	120	HzFoldRo	1920	Anticomar	5.4	76mm	Automat	25-100	HK209	50
Nestor	6x6cm	120	HzFoldRo	1920	Anticomar	4.2	76mm	Compur			50
Präzisions Kronos	9x12cm	plate	HzFoldPl	1920	Heli-Orthar	5.2	135mm	Compur	1-250	HK167	70
...KUEHN (W.D. Kuehn) - Berlin											
Lomara	9x12cm	plate	LgSLR	1921	Tessar	4.5	180mm	focal plane			210
Lomara Passbild		plate	MultLns	1910	13 lenses					HK654	1400
Lomaraskop	45x107	127	SterBox	1933	Lomara Anast.	4.5	5cm	focal plane		HK524	900
...KÜHN (Kurt Kühn) - Wetzlar											
Nova	3x4cm	127	MiniatRo	1938	Special Anst.	4.5	50mm		25-100		200
Reflexa	6x6cm	120	TLR	1946	Cassar	3.5	75mm				70
Reka	24x36mm	35mm	35vf	1950	Rekagon	2.8	50mm	Compur	1-300	A2102	70
Tex	3x4cm	127	MiniatRo	1949	Helur	4.5	50mm	Singlo	25-75	Mc400	120
...KUHNERT (Fritz Kuhnert) - Freiburg											
Efka 200	24x24mm	35mm	35vf	1949	Petar	3.5	40mm	Compur	1-200		370
Efka 500	24x24mm	35mm	35vf	1949	Evar	3.5	40mm	Compur-Rapid	1-500		490
...KUNIK (Walter Kunik K.G.) - Frankfurt											
Foto-Füller	10x10mm	Roll	Submin	1956						Mc267	370
Mickey Mouse Camera	14x14mm	16mm	Submin	1958	Meniscus			simple		Mc267	140
Ompex 16 (black)	14x14mm	16mm	Submin	1960	Meniscus			simple			70
Ompex 16 (red)	14x14mm	16mm	Submin	1960	Meniscus			simple			70
Petie	14x14mm	16mm	Submin	1958	Meniscus	11	25mm	simple		Mc267	60
Petie (gold)	14x14mm	16mm	Submin	1958	Meniscus	11	25mm	simple		Mc267	120
Petie Lighter	14x14mm	16mm	Submin	1956	Meniscus	11	25mm	simple		Mc267	700
Petie Vanity	14x14mm	16mm	Submin	1956	Meniscus	11	25mm	simple		Mc267	800
Petietux	14x14mm	16mm	Submin	1957	Optic	2.8	25mm	simple		Mc267	230
Petitax	14x14mm	16mm	Submin	1962	Meniscus	11	25mm	simple		Mc267	70
Petitux IV	14x14mm	16mm	Submin	1960	Wilon	2.8	28mm	7-speed		Mc267	640
Petitux IV	14x14mm	16mm	Submin	1960	Roeschl. Supronar	2.8	25mm	7-speed			640
Tuxi	14x14mm	16mm	Submin	1960	Achrom. Röschlei	7.7	25mm	synch	B,M	Mc267	80
Tuximat	14x14mm	16mm	Submin	1959	Meniscus	7.7	25mm	synch		Mc267	170
KÜRBI & NIGGELOH ☛ BILORA											
...KURIBAYASHI CAMERA WORKS - Tokyo											
1919 Speed Reflex 6x9	6x9cm	plate	LgSLR	1919	Tessar	3.5	105mm	focal plane	20-1000	KP40	640
1919 Speed Refl. 3¼x4¼"	3¼x4¼"	plate	LgSLR	1919	Tessar	4.5	135mm	focal plane	20-1000	KP40	640
Anscomatic 726	28x28mm	126	126	1966	Anscomatic	2.8	38mm	Petri VE	30-500	Mc271	30
Auto Semi First	4.5x6cm	120	FoldRo	1940	First Anast.	4.5	75mm			Mc269	170
Baby Semi First	4.5x6cm	120	FoldRo	1936	Toko Anast.	4.5	75mm	Compur	1-250	Mc269	160
BB Baby Semi First	4.5x6cm	120	FoldRo	1940	First Anast.	3.5	75mm	Rotte	1-200	Mc269	180
BB Semi First	4.5x6cm	120	FoldRo	1940	Toko	3.5	75mm	Seikosha	1-250	Mc269	180

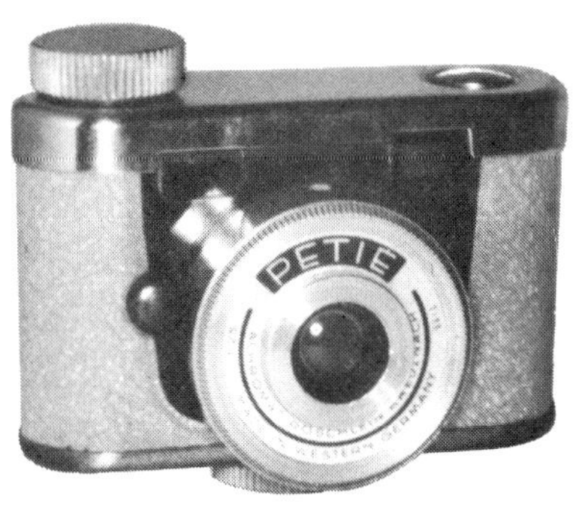

Petie (gold)

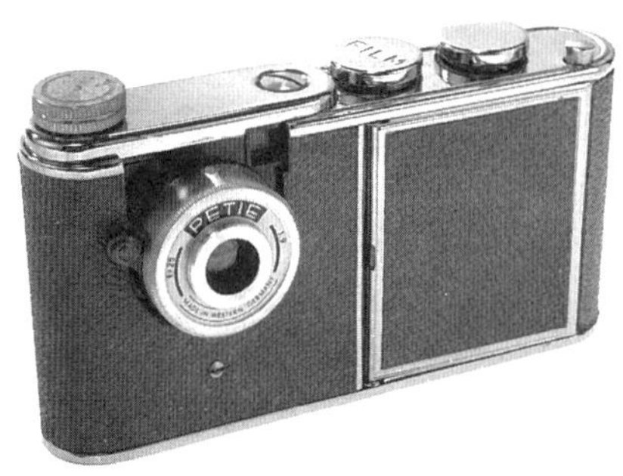

Petie Vanity

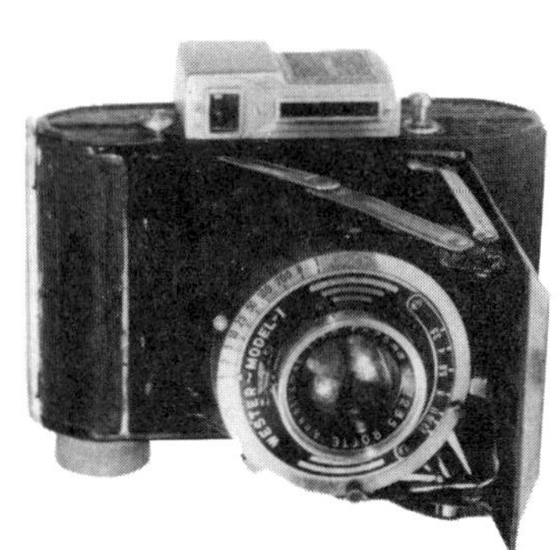

BB Semi First

MODEL	FORMAT	FILM	TYPE	Year	LENS	Apert	FL	SHUTTER	SPEEDS	ILLUS	U.S.$
First Center	6x9cm	120	FoldRo	1936	State Anast.	4.5	105mm	Seikosha	1-250	KP94	90
First Etui	2¼x3¼"	plate	FoldPl	1934	Toko Anast.	4.5	105mm	Magna	25-100	Mc268	220
First Hand	2¼x3¼"	plate	FoldPl	1929	Toko Anast.	6.3	105mm	Magna	25-100	Mc268	160
First Hand	2¼x3¼"	plate	FoldPl	1929	Tessar	4.5	105mm	Vario	25-100	KP48	160
First Reflex	6x6cm	120	TLR	1937	First Anast.	4.5	75mm	First	1-200	Mc269	350
First Reflex (model 2)	6x6cm	120	TLR	1940	Hit Anast.	3.2	7.5cm	Hit Rapid	-1/500	KP106	140
First Roll	6x9cm	120	VtFoldRo	1933	Radionar	4.5	105mm	Compur	1-250	Mc268	220
First Roll	6x9cm	120	FoldRo	1933	Toko Anast.	4.5	105mm	Compur	1-250	KP65	220
First Six	6x6cm	120	FoldRo	1936	Toko Anast.	3.5	75mm	Seikosha	T,B,1-250	Mc269	90
First Speed Pocket	4x6cm	127	FoldRo	1936	Toko Anast.	4.5	75mm	Seikosha	1-250	Mc269	110
First Speed Pocket	4x6cm	127	FoldRo	1936	Baron Anast.	4.5	75mm	Kerio	25-150	KP99	110
Karoron	4.5x6cm	120	FoldRo	1949	Orikon	3.5	75mm	Carperu	1-200	Mc270	110
Karoron RF	4.5x6cm	120	FoldRo	1951	Orikon	3.5	75mm	Carperu	1-200	KP131	120
Karoron S	4.5x6cm	120	FoldRo	1951	Orikon	3.5	75mm	Carperu	1-200	KP129	100
Karoron S-II	4.5x6cm	120	FoldRo	1951	Orikon	3.5	75mm	Carperu	1-200	KP130	120
Kokka Hand	2¼x3¼"	plate	FoldPl	1930	State Anast.	4.5	105mm	Magna	25-100	Mc268	160
Kokka Hand	2¼x3¼"	plate	FoldPl	1930	Trinar	6.3	105mm	Vario	25-100	KP54	160
Petri 1.8 Color Super	24x36mm	35mm	35rf	1959	Orikkor	1.8	45mm	Carperu	10-200	KP153	20
Petri 1.9 Color Super	24x36mm	35mm	35rf	1960	Orikkor	1.9	45mm	Carperu	10-200	Mc270	20
Petri 2.8 Color Super	24x36mm	35mm	35rf	1958	Orikkor	2.8	45mm	Carperu	10-200	Mc270	20
Petri 35 (original)	24x36mm	35mm	35rf	1954	Orikkor	3.5	45mm	Carperu	10-200	Mc270	40
Petri 35 (original)	24x36mm	35mm	35rf	1954	Orikkor	2.8	45mm	Carperu	10-200	KP140	40
Petri 35 1.9	24x36mm	35mm	35rf	1957	Orikkor	1.9	45mm	Copal	1-500	KP150	30
Petri 35 2.0	24x36mm	35mm	35rf	1957	Orikkor	2	45mm	Copal	1-500	KP149	30
Petri 35 2.8	24x36mm	35mm	35rf	1957	Orikkor	2.8	45mm	Carperu	10-200	Mc270	20
Petri 35 2.8	24x36mm	35mm	35rf	1957	Orikkor	2.8	45mm	Copal		KP145	20
Petri 35 RE	24x36mm	35mm	35rf	1977	Petri	2.7	38mm	Petri	2-1/500	KP176	20
Petri Auto Rapid	24x36mm	Rapid	35vf	1965	Petri	2.8	45mm	Petri MVE	1-500	Mc271	30
Petri Automate	24x36mm	35mm	35rf	1956	Orikkor	1.9	45mm	Carperu	1-300	Mc270	30
Petri Automate	24x36mm	35mm	35rf	1956	Orikkor	1.9	45mm	Copal	1-500	KP147	30
Petri Color 35	24x36mm	35mm	35rf	1968	Petri-Orikkor	2.8	40mm	Petri MS	15-250	Mc271	40
Petri Color 35E	24x36mm	35mm	35rf	1970	Petri-Orikkor	2.8	40mm	Petri MS	15-250	KP189	50
Petri Compact	18x24mm	35mm	35Half	1960	Petri-Orikkor	2.8	28mm	Carperu	15-250		40
Petri Compact 17	18x24mm	35mm	35Half	1962	Petri-Orikkor	2.8	28mm	Carperu	15-250	KP182	40
Petri Compact E	18x24mm	35mm	35Half	1960	Petri-Orikkor	2.8	28mm	Carperu	15-250	Mc271	50
Petri Computor 35 (black)	24x36mm	35mm	35rf	1971	Petri	2.8	40mm	Petri	2-250	KP172	20
Petri Computor 35 (chrome	24x36mm	35mm	35rf	1971	Petri	2.8	40mm	Petri	2-250		20
Petri EBn	24x36mm	35mm	35rf	1960	Orikkor	1.9	45mm	Copal	-1/500	Mc270	50
Petri EBn	24x36mm	35mm	35rf	1960	Orikkor	2.8	45mm	Carperu MVE	1-500	Mc270	50
Petri ES Auto 1.7	24x36mm	35mm	35rf	1974	Petri	1.7	40mm	Seiko	2-1/1000	Mc271	30
Petri ES Auto 2.8	24x36mm	35mm	35rf	1976	Petri	2.7	38mm	Seiko	8-800	KP175	20
Petri FA-1	24x36mm	35mm	35slr	1975	Petri	1.7	55mm	focal plane	1-1000	Mc272	100

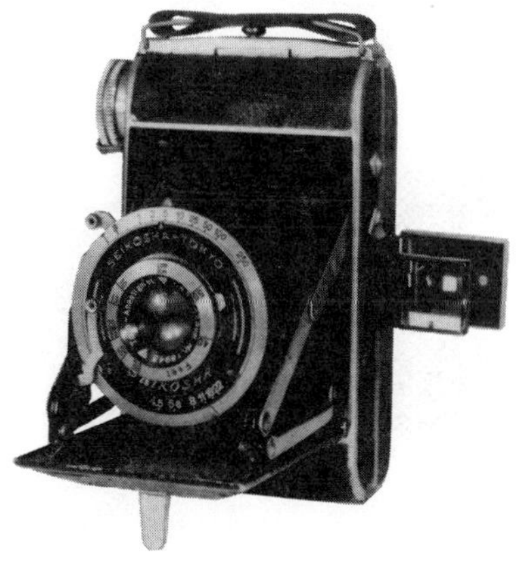

First Six

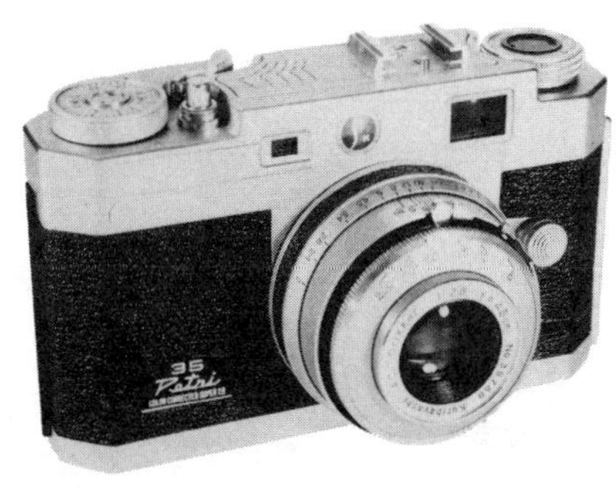

Petri 35 (original)

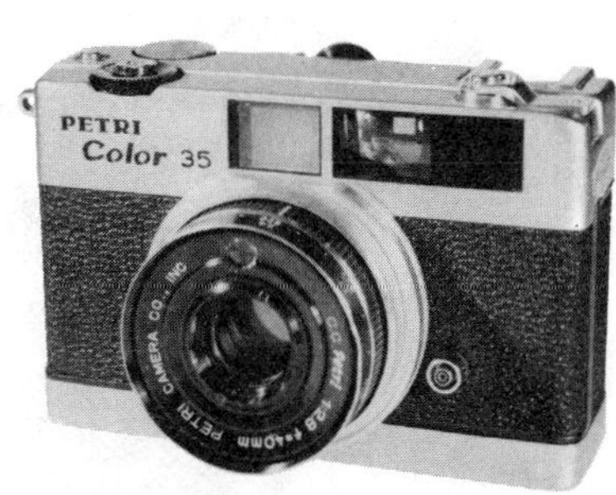

Petri Color 35

MODEL	FORMAT	FILM	TYPE	Year	LENS	Apert	FL	SHUTTER	SPEEDS	ILLUS	U.S.$
Petri Flex Seven	24x36mm	35mm	35slr	1964	Petri	1.8	55mm	focal plane	1-1000	Mc271	330
Petri Flex V	24x36mm	35mm	35slr	1961	Petri Orikkor	2	50mm	focal plane	½-500	KP199	80
Petri Flex V3	24x36mm	35mm	35slr	1964	Petri Orikkor	2	50mm	focal plane	½-500	KP202	70
Petri Flex V6	24x36mm	35mm	35slr	1965	Petri Orikkor	2	50mm	focal plane	½-500	KP204	70
Petri Flex V6-II	24x36mm	35mm	35slr	1970	Petri Orikkor	2	50mm	focal plane	½-500	KP205	70
Petri FT	24x36mm	35mm	35slr	1967	Petri	1.8	55mm	focal plane	1-1000	Mc271	90
Petri FT-II	24x36mm	35mm	35slr	1970	Petri	1.8	55mm	focal plane	1-1000	KP211	90
Petri FT 500	24x36mm	35mm	35slr	1976	Petri	2.8	55mm	focal plane	1-500	Mc272	90
Petri FT 1000	24x36mm	35mm	35slr	1976	Petri	1.7	55mm	focal plane	1-1000	Mc271	100
Petri FT EE	24x36mm	35mm	35slr	1969	Petri	1.7	55mm	focal plane	½-500	Mc272	100
Petri FTE	24x36mm	35mm	35slr	1973	Petri	1.7	55mm	focal plane	½-500	Mc271	90
Petri FTX	24x36mm	35mm	35slr	1974	Petri	1.8	55mm	focal plane	1-1000	KP212	90
Petri Grip-Pack 110	13x17mm	110	110	1977	Petri	11			70	KP241	30
Petri Half (original)	18x24mm	35mm	35Half	1960	Petri-Orikkor	2.8	28mm	Carperu	15-250	Mc271	40
Petri Half 7	18x24mm	35mm	35Half	1962	Petri-Orikkor	2.8	28mm	Carperu	15-250	KP183	40
Petri Hi-Lite	24x36mm	35mm	35rf	1964	Petri	2.8	45mm	Carperu S-EE	30-250	Mc271	20
Petri Instant Back	28x28mm	126	126	1966	Anscomatic	2.8	38mm	Petri VE	30-500	KP236	30
Petri Junior	18x24mm	35mm	35Half	1960	Petri-Orikkor	2.8	28mm	Carperu	15-250		40
Petri M 35	24x36mm	35mm	35rf	1973	Petri	2.7	38mm	Copal	30-650		20
Petri MFT 1000	24x36mm	35mm	35slr	1976	Petri	1.7	50mm	focal plane	1-1000	KP214	100
Petri Micro Compact	24x36mm	35mm	35rf	1976	Petri-Orikkor	2.8	40mm	Petri MS	15-250	KP190	40
Petri Micro MF-1	24x36mm	35mm	35slr	1977	Petri	1.7	50mm	focal plane	1-1000	Mc272	100
Petri Penta	24x36mm	35mm	35slr	1959	Petri Orikkor	2	50mm	focal plane	½-500	Mc271	70
Petri Penta V2	24x36mm	35mm	35slr	1961	Petri Orikkor	2	50mm	focal plane	½-500	KP198	80
Petri Penta V3	24x36mm	35mm	35slr	1964	Petri Orikkor	2	50mm	focal plane	½-500	Mc271	70
Petri Penta V6	24x36mm	35mm	35slr	1965	Petri Orikkor	2	50mm	focal plane	½-500	KP203	70
Petri Penta V6-II	24x36mm	35mm	35slr	1970	Petri Orikkor	2	50mm	focal plane	½-500	KP204	70
Petri Pocket 2	13x17mm	110	110	1975	Petri	11	25/42		100	KP239	30
Petri Prest	24x36mm	35mm	35rf	1961	Petri	2.8	45mm	Carperu VE	30-500	Mc271	20
Petri Pro Seven	24x36mm	35mm	35rf	1963	Petri	1.8	45mm	Carperu MVE	1-500	Mc270	20
Petri Push-Pull 110	13x17mm	110	110	1977	Petri	9.5			70		30
Petri Racer	24x36mm	35mm	35rf	1966	Petri	1.8	45mm	Carperu MVE	1-500	Mc270	20
Petri Racer	24x36mm	35mm	35rf	1966	Petri	2.8	45mm	Carperu MVE	1-500	KP165	20
Petri RF	4.5x6cm	120	FoldRo	1952	Orikon	3.5	75mm	Carperu	1-200	Mc269	140
Petri RF 120	4.5x6cm	120	FoldRo	1955	Orikon	3.5	75mm	Petri	1-200	KP123	240
Petri Semi	4.5x6cm	120	FoldRo	1948	Petri	3.5	75mm	Petri	1-200	Mc269	120
Petri Semi	4.5x6cm	120	FoldRo	1948	Orikon	3.5	75mm	Petri	1-200	KP116	120
Petri Semi II	4.5x6cm	120	FoldRo	1948	Petri	3.5	75mm	Petri	1-200		120
Petri Semi II	4.5x6cm	120	FoldRo	1948	Orikon	3.5	75mm	Petri	1-200	KP120	120
Petri Semi III	4.5x6cm	120	FoldRo	1948	Petri	3.5	75mm	Petri	1-200	KP122	120
Petri Semi III	4.5x6cm	120	FoldRo	1948	Orikon	3.5	75mm	Petri	1-200	KP121	120
Petri Seven	24x36mm	35mm	35rf	1961	Petri	1.8	45mm	Carperu MVE	1-500	Mc270	20

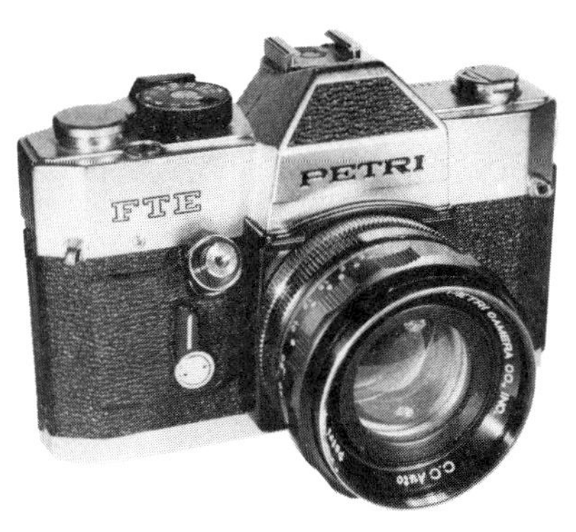

Petri FTE

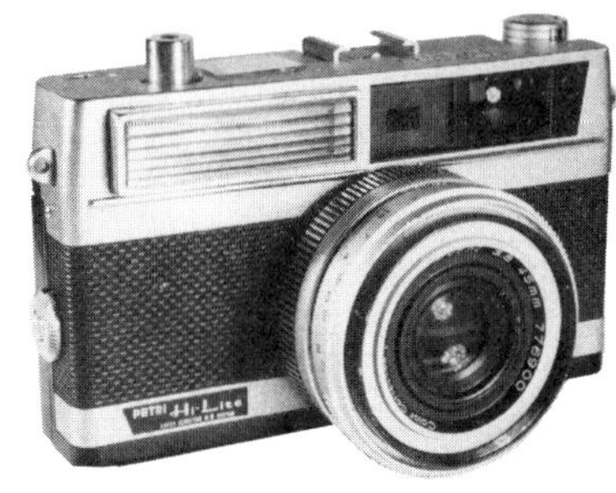
Petri Hi-Lite

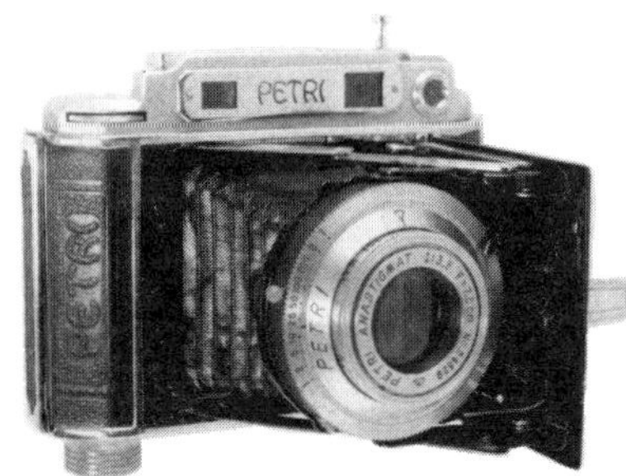

Petri Semi

MODEL	FORMAT	FILM	TYPE	Year	LENS	Apert	FL	SHUTTER	SPEEDS	ILLUS	U.S.$
Petri Seven	24x36mm	35mm	35rf	1961	Petri	2.8	45mm	Citizen	1-500	KP159	20
Petri Seven S	24x36mm	35mm	35rf	1962	Petri	1.8	45mm	Carperu MVE	1-500	KP162	20
Petri Seven S	24x36mm	35mm	35rf	1962	Petri	2.8	45mm	Citizen	1-500	KP161	20
Petri Seven S-II	24x36mm	35mm	35rf	1977	Petri	1.8	45mm	Carperu MVE	1-500		20
Petri Seven S-II	24x36mm	35mm	35rf	1977	Petri	2.8	45mm	Citizen	1-500		20
Petri Super	4.5x6cm	120	FoldRo	1955	Orikkor	3.5	75mm	Carperu	1-200	Mc269	350
Petri Super V	4.5x6cm	120	FoldRo	1956	Orikkor	3.5	75mm	Seikosha-Rapid	1-500		350
Petri Super V	4.5x6cm	120	FoldRo	1956	Orikkor	2.9	75mm	Seikosha-Rapid	1-500		350
Petriflex	6x6cm	120	TLR	1953	Orikkor	3.5	75mm	Carperu	1-200	Mc270	140
Romax Hand	2¼x3¼"	plate	FoldPl	1934	Trinar	6.3	105mm	Vario	25-100	KP59	160
Romax Hand	2¼x3¼"	plate	FoldPl	1934	Tessar	4.5	105mm	Compur	1-250	Mc268	160
Semi First	4.5x6cm	120	FoldRo	1935	Toko Anast.	4.5	75mm	Magna	25-100	KP70	170
Tokiwa Hand	2¼x3¼"	plate	FoldPl	1930	Trioplan	6.3	105mm	Velio	25-100	Mc268	160
Tokiwa Hand	2¼x3¼"	plate	FoldPl	1930	Trinar	6.3	105mm	Vario	25-100	KP57	160
...KAMERA WERKSTÄTTEN MÜNCHEN											
Jolly	10x15mm	Roll	Submin	1950	Achromat		25mm		T,I	Mc272	800
...K.W. - Kamera-Werkstätten Guthe & Thorsch - Dresden											
Astra 35F-X (1953)	24x36mm	35mm	35slr	1953	Westanar	3.5		focal plane	2-500		60
Astra 35F-X (1955)	24x36mm	35mm	35slr	1955	Tessar	3.5		focal plane	2-500		60
Astra 35F-X (1957)	24x36mm	35mm	35slr	1957	Tessar	2.8		focal plane	2-500		60
Cavalier II	24x36mm	35mm	35slr	1965	Domiplan	2.8		focal plane	2-500		30
Hanimex Praktica Nova I	24x36mm	35mm	35slr	1967	Domiplan	2.8	50mm	focal plane	2-500	Hu158	50
Hanimex Praktica Nova IB	24x36mm	35mm	35slr	1967	Domiplan	2.8	50mm	focal plane	2-500	Hu160	60
Hanimex Praktica Super TL	24x36mm	35mm	35slr	1969	Meyer Oreston	1.8	50mm	focal plane	1-500	Hu166	50
Happy	6.5x9cm	plate	FoldPl	1931	Radionar	6.3	105mm	Vario			100
Jenaflex AC-1	24x36mm	35mm	35slr	1987	WO	1.8	50mm	programmed	1-1000	Hu229	80
Jenaflex AM-1	24x36mm	35mm	35slr	1985	WO	1.8	50mm	programmed	1-1000	Hu223	110
Kawenda	24x36mm	35mm	35slr	1954	Tessar	2	50mm	focal plane	2-500	Hu130	90
Patent Etui (black) 6.5x9	6.5x9cm	plate	FoldPl	1924	Tessar	4.5	105mm	Vario			130
Patent Etui (black) 9x12	9x12cm	plate	FoldPl	1924	Zeiss Tessar	4.5		Compur		Mc273	70
Patent Etui (blue) 6.5x9	6.5x9cm	plate	FoldPl	1924	Radionar	6.3	105mm	Ibsor			450
Patent Etui (blue) 9x12	9x12cm	plate	FoldPl	1924	Radionar	6.3		Vario			370
Patent Etui (brown) 6.5x9	6.5x9cm	plate	FoldPl	1924	Radionar	6.3	105mm	Vario			310
Patent Etui (brown) 9x12	9x12cm	plate	FoldPl	1924	Isconar	6.3		Ibsor			270
Patent Etui (grey) 6.5x9	6.5x9cm	plate	FoldPl	1924	Radionar	6.3	105mm	Vario			310
Patent Etui (grey) 9x12	9x12cm	plate	FoldPl	1924	Eurynar	4.5		Vario			270
Patent Etui (red) 6.5x9	6.5x9cm	plate	FoldPl	1924	Radionar	6.3	105mm	Vario			450
Patent Etui (red) 9x12	9x12cm	plate	FoldPl	1924	Zeiss Tessar	4.5		Compur			410
Pentaflex	24x36mm	35mm	35slr	1965	Domiplan	2.8	50mm	focal plane	2-500		50
Pentaflex SL	24x36mm	35mm	35slr	1967	Domiplan	2.8	50mm	focal plane	2-500	Hu155	40
Pentor IB	24x36mm	35mm	35slr	1968	Domiplan	2.8	50mm	focal plane	2-500	Hu161	50
Pilot 6	6x6cm	120	MedSLR	1936	Laack Pololyt	3.5	75mm	guillotine		Mc273	130

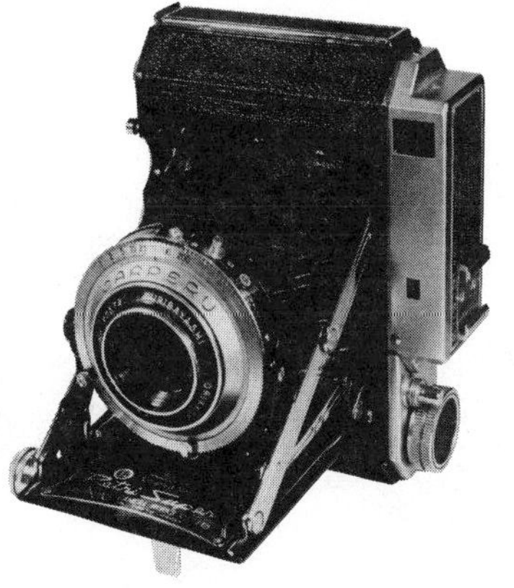

Petri Super

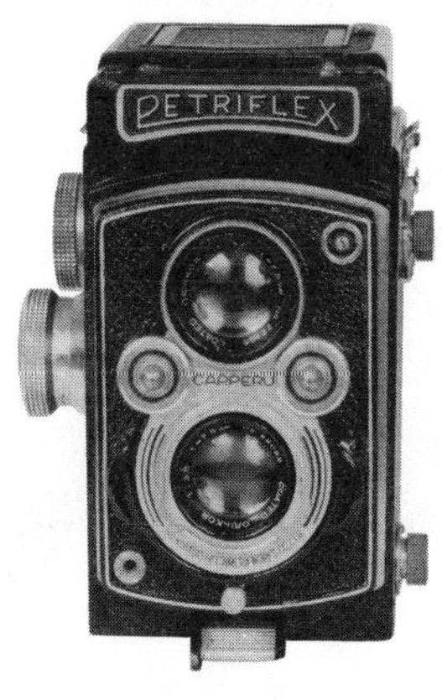

Petriflex

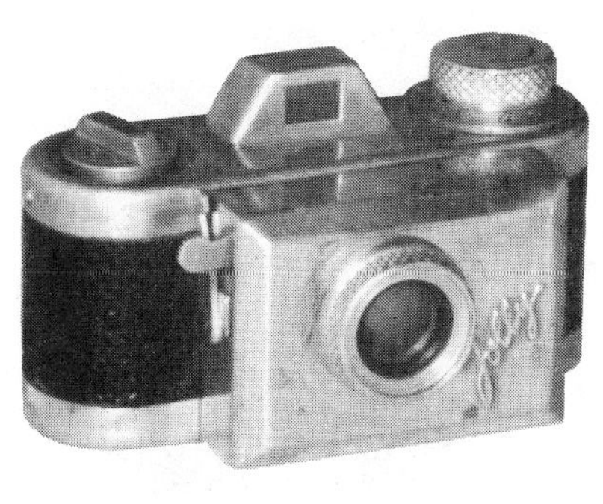

Jolly

MODEL	FORMAT	FILM	TYPE	Year	LENS	Apert	FL	SHUTTER	SPEEDS	ILLUS	U.S.$
Pilot 6	6x6cm	120	MedSLR	1936	KW Anastigmat	6.3	75mm	guillotine			130
Pilot Reflex	3x4cm	127	StrutTLR	1931	Xenar	2.9	50mm	Compur	1-300	Mc273	350
Pilot Super	6x6cm	120	MedSLR	1939	Pilotar	4.5		focal plane	20-200,T,B	Mc273	140
Pocket Dalco (black)	6x9cm	plate	FoldPl	1932	Tessar	4.5	105mm	Compur	1-300		90
Pocket Dalco (blue)	6x9cm	plate	FoldPl	1932	Tessar	4.5	105mm	Compur	1-300		190
Praktica (1949)	24x36mm	35mm	35slr	1949	Tessar	2.8	50mm	focal plane	2-500	Mc273	70
Praktica (1950)	24x36mm	35mm	35slr	1950	Westanar	3.5	50mm	focal plane	2-500	Hu083	70
Praktica (1951)	24x36mm	35mm	35slr	1951	Tessar	2.8	50mm	focal plane	2-500	Hu084	70
Praktica (1952)	24x36mm	35mm	35slr	1952	Tessar	2.8	50mm	focal plane	2-500	Hu085	70
Praktica (1955)	24x36mm	35mm	35slr	1955	Tessar	2.8	50mm	focal plane	2-500	Hu132	70
Praktica IV ("KW")	24x36mm	35mm	35slr	1959	Primotar	2.8	50mm	focal plane	2-500	Hu139	80
Praktica IV (no "KW")	24x36mm	35mm	35slr	1959	Tessar	2.8	50mm	focal plane	2-500	Mc273	50
Praktica IVB	24x36mm	35mm	35slr	1961	Domiplan	2.8	50mm	focal plane	2-500	Mc273	50
Praktica IVBM	24x36mm	35mm	35slr	1961	Domiplan	2.8	50mm	focal plane	2-500	Hu144	60
Praktica IVF	24x36mm	35mm	35slr	1962	Domiplan	2.8	50mm	focal plane	2-500	Mc274	50
Praktica IVFB	24x36mm	35mm	35slr	1961	Domiplan	2.8	50mm	focal plane	2-500	Mc273	60
Praktica IVM	24x36mm	35mm	35slr	1961	Tessar	2.8	50mm	focal plane	2-500	Hu143	60
Praktica VF	24x36mm	35mm	35slr	1964	Domiplan	2.8	50mm	focal plane	2-500	Mc274	70
Praktica VFB	24x36mm	35mm	35slr	1965	Domiplan	2.8	50mm	focal plane	2-500	Hu148	70
Praktica VLC	24x36mm	35mm	35slr	1974	Pentacon	1.8	50mm	focal plane	1-1000	Hu184	130
Praktica VLC2	24x36mm	35mm	35slr	1976	Pentacon	1.8	50mm	focal plane	1-1000	Hu196	120
Praktica VLC3	24x36mm	35mm	35slr	1978	Pentacon	1.8	50mm	focal plane	1-1000	Hu204	100
Praktica Autoreflex S	24x36mm	35mm	35slr	1975	Pentacon Auto	2.8	50mm	focal plane	1-1000	Hu172	70
Praktica Autoreflex S-TL	24x36mm	35mm	35slr	1975	Pentacon Auto	1.8	50mm	focal plane	1-1000	Hu177	70
Praktica Autoreflex SL	24x36mm	35mm	35slr	1975	Pentacon Auto	1.8	50mm	focal plane	1-1000	Hu182	70
Praktica B 100	24x36mm	35mm	35slr	1981	Prakticar	1.8	50mm	electronic	1-1000	A3215	90
Praktica B 100 (Type 2)	24x36mm	35mm	35slr	1983	Prakticar	1.8	50mm	electronic	1-1000	Hu226	90
Praktica B 200 (black)	24x36mm	35mm	35slr	1979	Prakticar	1.8	50mm	electronic	40-1/1000	A1648	100
Praktica B 200 (chrome)	24x36mm	35mm	35slr	1982	Prakticar	1.8	50mm	electronic	40-1/1000	Hu219	100
Praktica BC 1	24x36mm	35mm	35slr	1984	Prakticar	1.8	50mm	electronic	40-1/1000	A3214	100
Praktica BC 3	24x36mm	35mm	35slr	1987	Prakticar	1.8	50mm	electronic	40-1/1000	Hu224	90
Praktica BC Auto	24x36mm	35mm	35slr	1985	Prakticar	2.4	50mm	electronic	1-1000	Hu227	50
Praktica BCA	24x36mm	35mm	35slr	1986	Prakticar	1.8	50mm	programmed	1-1000	Hu228	100
Praktica BCC	24x36mm	35mm	35slr	1989	Prakticar	1.8	50mm	programmed	1-1000	Hu231	70
Praktica BCS	24x36mm	35mm	35slr	1989	Prakticar	1.8	50mm	programmed	1-1000	Hu230	70
Praktica BCX	24x36mm	35mm	35slr	1983	Prakticar	1.8	50mm	electronic	40-1/1000	Hu220	90
Praktica BM	24x36mm	35mm	35slr	1989	Prakticar	2.4	50mm	electronic	4-1/1000	Hu234	90
Praktica BMS	24x36mm	35mm	35slr	1989	Prakticar	1.8	50mm	electronic	4-1/1000	Hu232	90
Praktica BX 10 DX	24x36mm	35mm	35slr	1989	Prakticar	1.8	50mm	programmed	1-1000	Hu236	350
Praktica BX 20	24x36mm	35mm	35slr	1987	Prakticar	1.8	50mm	programmed	1-1000	Hu235	120
Praktica BX 20s	24x36mm	35mm	35slr	1990	Prakticar	3.3-4.5	35-70	programmed	1-1000	Hu238	500
Praktica BX 21	24x36mm	35mm	35slr	1990	Prakticar	1.8	50mm	programmed	1-1000	Hu237	390

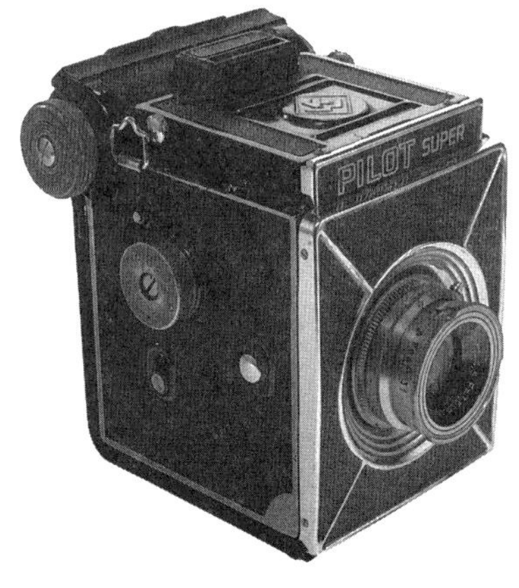

Pilot Super

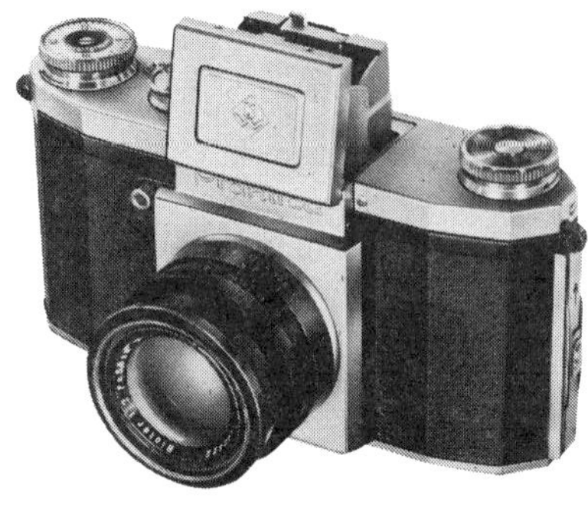

Praktica (1949)

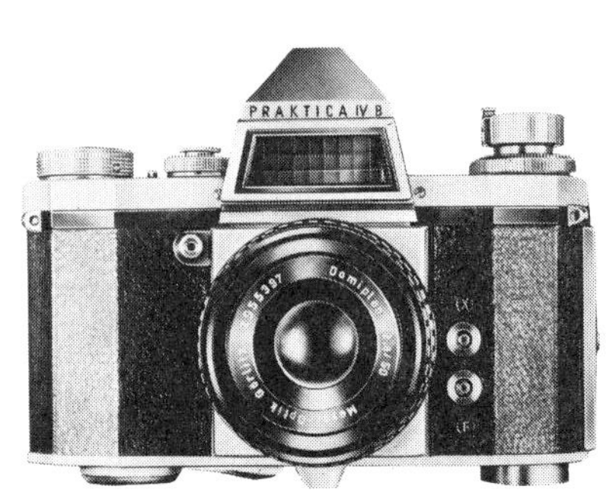

Praktica IVB

MODEL	FORMAT	FILM	TYPE	Year	LENS	Apert	FL	SHUTTER	SPEEDS	ILLUS	U.S.$
Praktica DTL2	24x36mm	35mm	35slr	1978	Pentacon	1.8	50mm	focal plane	1-1000	Hu198	430
Praktica DTL3	24x36mm	35mm	35slr	1979	Domiplan	2.8	50mm	focal plane	1-1000	Hu206	70
Praktica EE2	24x36mm	35mm	35slr	1977	Pentacon	1.8	50mm	focal plane	1-1000	Hu197	90
Praktica EE3	24x36mm	35mm	35slr	1979	Domiplan	2.8	50mm	focal plane	1-1000	Hu205	50
Praktica FX (3 Sync)	24x36mm	35mm	35slr	1952	Tessar	3.5	50mm	focal plane	2-500	Mc273	60
Praktica FX (2 Sync)	24x36mm	35mm	35slr	1953	Tessar	2.8	50mm	focal plane	2-500	Hu127	80
Praktica FX (1 Coax)	24x36mm	35mm	35slr	1954	Tessar	2.8	50mm	focal plane	2-500	A613	70
Praktica FX (2 Coax)	24x36mm	35mm	35slr	1954	Tessar	2.8	50mm	focal plane	2-500	Hu129	60
Praktica FX2 (1 Coax)	24x36mm	35mm	35slr	1956	Tessar	2.8	50mm	focal plane	2-500	Mc273	80
Praktica FX2 (2 Coax)	24x36mm	35mm	35slr	1956	Tessar	2.8	50mm	focal plane	2-500	Hu135	50
Praktica FX3	24x36mm	35mm	35slr	1956	Tessar	2.8	50mm	focal plane	2-500	Hu136	50
Praktica L	24x36mm	35mm	35slr	1969	Pentacon Auto	2.8	50mm	focal plane	1-1000	Mc274	40
Praktica L2	24x36mm	35mm	35slr	1975	Domiplan	2.8	50mm	focal plane	1-1000	Hu192	50
Praktica LB	24x36mm	35mm	35slr	1972	Oreston	1.8	50mm	focal plane	1-1000	Mc274	50
Praktica LB 2	24x36mm	35mm	35slr	1976	Domiplan	2.8	50mm	focal plane	1-1000	Hu194	70
Praktica LLC	24x36mm	35mm	35slr	1969	Pentacon	1.8	50mm	focal plane	1-1000	Hu173	70
Praktica LTL	24x36mm	35mm	35slr	1970	Pentacon	1.8	50mm	focal plane	1-1000	Hu175	70
Praktica LTL2	24x36mm	35mm	35slr	1975	Tessar	2.8	50mm	focal plane	1-1000	Hu186	60
Praktica LTL3	24x36mm	35mm	35slr	1975	Tessar	2.8	50mm	focal plane	1-1000	Hu189	70
Praktica MTL3	24x36mm	35mm	35slr	1978	Pancolar	1.8	50mm	focal plane	1-1000	A3213	70
Praktica MTL5	24x36mm	35mm	35slr	1983	Pentacon Auto	1.8	50mm	focal plane	1-1000	A3216	60
Praktica MTL50	24x36mm	35mm	35slr	1985	Pentacon Auto	1.8	50mm	focal plane	1-1000	Hu217	60
Praktica MTL5B	24x36mm	35mm	35slr	1985	Pentacon Auto	1.8	50mm	focal plane	1-1000	Hu214	60
Praktica Nova	24x36mm	35mm	35slr	1965	Domiplan	2.8	50mm	focal plane	2-500	A1644	40
Praktica Nova	24x36mm	35mm	35slr	1966	Tessar	2.8	50mm	focal plane	2-500	Mc274	40
Praktica Nova B	24x36mm	35mm	35slr	1965	Domiplan	2.8	50mm	focal plane	2-500	Mc274	40
Praktica PL electronic	24x36mm	35mm	35slr	1968	Domiplan	2.8	50mm	ElecFP	30-1/500	Hu163	80
Praktica PL Nova I	24x36mm	35mm	35slr	1967	Pancolar	1.8	50mm	focal plane	2-500	Mc274	50
Praktica PL Nova IB	24x36mm	35mm	35slr	1967	Domiplan	2.8	50mm	focal plane	2-500	Mc274	60
Praktica PLC2	24x36mm	35mm	35slr	1975	Pentacon	1.8	50mm	focal plane	1-1000	Hu191	100
Praktica PLC3	24x36mm	35mm	35slr	1978	Pentacon	1.8	50mm	focal plane	1-1000	Hu203	100
Praktica Super TL	24x36mm	35mm	35slr	1968	Meyer Oreston	1.8	50mm	focal plane	1-500	Mc274	50
Praktica Super TL2	24x36mm	35mm	35slr	1976	Domiplan	2.8	50mm	focal plane	1-500	Hu188	50
Praktica Super TL3	24x36mm	35mm	35slr	1978	Domiplan	2.8	50mm	focal plane	1-500	Hu199	50
Praktica Super TL 500	24x36mm	35mm	35slr	1981	Tessar	2.8	50mm	focal plane	1-1000	Hu208	80
Praktica Super TL 1000	24x36mm	35mm	35slr	1980	Tessar	2.8	50mm	focal plane	1-500	Hu207	50
Praktica TL	24x36mm	35mm	35slr	1976	Domiplan	2.8	50mm	focal plane	1-1000	Hu187	120
Prakticamat	24x36mm	35mm	35slr	1965	Pancolar	2	50mm	focal plane	1-1000,B	Mc274	70
Praktiflex (black)	24x36mm	35mm	35slr	1940	Victor	2.9	50mm	focal plane	20-500	Hu075	160
Praktiflex (chrome)	24x36mm	35mm	35slr	1940	Tessar	3.5	50mm	focal plane	20-500	Hu074	150
Praktiflex (post-war)	24x36mm	35mm	35slr	1946	Tessar	3.5	50mm	focal plane	20-500	A611	100
Praktiflex (bold script)	24x36mm	35mm	35slr	1938	Victor	2.9	50mm	focal plane	20-500	Hu072	310

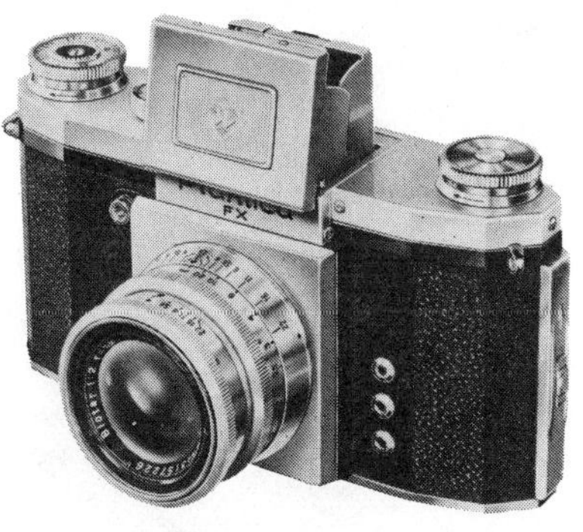

Praktica FX (3 Sync)

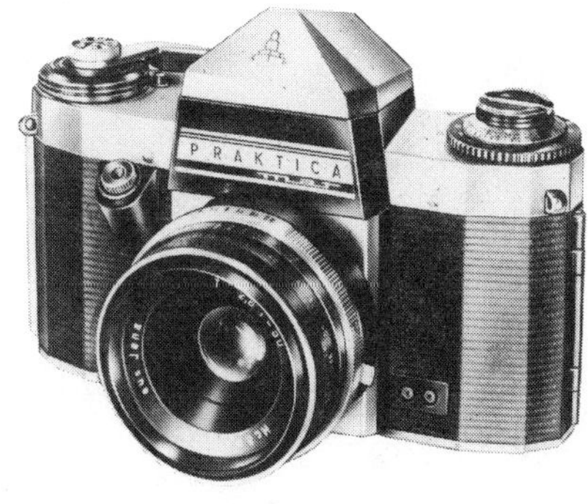

Prakticamat

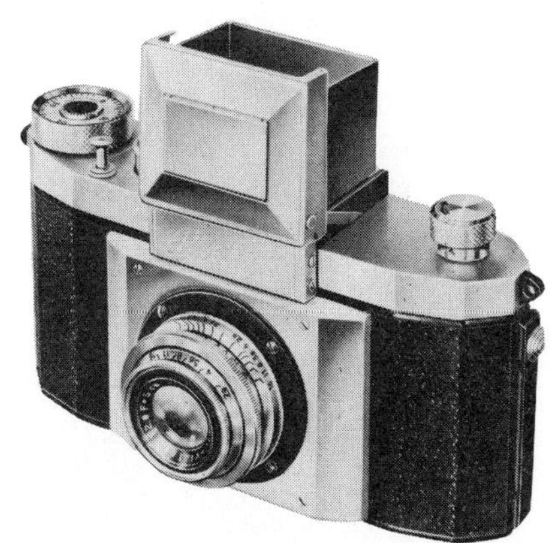

Prakticaflex

MODEL	FORMAT	FILM	TYPE	Year	LENS	Apert	FL	SHUTTER	SPEEDS	ILLUS	U.S.$
Praktiflex (no lugs)	24x36mm	35mm	35slr	1939	Tessar	3.5	50mm	focal plane	20-500	Hu073	240
Praktiflex II (M 40)	24x36mm	35mm	35slr	1947	Victor	2.9	50mm	focal plane	25-500	Hu079	70
Praktiflex II (M 42)	24x36mm	35mm	35slr	1948	Tessar	3.5	50mm	focal plane	2-500	Mc274	70
Praktiflex FX	24x36mm	35mm	35slr	1953	Primoplan	1.9	50mm	focal plane	2-500	Mc275	70
Praktina	24x36mm	35mm	35slr	1952	Tessar	2.8	58mm	focal plane	1-1000,B	Hu108	130
Praktina IIa	24x36mm	35mm	35slr	1959	Jena Flexon	2	50mm	focal plane	1-1000,B	Mc275	120
Praktina FX	24x36mm	35mm	35slr	1956	Biotar	2	58mm	focal plane	1-1000,B	Hu109	80
Praktisix	6x6cm	plate	MedSLR	1957	Primotar	3.5	80mm	focal plane	1-1000		210
Praktisix II	6x6cm	plate	MedSLR	1965	Meyer Primotar	3.5	80mm	focal plane	1-1000	Mc275	180
Reflex-Box	6x9cm	120	MedSLR	1933	KW Anastigmat	6.3	105mm		25-100,B		140
Reflex-Box	6x9cm	120	MedSLR	1933	Steinheil	4.5	105mm		25-100,B	Mc275	160
Rival Reflex	24x36mm	35mm	35slr	1955	Wetzlar Vastar	2.8	50mm	focal plane			120
...KYOTO PRECISION MFG. - Japan											
Cine Vero	24x35mm	35mm	35vf	1947	Lausar	4.5	50mm	Presto	T,B,1-500	Mc275	140
...LAACK (Julius Laack & Sons) - Rathenow											
Ferrotype camera	25mm	Ferro	Button	1895		3.5	60mm				1100
Merkur	10x15cm	plate	FoldPl		Polyxentar	6.8	150mm	Koilos			70
Padie	9x12cm	plate	FoldPl		Pololyt	6.8	135mm	Rulex	1-300		50
Tropical camera (brass)	9x12cm	plate	FoldPl		Pololyt	4.5	135mm	Ibsor			510
Tropical camera (brass)	9x12cm	plate	FoldPl		Dialytar	4.5	135mm	Compur			510
Tropical camera (gold)	9x12cm	plate	FoldPl		Pololyt	4.5	135mm	Ibsor			630
Wanderer	6.5x9cm	plate	FoldPl		Pololyt	4.5					50
...LAMPERTI & GARBAGNATI - Milan, Italy											
Carte de visite	13x18cm	plate	MultiLens	1885	Darlot 6-lens			flap		A1854	330
Detective camera	9x12cm	plate	MagBox	1890							350
Spiegamento rapido	9x14cm	plate	FoldPl	1900						Mc276	220
Stereo Detective	9x18cm	plate	StMagBox	1895	Cooke						400
Wet plate camera	18x18cm	WetPl	WetPlate	1870	Darlot Petzval						2100
...LANCART (Etablissements Lancart) - Paris											
Xyz	12x15mm	Roll	Submin	1935	Roussel Xyzor	7	22mm		25,B,I	Mc276	800
...LANCASTER (J. Lancaster) - Birmingham, England											
Alum.Bound Instantograph	3¼x4¼"	plate	Field	1892	Lancaster						350
Amateur's Camera 3¼x4¼"	3¼x4¼"	plate	Tailboard	1891	Lancaster					A2930	140
Amateur's Camera 4¼x6½"	4¼x6½"	plate	Tailboard	1891	Lancaster					A2928	150
Amateur's Camera 6½x8½"	6½x8½"	plate	Tailboard	1891	Lancaster						150
BrassBound Instantograph	3¼x4¼"	plate	Field	1908	Lancaster			Lancaster			320
Gem Apparatus	9x12cm	plate	MultiLens	1880	12-lens					A3227	2000
Instantograph View 3¼x4¼	3¼x4¼"	plate	Field	1886	Lancaster	8		Lancaster		A151	350
Instantograph 3¼x4¼"	3¼x4¼"	plate	Field	1886	Lancaster	10		Lancaster		A152	350
Instantograph 4¼x6½"	4¼x6½"	plate	Field	1880	Lancaster			Lancaster		Mc276	330
Instantograph 6½x8½"	6½x8½"	plate	Field	1880	Lancaster			Lancaster			330
International Pat. 3¼x4¼"	3¼x4¼"	plate	Tailboard	1885	Lancaster			Lancaster			310

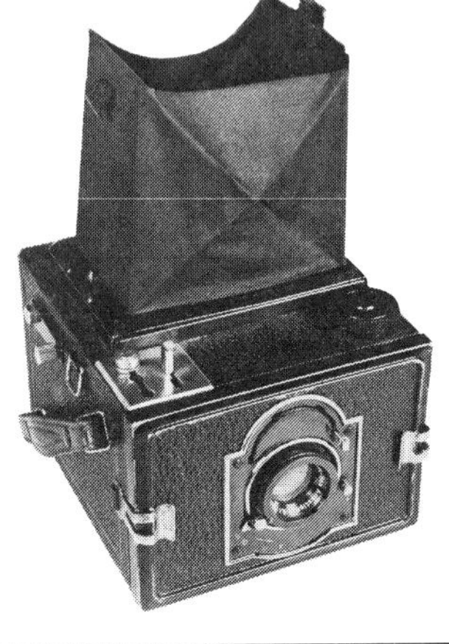

K.W. Reflex-Box

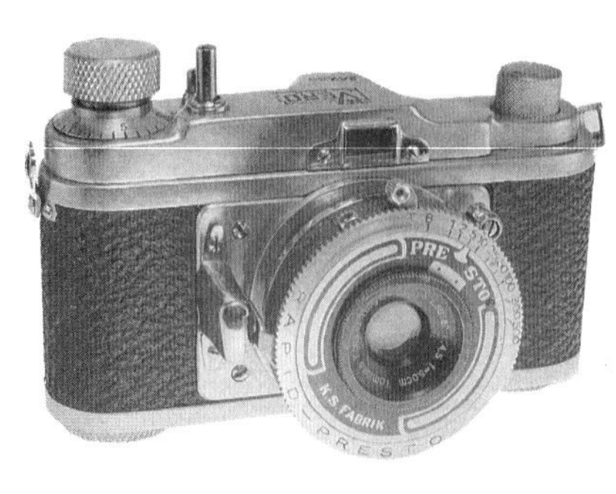

Kyoto Cine Vero

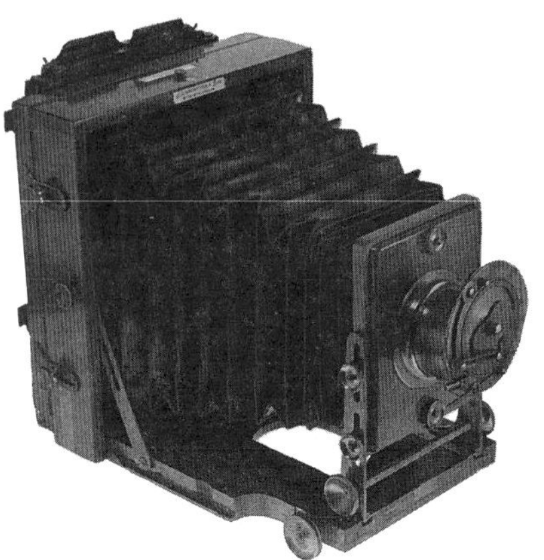

Instantograph View 4¼x6½

MODEL	FORMAT	FILM	TYPE	Year	LENS	Apert	FL	SHUTTER	SPEEDS	ILLUS	U.S.$
International Pat. 4¼x6½"	4¼x6½"	plate	Tailboard	1885	Lancaster			Lancaster			310
Kamrex 3¼x4¼"	3¼x4¼"	plate	FoldPl	1900	Rapid Rectilinear			Iris	I,T		250
Kamrex 4¼x6½"	4¼x6½"	plate	FoldPl	1900	Rapid Rectilinear			Iris	I,T	Mc276	250
Ladies (purse style) 3¼x4¼	3¼x4¼"	plate	Disguised	1894	Achromat					Mc276	1900
Ladies (purse style) 4¼x6½	4¼x6½"	plate	Disguised	1894	Achromat					A3285	1900
Ladies (purse style) 6½x8½	6½x8½"	plate	Disguised	1894	Achromat					A3285	1900
Ladies (tailboard style)	4¼x6½"	plate	Tailboard	1880	Achromat					Mc276	540
Ladies Gem Camera	3¼x4¼"	plate	FoldPl	1900		8	105mm	Vario		Mc277	12000
le Meritoire 3¼x4¼"	3¼x4¼"	plate	FoldPl	1880	Lancaster						330
le Meritoire 6½x8½"	6½x8½"	plate	FoldPl	1880	Lancaster					Mc277	330
le Meritoire 10x12"	10x12"	plate	FoldPl	1880	Lancaster						330
le Merveilleux 3¼x4¼"	3¼x4¼"	plate	FoldPl	1880	Aplanat					Mc277	270
le Merveilleux 4¼x6½"	4¼x6½"	plate	FoldPl	1880	Aplanat					A153	270
le Merveilleux Stereo	3¼x4¼"	plate	StFoldPl	1895	Aplanat					A2653	330
Omnigraph	3¼x4¼"	plate	DetectivBox	1890	achromatic			See-Saw		Mc277	280
Portable Instantograph	3¼x4¼"	plate	FoldPl	1893	Instantograh			See-Saw		Mc277	490
Portable Instantograph	4¼x6½"	plate	FoldPl	1893	Instantograh			See-Saw			490
Portable Instantograph	6½x8½"	plate	FoldPl	1893	Instantograh			See-Saw			490
Postage Stamp Camera	2½x4¼"	plate	MultiLens	1896	4-lens			flap		A3231	1400
Postage Stamp Camera		plate	MultiLens	1896	6-lens					A1852	2300
Postage Stamp Camera		plate	MultiLens	1896	9-lens					A1885	270
Rover	3¼x4¼"	plate	MagBox	1891	Rectilinear			See-Saw		Mc277	580
Special Brass Bound Inst.	3¼x4¼"	plate	Tailboard	1891	Lancaster			See-Saw		Mc277	330
Special Brass Bound Inst.	4¼x6½"	plate	Tailboard	1891	Rectigraph			See-Saw		A2935	350
Stereo Instantograph	8x17cm	plate	StFoldPl	1891	Lancaster			Instant		Mc277	630
Stereo Instantograph	8x17cm	plate	StFoldPl	1891	Rectigraph			See-Saw		A695	630
Watch Camera, Ladies	1x1½"	plate	Submin	1886	Achromat	22		rotary			45000
Watch Camera, Men's	1½x2"	plate	Submin	1886	Achromat	22		rotary		Mc277	35000
Watch Camera (Replica)	1½x2"	plate	Submin	1982	Achromat	22		rotary			1500
...LECHNER (R. Lechner) - Vienna											
Dreifarben-Kamera	9x12cm	plate	3-Color	1911	Goerz					A2031	270
Field camera 9x12	9x12cm	plate	Field	1895	Steinheil						150
Field camera 13x18	13x18cm	plate	Field	1895	Zeiss Anastigmat	7.2	195mm				270
Field camera 18x24	18x24cm	plate	Field	1900	Zeiss Anastigmat	8				A1367	190
Juwel	45x107	plate	SterStrut	1909	Achromat				T,I		350
Nanna IA	6x13cm	plate	StFoldPl	1909	Nanna Aplanat	8		guillotine			340
Nanna IA	6x13cm	plate	StFoldPl	1909	Dagor	6.8		guillotine			340
Sport-Kamera	13x18cm	plate	StrutPl	1895	Planastigmat					A3006	160
Spreizenkamera	9x12cm	plate	StrutPl	1905	Busch Anastigmat	5.5	130mm	focal plane		A298	300
Spreizenkamera	9x12cm	plate	StrutPl	1905	Doppel Anastigma	6	120mm	focal plane		A298	300
Stereo-Taschenkamera	45x107	plate	SterStrut	1910	Achromat				M,Z	A1780	240
Universal	9x12cm	plate	StrutPl	1899	Doppel Anastigma	6	120mm	focal plane			260

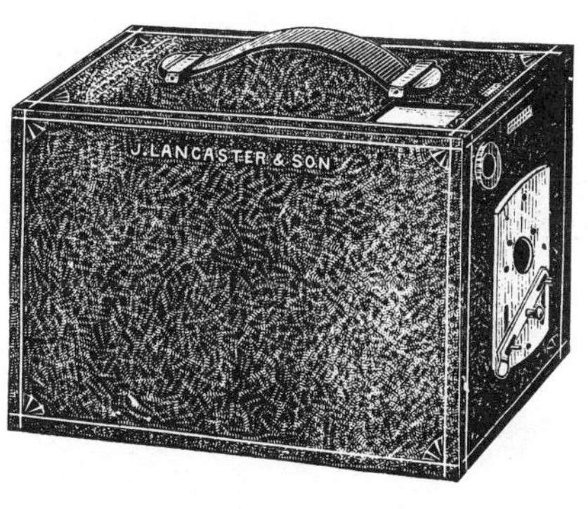

Omnigraph

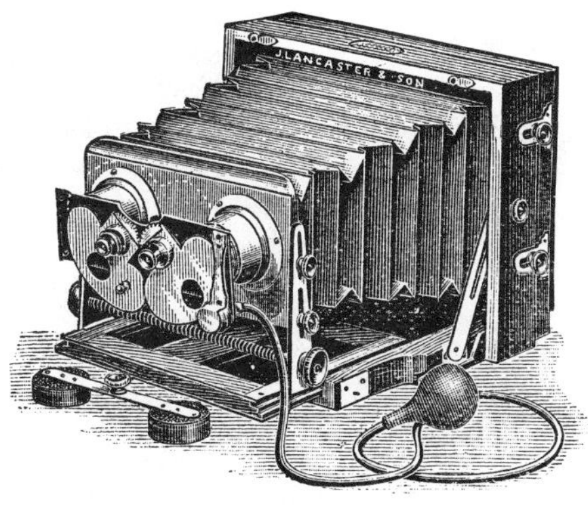

Stereo Instantograph

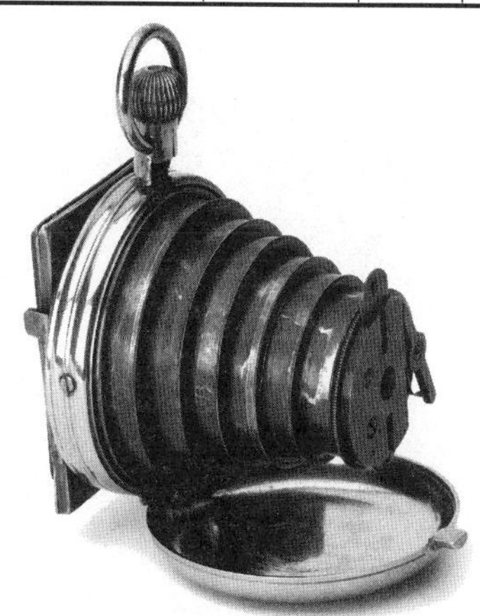

Lancaster Watch Camera, Men

MODEL	FORMAT	FILM	TYPE	Year	LENS	Apert	FL	SHUTTER	SPEEDS	ILLUS	U.S.$
Universal	9x12cm	plate	StrutPl	1899	Protar	6.3	140mm	focal plane		A1419	200
Universal	9x12cm	plate	StrutPl	1899	Zeiss Anastigmat	6.3	105mm	focal plane		A1419	220
...LEHMAN (Gebr. Lehman) - Berlin											
Pelar-Camera	24x36mm	35mm	35vf	1947	Ludwig Pelar	2.9	50mm	Vario	25-100		460
...LEHMANN (A. Lehmann) - Berlin											
Ben Akiba	13x25mm		Submin	1903	Meniscus	9	35mm		T,I	Mc278	6700
Ben Akiba Replica	13x25mm		Submin		Meniscus	9	35mm		T,I		2300
...LEIDOLF - Wetzlar											
Auto Malik	24x36mm	35mm	35vf		Lordonar	2.8	5cm	Prontor-Matic	30-500	Mc278	60
Leidox	4x4cm	127	RigidRo	1951	Triplet	3.8	50mm	Prontor-S	-300	A1057	50
Leidox II	4x4cm	127	RigidRo	1951	Triplet	3.8	50mm	Prontor-S	-300	A1058	50
Lordomat	24x36mm	35mm	35rf	1954	Lordonar	2.8	50mm	Prontor-SVS	1-500	Mc278	70
Lordomat	24x36mm	35mm	35rf	1954	Lordonar	1.9	50mm	Prontor-SVS	1-500		70
Lordomat II	24x36mm	35mm	35rf	1954	Lordonar	1.9	50mm	Prontor-SVS	1-500		70
Lordomat C-35	24x36mm	35mm	35rf	1954	Lordonar	2.8	50mm	Prontor-SVS	1-500	A1043	80
Lordomat SE	24x36mm	35mm	35rf	1954	Lordonar	1.9	50mm	Prontor-SVS	1-500		140
Lordomat SLE	24x36mm	35mm	35rf	1954	Lordonar	2.8	50mm	Prontor-SVS	1-500		90
Lordomatic	24x36mm	35mm	35rf	1954	Lordonar	2.8	50mm	Prontor-SVS	1-500		70
Lordomatic II	24x36mm	35mm	35rf	1954	Lordonar	2.8	50mm	Prontor-SVS	1-500		70
Lordox	24x36mm	35mm	35vf	1952	Lordon	2.8	50mm	Pronto	30-250	Mc279	50
Lordox II	24x36mm	35mm	35vf	1952	Triplon	2.8	50mm	Prontor-SV	1-300	A1041	40
Lordox II	24x36mm	35mm	35vf	1952	Triplon	2.8	50mm	Prontor-SVS	1-500		40
Lordox Automat	24x36mm	35mm	35vf	1962	Lordonar	2.8	50mm	Prontormatic	30-500		70
Lordox Blitz	24x36mm	35mm	35vf	1954	Triplon	2.8	5cm	Pronto	30-250	Mc279	30
Lordox Junior	24x36mm	35mm	35vf	1954	Triplon	2.8	50mm	Prontor-SVS	1-500		90
Lordox Junior B	24x36mm	35mm	35vf	1954	Triplon	2.8	50mm	Prontor-SVS	1-500		30
Lordox Super Automat	24x36mm	35mm	35vf	1960	Lordonar	2.8	50mm	Prontormatic	30-500	A2097	50
...LEITZ (Ernst Leitz GmbH) - Wetzlar											
Ur-Leica (Replica)	24x36mm	35mm	35vf							Mc279	1100
Leica 0-Series	24x36mm	35mm	35vf	1923	Leitz Anast.	3.5	50mm	focal plane		A957	55000
Leica I (A) (Anastigmat)	24x36mm	35mm	35vf	1925	Leitz Anast.	3.5	50mm	focal plane	25-500	A960	22000
Leica I (A) (Elmax)	24x36mm	35mm	35vf	1925	Elmax	3.5	50mm	focal plane	25-500	Mc281	6300
Leica I (A) (Hektor)	24x36mm	35mm	35vf	1930	Hektor	2.5	50mm	focal plane	25-500	A2191	3900
Leica I (A) 4-digit	24x36mm	35mm	35vf	1926	Elmar	3.5	50mm	focal plane	25-500	Mc281	2000
Leica I (A) 5-digit	24x36mm	35mm	35vf	1926	Elmar	3.5	50mm	focal plane	25-500	A2187	1500
Leica I (A) Luxus	24x36mm	35mm	35vf	1926	Elmar	3.5	50mm	focal plane	25-500	A969	36000
Leica I (A) Luxus Replica	24x36mm	35mm	35vf		Elmar	3.5	50mm	focal plane	25-500	A2192	1800
Leica I (B) (Dial Compur)	24x36mm	35mm	35vf	1926	Elmar	3.5	50mm	Dial-Compur	1-300	Mc281	8000
Leica I (B) (Rim Compur)	24x36mm	35mm	35vf	1926	Elmar	3.5	50mm	Rim-Compur	1-300	Mc281	7000
Leica I (C) (early)	24x36mm	35mm	35vf	1930	Elmar	3.5	50mm	focal plane	20-500	A2193	1500
Leica I (C) + Hektor	24x36mm	35mm	35vf	1930	Hektor	2.5	50mm	focal plane	20-500		2600
Leica I (C) "0"	24x36mm	35mm	35vf	1930	Elmar	3.5	50mm	focal plane	20-500		630

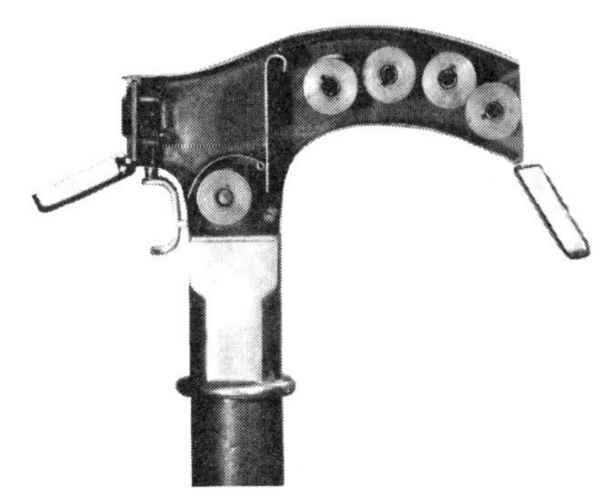

Ben Akiba

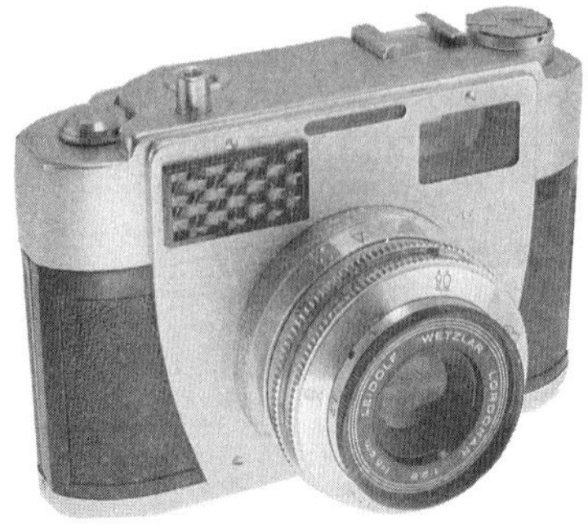

Auto Malik

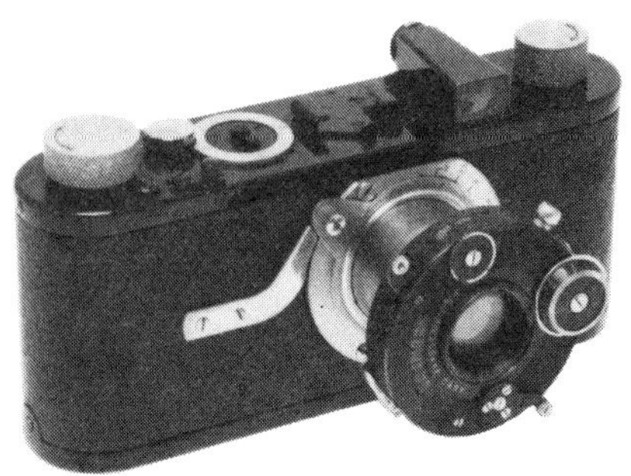

Leica I (B) (Dial-Compur)

MODEL	FORMAT	FILM	TYPE	Year	LENS	Apert	FL	SHUTTER	SPEEDS	ILLUS	U.S.$
Leica I (C) (Luxus)	24x36mm	35mm	35vf	1931	Elmar	3.5	50mm	focal plane	20-500	Mc281	41000
Leica Ic	24x36mm	35mm	35vf	1949	interchangeable			focal plane	30-500	A2209	560
Leica If (Black-dial)	24x36mm	35mm	35rf	1952	interchangeable			focal plane	30-500	A2210	1500
Leica If (Red-dial)	24x36mm	35mm	35vf	1952	interchangeable			focal plane	30-500	A2211	660
Leica Ig	24x36mm	35mm	35vf	1957	interchangeable			focal plane	1-1000	Mc283	1300
Leica II (D) (black)	24x36mm	35mm	35rf	1932	Elmar	3.5	50mm	focal plane	20-500	Mc282	520
Leica II (D) (chrome)	24x36mm	35mm	35rf	1932	Elmar	3.5	50mm	focal plane	20-500		480
Leica IIc body	24x36mm	35mm	35rf	1948	interchangeable			focal plane	30-500	Mc283	500
Leica IIf (Black-dial)	24x36mm	35mm	35rf	1951	interchangeable			focal plane	30-500	Mc283	460
Leica IIf (Red-dial)	24x36mm	35mm	35rf	1951	interchangeable			focal plane	30-500	A2218	550
Leica Standard (E) (black)	24x36mm	35mm	35vf	1932	Elmar	3.5	50mm	focal plane	20-500	Mc282	800
Leica Standard (E) (chrome	24x36mm	35mm	35vf	1932	Elmar	3.5	50mm	focal plane	20-500	A2206	490
Leica III (F) (black)	24x36mm	35mm	35rf	1933	Elmar	3.5	50mm	focal plane	1-500	Mc282	630
Leica III (F) (chrome)	24x36mm	35mm	35rf	1933	Elmar	3.5	50mm	focal plane	1-500	A2202	410
Leica IIIa (G)	24x36mm	35mm	35rf	1935	Elmar	3.5	50mm	focal plane	1-1000	Mc282	350
Leica IIIa "Monté en Sarre"	24x36mm	35mm	35rf	1950	Elmar	3.5	50mm	focal plane	1-1000	Mc282	4300
Leica IIIb (G)	24x36mm	35mm	35rf	1938	Elmar	3.5	50mm	focal plane	1-1000	Mc282	420
---IIIb Luftwaffen Eigentum	24x36mm	35mm	35rf	1938	Elmar	3.5	50mm	focal plane	1-1000		3500
Leica IIIc (-Nr.400,000)	24x36mm	35mm	35rf	1940	Elmar	3.5	50mm	focal plane	1-1000	Mc282	600
Leica IIIc (Nr.400,000+)	24x36mm	35mm	35rf	1945	Elmar	3.5	50mm	focal plane	1-1000	A2214	400
Leica IIIc (grey)	24x36mm	35mm	35rf	1940	Elmar	3.5	50mm	focal plane	1-1000	A2221	1600
---IIIc "K-Mod." (blue-grey)	24x36mm	35mm	35rf	1940	Elmar	3.5	50mm	focal plane	1-1000	A2222	2200
---IIIc "K-Mod." (chrome)	24x36mm	35mm	35rf	1940	Elmar	3.5	50mm	focal plane	1-1000		2100
---IIIc Luftwaffe (chrome)	24x36mm	35mm	35rf	1940	Elmar	3.5	50mm	focal plane	1-1000	Mc282	3100
---IIIc Luftwaffe (grey)	24x36mm	35mm	35rf	1940	Elmar	3.5	50mm	focal plane	1-1000		3400
---IIIc Wehrmacht (chrome)	24x36mm	35mm	35rf	1940	Elmar	3.5	50mm	focal plane	1-1000		2500
---IIIc Wehrmacht (grey)	24x36mm	35mm	35rf	1940	Elmar	3.5	50mm	focal plane	1-1000	A2221	3400
Leica IIId	24x36mm	35mm	35rf	1940	Elmar	3.5	50mm	focal plane	1-1000	A2213	7000
Leica IIIf (Black-dial)	24x36mm	35mm	35rf	1950	interchangeable			focal plane	1-1000	A2224	460
Leica IIIf (Red-dial)	24x36mm	35mm	35rf	1950	interchangeable			focal plane	1-1000	Mc283	500
Leica IIIf (Red-dial / ST)	24x36mm	35mm	35rf	1950	interchangeable			focal plane	1-1000	A2226	800
Leica IIIf Swedish Army	24x36mm	35mm	35rf	1950	interchangeable			focal plane	1-1000		7000
Leica IIIg	24x36mm	35mm	35rf	1956	interchangeable			focal plane	30-500	Mc283	1200
Leica IIIg Swedish Crown	24x36mm	35mm	35rf	1960	interchangeable			focal plane	30-500	Mc283	9000
Leica 72 (Midland)	18x24mm	35mm	35Half	1954	Elmar	3.5	50mm	focal plane	1-1000		14000
Leica 72 (Wetzlar)	18x24mm	35mm	35Half	1954	Elmar	3.5	50mm	focal plane	1-1000	Mc283	15000
Leica 250 Reporter (FF)	24x36mm	35mm	35rf	1934	Elmar	3.5	50mm	focal plane	1-500	Mc282	11000
Leica 250 Reporter (GG)	24x36mm	35mm	35rf	1935	Elmar	3.5	50mm	focal plane	1-1000	A2201	9000
Leica AF-C1	24x36mm	35mm	35AF-BiF	1990	bi-focal	2.8,5.6	40/80	programmed	8-400		260
Leica C2-Zoom	24x36mm	35mm	35afz	1992		3.5-7.7	40-90	programmed	4-350		240
Leica C2-Zoom Data-Back	24x36mm	35mm	35afz	1992		3.5-7.7	40-90	programmed	4-350		240
Leica CL body	24x36mm	35mm	35rf	1973	body only	---	---	focal plane	1-1000		610

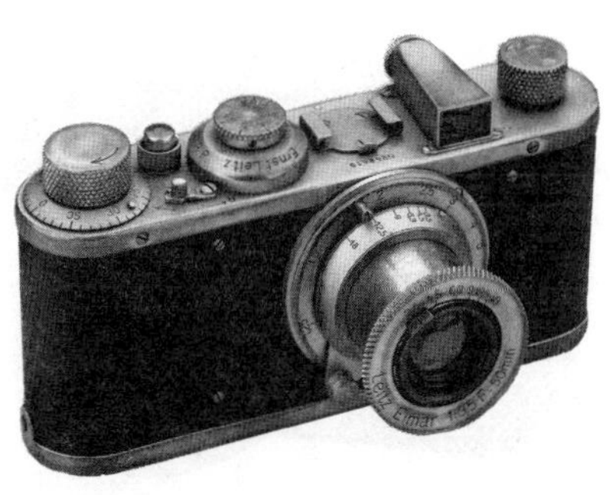

Leica I (C) (Luxus)

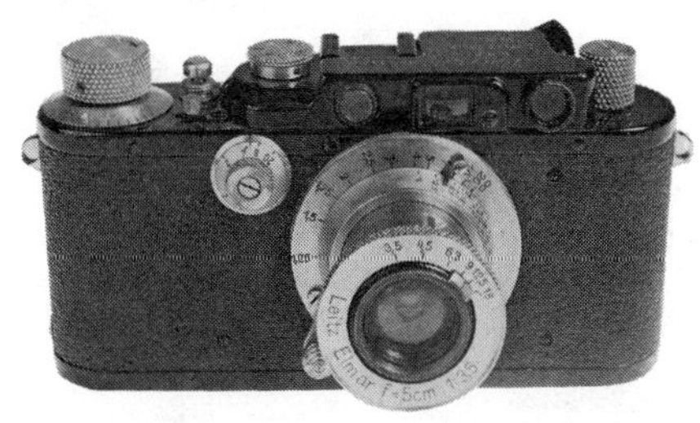

Leica III (F) (black)

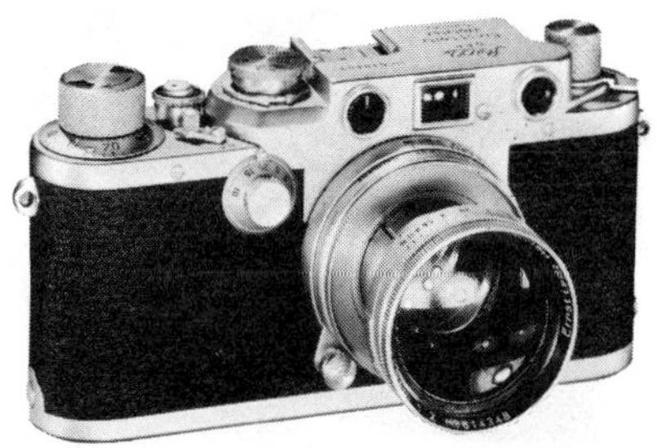

Leica IIIf (Red-dial)

MODEL	FORMAT	FILM	TYPE	Year	LENS	Apert	FL	SHUTTER	SPEEDS	ILLUS	U.S.$
Leica CL + 40/2	24x36mm	35mm	35rf	1973	Summicron	2	40mm	focal plane	1-1000		800
Leica CL 50 Jahre + Summ.	24x36mm	35mm	35rf	1975	Summicron	2	40mm	focal plane	1-1000	Mc285	1300
Leica CL 50 Jahre + Rokkor	24x36mm	35mm	35rf	1975	Rokkor	2	40mm	focal plane	1-1000		900
Leica KE-7A	24x36mm	35mm	35rf	1972	Elcan	2	50mm	focal plane	1-1000		5600
Leica M1	24x36mm	35mm	35vf	1959	interchangeable			focal plane	1-1000	Mc284	900
Leica M1 (green)	24x36mm	35mm	35vf	1959	interchangeable			focal plane	1-1000		5400
Leica M2 (black)	24x36mm	35mm	35rf	1957	interchangeable			focal plane	1-1000	A2239	1800
Leica M2 (chrome)	24x36mm	35mm	35rf	1957	interchangeable			focal plane	1-1000	Mc284	900
Leica M2 (grey)	24x36mm	35mm	35rf	1957	interchangeable			focal plane	1-1000		5100
Leica M2 MOT	24x36mm	35mm	35rf	1957	interchangeable			focal plane	1-1000	Mc284	4400
Leica M2M	24x36mm	35mm	35rf	1957	interchangeable			focal plane	1-1000		4600
Leica M2S	24x36mm	35mm	35rf	1966	interchangeable			focal plane	1-1000		2000
Leica M3 (Double-stroke)	24x36mm	35mm	35rf	1954	interchangeable			focal plane	1-1000	Mc283	800
Leica M3 (Single-stroke)	24x36mm	35mm	35rf	1954	interchangeable			focal plane	1-1000	A2232	900
Leica M3 (black)	24x36mm	35mm	35rf	1954	interchangeable			focal plane	1-1000	A2233	3100
Leica M3 (gold)	24x36mm	35mm	35rf	1954	Gold Summicron	2	50mm	focal plane	1-1000		2700
Leica M3 (gold)	24x36mm	35mm	35rf	1954	Gold Summilux	1.4	50mm	focal plane	1-1000		2900
Leica M3 (olive)	24x36mm	35mm	35rf	1968	interchangeable			focal plane	1-1000		3400
Leica M4 (black chrome)	24x36mm	35mm	35rf	1974	interchangeable			focal plane	1-1000	A3463	2100
Leica M4 (black enamel)	24x36mm	35mm	35rf	1968	interchangeable			focal plane	1-1000	Mc284	2200
Leica M4 (olive)	24x36mm	35mm	35rf		interchangeable			focal plane	1-1000		7000
Leica M4 (silver chrome)	24x36mm	35mm	35rf	1967	interchangeable			focal plane	1-1000	Mc284	1100
Leica M4 50 Jahre	24x36mm	35mm	35rf	1975	interchangeable			focal plane	1-1000	Mc284	2900
Leica M4 MOT	24x36mm	35mm	35rf	1968	interchangeable			focal plane	1-1000		4200
Leica M4-2 (black)	24x36mm	35mm	35rf	1978	interchangeable			focal plane	1-1000	A2248	900
Leica M4-2 (gold)	24x36mm	35mm	35rf	1979	Summilux	1.4	50mm	focal plane	1-1000		5100
Leica M4-P	24x36mm	35mm	35rf	1981	interchangeable			focal plane	1-1000	A2250	1100
Leica M4-P 70 Years	24x36mm	35mm	35rf	1983	body only			focal plane	1-1000		1800
Leica M4M	24x36mm	35mm	35rf	1968	interchangeable			focal plane	1-1000		3800
Leica M5 (black)	24x36mm	35mm	35rf	1971	interchangeable			focal plane	1-1000	Mc285	1400
Leica M5 (chrome)	24x36mm	35mm	35rf	1971	interchangeable			focal plane	1-1000	Mc285	1400
Leica M5 50 Jahre (black)	24x36mm	35mm	35rf	1975	interchangeable			focal plane	1-1000	A2245	2900
Leica M5 50 Jahre (chrome)	24x36mm	35mm	35rf	1975	interchangeable			focal plane	1-1000	A2246	3200
Leica M6 (black)	24x36mm	35mm	35rf	1984	interchangeable			focal plane	1-1000	A3458	1900
Leica M6 (chrome)	24x36mm	35mm	35rf	1984	interchangeable			focal plane	1-1000		2000
Leica M6 (cutaway) body	24x36mm	35mm	35rf	1984	body only	---	---	focal plane	1-1000		2800
Leica M6 Colombo '92	24x36mm	35mm	35rf	1993	Summicron	1.2	50mm	focal plane	1-1000		7000
Leica M6 LHSA Set	24x36mm	35mm	35rf	1993	Summicron 35, 50, 90mm			focal plane	1-1000		13000
Leica M6 Rooster	24x36mm	35mm	35rf	1993	Summicron	1.2	50mm	focal plane	1-1000		9000
Leica M6 Royal-Foto (black	24x36mm	35mm	35rf	1993	body only, w/box, papers.			focal plane	1-1000		8200
Leica M6 Royal-Foto (silver	24x36mm	35mm	35rf	1993	body only, w/box, papers.			focal plane	1-1000		7800
Leica M6 RPS 100 Jahre '94	24x36mm	35mm	35rf	1994	Summicron-M	2	50mm	focal plane	1-1000		9000

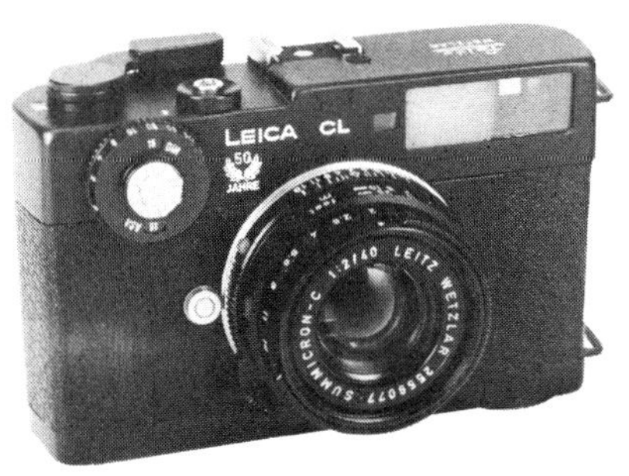

Leica CL 50 Jahre

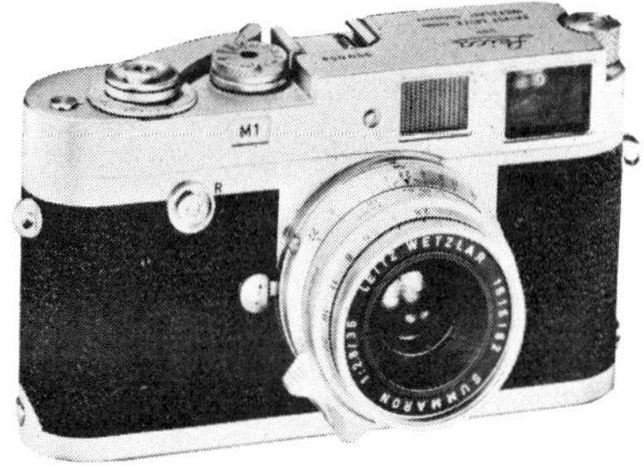

Leica M1

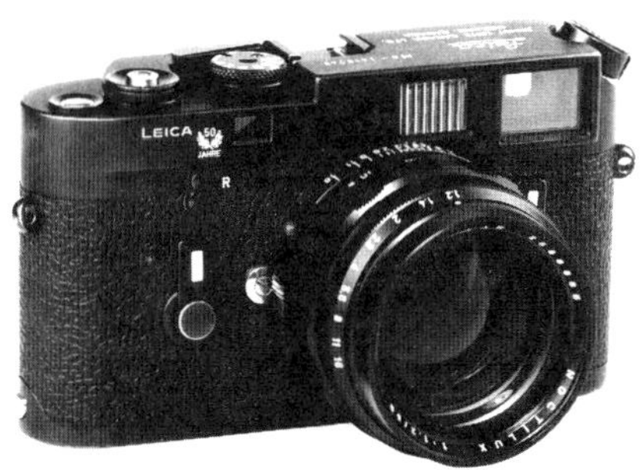

Leica M4 50 Jahre

MODEL	FORMAT	FILM	TYPE	Year	LENS	Apert	FL	SHUTTER	SPEEDS	ILLUS	U.S.$
Leica M6 Titanium body	24x36mm	35mm	35rf	1989	body only	---	---	focal plane	1-1000		2500
Leica M6 Titanium + 50/1.4	24x36mm	35mm	35rf	1989	Summilux	1.4	50mm	focal plane	1-1000		5600
Leica M6 Traveller Set	24x36mm	35mm	35rf	1994	Summilux-M	1.4	50mm	focal plane	1-1000		3700
Leica M6J	24x36mm	35mm	35rf	1995	Elmar-M	2.8	50mm	focal plane	1-1000		4800
Leica MD	24x36mm	35mm	35vf	1965	interchangeable			focal plane	1-1000	A2240	1000
Leica MD-2	24x36mm	35mm	35vf	1980	interchangeable			focal plane	1-1000	A2251	1000
Leica MDa	24x36mm	35mm	35vf	1966	interchangeable			focal plane	1-1000	A2241	1000
Mifilmca (detachable tube)	24x36mm	35mm	SciMed	1927				Ibsor			4600
Mifilmca (fixed tube)	24x36mm	35mm	SciMed	1927				Ibsor		Mc281	5000
Leica Mini	24x36mm	35mm	35af	1991	Elmar	3.5	35mm	programmed	5-250		200
Leica Mini Data-Back	24x36mm	35mm	35af	1991	Elmar	3.5	35mm	programmed	5-250		180
Leica Mini II	24x36mm	35mm	35af	1992	Elmar	3.5	35mm	programmed	5-250		190
Leica Mini II Data-Back	24x36mm	35mm	35af	1992	Elmar	3.5	35mm	programmed	5-250		210
Leica Mini Zoom	24x36mm	35mm	35afz	1994	Vario Elmar	4-7.6	35-70	programmed	4-300		260
Leica Mini Zoom Data-Back	24x36mm	35mm	35afz	1994	Vario Elmar	4-7.6	35-70	programmed	4-300		280
Leica MP (black)	24x36mm	35mm	35rf	1956	interchangeable			focal plane	1-1000	Mc284	12000
Leica MP (chrome)	24x36mm	35mm	35rf	1956	interchangeable			focal plane	1-1000	Mc284	9000
Leica MP2	24x36mm	35mm	35rf	1958	interchangeable			focal plane	1-1000		10000
Leica R-E	24x36mm	35mm	35slr	1990	interchangeable			electronic	15-1/2000		1000
Leica R-E Olympic	24x36mm	35mm	35slr	1992	interchangeable			electronic	15-1/2000		2300
Leica R3 (Germany, black)	24x36mm	35mm	35slr	1976	interchangeable			electronic	4-1/1000	A2262	650
LeicaR3 (Germany, chrome	24x36mm	35mm	35slr	1976	interchangeable			electronic	4-1/1000		700
Leica R3 (Portugal, black)	24x36mm	35mm	35slr	1976	interchangeable			electronic	4-1/1000		330
Leica R3 (Portugal, chrome	24x36mm	35mm	35slr	1976	interchangeable			electronic	4-1/1000	Mc286	440
Leica R3 (gold)	24x36mm	35mm	35slr	1979	Summilux-R	1.4	50mm	electronic	4-1/1000	A2264	3600
Leica R3 Mot	24x36mm	35mm	35slr	1978	interchangeable			electronic	4-1/1000	A2263	480
Leica R3 Mot (gold)	24x36mm	35mm	35slr	1979	Gold Summilux	1.4	50mm	electronic	4-1/1000		2800
Leica R3 Safari	24x36mm	35mm	35slr	1976	Summilux-R	1.4	50mm	electronic	4-1/1000	A2265	1900
Leica R4 (black)	24x36mm	35mm	35slr	1981	interchangeable			electronic	8-1/1000	Mc286	700
Leica R4 (chrome)	24x36mm	35mm	35slr	1981	interchangeable			electronic	8-1/1000		800
Leica R4 (gold)	24x36mm	35mm	35slr	1984	Gold Summilux	1.4	50mm	electronic	8-1/1000	Mc286	3800
Leica R4 Mot (black)	24x36mm	35mm	35slr	1980	interchangeable			electronic	1-1000	A2267	900
Leica R4 Mot (chrome)	24x36mm	35mm	35slr	1980	interchangeable			electronic	1-1000		700
Leica R4S	24x36mm	35mm	35slr	1983	interchangeable			electronic	8-1/1000	A3208	580
Leica R4S II (R4S-P)	24x36mm	35mm	35slr	1985	interchangeable			electronic	8-1/1000		800
Leica R5 (black)	24x36mm	35mm	35slr	1987	interchangeable			electronic	15-1/2000		1500
Leica R5 (chrome)	24x36mm	35mm	35slr	1987	interchangeable			electronic	15-1/2000		1200
Leica R6	24x36mm	35mm	35slr	1988	interchangeable			focal plane	1-1000		1500
Leica R6.2 (black)	24x36mm	35mm	35slr	1992	interchangeable			focal plane	1-2000		1900
Leica R6.2 (chrome)	24x36mm	35mm	35slr	1992	interchangeable			focal plane	1-2000		1900
Leica R7 (black)	24x36mm	35mm	35slr	1992	interchangeable			programmed	16-1/2000		1900
Leica R7 (chrome)	24x36mm	35mm	35slr	1992	interchangeable			programmed	16-1/2000		1900

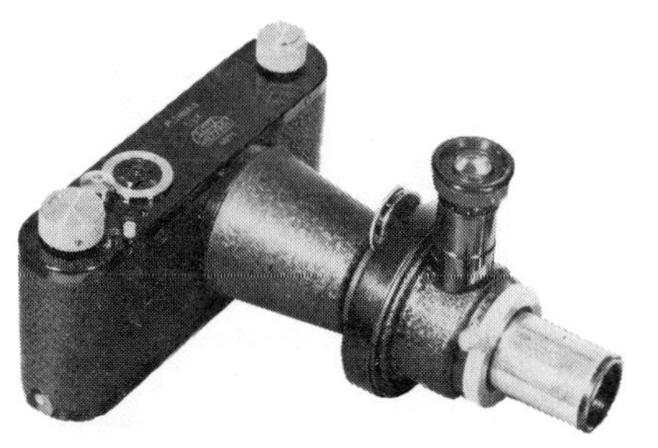

Mifilmca (fixed tube)

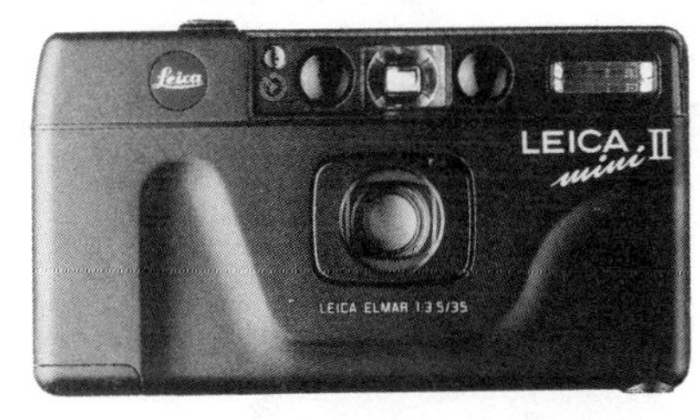

Leica Mini II

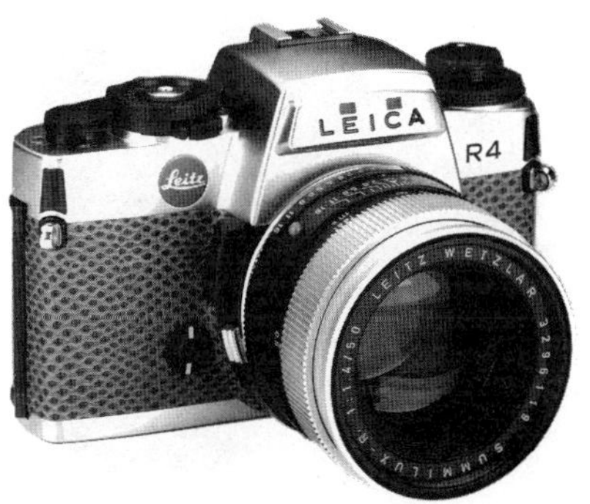

Leica R4 (gold)

MODEL	FORMAT	FILM	TYPE	Year	LENS	Apert	FL	SHUTTER	SPEEDS	ILLUS	U.S.$
Leicaflex (black)	24x36mm	35mm	35slr	1964	interchangeable			focal plane	1-2000	Mc285	1000
Leicaflex (chrome)	24x36mm	35mm	35slr	1964	interchangeable			focal plane	1-2000	Mc285	410
Leicaflex SL (black)	24x36mm	35mm	35slr	1968	interchangeable			focal plane	1-2000	Mc285	580
Leicaflex SL (chrome)	24x36mm	35mm	35slr	1968	interchangeable			focal plane	1-2000	Mc285	450
Leicaflex SL Mot	24x36mm	35mm	35slr	1969	interchangeable			focal plane	1-2000	Mc285	1300
Leicaflex SL Olympic	24x36mm	35mm	35slr	1972	interchangeable			focal plane	1-2000	A2257	1300
Leicaflex SL2 (black)	24x36mm	35mm	35slr	1974	interchangeable			focal plane	1-2000	A2260	1100
Leicaflex SL2 (chrome)	24x36mm	35mm	35slr	1974	interchangeable			focal plane	1-2000	Mc286	1100
SL2 50 Jahre (black)	24x36mm	35mm	35slr	1975	interchangeable			focal plane	1-2000	Mc286	2000
SL2 50 Jahre (chrome)	24x36mm	35mm	35slr	1975	interchangeable			focal plane	1-2000	A2261	2000
Leicaflex SL2 Mot	24x36mm	35mm	35slr	1974	interchangeable			focal plane	1-2000		1900
...LENINGRAD (Leningrad Optical-Mechanical Union) - Leningrad, USSR											
Leningrad	24x36mm	35mm	35rf	1955	Jupiter-8	2	50mm	focal plane	1-1000	Mc289	220
...LENNOR ENGINEERING CO. - Illinois, USA											
Delta Stereo	24x36mm	35mm	35Ster	1955	La Croix	6.3		guillotine	25-100	Mc289	130
...LEONAR KAMERAWERK - Hamburg											
Filmos	8x10.5cm	124	FoldRo	1910	Periscop Aplanat	11	130mm	Koilos		Mc289	60
Filmos	8x10.5cm	124	FoldRo	1910	Leonar Aplanat	8	130mm	Koilos			60
Leonar 9x12	9x12cm	plate	FoldPl	1910	Periscop	11	130mm		I,T	Mc289	40
Leonar 10x15	10x15cm	plate	FoldPl	1910	Leonar Anast.	8	140mm	Dial-Compur	1-200		120
Leonar 10x15	10x15cm	plate	FoldPl	1910	Leonar Anast.	6.8	170mm	Dial-Compur	1-200		120
Perkeo Mod. IV	9x12cm	plate	FoldPl	1910	Achromat	16		B&L Auto			50
Perkeo Mod. IV	9x12cm	plate	FoldPl	1910	Aplanat	11		B&L Auto			50
Perkeo Mod. IV	9x12cm	plate	FoldPl	1910	Extra Rap. Aplan.	8		B&L Auto			50
...LEREBOURS - Paris											
Gaudin Daguerreotype		Dag	Dag	1841						F78	10000
...LEROY (Lucien LeRoy) - Paris											
Minimus	6x13cm	plate	StJumelle	1924						Mc289	280
Néovues 6x13	6x13cm	plate	StJumelle	1919	Berthiot	6.3	70mm	guillotine	1-100		340
Stereo Panoramique	6x13cm	plate	Stereo	1905	Krauss Protar	9	82mm	5-speed		Mc289	330
Stereo Panoramique	6x13cm	plate	Stereo	1905	Goerz Doppel An.	8.5	80mm	5-speed		F1399	330
...LEULLIER (Louis Leullier) - Paris											
Summum	6x13cm	plate	Stereo	1924	Berthiot Flor	4.5	75mm	Compur	1-150	F1422	200
Summum	6x13cm	plate	Stereo	1925	Roussel Stylor	4.5	75mm	Stereo	25-100	Mc289	220
Summum Sterechrome	24x30mm	35mm	35Ster	1940	Berthiot Flor	3.5	40mm		1-300	F1462	440
...LEVI (S.J. Levi) - London											
Leviathan Surprise Detectiv	3¼x4¼"	plate	DetectivBox	1892							1000
Minia Camera	3¼x4¼"	plate	FoldPl	1896	Goerz Doppel An.	7.7	5"	Thornton-Pickard			200
Pullman Detective 3¼x4¼"	3¼x4¼"	plate	Disguised	1896	Archer & Sons			Thornton-Pickard			3900
Pullman Detective 4x5"	4x5"	plate	Disguised	1896	Archer & Sons			Thornton-Pickard			3900
Pullman Detective 5x7"	5x7"	plate	Disguised	1896	Archer & Sons			Thornton-Pickard			3900
Pullman Detective Stereo	5x7"	plate	StFoldPl	1896	Archer & Sons			Thornton-Pickard			2400

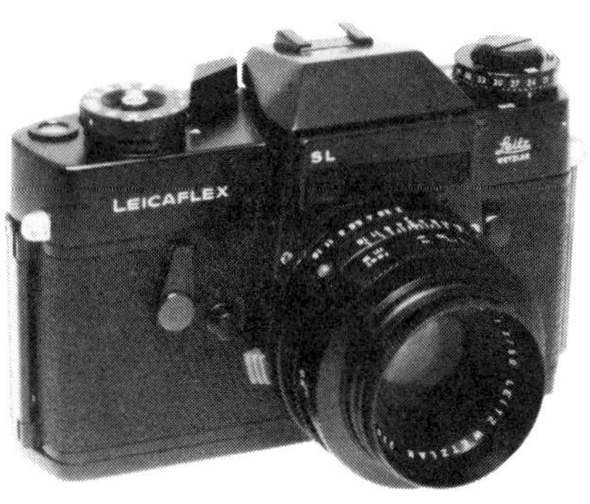

Leicaflex SL

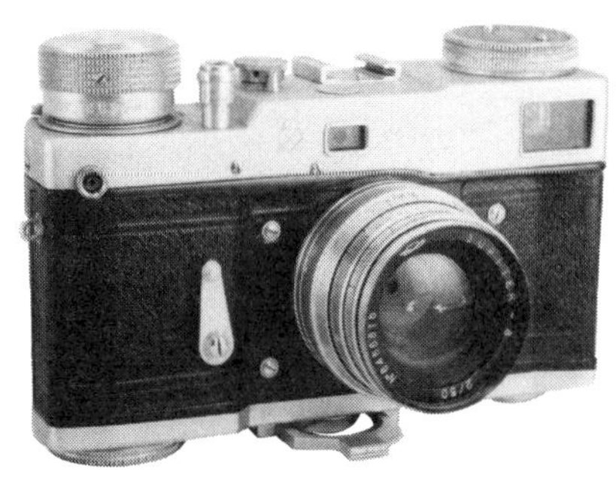

Leningrad

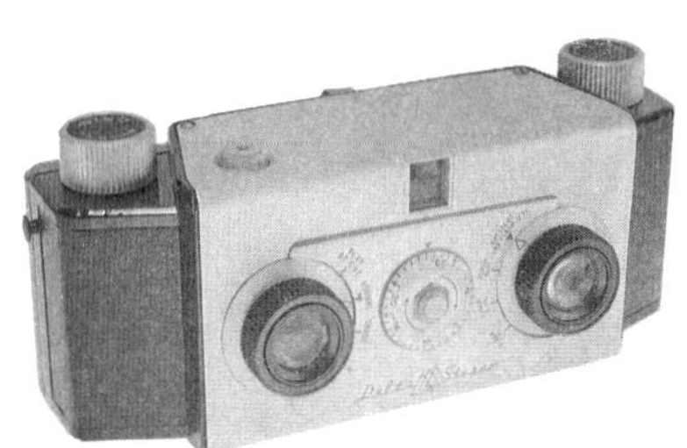

Delta Stereo

MODEL	FORMAT	FILM	TYPE	Year	LENS	Apert	FL	SHUTTER	SPEEDS	ILLUS	U.S.$
...LEVY-ROTH - Berlin											
Minnigraph	18x24mm	35mm	35Half	1915	Minnigraph Anast.	3.5	54mm			Mc290	1100
...L.F.G. & CO. - Paris											
Français	4x5cm	plate	MetBx	1910	Meniscus	11	55mm			Mc290	160
Franceville (cardboard)	4x4cm	plate	CardBox	1908	Meniscus			guillotine		Mc290	180
Franceville (plastic)	4x4cm	plate	PlasBx	1908	Meniscus			guillotine		Mc290	180
...LIEBE (V. Liebe) - Paris											
Monobloc	6x13cm	plate	StJumelle	1920	Tessar	6.3	85mm	pneumatic		A709	260
Monobloc	6x13cm	plate	StJumelle	1920	Boyer Saphir	4.5	85mm	pneumatic		F1319	260
Monobloc (rollfilm)	6x13cm	116	StJumelle	1920	Berthiot	4.5	85mm	pneumatic		F1321	330
...LIEBERMAN & GORTZ - Germany											
Dual-finder rollfilm camera	4x4cm	127	BakeliteRoll	1950	Achromat	9	6cm				50
...LIESEGANG - Düsseldorf											
Atelier (Studio) camera	30x40cm	plate	Studio	1861	Liesegang					A2959	1300
Künstlerkamera	3x3cm	plate	MagBox	1884						A1861	2600
Reisekamera (Field camera	10x15cm	plate	Field	1900				Unicum			220
...LIFE-O-RAMA CORP.											
Life-O-Rama	6x6cm	120	HzFoldRo		Foinar	4.5	75mm	Vario		Mc290	30
Life-O-Rama III	6x6cm	120	HzFoldRo	1953	Ennar	5.6	75mm	Vario			30
Life-O-Rama III	6x6cm	120	HzFoldRo	1953	Ennar	3.5	75mm	Vario			30
...LIGHT INDUSTRIAL PRODUCTS - China											
Seagull 4	6x6cm	120	TLR	1970	Haiou	3.5	75mm		1-300	Mc290	60
Seagull 4A	6x6cm	120	TLR	1970	Haiou	3.5	75mm		1-300		60
Seagull 4B	6x6/4.5x6	120	TLR	1970	Haiou	3.5	75mm		1-300		60
Seagull 4C	6x6cm	120	TLR	1970	Haiou	3.5	75mm		1-300		80
Seagull No. 203	6x6cm	120	HzFoldRo	1970		3.5	75mm			Mc291	80
Seagull DF-300	24x36mm	35mm	35slr	1994	Seagull-610	1.8	50mm	focal plane	4-1/1000		130
...LINDEN (Friedrich Linden) - Lüdenscheid, Germany											
Lindar	6x6cm	120	MetBx	1950	Meniscus	9.5	80mm		T,I	HK122	50
Lindi (black)	6x6cm	120	MetBx	1950	Meniscus	10.5	80mm				50
Lindi (grey)	6x6cm	120	MetBx	1950	Meniscus	10.5	80mm				70
Reporter 66	6x6cm	120	MetBx	1952	Meniscus	9.5	80mm				50
...LINHOF PRÄZISIONS-KAMERA-WERKE (V. Linhof) - Munich											
Aero Electric	56x72mm	Roll	Aerial	1976	Planar	2.8	80mm	Sync-Compur		A2023	1600
Aero Press	56x72mm	70mm	Aerial	1963	Schneider		80mm				1400
Aero Technika 9x12	9x12cm	cfh	Aerial	1958	Biogon	4.5	75mm	Sync-Compur	1-500		1400
Aero Technika 4x5"	4x5"	cfh	Aerial	1958	Planar	3.5	135mm	Sync-Compur	1-400		1400
Aero Technika 45	4x5"	cfh	Aerial	1972	interchangeable			Sync-Compur	1-500	A2024	2300
Aero Technika 45 EL	4x5"	cfh	Aerial	1976	interchangeable			Sync-Compur	1-500		4000
Aerotronica 69	58x85mm	70mm	Aerial	1985	interchangeable			rotary	-1500	A3446	8000
Color 6.5x9	6.5x9cm	cfh	Monorail	1958	interchangeable						240
Color 9x12	9x12cm	cfh	Monorail	1958	interchangeable						390

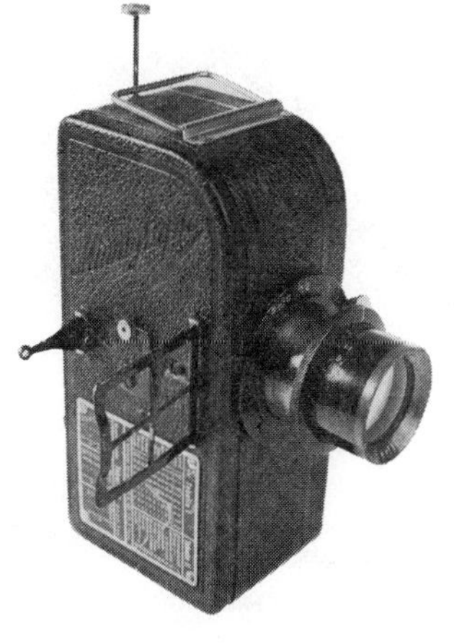

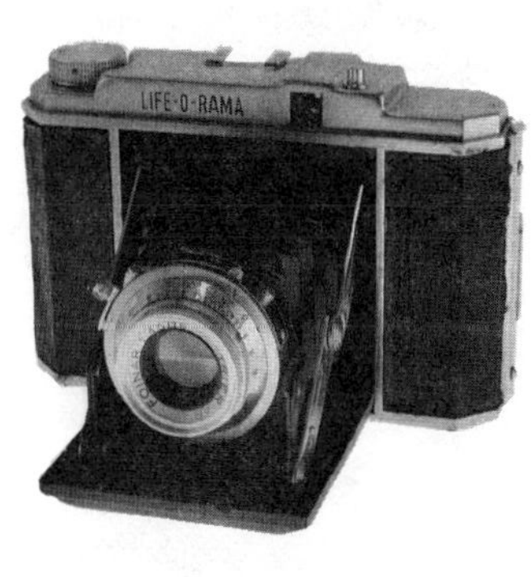

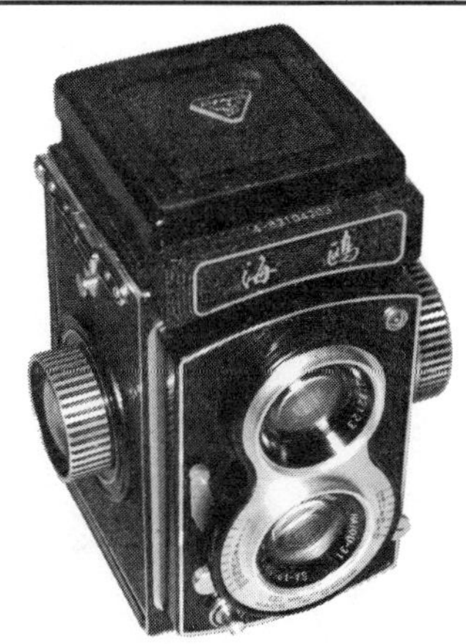

Minnigraph **Life-O-Rama** **Seagull 4**

MODEL	FORMAT	FILM	TYPE	Year	LENS	Apert	FL	SHUTTER	SPEEDS	ILLUS	U.S.$
Handkammer Hk12.5	7x9cm	Roll	Aerial	1940	Xenon	2	125mm				670
Kardan B (Kardan Bi) 9x12	9x12cm	cfh	Monorail	1970	interchangeable			Central			900
Kardan B (Kardan Bi) 13x18	13x18cm	cfh	Monorail	1970	interchangeable			Central			900
Kardan B (Kardan Bi) 18x24	18x24cm	cfh	Monorail	1970	interchangeable			Central			1000
Kardan Color 9x12	9x12cm	cfh	Monorail	1965	interchangeable			Central			670
Kardan Color 13x18	13x18cm	cfh	Monorail	1956	interchangeable			Central			700
Kardan Color 18x24	18x24cm	cfh	Monorail	1956	interchangeable			Central			800
Kardan Color 45S	4x5"	cfh	Monorail	1969	interchangeable			Central			620
Kardan E	4x5"	cfh	Monorail	1990	interchangeable			Central			1200
Kardan GT 4x5"	4x5"	cfh	Monorail	1987	interchangeable			Central			1500
Kardan GT 5x7"	5x7"	cfh	Monorail	1987	interchangeable			Central			2000
Kardan GT 8x10"	8x10"	cfh	Monorail	1987	interchangeable			Central			2600
Kardan Master GTL 45	4x5"	cfh	Monorail	1987	interchangeable			Central			3400
Kardan Master GTL 57	5x7"	cfh	Monorail	1987	interchangeable			Central			4200
Kardan Master GTL 810	8x10"	cfh	Monorail	1987	interchangeable			Central			4700
Kardan Master L 9x12	9x12cm	cfh	Monorail	1975	interchangeable			Central			800
Kardan Master L 13x18	13x18cm	cfh	Monorail	1975	interchangeable			Central			800
Kardan Master TE 4x5"	4x5"	cfh	Monorail	1982	interchangeable			Central			1000
Kardan Master TE 5x7"	5x7"	cfh	Monorail	1983	interchangeable			Central			1100
Kardan Master TE 8x10"	8x10"	cfh	Monorail	1983	interchangeable			Central			1500
Kardan Master TL 4x5"	4x5"	cfh	Monorail	1981	interchangeable			Central			1600
Kardan Master TL 5x7"	5x7"	cfh	Monorail	1981	interchangeable			Central			1700
Kardan Master TL 8x10"	8x10"	cfh	Monorail	1981	interchangeable			Central			2000
Kardan Standard 9x12	9x12cm	cfh	Monorail	1975	interchangeable			Central		A1440	490
Kardan Standard 13x18	13x18cm	cfh	Monorail	1977	interchangeable			Central			800
Kardan Standard 18x24	18x24cm	cfh	Monorail	1977	interchangeable			Central			1200
Kardan Super Color 9x12	9x12cm	cfh	Monorail	1976	interchangeable			Central			540
Kardan Super Color 13x18	13x18cm	cfh	Monorail	1976	interchangeable			Central			560
Kardan Super Color 18x24	18x24cm	cfh	Monorail	1976	interchangeable			Central			900
Kardan Super Color JBL	9x12cm	cfh	Monorail	1977	interchangeable			Central			610
Kardan Super Color JBL	13x18cm	cfh	Monorail	1981	interchangeable			Central			1100
Kardan Super Color JBL	18x24cm	cfh	Monorail	1977	interchangeable			Central			2100
Kardan Super Color ST	9x12cm	cfh	Monorail	1982	interchangeable			Central			700
Linhof 6.5x9 (1910)	6.5x9cm	plate	VtFoldPl	1910	Orthostigmat	6.8	105mm	Linhof	25-250	A278	180
Linhof 9x12 (1903)	9x12cm	plate	HzFoldPl	1903	Collinear	5.4	135mm	Linhof	1/250	A277	160
Linhof 9x12 (1920)	9x12cm	plate	VtFoldPl	1920	Tessar	4.5	150mm	Compound	½-150	A280	160
Linhof 10x15 (1920)	10x15cm	plate	VtFoldPl	1920	Tessar	4.8	180mm	Linhof	25-250		170
Linhof 220	56x72mm	220	Press	1967	Technikar	3.5	95mm	Sync-Compur	1-500	A827	1000
Linhof 220 PL	56x72mm	220	Aerial	1976	Technikar	3.5	95mm	Sync-Compur	1-500		1000
Linhof 220 RS	56x72mm	220	Press	1975	Technikar	3.5	95mm	Sync-Compur	1-500		1000
Master Technika	9x12cm	Roll	FoldPress	1972	Super Angulon	5.6	90mm	Compur		A2991	2100
Master Technika 2000	9x12cm	Roll	FoldPress	1994	interchangeable						4600

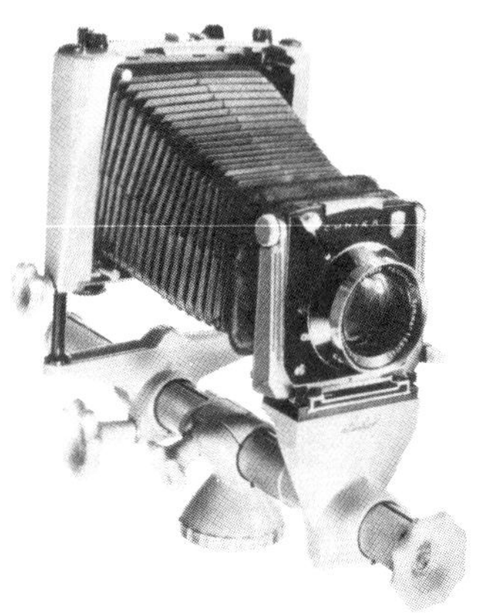

Kardan Color 9x12

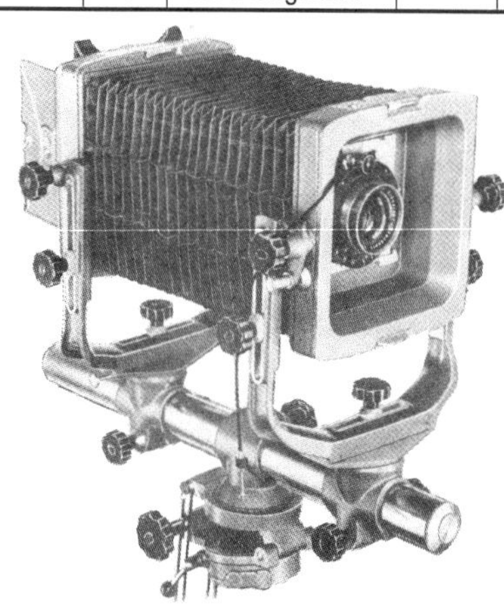

Kardan Color 13x18

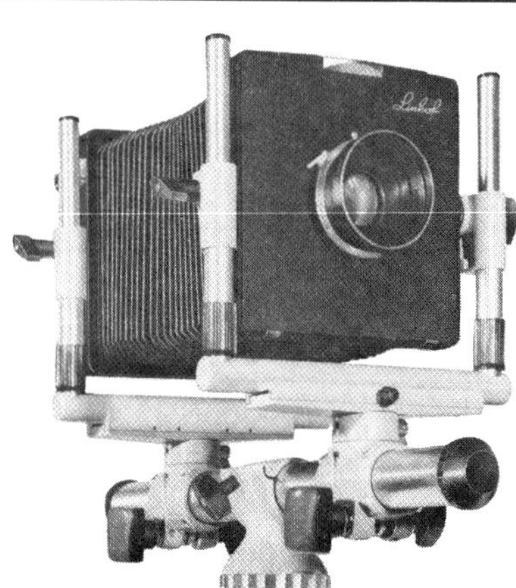

Kardan Color 45S

MODEL	FORMAT	FILM	TYPE	Year	LENS	Apert	FL	SHUTTER	SPEEDS	ILLUS	U.S.$
Präzisions-Kamera 4.5x6	4.5x6cm	plate	FoldPl	1933	Steinheil	3.5	75mm	Compur	1-300	A2990	1000
Präzisions-Kamera 6.5x9	6.5x9cm	plate	FoldPl	1929	Xenar	3.5	120mm	Compur	1-300	A1397	230
Präzisions-Kamera 6.5x9	6.5x9cm	plate	FoldPl	1929	Tessar	4.5	120mm	Compur	1-300	Mc291	220
Präzisions-Kamera 9x12	9x12cm	plate	FoldPl	1933	Cassar	3.5	150mm	Compur	1-300		230
Präzisions-Kamera 10x15	10x15cm	plate	FoldPl	1929	Xenar	3.5	165mm	Compur	1-300		220
Präzisions-Kamera 13x18	13x18cm	plate	FoldPl	1929	Tessar	4.5	210mm	Compur	1-300	A281	220
Präzisions-Kamera 13x18	13x18cm	plate	FoldPl	1933	Steinheil Unofocal	4.5	210mm	Compur	1-300		220
Press 70	56x72mm	cfh	Press	1964	Super Angulon	4	53mm	Sync-Compur	1-500	A1406	1300
Press 70	56x72mm	cfh	Press	1964	Xenotar	4	100mm	Sync-Compur	1-500	A1406	1300
Standard 6.5x9	6.5x9cm	plate	FoldPl	1936	Tessar	4.5	12cm	Compur			210
Standard 9x12	9x12cm	plate	FoldPl	1936	Tessar	4.5	15cm	Compur			180
Standard 9x12	9x12cm	plate	FoldPl	1936	WW Orthar	9		Compur			180
Standard 10x15	10x15cm	plate	FoldPl	1936	Tessar	4.5	18cm	Compur			160
Standard 12x16.5	12x16.5	plate	FoldPl	1936	Tessar	4.5	21cm	Compur			260
Standard Press	9x12cm	plate	FoldPress	1951	Xenar	3.5	150mm	Compur	1-200		1000
Standard Press	9x12cm	plate	FoldPress	1951	Apo-Lanthar	4.5	150mm	Sync-Compur	1-400		1000
Stereo-Panorama-K. 6x13	6x13cm	plate	StFoldPl	1920	Rietzschel Sextar	6.8	120mm	Compound		Mc291	460
Stereo-Panorama-K. 9x14	9x14cm	plate	StFoldPl	1910	Mofokar	5.4	105mm	Linhof			460
Super Technika 23	6.5x9cm	plate	FoldPress	1952	Xenotar	2.8	105mm	Compur	1-200	A1407	200
Super Technika 4x5	4x5"	plate	FoldPress	1950	Xenar	4.5	150mm	Compur	1-200		540
Super Technika 5x7	13x18cm	plate	FoldPress	1950	Xenar	4.5	210mm	Compur	1-200		800
Super Technika III 6.5x9	6.5x9cm	plate	FoldPress	1951	Xenotar	2.8	120mm	Compur	1-200		390
Super Technika III 9x12	9x12cm	plate	FoldPress	1951	Xenar	4.5	150mm	Compur	1-200		490
Super Technika IV 6.5x9	6.5x9cm	plate	FoldPress	1956	Planar	2.8	100mm	Compur	1-400		800
Super Technika IV 9x12	9x12cm	plate	FoldPress	1956	Planar	3.5	135mm	Compur	1-400		1500
Super Technika IV 13x18	13x18cm	plate	FoldPress	1956	Planar	3.5	210mm	Compur	1-400		900
Super Technika V 6.5x9	6.5x9cm	plate	FoldPress	1963	Planar	2.8	100mm	Compur	1-400		1100
Super Technika V 9x12	9x12cm	plate	FoldPress	1963	Planar	3.5	135mm	Compur	1-400		1100
Super Technika V 13x18	13x18cm	plate	FoldPress	1963	Planar	3.5	210mm	Compur	1-400		1600
Technar	4x5"	Pl/Ro	WideAng	1978	Super Angulon	5.6	75mm				2000
Technika 70	6.5x9cm	cfh	FoldPress	1963	Planar	2.8	100mm	Sync-Compur			1200
Technika II 6.5x9	6.5x9cm	plate	FoldPress	1936	Tessar	4.5		Compur			580
Technika II 9x12	9x12cm	plate	FoldPress	1936	Tessar	4.5		Compur		A282	470
Technika II 13x18	13x18cm	plate	FoldPress	1936	Tessar	4.5		Compur			470
Technika III 6.5x9	6.5x9cm	plate	FoldPress	1946	Xenar	4.5		Compound			340
Technika III 9x12	9x12cm	plate	FoldPress	1946	Xenar	4.5		Compound		A283	500
Technika III 13x18	13x18cm	plate	FoldPress	1946	Xenar	4.5		Compound		Mc291	460
Technika IV 6.5x9	6.5x9cm	plate	FoldPress	1956	Symmar	5.6		Sync-Compur			630
Technika IV 9x12	9x12cm	plate	FoldPress	1956	Symmar	5.6	150mm	Sync-Compur		A285	800
Technika IV 13x18	13x18cm	plate	FoldPress	1956	Symmar	5.6		Sync-Compur			700
Technika V 6.5x9	6.5x9cm	plate	FoldPress		Heliar	4.5		Sync-Compur			900
Technika V 9x12	9x12cm	plate	FoldPress	1964	Heliar	4.5		Sync-Compur			900

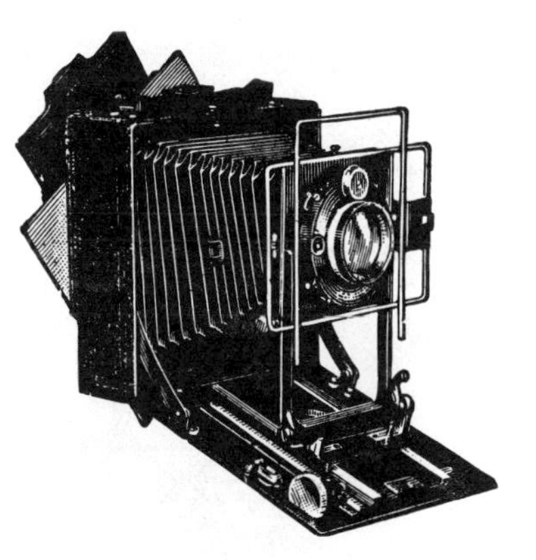

Präzisions-Kamera 6.5x9

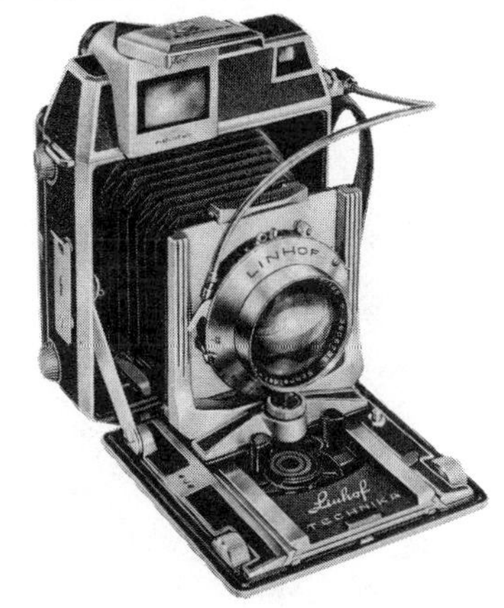

Super Technika IV 6.5x9

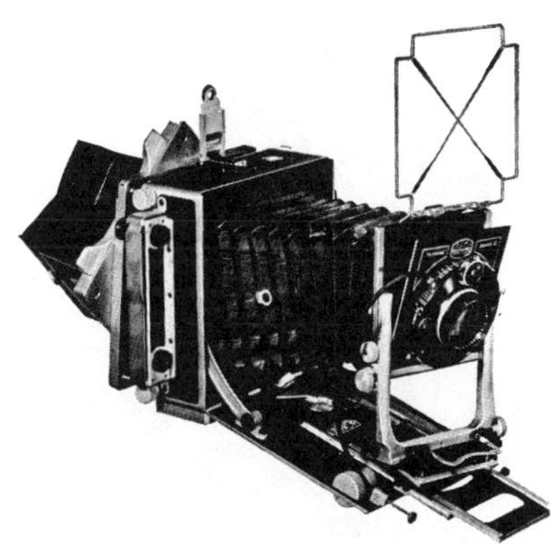

Technika III 13x18

MODEL	FORMAT	FILM	TYPE	Year	LENS	Apert	FL	SHUTTER	SPEEDS	ILLUS	U.S.$
Technika V 13x18	13x18cm	plate	FoldPress	1964	Heliar	4.5		Sync-Compur			700
Technika Press 23	6x9cm	Roll	Press	1958				Compur	1-400	Mc291	440
Technikardan 6x9	6x9cm	Roll	Monorail	1984	interchangeable			Central		A2992	1600
Technikardan 9x12	9x12cm	Roll	Monorail	1984	interchangeable			Central			2100
Technorama	6x17cm	120	Panoramic	1976	Super Angulon	5.6	90mm	Compur	1-500	A2020	2500
Technorama 612 II	6x12cm	120	Panoramic	1990	Super Angulon	5.6	65mm	Compur	1-500		2800
Technorama 612 PC	6x12cm	120	Panoramic	1983	Super Angulon	5.6	65mm	Compur	1-500	A3410	1700
Technorama 617 S	6x17cm	120	Panoramic	1989	Super Angulon	5.6	90mm	Copal	1-500		3700
...LIONEL MFG. CO. - New York											
Linex	16x20mm	Roll	Stereo	1954		8	30mm	guillotine			140
...LIPPISCHE CAMERAFABRIK - Barntrup											
Flexo	6x6cm	120	TLR	1950	Ennar	4.5	75mm	Vario		Mc292	50
Flexo	6x6cm	120	TLR	1950	Ennagon	3.5	75mm	Prontor II		HK421	50
Flexo I	6x6cm	120	TLR	1950	Ennar	3.5	75mm	Pronto S		HK420	50
Flexo Richard	6x6cm	120	TLR	1950	Ennar	4.5	75mm	Vario			70
Flexo Richard	6x6cm	120	TLR	1950	Ennagon	3.5	75mm	Prontor II			70
Flexo Richard I	6x6cm	120	TLR	1950	Ennar	3.5	75mm	Pronto S			80
Flexora I	6x6cm	120	TLR	1953	Ennar	4.5	75mm	Vario	25-200		70
Flexora II	6x6cm	120	TLR	1953	Ennar	3.5	75mm	Prontor-S	1-300		70
Flexora IIA	6x6cm	120	TLR	1953	Ennar	3.5	75mm	Prontor-SV	1-250	Mc292	70
Flexora III	6x6cm	120	TLR	1953	Ennagon	3.5	75mm	Prontor-S	1-300		70
Flexora IIIA	6x6cm	120	TLR	1953	Ennagon	3.5	75mm	Prontor-SV	1-250		70
Optimet (I)	6x6cm	120	TLR	1958	Ennagon	3.5	75mm	Prontor-SVS	1-300		90
Richard Reflex	6x6cm	120	TLR	1953	Ennar	3.5	75mm	Prontor-S	1-300	A1708	90
Rollop	6x6cm	120	TLR	1954	Ennagon	3.5	75mm	Prontor-SVS	1-300	Mc292	100
Rollop II	6x6cm	120	TLR	1954	Ennagon	3.5	80mm	Prontor-SVS	1-300	HK431	90
Rollop Automatic	6x6cm	120	TLR	1956	Ennit	2.8	80mm	Prontor-SVS	1-300		150
... (Spain)											
Lirba	35x35mm	Roll	MetBx	1950	Meniscus			rotary		Mc292	50
...LIZARS (J. Lizars) - Glasgow											
Challenge 3¼x4¼"	3¼x4¼"	plate	FoldPl	1905	Aldis	8					240
Challenge 3¼x4¼"	3¼x4¼"	plate	FoldPl	1905	Goerz	6.8				A355	240
Challenge 4¼x6½"	4¼x6½"	plate	FoldPl	1905	Beck	8					240
Challenge 5x7"	5x7"	plate	FoldPl	1905	Rapid Rectilinear			rollerblind			320
Challenge 6½x8½"	6½x8½"	plate	FoldPl	1905	Rapid Rectilinear			rollerblind			320
Challenge Dayspool	3¼x4¼"	124	FoldRo	1905	Aldis	8				Mc292	230
Challenge Dayspool	3¼x4¼"	124	FoldRo	1905	Goerz	6.8					230
Challenge Dayspool No. 1	4¼x6½"	Roll	FoldRo	1900	Beck Symmetrical					Mc292	240
Challenge Day. Stereo Trop	2¼x6¾"	plate	StFoldRo	1905							1100
Challenge Dayspool Trop.	3¼x4¼"	124	FoldRo	1905	Beck	6					1000
Challenge Dayspool Trop.	3¼x4¼"	124	FoldRo	1905	Goerz	6.8					1000
Challenge Deluxe Tropical	4x5"	plate	FoldPl	1911	Cooke	6.5		B&L pneumatic		A1381	1000

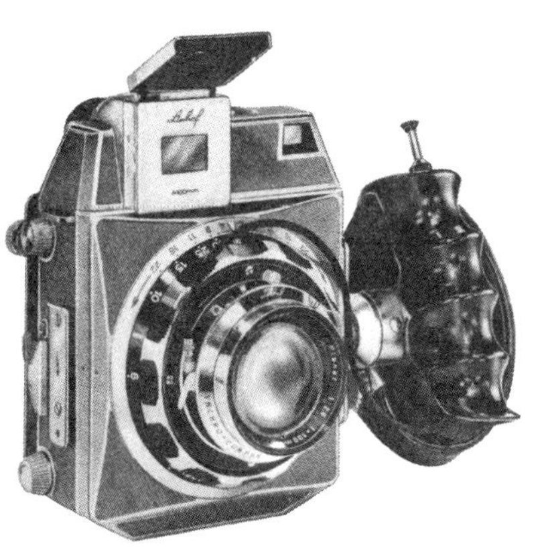

Technika Press 23

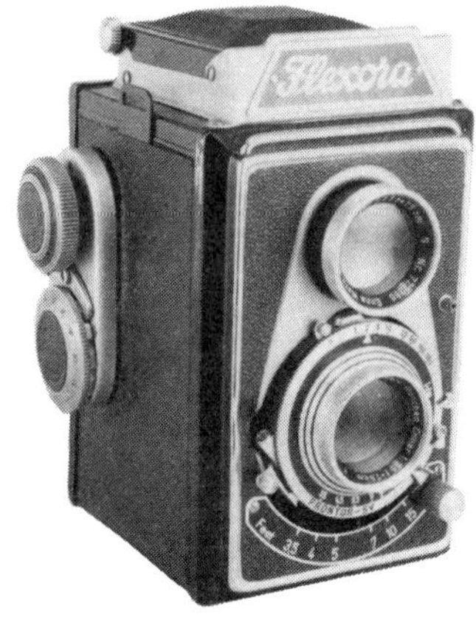

Flexora IIIA

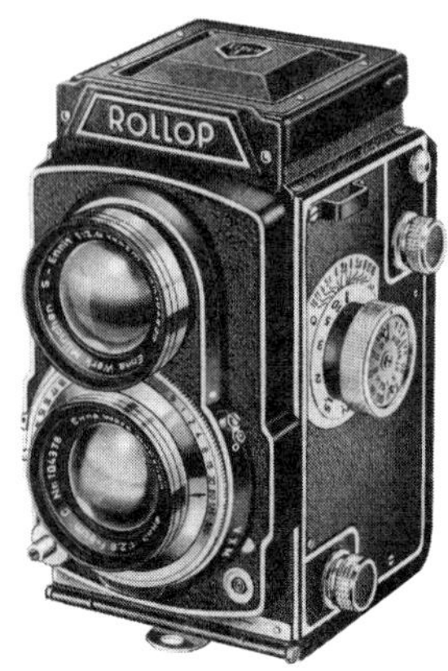

Rollop

MODEL	FORMAT	FILM	TYPE	Year	LENS	Apert	FL	SHUTTER	SPEEDS	ILLUS	U.S.$
Challenge Deluxe Tropical	4¼x6½"	plate	FoldPl	1911	Dagor	6.8		B&L pneumatic			1100
Challenge Jr Dayspool A	2¼x2¼"	120	HzFoldRo	1903	Beck Symmetrical			B&L pneumatic			350
Challenge Jr Dayspool B	2¼x3¼"	120	HzFoldRo	1903	Beck Symmetrical			B&L pneumatic			270
Challenge Jr Dayspool C	2½x4¼"	116	HzFoldRo	1903	Beck Symmetrical			B&L pneumatic			270
Challenge Magazine	3¼x4¼"	plate	MagBox	1903	Beck Symmetrical			Unicum			60
Challenge Stereo Mod. 1B	8x17cm	plate	StFoldPl	1905	Beck			Thornton-Pickard			500
Challenge Stereo Mod. 1B	8x17cm	plate	StFoldPl	1905	Goerz			Anschütz		A1761	500
Challenge Stereo Mod. B	3¼x6¾"	plate	StFoldPl	1905	B&L Rapid Rect.			B&L Stereo		Mc292	540
Challenge Stereo B Trop.	3¼x6¾"	plate	StFoldPl	1905	Aldis Anastigmat			B&L Stereo			800
Rambler	8x10.5cm	plate	Field	1898				Thornton-Pickard			350
...LOEBER (Eugene Loeber) - Dresden											
Field camera 13x18	13x18cm	plate	Field	1895	Rod. Bistigmat		13x18				240
Field camera 18x24	18x24cm	plate	Field	1895	Collinear	12.5					190
Klapp camera	9x12cm	plate	StrutPl	1915	Anastigmat	6.8	135mm				130
Magazine Camera	9x12cm	plate	MagBox	1905		8		3-speed			180
...LOMAN & CO. - Amsterdam											
Amsterdam Reflex-Box	9x12cm	plate	SLR-Box	1906	Berthiot ExtraRap.			focal plane	8-1300		310
Loman's Reflex 6.5x9	6.5x9cm	plate	LgSLR	1895	Loman Aplanat			focal plane	3-200	A3137	620
Loman's Reflex 9x9	9x9cm	plate	LgSLR	1900	Loman Aplanat					A3141	440
Loman's Reflex 3¼x4¼"	3¼x4¼"	plate	LgSLR	1890	Loman Aplanat	8	140mm	focal plane	3-200		1500
Loman's Reflex 4¼x6½"	4¼x6½"	plate	LgSLR	1890	Loman Aplanat	8	140mm	focal plane	3-200	Mc293	1700
Loman Reflex	3¼x4¼"	plate	LgSLR	1906	Eurynar Anastig.	4	135mm	focal plane	8-1300		180
...LOMO - Leningrad, USSR											
Lomo 135 BC (VS)	24x36mm	35mm	35vf	1975	Industar	2.8	50mm		-250	Ru43	50
Lomo 135 M	24x36mm	35mm	35vf	1980	Jupiter	2.8	50mm		-250	Ru43	50
...LONDON & PARIS OPTIC & CLOCK CO.											
Countess	4¼x6½"	plate	Field	1890						Mc293	320
Duchess	4¼x6½"	plate	Field	1887	Rapid Rectilinear						460
Princess May	4¼x6½"	plate	Field	1895	Ross Anastigmat	8	7.5"				340
...LONDON STEREOSCOPIC & PHOTO CO.											
Artist Hand Camera 9x12	9x12cm	plate	TLR	1889	Euryscope	6				Mc293	1800
Artist Hand Cam. 4¼x6½"	4¼x6½"	plate	TLR	1892	Optimus			focal plane			1800
Artist Hand Camera 5x7"	5x7"	plate	TLR	1898	Zeiss Anast.	6.3	250mm	Sector		A3140	1800
Artist Reflex	4¼x6½"	plate	TLR	1898	Optimus			focal plane	-800		1300
Artist Reflex, Tropical	3¼x4¼"	plate	TLR	1910	Heliar	4.5	150mm	focal plane	-1000	Mc293	2600
Binocular camera No. 1	1½x2½"	plate	StJumelle	1898	Krauss-Z. Anast.	6.3	110mm	guillotine		Mc293	240
Binocular camera No. 1	1½x2½"	plate	StJumelle	1898	Krauss-Z. Anast.	8	110mm	guillotine			240
Binocular camera No. 2	2½x3½"	plate	StJumelle	1898	Krauss-Z. Anast.	6.3	110mm	guillotine			240
Binocular camera No. 2	2½x3½"	plate	StJumelle	1898	Krauss-Z. Anast.	8	110mm	guillotine			240
Carlton 3¼x4¼"	3¼x4¼"	plate	TLR	1895	Rapid Rectilinear				1-100,T,I	Mc294	500
Carlton 4¼x6½"	4¼x6½"	plate	TLR	1895	Euryscope	5.6			1-100,T,I		500
Carlton 4x5"	4x5"	plate	TLR	1895	Ross Goerz D.A.	7.7			1-100,T,I		500

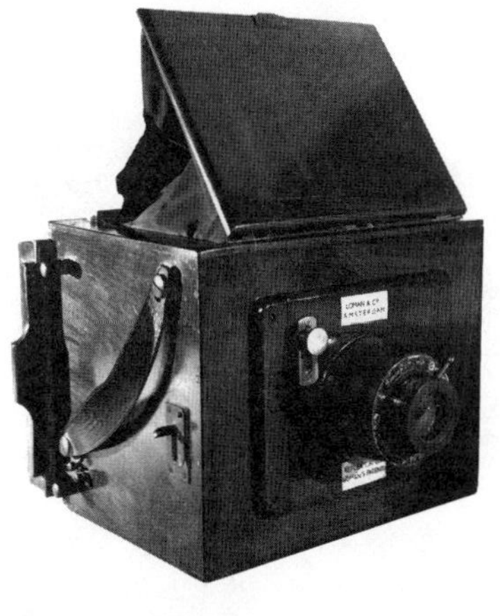

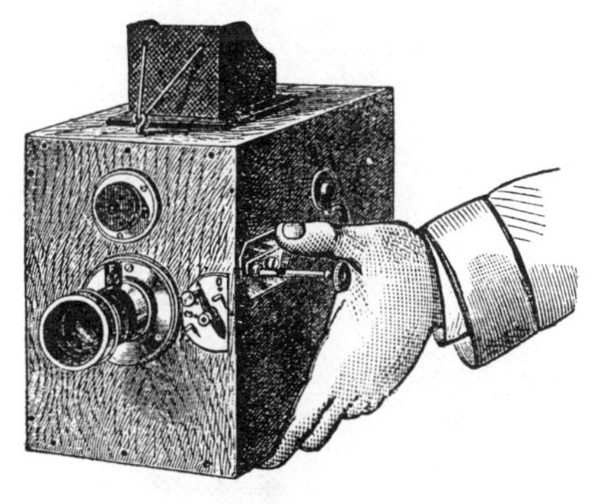

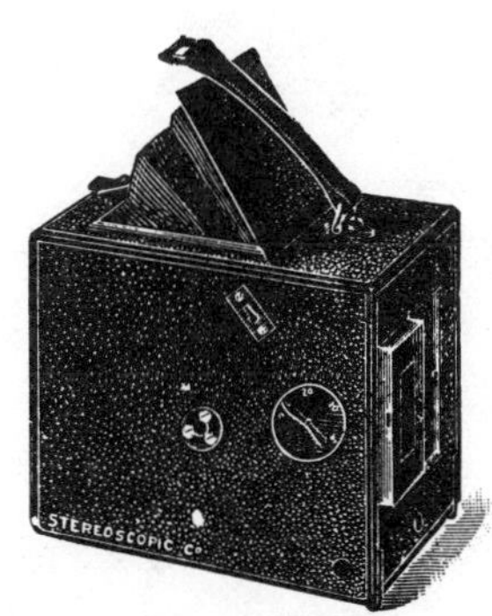

Loman's Reflex **Artist's Hand Camera** **Carlton**

MODEL	FORMAT	FILM	TYPE	Year	LENS	Apert	FL	SHUTTER	SPEEDS	ILLUS	U.S.$
Dispatch Detective	9x12cm	plate	DetectivBox	1888						Mc294	900
Field camera 3¼x4¼"	3¼x4¼"	plate	Field	1885	Rapid Rectilinear	8				A148	300
Field camera 4¼x6½"	4¼x6½"	plate	Field	1885	Portrait	8					300
Field camera 6½x8½"	6½x8½"	plate	Field	1885	Rapid Rectilinear	8				Mc294	330
King's Own Trop. 2½x4¼"	2½x4¼"	plate	HzFoldPl	1905	Goerz Dagor	6.8	120mm	Koilos	1-300	Mc294	1600
King's Own Trop. 3¼x4¼"	3¼x4¼"	plate	HzFoldPl	1907	Dagor	4.6	105mm		25-100	A3028	1000
King's Own Trop. 4¼x6½"	4¼x6½"	plate	HzFoldPl	1905	Doppel Anast.	9	180mm	B&L			1600
Parvex	2¼x3¼"	120	StrutRo	1911	TTH Cooke			dialset			200
Tailboard stereo 3½x6¼"	3½x6¼"	plate	StFoldPl	1885	Swift & Son		4"	Thornton-Pickard			630
Tailboard stereo 4¼x6½"	4¼x6½"	plate	StFoldPl	1899	Rapid Rectilinear			Thornton-Pickard		A694	610
Tailboard stereo 5x7"	5x7"	plate	StFoldPl	1885	Clement & Gllmer			Thornton-Pickard			900
Twin Lens Artist Hand C.	9x12cm	plate	TLR	1889						Mc294	470
Twin Lens Artist Hand C.	4x5"	plate	TLR	1889							470
Twin Lens Artist Hand C.	4¼x6½"	plate	TLR	1889							470
Twin Lens Reflex 2¾x4"	2¾x4"	plate	TLR	1890						A545	440
Twin Lens Reflex 2¾x4"	2¾x4"	plate	TLR	1890		6		B&L pneumatic	25-100	A548	420
Twin Lens Reflex 4x5"	4x5"	plate	TLR	1890							440
Vesca (black)	4.5x6cm	plate	StrutPl		Goerz Dagor	6.8	75mm				330
Vesca (green)	4.5x6cm	plate	StrutPl		Goerz Dagor	6.8	75mm				450
Vesca Stereo (black)	4.5x10.7	plate	SterStrut		Goerz Celor	4.5	60mm				320
Vesca Stereo (green)	4.5x10.7	plate	SterStrut		Goerz Celor	4.5	60mm				500
Wet plate camera	4x5"	WetPl	WetPlate	1855	Petzval-type						2700
...LORENZ (Ernst Lorenz) - Berlin											
Clarissa	4.5x6cm	plate	StrutPl	1929	Trioplan	3	75mm	focal plane	1/20-1000	A296	1300
Clarissa (teak)	4.5x6cm	plate	StrutPl	1929	Helioplan	4.5	75mm	focal plane	1/20-1000	Mc294	1800
...LORILLON (E. Lorillon) - Paris											
Field camera 13x18	13x18cm	plate	Field	1905	TTH			rollerblind		F115	320
Field camera 18x24	18x24cm	plate	Field	1905	TTH			rollerblind			610
...LUMIÈRE & CIE. - Lyon, France											
Box camera	4x4cm	127	MetBx							Mc294	20
Box camera No. 49	3¼x5½"	122	RollBox								20
Elax I	3x4cm	127	StrutRo	1933	Flor	3.5	50mm	focal plane	1-1000	F729	560
Elax II	3x4cm	127	StrutRo	1946	Flor	3.5	50mm	focal plane	1-1000	F731	640
Eljy	24x36mm	35mm	TelescRo	1937	Lypar	3.5	50mm	Eljy	10-150	Mc294	90
Eljy Club (meter)	24x36mm	35mm	TelescRo	1951	Lypar	3.5	40mm	Synchro	1-300	A1538	130
Eljy Club (meter), (colored)	24x36mm	35mm	TelescRo	1951	Lypar	3.5	40mm	Synchro	1-300	Mc294	220
Eljy Club (no meter)	24x36mm	35mm	TelescRo	1951	Lypar	3.5	40mm	Synchro	1-300	F562	140
Eljy Club Luxus	24x36mm	35mm	TelescRo	1951	Lypar	3.5	40mm	Synchro	1-300	F561	280
Ludax	6x9cm	120	FoldRo	1953	Fidor	6.3	150mm	Ludax	10-150	F366	10
Lumière 6x6	6x6cm	120/6	HzFoldRo	1954	Spector	4.5	80mm		10-250	F353	120
Lumière 6x9	6x9cm	120/6	VtFoldRo	1953	Fidor	6.3	105mm		1-125	F352	70
Lumière 6.5x11	6.5x11cm	116	VtFoldRo	1956	Berthiot	4.5	125mm	Lumiere	1-300	F354	70

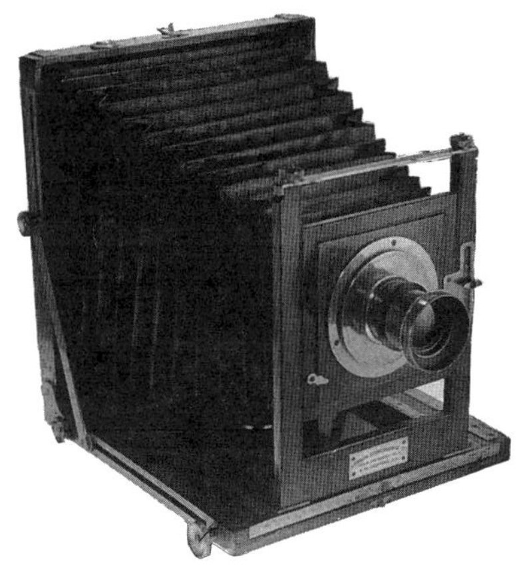

London Field Camera

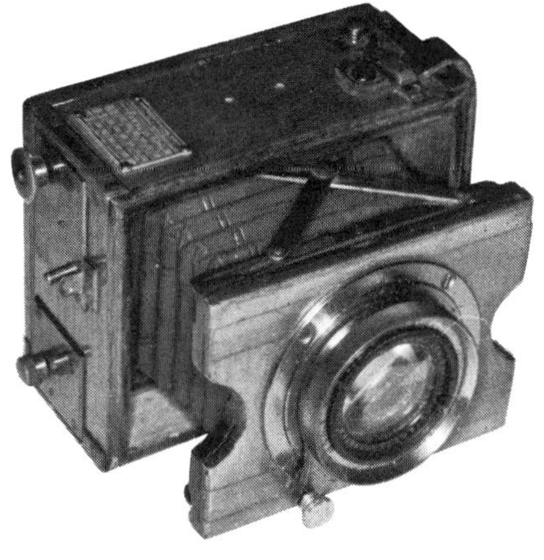

Lorenz Clarissa

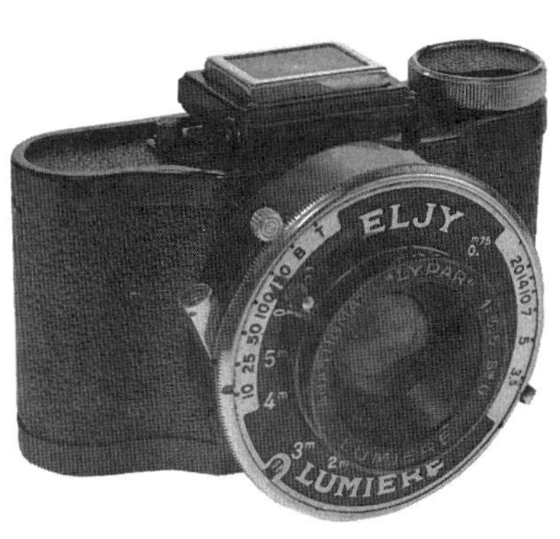

Eljy

MODEL	FORMAT	FILM	TYPE	Year	LENS	Apert	FL	SHUTTER	SPEEDS	ILLUS	U.S.$
Lumibox	6x9cm	120	MetBx	1934	achromatic				P,I	F850	20
Lumiclub	6x6/4.5x6	120/6	TelescRo	1951	Flor-Berthiot	3.5	75mm	Royer	1-300	Mc295	260
Lumiflex	6x6cm	Roll	TLR	1950	Spector	4.5	80mm	Atos 2	1-300	F455	40
Lumireflex	6x6cm	Roll	TLR	1951	Spector	4.5	80mm	Atos 2	1-300	F457	80
Lumirex	6x9cm	620	FoldRo	1946	Fidor	6.3	105mm		10-200	Mc295	30
Lumirex	6x9cm	620	FoldRo	1946	Spector	4.5	105mm		10-200	F359	30
Lumirex III	6x9cm	620	FoldRo	1956	Angenieux	3.5	100mm	Lumiere	1-300	F361	60
Lumirex III	6x9cm	620	FoldRo	1956	Angenieux	4.5	100mm	Prontor-S	1-250	F362	60
Lumix F	6x9cm	620	FoldRo	1946	Meniscus				P,I	F365	30
Lutac	6x9cm	620	RigidRo	1953	Fidor	6.3	105mm		10-150	A3109	20
Lux-Box	6x9cm	620	MetBx	1939		6.3			25,75,B	Mc295	30
Optax (early)	24x36mm	35mm	35vf	1948	Lypar	3.5	50mm		10-200	F634	140
Optax (later)	24x36mm	35mm	35vf	1949	Altar	3.5	40mm		10-200	Mc295	80
Periphote	7x38cm	Roll	Panoramic	1901						Mc295	6300
Scout-Box	6x9cm	120	MetBx	1935						A2868	30
Sinox	6x9cm	120	FoldRo		Nacor Anastigmat	6.3	105mm	Central	25-100		30
Starter	24x36mm	35mm	35vf	1955	Lypar	3.5	45mm			Mc295	50
Sterelux	6x13cm	116	StFoldRo	1920	Spector Anast.	4.5	80mm		25-100	F1457	270
Sterelux	6x13cm	116	StFoldRo	1920	Spector Anast.	4.5	80mm		1-100	Mc295	270
Super Eljy	24x36mm	35mm	TelescRo	1937	Lypar	3.5	50mm	Eljy	10-150		80
...LÜTTKE (Dr. Lüttke & Arndt) - Wandsbek, Hamburg, Berlin, Germany											
Cobra	9x12cm	plate	HzFoldPl	1900	Extra Rap. Aplan.	7.5					240
Field camera	9x12cm	plate	Field	1900	Periscop	16		Junior			180
Filmos	8x10.5cm	plate	FoldPl	1902	Periscop	10		pneumatic			200
Folding plate camera 9x12	9x12cm	plate	VtFoldPl	1902	Periscop						140
Folding plate camera 9x12	9x12cm	plate	VtFoldPl	1902	Extra Rap. Aplan.					A187	160
Folding plate camera 13x18	13x18cm	plate	FoldPl	1900	Periscop						160
Folding plate/rollfilm camer	9x12cm	pl/118	FoldPl	1900							300
Folding rollfilm camera	8x10.5cm	118	FoldRo		Periplanat						70
Linos (horizontal) 9x12	9x12cm	plate	HzFoldPl	1898	Meniscus			pneumatic		U0220	440
Linos (horizontal) 13x18	13x18cm	plate	HzFoldPl	1898	Meniscus			pneumatic		U0221	440
Linos (square) 9x12	9x12cm	plate	FoldPl	1898	Aplanat	8	165mm	pneumatic			390
Linos Stereo	9x18cm	plate	StFoldPl	1898	Aplanat	8	165mm			A2664	620
Magazinkamera	9x12cm	plate	MagBox	1905	Aplanat	8					70
Transvaal	9x9cm	Pl+Ro	FoldRo	1900		8			M,Z		340
Vidol	8x14cm	Roll	FoldRo								220
...MACKENSTEIN (H. Mackenstein) - Paris											
Chambre à Joues	9x12cm	plate	StrutPl	1889	Darlot R.R.					F156	220
Detective Box	9x12cm	plate	MagBox	1897	Rapid Rectilinear			guillotine		A1315	440
Detective Box	9x12cm	plate	MagBox	1897	Aplanat			rotary		A2813	440
Field camera	13x18cm	plate	Field	1900	Zeiss Anastigmat			Mattioli		F22	290
Folding camera	9x12cm	plate	StrutPl	1890	Aplanat	9	150mm			F185	370

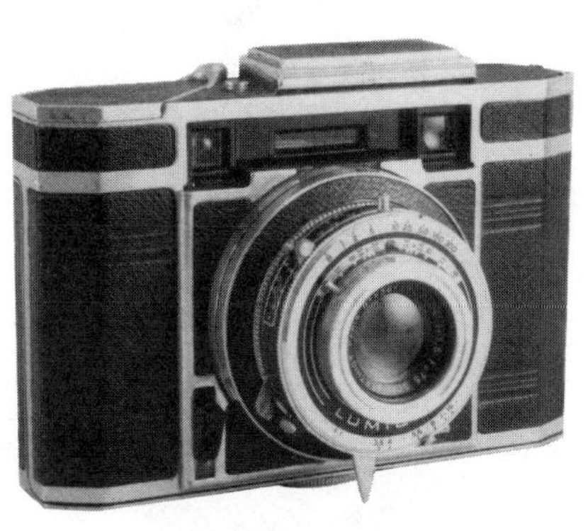

Lumiclub

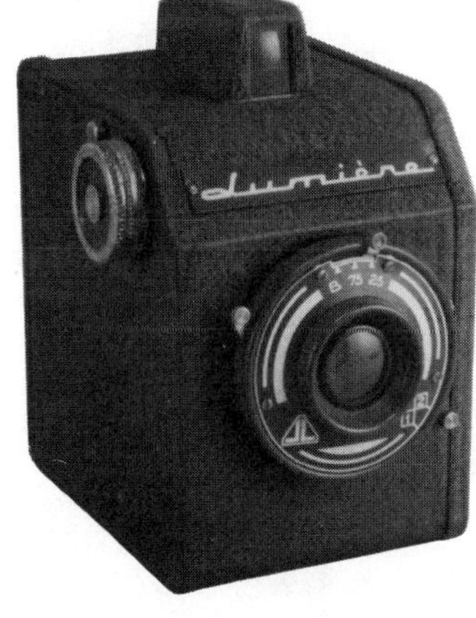

Lux-Box

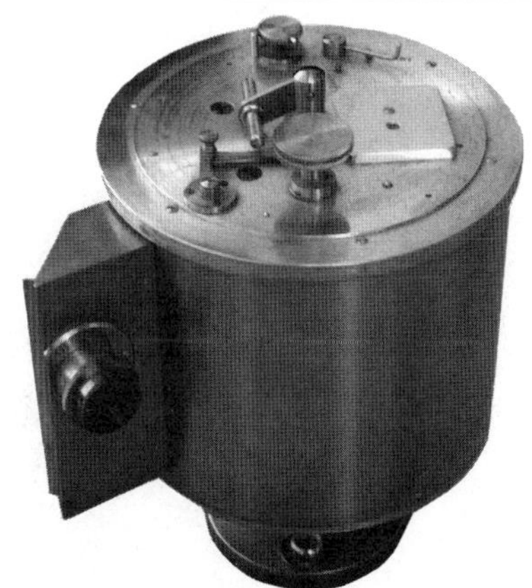

Periphote

MODEL	FORMAT	FILM	TYPE	Year	LENS	Apert	FL	SHUTTER	SPEEDS	ILLUS	U.S.$
Francia	9x12cm	plate	StrutPl	1910	Dagor	6.8	120mm	focal plane	15-2000		280
Francia Stéréo (folding)	45x107	plate	SterStrut	1906	Max Balbreck			guillotine		A706	310
Francia Stéréo (folding)	6x13cm	plate	SterStrut	1906	Sumo Aplanat			guillotine		F1241	290
Francia Stéréo (jumelle)	6x13cm	plate	StJumelle	1900	Goerz Doppel An.	6.8		guillotine		Mc296	330
Francia Stéréo (jumelle)	6x13cm	plate	StJumelle	1900	Dagor	6.8		guillotine		F1242	330
Francia Stéréo (jumelle)	9x18cm	plate	StJumelle	1900	Goerz Doppel An.	6.8		guillotine		F1242	330
Jumelle Photographique	6.5x9cm	plate	Jumelle	1895	Goerz Doppel An.	8		guillotine		F1063	220
Jumelle Photographique	9x12cm	plate	Jumelle	1895	Goerz Doppel An.	8		guillotine		A839	240
Jumelle Photographique	9x12cm	plate	Jumelle	1903	Zeiss Anastigmat	8	136mm	guillotine		F1058	210
Jumelle Stéréo Panoram.	45x107	plate	StJumelle	1900	Goerz Anastigmat		54mm	guillotine		F1301	380
Jumelle Stéréo Panoram.	6x13cm	plate	StJumelle	1905	Goerz Doppel An.	6.4	90mm	guillotine		F1302	350
Jumelle Stéréo Panoram.	9x18cm	plate	StJumelle	1899	Zeiss Anastigmat	8	110mm	guillotine		F1299	350
Jumelle Stéréoscopique	8x16cm	plate	StJumelle	1893	Protar	6.3	110mm	guillotine		A697	260
Jumelle Stéréoscopique	9x18cm	plate	StJumelle	1893	Goerz Doppel An.		110mm	guillotine			260
Kallista	6x13cm	plate	StJumelle	1896	Boyer-Saphir	6.3	54mm	guillotine		F1304	270
Photo Livre	4x4cm	plate	Disguised	1890	achromatic	12	65mm	guillotine		F1480	4800
Stereo Français 9x12	9x12cm	plate	SterField	1896	Z.-Krauss Protar			Thornton-Pickard		F1392	290
Stereo Français 13x18	13x18cm	plate	SterField	1896	Z.-Krauss Protar			Thornton-Pickard			320
...MACRIS-BOUCHER - Paris											
Nil Mélior Stéréo	6x13cm	plate	StJumelle	1920	Krauss Tessar	4.5	65mm			Mc296	190
...MACVAN MFG. CO.											
Macvan Reflex 5-7 Studio	5x7"	plate	LgTLR	1948	Ilex Paragon	4.5	8.5"	Ilex Universal		Mc296	350
...MADER (H. Mader) - Isny, Württemberg											
Invincibel 10x15	10x15cm	plate	Field	1889	Rapid Aplanat	8					1600
Invincibel 13x18	13x18cm	plate	Field	1889	Aplanat	6	180mm			A1417	1100
Invincibel Mod. III	12x16.5	plate	Field	1893	Rapid Aplanat	8					1300
...MAGIC INTRODUCTION CO. - New York											
Photoret Watch Camera	½x½"	Disc	Disguised	1894	Meniscus			rotary		Mc296	900
Presto	28x28mm	Roll	RigidRo	1896	Meniscus				I	Mc296	610
...MAMIYA CAMERA CO. - Tokyo											
Auto Deluxe	24x36mm	35mm	35rf	1961	Sekor	1.7	48mm	Seikosha-SLV	1-500		50
Auto Deluxe 2	24x36mm	35mm	35rf	1962	Sekor	1.7	48mm	Copal	1-500		50
Auto-Lux 35	24x36mm	35mm	35slr	1964	Sekor	2.8	48mm	Copal	15-500		120
Auto-Metra	24x36mm	35mm	35rf	1958	Sekor	1.9	48mm	Copal	1-500		70
Auto-Metra II	24x36mm	35mm	35rf	1959	Sekor	1.7	48mm	Copal	1-500		70
Automatic 35 EEF	24x36mm	35mm	35vf	1961	Kominar	3.8	45mm	Seikosha	60-250		80
C220 Professional body	6x6cm	120/2	TLR	1968	body only	---	---	Seiko	1-500		180
C220 Professional + 80/2.8	6x6cm	120/2	TLR	1968	Sekor	2.8	80mm	Seiko	1-500		330
C220 Professional f body	6x6cm	120/2	TLR	1983	body only	---	---	Seiko	1-500		200
C220 Professional f + 80/2.8	6x6cm	120/2	TLR	1983	Sekor	2.8	80mm	Seiko	1-500		400
C330 Professional body	6x6cm	120/2	TLR	1969	body only	---	---	Seiko	1-500		260
C330 Professional + 105/3.5	6x6cm	120/2	TLR	1969	Sekor	3.5	105mm	Seiko	1-500		440

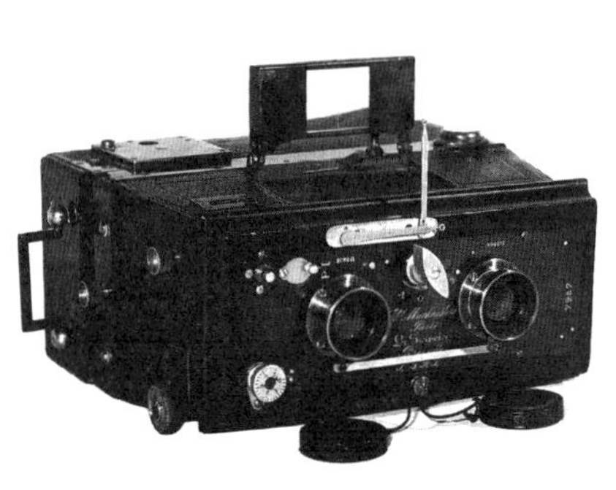

Francia Stéréo (jumelle)

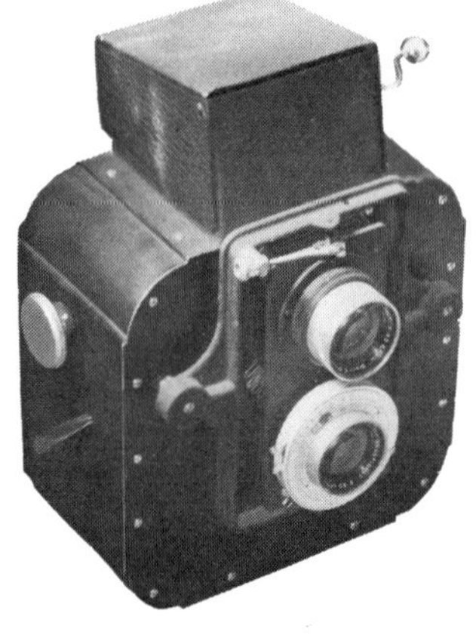

Macvan Reflex 5-7 Studio

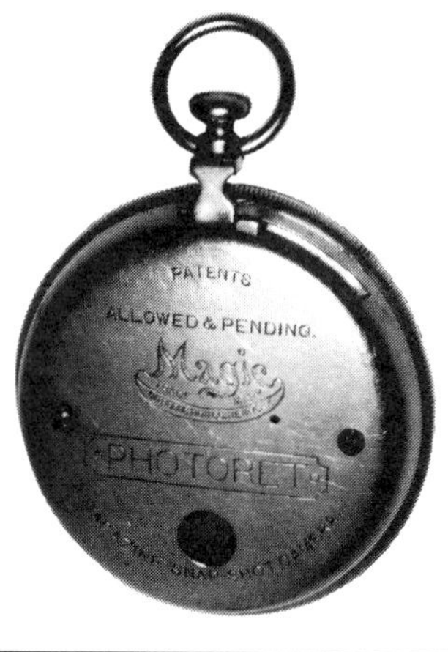

Photoret Watch Camera

MODEL	FORMAT	FILM	TYPE	Year	LENS	Apert	FL	SHUTTER	SPEEDS	ILLUS	U.S.$
C330 Professional f body	6x6cm	120/2	TLR	1975	body only	---	---	Seiko	1-500		310
C330 Professional f + 80/2.8	6x6cm	120/2	TLR	1975	Sekor	2.8	80mm	Seiko	1-500		530
C330 Professional S body	6x6cm	120/2	TLR	1983	body only	---	---	Seiko	1-500		540
C330 Profession. S +80/2.8	6x6cm	120/2	TLR	1983	Sekor	2.8	80mm	Seiko	1-500		660
Camex Six	6x6cm	120	HzFoldRo	1950	Zuiko	3.5	75mm	Seikosha-Rapid	1-500		390
Crown	24x36mm	35mm	35rf	1958	Sekor	1.9	4.8cm	Seikosha-MXL	1-500		270
EE Merit	24x36mm	35mm	35rf	1962		2.8	40mm	Seikosha	30-250		60
EE Super Merit	24x36mm	35mm	35rf	1962		2.8	40mm	Seikosha	30-250		70
EF2	24x36mm	35mm	35C	1982		4	38mm		1/125		30
Elca	24x36mm	35mm	35rf	1958	Sekor	2.8	5cm	Copal-MXV	1-500		70
Family	24x36mm	35mm	35slr	1962	Sekor	2.8	48mm	Copal	15-250		50
Junior	24x36mm	35mm	35slr	1962	Sekor	2.8	48mm		15-250		60
Korvette	24x36mm	35mm	35slr	1963	Sekor	2.8	48mm	Copal	15-250		70
M645 body	4.5x6cm	120	MedSLR	1983	body only	---	---	electronic	8-1/500		320
M645 + 80/2.8	4.5x6cm	120	MedSLR	1983	Sekor C	2.8	80mm	electronic	8-1/500		510
M645 1000S body	4.5x6cm	120	MedSLR	1977	body only	---	---	electronic	8-1/1000		420
M645 1000S + 80/2.8	4.5x6cm	120	MedSLR	1977	Sekor C	2.8	80mm	electronic	8-1/1000		650
M645J body	4.5x6cm	120	MedSLR	1979	body only	---	---	electronic	8-1/1000		290
M645J + 80/2.8	4.5x6cm	120	MedSLR	1979	Sekor C	2.8	80mm	electronic	8-1/1000		530
M645 Pro body	4.5x6cm	120	MedSLR	1992	body only	---	---	electronic	4-1/1000		1000
M645 Pro + 80/2.8	4.5x6cm	120	MedSLR	1992	Sekor C	2.8	80mm	electronic	4-1/1000		1200
M645 Super body	4.5x6cm	120	MedSLR	1985	body only	---	---	electronic	4-1/1000		670
M645 Super + 80/2.8	4.5x6cm	120	MedSLR	1985	Sekor C	2.8	80mm	electronic	4-1/1000		1000
Magazine 35	24x36mm	35mm	35rf	1957	Sekor	2.8	50mm	Seikosha-MXL	1-500	Mc297	180
Mamiya 6	6x6cm	120	HzFoldRo	1940	K.O.L. Special	3.5	75mm	NKS	1-200		240
Mamiya 6 (1993)	6x6cm	120/2	MedRF	1989		3.5	75mm	electronic	4-1/500		1000
Mamiya 6 Ia	6x6cm	120	HzFoldRo	1940	K.O.L. Special	3.5	75mm	NKS	1-200		270
Mamiya 6 II	6x6cm	120	HzFoldRo	1941	K.O.L. Special	3.5	75mm	NKS	1-200		280
Mamiya 6 III	6x6cm	120	HzFoldRo	1941	K.O.L. Special	3.5	75mm	NKS	1-200		240
Mamiya 6 IV	6x6cm	120	HzFoldRo	1947	Zuiko	3.5	75mm	Copal	1-200		140
Mamiya 6 IV	6x6cm	120	HzFoldRo	1947	Zuiko	3.5	75mm	Seikosha-Rapid	1-500	Mc297	140
Mamiya 6 IVB	6x6cm	120	HzFoldRo	1955	Zuiko	3.5	75mm	Seikosha-Rapid	1-500		120
Mamiya 6 IVS	6x6cm	120	HzFoldRo	1957	Sekor	3.5	75mm	Seikosha-Rapid	1-500		110
Mamiya 6 V	6x6cm	120	HzFoldRo	1953	Zuiko	3.5	75mm	Seikosha-Rapid	1-500		110
Mamiya 6 Automat	6x6cm	120	HzFoldRo	1955	Zuiko	3.5	75mm	Seikosha	1-500		90
Mamiya 6 Automat 2	6x6cm	120	HzFoldRo	1958	Sekor	3.5	75mm	Seikosha	1-500		90
Mamiya 6 K	6x6/4.5x6	120	HzFoldRo	1954	Sekor	3.5	75mm	Copal	1-300		100
Mamiya 6 K II	6x6cm	120	HzFoldRo	1956	Sekor	3.5	75mm	Copal	1-300		100
Mamiya 6 MF (New) body	6x6cm	120/2	MedRF	1995	body only	---	---	electronic	4-1/500		1200
Mamiya 6 MF (New) +75/3.5	6x6cm	120/2	MedRF	1995	Sekor C	3.5	75mm	electronic	4-1/500		2000
Mamiya 6 P	6x6cm	120	HzFoldRo	1957	Sekor	3.5	75mm	Copal	1-300		100
Mamiya-16	10x14mm	16mm	Submin	1950		3.5	25mm		25-100		100

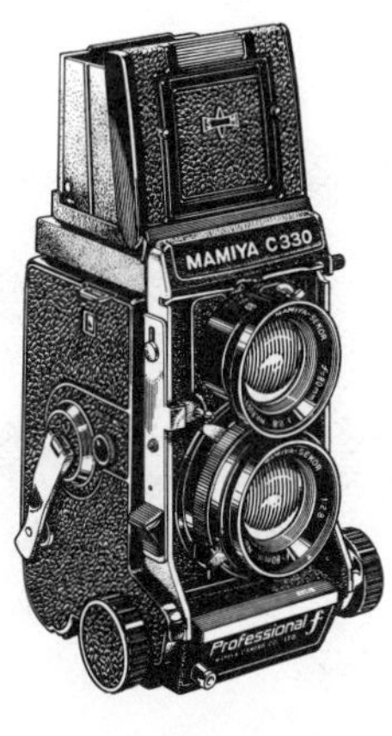

Mamiya C330 Professional f

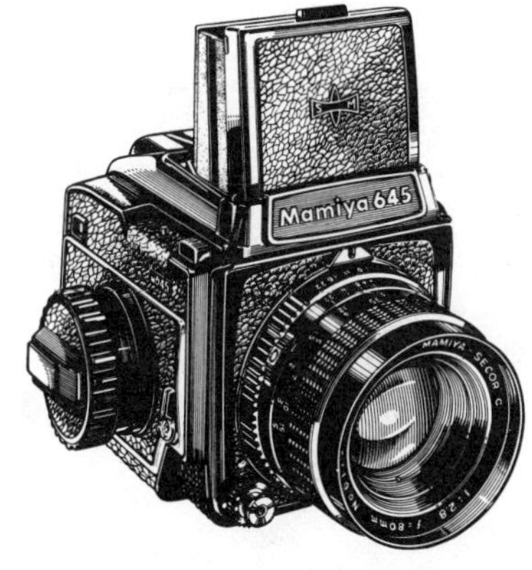

Mamiya M645

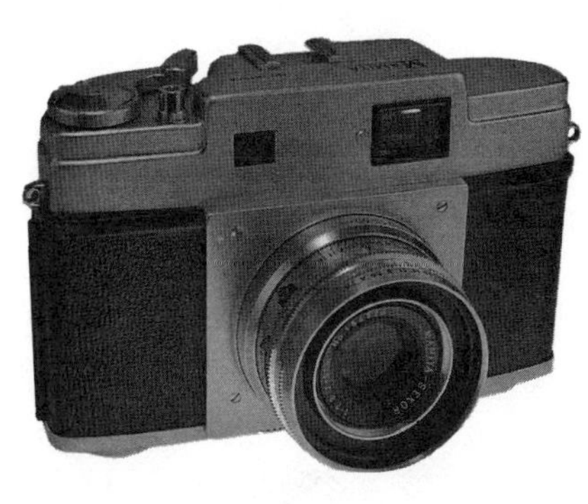

Mamiya Magazine 35

MODEL	FORMAT	FILM	TYPE	Year	LENS	Apert	FL	SHUTTER	SPEEDS	ILLUS	U.S.$
Mamiya-16 Automatic	10x14mm	16mm	Submin	1950	Sekor	2.8	25mm		2-200		60
Mamiya-16 Automatic RS	10x14mm	16mm	Submin	1960	Sekor	2.8	25mm		1/5-200		90
Mamiya-16 Deluxe	10x14mm	16mm	Submin	1950	Sekor	2.8	25mm		25-200		60
Mamiya-16 EE	10x14mm	16mm	Submin	1962	Sekor	2.8	25mm		1/5-200		30
Mamiya-16 EE Deluxe	10x14mm	16mm	Submin	1962	Sekor	2.8	25mm		1/5-200		100
Mamiya-16 Police	10x14mm	16mm	Submin	1949		3.5	25mm		25-100		490
Mamiya-16 Super	10x14mm	16mm	Submin	1950		3.5	25mm		½-200	Mc297	60
Mamiya-16 Super II	10x14mm	16mm	Submin	1957		3.5	25mm		½-200		70
Mamiya-16 Super Mod. III	10x14mm	16mm	Submin	1958		3.5	25mm		½-200		90
Mamiya 23 Standard body	6x9cm	120	MedRF	1965	body only	---	---	Seikosha	1-500		100
Mamiya 23 Stand. + 90/3.5	6x9cm	120	MedRF	1965	Sekor	3.5	90mm	Seikosha	1-500		230
Mamiya 35 (I)	24x36mm	35mm	35rf	1949	Hexar	3.5	50mm	Copal	1-200		270
Mamiya 35 II 2.8 (Deluxe)	24x36mm	35mm	35rf	1955	Sekor	2.8	5cm	Seikosha-MX	1-500		120
Mamiya 35 II 3.5	24x36mm	35mm	35rf	1955	Sekor	3.5	45mm	Seikosha-MX	1-500		120
Mamiya 35 IIi 2.0	24x36mm	35mm	35rf	1957	Sekor	2.0	4.8cm	Seikosha-MXL	1-500		50
Mamiya 35 III 2.8	24x36mm	35mm	35rf	1957	Sekor	2.8	5cm	Seikosha-MXL	1-500		130
Mamiya 35 M3	24x36mm	35mm	35rf	1962	Sekor	2	48mm	Copal-SV			50
Mamiya 35 S	24x36mm	35mm	35rf	1959	Sekor	1.9	4.8cm	Seikosha-MXL	1-500		70
Mamiya 35 S2	24x36mm	35mm	35rf	1959	Sekor	2.8	48mm	Copal-SV	1-500		50
Mamiya 35 Wide	24x36mm	35mm	35rf	1957	Sekor	2.8	3.5cm	Seikosha-MXL	1-500		110
Mamiya 35 Wide E	24x36mm	35mm	35rf	1959	Sekor	2.8	3.5cm	Seikosha-MXL	1-500		140
Mamiya 135	24x36mm	35mm	35rf	1977	Sekor	2.8	38mm		30-650		50
Mamiya 135AF	24x36mm	35mm	35af	1981	Sekor	2.8	38mm		8-450		70
Mamiya 135EF	24x36mm	35mm	35vf	1981	Sekor	2.8	38mm		60-250		50
Mamiya CP	24x36mm	35mm	35slr	1964	Sekor	1.7	58mm		1-1000		90
Mamiya M	24x36mm	35mm	35af	1983		2.8	35mm	programmed	8-500		70
Mamiya M Time Memory	24x36mm	35mm	35af	1983		2.8	38mm	programmed			110
Mamiya Press	6x9cm	120	MedRF	1962	Sekor	3.5	90mm	Seikosha	1-500		300
Mamiya Press G	6x9cm	120	MedRF	1963	Sekor	3.5	90mm	Seikosha	1-500		340
Mamiya Press S	6x9cm	120	MedRF	1964	Sekor	3.5	105mm	Seikosha	1-500		390
Mam. Press Super 23 body	6x9cm	120	MedRF	1967	body only	---	---	Seiko	1-500		330
Mam. Press S. 23 +100/3.5	6x9cm	120	MedRF	1967	Sekor	3.5	100mm	Seiko	1-500		370
Mamiya SLR	24x36mm	35mm	35SLR	1963	Canon	1.9		focal plane	1-1000		90
Mamiya/Sekor (CWP)	24x36mm	35mm	35slr	1964	Sekor	1.7	58mm	focal plane	1-1000		70
Mamiya/Sekor 500 DTL	24x36mm	35mm	35slr	1969	Sekor	2	55mm	focal plane	1-500		70
Mamiya/Sekor 500 TL	24x36mm	35mm	35slr	1966	Sekor	2.8	55mm	focal plane	1-500	Mc298	50
Mamiya/Sekor 528 AL	24x36mm	35mm	35slr	1975	Sekor	2.8	48mm	Copal			70
Mamiya/Sekor 528 TL	24x36mm	35mm	35slr	1967	Sekor	2.8	48mm	Copal			60
Mamiya/Sekor 1000 DTL	24x36mm	35mm	35slr	1968	Sekor	1.8	55mm	focal plane	1-1000		80
Mamiya/Sekor 1000 TL	24x36mm	35mm	35slr	1966	Sekor	1.8	55mm	focal plane	1-1000		60
Mamiya/Sekor Auto X1000	24x36mm	35mm	35slr	1975	Auto Sekor	1.8	55mm	focal plane			70
Mamiya/Sekor Auto XTL	24x36mm	35mm	35slr	1971	Auto Sekor	1.8	55mm	focal plane	1-1000	Mc298	130

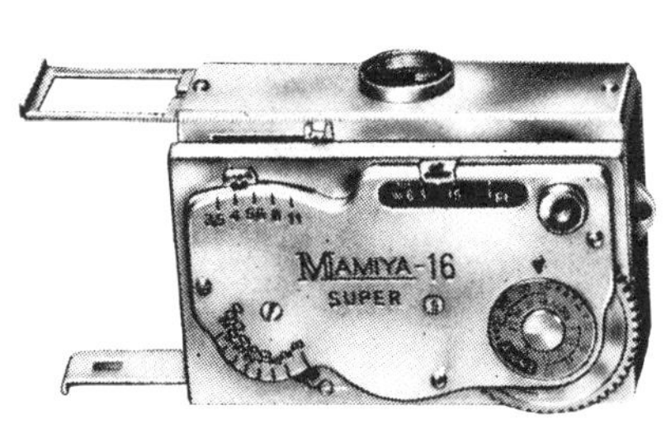

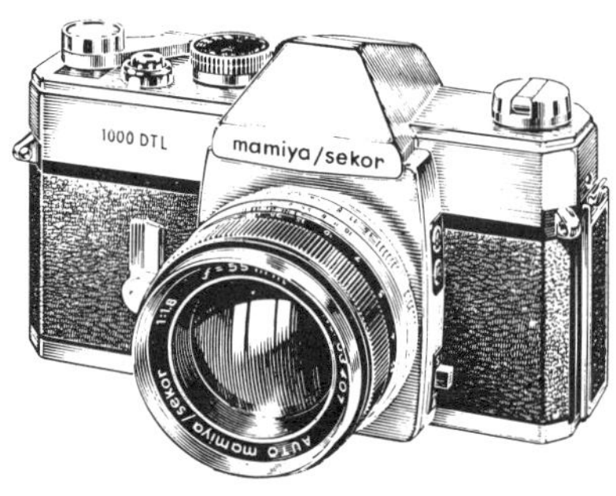

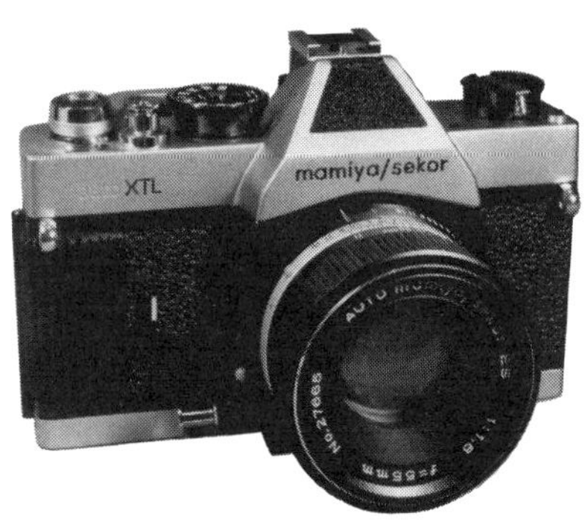

Mamiya-16 Super | **Mamiya/Sekor 1000 DTL** | **Mamiya/Sekor Auto XTL**

MODEL	FORMAT	FILM	TYPE	Year	LENS	Apert	FL	SHUTTER	SPEEDS	ILLUS	U.S.$
Mamiya/Sekor DSX 500	24x36mm	35mm	35slr	1974	Auto Sekor	1.8	55mm	focal plane	1-500		100
Mamiya/Sekor DSX 1000	24x36mm	35mm	35slr	1974	Auto Sekor	1.8	55mm	focal plane	1-1000		120
Mamiya/Sekor MSX 500	24x36mm	35mm	35slr	1974	Auto Sekor	1.8	55mm	focal plane	1-500		80
Mamiya/Sekor MSX 1000	24x36mm	35mm	35slr	1975	Auto Sekor	1.8	55mm	focal plane	1-1000		100
Mamiyaflex I	6x6cm	120	TLR	1951	Sekor	3.5	7.5cm	Merit	1-300	Mc298	140
Mamiyaflex II	6x6cm	120	TLR	1952	Sekor	3.5	7.5cm	Merit	1-300	Mc298	140
Mamiyaflex Automatic-A	6x6cm	120	TLR	1949	Zuiko	3.5	75mm	Seikosha-Rapid			140
Mamiyaflex Aut.-A (Type 2)	6x6cm	120	TLR	1949	Zuiko	3.5	75mm	Seikosha-Rapid		Mc297	180
Mamiyaflex Aut.-A (Type 3)	6x6cm	120	TLR	1949	Zuiko	3.5	75mm	Seikosha-Rapid			180
Mamiyaflex Automatic A-II	6x6cm	120	TLR	1954	Zuiko	3.5	75mm	Seikosha-Rapid	1-500		110
Mamiyaflex Automatic B	6x6cm	120	TLR	1953	Sekor	3.5	75mm	Seikosha-Rapid	1-500		90
Mamiyaflex Automatic B II	6x6cm	120	TLR	1956	Sekor	3.5	75mm	Seikosha-Rapid	1-500		100
Mamiyaflex C body	6x6cm	120	TLR	1956	body only	---	---	Seikosha	1-500		120
Mamiyaflex C + 80/2.8	6x6cm	120	TLR	1956	Sekor	2.8	80mm	Seikosha	1-500		220
Mamiyaflex C2 body	6x6cm	120	TLR	1958	body only	---	---	Seikosha	1-500		80
Mamiyaflex C2 + 80/2.8	6x6cm	120	TLR	1958	Sekor	2.8	80mm	Seikosha	1-500		190
Mamiya(flex) C3 body	6x6cm	120	TLR	1962	body only	---	---	Seikosha	1-500		150
Mamiya(flex) C3 + 80/2.8	6x6cm	120	TLR	1962	Sekor	2.8	80mm	Seikosha	1-500		240
Mamiya(flex) C22 body	6x6cm	120	TLR	1966	body only	---	---	Seikosha	1-500		100
Mamiya(flex) C22 + 105/3.5	6x6cm	120	TLR	1966	Sekor	3.5	105mm	Seikosha	1-500		230
Mamiya(flex) C33 body	6x6cm	120	TLR	1965	body only	---	---	Seikosha	1-500		120
Mamiya(flex) C33 + 105/3.5	6x6cm	120	TLR	1965	Sekor	3.5	105mm	Seikosha	1-500		280
Mamiyaflex Junior (early)	6x6cm	120	TLR	1948	Neocon	3.5	75mm	Stamina	1-200	Mc298	210
Mamiyaflex Junior (later)	6x6cm	120	TLR	1948	Neocon	3.5	75mm	Stamina	1-200	Mc298	150
Mamiyaflex Junior 300	6x6cm	120	TLR	1948	Neocon	3.5	75mm	Stamina	1-300		100
Mamiya(flex) PF	6x6cm	120	TLR	1957	Sekor	2.8	80mm	Seikosha-Rapid	1-500		270
Mammy	24x28mm	828	RigidRo	1953	Cute Anastigmat	3.5	45mm		25-100	Mc298	100
Metra	24x36mm	35mm	35rf	1958	Sekor	1.9	48mm	Seikosha-MXL	1-500		70
Metra II	24x36mm	35mm	35rf	1959	Sekor	1.9	48mm	Seikosha-MXL	1-500		70
Myrapid	18x24mm	35mm	35rf	1965	Tominon	1.7	32mm	Auto Copal	30-800		40
NC1000	24x36mm	35mm	35slr	1977	Sekor	1.4	50mm	electronic	1-1000		150
NC1000S	24x36mm	35mm	35slr	1977	Sekor	1.4	50mm	electronic	1-1000		120
Pistol camera	18x24mm	35mm	Special	1954	Sekor	5.6	45mm		I	Mc298	4200
Prismat NP	24x36mm	35mm	35slr	1961	Sekor	1.7	58mm		1-1000		120
Prismat PH	24x36mm	35mm	35slr	1961	Sekor	1.9	48mm	Seikosha	1-500		120
Prismat WP	24x36mm	35mm	35slr	1962	Sekor	1.7	48mm	focal plane	1-1000		110
RB67 body	6x7cm	120	MedSLR	1969	body only	---	---	Seiko	1-400		470
RB67 + 90/3.8	6x7cm	120	MedSLR	1969	Sekor	3.8	90mm	Seiko	1-400		700
RB67 Pro S body	6x7cm	120	MedSLR	1983	body only	---	---	Seiko	1-400		500
RB67 Pro S + 90/3.8	6x7cm	120	MedSLR	1983	Sekor C	3.8	90mm	Seiko	1-400		900
RB67 Pro SD body	6x7cm	120	MedSLR	1991	body only	---	---	Seiko	1-400		1000
RB67 Pro SD + 90/3.5	6x7cm	120	MedSLR	1991	Mamiya KL	3.5	90mm	Seiko	1-400		2300

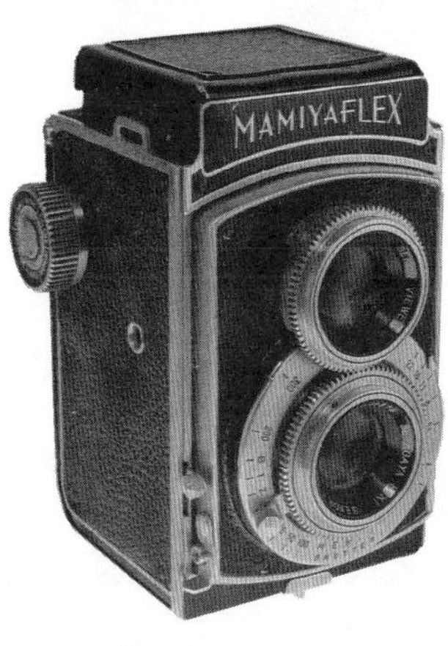

Mamiyaflex I

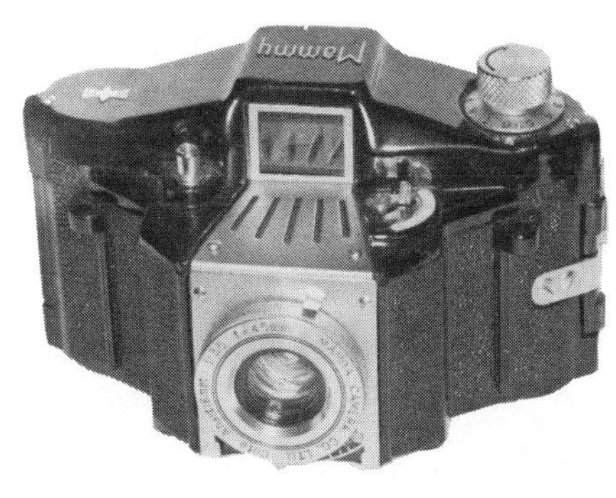

Mammy

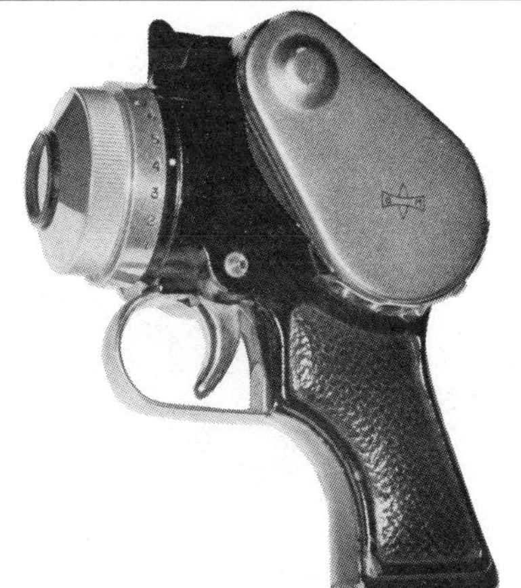

Mamiya Pistol camera

MODEL	FORMAT	FILM	TYPE	Year	LENS	Apert	FL	SHUTTER	SPEEDS	ILLUS	U.S.$
RB67 Pro SD Gold Set	6x7cm	120	MedSLR	1990	Mamiya KL	3.5	127mm	Seiko	1-400		5200
Ruby 1.9	24x36mm	35mm	35rf	1960	Sekor	1.9	48mm	Copal	1-500		90
Ruby 2.8	24x36mm	35mm	35rf	1959	Sekor	2.8	48mm	Copal	1-500		50
Ruby Standard 2.0	24x36mm	35mm	35rf	1962		2	48mm	Copal	1-500		70
RZ67 Professional body	6x7cm	120	MedSLR	1983	body only	---	---	Seiko	8-1/400		1000
RZ67 Professional + 110/2.8	6x7cm	120	MedSLR	1983	Sekor Z	2.8	110mm	Seiko	8-1/400		1700
RZ67 Professional II body	6x7cm	120	MedSLR	1994	body only	---	---	Seiko	8-1/400		1300
RZ67 Prof. II + 110/2.8	6x7cm	120	MedSLR	1994	Sekor Z	2.8	110mm	Seiko	8-1/400		2000
Saturn	24x36mm	35mm	35slr	1963	Sekor	2.8	48mm	Copal	15-250		70
Sketch	24x24mm	35mm	35rf	1959	Sekor	2.8	35mm	Copal	1-300		120
Super Deluxe 1.5	24x36mm	35mm	35rf	1964	Sekor	1.5	48mm	Copal-SVE	1-500		100
Super Deluxe 1.7	24x36mm	35mm	35rf	1964	Sekor	1.7	48mm	Copal-SVE	1-500		70
U (black)	24x36mm	35mm	35vf	1981	Sekor	2.8	35mm	programmed	8-500		60
U (silver)	24x36mm	35mm	35vf	1981	Sekor	2.8	35mm	programmed	8-500		60
U Autofocus (black)	24x36mm	35mm	35af	1983	Sekor	2.8	35mm	programmed	8-450		70
U Autofocus (red)	24x36mm	35mm	35af	1983	Sekor	2.8	35mm	programmed	8-450		70
U Autofocus (silver)	24x36mm	35mm	35af	1983	Sekor	2.8	35mm	programmed	8-450		70
Universal Press body	6x9cm	120/2	MedRF	1969	body only	---	---	Seiko	1-500		210
Universal Press + 100/3.5	6x9cm	120/2	MedRF	1969	Sekor	3.5	100mm	Seiko	1-500		470
ZE	24x36mm	35mm	35slr	1980	Sekor	1.7	50mm	Seiko	1-1000		70
ZE-2 Quartz	24x36mm	35mm	35slr	1981	Sekor	1.7	50mm	Seiko	1-1000		140
ZE-X	24x36mm	35mm	35slr	1981	Sekor	1.7	50mm	Seiko	8-1/1000		210
ZM Quartz	24x36mm	35mm	35slr	1982	Sekor	1.7	50mm	Seiko	4-1/1000		120
...MANHATTAN OPTICAL CO. - New York											
Bo-Peep, Mod. B 4x5"	4x5"	plate	HzFoldPl	1898						Mc299	110
Bo-Peep, Mod. B 5x7"	5x7"	plate	HzFoldPl	1898							120
Cycle Wizard 4x5"	4x5"	plate	FoldPl	1900							130
Cycle Wizard 5x7"	5x7"	plate	FoldPl	1900							140
Long Focus Wizard	5x7"	plate	FoldPl	1900	Rapid Rectilinear			Unicum		Mc299	180
Night Hawk Det. (leather)	4x5"	plate	PlateBox	1895	Rapid Achromatic				T,I		420
Night Hawk Detect. (wood)	4x5"	plate	PlateBox	1895	Rapid Achromatic				T,I	Mc299	590
Wizard A 4x5"	4x5"	plate	FoldPl	1900							130
Wizard B 4x5"	4x5"	plate	FoldPl	1900							130
Wizard B 5x7"	5x7"	plate	FoldPl	1900							140
Wizard Baby	4x5"	plate	FoldPl	1900							130
Wizard Duplex No. 1	3¼x4¼"	plate	FoldRo	1902							450
Wizard Duplex No. 2	3¼x4¼"	plate	FoldRo	1902							450
Wizard Junior	4x5"	plate	FoldPl	1900							130
Wizard Senior 4x5"	4x5"	plate	FoldPl	1900						Mc299	130
Wizard Senior 5x7"	5x7"	plate	FoldPl	1900							140
Wizard Special 3¼x4¼"	3¼x4¼"	plate	FoldPl	1900							180
Wizard Special 4x5"	4x5"	plate	FoldPl	1900							180

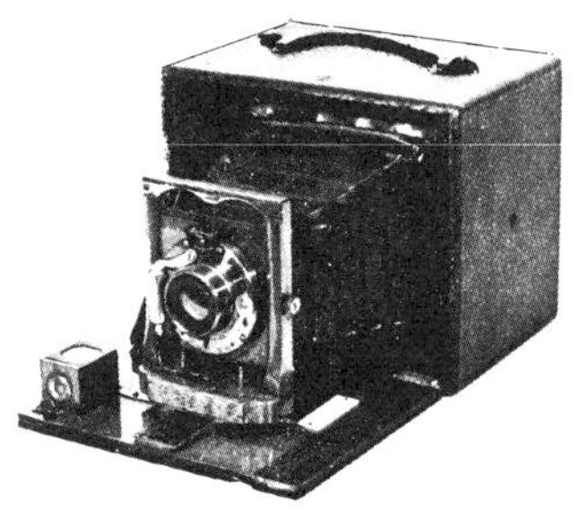

Bo-Peep, Model B 4x5"

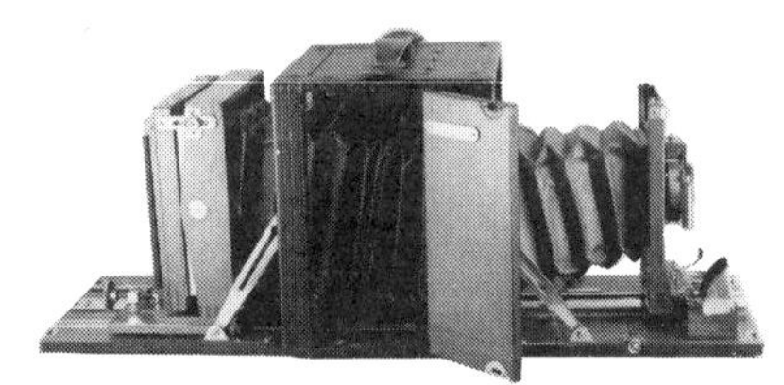

Long Focus Wizard

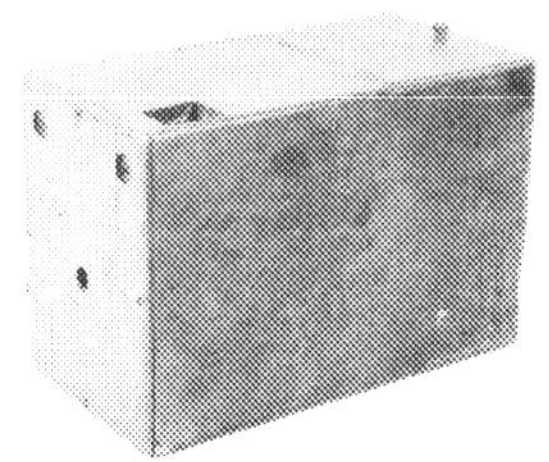

Night Hawk Detective (wood)

MODEL	FORMAT	FILM	TYPE	Year	LENS	Apert	FL	SHUTTER	SPEEDS	ILLUS	U.S.$
Wizard Wide Angle	4x5"	plate	FoldPl	1900							130
...(unknown)											
Maniga 13x14mm	13x14mm	Roll	Submin	1930	Meniscus				I	Mc299	290
Maniga 3x4	3x4cm	127	RigidRo	1930				Maniga		Mc299	250
Maniga Manetta	3x4cm	127	RigidRo	1930	Laack Poloyt	4.5	50mm	Manetta	25-100		300
...MARION & CO., LTD. - London											
Academy 1¼x1¼"	1¼x1¼"	plate	MagBox	1885	Rapid Rectilinear				T,I	A3247	3200
Academy 3¼x4¼"	3¼x4¼"	plate	MagBox	1885	Rapid Rectilinear				T,I		3200
Cambridge 3¼x4¼"	3¼x4¼"	plate	Field	1901	Rapid Rectilinear			Thornton-Pickard			310
Cambridge 4¼x6½"	4¼x6½"	plate	Field	1901	Rapid Rectilinear			Thornton-Pickard			310
Cambridge 6½x8½"	6½x8½"	plate	Field	1901	Rapid Rectilinear			Thornton-Pickard			310
Durham 4¼x6½"	4¼x6½"	plate	Field	1904	Rapid Rectilinear			Thornton-Pickard			310
Durham 6½x8½"	6½x8½"	plate	Field	1904	Rapid Rectilinear			Thornton-Pickard			310
Field camera	6½x8½"	plate	Tailboard	1887	Rapid Rectilinear					A1365	400
Krugener's Book Camera	4x4cm	plate	Disguised	1889	achromatic	12	65mm	guillotine	T,I		5000
Metal Miniature 3x3	3x3cm	plate	Submin	1884	Petzval	5.6	55mm	guillotine	T,I	A3244	4000
Metal Miniature 5x5	5x5cm	plate	NFPl	1884	Petzval	5.6		guillotine	T,I	A3250	3600
Metal Miniature 4¼x6½"	4¼x6½"	plate	NFPl	1884	Petzval	5.6		guillotine	T,I		3500
Modern	3½x4¾"	plate	FoldPl	1898	achromatic				T,I		200
Modern	3½x4¾"	plate	FoldPl	1898	Rapid Rectilinear				T,I		200
Parcel Detective	3¼x4¼"	plate	Disguised	1885	achromatic					Mc300	6100
Perfection 6½x8½"	6½x8½"	plate	Field	1890	Dallm. R.R.	8					540
Perfection 10x12"	10x12"	plate	Field	1890	Dallm. R.R.	8		Thornton-Pickard			540
Perfection 12x15"	12x15"	plate	Field	1890	Dallm. R.R.	8					540
Radial Hand Camera	3¼x4¼"	plate	MagBox	1890				guillotine		Mc300	900
Soho Reflex 4.5x6	4.5x6cm	plate	LgSLR	1909	Ross Xpres	4.5	3.5"	focal plane			670
Soho Reflex 2½x3½"	2½x3½"	plate	LgSLR	1909	Tessar	4.5	4"	focal plane			250
Soho Reflex 3¼x4¼"	3¼x4¼"	plate	LgSLR	1909	Ross Xpres	3.5	5.5"	focal plane		A556	250
Soho Reflex 3½x5½"	3½x5½"	plate	LgSLR	1909	Ross Xpres	4.5		focal plane			250
Soho Reflex 4¾x6½"	4¾x6½"	plate	LgSLR	1909	Dagor	6.8	210mm	focal plane			250
Soho Stereo Reflex	9x14cm	plate	SterRefl	1909	Goerz			focal plane		Mc300	1000
Soho Stereo Trop. Reflex	3½x5½"	plate	SterRefl	1909	Ross Homocentric	6.8	5"	focal plane			11000
Soho Tropical Reflex	2½x3½"	plate	LgSLR	1909	Dalmac	3.5		focal plane			2500
Soho Tropical Reflex	3¼x4¼"	plate	LgSLR	1909	Dalmac	3.5		focal plane		Mc300	2600
Soho Tropical Reflex	3½x4¾"	plate	LgSLR	1909	Dalmac	3.5		focal plane			2600
...(unknown)											
Marlboro	13x17mm	110	Disguised	1989	Meniscus				I	Mc300	50
...MARSHAL OPTICAL WORKS - Japan											
Marshall Press	6x9cm	120/2	MedRF	1966	Nikkor-Q	3.5	105mm	Seiko	1-500	Mc301	650
...MARUSO TRADING CO. - Japan											
Spy-14	14x14mm	Roll	Submin	1965	Meniscus				I,B		90
Top Camera	14x14mm	Roll	Submin	1965	Meniscus				I,B	Mc301	60

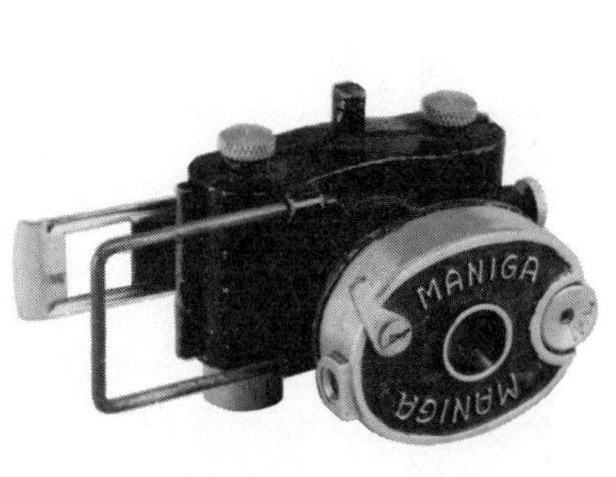

Maniga 13x14mm

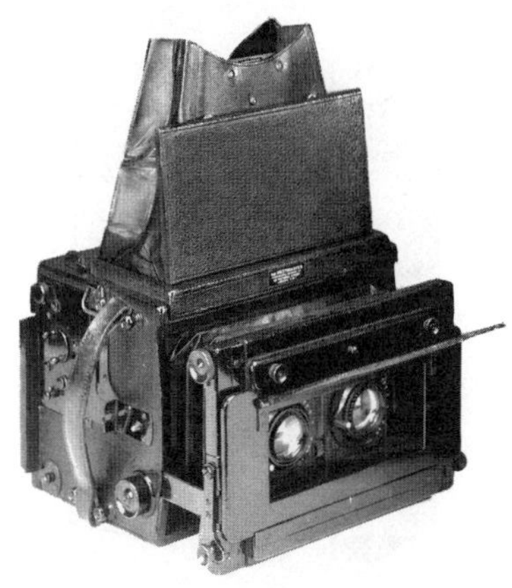

Soho Stereo Reflex

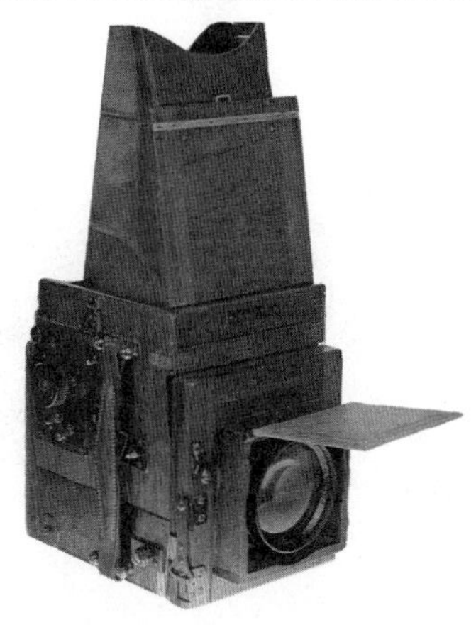

Soho Tropical Reflex

MODEL	FORMAT	FILM	TYPE	Year	LENS	Apert	FL	SHUTTER	SPEEDS	ILLUS	U.S.$
Top II Camera (black)	14x14mm	Roll	Submin	1965	Meniscus				I,B		70
Top II Camera (grey)	14x14mm	Roll	Submin	1965	Meniscus				I,B	Mc301	60
...MARYNEN - Brussels											
Studio camera	18x24cm	plate	Studio	1910	Eurynar	4.5	360mm				1100
...MASON (Perry Mason & Co.) - Boston											
Argus Repeating Camera	3¼x4¼"	plate	Disguised	1890						Mc301	2500
Companion	4x5"	plate	Tailboard	1886	achromatic						180
Harvard	2½x3½"	plate	MetBx	1890	Meniscus						150
Phoenix Dollar Camera	4.5x6cm	plate	MetBx	1890						Mc301	150
...MATSUSHITA ELECTRIC - Japan											
National C-300 EF	24x36mm	35mm	35vf	1985		5.6	38mm		1/150		30
National C-310 EF	24x36mm	35mm	35vf	1987	Panasonic	5.6	38mm		1/150		40
National C-320 EF	24x36mm	35mm	35vf	1987	Panasonic	5.6	35mm		1/150		50
National C-500 AF (black)	24x36mm	35mm	35AF	1985		3.8	35mm	programmed	30-500		70
National C-500 AF (red)	24x36mm	35mm	35AF	1985		3.8	35mm	programmed	30-500		70
National C-510 AF	24x36mm	35mm	35AF	1987	Panasonic	3.8	35mm	programmed	30-500		50
National C-600 AF	24x36mm	35mm	35AF	1985	Panasonic	3.2	35mm	programmed	30-500		50
National C-600 AF DX	24x36mm	35mm	35AF	1987	Panasonic	3.2	35mm	programmed	30-500		50
National C-700 AF	24x36mm	35mm	35AF	1985		2.8	35mm	programmed	2-500		40
National C-D700 AF	24x36mm	35mm	35AF	1985		2.8	35mm	programmed	2-500		50
Panasonic C-225 EF (black)	24x36mm	35mm	35vf	1990	Panasonic	5.6	38mm		1/150		30
Panasonic C-225 EF (red)	24x36mm	35mm	35vf	1990	Panasonic	5.6	38mm		1/150		30
Panasonic C-300 EF	24x36mm	35mm	35vf	1985		5.6	38mm		1/150		30
Panasonic C-310 EF	24x36mm	35mm	35vf	1987	Panasonic	5.6	38mm		1/150		40
Panasonic C-320 EF	24x36mm	35mm	35vf	1987	Panasonic	5.6	35mm		1/150		50
Panasonic C-325 EF	24x36mm	35mm	35vf	1990	Panasonic	5.6	34mm		1/130		30
Panasonic C-D325 EF	24x36mm	35mm	35vf	1990	Panasonic	5.6	34mm		1/130		40
Panasonic C-330 EF	24x36mm	35mm	35vf	1988	Panasonic	5.6	35mm		1/150		30
Panasonic C-335 EF	24x36/pan	35mm	35vf	1991	Panasonic	8	28mm		1/130		50
Panasonic C-D335 EF	24x36/pan	35mm	35vf	1991	Panasonic	8	28mm		1/130		60
Panasonic C-340 EF (black)	24x36mm	35mm	35vf	1988	Panasonic	4.5	35mm	programmed	30-250		40
Panasonic C-340 EF (red)	24x36mm	35mm	35vf	1988	Panasonic	4.5	35mm	programmed	30-250		40
Panasonic CD340EF (black)	24x36mm	35mm	35vf	1988	Panasonic	4.5	35mm	programmed	30-250		60
Panasonic CD340EF (red)	24x36mm	35mm	35vf	1988	Panasonic	4.5	35mm	programmed	30-250		60
Panasonic C-410 AF	24x36mm	35mm	35AF	1988	Panasonic	3.8	34mm		1/200,1/300		40
Panasonic C-425 AF	24x36mm	35mm	35CAF	1990	Panasonic	3.5	34mm		1/130		50
Panasonic C-D425 AF	24x36mm	35mm	35CAF	1990	Panasonic	3.5	34mm		1/130		60
Panasonic C-426 AF	24x36mm	35mm	35CAF	1993	Panasonic	3.5	34mm		1/130		60
Panasonic C-D426 AF	24x36mm	35mm	35CAF	1993	Panasonic	3.5	34mm		1/130		60
Panasonic C-500 AF (black)	24x36mm	35mm	35AF	1985		3.8	35mm	programmed	30-500		70
Panasonic C-500 AF (red)	24x36mm	35mm	35AF	1985		3.8	35mm	programmed	30-500		70
Panasonic C-510 AF	24x36mm	35mm	35AF	1987	Panasonic	3.8	35mm	programmed	30-500		50

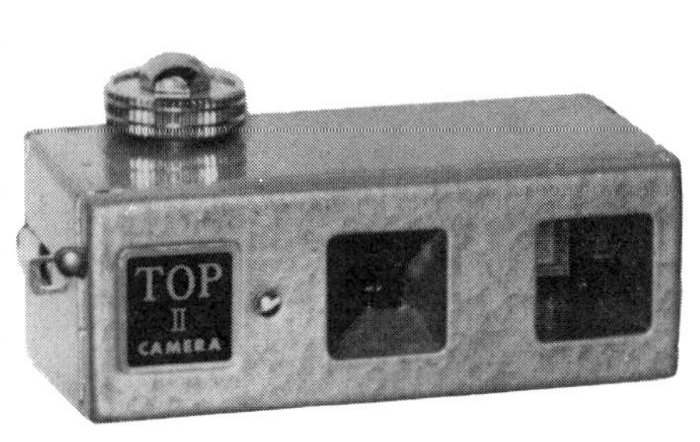

Top II Camera (grey)

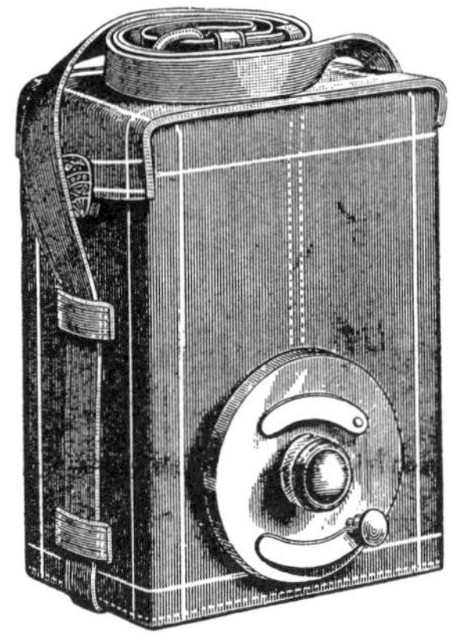

Argus Repeating Camera

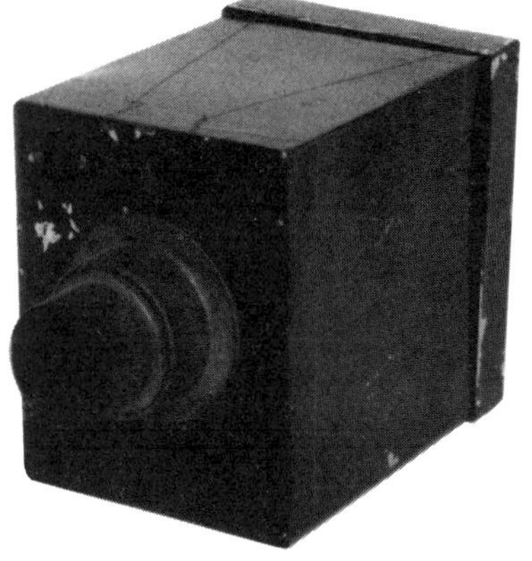

Phoenix Dollar Camera

MODEL	FORMAT	FILM	TYPE	Year	LENS	Apert	FL	SHUTTER	SPEEDS	ILLUS	U.S.$
Panasonic C-520 AF (black)	24x36mm	35mm	35CAF	1988	Panasonic	3.5	35mm	programmed	40-250		50
Panasonic C-520 AF (red)	24x36mm	35mm	35CAF	1988	Panasonic	3.5	35mm	programmed	40-250		50
Panasonic CD520AF (black	24x36mm	35mm	35CAF	1988	Panasonic	3.5	35mm	programmed	40-250		60
Panasonic CD520AF (red)	24x36mm	35mm	35CAF	1988	Panasonic	3.5	35mm	programmed	40-250		60
Panasonic C-525 AF	24x36mm	35mm	35CAF	1990	Panasonic	3.5	35mm	programmed	40-400		70
Panasonic C-D525 AF	24x36mm	35mm	35CAF	1990	Panasonic	3.5	35mm	programmed	40-400		70
Panasonic C-535 AF	24x36/pan	35mm	35CAF	1993	Panasonic	4.5	32mm	programmed	50-125		80
Panasonic C-D535 AF	24x36/pan	35mm	35CAF	1993	Panasonic	4.5	32mm	programmed	50-125		100
Panasonic C-600 AF	24x36mm	35mm	35AF	1985	Panasonic	3.2	35mm	programmed	30-500		50
Panasonic C-600 AF DX	24x36mm	35mm	35AF	1987	Panasonic	3.2	35mm	programmed	30-500		50
Panasonic C-625 AF	24x36mm	35mm	35CAF	1990	Panasonic	3.5	34mm	programmed	80-350		120
Panasonic C-D625 AF	24x36mm	35mm	35CAF	1990	Panasonic	3.5	34mm	programmed	80-350		120
Panasonic C-700 AF	24x36mm	35mm	35AF	1985		2.8	35mm	programmed	2-500		40
Panasonic C-D700 AF	24x36mm	35mm	35AF	1985		2.8	35mm	programmed	2-500		50
Panasonic C-900 ZM	24x36mm	35mm	35afz	1988	Panasonic Zoom	3.5-6.7	35-70	programmed	2-250		160
Panasonic C-D900 ZM	24x36mm	35mm	35afz	1988	Panasonic Zoom	3.5-6.7	35-70	programmed	2-250		190
Panasonic C-2000 ZM	24x36mm	35mm	35afz	1989	Panasonic Zoom	3.8-7.6	38-80	programmed	80-250		150
Panasonic C-D2000 ZM	24x36mm	35mm	35afz	1989	Panasonic Zoom	3.8-7.6	38-80	programmed	80-250		160
Panasonic C-2100 ZM	24x36mm	35mm	35afz	1991	Panasonic Zoom	3.8-7.6	38-80	programmed	5-250		160
Panasonic C-D2100 ZM	24x36mm	35mm	35afz	1991	Panasonic Zoom	3.8-7.6	38-80	programmed	5-250		170
Panasonic C-2200 ZM	24x36mm	35mm	35afz	1993	Panasonic Zoom	4.0-7.6	35-70	programmed	4-300		180
Panasonic C-D2200 ZM	24x36mm	35mm	35afz	1993	Panasonic Zoom	4.0-7.6	35-70	programmed	4-300		180
Panasonic C-3000 ZM	24x36mm	35mm	35afz	1991	Panasonic	3.2-7.7	28-80	programmed	30-250		220
Panasonic C-D3000 ZM	24x36mm	35mm	35afz	1991	Panasonic	3.2-7.7	28-80	programmed	30-250		230
...MAW OF LONDON											
Nustyle	6x9cm	120	FoldRo		achromatic				T,I	Mc301	40
Nustyle Alpha	6x9cm	120	FoldRo		Alphar	11			T,I		50
Nustyle DeLuxe	6x9cm	120	MetBx		Meniscus						30
...MAY, ROBERTS & CO. - London											
Sandringham	8x10.5cm	plate	Field	1900	Wray		5"				270
...MAYFIELD COBB & CO. - London											
Companion	4¼x6½"	plate	Field		Lancaster Portrait			Thornton-Pickard			290
...MAZO (E. Mazo) - Paris											
Field & Studio Camera	9x12cm	plate	Field	1900	Mazo & Magenta	8		Thornton-Pickard		F33	330
Field & Studio Camera	13x18cm	plate	Field	1900	Orthoscope Rapid	8		Thornton-Pickard			330
Foldette	8x11cm	plate	FoldPl	1905	Anastigmat	9	130mm			A1325	370
Graphostéréochrome	6x13cm	plate	StFoldPl	1910	Rapid Rectilinear			guillotine		A2032	2100
Graphostéréochrome	10x15cm	plate	StFoldPl	1910	Rapid Rectilinear			guillotine		F1255	2100
Jumelle Réclame	9x12cm	plate	Jumelle	1903	Extra Rapide Rectinlineare					F1071	130
Stereo camera		plate	StFoldPl		Mazo			Thornton-Pickard			670
...McBEAN - Edinburgh											
Stereo Tourist	9x18cm	plate	Field		Steinh. Antiplanat			Thornton-Pickard	1-225	Mc302	650

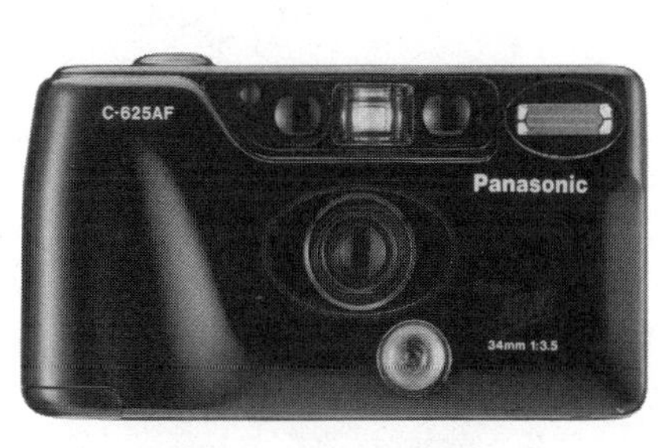

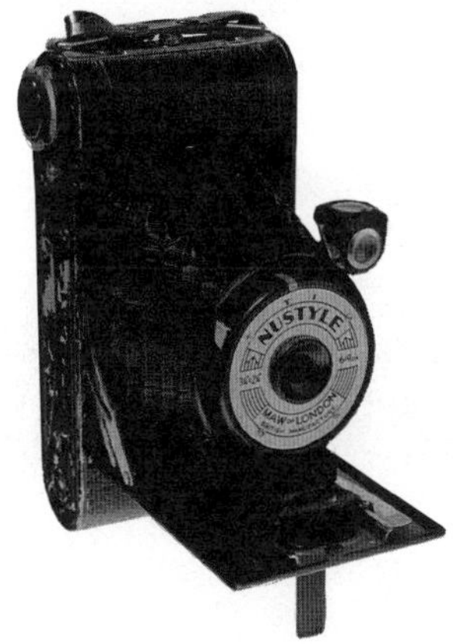

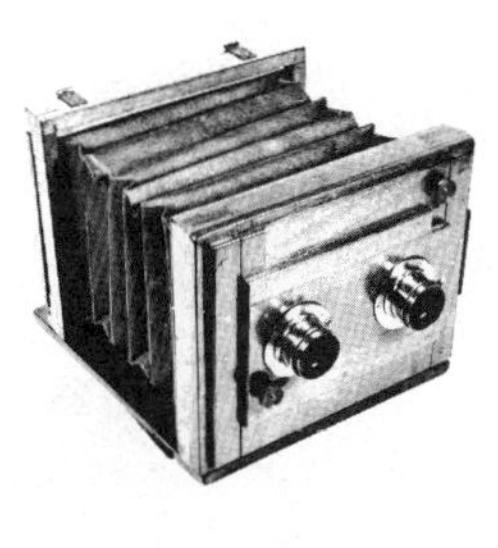

Panasonic C-625 AF | **Nustyle** | **McBean Stereo Tourist**

MODEL	FORMAT	FILM	TYPE	Year	LENS	Apert	FL	SHUTTER	SPEEDS	ILLUS	U.S.$
...McGHIE and CO. - Glasgow, Scotland											
Detective camera	3¼x4¼"	plate	DetectivBox	1885	Wray						1000
Field camera	4¼x6½"	plate	Field								370
Studio View		plate	Studio	1890	Wray						330
...MEAGHER - London											
Field camera	13x18cm	plate	Field	1910	Ross					A2948	550
Tailboard camera 3¼x4¼"	3¼x4¼"	plate	Field	1870	Voigtländer					Mc302	560
Tailboard camera 6½x8½"	6½x8½"	plate	Field	1870	Voigtländer						650
Tourist Binocular (stereo)	8x16cm	plate	StFoldPl	1900	Thornton-Pickard					A1758	630
Tourist Binocular (stereo)	9x18cm	plate	StFoldPl	1870	Dallmeyer						650
Wet plate bellows camera	4¼x6½"	WetPl	WetPlate	1860	Dallmeyer					A1363	1300
Wet plate bellows camera	6½x8½"	WetPl	WetPlate	1860	Dallmeyer						1200
Wet plate bellows camera	10x12"	WetPl	WetPlate	1860	Ross						1200
Wet plate sliding-box ¼-pl.	3¼x4¼"	WetPl	WetPlate	1860						Mc303	2200
Wet plate sliding-box ½-pl.	5½x7½"	WetPl	WetPlate	1860							2300
Wet plate studio camera	18x24cm	WetPl	WetPlate	1865	Dallmeyer					A2960	1200
...(unknown)											
Mecum	9x12cm	plate	SterBox	1910	Mensicus				I,T		180
...MEGURO KOGAKU KOGYO CO. - Japan											
Melcon	24x36mm	35mm	35rf	1955	Hexar	3.5	50mm	focal plane	1-500	Mc303	1700
...MEJIRO OPTICAL WORKS											
Honor S1 500	24x36mm	35mm	35rf	1956	Hexar	3.5	50mm	focal plane	1-500		1100
Honor S1 1000	24x36mm	35mm	35rf	1957	Honor	1.9	50mm	focal plane	1-1000		1200
...MENDEL (Georges Mendel) - Paris											
Detective camera	3¼x4¼"	plate	DetectivBox		Rapid Rectilinear						200
Triomphant	9x12cm	plate	MagBox	1900	Ortho-Symmetrical			Extra Rapid			200
...MENDOZA (Marco Mendoza) - Paris											
Argus	9x12cm	plate	MagBox	1895	achromatic					F895	420
Field camera 6.5x9	6.5x9cm	plate	Field	1887	achromatic					F106	310
Field camera 9x12	9x12cm	plate	Field	1887	achromatic					F106	240
Field camera 11x16.5	11x16.5	plate	Field	1910	achromatic						160
Field camera 12x18	12x18cm	plate	Field	1910	achromatic						160
...MEOPTA - Prerov, Czechoslovakia											
Flexaret	6x6cm	120	TLR	1948	Mirar	3.5	80mm	Prontor II			100
Flexaret Automat	6x6cm	120	TLR	1962	Belar	3.5	80mm	Prestor	1-500		100
Flexaret II	6x6cm	120	TLR	1953	Mirar	3.5	80mm	Prontor II			70
Flexaret III	6x6cm	120	TLR	1950	Belar	3.5	80mm	Prontor II			70
Flexaret IIIa	6x6cm	120	TLR	1950	Belar	3.5	80mm	Prontor-SVS			70
Flexaret IV	6x6cm	120	TLR	1953	Belar	3.5	80mm	Prontor-SVS			70
Flexaret IVa	6x6cm	120	TLR	1953	Belar	3.5	80mm	Prontor-SVS		Mc303	70
Flexaret V	6x6cm	120	TLR	1958	Belar	3.5	80mm	Prontor-SVS			80
Flexaret Va	6x6cm	120	TLR	1959	Belar	3.5	80mm	Prontor-SVS			90

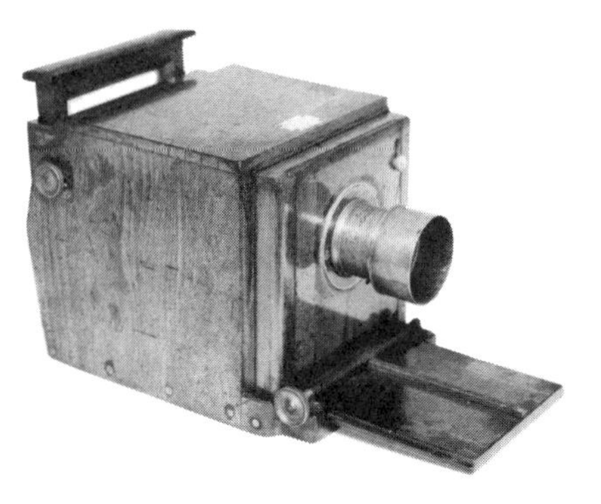

Meagher Wet Plate sliding box

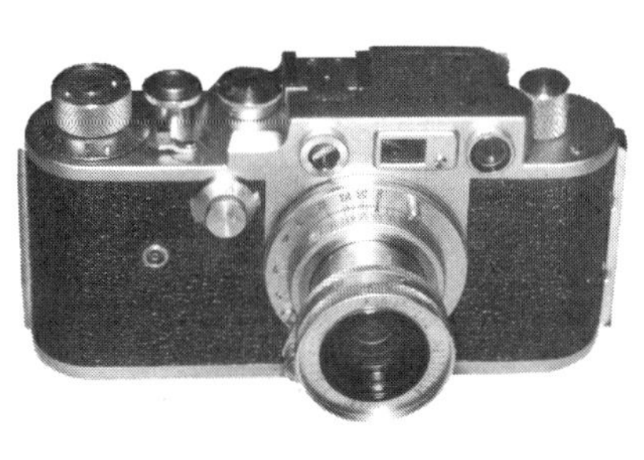

Meguro Melcon

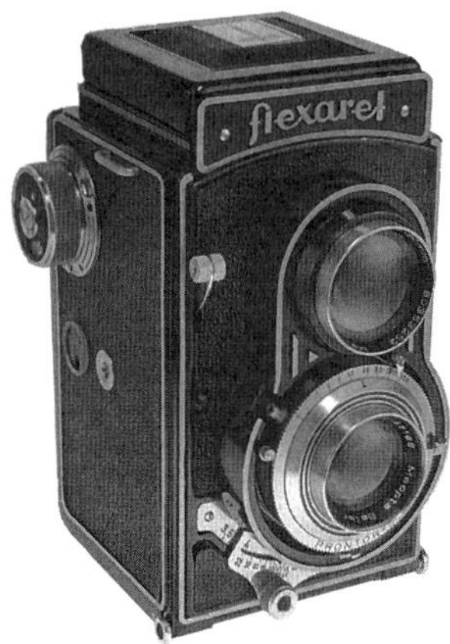

Meopta Flexaret IVa

MODEL	FORMAT	FILM	TYPE	Year	LENS	Apert	FL	SHUTTER	SPEEDS	ILLUS	U.S.$
Flexaret VI	6x6cm	120	TLR	1959	Belar	3.5	80mm	Prontor-SVS		HK445	100
Flexaret VII	6x6cm	120	TLR	1960	Belar	3.5	80mm	Prontor-SVS			100
Iskra	6x6cm	120	HzFoldRo	1948	Mirar	4.4	80mm	Compur-Rapid			80
Magnola	13x18cm	plate	FoldPl	1960	Belar	4.5	210mm				350
Mikroma	11x14mm	16mm	Submin	1949	Mirar	3.5	20mm		25-200	Mc303	120
Mikroma (black)	11x14mm	16mm	Submin	1960	Mirar	3.5	20mm		25-200	Mc303	540
Mikroma II (beige)	11x14mm	16mm	Submin	1964	Mirar	3.5	20mm		5-400	HK641	160
Mikroma II (green)	11x14mm	16mm	Submin	1964	Mirar	3.5	20mm		5-400	Mc303	160
Mikronette	11x14mm	16mm	Submin	1956	Mirar	3.5	20mm		25-200	HK640	340
Mikronette 240	11x14mm	16mm	Submin	1958	Mirar	3.5	20mm		25-200		1700
Milona I	6x6cm	120	HzFoldRo	1950	Mirar	4.5	80mm	Compur-Rapid	1-500		50
Milona II	6x6cm	120	HzFoldRo	1950	Mirar	4.5	80mm	Prontor II			50
Opema + 50/2	24x32mm	35mm	35rf	1950	Opemar	2	50mm	focal plane	25-500		160
Opema + 50/2.8	24x32mm	35mm	35rf	1950	Belar	2.8	50mm	focal plane	25-500		200
Opema II	24x32mm	35mm	35rf	1951	Belar	2.8	50mm	focal plane	25-500		120
Optineta	24x36mm	35mm	35vf	1960	Belar	3.5	45mm	Metax	1-400		50
Pankopta	55x237	120	Panoramic	1961	Belar	4.5	105mm	Spezial	2-200	HK707	900
Stereo 35	12x13mm	35mm	35Ster	1960	Mirar	3.5	25mm	Spezial	1/60	Mc303	180
Stereo Mikroma	12x13mm	16mm	SterMiniat	1961	Mirar	3.5	25mm		5-100	HK531	210
Stereo Mikroma II (black)	12x13mm	16mm	SterMiniat	1965	Mirar	3.5	25mm		5-100		220
Stereo Mikroma II (grey)	12x13mm	16mm	SterMiniat	1965	Mirar	3.5	25mm		5-100		220
...MERIDIAN INSTRUMENT CORP.											
Meridian	4x5"	plate	Press	1947	Kodak Ektar			Supermatic		Mc304	230
...MERKEL (Ferdinand Merkel) - Tharandt, Germany											
Elite	6.5x9cm	plate	FoldPl	1924	Anastigmat	6.8	120mm		1-100		70
Metharette	3x4cm	Roll	StrutRo	1931	Trinar	2.9	50mm	Rim-Compur			120
Metharis	9x12cm	plate	FoldPl	1938	Xenar	4.5	130mm				580
Minerva 6.5x9	6.5x9cm	plate	FoldPl	1925	Selar	4.5	105mm				520
Minerva 9x12	9x12cm	plate	FoldPl	1925	Trioplan	4.5	135mm	Ibsor			560
Phõnix Tropical	9x12cm	plate	FoldPl	1925	Tessar	4.5	135mm				420
Tropical Klapp	9x12cm	plate	FoldPl	1930	Sytar	4.5	135mm				370
...MERTEN (Gebr. Merten) - Gummersbach, Germany											
Merit Box (black)	4x6.5cm	127	BakeliteBox	1935	Rodenstock	11	75mm		T,I		120
Merit Box (brown)	4x6.5cm	127	BakeliteBox	1935	Rodenstock	11	75mm		T,I		280
Merit Box (red)	4x6.5cm	127	BakeliteBox	1935	Rodenstock	11	75mm		T,I		280
Merit Box 6x9	6x9cm	120	BakeliteBox	1935	Rodenstock	11			Z,M	HK89	70
...(unknown)											
Metascoflex	6x6cm		TLR	1950	Metar	3.5	80mm			Mc304	90
...METRO MFG. CO. - New Jersey											
Metro Flash	6x9cm	120	FoldRo								30
Metro Flash No. 1 Deluxe	6x9cm	120	FoldRo							Mc304	30
Metro Super Reflex	6x6cm	120	TLR-Box	1949	Supra Color	5.6		Skymatic	1-100		50

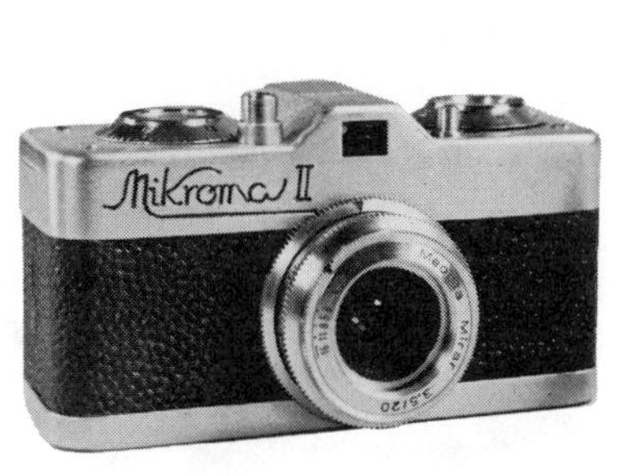

Mikroma II (green)

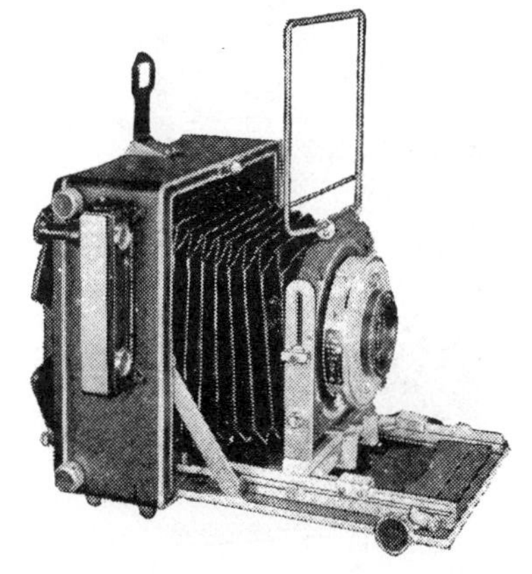
Meridian

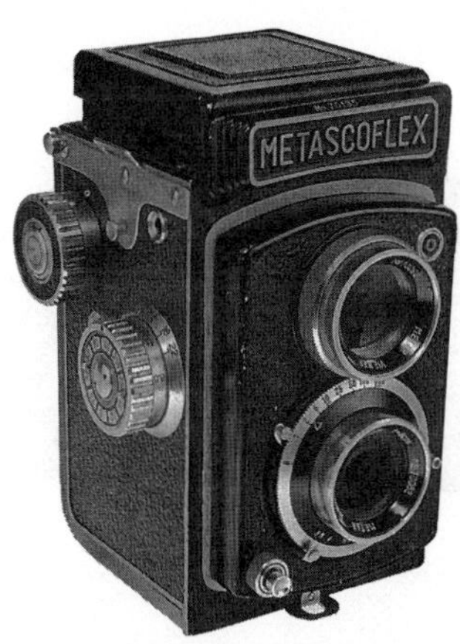

Metascoflex

MODEL	FORMAT	FILM	TYPE	Year	LENS	Apert	FL	SHUTTER	SPEEDS	ILLUS	U.S.$
...METROPOLITAN INDUSTRIES - Chicago, IL, USA											
Clix 120	6x9cm	120	MetBx						I,T		10
Clix 120 Elite	6x9cm	120	MetBx						I,T		10
Clix Deluxe	3x4cm	127	Minicam	1947						A3055	10
Clix Miniature	28x40mm	828	Minicam								10
Clix-Master	3x4cm	127	Minicam								10
Clix-O-Flex	3x4cm	127	TLR-Box	1947						A649	20
Clix-Supreme	4x4cm	127	Minicam	1946						Mc304	20
Metro-Cam	3x4cm	127	Minicam							Mc304	10
Metro-Flex	3x4cm	127	TLR-Box						I,T	Mc304	20
Rival 120 Elite	6x9cm	120	MetBx						I,T		10
...MEYER (Ferd. Franz Meyer) - Blasewitz-Dresden, Germany											
Field Camera (English style)		plate	Field	1900	Rapid Rectilinear						240
Field Camera (revolving bel	13x18cm	plate	Field	1900	Meyer Lysioskop						200
Field Camera (square bel.)	13x18cm	plate	Field	1900	Universal Aplanat	7.8					160
Field Camera 18x24	18x24cm	plate	Field	1900	Rod. Dopp. Anast.	7.7	360mm				200
Stereo field camera	8.5x17cm	plate	StFoldPl	1897	Rapid Aplanat						630
...MEYER (Hugo Meyer & Co.) Görlitz											
Megor	3x4cm	Roll	StrutRo	1931	Trioplan	3.5	50mm	Compur	1-300	Mc305	120
Silar 4.5x6	4.5x6cm	plate	FoldPl	1930	Plasmat			Compur			270
Silar 6.5x9	6.5x9cm	plate	FoldPl	1930	Plasmat			Compur			260
Silar 9x12	9x12cm	plate	FoldPl	1930	Plasmat			Compur			240
Silar 10x15	10x15cm	plate	FoldPl	1930	Plasmat			Compur			240
Silar 13x18	13x18cm	plate	FoldPl	1930	Plasmat			Compur			240
...MEYER & KASTE											
Field camera		plate	Field	1900	Universal Aplanat	8					220
...(unknown)											
MF Stereo Camera	45x107	plate	StFoldPl		Luminor	6.8					210
...(unknown)											
Micro 110	13x17mm	110	110snap	1986	Meniscus						10
Micro 110 "Baby 110"	13x17mm	110	110snap	1986	Meniscus						10
Micro 110 "Mini 110"	13x17mm	110	110snap	1986	Meniscus						10
Micro 110 (Cat & Fish)	13x17mm	110	110snap	1988	Meniscus					Mc305	30
Micro 110 (Cheeseburger)	13x17mm	110	110snap	1988	Meniscus						30
Micro 110 (Panda)	13x17mm	110	110snap	1988	Meniscus					Mc305	30
...MICRO PRECISION PRODUCTS - England											
Microcord, Mk 1	6x6cm	120	TLR	1952	Ross Xpres	3.5	75mm	Epsilon		Mc305	130
Microcord, Mk 2	6x6cm	120	TLR	1952	Ross Xpres	3.5	75mm	Prontor-SVS	1-300		120
Microflex	6x6cm	120	TLR	1959	Horinor	3.5	75mm	Prontor-SVS	1-300		140
...(unknown)											
Microntaflex	6x6cm	120	TLR	1955	Horinor	3.5	75mm	NKS			140
Microntaflex Special	6x6cm	120	TLR	1957	Alpha Anast.	3.5	75mm	NFG	1-250		200

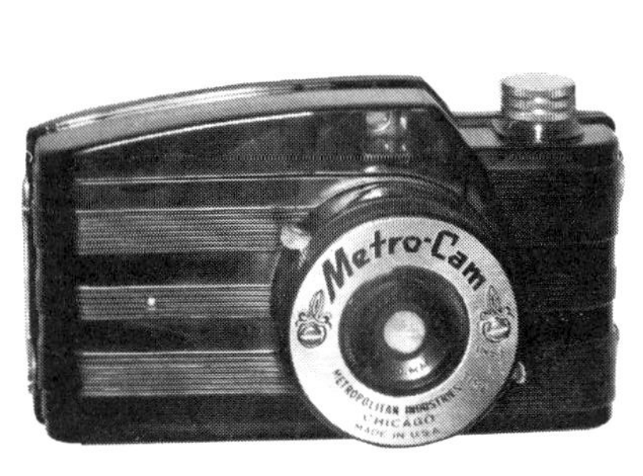

Metro-Cam

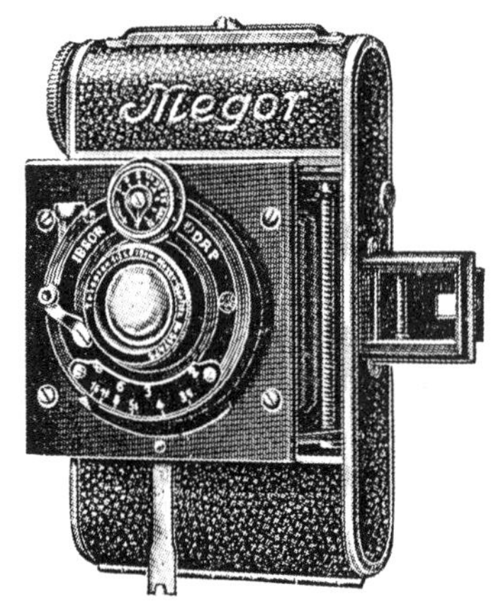

Megor

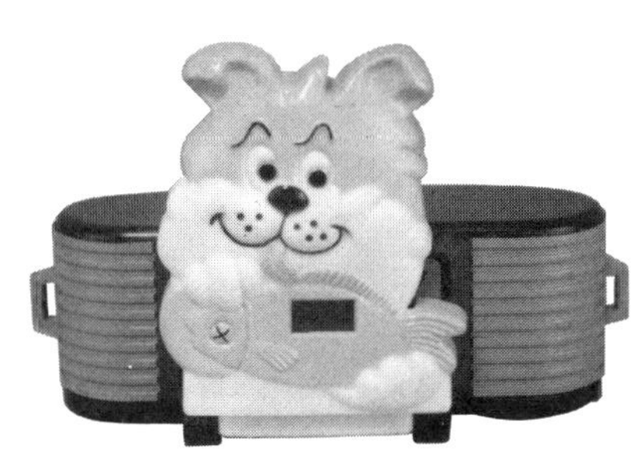
Micro 110 (Cat & Fish)

MODEL	FORMAT	FILM	TYPE	Year	LENS	Apert	FL	SHUTTER	SPEEDS	ILLUS	U.S.$
...MIDDL OPTICAL WORKS LTD. (OTOWA OPTICAL WORKS) - Japan											
Middl 120-A	4.5x6cm	120	HzFoldRo	1952	Seriter Anastigmat	3.5	80mm	NKS	1-200		90
...MIDDLEMISS (W. Middlemiss) - Bradford, England											
Middlemiss Patent Camera		plate	Field	1887						Mc305	380
...MIKUT (Oskar Mikut) - Dresden											
Mikut Color Camera	4x4cm	plate	3-Color	1937	Mikutar	3.5	130mm	Compur	1-200	Mc305	3700
...(unknown)											
Miloflex	6x6cm		TLR		Tri-Lausar	3.5	80mm				100
...MIMOSA AG - Dresden											
Mimosa I	24x36mm	35mm	35vf	1947	Trioplan	2.9	50mm	Compur-Rapid		Mc305	70
Mimosa II	24x36mm	35mm	35vf	1950	Meritar	2.9	50mm	Prontor-S		Mc306	60
Mimosa II	24x36mm	35mm	35vf	1950	Trioplan	2.9	50mm	Velax			60
...MINOLTA - Osaka, Japan											
Minolta 16 Mod. I (black)	10x14mm	16mm	Submin	1957	Rokkor	3.5	25mm		25-200		90
Minolta 16 Mod. I (blue)	10x14mm	16mm	Submin	1957	Rokkor	3.5	25mm		25-200		220
Minolta 16 Mod. I (chrome)	10x14mm	16mm	Submin	1957	Rokkor	3.5	25mm		25-200	Mc312	90
Minolta 16 Mod. I (gold)	10x14mm	16mm	Submin	1957	Rokkor	3.5	25mm		25-200		180
Minolta 16 Mod. I (green)	10x14mm	16mm	Submin	1957	Rokkor	3.5	25mm		25-200		180
Minolta 16 Mod. I (red)	10x14mm	16mm	Submin	1957	Rokkor	3.5	25mm		25-200		160
Minolta 16 Mod. II (black)	10x14mm	16mm	Submin	1957	Rokkor	3.5	25mm		25-200		70
Minolta 16 Mod. II (blue)	10x14mm	16mm	Submin	1957	Rokkor	3.5	25mm		25-200		220
Minolta 16 Mod. II (chrome)	10x14mm	16mm	Submin	1957	Rokkor	3.5	25mm		25-200	A928	100
Minolta 16 Mod. II (gold)	10x14mm	16mm	Submin	1957	Rokkor	3.5	25mm		25-200		180
Minolta 16 Mod. II (green)	10x14mm	16mm	Submin	1957	Rokkor	3.5	25mm		25-200		180
Minolta 16 Mod. II (red)	10x14mm	16mm	Submin	1957	Rokkor	3.5	25mm		25-200		160
Minolta 16 EE	10x14mm	16mm	Submin	1962	Rokkor	2.8	25mm		30-500	Mc313	40
Minolta 16 EE II	10x14mm	16mm	Submin	1963	Rokkor	2.8	25mm		50,200	Mc313	30
Minolta 16 MG	10x14mm	16mm	Submin	1966	Rokkor	2.8	20mm		30-250	Mc313	40
Minolta 16 MG-S (black)	12x17mm	16mm	Submin	1969	Rokkor	2.8	23mm		30-500		50
Minolta 16 MG-S (silver)	12x17mm	16mm	Submin	1969	Rokkor	2.8	23mm		30-500	A1946	50
Minolta 16 Mod. P	10x14mm	16mm	Submin	1960	Rokkor	3.5	25mm		100	Mc312	30
Minolta 16 PS	10x14mm	16mm	Submin	1964	Rokkor				30,100	Mc313	30
Minolta 16 QT (black)	12x17mm	16mm	Submin	1972	Rokkor	3.5	23mm		30-250	Mc313	40
Minolta 16 QT (chrome)	12x17mm	16mm	Submin	1972	Rokkor	3.5	23mm		30-250		50
Minolta 24 Rapid	24x24mm	35mm	35rf	1965	Rokkor	2.8	32mm		30-250	Mc310	100
Minolta 35 (Type A)	24x32mm	35mm	35rf	1947	Super Rokkor	2.8	45mm	focal plane	1-500		500
Minolta 35 (Type B)	24x33.5	35mm	35rf	1948	Super Rokkor	2.8	45mm	focal plane	1-500		360
Minolta 35 (Type C)	24x34mm	35mm	35rf	1949	Super Rokkor	2.8	45mm	focal plane	1-500		300
Minolta 35 (Type D)	24x34mm	35mm	35rf	1949	Super Rokkor	2.8	45mm	focal plane	1-500		300
Minolta 35 Mod. E	24x34mm	35mm	35rf	1951	Super Rokkor	2.8	45mm	focal plane	1-500	Mc308	310
Minolta 35 Mod. F	24x34mm	35mm	35rf	1952	Super Rokkor	2.8	45mm	focal plane	1-500		310
Minolta 35 Mod. II	24x34mm	35mm	35rf	1953	Super Rokkor	2.8	45mm	focal plane	1-500	A2134	310

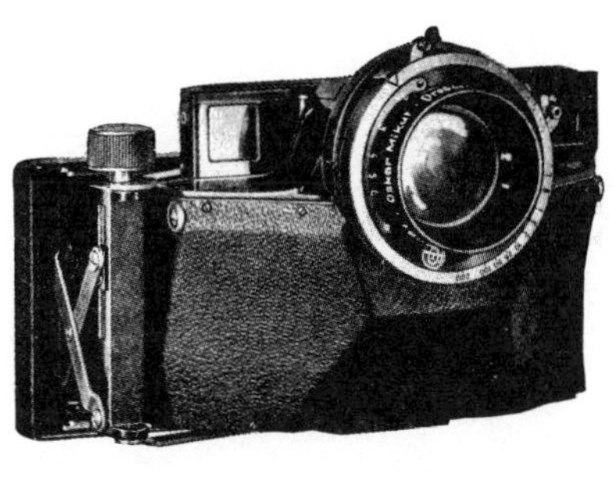

Mikut Color Camera

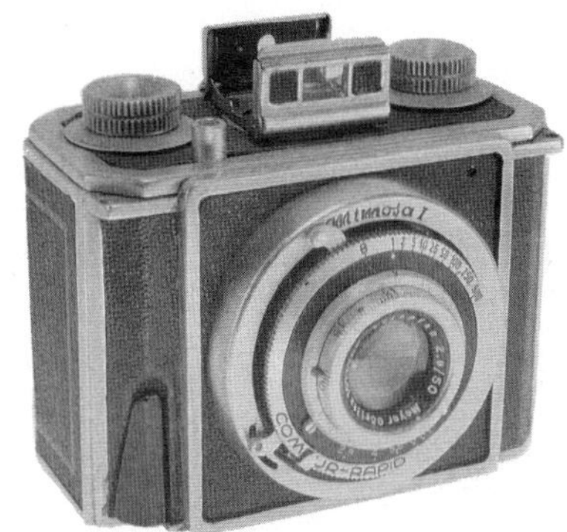

Mimosa I

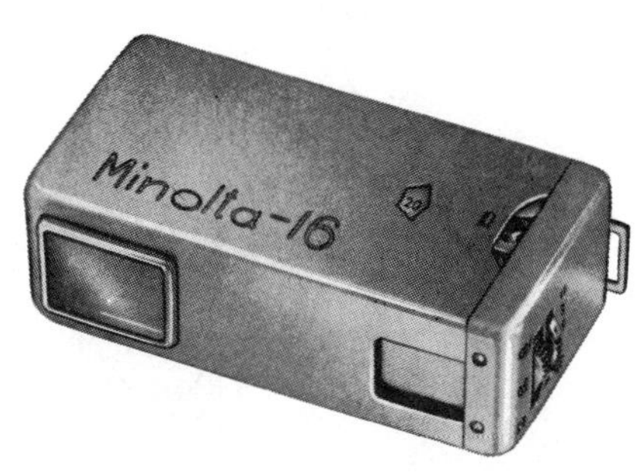

Minolta 16 Mod. I

MODEL	FORMAT	FILM	TYPE	Year	LENS	Apert	FL	SHUTTER	SPEEDS	ILLUS	U.S.$
Minolta 35 Mod. II	24x34mm	35mm	35rf	1953	Super Rokkor	2.0	5cm	focal plane	1-500	Mc308	220
Minolta 35 Mod. IIB	24x36mm	35mm	35rf	1958	Super Rokkor	1.8	50mm	focal plane	1-500	Mc308	460
Minolta 110 Zoom SLR	13x17mm	110	110SLR	1976	Rokkor	4.5	25-50	electronic	10-1/1000	Mc313	90
Minolta 110 Zoom Mark II	13x17mm	110	110SLR	1979	Z-Rokkor Macro	3.5	25-67	electronic	4-1000		220
Minolta 5000 body	24x36mm	35mm	35slr	1986	body only	---	---	electronic	4-1/2000		130
Minolta 5000 + 50/1.4	24x36mm	35mm	35slr	1986	AF	1.4	50mm	electronic	4-1/2000		220
Minolta 7000 body	24x36mm	35mm	35slr	1986	body only	---	---	electronic	30-1/2000		150
Minolta 7000 + 50/1.4	24x36mm	35mm	35slr	1986	AF	1.4	50mm	electronic	30-1/2000		230
Minolta 9000 body	24x36mm	35mm	35slr	1986	body only	---	---	electronic	30-1/4000		280
Minolta 9000 + 50/1.4	24x36mm	35mm	35slr	1986	AF	1.4	50mm	electronic	30-1/4000		350
Minolta A	24x36mm	35mm	35rf	1955	Rokkor	3.5	45mm	Optiper MX		Mc308	120
Minolta A	24x36mm	35mm	35rf	1955	Rokkor	3.5	45mm	Citizen MV			120
Minolta A2	24x36mm	35mm	35rf	1955	Rokkor	3.5	45mm	Citizen			70
Minolta A2	24x36mm	35mm	35rf	1957	Rokkor	3.5	45mm	Citizen MV			70
Minolta A2	24x36mm	35mm	35rf	1958	Rokkor	2.8	45mm	Optiper MXV		Mc308	70
Minolta A3	24x36mm	35mm	35rf	1959	Rokkor	2.8	45mm		1-500		60
Minolta A5 (1/500)	24x36mm	35mm	35rf	1960	Rokkor	2.8	45mm	Citizen MVL	1-500	Mc308	50
Minolta A5 (1/1000)	24x36mm	35mm	35rf	1960	Rokkor	2.8	45mm	Citizen MVL	1-1000		70
Minolta A5 (1/1000)	24x36mm	35mm	35rf	1960	Rokkor	2.0	45mm	Citizen MVL	1-1000		70
α-3xi body	24x36mm	35mm	35slr	1991	body only	---	---	electronic	30-1/2000		160
α-3xi + 28-80	24x36mm	35mm	35slr	1991	AF Zoom	4.0-5.6	28-80	electronic	30-1/2000		250
α-5xi body	24x36mm	35mm	35slr	1991	body only	---	---	electronic			260
α-5xi + 28-80	24x36mm	35mm	35slr	1991	AF Zoom	4.0-5.6	28-80	electronic			350
α-7xi body	24x36mm	35mm	35slr	1991	body only	---	---	electronic	30-1/8000		350
α-7xi + 28-105	24x36mm	35mm	35slr	1991	AF Zoom	3.5-4.5	28-105	electronic	30-1/8000		600
α-9xi body	24x36mm	35mm	35slr	1992	body only	---	---	electronic	30-1/12000		530
α-9xi + 24-85	24x36mm	35mm	35slr	1992	AF Zoom	3.5-4.5	24-85	electronic	30-1/12000		700
α-303si body	24x36mm	35mm	35slr	1994	body only	---	---	electronic	30-1/2000		220
α-303si + 50/1.4	24x36mm	35mm	35slr	1994	AF	1.4	50mm	electronic	30-1/2000		310
α-707si body	24x36mm	35mm	35slr	1994	body only	---	---	electronic	30-1/8000		480
α-707si + 24-85	24x36mm	35mm	35slr	1994	AF Zoom	3.5-4.5	24-85	electronic	30-1/8000		700
α-3700i body	24x36mm	35mm	35slr	1988	body only	---	---	electronic	4-1/1000		100
α-3700i + 50/1.7	24x36mm	35mm	35slr	1988	AF	1.7	50mm	electronic	4-1/1000		130
α-5000 body	24x36mm	35mm	35slr	1986	body only	---	---	electronic	4-1/2000		130
α-5000 + 50/1.4	24x36mm	35mm	35slr	1986	AF	1.4	50mm	electronic	4-1/2000		220
α-5700i body	24x36mm	35mm	35slr	1989	body only	---	---	electronic	4-1/2000		170
α-5700i + 50/1.7	24x36mm	35mm	35slr	1989	AF	1.7	50mm	electronic	4-1/2000		200
α-7000 body	24x36mm	35mm	35slr	1986	body only	---	---	electronic	30-1/2000		150
α-7000 + 50/1.4	24x36mm	35mm	35slr	1986	AF	1.4	50mm	electronic	30-1/2000		230
α-7700i body	24x36mm	35mm	35slr	1988	body only	---	---	electronic	30-1/4000		220
α-7700i + 50/1.7	24x36mm	35mm	35slr	1988	AF	1.7	50mm	electronic	30-1/4000		270
α-8700i body	24x36mm	35mm	35slr	1990	body only	---	---	electronic	30-1/8000		330

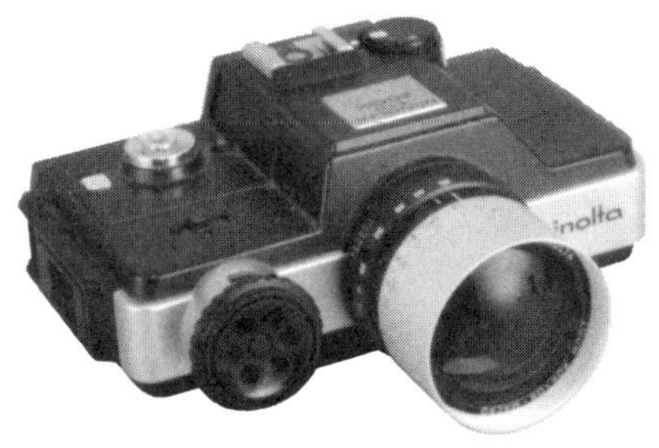

Minolta 110 Zoom SLR

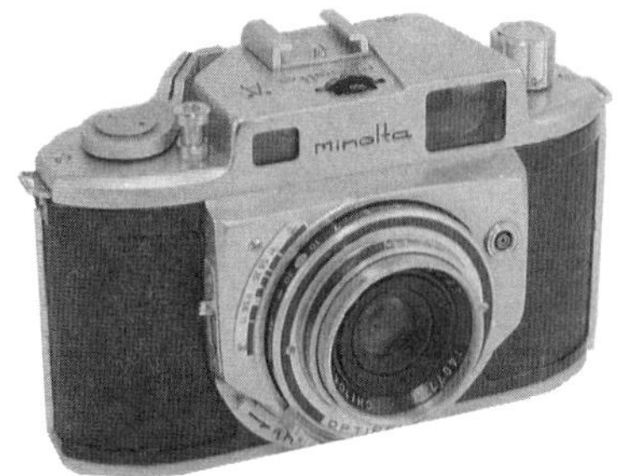

Minolta A

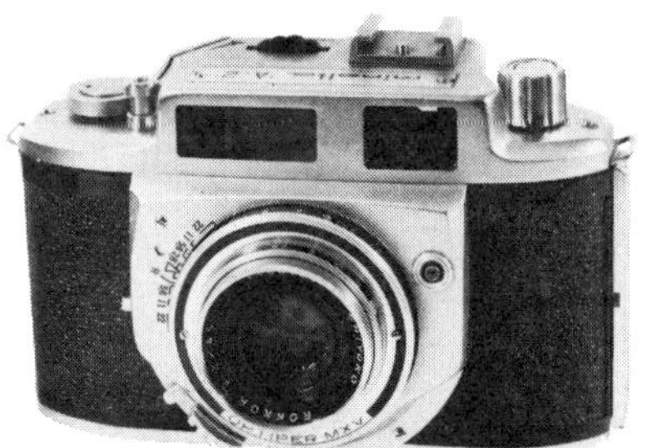

Minolta A2

MODEL	FORMAT	FILM	TYPE	Year	LENS	Apert	FL	SHUTTER	SPEEDS	ILLUS	U.S.$
α-8700i + 50/1.7	24x36mm	35mm	35slr	1990	AF	1.7	50mm	electronic	30-1/8000		360
α-9000 body	24x36mm	35mm	35slr	1986	body only	---	---	electronic	30-1/4000		280
α-9000 + 50/1.4	24x36mm	35mm	35slr	1986	AF	1.4	50mm	electronic	30-1/4000		350
Aerial camera 100-SK	11.5x16	Roll	Aerial	1940	Rokkor	4.5	200mm		1-400		900
AF-C	24x36mm	35mm	35CAF	1982	Minolta	2.8	35mm	programmed	8-430		100
AF-DL	24x36mm	35mm	35AF-BiF	1988	Minolta	3.5,5.6	35/50	programmed			120
AF-DL Quartz Date	24x36mm	35mm	35af	1988	Minolta	3.5,5.6	35/50	programmed			130
AF-E	24x36mm	35mm	35af	1984	Minolta	3.5	35mm	programmed			80
AF-EII	24x36mm	35mm	35af	1987	Minolta	4.5	35mm				90
AF-EII Date	24x36mm	35mm	35af	1988	Minolta	4.5	35mm				100
AF-S	24x36mm	35mm	35af	1983	Minolta	2.8	35mm	programmed	8-625		60
AF-SP	24x36mm	35mm	35af	1989	Minolta	4.5	35mm				70
AF-Sv	24x36mm	35mm	35af	1984	Minolta	2.8	35mm	programmed	8-625	A3503	100
AF-T	24x36mm	35mm	35AF-BiF	1986	Minolta	2.8,4.3	38/60	programmed	40-500		120
AF-Tele	24x36mm	35mm	35AF-BiF	1986	Minolta	2.8,4.3	38/60	programmed	40-500		120
AF-Tele 60	24x36mm	35mm	35AF-BiF	1989	Minolta	4.0,7.0	38/60				110
AF-Tele Super	24x36mm	35mm	35AF-BiF	1988	Minolta	2.8,5.6	38/80	programmed	8-400		130
AF-Z	24x36mm	35mm	35af	1986	Minolta	2.8	35mm	programmed	40-800		70
AF-Zoom 65	24x36mm	35mm	35afz	1989	Minolta	4.5-7.2	38-65				130
AF-Zoom 90	24x36mm	35mm	35afz	1989	Minolta	3.5-7.5	38-90	programmed	8-400		170
AF101R	24x36mm	35mm	35CAF	1994	Minolta	5.6	28mm		1/125		70
Minolta AL	24x36mm	35mm	35rf	1961	Rokkor	2.0	45mm	Citizen	1-1000	Mc309	60
Minolta AL-2	24x36mm	35mm	35rf	1963	Rokkor	1.8	45mm	Citizen	1-500		60
Minolta AL-E	24x36mm	35mm	35rf	1969	Rokkor	1.8	40mm	Citizen	8-500		80
Minolta AL-F	24x36mm	35mm	35rf	1968	Rokkor	2.7	38mm	Citizen	30-500	Mc309	70
Minolta AL-S	24x36mm	35mm	35rf	1965	Rokkor	1.8	40mm	Citizen	1-500		140
Apex 90	24x36mm	35mm	35afz	1993	Minolta	3.5-7.7	38-90	programmed			140
Apex 90 Date	24x36mm	35mm	35afz	1993	Minolta	3.5-7.7	38-90	programmed			140
Apex 105	24x36mm	35mm	35afz	1990	Minolta	4-6.7	35-105	programmed	2-500		170
Apex 105 Date	24x36mm	35mm	35afz	1991	Minolta	4-6.7	35-105	programmed	2-500		200
Apex ZF900	24x36mm	35mm	35afz	1993	Minolta	3.5-7.7	38-90	programmed			150
Apex Zoom 70c	24x36mm	35mm	35afz	1992	Minolta	3.5-6.5	35-70	programmed			130
Apex Zoom 70c Date	24x36mm	35mm	35afz	1992	Minolta	3.5-6.5	35-70	programmed			130
Arcadia	6.5x9cm	plate	VtFoldPl	1931	Helostar	4.5	105mm	Lidex	1-200	Mc306	350
Auto Minolta (1/200)	6.5x9cm	plate	StrutPl	1934	Actiplan Anast.	4.5	105mm	Crown	1-200	Mc308	260
Auto Minolta (1/400)	6.5x9cm	plate	StrutPl	1934	Tessar	4.5	105mm	Crown Rapid	1-400		340
Auto Semi Minolta	4.5x6cm	120	FoldRo	1937	Promar Anast.	3.5	75mm	Crown	1-400	Mc307	170
Autocord	6x6cm	120	TLR	1955	Rokkor	3.5	75mm	Optiper MX	1-500	Mc312	100
Autocord CdS I	6x6cm	120	TLR	1964	Rokkor	3.5	75mm	Citizen	1-500	Mc312	180
Autocord CdS II	6x6cm	120/2	TLR	1965	Rokkor	3.5	75mm	Citizen MVL	1-500		180
Autocord CdS III	6x6cm	120	TLR	1965	Rokkor	3.5	75mm	Citizen MVL	1-500		160
Autocord II	6x6cm	120/2	TLR	1965	Rokkor	3.5	75mm	Citizen MVL	1-500		200

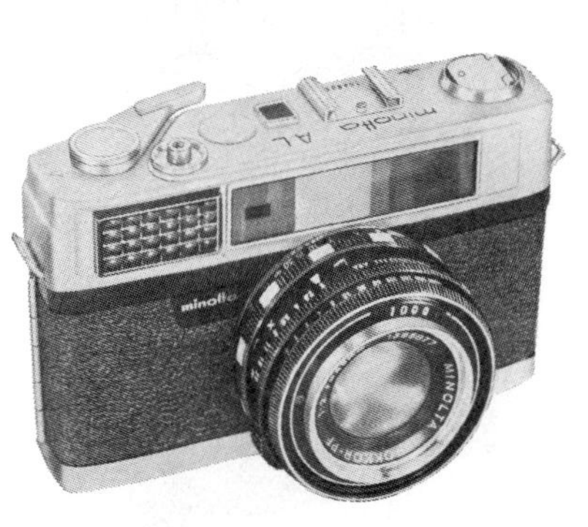

Minolta AL

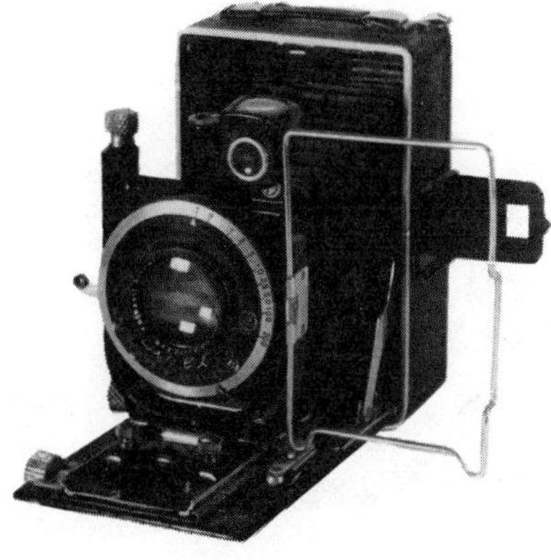

Arcadia

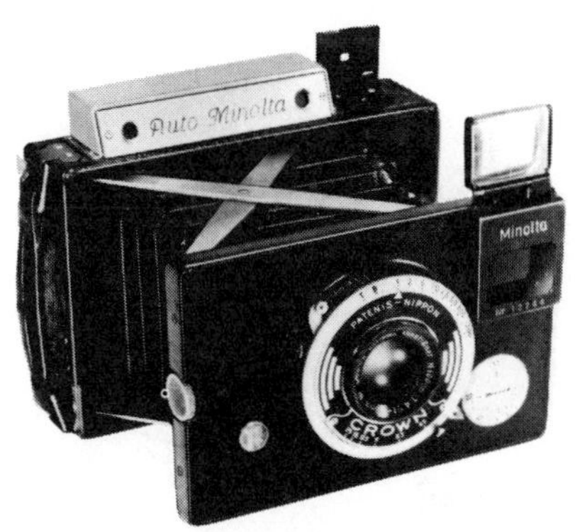

Auto Minolta (1/200)

MODEL	FORMAT	FILM	TYPE	Year	LENS	Apert	FL	SHUTTER	SPEEDS	ILLUS	U.S.$
Autocord III	6x6cm	120	TLR	1965	Rokkor	3.5	75mm	Citizen MVL	1-500		270
Autocord L	6x6cm	120	TLR	1955	Rokkor	3.5	75mm	Seikosha-MX	1-500	Mc312	100
Autocord LMX	6x6cm	120	TLR	1955	Rokkor	3.5	75mm	Seikosha-MX	1-500		100
Autocord RA	6x6cm	120	TLR	1955	Rokkor	3.5	75mm	Optiper MX	1-500		100
Minolta Automat	6x6cm	120	TLR	1939	Promar	3.5	75mm	Crown	1-300	Mc312	160
Autopak 400-X	28x28mm	126	126vf	1972	Rokkor	8	34mm	programmed	45,90		30
Autopak 500	28x28mm	126	126vf	1966	Rokkor	2.8	38mm	programmed	40,90		30
Autopak 550	28x28mm	126	126vf	1969	Rokkor	2.8	38mm	programmed	40,90		30
Autopak 600-X	28x28mm	126	126vf	1971	Rokkor	2.8	38mm	programmed	40,90		30
Autopak 700	28x28mm	126	126vf	1966	Rokkor	2.8	38mm	programmed	30-250		20
Autopak 800	28x28mm	126	126vf	1969	Rokkor	2.8	38mm	programmed	40,90	A1174	50
Minolta Autopress	6.5x9cm	plate	StrutPl	1937	Promar Anast.	3.5	105mm	Crown Rapid	1-400	Mc308	260
Minolta Autowide	24x36mm	35mm	35rf	1958	Rokkor	2.8	35mm	Optiper MVL	1-500	Mc309	80
Baby Minolta	4x6.5cm	127	TelescRo	1935	Coronar Anast.	8	80mm		25-100	Mc307	120
Minolta Best Mod. I	4x6.5cm	127	TelescRo	1934	Coronar Anast.	8	75mm	Marble	25-100	A3049	100
Minolta Best Mod. II	4x6.5cm	127	TelescRo	1934	Coronar Anast.	5.6	75mm	Marble	25-100	Mc307	100
Minolta Best Mod. III	4x6.5cm	127	TelescRo	1934	Coronar Anast.	4.5	80mm	Marble	25-100		100
CL	24x36mm	35mm	35rf	1973	Rokkor	2	40mm	electronic	1-1000		510
CLE	24x36mm	35mm	35rf	1983	M-Rokkor	2	40mm	electronic	1-1000	A2169	900
Courrèges ac101	8x10mm	Disc	Disc	1983	Minolta	2.8	12.5mm		1/100,1/20	A3385	100
Courrèges ac301	8x10mm	Disc	Disc	1983	Minolta	2.8	12.5mm		1/100,1/20	A3384	80
Disc-5	8x10mm	Disc	Disc	1983	Minolta	2.8	12.5mm		1/100,1/200		30
Disc-7	8x10mm	Disc	Disc	1983	Minolta	2.8	12.5mm		1/100,1/200		40
Disc-K	8x10mm	Disc	Disc	1983	Minolta	2.8	12.5mm		1/100,1/200		50
Disc-S	8x10mm	Disc	Disc	1983	Minolta	2.8	12.5mm		1/100,1/200		50
Dynax 2xi body	24x36mm	35mm	35slr	1991	body only	---	---	electronic	30-1/2000		140
Dynax 2xi + 28-80	24x36mm	35mm	35slr	1991	AF Zoom	4.0-5.6	28-80	electronic	30-1/2000		220
Dynax 3xi body	24x36mm	35mm	35slr	1991	body only	---	---	electronic	30-1/2000		160
Dynax 3xi + 28-80	24x36mm	35mm	35slr	1991	AF Zoom	4.0-5.6	28-80	electronic	30-1/2000		250
Dynax 5xi body	24x36mm	35mm	35slr	1991	body only	---	---	electronic			260
Dynax 5xi + 28-80	24x36mm	35mm	35slr	1991	AF Zoom	4.0-5.6	28-80	electronic			350
Dynax 7xi body	24x36mm	35mm	35slr	1991	body only	---	---	electronic	30-1/8000		350
Dynax 7xi + 28-105	24x36mm	35mm	35slr	1991	AF Zoom	3.5-4.5	28-105	electronic	30-1/8000		600
Dynax 9xi body	24x36mm	35mm	35slr	1992	body only	---	---	electronic	30-1/12000		530
Dynax 9xi + 24-85	24x36mm	35mm	35slr	1992	AF Zoom	3.5-4.5	24-85	electronic	30-1/12000		700
Dynax 500si body	24x36mm	35mm	35slr	1994	body only	---	---	electronic	30-1/2000		220
Dynax 500si + 50/1.4	24x36mm	35mm	35slr	1994	AF	1.4	50mm	electronic	30-1/2000		310
Dynax 700si body	24x36mm	35mm	35slr	1994	body only	---	---	electronic	30-1/8000		480
Dynax 700si + 24-85	24x36mm	35mm	35slr	1994	AF Zoom	3.5-4.5	24-85	electronic	30-1/8000		700
Dynax 3000i body	24x36mm	35mm	35slr	1988	body only	---	---	electronic	4-1/1000		100
Dynax 3000i + 50/1.7	24x36mm	35mm	35slr	1988	AF	1.7	50mm	electronic	4-1/1000		130
Dynax 5000i body	24x36mm	35mm	35slr	1989	body only	---	---	electronic	4-1/2000		170

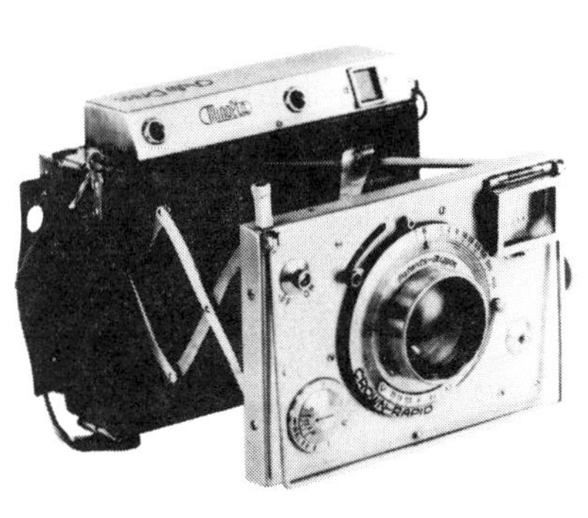

Minolta Autopress

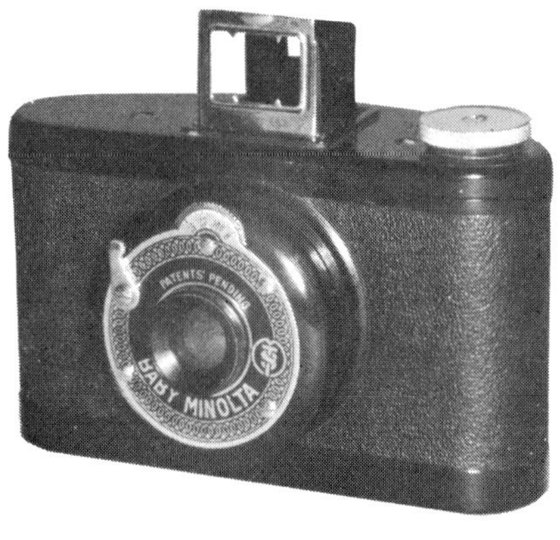

Baby Minolta

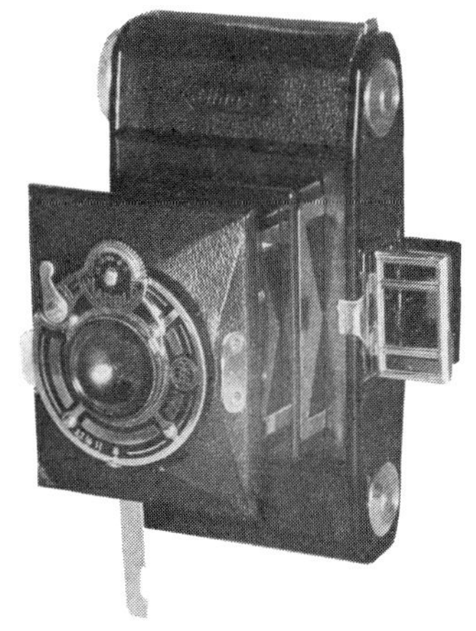

Minolta Best Mod. II

MODEL	FORMAT	FILM	TYPE	Year	LENS	Apert	FL	SHUTTER	SPEEDS	ILLUS	U.S.$
Dynax 5000i + 50/1.7	24x36mm	35mm	35slr	1989	AF	1.7	50mm	electronic	4-1/2000		200
Dynax 7000i body	24x36mm	35mm	35slr	1988	body only	---	---	electronic	30-1/4000		220
Dynax 7000i + 50/1.7	24x36mm	35mm	35slr	1988	AF	1.7	50mm	electronic	30-1/4000		270
Dynax 8000i body	24x36mm	35mm	35slr	1990	body only	---	---	electronic	30-1/8000		330
Dynax 8000i + 50/1.7	24x36mm	35mm	35slr	1990	AF	1.7	50mm	electronic	30-1/8000		360
Dynax SPxi body	24x36mm	35mm	35slr	1991	body only	---	---	electronic	30-1/2000		170
Dynax SPxi + 28-80	24x36mm	35mm	35slr	1991	AF Zoom	4.0-5.6	28-80	electronic	30-1/2000		290
Eaton	6.5x9cm	plate	VtFoldPl	1931	Coronar	4.5	105mm	Crown-A	1-200		270
Electro Shot	24x36mm	35mm	35rf	1965	Rokkor QF	1.8	40mm		16-500	Mc310	50
Minolta ER body	24x36mm	35mm	35slr	1963	body only	---	---		30-500		150
Minolta ER + 45/2.8	24x36mm	35mm	35slr	1963	Rokkor	2.8	45mm		30-500	Mc311	160
F10	24x36mm	35mm	35C	1995	Minolta	5.6	35mm		1/125		40
F20R	24x36mm	35mm	35C	1995	Minolta	5.6	28mm		1/125		50
Freedom I	24x36mm	35mm	35vf	1985	Minolta	4.5	35mm	programmed			70
Freedom II	24x36mm	35mm	35af	1984	Minolta	3.5	35mm	programmed			80
Freedom III	24x36mm	35mm	35af	1986	Minolta	2.8	35mm	programmed	40-800		70
Freedom 50N	24x36mm	35mm	35C	1993	Minolta	4.5	35mm	programmed	1/125		40
Freedom 100	24x36mm	35mm	35vf	1987	Minolta	4.5	35mm				60
Freedom 100 Date	24x36mm	35mm	35vf	1987	Minolta	4.5	35mm				60
Freedom 101	24x36mm	35mm	35vf	1989	Minolta	4.5	35mm				60
Freedom 101 Date	24x36mm	35mm	35vf	1989	Minolta	4.5	35mm				70
Freedom 200	24x36mm	35mm	35af	1987	Minolta	4.5	35mm				90
Freedom 200 Date	24x36mm	35mm	35af	1988	Minolta	4.5	35mm				100
Freedom 202	24x36mm	35mm	35af	1989	Minolta	4.5	35mm				70
Freedom Action Zoom	24x36mm	35mm	35afz	1993	Minolta	4.3-6.4	38-60	programmed			100
Freedom AF10R	24x36mm	35mm	35CAF	1995	Minolta	4.5	30mm	programmed			50
Freedom AF35	24x36mm	35mm	35af	1990	Minolta	4.5	35mm	programmed			80
Freedom AF35 Date	24x36mm	35mm	35af	1990	Minolta	4.5	35mm	programmed			100
Freedom AF35R	24x36mm	35mm	35af	1993	Minolta	4.5	35mm	programmed			60
Freedom Dual	24x36mm	35mm	35AF-BiF	1988	Minolta	3.5,5.6	35/50	programmed			120
Freedom Dual 60	24x36mm	35mm	35AF-BiF	1989	Minolta	4.0,7.0	38/60				110
Freedom Dual C	24x36mm	35mm	35AF-BiF	1992	Minolta	4.0,5.6	28/40	programmed			110
Freedom Dual Quartz Date	24x36mm	35mm	35af	1988	Minolta	3.5,5.6	35/50	programmed			130
Freedom Escort	24x36mm	35mm	35CAF	1993	Minolta	3.5	34mm	programmed			70
Freedom Holiday	24x36mm	35mm	35C	1995	Minolta	4.5	35mm	programmed	1/35,1/100		50
Freedom Tele	24x36mm	35mm	35AF-BiF	1988	Minolta	2.8,5.6	38/80	programmed	8-400		130
Freedom Vista	24x36mm	35mm	35Pan	1993	Minolta	4.5	24mm	programmed	4-200		110
Freedom Zoom 65	24x36mm	35mm	35afz	1989	Minolta	4.5-7.2	38-65				130
Freedom Zoom 70c	24x36mm	35mm	35afz	1992	Minolta	3.5-6.5	35-70	programmed			130
Freedom Zoom 70c Date	24x36mm	35mm	35afz	1992	Minolta	3.5-6.5	35-70	programmed			130
Freedom Zoom 70EX	24x36mm	35mm	35afz	1995	Minolta	3.8-7.2	35-70	programmed			110
Freedom Zoom 90	24x36mm	35mm	35afz	1989	Minolta	3.5-7.5	38-90	programmed	8-400		170

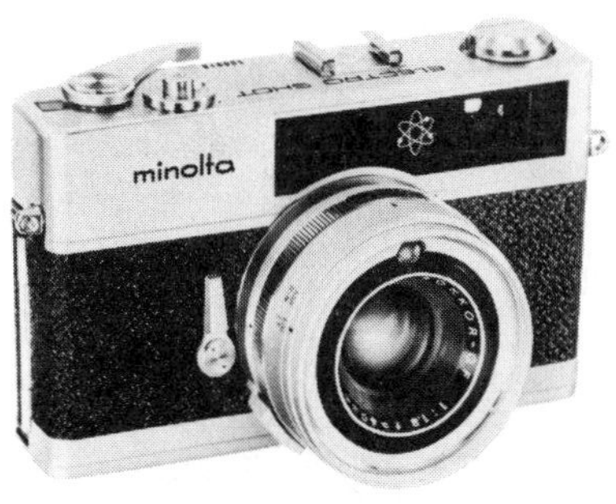

Electro Shot

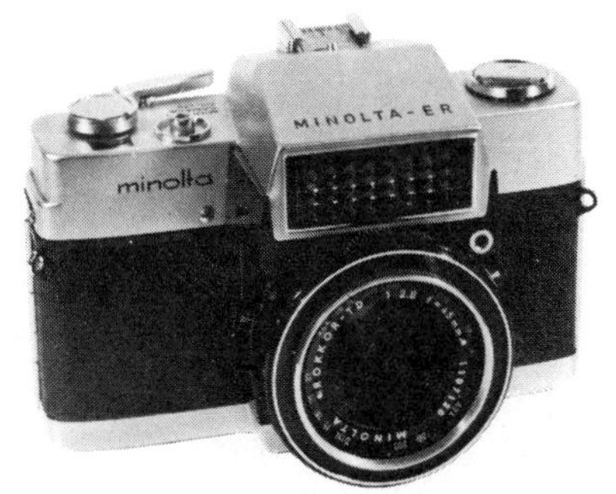

Minolta ER

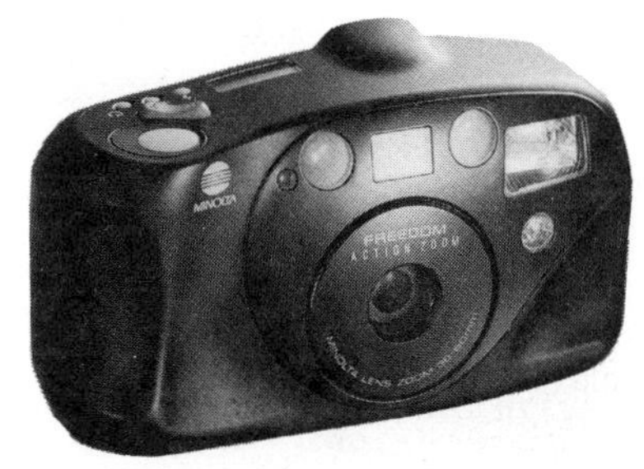

Freedom Action Zoom

MODEL	FORMAT	FILM	TYPE	Year	LENS	Apert	FL	SHUTTER	SPEEDS	ILLUS	U.S.$
Freedom Zoom 90c	24x36mm	35mm	35afz	1993	Minolta	3.5-7.7	38-90	programmed			140
Freedom Zoom 90c Date	24x36mm	35mm	35afz	1993	Minolta	3.5-7.7	38-90	programmed			140
Freedom Zoom 90EX	24x36mm	35mm	35afz	1993	Minolta	3.5-7.7	38-90	programmed			150
Freedom Zoom 105EX	24x36mm	35mm	35afz	1994	Minolta	3.5-9.2	38-105	programmed			190
Freedom Zoom 105i	24x36mm	35mm	35afz	1990	Minolta	4-6.7	35-105	programmed	2-500		170
Freedom Zoom 105i Date	24x36mm	35mm	35afz	1991	Minolta	4-6.7	35-105	programmed	2-500		200
Freedom Zoom 135EX	24x36mm	35mm	35afz	1994	Minolta	3.5-9.2	38-135	programmed			240
FS-35	24x36mm	35mm	35vf	1990	Minolta	4.5	35mm		1/125		50
FS-35II	24x36mm	35mm	35C	1993	Minolta	4.5	35mm	programmed	1/125		40
FS-E	24x36mm	35mm	35vf	1985	Minolta	4.5	35mm	programmed			70
FS-EII	24x36mm	35mm	35vf	1987	Minolta	4.5	35mm				60
FS-EII Date	24x36mm	35mm	35vf	1987	Minolta	4.5	35mm				60
FS-EIII	24x36mm	35mm	35vf	1989	Minolta	4.5	35mm				60
FS-EIII Date	24x36mm	35mm	35vf	1989	Minolta	4.5	35mm				70
Happy	6.5x9cm	plate	VtFoldPl	1931	Zeiss Anastigmat	4.5	105mm	Compur	1-200		350
Hi-Matic	24x36mm	35mm	35rf	1962	Rokkor PF	2.0	45mm	Citizen	30-500	Mc309	50
Hi-Matic (Ansco Autoset)	24x36mm	35mm	35rf	1962	Rokkor PF	2.8	45mm	Citizen	30-500	Mc310	40
Hi-Matic 5	24x36mm	35mm	35vf	1971	Rokkor	2.7	40mm	Seiko	30-250		50
Hi-Matic 7	24x36mm	35mm	35rf	1963	Rokkor PF	1.8	45mm	Citizen	4-500	Mc310	40
Hi-Matic 7s	24x36mm	35mm	35rf	1966	Rokkor	1.8	45mm	Seiko	4-500		50
Hi-Matic 7sII	24x36mm	35mm	35rf	1977	Rokkor	1.7	40mm	Copal	8-500		70
Hi-Matic 9	24x36mm	35mm	35rf	1966	Rokkor PF	1.7	45mm			Mc310	60
Hi-Matic 11	24x36mm	35mm	35rf	1969	Rokkor	1.7	45mm	Seiko	30-250		80
Hi-Matic AF	24x36mm	35mm	35af	1979	Rokkor	2.8	38mm	Seiko	8-430		60
Hi-matic AF2	24x36mm	35mm	35af	1981	Rokkor	2.8	38mm	programmed	8-430		50
Hi-matic AF2-M	24x36mm	35mm	35af	1982	Rokkor	2.8	38mm	programmed	8-430		80
Hi-matic C	24x36mm	35mm	35vf	1969	Rokkor	2.7	40mm	Seiko	30-250		30
Hi-matic E	24x36mm	35mm	35rf	1971	Rokkor	1.7	40mm	Seiko	2-1/1000		70
Hi-matic F	24x36mm	35mm	35rf	1972	Rokkor	2.7	38mm	programmed	4-1/724		40
Hi-matic G	24x36mm	35mm	35vf	1974	Rokkor	2.8	38mm	programmed	30-650		40
Hi-matic G2	24x36mm	35mm	35vf	1981	Rokkor	2.8	38mm	programmed	60-250		40
Hi-matic GF	24x36mm	35mm	35vf	1982	Rokkor	4	38mm		1/125		60
Hi-matic S	24x36mm	35mm	35vf	1981	Minolta	2.7	38mm	programmed	4-450	A2168	50
Hi-matic S2	24x36mm	35mm	35vf	1981	Minolta	2.8	38mm	programmed	8-430		70
Hi-matic SD	24x36mm	35mm	35vf	1978	Minolta	2.7	38mm	programmed	4-450		100
Hi-matic SD2	24x36mm	35mm	35vf	1979	Minolta	2.8	38mm	programmed	8-430		120
Konan 16	10x14mm	16mm	Submin	1950	Rokkor	3.5	25mm		25-200		140
Konan 16 Stereo	10x14mm	16mm	Submin	1952	Rokkor	3.5	25mm		25-200		1600
Mac 7	24x36mm	35mm	35af	1986	Minolta	2.8	35mm	programmed	40-800		70
Mac-35	24x36mm	35mm	35af	1990	Minolta	4.5	35mm	programmed			80
Mac-35 Date	24x36mm	35mm	35af	1990	Minolta	4.5	35mm	programmed			100
Mac-Auto	24x36mm	35mm	35af	1987	Minolta	4.5	35mm				90

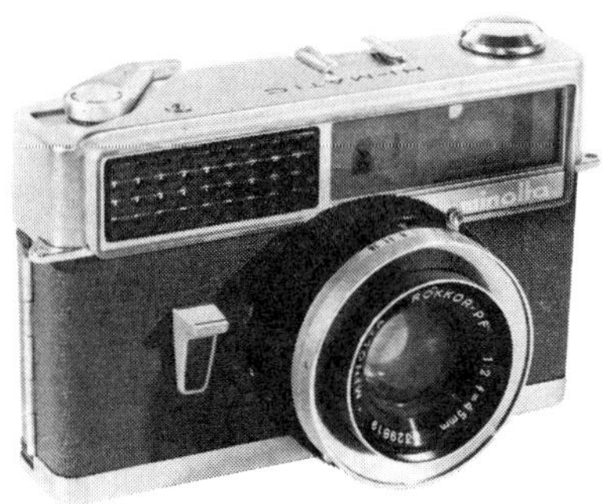

Hi-Matic

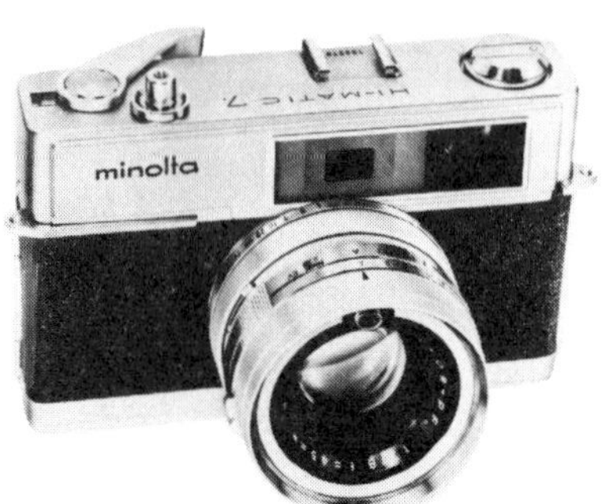

Hi-Matic 7

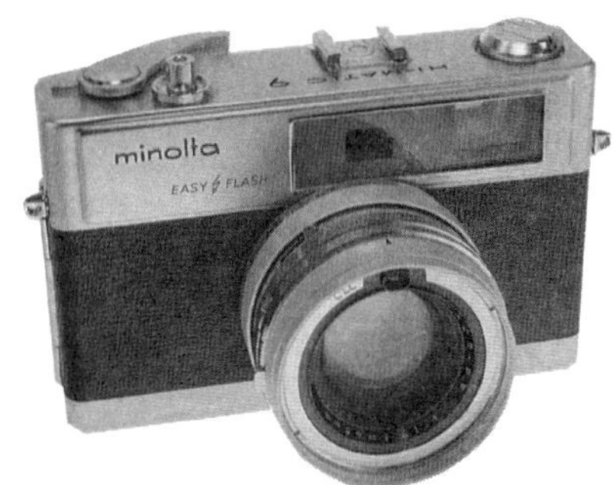

Hi-Matic 9

MODEL	FORMAT	FILM	TYPE	Year	LENS	Apert	FL	SHUTTER	SPEEDS	ILLUS	U.S.$
Mac-Auto Date	24x36mm	35mm	35af	1988	Minolta	4.5	35mm				100
Mac-Dual	24x36mm	35mm	35AF-BiF	1988	Minolta	3.5,5.6	35/50	programmed			120
Mac-Mate	24x36mm	35mm	35af	1989	Minolta	4.5	35mm				70
Mac-Tele	24x36mm	35mm	35AF-BiF	1988	Minolta	2.8,5.6	38/80	programmed	8-400		130
Mac-Tele 60	24x36mm	35mm	35AF-BiF	1989	Minolta	4.0,7.0	38/60				110
Mac-Zoom 65	24x36mm	35mm	35afz	1989	Minolta	4.5-7.2	38-65				130
Mac-Zoom 90	24x36mm	35mm	35afz	1989	Minolta	3.5-7.5	38-90	programmed	8-400		170
Maxxum 2xi body	24x36mm	35mm	35slr	1991	body only	---	---	electronic	30-1/2000		140
Maxxum 2xi + 28-80	24x36mm	35mm	35slr	1991	AF Zoom	4.0-5.6	28-80	electronic	30-1/2000		220
Maxxum 3xi body	24x36mm	35mm	35slr	1991	body only	---	---	electronic	30-1/2000		160
Maxxum 3xi + 28-80	24x36mm	35mm	35slr	1991	AF Zoom	4.0-5.6	28-80	electronic	30-1/2000		250
Maxxum 5xi body	24x36mm	35mm	35slr	1991	body only	---	---	electronic			260
Maxxum 5xi + 28-80	24x36mm	35mm	35slr	1991	AF Zoom	4.0-5.6	28-80	electronic			350
Maxxum 7xi body	24x36mm	35mm	35slr	1991	body only	---	---	electronic	30-1/8000		350
Maxxum 7xi + 28-105	24x36mm	35mm	35slr	1991	AF Zoom	3.5-4.5	28-105	electronic	30-1/8000		600
Maxxum 9xi body	24x36mm	35mm	35slr	1992	body only	---	---	electronic	30-1/12000		530
Maxxum 9xi + 24-85	24x36mm	35mm	35slr	1992	AF Zoom	3.5-4.5	24-85	electronic	30-1/12000		700
Maxxum 400si body	24x36mm	35mm	35slr	1994	body only	---	---	electronic	30-1/2000		220
Maxxum 400si + 50/1.4	24x36mm	35mm	35slr	1994	AF	1.4	50mm	electronic	30-1/2000		310
Maxxum 700si	24x36mm	35mm	35slr	1994	body only	---	---	electronic	30-1/8000		480
Maxxum 700si + 24-85	24x36mm	35mm	35slr	1994	AF Zoom	3.5-4.5	24-85	electronic	30-1/8000		700
Maxxum 3000i body	24x36mm	35mm	35slr	1988	body only	---	---	electronic	4-1/1000		100
Maxxum 3000i + 50/1.7	24x36mm	35mm	35slr	1988	AF	1.7	50mm	electronic	4-1/1000		130
Maxxum 5000 body	24x36mm	35mm	35slr	1986	body only	---	---	electronic	4-1/2000		130
Maxxum 5000 + 50/1.4	24x36mm	35mm	35slr	1986	AF	1.4	50mm	electronic	4-1/2000		220
Maxxum 5000i body	24x36mm	35mm	35slr	1989	body only	---	---	electronic	4-1/2000		170
Maxxum 5000i + 50/1.7	24x36mm	35mm	35slr	1989	AF	1.7	50mm	electronic	4-1/2000		200
Maxxum 7000 body	24x36mm	35mm	35slr	1986	body only	---	---	electronic	30-1/2000		150
Maxxum 7000 + 50/1.4	24x36mm	35mm	35slr	1986	AF	1.4	50mm	electronic	30-1/2000		230
Maxxum 7000i body	24x36mm	35mm	35slr	1988	body only	---	---	electronic	30-1/4000		220
Maxxum 7000i + 50/1.7	24x36mm	35mm	35slr	1988	AF	1.7	50mm	electronic	30-1/4000		270
Maxxum 8000i body	24x36mm	35mm	35slr	1990	body only	---	---	electronic	30-1/8000		330
Maxxum 8000i + 50/1.7	24x36mm	35mm	35slr	1990	AF	1.7	50mm	electronic	30-1/8000		360
Maxxum 9000 body	24x36mm	35mm	35slr	1986	body only	---	---	electronic	30-1/4000		280
Maxxum 9000 + 50/1.4	24x36mm	35mm	35slr	1986	AF	1.4	50mm	electronic	30-1/4000		350
Maxxum SPxi body	24x36mm	35mm	35slr	1991	body only	---	---	electronic	30-1/2000		170
Maxxum SPxi + 28-80	24x36mm	35mm	35slr	1991	AF Zoom	4.0-5.6	28-80	electronic	30-1/2000		290
Memo 1949	24x36mm	35mm	35vf	1949	Rokkor	4.5	50mm		25-100	Mc308	120
Memo 1993	24x36mm	35mm	35af	1993	Minolta	4.5	35mm	programmed			60
Memory Maker	24x36mm	35mm	35C	1995	Minolta	4.5	35mm		1/125		30
Miniflex	4x4cm	127	TLR	1959	Rokkor	3.5	60mm	Citizen	1-500	Mc312	550
Minolta	6.5x9cm	225	StrutPl	1933	Coronar Anast.	4.5	105mm	Crown	1-200	Mc307	290

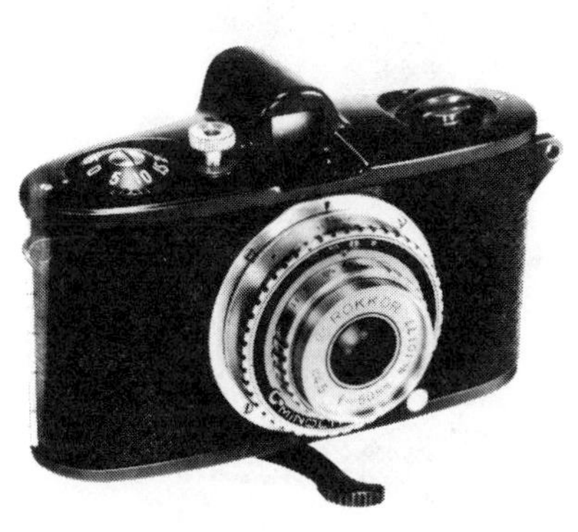

Memo 1949

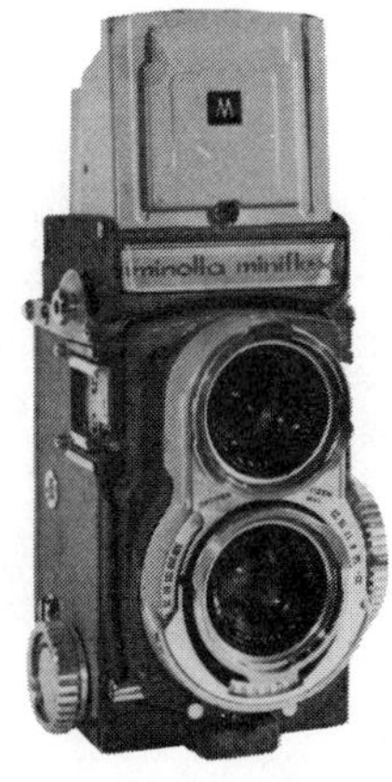

Miniflex

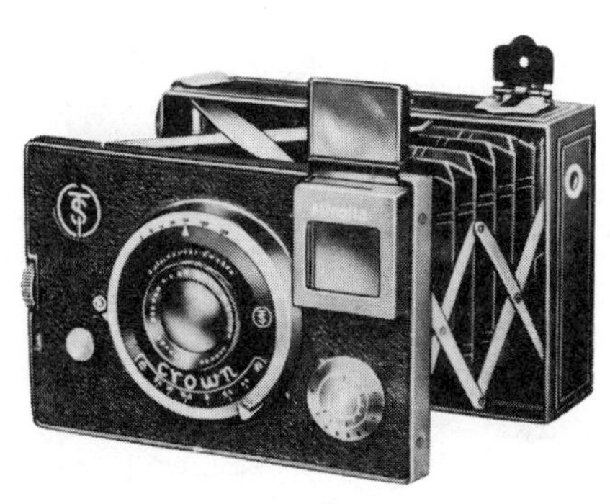

Minolta

MODEL	FORMAT	FILM	TYPE	Year	LENS	Apert	FL	SHUTTER	SPEEDS	ILLUS	U.S.$
Minoltacord	6x6cm	120	TLR	1953	Rokkor	3.5	75mm	Citizen	1-400	Mc312	140
Minoltacord Automat	6x6cm	120	TLR	1955	Rokkor	3.5	75mm	Citizen	1-400		100
Minoltaflex (I)	6x6cm	120	TLR	1936	Promar Anast.	3.5	75mm	Crown-II	1-300	Mc312	180
Minoltaflex II	6x6cm	120	TLR	1950	Rokkor	3.5	75mm	S-Konan Rapid	1-500	Mc312	140
Minoltaflex IIB	6x6cm	120	TLR	1952	Rokkor	3.5	75mm	S-Konan Rapid	1-500		80
Minoltaflex III	6x6cm	120	TLR	1950	Rokkor	3.5	75mm	S-Konan Rapid	1-500		80
Minoltina-P	24x36mm	35mm	35rf	1964	Rokkor PF	2.8	38mm	Citizen	30-250	Mc310	50
Minoltina-S	24x36mm	35mm	35rf	1964	Rokkor QF	1.8	40mm	Seikosha	1-500	Mc310	50
Nifca-Dox	6.5x9cm	plate	StrutPl	1930	Nifca Anastigmat	6.8	105mm	Koilos	25-100	Mc306	610
Nifca-Dox	6.5x9cm	plate	StrutPl	1930	Wekar Anastigmat	6.3	105mm	Koilos	25-100		610
Nifca-Klapp	6.5x9cm	plate	VtFoldPl	1930	Zeiss Anastigmat	6.3	105mm	Compur	25-200		310
Nifca-Klapp	6.5x9cm	plate	VtFoldPl	1930	Wekar Anastigmat	6.3	105mm	Vario	25-100	Mc306	310
Nifca-Sport	6.5x9cm	plate	VtFoldPl	1930	Wekar Anastigmat	4.5	105mm	Compur	1-200	Mc306	310
Nifcalette	4x6.5cm	127	FoldRo	1929	Hellostar Anast.	6.3	75mm	Koilos	25-100	Mc306	410
Minolta P's	24x36mm	35mm	35Pan	1993	Minolta	4.5	24mm	programmed	4-200		110
Panorama Zoom 5	24x36mm	35mm	35afz	1993	Minolta	4.3-6.4	38-60	programmed			100
Panorama Zoom 7	24x36mm	35mm	35afz	1995	Minolta	3.8-7.2	35-70	programmed			110
Panorama Zoom 28	24x36mm	35mm	35afz	1994	Minolta	3.5-8.4	28-70	programmed			170
Panorama Zoom 105	24x36mm	35mm	35afz	1994	Minolta	3.5-9.2	38-105	programmed			190
Panorama Zoom 135	24x36mm	35mm	35afz	1994	Minolta	3.5-9.2	38-135	programmed			240
Pico	24x36mm	35mm	35CAF	1993	Minolta	3.5	34mm	programmed			70
Pocket Autopak 50	13x17mm	110	110VF	1973	Rokkor	8	26mm	electronic	10-1/330		30
Pocket Autopak 70	13x17mm	110	110VF	1973	Rokkor	3.5	26mm	electronic	10-1/330		80
Pocket Autopak 200 (USA)	13x17mm	110	110VF	1975	Rokkor	8	26mm		1/50,1/125		30
Pocket Autopak 230 (Eur)	13x17mm	110	110VF	1975	Rokkor	8	26mm		1/50,1/125		30
Pocket Autopak 250	13x17mm	110	110VF	1975	Rokkor	8	26mm	electronic	10-1/330	A1980	40
Pocket Autopak 270	13x17mm	110	110VF	1975	Rokkor	3.5	26mm	electronic	10-1/330		50
Pocket Autopak 430E	13x17mm	110	110VF	1976	Rokkor	5.6	26mm		1/200	A1986	50
Pocket Autopak 430EX	13x17mm	110	110VF	1980	Rokkor	5.6	26mm		1/200	A3370	50
Pocket Autopak 440E	13x17mm	110	110VF	1976	Rokkor	5.6	26mm		1/200		40
Pocket Autopak 440EX	13x17mm	110	110VF	1980	Rokkor	5.6	26mm		1/200		50
Pocket Autopak 450E	13x17mm	110	110VF	1976	Rokkor	3.5	26mm		1/200	A1986	50
Pocket Autopak 450EX	13x17mm	110	110VF	1980	Rokkor	3.5	26mm		1/200	A3371	40
Pocket Autopak 460T	13x17mm	110	110BiFoc	1978	Rokkor	3.5,4.7	26/43		1/200	A1978	60
Pocket Autopak 460TX	13x17mm	110	110BiFoc	1980	Rokkor	3.5,4.7	26/43		1/200	A3372	60
Pocket Autopak 470	13x17mm	110	110VF	1977	Rokkor	3.5	26mm	electronic	2-1/1000	A3373	70
Prod-20's	24x36mm	35mm	35af	1990	Rokkor	4.5	35mm	programmed			220
Repo	18x24mm	35mm	35Half	1962	Rokkor	2.8	30mm	Citizen L		Mc309	50
Repo-S (black)	18x24mm	35mm	35Half	1964	Rokkor	1.8	32mm		8-500		70
Repo-S (chrome)	18x24mm	35mm	35Half	1964	Rokkor PF	1.8	32mm		8-500	Mc309	70
Riva 35	24x36mm	35mm	35C	1993	Minolta	4.5	35mm	programmed	1/125		40
Riva 35ST	24x36mm	35mm	35C	1995	Minolta	4.5	35mm	programmed	1/35,1/100		50

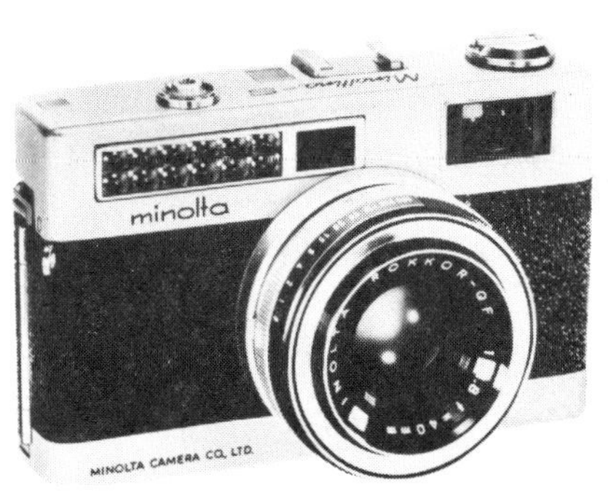

Minoltina-S

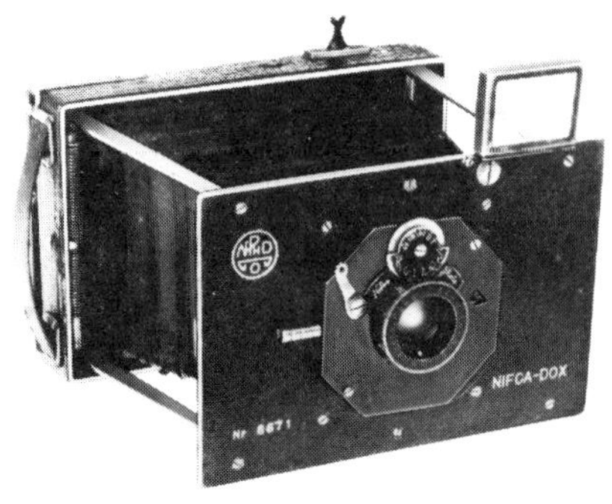

Nifca-Dox

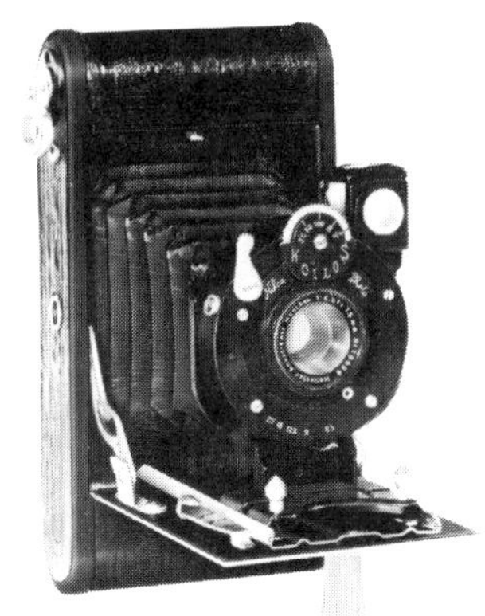
Nifcalette

MODEL	FORMAT	FILM	TYPE	Year	LENS	Apert	FL	SHUTTER	SPEEDS	ILLUS	U.S.$
Riva AF35	24x36mm	35mm	35af	1990	Minolta	4.5	35mm	programmed			80
Riva AF35 Date	24x36mm	35mm	35af	1990	Minolta	4.5	35mm	programmed			100
Riva AF35c	24x36mm	35mm	35af	1993	Minolta	4.5	35mm	programmed			60
Riva AF35EX	24x36mm	35mm	35CAF	1995	Minolta	4.5	30mm	programmed			50
Riva Mini	24x36mm	35mm	35CAF	1993	Minolta	3.5	34mm	programmed			70
Riva Panorama	24x36mm	35mm	35Pan	1993	Minolta	4.5	24mm	programmed	4-200		110
Riva Twin 28	24x36mm	35mm	35AF-BiF	1992	Minolta	4.0,5.6	28/40	programmed			110
Riva Zoom 70c	24x36mm	35mm	35afz	1992	Minolta	3.5-6.5	35-70	programmed			130
Riva Zoom 70c Date	24x36mm	35mm	35afz	1992	Minolta	3.5-6.5	35-70	programmed			130
Riva Zoom 70EX	24x36mm	35mm	35afz	1995	Minolta	3.8-7.2	35-70	programmed			110
Riva Zoom 90c	24x36mm	35mm	35afz	1993	Minolta	3.5-7.7	38-90	programmed			140
Riva Zoom 90c Date	24x36mm	35mm	35afz	1993	Minolta	3.5-7.7	38-90	programmed			140
Riva Zoom 90EX	24x36mm	35mm	35afz	1993	Minolta	3.5-7.7	38-90	programmed			150
Riva Zoom 105EX	24x36mm	35mm	35afz	1994	Minolta	3.5-9.2	38-105	programmed			190
Riva Zoom 105i	24x36mm	35mm	35afz	1990	Minolta	4-6.7	35-105	programmed	2-500		170
Riva Zoom 105i Date	24x36mm	35mm	35afz	1991	Minolta	4-6.7	35-105	programmed	2-500		200
Riva Zoom 135EX	24x36mm	35mm	35afz	1994	Minolta	3.5-9.2	38-135	programmed			240
Riva Zoom PICO	24x36mm	35mm	35afz	1993	Minolta	4.3-6.4	38-60	programmed			100
Semi-Minolta I	4.5x6cm	120	FoldRo	1934	Coronar Anast.	4.5	75mm	Crown	5-200	Mc307	180
Semi-Minolta II	4.5x6cm	120	FoldRo	1937	Coronar Anast.	4.5	75mm	Crown	5-200	Mc307	70
Semi-Minolta IIIA	4.5x6cm	120	FoldRo	1946	Rokkor	3.5	75mm	Konan-Rapid	1-500	Mc307	130
Semi-Minolta IIIB	4.5x6cm	120	FoldRo	1947	Rokkor	3.5	75mm	Konan-Rapid	1-500		130
Semi-Minolta IIIC	4.5x6cm	120	FoldRo	1948	Rokkor	3.5	75mm	Konan-Rapid	1-500		130
Semi-Minolta P	4.5x6cm	120	FoldRo	1951	Promar SII	3.5	75mm	Konan Flicker	2-200	Mc307	80
Sirius	6.5x9cm	plate	VtFoldPl	1931	Helostar	6.3	105mm	Koilos	25-100		150
Minolta Six	6x6cm	120	TelescRo	1935	Coronar Anast.	5.6	80mm	Crown	25-150	Mc307	120
Minolta Sky	24x36mm	35mm	35rf	1957	Rokkor	1.8	50mm			Mc309	10000
Sonocon 16mm MB-ZA	10x14mm	16mm	Disguised	1962	Rokkor	2.8	22mm		30-500	A3319	1000
SR-1 (early) body	24x36mm	35mm	35slr	1959	body only	---	---	focal plane	1-500	Mc310	70
SR-1 (early) + 55/2.0	24x36mm	35mm	35slr	1959	Rokkor PF	2.0	55mm	focal plane	1-500	Mc310	90
SR-1 (new) body	24x36mm	35mm	35slr	1964	body only	---	---	focal plane	1-500	Mc310	70
SR-1 (new) + 55/2.0	24x36mm	35mm	35slr	1964	Rokkor PF	2.0	55mm	focal plane	1-500	Mc310	100
SR-1S body	24x36mm	35mm	35slr	1964	body only	---	---	focal plane	1-1000	Mc310	70
SR-1S + 55/2.0	24x36mm	35mm	35slr	1964	Rokkor PF	2.0	55mm	focal plane	1-1000	Mc310	90
SR-2 body	24x36mm	35mm	35slr	1958	body only	---	---	focal plane	1-1000	Mc310	60
SR-2 + 55/1.8	24x36mm	35mm	35slr	1958	Rokkor PF	1.8	55mm	focal plane	1-1000	Mc310	100
SR-3 body	24x36mm	35mm	35slr	1960	body only	---	---	focal plane	1-1000	Mc310	80
SR-3 + 55/1.8	24x36mm	35mm	35slr	1960	Auto Rokkor	1.8	55mm	focal plane	1-1000	Mc310	120
SR-7 (early) body	24x36mm	35mm	35slr	1962	body only	---	---	focal plane	1-1000	Mc311	90
SR-7 (early) + 58/1.4	24x36mm	35mm	35slr	1962	Rokkor PF	1.4	58mm	focal plane	1-1000	Mc311	120
SR-7 (later) body	24x36mm	35mm	35slr	1964	body only	---	---	focal plane	1-1000		100
SR-7 (later) + 58/1.4	24x36mm	35mm	35slr	1964	Rokkor PF	1.4	58mm	focal plane	1-1000		130

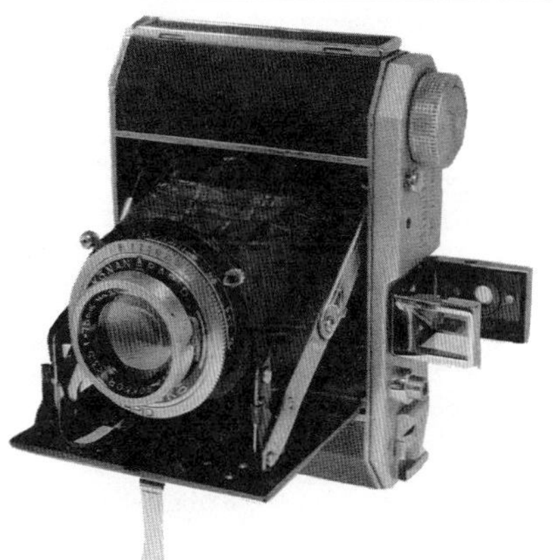

Semi-Minolta IIIA

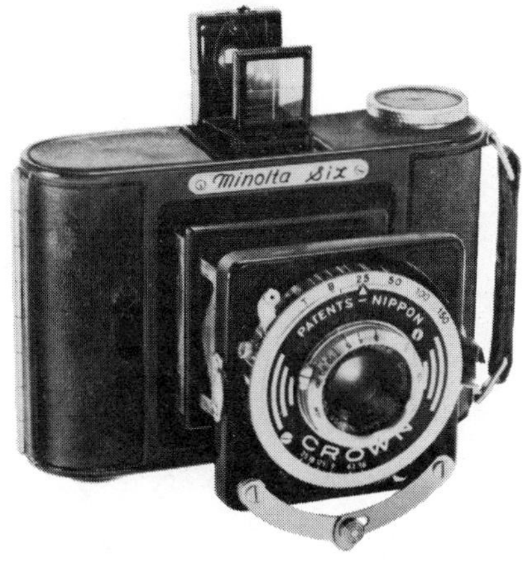

Minolta Six

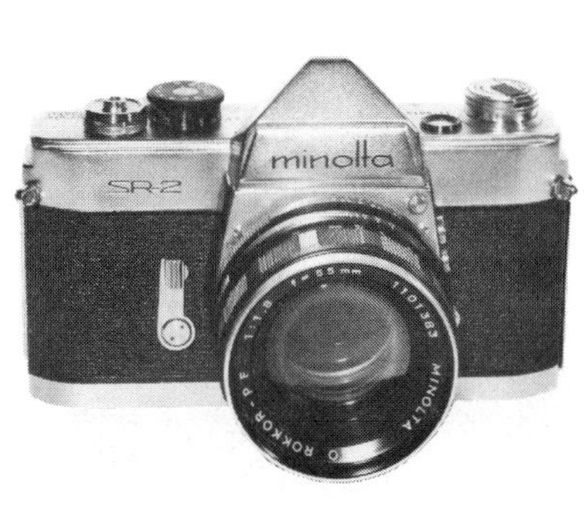

Minolta SR-2

MODEL	FORMAT	FILM	TYPE	Year	LENS	Apert	FL	SHUTTER	SPEEDS	ILLUS	U.S.$
SR-101 body	24x36mm	35mm	35slr	1975	body only	---	---	focal plane	1-1000		120
SR-101 + 50/1.7	24x36mm	35mm	35slr	1975	Rokkor	1.7	50mm	focal plane	1-1000		140
SR-505 body	24x36mm	35mm	35slr	1973	body only	---	---	focal plane	1-1000		170
SR-505 + 50/1.4	24x36mm	35mm	35slr	1973	Rokkor	1.4	50mm	focal plane	1-1000		210
SR-M body	24x36mm	35mm	35slr	1970	body only	---	---	focal plane	1-1000		340
SR-M + 55/1.7	24x36mm	35mm	35slr	1970	Rokkor RF	1.7	55mm	focal plane	1-1000	Mc311	380
SRT Super body	24x36mm	35mm	35slr	1973	body only	---	---	focal plane	1-1000		130
SRT Super + 50/1.7	24x36mm	35mm	35slr	1973	Rokkor	1.7	50mm	focal plane	1-1000		160
SRT-100 (black) body	24x36mm	35mm	35slr	1971	body only	---	---	focal plane	1-500		80
SRT-100 (black) + 55/1.9	24x36mm	35mm	35slr	1971	Rokkor	1.9	55mm	focal plane	1-500		120
SRT-100 (chrome) body	24x36mm	35mm	35slr	1971	body only	---	---	focal plane	1-500		80
SRT-100 (chrome) + 55/1.9	24x36mm	35mm	35slr	1971	Rokkor	1.9	55mm	focal plane	1-500		100
SRT-100b body	24x36mm	35mm	35slr	1975	body only	---	---	focal plane	1-500		110
SRT-100b + 55/1.9	24x36mm	35mm	35slr	1975	Rokkor	1.9	55mm	focal plane	1-500		120
SRT-100X body	24x36mm	35mm	35slr	1977	body only	---	---	focal plane	1-1000		90
SRT-100X + 50/2.0	24x36mm	35mm	35slr	1977	Rokkor	2.0	50mm	focal plane	1-1000		130
SRT-101 (black) body	24x36mm	35mm	35slr	1966	body only	---	---	focal plane	1-1000		100
SRT-101 (black) + 50/1.7	24x36mm	35mm	35slr	1966	Rokkor	1.7	50mm	focal plane	1-1000		140
SRT-101 (chrome) body	24x36mm	35mm	35slr	1966	body only	---	---	focal plane	1-1000		100
SRT-101 (chrome) + 50/1.7	24x36mm	35mm	35slr	1966	Rokkor	1.7	50mm	focal plane	1-1000	A1701	130
SRT-101b (black) body	24x36mm	35mm	35slr	1975	body only	---	---	focal plane	1-1000		130
SRT-101b (black) + 50/1.7	24x36mm	35mm	35slr	1975	Rokkor	1.7	50mm	focal plane	1-1000		160
SRT-101b (chrome) body	24x36mm	35mm	35slr	1975	body only	---	---	focal plane	1-1000		120
SRT-101b (chrome) + 50/1.7	24x36mm	35mm	35slr	1975	Rokkor	1.7	50mm	focal plane	1-1000		140
SRT-102 body	24x36mm	35mm	35slr	1973	body only	---	---	focal plane	1-1000		130
SRT-102 + 50/1.7	24x36mm	35mm	35slr	1973	Rokkor	1.7	50mm	focal plane	1-1000		160
SRT-200 body	24x36mm	35mm	35slr	1975	body only	---	---	focal plane	1-500		110
SRT-200 + 50/1.4	24x36mm	35mm	35slr	1975	Rokkor	1.4	50mm	focal plane	1-500		120
SRT-201 (black) body	24x36mm	35mm	35slr	1975	body only	---	---	focal plane	1-1000		130
SRT-201 (black) + 50/1.7	24x36mm	35mm	35slr	1975	Rokkor	1.7	50mm	focal plane	1-1000		160
SRT-201 (chrome) body	24x36mm	35mm	35slr	1975	body only	---	---	focal plane	1-1000		120
SRT-201 (chrome) + 50/1.7	24x36mm	35mm	35slr	1975	Rokkor	1.7	50mm	focal plane	1-1000		140
SRT-202 body	24x36mm	35mm	35slr	1975	body only	---	---	focal plane	1-1000		170
SRT-202 + 50/1.4	24x36mm	35mm	35slr	1975	Rokkor	1.4	50mm	focal plane	1-1000		210
SRT-303 body	24x36mm	35mm	35slr	1973	body only	---	---	focal plane	1-1000		130
SRT-303 + 50/1.7	24x36mm	35mm	35slr	1973	Rokkor	1.7	50mm	focal plane	1-1000		160
SRT-303b body	24x36mm	35mm	35slr	1973	body only	---	---	focal plane	1-1000		170
SRT-303b + 50/1.4	24x36mm	35mm	35slr	1973	Rokkor	1.4	50mm	focal plane	1-1000		210
SRT-MC body	24x36mm	35mm	35slr	1975	body only	---	---	focal plane	1-1000		100
SRT-MC + 50/1.4	24x36mm	35mm	35slr	1975	Rokkor	1.4	50mm	focal plane	1-1000		130
SRT-MCII body	24x36mm	35mm	35slr	1975	body only	---	---	focal plane	1-1000		100
SRT-MCII + 50/1.4	24x36mm	35mm	35slr	1975	Rokkor	1.4	50mm	focal plane	1-1000		130

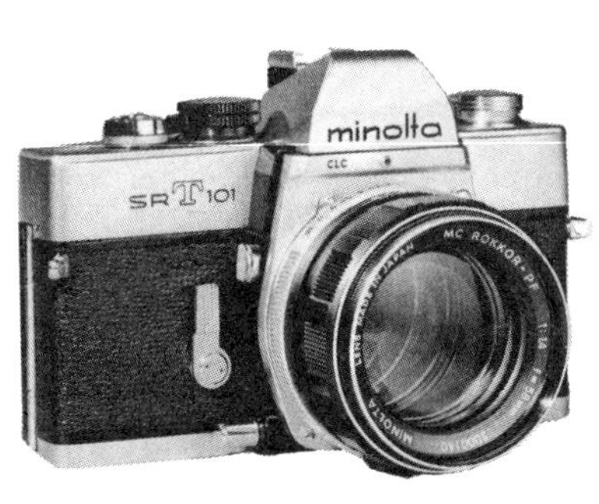

Minolta SRT-101

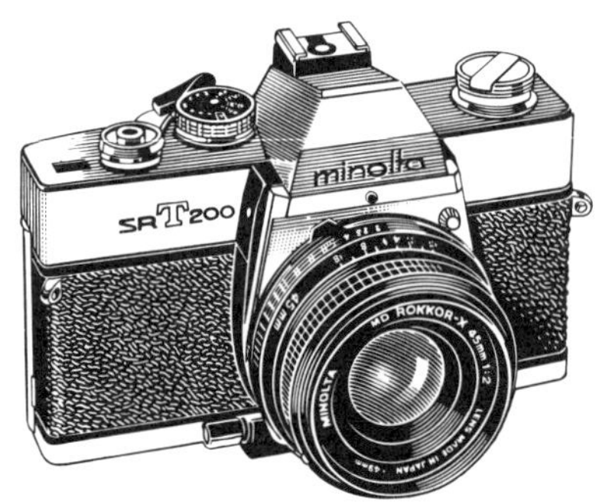

Minolta SRT-200

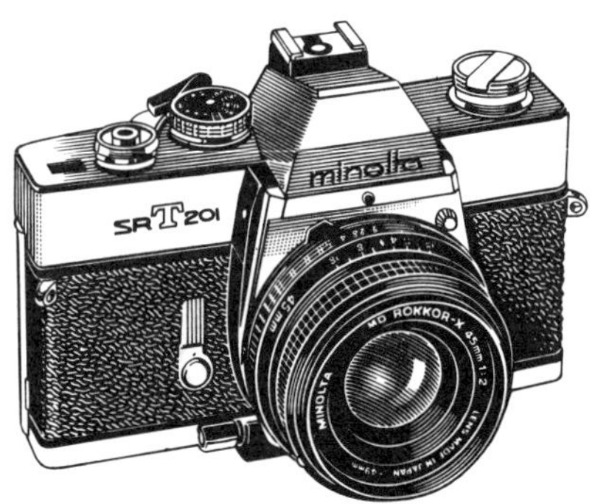

Minolta SRT-201

MODEL	FORMAT	FILM	TYPE	Year	LENS	Apert	FL	SHUTTER	SPEEDS	ILLUS	U.S.$
SRT-SC body	24x36mm	35mm	35slr	1975	body only	---	---	focal plane	1-1000		100
SRT-SC + 50/1.4	24x36mm	35mm	35slr	1975	Rokkor	1.4	50mm	focal plane	1-1000		130
SRT-SCII body	24x36mm	35mm	35slr	1975	body only	---	---	focal plane	1-1000		100
SRT-SCII + 50/1.4	24x36mm	35mm	35slr	1975	Rokkor	1.4	50mm	focal plane	1-1000		130
Minolta Super A	24x36mm	35mm	35rf	1957	Super Rokkor	1.8	50mm	Seikosha-MX	1-400	Mc309	180
Twin 28	24x36mm	35mm	35AF-BiF	1992	Minolta	4.0,5.6	28/40	programmed			110
Uniomat	24x36mm	35mm	35rf	1960	Rokkor	2.8				Mc309	60
Uniomat III	24x36mm	35mm	35rf	1964	Rokkor	2.8	45mm				60
Minolta V2	24x36mm	35mm	35rf	1958	Rokkor	2.0	45mm	Optiper HS	1-2000	Mc309	110
Minolta V3	24x36mm	35mm	35rf	1960	Rokkor	1.8	45mm	Optiper HS	1-3000		140
Weathermatic 35DL	24x36mm	35mm	35uw	1987	Minolta	3.5,5.6	35/50	programmed	30-150		180
Weathermatic-A	13x17mm	110	110UW	1980	Minolta	3.5	26mm		1/200	A3449	70
Weathermatic Dual 35	24x36mm	35mm	35uw	1987	Minolta	3.5,5.6	35/50	programmed	30-150		180
X-1 body	24x36mm	35mm	35slr	1972	body only	---	---	electronic	16-1/2000		310
X-1 + 50/1.2	24x36mm	35mm	35slr	1972	MD	1.2	50mm	electronic	16-1/2000		470
X-1 Motor body	24x36mm	35mm	35slr	1983	body only	---	---	electronic	16-1/2000		570
X-1 Motor + 50/1.4	24x36mm	35mm	35slr	1983	MD	1.4	50mm	electronic	16-1/2000		670
X-7A body	24x36mm	35mm	35slr	1984	body only	---	---	electronic	4-1/1000		120
X-7A + 50/1.2	24x36mm	35mm	35slr	1984	MD	1.2	50mm	electronic	4-1/1000		220
X-9 body	24x36mm	35mm	35slr	1992	body only	---	---	electronic	4-1/1000		140
X-9 + 50/1.7	24x36mm	35mm	35slr	1992	MD	1.7	50mm	electronic	4-1/1000		170
X-300 body	24x36mm	35mm	35slr	1984	body only	---	---	electronic	4-1/1000		120
X-300 + 50/1.2	24x36mm	35mm	35slr	1984	MD	1.2	50mm	electronic	4-1/1000		220
X-300S body	24x36mm	35mm	35slr	1990	body only	---	---	electronic	4-1/1000		150
X-300S + 50/1.7	24x36mm	35mm	35slr	1990	MD	1.7	50mm	electronic	4-1/1000		200
X-370 body	24x36mm	35mm	35slr	1984	body only	---	---	electronic	4-1/1000		120
X-370 + 50/1.2	24x36mm	35mm	35slr	1984	MD	1.2	50mm	electronic	4-1/1000		220
X-370N body	24x36mm	35mm	35slr	1990	body only	---	---	electronic	4-1/1000		150
X-370N + 50/1.7	24x36mm	35mm	35slr	1990	MD	1.7	50mm	electronic	4-1/1000		200
X-500 body	24x36mm	35mm	35slr	1983	body only	---	---	electronic	4-1/1000		150
X-500 + 50/1.2	24x36mm	35mm	35slr	1983	MD	1.2	50mm	electronic	4-1/1000		200
X-570 body	24x36mm	35mm	35slr	1983	body only	---	---	electronic	4-1/1000		150
X-570 + 50/1.7	24x36mm	35mm	35slr	1983	MD	1.7	50mm	electronic	4-1/1000		170
X-700 body	24x36mm	35mm	35slr	1981	body only	---	---	electronic	4-1/1000		170
X-700 + 50/1.7	24x36mm	35mm	35slr	1981	MD	1.7	50mm	electronic	4-1/1000		200
XD (black) body	24x36mm	35mm	35slr	1977	body only	---	---	electronic	1-1000		260
XD (black) + 50/1.2	24x36mm	35mm	35slr	1977	MD	1.2	50mm	electronic	1-1000		320
XD (chrome) body	24x36mm	35mm	35slr	1977	body only	---	---	electronic	1-1000		210
XD (chrome) + 50/1.2	24x36mm	35mm	35slr	1977	MD	1.2	50mm	electronic	1-1000		290
XD-5 body	24x36mm	35mm	35slr	1979	body only	---	---	electronic	1-1000		150
XD-5 + 50/1.2	24x36mm	35mm	35slr	1979	MD	1.2	50mm	electronic	1-1000		220
XD-7 (black) body	24x36mm	35mm	35slr	1977	body only	---	---	electronic	1-1000	Mc311	260

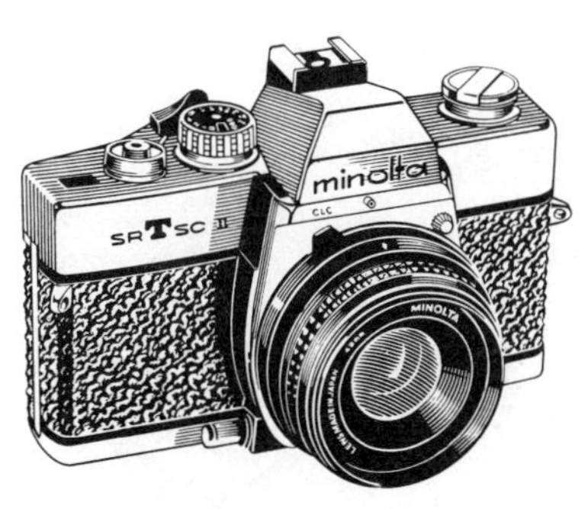

Minolta SRT-SCII

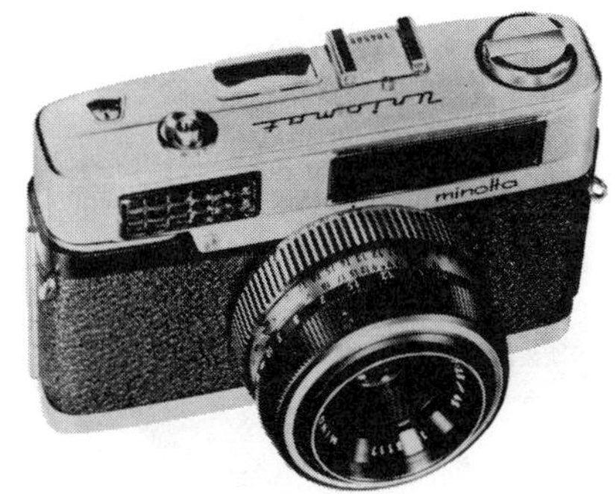

Minolta Uniomat

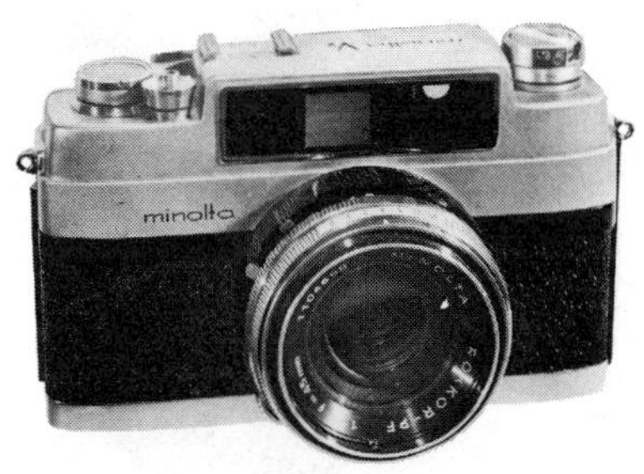

Minolta V2

MODEL	FORMAT	FILM	TYPE	Year	LENS	Apert	FL	SHUTTER	SPEEDS	ILLUS	U.S.$
XD-7 (black) + 50/1.2	24x36mm	35mm	35slr	1977	MD	1.2	50mm	electronic	1-1000	Mc311	320
XD-7 (chrome) body	24x36mm	35mm	35slr	1977	body only	---	---	electronic	1-1000		210
XD-7 (chrome) + 50/1.2	24x36mm	35mm	35slr	1977	MD	1.2	50mm	electronic	1-1000		290
XD-11 (black) body	24x36mm	35mm	35slr	1977	body only	---	---	electronic	1-1000		260
XD-11 (black) + 50/1.2	24x36mm	35mm	35slr	1977	MD	1.2	50mm	electronic	1-1000		320
XD-11 (chrome) body	24x36mm	35mm	35slr	1977	body only	---	---	electronic	1-1000		210
XD-11 (chrome) + 50/1.2	24x36mm	35mm	35slr	1977	MD	1.2	50mm	electronic	1-1000		290
XE body	24x36mm	35mm	35slr	1975	body only	---	---	focal plane	4-1/1000		170
XE + 50/1.4	24x36mm	35mm	35slr	1975	MD	1.4	50mm	focal plane	4-1/1000		300
XE-1 (black) body	24x36mm	35mm	35slr	1975	body only	---	---	focal plane	4-1/1000		210
XE-1 (black) + 50/1.4	24x36mm	35mm	35slr	1975	MD	1.4	50mm	focal plane	4-1/1000		380
XE-1 (chrome) body	24x36mm	35mm	35slr	1975	body only	---	---	focal plane	4-1/1000		170
XE-1 (chrome) + 50/1.4	24x36mm	35mm	35slr	1975	MD	1.4	50mm	focal plane	4-1/1000		300
XE-5 body	24x36mm	35mm	35slr	1975	body only	---	---	focal plane	4-1/1000		140
XE-5 + 50/1.4	24x36mm	35mm	35slr	1975	MD	1.4	50mm	focal plane	4-1/1000		190
XE-7 body	24x36mm	35mm	35slr	1975	body only	---	---	focal plane	4-1/1000		170
XE-7 + 50/1.4	24x36mm	35mm	35slr	1975	MD	1.4	50mm	focal plane	4-1/1000		300
XE-b body	24x36mm	35mm	35slr	1975	body only	---	---	focal plane	4-1/1000		140
XE-b + 50/1.4	24x36mm	35mm	35slr	1975	MD	1.4	50mm	focal plane	4-1/1000		190
XG-1 body	24x36mm	35mm	35slr	1980	body only	---	---	electronic	1-1000		100
XG-1 + 50/1.4	24x36mm	35mm	35slr	1980	MD	1.4	50mm	electronic	1-1000		140
XG-2 body	24x36mm	35mm	35slr	1977	body only	---	---	electronic	1-1000		100
XG-2 + 50/1.4	24x36mm	35mm	35slr	1977	MD	1.4	50mm	electronic	1-1000		150
XG-7 body	24x36mm	35mm	35slr	1978	body only	---	---	electronic	1-1000		100
XG-7 + 50/1.4	24x36mm	35mm	35slr	1978	MD	1.4	50mm	electronic	1-1000		150
XG-9 body	24x36mm	35mm	35slr	1979	body only	---	---	electronic	1-1000		120
XG-9 + 50/1.4	24x36mm	35mm	35slr	1979	MD	1.4	50mm	electronic	1-1000		170
XG-A body	24x36mm	35mm	35slr	1982	body only	---	---	electronic	1-1000		80
XG-A + 50/1.4	24x36mm	35mm	35slr	1982	MD	1.4	50mm	electronic	1-1000		140
XG-E body	24x36mm	35mm	35slr	1977	body only	---	---	electronic	1-1000		100
XG-E + 50/1.4	24x36mm	35mm	35slr	1977	MD	1.4	50mm	electronic	1-1000		150
XG-M body	24x36mm	35mm	35slr	1981	body only	---	---	electronic	1-1000		120
XG-M + 50/1.4	24x36mm	35mm	35slr	1981	MD	1.4	50mm	electronic	1-1000		160
XG-S body	24x36mm	35mm	35slr	1979	body only	---	---	electronic	1-1000		120
XG-S + 50/1.4	24x36mm	35mm	35slr	1979	MD	1.4	50mm	electronic	1-1000		170
XG-SE body	24x36mm	35mm	35slr	1978	body only	---	---	electronic	1-1000		100
XG-SE + 50/1.4	24x36mm	35mm	35slr	1978	MD	1.4	50mm	electronic	1-1000		160
XK body	24x36mm	35mm	35slr	1973	body only	---	---	electronic	16-1/2000		310
XK + 50/1.2	24x36mm	35mm	35slr	1973	MD	1.2	50mm	electronic	16-1/2000		470
XK Motor body	24x36mm	35mm	35slr	1977	body only	---	---	electronic	16-1/2000		570
XK Motor + 50/1.4	24x36mm	35mm	35slr	1977	MD	1.2	50mm	electronic	16-1/2000		670
XM body	24x36mm	35mm	35slr	1972	body only	---	---	electronic	16-1/2000		310

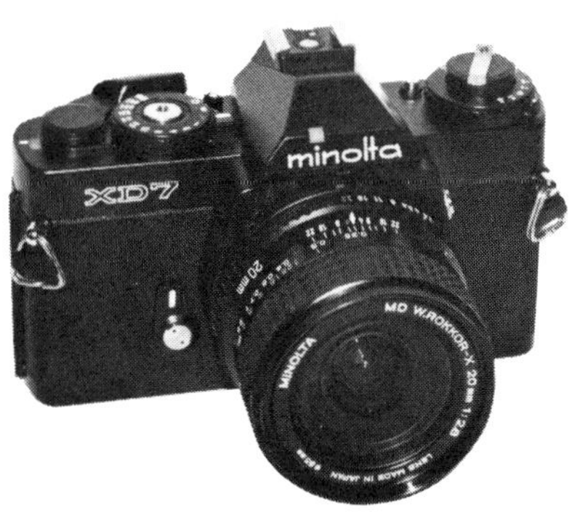

Minolta XD-7

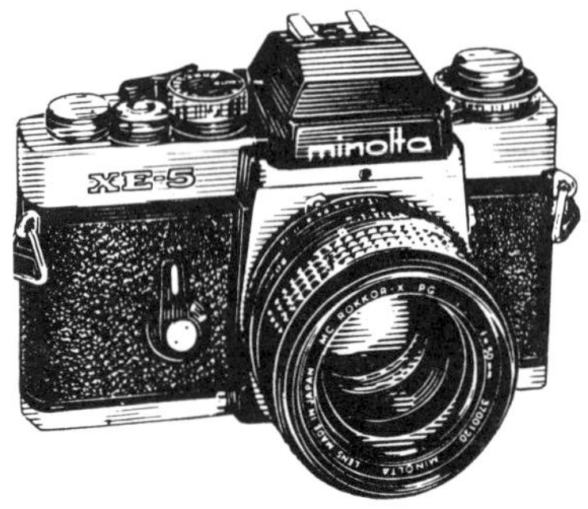

Minolta XE-5

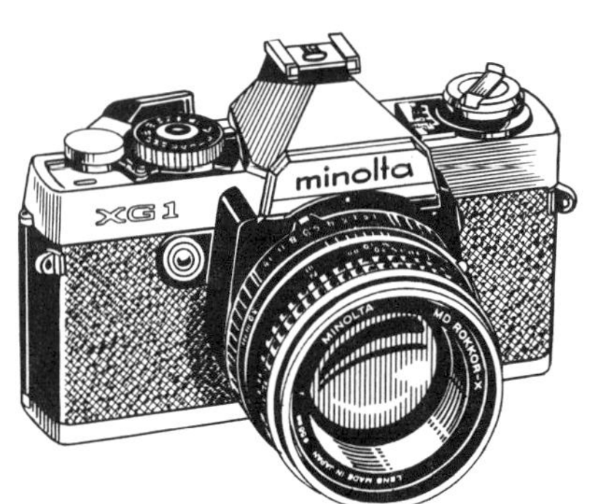

Minolta XG-1

MODEL	FORMAT	FILM	TYPE	Year	LENS	Apert	FL	SHUTTER	SPEEDS	ILLUS	U.S.$
XM + 50/1.2	24x36mm	35mm	35slr	1972	MD	1.2	50mm	electronic	16-1/2000		470
XM Motor body	24x36mm	35mm	35slr	1983	body only	---	---	electronic	16-1/2000		570
XM Motor + 50/1.4	24x36mm	35mm	35slr	1983	MD	1.4	50mm	electronic	16-1/2000		670
...MINOX											
Minox "Latvia, Pat.app."	8x11mm	9.5mm	Submin	1937	Minostigmat	3.5	15mm	guillotine	½-1/1000		1400
Minox "RIGA"	8x11mm	9.5mm	Submin	1937	Minostigmat	3.5	15mm	guillotine	½-1/1000	Mc313	1000
Minox "RIGA" (w/ eyelet)	8x11mm	9.5mm	Submin	1937	Minostigmat	3.5	15mm	guillotine	½-1/1000		1000
Minox "Made in USSR"	8x11mm	9.5mm	Submin	1940	Minostigmat	3.5	15mm	guillotine	½-1/1000	Mc313	1300
Minox 35 AF	24x36mm	35mm	35af	1988	Minoxar	3.5	32mm	electronic	30-500		130
Minox 35 AL (black)	24x36mm	35mm	35C	1987	Minotar	4	35mm		1-300		110
Minox 35 AL (white)	24x36mm	35mm	35C	1987	Minotar	4	35mm		1-300		120
Minox 35 EL	24x36mm	35mm	35C	1974	Minotar	2.8	35mm	electronic	30-500		120
Minox 35 GL	24x36mm	35mm	35C	1979	Minotar	2.8	35mm	electronic	30-1/500		140
Minox 35 GSE	24x36mm	35mm	35C	1992	Minotar	2.8	35mm	electronic	8-1/500		210
Minox 35 GT	24x36mm	35mm	35C	1981	Minotar	2.8	35mm	electronic	30-1/500		180
Minox 35 GT "Golf"	24x36mm	35mm	35C	1984	Minotar	2.8	35mm	electronic	30-1/500		290
Minox 35 GT-E	24x36mm	35mm	35C	1988	Minoxar	2.8	35mm	electronic	8-1/500		240
---35 GT-E 'Goldknopf'	24x36mm	35mm	35C	1993	Minoxar	2.8	35mm	electronic	8-1/500		300
Minox 35 MB	24x36mm	35mm	35C	1986	Minotar	2.8	35mm	electronic	1-500		170
Minox 35 ML	24x36mm	35mm	35C	1985	Minoxar	2.8	35mm	programmed	1-500	A3501	240
Minox 35 PE	24x36mm	35mm	35C	1982	Minotar	2.8	35mm	programmed	4-1/500		160
Minox 35 PL	24x36mm	35mm	35C	1982	Minotar	2.8	35mm	programmed	4-1/500		140
Minox 110 S	13x17mm	110	110RF	1976		2.8	25mm	electronic	4-1/1000		100
Minox A (chrome)	8x11mm	9.5mm	Submin	1948	Complan	3.5	15mm	guillotine	½-1/1000	Mc313	540
Minox A (gold)	8x11mm	9.5mm	Submin	1948	Complan	3.5	15mm	guillotine	½-1/1000		3200
Minox AF Mini	24x36mm	35mm	35CAF	1994	Minoxar	3.5	34mm	electronic	4-250		90
Minox AX (chrome)	8x11mm	9.5mm	Submin	1993		3.5	15mm	guillotine	½-1/1000		1400
Minox AX (gold)	8x11mm	9.5mm	Submin	1993		3.5	15mm	guillotine	½-1/1000		2200
Minox B (black)	8x11mm	9.5mm	Submin	1958	Complan	3.5	15mm	guillotine	½-1/1000		390
Minox B (chrome)	8x11mm	9.5mm	Submin	1958	Complan	3.5	15mm	guillotine	½-1/1000	Mc314	180
Minox B (gold)	8x11mm	9.5mm	Submin	1958	Complan	3.5	15mm	guillotine	½-1/1000		3300
Minox BL (black)	8x11mm	9.5mm	Submin	1971	Complan	3.5	15mm	guillotine	½-1/1000		490
Minox BL (chrome)	8x11mm	9.5mm	Submin	1971	Complan	3.5	15mm	guillotine	½-1/1000	A1952	350
Minox BL (gold)	8x11mm	9.5mm	Submin	1971	Complan	3.5	15mm	guillotine	½-1/1000		1000
Minox C (black)	8x11mm	9.5mm	Submin	1969	Complan	3.5	15mm	electronic	7-1/1000		270
Minox C (chrome)	8x11mm	9.5mm	Submin	1969	Complan	3.5	15mm	electronic	7-1/1000	Mc314	200
Minox EC	8x11mm	9.5mm	Submin	1981		5.6	15mm	guillotine	8-1/500	A3329	160
Minox II	8x11mm	9.5mm	Submin	1949	Complan	3.5	15mm	guillotine	½-1/1000	A923	640
Minox III	8x11mm	9.5mm	Submin	1951	Complan	3.5	15mm	guillotine	½-1/1000	Mc313	240
Minox III (gold)	8x11mm	9.5mm	Submin	1951	Complan	3.5	15mm	guillotine	½-1/1000		1800
Minox III-S (black)	8x11mm	9.5mm	Submin	1954	Complan	3.5	15mm	guillotine	½-1/1000		620
Minox III-S (chrome)	8x11mm	9.5mm	Submin	1954	Complan	3.5	15mm	guillotine	½-1/1000		200

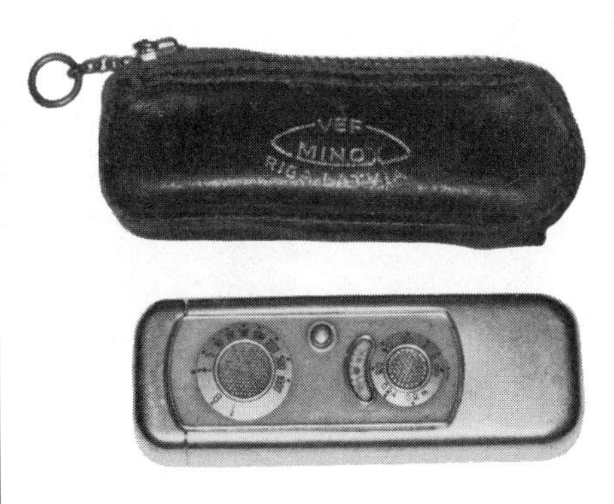

Minox "RIGA"

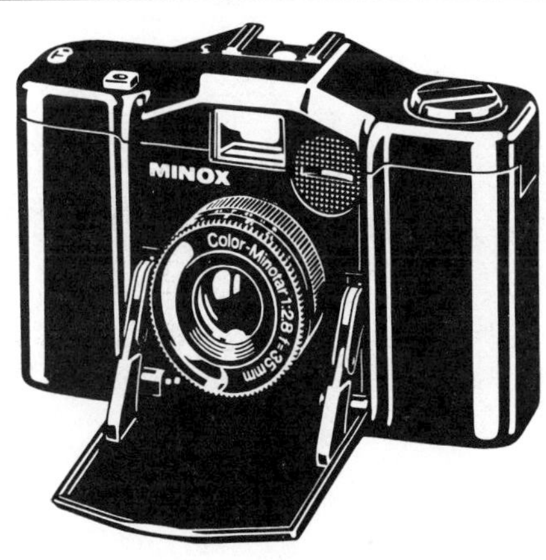

Minox 35 GT

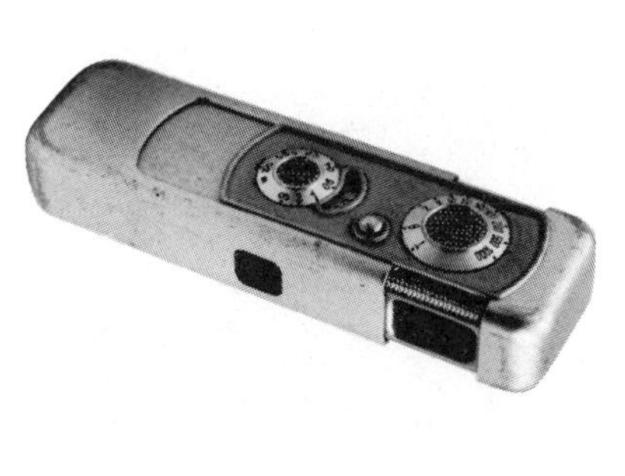

Minox III

MODEL	FORMAT	FILM	TYPE	Year	LENS	Apert	FL	SHUTTER	SPEEDS	ILLUS	U.S.$
Minox III-S (gold)	8x11mm	9.5mm	Submin	1954	Complan	3.5	15mm	guillotine	½-1/1000	A1948	2900
Minox LX (black)	8x11mm	9.5mm	Submin	1978		3.5	15mm	electronic	15-1/2000		610
Minox LX (chrome)	8x11mm	9.5mm	Submin	1978		3.5	15mm	electronic	15-1/2000	A1953	540
Minox LX (gold)	8x11mm	9.5mm	Submin	1988		3.5	15mm	electronic	15-1/2000		1500
Minox LX (platin)	8x11mm	9.5mm	Submin	1991	Minox	3.5	15mm	electronic	15-1/2000		1900
Minox LX (sterling)	8x11mm	9.5mm	Submin	1992	Minox	3.5	15mm	electronic	15-1/2000		4300
Minox M.D.C.	24x36mm	35mm	35C	1992	Minoxar	2.8	35mm	programmed	1-500		460
Minox Touring	24x36mm	35mm	35C	1990	Minotar	2.8	35mm	programmed			270
...M.I.O.M. (Manufacture d'Isolants et d'Objets Moulés) - Vitry-sur-Seine, France											
Astra	6x9cm	120	TelescRo	1937	Boyer				P,I	Mc314	60
Jacky	6x9cm	120	TelescRo	1937	Boyer				P,I	Mc314	60
Lec Junior (black)	4x6.5cm	127	RigidRo	1937	Duxor				T,I	Mc314	30
Lec Junior (brown)	4x6.5cm	127	RigidRo	1937	Duxor				T,I		30
Loisirs	6x9cm	120	RigidRo	1938	Radior				T,I		30
Miom 4x6.5	4x6.5cm	127	RigidRo	1937						F708	30
Miom 6x9	6x9cm	120	TelescRo	1938	Boyer				P,I	A1090	30
Photax (original)	6x9cm	120	TelescRo	1937	Boyer				P,I	Mc314	60
Photax "Blindé"	6x9cm	120	TelescRo	1938	Boyer					Mc314	30
Photax V	6x9cm	120	TelescRo		Heanar					Mc314	70
Rex	4x6.5cm	127	RigidRo	1937	Reginor				P,I	Mc315	30
...(unknown)											
Mirage	6x6cm	120	RigidRo							Mc315	10
...MIRANDA CAMERA CO. LTD. - Tokyo, Japan											
Miranda A	24x36mm	35mm	35slr	1957	Miranda	1.9	5cm	focal plane	1-1000	Mc315	130
Miranda A II	24x36mm	35mm	35slr	1957	Miranda	1.9	5cm	focal plane	1-1000	Mc315	130
Miranda Auto Sensorex EE	24x36mm	35mm	35slr	1971	Auto Miranda E	1.8	50mm	focal plane	1-1000		90
Miranda Auto Sens. EE-2	24x36mm	35mm	35slr	1971	Auto Miranda E	1.8	50mm	focal plane	1-1000		80
Miranda Automex	24x36mm	35mm	35slr	1959	Miranda	1.9	5cm	focal plane	1-1000		90
Miranda Automex II	24x36mm	35mm	35slr	1963	Miranda	1.9	5cm	focal plane	1-1000	Mc316	90
Miranda Automex III	24x36mm	35mm	35slr	1965	Miranda	1.9	5cm	focal plane	1-1000		80
Miranda B	24x36mm	35mm	35slr	1957	Miranda	1.9	5cm	focal plane	1-1000		140
Miranda C	24x36mm	35mm	35slr	1959	Miranda	1.9	5cm	focal plane	1-1000	Mc316	140
Miranda D	24x36mm	35mm	35slr	1960	Miranda	1.9	5cm	focal plane	1-500	Mc316	70
Miranda DR	24x36mm	35mm	35slr	1962	Miranda	1.9	5cm	focal plane	1-500		70
Miranda DX-3 (black)	24x36mm	35mm	35slr	1976	Auto Miranda EC	1.8	50mm	focal plane	1-1000		60
Miranda DX-3 (chrome)	24x36mm	35mm	35slr	1976	Auto Miranda EC	1.8	50mm	focal plane	1-1000		110
Miranda F (500) (black)	24x36mm	35mm	35slr	1963	Miranda	1.9	5cm	focal plane	1-500		150
Miranda F (500) (chrome)	24x36mm	35mm	35slr	1963	Miranda	1.9	5cm	focal plane	1-500		70
Miranda F (1000) (black)	24x36mm	35mm	35slr	1963	Miranda	1.9	5cm	focal plane	1-1000		170
Miranda F (1000) (chrome)	24x36mm	35mm	35slr	1963	Miranda	1.9	5cm	focal plane	1-1000	Mc316	100
Miranda FM (black)	24x36mm	35mm	35slr	1963	Miranda	1.9	5cm	focal plane	1-1000		160
Miranda FM (chrome)	24x36mm	35mm	35slr	1963	Miranda	1.9	5cm	focal plane	1-1000		80

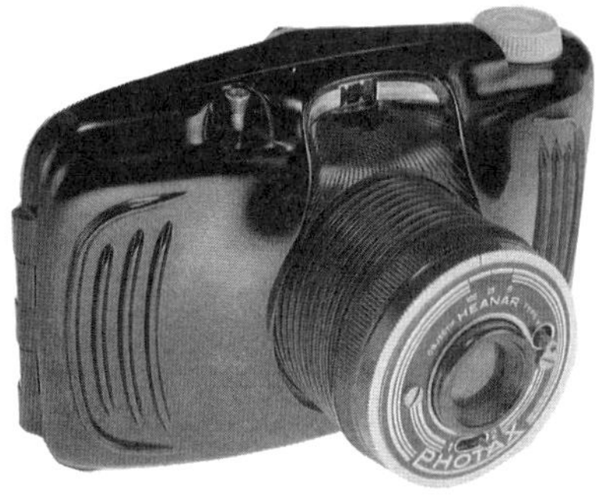

Photax V

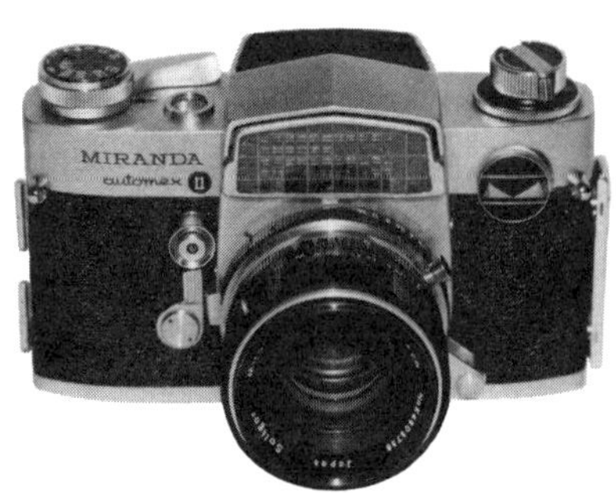

Miranda Automex II

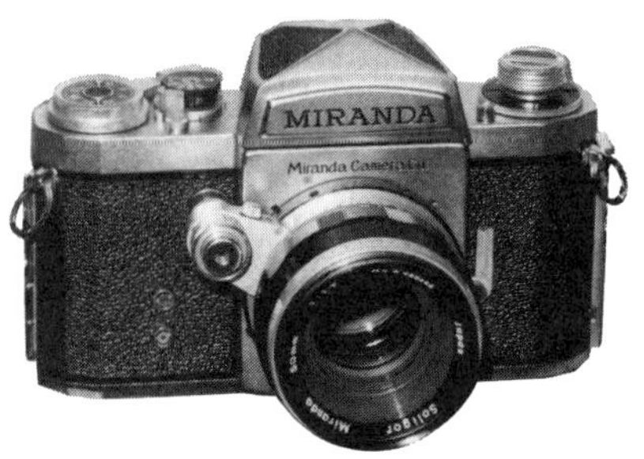

Miranda C

MODEL	FORMAT	FILM	TYPE	Year	LENS	Apert	FL	SHUTTER	SPEEDS	ILLUS	U.S.$
Miranda FT (black)	24x36mm	35mm	35slr	1963	Miranda	1.9	5cm	focal plane	1-1000		160
Miranda FT (chrome)	24x36mm	35mm	35slr	1963	Miranda	1.9	5cm	focal plane	1-1000		80
Miranda Fv (500) (black)	24x36mm	35mm	35slr	1966	Miranda	1.9	5cm	focal plane	1-500		110
Miranda Fv (500) (chrome)	24x36mm	35mm	35slr	1966	Miranda	1.9	5cm	focal plane	1-500		90
Miranda Fv (1000) (black)	24x36mm	35mm	35slr	1966	Miranda	1.9	5cm	focal plane	1-1000		110
Miranda Fv (1000) (chrome)	24x36mm	35mm	35slr	1966	Miranda	1.9	5cm	focal plane	1-1000		100
Miranda G (black)	24x36mm	35mm	35slr	1965	Miranda	1.9	5cm	focal plane	1-1000		100
Miranda G (chrome)	24x36mm	35mm	35slr	1965	Miranda	1.9	5cm	focal plane	1-1000		160
Miranda GT (black)	24x36mm	35mm	35slr	1965	Miranda	1.9	5cm	focal plane	1-1000		120
Miranda GT (chrome)	24x36mm	35mm	35slr	1965	Miranda	1.9	5cm	focal plane	1-1000		190
Miranda Laborec	24x36mm	35mm	35slr	1969	Macron	2.8	50mm		1-125		320
Miranda Laborec II	24x36mm	35mm	35slr		Macron	2.8			1-125		320
Miranda Laborec III	24x36mm	35mm	35slr	1976	Macron	2.8		focal plane	1-500		320
Mirax Laborec Electro-D	24x36mm	35mm	35slr	1976	Macron	2.8		focal plane	1-125		480
Miranda S	24x36mm	35mm	35slr	1959	Miranda	2.8	5cm	focal plane	30-500		150
Miranda Sensomat (black)	24x36mm	35mm	35slr	1969	Auto Miranda	1.8	50mm	focal plane	1-1000		70
Miranda Sensomat (chrome	24x36mm	35mm	35slr	1969	Auto Miranda	1.8	50mm	focal plane	1-1000		70
Miranda Sensomat RE	24x36mm	35mm	35slr	1971	Auto Miranda	1.8	50mm	focal plane	1-1000		90
Miranda Sensomat RE-II	24x36mm	35mm	35slr	1975	Auto Miranda	1.8	50mm	focal plane	1-1000		70
Miranda Sensomat RS	24x36mm	35mm	35slr	1972	Auto Miranda	1.8	50mm	focal plane	1-1000		80
Miranda Sensoret	24x36mm	35mm	35rf	1972	Soligor	2.8	38mm	Seiko Elect.	4-1/800		30
Miranda Sensorex (black)	24x36mm	35mm	35slr	1968	Auto Miranda	1.8	50mm	focal plane	1-1000		140
Miranda Sensorex (chrome)	24x36mm	35mm	35slr	1968	Auto Miranda	1.8	50mm	focal plane	1-1000		80
Miranda Sensorex II	24x36mm	35mm	35slr	1971	Auto Miranda	1.8	50mm	focal plane	1-1000		100
Miranda ST	24x36mm	35mm	35slr	1959	Miranda	1.9	5cm	focal plane	1-500		500
Miranda T (black) (Orion)	24x36mm	35mm	35slr	1953	Zunow	1.9	5cm	focal plane	1-500		1300
Miranda T (chrome) (Orion)	24x36mm	35mm	35slr	1953	Zunow	1.9	5cm	focal plane	1-500	Mc315	800
Miranda T	24x36mm	35mm	35slr	1956	Miranda	1.9	5cm	focal plane	1-500	Mc315	490
Miranda T II	24x36mm	35mm	35slr	1956	Arco	2.4	5cm	focal plane			500
Miranda TM	24x36mm	35mm	35slr	1974	Auto Miranda	1.8	50mm	focal plane	1-1000		80
Miranda TM (II)	24x36mm	35mm	35slr	1976	Auto Miranda	1.8	50mm	focal plane	1-1000		80
...(unknown)											
Mirroflex	6x6cm	120	TLR	1960	Tri-Lausar	3.5	80mm	Rectus			100
...MISUZU KOGAKU KOGYO CO. LTD. - Japan											
Alta	24x36mm	35mm	35rf	1957	Altanon	2	50mm	focal plane	1-500		1500
Bower	24x36mm	35mm	SciMed					focal plane	1-500		800
...MISUZU TRADING CO. - Japan											
Midget Jilona (I)	14x14mm	Roll	Submin	1937	Doublet	6.8	22mm		B,1/25	Mc317	220
Midget Jilona Mod. No. 2	14x14mm	Roll	Submin	1949	Midget Anastig.	4.5	20mm		B, 1/50		100
Midget Mod. III	14x14mm	Roll	Submin	1950	Midget Anastig.	4.5	20mm		25-100	Mc317	160
Misuzu Six	6x6cm	120	FoldRo	1950	Alpha Anast.	6.3	75mm	NFG	25-100		100
Vest Alex	4x6cm	127	TelescRo	1936	[fith Anastigmat	6.3	75mm		25-100	Mc317	70

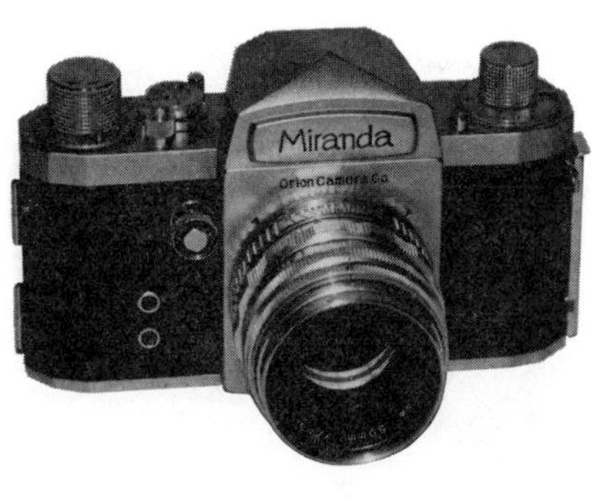

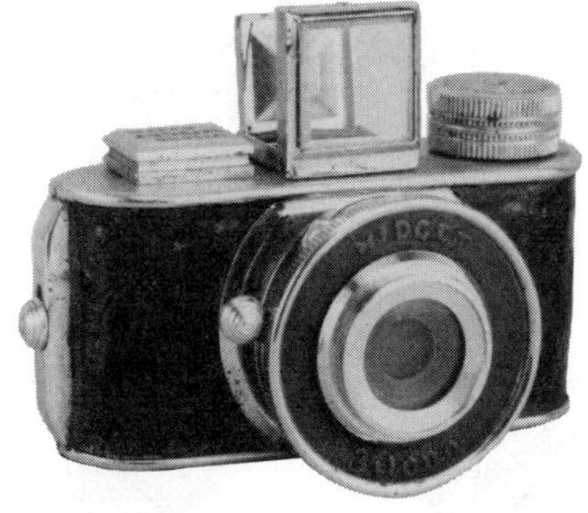

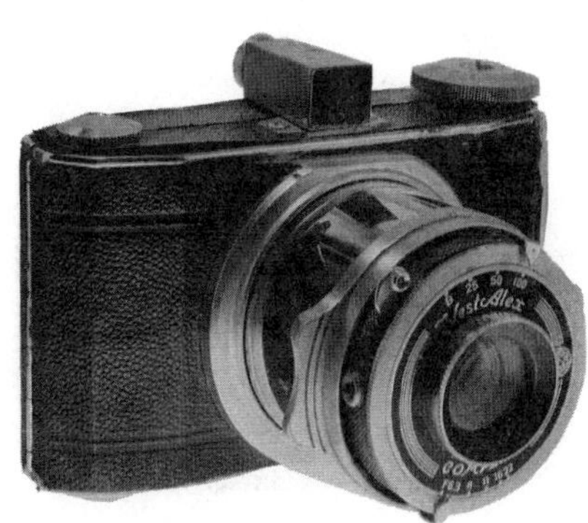

Miranda T (chrome) (Orion) **Midget Jilona (I)** **Misuzu Vest Alex**

MODEL	FORMAT	FILM	TYPE	Year	LENS	Apert	FL	SHUTTER	SPEEDS	ILLUS	U.S.$
...(unknown)											
Mithra 47	6x9cm	120	MetBx	1950	Meniscus				I,B	Mc317	50
...MIYAGAWA SEISAKUSHO - Tokyo, Japan											
Boltax I	24x24mm	Bolta	MiniatRo	1938	Picner Anast.	4.5	40mm	Picny-D	25-100	Mc317	150
Boltax II	24x24mm	Bolta	MiniatRo	1940	Picner Anast.	4.5	40mm	Boltax	25-100		150
Boltax III	24x24mm	Bolta	MiniatRo	1940	Picner Anast.	4.5	40mm	Picny	25-100		150
Picny (black)	3x4cm	127	TelescRo	1940	Picny Anastigmat	4.5	40mm	Picny	25-100		300
Picny (chrome)	3x4cm	127	TelescRo	1935	Picny Anastigmat	4.5	40mm	Picny	25-100		150
Picny 35	24x36mm	35mm	35vf	1950	Picny Anastigmat	3.5	44mm		25-100		140
...MIZUHO KOKI - Japan											
Mizuho-Six	6x6/4.5x6	120	FoldRo	1952	Militar Special	3.5	80mm	NKS	1-200		80
Mizuho-Six Mod. V	6x6cm	120	FoldRo	1952	Militar Special						90
...MÖLLER (J. D. Möller) - Hamburg, Germany											
Cambinox (I)	10x14mm	16mm	Disguised	1954	Idemar	3.5	90mm	focal plane	30-1000	Mc317	1100
Cambinox II "N"	10x14mm	16mm	Disguised	1956	Idemar	3.5	90mm	focal plane	30-800	HK632	1000
Cambinox II "S"	10x14mm	16mm	Disguised	1957	Idemar	3.5	90mm	focal plane	30-800	A3277	1800
...MOESSARD & FAUVEL											
Cylindrographe	12x42cm		Panoramic	1885	Hermagis	8				F1546	26000
...MOLLIER (Etablissements Mollier) - Paris, France											
Le Cent Vues	18x24mm	35mm	35vf	1924	Hermagis Anast.	3.5	40mm	Compur	1-300	F547	2200
Le Cent Vues (second mod	18x24mm	35mm	35vf	1926	Hermagis Anast.	3.5	40mm	Compur	1-300	F548	2000
...MOLTENI - Paris, France											
Detective camera	9x12cm	plate	DetectivBox	1885	Molteni Aplanat					F902	1600
...MOM (Magyar Optikai Müvek) - Budapest, Hungary											
Fotobox	6x6cm	120	MetBx	1950	Achromat	7.7	75mm		25-100	Mc318	70
Mometta	24x36mm	35mm	35rf	1950	Ymmar	3.5	50mm	focal plane	25-500	Mc318	140
Mometta II	24x36mm	35mm	35rf	1953	Ymmar	3.5	50mm	focal plane	25-500		140
Mometta III	24x36mm	35mm	35rf	1957	Ymmar	3.5	50mm	focal plane	25-500	Mc318	410
Momikon	24x36mm	35mm	35rf	1950	Ymmar	3.5	50mm	focal plane	25-500	A2129	140
...MONARCH MFG. CO. - Chicago, IL, USA											
Churchill	3x4cm	127	RigidRo	1939	Graf		50mm		I,T		20
Dasco	3x4cm	127	RigidRo	1939	Graf		50mm		I,T		20
Flash Master	3x4cm	127	RigidRo	1939	Graf		50mm		I,T		20
Fleetwood	3x4cm	127	RigidRo	1939	Alphar		50mm		I,T		20
Flex-Master	3x4cm	127	TLR-Box	1939	Graf		50mm		I,T		10
Kando Reflex	3x4cm	127	TLR-Box	1939	Alphar		50mm		I,T		20
Majestic	3x4cm	127	RigidRo	1939	Graf		50mm		I,T		20
Monarch 620	4.5x6cm	620	RigidRo	1939	Meniscus						30
Pickwik	3x4cm	127	RigidRo	1939	Graf		50mm		I,T		10
Pickwik Reflex	3x4cm	127	TLR-Box	1939	Graf		50mm		I,T		20
Remington	3x4cm	127	RigidRo	1939	Alphar		50mm		I,T		10
Royal Reflex	3x4cm	127	TLR-Box	1939	Graf		50mm		I,T		20

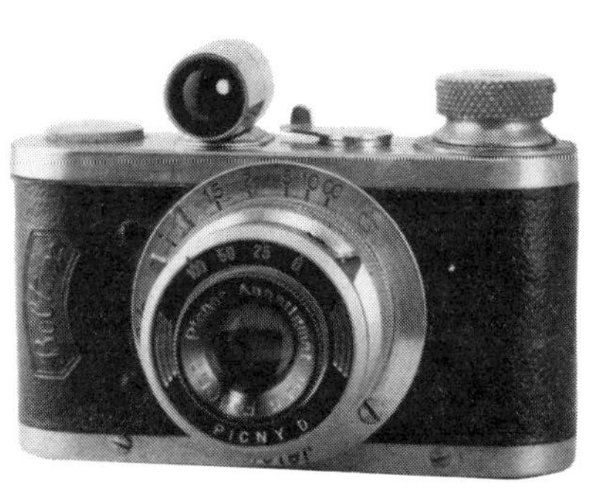

Boltax I

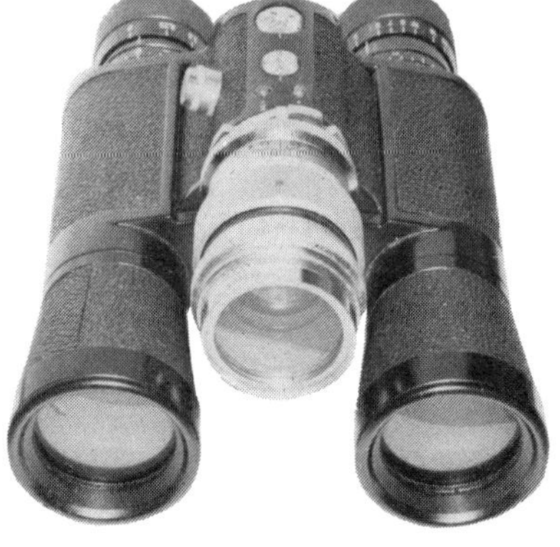

Cambinox (I)

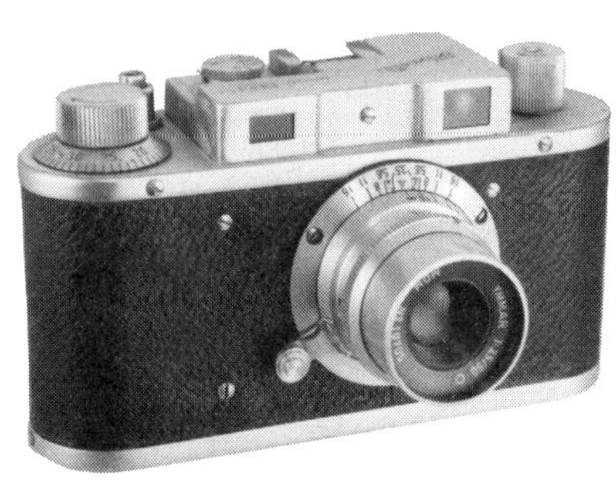

Mometta

MODEL	FORMAT	FILM	TYPE	Year	LENS	Apert	FL	SHUTTER	SPEEDS	ILLUS	U.S.$
...MONO-WERK (Rudolph Chaste) - Magdeburg, Germany											
Mono 00	6.5x9cm	plate	FoldPl	1913	Monar Anast.	6.8		Vario		Mc318	50
Mono XXVI	13x18cm	plate	FoldPl	1913	Monar Anast.	6.8		Vario			140
Mono XXVIII	13x18cm	plate	FoldPl	1913	Mono Dopp. An.	6.3		FP, Ibso	1-1000		160
Mono Spiegel-Reflex	6.5x9cm	plate	MedSLR	1915	Monar Anast.	6.8	120mm	Vario			300
Mono-Trumpf	9x12cm	plate	FoldPl	1914	Mono Dopp. An.	6.3	136mm	Ibsor		HK162	50
...MONROE CAMERA CO. - Rochester, NY, USA											
Folding plate camera 4x5"	4x5"	plate	FoldPl	1897	Single Achromatic						90
Folding plate camera 5x7"	5x7"	plate	FoldPl	1897	Single Achromatic						270
Monroe No. 4C	4x5"	plate	FoldPl	1898	achromatic			Royal			90
Monroe No. 5		plate	FoldPl	1898	Rapid Rectilinear			Unicum			110
Monroe No. 7	5x7"	plate	FoldPl	1898	Rapid Rectilinear			Gundlach		Mc318	140
Pocket Monroe A	3¼x4¼"	plate	StrutPl	1898	Single Achromatic					Mc318	260
Pocket Monroe No. 2	3½x3½"	plate	StrutPl	1898	Single Achromatic					Mc318	230
Vest Pocket Monroe	2x2½"	plate	StrutPl	1898	Single Achromatic					Mc318	370
...MONROE SALES CO.											
Color-flex	1¼x1½"	127	TLR-Box	1947	Meniscus						60
...MONTANUS CAMERABAU - Solingen, Germany											
Delmonta	6x6cm	120	TLR	1953	Pluscanar	3.5	75mm	Vario		A642	70
Delmonta	6x6cm	120	TLR	1953	Pluscanar	3.5	75mm	Prontor-SVS		HK434	70
Montana (black)	24x36mm	35mm	35vf	1956	Deltamon Anast.	3.5	45mm		50-200	A1114	60
Montana (reptile)	24x36mm	35mm	35vf	1956	Deltamon Anast.	3.5	45mm		50-200	Mc319	160
Montiflex	6x6cm	120	TLR	1955	Pluscanar	3.5	75mm	Prontor-SVS		Mc319	100
Montiflex	6x6cm	120	TLR	1955	Cassar	2.8	80mm	Prontor-SVS			100
Rocca Automatic	6x6cm	120	TLR	1954	Cassar	2.8	80mm	Prontor-SVS		Mc319	110
Rocca Super Reflex	6x6cm	120	TLR	1955	Cassar	2.8	80mm	Prontor	1-300		100
...MONTGOMERY WARD & CO. - USA											
Long Focus Thornward	4x5"	plate	FoldPl								100
Mod. B	4x5"	plate	FoldPl		Rapid Convertible			Wollensak			80
MW		Roll	BakFoldRo								40
Thornward Dandy	4x5"	plate	PlateBox								80
Wardette	6x6cm	120	MetBx	1953	Meniscus	11				Mc319	20
Wardflex	6x6cm	120	TLR	1955	Telmer	3.5	80mm	TKK			80
Wardflex	6x6cm	120	TLR-Box	1941	Argus Varex	6.3	75mm		25-150		30
Wardflex II	6x6cm	120	TLR	1957	Biokor	3.5		Synchro MX	1-300	Mc319	110
Wards 25	4x4cm	127	PlasticBox							Mc319	10
Wards 35	24x36mm	35mm	35vf	1956	Adoxar	3.5	45mm		1-300		30
Wards 35-EE	24x36mm	35mm	35vf	1963		4.0	50mm		1/60	Mc319	30
Wards x100	24x36mm	35mm	35vf	1964	Adoxon	2.8	45mm			Mc320	10
Wards xp400	24x36mm	35mm	35vf	1963							20
...MONTI (Charles Monti) - France											
L'Automatique	9x12cm	plate	MagBox	1890	Rapid Rectilinear	11	135mm	leaf		F808	670

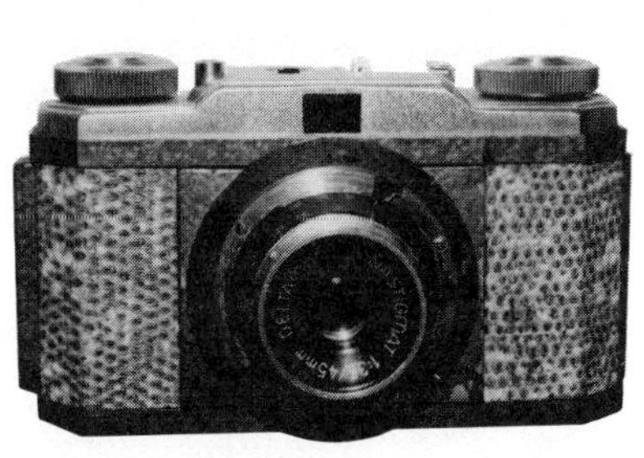

Montana (reptile)

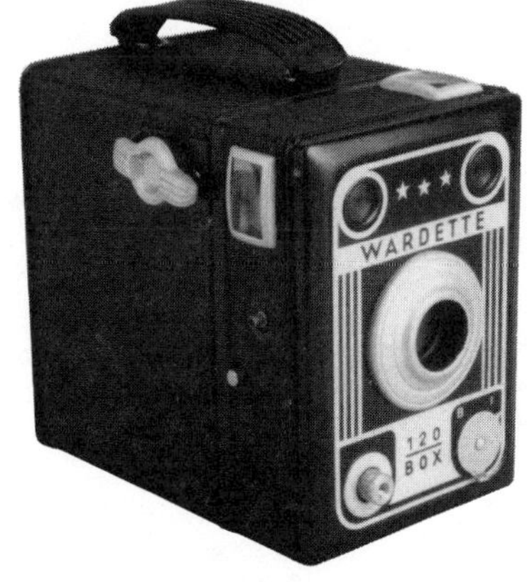

Wardette

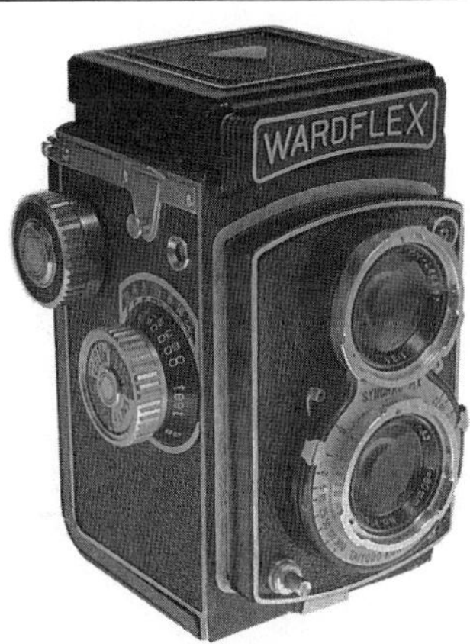

Wardflex II

MODEL	FORMAT	FILM	TYPE	Year	LENS	Apert	FL	SHUTTER	SPEEDS	ILLUS	U.S.$
...MONTENEGRO - Carlos											
Monte Carlo	6x9cm	120	FoldRo	1947		4.5	90mm				30
Monte Carlo Mini	4.5x6cm	120	FoldRo	1947	Manar	3.5	75mm	Gaumet	1-250		30
Monte Carlo Special	6x9cm	120	FoldRo	1947		3.5	90mm				30
...(unknown)											
Moonflex	6x6cm	120	TLR	1957	Tri-Lausar	3.5	80mm		1-300	Mc320	90
...MOORE & CO. - Liverpool, England											
Aptus Ferrotype Camera	4.5x6.3cm	Ferro	Ferrotype	1895	Meniscus					Mc320	420
...MOORSE (H. Moorse) - London, England											
Single-lens Stereo	9x18cm	WetPl	StWetPl	1865	Meniscus						5000
...MORITA TRADING CO. - Japan											
Gem 16, Mod. II	14x14mm	16mm	Submin	1956	Meniscus	8	25mm		B,I	Mc320	110
Kiku 16, Mod. I	14x14mm	16mm	Submin	1955	Meniscus	8	25mm		B,I		500
Kiku 16, Mod. II	14x14mm	16mm	Submin	1956	Meniscus	8	25mm		B,I		130
Saica	14x14mm	16mm	Submin	1954	Meniscus	8	25mm		B,I		240
...MORLEY (W. Morley, Ltd.) - London, England											
Wet plate camera	3¼x4¼"	WetPl	WetPlate	1860	Jamin-Darlot						1000
Wet plate camera	16x18cm	WetPl	WetPlate	1860	Jamin						1800
Wet plate stereo camera		WetPl	StWetPl	1860	Negretti & Zambra						2800
...MOTOSHIMA OPTICAL WORKS - Japan											
Zeitax (early)	4.5x6cm	120	FoldRo	1939	Zeitax Anastigmat	3.5	75mm		-200	Mc320	90
Zeitax (later)	4.5x6cm	120	FoldRo	1941	Zeitax Anastigmat	3.5	75mm	Shinko	-300		130
...MOZAR (Dr. Paul Mozar) - Düsseldorf, Germany											
Diana	6x9cm	120	BakeliteBox	1950		11			M,Z	Mc320	80
...MÜLLER (Conrad Müller) - Strengenberg, Germany											
Noris 4.5x6	4.5x6cm	120	FoldRo	1930	Cassar	2.9	75mm	Compur		Mc320	70
Noris 6x6	6x6cm	120	FoldRo	1935	Corygon	4.5	80mm	Compur			30
Noris 6x9	6x9cm	120	FoldRo	1935	Corygon	4.5	105mm	Compur			30
...MULTI-PHOTO (Société Multiphoto) - Lyon, France											
Multi-Photo 26x36	26x36mm	plate	MultiLens	1924	Saphir-Boyer	4.5	40mm	guillotine		F1511	2200
Multi-Photo 27x27	27x27mm	plate	MultiLens	1924	Saphir-Boyer	4.5	40mm	guillotine			2200
...MULTI-SPEED SHUTTER CO. - New York, NY, USA											
Multi-Speed Precision Cam.	3¼x4¼"	plate	FoldPl	1920	Busch Leukar	6.8	6.5"	Multi-Speed			140
Simplex	24x36mm	35mm	35Early	1914	B&L Tessar	3.5	50mm		1-300		3400
Simplex (dual-format)	24x36mm	35mm	35Early	1914	B&L Tessar	3.5	50mm		1-300	A3292	4400
...MULTIPOSE PORTABLE CAMERAS LTD. - France											
Maton	24x30mm	35mm	BakeliteBox	1930	Rousell Trylor	4.5	85mm	Gitzo		F1669	410
...MULTISCOPE & FILM CO. - Burlington, WI, USA											
Al-Vista 3B	3½x9"	118	Panoramic	1900	Extra Rap. Rectil.						330
Al-Vista 4B	4x12"	109	Panoramic	1900	Extra Rap. Rectil.					A934	370
Al-Vista 4G	4x10"	123	Panoramic	1904	Rapid Rectilinear						360
Al-Vista 5B	5x12"	110	Panoramic	1900	Extra Rap. Rectil.					Mc321	390

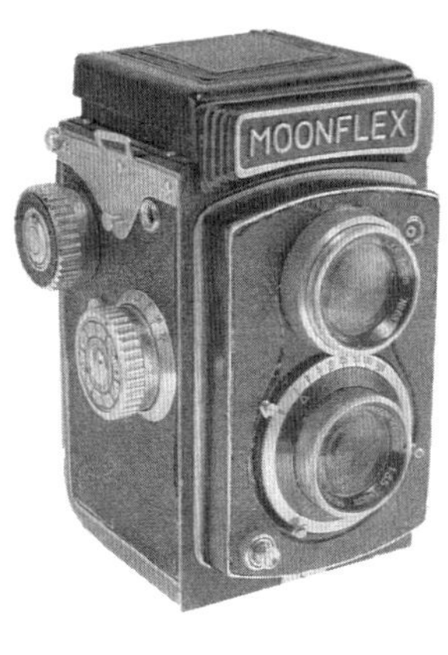

Moonflex

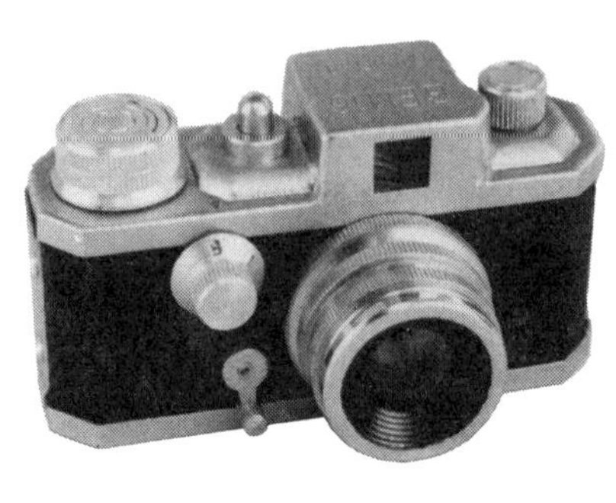
Gem 16, Mod. II

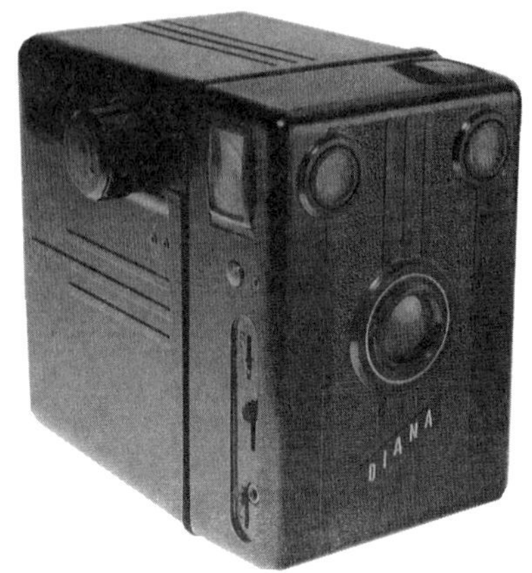

Mozar Diana

MODEL	FORMAT	FILM	TYPE	Year	LENS	Apert	FL	SHUTTER	SPEEDS	ILLUS	U.S.$
Al-Vista 5C	5x12"	110	Panoramic	1900	Extra Rap. Rectil.						390
Al-Vista 5D	5x16"	110	Panoramic	1900	Extra Rap. Rectil.					Mc321	350
Al-Vista 5F	5x12"	110	Panoramic	1900	Extra Rap. Rectil.					Mc321	670
Al-Vista 7D	7x15"	112	Panoramic	1901	Rapid Rectilinear						500
Al-Vista 7E	7x21"	112	Panoramic	1901	Appoplanat					A3398	500
Al-Vista 7F	7x15"	112	Panoramic	1901	Extra Rap. Rectil.					Mc321	900
Al-Vista Senior	8½x26"		Panoramic	1899							1500
Baby Al-Vista	2¼x6¾"	120	Panoramic	1906	Rapid Rectilinear					Mc321	440
...MUNDUS - France											
Mundus Color	8x14mm	8mm	Submin	1958	Berthiot	2.8	20mm		1-300	F736	310
Mundus Color 60	8x14mm	8mm	Submin	1960	Som-Berthiot	2.8	20mm			F737	270
Mundus Color 65	8x14mm	8mm	Submin	1974	Som-Berthiot	2.8	25mm			F738	240
...MÜNSTER KAMERABAU - Germany											
Phips	6x9cm	120	MetBx	1949	Achromat	9			T,I	HK103	100
...MURER & DURONI - Milan, Italy											
Express (strut-fold) 4.5x6	4.5x6cm	plate	StrutPl	1905	Murer Aplanat			focal plane			160
Express (strut-fold) 6x9	6x9cm	plate	StrutPl	1905	Murer Aplanat			focal plane			160
Express (strut-fold) 7x8	7x8cm	plate	StrutPl	1905	Murer Aplanat			focal plane		Mc322	160
Express (strut-fold) 8.5x11	8.5x11cm	plate	StrutPl	1905	Murer Aplanat			focal plane			160
Express (strut-fold) 9x12	9x12cm	plate	StrutPl	1905	Murer Aplanat			focal plane			160
Express Magazine Camera	9x12cm	plate	MagBox	1905	Aplanat	12	135mm	guillotine		A1319	90
Express Stereo 45x107	45x107	plate	StFoldPl	1905	Murer Anastigmat	4.5	60mm	guillotine			380
Express Stereo 6x13	6x13cm	plate	StFoldPl	1905	Murer Aplanat	8	80mm	guillotine			400
Folding pocket camera	4.5x6cm	plate	FoldPl	1910	Murer Aplanat			guillotine	T,I		120
Murer DH	13x18cm	plate	StrutPl	1908	Aplanat			focal plane			120
Murer DO-R	6.5x9cm	plate	StrutPl	1920	Murer Anastigmat	4.5	105mm	focal plane			120
Murer NL 6.5x9	6.5x9cm	plate	StrutPl	1905	Aplanat	8	90mm				80
Murer NL 9x12	9x12cm	plate	StrutPl	1905	Aplanat	8					100
Murer SL Box	4x5.5cm	Roll	RollBox	1900					P,L		120
Murer SL Special 45x107	45x107	plate	SterStrut	1910	Murer Aplanat	8	56mm	guillotine		A1783	200
Murer SL Stereo 6x13	6x13cm	plate	SterStrut	1910	Rapide Aplanat	8	80mm	guillotine			190
Murer UF	4.5x6cm	pack	StrutPl	1910	Aplanat				25-100		120
Murer UL	4.5x6cm	pack	StrutPl	1910	Aplanat				25-100		140
Murer UP-M	4.5x6cm	plate	StrutPl	1924	Rapid Aplanat	8	70mm	focal plane			120
Murer VL	4.5x6cm	plate	StrutPl	1910	Aplanat	8			25-100		50
Muro	4.5x6cm	plate	StrutPl	1914	Suter Anastigmat	5	70mm	focal plane	-1000		250
Newness Express 4.5x6	4.5x6cm	plate	MagBox	1900	Murer Anastigmat	4.5		focal plane			50
Newness Express 6x9	6x9cm	plate	MagBox	1900	Murer Anastigmat	4.5		focal plane			50
Newness Express 7x8	7x8cm	plate	MagBox	1900	Murer Anastigmat	4.5		focal plane			60
Newness Express 8.5x11	8.5x11cm	plate	MagBox	1900	Murer Anastigmat	4.5		focal plane			50
Newness Express 9x12	9x12cm	plate	MagBox	1900	Murer Anastigmat	4.5		focal plane			70
Newness Express Stereo	6x13cm	plate	StMagBox	1900	Rapide Rectilinear	10					280

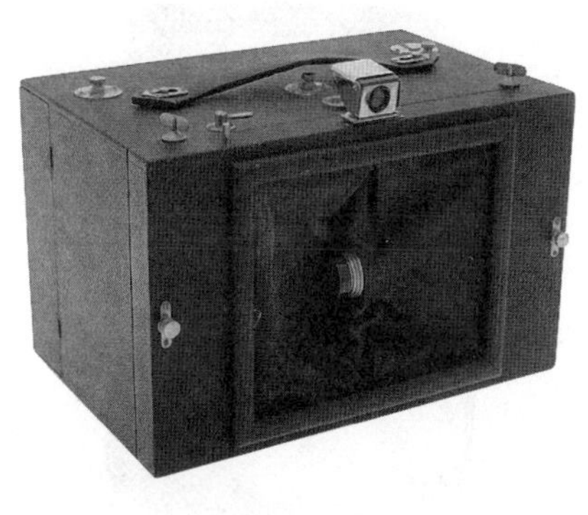

Al-Vista 7F

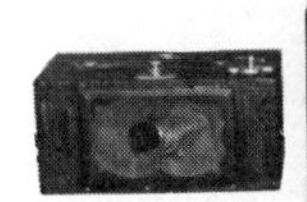

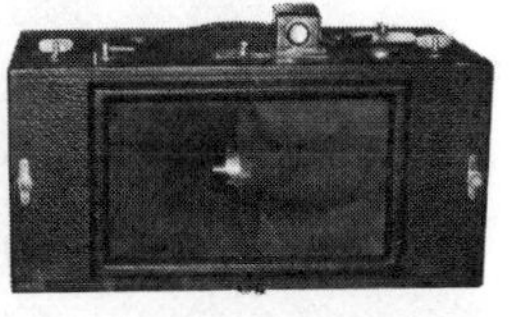

Baby Al-Vista

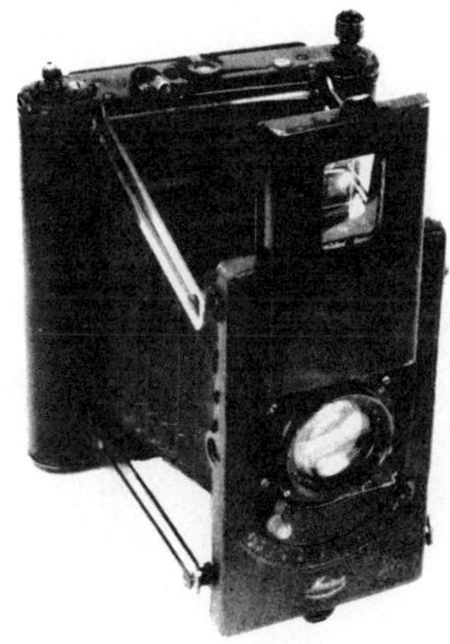

Murer Express (strut)

MODEL	FORMAT	FILM	TYPE	Year	LENS	Apert	FL	SHUTTER	SPEEDS	ILLUS	U.S.$
Newness Express Stereo	9x18cm	plate	StMagBox	1900	Murer Aplanat	10	110mm	guillotine			290
Piccolo	4x5cm	Roll	Jumelle	1900						Mc322	160
Reflex	6.5x9cm	plate	MedSLR	1925	Murer Anastigmat	4.5	120mm	focal plane	15-1000		160
Sprite (plate)	4.5x6cm	plate	StrutPl	1915	Rapide Aplanat	8	70mm		25-100		120
Sprite (rollfilm)	4.5x6cm	127	StrutRo	1915	Rapide Aplanat	8	70mm		25-100		120
Stereo DP-R	45x107	plate	SterStrut	1920	Murer Anastigmat	8	60mm	focal plane	15-1000	A1781	230
Stereo Reflex 45x107	45x107	plate	SterRefl	1925	Murer Anastigmat	4.5					590
Stereo Reflex 6x13	6x13cm	plate	SterRefl	1924	Murer Anastigmat	4.5	90mm	focal plane			280
...MURRAY & HEATH - London, England											
Stereoscopic camera	9x17cm	WetPl	StWetPl	1865	Ross						2800
Tailboard camera	11.5x18	plate	Tailboard	1905	Ross	8					270
...MUSASHINO KOKI - Japan											
Graphic 6x6	6x6cm	120/2	MedSLR	1968	Rittron	2	80mm	focal plane	1-500		590
Norita 6x6	6x6cm	120/2	MedSLR	1968	Rittron	2	80mm	focal plane	1-500		460
Optika IIa	6x9cm	120	MedSLR	1956	Luminor	3.5	105mm	focal plane	20-400	Mc322	330
Optika Pro	6x9cm	120	MedSLR	1963	Luminor	3.5	105mm	focal plane	½-400		230
Rittreck 6x6	6x6cm	120/2	MedSLR	1968	Rittron	2	80mm	focal plane	1-500	Mc322	590
Rittreck IIa	6x9cm	120	MedSLR	1956	Luminant	3.5	105mm	focal plane	20-500	A1620	330
Rittreck SP	6x9cm	120	MedSLR	1961	Luminant	3.5	105mm	focal plane	2-500		330
Warner 6x6	6x6cm	120/2	MedSLR	1968	Rittron	2	80mm	focal plane	1-500	Mc322	590
...MUSE OPTICAL CO. - Tokyo, Japan											
Museflex	3x3cm	Bolta	TLR	1950	Meica	4.5	50mm		B,25-150		120
Museflex IIa	3x3cm	Bolta	TLR	1951	Muse Anast	3.8	50mm		B,25-150		120
Museflex Mod.-M	3x3cm	Bolta	TLR	1949	Alphar-T	5.6	55mm		B,25,50	Mc322	130
Museflex Mod.-M II	3x3cm	Bolta	TLR	1950	Alphar-T	5.6	55mm		I,B	A1735	120
...(unknown)											
Mykey-4	4x4cm	127	RigidRo	1960	Tokinon	3.5	60mm		25-300	Mc322	70
...NADAR (Paul Nadar) - Paris											
Express Détective Nadar	9x12cm	plate	DetectivBox	1890	Antiplanat	6.8	150mm		I,T	F950	3900
Express Détective Nadar	13x18cm	plate	DetectivBox	1890	Antiplanat	6.8	150mm		I,T	F951	1400
...NAGEL (Dr. August Nagel Camerawerk) - Stuttgart											
Anca 10 a	6.5x9cm	plate	VtFoldPl	1928	Nagel Anastigmat	6.8	10.5cm	Nagel	25-100		140
Anca 10 b	6.5x9cm	plate	VtFoldPl	1928	Nagel Anastigmat	6.3	10.5cm	Ibsor	1-125		140
Anca 10 c	6.5x9cm	plate	VtFoldPl	1928	Nagel Anastigmat	4.5	10.5cm	Pronto	25-100		140
Anca 14 b	6.5x9cm	plate	VtFoldPl	1928	Nagel Anastigmat	6.3	10.5cm	Ibsor	1-125		140
Anca 14 g	6.5x9cm	plate	VtFoldPl	1928	Laudar	4.5	10.5cm	Compur	1-250		140
Anca 25 b	9x12cm	plate	VtFoldPl	1928	Nagel Anastigmat	6.3	13.5cm	Ibsor	1-125		140
Anca 25 g	9x12cm	plate	VtFoldPl	1928	Laudar	4.5	13.5cm	Ibsor	1-125		140
Anca 28 b	9x12cm	plate	VtFoldPl	1928	Nagel Anastigmat	6.3	13.5cm	Pronto	25-100		140
Anca 28 g	9x12cm	plate	VtFoldPl	1928	Laudar	4.5	13.5cm	Compur	1-250		140
Fornidar 30 e	9x12cm	plate	VtFoldPl	1930	Xenar	4.5	13.5cm	Compur	1-250		120
Fornidar 30 u	9x12cm	plate	VtFoldPl	1930	Elmar	4.5	13.5cm	Compur-S	1-250		120

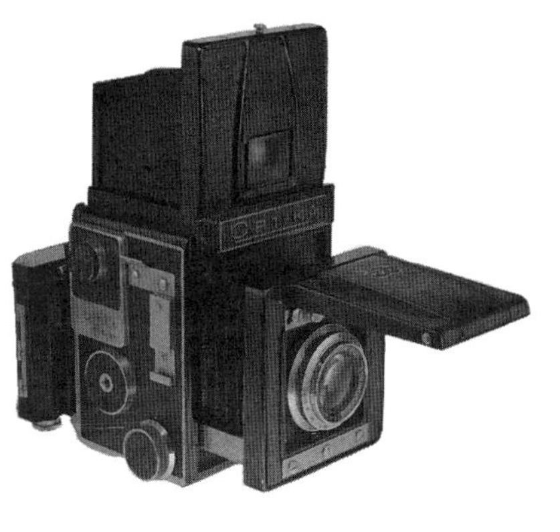

Musashino Optika IIa

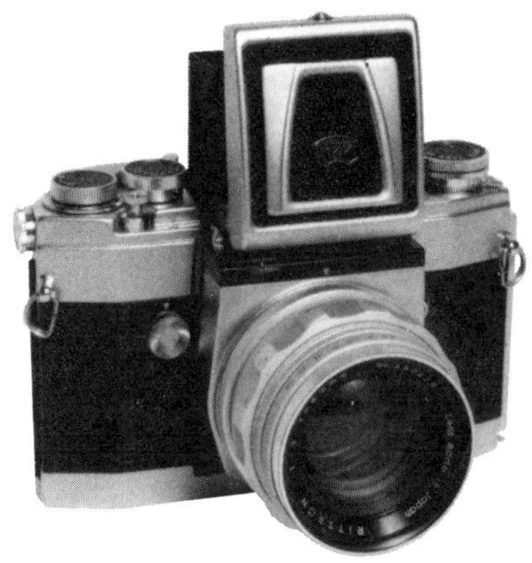

Rittreck 6x6

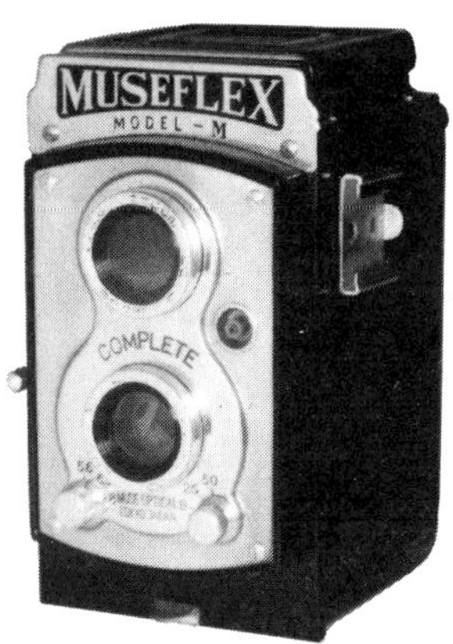

Museflex Mod.-M

MODEL	FORMAT	FILM	TYPE	Year	LENS	Apert	FL	SHUTTER	SPEEDS	ILLUS	U.S.$
Librette 65 a	6x9cm	120	VtFoldRo	1928	Nagel Anastigmat	6.8	10.5cm	Nagel	25-100		70
Librette 65 c	6x9cm	120	VtFoldRo	1928	Nagel Anastigmat	4.5	10.5cm	Pronto	25-100		70
Librette 74 b	6x9cm	120	VtFoldRo	1928	Nagel Anastigmat	6.8	10.5cm	Pronto	25-100		70
Librette 74 e	6x9cm	120	VtFoldRo	1928	Xenar	4.5	10.5cm	Compur	1-250		70
Librette 74 g	6x9cm	120	VtFoldRo	1928	Laudar	4.5	10.5cm	Ibsor	1-125		70
Librette 74 u	6x9cm	120	VtFoldRo	1928	Elmar	4.5	12cm	Compur	1-250		70
Librette 74/1 Luxus	6x9cm	120	VtFoldRo	1928	Xenar	4.5	10.5cm	Compur	1-250		210
Librette 74/1 Luxus (Elmar)	6x9cm	120	VtFoldRo	1928	Elmar	4.5	12cm	Compur	1-250		270
Librette 75	6x9cm	120	VtFoldRo	1933	Radionar	4.5	10.5cm	Pronto	25-100		70
Librette 75	6x9cm	120	VtFoldRo	1933	Tessar	4.5	10.5cm	Compur-S	1-250		70
Librette 79 b	6.5x11cm	118	VtFoldRo	1930	Anastigmat	6.3	12cm	Pronto	25-100		80
Librette 79 e	6.5x11cm	118	VtFoldRo	1930	Xenar	4.5	12cm	Compur	1-250		80
Librette 79/1 g Luxus	6.5x11cm	118	VtFoldRo	1930	Laudar	4.5	12cm	Compur	1-250		80
Pupille M	3x4cm	127	RigidRo	1931	Leitz Elmar	3.5	5cm	Compur	1-300		490
Pupille P	3x4cm	127	RigidRo	1931	Xenar	2.9	5cm	Compur	1-300		260
Pupille Z	3x4cm	127	RigidRo	1931	Xenon	2	5cm	Compur	1-300		310
Ranca 46	3x4cm	127	RigidRo	1930	Nagel Anastigmat	4.5	50mm	Prontor	25-100	Mc323	190
Ranca 46/1	3x4cm	127	RigidRo	1930	Nagel Anastigmat	4.5	50mm	Ibsor	1-150		190
Recomar 18 b	6.5x9cm	plate	VtFoldPl	1929	Nagel Anastigmat	6.3	10.5cm	Ibsor	1-150		80
Recomar 18 e	6.5x9cm	plate	VtFoldPl	1929	Xenar	4.5	10.5cm	Compur	1-250		80
Recomar 18 u	6.5x9cm	plate	VtFoldPl	1929	Leitz Elmar	4.5	12cm	Compur	1-250		160
Recomar 33 e	9x12cm	plate	VtFoldPl	1929	Xenar	4.5	13.5cm	Ibsor	1-150		90
Recomar 33 g	9x12cm	plate	VtFoldPl	1929	Laudar	4.5	13.5cm	Compur	1-250		90
Recomar 33 u	9x12cm	plate	VtFoldPl	1929	Leitz Elmar	4.5	13.5cm	Compur	1-250		190
Rolloroy	3x4cm	127	RigidRo	1931	Tessar	2.8	5cm	Compur	1-300		260
Rolloroy L	3x4cm	127	RigidRo	1931	Xenar	3.5	5cm	Compur	1-300		260
Vollenda 48	3x4cm	127	HzFoldRo	1931	Radionar	4.5	5cm	Pronto-S	25-100		100
Vollenda 48 u	3x4cm	127	HzFoldRo	1931	Elmar	3.5	5cm	Compur	1-300		180
Vollenda 52	4x6.5cm	127	VtFoldRo	1932	Radionar	4.5	7.5cm	Prontor-S		Mc323	60
Vollenda 60/0 b	5x7.5cm	129	VtFoldRo	1930	Nagel Anastigmat	6.3	9cm	Nagel	25-100		80
Vollenda 60/0 c	5x7.5cm	129	VtFoldRo	1930	Nagel Anastigmat	4.5	9cm	Pronto	25-100		70
Vollenda 60/1 e	5x7.5cm	129	VtFoldRo	1930	Xenar	4.5	9cm	Compur	1-300		70
Vollenda 60/1 g	5x7.5cm	129	VtFoldRo	1930	Laudar	4.5	9cm	Compur	1-300		70
Vollenda 68	6x9cm	120	VtFoldRo	1930	Xenar	6.3	10.5cm	Nagel			50
Vollenda 70/0 b	6x9cm	120	VtFoldRo	1930	Nagel Anastigmat	6.3	10.5cm	Pronto	25-100		70
Vollenda 70/0 c	6x9cm	120	VtFoldRo	1930	Nagel Anastigmat	4.5	10.5cm	Pronto	25-100		70
Vollenda 70/1	6x9cm	120	VtFoldRo	1930	Elmar	4.5	12cm	Compur	1-250		60
Vollenda 70/1 c	6x9cm	120	VtFoldRo	1930	Nagel Anastigmat	4.5	10.5cm	Pronto	25-100		60
Vollenda 70/1 e	6x9cm	120	VtFoldRo	1930	Xenar	4.5	10.5cm	Compur	1-250		60
Vollenda 70/1 g	6x9cm	120	VtFoldRo	1930	Laudar	4.5	10.5cm	Ibsor	1-150		60
Vollenda 70/2 e Luxus	6x9cm	120	VtFoldRo	1930	Xenar	4.5	10.5cm	Compur	1-250		120
Vollenda 70/2 g Luxus	6x9cm	120	VtFoldRo	1930	Laudar	4.5	10.5cm	Compur	1-250		120

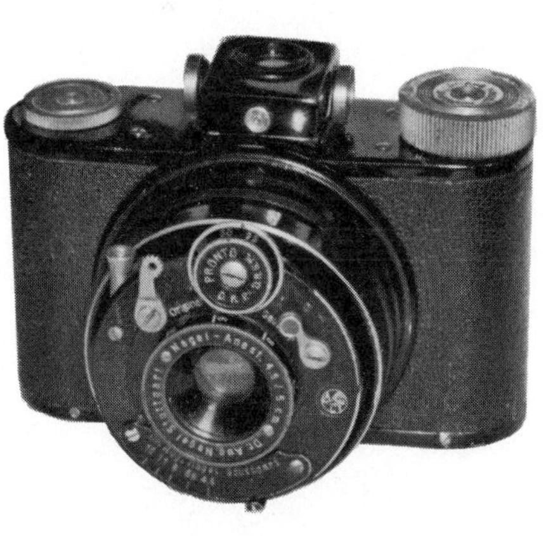

Ranca 46

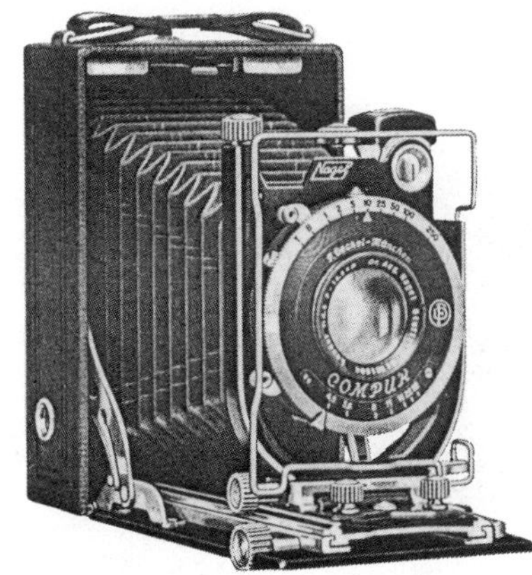

Recomar 18

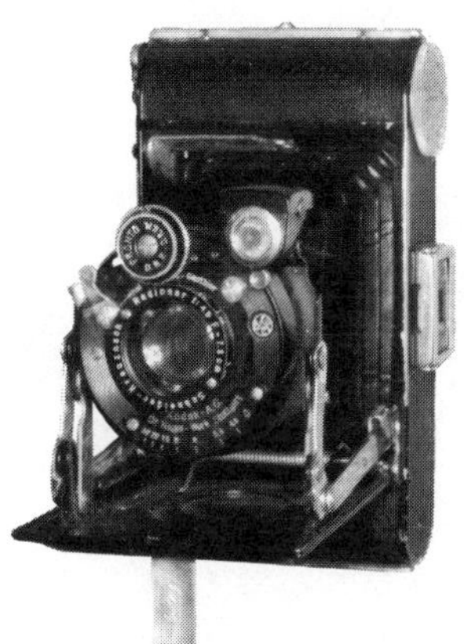

Vollenda 52

MODEL	FORMAT	FILM	TYPE	Year	LENS	Apert	FL	SHUTTER	SPEEDS	ILLUS	U.S.$
Vollenda 70/2 Luxus	6x9cm	120	VtFoldRo	1930	Elmar	4.5	12cm	Compur	1-250		120
Vollenda 72	6x9cm	120	VtFoldRo	1930	Radionar	4.5	10.5cm	Pronto-S			80
Vollenda 72	6x9cm	120	VtFoldRo	1930	Xenar	4.5	10.5cm	Compur	1-250		80
Vollenda 72	6x9cm	120	VtFoldRo	1930	Tessar	4.5	10.5cm	Compur	1-250		80
Vollenda 80 c	6.5x11cm	118	VtFoldRo	1930	Nagel Anastigmat	6.3	12cm	Pronto	25-100		70
Vollenda 80 e	6.5x11cm	118	VtFoldRo	1930	Xenar	4.5	12cm	Compur	1-250		70
Vollenda 80 h	6.5x11cm	118	VtFoldRo	1930	Laudar	4.5	12cm	Compur	1-250		70
Vollenda 80/1 c	6.5x11cm	118	VtFoldRo	1930	Nagel Anastigmat	6.3	12cm	Pronto	25-100		70
Vollenda 80/1 e	6.5x11cm	118	VtFoldRo	1930	Xenar	4.5	12cm	Compur	1-250		70
Vollenda 80/1 g	6.5x11cm	118	VtFoldRo	1930	Laudar	4.5	12cm	Compur	1-250		70
Vollenda 80/2 e Luxus	6.5x11cm	118	VtFoldRo	1930	Xenar	4.5	12cm	Compur	1-250		140
Vollenda 80/2 g Luxus	6.5x11cm	118	VtFoldRo	1930	Laudar	4.5	12cm	Compur	1-250		140
...NATIONAL - Osaka, Japan											
Radicame CR-1	13x17mm	110	110VF	1978	Fujinon				I	Mc323	140
Radio/Flash CR-1	13x17mm	110	110VF	1978	Fujinon				I	HK648	130
Radio/Flash CR-2	13x17mm	110	110VF	1979	Fujinon	5.6	24mm		I		140
...NATIONAL CAMERA CO. - N.Y.C.											
Baldwin-Flex	3x4cm	127	TLR-Box						I,T	Mc323	20
...NATIONAL CAMERA CO. - St. Louis, Missouri											
Naco	8x14cm	122	HzFoldRo		Rapid Rectilinear	4		Ilex	25-100	Mc323	50
...NATIONAL INSTRUMENT CORP. - Houston, Texas											
Camflex	6x6cm	620	MetBx	1948	Meniscus				I	Mc323	30
Colonel	6x6cm	620	MetBx	1947	Meniscus		85mm		I	Mc323	40
Major	6x6cm	620	MetBx	1947	Meniscus		85mm		I	Mc324	40
...NATIONAL PHOTOCOLOR CORP. - New York, NY											
Daylight Color Camera	3¼x4¼"	plate	3-Color	1942	Goerz Dogmar	4.5	8 1/4"	Compound	1-100		520
Lerochrome 3¼x4¼"	3¼x4¼"	plate	3-Color	1939	Velostigmat	4.5	8 1/4"	Compound	1-100	Mc324	550
Lerochrome 5x7"	5x7"	plate	3-Color	1939	Velostigmat	4.5	12"	Compound	1-100		490
One-Shot Color Camera	3¼x4¼"	plate	3-Color	1939	Goerz Dogmar	4.5	8 1/4"	Compound	1-100	Mc324	480
One-Shot Color Camera	5x7"	plate	3-Color	1939	Goerz Dogmar	4.5	12"	Compound	1-100		440
...NAYLOR (T. Naylor) - England											
Field Camera	6½x8½"	plate	Field		Brass barrel						230
...NEBRO - Argentina											
Baby Nebro	6x6cm	620	RigidRo						I,T	Mc324	30
Box-Nebro	6x9cm	620	MetBx	1930					I	Mc324	20
Nebro Flash	6x9cm	620/1	RigidRo						I,T	Mc324	30
Super Nebro	6x9cm	620	RigidRo						I,T	Mc324	30
...NEGRETTI & ZAMBRA - London, England											
Binocular camera	4.5x6cm	plate	Disguised	1910	Negretti					A3275	2500
Cosmos	45x105m	plate	StMagBox	1903	Extra Rapid						660
Field Camera	4¼x6½"	plate	Field		Brass barrel			roller-blind			390
One-Lens Stereo Camera	8x8cm	WetPl	StWetPl	1865	Negretti			Negretti & Zambra			11000

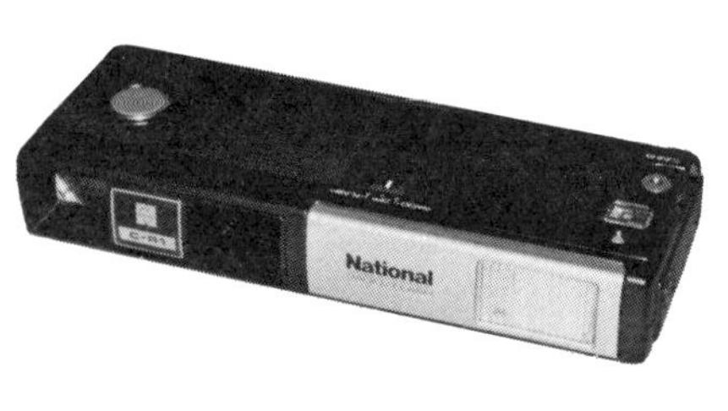

Radicame CR-1

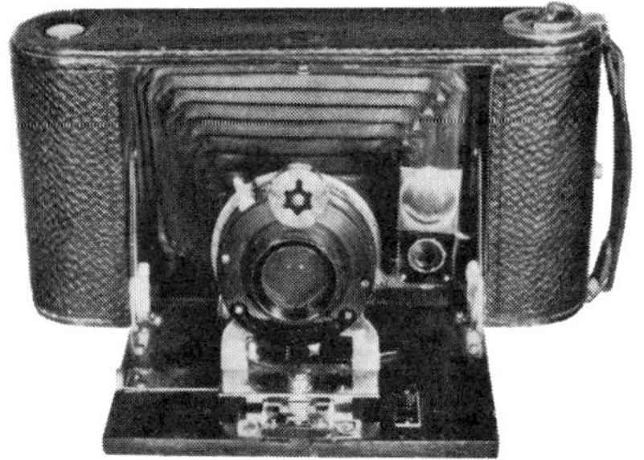

Naco

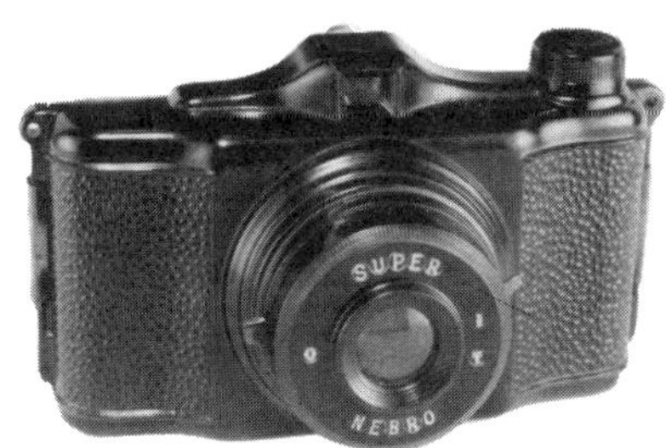

Super Nebro

MODEL	FORMAT	FILM	TYPE	Year	LENS	Apert	FL	SHUTTER	SPEEDS	ILLUS	U.S.$
Stereo		WetPl	StWetPl	1862	Negretti						4700
...NEIDIG (Richard Neidig Kamera-Werk) - Plankstadt, Germany											
Perlux 24x24	24x24mm	35mm	35vf	1950	Radionar	3.5	38mm	Prontor-S			110
Perlux 24x36	24x36mm	35mm	35vf	1952	Kataplast	2.8	45mm	Vario	25-200		70
...NEITHOLD (Carl Neithold) - Frankfurt/Main											
Ce-Nei-Fix	6x9cm	120	FoldRo	1930		11		AGC	25,50	Mc324	50
Ce-Nei Indopor I	9x18cm	plate	SterBox	1926	Laack						200
Ce-Nei Knirps	3x3cm	Roll	TelescRo	1930	Polynar	6.8	42mm		M,Z	A3302	370
Ce-Nei Knirps	3x3cm	Roll	TelescRo	1930	Dialytar	3.5	42mm		M,Z		380
...(unknown)											
Neo Fot A	4.5x6cm	120	RigidRo	1950					I	Mc325	30
...NEOCA CO. - Japan											
Neoca 1S	24x36mm	35mm	35rf	1955	Neokor	3.5	45mm	Ceres	5-300		50
Neoca 2S	24x36mm	35mm	35rf	1955	Neokor	3.5	45mm	Rectus	1-300	Mc325	60
Neoca IVS	24x36mm	35mm	35rf	1958	Neokor	2.8	45mm	Citizen MV B	1-400	Mc325	70
Robin	24x36mm	35mm	35rf	1962	Neokar	2.8	45mm	Citizen MV	-500		50
...NETTEL KAMERAWERK - Sontheim-Heilbronn, Germany											
Argus	4.5x6cm	plate	Disguised	1911						A855	1300
Deckrullo-Nettel	18x24cm	plate	StrutPl	1908	Dagor	6.8	210mm	focal plane	1-2800		260
Deckrullo-Nettel	18x24cm	plate	StrutPl	1908	Xenar	4.5	210mm	focal plane	1-2800		260
Deckrullo-Nettel 101	9x12cm	plate	StrutPl	1908	Rapid-Aplanat	8	150mm	focal plane	½-2800		140
Deckrullo-Nettel 105	9x12cm	plate	StrutPl	1908	Dagor	6.8	150mm	focal plane	½-2800		140
Deckrullo-Nettel 116	9x12cm	plate	StrutPl	1908	Tessar	4.5	150mm	focal plane	½-2800	A311	140
Deckrullo-Nettel 121	10x15cm	plate	StrutPl	1908	Rapid-Aplanat	8	165mm	focal plane	½-2800		200
Deckrullo-Nettel 125	10x15cm	plate	StrutPl	1908	Dagor	6.8	165mm	focal plane	½-2800		200
Deckrullo-Nettel 135	10x15cm	plate	StrutPl	1908	Tessar	4.5	180mm	focal plane	½-2800		200
Deckrullo-Nettel 142	13x18cm	plate	StrutPl	1908	Nettel Anastigmat	6.5	18cm	focal plane	1-2800		180
Deckrullo-Nettel 145	13x18cm	plate	StrutPl	1908	Dagor	6.8	18cm	focal plane	1-2800		180
Deckrullo-Nettel 156	13x18cm	plate	StrutPl	1908	Tessar	4.5	210mm	focal plane	1-2800		180
Deckrullo-Nettel 316	6.5x9cm	plate	StrutPl	1910	Tessar	6.3	120mm	focal plane	1-1500		140
Deckrullo-Nettel 317	6.5x9cm	plate	StrutPl	1910	Tessar	4.5	120mm	focal plane	1-1500		140
Folding plate camera 9x12	9x12cm	plate	FoldPl		Tessar	6.3	135mm	Dial-Compur	1-250		80
Folding plate camera 5x7"	5x7"	plate	FoldPl		Zeiss Anastigmat	8	210mm	Dial-Compur	1-250		130
Sonnet 6x9	6x9cm	plate	FoldPl	1919	Tessar	4.5	120mm				160
Sonnet 10x15	10x15cm	plate	FoldPl	1913	Tessar	6.3	165mm	Compur	1-200		120
Sonnet (Tropical) 4.5x6	4.5x6cm	plate	FoldPl		Tessar	4.5	75mm	Compound	1-300	A258-9	650
Sonnet (Tropical) 6x9	6x9cm	plate	FoldPl		Tessar	4.5	120mm	Compound			350
Stereax 45x107	45x107	plate	SterStrut	1915	Tessar	4.5	62mm	focal plane			420
Stereax 6x13	6x13cm	plate	SterStrut	1909	Tessar	6.3	84mm	focal plane			270
Stereax 231	6x13cm	plate	SterStrut	1915	Tessar	4.5	120mm	focal plane			420
Stereo-Deckrullo-Nettel	6x13cm	plate	SterStrut	1910	Tessar	4.5	90mm	focal plane			280
Stereo-Deckrullo-Nettel	10x15cm	plate	SterStrut	1910	Tessar	4.5	120mm	focal plane	½-2800		360

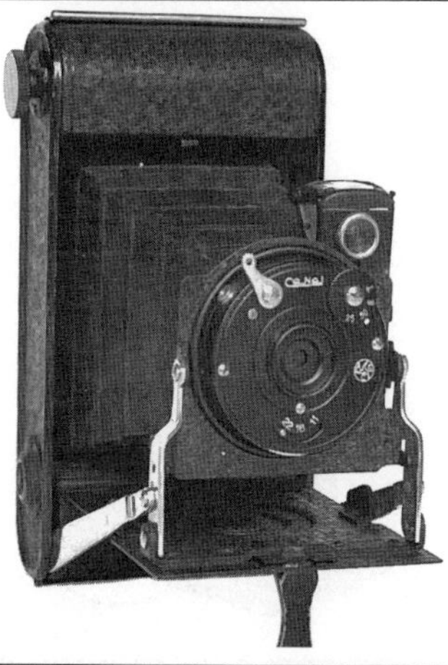

Ce-Nei-Fix

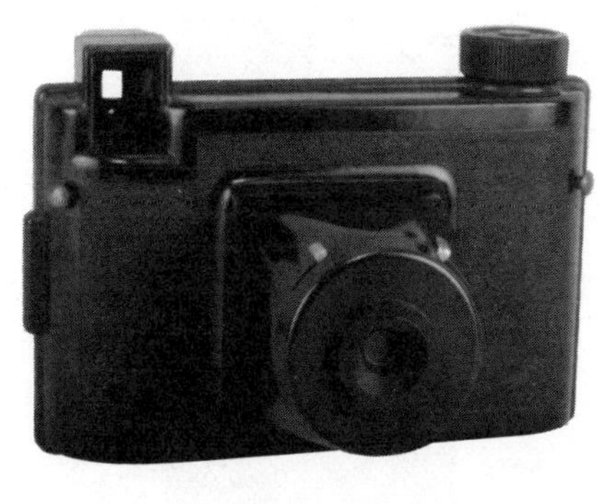

Neo Fot A

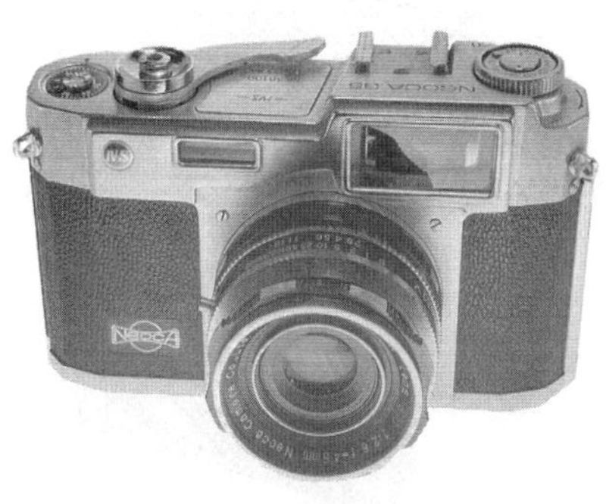

Neoca IVS

MODEL	FORMAT	FILM	TYPE	Year	LENS	Apert	FL	SHUTTER	SPEEDS	ILLUS	U.S.$
Stereo-Deckrullo-Nettel	13x18cm	plate	SterStrut	1910	Dagor	6.8		focal plane	1-2800		360
Stereo-Deckrullo-Nettel	13x18cm	plate	SterStrut	1910	Tessar	4.5		focal plane	1-2800		360
Stereo-Deckrullo-Nettel 166	10x15cm	plate	SterStrut	1910	Dagor	6.8	120mm	focal plane	½-2800		360
Stereo-Deckrullo-N. Trop.	9x14cm	plate	SterStrut	1912	Tessar	4.5		focal plane	½-2800		900
Stereo-Deckrullo-N. Trop.	9x18cm	plate	SterStrut	1912	Tessar	4.5		focal plane	1-2800		900
Stereo-Deckrullo-N. Trop.	10x15cm	plate	SterStrut	1912	Tessar	4.5		focal plane	½-2800		900
Tropen-Deckrullo-Nettel	6.5x9cm	plate	StrutPl	1918	Nettel Anastigmat	4.5	120mm	focal plane	½-2800	A313	1000
Tropen-Deckrullo-Nettel	10x15cm	plate	StrutPl	1910	Nettel Anastigmat	4.5	165mm	focal plane	½-2800	Mc325	900
...NEUBERT (Franz Robert Neubert) - Jena											
Neuca	24x36mm	35mm	35rf	1949	Triplar	2.8	50mm	focal plane	20-500		1500
Neucaflex	24x36mm	35mm	35slr	1949	Primoplan	1.9	58mm	focal plane	1-1000	A1642	2900
Neucaflex	24x36mm	35mm	35slr	1949	Primoplan	1.9	58mm	focal plane	20-1000	A1059	2500
...NEUE GÖRLITZER KAMERAWERKE (GÖRLITZER KAMERAWERKE) - Görlitz											
Field camera 13x18	13x18cm	plate	Tailboard	1920	various			various			300
Field camera 18x24	18x24cm	plate	Tailboard	1920	various			various			300
Globus Stella	13x18cm	plate	Studio	1922	various			various			1400
Globus Studio camera	13x18cm	plate	Studio	1922	Eurygon	4.5	240mm				1100
Globus Studio camera	18x24cm	plate	Studio	1922	various			various			1100
Studio camera 13x18	13x18cm	plate	Studio	1920	various			various			240
Studio camera 18x24	18x24cm	plate	Studio	1920	various			various			240
...NEUMANN (Felix Neumann) - Vienna, Austria											
Field Camera		plate	Tailboard	1900							220
Helios 6x9	6x9cm	plate	Box	1890	fixed focus				Z,M		3800
Helios 9x12	9x12cm	plate	Box	1890	fixed focus				Z,M	HK38	3800
Magazine camera	9x12cm	plate	MagBox	1895	Meniscus						310
...NEUMANN & HEILEMANN - Japan											
Condor	4.5x6cm	120	FoldRo								90
...NEW IDEAS MFG. CO. - New York											
Magazine camera		plate	DetectivBox	1898				string-set		Mc325	410
Tourist Multiple	18x24mm	35mm	35Early	1913	Tessar	3.5		guillotine		Mc325	2200
...NEW YORK FERROTYPE CO.											
Tintype camera	1½x2½"	Ferro	Ferrotype	1906				Wollensak			240
...NEWMAN & GUARDIA, LTD. - London											
Baby Sibyl (plate)	4.5x6cm	plate	FoldPl	1912	Tessar	4.5	75mm	N&G	2-200	Mc326	700
Baby Sibyl (rollfilm)	1⅝x2⅝"	127	FoldRo	1912	Ross Xpress	4.5	75mm	N&G	2-200		560
Deluxe	3¼x4¼"	plate	PlateBox	1896	Zeiss Protar	9	220mm	N&G	½-100	Mc326	350
Folding Reflex + f2.9	6.5x9cm	plate	LgSLR	1921	Ross Xpress	2.9	5.5"	focal plane	10-800	A557	260
Folding Reflex	6.5x9cm	plate	LgSLR	1921	Ross Xpress	4.5	5.5"	focal plane	10-800	Mc326	350
High Speed Pattern	3½x4¾"	plate	MagBox	1911	Zeiss Tessar	4.5		focal plane	2-800		470
New Ideal Sibyl	3x4⅝"	124	FoldRo	1913	Tessar	4.5	135mm	N&G Special			240
New Ideal Sibyl	3¼x4¼"	plate	FoldPl	1913	Tessar	4.5	135mm	N&G Special			260
New Special Sibyl (plate)	6.5x9cm	plate	FoldPl	1914	Ross Xpress	4.5	112mm	N&G Special			290

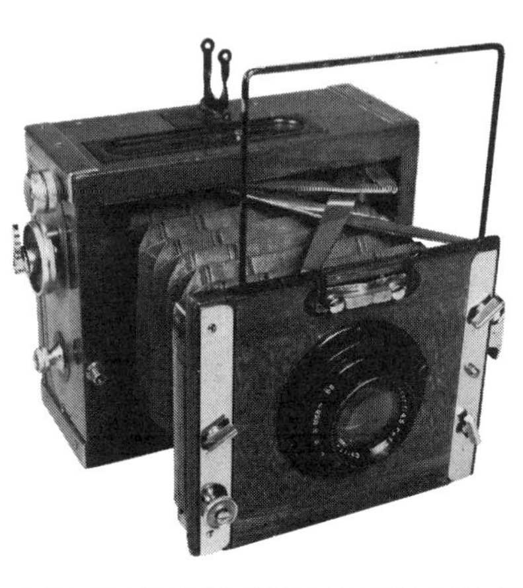
Tropen-Deckrullo-Nettel

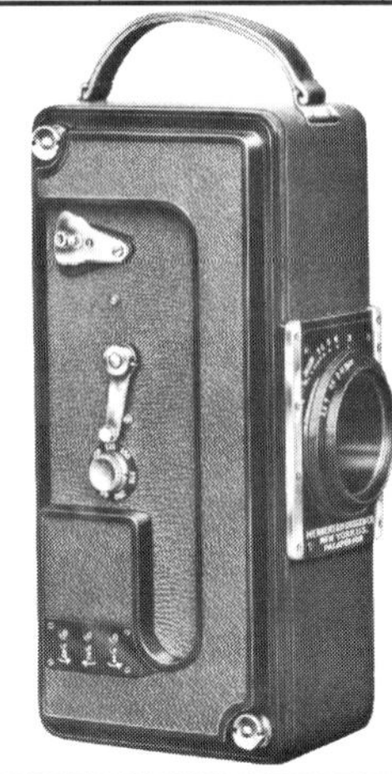
Tourist Multiple

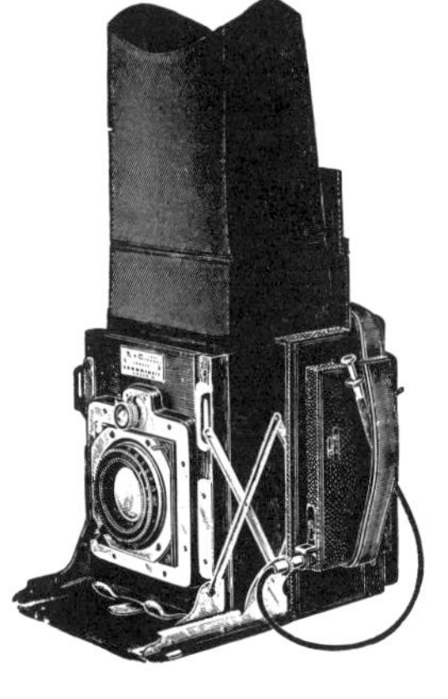
Folding Reflex

MODEL	FORMAT	FILM	TYPE	Year	LENS	Apert	FL	SHUTTER	SPEEDS	ILLUS	U.S.$
New Special Sibyl (plate)	6.5x9cm	plate	FoldPl	1914	Tessar	4.5	112mm	N&G Special			290
New Special Sibyl (rollfilm)	2¼x3¼"	120	FoldRo	1914	Ross Xpress	4.5	112mm	N&G Special			240
New Special Sibyl (rollfilm)	2¼x3¼"	120	FoldRo	1914	Tessar	4.5	112mm	N&G Special			240
Nydia 9x12	9x12cm	plate	StrutPl	1900	Wray R.R.			guillotine	2-100	Mc326	700
Nydia 10x13	10x13cm	plate	StrutPl	1900	Wray R.R.			guillotine	2-100	A290	900
Nydia 10x13	10x13cm	plate	StrutPl	1900	Ross	8		guillotine	2-100		900
Postcard Sibyl	3½x5½"	plate	FoldPl	1912	Zeiss Tessar	4.5	150mm	N&G Pneum.	½-100		320
Sibyl (plate) 6.5x9	6.5x9cm	plate	FoldPl	1907	Tessar	6.3	120mm	N&G Special		A2982	140
Sibyl (plate) 6.5x9	6.5x9cm	plate	FoldPl	1907	Ross	4.5	112mm	N&G Special			140
Sibyl (plate) 3¼x4¼"	3¼x4¼"	plate	FoldPl	1907	Ross	3.5		N&G Special			160
Sibyl (rollfilm) 6.5x9	6.5x9cm	120	FoldRo	1907	Ross	3.5	112mm	N&G Special			140
Sibyl (rollfilm) 3¼x4¼"	3¼x4¼"	124	FoldRo	1907	Tessar	6.3	135mm	N&G Special			160
Sibyl (rollfilm) 3¼x4¼"	3¼x4¼"	124	FoldRo	1907	Ross	4.5		N&G Special			160
Sibyl Deluxe	3¼x4¼"	plate	FoldPl	1909	Zeiss Protar	6.3	5"	N&G	2-100	Mc326	460
Sibyl Deluxe	3¼x4¼"	plate	FoldPl	1909	Ross Convertible	6.3	5"	N&G	2-100		460
Sibyl Excelsior	2½x4¼"	116	FoldRo	1933	Ross Xpres	4.5	136mm	N&G Patent		Mc326	270
Sibyl Stereo	6x13cm	plate	StFoldPl	1912	Zeiss Tessar	4.5	120mm		2-100		1500
Special Ster. Rollfilm Sibyl	1¾x4¼"	116	StFoldPl	1920	Ross Xpres	4.5	75mm	N&G	½-100		2700
Stereoscopic Pattern	4¼x6½"	plate	StMagBox	1896		6.3		N&G Pneum.			1000
Trellis 3¼x4¼"	3¼x4¼"	plate	FoldPl	1910	Protar			N&G		Mc326	370
Trellis 4¼x6½"	4¼x6½"	plate	FoldPl	1010	Protar			N&G			510
Twin Lens Pattern	9x12cm	plate	TLR	1895				Newman Pat.	½-100	Mc326	700
Universal Pattern B	3¼x4¼"	plate	MagBox	1905	Zeiss Anastigmat	6.3		N&G Pneum.	2-100		410
Universal Pattern B	4x5"	plate	MagBox	1905	Zeiss Anastigmat	6.3		N&G Pneum.	2-100		410
Universal Special Patt. B	3¼x4¼"	plate	MagBox	1905	Zeiss Anastigmat	6.3		N&G Pneum.	2-100		410
Universal Special Patt. B	4x5"	plate	MagBox	1905	Zeiss Anastigmat	6.3		N&G Pneum.	2-100		410
...NEWTON & CO. - London											
Tailboard camera 4¼x6½"	4¼x6½"	plate	Tailboard	1887	various			various			250
Tailboard camera 10x12"	10x12"	plate	Tailboard	1887	various			various			250
...NEWTON PHOTO PRODUCTS - Los Angeles, CA											
Newton New Vue	4x5"	plate	2-Rail	1947	various			various		Mc327	200
...NIAGARA CAMERA CO. - Buffalo, NY											
Niagara No. 2	3½x3½"	plate	PlateBox	1899	achromatic			Automatic	I,T	Mc327	50
...NIC - Barcelona, Spain											
Foto Nic			Instant	1935						Mc327	310
...NICCA CAMERA WORKS - Japan											
Nicca (original)	24x36mm	35mm	35rf	1948	Nikkor-QC	3.5	5cm	focal plane	1-500		1300
Nicca III (Type-3)	24x36mm	35mm	35rf	1949	Nikkor-HC	2	5cm	focal plane	1-500		320
Nicca IIIA	24x36mm	35mm	35rf	1951	Nikkor-HC	2	5cm	focal plane	1-500		410
Nicca IIIA	24x36mm	35mm	35rf	1951	Nikkor-QC	3.5	5cm	focal plane	1-500		340
Nicca IIIB	24x36mm	35mm	35rf	1951	Nikkor-SC	1.5	5cm	focal plane	1-500		350
Nicca IIIL	24x36mm	35mm	35rf	1958	Nikkor-H	2	5cm	focal plane	1-1000		400

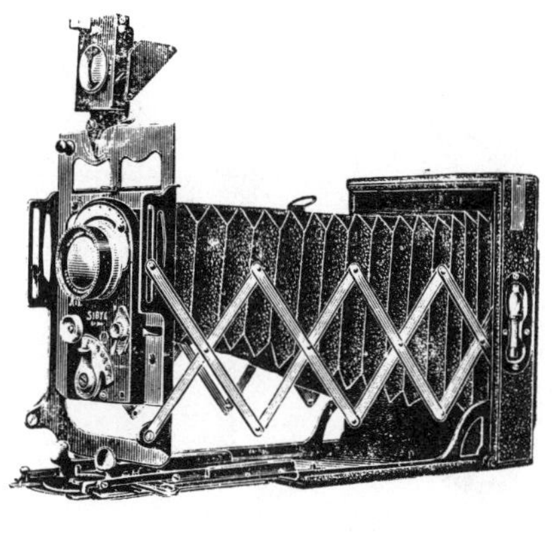

Sibyl Deluxe

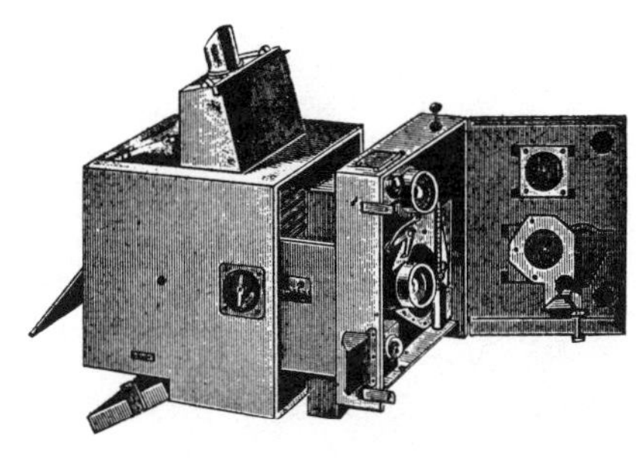

Twin Lens Pattern

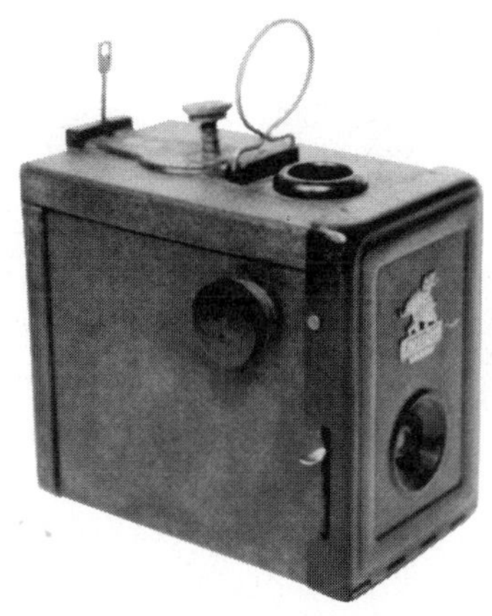

Foto Nic

MODEL	FORMAT	FILM	TYPE	Year	LENS	Apert	FL	SHUTTER	SPEEDS	ILLUS	U.S.$
Nicca IIIS	24x36mm	35mm	35rf	1952	Nikkor-QC	3.5	5cm	focal plane	1-500		390
Nicca IIIS	24x36mm	35mm	35rf	1952	Nikkor	2	5cm	focal plane	1-500		390
Nicca 3-F (knob)	24x36mm	35mm	35rf	1956	Nikkor-H	2.5	5cm	focal plane	1-500		460
Nicca 3-F (lever)	24x36mm	35mm	35rf	1957	Nikkor-H	2.5	5cm	focal plane	1-500		460
Nicca 3-S	24x36mm	35mm	35rf	1954	Nikkor-QC	3.5	5cm	focal plane	1-500		320
Nicca 4	24x36mm	35mm	35rf	1953	Nikkor-SC	1.5	5cm	focal plane	1-1000		440
Nicca 5	24x36mm	35mm	35rf	1955	Nikkor-H	2	5cm	focal plane	1-1000		550
Nicca 5L	24x36mm	35mm	35rf	1957	Nikkor-H	2	5cm	focal plane	1-1000		440
Nicca 33	24x36mm	35mm	35rf	1957	Nicca	2.8	5cm	focal plane	2-500		1700
Nicca 33	24x36mm	35mm	35rf	1957	Nicca	2	5cm	focal plane	2-500		400
Nippon	24x36mm	35mm	35vf	1942	K.O.L. Xebec	2	5cm	focal plane	20-500		2400
Nippon + Nikkor	24x36mm	35mm	35vf	1942	Nikkor	4	5cm	focal plane	20-500		2800
Nippon (RF)	24x36mm	35mm	35rf	1942	Sun Xebec	2	5cm	focal plane	1-500		2400
Nippon (RF) + Nikkor	24x36mm	35mm	35rf	1942	Nikkor	4	5cm	focal plane	1-500		2800
Snider 35	24x36mm	35mm	35rf	1956	Schneider Xenon	2	50mm	focal plane	1-1000		1300
...NICHIRYO TRADING CO. - Japan											
Nicnon Binocular Camera	18x24mm	35mm	Special	1968	Nicnon	3.5	165mm		60-250	Mc328	600
...NICHOLLS (H. Nicholls) - Liverpool, England											
Detective Camera	3¼x4¼"	plate	DetectivBox		Eureka R.R.			Thornton-Pickard			130
...NIELL & SIMONS - Cologne											
Lopa	6.5x9cm	plate	FoldPl	1902	Meniscus	11	120mm	guillotine		A3009	1400
...NIHON KOKI CO. - Japan											
Well Standard Mod. I	4x5cm	127	TelescRo	1939	Well Anastigmat	4.5	65mm	NKK	25-150		200
Well Standard Mod. I	4x5cm	127	TelescRo	1939	Well Anastigmat	3.5	65mm	Well-Rapid	1-500		200
...NIHON SEIMITSU KOGYO (NIHON PRECISION INDUSTRY) - Japan											
Zany "N.D.K."	10x14mm	16mm	Submin	1950	Gemmy Anast.	4.5	25mm		I	Mc328	450
Zany "N.S.K."	10x14mm	16mm	Submin	1950	Gemmy Anast.	4.5	25mm		I		450
...NIHON SEIKI - Japan											
Nescon 35	24x36mm	35mm	35vf	1956	Nescor	3.5	40mm		25-200	Mc328	70
Ranger 35	24x36mm	35mm	35vf	1956	Nescor	3.5	40mm		25-200	Mc328	70
Soligor 45	24x36mm	35mm	35vf	1956	Nescor	3.5	40mm		25-200		80
...NIKOH CO. LTD. - Japan											
Enica-SX	8x11mm	Minox	Submin	1983	Suzunon	3.8	14.3mm		1/60		120
Minimax-lite	8x11mm	Minox	Submin	1981		8	14.3mm		1/60	Mc328	80
Supra Photolite	8x11mm	Minox	Submin	1981		8	14.3mm		1/60	A3324	80
...NIMSLO LTD - London											
Nimslo 3D	18x22mm	35mm	35Ster	1980	Quadra	5.6	30mm	programmed	1/30-500		140
...NIPPON KOGAKU K.K. - Tokyo											
Calypso/Nikkor II	24x36mm	35mm	35uw	1968	Nikkor	3.5	35mm	focal plane	1/30-500	A2026	200
Nikkorex 35	24x36mm	35mm	35SLR	1960	Nikkor	2.5	50mm	Citizen	1-500		110
Nikkorex 35-2	24x36mm	35mm	35SLR	1960	Nikkor	2.5	50mm	Citizen	1-500		110
Nikkorex Auto 35	24x36mm	35mm	35SLR	1964	Nikkor	2	48mm	Citizen	1-500		160

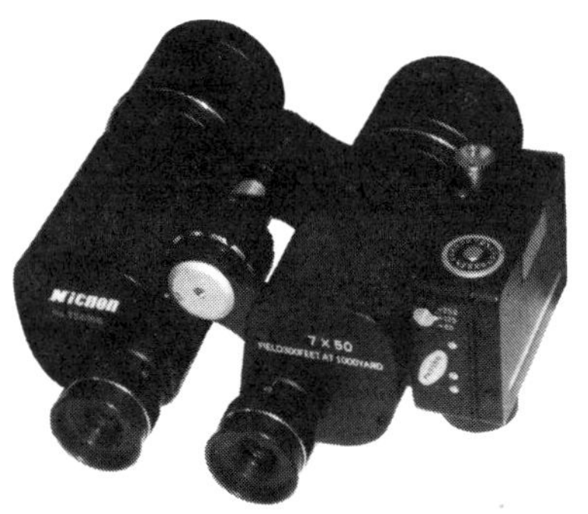

Nicnon Binocular Camera

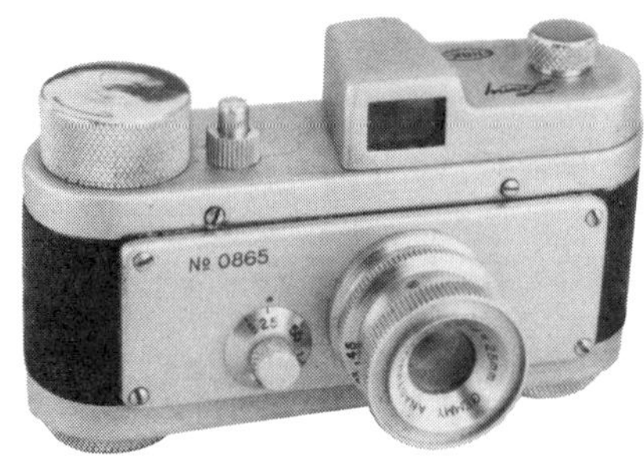

Zany "N.D.K."

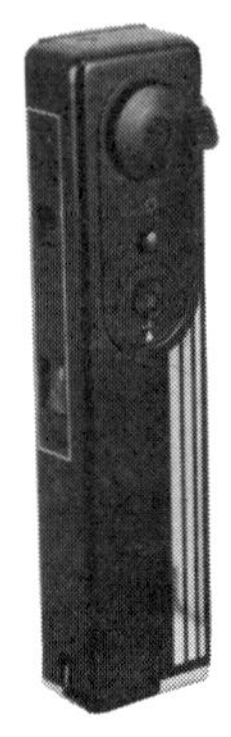
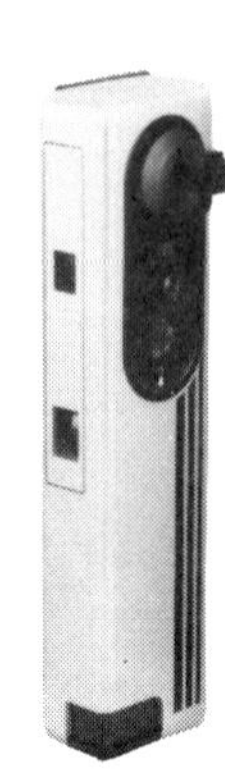
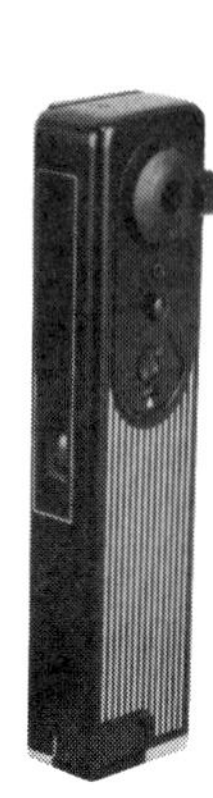

Minimax-lite

MODEL	FORMAT	FILM	TYPE	Year	LENS	Apert	FL	SHUTTER	SPEEDS	ILLUS	U.S.$
Nikkorex F	24x36mm	35mm	35SLR	1962	Nikkor	2	50mm	focal plane	1-1000,B	Mc329	140
Nikkorex Zoom 35	24x36mm	35mm	35SLR	1963	Zoom Nikkor Auto	3.5	43-86	focal plane	1-1000	Mc329	180
Nikkormat EL (black) body	24x36mm	35mm	35SLR	1973	body only	---	---	focal plane	4-1000		200
---EL (black) + 50/1.4	24x36mm	35mm	35SLR	1973	Nikkor SC Auto	1.4	50mm	focal plane	4-1000		310
---EL (chrome) body	24x36mm	35mm	35SLR	1973	body only	---	---	focal plane	4-1000		170
---EL (chrome) + 50/1.4	24x36mm	35mm	35SLR	1973	Nikkor SC Auto	1.4	50mm	focal plane	4-1000		280
---ELW (black) body	24x36mm	35mm	35SLR	1976	body only	---	---	focal plane	4-1000		210
---ELW (black) + 50/1.4	24x36mm	35mm	35SLR	1976	Nikkor SC Auto	1.4	50mm	focal plane	4-1000		300
Nikkormat FS body	24x36mm	35mm	35SLR	1965	body only	---	---	focal plane	1-1000		340
Nikkormat FS + 50/2	24x36mm	35mm	35SLR	1965	Nikkor H-Auto	2	50mm	focal plane	1-1000		410
Nikkormat FT body	24x36mm	35mm	35SLR	1965	body only	---	---	focal plane	1-1000		140
Nikkormat FT + 50/2	24x36mm	35mm	35SLR	1965	Nikkor S Auto	2	50mm	focal plane	1-1000		170
--- FT2 (black) body	24x36mm	35mm	35SLR	1975	body only	---	---	focal plane	1-1000		200
--- FT2 (black) + 50/2	24x36mm	35mm	35SLR	1975	Nikkor	2	50mm	focal plane	1-1000		220
--- FT2 (chrome) body	24x36mm	35mm	35SLR	1975	body only	---	---	focal plane	1-1000		180
--- FT2 (chrome) + 50/2	24x36mm	35mm	35SLR	1975	Nikkor	2	50mm	focal plane	1-1000		220
--- FT3 (black) body	24x36mm	35mm	35SLR	1977	body only	---	---	focal plane	1-1000		220
--- FT3 (black) + 50/2	24x36mm	35mm	35SLR	1977	Nikkor	2	50mm	focal plane	1-1000		260
--- FT3 (chrome) body	24x36mm	35mm	35SLR	1977	body only	---	---	focal plane	1-1000		210
--- FT3 (chrome) + 50/2	24x36mm	35mm	35SLR	1977	Nikkor	2	50mm	focal plane	1-1000		260
--- FTN (black) body	24x36mm	35mm	35SLR	1967	body only	---	---	focal plane	1-1000		180
--- FTN (black) + 50/1.4	24x36mm	35mm	35SLR	1967	Nikkor S Auto	1.4	50mm	focal plane	1-1000		280
--- FTN (chrome) body	24x36mm	35mm	35SLR	1967	body only	---	---	focal plane	1-1000		150
--- FTN (chrome) + 50/1.4	24x36mm	35mm	35SLR	1967	Nikkor S Auto	1.4	50mm	focal plane	1-1000		220
Nikomat FT body	24x36mm	35mm	35SLR	1965	body only	---	---	focal plane	1-1000		140
Nikomat FT + 50/2	24x36mm	35mm	35SLR	1965	Nikkor S Auto	2	50mm	focal plane	1-1000		170
Nikon I	24x32mm	35mm	35RF	1948	Nikkor	3.5	50mm	focal plane	1-500	Mc329	15000
Nikon I	24x32mm	35mm	35RF	1948	Nikkor	2. 0	50mm	focal plane	1-500	Mc329	15000
Nikon 28 Ti Quartz Date	24x36mm	35mm	35AF	1994	AF Nikkor	2.8	28mm	programmed	2-1/500		1000
Nikon 35 Ti Quartz Date	24x36mm	35mm	35AF	1993	NIkkor	2.8	35mm	programmed	2-1/500		900
Nikon Action Touch	24x36mm	35mm	35aw	1983	Nikon	2.8	35mm	programmed	1/8-430		260
Nikon AD3	24x36mm	35mm	35AF	1987	Nikon	2.8	35mm	programmed			170
Nikon AF 200	24x36mm	35mm	35AF	1993	Nikon	4.5	35mm		1/130		70
Nikon AF 210	24x36mm	35mm	35CAF	1993	Nikon	4.5	32mm	programmed			50
Nikon AF 400	24x36mm	35mm	35CAF	1993	Nikon	4.3	31mm	programmed			70
Nikon AF 600	24x36mm	35mm	35CAF	1993	Nikon	3.5	28mm	programmed			150
Nikon AF3	24x36mm	35mm	35AF	1987	Nikon	2.8	35mm	programmed			120
Nikon AW35	24x36mm	35mm	35aw	1993	Nikon	3.5	35mm	programmed			100
Nikon EF 100	24x36mm	35mm	35vf	1993	Nikon	4.5	35mm		1/125		40
Nikon EL-2 (black) body	24x36mm	35mm	35SLR	1977	body only	---	---				260
Nikon EL-2 (black) + 50/2	24x36mm	35mm	35SLR	1977	Auto Nikkor	2.0	50mm				340
Nikon EL-2 (chrome) body	24x36mm	35mm	35SLR	1977	body only	---	---				240

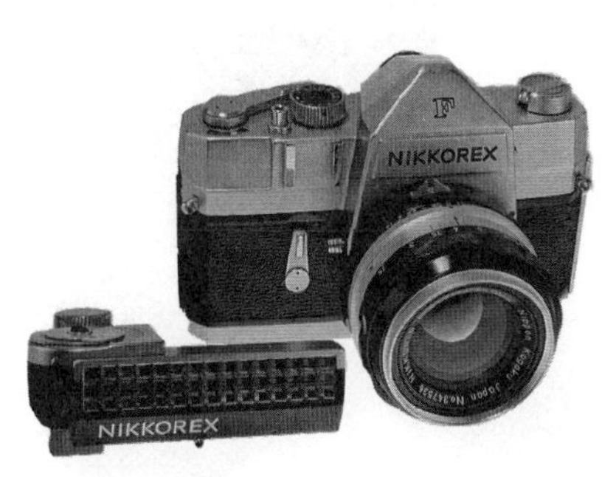

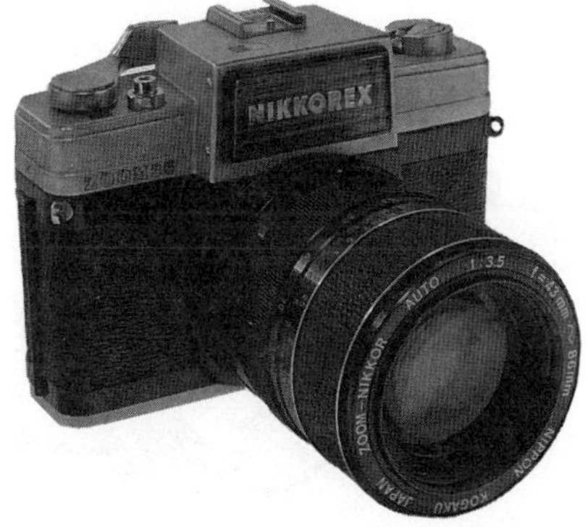

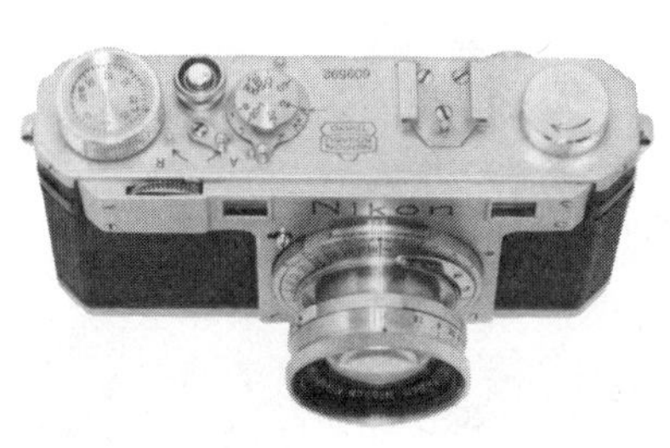

Nikkorex F | Nikkorex Zoom 35 | Nikon I

MODEL	FORMAT	FILM	TYPE	Year	LENS	Apert	FL	SHUTTER	SPEEDS	ILLUS	U.S.$
Nikon EL-2 (chrome) +50/2	24x36mm	35mm	35SLR	1977	Auto Nikkor	2.0	50mm				310
Nikon EM body	24x36mm	35mm	35SLR	1979	body only	---	---	focal plane	1-1000		120
Nikon EM + 50/1.8	24x36mm	35mm	35SLR	1979	Nikon	1.8	50mm	focal plane	1-1000		160
Nikon F "Nikkor F" (black)	24x36mm	35mm	35SLR	1959	body only	---	---	focal plane	1-1000		520
Nikon "Nikkor F" (chrome)	24x36mm	35mm	35SLR	1959	body only	---	---	focal plane	1-1000		520
Nikon F (black)	24x36mm	35mm	35SLR	1959	body only	---	---	focal plane	1-1000		370
Nikon F (chrome)	24x36mm	35mm	35SLR	1959	body only	---	---	focal plane	1-1000		290
Nikon F Photomic (black)	24x36mm	35mm	35SLR	1962	body only	---	---	focal plane	1-1000		350
Nikon F Photomic (chrome)	24x36mm	35mm	35SLR	1962	body only	---	---	focal plane	1-1000		270
F Photomic FTn (black)	24x36mm	35mm	35SLR	1968	body only	---	---	focal plane	1-1000		330
F Photomic FTn (chrome)	24x36mm	35mm	35SLR	1968	body only	---	---	focal plane	1-1000		290
Nikon F Photomic T (black)	24x36mm	35mm	35SLR	1965	body only	---	---	focal plane	1-1000		190
F Photomic T (chrome)	24x36mm	35mm	35SLR	1965	body only	---	---	focal plane	1-1000		180
F Photomic Tn (black)	24x36mm	35mm	35SLR	1967	body only	---	---	focal plane	1-1000		180
F Photomic Tn (chrome)	24x36mm	35mm	35SLR	1967	body only	---	---	focal plane	1-1000		170
Nikon F2 "Titan"	24x36mm	35mm	35SLR	1978	Nikkor	1.4	50mm	focal plane	10-2000		1400
Nikon F2 (black)	24x36mm	35mm	35SLR	1971	body only	---	---	focal plane	10-2000		410
Nikon F2 (chrome)	24x36mm	35mm	35SLR	1971	body only	---	---	focal plane	10-2000		350
Nikon F2 Photomic (black)	24x36mm	35mm	35SLR	1971	body only	---	---	focal plane	10-2000		420
---F2 Photomic (chrome)	24x36mm	35mm	35SLR	1971	body only	---	---	focal plane	10-2000		350
Nikon F2 T body	24x36mm	35mm	35SLR	1976	body only	---	---	focal plane	10-2000		900
Nikon F2 T + 50/1.4	24x36mm	35mm	35SLR	1976	Nikkor	1.4	50mm	focal plane	10-2000		1200
Nikon F2A "25 Years"	24x36mm	35mm	35SLR	1979	Nikkor	1.4	50mm	focal plane	10-2000		1800
Nikon F2A (black)	24x36mm	35mm	35SLR	1977	body only	---	---	focal plane	10-2000		520
Nikon F2A (chrome)	24x36mm	35mm	35SLR	1977	body only	---	---	focal plane	10-2000		520
Nikon F2AS (black)	24x36mm	35mm	35SLR	1978	body only	---	---	focal plane	10-2000		680
Nikon F2AS (chrome)	24x36mm	35mm	35SLR	1978	body only	---	---	focal plane	10-2000		700
---F2AS Data Set (MF10)	24x36mm	35mm	35SLR	1978	body only	---	---	focal plane	10-2000		2200
Nikon F2H	24x36mm	35mm	35SLR	1978	body only	---	---	focal plane	10-2000		2600
Nik. F2S Photomic (black)	24x36mm	35mm	35SLR	1973	body only	---	---	focal plane	10-2000		430
---F2S Photomic (chrome)	24x36mm	35mm	35SLR	1973	body only	---	---	focal plane	10-2000		360
Nikon F2SB (black)	24x36mm	35mm	35SLR	1977	body only	---	---	focal plane	10-2000		610
Nikon F2SB (chrome)	24x36mm	35mm	35SLR	1977	body only	---	---	focal plane	10-2000		550
Nikon F3	24x36mm	35mm	35SLR	1980	body only	---	---	focal plane	8-1/2000		570
Nikon F3 HP body	24x36mm	35mm	35SLR	1982	body only	---	---	focal plane	8-1/2000		700
Nikon F3 HP + 50/1.4	24x36mm	35mm	35SLR	1982	Nikkor	1.4	50mm	focal plane	8-1/2000		1100
Nikon F3 P body	24x36mm	35mm	35SLR	1983	body only	---	---	focal plane	8-1/2000		1000
Nikon F3 P + 50/1.8	24x36mm	35mm	35SLR	1983	Nikkor	1.8	50mm	focal plane	8-1/2000		1100
Nikon F3/T body	24x36mm	35mm	35SLR	1983	body only	---	---	focal plane	8-1/2000		900
Nikon F3/T + 50/1.4	24x36mm	35mm	35SLR	1983	Nikkor	1.4	50mm	focal plane	8-1/2000		1100
Nikon F3AF body	24x36mm	35mm	35SLR	1982	body only	---	---	focal plane	8-1/2000	A3212	570
Nikon F3AF +80/2.8	24x36mm	35mm	35SLR	1982	Auto Nikkor	2.8	80mm	focal plane	8-1/2000	Mc332	1500

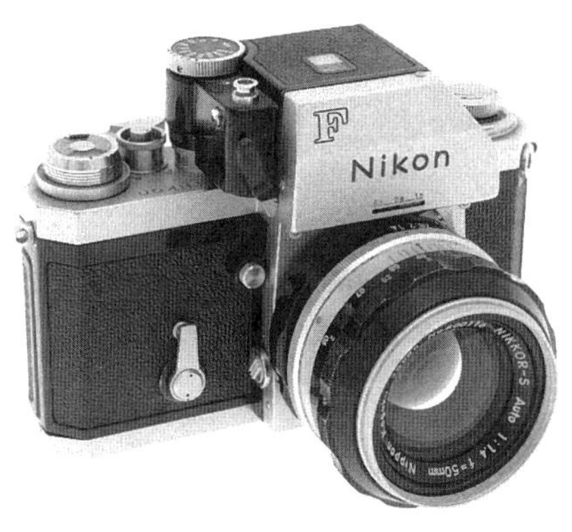

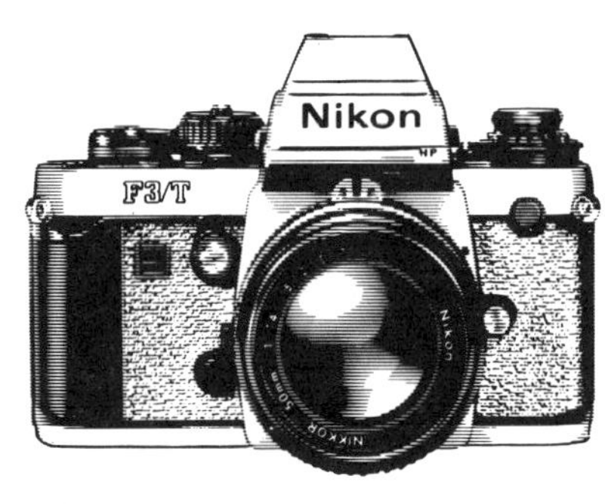

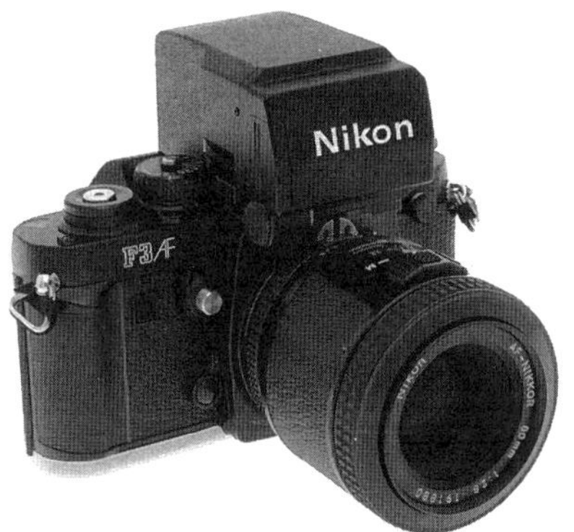

NIkon F Photomic FTn | Nikon F3/T | Nikon F3AF

MODEL	FORMAT	FILM	TYPE	Year	LENS	Apert	FL	SHUTTER	SPEEDS	ILLUS	U.S.$
Nikon F4 body	24x36mm	35mm	35SLR	1988	body only	---	---	focal plane	30-8000		1100
Nikon F4 + 50/1.8	24x36mm	35mm	35SLR	1988	AF Nikkor	1.8	50mm	focal plane	30-8000		1500
Nikon F4E body	24x36mm	35mm	35SLR	1994	body only	---	---	focal plane	30-8000		1400
Nikon F4E + 50/1.8	24x36mm	35mm	35SLR	1994	AF Nikkor	1.8	50mm	focal plane	30-8000		1500
Nikon F4s body	24x36mm	35mm	35SLR	1988	body only	---	---	focal plane	30-8000		1300
Nikon F4s + 50/1.8	24x36mm	35mm	35SLR	1988	AF Nikkor	1.8	50mm	focal plane	30-8000		1500
Nikon F50 body	24x36mm	35mm	35AFSLR	1994	body only	---	---	focal plane	30-2000		330
Nikon F50 + 50/1.8	24x36mm	35mm	35AFSLR	1994	AF Nikkor	1.8	50mm	focal plane	30-2000		500
Nikon F50 D Pan. body	24x36mm	35mm	35AFSLR	1994	body only	---	---	focal plane	30-2000		330
Nikon F50 D Pan. + 50/1.8	24x36mm	35mm	35AFSLR	1994	AF Nikkor	1.8	50mm	focal plane	30-2000		500
Nikon F70 body	24x36mm	35mm	35AFSLR	1994	body only	---	---	focal plane	30-4000		600
Nikon F70D body	24x36mm	35mm	35AFSLR	1994	body only	---	---	focal plane	30-4000		680
Nikon F70D + 28-70	24x36mm	35mm	35AFSLR	1994	AF Nikkor	3.5-4.5	28-70	focal plane	30-4000		880
Nikon F90 body	24x36mm	35mm	35AFSLR	1992	body only	---	---	focal plane	30-8000		700
Nikon F90D body	24x36mm	35mm	35AFSLR	1992	body only	---	---	focal plane	30-8000		1000
Nikon F90D + 28-70	24x36mm	35mm	35AFSLR	1992	AF Nikkor	3.5-4.5	28-70	focal plane	30-8000		1160
Nikon F90S body	24x36mm	35mm	35AFSLR	1992	body only	---	---	focal plane	30-8000		700
Nikon F90S + 28-70	24x36mm	35mm	35AFSLR	1992	AF Nikkor	3.5-4.5	28-70	focal plane	30-8000		950
Nikon F90X body	24x36mm	35mm	35AFSLR	1994	body only	---	---	focal plane	30-8000		1200
Nikon F90X + 28-70	24x36mm	35mm	35AFSLR	1994	AF Nikkor	3.5-4.5	28-70	focal plane	30-8000		1400
Nikon F-301 body	24x36mm	35mm	35SLR	1985	body only	---	---	focal plane	1-2000		220
Nikon F-301 + 50/1.8	24x36mm	35mm	35SLR	1985	Nikkor	1.8	50mm	focal plane	1-2000		310
Nikon F-401 body	24x36mm	35mm	35AFSLR	1986	body only	---	---	focal plane	1-2000		220
Nikon F-401 + 35-70	24x36mm	35mm	35AFSLR	1986	AF Nikkor	3.3-4.5	35-70	focal plane	1-2000		360
Nikon F-401s body	24x36mm	35mm	35AFSLR	1989	body only	---	---	focal plane	1-2000		200
Nikon F-401s + 35-70	24x36mm	35mm	35AFSLR	1989	AF Nikkor	3.3-4.5	35-70	focal plane	1-2000		330
Nikon F-401x body	24x36mm	35mm	35AFSLR	1991	body only	---	---	focal plane	30-2000		270
Nikon F-401x + 35-70	24x36mm	35mm	35AFSLR	1991	AF Nikkor	3.3-4.5	35-70	focal plane	30-2000		360
Nikon F-401x + 50/1.8	24x36mm	35mm	35AFSLR	1991	AF Nikkor	1.8	50mm	focal plane	30-2000		330
Nikon F-501 body	24x36mm	35mm	35AFSLR	1986	body only	---	---	focal plane	1-2000		280
Nikon F-501 + 50/1.4	24x36mm	35mm	35AFSLR	1986	AF Nikkor	1.4	50mm	focal plane	1-2000		370
Nikon F-601 body	24x36mm	35mm	35AFSLR	1990	body only	---	---	focal plane	30-2000		330
Nikon F-601 + 35-70	24x36mm	35mm	35AFSLR	1990	AF Nikkor	3.3-4.5	35-70	focal plane	30-2000		480
---F-601 Quartz Date body	24x36mm	35mm	35AFSLR	1989	body only	---	---	focal plane	30-2000		370
---F-601 Quartz D. + 35-70	24x36mm	35mm	35AFSLR	1989	AF Nikkor	3.3-4.5	35-70	focal plane	30-2000		580
Nikon F-601M body	24x36mm	35mm	35SLR	1989	body only	---	---	focal plane	30-2000		280
Nikon F-601M + 50/1.8	24x36mm	35mm	35SLR	1989	Nikkor	1.8	50mm	focal plane	30-2000		350
Nikon F-801 body	24x36mm	35mm	35AFSLR	1988	body only	---	---	focal plane	30-8000		390
Nikon F-801 + 35-70	24x36mm	35mm	35AFSLR	1988	AF Nikkor	3.3-4.5	35-70	focal plane	30-8000		800
Nikon F-801s body	24x36mm	35mm	35AFSLR	1991	body only	---	---	focal plane	30-8000		520
Nikon F-801s + 35-70	24x36mm	35mm	35AFSLR	1991	AF Nikkor	3.3-4.5	35-70	focal plane	30-8000		920
Nikon F-801s + 50/1.8	24x36mm	35mm	35AFSLR	1991	AF Nikkor	1.8	50mm	focal plane	30-8000		630

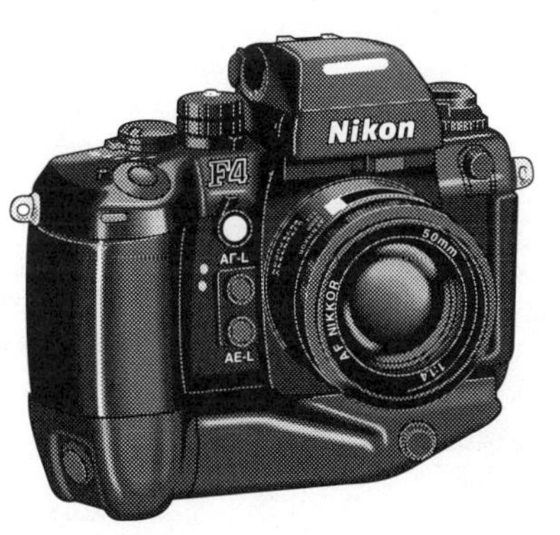

Nikon F4s

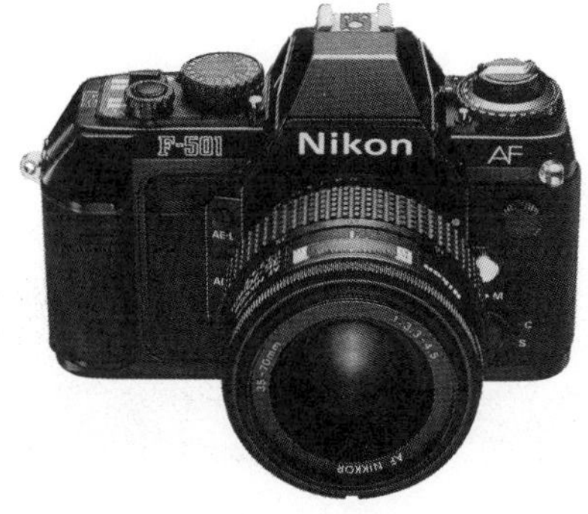

Nikon F-501

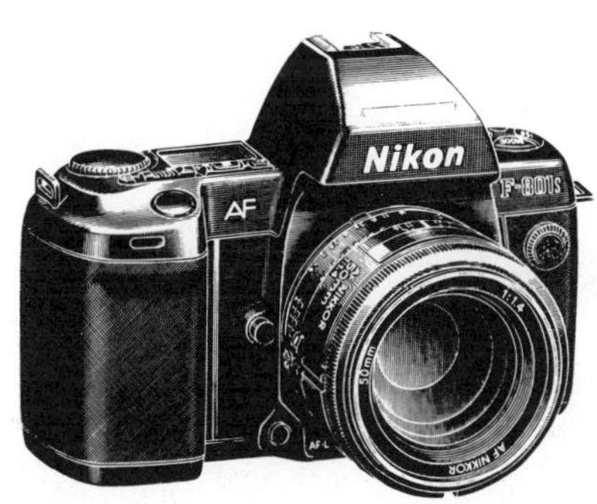

Nikon F-801s

MODEL	FORMAT	FILM	TYPE	Year	LENS	Apert	FL	SHUTTER	SPEEDS	ILLUS	U.S.$
Nikon FA (black) body	24x36mm	35mm	35SLR	1983	body only	---	---	focal plane	1-4000		410
Nikon FA (black) + 50/1.8	24x36mm	35mm	35SLR	1983	Nikkor	1.8	50mm	focal plane	1-4000		510
Nikon FA (chrome) body	24x36mm	35mm	35SLR	1983	body only	---	---	focal plane	1-4000		370
---FA (chrome) + 50/1.8	24x36mm	35mm	35SLR	1983	Nikkor	1.8	50mm	focal plane	1-4000		410
Nikon FE (black) body	24x36mm	35mm	35SLR	1978	body only	---	---	focal plane	8-1000		310
Nikon FE (black) + 50/1.8	24x36mm	35mm	35SLR	1978	Nikkor	1.8	50mm	focal plane	8-1000		380
Nikon FE (chrome) body	24x36mm	35mm	35SLR	1978	body only	---	---	focal plane	8-1000		270
---FE (chrome) + 50/1.8	24x36mm	35mm	35SLR	1978	Nikkor	1.8	50mm	focal plane	8-1000		370
Nikon FE2 (black) body	24x36mm	35mm	35SLR	1983	body only	---	---	focal plane	8-4000		420
---FE2 (black) + 50/1.8	24x36mm	35mm	35SLR	1983	Nikkor	1.8	50mm	focal plane	8-4000		490
---FE2 (chrome) body	24x36mm	35mm	35SLR	1983	body only	---	---	focal plane	8-4000		390
---FE2 (chrome) + 50/1.8	24x36mm	35mm	35SLR	1983	Nikkor	1.8	50mm	focal plane	8-4000		460
Nikon FG (black) body	24x36mm	35mm	35SLR	1982	body only	---	---	focal plane	1-1000		200
Nikon FG (black) + 50/1.8	24x36mm	35mm	35SLR	1982	Nikkor	1.8	50mm	focal plane	1-1000		280
Nikon FG (chrome) body	24x36mm	35mm	35SLR	1982	body only	---	---	focal plane	1-1000		180
---FG (chrome) + 50/1.8	24x36mm	35mm	35SLR	1982	Nikkor	1.8	50mm	focal plane	1-1000		270
Nikon FG-20 body	24x36mm	35mm	35SLR	1984	body only	---	---	focal plane	1-1000		160
Nikon FG-20 + 50/1.8	24x36mm	35mm	35SLR	1984	Nikkor	1.8	50mm	focal plane	1-1000		240
Nikon FM (black) body	24x36mm	35mm	35SLR	1977	body only	---	---	focal plane	1-1000		240
Nikon FM (black) + 50/1.8	24x36mm	35mm	35SLR	1977	Nikkor	1.8	50mm	focal plane	1-1000		330
Nikon FM (chrome) body	24x36mm	35mm	35SLR	1977	body only	---	---	focal plane	1-1000		240
Nik. FM (chrome) + 50/1.8	24x36mm	35mm	35SLR	1977	Nikkor	1.8	50mm	focal plane	1-1000		330
Nikon FM2 (black) body	24x36mm	35mm	35SLR	1982	body only	---	---	focal plane	1-4000		340
Nikon FM2 (black) + 50/1.8	24x36mm	35mm	35SLR	1982	Nikkor AI	1.8	50mm	focal plane	1-4000		370
Nikon FM2 (chrome) body	24x36mm	35mm	35SLR	1982	body only	---	---	focal plane	1-4000		300
---FM2 (chrome) + 50/1.8	24x36mm	35mm	35SLR	1982	Nikkor AI	1.8	50mm	focal plane	1-4000		350
Nikon FM2N (black) body	24x36mm	35mm	35SLR	1990	body only	---	---	focal plane	1-4000		310
---FM2N (black) + 50/1.8	24x36mm	35mm	35SLR	1990	Nikkor	1.8	50mm	focal plane	1-4000		460
---FM2N (chrome) body	24x36mm	35mm	35SLR	1990	body only	---	---	focal plane	1-4000		290
---FM2N (chrome) + 50/1.8	24x36mm	35mm	35SLR	1990	Nikkor	1.8	50mm	focal plane	1-4000		420
Nikon FM2T	24x36mm	35mm	35SLR	1994	Nikkor	1.8	50mm	focal plane	1-4000		900
Nikon Fun-Touch	24x36mm	35mm	35CAF	1987	Nikon	3.5	35mm	programmed			70
Nikon Fun-Touch 2	24x36mm	35mm	35AF	1993	Nikon	4.5	35mm		1/130		70
Nikon Fun-Touch 3	24x36mm	35mm	35CAF	1993	Nikon	4.5	32mm	programmed			50
Nikon L35 AD	24x36mm	35mm	35af	1983	Nikon	2.8	35mm	programmed	1/8-430		120
Nikon L35 AD2	24x36mm	35mm	35af	1985	Nikon	2.8	35mm	programmed	1/8-430		660
Nikon L35 AF	24x36mm	35mm	35af	1983	Nikon	2.8	35mm	programmed	1/8-430		100
Nikon L35 AF2	24x36mm	35mm	35af	1985	Nikon	2.8	35mm	programmed	1/8-430		150
Nikon L35 AWAD	24x36mm	35mm	35aw	1983	Nikon	2.8	35mm	programmed	1/8-430		350
Nikon L35 AWAF	24x36mm	35mm	35aw	1983	Nikon	2.8	35mm	programmed	1/8-430		260
Nikon L35 TWAD	24x36mm	35mm	35AF-BiF	1986	Nikon	3.5	38/65	programmed			310
Nikon L35 TWAF	24x36mm	35mm	35AF-BiF	1986	Nikon	3.5	38/65	programmed			210

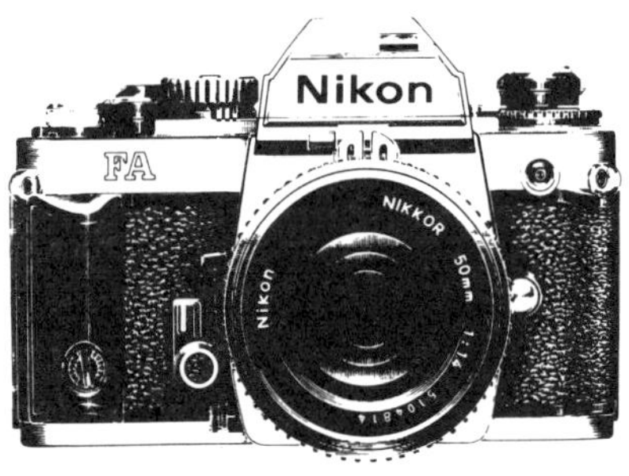

Nikon FA

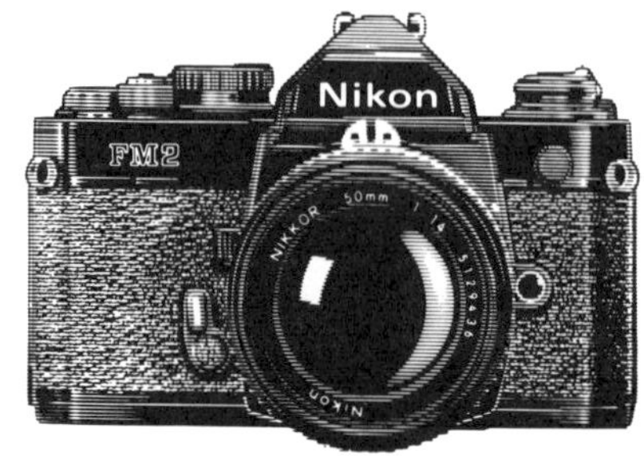

Nikon FM2

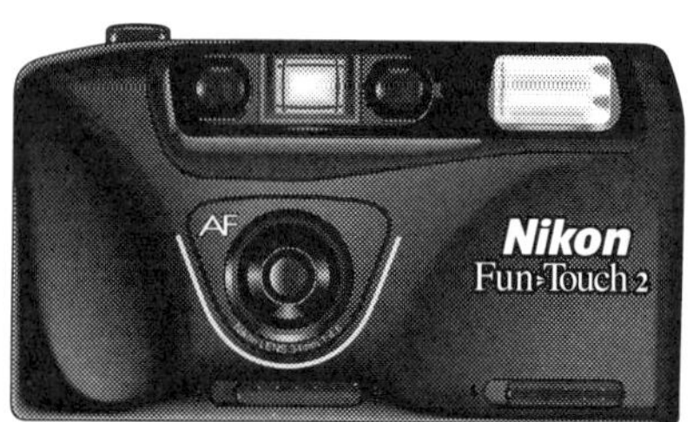

Nikon Fun-Touch 2

MODEL	FORMAT	FILM	TYPE	Year	LENS	Apert	FL	SHUTTER	SPEEDS	ILLUS	U.S.$
Nikon L135 AF	24x36mm	35mm	35af	1984	NIkon	3.5	35mm	programmed	1/37-700		80
Nikon Lite-Touch	24x36mm	35mm	35CAF	1993	Nikon	3.5	28mm	programmed			150
Nikon Lite-Touch Zoom	24x36mm	35mm	35afz	1993	Nikon Zoom	3.5-6.5	35-70	programmed			190
Nikon M (no sync)	24x34mm	35mm	35RF	1949	Nikkor	2. 0	5cm	focal plane	1-500	Mc329	5300
Nikon M (sync)	24x34mm	35mm	35RF	1950	Nikkor	1.4	5cm	focal plane	1-500		1700
Nikon N50 body	24x36mm	35mm	35AFSLR	1994	body only	---	---	focal plane	30-2000		330
Nikon N50 + 50/1.8	24x36mm	35mm	35AFSLR	1994	AF Nikkor	1.8	50mm	focal plane	30-2000		500
Nikon N70 body	24x36mm	35mm	35AFSLR	1994	body only	---	---	focal plane	30-4000		600
Nikon N90 body	24x36mm	35mm	35AFSLR	1992	body only	---	---	focal plane	30-8000		700
Nikon N90S body	24x36mm	35mm	35AFSLR	1994	body only	---	---	focal plane	30-8000		1200
Nikon N90S + 28-70	24x36mm	35mm	35AFSLR	1994	AF Nikkor	3.5-4.5	28-70	focal plane	30-8000		1400
Nikon N2000 body	24x36mm	35mm	35SLR	1985	body only	---	---	focal plane	1-2000		220
Nikon N2020 body	24x36mm	35mm	35AFSLR	1986	body only	---	---	focal plane	1-2000		280
Nikon N4000 body	24x36mm	35mm	35AFSLR	1986	body only	---	---	focal plane	1-2000		220
Nikon N4004 body	24x36mm	35mm	35AFSLR	1989	body only	---	---	focal plane	1-2000		200
Nikon N5005 body	24x36mm	35mm	35AFSLR	1991	body only	---	---	focal plane	30-2000		270
Nikon N6000 body	24x36mm	35mm	35SLR	1989	body only	---	---	focal plane	30-2000		280
Nikon N6006 body	24x36mm	35mm	35AFSLR	1990	body only	---	---	focal plane	30-2000		330
Nikon N8008 body	24x36mm	35mm	35AFSLR	1988	body only	---	---	focal plane	30-8000		390
Nikon N8008s body	24x36mm	35mm	35AFSLR	1991	body only	---	---	focal plane	30-8000		520
Nikon Nice-Touch 2	24x36mm	35mm	35vf	1993	Nikon	4.5	35mm		1/125		40
Nikon Nice-Touch Zoom	24x36mm	35mm	35afz	1994	Nikon Zoom	5.7-9.3	35-60		1/90		70
Nikon One Touch	24x36mm	35mm	35AF	1987	Nikon	2.8	35mm	programmed			120
Nikon One Touch	24x36mm	35mm	35af	1985	Nikon	2.8	35mm	programmed	1/8-430		150
Nikon One Touch 100	24x36mm	35mm	35CAF	1988		3.5	35mm	programmed			80
Nikon One Touch 200	24x36mm	35mm	35CAF	1992	Nikon	3.5	35mm	programmed			90
Nikon One Touch 200 QD	24x36mm	35mm	35CAF	1992	Nikon	3.5	35mm	programmed			100
Nikon One Touch 300	24x36mm	35mm	35CAF	1993	Nikon	4.3	31mm	programmed			70
Nikon RD	24x36mm	35mm	35CAF	1987	Nikon	3.5	35mm	programmed			90
Nikon RD2	24x36mm	35mm	35CAF	1988		3.5	35mm	programmed			100
Nikon RF	24x36mm	35mm	35CAF	1987	Nikon	3.5	35mm	programmed			70
Nikon RF 2	24x36mm	35mm	35CAF	1988		3.5	35mm	programmed			80
Nikon RF 10	24x36mm	35mm	35af	1993		4.5	34mm		1/130		50
Nikon S + 5cm/2	24x34mm	35mm	35RF	1951	Nikkor-S	2	5cm	focal plane	1-500	Mc329	480
Nikon S + 5cm/1.4	24x34mm	35mm	35RF	1951	Nikkor-S	1.4	5cm	focal plane	1-500		650
Nikon S2 (black) + 5cm/2	24x36mm	35mm	35RF	1954	Nikkor-S	2	5cm	focal plane	1-1000	Mc330	900
Nikon S2 (black) + 5cm/1.4	24x36mm	35mm	35RF	1954	Nikkor-S	1.4	5cm	focal plane	1-1000		1100
Nikon S2 (chrome) +5cm/2	24x36mm	35mm	35RF	1954	Nikkor-S	2	5cm	focal plane	1-1000		650
Nikon S2 (chrome)+5cm/1.4	24x36mm	35mm	35RF	1954	Nikkor-S	1.4	5cm	focal plane	1-1000	Mc330	900
Nikon S3 (black) + 5cm/2	24x36mm	35mm	35RF	1958	Nikkor-HC	2	5cm	focal plane	1-1000		1000
Nikon S3 (black) + 50/1.4	24x36mm	35mm	35RF	1958	Nikkor-S	1.4	50mm	focal plane	1-1000	Mc330	1300
Nikon S3 (chrome) + 5cm/2	24x36mm	35mm	35RF	1958	Nikkor-HC	2	5cm	focal plane	1-1000	Mc330	1100

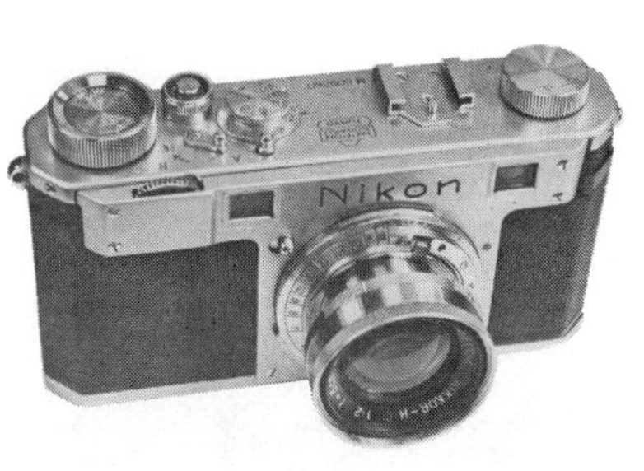

Nikon M (unsync)

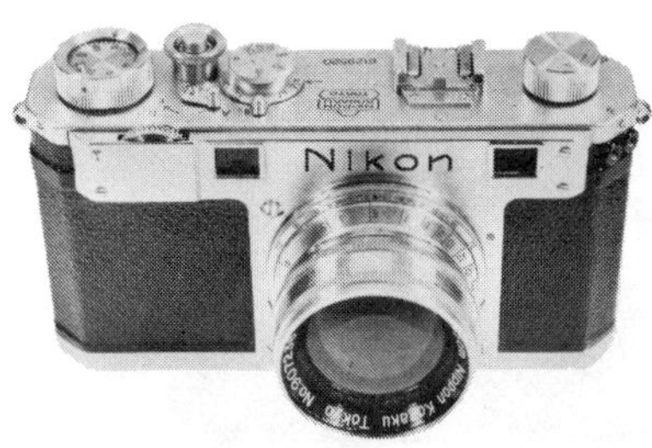

Nikon S

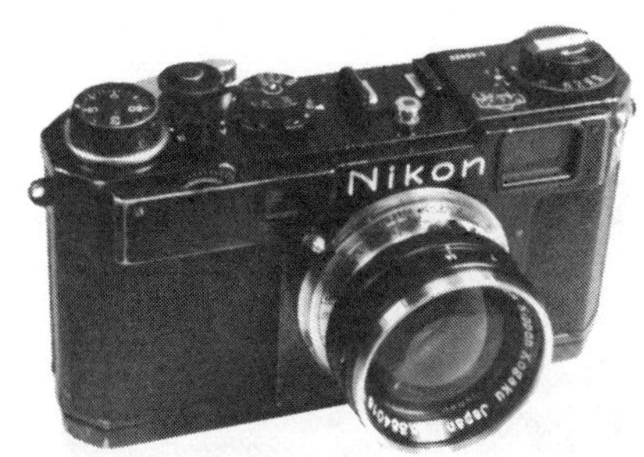

Nikon S2

MODEL	FORMAT	FILM	TYPE	Year	LENS	Apert	FL	SHUTTER	SPEEDS	ILLUS	U.S.$
Nikon S3 (chrome) + 50/1.4	24x36mm	35mm	35RF	1958	Nikkor-S	1.4	50mm	focal plane	1-1000	A2069	1300
Nikon S3M (black)	18x24mm	35mm	35Half	1960	Nikkor-H	2	5cm	focal plane	1-1000		14000
Nikon S3M (black)	18x24mm	35mm	35Half	1960	Nikkor-S	1.4	50mm	focal plane	1-1000		14000
Nikon S3M (chrome)	18x24mm	35mm	35Half	1960	Nikkor-H	2	5cm	focal plane	1-1000	Mc330	14000
Nikon S3M (chrome)	18x24mm	35mm	35Half	1960	Nikkor-S	1.4	50mm	focal plane	1-1000		14000
Nikon S4 + 5cm/2	24x36mm	35mm	35RF	1959	Nikkor-H	2	5cm	focal plane	1-1000		1000
Nikon S4 + 50/1.4	24x36mm	35mm	35RF	1959	Nikkor-S	1.4	50mm	focal plane	1-1000	Mc330	2200
Nikon Smile Taker	24x36mm	35mm	35af	1993		4.5	34mm		1/130		50
Nikon SP (black)	24x36mm	35mm	35RF	1957	Nikkor-N	2	5cm	focal plane	1-1000		1600
Nikon SP (black)	24x36mm	35mm	35RF	1957	Nikkor-S	1.4	50mm	focal plane	1-1000	Mc330	1600
Nikon SP (chrome)	24x36mm	35mm	35RF	1957	Nikkor-N	2	5cm	focal plane	1-1000		1300
Nikon SP (chrome)	24x36mm	35mm	35RF	1957	Nikkor-S	1.4	50mm	focal plane	1-1000	Mc330	1300
Nikon Sport Touch	24x36mm	35mm	35aw	1993	Nikon	3.5	35mm	programmed			100
Nikon Tele Touch	24x36mm	35mm	35AF-BiF	1986	Nikon	3.5	38/65	programmed			210
Nikon Tele Touch 300	24x36mm	35mm	35AF-BiF	1988		3.8	35mm	programmed			100
Nikon Tele Touch 300 QD	24x36mm	35mm	35AF-BiF	1988		3.8	35mm	programmed			110
Nikon Tele Touch Deluxe	24x36mm	35mm	35AF-BiF	1987		3.5	35mm	programmed			100
Nikon Tele Touch Del. QD	24x36mm	35mm	35AF-BiF	1987		3.5	35mm	programmed			100
Nikon TW Zoom	24x36mm	35mm	35afz	1988	Nikon Zoom	3.5-7.8	35-80	programmed			120
Nikon TW Zoom QD	24x36mm	35mm	35afz	1988	Nikon Zoom	3.5-7.8	35-80	programmed			140
Nikon TW Zoom 35-70	24x36mm	35mm	35afz	1989	Nikon Zoom	4-7.6	35-70	programmed			130
Nikon TW Zoom 35-70 QD	24x36mm	35mm	35afz	1989	Nikon Zoom	4-7.6	35-70	programmed			140
Nikon TW Zoom 35-80	24x36mm	35mm	35afz	1992	Nikon Zoom	3.5-7.8	35-80	programmed			150
Nikon TW Zoom 35-80 Data	24x36mm	35mm	35afz	1992	Nikon Zoom	3.5-7.8	35-80	programmed			160
Nikon TW Zoom 85	24x36mm	35mm	35afz	1993	Nikon Zoom	4.5-11	32-85	programmed			160
Nikon TW Zoom 85 QD	24x36mm	35mm	35afz	1993	Nikon Zoom	4.5-11	32-85	programmed			170
Nikon TW Zoom 105	24x36mm	35mm	35afz	1993	Nikon Zoom	3.7-9.9	37-105	programmed			290
Nikon TW Zoom 105 (WT)	24x36mm	35mm	35afz	1993	Nikon Zoom	3.7-9.9	37-105	programmed			270
Nikon TW2	24x36mm	35mm	35AF-BiF	1987		3.5	35mm	programmed			100
Nikon TW2 D	24x36mm	35mm	35AF-BiF	1987		3.5	35mm	programmed			100
Nikon TW20	24x36mm	35mm	35AF-BiF	1988		3.8	35mm	programmed			100
Nikon TW20 Quartz Date	24x36mm	35mm	35AF-BiF	1988		3.8	35mm	programmed			130
Nikon W35	24x36mm	35mm	35CAF	1992	Nikon	3.5	35mm	programmed			90
Nikon W35 Quartz Date	24x36mm	35mm	35CAF	1992	Nikon	3.5	35mm	programmed			100
Nikon Zoom 60	24x36mm	35mm	35afz	1994	Nikon Zoom	5.7-9.3	35-60		1/90		70
Nikon Zoom 100 AF (QD)	24x36mm	35mm	35afz	1993	Nikon Zoom	4-7.6	35-70	programmed			130
Nikon Zoom 300 AF (QD)	24x36mm	35mm	35afz	1993	Nikon Zoom	3.5-6.5	35-70	programmed			190
Nikon Zoom 700 VR (QD)	24x36mm	35mm	35afz	1994	Nikon Zoom	4-7.8	38-105	programmed			300
Nikon Zoom-Touch 105 VR	24x36mm	35mm	35afz	1994	Nikon Zoom	4-7.8	38-105	programmed			300
Nikon Zoom-Touch 400	24x36mm	35mm	35afz	1989	Nikon Zoom	4-7.6	35-70	programmed			130
Nikon Zoom-Touch 400 QD	24x36mm	35mm	35afz	1989	Nikon Zoom	4-7.6	35-70	programmed			140
Nikon Zoom-Touch 470	24x36mm	35mm	35afz	1993	Nikon Zoom	4-7.6	35-70	programmed			130

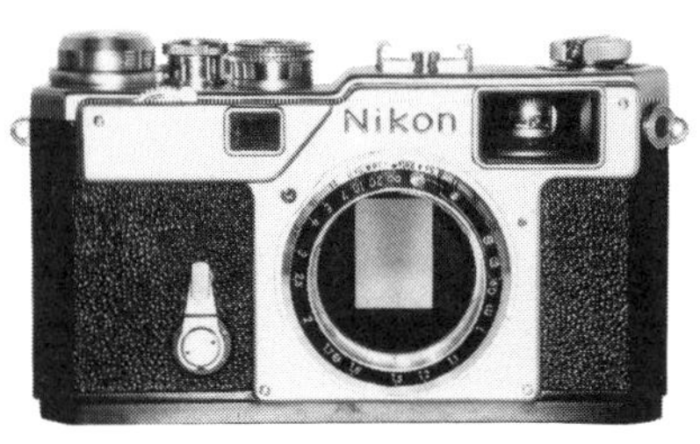

Nikon S3M

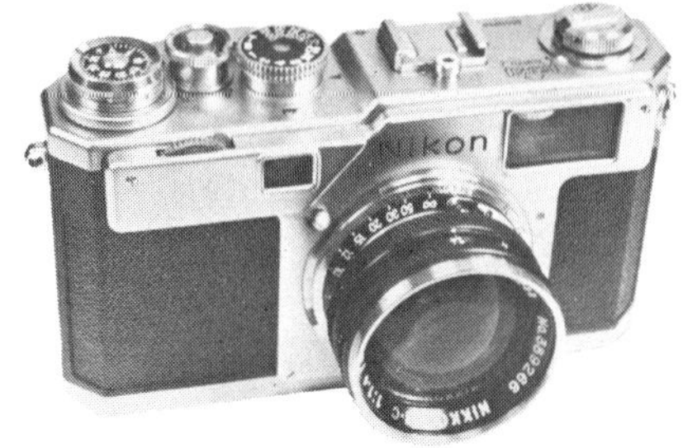

Nikon S4

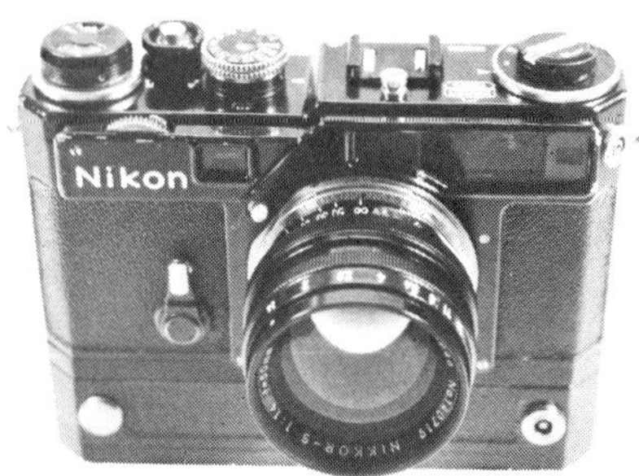

Nikon SP

MODEL	FORMAT	FILM	TYPE	Year	LENS	Apert	FL	SHUTTER	SPEEDS	ILLUS	U.S.$
Nikon Zoom-Touch 500	24x36mm	35mm	35afz	1988	Nikon Zoom	3.5-7.8	35-80	programmed			120
Nikon Zoom-Touch 500s	24x36mm	35mm	35afz	1992	Nikon Zoom	3.5-7.8	35-80	programmed			150
Nikon Zoom-Touch 600	24x36mm	35mm	35afz	1993	Nikon Zoom	4.5-11	32-85	programmed			160
Nikon Zoom-Touch 800	24x36mm	35mm	35afz	1993	Nikon Zoom	3.7-9.9	37-105	programmed			290
Nikonos	24x36mm	35mm	35uw	1963	Nikkor	2.5	35mm	focal plane	1/20-1000	A2025	280
Nikonos II	24x36mm	35mm	35uw	1968	Nikkor	3.5	35mm	focal plane	1/30-500	A2026	170
Nikonos III	24x36mm	35mm	35uw	1976	Nikkor	2.5	35mm	focal plane	1/30-500		320
Nikonos IV-A	24x36mm	35mm	35uw	1980	Nikkor	2.5	35mm	focal plane	1/30-1000	A2027	370
Nikonos V	24x36mm	35mm	35uw	1984	UW NIkkor	2.8	15mm	focal plane	1/30-1000		470
Nikonos RS AF	24x36mm	35mm	35uw	1991	R-UW AF Nikkor	2.8	28mm	focal plane	1-2000		1900
...NIPPON KOSOKKI SEISAKUSHO - Japan											
Taroflex	6x6cm	120	TLR	1943	Taro Anastigmat	3.5	75mm	NKS	1-200		250
...NISHIDA KOGAKU - Japan											
Apollo 120	42x55mm	120	HzFoldRo	1951	S.O.W.	3.5		Newman Pat.	1-200		70
Apollo 120	42x55mm	120	HzFoldRo	1951	Wester Anastigma	3.5		Newman Pat.	1-200		70
Apollo Semi II	42x55mm	120	HzFoldRo	1951	C.O.W.	3.5		Newman Pat.	1-200		70
Mikado	4.5x6cm	120	HzFoldRo	1951	Wester Anastigma	3.5	75mm	Northter Model II	200		60
Wester Autorol	6x6cm	120	HzFoldRo	1956	Wescon	3.5	75mm	NKK	1-400,B		60
...NITTO SEIKO - Japan											
Elega-35	24x36mm	35mm	35vf	1952	Eleger	3.5	45mm	rotary	1-200,B	Mc336	660
Elega-35	24x36mm	35mm	35vf	1952	Elega	3.5	45mm	rotary	1-200,B	Mc336	650
...NIXON CAMERA-WERK - Germany											
Ideal Color 35	24x36mm	35mm	35vf	1955	Nixon Anastigmat	3.5	45mm	Spezial	25-200		50
Ideal Color 35	24x36mm	35mm	35vf	1955	Nixon Anast.	3.5	45mm	Spezial	25-200		50
Nixette	6x6cm	120	HzFoldRo		Supra Anastigmat	5.6	75mm	Vario	25-100	Mc336	80
Trixette	6x6cm	120	HzFoldRo		Supra Anastigmat	5.6	75mm	Spezial	25-200		80
Trixette II	6x6cm	120	HzFoldRo		Supra Anastigmat	5.6	75mm	Vario	25-100		80
...NOBLEX (KAMERA WERKE NOBLE GmbH) - Dresden											
Noblex 135 N	24x66mm	35mm	Panoramic	1994	Noblar T	4.5	29mm				1000
Noblex 135 S	24x66mm	35mm	Panoramic	1994	Noblar T	4.5	29mm		30-500		1300
Noblex 135 U	24x66mm	35mm	Panoramic	1994	Noblar T	4.5	29mm				1700
Noblex Pro 06/150	5x12cm	120	Panoramic	1992	Tessar	4.5	50mm		30-250		1900
Noblex Pro 06/150 F	5x12cm	120	Panoramic	1993	Tessar	4.5	50mm		30-250		2600
Noblex Pro 06/150 HS	5x12cm	120	Panoramic	1993	Tessar	4.5	50mm		30-250		2700
Noblex Pro 06/150 L	5x12cm	120	Panoramic	1993	Tessar	4.5	50mm		30-250		6700
Noblex Pro 06/150 S	5x12cm	120	Panoramic	1993	Tessar	4.5	50mm		30-250		2600
...NORISAN APPARATEBAU GmbH - Nürnberg, Germany											
Afex	25x25mm	828	MiniatRo	1936		8	35mm		M,Z		50
Hacon	25x25mm	828	MiniatRo	1935		8	35mm		M,Z		50
Nori 0	25x25mm	35mm	MiniatRo	1935	Meniscus	11	37mm		M,Z	HK616	50
Nori (folding finder)	25x25mm	35mm	MiniatRo	1935	Nori	6.3	37mm		M,Z	Mc336	50
Nori (rigid finder)	25x25mm	35mm	MiniatRo	1937	Meniscus	8	40mm		M,Z	A918	50

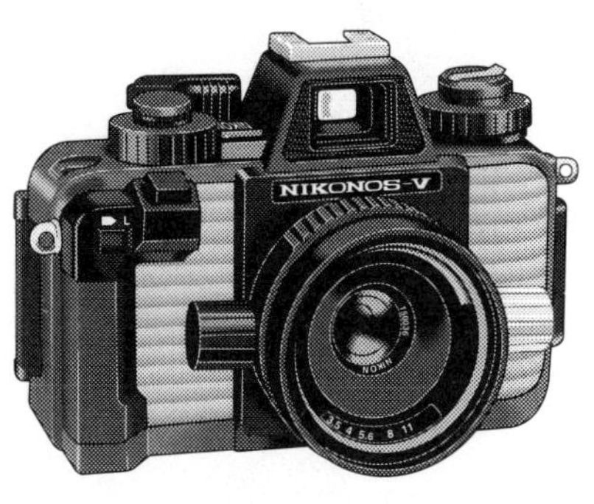

Nikonos V

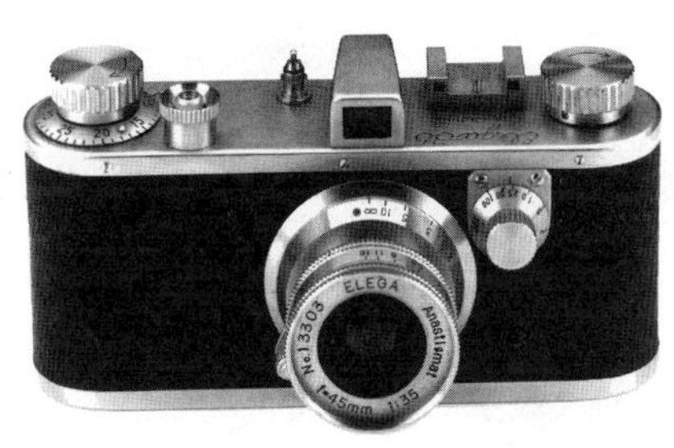

Nitto Elega-35

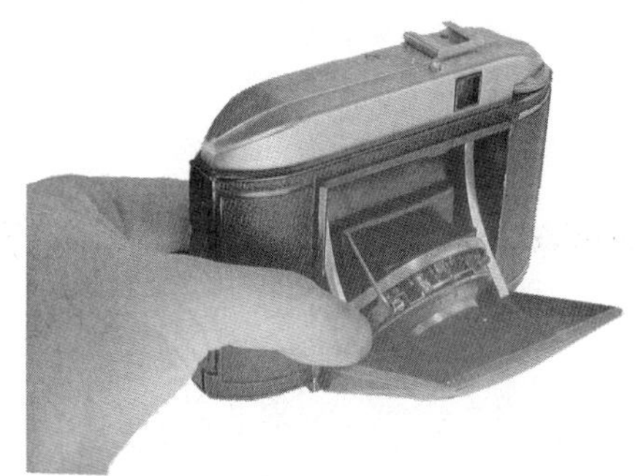

Nixette

MODEL	FORMAT	FILM	TYPE	Year	LENS	Apert	FL	SHUTTER	SPEEDS	ILLUS	U.S.$
...NORTH AMERICAN MFG. CO. - Chicago											
Namco Multi-Flex	3x4cm	127	TLR-Box	1939	Graf		75mm		I,T		20
...NORTON LABORATORIES											
Norton	1$^1/_8$x1½"	Roll	MiniatRo	1934							40
Norton Century of Progress	1$^1/_8$x1½"	Roll	MiniatRo	1934						Mc336	140
...NOVO CAMERA CO.											
Novo 35 Super 2.8	24x36mm	35mm	35rf	1950	Novo Avigon	2.8	45mm	Copal			60
...(unknown)											
Nymco	3x5cm	Sheet	Yen	1938	Meniscus				I	Mc337	30
Nymco Folding Camera	3x5cm	Sheet	Yen	1938					I	Mc337	60
...OBERGASSNER - Munich											
Oga	24x36mm	35mm	35vf	1960	Ennit	2.8	45mm	Prontor-SVS	1-300		40
Ogamatic	24x36mm	35mm	35vf	1960	Color Isconar	2.8	45mm	Prontormat	1-300		30
...OEHLER (B.J. Oehler) - Wetzlar											
Infra	24x24mm	35mm	35vf	1951	Punktar	2.8	35mm	Prontor	25-200	Mc337	60
...OKADA OPTICAL INDUSTRIAL CO. LTD. - Tokyo, Japan											
Gemmy	10x14mm	16mm	Submin	1950	Fixed Focus	4.5	35mm		25-100		1200
Kolt	13x13mm	16mm	Submin	1950	Kolt Anastigmat	4.5	25mm		25-100		240
Waltax (I)	4.5x6cm	120	FoldRo	1940	Kolex Anastigmat	3.5	75mm	Dabit	1-500		100
Walz Baby	3x4cm	127	StrutRo	1936	Walz Anastigmat	4.5	50mm	Walz	25-100		110
...OKAM - Slatinany, Czechoslovakia											
Okam	4.5x6cm	plate	PlateBox	1926	Meyer Helioplan	6	105mm		1/5-1000	Mc337	350
Okam (simple model)	4.5x6cm	plate	PlateBox	1926				1-speed	1/40		370
...OKAYA OPTICAL WORKS - Japan											
Lord IVB	24x36mm	35mm	35rf	1958	Highkor	2.8	40mm	Seikosha-MX	1-500,B		90
Lord 5D	24x36mm	35mm	35rf	1958	Highkor	1.9	40mm	Seikosha-MX	B,1-500		90
...OLBIA - Paris											
Clartex 6/6	6x6cm	620	BakeliteRoll		Meniscus				I,T	F1592	40
Olbia BX (black)	6x6cm	620	BakeliteRoll		Meniscus				I,T	F1628	40
Olbia BX (maroon)	6x6cm	620	BakeliteRoll		Meniscus				I,T	F1628	40
...OLYMPIC CAMERA WORKS - Japan											
New Olympic	3x4cm	127	BakeliteRoll	1934	Alphar	6.3	50mm	Olympic	25,50,B		100
Olympic Junior	3x4cm	127	BakeliteRoll	1934	Olynar	6.3	50mm	Olympic	25,50,B		100
Semi-Olympic	4.5x6cm	120	BakeliteRoll	1937	Ukas	4.5	75mm	Fiskus	25-150,T,B		90
Super-Olympic	24x36mm	35mm	35vf	1935	Ukas	4.5	50mm		25-150,T,B		160
Vest Olympic	3x4cm	127	BakeliteRoll	1938	Ukas	4.5	75mm	Fiskus	25-150,T,B		90
...OLYMPUS KOGAKU - Japan											
Olympus 35 I	24x32mm	35mm	35VF	1948	Zuiko	3.5	40mm	Seikosha-Rap.		Mc341	90
Olympus 35 III	24x36mm	35mm	35VF	1949	Zuiko	3.5	40mm	Seikosha-Rap.		Mc341	120
Olympus 35 IV	24x36mm	35mm	35VF	1949	Zuiko	3.5	4cm	Copal	B, 1-200	Mc341	120
Olympus 35 IVa	24x36mm	35mm	35VF	1953	Zuiko	3.5	4cm	Copal	1-300	Mc342	50
Olympus 35 IVb	24x36mm	35mm	35VF	1954	Zuiko	3.5	4cm	Seikosha-Rap.	1-500	Mc342	70

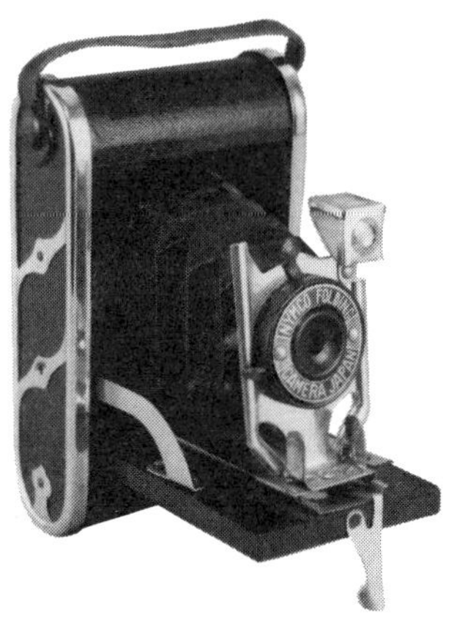

Nymco Folding Camera

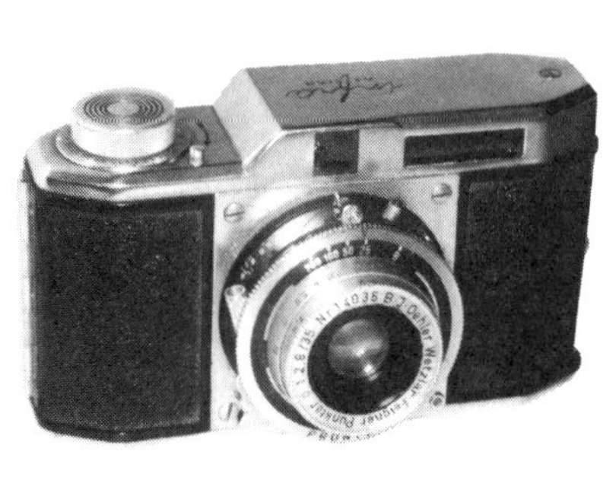

Oehler Infra

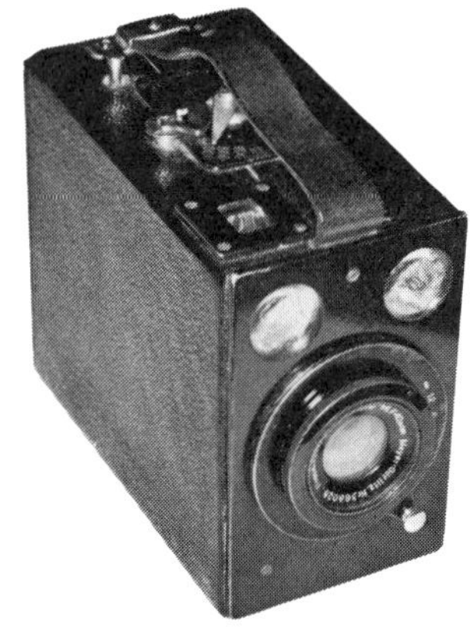

Okam

MODEL	FORMAT	FILM	TYPE	Year	LENS	Apert	FL	SHUTTER	SPEEDS	ILLUS	U.S.$
Olympus 35 Va	24x36mm	35mm	35VF	1955	Zuiko	3.5	4cm	Copal	1-300	Mc342	30
Olympus 35 Vb	24x36mm	35mm	35VF	1955	Zuiko	3.5	4cm	Seikosha-Rapdi	1-500	Mc342	30
Olympus 35 EC	24x36mm	35mm	35C	1969	Zuiko	2.8	42mm	Seiko Electr.	4-1/800	OL146	30
Olympus 35 EC-2	24x36mm	35mm	35C	1971	Zuiko	2.8	42mm	Seiko Electr.	4-1/800	OL146	40
Olympus 35 ECR	24x36mm	35mm	35rf	1972	Zuiko	2.8	42mm	Seiko Electr.	4-1/800	OL146	40
Olympus 35 ED	24x36mm	35mm	35rf	1974	Zuiko	2.8	38mm	Seiko Electr.	4-1/800	OL152	50
Olympus 35-K	24x36mm	35mm	35rf	1957	Zuiko	3.5	4cm	Copal MX	1-500	Mc342	60
Olympus 35 RC	24x36mm	35mm	35rf	1970	Zuiko	2.8	42mm	electronic	1/15-500	OL148	140
Olympus 35 RD	24x36mm	35mm	35rf	1975	Zuiko	1.7	40mm	Seiko Electr.	½-500	OL153	90
Olympus 35-S 1.9	24x36mm	35mm	35rf	1956	Zuiko	1.9	4.5cm	Seikosha-MX	1-500	Mc342	90
Olympus 35-S 2.8	24x36mm	35mm	35rf	1955	Zuiko	2.8	4.8cm	Seikosha-Rap.	1-500	Mc342	60
Olympus 35-S 3.5	24x36mm	35mm	35rf	1955	Zuiko	3.5	4cm	Seikosha-Rap.	1-500	Mc342	60
Olympus 35-S II -f1.8 (I)	24x36mm	35mm	35rf	1957	Zuiko	1.8	4.2cm	Seikosha	1-500	Mc342	80
Olympus 35-S II -f1.8 (II)	24x36mm	35mm	35rf	1958	Zuiko	1.8	4.2cm	Seikosha	1-500	Mc342	80
Olympus 35-S II -f2	24x36mm	35mm	35rf	1958	Zuiko	2	4.2cm	Seikosha	1-500	Mc342	80
Olympus 35-S II -f2.8	24x36mm	35mm	35rf	1957	Zuiko	2.8	4.5cm	Seikosha	1-500	Mc342	50
Olympus 35-SP	24x36mm	35mm	35rf	1969	Zuiko	1.7	42mm	programmed	1-500	OL145	150
Olympus 35-SPn	24x36mm	35mm	35rf	1972	Zuiko	1.7	42mm	programmed	1-500	OL150	150
Olympus Ace	24x36mm	35mm	35rf	1958	E.Zuiko	2.8	45mm	Copal-SV	1-500	Mc343	200
Olympus Ace E	24x36mm	35mm	35rf	1958	E.Zuiko	2.8	4.5cm	Seikosha	1-500	Mc343	100
AF-1 (Infinity)	24x36mm	35mm	35aw-af	1988	Zuiko	2.8	35mm	programmed	1/30-750		140
AF-1 Mini	24x36mm	35mm	35aw-af	1994	Olympus	3.5	35mm	programmed			80
AF-1 Super	24x36mm	35mm	35aw-af	1989	Olympus	2.8	35mm	programmed	1/15-750		130
AF-1 Twin	24x36mm	35mm	35AF-BiF	1989	Olympus	3.5/6.3	35/70	programmed	1/15-730		160
AF-10	24x36mm	35mm	35caf	1988	Olympus	3.5	35mm	programmed	1/45-400		120
AF-10 Mini	24x36mm	35mm	35caf	1994	Olympus	4.5	35mm	programmed			100
AF-10 Super	24x36mm	35mm	35caf	1991	Olympus	3.5	35mm	programmed	1/45-400		90
AF-10 Twin	24x36mm	35mm	35AF-BiF	1992	Olympus	3.5	35mm	programmed			110
AFL	24x36mm	35mm	35af	1983	Zuiko	2.8	38mm	programmed	1/8-500		100
AFL-S	24x36mm	35mm	35af	1986	Olympus	2.8	38mm	programmed	1/8-500		220
AFL-T	24x36mm	35mm	35AF-BiF	1986	Olympus	2.8/4.5	36/60	programmed	1/30-500		110
AM-100	24x36mm	35mm	35vf	1989	Olympus	3.5	35mm	programmed	1/45-400		70
Olympus Auto	24x36mm	35mm	35rf	1958	E.Zuiko	1.8	42mm	Seikosha	1-500	Mc343	50
Olympus Auto B	24x36mm	35mm	35rf	1959	E.Zuiko	2.8	35mm	Seikosha	1-500		50
Olympus Auto Eye	24x36mm	35mm	35rf	1960	D.Zuiko	2.8	45mm	Copal-SV	1-500	Mc343	110
Olympus Auto Eye II	24x36mm	35mm	35rf	1962	D.Zuiko	2.5	43mm		1-500		90
AZ-1 Zoom	24x36mm	35mm	35afz	1988	Zoom	3.5-6.7	35-70	programmed	1/45-250		210
AZ-100	24x36mm	35mm	35afz	1990	Zoom	4-7.7	35-70	programmed	1/40-250		150
AZ-200 Super Zoom	24x36mm	35mm	35afz	1990	Zoom	4.5-6.4	38-80	programmed	1-500		190
AZ-210 Super Zoom	24x36mm	35mm	35afz	1992	Zoom	4.5-6.2	38-76	programmed			120
AZ-220 Wide Zoom	24x36mm	35mm	35afz	1992	Zoom	3.5-6.5	28-56	programmed			190
AZ-230 Super Zoom	24x36mm	35mm	35afz	1992	Zoom	4.5-7.2	38-90	programmed	2-1/500		160

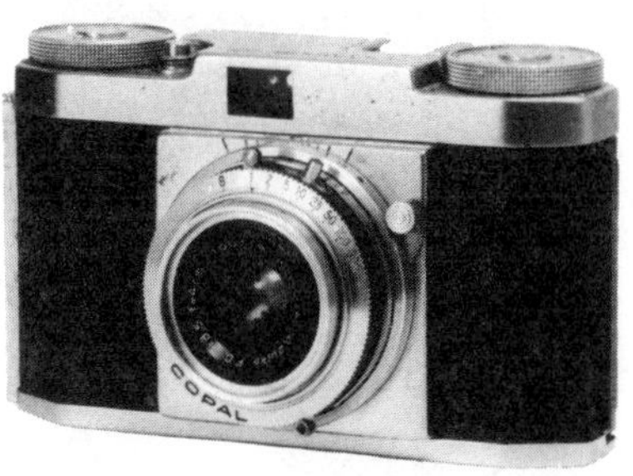

Olympus 35 Va

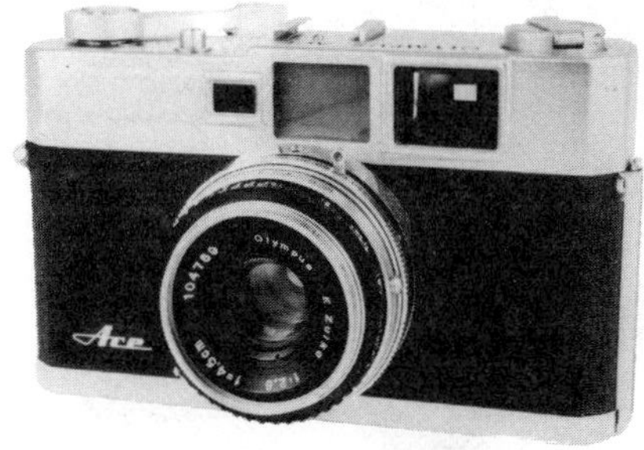

Olympus Ace

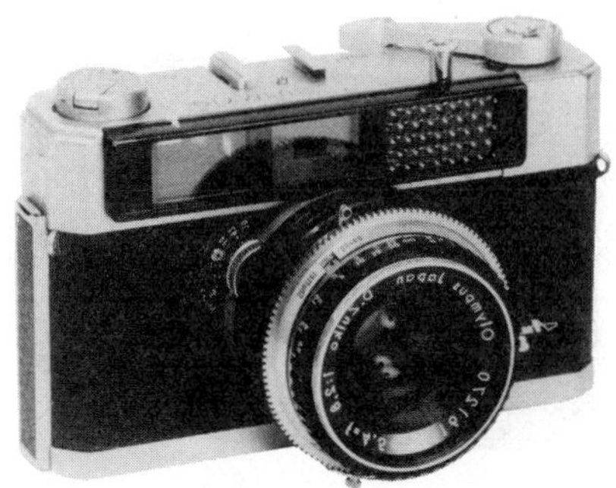

Olympus Auto Eye

MODEL	FORMAT	FILM	TYPE	Year	LENS	Apert	FL	SHUTTER	SPEEDS	ILLUS	U.S.$
AZ-300 Super Zoom	24x36mm	35mm	35afz	1988	Zoom	4.5-6	38-105	programmed	2-1/500		240
AZ-330 Super Zoom	24x36mm	35mm	35afz	1993	Zoom	4.5-6	38-105	programmed	2-1/500		250
Chrome Six I	6x6cm	120	HzFoldRo	1948	Zuiko	3.5	7.5cm	Copal	1-200	Mc338	130
Chrome Six II	6x6cm	120	HzFoldRo	1948	Zuiko	2.8	7.5cm	Copal	1-200	Mc338	130
Chrome Six IIIA	6x6cm	120	HzFoldRo	1950	Zuiko	3.5	7.5cm	Copal	1-200	Mc339	110
Chrome Six IIIB	6x6cm	120	HzFoldRo	1950	Zuiko	2.8	7.5cm	Copal	1-200	OL64	110
Chrome Six IVA	6x6cm	120	HzFoldRo	1954	Zuiko	3.5	7.5cm	Copal	1-200		130
Chrome Six IVB	6x6cm	120	HzFoldRo	1954	Zuiko	2.8	7.5cm	Copal	1-200	OL66	130
Chrome Six VA	6x6cm	120	HzFoldRo	1955	Zuiko	3.5	7.5cm	Copal	1-200		110
Chrome Six VB	6x6cm	120	HzFoldRo	1955	Zuiko	2.8	7.5cm	Copal	1-200	Mc339	110
Chrome Six RIIA	6x6cm	120	HzFoldRo	1956	Zuiko	3.5	7.5cm	Copal	1/300	OL68	110
Chrome Six RIIB	6x6cm	120	HzFoldRo	1956	Zuiko	2.8	7.5cm	Copal	1/300	OL68	110
Olympus Flex A2.8	6x6cm	120	TLR	1955	Zuiko	2.8	7.5cm	Seikosha-Rap.	1-500	Mc339	130
Olympus Flex A3.5	6x6cm	120	TLR	1954	Zuiko	3.5	7.5cm	Seikosha-Rap.	1-500	Mc339	100
Olympus Flex A3.5II	6x6cm	120	TLR	1956	Zuiko	3.5	7.5cm	Seikosha-Rap.	1-500	Mc339	100
Olympus Flex B I	6x6cm	120	TLR	1952	Zuiko	2.8	7.5cm	Seikosha-Rap.	1-400	Mc339	160
Olympus Flex BII	6x6cm	120	TLR	1953	Zuiko	2.8	7.5cm	Seikosha-Rap.	1-500	Mc339	140
Olympus FTL	24x36mm	35mm	35slr	1971	Zuiko	1.4	50mm	focal plane		Mc343	100
Olympus FTL	24x36mm	35mm	35slr	1971	Zuiko	1.8	50mm	focal plane			120
Infinity II	24x36mm	35mm	35aw-af	1989	Olympus	2.8	35mm	programmed	1/15-750		130
Infinity Hi-Lite	24x36mm	35mm	35caf	1994	Olympus	4.5	35mm	programmed			100
Infinity Jr	24x36mm	35mm	35caf	1988	Olympus	3.5	35mm	programmed	1/45-400		120
Infinity Mini	24x36mm	35mm	35aw-af	1994	Olympus	3.5	35mm	programmed			80
Infinity S	24x36mm	35mm	35vf	1989	Olympus	3.5	35mm	programmed	1/45-400		70
Infinity Stylus	24x36mm	35mm	35caf	1991	Olympus	3.5	35mm	programmed	1/15-500		100
Infinity Stylus Zoom	24x36mm	35mm	35afz	1992	Zoom	4.5-6.9	35-70	programmed	4-1/500		170
Infinity Super Zoom 300	24x36mm	35mm	35afz	1988	Zoom	4.5-6	38-105	programmed	2-1/500		240
Infinity Super Zoom 330	24x36mm	35mm	35afz	1993	Zoom	4.5-6	38-105	programmed	2-1/500		250
Infinity Superzoom 2800	24x36mm	35mm	35afz	1994	Zoom	4.5-7.8	28-80	programmed			210
Infinity Superzoom 3000	24x36mm	35mm	35afz	1993	Zoom	3.8-8.1	38-110	programmed			210
Infinity Superzoom 3500	24x36mm	35mm	35aw-af	1994	Zoom	4.5-8.7	35-120	programmed			260
Infinity Tele	24x36mm	35mm	35AF-BiF	1992	Olympus	3.5	35mm	programmed			110
Infinity Twin	24x36mm	35mm	35AF-BiF	1989	Olympus	3.5/6.3	35/70	programmed	1/15-730		160
Infinity Zoom 200	24x36mm	35mm	35afz	1990	Zoom	4.5-6.4	38-80	programmed	1-500		190
Infinity Zoom 210	24x36mm	35mm	35afz	1992	Zoom	4.5-6.2	38-76	programmed			120
Infinity Z. 220 Panorama	24x36mm	35mm	35afz	1992	Zoom	3.5-6.5	28-56	programmed			190
Infinity Zoom 230	24x36mm	35mm	35afz	1992	Zoom	4.5-7.2	38-90	programmed	2-1/500		160
Infinity Zoom 2000	24x36mm	35mm	35afz	1994	Zoom	4.5-7.8	38-70	programmed			120
Olympus IS-1	24x36mm	35mm	35ZLR	1991	Zoom	4.5-5.6	35-135	focal plane	15-2000		330
Olympus IS-10	24x36mm	35mm	35ZLR	1994	Zoom	4.5-5.6	28-110	focal plane	2-2000		340
Olympus IS-100	24x36mm	35mm	35ZLR	1994	Zoom	4.5-5.6	28-110	focal plane	2-2000		340
Olympus IS-1000	24x36mm	35mm	35ZLR	1991	Zoom	4.5-5.6	35-135	focal plane	15-2000		330

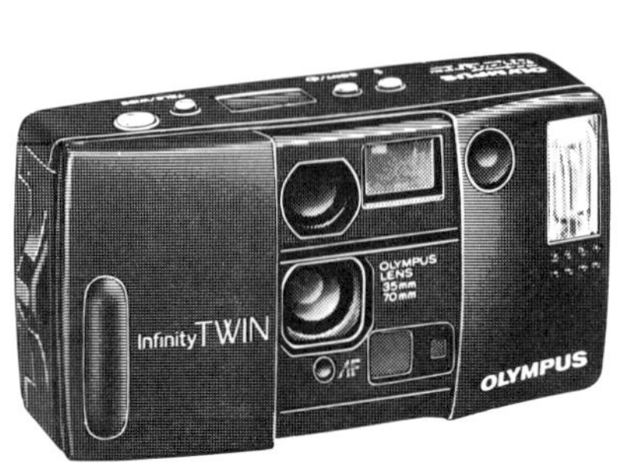

Olympus Infinity Twin

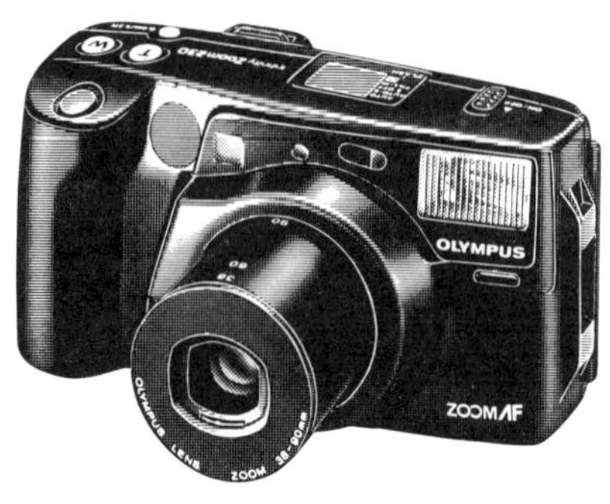

Olympus Infinity Zoom 230

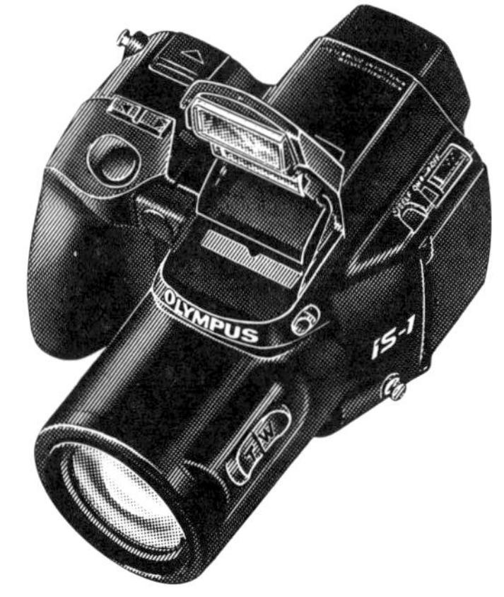

Olympus IS-1

MODEL	FORMAT	FILM	TYPE	Year	LENS	Apert	FL	SHUTTER	SPEEDS	ILLUS	U.S.$
Olympus IS-2	24x36mm	35mm	35ZLR	1993	Zoom	4.5-5.6	35-135	focal plane	15-2000		410
Olympus IS-2000	24x36mm	35mm	35ZLR	1993	Zoom	4.5-5.6	35-135	focal plane	15-2000		410
Olympus IS-3 DLX	24x36mm	35mm	35ZLR	1993	Zoom	4.5-5.6	35-180	focal plane	15-2000		500
Olympus IS-3000	24x36mm	35mm	35ZLR	1993	Zoom	4.5-5.6	35-180	focal plane	15-2000		500
IZM200	24x36mm	35mm	35afz	1990	Zoom	4.5-6.4	38-80	programmed	1-500		190
IZM210	24x36mm	35mm	35afz	1992	Zoom	4.5-6.2	38-76	programmed			120
IZM220 Panorama Z. QD	24x36mm	35mm	35afz	1992	Zoom	3.5-6.5	28-56	programmed			190
IZM230	24x36mm	35mm	35afz	1992	Zoom	4.5-7.2	38-90	programmed	2-1/500		160
IZM300	24x36mm	35mm	35afz	1988	Zoom	4.5-6	38-105	programmed	2-1/500		240
IZM330	24x36mm	35mm	35afz	1993	Zoom	4.5-6	38-105	programmed	2-1/500		250
Olympus L-1	24x36mm	35mm	35ZLR	1991	Zoom	4.5-5.6	35-135	focal plane	15-2000		330
Olympus L-2	24x36mm	35mm	35ZLR	1993	Zoom	4.5-5.6	35-135	focal plane	15-2000		410
Olympus L-3	24x36mm	35mm	35ZLR	1993	Zoom	4.5-5.6	35-180	focal plane	15-2000		500
Olympus L-10 Panorama	24x36mm	35mm	35ZLR	1994	Zoom	4.5-5.6	28-110	focal plane	2-2000		340
Olympus M-1 body	24x36mm	35mm	35slr	1972	body only	---	---	focal plane	1-1000,B	OL166	270
Olympus M-1 + 50/1.4	24x36mm	35mm	35slr	1972	Zuiko	1.4	50mm	focal plane	1-1000,B	Mc343	380
mju (μ) Panorama QD	24x36mm	35mm	35caf	1991	Olympus	3.5	35mm	programmed	1/15-500		100
mju (μ) Zoom	24x36mm	35mm	35afz	1992	Zoom	4.5-6.9	35-70	programmed	4-1/500		170
mju-1 (μ-1)	24x36mm	35mm	35caf	1991	Olympus	3.5	35mm	programmed	1/15-500		100
New Infinity. Jr	24x36mm	35mm	35caf	1991	Olympus	3.5	35mm	programmed	1/45-400		90
O-Product	24x36mm	35mm	35AF	1988	Olympus	3.5	35mm	programmed	1/45-400	Mc343	700
OM-1 (black) body	24x36mm	35mm	35slr	1973	body only	---	---	focal plane	1-1000,B		200
OM-1 (black) + 50/1.4	24x36mm	35mm	35slr	1973	Zuiko	1.4	50mm	focal plane	1-1000,B		240
OM-1 (chrome) body	24x36mm	35mm	35slr	1973	body only	---	---	focal plane	1-1000,B	OL166	160
OM-1 (chrome) + 50/1.4	24x36mm	35mm	35slr	1973	Zuiko	1.4	50mm	focal plane	1-1000,B	Mc343	230
OM-1 MD (black) body	24x36mm	35mm	35slr	1974	body only	---	---	focal plane	1-1000,B		170
OM-1 MD (black) + 50/1.8	24x36mm	35mm	35slr	1974	Zuiko	1.8	50mm	focal plane	1-1000,B		220
OM-1 MD (chrome) body	24x36mm	35mm	35slr	1974	body only	---	---	focal plane	1-1000,B		170
---1 MD (chrome) + 50/1.8	24x36mm	35mm	35slr	1974	Zuiko	1.8	50mm	focal plane	1-1000,B	OL168	200
OM-1N MD (black) body	24x36mm	35mm	35slr	1979	body only	---	---	focal plane	1-1000		200
---1N MD (black) + 50/1.4	24x36mm	35mm	35slr	1979	Zuiko	1.4	50mm	focal plane	1-1000		250
OM-1N MD (chrome) body	24x36mm	35mm	35slr	1979	body only	---	---	focal plane	1-1000	OL170	190
---1N MD (chrome) + 50/1.4	24x36mm	35mm	35slr	1979	Zuiko	1.4	50mm	focal plane	1-1000	Mc344	250
OM-2 (black) body	24x36mm	35mm	35slr	1975	body only	---	---	focal plane	120-1000		190
OM-2 (black) + 50/1.4	24x36mm	35mm	35slr	1975	Zuiko	1.4	50mm	focal plane	120-1000		310
OM-2 (chrome) body	24x36mm	35mm	35slr	1975	body only	---	---	focal plane	120-1000		200
OM-2 (chrome) + 50/1.4	24x36mm	35mm	35slr	1975	Zuiko	1.4	50mm	focal plane	120-1000	OL169	300
OM-2 MD body	24x36mm	35mm	35slr	1975	body only	---	---	focal plane			230
OM-2 MD + 35/2.8	24x36mm	35mm	35slr	1975	Zuiko	2.8	35mm	focal plane		Mc344	350
OM-2N MD (black) body	24x36mm	35mm	35slr	1979	body only	---	---	focal plane		OL171	270
---2N MD (black) + 50/1.4	24x36mm	35mm	35slr	1979	Zuiko	1.4	50mm	focal plane		Mc344	330
OM-2N MD (chrome) body	24x36mm	35mm	35slr	1979	body only	---	---	focal plane			230

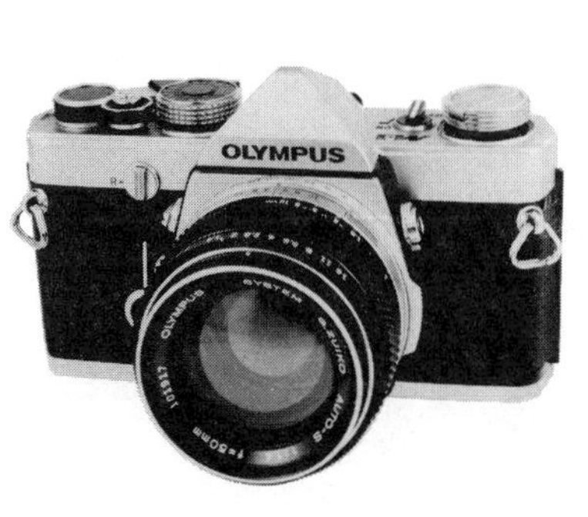

Olympus M-1

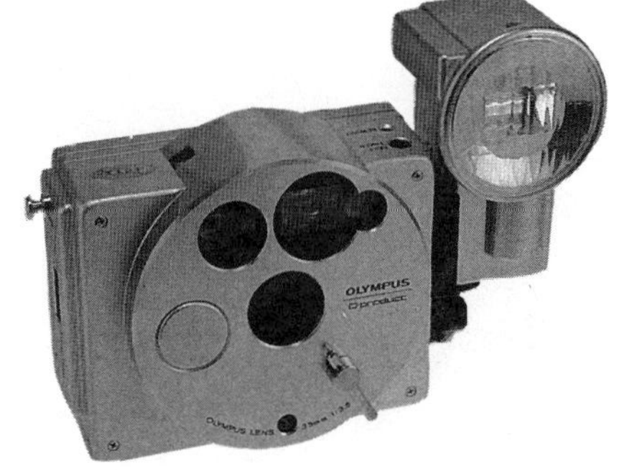

O-Product

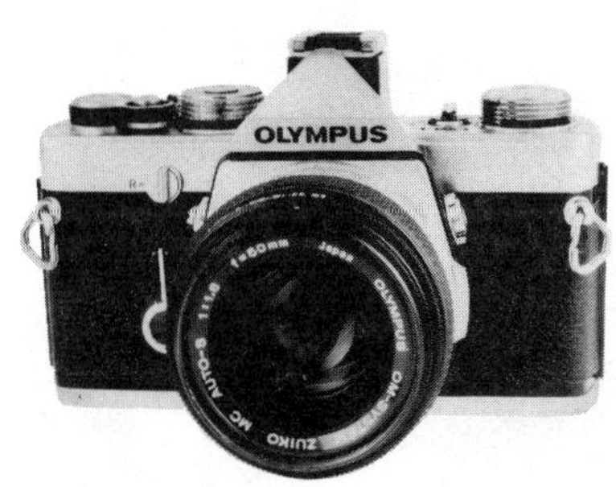

Olympus OM-1

MODEL	FORMAT	FILM	TYPE	Year	LENS	Apert	FL	SHUTTER	SPEEDS	ILLUS	U.S.$
---2N MD (chrome) + 50/1.4	24x36mm	35mm	35slr	1979	Zuiko	1.4	50mm	focal plane			320
OM-2S Program body	24x36mm	35mm	35slr	1984	body only	---	---	focal plane	60-1/1000		290
OM-2S Program + 50/1.4	24x36mm	35mm	35slr	1984	Zuiko	1.4	50mm	focal plane	60-1/1000		370
OM-3 body	24x36mm	35mm	35slr	1983	body only	---	---	focal plane	1-2000		540
OM-3 + 50/1.4	24x36mm	35mm	35slr	1983	Zuiko	1.4	50mm	focal plane	1-2000	OL176	660
OM-3 Ti body	24x36mm	35mm	35slr	1994	body only	---	---	focal plane	1-2000		1500
OM-3 Ti + 50/1.2	24x36mm	35mm	35slr	1994	Zuiko	1.2	50mm	focal plane	1-2000		1800
OM-4 (black) body	24x36mm	35mm	35slr	1983	body only	---	---	focal plane	180-1/2000		440
OM-4 (black) + 50/1.4	24x36mm	35mm	35slr	1983	Zuiko	1.4	50mm	focal plane	180-1/200	OL176	530
OM-4 (chrome) body	24x36mm	35mm	35slr	1983	body only	---	---	focal plane	180-1/2000		410
OM-4 (chrome) + 50/1.4	24x36mm	35mm	35slr	1983	Zuiko	1.4	50mm	focal plane	180-1/2000		470
OM-4T (black) body	24x36mm	35mm	35slr	1993	body only	---	---	focal plane	240-1/2000		700
OM-4T (black) + 50/1.2	24x36mm	35mm	35slr	1993	Zuiko	1.2	50mm	focal plane	240-1/2000		900
OM-4T (chrome) body	24x36mm	35mm	35slr	1985	body only	---	---	focal plane	240-1/2000		530
OM-4T (chrome) + 50/1.2	24x36mm	35mm	35slr	1985	Zuiko	1.2	50mm	focal plane	240-1/2000		700
OM-4Ti (black) body	24x36mm	35mm	35slr	1993	body only	---	---	focal plane	240-1/2000		700
OM-4Ti (black) + 50/1.2	24x36mm	35mm	35slr	1993	Zuiko	1.2	50mm	focal plane	240-1/2000		900
OM-4Ti (chrome) body	24x36mm	35mm	35slr	1985	body only	---	---	focal plane	240-1/2000		530
OM-4Ti (chrome) + 50/1.2	24x36mm	35mm	35slr	1985	Zuiko	1.2	50mm	focal plane	240-1/2000		700
OM-10 body	24x36mm	35mm	35slr	1979	body only	---	---	focal plane	1-1000	OL172	100
OM-10 + 50/1.8	24x36mm	35mm	35slr	1979	Zuiko	1.8	50mm	focal plane	1-1000	Mc343	140
OM-10 Quartz body	24x36mm	35mm	35slr	1979	body only	---	---	focal plane	2-1/1000		110
OM-10 Quartz + 50/1.8	24x36mm	35mm	35slr	1979	Zuiko	1.8	50mm	focal plane	2-1/1000	OL172	150
OM-20 body	24x36mm	35mm	35slr	1981	body only	---	---	focal plane	2-1/1000		130
OM-20 + 50/1.4	24x36mm	35mm	35slr	1981	Zuiko	1.4	50mm	focal plane	2-1/1000	OL174	210
OM-30 body	24x36mm	35mm	35AFSLR	1982	body only	---	---	focal plane	2-1/1000		140
OM-30 + 50/1.4	24x36mm	35mm	35AFSLR	1982	Zuiko	1.4	50mm	focal plane	2-1/1000	OL175	210
OM-40 body	24x36mm	35mm	35slr	1985	body only	---	---	focal plane	2-1/1000		160
OM-40 + 50/1.4	24x36mm	35mm	35slr	1985	Zuiko	1.4	50mm	focal plane	2-1/1000		240
OM-77AF body	24x36mm	35mm	35AFSLR	1986	body only	---	---	focal plane	2-1/2000		140
OM-77AF + 50/1.8	24x36mm	35mm	35AFSLR	1986	Olympus	1.8	50mm	focal plane	2-1/2000		220
OM-88 body	24x36mm	35mm	35slr	1988	body only	---	---	focal plane	2-1/2000		150
OM-88 + 50/1.2	24x36mm	35mm	35slr	1988	AF	1.2	50mm	focal plane	2-1/2000		230
OM-101 body	24x36mm	35mm	35slr	1988	body only	---	---	focal plane	2-1/2000		150
OM-101 + 50/1.2	24x36mm	35mm	35slr	1988	AF	1.2	50mm	focal plane	2-1/2000		230
OM-707 AF body	24x36mm	35mm	35AFSLR	1986	body only	---	---	focal plane	2-1/2000		140
OM-707 AF + 50/1.8	24x36mm	35mm	35AFSLR	1986	Olympus	1.8	50mm	focal plane	2-1/2000		220
OM-F body	24x36mm	35mm	35AFSLR	1982	body only	---	---	focal plane	2-1/1000		140
OM-F + 50/1.4	24x36mm	35mm	35AFSLR	1982	Zuiko	1.4	50mm	focal plane	2-1/1000	OL175	210
OM-G body	24x36mm	35mm	35slr	1981	body only	---	---	focal plane	2-1/1000		130
OM-G + 50/1.4	24x36mm	35mm	35slr	1981	Zuiko	1.4	50mm	focal plane	2-1/1000	OL174	210
OM-PC body	24x36mm	35mm	35slr	1985	body only	---	---	focal plane	2-1/1000		160

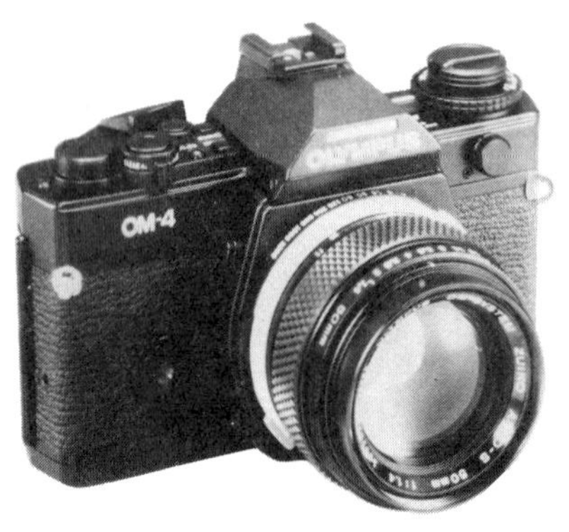

Olympus OM-4

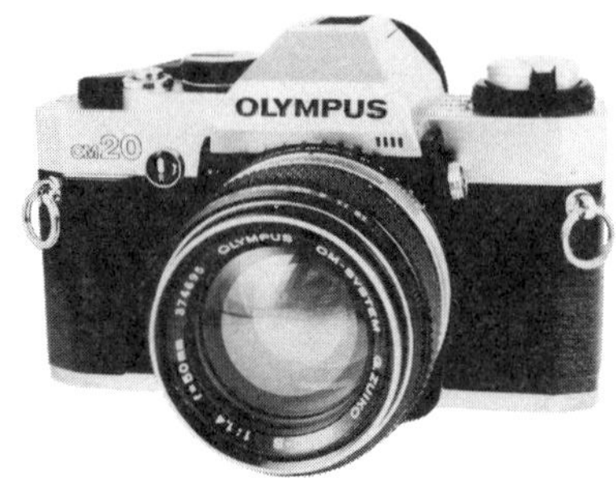

Olympus OM-20

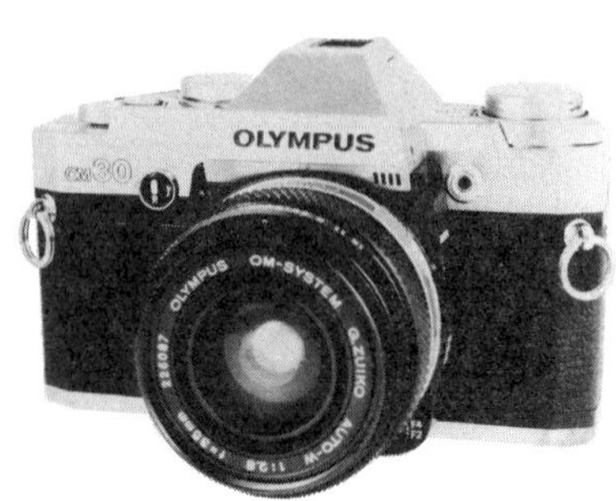

Olympus OM-30

MODEL	FORMAT	FILM	TYPE	Year	LENS	Apert	FL	SHUTTER	SPEEDS	ILLUS	U.S.$
OM-PC + 50/1.4	24x36mm	35mm	35slr	1985	Zuiko	1.4	50mm	focal plane	2-1/1000		240
OZ1 Panorama	24x36mm	35mm	35aw-af	1994	Olympus	3.5	35mm	programmed			80
OZ70 Panorama Zoom QD	24x36mm	35mm	35afz	1994	Zoom	4.5-7.8	38-70	programmed			120
OZ-110 Zoom	24x36mm	35mm	35afz	1993	Zoom	3.8-8.1	38-110	programmed			210
OZ120 Zoom	24x36mm	35mm	35aw-af	1994	Zoom	4.5-8.7	35-120	programmed			260
OZ280 P Zoom QD	24x36mm	35mm	35afz	1994	Zoom	4.5-7.8	28-80	programmed			210
Pen	18x24mm	35mm	35Half	1959	Zuiko	3.5	28mm	Copal-X	25-200	Mc340	60
Pen D	18x24mm	35mm	35Half	1962	Zuiko	1.9	32mm	Copal-X	1/8-500	Mc340	80
Pen D2	18x24mm	35mm	35Half	1964	Zuiko	1.9	32mm	Copal-X	1/8-500		50
Pen D3	18x24mm	35mm	35Half	1965	Zuiko	1.7	32mm	Copal-X	1-500	Mc340	70
Pen EE	18x24mm	35mm	35Half	1961	Fixed focus	3.5	28mm	Automatic		Mc340	50
Pen EE-2	18x24mm	35mm	35Half	1968	Zuiko	3.5	28mm	Olympus	30-250	Mc341	50
Pen EE-3	18x24mm	35mm	35Half	1973	Zuiko	3.5	28mm	Auto	30-250	Mc341	60
Pen EED	18x24mm	35mm	35Half	1967	Zuiko	1.7	32mm	Auto	15-500	Mc341	70
Pen EE-EL	18x24mm	35mm	35Half	1966	Zuiko	3.5	28mm	Auto	15-500	Mc340	40
Pen EES	18x24mm	35mm	35Half	1962	Zone-focusing	2.8	30mm	Olympus	30-250	Mc340	50
Pen EES-EL	18x24mm	35mm	35Half	1966	Zuiko	2.8	30mm	Auto	15-500		40
Pen EES2	18x24mm	35mm	35Half	1968	Zuiko	2.8	30mm	Auto	15-500	Mc341	50
Pen EF	18x24mm	35mm	35Half	1981	Zuiko	3.5	28mm	Copal-X	1/30-250	OL98	100
Pen EM	18x24mm	35mm	35Half	1965	Zuiko	2	35mm	Copal-X		Mc340	60
Pen F	18x24mm	35mm	35SLR	1963	Zuiko	1.4	40mm	focal plane	1-500	Mc341	200
Pen F	18x24mm	35mm	35SLR	1963	Zuiko	1.8	38mm	focal plane	1-500	OL100	200
Pen FT (black)	18x24mm	35mm	35SLR	1966	Zuiko	1.8	38mm	focal plane	1-500	OL100	310
Pen FT (chrome)	18x24mm	35mm	35SLR	1966	Zuiko	1.8	38mm	focal plane	1-500	Mc341	240
Pen FT Gastro	18x24mm	35mm	35SLR	1967	Endoscope			focal plane	1-500	OL103	200
Pen FV	18x24mm	35mm	35SLR	1967	Zuiko	1.8	38mm	focal plane	1-500	OL102	180
Pen Rapid EED	18x24mm	35mm	35Half	1965	Zuiko	1.7	32mm	Auto	15-500	Mc340	130
Pen Rapid EES	18x24mm	35mm	35Half	1965	Zuiko	3.5	38mm	Olympus	30-250	Mc340	90
Pen S 2.8	18x24mm	35mm	35Half	1960	Zuiko	2.8	30mm	Copal-X	8-250	Mc340	80
Pen S 3.5	18x24mm	35mm	35Half	1965	Zuiko	3.5	30mm	Copal-X	8-250		80
Pen W (Wide)	18x24mm	35mm	35Half	1964	Zuiko	2.8	25mm	Copal-X	1/8-250	Mc340	100
Quick Shooter	24x36mm	35mm	35af	1986	Olympus	2.8	38mm	programmed	1/8-500		220
Quick Shooter Tele	24x36mm	35mm	35AF-BiF	1986	Olympus	2.8/4.5	36/60	programmed	1/30-500		110
Quick Shooter Zoom	24x36mm	35mm	35afz	1988	Zoom	3.5-6.7	35-70	programmed	1/45-250		210
Quick Shooter Zoom 2	24x36mm	35mm	35afz	1990	Zoom	4-7.7	35-70	programmed	1/40-250		150
Olympus-S "Electro Set"	24x36mm	35mm	35rf	1962	G.Zuiko	1.8	42mm	Copal	1-500	Mc343	60
Olympus-S (CdS)	24x36mm	35mm	35rf	1963	Zuiko	1.8	42mm	Copal-X	1-500	Mc343	60
Semi-Olympus Mod. I C	4.5x6cm	120	VtFoldRo	1936	Zuiko	4.5	75mm	Compur	1-250	Mc338	440
Semi-Olympus Mod. I K	4.5x6cm	120	VtFoldRo	1937	Zuiko	4.5	75mm	Koho	1/150	OL57	440
Semi-Olympus Mod. II	4.5x6cm	120	HzFoldRo	1938	Zuiko	4.5	75mm	Koho	150	Mc338	340
Olympus Six (1939)	6x6cm	120	HzFoldRo	1939	Zuiko	4.5	75mm	Koho	200		200
Olympus Six (1940)	6x6cm	120	HzFoldRo	1940	Zuiko	3.5	75mm	Koho	200	Mc338	200

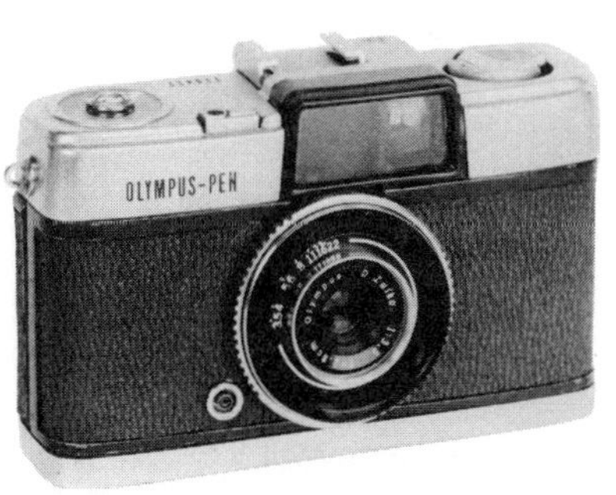

Olympus Pen

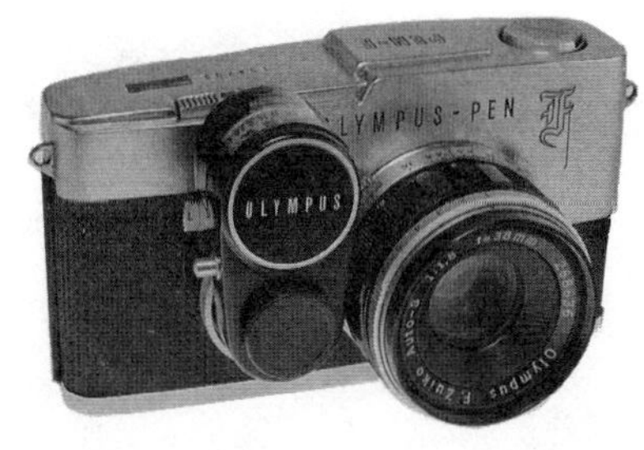

Olympus Pen F

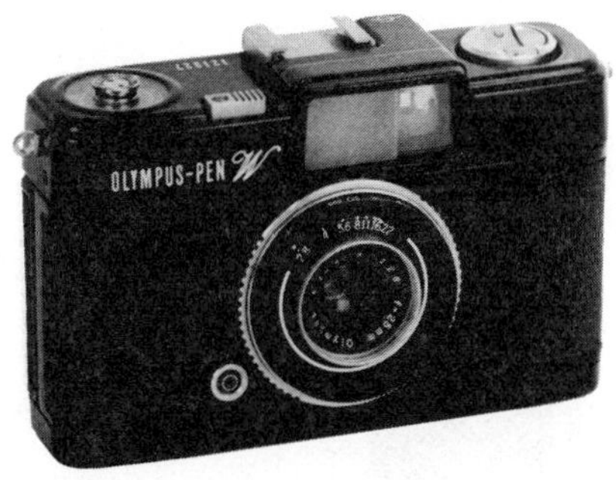

Olympus Pen W (Wide)

MODEL	FORMAT	FILM	TYPE	Year	LENS	Apert	FL	SHUTTER	SPEEDS	ILLUS	U.S.$
Olympus Standard	4x5cm	127	MedRF	1937	Zuiko	3.5	65mm	focal plane	25-500	Mc338	6100
Supertrip	24x36mm	35mm	35vf	1986	Zuiko	4.3	35mm				40
Superzoom 70	24x36mm	35mm	35afz	1994	Zoom	4.5-7.8	38-70	programmed			120
Superzoom 80 Wide	24x36mm	35mm	35afz	1994	Zoom	4.5-7.8	28-80	programmed			210
Superzoom 110	24x36mm	35mm	35afz	1993	Zoom	3.8-8.1	38-110	programmed			210
Superzoom 120	24x36mm	35mm	35aw-af	1994	Zoom	4.5-8.7	35-120	programmed			260
Trip 10	24x36mm	35mm	35vf	1994	Olympus	4.5	33mm		1/125		50
Trip 35	24x36mm	35mm	35vf	1977	Zuiko	2.8	40mm	programmed	1/40-200		50
Trip AF	24x36mm	35mm	35af	1982	Zuiko	3.5	35mm	programmed	1/85-250	OL159	60
Trip AF Motor	24x36mm	35mm	35af	1982	Zuiko	3.8	35mm	programmed			100
Trip AF S-2	24x36mm	35mm	35af	1992	Olympus	4.5	34mm		1/130		50
Trip AF Super	24x36mm	35mm	35af	1991	Olympus	4.5	35mm		1/125		60
Trip Junior	24x36mm	35mm	35vf	1991	Olympus	4.5	33mm		1/125		40
Trip MD	24x36mm	35mm	35vf	1989	Olympus	4	35mm		1/125		40
Trip MD2	24x36mm	35mm	35vf	1991	Olympus	4.5	35mm		1/125		50
Trip Panorama	24x36mm	35mm	35vf	1990	Olympus	4.5	33mm		1/125		50
Trip Panorama 2	24x36mm	35mm	35vf	1993	Olympus	4.5	33mm		1/125		60
Trip S	24x36mm	35mm	35vf	1990	Olympus	4.5	35mm		1/125		40
Olympus Wide	24x36mm	35mm	35VF	1955	Zuiko	3.5	35mm	Copal MX	1-300	Mc342	50
Olympus Wide II	24x36mm	35mm	35VF	1958	Zuiko	3.5	35mm	Copal MX	1-300	Mc342	70
Olympus Wide E	24x36mm	35mm	35VF	1957	Zuiko	3.5	35mm	Copal MX	1-300	Mc342	70
Olympus Wide S	24x36mm	35mm	35rf	1957	Zuiko	2	35mm	Seikosha-Rap.	1-500	Mc342	70
XA	24x36mm	35mm	35rf	1979	Zuiko	2.8	35mm		10-1/500	OL154	140
XA-1	24x36mm	35mm	35vf	1982	Zuiko	4	35mm	programmed	1/30-250	OL157	60
XA-2	24x36mm	35mm	35vf	1980	Zuiko	3.5	35mm	programmed	2-1/750	OL154	80
XA-3	24x36mm	35mm	35vf	1982	Zuiko	3.5	35mm	programmed	2-1/750		120
XA4 Macro	24x36mm	35mm	35C	1982	Zuiko	3.5	28mm	programmed	2-1/750		160
...OMI (OTTICO MECCANICA ITALIANA) - Rome											
Sunshine	10x12mm	35mm	3-Color	1947	Omiterna	3.5	35mm			Mc344	1100
...O.P.L.-FOCA (OPTIQUE ET PRÉCISION DE LEVALLOIS S.A.) - France											
Foca (*) (1946 type)	24x36mm	35mm	35vf	1946	Foca	3.5	3.5cm	focal plane	20-500	Mc344	220
Foca (**) (1945 type)	24x36mm	35mm	35rf	1945	Foca	3.5	5cm	focal plane	20-500	Mc344	200
Foca (**) PF2B	24x36mm	35mm	35rf	1947	Oplar	2.8	5cm	focal plane	25-1000	Mc344	130
F. PF2B Marine Nationale	24x36mm	35mm	35rf		Oplar	1.9	5cm	focal plane	25-1000	F574	300
Foca (***) PF3	24x36mm	35mm	35rf	1951	Oplar	3.5	5cm	focal plane	1-1000	Mc344	200
Foca (***) PF3L	24x36mm	35mm	35rf	1958	Oplar	2.8	5cm	focal plane	1-1000	F579	190
Foca Marly	4x4cm	127	RigidRo	1964	Meniscus				I	F689	30
Foca-Sport	24x36mm	35mm	35rf	1955	Neoplar	2.8	45mm	Atos-2	1-300	F580	80
Foca-Sport I	24x36mm	35mm	35rf	1958	Neoplar	2.8	45mm	Atos-2	1/15-500	F581	100
Foca-Sport Ib	24x36mm	35mm	35rf	1959	Neoplar	3.5	45mm	Atos-2	1-300	F582	100
Foca-Sport Ic	24x36mm	35mm	35rf	1957	Neoplar	3.5	45mm	Atos-2	1-300	F583	100
Foca-Sport Id	24x36mm	35mm	35rf	1959	Neoplar	2.8	45mm	Atos-2	1-300	F584	100

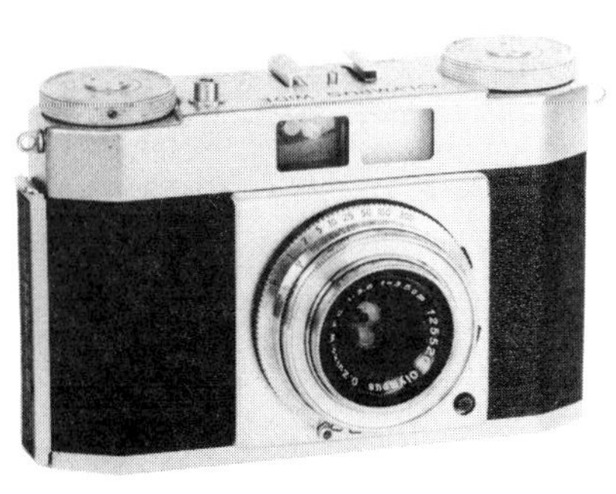

Olympus Wide

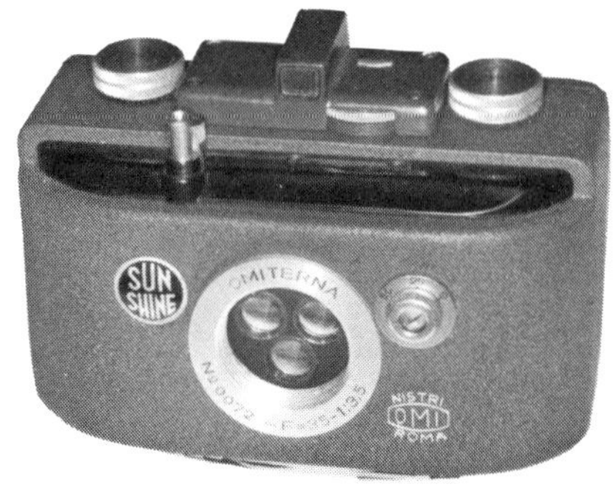

Omi Sunshine

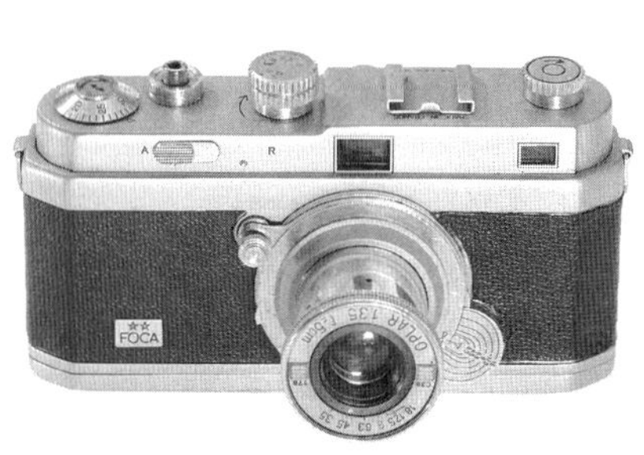

Foca (**) PF2B

MODEL	FORMAT	FILM	TYPE	Year	LENS	Apert	FL	SHUTTER	SPEEDS	ILLUS	U.S.$
Foca-Sport II	24x36mm	35mm	35rf	1957	Oplar	2.8	50mm	Atos-2	1-300	Mc345	90
Foca Standard (*)	24x36mm	35mm	35vf	1947	Oplar	3.5	3.5cm	focal plane	25-500	Mc344	140
Foca U.R.	24x36mm	35mm	35rf	1955	Oplex	2.8	5cm	focal plane	1-1000	Mc344	310
Foca Universel	24x36mm	35mm	35rf	1948	Oplar	2.8	5cm	focal plane	1-1000	F600	140
Foca Universel R	24x36mm	35mm	35rf	1948	Oplar	2.8	5cm	focal plane	1-1000	F602	140
Foca Universel RC (URC)	24x36mm	35mm	35rf	1959	Oplar	2.8	5cm	focal plane	1-1000	F604	270
Focaflex	24x36mm	35mm	35slr	1960	Oplar Color	2.8	50mm	Leaf	B, 1-250	Mc345	230
Focaflex II	24x36mm	35mm	35slr	1962	Néoplex	2.8	50mm	Prontor-Refl.		F409	230
Focaflex Automatic	24x36mm	35mm	35slr	1962	Oplar-Color	2.8	5cm	Atom-1	1-250	Mc345	120
...OPTIKOTECHNA - Prague & Prerov, C.S.S.R.											
Autoflex	6x6cm	120	TLR	1938	Trioplan	2.9	75mm	Compur S			100
Coloreta	24x36mm	35mm	3-Color	1939	Spektar	2.9	70mm	Compur	1-250		3600
Flexette	6x6cm	120	TLR	1938	Trioplan	2.9	75mm	Compur	1-250		120
Flexette	6x6cm	120	TLR	1938	Trioplan	4.5	75mm	Prontor II			120
Optiflex	6x6cm	120	TLR	1938	Mirar T3	2.9	75mm	Compur S.			100
Spektareta	24x36mm	35mm	3-Color	1939	Spektar	2.9	70mm	Compur	1-250	A2012	4100
...ORION WERK - Hannover											
Daphne	4x6.5cm	127	FoldRo		F.Corygon Anast.	6.3	85mm	Pronto	25-100		60
Orion (box)	6x9cm	plate	RollBox	1922	Meniscus	17		simple			70
Orion Klappreflex 6.5x9	6.5x9cm	plate	FoldSLR	1924	Tessar	4.5	120mm	focal plane	1/15-500	A3150	270
Orion Klappreflex 9x12	9x12cm	plate	FoldSLR	1924	Tessar	4.5	150mm	focal plane	1/15-500	HK328	530
Rio 8 C	9x12cm	plate	VtFoldPl	1925	Corygon	6.3	135mm	Vario			60
Rio 10 C	9x12cm	plate	VtFoldPl	1921	Helioplan	6.8	135mm	Vario			60
Rio 11 B	6.5x9cm	plate	VtFoldPl	1921	E.R.Aplanat	8	10.5cm	Pronto			70
Rio 12 C	9x12cm	plate	VtFoldPl	1921	Hemi Anast	7.2	135mm	Vario			70
Rio 14 C	9x12cm	plate	VtFoldPl	1921	Trioplan	6.3	135mm	Vario			70
Rio 15 B	6.5x9cm	plate	VtFoldPl	1921	Eurynar	6.8	10.5cm	Compur	1-200		70
Rio 16 C	9x12cm	plate	VtFoldPl	1921	Dagor	6.8	13cm	Ibso			70
Rio 22 C	9x12cm	plate	VtFoldPl	1921	Tessar	6.3	13,5cm	Compur			70
Rio 22 D	10x15cm	plate	VtFoldPl	1923	Trioplan	6.8	16.5cm	Compur	1-200		70
Rio 25 C Luxus	9x12cm	plate	VtFoldPl	1923	Tessar	4.5	135mm	Compur	1-200		270
Rio 25 D	10x15cm	plate	VtFoldPl	1923	Trioplan	4.5	165mm	Vario			160
Rio 26 C	9x12cm	plate	VtFoldPl	1923	Unofocal	5.4	135mm	Ibsor	1-100		80
Rio 28 C	9x12cm	plate	VtFoldPl	1923	Xenar	4.5	135mm	Compur	1-200		140
Rio 44 C	9x12cm	plate	HzFoldPl	1921	Corygon	6.3	135mm	Vario			120
Rio 73 B	6.5x9cm	plate	PlateBox	1923	Meniscus				M,Z		200
Rio 74 B	6x6cm	120	RollBox	1923	Meniscus				M,Z		270
Rio 79 C	6x9cm	120	FoldRo	1923	Spezial Aplanat	8	105mm	Pronto	25-100		70
Rio 83	6x9cm	120	FoldRo	1923	Helioplan	6.8	105mm	Pronto	25-100		90
Rio 84 A	4x6.5cm	127	StrutRo	1925	Xenar	4.5	75mm	Compur	1-200	A403	90
Rio 84 C	6x9cm	120	FoldRo	1925	Helioplan	4.5	75mm	Ibsor	1-100	Mc346	40
Rio 84 E	8x10.5cm	124	FoldRo	1925	Trioplan	6.3	135mm	Vario			80

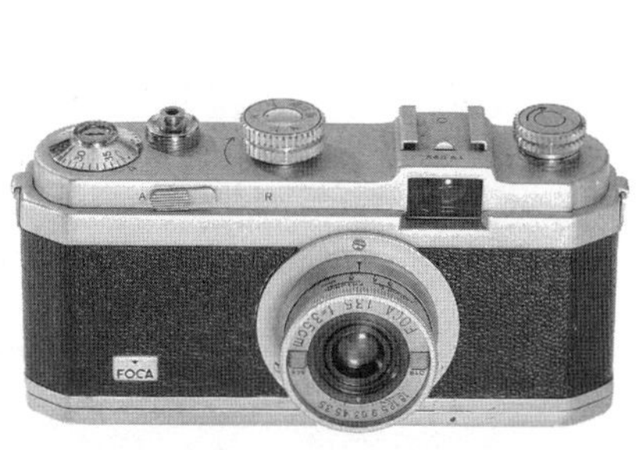

Foca Standard (*)

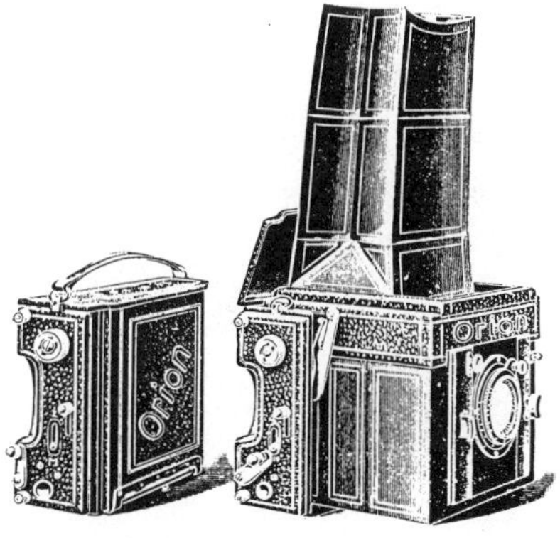

Orion Klappreflex

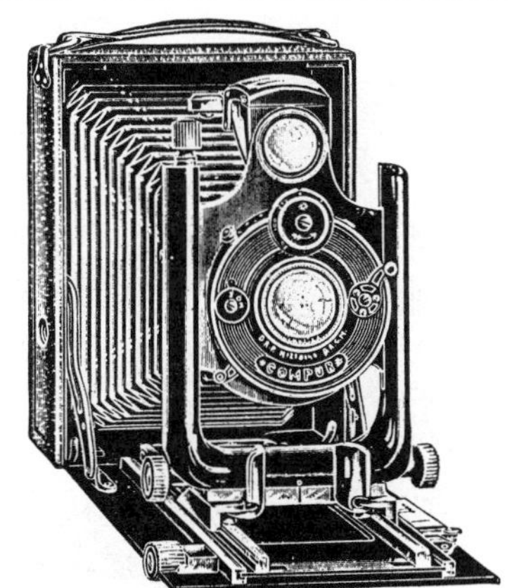

Orion Rio 22 C

MODEL	FORMAT	FILM	TYPE	Year	LENS	Apert	FL	SHUTTER	SPEEDS	ILLUS	U.S.$
Tropen Rio 2C	9x12cm	plate	VtFoldPl	1920	Triotar	6.3	135mm	Compur	1-150		480
Tropen Rio 5C	9x12cm	plate	VtFoldPl	1920	Xenar	4.5	150mm	Compur	1-150		420
...OSHIRO OPTICAL WORKS - Japan											
Emi 35A	24x36mm	35mm	35vf	1956	Tri-Lausar	3.5	45mm		B,1-300		330
Emi K 35	24x36mm	35mm	35vf	1956	Eminent Color	2.8	50mm		B,25-300	Mc346	60
Lumica	24x36mm	35mm	35vf	1956	Tri-Lausar	3.5	45mm		B,1-300		50
Sierra 35	24x36mm	35mm	35vf	1956	Tokina	3.5	45mm		B,S,M,F,H	Mc346	50
Spinney	24x36mm	35mm	35vf	1956	Eminent Color	2.8	50mm		B,25-300	Mc346	60
...O.T.A.G. (ÖSTERREICHISCHE TELEFON A.G.) - Vienna, Austria											
Amourette	24x30mm	35mm	35Early	1925	Trioplan	6.3		Compur	25-100		390
Amourette	24x30mm	35mm	35Early	1930	Trioplan	6.3		Compur	300		390
CIM	24x30mm	35mm	35Early	1925	Extra Rapid	6.3	35mm	Compur	25-100		490
Lutin	24x30mm	35mm	35Early	1925	Trioplan	6.3		Compur	25-100	Mc346	400
...OTTEWILL (Thomas Ottewill) - London											
Sliding-box camera 8x10"	8x10"	WetPl	WetPlate	1851	Petzval-type						4100
Sliding-box camera 9x11"	9x11"	WetPl	WetPlate	1851	Ross					A2956	8000
...OWLA KOKI - Japan											
Owla Stereo (black)	24x23mm	35mm	Ster35	1960	Owla	3.5	35mm		10-200,B	A1836	320
Owla Stereo (chrome)	24x23mm	35mm	Ster35	1958	Owla	3.5	35mm		10-200,B	A2717	390
...PALMER & LONGKING											
Lewis-style Daguerreotype	4¼x6½"	Dag	Dag	1855	Brass barrel					Mc346	8000
...PANON CAMERA CO. LTD. - Japan											
Panon Wide Angle f2.8	2x4½"	120	Panoramic	1952	Hexanon	2.8	50mm		2-200	A2019	1100
Panon Wide Angle f3.5	2x4½"	120	Panoramic	1952	Hexar	3.5	50mm		2-200	Mc346	1100
Panophic	5x12cm	120	Panoramic	1963	Hexanon	2.8	50mm		8-250		1500
Widelux	24x59mm	35mm	Panoramic	1959	Lux	2.8	26mm				900
Widelux F6	24x59mm	35mm	Panoramic	1959	Lux	2.8	26mm		10-250		700
Widelux F6B	24x59mm	35mm	Panoramic	1973	Lux	2.8	26mm		10-250	A941	900
Widelux F7	24x59mm	35mm	Panoramic	1974	Lux	2.8	26mm		15-250	A3405	900
Widelux F8	24x59mm	35mm	Panoramic	1988	Lux	2.8	26mm				1000
Widelux FV	24x59mm	35mm	Panoramic	1959	Lux	2.8	26mm		10-250	A3404	800
...PAPIGNY - Paris											
Jumelle Stereo	8x8cm	plate	StJumelle	1890	Chevalier	6.5	100mm	Guillotine		F1275	270
...PARIS (Georges Paris)											
GAP Box 3x4 (black)	3x4cm	127	RollBox	1949					M,Z	F834	50
GAP Box 3x4 (colors)	3x4cm	127	RollBox	1949					M,Z	Mc347	70
GAP Box 3x4 (advertising)	3x4cm	127	RollBox	1949					M,Z	F836	50
GAP Box 6x9 (black)	6x9cm	120	RollBox	1947					M,Z	Mc347	30
GAP Box 6x9 (colors)	6x9cm	120	RollBox	1947					M,Z		20
GAP Super (black)	6x9cm	120	TelescRo	1950	Meniscus				P&I	Mc347	50
GAP Super (chrome)	6x9cm	120	TelescRo	1950	Meniscus				P&I	Mc347	50
Vog	6x9cm	120	TelescRo	1950	Meniscus				P&I	F1659	50

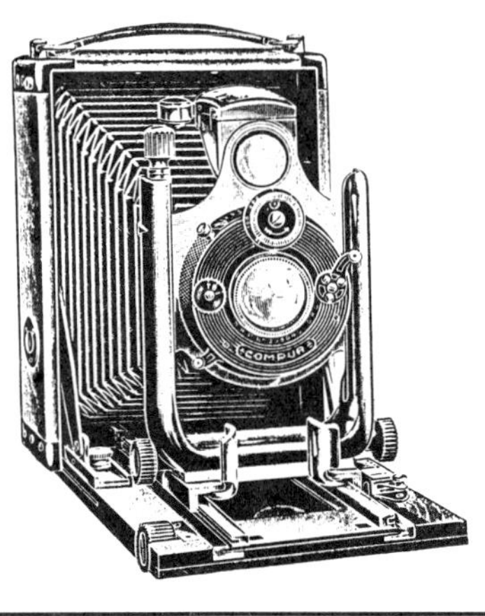

Orion Tropen Rio 2C

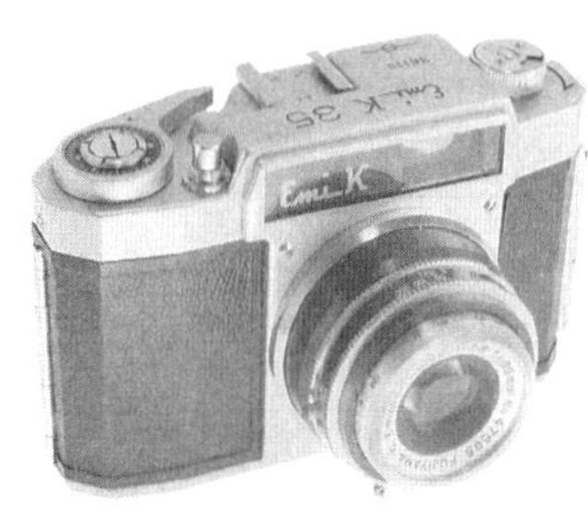

Oshiro Emi K 35

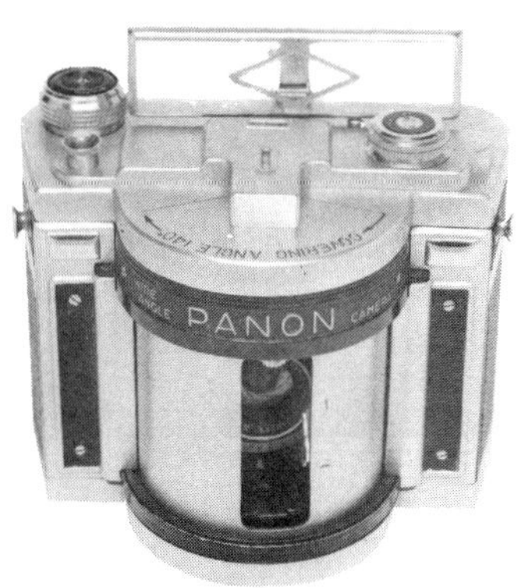

Panon Wide Angle f3.5

MODEL	FORMAT	FILM	TYPE	Year	LENS	Apert	FL	SHUTTER	SPEEDS	ILLUS	U.S.$
...PARK (Henry Park) - London											
Tailboard camera 1/1-pl	6½x8½"	plate	Tailboard	1890	various		22"	various			330
Tailboard camera 10x12"	10x12"	plate	Tailboard	1890	various			various			330
Twin Lens Reflex	3¼x4¼"	plate	LgTLR	1890	T.T. & Hobson		5"				1500
Victoria	6½x8½"	plate	Field	1892	various			various		Mc347	350
...PARKER PEN CO. - Janesville, Wisconsin USA											
Parker Camera	13x16mm	16mm	Submin	1949	Stellar	4.5	37mm	rotary	30-50	Mc347	800
...PARSELL (H.V. Parsell & Fils) - Paris											
Détective camera	6.5x6.5cm	plate	Disguised	1885	Rapid Rectilinear						240
...PCA (Photronic Corp. of America)											
Prismat V-90	24x36mm	35mm	35slr	1960	Mamiya-Sekor	1.9	48mm	Leaf	1-500,B		100
...PDQ CAMERA CO. - Chicago											
Mandel Autom.PDQ Mod.G	6x9cm	120	Street	1935	Rapid Rectilinear	6	135mm				330
PDQ Mod. H	2½x3½"	120	Street		Steinheil	3.8	105mm	sync			140
PDQ Photo Button			Button	1930	Echo Anastigmat						1100
...PEACE											
Peace	14x14mm	Roll	Submin	1949	Achromat				B,I		200
Peace (TLR)	12x14mm	Roll	Submin	1949	Achromat				B,I		2600
Peace III	14x14mm	Roll	Submin	1950	Kowa	4.5		R.K.		Mc347	210
Peace Baby Flex	12x14mm	Roll	Submin	1949	Achromat				B,I		2100
...PEARSALL (G. Frank E. Pearsall) - Brooklyn, NY											
Compact	6½x8½"	plate	FoldPl	1883							3900
...PECK (Samuel Peck & Co.) - New Haven, Conn. USA											
Four-tube Ferrotype	2¼x2¾"	plate	MultiLens	1865							1300
Wet plate camera	6½x8½"	WetPl	WetPlate	1859							1300
...(unknown)											
PEER 100	13x17mm	110	Disguised	1973							400
...PEERLESS MFG. CO.											
Box camera	2½x2½"	plate	PlateBox						I		100
...PENROSE (A.W. Penrose & Co. Ltd.) - England											
Studio camera	19x19"	plate	Studio	1915	various			various			320
...PENTACON (VEB Pentacon) - Dresden, Germany											
Astraflex Auto 35	24x36mm	35mm	35slr	1965	Meyer Primotar	3.5	50mm	focal plane			80
Consul	24x36mm	35mm	35slr	1955	Tessar	2.8	50mm	focal plane	1000		170
Contax D	24x36mm	35mm	35slr	1953	Biotar	2	50mm	focal plane	1-1000	Hu093	220
Contax D "VEB"	24x36mm	35mm	35slr	1953	Biotar	2	50mm	focal plane	1-1000	A1000	80
Contax d	24x36mm	35mm	35slr	1953	Tessar	2.8	50mm	focal plane	1-1000		90
Contax d (ST)	24x36mm	35mm	35slr	1953	Biotar	2	50mm	focal plane	1-1000		80
Contax E	24x36mm	35mm	35slr	1955	Primoplan	1.9	50mm	focal plane	1-1000	Hu097	140
Contax F	24x36mm	35mm	35slr	1957	Biotar	2	50mm	focal plane	1-1000	Hu100	90
Contax FB	24x36mm	35mm	35slr	1957	Biotar	2	58mm	focal plane	1-1000	Mc348	90
Contax FBM	24x36mm	35mm	35slr	1957	Biotar	2	58mm	focal plane	1-1000	Hu106	100

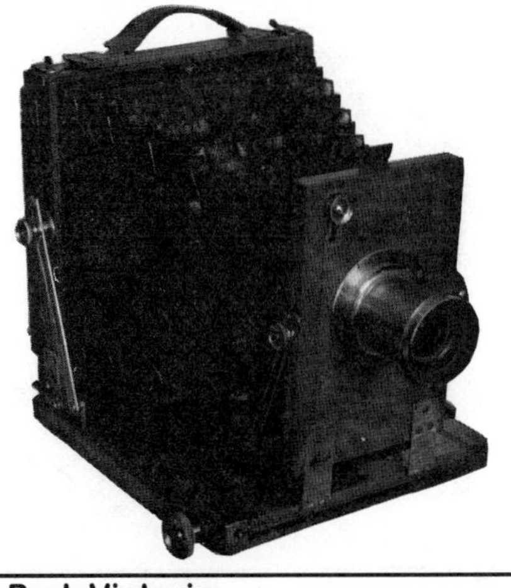

Park Victoria

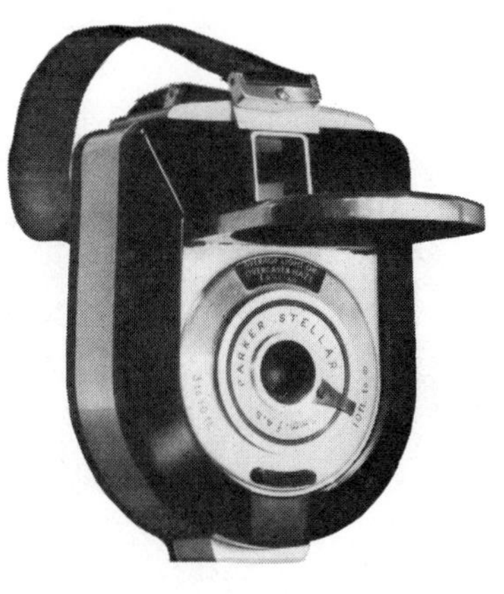

Parker Camera

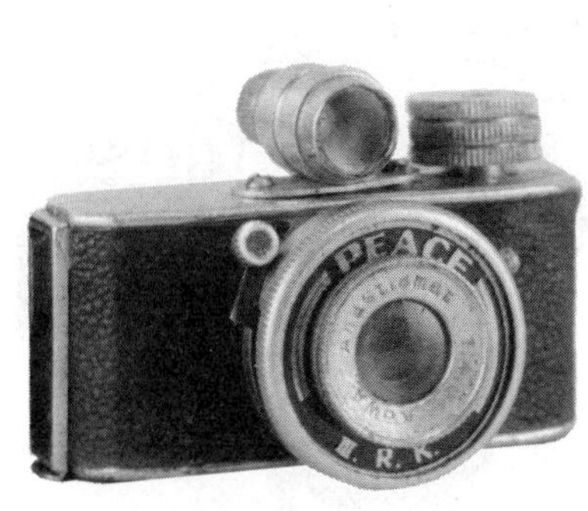

Peace III

MODEL	FORMAT	FILM	TYPE	Year	LENS	Apert	FL	SHUTTER	SPEEDS	ILLUS	U.S.$
Contax FM	24x36mm	35mm	35slr	1957	Zeiss Biotar	2	58mm	focal plane	1-1000	Hu104	150
Contax S (black prism)	24x36mm	35mm	35slr	1949	Biotar	2	50mm	focal plane	1-1000,B	Hu086	290
Contax S (chrome prism)	24x36mm	35mm	35slr	1949	Biotar	2	50mm	focal plane	1-1000,B	Hu087	290
Contax S (self-timer)	24x36mm	35mm	35slr	1950	Biotar	2	50mm	focal plane	1-1000,B	Mc348	220
Ercona (I)	6x9cm	120	FoldRo	1949	Tessar	3.5	105mm	Tempor	1-250		40
Ercona II	6x9cm	120	FoldRo	1956	Tessar	3.5	105mm	Tempor	1-250	Mc348	70
Exona 12/2034	6x9cm	120	FoldRo	1956	Tessar	3.5	105mm	Prontor-SVS	1-250		140
Geheimkamera (Disguised)		15mm	Submin	1960	Biotar	1.8	10mm				1360
Hexacon	24x36mm	35mm	35slr	1954	Biotar	2	50mm	focal plane	1-1000	Mc348	110
Orix	18x24mm	35mm	35vf	1958	Trioplan	3.5	50mm		125	U993	100
Pentacon	24x36mm	35mm	35slr	1948	Tessar	2.8	50mm	focal plane	1-1000	Hu094	120
Pentacon "No-Name"	24x36mm	35mm	35slr	1962	Tessar	3.5	50mm	focal plane	1-1000		250
Pentacon (logo & ZI)	24x36mm	35mm	35slr	1948	Tessar	3.5	50mm	focal plane	1-1000	Mc348	100
Pentacon (ZI)	24x36mm	35mm	35slr	1948	Tessar	2.8	50mm	focal plane	1-1000	Hu095	100
Pentacon E	24x36mm	35mm	35slr	1955	Biotar	2	58mm	focal plane	1-1000	A1001	100
Pentacon Electra	24x36mm	35mm	35VF	1988	Domiplan	2.8	45mm	programmed			50
Pentacon Electra 2	24x36mm	35mm	35VF	1988	Domiplan	2.8	45mm	programmed			50
Pentacon F	24x36mm	35mm	35slr	1957	Tessar	2.8	50mm	focal plane	1-1000	Mc349	50
Pentacon FB	24x36mm	35mm	35slr	1959	Tessar	2.8	50mm	focal plane	1-1000	Hu103	90
Pentacon FBM	24x36mm	35mm	35slr	1957	Tessar	2.8	50mm	focal plane	1-1000	Hu107	100
Pentacon FM	24x36mm	35mm	35slr	1957	Biotar	2	50mm	focal plane	1-1000	Hu105	100
Pentacon K16	13x17mm	110	110VF	1988	Pentacon	8	27mm		30-250		50
Pentacon Six	6x6cm	120	MedSLR	1967	Biometar	2.8	80mm	focal plane	1-1000		250
Pentacon Six TL	6x6cm	120	MedSLR	1968	Biometar	2.8	80mm	focal plane	1-1000		280
Pentacon Super	24x36mm	35mm	35slr	1966	Pancolar	1.8	50mm	focal plane	8-1/2000	Hu119	390
Pentina	24x36mm	35mm	35slr	1960	Tessar	2.8	50mm	leaf	1-500	Mc349	70
Pentina E	24x36mm	35mm	35slr	1960	Tessar	2.8	50mm	leaf	1-500	Hu117	50
Pentina FM	24x36mm	35mm	35slr	1960	Tessar	2.8	50mm	leaf	1-500	A1122	50
Pentina M	24x36mm	35mm	35slr	1962	Tessar	2.8	50mm	leaf	1-500	Hu115	70
Pentona	24x36mm	35mm	35vf	1956	Trioplan	3.5	45mm	Priomat	30-125	Mc349	40
Pentona II	24x36mm	35mm	35vf	1960	Trioplan	3.5	45mm	Priomat	30-125		30
Pentor I B	24x36mm	35mm	35slr	1968	Tessar	2.8	50mm	focal plane	1-500		50
Pentor Super TL	24x36mm	35mm	35slr	1968	Tessar	2.8	50mm	focal plane	1-500	Mc349	40
Prakti (black)	24x36mm	35mm	35vf	1960	Meyer Domiton	3.5	40mm	Prestor	30-250		50
Prakti (grey)	24x36mm	35mm	35vf	1962	Meyer Domiton	3.5	40mm	Prestor	30-250	Mc349	90
Ritacon F	24x36mm	35mm	35slr	1961	Primotar	3.5	50mm	focal plane	1-1000		120
Taxona	24x24mm	35mm	35vf	1952	Tessar	3.5	37.5mm	Tempor	1-300	Mc349	50
Verikon	24x36mm	35mm	35slr	1961	Primotar	3.5	50mm	focal plane	1-1000		100
...PERKA PRÄZISIONS KAMERAWERK - Munich, Germany											
Perka 6.5x9	6.5x9cm	plate	FoldPl	1922	Xenar	3.5	105mm	Compound		Mc349	180
Perka 9x12	9x12cm	plate	FoldPl	1922	Symmar	5.6	135mm	Compound			200
Perka 10x15	10x15cm	plate	FoldPl	1922	Tessar	4.5	150mm	Compur-Rap.			190

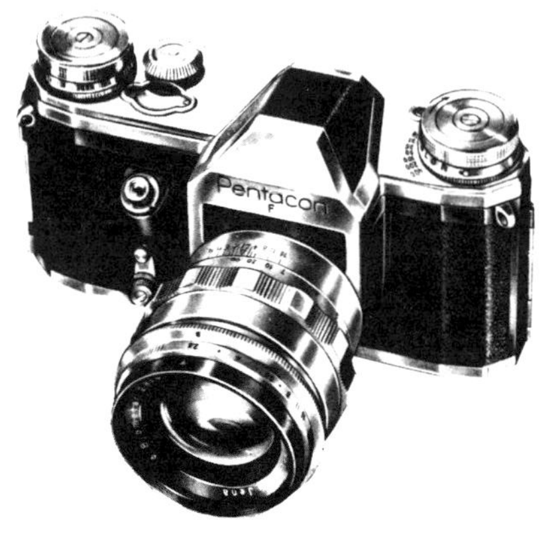

Pentacon F

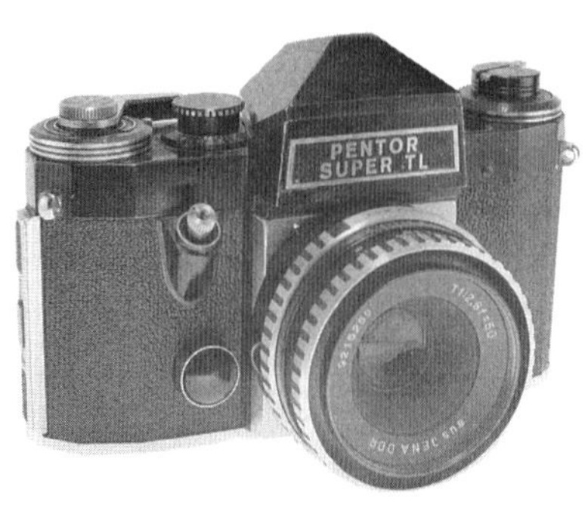

Pentor Super TL

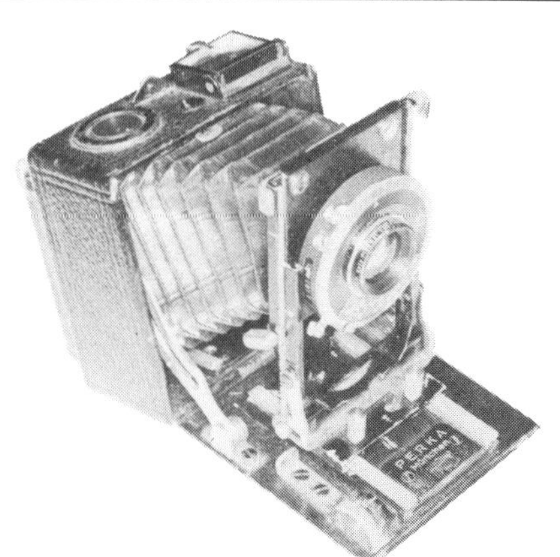

Perka

MODEL	FORMAT	FILM	TYPE	Year	LENS	Apert	FL	SHUTTER	SPEEDS	ILLUS	U.S.$
...PERKEN, SON, & RAYMENT - London											
Optimus Camera DeLuxe	3¼x4¼"	plate	FoldPl	1894	Euryscope	6		roller-blind		Mc350	470
Optimus Detective	3¼x4¼"	plate	DetectivBox	1888	Rapid Rectilinear	8		roller-blind		Mc350	620
Optimus Folding Camera	4¼x6½"	plate	Field	1890	Optimus						290
Optimus Long Focus	4¼x6½"	plate	Tailboard	1892	Rap. Symmetrical					Mc350	380
Rayment's Patent ¼-pl	3¼x4¼"	plate	Field	1886							370
Rayment's Patent 8x10"	8x10"	plate	Field	1886						Mc350	480
Studio camera	6½x8½"	plate	Tailboard	1890						Mc350	310
Tailboard camera ¼-pl	3¼x4¼"	plate	Tailboard	1886	various			roller-blind			270
Tailboard camera ½-pl	4¼x6½"	plate	Tailboard	1886	various			roller-blind			270
Tailboard camera 1/1-pl	6½x8½"	plate	Tailboard	1886	various			roller-blind			270
...PHILIPS - Netherlands											
Philips Box Flash	6x6cm	620	BakeliteBox	1955						Mc350	80
...PHOBA A.G. - Basel, Switzerland											
Diva	6x9cm	plate	FoldPl	1925	Titar	4.5	105mm	Compur			60
...PHO-TAK CORP. - Chicago											
Eagle Eye	2¼x3¼"	120	MetalBox	1950	Precision		110mm	T&I			20
Foldex	2¼x3¼"	120	FoldRo	1950	Steinheil	6.3		Vario	25-200	Mc350	20
Foldex 20	2¼x3¼"	120	FoldRo	1950	Octvar		85mm				20
Foldex 30	2¼x3¼"	120	FoldRo	1950	Steinheil						20
Macy 120	2¼x3¼"	120	MetalBox	1950	Meniscus				I,T		20
Marksman	2¼x3¼"	120	MetalBox	1950	Meniscus				I,T	Mc350	20
Reflex I	2¼x3¼"	120	TLR-Box	1953	Achromat		74mm		I,T		20
Scout 120 Flash	2¼x3¼"	120	MetalBox	1950							30
Spectator Flash	2¼x3¼"	120	MetalBox	1950	Zellar				I,T		20
Traveler 120	2¼x3¼"	120	MetalBox	1950	Zellar Meniscus	11			I,T		20
...PHOTAVIT-WERK - Nürnberg, Germany											
Photina	6x6cm	120	TLR	1953	Cassar	3.5	75mm	Prontor-SVS		Mc351	80
Photina II	6x6cm	120	TLR	1953	Cassar	3.5	75mm	Prontor-SVS			80
Photina II	6x6cm	120	TLR	1953	Westar	3.5	75mm	Pronto		HK428	80
Photina III	6x6cm	120	TLR	1954	Westar	3.5	75mm	Prontor-SVS			110
...PHOTO HALL - Paris											
Perfect Detective	9x12cm	plate	DetectivBox	1910	Extra Rap. Rectil.						240
Perfect Jumelle	6.5x9cm	plate	Jumelle	1900	Zeiss Protar	8	110mm			Mc351	240
Perfect Pliant No. 1	9x12cm	plate	FoldPl	1905	Extra Rap. Aplan.		135mm	Central		F266	150
Perfect Pliant No. 4	9x12cm	plate	FoldPl	1905	Berthiot	4.5	135mm	Gauthier		F267	150
Stereo camera	6x13cm	plate	StJumelle	1905				guillotine	1/50		130
...PHOTO-IT MFG. CO. - LaCrosse, WI											
The Photo-It	12x18mm	12mm	Submin							Mc351	2400
The Secret Eye	12x18mm	12mm	Submin								0
...PHOTO MARS - Augsburg											
Stereo camera	9x18cm	plate	SterStrut	1902		8	105mm	guillotine		A750	440

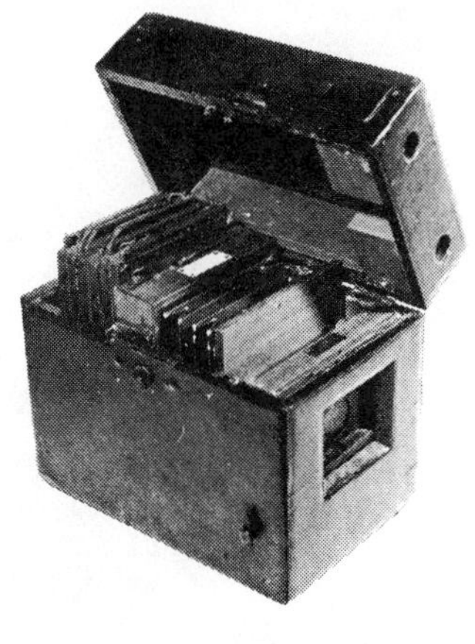

Optimus Detective

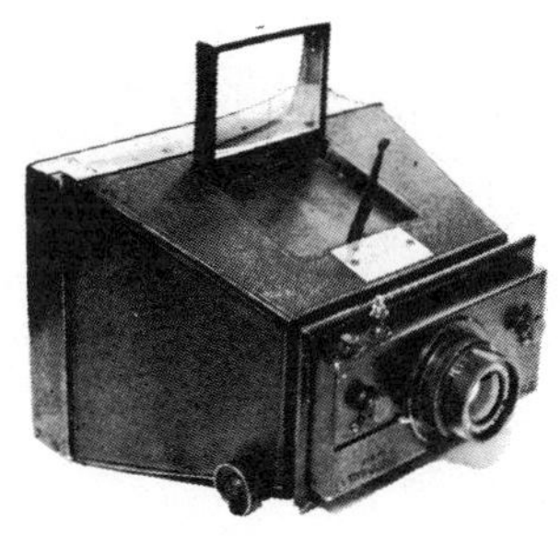

Perfect Jumelle

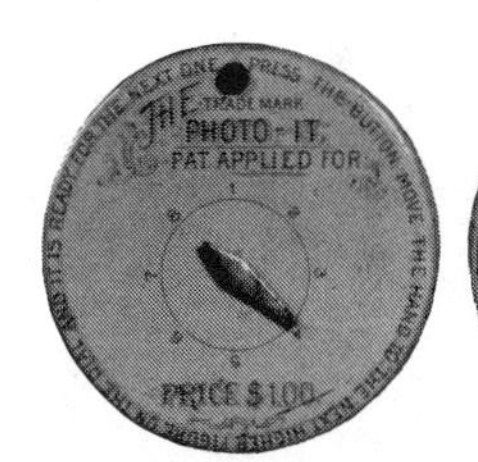

The Photo-It

MODEL	FORMAT	FILM	TYPE	Year	LENS	Apert	FL	SHUTTER	SPEEDS	ILLUS	U.S.$
...PHOTO MASTER											
Photo Master	3x4cm	127	RigidRo	1948	Rollax		50mm	rotary	I	Mc351	10
Photo Master Super 16	4x5.5cm	620	RigidRo		Rollax		62mm		T,I	Mc351	30
Photo Master Twin 620	4x5.5cm	620	RigidRo	1940	Rollax		62mm		I,T		30
...PHOTO MATERIALS CO. - Rochester, NY											
Trokonet	4x5"	plate	MagBox	1893	Gundlach R.R.					Mc351	700
...PHOTO MIAMI - France											
Photo Miami	4x6.5cm	127	RigidRo	1948					I,P	Mc351	40
...PHOTO-OPERA - Paris											
Piccolo	3x4cm	102	Jumelle					guillotine	I,T	F1108	560
...PHOTO-PAC CAMERA MFG. CO. , INC. - New York City & Dallas, TX											
Photo-Pac			Dispose	1950						Mc351	50
...PHOTO-PLAIT - Paris											
Mixo (red)	6x9cm	Ro+Pl	PlateBox	1925	Achromat					F982	100
Mixo (black)	6x9cm	120	RollBox	1925	Achromat					A2835	60
No. 2 Plait Pliant	9x12cm	plate	FoldPl	1920	Anastigmat	6.3	135mm	Woll. Ultex			40
...PHOTO-PORST - Hanns Porst, Nürnberg											
Blitzpocket 300	13x17mm	110	110VF	1977	Porst	9.5			I		30
Blitzpocket 400E	13x17mm	110	110VF	1977	Porst	5.6		programmed			30
Blitzpocket 500EE	13x17mm	110	110VF	1977	Porst	5.6		programmed			30
Compact Reflex	24x36mm	35mm	35SLR	1977	Color-Reflex	1.8	50mm	focal plane	4-1000		80
Compact Reflex	24x36mm	35mm	35SLR	1977	Color-Reflex	2.8	50mm	focal plane	4-1000		80
Compact Reflex OC	24x36mm	35mm	35SLR	1977	Color-Reflex	1.8	50mm	focal plane	4-1000		60
Compact Reflex OC	24x36mm	35mm	35SLR	1977	Color-Reflex	2.8	50mm	focal plane	4-1000		60
Compact Reflex OS	24x36mm	35mm	35SLR	1977		1.7	50mm	focal plane	4-1000		70
Compact Reflex OS	24x36mm	35mm	35SLR	1977		2.8	50mm	focal plane	4-1000		70
Compact Reflex SP	24x36mm	35mm	35SLR	1977		1.7	55mm	focal plane	4-1000		50
Compact Reflex SP	24x36mm	35mm	35SLR	1977		1.4	55mm	focal plane	4-1000		50
CR-3	24x36mm	35mm	35SLR	1980		1.7	50mm	focal plane			70
CR-3	24x36mm	35mm	35SLR	1980		1.4	50mm	focal plane			70
CR-5	24x36mm	35mm	35SLR	1980		1.7	50mm	focal plane			70
CR-5	24x36mm	35mm	35SLR	1980		1.4	50mm	focal plane			70
CR-7	24x36mm	35mm	35SLR	1980		1.7	50mm	focal plane			240
CR-7	24x36mm	35mm	35SLR	1980		1.2	50mm	focal plane			240
Hapo 5	6x9cm	120	VtFoldRo	1930	Schn. Radionar	4.5	105mm	Compur		A1469	30
Hapo 5	6x9cm	120	VtFoldRo	1930	Trioplan	3.8	105mm	Compur-Rap.			30
Hapo 10	6x9cm	120	VtFoldRo	1930	Schn. Radionar	4.5	105mm	Compur-Rap.			40
Hapo 10	6x9cm	120	VtFoldRo	1930	Trioplan	3.8	105mm	Compur			40
Hapo 35	24x36mm	35mm	35fold	1955	Enna Haponar	2.9	50mm	Prontor-SVS	1-300		60
Hapo 36	24x36mm	35mm	35RF	1955	Steinheil	2.8	50mm	Prontor			40
Hapo 45	6x9cm	120	VtFoldRo	1930	Schn. Radionar	4.5	105mm	Compur			30
Hapo 45	6x9cm	120	VtFoldRo	1930	Trioplan	3.8	105mm	Compur-Rap.			30

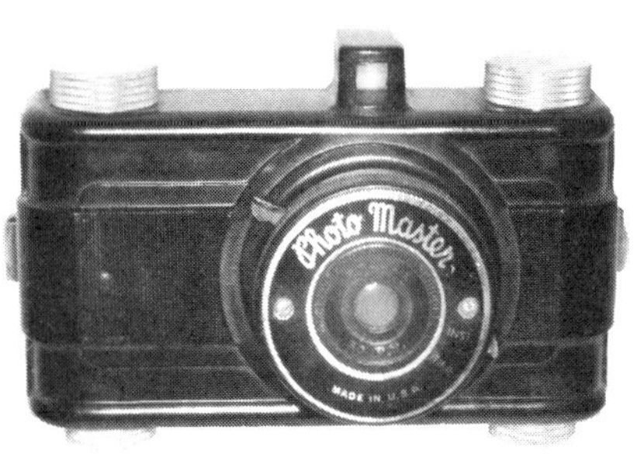

Photo Master

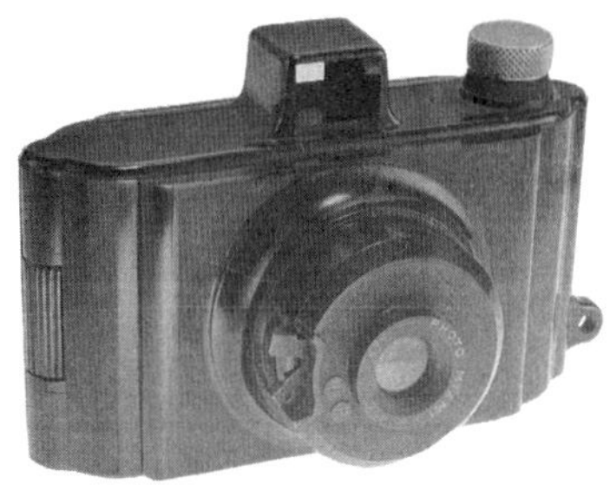
Photo Miami

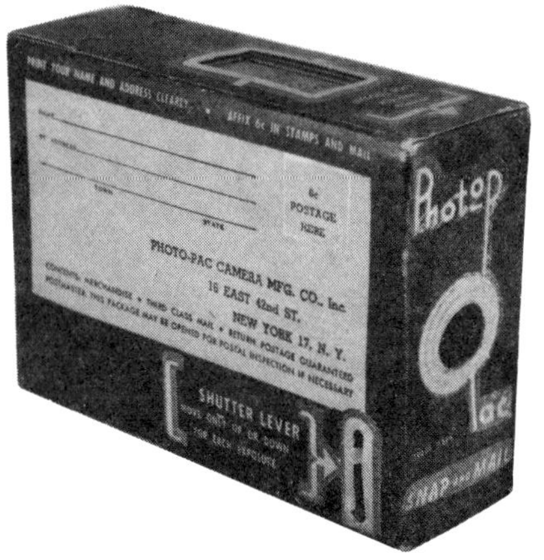

Photo-Pac

MODEL	FORMAT	FILM	TYPE	Year	LENS	Apert	FL	SHUTTER	SPEEDS	ILLUS	U.S.$
Hapo 66	6x6cm	120	FoldRo	1950	Enna Haponar	4.5	75mm	Pronto sync.	½-200		30
Hapo 66E	6x6cm	120	FoldRo	1950	Enna Haponar	4.5	75mm	Pronto sync.	½-200	A1508	50
Hapomatic 4/4	4x4cm	127	RigidRo	1965	Haponar	4.5	50mm				30
Haponette B	24x36mm	35mm	35VF	1960	Color Isconar	2.8	45mm	Prontor			20
Haponette EB	24x36mm	35mm	35RF	1960	Color Isconar	2.8	45mm	Prontor			30
Motorpocket 401	13x17mm	110	110VF	1980				programmed			30
Motorpocket 501E	13x17mm	110	110VF	1982				programmed		A3366	50
Pocketpak 1000	13x17mm	110	110VF	1976		11			1/70		20
Pocketpak 1002	13x17mm	110	110VF	1978		11			1/70		30
Pocketpak 2000	13x17mm	110	110VF	1976				2-speed	50-100		30
Pocketpak 2001	13x17mm	110	110VF	1978							30
Pocketpak 3000	13x17mm	110	110VF	1976		4.5			30-500		30
Pocketpak 4000	13x17mm	110	110VF	1976		4.5			30-500		30
Pocketpak 6000	13x17mm	110	110VF	1978				electronic			30
Pocketpak EB-S	13x17mm	110	110VF	1976		8			1/60		50
Pocketpak Electronic Blitz	13x17mm	110	110VF	1976		5.6		electronic	10-1/125		60
Pocketpak ET	13x17mm	110	110VF	1976		6.3		electronic	30-500		40
Pocketpak Tele	13x17mm	110	110VF	1978							30
Pocketpak XF 22	13x17mm	110	110VF	1978				electronic			50
Porst 126	28x28mm	126	126VF	1975				2-speed			30
Porst 126 Luxus	28x28mm	126	126VF	1976				2-speed			30
Porst 135 C	24x36mm	35mm	35VF	1976	Color-Spezial	2.7	38mm	programmed	30-650		60
Porst 135 CM Auto	24x36mm	35mm	35VF	1978	Color-Spezial						30
Porst 135 E	24x36mm	35mm	35VF	1978	Color-Spezial	2.7	38mm	programmed			30
Porst 135 L	24x36mm	35mm	35VF	1978	Color-Spezial						30
Porst 135 S	24x36mm	35mm	35RF	1976	Color-Spezial	2.7	38mm	programmed	30-650		70
Porst Autoflex	24x36mm	35mm	35slr	1961	Porst-Sekor	2.8	48mm	Copal	15-500	A1674	60
Porst EX55 Electronic	8x11mm	Minox	Submin	1970	Yashinon	2.8	18mm	programmed	8-350	Mc352	70
Porst KX50	8x11mm	Minox	Submin	1965	Yashinon	2.8	18mm		45-250		100
Porst Reflex C-EE	24x36mm	35mm	35SLR	1975	Color Reflex	2.8	55mm	focal plane			70
Porst Reflex CX 3	24x36mm	35mm	35SLR	1975	Color Reflex	2.8	50mm	focal plane	1-1000	Hu171	50
Porst Reflex CX 4	24x36mm	35mm	35SLR	1976	Color Reflex	2.8	50mm	focal plane	1-1000	Hu181	90
Porst Reflex CX 6	24x36mm	35mm	35SLR	1977	Color Reflex			focal plane	1-1000	Hu176	50
Porst Reflex FX 2	24x36mm	35mm	35SLR	1957	Color Reflex	1.9	58mm	focal plane	1-500	Hu134	60
Porst Reflex FX 3	24x36mm	35mm	35SLR	1976	Color Reflex	2.8	50mm	focal plane	1-500	Hu156	50
Porst Reflex FX 4	24x36mm	35mm	35SLR	1968	Color Reflex	2.8	50mm	focal plane	500	Hu162	50
Porst Reflex FX 6	24x36mm	35mm	35SLR	1969	Color Reflex	1.8	50mm	focal plane	500	Hu167	50
Porst Reflex M-CE	24x36mm	35mm	35SLR	1976	Color Reflex	1.4	55mm	focal plane	2-2000		20
Porst Reflex TL	24x36mm	35mm	35SLR	1971	Color Reflex	2.8	55mm	focal plane	1-1000		60
Porst Zoompocket	13x17mm	110	110VF	1977		5.6					60
Uniflex 1000 S	24x36mm	35mm	35SLR	1977	Color Reflex	1.4	55mm	focal plane			50
Uniflex 1000 S	24x36mm	35mm	35SLR	1977	Color Reflex	2.8	55mm	focal plane			50

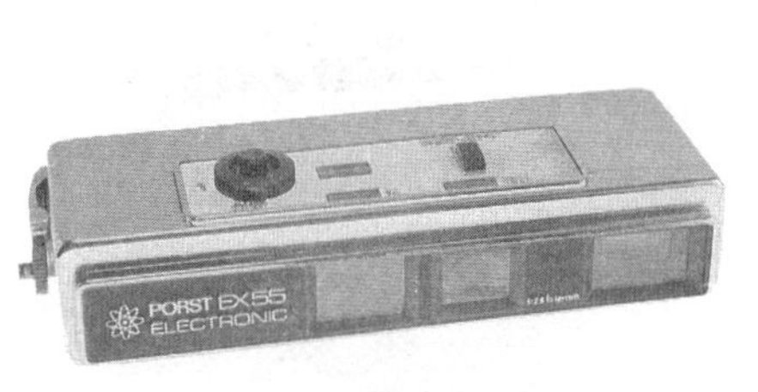

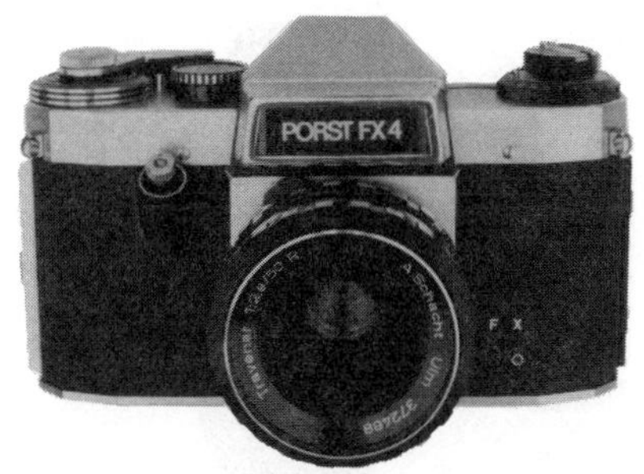

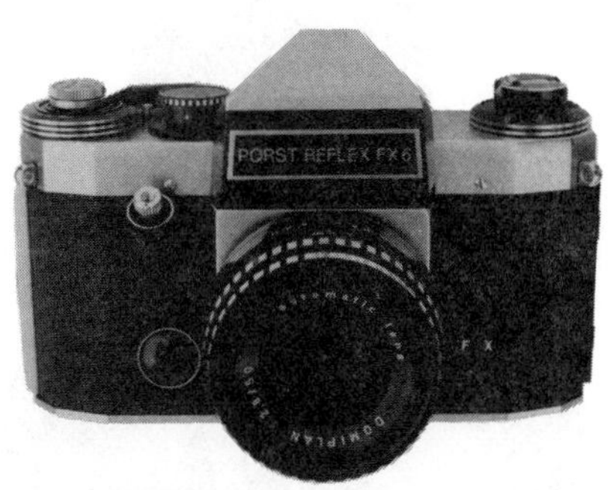

Porst EX55 Electronic

Porst Reflex FX 4

Porst Reflex FX 6

MODEL	FORMAT	FILM	TYPE	Year	LENS	Apert	FL	SHUTTER	SPEEDS	ILLUS	U.S.$
...PHOTO QUINT - Offenstadt, Paris											
Photo Quint	4x5cm	plate	PlateBox	1911						Mc352	800
...PHOTO SEE CORP. - N.Y.C.											
Photo-See	1¾x2¾"	plate	Instant	1936						Mc352	70
...PHOTOLET											
Photolet	2x2cm	Roll	Submin	1932	Meniscus	8	31mm			Mc352	110
...PHOTOPRINT A.G. - Germany											
Ernos	25x25mm	35mm	BakeliteRoll	1949	Meniscus						60
...PHOTOREX (Societe Francaise Photorex) - St. Etienne, France											
Rex Reflex B1	6x6cm	120	TLR	1949	Flor	3.5	75mm	Atos	1-300	Mc352	170
Rex Reflex B2	6x6cm	120	TLR	1951	Flor	3.5	75mm	Atos	1-300	F477	150
Rex Reflex Standard	6x6cm	120	TLR	1951	Angenieux	4.5	75mm	Atos 1	25-150	F480	140
...PIC											
Pic	3x4cm	127	RigidRo	1950	Meniscus			rotary		Mc352	100
...PIERRAT (André Pierrat) - France											
Drepy		120	FoldRo	1946	Drestar Anast.	4.5	105mm	Drestop	B,1-250	Mc352	50
...PIGGOTT (John Piggott) - London											
Sliding-box Wet Plate	8x8"	WetPl	WetPlate	1860	Petzval						1900
...PIGNONS AG - Ballaigues, Switzerland											
Alpa (Standard)	24x36mm	35mm	35rf	1946	Angenieux	2.9	50mm		25-1000	Mc353	1400
Alpa 4	24x36mm	35mm	35slr	1952	Spektros	3.5	50mm	focal plane	1-1000	Mc353	680
Alpa 4a	24x36mm	35mm	35slr	1952	Spektros	3.5	50mm				700
Alpa 4b	24x36mm	35mm	35slr	1959	Old Delft	2.8	50mm				800
Alpa 4b Omega	24x36mm	35mm	35slr	1963							900
Alpa 5	24x36mm	35mm	35slr	1952	Old Delft	2.8	50mm				460
Alpa 5a	24x36mm	35mm	35slr	1955	Old Delft	2.8	50mm				520
Alpa 5b	24x36mm	35mm	35slr	1959	Macro Switar	1.8	50mm	focal plane	1-1000		440
Alpa 6	24x36mm	35mm	35slr	1956	Old Delft	2.8	50mm	focal plane	1-1000		460
Alpa 6b	24x36mm	35mm	35slr	1959	Macro Switar	1.8	50mm	focal plane	1-1000		480
Alpa 6c	24x36mm	35mm	35slr	1960	Macro Switar	1.8	50mm	focal plane	1-1000		480
Alpa 7	24x36mm	35mm	35slr	1952	Kern Switar	1.8	50mm	focal plane	1-1000	Mc353	410
Alpa 7b	24x36mm	35mm	35slr	1959	Macro Switar	1.8	50mm	focal plane	1-1000		700
Alpa 7s	18x24mm	35mm	35slr	1957	Kern Switar	1.8	50mm	focal plane	1-1000		800
Alpa 8	24x36mm	35mm	35slr	1957	Alfinon		50mm				660
Alpa 8b	24x36mm	35mm	35slr	1959	Macro Switar	1.8	50mm	focal plane	1-1000		580
Alpa 9d	24x36mm	35mm	35slr	1965	Macro Switar	1.8	50mm	focal plane	1-1000	Mc353	600
Alpa 9d (gold)	24x36mm	35mm	35slr	1965	Macro Switar	1.8	50mm	focal plane	1-1000		220
Alpa 9f	24x36mm	35mm	35slr	1965	Macro Switar	1.8	50mm	focal plane	1-1000		700
Alpa 10d	24x36mm	35mm	35slr	1968	Macro Switar	1.9	50mm	focal plane	1-1000		600
Alpa 10d (gold)	24x36mm	35mm	35slr	1968	Macro Switar	1.9	50mm	focal plane	1-1000		630
Alpa 10d (red or green)	24x36mm	35mm	35slr	1968	Macro Switar	1.9	50mm	focal plane	1-1000		900
Alpa 10f	24x36mm	35mm	35slr	1969	Macro Kern	1.9	50mm	focal plane	1-1000		700

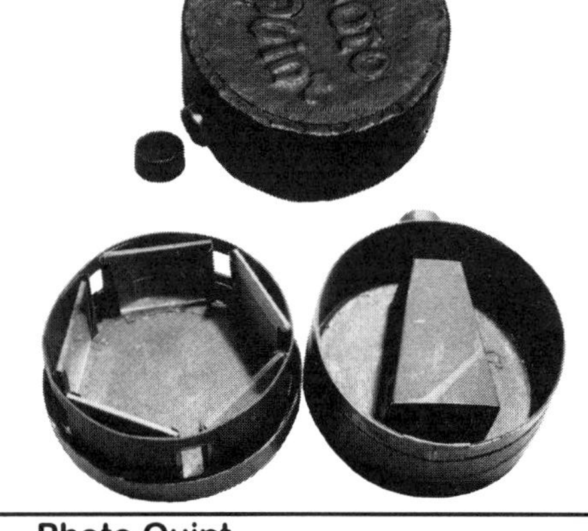

Photo Quint

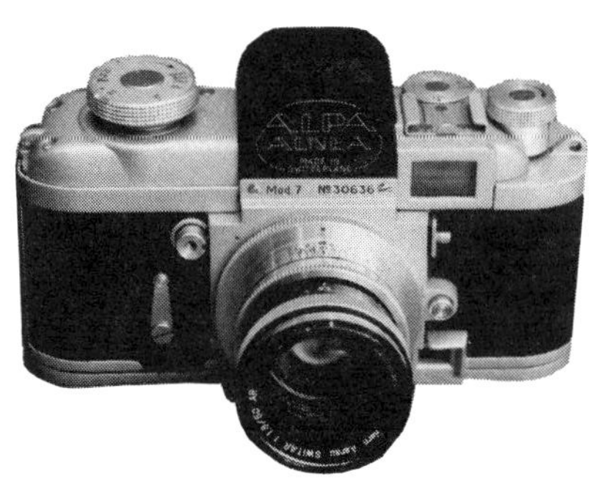

Alpa 7

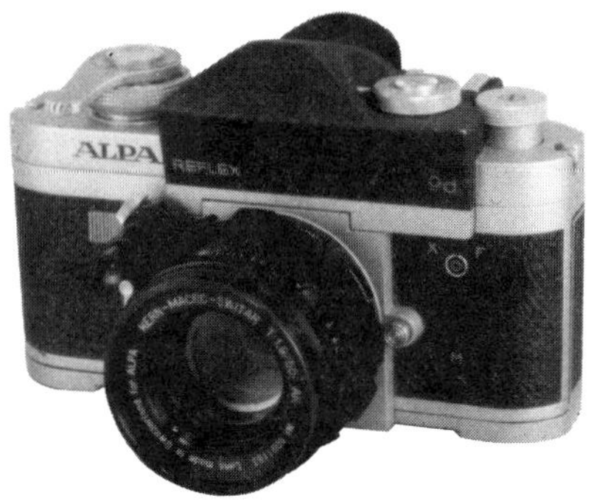

Alpa 9d

MODEL	FORMAT	FILM	TYPE	Year	LENS	Apert	FL	SHUTTER	SPEEDS	ILLUS	U.S.$
Alpa 10s	24x36mm	35mm	35slr	1972	Macro Switar	1.9	50mm	focal plane	1-1000		800
Alpa 11a	24x24mm	35mm	35mm	1973					1/60		1000
Alpa 11a	24x27mm	35mm	35slr	1973					1/60		1000
Alpa 11a	24x36mm	35mm	35slr	1973					1/60		900
Alpa 11e	24x36mm	35mm	35slr	1971	Macro Switar	1.9	50mm	focal plane	1-1000		670
Alpa 11e (gold)	24x36mm	35mm	35slr	1971	Macro Switar	1.9	50mm	focal plane	1-1000		800
Alpa 11e (red or green)	24x36mm	35mm	35slr	1971	Macro Switar	1.9	50mm	focal plane	1-1000		900
Alpa 11 el	24x36mm	35mm	35slr	1972	Macro Switar	1.9	50mm	focal plane	1-1000		800
Alpa 11 el (red or green)	24x36mm	35mm	35slr	1972	Macro Switar	1.9	50mm	focal plane	1-1000		900
Alpa 11f	24x36mm	35mm	35slr	1973					1/60		1100
Alpa 11m	10x15mm	35mm	35slr	1977	Mercure Takumar		35mm		1/60, B		1300
Alpa 11p	24x36mm	35mm	35slr	1973					1/60		900
Alpa 11 si	24x36mm	35mm	35slr	1976	Macro Switar	1.9	50mm	focal plane	1-1000	Mc354	900
Alpa 11 si (gold)	24x36mm	35mm	35slr	1976	Macro Switar	1.9	50mm	focal plane	1-1000		2800
Alpa 11z	18x24mm	35mm	35slr	1978	Micro Switar	1.9	60mm		1/60		1100
Alpa Prisma Reflex (III)	24x36mm	35mm	35slr	1948	Angenieux	2.9	50mm	focal plane	1-1000		700
Alpa Reflex (I)	24x36mm	35mm	35slr	1944	Angenieux	2.9	50mm	focal plane	1-1000	HK367	1200
Alpa Reflex (II)	24x36mm	35mm	35slr	1945	Angenieux	1.8	50mm	focal plane	1-1000		700
Bolca (Standard)	24x36mm	35mm	35rf	1942	Berthiot	2.9	50mm	Cloth FP	1-1000		1800
Bolca I	24x36mm	35mm	35slr	1942	Berthiot	2.9	50mm	Cloth FP	1-1000	Mc353	1600
Bolca A	24x36mm	35mm	35slr	1942	Berthiot	2.9	50mm	Cloth FP	1-1000		2000
...PIONIER DEKO - Berlin-Köpenick											
Pionier Deko (black)	3x4cm	127	BakeliteRoll	1955	Meniscus	11			I,T		130
Pionier Deko (blue)	3x4cm	127	BakeliteRoll	1955	Meniscus	11			I,T		140
Pionier Deko (red)	3x4cm	127	BakeliteRoll	1955	Meniscus	11			I,T	Mc354	140
...PIPON - Paris											
Jumelle	9x12cm	plate	Jumelle	1900	Goerz Doppel An.		120mm	guillotine	6 Zeiten	A841	200
Magazine camera	9x12cm	plate	MagBox	1900	Aplanoscope	9				Mc354	100
Self-Worker 8x16	8x16cm	plate	StJumelle	1895	Goerz Doppel An.		120mm	guillotine	6 Zeiten	F1369	410
Self-Worker 9x12	9x12cm	plate	Jumelle	1895	Goerz Doppel An.		120mm	guillotine	6 Zeiten	F1115	220
...PLASMAT GmbH - Berlin-Halensee, Germany											
Roland	4.5x6cm	120	TelescRo	1934	Plasmat	2.7	70mm	Compur-Rap.	400	Mc355	1100
Roland (no meter)	4.5x6cm	120	TelescRo	1934	Plasmat	2.7	70mm	Compur	1-250	A1529	1000
...PLAUBEL & CO. - Frankfurt, Germany											
69W Proshift Superwide	6x9cm	120	WideAng	1981	Super-Angulon	5.6	47mm	Copal	1-500	A3409	1700
Baby Makina	4.5x6cm	plate	StrutPl	1912	Anticomar	2.8	75mm	Compur			480
Folding plate camera	6x9cm	plate	FoldPl	1915	Anticomar			Ibso			70
Luftbild (Aerial) Camera	6x9cm	120	Aerial	1955	Anticomar	3.5	100mm	focal plane	20-1000		1400
Makiflex 6x6 (prototype)	6x6cm	120	MedSLR	1956	Suprasomar	2.5	80mm	focal plane	30-1000	A1622	2900
Makiflex 9x9	9x9cm	120	LgSLR	1967	Xenar	4.5	150mm	focal plane	4-500	A1621	510
Makiflex Standard 9x9	9x9cm	120	LgSLR	1967	Tessar	4.5	150mm	focal plane	4-500		420
Makina (I)	6.5x9cm	Sheet	StrutPl	1920	Anticomar	2.9	10cm	Compur		Mc355	220

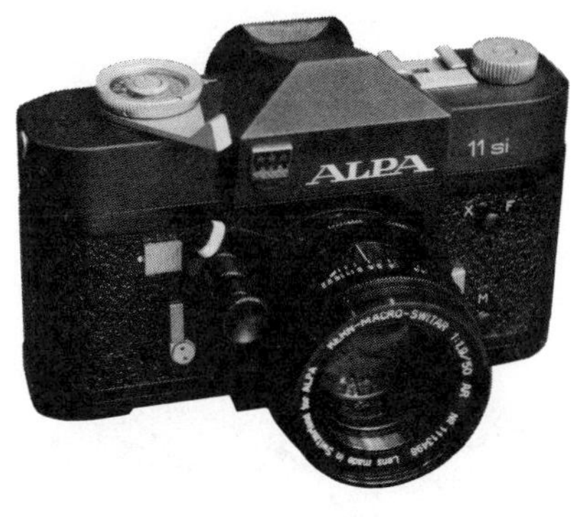

Alpa 11 si

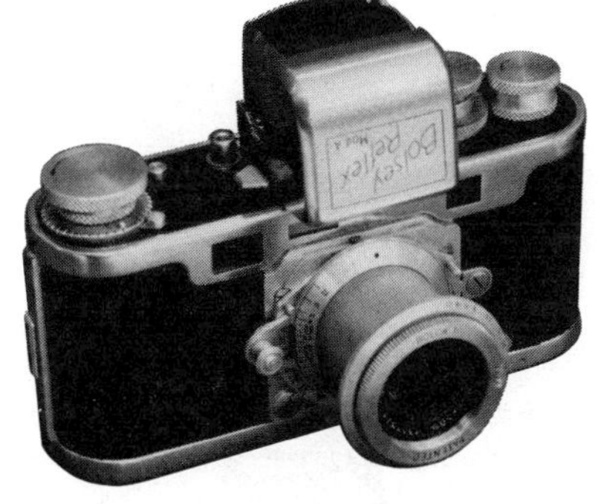

Bolca I

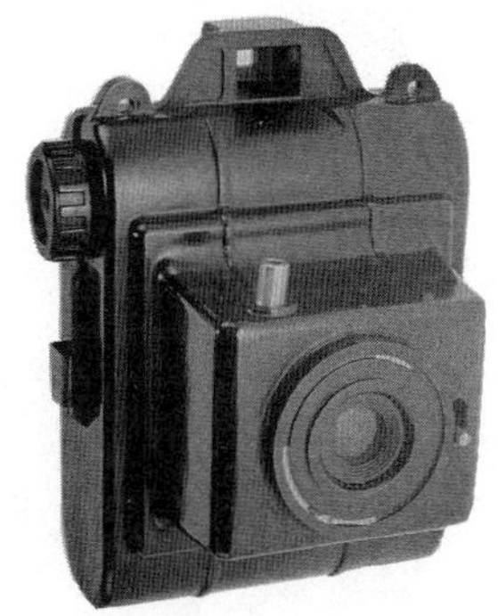

Pionier Deko

MODEL	FORMAT	FILM	TYPE	Year	LENS	Apert	FL	SHUTTER	SPEEDS	ILLUS	U.S.$
Makina II	6.5x9cm	Sheet	StrutPl	1933	Anticomar	2.9	100mm	Compur		Mc355	220
Makina IIa	6.5x9cm	Sheet	StrutPl	1946	Anticomar	4.2	100mm	Compur	1/400,ST		250
Makina IIa	6.5x9cm	Sheet	StrutPl	1946	Xenar	4.5	105mm	Compur	1/400,ST		250
Makina IIb	6.5x9cm	Sheet	StrutPl	1946	Anticomar	4.2	100mm	Compur	1-200		210
Makina IIS	6.5x9cm	Sheet	StrutPl	1936	Anticomar	2.9	50mm	Compur	1-200	Mc355	280
Makina III	6.5x9cm	Sheet	StrutPl	1949	Anticomar	2.9	100mm	Rim-Compur	1-200	Mc355	320
Makina 67	6x7cm	120	StrutRo	1979	Nikkor	3.5	80mm	Copal	1-500	A1571	900
Makina W67	6x7cm	120	StrutRo	1982	Wide-Nikkor	4.5	55mm	Copal	1-500	A3408	1500
Makinette	3x4cm	127	StrutRo	1931	Supracomar	2	50mm	Compur	1-300	Mc355	700
Normal Peco 9x12	9x12cm	plate	FoldPl	1926	Anticomar	4.5	150mm	Compur			130
Peco Junior 6.5x9	6.5x9cm	Sheet	Monorail	1958	Symmar	4.5	100mm	Compur			700
Peco Junior 9x12	9x12cm	Sheet	Monorail	1958	various		150mm	Compur			410
Peco Junior 10x15	10x15cm	Sheet	Monorail	1958	various		150mm	Compur			550
Peco Profia 10x13	10x13cm	Sheet	Monorail	1967	various			various			900
Peco Profia 13x18	13x18cm	Sheet	Monorail	1969	various			various			1500
Peco Profia V	10x13cm	Sheet	Monorail	1979	various			various			700
Peco Studiokamera		Sheet	Monorail	1952	various			various			490
Peco Supra	13x18cm	Sheet	Monorail	1958	various			various			500
Peco Supra II	10x13cm	Sheet	Monorail	1958	various			various			420
Peco Universal I	10x13cm	Sheet	Monorail	1954	various			various			390
Peco Universal II	10x13cm	Sheet	Monorail	1958	various			various			480
Peco Universal III	18x24cm	Sheet	Monorail	1960	various			various			590
Peconette 6x6	6x6cm	120	FoldRo	1922	Anticomar	4.2	75mm	Compur			160
Peconette 6x9	6x9cm	120	FoldRo	1929	Anticomar	4.2	100mm	Compur			180
Peconette II	6x9cm	120	FoldRo	1930	Supracomar	3.9	100mm	Compur			180
Präzisions-Peco 9x12 H	9x12cm	plate	HzFoldPl	1910	Dopp.Anast	6.8		Compound	1-200	A1396	280
Präzisions-Peco 9x12 V	9x12cm	plate	VtFoldPl	1922	Anticomar	3.2	135mm	Compound			330
Präzisions-Peco 10x15 V	10x15cm	plate	VtFoldPl	1922	Anticomar	3.2	165mm	Compound			310
Roll-Op (II)	4.5x6cm	120	FoldRo	1935	Anticomar	2.8	75mm	Compur-Rap.	1-250	Mc355	210
Sportkamera 1955	6x9cm	120	RigidRo	1955	various			focal plane	1/30-1000	A1908	410
Stereo Makina 45x107	45x107	plate	SterStrut	1912	Orthar	6	60mm	Compur		HK473	1000
Stereo Makina 6x13	6x13cm	plate	SterStrut	1926	Anticomar	2.9	90mm	Compur	1-100	Mc356	1000
Superwide Polaroid	6x9cm	Roll	WideAng	1960	Super-Angulon	8	65mm	Compur		A1569	500
Veriwide 100	6x9cm	120	WideAng	1960	Super-Angulon	8	47mm	Sync-Compur	1-500,B,M	Mc356	700
...PLAUL (Carl Plaul) - Dresden											
Field camera 9x12	9x12cm	plate	Field	1900	Prima Aplanat						200
Field camera 10x15	10x15cm	plate	Field	1900	Prima Aplanat						220
Field camera 13x18	13x18cm	plate	Field	1900	Doppel-Anastigmat						190
...PLAYTIME PRODUCTS INC. - New York											
Cabbage Patch Kids 100	13x17mm	110	110VF	1984						Mc356	30
Go Bots 110 Camera	13x17mm	110	110VF	1984							30
Ninja Warrier Camera	13x17mm	110	110VF	1984							0

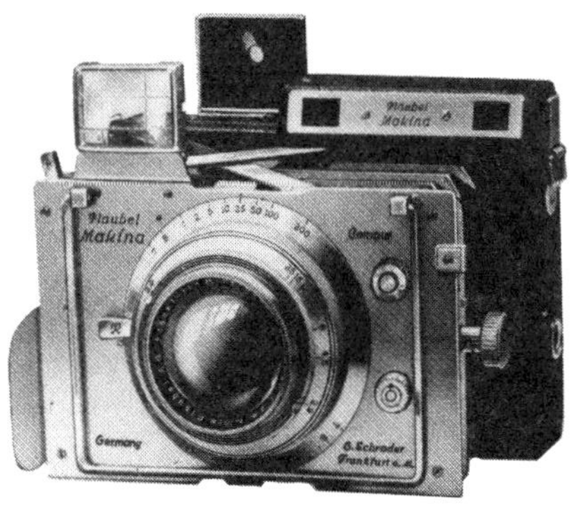

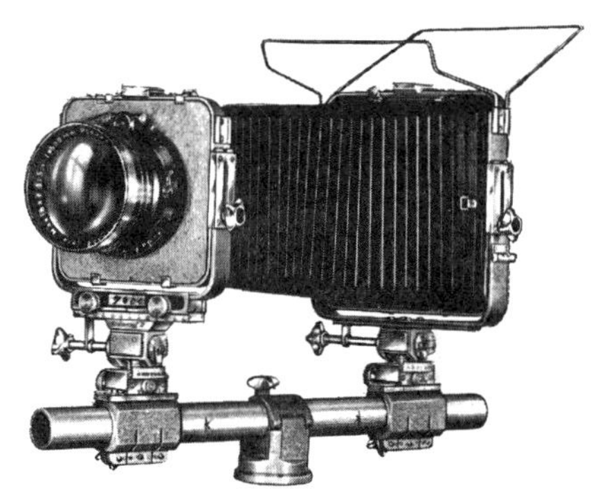

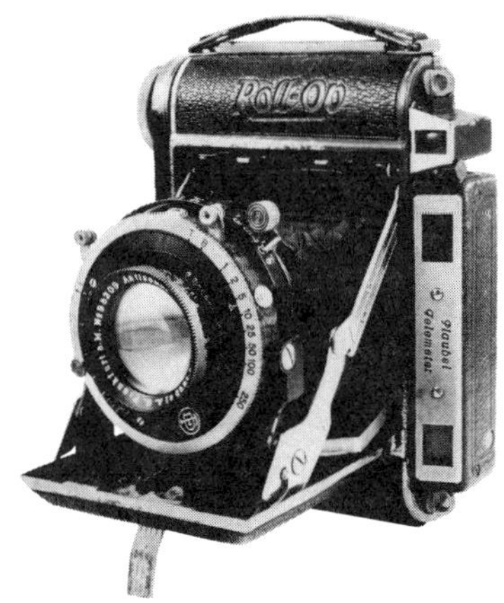

Makina III **Peco Universal II** **Roll-Op (II)**

MODEL	FORMAT	FILM	TYPE	Year	LENS	Apert	FL	SHUTTER	SPEEDS	ILLUS	U.S.$
...PÖCK (Hans Pöck) - Munich, Germany											
Detective Camera	6x9cm		DetectivBox	1888	Voigtländer Euryskop			guillotine	1-100		3100
Repetir Geheimkamera	6x9cm		DetectivBox	1888	Voigtländer Euryskop			guillotine	1-100		3100
...POLAROID - Cambridge, MA											
35 Autofocus	24x36mm	35mm	35AF	1994							60
35 Fixfocus	24x36mm	35mm	35VF	1994							50
80 (Highlander)	2¾x3½"	inst	Instant	1954	Triplet	8.8	100mm		25-100	Mc356	20
80A (Highlander)	2¾x3½"	inst	Instant	1957	Triplet	8.8	100mm		25-100	A3386	30
80B	2¾x3½"	inst	Instant	1959	Triplet	8.8	100mm		25-100	Mc356	20
95	3¼x4¼"	inst	Instant	1948	Triplet	11	135mm		8-160	Mc357	50
95A	3¼x4¼"	inst	Instant	1954	Triplet	8	130mm		12-100	Mc357	50
95B (Speedliner)	3¼x4¼"	inst	Instant	1957	Triplet	8	130mm		12-100		50
100 ("Automatic 100")	3¼x4¼"	inst	Instant	1963		8.8	114mm		10-1200		40
100 (rollfilm)	3¼x4¼"	inst	Instant	1954	Triplet	8	130mm		12-100	A1992	30
101	3¼x4¼"	inst	Instant	1964		8.8	114mm		1-1200	A1993	20
102	3¼x4¼"	inst	Instant	1964		8.8	114mm		1-1000		20
103	3¼x4¼"	inst	Instant	1964	Triplet	8.8	114mm		1-1000		30
104	3¼x4¼"	inst	Instant	1964		8.8	114mm		1-1000		30
110 (Pathfinder)	3¼x4¼"	inst	Instant	1952	Wollensak Raptar	4.5	127mm	Rapax II	1-400		70
110A (Pathfinder)	3¼x4¼"	inst	Instant	1957	Rod. Ysarex	4.7	125mm	Prontor-SVS	1-300		60
110A (Pathfinder)	3¼x4¼"	inst	Instant	1957	Enna-Werk Ennit	4.7	127mm	Prontor-SVS	1-300		60
110B (Pathfinder)	3¼x4¼"	inst	Instant	1960	Rodenstock	4.7	127mm		1-300		120
120	3¼x4¼"	inst	Instant	1961	Yashica	4.7	127mm	Seikosha-SLV	1-500,B		50
125	3¼x4¼"	inst	Instant	1964		8.8	114mm		1-1000		30
135	3¼x4¼"	inst	Instant	1964		8.8	114mm		1-1000		30
150	3¼x4¼"	inst	Instant	1957	Triplet	8	130mm		12-100		30
160	3¼x4¼"	inst	Instant	1962	Triplet	8	130mm		12-100		20
180	3¼x4¼"	inst	Instant	1965	Tominon	4.5	114mm	Seiko	1-500		260
185	3¼x4¼"	inst	Instant	1965	Mamiya Sekor	5.6					290
190	3¼x4¼"	inst	Instant	1974		3.8					240
195	3¼x4¼"	inst	Instant	1974	Tominon	3.8	114mm	Automatic	1-500		180
210	3¼x4¼"	inst	Instant	1967						A1994	50
215	3¼x4¼"	inst	Instant	1968							50
220	3¼x4¼"	inst	Instant	1967							30
230	3¼x4¼"	inst	Instant	1967							40
250	3¼x4¼"	inst	Instant	1967							40
320	3¼x4¼"	inst	Instant	1969						A1995	30
330	3¼x4¼"	inst	Instant	1969							30
340	3¼x4¼"	inst	Instant	1969						A1996	50
350	3¼x4¼"	inst	Instant	1969							20
355	3¼x4¼"	inst	Instant	1975							20
415	3¼x4¼"	inst	Instant	1965							10

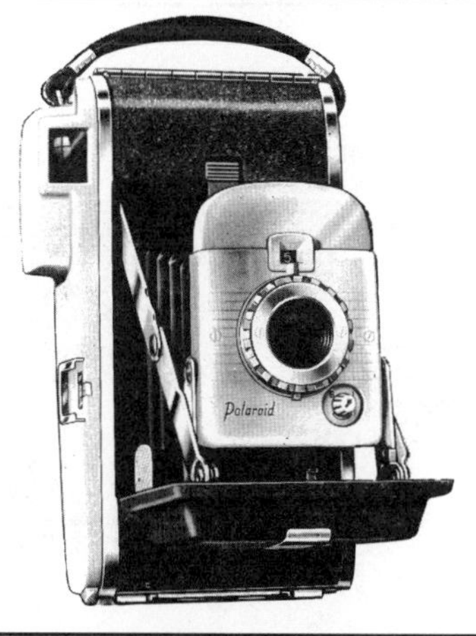

Polaroid 80 (Highlander)

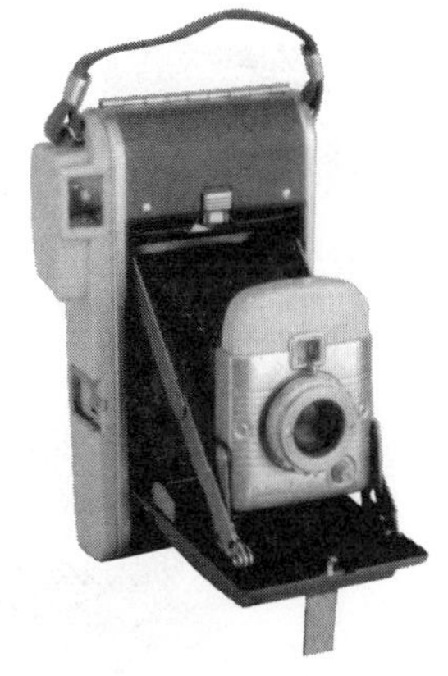
Polaroid 80B

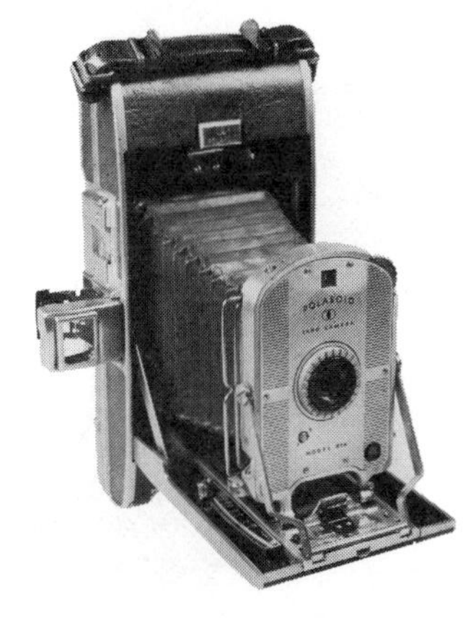

Polaroid 95A

MODEL	FORMAT	FILM	TYPE	Year	LENS	Apert	FL	SHUTTER	SPEEDS	ILLUS	U.S.$
420	3¼x4¼"	inst	Instant	1971							10
450	3¼x4¼"	inst	Instant	1971							20
600 SE	8x8cm	inst	Instant	1978		5.6	150mm				510
636 CL	8x8cm	inst	Instant	1993		14.6	109mm				30
700	3¼x4¼"	inst	Instant	1955	Triplet	8.8	130mm		12-100	Mc357	30
800	3¼x4¼"	inst	Instant	1957	Triplet	8.8	130mm		12-100		30
850	3¼x4¼"	inst	Instant	1961	Triplet	8.8	130mm	pneumatic	10-600	Mc357	20
900	3¼x4¼"	inst	Instant	1960		8.8	130mm	Automatic	1/12-600		30
1000	8x8cm	inst	Instant	1977							10
2000	8x8cm	inst	Instant	1976							30
3000	8x8cm	inst	Instant	1977						A2006	30
5000 Sonar	8x8cm	inst	Instant	1960							30
Big Shot	3¼x4¼"	inst	Instant	1971						A2003	30
Captiva SLR SE	53x72mm	inst	Instant	1993			106mm	program	¼-1/180		100
Colorpack 80	83x86mm	inst	Instant	1971						A1999	20
Colorpack 88	83x86mm	inst	Instant	1971						A2002	10
EE 33	83x86mm	inst	Instant	1976							10
EE 44	83x86mm	inst	Instant	1976						A2000	20
EE 100	8x8cm	inst	Instant	1977						A1997	50
Image	8x8cm	inst	Instant	1992							80
Image II	8x8cm	inst	Instant	1993							70
Image A	8x8cm	inst	Instant	1993							120
Image Pro	8x8cm	inst	Instant	1993							140
Impulse AF (black)	8x8cm	inst	Instant	1993		10	113mm				30
Impulse AF (gray)	8x8cm	inst	Instant	1993		10	113mm				40
Impulse AF SE	8x8cm	inst	Instant	1994		10	113mm				50
Impulse Portrait (black)	8x8cm	inst	Instant	1993		14.6	113mm				30
Impulse Portrait (gray)	8x8cm	inst	Instant	1993		14.6	113mm				30
Instant 10	83x86mm	inst	Instant	1960							20
J-33	2¼x3¼"	inst	Instant	1961		32	101mm	pneumatic	15-1000		10
J-66	3¼x4¼"	inst	Instant	1961		19	114.5	pneumatic	15-1000		20
Miniportrait 452	3¼x4¼"	inst	Instant	1976						A2008	350
ProCam	8x8cm	inst	Instant	1993		10	95mm		2.8-1/245		210
Propack	3¼x4¼"	inst	Instant	1993							200
Spectra SE	72x91mm	inst	Instant	1994							80
Super Swinger	83x86mm	inst	Instant	1975						A2001	10
Swinger Mod. 20	3¼x4¼"	inst	Instant	1965		17	100mm	Universal	200	A1998	10
Swinger Sentinel M15	2¼x3¼"	inst	Instant	1965							10
SX-70 (Deluxe Mod.)	8x8cm	inst	Instant	1972		8	117mm		18-180	A2004	90
SX-70 Alpha 1	8x8cm	inst	Instant	1977						A2005	100
SX-70 II	8x8cm	inst	Instant	1974							90
SX-70 III	8x8cm	inst	Instant	1975							80

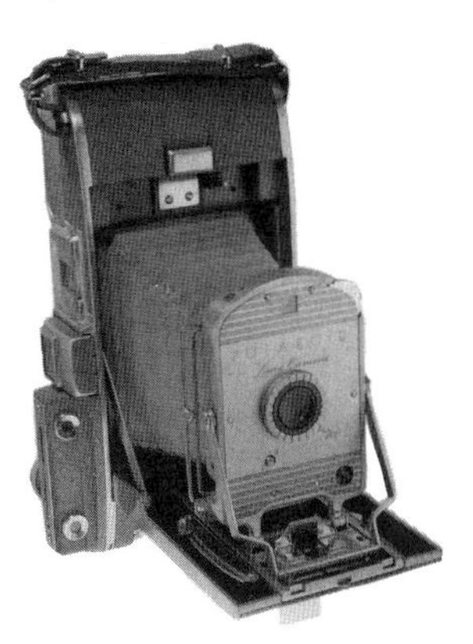

Polaroid 700

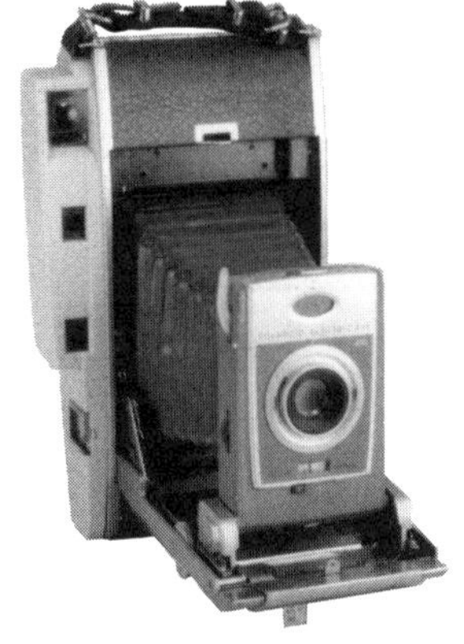

Polaroid 850

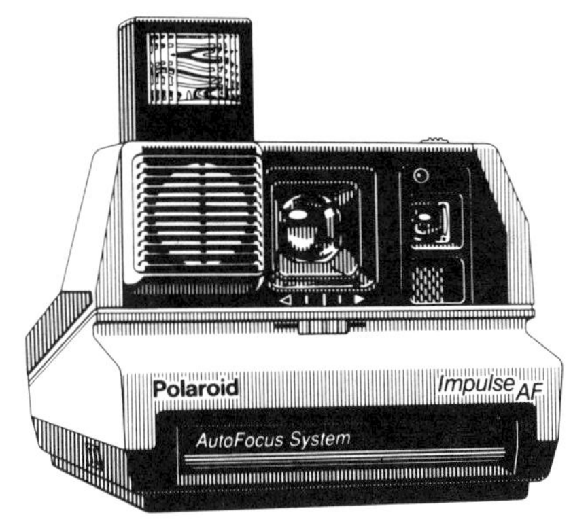

Polaroid Impulse AF

MODEL	FORMAT	FILM	TYPE	Year	LENS	Apert	FL	SHUTTER	SPEEDS	ILLUS	U.S.$
SX-70 Sonar	8x8cm	inst	Instant	1978							120
SX-70 Sonar AF	8x8cm	inst	Instant	1960							160
Vision	8x8cm	inst	Instant	1993							80
...PONTIAC - Paris											
Baby-Lynx	24x36mm	35mm	35VF	1950	Flor	3.5	50mm	Prontor II	1-250	F532	200
Baby-Lynx	24x36mm	35mm	35VF	1950	Flor	3.5	50mm	Atos 2	1-250	F534	200
Baby-Lynx	24x36mm	35mm	35VF	1952	Berthiot	2.8	50mm	Prontor-S		F535	200
Baby Standard	24x36mm	35mm	35VF	1950	Trylor	3.9	50mm	Prontor		F544	120
Bakélite A	6x9cm	120	BakFoldRo	1938	Berthiot	4.5	105mm	Gitzo	25-150	Mc358	100
Bakélite B	6x9cm	120	BakFoldRo	1938	Berthiot	4.5	105mm	MFAP	25-100	F372	100
Bakélite C	6x9cm	120	BakFoldRo	1938	achromatic	11			I,P	F371	100
Bakélite (brown)	6x9cm	120	BakFoldRo	1938	Berthiot	4.5	105mm	MFAP	25-100	F371	120
Bloc-Metal 41	6x9cm	120	VtFoldRo	1941	Anastigmat	4.5		MFAP	25-100	Mc358	60
Bloc-Metal 41	6x9cm	120	VtFoldRo	1942	Pontiac	4.5	105mm	Prontor II	1-250	F288	60
Bloc-Metal 45A	6x9cm	120	VtFoldRo	1946	Trylor Roussel	4.5	105mm	Prontor II		Mc358	60
Bloc-Metal 45AF	6x9cm	120	VtFoldRo	1946	Special Berthiot	4.5	105mm	Prontor II		F291	60
Bloc-Metal 45B	6x9cm	120	VtFoldRo	1946	Flor Berthiot	4.5	105mm	Prontor II		F290	60
Bloc-Metal 145	6x9cm	120	VtFoldRo	1946	Trylor Roussel	4.5	105mm	Compur-Rap.		F292	130
Bloc-Metal 145	6x9cm	120	VtFoldRo	1946	Special Berthiot	4.5	105mm	Compur-Rap.		F292	130
Bloc-Metal 145	6x9cm	120	VtFoldRo	1946	Flor Berthiot	4.5	105mm	Compur-Rap.		F292	130
Lynx	3x4cm	127	RigidRo	1948	Flor Berthiot	2.8	50mm	focal plane		Mc358	140
Lynx II	3x4cm	127	RigidRo	1948	Flor Berthiot	2.8	50mm	focal plane		Mc358	120
Lynx Compur	3x4cm	127	RigidRo	1948	Flor Berthiot	2.8	50mm	Compur	1-300	F704	320
Lynx De Nuit	3x4cm	127	RigidRo	1948	Flor Berthiot	1.5	50mm	focal plane		F696	340
Lynx Standard	3x4cm	127	RigidRo	1948	Trylor Roussel	3.5	50mm	focal plane		F706	310
Lynx Standard	3x4cm	127	RigidRo	1948	Flor Berthiot	2.8	50mm	focal plane		F706	310
Super Lynx	24x36mm	35mm	35VF	1950	Flor Berthiot	2.8		focal plane	25-500	F675	320
Super Lynx	24x36mm	35mm	35VF	1950	Flor Berthiot	3.5		focal plane	25-500	F675	320
Super Lynx I	24x36mm	35mm	35VF	1950	Flor Berthiot	2.8		focal plane	25-500	F676	220
Super Lynx I	24x36mm	35mm	35VF	1950	Flor Berthiot	3.5		focal plane	25-500	F677	220
Super Lynx II a	24x36mm	35mm	35VF	1950	Flor Berthiot	2.8		focal plane	25-500	F678	390
Super Lynx II b	24x36mm	35mm	35VF	1950	Flor Berthiot	3.5		focal plane	25-500	F678	390
Super Lynx II c	24x36mm	35mm	35VF	1950	Sacem Hexar	2		focal plane	25-500		390
Super Lynx Standard	24x36mm	35mm	35VF	1951	Flor Berthiot	3.5	50mm	focal plane	25-500	F674	300
...POPULAR PHOTOGRAPH CO. - New York											
Nodark Tintype Camera	2½x3½"	Ferro	Ferrotype	1899							900
...PORTAFAX - France											
Photo-Volume	9x12cm	plate	Disguised	1891	Rapid Rectilinear			guillotine		F1485	1300
Photo-Volume	9x12cm	plate	Disguised	1891	Anastigmat			guillotine		F1485	1300
...POTTHOFF (Kamerafabrik Potthoff & Co.) - Solingen, Germany											
Amplion-Reflex	6x6cm	120	TLR	1952	Pluscanar	3.5	75mm	Prontor-SVS		Mc358	70
Plascaflex PS 35	6x6cm	120	TLR	1952	Plascanar	3.5	75mm	Prontor		A3169	70

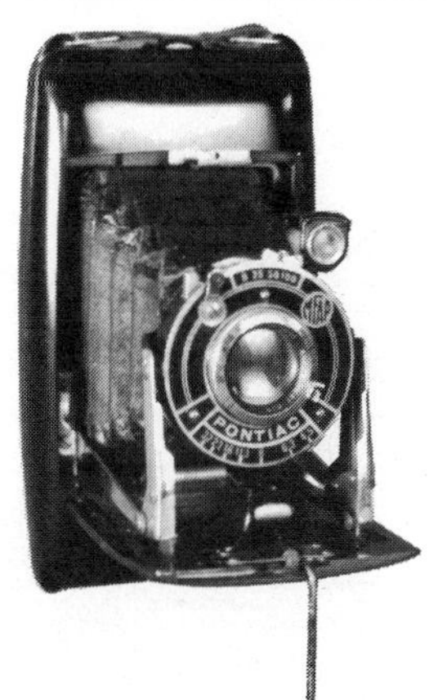

Pontiac Bakélite A

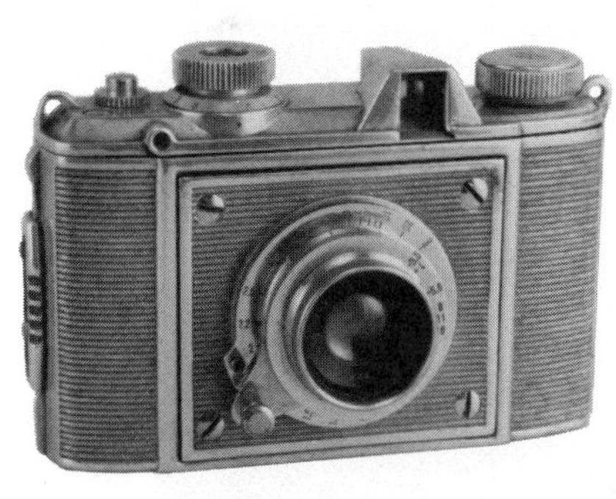

Pontiac Lynx

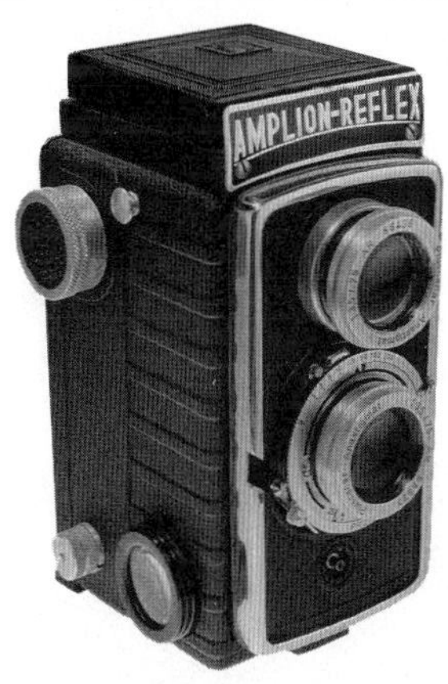

Potthoff Amplion-Reflex

MODEL	FORMAT	FILM	TYPE	Year	LENS	Apert	FL	SHUTTER	SPEEDS	ILLUS	U.S.$
Plascaflex PS 35	6x6cm	120	TLR	1952	Plascanar	3.5	75mm	Compur		A3169	70
Plascaflex V 45	6x6cm	120	TLR	1952	Plascanar	4.5	75mm	Vario		A640	70
...POUVA (Karl Pouva) - Freital, Germany											
Start 24x36	24x36mm	35mm	35VF	1971	Chromar				M,Z		10
Start 6x6	6x6cm	120	BakFoldRo	1952		8			M,Z	A1615	30
Start SL 100	24x36mm	35mm	35VF	1973	Chromar				M,Z		10
...PREMIER INSTRUMENT CO. - New York											
Kardon (civilian)	24x36mm	35mm	35VF	1945	Ektar	2	47mm	focal plane	1-1000	A977	540
Kardon Signal Corps	24x36mm	35mm	35VF	1945	Ektar	2	47mm	focal plane	1-1000	Mc359	430
...PRESCOTT & CO. - Glasgow											
Field camera	4¼x6½"	plate	Field		various			Challenge			330
...PRIMO - Netherlands											
Primo	24x35mm	35mm	35VF	1950	Nedinsco-Venio	3.5	45mm		25-200	Mc359	50
...(unknown)											
Prince	14x16mm	Roll	Submin	1960	Fixed focus	10			B,I	Mc359	310
...PRINTEX PRODUCTS - Pasadena, CA											
Printex 2¼x3¼"	2¼x3¼"	Sheet	Press	1946	various						130
Printex 4x5"	4x5"	Sheet	Press	1946	various						130
...(unknown)											
Prona Tropical	6.5x9cm	plate	VtFoldPl	1925	Prona Anastigmat	6.3	105mm	Vario			130
...PROUD CO. - Japan											
Rosen Semi	4.5x6cm	120	VtFoldRo	1937	Rosen Anastigmat	4.5	75mm	Rosen			80
...PUTMAN (F. Putnam) - N.Y.											
Marvel	5x8"	plate	Field	1885	Scovill Waterbury					Mc359	250
...PYNE - Manchester, England											
Stereoscopic Camera	8x17cm	plate	SterTail	1860	Ross						5500
...Q.R.S.-DeVRY CORP. - Chicago											
Q.R.S. Kamra	24x32mm	35mm	35Early	1928	Graf Anastigmat	7.7	40mm			Mc359	140
...RAACO Strasbourg, France											
Mignon	4.5x6cm	plate	CardBox	1929	Meniscus			Sector		Mc360	130
...(unknown)											
Radix	3¼x4¼"	plate	PlateBox	1897						Mc360	70
...(unknown)											
Randorflex	4x4cm	127	TLR			8		simple	1/50		20
...RANKOLOR LABORATORIES - U.S.A.											
Rank	13x17mm	110	Dispose	1975		11		simple	1/80		10
...RAY CAMERA CO. - Rochester, N.Y.											
Box camera	3½x3½"	plate	PlateBox		Single Achromatic			rotary			50
Pocket Ray	3¼x4¼"	plate	VtFoldPl	1904	Rapid Rectilinear			Ray Autom.			80
Ray A	4x5"	plate	FoldPl	1898	Roch.Symmetrical					Mc360	120
Ray A	4x5"	plate	FoldPl	1898	Zeiss Anastigmat					Mc360	120
Ray C	4x5"	plate	FoldPl	1899	Meniscus			rotary	I,T		80

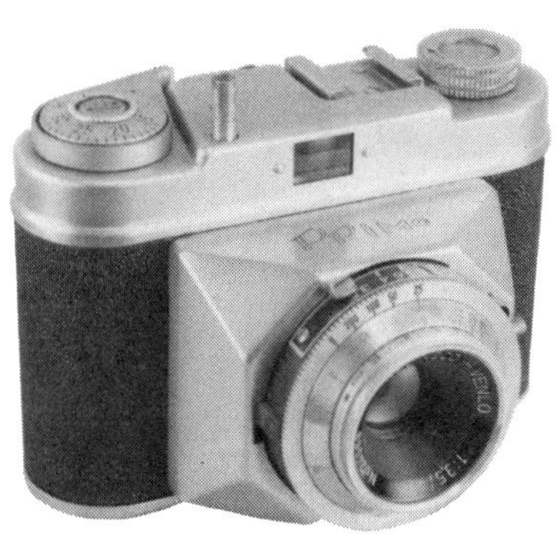

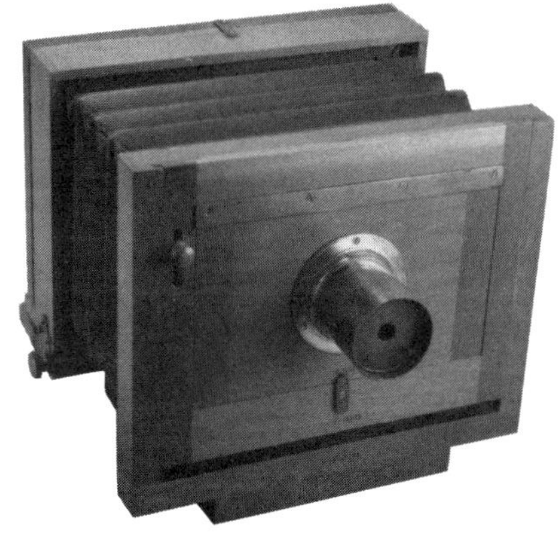

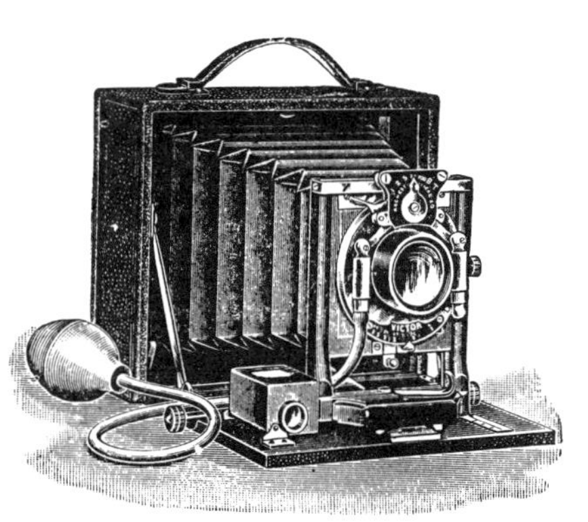

Primo **Putman Marvel** **Ray A**

MODEL	FORMAT	FILM	TYPE	Year	LENS	Apert	FL	SHUTTER	SPEEDS	ILLUS	U.S.$
Ray Jr.	2½x2½"	plate	PlateBox	1897	Single Achromatic			rotary	I,T	Mc360	80
Ray No. 1	4x5"	plate	FoldPl	1899	Single Achromatic			Ray	I,T	Mc360	140
Ray No. 2	5x7"	plate	FoldPl	1899	Brass barrel			Unicum		Mc360	270
Ray No. 4	4x5"	plate	FoldPl	1899	Rapid Rectilinear			Ray	I,T	Mc360	140
Ray No. 6	4x5"	plate	FoldPl	1899	Rap. Symmetrical			Unicum	I,T	Mc360	140
Ray No. 7	5x7"	plate	FoldPl	1899	Brass barrel			Unicum		Mc360	130
Telephoto Ray Mod. C	4x5"	plate	FoldPl	1901				Woll. Auto			120
...RECKMEIER & SCHUNEMANN											
Dreifarben	6.5x9cm	plate	3-Color	1935	Heliar	3.5		Compur		A948	590
...RECORD CAMERA											
Record Camera	3¼x4"	plate	LgTLR	1890	Achromat				T,I		1300
...RECTAFLEX - Rome, Italy											
Director	24x36mm	35mm	35VF	1952	Angenieux	2.9	50mm	focal plane			2600
Recta	24x36mm	35mm	35RF	1952	Angenieux	2.9	50mm	focal plane			3000
Rectaflex 1000	24x36mm	35mm	35SLR	1949	Schneider Xenon	2	50mm	focal plane	1-1000	Mc360	350
Rectaflex 1000	24x36mm	35mm	35SLR	1949	Angenieux	1.8	50mm	focal plane	1-1000	Mc360	350
Rectaflex 1300	24x36mm	35mm	35SLR	1952	Schneider Xenon	2.8	50mm	focal plane	1-1300	A621	370
Rectaflex 1300	24x36mm	35mm	35SLR	1952	Biotar	2	58mm	focal plane	1-1300	A621	360
Rectaflex Junior	24x36mm	35mm	35SLR	1952	Angenieux	2.9	50mm	focal plane	25-500	Mc360	260
Rectaflex Rotor	24x36mm	35mm	35SLR	1952	Xenar		50mm	focal plane	1-1300	Mc360	1800
...REFLEX CAMERA CO. - Newark, NJ & Yonkers, NY											
Focal plane postcard cam.	3¼x4¼"	plate	VtFoldPl	1912	Cooke Anastigmat			focal plane		Mc361	230
Focal plane postcard cam.	3¼x4¼"	plate	VtFoldPl	1912	Ilex R.R.			focal plane		Mc361	230
Junior Reflex	3¼x4¼"	plate	LgSLR	1911				sector		Mc361	160
Patent Reflex Hand camera	4x5"	plate	LgSLR	1902				focal plane		Mc361	370
Reflex camera 4x5"	4x5"	plate	LgSLR	1900	Euryplan Anast.		7"	focal plane		Mc361	200
Reflex camera 5x7"	5x7"	plate	LgSLR	1900	Anastigmat	16	210mm	focal plane		A1585	400
...REICHENBACH, MOREY & WILL CO. - Rochester, N.Y.											
Alta Automatic	4x5"	plate	FoldPl	1896				R.M.&W.	I&T	Mc361	160
Alta D	5x7"	plate	FoldPl	1896							140
...REID & SIGRIST - Leicester, England											
Reid I	24x36m	35mm	35VF	1958	Taylor Hobson	2	2"	focal plane	1/20-1000	Mc362	350
Reid I Military	24x36m	35mm	35VF	1958	Taylor Hobson	2	2"	focal plane	1/20-1000		540
Reid Ia	24x36m	35mm	35VF	1958	Taylor Hobson	2	2"	focal plane	1/20-1000		310
Reid Ia Military	24x36m	35mm	35VF	1958	Taylor Hobson	2	2"	focal plane	1/20-1000		590
Reid II	24x36m	35mm	35RF	1958	Taylor Hobson	2	2"	focal plane	1/20-1000		370
Reid III	24x36m	35mm	35RF	1947	Taylor Hobson	2	2"	focal plane	1-1000	A3466	440
Reid III (sync)	24x36m	35mm	35RF	1947	Taylor Hobson	2	2"	focal plane	1-1000		380
...REVERE											
Automatic-1034	28x28mm	126	126VF	1969							10
Eyematic EE 127	1½x1½"	127	RigidRo	1958	Wollensak	2.8	58mm			Mc362	40
Stereo 33	22x24mm	35mm	35Ster	1953	Wollensak	3.5	35mm		2-200	Mc362	270

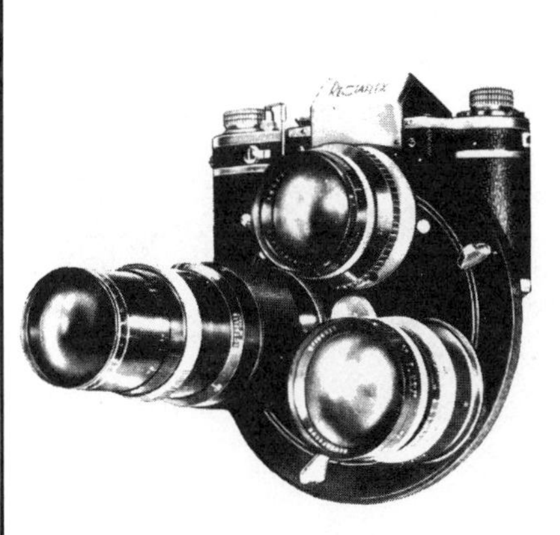
Rectaflex Rotor

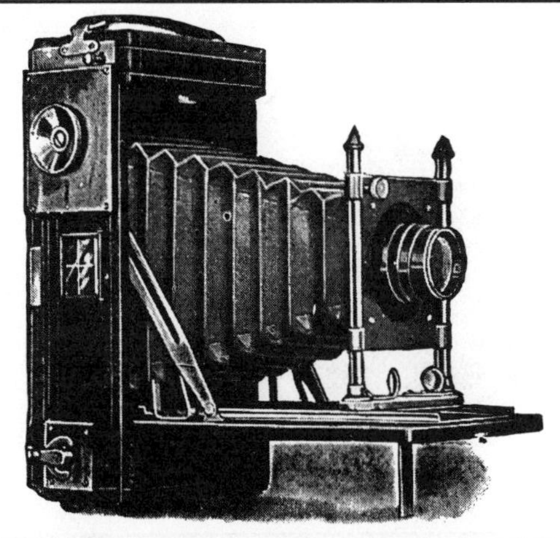
Reflex Focal plane postcard cam.

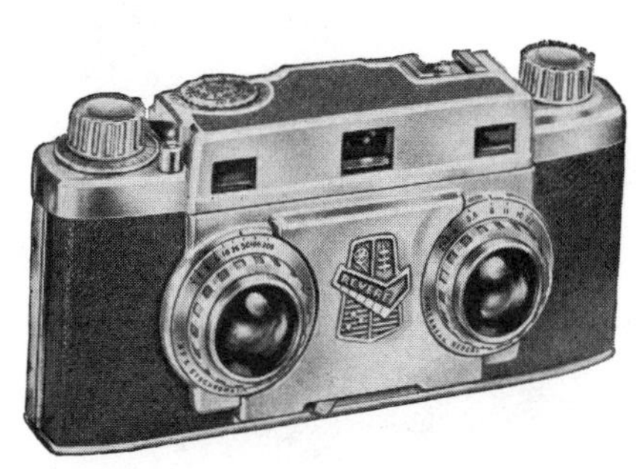

Revere Stereo 33

MODEL	FORMAT	FILM	TYPE	Year	LENS	Apert	FL	SHUTTER	SPEEDS	ILLUS	U.S.$
...REWO - Delft, Netherlands											
Rewo Louise	4x6.5cm	127	MetalBox	1950	Meniscus				M,T	Mc362	30
...REX											
Baby Powell	3x4cm	127	VtFoldRo		Hexar	4.5	50mm	Konishiroku			130
Powell Senior	6x9cm	120	VtFoldRo		Alphar	4.5	105mm	NFG			0
...REX MAGAZINE CAMERA CO. - Chicago											
Rex Magazine 2x2"	2x2"	plate	MagBox	1899	Meniscus				I		310
Rex Magazine 3¼x4¼"	3¼x4¼"	plate	MagBox	1899	Meniscus				I	Mc362	290
Rex Magazine 4x5"	4x5"	plate	MagBox	1899	Meniscus				I	Mc362	240
...REYGONAUD - Paris											
Stand Camera	8x11cm	plate	Tailboard	1870	Jamin Darlot					F24	900
...REYNOLDS & BRANSON - Leeds, England											
Field camera 4¼x6½"	4¼x6½"	plate	Tailboard	1890	Rapid Rectilinear					A2671	390
Field camera 6½x8½"	6½x8½"	plate	Tailboard	1890	Rapid Rectilinear						340
...RHEINMETALL (VEB Rheinmetall) - Sömmerda, East Germany											
Exa System	24x36mm	35mm	35SLR	1955	Tessar	2.8	50mm	focal plane			130
Perfekta	6x6cm	120	BakeliteRoll	1955	Chromat	7.7	80mm		M,Z	Mc362	30
Perfekta II	6x6cm	120	TelescRo	1956	Achromat	7.7	80mm		25-100	Mc363	30
...RICH-RAY TRADING CO. - Japan											
Rich-Ray	24x24mm	Bolta	BakeliteRoll	1951	fixed focus	5.6			B,I	Mc363	50
Richlet 35	24x36mm	Bolta	BakeliteRoll	1954		5.6			B,25-100	Mc363	50
...RICHARD (F.M. Richard)											
Detective	13x18cm	plate	MagBox	1895							800
...RICHARD (Jules Richard) - Paris, France											
Glyphoscope	45x107	plate	StJumelle	1905	Meniscus			guillotine		Mc363	140
Homeos	19x24mm	35mm	35Ster	1914	Optis	4.5	28mm	guillotine		Mc363	1800
Homeos	19x24mm	35mm	35Ster	1914	Z. Krauss Anast.	4.5	28mm	guillotine		Mc363	1800
Homeoscope 6x13	6x13cm	plate	StJumelle	1900	Zeiss Anastigmat	6.3	124mm	guillotine		F1260	270
Homeoscope 9x18	9x18cm	plate	StJumelle	1900	Zeiss Anastigmat	6.3	124mm	guillotine		F1258	270
Verascope 45x107	45x107	plate	StJumelle	1895	Rapid Rectilinear	10			P,I	F1427	160
Verascope 45x107	45x107	127	StJumelle	1895	Rapid Rectilinear	10			P,I	F1427	240
Verascope 45x107	45x107	plate	StJumelle	1908	Krauss Tessar	4.5	55mm	Chronomos	1/9-150	F1429	260
Verascope 45x107	45x107	127	StJumelle	1908	Krauss Tessar	4.5	55mm	Chronomos	1/9-150	F1429	270
Verascope 6x13	6x13cm	plate	StJumelle	1905	Zeiss Anastigmat	4.5	85mm	guillotine	20-142	F1430	180
Verascope 6x13	6x13cm	120	StJumelle	1905	Zeiss Anastigmat	4.5	85mm	guillotine	20-142	F1430	240
Verascope 7x13	7x13cm	plate	StJumelle	1905	Zeiss Anastigmat	4.5	85mm	guillotine	20-142	F1434	180
Verascope 7x13	7x13cm	116	StJumelle	1905	Zeiss Anastigmat	4.5	85mm	guillotine	20-142	F1434	240
Verascope F40	24x30mm	35mm	35Ster	1950	Berthiot	3.5	40mm	guillotine	1-250	F1464	560
...RICHTER - Tharandt, Germany											
Reflecta	6x6cm	120	TLR	1948	Meritare	3.5	7.5cm		1/25,1/75	A1711	50
Rica-Flex	6x6cm	120	TLR	1937	Pololyt	3.5	75mm	Stelo			100
Trumpf Reflex	6x6cm	120	TLR	1936	Trioplan	3.5	75mm				100

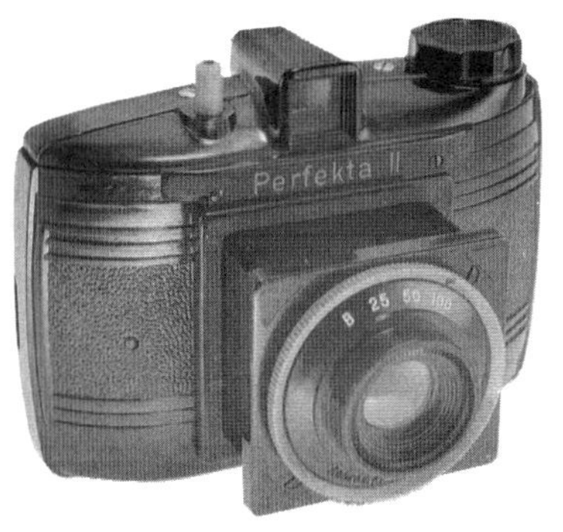

Perfekta II

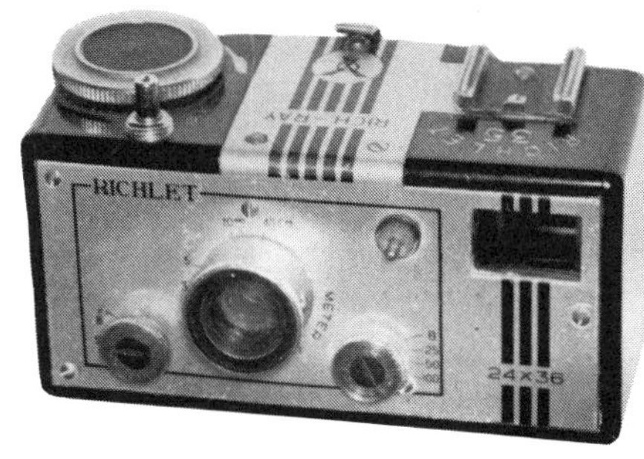

Richlet 35

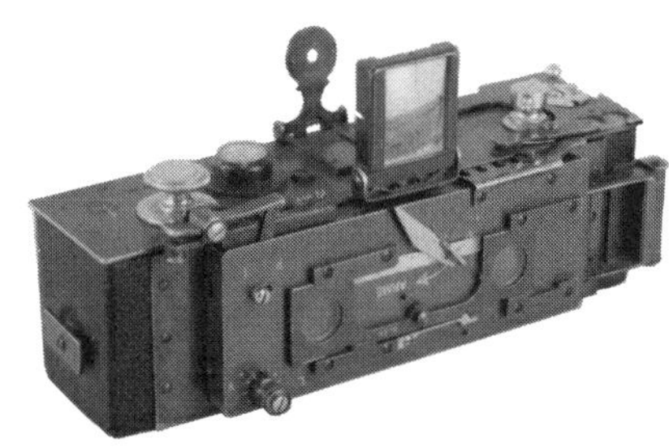

Richard Homeos

MODEL	FORMAT	FILM	TYPE	Year	LENS	Apert	FL	SHUTTER	SPEEDS	ILLUS	U.S.$
...RICHTER - Berlin											
Germania	9x12cm	plate	DetectivBox	1900							700
...RIDDELL (A. Riddell) - Glasgow											
Folding plate camera	9x12cm	plate	FoldPl	1880				roller-blind			270
...RIETZSCHEL (A. Heinrich Rietzschel GmbH Optische Fabrik) - Munich, Germany											
Clack I 9x12	9x12cm	plate	HzFoldPl	1900	Anastigmat	8		Brass			650
Clack I 9x12	9x12cm	plate	HzFoldPl	1910		6.3		Dbl. Pneum.		Mc363	140
Clack I 10x15	10x15cm	plate	HzFoldPl	1900		6.3		Brass			650
Clack I 10x15	10x15cm	plate	HzFoldPl	1910	Anastigmat	8		Dbl. Pneum.		A1398	140
Clack Luxus 6.5x9	6.5x9cm	plate	HzFoldPl	1910	Solinar	4.5	120mm	Compur			360
Clack Luxus 9x12	9x12cm	plate	HzFoldPl	1910	Linear	4.8	135mm	Compur			340
Condor Luxus	9x12cm	plate	FoldPl	1925	Solinear	4.5	135mm	Compur			310
Heli-Clack 9x12	9x12cm	plate	HzFoldPl	1910	Dopp. Anast.	6.8		Compound		A237	160
Heli-Clack 9x12	9x12cm	plate	HzFoldPl	1910	Tri-Linear	4.5		Compound		A237	160
Heli-Clack 9x18	9x18cm	plate	StFoldPl	1920	Tri-Linear	4.5		Compound			640
Heli-Clack 10x15	10x15cm	plate	HzFoldPl	1910	Dopp. Anast.	6.8		Compound		Mc363	140
Heli-Clack 10x15	10x15cm	plate	HzFoldPl	1910	Tri-Linear	4.5		Compound		Mc363	140
Heli-Tip	6.5x9cm	plate	VtFoldRo	1910	Tri-Linear	4.5		Compound			80
Heli-Tip I	9x12cm	plate	VtFoldRo	1910	Rectigraph	8		Compound			160
Heli-Tip I	9x12cm	plate	VtFoldRo	1910	Tri-Linear	4.5		Compound			160
Heli-Tip 102	9x12cm	plate	VtFoldRo	1910	Tri-Linear	4.5		Compound			90
Kosmo-Clack Stereo	45x107	plate	StJumelle	1914	Dopp. Anast.	6.3		Compur	1-250	Mc363	350
Kosmo-Clack Stereo	45x107	plate	StJumelle	1914	Rietzschel	4.5	60mm	Compur	1-250	A743	350
Ladies Hand camera	9x12cm	plate	FoldPl	1900	Rietzschel Anast.	8		Dbl. Pneum.	1-100		3800
Miniatur-Clack 109	4.5x6cm	plate	FoldPl	1924	Linear Anastigmat	4.5	165mm	Compound		Mc364	200
Miniatur-Clack 109	4.5x6cm	plate	FoldPl	1924	Linear Anastigmat	4.5	165mm	Compur		Mc364	200
Platten-Clack 9x12	9x12cm	plate	FoldPl	1901	Anastigmat	8	140mm	Unicum			150
Platten-Clack 9x12	9x12cm	plate	FoldPl	1901	Linear C	6.8	120mm	Unicum			150
Platten-Clack 13x18	13x18cm	plate	FoldPl	1901	Anastigmat	9	200mm	Unicum			370
Platten-Clack 13x18	13x18cm	plate	FoldPl	1901	Linear C	6.8	180mm	Auto Rapid			370
Reform-Clack 111	6.5x9cm	plate	FoldPl	1910	Dialyt	6.8	108mm	Compound	1-250	Mc364	100
Reform-Clack 111	6.5x9cm	plate	FoldPl	1910	Dialyt	6.8	108mm	Dial-Compur	1-250		100
Roll-Tip 6x9	6x9cm	120	VtFoldRo	1923	Trilnear	7.5		Pronto			30
Roll-Tip 8x10.5	8x10.5cm	124	VtFoldRo	1923	Rapid Aplanat			Simplex			120
Taschen Clack 8x10.5	8x10.5cm	124	VtFoldRo	1920	Sextar	6.8	90mm	Compur			80
Taschen Clack 128 4.5x6	4.5x6cm	120	VtFoldRo	1920	Sextar	6.8	90mm	Compur			100
Taschen Clack 128 6x6	6x6cm	120	VtFoldRo	1920	Dialyt	6.8	90mm	Compur			100
Taschen Clack 129 6x9	6x9cm	120	VtFoldRo	1920	Sextar	6.8	90mm	Compur			120
Taschen Clack 129 6x9	6x9cm	120	VtFoldRo	1920	Linear	4.5	90mm	Compur			120
Universal Heli-Clack I	8x14cm	plate	HzFoldPl	1910	Linear Anastigmat	4.8	210mm	Compound			110
Universal Heli-Clack I	10x15cm	plate	HzFoldPl	1910	Linear Anastigmat	4.8	150mm	Compound			160
Universal Heli-Clack I	13x18cm	plate	HzFoldPl	1910	Linear Anastigmat	4.8	210mm	Compound		Mc364	160

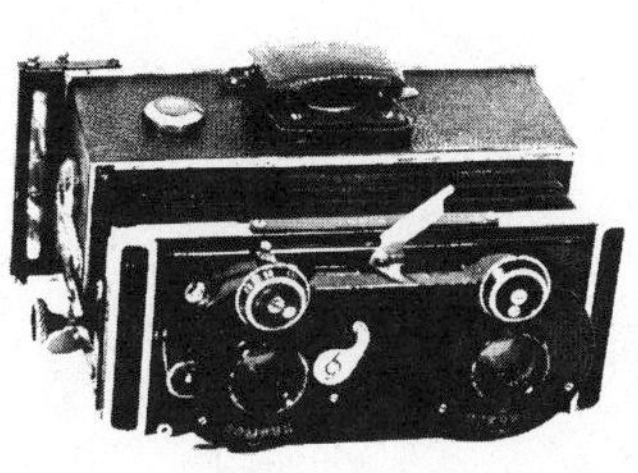

Kosmo-Clack Stereo

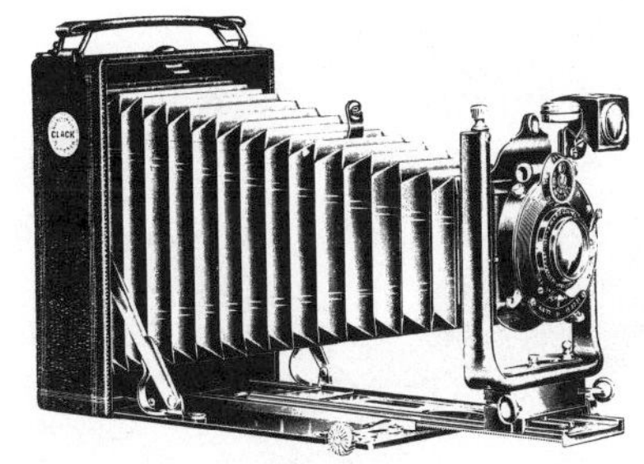

Reform-Clack 111

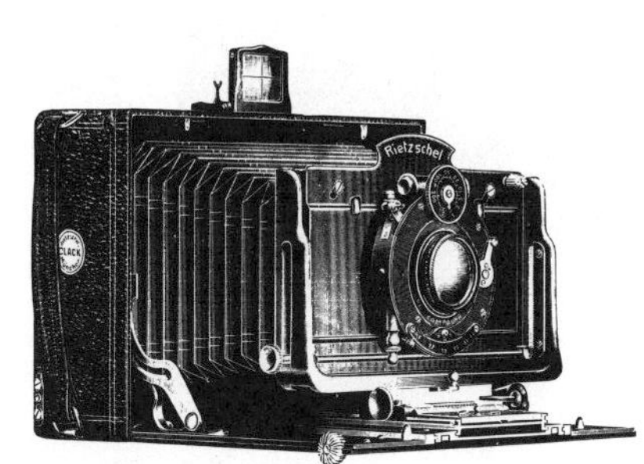

Universal Heli-Clack I

MODEL	FORMAT	FILM	TYPE	Year	LENS	Apert	FL	SHUTTER	SPEEDS	ILLUS	U.S.$
Univ. Heli-Clack II (stereo)	8x14cm	plate	StFoldPl	1910	Doppel Apotar	6.3	120mm	Compound			350
Univ. Heli-Clack II (stereo)	13x18cm	plate	StFoldPl	1910	Doppel Apotar	6.3	120mm	Compound		Mc364	350
Universal Heli-Clack III	13x18cm	plate	HzFoldPl	1910	Linear Anastigmat	4.8	210mm	Compound		Mc364	510
Universal Heli-Clack III	13x18cm	plate	HzFoldPl	1910	Linear Anastigmat	6.3	210mm	Compound			510
...RIKEN OPTICAL - Japan											
Adler Semi	4.5x6cm	120	VtFoldRo	1938	Adler Anastigmat	3.5		Automat		Mc364	90
Adler Semi	4.5x6cm	120	VtFoldRo	1938	Adler Anastigmat	4.5		Newmann-Heilemann			90
Baby Kinsi	3x4cm	127	StrutRo	1941	Kinsi Anastigmat	4.5	5cm	Seikosh.Licht		Mc364	290
Gokoku	24x36mm	35mm	35VF	1939		3.5	50mm				630
Golden Ricoh 16	10x14mm	16mm	Submin	1957	Ricoh	3.5	25mm		50-200,B	Mc364	220
Golden Steky	10x14mm	16mm	Submin	1957	Stekinar	3.5	25mm		50-200,B	Mc364	280
Hanken	10x14mm	16mm	Submin	1952	Stekinar	3.5	25mm		25-100		3200
Ricoh 16	10x14mm	16mm	Submin	1958	Ricoh	2.8	25mm		50-200,B	Mc364	230
Ricoh 35	24x36mm	35mm	35RF	1955	Ricomat	3.5	45mm	Riken	10-200,B		70
Ricoh 35	24x36mm	35mm	35RF	1955	Ricomat	2.8	45mm	Seikosha-Rap.	1-500,B	A3487	70
Ricoh 35 Deluxe	24x36mm	35mm	35RF	1956	Ricomat	2.8	45mm	Seikosha-MX	1-500,B	Mc365	70
Ricoh 35 Deluxe	24x36mm	35mm	35RF	1955	Ricomat	2	45mm	Seikosha-MX	1-500,B		70
Ricoh 35 Deluxe II	24x36mm	35mm	35RF	1956	Ricomat	2.8	45mm				70
Ricoh 35 EF	24x36mm	35mm	35VF	1979	Color Rikenon	3.8	40mm		1/125		50
Ricoh 35 EFL	24x36mm	35mm	35VF	1983	Color Rikenon	3.8	40mm		1/125		60
Ricoh 35 EFS	24x36mm	35mm	35VF	1983	Color Rikenon	2.8	40mm		1/125		60
Ricoh 35 Electronic	24x36mm	35mm	35RF	1972	Rikenon	1.8	40mm	programmed	2-1/1000		30
Ricoh 35 Flex	24x36mm	35mm	35SLR	1963	Ricoh	2.8	50mm	Seikosha	30-300		70
Ricoh 35 Flex CdS	24x36mm	35mm	35SLR	1960	Ricoh	2.8	50mm	Seikosha	30-300		70
Ricoh 35 FM	24x36mm	35mm	35VF	1981	Ricoh	2.8	50mm		1/20-300,B		70
Ricoh 35 K Rapid	24x36mm	35mm	35VF	1960	Rikenon	2.8	40mm	Copal-X	25-200		70
Ricoh 35 S	24x36mm	35mm	35RF	1957	Ricoh	2.8	45mm			Mc365	70
Ricoh 35 ZF ST (black)	24x36mm	35mm	35VF	1977	Rikenon	2.8	40mm				60
Ricoh 35 ZF ST (chrome)	24x36mm	35mm	35VF	1977	Rikenon	2.8	40mm				60
Ricoh 126-C Auto CdS	28x28mm	126	126VF	1967	Rikenon	2.8	50mm				90
Ricoh 126 C Automatic	28x28mm	126	126VF	1960	Rikenon	2.8	40mm	Copal	1/30, 125		100
Ricoh 126 C Deluxe	28x28mm	126	126VF	1967	Rikenon	2.8	40mm		1/30-500		110
Ricoh 126-C EE	28x28mm	126	126VF	1967	Rikenon						90
Ricoh 126-C EES	28x28mm	126	126VF	1971	Rikenon						70
Ricoh 126C-Flex TLS	28x28mm	126	35SLR	1969	Rikenon	2.8	55mm		B,30-300	Mc365	110
Ricoh 300	24x36mm	35mm	35RF	1959	Rikenon	2.8	45mm	Riken leaf	1/10-300	Mc365	40
Ricoh 300S	24x36mm	35mm	35RF	1962	Rikenon	2.8	45mm	Riken leaf	1/8-300		30
Ricoh 500	24x36mm	35mm	35RF	1957	Ricomat	2.8	45mm	Seikosha-MXL	1-500		60
Ricoh 500 Deluxe	24x36mm	35mm	35RF								30
Ricoh 500 G	24x36mm	35mm	35RF	1972	Rikenon	2.8	40mm				30
Ricoh 500 GX	24x36mm	35mm	35RF	1977	Rikenon	2.8	40mm				30
Ricoh 500 ME	24x36mm	35mm	35RF	1983	Color Rikenon	2.8	40mm		1/8-500		60

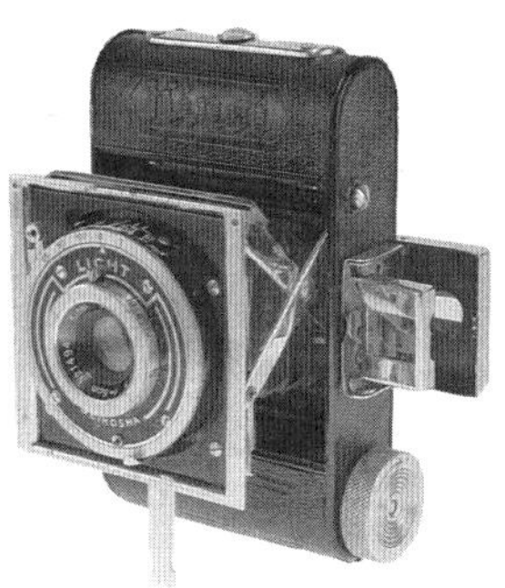

Baby Kinsi

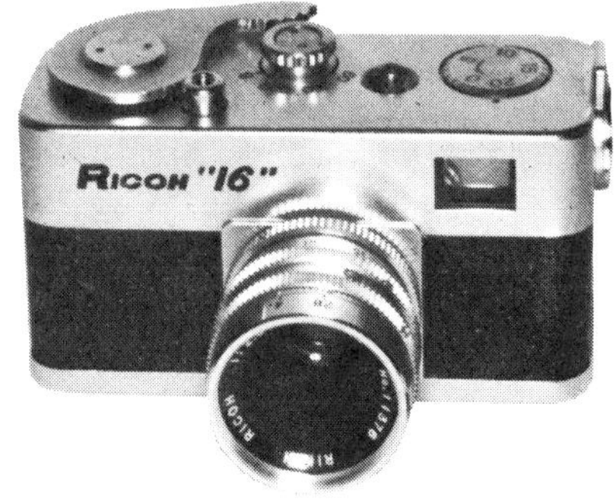

Ricoh 16

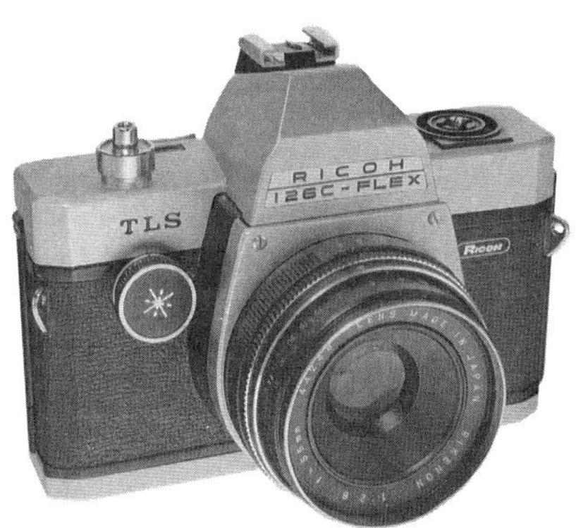

Ricoh 126C-Flex TLS

MODEL	FORMAT	FILM	TYPE	Year	LENS	Apert	FL	SHUTTER	SPEEDS	ILLUS	U.S.$
Ricoh 500 RF	24x36mm	35mm	35RF	1983	Color Rikenon	2.8	40mm		1/8-500		40
Ricoh 500 ST	24x36mm	35mm	35VF	1983	Color Rikenon	2.8	40mm		1/8-500		30
Ricoh 500 ZF	24x36mm	35mm	35VF	1983	Color Rikenon	2.8	40mm		1/8-500		30
Ricoh 519 Deluxe	24x36mm	35mm	35RF	1958	Rikenon	1.9	45mm				50
Ricoh 520 M	24x36mm	35mm	35RF	1965	Rikenon	2					50
Ricoh 520 M CdS	24x36mm	35mm	35RF	1960	Rikenon	2	48mm	Seikosha	1-500		50
Ricoh 800 EES	24x36mm	35mm	35RF	1975	Rikenon						60
Ricoh 999	24x36mm	35mm	35RF	1960	Rikenon	1.9	50mm				30
Ricoh A-2	24x36mm	35mm	35VF	1983	Color Rikenon	2.8	35mm	programmed	30-250		70
RIcoh AD-1	24x36mm	35mm	35VF	1983	Color Rikenon	2.8	38mm	programmed	30-250		70
Ricoh AF-2	24x36mm	35mm	35AF	1983	Color Rikenon	2.8	38mm	programmed	1/8-500		70
Ricoh AF-2D	24x36mm	35mm	35AF	1983	Color Rikenon	2.8	38mm	programmed	1/8-500		100
Ricoh AF-5	24x36mm	35mm	35AF	1985	Color Rikenon	2.8	38mm	programmed	1/8-500		70
Ricoh AF-5D	24x36mm	35mm	35AF	1985	Color Rikenon	2.8	38mm	programmed	1/8-500		70
Ricoh AF-7	24x36mm	35mm	35AF	1985	Color Rikenon	2.8	38mm	programmed	1/8-500		60
Ricoh AF-9	24x36mm	35mm	35AF	1985	Ricoh	3.2	35mm	programmed	1/6-500		50
Ricoh AF-40	24x36mm	35mm	35AF	1987		2.8	38mm	programmed	1/8-500		70
Ricoh AF-50	24x36mm	35mm	35AF	1987		3.5	35mm	programmed	30-500		90
Ricoh AF-50D	24x36mm	35mm	35AF	1987		3.5	35mm	programmed	30-500		110
Ricoh AF-55	24x36mm	35mm	35AF	1989		3.9	35mm	programmed	30-500		50
Ricoh AF-55D	24x36mm	35mm	35AF	1989		3.9	35mm	programmed	30-500		60
Ricoh AF-60	24x36mm	35mm	35AF	1985		3.5	35mm	programmed	30-500		50
Ricoh AF-66	24x36mm	35mm	35AF	1993		3.9	35mm	programmed	125-600		50
Ricoh AF-70	24x36mm	35mm	35AF	1987		3.5	35mm	programmed	30-500		90
Ricoh AF-70D	24x36mm	35mm	35AF	1987		3.5	35mm	programmed	30-500		110
Ricoh AF-77	24x36mm	35mm	35AF	1994		4.5	34mm	programmed	50-100		60
Ricoh AF-77 Data	24x36mm	35mm	35AF	1994		4.5	34mm	programmed	50-100		70
Ricoh AF-303	24x36mm	35mm	35AF	1987		2.8	38mm	programmed	1/8-500		50
Ricoh AF-500	24x36mm	35mm	35AF	1988		3.5	35mm	programmed	30-500		50
Ricoh AF-500D	24x36mm	35mm	35AF	1988		3.5	35mm	programmed	30-500		50
Ricoh AF-505	24x36mm	35mm	35AF	1987		3.5	35mm	programmed	30-500		50
Ricoh AF-505D	24x36mm	35mm	35AF	1994		4.5	34mm	programmed	50-100		50
Ricoh Auto 35	24x36mm	35mm	35VF	1960	Ricoh	4	40mm		1/25-170		40
Ricoh Auto 35-L	24x36mm	35mm	35VF	1960	Ricoh	4	40mm		1/25-170		40
Ricoh Auto 35-V	24x36mm	35mm	35VF	1961							50
Ricoh Auto 66	6x6cm	120	TLR	1960	Ricoh	3.5	80mm	Seikosha-L	1-250	Mc365	200
Ricoh Auto 126	28x28mm	126	126VF	1960	Rikenon	2.8	35mm	Copal	1/30, 125		50
Ricoh Auto Half	18x24mm	35mm	35Half	1960	Ricoh	2.8	25mm	Seikosha	1/30, 125		50
Ricoh Auto Half E	18x24mm	35mm	35Half	1960	Ricoh	2.8	25mm	Seikosha	1/30, 125	A2151	50
Ricoh Auto Half E2	18x24mm	35mm	35Half	1960	Ricoh	2.8	25mm	Seikosha	1/30, 125		70
Ricoh Auto Half EF	18x24mm	35mm	35Half	1960	Ricoh	2.8	25mm	Seikosha	1/30, 125		60
Ricoh Auto Half EF2	18x24mm	35mm	35Half	1960	Ricoh	2.8	25mm	Seikosha	1/30, 125		60

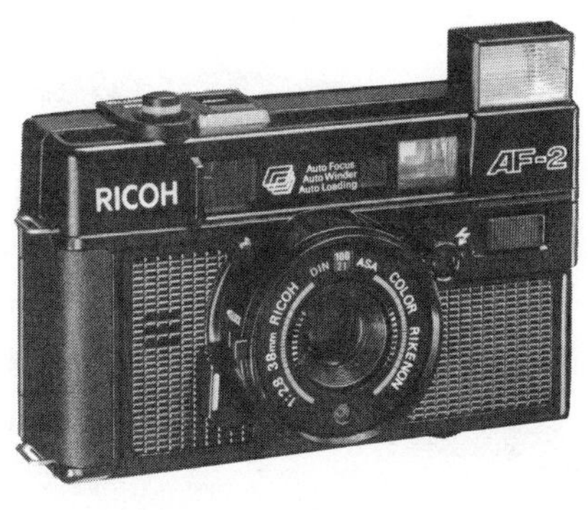

Ricoh AF-2

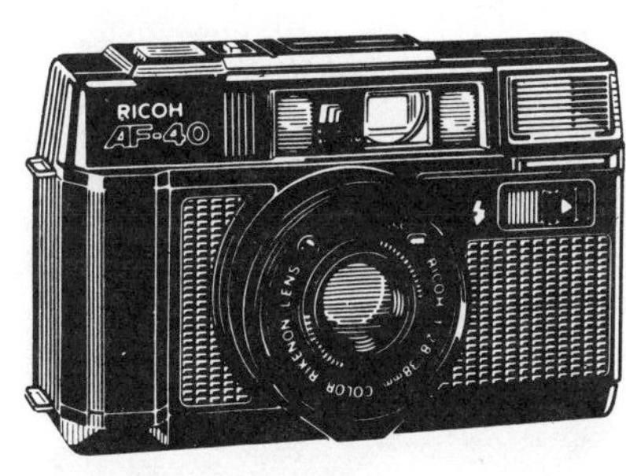

Ricoh AF-40

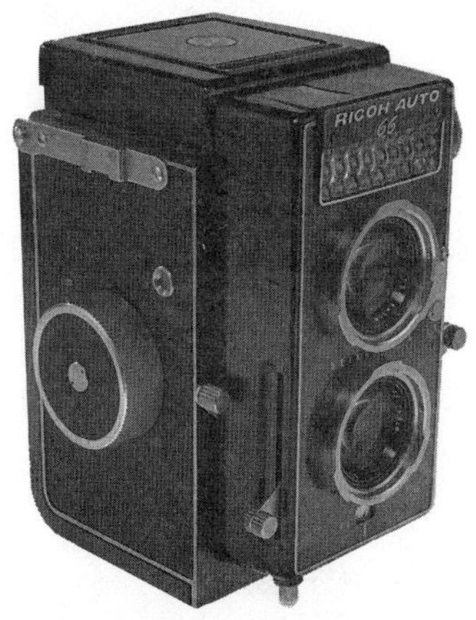

Ricoh Auto 66

MODEL	FORMAT	FILM	TYPE	Year	LENS	Apert	FL	SHUTTER	SPEEDS	ILLUS	U.S.$
Ricoh Auto Half Pro	18x24mm	35mm	35Half	1960	Ricoh	2.8	25mm	Seikosha	1/30, 125		70
Ricoh Auto Half S	18x24mm	35mm	35Half	1960	Ricoh	2.8	25mm	Seikosha	1/30, 125		50
Ricoh Auto Half SE	18x24mm	35mm	35Half	1967	Ricoh	2.8	25mm	Seikosha	1/30, 125		60
Ricoh Auto Half SE2	18x24mm	35mm	35Half	1960	Ricoh	2.8	25mm	Seikosha	1/30, 125		70
Ricoh Auto Half SL	18x24mm	35mm	35Half	1960	Ricoh	2.8	25mm	Seikosha	1/30, 125	A902	50
Ricoh Auto Half Zone Foc.	18x24mm	35mm	35Half	1960	Ricoh	2.8	25mm	Seikosha	1/30, 125		70
Ricoh Auto Shot	24x36mm	35mm	35VF	1960	Rikenon	2.8	35mm	Copal	1/30, 125		60
Ricoh Auto TLS EE	24x36mm	35mm	35SLR	1973	Auto Rikenon	1.7	50mm	TTL CdS	1-1000,B		50
Ricoh Caddy	18x24mm	35mm	35Half	1962							60
Ricoh CR-5	24x36mm	35mm	35SLR	1983	Rikenon	2	50mm	focal plane	1/8-1000		70
Ricoh Diacord G	6x6cm	120	TLR	1958	Ricoh	3.5	8cm	Citizen-MV	B,1-300		50
Ricoh Diacord L	6x6cm	120	TLR	1958	Rikenon	3.5	8cm	Seiko. MXL		Mc365	60
Ricoh FF-1	24x36mm	35mm	35Fold	1980	Rikenon	2.8					80
Ricoh FF-1S	24x36mm	35mm	35Fold	1983	Color Rikenon	2.8	36mm	programmed	2-1/500		70
Ricoh FF-3AF	24x36mm	35mm	35AF	1983	Ricoh			programmed	1/6-500		90
Ricoh FF-3AF Super	24x36mm	35mm	35AF	1985	Ricoh	3.2	35mm	programmed	1/6-500		100
Ricoh FF-3DAF	24x36mm	35mm	35AF	1985	Ricoh	3.2	35mm	programmed	1/6-500		50
Ricoh FF-8 WR	24x36mm	35mm	35AF	1993			28mm				70
Ricoh FF-8 WR Date	24x36mm	35mm	35AF	1993			28mm				70
Ricoh FF-9	24x36mm	35mm	35AF	1989		3.5	35mm	programmed	¼-400		70
Ricoh FF-9D	24x36mm	35mm	35AF	1989		3.5	35mm	programmed	¼-400		90
Ricoh FF-9s	24x36mm	35mm	35AF	1991		3.5	35mm	programmed	¼-400		70
Ricoh FF-10 Twin	24x36mm	35mm	35AF-Bif	1993	Ricoh	4.5	35mm	programmed	1/3-350		70
Ricoh FF-10 Twin Data	24x36mm	35mm	35AF-Bif	1993	Ricoh	4.5	35mm	programmed	1/3-350		70
Ricoh FF-10 Twin Super	24x36mm	35mm	35AF-Bif	1994	Ricoh	4.5	35mm	programmed	1/3-350		140
Ricoh FF-10 Zoom	24x36mm	35mm	35AFZ	1993		4.5-6.9	38-60	programmed	¼-300		70
Ricoh FF-10s	24x36mm	35mm	35AFZ	1994		4.5-6.9	38-60	programmed	¼-300		70
Ricoh FF-20 Wide Zoom	24x36mm	35mm	35AFZ	1994	Ricoh Zoom	4.8-8.8	32-64	programmed	1/3-300		220
Ricoh FF-20 Wide Zoom D	24x36mm	35mm	35AFZ	1994	Ricoh Zoom	4.8-8.8	32-64	programmed	1/3-300		230
Ricoh FF-70	24x36mm	35mm	35AF	1987		2.8	35mm	programmed	2-1/500		130
Ricoh FF-70D	24x36mm	35mm	35AF	1987		2.8	35mm	programmed	2-1/500		90
Ricoh FF-90	24x36mm	35mm	35AF	1987		2.8	35mm	programmed	2-1/500		130
Ricoh FF-90D	24x36mm	35mm	35AF	1987		2.8	35mm	programmed	2-1/500		90
Ricoh FF-300	24x36mm	35mm	35AF	1987		2.8	35mm	programmed	2-1/500		120
Ricoh FF-700	24x36mm	35mm	35AF	1987		2.8	35mm	programmed	2-1/500		120
Ricoh FF-700D	24x36mm	35mm	35AF	1987		2.8	35mm	programmed	2-1/500		120
Ricoh Hi-Color 35	18x24mm	35mm	35Half	1968	Rikenon	2.8			30-300		70
Ricoh Hi-Color 35S	18x24mm	35mm	35Half	1970	Rikenon	2.8					70
Ricoh Jet	24x36mm	35mm	35RF	1960	Rikenon	1.9					50
Ricoh KR-5	24x36mm	35mm	35SLR	1979	Rikenon	2.2	55mm	focal plane	1/8-500		100
Ricoh KR-5 III	24x36mm	35mm	35SLR	1994	Rikenon	1.7	50mm	focal plane	1-2000		220
Ricoh KR-5 Super	24x36mm	35mm	35SLR	1983	Rikenon	2	50mm	focal plane	1/8-1000		100

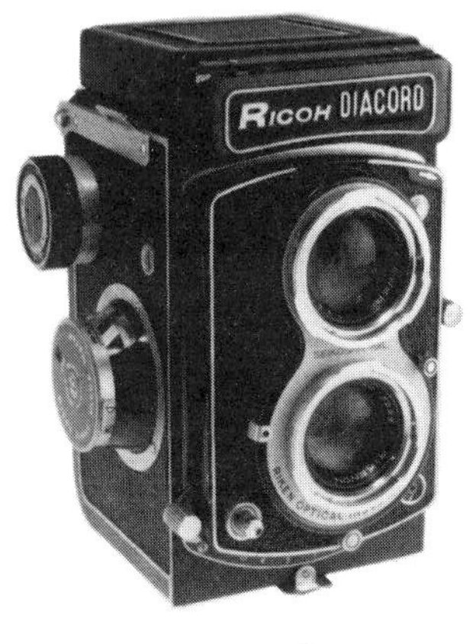

Ricoh Diacord L

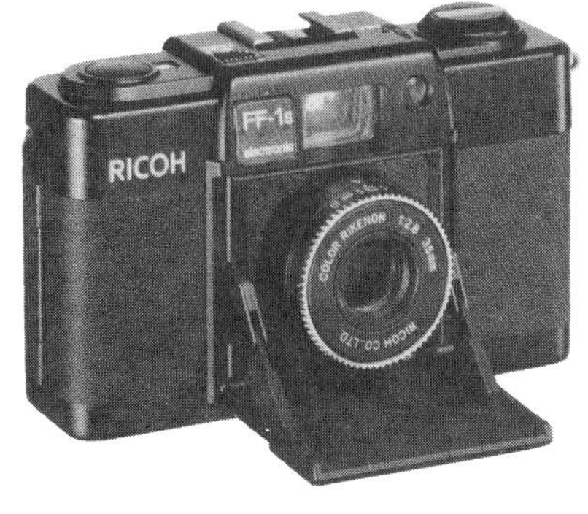

Ricoh FF-1S

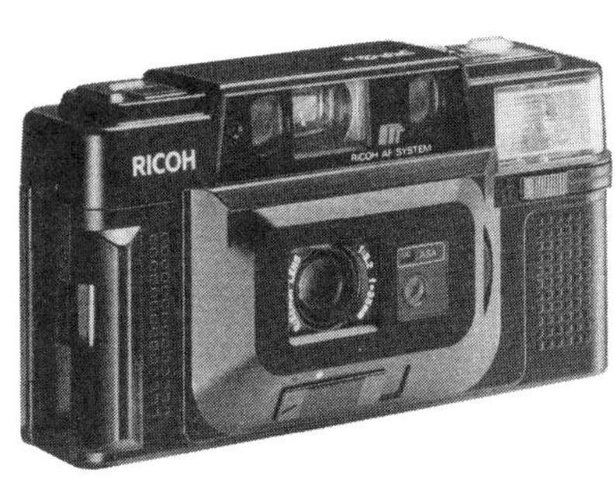

Ricoh FF-3AF

MODEL	FORMAT	FILM	TYPE	Year	LENS	Apert	FL	SHUTTER	SPEEDS	ILLUS	U.S.$
Ricoh KR-5 Super II	24x36mm	35mm	35SLR	1991	Rikenon	1.7	50mm	focal plane	1-2000		150
Ricoh KR-10	24x36mm	35mm	35SLR	1983	Rikenon	1.7	50mm	focal plane	4-1000		140
Ricoh KR-10 M	24x36mm	35mm	35SLR	1991	Rikenon	1.7	50mm	focal plane	16-2000		200
Ricoh KR-10 Super	24x36mm	35mm	35SLR	1983	Rikenon	1.7	50mm	focal plane	16-1000		170
Ricoh KR-10 X	24x36mm	35mm	35SLR	1987	Rikenon	1.7	50mm	focal plane	16-1000		140
Ricoh KR-30 SP	24x36mm	35mm	35SLR	1987	Rikenon	1.7	50mm	focal plane	16-2000		150
Ricoh L-20	24x36mm	35mm	35VF	1990	Ricoh	4.5	35mm		1/125		40
Ricoh LX-22	24x36mm	35mm	35VF	1993	Ricoh	4.5	35mm		1/125		60
Ricoh LX-25	24x36mm	35mm	35VF	1994	Ricoh	4.5	35mm		50-100		40
Ricoh LX-33 W	24x36mm	35mm	35AW	1994		4.5	35mm		50-100		50
Ricoh LX-33 W Data	24x36mm	35mm	35AW	1994		4.5	35mm		50-100		60
Ricoh Mate	24x36mm	35mm	35RF	1960	Ricoh	2.8					50
Ricoh Max	24x36mm	35mm	35RF	1959	Ricoh	2					50
Ricoh Mirai	24x36mm	35mm	35AFSLR	1989	Ricoh	4.2-5.6	35-135	focal plane	32-2000		290
Ricoh Mirai 105	24x36mm	35mm	35AFSLR	1990	Ricoh	4.5-6	38-105	focal plane	2-1/500		190
Ricoh Mirai Zoom 3	24x36mm	35mm	35AFSLR	1993	Ricoh	3.8-7.5	35-105	programmed	¼-500		130
Ricoh R 1	24x36mm	35mm	35VF	1994	Ricoh	3.5	30mm	programmed	2-1/400		180
Ricoh RT-550	24x36mm	35mm	35AF-BiF	1990	Ricoh AF	3.5/6.6	35/70	programmed	1-500		110
Ricoh RT-550 Date	24x36mm	35mm	35AF-BiF	1990		3.5/6.6	35/70	programmed	1-500		120
Ricoh RW-1	24x36mm	35mm	35AW-AF	1994	Ricoh	4.5	34mm	programmed	50-100		70
Ricoh RW-1 Data	24x36mm	35mm	35AW-AF	1994	Ricoh	4.5	34mm	programmed	50-100		100
Ricoh RZ 105 Zoom	24x36mm	35mm	35AFZ	1993	Ricoh Zoom	3.6-5.5	38-105	programmed	1-500		200
Ricoh RZ 105 Zoom Date	24x36mm	35mm	35AFZ	1993	Ricoh Zoom	3.6-5.5	38-105	programmed	1-500		240
Ricoh RZ-700	24x36mm	35mm	35AFZ	1991	Ricoh Zoom	4-7.6	35-70	programmed			140
Ricoh RZ-750	24x36mm	35mm	35AFZ	1990	Ricoh Zoom	3.5-6.7	38-76	programmed			190
Ricoh RZ-800	24x36mm	35mm	35AFZ	1992	Ricoh Zoom	4.5-6.4	38-80	programmed	½-400		100
Ricoh RZ-800 Data	24x36mm	35mm	35AFZ	1992	Ricoh Zoom	4.5-6.4	38-80	programmed	½-400		120
Ricoh RZ-900	24x36mm	35mm	35AFZ	1994	Ricoh Zoom	4.5-7.2	38-90	programmed	1-400		120
Ricoh RZ-900 Data	24x36mm	35mm	35AFZ	1994	Ricoh Zoom	4.5-7.2	38-90	programmed	1-400		140
Ricoh RZ-1000	24x36mm	35mm	35AFZ	1994	Ricoh Zoom		38-105	programmed	½-400		200
Ricoh S-3	24x36mm	35mm	35RF	1959		2.8	45mm				50
Ricoh S-30	24x36mm	35mm	35AF	1989		3.9	35mm		1/125		70
Ricoh S-30D	24x36mm	35mm	35AF	1989		3.9	35mm		1/125		90
Ricoh Singlex	24x36mm	35mm	35SLR	1964	Auto Rikenon	1.4	55mm	focal plane	1-1000,B	Mc365	90
Ricoh Singlex II	24x36mm	35mm	35SLR	1976	Rikenon Auto	1.4	50mm	focal plane	1-1000		110
Ricoh Singlex TLS	24x36mm	35mm	35SLR	1968	Rikenon Auto	1.4	50mm	focal plane	1-1000	A1684	80
Ricoh Six	6x6cm	120	HzFoldRo	1952	Orinar	3.5	80mm	Riken	25-100,B	Mc365	80
Ricoh SLX 500	24x36mm	35mm	35SLR	1976					1/500		70
Ricoh Super 44	4x4cm	127	TLR	1958	Riken	3.5	60mm	Citizen-MV	1-400,B		50
Ricoh Super Shot	24x36mm	35mm	35VF	1960	Rikenon	1.7	43mm	programmed	15-500		50
Ricoh Teleca 240	18x24mm	35mm	35Half	1971	Rikenon	3.5	163mm	Copal	60-250		540
Ricoh TF-200	24x36mm	35mm	35AF-BiF	1987	Rikenon	3.5/6	38/65	programmed	1/6-500		100

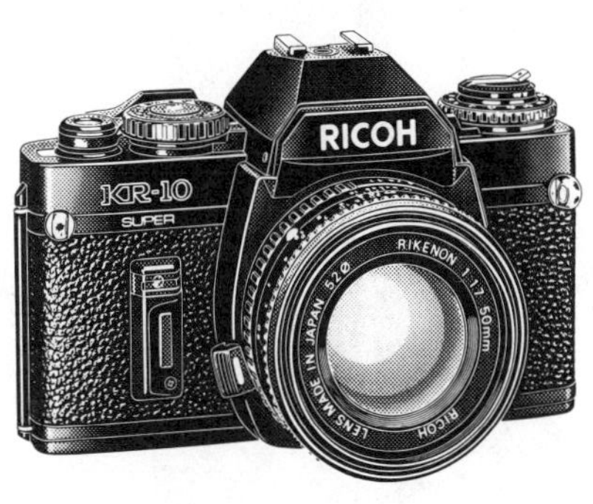

Ricoh KR-10 Super

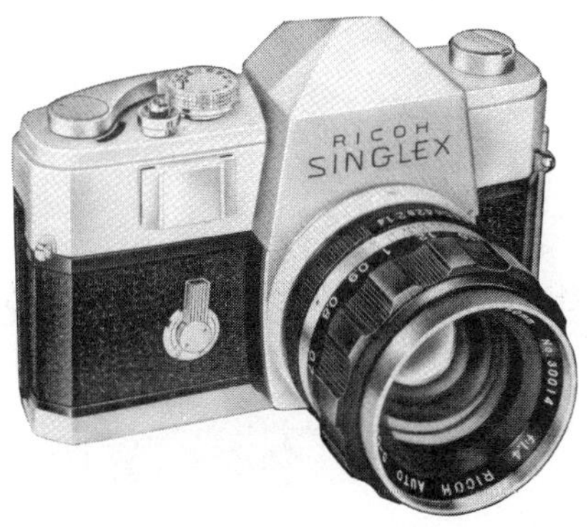

Ricoh Singlex

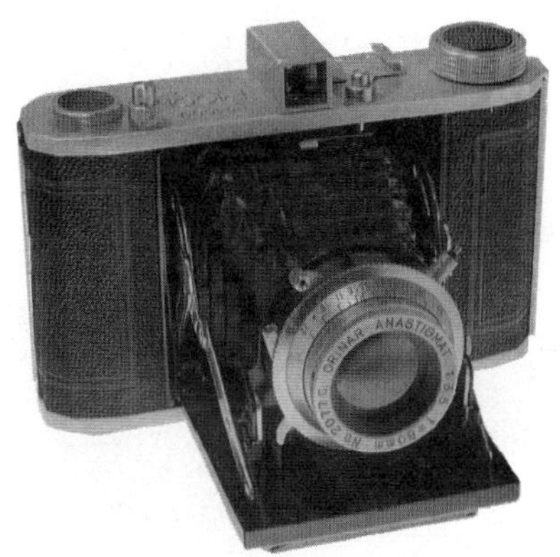

Ricoh Six

MODEL	FORMAT	FILM	TYPE	Year	LENS	Apert	FL	SHUTTER	SPEEDS	ILLUS	U.S.$
Ricoh TF-200 D	24x36mm	35mm	35AF-BiF	1987	Rikenon	3.5/6	38/65	programmed	1/6-500		100
Ricoh TF-500	24x36mm	35mm	35AF-BiF	1987	Rikenon	2.8	35mm	programmed	1-500		220
Ricoh TF-900	24x36mm	35mm	35AF-BiF	1987	Rikenon	2.8	35mm	programmed	1-500		220
Ricoh TF-900D	24x36mm	35mm	35AF-BiF	1987	Rikenon	2.8	35mm	programmed	1-500		180
Ricoh Wide	24x36mm	35mm	35RF	1960		2.4	35mm	Seiko. MXL			70
Ricoh XF-20	24x36mm	35mm	35VF	1994		4.5	35mm				40
Ricoh XF-30	24x36mm	35mm	35VF	1986	Color Rikenon	4	35mm	programmed	30-500		70
Ricoh XF-30 Super	24x36mm	35mm	35VF	1991	Color Rikenon	3.9	35mm	programmed	30-500		80
Ricoh XF-30D	24x36mm	35mm	35VF	1986	Color Rikenon	4	35mm	programmed	30-500		30
Ricoh XR-1	24x36mm	35mm	35SLR	1977	Rikenon	1.7	50mm	focal plane	1-1000		150
Ricoh XR-01	24x36mm	35mm	35SLR	1977	Rikenon	1.4	50mm	focal plane	1-1000		160
Ricoh XR-1s	24x36mm	35mm	35SLR	1979	Rikenon	1.7	50mm	focal plane	1-1000		140
Ricoh XR-1s	24x36mm	35mm	35SLR	1979	Rikenon	1.4	50mm	focal plane	1-1000		140
Ricoh XR-2	24x36mm	35mm	35SLR	1979	Rikenon	1.7	50mm	focal plane	8-1/1000		140
Ricoh XR-2	24x36mm	35mm	35SLR	1979	Rikenon	1.4	50mm	focal plane	8-1/1000		170
Ricoh XR-2s	24x36mm	35mm	35SLR	1979	Rikenon	1.7	50mm	focal plane	8-1/1000		170
Ricoh XR-2s	24x36mm	35mm	35SLR	1979	Rikenon	1.4	50mm	focal plane	8-1/1000		170
Ricoh XR-6	24x36mm	35mm	35AFSLR	1979	AF Rikenon	2	50mm	focal plane	1-1000		100
Ricoh XR-7	24x36mm	35mm	35SLR	1979	Rikenon	1.7	50mm	focal plane	16-1000		140
Ricoh XR-7	24x36mm	35mm	35SLR	1979	Rikenon	1.4	50mm	focal plane	16-1000		170
Ricoh XR-7M II	24x36mm	35mm	35SLR	1995	XR Rikenon	2.8	50mm	focal plane	8-1000		190
Ricoh XR-8	24x36mm	35mm	35SLR	1991	Rikenon	1.7	50mm	focal plane	1-2000		150
Ricoh XR-8 Super	24x36mm	35mm	35SLR	1994	Rikenon	1.7	50mm	focal plane	1-2000		180
Ricoh XR-10	24x36mm	35mm	35SLR	1987	Rikenon	1.7	50mm	focal plane	16-1000		140
Ricoh XR-10 Super	24x36mm	35mm	35SLR	1984	Rikenon	1.7	50mm	focal plane	16-1000		140
Ricoh XR-10M	24x36mm	35mm	35SLR	1991	Rikenon	1.7	50mm	focal plane	16-2000		200
Ricoh XR-20 SP	24x36mm	35mm	35SLR	1985	Rikenon	1.7	50mm	focal plane	16-2000		150
Ricoh XR-500	24x36mm	35mm	35SLR	1979	Rikenon	2.8	50mm	focal plane	1/8-500		170
Ricoh XR-500	24x36mm	35mm	35SLR	1979	Rikenon	2	50mm	focal plane	1/8-500		140
Ricoh XR-F	24x36mm	35mm	35SLR	1983	Rikenon	1.7	50mm	focal plane	1-1000		200
Ricoh XR-M	24x36mm	35mm	35SLR	1988	Rikenon	1.4	50mm	focal plane	16-2000		260
Ricoh XR-P	24x36mm	35mm	35SLR	1986	Rikenon	1.7	50mm	focal plane	4-2000		330
Ricoh XR-S	24x36mm	35mm	35SLR	1983	Rikenon	1.4	50mm	focal plane	16-1000	A1705	220
Ricoh XR Solar	24x36mm	35mm	35SLR	1994	Rikenon	1.4	50mm	focal plane	1-2000		240
Ricoh XR-X	24x36mm	35mm	35SLR	1988	Rikenon	1.4	50mm	focal plane	16-2000		260
Ricoh XR-X 3PF	24x36mm	35mm	35SLR	1995	Rikenon	1.7	50mm	focal plane	32-3000		330
Ricoh YF-20	24x36mm	35mm	35VF	1987		4	35mm		1/125		40
Ricoh YF-20D	24x36mm	35mm	35VF	1988		4	35mm		1/125		50
Ricoh YF-20X	24x36mm	35mm	35VF	1994	Rikenon	4.5	35mm		1/125		50
Ricohflex III	6x6cm	120	TLR	1950	Ricoh Anastigmat	3.5	80mm	Riken	25-100,B		90
Ricohflex IIIB	6x6cm	120	TLR	1951	Ricoh Anastigmat	3.5	80mm	Riken	25-100,B		70
Ricohflex IV	6x6cm	120	TLR	1952	Ricoh Anastigmat	3.5	80mm	Riken	25-100,B		80

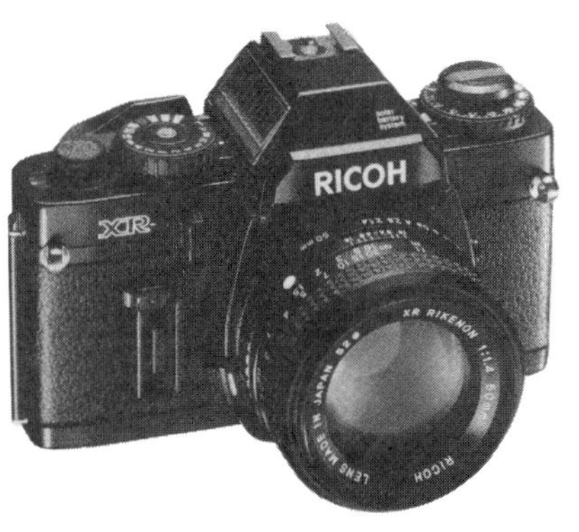

Ricoh XR-S

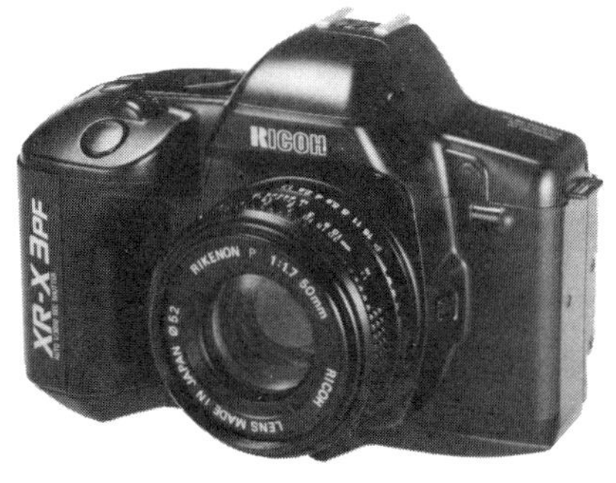

Ricoh XR-X 3PF

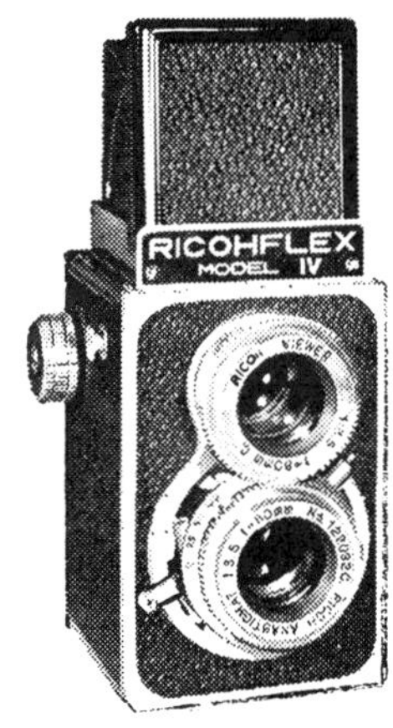

Ricohflex IV

MODEL	FORMAT	FILM	TYPE	Year	LENS	Apert	FL	SHUTTER	SPEEDS	ILLUS	U.S.$
Ricohflex VI	6x6cm	120	TLR	1953	Ricoh Anastigmat	3.5	80mm	Riken	25-100,B	Mc366	60
Ricohflex VII	6x6cm	120	TLR	1954	Ricoh Anastigmat	3.5	80mm	Riken	25-100,B		70
Ricohflex VIIM	6x6cm	120	TLR	1956	Ricoh Anastigmat	3.5	80mm				80
Ricohflex VIIS	6x6cm	120	TLR	1955	Ricoh Anastigmat	3.5	80mm	Riken	25-100,B		60
Ricohflex B	6x6cm	120	TLR	1941		4.5	75mm				130
Ricohflex Dia	6x6cm	120	TLR	1955	Ricoh	3.5	80mm	Citizen-MXV	1-400,B		70
Ricohflex Dia L	6x6cm	120	TLR	1957		3.5	80mm				60
Ricohflex Dia M	6x6cm	120	TLR	1956		3.5	80mm				90
Ricohflex Diacode G	6x6cm	120	TLR	1958		3.5	80mm				70
Ricohflex Holiday	6x6cm	120	TLR	1956		3.5	80mm				70
Ricohflex Million	6x6cm	120	TLR	1957	Ricoh	3.5	80mm				70
Ricohflex New Dia	6x6cm	120	TLR	1956		3.5	80mm				90
Ricohflex TLS-401	24x36mm	35mm	35SLR	1970	Auto Rikenon	1.7	50mm	Copal	1-1000		130
Ricohl	3x4cm	127	RigidRo	1941		3.5	50mm			Mc366	380
Ricohlet II	24x36mm	35mm	35RF	1955	Ricoh	3.5	45mm				30
Ricohmatic 35	24x36mm	35mm	35RF	1961		2.8	40mm		200		50
Ricohmatic 44	4x4mm	127	TLR	1956	Riken	3.5	60mm	Riken	32-170,B		70
Ricohmatic 126	28x28mm	126	126VF	1965	Rikenon	2.8	35mm	Copal	1/30, 125		50
Ricohmatic 225	6x6cm	120	TLR	1959	Rikenon	3.5	80mm	Seikosha-SLV	1-500,B		90
Ricolet	24x36mm	35mm	35VF	1954	Ricoh	3.5	45mm	Riken	25-50-100		50
Ricolet S	24x36mm	35mm	35VF	1955	Ricoh	3.5	4.5cm	Riken	10-200	Mc366	30
Ricomatic 110 X	13x17mm	110	110VF	1974		2.8			30-250		50
Ricomatic 600 M	13x17mm	110	110VF	1976		2.8			30-250		50
Riken	3x4cm	127		1939							50
Riken 35 S	24x36mm	35mm	35RF	1957		2.8	4.5cm	Riken	10-300		50
Roico	4x4cm	127	TelecsRo	1940	Roico Anastigmat	3.5	60mm		1/5-200	Mc366	100
Roico	4x4cm	127	TelecsRo	1943	Roico Anastigmat	3.5	60mm	R.K.K.	T,B,1-200		100
Steky	10x14mm	16mm	Submin	1947	Stekinar Anast.	3.5	25mm		25-100	Mc366	130
Steky "Made in Tokyo"	10x14mm	16mm	Submin	1947	Stekinar Anast.	3.5	25mm		25-100	Mc366	300
Steky II	10x14mm	16mm	Submin	1950	Stekinar Anast.	3.5	25mm		25-100		130
Steky III	10x14mm	16mm	Submin	1950	Stekinar Anast.	3.5	25mm		25-100		120
Steky IIIa	10x14mm	16mm	Submin	1950	Stekinar Anast.	3.5	25mm		25-100		130
Steky IIIb	10x14mm	16mm	Submin	1950	Stekinar Anast.	3.5	25mm		25-100		140
Super Ricohflex	6x6cm	120	TLR	1955	Ricoh Anastigmat	3.5	80mm	Riken	10-300,B		120
...RILEY RESEARCH - Santa Monica, CA											
Rilex Press	2¼x3¼"	120	FoldPress	1948	Tessar	4.5	127mm			Mc367	180
Rilex Press	2¼x3¼"	120	FoldPress	1948	Woll. Velostigmat	4.5	127mm				180
...RINGFOTO - Germany											
Rallye	24x36mm	35mm	35SLR	1970	Iscovitar	2.8	50mm	focal plane	30-1000		110
Rallye	24x36mm	35mm	35SLR	1970	Westromat	1.9	50mm	focal plane	30-1000		110
...(unknown)											
Rival	1⅝x2¼"	620	VtFoldRo	1953		4.5		Vario	25-200		30

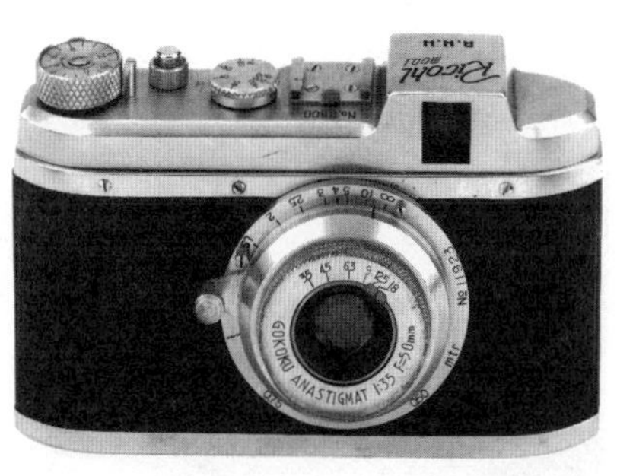
Ricohl

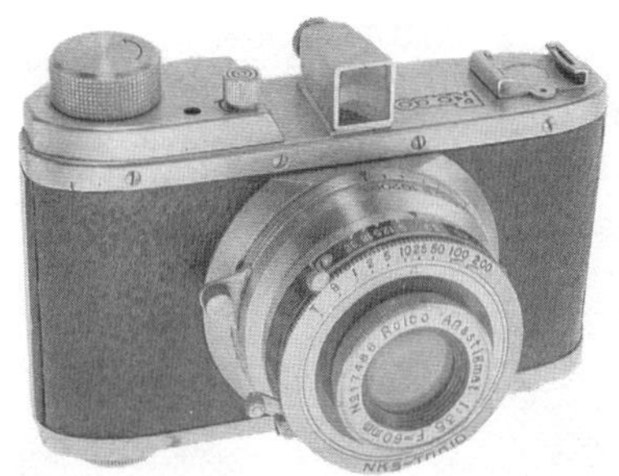
Roico

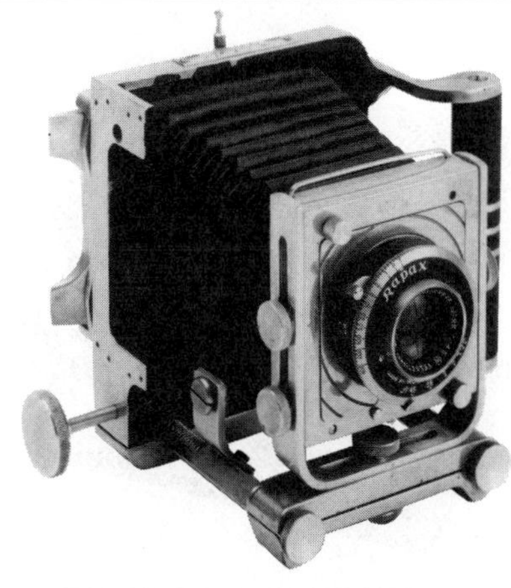
Rilex Press

MODEL	FORMAT	FILM	TYPE	Year	LENS	Apert	FL	SHUTTER	SPEEDS	ILLUS	U.S.$
Rival	1 5/8x2¼"	120	VtFoldRo	1953		4.5		Vario	25-200		30
Rival 2¼x3¼"	2¼x3¼"	620	VtFoldRo	1953		4.5		Vario	25-200		20
Rival 2¼x3¼"	2¼x3¼"	120	VtFoldRo	1953		4.5		Vario	25-200		20
Rival 35	24x36mm	35mm	35Fold	1950	Radionar	3.5	50mm	Prontor-S	1-300	Mc367	50
Rival 35	24x36mm	35mm	35Fold	1950	Ennagon	3.5	50mm	Prontor-S	1-300	Mc367	50
Rival 120	6x9cm	120	RollBox	1950		4.5		Vario	25-200		20
...RO-TO - Turin, Italy											
Elvo	3x4cm	127	BakFoldRo	1938	achromatic	8					70
Nea Fotos	24x36mm	35mm	35RF	1948	achromatic	7.7	54mm		25-100,B		30
OK	6x9cm	120	MetalBox	1950							120
...ROBERTS (John Roberts) - Boston											
Daguerreotype Camera	3¼x4¼"	Dag	Dag	1852	various						7000
Daguerreotype Camera	8x10"	Dag	Dag	1850	various						10000
...ROBINSON (J. Robinson & Sons)											
Field camera	12x16.5	plate	Field	1900	Rapid Rectilinear					A1379	570
Luzo	6x6cm	plate	DetectivBox	1889	Aplanat	8	75	rotary		Mc367	1200
Luzo	6x6cm	120	DetectivBox	1889	Aplanat	8	75	rotary		Mc367	1300
...ROCAMCO PRODUCTS - Boonton, NJ											
Rocamco	2.5x3cm	35mm	MetalBox	1936	Meniscus					Mc368	160
Rocamco No. 3 Daylight	32x32mm	35mm	BakeliteRoll	1938						Mc368	50
...ROCHE (J. Roche) - Villeurbanne, France											
Allox	6x9cm	120	RigidRo	1948	achromatic	11			I,P	F777	70
Rox	6x9cm	120	RigidRo	1948	Aplanat	8	105mm	Gitzo	25-200	Mc368	140
Rox	6x9cm	120	RigidRo	1948	Trylor	4.5		Gitzo	25-200	F797	140
...ROCHECHOUARD - Paris											
Le Multicolore	9x12cm	plate	MagBox	1912	Rapid Rectilinear			guillotine			1300
...ROCHESTER CAMERA MFG. CO.											
Cycle Poco No. 1 4x5"	4x5"	plate	HzFoldPl	1893	B&L Rapid Rect.			Unicum			100
Cycle Poco No. 1 5x7"	5x7"	plate	HzFoldPl	1893	Rapid Rectilinear			Unicum			140
Cycle Poco No. 2 4x5"	4x5"	plate	HzFoldPl	1893	B&L Rapid Rect.			Unicum			100
Cycle Poco No. 2 5x7"	5x7"	plate	HzFoldPl	1893	Rapid Rectilinear			Unicum			140
Cycle Poco No. 3 4x5"	4x5"	plate	HzFoldPl	1893	B&L Rapid Rect.			Unicum			100
Cycle Poco No. 3 5x7"	5x7"	plate	HzFoldPl	1893	Rapid Rectilinear			Unicum			140
Cycle Poco No. 4 4x5"	4x5"	plate	HzFoldPl	1893	B&L Rapid Rect.			Unicum		Mc368	100
Cycle Poco No. 4 5x7"	5x7"	plate	HzFoldPl	1893	Rapid Rectilinear			Unicum			140
Cycle Poco No. 5 4x5"	4x5"	plate	HzFoldPl	1893	B&L Rapid Rect.			Unicum			100
Cycle Poco No. 5 5x7"	5x7"	plate	HzFoldPl	1893	Rapid Rectilinear			Unicum			140
Cycle Poco No. 6 4x5"	4x5"	plate	HzFoldPl	1893	B&L Rapid Rect.			Unicum			100
Cycle Poco No. 7 4x5"	4x5"	plate	HzFoldPl	1893	B&L Rapid Rect.			Unicum			100
Favorite 5x8"	5x8"	plate	Tailboard	1890	Brass Emile		15 5/8"				290
Favorite 8x10"	8x10"	plate	Tailboard	1890	Brass Emile		18¼"				290
Folding Gem Poco 3¼x4¼"	3¼x4¼"	plate	FoldPl	1895							130

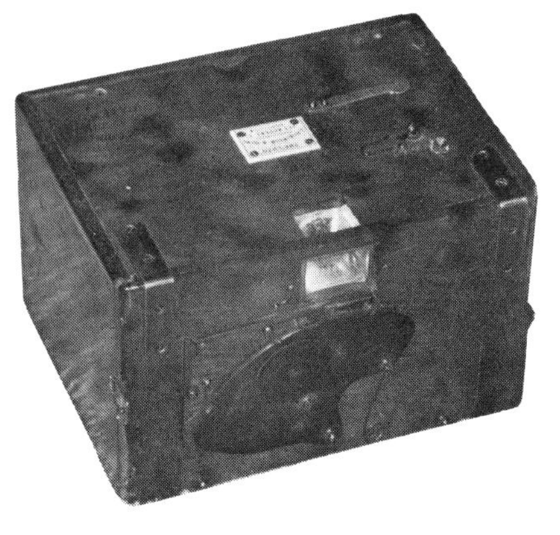

Robinson Luzo

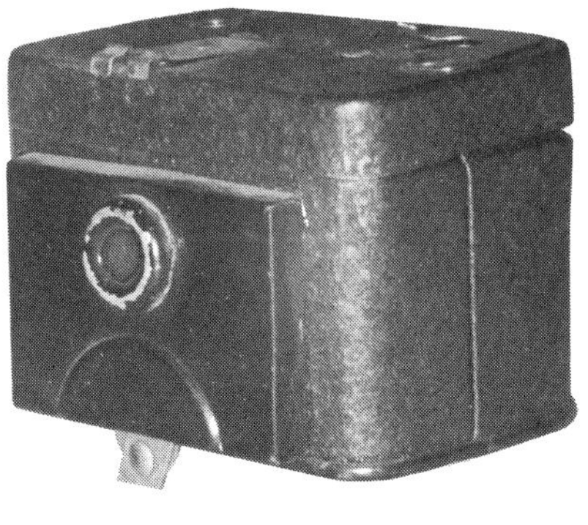

Rocamco

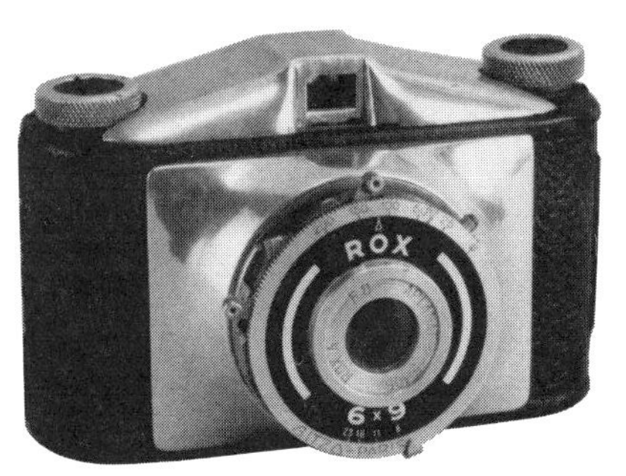

Roche Rox

MODEL	FORMAT	FILM	TYPE	Year	LENS	Apert	FL	SHUTTER	SPEEDS	ILLUS	U.S.$
Folding Gem Poco 4x5"	4x5"	plate	FoldPl	1895							140
Folding Poco Series A	4x5"	plate	HzFoldPl	1893	B&L Rapid Rect.			Unicum			100
Folding Poco Series B	4x5"	plate	HzFoldPl	1893	B&L Rapid Rect.			Unicum			100
Folding Poco Series C	4x5"	plate	HzFoldPl	1893	B&L Rapid Rect.			Unicum			100
Folding Rochester 4x5"	4x5"	plate	FoldPl	1892							470
Folding Rochester 5x7"	5x7"	plate	FoldPl	1892							470
Gem Poco	4x5"	plate	PlateBox	1897						Mc368	80
King 5x7"	5x7"	plate	Field	1898	various			various			300
King 6½x8½"	6½x8½"	plate	Field	1898	various			various			300
King 8x10"	8x10"	plate	Field	1898	various			various			300
King 11x14"	11x14"	plate	Field	1898	various			various			300
King Poco 4x5"	4x5"	plate	FoldPl	1899	Symmetrical			Unicum			200
King Poco 5x7"	5x7"	plate	FoldPl	1899	Symmetrical			Unicum		Mc368	230
King Poco 8x10"	8x10"	plate	FoldPl	1899	Symmetrical			Unicum			220
Pocket Poco	3¼x4¼"	plate	VtFoldPl	1893	Rapid Rectilinear			pneumatic		Mc368	90
Pocket Poco A	3¼x4¼"	plate	StrutPl	1903	B&L Achromatic			Automatic			200
Poco 8x10"	8x10"	plate	HzFoldPl	1893	B&L Symmetrical						140
Stereo Poco	5x7"	plate	StFoldPl	1898	Rapid Rectilinear			pneumatic			390
Telephoto Cycle Poco 4x5"	4x5"	plate	FoldPl	1891	B&L			Auto		Mc368	140
Telephoto Cycle Poco 4x5"	4x5"	plate	FoldPl	1891	B&L			Victor			140
Telephoto Cycle Poco 5x7"	5x7"	plate	FoldPl	1902	B&L Rapid Rect.			Auto			150
Telephoto C. Poco 6½x8½"	6½x8½"	plate	FoldPl	1902	B&L Rapid Rect.			Auto			220
Telephoto Poco 4x5"	4x5"	plate	H&S	1891	B&L			Auto			140
Telephoto Poco 4x5"	4x5"	plate	H&S	1891	B&L			Victor			140
Telephoto Poco 5x7"	5x7"	plate	H&S	1902	B&L Rapid Rect.			Auto			150
Telephoto Poco 6½x8½"	6½x8½"	plate	H&S	1902	B&L Rapid Rect.			Auto			220
Tuxedo	4x5"	plate	FoldPl	1892	B&L Rapid Rect.						310
View 5x7"	5x7"	plate	Tailboard	1899	various			various			250
View 6½x8½"	6½x8½"	plate	Tailboard	1899	various			various			250
View 8x10"	8x10"	plate	Tailboard	1899	various			various			250
...ROCHESTER OPTICAL CO.											
Carlton 4x5"	4x5"	plate	Field	1893	various			various		Mc369	290
Carlton 5x7"	5x7"	plate	Field	1893	various			various		Mc369	300
Carlton 6½x8½"	6½x8½"	plate	Field	1893	various			various		Mc369	290
Carlton 11x14"	11x14"	plate	Field	1893	various			various		Mc369	340
Cyclone Junior	3½x3½"	plate	PlateBox	1902	achromatic			Automatic	I,T		50
Cyclone Senior	4x5"	plate	PlateBox	1902	achromatic			Automatic	I,T		50
Cyko Reko	4x5"	plate	FoldPl	1900	Meniscus Achrom.			Unicum			130
Empire State View 5x7"	5x7"	plate	Field	1895	various		15.25"	various		Mc369	130
Empire State View 6½x8½"	6½x8½"	plate	Field	1895	various		16.25"	various		Mc369	130
Empire State View 8x10"	8x10"	plate	Field	1895	various		19"	various		Mc369	160
Empire State View 11x14"	11x14"	plate	Field	1895	various		23.5"	various		Mc369	260

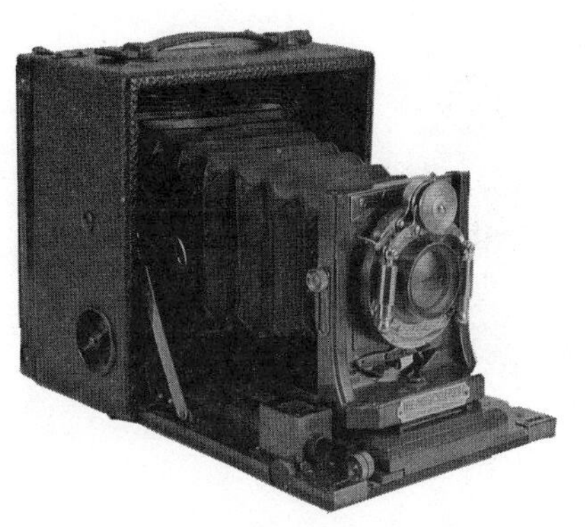

Roch. Telephoto Cycle Poco

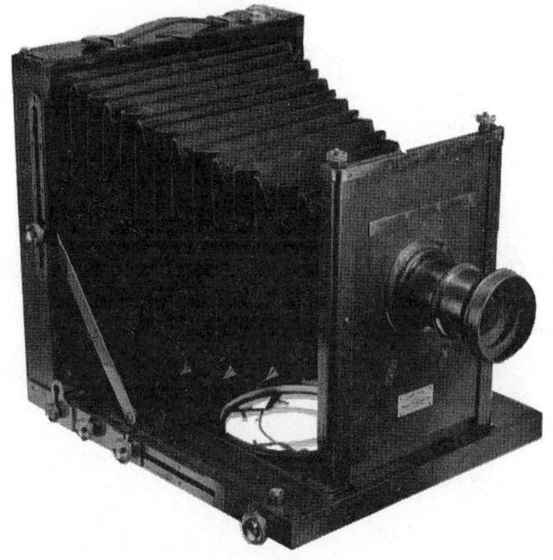

Rochester Carlton

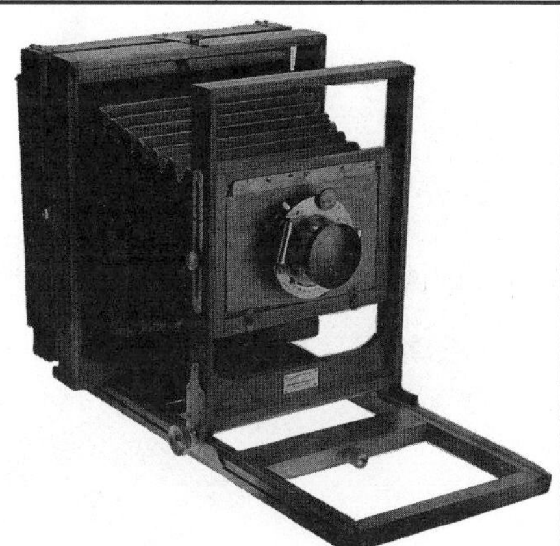

Empire State View

MODEL	FORMAT	FILM	TYPE	Year	LENS	Apert	FL	SHUTTER	SPEEDS	ILLUS	U.S.$
Folding Pocket Cyko No. 1	3¼x4⅓"	plate	FoldPl		Meniscus			Sector	I,T		350
Folding Premo Camera	4x5"	plate	FoldPl	1893	Rapid Rectilinear			Star		Mc370	170
Folding Premo Camera	5x7"	plate	FoldPl	1893	Rapid Rectilinear			Star			170
Folding Premo Camera	6½x8½"	plate	FoldPl	1893	Rapid Rectilinear			Star			170
Handy	4x5"	plate	DetectivBox	1892							150
Ideal 4x5"	4x5"	plate	Field	1885	various			various		Mc369	200
Ideal 5x7"	5x7"	plate	Field	1885	various			various			200
Ideal 6½x8½"	6½x8½"	plate	Field	1885	various			various			200
Ideal 8x10"	8x10"	plate	Field	1885	various			various			180
Long Focus Premo 4x5"	4x5	plate	FoldPl	1895						Mc370	230
Long Focus Premo 5x7"	5x7	plate	FoldPl	1895						Mc370	230
Long Focus Premo 6½x8½"	6½x8½"	plate	FoldPl	1895						Mc370	230
Magazine Cyclone 2	3¼x4¼"	plate	MagBox	1898	Meniscus			Sector		Mc369	80
Magazine Cyclone 2	4x5"	plate	MagBox	1898	Meniscus			Sector			80
Magazine Cyclone 4	3¼x4¼"	plate	MagBox	1898	Meniscus			Sector		Mc369	80
Magazine Cyclone 4	4x5"	plate	MagBox	1898	Meniscus			Sector			80
Magazine Cyclone 5	3¼x4¼"	plate	MagBox	1898	Meniscus			Sector		Mc369	80
Magazine Cyclone 5	4x5"	plate	MagBox	1898	Meniscus			Sector			80
Midget Pocket	6½x8½"	plate	Field	1886	various		20.25"	various			180
Monitor 6½x8½"	6½x8½"	plate	Field	1886	various		20.25"	various			220
Monitor 8x10"	8x10"	plate	Field	1886	various		24"	various		Mc369	260
New Model Impr. Stereo	5x7"	plate	SterTail	1895	various			various			480
New Model Impr. 4x5"	4x5"	plate	Tailboard	1895	various			various			220
New Model Impr. 5x7"	5x7"	plate	Tailboard	1895	various			various			230
New Model Impr. 6½x8½"	6½x8½"	plate	Tailboard	1895	various			various			220
New Model Impr. 8x10"	8x10"	plate	Tailboard	1895	various			various			250
New Model View 4x5"	4x5"	plate	Tailboard	1895	various			various		Mc369	230
New Model View 5x7"	5x7"	plate	Tailboard	1895	various			various			220
New Model View 6½x8½"	6½x8½"	plate	Tailboard	1895	various			various			220
New Model View 8x10"	8x10"	plate	Tailboard	1895	various			various			220
Peerless (view)	5x7"	plate	Field	1897	various			Wollensak			230
Pocket Premo	3¼x4¼"	plate	VtFoldPl	1903				B&L Automatic		Mc370	90
Pocket Premo	3¼x4¼"	plate	VtFoldPl	1903				Volute			90
Pony Premo No. 2	3¼x4¼"	plate	FoldPl	1905	Rapid Rectilinear			Gem		Mc369	130
Pony Premo No. 4 4x5"	4x5"	plate	FoldPl	1900	Rapid Rectilinear			Victor			160
Pony Premo No. 4 5x7"	5x7"	plate	FoldPl	1900	Dopp. Anast.			B&L Automatic			160
Pony Premo No. 5 4x5"	4x5"	plate	FoldPl	1898	Zeiss Anastigmat			B&L Automatic			120
Pony Premo No. 5 5x7"	5x7"	plate	FoldPl	1898	Zeiss Anastigmat			B&L Automatic			140
Pony Premo No. 5 6½x8½"	6½x8½"	plate	FoldPl	1898	Zeiss Anastigmat			B&L Automatic			160
Pony Premo No. 6 5x7"	5x7"	plate	FoldPl	1900	Dopp. Anast.			B&L Automatic			140
Premaret	4x5"	plate	PlateBox	1895							100
Premier (box) 4x5"	4x5"	plate	PlateBox	1891						Mc369	210

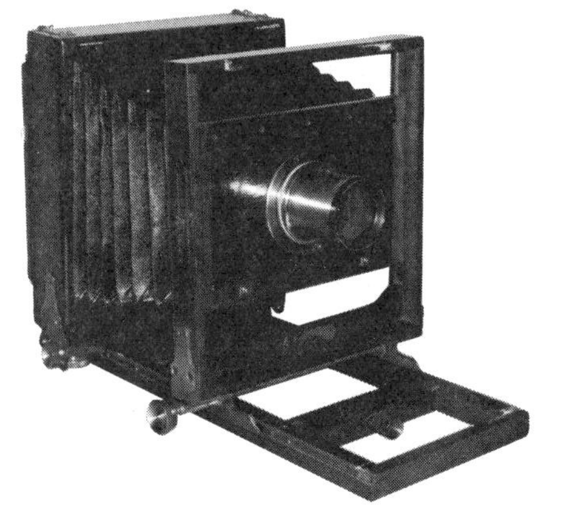

Rochester Ideal

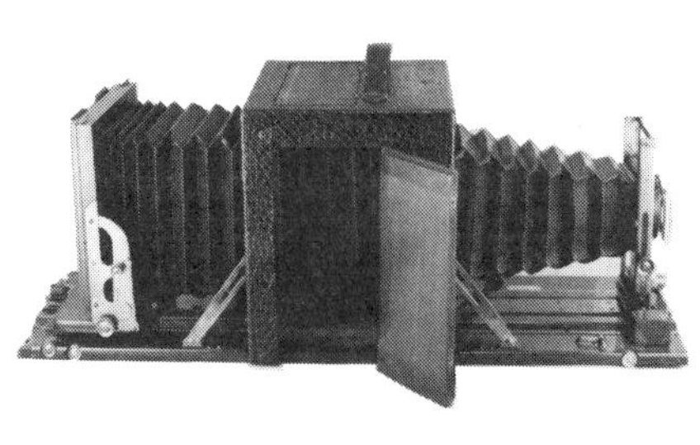

Roch. Long Focus Premo

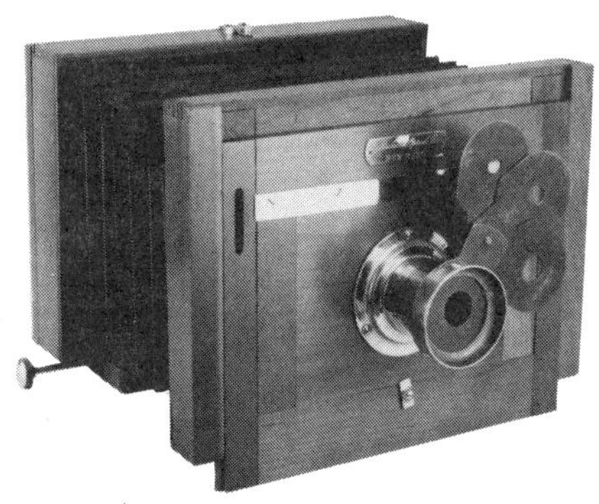

Roch. New Mod. View

MODEL	FORMAT	FILM	TYPE	Year	LENS	Apert	FL	SHUTTER	SPEEDS	ILLUS	U.S.$
Premier (box) 5x7"	5x7"	plate	PlateBox	1891						Mc369	210
Premier (folding) 4x5"	4x5"	plate	H&S	1892				built-in		Mc369	340
Premier (folding) 5x7"	5x7"	plate	H&S	1892				B&L pneumatic		Mc369	270
Premo (box)	4x5"	plate	PlateBox	1893	achromatic						30
Premo (folding) 4x5"	4x5"	plate	FoldPl	1893	Rapid Rectilinear						110
Premo (folding) 5x7"	5x7"	plate	FoldPl	1893	Rapid Rectilinear						150
Premo Folding Film No. 1	3¼x4¼"	pack	FoldPack	1904	Rapid Rectilinear			Gem Autom.		Mc370	90
Premo Folding Film No. 1	3¼x5½"	pack	FoldPack	1904	Rapid Rectilinear			Gem Autom.			90
Premo Folding Film No. 1	4x5"	pack	FoldPack	1904	Rapid Rectilinear			Gem Autom.			90
Premo Folding Film No. 3	3¼x4¼"	pack	FoldPack	1905	B&L Plastigmat	6.8		Volute			120
Premo Folding Film No. 3	3¼x4¼"	pack	FoldPack	1905	B&L Plastigmat	6.8		B&L Automatic			120
Premo Folding Film No. 3	3¼x5½"	pack	FoldPack	1905	B&L Zeiss Protar			B&L Automatic			120
Premo Folding Film No. 3	3¼x5½"	pack	FoldPack	1905	Goerz Doppel An.	6.8		Volute			120
Premo Folding Film No. 3	4x5"	pack	FoldPack	1905	Goerz Doppel An.	6.8		B&L Automatic			120
Premo No. 6	5x7"	plate	FoldPl	1900	Zeiss Anastigmat			B&L Automatic			140
Premo Reflecting Camera	4x5"	plate	LgSLR	1905	B&L Plastigmat	6.8		focal plane		Mc370	1000
Premo Reflecting Camera	4x5"	plate	LgSLR	1905	Goerz Doppel An.	6.8		focal plane		A3145	1000
Premo Sr. Stereo 5x7"	5x7"	plate	StFoldPl	1895	Rapid Rectilinear			B&L Stereo		Mc370	410
Premo Sr. Stereo 6½x8½"	6½x8½"	plate	StFoldPl	1895	Rapid Rectilinear			B&L Stereo		Mc370	410
Premograph	3¼x4¼"	plate	LgSLR	1908	Rapid Rectilinear			Compound		A3142	300
Reko	4x5"	plate	FoldPl	1899	Sp. Reko Rectil.			Unicum			120
Reversible Back Premo	4x5"	plate	FoldPl	1897	Rapid Rectilinear			Victor		Mc370	240
Reversible Back Premo	5x7"	plate	FoldPl	1897	Rapid Rectilinear			Victor		Mc370	240
Reversible Back Premo	6½x8½"	plate	FoldPl	1897	Rapid Rectilinear			Victor		Mc370	240
Reversible Back Premo	8x10"	plate	FoldPl	1897	Rapid Rectilinear			Victor		Mc370	240
Rochester Stereo 5x7"	5x7"	plate	SterField	1891				B&L			340
Rochester Stereo 6½x8½"	6½x8½"	plate	SterField	1891				B&L			340
Rochester View	3¼x4¼"	plate	Field	1902	various			various			260
Snappa	3¼x4¼"	plate	HzFoldPl	1902	Rapid Rectilinear					Mc370	220
Twin Lens Carlton	4x5"	plate	LgTLR	1895	various			various			540
Universal 3¼x4¼"	3¼x4¼"	plate	Field	1888	Brass barrel						230
Universal 5x7"	5x7"	plate	Field	1888	Brass barrel					Mc370	220
Universal 6½x8½"	6½x8½"	plate	Field	1888	Brass barrel					Mc370	230
Universal 17x20"	17x20"	plate	Field	1888	Brass barrel						230
...ROCKET CAMERA CO. LTD. - Japan											
General	4x5cm	120	MetalBox	1955					B,I		20
New Rocket	14x14mm		Submin		Rocket	4.5	20mm		I	Mc371	210
Palmer	4x5cm	120	MetalBox	1955					B,I	Mc370	20
Rocket Camera	4x5cm	120	MetalBox	1955					B,I		20
...RODEHÜSER (Dr. Rodehüser) - Bergkamen, Westf., Germany											
Panta 4x6.5	4x6.5cm	127	TelescRo	1950	Enna	4.5		Vario		A543	80
Panta 5x5.5	5x5.5cm	120	TelescRo	1950	Enna	4.5		Prontor		A1566	60

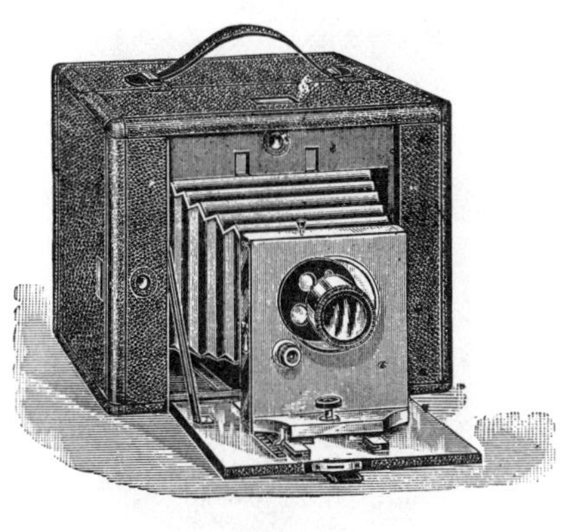

Rochester Premier (folding)

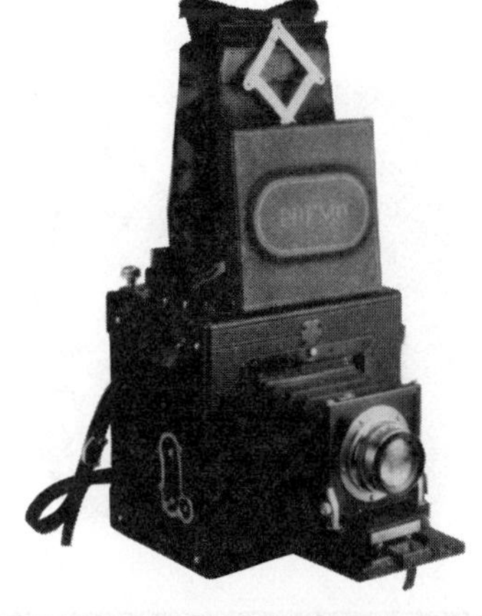

Roch. Premo Reflecting Camera

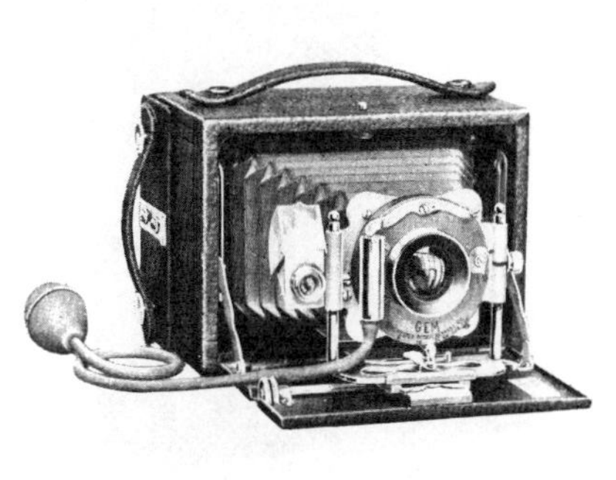

Rochester Snappa

MODEL	FORMAT	FILM	TYPE	Year	LENS	Apert	FL	SHUTTER	SPEEDS	ILLUS	U.S.$
...RODENSTOCK (Optische Werke G.Rodenstock) - Munich											
Astra	6.5x9cm	plate	FoldPl		Eurynar	6.8	90mm	Compound			50
Bafo	4x6cm	127	VtFoldRo	1931	Zecanar	4.5	70mm	Vario	25-100	A405	290
Citoklapp	6x9cm	120	VtFoldRo	1930	Trinar	4.9	100mm	Pronto		Mc371	50
Citonette	4.5x6cm	120	VtFoldRo	1933	Trinar	2.9		Pronto S		Mc371	40
Clarovid	6x9/4.5x6	120	VtFoldRo	1932	Trinar Anastigmat	4.5		Rim-Compur	1-250	Mc371	120
Clarovid	6x9/4.5x6	120	VtFoldRo	1932	Trinar Anastigmat	3.8	105mm	Rim-Compur	1-250	A433	120
Clarovid II	6x9/4.5x6	120	VtFoldRo	1932	Trinar Anastigmat	4.5		Rim-Compur	1-250		120
Folding plate camera 6.5x9	6.5x9cm	plate	FoldPl	1932	Trinar	2.9		Compur			50
Folding plate camera 9x12	9x12cm	plate	FoldPl	1932	Trinar	4.5		Compur			60
Folding rollfilm camera	4.5x6cm	120	VtFoldRo	1932	Rodenstock Trinar	2.9		Rim-Compur	1-250	Mc371	40
Folding rollfilm camera	6x6cm	120	VtFoldRo	1932	Eurynar	4.5		Rim-Compur	1-250	Mc371	30
Folding rollfilm camera	6x9cm	120	VtFoldRo	1932	Eurynar	4.5		Rim-Compur	1-250		50
Folding rollfilm camera	6.5x11cm	116	VtFoldRo	1932	Rodenstock Trinar	2.9		Rim-Compur	1-250	Mc371	40
Imagon Special	9x12cm	plate	HzFoldPl	1932	Imagon	5.4	20cm	focal plane	1/10-1000	A245	100
Planitta	6x9cm	Sheet	VtFoldPl	1932	Xenar	4.5	105mm	Rim-Compur	1-250		60
Prontoklapp	6x9cm	120	VtFoldRo	1932	Trinar Anastigmat	4.5		Compur			40
Robra	4.5x6cm	120	VtFoldRo	1937	Robra Anastigmat	3.5	75mm	Compur			60
Rodar I	6.5x9cm	plate	FoldPl	1937	Trinar	4.5		Compur			50
Rodar II	6.5x9cm	plate	FoldPl	1937	Trinar	4.5		Compur			50
Rodella	3x4cm	127	StrutRo	1932	Trinar	4.5		Prontor II			80
Rodinett	3x4cm	127	StrutRo	1932	Rodenstock Ysar	3.5	50mm				220
Rofina II	4x6.5cm	127	StrutRo	1932	Trinar	2.9	75mm	Compur		HK242	150
Stereo Wet plate	6.5x9cm	WetPl	StWetPl	1925	Eurynar	5.4	105mm				700
Wedar 6.5x9	6.5x9cm	plate	FoldPl	1929	various			various			50
Wedar 9x12	9x12cm	plate	FoldPl	1929	various			various			60
Wedar II 6.5x9	6.5x9cm	plate	FoldPl	1929	various			various			50
Wedar II 9x12	9x12cm	plate	FoldPl	1929	various			various			60
Werol I	6.5x11cm	116	FoldRo	1932	Eurynar	4.5	120mm	Rim-Compur	1-250		50
Ysella	3x4cm	127	VtFoldRo	1932	Trinar	2.8	50mm	Compur		Mc371	100
Ysella	3x4cm	127	VtFoldRo	1932	Trinar	4.5	50mm	Compur		Mc371	100
...ROKUWA CO. - Japan											
Stereo Rocca	23x24mm	120	Stereo	1955	Fixed focus	8			30,B	Mc371	170
...ROLAND (Alphonse Roland) - Brüssel, Belgien											
Folding plate camera	9x12cm	plate	VtFoldPl	1895		11					280
...(unknown)											
Rollo-Frex		Roll	TLR	1941						Mc371	230
...ROLLS CAMERA MFG. CO. - Chicago											
Beauta Miniature Candid	1¼x1½"	127	Minicam							Mc372	10
Picta Twin 620	1¼x1⅝"	620	RigidRo		Rollax		62mm		I,T	Mc372	30
Rolls	1¼x1½"	127	Minicam	1939	Rollax		50mm		I,T	Mc372	10
Rolls Twin 620	1⅝x2¼"	620	RigidRo	1939	Rollax Anastigmat	7.7			I,T		20

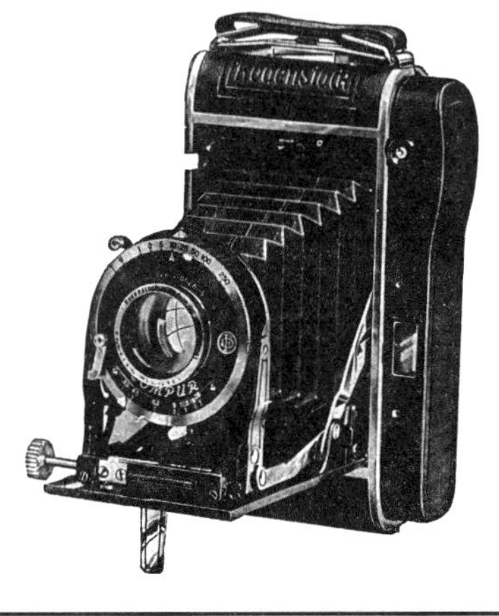

Rodenstock Clarovid

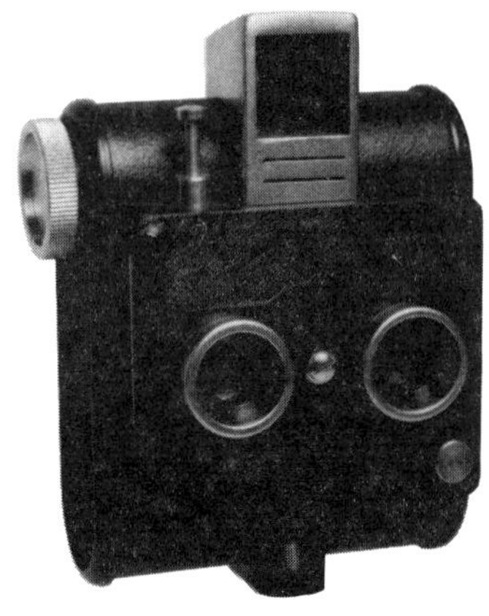
Rokuwa Stereo Rocca

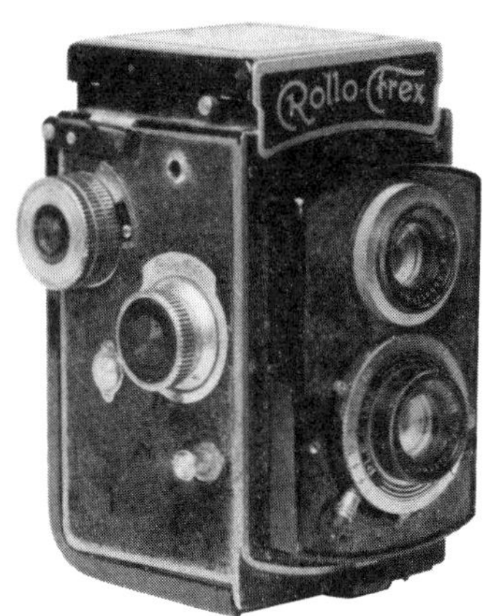

Rollo-Frex

MODEL	FORMAT	FILM	TYPE	Year	LENS	Apert	FL	SHUTTER	SPEEDS	ILLUS	U.S.$
Super Rolls	24x36mm	35mm	35VF		Achromatic Rollax	3.5		Alphax Jr	25-200	Mc372	30
Super Rolls	24x36mm	35mm	35VF		Anastigmat	4.5		Alphax Jr	25-200	Mc372	30
Super Rolls Seven Seven	4x5.5cm	620	RigidRo		Achromatic Rollax	7.7		Automatic	T,B,I	Mc372	30
...ROSS (Thomas Ross & Co.)											
Field Camera	4¼x6½"	plate	Field	1890	Rap. Symmetrical						340
Folding Twin Lens Camera		plate	LgTLR	1895	Goerz Doppel An.	7.7	5'			Mc372	800
Kinnear's Patent	6x7"	WetPl	WetPlate	1860	landscape						800
Kinnear's Patent	10x12"	WetPl	WetPlate	1860	landscape						800
Photoscope	1⅜x1½"	Roll	Disguised	1897	Rap. Symmetrical						700
Portable Divided Camera	3¼x4¼"	plate	LgTLR	1891	Rap. Symmetrical						650
Reflex 3¼x4¼"	3¼x4¼"	plate	LgTLR	1912	Single reflex			focal plane	1/14-800	Mc372	230
Reflex 5x7"	5x7"	plate	LgTLR	1912	Single reflex			focal plane	1/14-800	Mc372	260
Sliding-box Wet Plate		WetPl	WetPlate	1855						A1296	1300
Stereo camera	4¼x6½"	plate	StFoldPl	1900	Ross			Thornton-Pickard			800
Stereo sliding-box (wet pl.)		WetPl	WetPlate	1855	Grubb						4000
Stereo sliding-box (wet pl.)		WetPl	WetPlate	1855	Dallmeyer						4000
Stereo tailboard (wet plate)	6½x8½"	WetPl	WetPlate	1865	Ross Petzval		6"				3200
Sutton Panoramic Camera		WetPl	WetPlate	1861						Mc372	15000
Tailboard camera 4¼x6½"	4¼x6½"	plate	Tailboard	1888	Ross			Thornton-Pickard			380
Tailboard camera 6½x8½"	6½x8½"	plate	Tailboard	1888	Ross			Thornton-Pickard			330
Tailboard camera 10x12"	10x12"	plate	Tailboard	1888	Ross			Thornton-Pickard			330
Tailboard Wet Plate		WetPl	WetPlate	1865	Brassbound Ross						1800
Tailboard Wet Plate		WetPl	WetPlate	1865	Euryscop						1800
Twin Lens Reflex 3¼x4¼"	3¼x4¼"	plate	LgTLR	1912	RossSymmetrical			Thornton-Pickard			700
Twin Lens Reflex 4x5"	4x5"	plate	LgTLR	1912	RossSymmetrical			Thornton-Pickard		A546	800
...ROSS ENSIGN LTD.											
Ful-Vue Super	6x9cm	620	TLR-Box	1950							30
Fulvueflex Synchroflash	6x6cm	120	TLR-Box	1950	Astaross				I,B	Mc373	30
Snapper	6x9cm	620	VtFoldRo							Mc373	30
...ROTH (A.O. Roth) - London											
Reflex 4.5x6	4.5x6cm	plate	LgSLR	1926	Meyer Trioplan	6.3	75mm	focal plane	10-1000	A1616	420
Reflex 4.5x6	4.5x6cm	plate	LgSLR	1926	Tessar	1.5	75mm	focal plane	10-1000		420
Reflex 8x10.5	8x10.5cm	plate	LgSLR	1920	Meyer Trioplan	2.8	95mm	focal plane	10-1000		290
...ROUCH (W.W. Rouch & Co.) - London, England											
Eureka 8x8cm	8x8cm	plate	MagBox	1888	Rouch		150mm	roller-blind		A1306	460
Eureka 3¼x4¼"	3¼x4¼"	plate	MagBox	1888	Rouch		150mm	roller-blind			460
Excelsior	3¼x4¼"	plate	MagBox	1890						Mc373	510
Patent Portable Camera	4¾x6½"	plate	Field	1885	Rap. Symmetrical					Mc373	440
Patent Portable Camera	6½x8½"	plate	Field	1885	Rap. Symmetrical					Mc373	440
Patent Portable Camera	7½x7½"	WetPl	WetPlate	1880	Rap. Symmetrical					Mc373	650
Patent Portable Camera	12x15"	plate	Field	1885	Rap. Symmetrical					Mc373	700
Stereo Wet plate	10.5x19	WetPl	StWetPl	1863	Petzval						3900

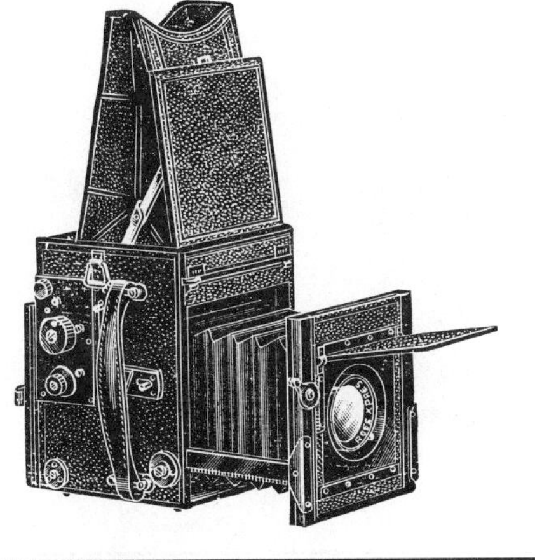

Ross Reflex

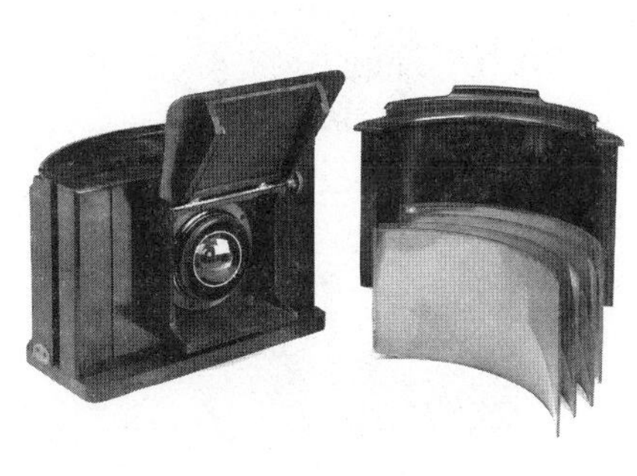

Ross Sutton Panoramic Camera

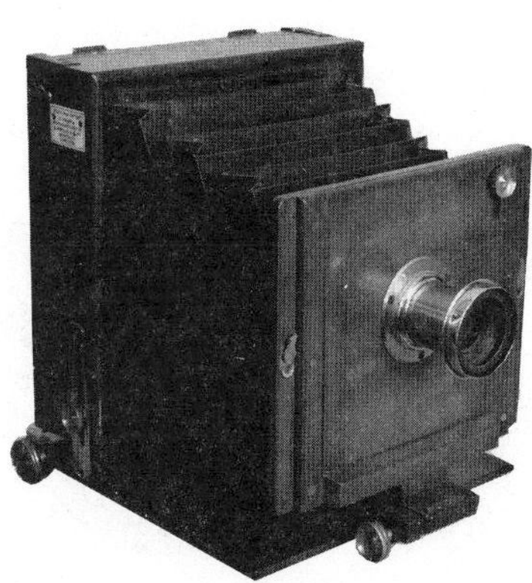

Rouch Patent Portable Camera

MODEL	FORMAT	FILM	TYPE	Year	LENS	Apert	FL	SHUTTER	SPEEDS	ILLUS	U.S.$
Tailboard camera	3¼x4¼"	plate	Tailboard	1888	Rouch						290
Universal Camera 4¾x6½"	4¾x6½"	plate	Field	1885	Rap. Symmetrical						390
Universal Camera 6½x8½"	6½x8½"	plate	Field	1885	Rap. Symmetrical						490
...ROUSSEL (H. Roussel) - Paris											
Folding camera	9x12cm	plate	FoldPl	1899	Anti-Spectroscop.					F262	180
Stella Jumelle	9x12cm	plate	Jumelle	1900	Anti-Spectroscop.	7.7	130mm	guillotine	7 Zeiten	Mc373	370
...ROYAL CAMERA CO. - Japan											
Royal 35	24x36mm	35mm	35RF	1960	Tominor	2.8	50mm	Copal	1-300		110
Royal 35M	24x36mm	35mm	35RF	1957	Tominor	2.8	45mm	Copal MXV			100
...ROYAL-HAMILTON INDUSTRIES INC. - New York & Chicago											
Royal #1	2¼x3¼"	120	BakeliteRoll		Meniscus				I,T	Mc374	30
...(unknown)											
Royalcord	6x6cm	120	TLR	1956	Horinor Anast.	3.5	75mm	Ceres synchro	1-300		120
...ROYCE MFG. CO.											
Royce Reflex	6x6cm	120	TLR	1946		4.5	75mm	Alphax	25-150,T,B		30
...ROYER (René Royer) - Fontenay-sous-Bois, France											
Altessa	6x9cm	120	TelescRo	1952	Angenieux	3.5	105mm			A1567	90
Royer	6x9cm	120	VtFoldRo	1948		4.5	105mm	Sito	10-200	A1473	70
Royer A	6x9cm	120	VtFoldRo	1949	Angenieux Type V	4.5	105mm	Sito	10-200		30
Royflex	6x6cm	120	TLR	1960		3.5	75mm	Royer	1-300	A1730	100
Savoy	24x36mm	35mm	35VF	1960	Berthiot	2.8	50mm	Royer	1-300	F655	50
Savoy II	24x36mm	35mm	35VF	1960	Berthiot	2.8	50mm	Royer	1-300	Mc374	50
Savoyflex	24x36mm	35mm	35SLR	1959	Som Berthiot	2.8	50mm	Prontor-Refl.	1-500	A1672	70
Savoyflex Automatique	24x36mm	35mm	35SLR	1959	Som Berthiot	2.8	50mm	Prontor-Refl.	B, 1-300	F418	110
Savoyflex II	24x36mm	35mm	35SLR							Mc374	70
Teleroy	6x9cm	120	VtFoldRo	1950	Angenieux X1	3.5	105mm		B,1-300	Mc374	160
Teleroy	6x9cm	120	VtFoldRo	1950	Flor	3.5	105mm		B,1-300	A3048	160
...ROYET (Paul Royet) - St. Etienne, France											
Reyna Cross III	24x36mm	35mm	35VF	1943	Berthiot	3.5		2-blade	25-200,B	Mc374	50
Reyna Cross III	24x36mm	35mm	35VF	1943	Cross	2.9	45mm	2-blade	25-200,B	F648	50
...RUBERG & RENNER											
Adickes	4x6cm	127	BakFoldRo	1933	Rodenstock				I,T		50
Allbright	4x6cm	127	TelescRo							Mc374	70
Baby Ruby	3x4cm	127	BakFoldRo	1939	Rod. Periscop	11			I,T	Mc374	50
Dixi	4x5.5cm	127	TelescRo							Mc374	70
Fibiru	4x6cm	127	TelescRo							Mc374	60
Fibituro	4x6/3x4	127	TelescRo	1934	Rod. Periscop	11			M,Z	A1088	60
Hollywood	40x55mm	127	BakFoldRo	1932						Mc375	30
Hollywood Duplo	4x6/3x4	127	TelescRo		Meniscus					Mc375	40
Little Wonder	40x55mm	127	TelescRo	1932	Meniscus				I,T	Mc375	70
Neñita	4x6cm	127	TelescRo	1950						Mc375	100
Popular	3x4cm	127	TelescRo	1939	Rod. Periscop	11			I,T	A1515	90

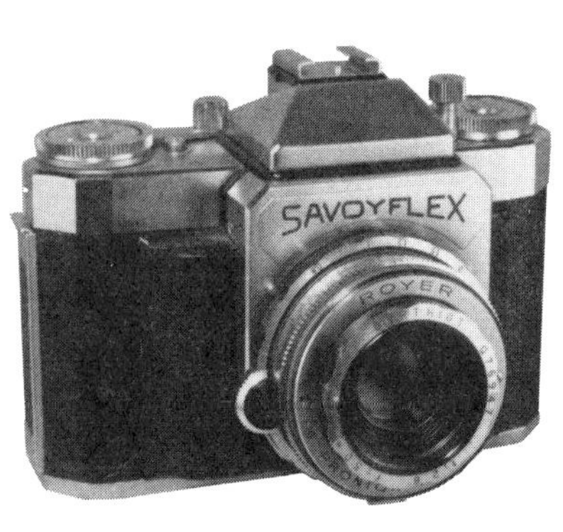

Savoyflex II

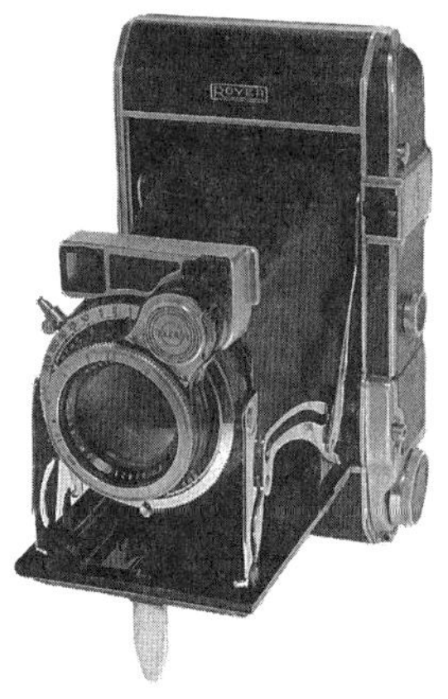
Teleroy

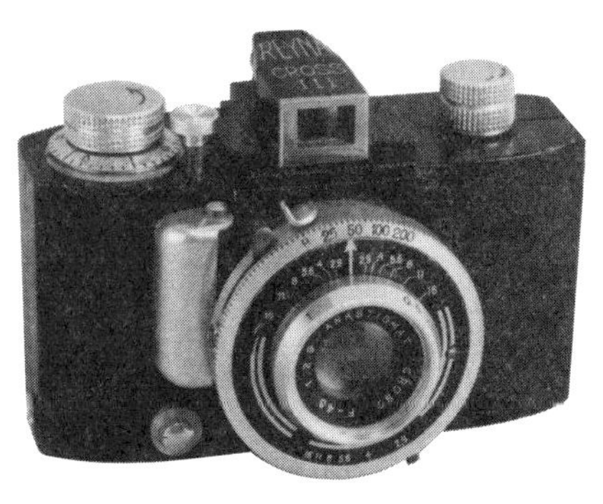
Reyna Cross III

MODEL	FORMAT	FILM	TYPE	Year	LENS	Apert	FL	SHUTTER	SPEEDS	ILLUS	U.S.$
Ruberg (black)	4x6cm	127	TelescRo	1953	Rod. Periscop	11			I,T	Mc375	40
Ruberg (red)	4x5.5cm	127	TelescRo	1953	Rod. Periscop	11			I,T		120
Ruberg Futuro (black)	4x6cm	127	TelescRo	1935	Rod. Periscop	11			I,T	Mc375	50
Ruberg Futuro (red)	4x6cm	127	TelescRo	1935	Rod. Periscop	11			I,T		50
Rubette	3x4cm	127	TelescRo	1933	Rodenstock						60
...SACHS (Johann Sachs & Co.) - Berlin											
Field camera 9x12	9x12cm	plate	Tailboard	1905	Brass barrel					A136	240
Field camera 13x18	13x18cm	plate	Tailboard	1905	Brass barrel						240
Field camera 18x24	18x24cm	plate	Tailboard	1905	Brass barrel						240
Stereo Field camera	9x18cm	plate	SterTail	1905	Brass barrel					A1760	400
...SAINT-ETIENNE - France											
Universelle 8.5x11	8.5x11cm	Ro+Pl	FoldRo	1908	Rapid Rectilinear		150mm	B&L Unicum			160
Universelle 9x12	9x12cm	Ro+Pl	FoldRo	1908	Beckers Anast.	6.8	150mm	B&L Unicum		A377	220
...SAKURA SEIKI CO. - Japan											
Petal (octagonal)	6mm dia.	25mm	Submin	1948		5.6	12mm		1/25	Mc375	270
Petal (round)	6mm dia.	25mm	Submin	1948		5.6	12mm		1/25	Mc375	330
...SAMSUNG - Seoul, Korea											
AF Slim	24x36mm	35mm	35AF	1990	Samsung Macro	3.5	35mm	programmed	2-500		160
AF Slim Dual	24x36mm	35mm	35AF-BI	1994	Samsung	3.8/6	28/48	programmed	60-400		110
AF Slim Zoom	24x36mm	35mm	35AFZ	1993	Samsung Macro	3.5	35-70	programmed	3-400		140
AF Slim-R	24x36mm	35mm	35AF	1993	Samsung	4.5	38mm	programmed	64-300		80
AF Zoom 700	24x36mm	35mm	35AFZ	1989	Samsung	3.5	35-70	programmed	4-250		170
AF Zoom 800	24x36mm	35mm	35AFZ	1990	Samsung		38-80				140
AF Zoom 1050	24x36mm	35mm	35AFZ	1992	Samsung	4	38-105	programmed	3-250		150
ECX 1 Panorama	24x36mm	35mm	35AFZ	1994	Samsung	3.8	38-140	programmed	3-400		290
Slim Zoom 1150	24x36mm	35mm	35AFZ	1994	Samsung Macro	3.9	38-115	programmed	3-400		160
...SAN GIORGIO - Genova, Italy											
Janua		35mm	35RF	1949	Essegi	3.5	50mm	focal plane	50-1000	HK577	800
Parva		16mm	Submin	1947							16000
...SANDERS & CROWHURST - Brighton, England											
Birdland	3¼x4¼"	plate	LgSLR	1904	Dagor	6.8		focal plane	1000		370
...SANDERSON CAMERA WORKS - England											
Deluxe 3¼x4¼"	3¼x4¼"	plate	H&S	1903	Ross Homocentric	6.3		Unicum		Mc376	350
Deluxe 4x5"	4x5"	plate	H&S	1903	Ross Homocentric	6.3		Unicum			350
Deluxe 4¼x6½"	4¼x6½"	plate	H&S	1903	Ross Homocentric	6.3		Unicum			350
Deluxe 5x7"	5x7"	plate	H&S	1903	Ross Homocentric	6.3		Unicum			350
Field camera (alum. bound)	6½x8½"	plate	Field	1896	Triple Convertible					Mc376	550
Field camera 3¼x4¼"	3¼x4¼"	plate	Field	1898	various			Thornton-Pickard			410
Field camera 4¼x6½"	4¼x6½"	plate	Field	1898	various			Thornton-Pickard		A2968	500
Field camera 6½x8½"	6½x8½"	plate	Field	1898	various			Thornton-Pickard			500
Field camera 8x10"	8x10"	plate	Field	1898	various			Thornton-Pickard			470
Field camera 10x12"	10x12"	plate	Field	1898	various			Thornton-Pickard			500

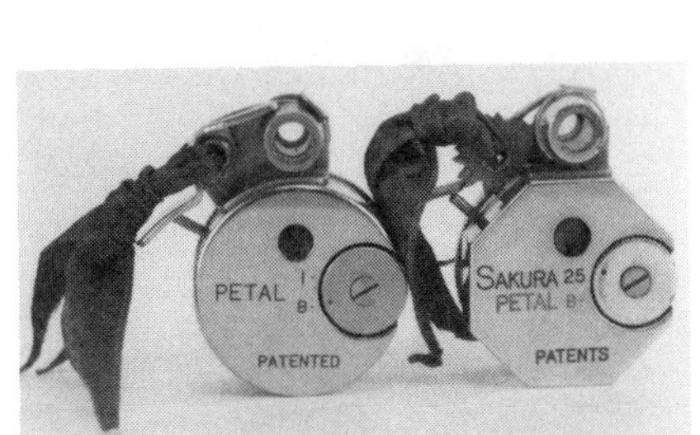

Petal (octagonal/round)

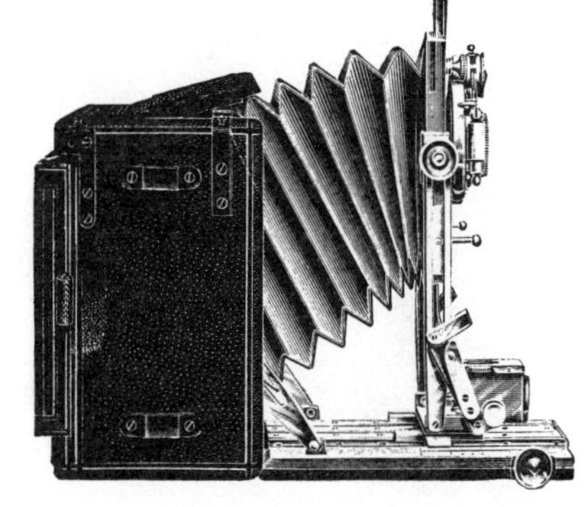

Sanderson Deluxe

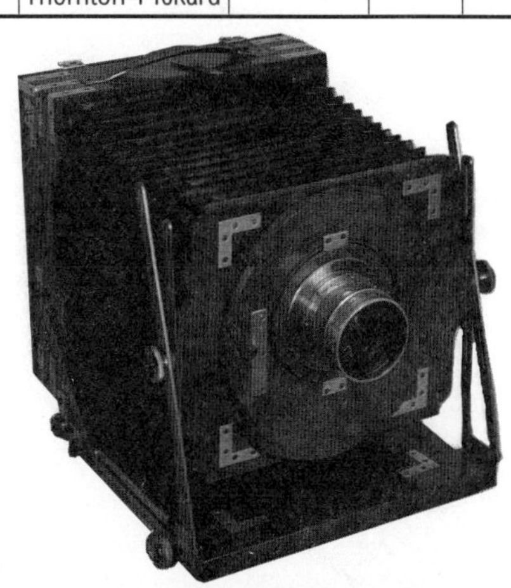

Sander.Field Cam. Alum. Bound

MODEL	FORMAT	FILM	TYPE	Year	LENS	Apert	FL	SHUTTER	SPEEDS	ILLUS	U.S.$
Junior 3¼x4¼"	3¼x4¼"	plate	H&S	1903	Goerz Dagor	6.8	125mm	Koilos	1-250	Mc376	330
Junior 4x5"	4x5"	plate	H&S	1903	Goerz Dagor	6.8		Koilos	1-250		320
Junior 4¼x6½"	4¼x6½"	plate	H&S	1903	Goerz Dagor	6.8		Koilos	1-250		330
Junior 5x7"	5x7"	plate	H&S	1903	Goerz Dagor	6.8		Koilos	1-250		320
Regular 3¼x4¼"	3¼x4¼"	plate	H&S	1903	Goerz Doppel An.					Mc376	330
Regular 4x5"	4x5"	plate	H&S	1903	Goerz Doppel An.						370
Regular 4¼x6½"	4¼x6½"	plate	H&S	1903	Rapid Rectilinear			Thornton-Pickard			350
Regular 5x7"	5x7"	plate	H&S	1903	Rapid Rectilinear			Thornton-Pickard			350
Stereo Half Plate	4¼x6½"	plate	SterField	1904	Goerz Doppel An.						390
Stereo Full Plate	6½x8½"	plate	SterField	1904	Goerz Doppel An.					A696	440
Tourist 3¼x4¼"	3¼x4¼"	plate	H&S	1903	B&L Rapid Rect.			Unicum		A176	400
Tourist 4¼x6½"	4¼x6½"	plate	H&S	1903	B&L Rapid Rect.			Unicum			540
Tropical Field Camera	3¼x4¼"	plate	Field	1920	Zeiss Tessar	4.9		Compur	1-200		800
Tropical Field Camera	6½x8½"	plate	Field	1920	Zeiss Tessar	4.9	13cm	Compur	1-200	Mc376	800
Tropical H&S 3¼x4¼"	3¼x4¼"	plate	H&S	1920	Goerz Dagor	6.8		Compur		Mc376	900
Tropical H&S 3¼x4¼"	3¼x4¼"	plate	H&S	1920	Aldis	6.3		Compur		Mc376	900
Tropical H&S 4¼x6½"	4¼x6½"	plate	H&S	1920	Goerz Dagor	6.8		Compur		Mc376	900
Tropical H&S 4¼x6½"	4¼x6½"	plate	H&S	1920	Beck	7.7		Compur		Mc376	900
...SANDS, HUNTER & CO., LTD. (The Strand) - London, England											
Field camera 4¼x6½"	4¼x6½"	plate	Field	1880	Anastigmat					Mc376	380
Field camera 4¼x6½"	4¼x6½"	plate	Field	1880	Rapid Rectilinear						380
Field camera 6½x8½"	6½x8½"	plate	Field	1880	Anastigmat						380
Field camera 6½x8½"	6½x8½"	plate	Field	1880	Rapid Rectilinear						380
Field camera 10x12"	10x12"	plate	Field	1880	Anastigmat						380
Field camera 10x12"	10x12"	plate	Field	1880	Rapid Rectilinear						380
...SANEI SANGYO - Japan											
Samoca 35	24x36mm	35mm	35VF	1950	Ezumar	3.5	50mm		25-100		40
Samoca 35II	24x36mm	35mm	35VF	1950	Ezumar	3.5	50mm		25-100		40
Samoca 35III	24x36mm	35mm	35VF	1950	Ezumar	3.5	50mm		25-100	Mc376	40
Samoca 35 M-28	24x36mm	35mm	35RF	1960	Ezumar	3.5	50mm	Samoca Sync.	1-300		50
Samoca 35 Super	24x36mm	35mm	35RF	1956	Ezumar	3.5	50mm		10-200	Mc376	50
Samoca 35 V	24x36mm	35mm	35VF	1955	Ezumar Anast.	3.5	50mm		10-200		70
Samoca EM	24x36mm	35mm	35RF	1956	Ezumar	3.5	50mm		200		70
Samoca LE	24x36mm	35mm	35RF	1957	Ezumar	2.8	50mm	Samoca Sync.	1-300,B	A2137	30
Samoca LE-II	24x36mm	35mm	35RF	1957	Ezumar	2.8	50mm	Samoca Sync.	1-300,B	A1167	30
Samocaflex 35	24x36mm	35mm	35TLR	1955	Ezumar	2.8	50mm	Seikosha-Rap.	1-500,B	Mc376	520
Samocaflex 35II	24x36mm	35mm	35TLR	1956	Ezumar	2.8	50mm	Seikosha-MX	B,1-500		470
...SANEIKOKI - Japan											
Sanei Baby 35	24x36mm	Bolta	MiniatRo								70
Starrich 35	24x36mm	Bolta	MiniatRo							Mc377	70
...SANGER-SHERPHERD - London, England											
Three-color camera	2¼x3¼"	plate	3-Color	1907	Anastigmat	6.8	140mm				440

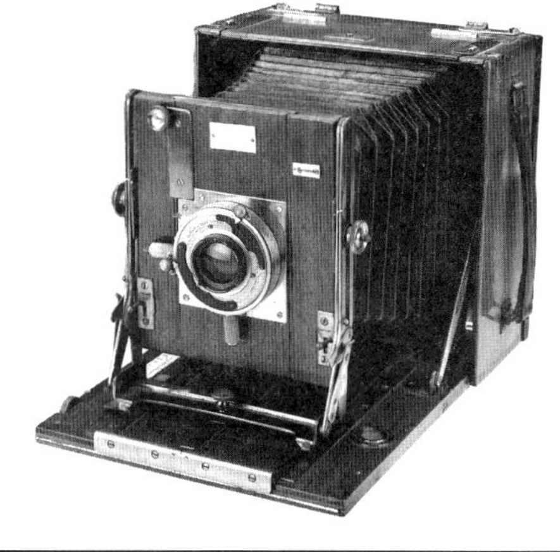

Sanderson Tropical H&S

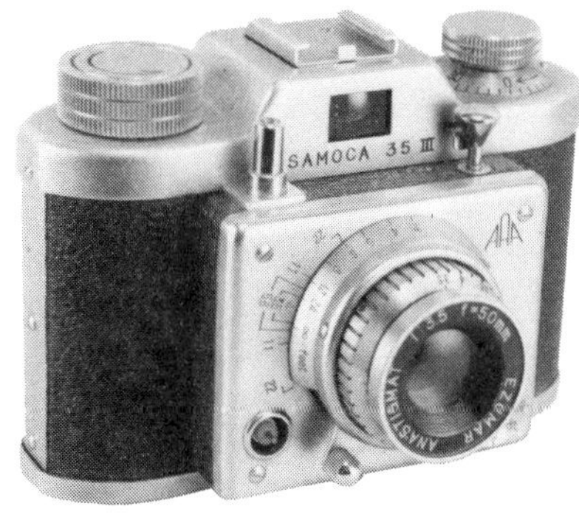

Sanei Samoca 35III

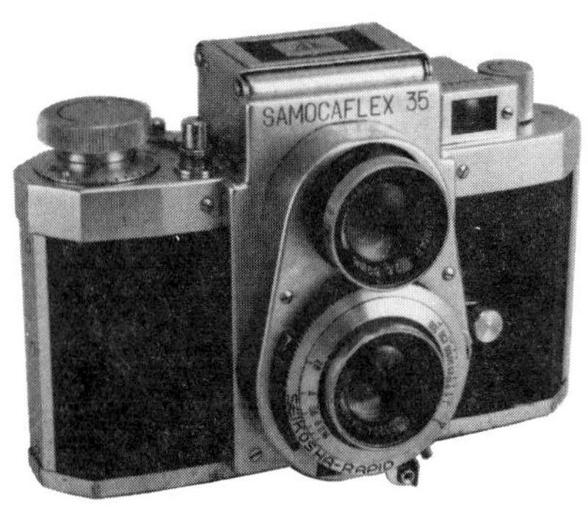

Sanei Samocaflex 35

MODEL	FORMAT	FILM	TYPE	Year	LENS	Apert	FL	SHUTTER	SPEEDS	ILLUS	U.S.$
...SANWA CO. LTD., SANWA SHOKAI - Japan											
Mycro (original)	14x14mm	17.5	Submin	1938	Doublet	4.5	20mm		25-100		200
Mycro	14x14mm	17.5	Submin	1940	Mycro Una	4.5	20mm		25-100	Mc377	60
Mycro II	14x14mm	17.5	Submin	1948	Mycro Una	4.5	20mm		25-100		60
Mycro IIIA	14x14mm	17.5	Submin	1950	Mycro Una	4.5	20mm		25-100	Mc377	70
Suzuki Baby I	3x4cm	127	FoldRo	1951	Teriotar	4.5	50mm	STK			140
...SAS GmbH - Vlotho, Germany											
Sassex	6x6cm	120	RigidRo	1951	Sas-Siagon	9	80mm		T,B,M	A3107	50
...SAWYERS INC. - Portland, Ore.											
Mark IV	4x4cm	127	TLR	1958	Topcor	2.8	60mm	Seikosha-MX	1-500,B		120
Nomad 127	4x6.5cm	127	BakeliteRoll	1957					1/50	Mc377	20
Nomad 620	6x6cm	620	BakeliteRoll	1957					1/50		20
V-M Personal Ster. (black)	12x13mm	35mm	35Ster	1952	Anastigmat	3.5	25mm		10-100	Mc377	220
V-M Personal Ster. (brown)	12x13mm	35mm	35Ster	1952	Anastigmat	3.5	25mm		10-100		340
View-master Stereo Color	12x13mm	35mm	35Ster	1961	Rodenstock Trinar	2.8	20mm		I	A792	200
Viewmaster Mark II	12x13mm	35mm	35Ster	1961	Rodenstock Trinar	2.8	20mm		I		220
Viewmaster Stereo	12x13mm	35mm	35Ster	1961	Rodenstock Trinar	2.8	20mm		I		180
...SCAPEC - France											
Rollex	6x9cm	120	MetalBox	1950	Meniscus			Synchro	I,T	Mc377	50
...S.C.A.T. (Societa Construzioni Articoli Technici) - Rome											
Scat	7x10mm	16mm	Submin	1950		3.5			I	Mc378	180
...SCHAAP & CO. - Amsterdam											
Van Albada Stereo	6x13cm	plate	SterBox	1900				focal plane			900
...SCHAEFFNER (A. Schaeffner) - Paris											
Photo-Album	9x12cm	plate	Special	1890	Achromat			guillotine			2700
Photo-Album	9x12cm	plate	Special	1890	Rapid Rectilinear			guillotine			2700
...SCHAJA (Photo-Schaja) - Munich											
Schaja 6x9/4.5x6	6x9/4.5x6	120	VtFoldRo	1938	Corygon	4.5	105mm	Prontor II			60
Schaja 9x12	9x12cm	plate	VtFoldPl	1927	Tessar	4.5	135mm	Compur			50
...SCHATZ & SONS - Germany											
Sola	13x18mm		Submin	1938	Schn. Kinoplan	3	25	Behind-the-lens	1-500	Mc378	1900
...SCHAUB (Jacob Schaub) - Logan, Utah											
Multiplying Camera	4x5"	plate	Multiply	1899						Mc378	2000
...SCHIANSKY											
Universal Studio	7x9¼"	Sheet	Studio	1950	Zeiss Apo-Tessar	9	450mm				610
...SCHIFFMACHER (Eusebius Schiffmacher) - Munich											
Box-Kamera	9x12cm	plate	PlateBox	1897	Anastigmat	7.2				A1310	120
Field camera 13x18	13x18cm	plate	Field	1900	various						240
Field camera 18x24	18x24cm	plate	Field	1900	various						270
Reflex	9x9cm	plate	LgSLR	1897	Anastigmat	7.2				A1576	600
Stereo Reflex	9x18cm	plate	SterRefl	1897	Anastigmat	7.2				A688	2000
Strut camera	13x18cm	plate	StrutPl	1900	various					A1413	220

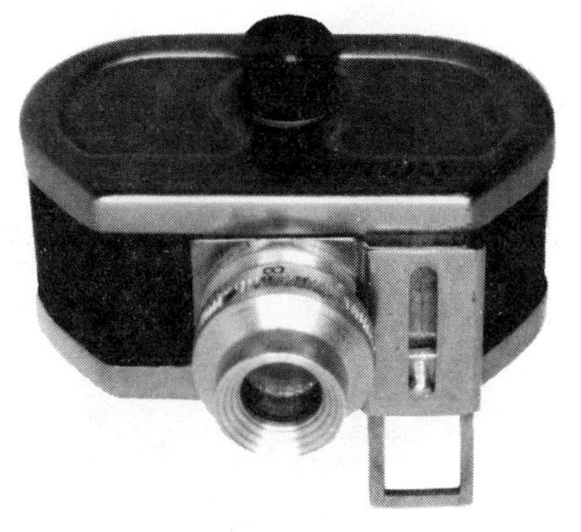

Scat

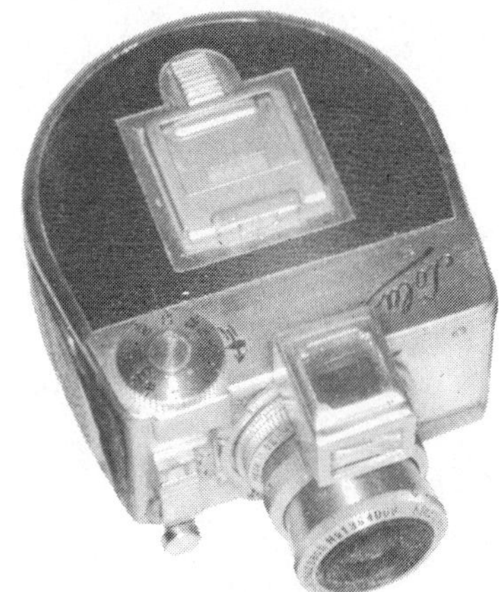

Schatz Sola

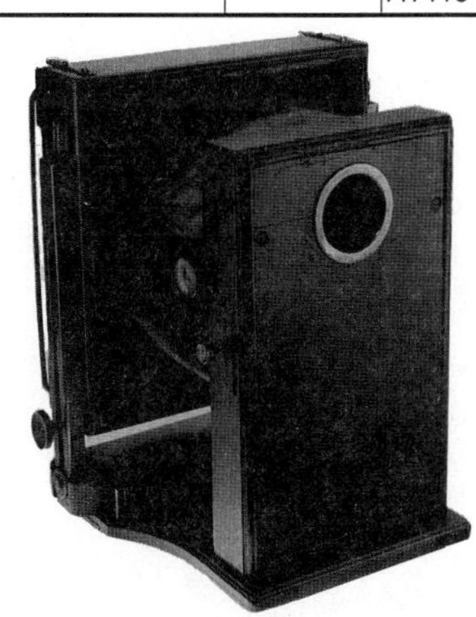

Schaub Multiplying Camera

MODEL	FORMAT	FILM	TYPE	Year	LENS	Apert	FL	SHUTTER	SPEEDS	ILLUS	U.S.$
...SCHLESICKY & STROHLEN - Frankfurt											
Comfort	6x7.5cm	plate	MagBox	1890	Achromat			guillotine	M,Z	HK32	440
Field camera 18x24	18x24cm	plate	Field	1890	various			various			270
Field camera 24x30	24x30cm	plate	Field	1890	various			various			230
...SCHMITZ & THIENEMANN - Dresden											
Patent-Sport-Reflex	6.5x9cm	plate	LgSLR	1931	Trioplan	4.5	105mm	Pronto		A587	280
Uniflex 4x6.5	4x6.5/3x4	127	LgSLR	1933	Trioplan	3.5	75mm	Pronto	25-100		700
Uniflex 6x9	6x9cm	120	LgSLR	1933	Trioplan	3.5	75mm	Pronto	25-100		250
Uniflex Reflex Meteor	6.5x9cm	plate	LgSLR	1931	Trioplan	4.5	105mm	Pronto	25-100		180
...SCHRAMBACH (C. Schrambach) - Paris											
Jumelle 6.5x9	6.5x9cm	plate	Jumelle	1903	Anastigmat			guillotine		F1109	140
Jumelle 9x12	9x12cm	plate	Jumelle	1903	Anastigmat			guillotine		A836	110
...SCHUNEMAN & EVANS - St. Paul, MN											
Lightning	4x5"	plate	VtFold Pl					B&L Unicum			90
...SCOTT-ATWATER MFG. CO. - Minneapolis, Minn.											
Photopal 3x3.5	3x3.5cm	127	RigidRo							Mc378	50
Photopal 4x6	4x6cm	127	RigidRo							Mc378	50
...SCOVILL MANUFACTURING CO. - N.Y.											
Antique Oak Detective	4x5"	plate	DetectivBox	1890	Dbl Combination			string-set		Mc378	700
Book Camera	4x5"	plate	Disguised	1892	Periscopic Achr.	12	75mm	guillotine		Mc378	12000
Field camera 4x5"	4x5"	plate	Field	1880	Waterbury						200
Field camera 8x10"	8x10"	plate	Field	1880	Waterbury						200
Irving	11x14'	plate	Field	1890	Rapid Rectilinear					Mc379	410
Knack Detective		plate	DetectivBox	1891							630
Mascot	4x5"	plate	DetectivBox	1890				string-set			460
Scovill Detective 3¼x4¼"	3¼x4¼"	plate	DetectivBox	1886							900
Scovill Detective 4x5"	4x5"	plate	DetectivBox	1886						Mc379	800
Scovill Detective 4¼x6½"	4¼x6½"	plate	DetectivBox	1886							800
Scovill Detective 5x7"	5x7"	plate	DetectivBox	1886							800
St. Louis	8x10"	plate	Field	1888							230
Stereo Field camera	5x8"	plate	SterField	1894	Anastigmat					A2654	420
Stereo Solograph	4x6½"	plate	StFoldPl	1899	Stereo R.R.			Stereo Auto			460
Triad Detective	4x5"	plate	DetectivBox	1892				Instant		Mc379	380
View 4x5"	4x5"	plate	Field	1882	various			various			260
View 5x8"	5x8"	plate	Field	1882	various			various			260
Waterbury Det. (original)	4x5"	plate	DetectivBox	1888	Wale				I,T		510
Waterbury Det. (original)	5x7"	plate	DetectivBox	1888	Wale				I,T		700
Waterbury Det. (improved)	4x5"	plate	DetectivBox	1892	Wale				I,T	Mc379	410
Waterbury Det. (improved)	5x7"	plate	DetectivBox	1892	Wale				I,T	Mc379	410
Waterbury Stereo	5x8"	plate	SterTail	1885	Scovill Waterbury					Mc379	520
Waterbury View 4x5"	4x5"	plate	Tailboard	1886	Eurygraph			Prosch Dupl.		Mc379	180
Waterbury View 4x5"	4x5"	plate	Tailboard	1886	Rapid Rectilinear			Prosch Dupl.		Mc379	180

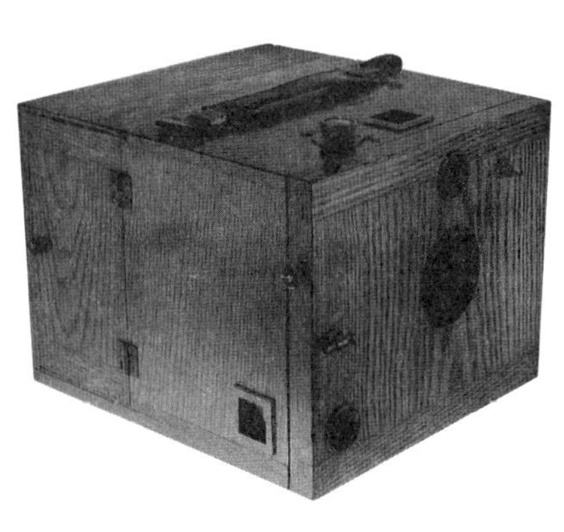

Scovill Antique Oak Detective

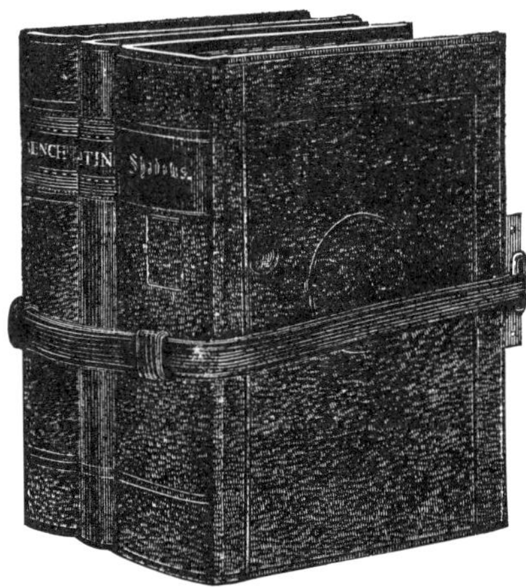

Scovill Book Camera

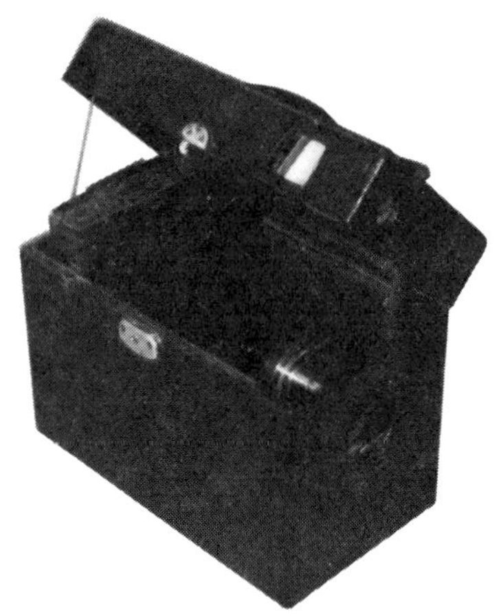

Scovill Detective

MODEL	FORMAT	FILM	TYPE	Year	LENS	Apert	FL	SHUTTER	SPEEDS	ILLUS	U.S.$
Waterbury View 5x8"	5x8"	plate	Tailboard	1886	Waterbury						240
Waterbury View 6½x8½"	6½x8½"	plate	Tailboard	1886	Waterbury						200
Wet plate camera	5x7"	WetPl	WetPlate	1860							1900
...SEARS ROEBUCK & CO. (Seroco)											
Delmar 3¼x4¼"	3¼x4¼"	plate	PlateBox								30
Delmar 4x5"	4x5"	plate	PlateBox								30
Marvel S-16	2½x4¼"	116	RollBox	1940				leaf	I,T		10
Marvel S-20	6x9cm	120	RollBox	1940				leaf	I,T		10
Marvel-flex	6x6cm	120	TLR	1941	Woll. Velostigmat	4.5	83mm	Alphax	10-200,T,B	Mc379	30
Perfection	4x5"	plate	FoldPl								50
Plate Camera	4x5"	plate	H&S							Mc379	120
Seroco (folding plate)	4x5"	plate	H&S	1901	Seroco Symmetr.			Wollensak		Mc380	120
Seroco (folding plate)	5x7"	plate	H&S								140
Seroco (folding plate)	6½x8½"	plate	H&S								160
Seroco (view)	8x10"	plate	Field	1915	various			various			180
Seroco Magazine	4x5"	plate	MagBox	1902	achromatic						70
Seroco Magazine	4x5"	plate	MagBox	1902	Meniscus						70
Seroco Stereo	5x7"	plate	StFoldPl					Woll. Stereo			460
Tower (Iloca Quick B)	24x36mm	35mm	35VF	1955	Tower Anastigmat	2.9	50mm	Prontor-S	1-300		30
Tower, Type 3	24x36mm	35mm	35RF	1949	Nikkor	2	50mm			Mc380	330
Tower No. 5	4x4cm	127	RigidRo	1960	Meniscus					Mc380	30
Tower 10A	24x36mm	35mm	35RF	1960	Mamiya-Sekor	2.8	48mm		B,1-500		30
Tower 16	10x14mm	16mm	Submin	1959	Mamiya	3.5	25mm		2-200	Mc380	140
Tower 18A	24x36mm	35mm	35RF	1960	Mamiya	1.9	48mm		1-500		30
Tower 18B	24x36mm	35mm	35RF	1962	Mamiya-Kominar	2	48mm	Copal SVK	B, 1-500		30
Tower 19	24x36mm	35mm	35RF	1960	E.Zuiko	2.8	45mm	Seikosha-SLV	1-500		100
Tower 22	24x36mm	35mm	35SLR	1954	Takumar	3.5	50mm	focal plane	500		170
Tower 23	24x36mm	35mm	35SLR	1954	Takumar	2.4	58mm	focal plane	500	Mc380	170
Tower 24	24x36mm	35mm	35SLR	1954	Takumar	3.5	50mm	focal plane	500	Mc380	170
Tower 26	24x36mm	35mm	35SLR	1958	Takumar	2.4	55mm	focal plane	500		170
Tower 29	24x36mm	35mm	35SLR	1959	Auto-Takumar	1.9	55mm	focal plane	1-1000		90
Tower 32A	24x36mm	35mm	35SLR	1963	Mamiya/Sekor	1.7	58mm	focal plane	1-1000,B		100
Tower 33	24x36mm	35mm	35SLR	1960	Reflex-Quinon	2.8	50mm	Sync-Compur	1-500,B,ST		70
Tower 34	24x36mm	35mm	35SLR	1960	Reflex-Quinon	1.9	50mm	Sync-Compur	1-500	Mc380	70
Tower 35	24x36mm	35mm	35SLR	1960	Nikkor	2.8	50mm	focal plane	1-1000		430
Tower 37	24x36mm	35mm	35SLR	1961	Mamiya	2.8	48mm	focal plane	1-500	Mc380	70
Tower 39 Automatic 35	24x36mm	35mm	35VF	1962	Mamiya	3.8			250		30
Tower 41	24x36mm	35mm	35RF	1962		2.8			250		30
Tower 45	24x36mm	35mm	35RF	1957	Nikkor	2	50mm	focal plane	1-1000	Mc381	210
Tower 46	24x36mm	35mm	35RF	1957	Nikkor	1.4		focal plane	1-1000		210
Tower 50 (35mm)	24x36mm	35mm	35VF	1954	Cassar	2.8	45mm		25-200,B	Mc381	30
Tower 51 (35mm)	24x36mm	35mm	35RF	1954	Cassar	2.8	50mm	Prontor-SVS	B, 1-300	Mc381	30

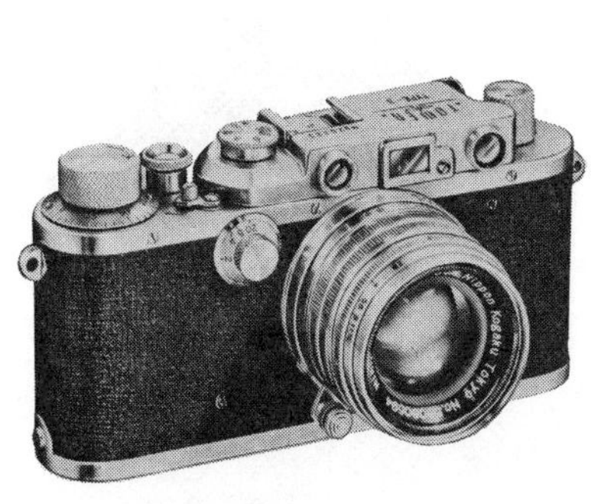

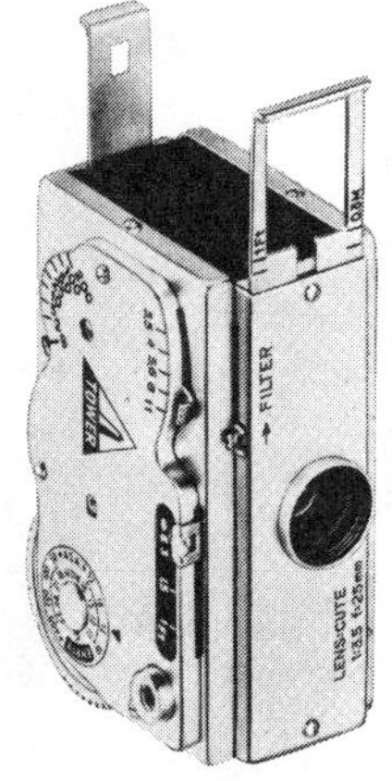

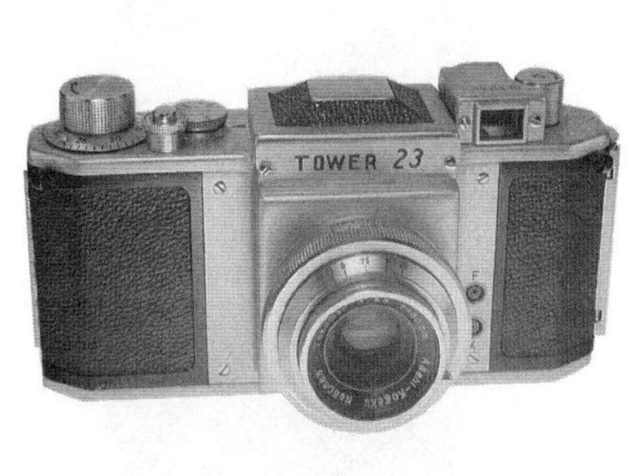

Sears Tower, Type 3 | **Sears Tower 16** | **Sears Tower 23**

MODEL	FORMAT	FILM	TYPE	Year	LENS	Apert	FL	SHUTTER	SPEEDS	ILLUS	U.S.$
Tower 51 (rollfilm)	6x9cm	120	VtFoldRo	1955	Crystar				I,B	Mc381	10
Tower 55	24x36mm	35mm	35VF	1959	Color Luna	3.5	45mm	Leaf	B,25-300	Mc381	30
Tower 127EF	$1\frac{5}{8}$x$1\frac{5}{8}$"	127	RigidRo		Meniscus					Mc381	50
Tower Automatic 127	4x4cm	127	RigidRo	1960	Meniscus	5.6					30
Tower Bonita Mod. 14	4x4cm	127	TLR-Box		Meniscus				I,T	Mc381	30
Tower Camflash 127	4x4cm	127	RigidRo		Meniscus						20
Tower Camflash II 127	4x4cm	127	RigidRo		Meniscus						20
Tower Companion	6x6cm	120	PlasticBox		Meniscus						10
Tower Hide Away	$3\frac{1}{2}$x$3\frac{1}{2}$"	127	PlasticBox	1960	Meniscus				I,T		10
Tower Jr	$1\frac{5}{8}$x$2\frac{1}{2}$"	127	BakeliteRoll	1953	Meniscus				I,T	Mc381	40
Tower One-Twenty	6x9cm	120	RollBox	1950	Meniscus	16	110mm	Leaf	I,T		10
Tower One-Twenty Flash	6x9cm	120	RollBox	1950	Meniscus	16	110mm	Leaf	I,T		10
Tower Phantom	4x4cm	127	TLR-Box	1960	Meniscus				I,T	Mc381	30
Tower Pixie 127	4x4cm	127	RigidRo		Meniscus						10
Tower Pixie II 127	4x4cm	127	RigidRo		Meniscus						10
Tower Reflex	6x6cm	120	TLR	1955	Westar Anast.	3.5	75mm	Pronto	25-200	Mc382	70
Tower Reflex	6x6cm	120	TLR	1957	Tri-Lauser Anast.	3.5	80mm		1/25-300,B		70
Tower Reflex (MV)	6x6cm	120	TLR	1960	Fujitar	3.5	80mm	Citizen-MV	1-500,B		120
Tower Skipper	4x4cm	127	PlasticBox								30
Tower Snappy	6x6cm	620	PlasticBox							Mc382	10
Tower Stereo	24x25mm	35mm	35Ster	1955	Isco-Westar	3.5	35mm	Prontor-S	1-300		220
Trumpfreflex	6x6cm	120	TLR	1940	Trioplan	3.5	75mm		1-300		70
...SECAM - Paris											
Stereophot	10x10mm	16mm	SterMiniat	1950						Mc382	1200
Stylophot "Deluxe"	10x10mm	16mm	Submin	1950	Roussel Anast.	3.5	27mm		1/75	Mc382	200
Stylophot "Standard"	10x10mm	16mm	Submin	1950		6.3			1/50	Mc382	150
...S.E.D.E. - Rome											
Kelvin Maior	24x36mm	35mm	35VF	1952	Duo-Kelvin Achr.	8	50mm		25-100		30
Kelvin Minor	24x36mm	35mm	35VF	1952	Duo-Kelvin Achr.	8	50mm	2-speed		Mc382	30
Vinkel 50	24x36mm	35mm	35VF	1960					1/50		30
Vinkel Deluxe	24x36mm	35mm	35VF	1960					25-100	Mc382	20
...SEEMAN (H. Seeman)											
Stereo camera			SterStrut		Goerz Dagor		120mm				460
...SEIKI KOGAKU CO.											
Seiki		16mm	Submin	1950	Seek Anastigmat	3.5	25mm		25,50,100	Mc383	800
...SEISCHAB (Otto Seischab) - Nürnberg, Germany											
Esco	18x24mm	35mm	35Half	1922	Steinheil Cassar	3.5	35mm	Dial-Compur	1-300	A2045	3700
Esco	18x24mm	35mm	35Half	1922	Steinheil Cassar	2.5	50mm	Dial-Compur	1-300	A2046	3700
...S.E.M. (Sociéte des Établissements Modernes) - Aurec, France											
Babysem (first type)	24x36mm	35mm	35VF	1949	Cross	2.9	45mm	Orec	25-200	F539	30
Babysem (new type)	24x36mm	35mm	35VF		Berthiot	2.8	45mm	Orec	15-250	Mc383	50
Challenger	4x4cm	620	RigidRo	1959	Angenieux				I	Mc383	30

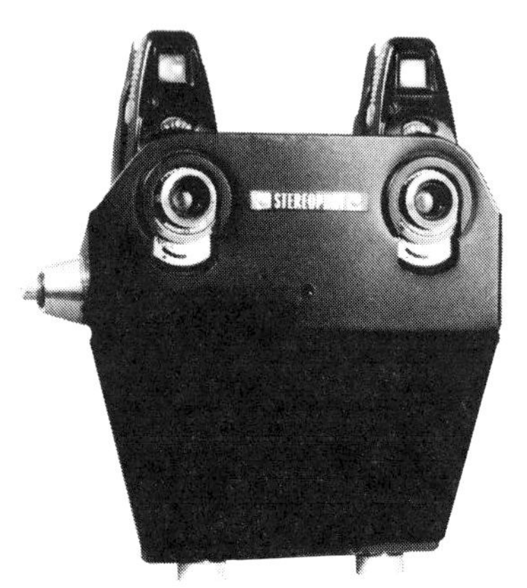

Secam Stereophot

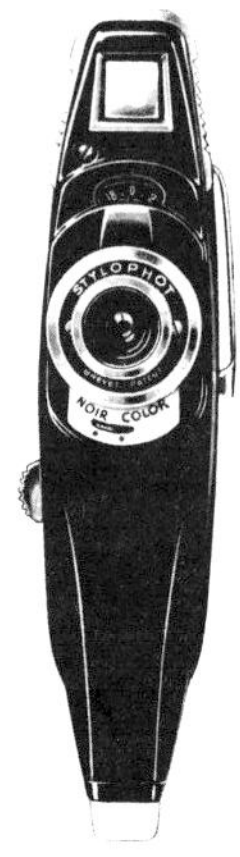

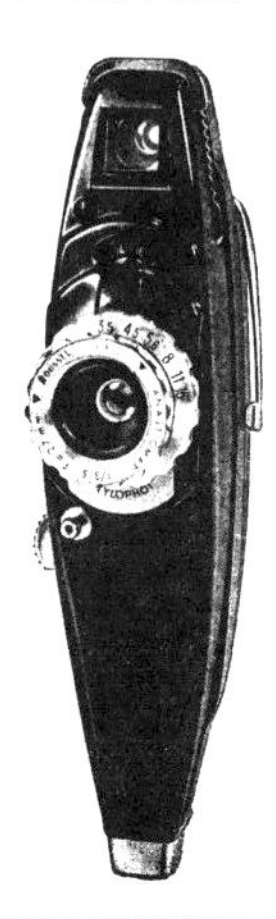

Secam Stylophot "Standard"

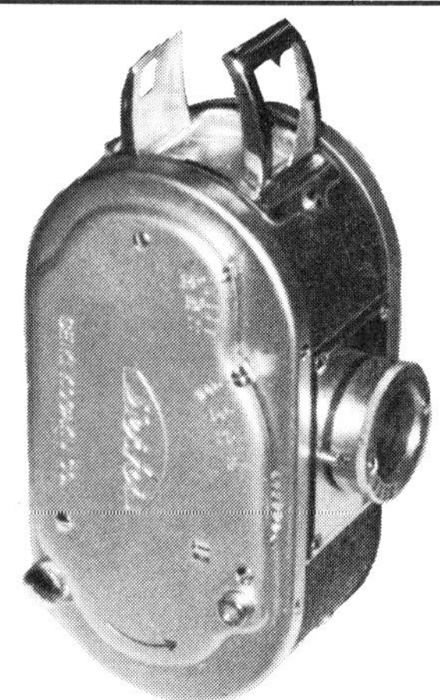

Seiki

MODEL	FORMAT	FILM	TYPE	Year	LENS	Apert	FL	SHUTTER	SPEEDS	ILLUS	U.S.$
Colorado	4x4cm	620	RigidRo	1959	Angenieux				I	Mc383	30
Grenaflex	6x6cm	120	TLR	1947	Angenieux				15-250		70
Kim	24x36mm	35mm	35VF	1947	Cross Anastigmat	2.9	45mm		25-200	Mc383	30
Kim	24x36mm	35mm	35VF	1947	Cross Anastigmat	2.9	45mm		1-200	Mc383	30
Orenac III	24x36mm	35mm	35VF	1950	Angenieux	2.9	50mm	Orec	1-400	F639	30
Orenac III	24x36mm	35mm	35VF	1950	Berthiot	2.8	50mm	Orec	1-400	F640	30
Semflex 154	6x6cm	120	TLR	1954	Angenieux	3.5	75mm	Orec	1-400	F521	90
Semflex Joie de Vivre 45	6x6cm	120	TLR	1958	Berthiot	4.5	75mm	Orec	1/50	F522	140
Semflex Joie de Vivre 45	6x6cm	120	TLR	1958	Berthiot	3.5	75mm	Orec	1/50	F523	140
Semflex Otomatic	6x6cm	120	TLR	1950	Berthiot	3.5	75mm	Orec	1-300	Mc383	70
Semflex Otomatic 2	6x6cm	120	TLR	1950	Flor Berthiot	3.5	75mm	Orec	1-300	F519	90
Semflex Otomatic 3	6x6cm	120	TLR	1955	Flor Berthiot	3.5	75mm	Compur	1-500	F520	120
Semflex S2	6x6cm	120	TLR	1950	Angenieux	3.5	75mm	Orec	1-400	F496	100
Semflex Standard	6x6cm	120	TLR	1950	Angenieux	3.5	75mm	Orec	1-400	Mc383	70
Semflex Studio Standard	6x6cm	120	TLR	1951	Berthiot	5.4	150mm	Orec	1-400	Mc383	300
Semflex Studio Standard	6x6cm	120	TLR	1972	Berthiot	5.4	150mm	Sync-Compur	1-500	Mc383	290
Semflex T950	6x6cm	120	TLR	1954	Berthiot	4.5	75mm	Orec	10-250	F503	60
...SEMMENDINGER (A. Semmendinger) - Ft. Lee, NJ											
Excelsior 5x5"	5x5"	WetPl	WetPlate	1870	Brass barrel						1000
Excelsior 6½x8½"	6½x8½"	WetPl	WetPlate	1870	Brass barrel						1000
Excelsior 12x12"	12x12"	WetPl	WetPlate	1870	Brass barrel						1000
...SENECA CAMERA CO. - Rochester, N.Y.											
Black Beauty 3¼x5½"	3¼x5½"	plate	H&S							Mc384	90
Black Beauty 4x5"	4x5"	plate	H&S							Mc384	90
Busy Bee	4x5"	plate	PlateBox	1903	Rapid Rectilinear			Uno			70
Camera City View 5x7"	5x7"	plate	Field	1907	Seneca Anast.			Ilex		Mc384	200
Camera City View 6½x8½"	6½x8½"	plate	Field	1907	Seneca Anast.			Ilex		Mc384	200
Camera City View 8x10"	8x10"	plate	Field	1907	Seneca Anast.			Ilex		Mc384	200
Camera City View 17x20"	17x20"	plate	Field	1907	Symmetrical	8		Autic			370
Chautauqua 4x5"	4x5"	plate	H&S		Wollensak			Seneca Uno		Mc384	90
Chautauqua 5x7"	5x7"	plate	H&S		Wollensak			Seneca Uno			100
Chief 1A	2½x4¼"	116	VtFoldRl	1918							30
Competitor View 5x7"	5x7"	plate	Field	1907	various			various		Mc384	130
Competitor View 8x10"	8x10"	plate	Field	1907	various			various		Mc384	130
Competitor View Stereo	5x7	plate	SterField		various			various			330
Filmett	3¼x4¼"	pack	FoldPack	1910	Woll. Achromatic			Uno		Mc384	40
Folding plate camera	3¼x4¼"	plate	VtFoldPl		Wollensak	16		Uno			50
Folding plate camera	3¼x5½"	plate	VtFoldPl		Triple convertible						50
Folding plate camera	4x5"	plate	VtFoldPl					Seneca Uno			50
Folding plate camera	4x5"	plate	VtFoldPl					Auto			50
Folding plate camera	5x7"	plate	VtFoldPl		Rogers		7"	Auto			80
Folding plate camera	5x7"	plate	VtFoldPl		Seneca Anast.		7"	Auto			80

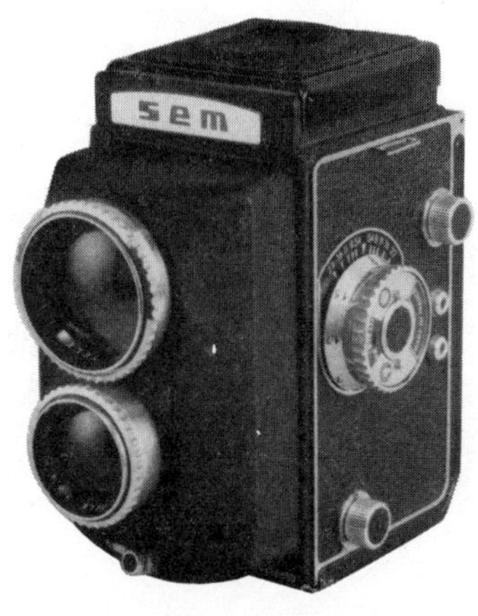

Semflex Studio Standard

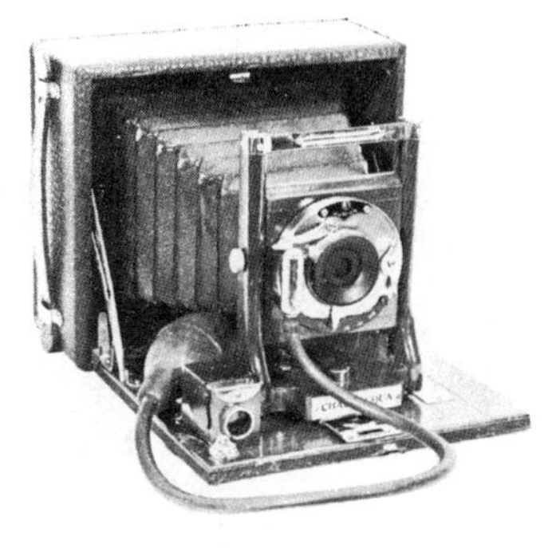

Seneca Chautauqua

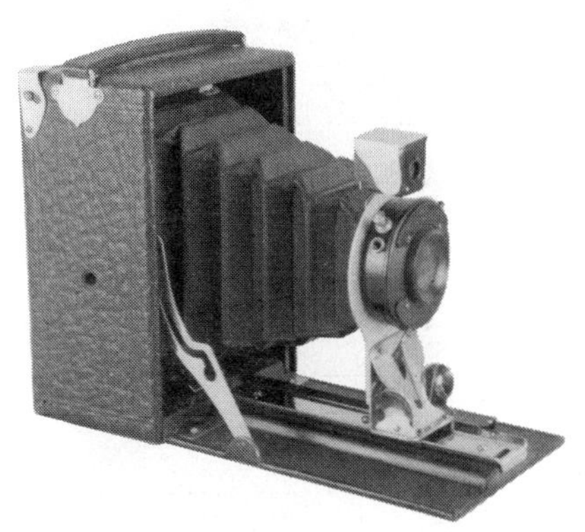

Seneca Filmett

MODEL	FORMAT	FILM	TYPE	Year	LENS	Apert	FL	SHUTTER	SPEEDS	ILLUS	U.S.$
Folding plate camera No. 8	4x5"	plate	VtFoldPl	1920	Symmetrical	8		Autic			70
Folding plate camera No. 9	3¼x4¼"	plate	VtFoldPl	1907	Convertible	4				Mc384	120
Folding plate camera No. 9	4x5"	plate	VtFoldPl	1907	Velostigmat			Compur		Mc384	120
Folding plate camera No. 9	5x7"	plate	VtFoldPl	1907	Velostigmat			Duo			130
Folding Scout No. 2A	2¼x4¼"	116	VtFoldRo	1915	Wollensak R.R.			Ultro			20
Folding Scout No. 2C	2⅞x4⅞"	130	VtFoldRo	1917	Wollensak R.R.			Ultro			20
Folding Scout No. 3	3¼x4¼"	124	VtFoldRo	1915	Wollensak R.R.			Ultro		Mc385	20
Folding Scout No. 3A	3¼x5½"	122	VtFoldRo	1915	Wollensak R.R.			Seneca Trio			20
Kao Jr.	3½x3½"	plate	PlateBox		Meniscus				I,T		50
Kao Sr.	4x5"	plate	PlateBox		Meniscus				I,T		70
No. 1 Seneca Junior	2¼x3¼"	120	StrutRo	1916				Ilex		Mc384	30
Pocket Seneca No. 3A	3¼x5½"	plate	VtFoldPl	1908	Rapid convertible			Auto	1-100	Mc384	50
Pocket Seneca No. 29	4x5"	plate	VtFoldPl	1905		8		Seneca Uno			60
Roll Film Seneca No. 1	2¼x3¼"	120	VtFoldRo	1914	Meniscus Achrom.			Trio			30
Roll Film Seneca No. 1A	2¼x4¼"	116	VtFoldRo	1914	Meniscus Achrom.			Trio			30
Scout box No. 2	2¼x3¼"	120	RollBox	1913	Meniscus			Auto	I,T	Mc384	20
Scout box No. 2A	2¼x4¼"	116	RollBox	1913	Meniscus Achrom.			Auto	I,T	Mc384	20
Scout box No. 3	3¼x4¼"	124	RollBox	1913	Meniscus Achrom.			Auto	I,T	Mc384	20
Scout box No. 3A	3¼x5½"	122	RollBox	1913	Meniscus Achrom.			Auto	I,T	Mc384	20
Senco No. 1		120	VtFoldRo	1912						Mc385	50
Stereo View	5x7"	plate	StFoldPl	1910	Wollensak			Stereo Uno		Mc385	370
Stereo View	5x7"	plate	StFoldPl	1910	Wollensak			Stereo Auto		Mc385	370
Vest Pocket	1½x2½"	127	StrutRo	1916	Seneca Anast.	7.7		Trio	25-100	Mc385	50
View Camera 5x7"	5x7"	plate	Field	1903	Rapid convertible			Ilex	1-100		140
View Camera 5x7"	5x7"	plate	Field	1903	Goerz Syntor	6.8		Ilex	1-100		140
View Camera 8x10"	8x10"	plate	Field	1902	Woll. Velostigmat	4.5	12"	Optimo			180
View Camera 8x10"	8x10"	plate	Field	1902	Double Anast.			Woll. Regular			180
View Camera Improved	5x7"	plate	Field	1905	Woll. Planatic			Auto		Mc385	160
View Camera Improved	6½x8½"	plate	Field	1905	Goerz Doppel An.	6.8	7"	Volute			140
View Camera Improved	8x10"	plate	Field	1902	Woll. Velostigmat	4.5	12"	Optimo			180
View Camera Improved	8x10"	plate	Field	1902	Double Anast.			Woll. Regular			180
...SEYMORE PRODUCTS CO. - Chicago, IL											
Brenda Starr Cub Reporter	3x4cm	127	Minicam						I,T	Mc385	100
Dick Tracy	3x4cm	127	Minicam	1942					I,T	Mc385	40
...SEYMOUR SALES CO. - Chicago											
Dick Tracy	3x4cm	127	Minicam	1942					I,T	Mc385	30
Flash-Master	3x4cm	127	Minicam						I,T	Mc385	10
...S.F.O.M. (Société Francaise d' Optique Méchanique)											
Sfomax	14x23mm	16mm	Submin	1949	S'fomar	3.5	30mm		25-400	Mc385	610
Sfomax	14x23mm	16mm	Submin	1949	S'fomar	3.5	30mm		30-400	Mc385	610
...SHACKMAN (D. Shackman and Sons) - London, England											
Auto Camera, Mark 3	24x24mm	35mm	SciMed	1953	Dallmeyer					A1912	140

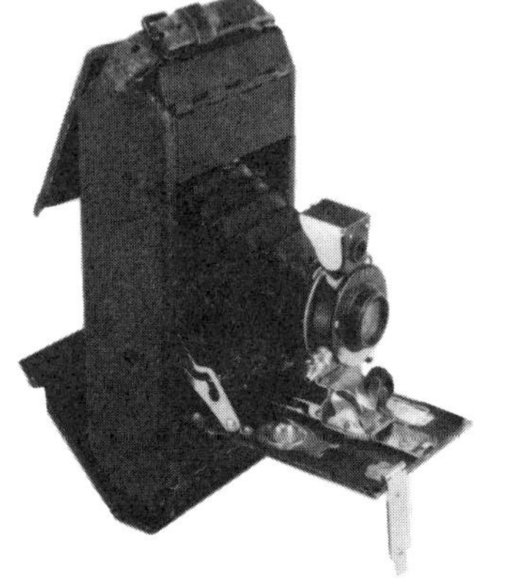

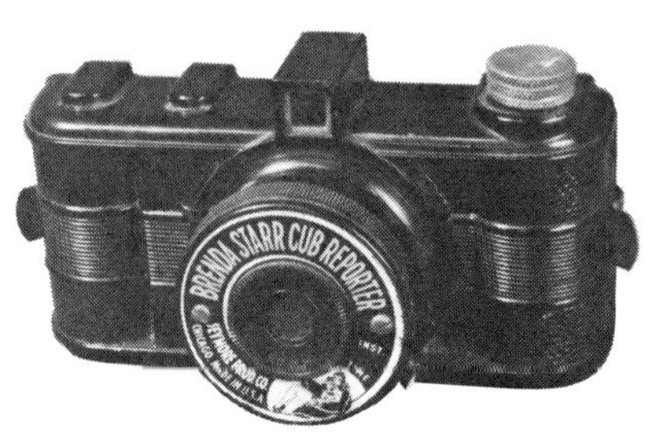

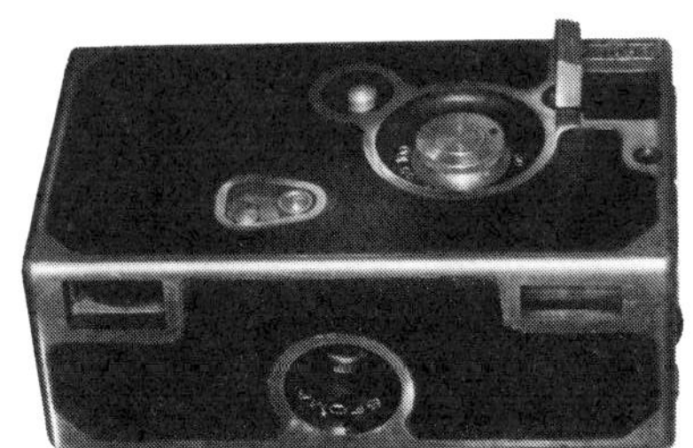

Senco No. 1 | Brenda Starr Cub Reporter | Sfomax

MODEL	FORMAT	FILM	TYPE	Year	LENS	Apert	FL	SHUTTER	SPEEDS	ILLUS	U.S.$
Multi-Shot Four X Four		Pola	MultiLens	1977	Wray					A3392	110
Multi-Shot Mini Four X Four		Pola	MultiLens	1977	Wray					A3392	140
...SHANGHAI CAMERA FACTORY											
East Wind	6x6cm	120	MedSLR	1970		2.8	80mm	focal plane			4200
Red Flag 20	24x36mm	35mm	35RF	1971		1.4	50mm	focal plane			4100
Shanghai	6x6cm	120	TLR	1950	Shanghai	3.5	75mm		300		230
Shanghai 58-I	24x36mm	35mm	35RF	1950	Shanghai	3.5	50mm	focal plane		Mc386	1700
Shanghai 58-II	24x36mm	35mm	35RF	1950	Shanghai	3.5	50mm	focal plane		Mc386	400
Shanghai 201	6x6/4.5x6	120	FoldRo	1950	Shanghai	3.5	75mm		300		210
Shanghai 203	6x6/4.5x6	120	FoldRo	1950	Shanghai	3.5	75mm		300		210
...SHAW (H.E. Shaw & Co.)											
Oxford Minicam	3x4cm	127	Minicam		Minivar				I,T	Mc386	10
...SHAW-HARRISON											
Sabre 620	6x6cm	620	PlasticBox	1956					I,T	A2848	10
Valiant 620	6x6cm	620	PlasticBox	1956					I,T		10
...SHEW (J.F. Shew & Co.) - London											
Aluminum Xit 3¼x4¼"	3¼x4¼"	plate	StrutPl	1900	Eclipse	8	5.5"	Central			270
Aluminum Xit 4¼x6½"	4¼x6½"	plate	StrutPl	1900	Eclipse	8	5.5"	Central			310
Day-Xit	3¼x4¼"	plate	StrutPl	1910	Cooke Anastigmat	6.5	5"	sector	1-100		220
Eclipse 3¼x4¼"	3¼x4¼"	plate	StrutPl	1890	Darlot R.R.			Eclipse		Mc386	270
Eclipse 4x5"	4x5"	plate	StrutPl	1890	Darlot R.R.			Eclipse		Mc386	300
Eclipse 4¼x6½"	4¼x6½"	plate	StrutPl	1890	Stigmatic			Eclipse		Mc386	300
Eclipse 5x7"	5x7"	plate	StrutPl	1890	Stigmatic			Eclipse		Mc386	240
Focal Plane Eclipse	3¼x4¼"	plate	StrutPl	1890	Darlot R.R.			focal plane	15-1000		290
Focal Plane Eclipse	5x7"	plate	StrutPl	1890	Darlot R.R.			focal plane	15-1000		280
Guinea Xit	8x10.5cm	plate	StrutPl	1906	achromatic		5.5"	Central rotary			230
Hand and Stand camera	3¼x4¼"	plate	H&S	1890	Darlot	8	100mm				410
Stereo camera	4¼x6½"	plate	SterStrut	1900	Shew					A1778	370
Stereo Field Camera	5x7"	plate	SterField	1900	Tessar	6.3	120mm	Dbl. Pneum.			1000
Tailboard camera 4x5"	4x5"	plate	Tailboard	1900	Shew						270
Tailboard camera 5x7"	5x7"	plate	Tailboard	1900	Beck Symmetrical	8					260
Xit 3¼x4¼"	3¼x4¼"	plate	StrutPl	1900	Eclipse	8	5.5"	Central		A287	280
Xit 9x12	9x12cm	plate	StrutPl	1900	Celor	4.8	125mm	Central			220
Xit 4¼x6½"	4¼x6½"	plate	StrutPl	1900	Eclipse	8	5.5"	Central			220
Xit Stereoscopic		plate	SterStrut	1900							800
...SHIMURA KOKI - Japan											
Mascot	14x14mm	Roll	Submin	1950	Mascot	4.5	25mm		25-100,B	HK622	400
...SHIN NIPPON - Japan											
Poppy			Submin		Erinor					Mc386	2700
...SHINANO CAMERA CO. LTD., SHINANO OPTICAL WORKS - Japan											
Pigeon	24x36mm	35mm	35VF	1952	Tri-Lausar	3.5	45mm	Synchro	1-200	Mc386	40
Pigeon III	24x36mm	35mm	35VF	1952	Tri-Lausar	3.5	45mm	TSK			50

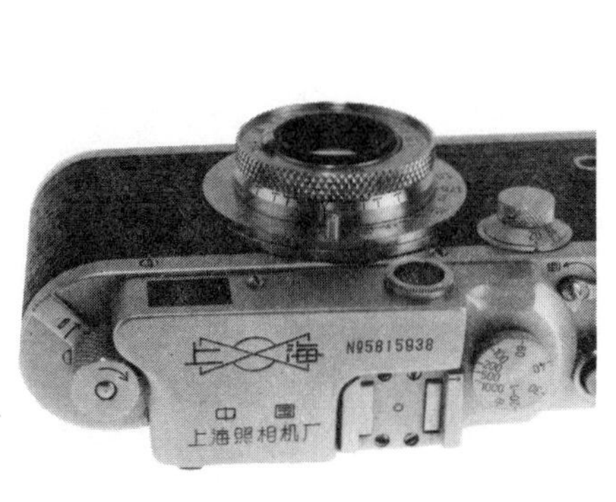

Shanghai 58-I

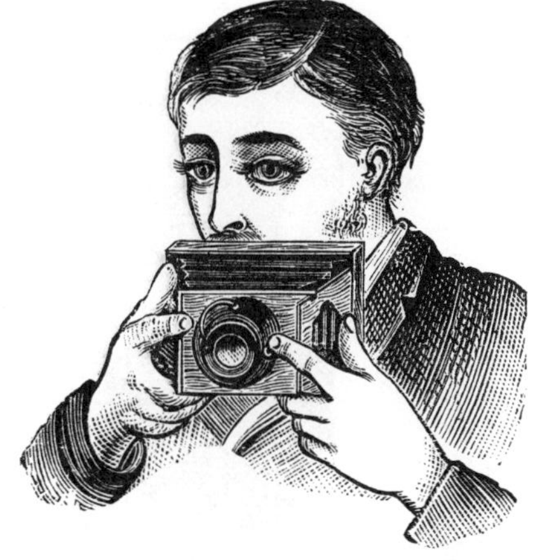

Shew Eclipse

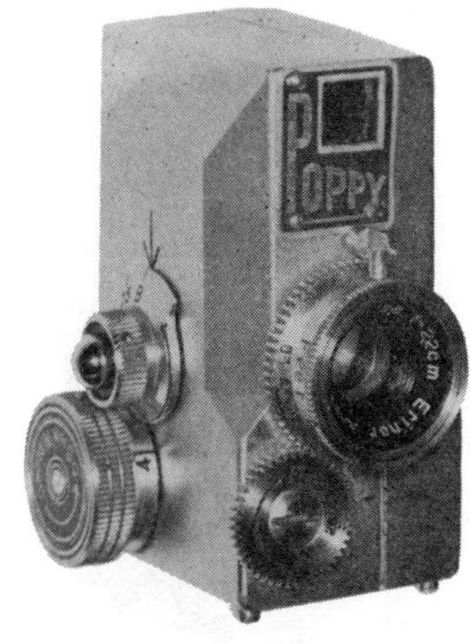

Shin Nippon Poppy

MODEL	FORMAT	FILM	TYPE	Year	LENS	Apert	FL	SHUTTER	SPEEDS	ILLUS	U.S.$
...SHINCHO SEIKI CO. LTD. - Japan											
Albert	10x12mm	16mm	Submin	1957	Normal-Arcus	1.9	10mm		I,B	Mc386	540
Darling-16	10x12mm	16mm	Submin	1957	Normal-Arcus	1.9	10mm		I,B	Mc386	400
...SHINSEI OPTICAL WORKS - Japan											
Monte 35	24x36mm	35mm	35VF	1953	Monte Anastigmat	3.5	50mm	Heilemann	1-200		50
...SHIRO PHOTO TRADING CO. LTD. - Osaka, Japan											
S&K 45MS 6x9	6x9cm	120	Field	1985	various			various		A2996	210
S&K 45MS 4x5"	4x5"	Sheet	Field	1985	various			various			210
...SHOEI MFG. CO. - Japan											
Ruvinal II	6x6cm	120	FoldRo	1951	Pentagon	3.5	80mm		1-200		40
Ruvinal III	6x6cm	620	FoldRo	1951	Seriter	3.5	75mm		1-200		40
...SHOWA KOGAKU - Japan											
Gemflex	14x14mm	Roll	Submin	1949	Gem	3.5	25mm	Swallow	25-100	Mc387	650
Leotax DIV	24x36mm	35mm	35RF	1950	C. Simlar	1.5	50mm	focal plane	1-500		390
Leotax F	24x36mm	35mm	35RF	1954	Topcor	1.5	50mm	focal plane	1-1000		290
Leotax FV	24x36mm	35mm	35RF	1958	Topcor	2	5cm	focal plane	1-500		340
Leotax G	24x36mm	35mm	35RF	1961	Topcor	1.8	5cm	focal plane	1-1000		520
Leotax K	24x36mm	35mm	35RF	1955	Topcor	3.5	50mm	focal plane	25-500		220
Leotax K3	24x36mm	35mm	35RF	1958	Fujinon	2.8	5cm	focal plane	8-500		330
Leotax NR III	24x36mm	35mm	35RF	1949	C. Simlar	3.5	50mm	focal plane	1-500		1700
Leotax S	24x36mm	35mm	35RF	1952	C. Simlar	1.5	50mm	focal plane	1-500	Mc387	220
Leotax Special	24x36mm	35mm	35RF	1946	State	3.5	50mm	focal plane	20-500		1500
Leotax Special A	24x36mm	35mm	35RF	1942	Letana Anastigmat	3.5	5cm	focal plane	20-500		1500
Leotax Special B	24x36mm	35mm	35RF	1942	Letana Anastigmat	3.5	5cm	focal plane	1-500		1500
Leotax Special DII	24x36mm	35mm	35RF	1947	C. Simlar	3.5	50mm	focal plane	20-500		530
Leotax Special DIII	24x36mm	35mm	35RF	1947	C. Simlar	3.5	50mm	focal plane	1-500		620
Leotax T	24x36mm	35mm	35RF	1955	Topcor	3.5	50mm	focal plane	1/500		220
Leotax T2	24x36mm	35mm	35RF	1958	Fujinon	2	50mm	focal plane	1-500		330
Leotax T2L	24x36mm	35mm	35RF	1959	Leonon	2	5cm	focal plane	1-500		440
Leotax TV	24x36mm	35mm	35RF	1957	Topcor	2	50mm	focal plane	1-500		310
Leotax TV2	24x36mm	35mm	35RF	1958	Topcor	2	5cm	focal plane	1-500		440
Semi-Leotax	4.5x6cm	120	VtFoldRo	1940	Reginon Anast.	3.5	75mm	Wester	1-200	Mc387	100
...SIAF - Argentina & Chile											
Amiga	6x9/4.5x6	120	RigidRo			7.5	135mm		I,P	Mc387	30
Gradosol	6x9/4.5x6	120	RigidRo			7.5	135mm		I,P	Mc387	30
Gradosol Lujo	6x9/4.5x6	120	RigidRo		Fixed focus	10	91mm		I,P	Mc387	30
...SIDA GmbH - Berlin-Charlottenburg											
Sida (black)	24x24mm	Roll	MiniatRo	1936						Mc387	50
Sida (green)	24x24mm	Roll	MiniatRo	1936						Mc387	70
Sida (England)	24x24mm	Roll	MiniatRo	1936						Mc387	60
Sida (France)	24x24mm	Roll	MiniatRo	1936						Mc387	70
Sida (Italy)	24x24mm	Roll	MiniatRo	1936						Mc387	70

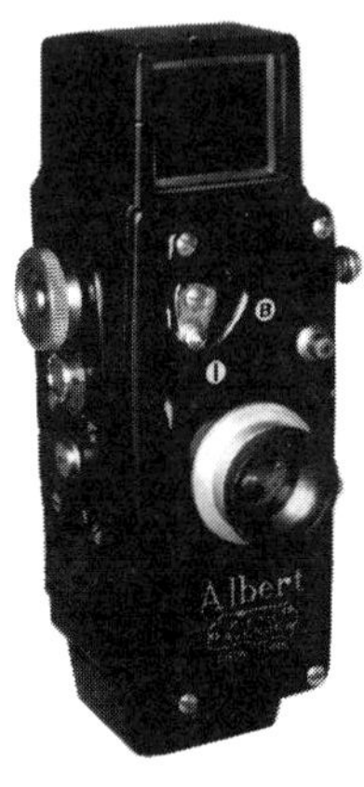

Shincho Albert

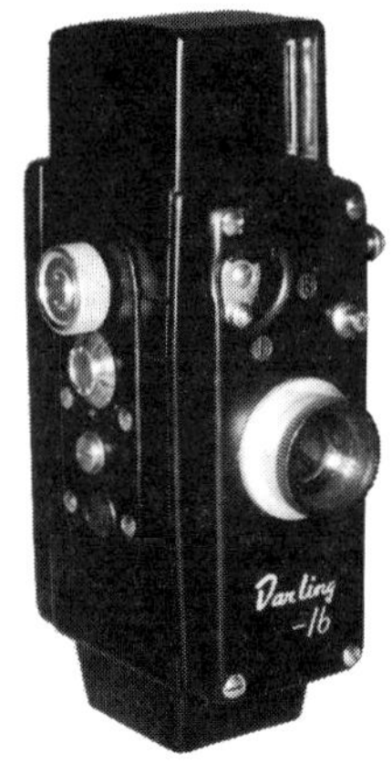

Shincho Darling-16

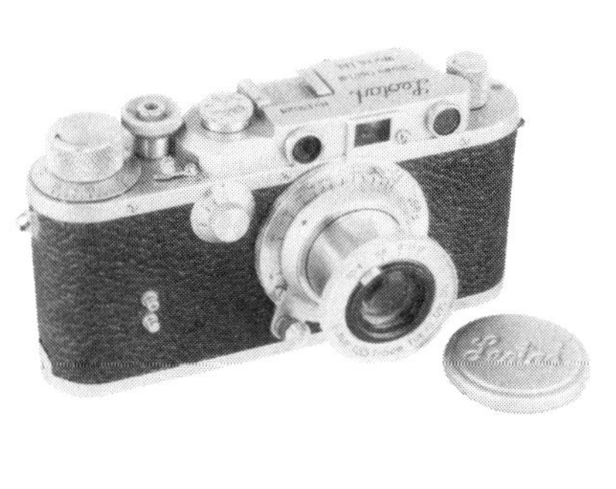
Showa Leotax S

MODEL	FORMAT	FILM	TYPE	Year	LENS	Apert	FL	SHUTTER	SPEEDS	ILLUS	U.S.$
Sida (Poland)	24x24mm	Roll	MiniatRo	1938	Sida Optik	8	35mm			Mc387	70
Sida Extra (black)	24x24mm	Roll	MiniatRo	1938	Sida Optik	8	35mm			Mc387	50
Sida Extra (brown)	24x24mm	Roll	MiniatRo	1938	Sida Optik	8	35mm			Mc387	70
Sida Standard	25x25mm	Roll	MiniatRo	1938	Sida Optik	8	35mm			Mc388	30
Sidax	25x25mm	Roll	MiniatRo	1948						Mc388	70
...SIGMA CORP. - Japan											
28 AF Zoom	24x36mm	35mm	35AFZ	1993	Sigma Zoom	4.2-7	28-50	programmed	2-1/500		180
35 AF Zoom	24x36mm	35mm	35AFZ	1988	Sigma Zoom	3.5-6.7	35-70	programmed	1-500		130
50 AF Zoom	24x36mm	35mm	35AFZ	1993	Sigma Zoom	4.3-8	50-100	programmed			140
AF Zoom Super 70	24x36mm	35mm	35AFZ		Sigma Zoom	3.5-6.7	35-70	programmed	1-500		130
AF Zoom Super 100	24x36mm	35mm	35AFZ		Sigma Zoom	4.3-8	50-100	programmed			140
Mark I	24x36mm	35mm	35SLR	1976	Tessar	2.8	50mm	focal plane			50
Mini-Zoom	24x36mm	35mm	35AFZ	1994	Sigma Zoom	3.8-8.5	38-105	programmed	8-1/500		290
SA-1	24x36mm	35mm	35SLR	1984	Sigma Zoom	2.8	35-70	focal plane	8-1/1000		280
SA-300	24x36mm	35mm	35AFSLR	1993	Sigma Zoom	4-5.6	35-80	programmed	30-1/4000		290
SA-300N	24x36mm	35mm	35AFSLR	1994	Sigma AF	4-5.6	28-70	focal plane	30-1/4000		340
...SIGRISTE (J.G. Sigriste) - Paris											
Sigriste 6.5x9	6.5x9cm	plate	Jumelle	1900	Zeiss Tessar	4.5		focal plane	1/10000	F1116	5100
Sigriste 9x12	9x12cm	plate	Jumelle	1900	Zeiss Tessar	4.5		focal plane	1/40-2500	A830	5100
Sigriste Stereo	6x13cm	plate	StJumelle	1900	Tele-Tessar	4.5	150mm	focal plane	60-4000	F1370	8000
Sigriste Stereo	6x13cm	plate	StJumelle	1900	Tessar	4.5	90mm	focal plane	1/2000	A1790	6800
...SIMDA - Le Perreux, France											
Panorascope	11.7x20m	16mm	SterMiniat	1955	Roussel Microcol	3.5	25mm	Stereo	1-250	Mc388	700
Panorascope	11.7x20m	16mm	SterMiniat	1955	Angenieux	3.5	25mm	Stereo	1-250	Mc388	700
...SIMMON BROTHERS, INC. - New York											
Omega 120	2¼x2¾"	120	MedRF	1954	Omicron	3.5	90mm	Rapax	1-400	Mc388	210
Signal Corps Combat Cam.	2¼x3¼"	pack	MedRF		Velostigmat	4.5	101mm	Rapax			250
...SIMONS (Wolfgang Simons & Co.) - Bern, Switzerland											
Sico 30x40	30x40mm	35mm	RigidRo	1923	Dagor Dop.Anast.	6.8		Dial-Compur	1-300	Mc388	4400
Sico 30x40	30x40mm	35mm	RigidRo	1923	Sico Rüdersdorf	3.5	60mm	Dial-Compur	1-300	Mc388	4400
Sico 4.5x6	4.5x6cm	120	RigidRo	1923	Dagor	6.8	90mm	Dial-Compur	1-250	Mc388	4400
...SINAR A.G. - Switzerland											
Sinar 4x5"	4x5"	plate	Monorail	1953	various			various			660
Sinar 5x7"	5x7"	plate	Monorail	1953	various			various			660
Sinar-f 4x5"	4x5"	plate	Monorail	1973	various			various			900
Sinar-f 8x10"	8x10"	plate	Monorail	1973	various			various			1700
Sinar-f2 4x5"	4x5"	plate	Monorail	1988	various			various			1500
Sinar-f2 5x7"	5x7"	plate	Monorail	1988	various			various			1500
Sinar-p 4x5"	4x5"	plate	Monorail	1971	various			various			2300
Sinar-p 5x7"	5x7"	plate	Monorail	1971	various			various			2300
Sinar-p 8x10"	8x10"	plate	Monorail	1971	various			various			3400
Sinar-p2 4x5"	4x5"	plate	Monorail	1988	various			various			3500

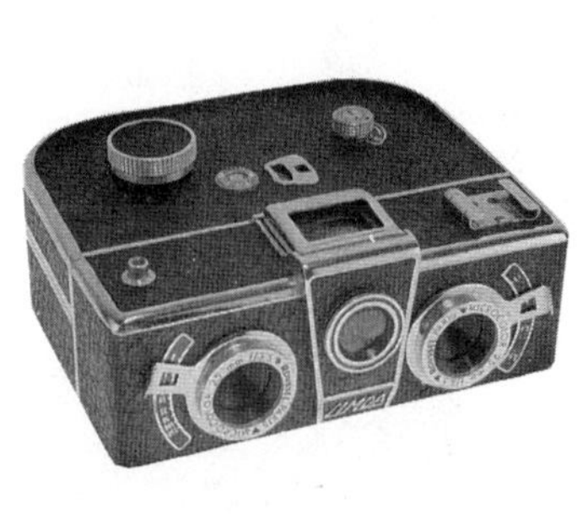

Simda Panorascope

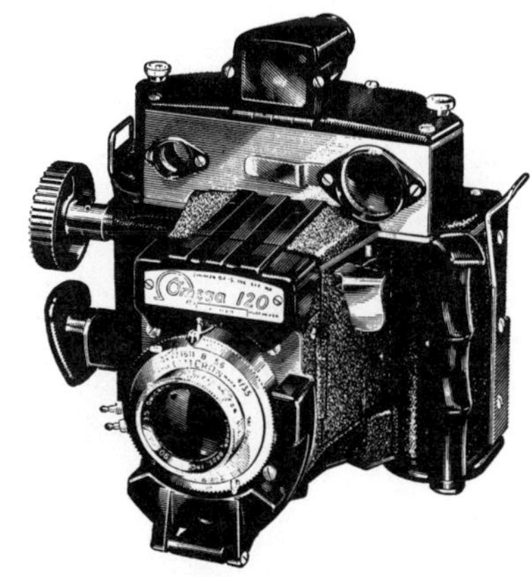

Simmon Omega 120

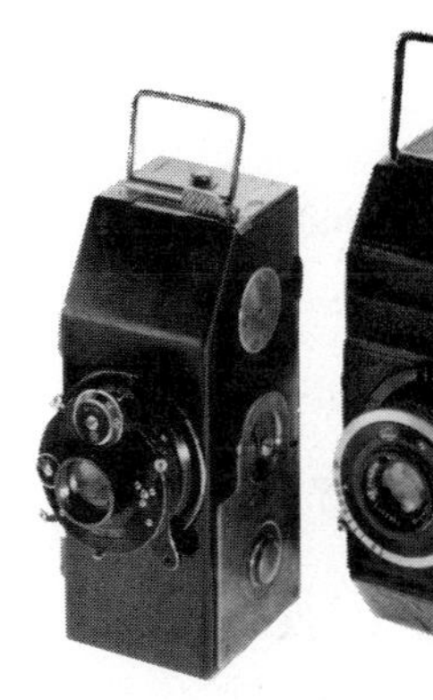

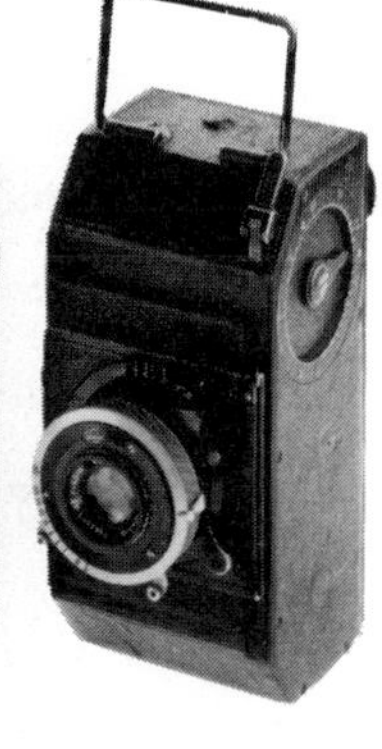

Simons Sico 30x40

MODEL	FORMAT	FILM	TYPE	Year	LENS	Apert	FL	SHUTTER	SPEEDS	ILLUS	U.S.$
Sinar-p2 5x7"	5x7"	plate	Monorail	1988	various			various			3300
Sinar-p2 18x24 cm	18x24cm	plate	Monorail	1988	various			various		A2997	4300
Sinar-x 4x5"	4x5"	plate	Monorail	1994	various						3800
Sinar-x 5x7"	5x7"	plate	Monorail	1994	various						3800
Sinar-x 18x24	18x24cm	plate	Monorail	1994	various						3800
...SINCLAIR (James A. Sinclair & Co., Ltd.) - London											
N&S Reflex	3¼x4¼"	plate	LgSLR	1910	Ross	4.5					410
Traveller Roll-Film	3¼x4¼"	118	RollBox	1910	Goerz Dagor	6.8		B&L Automat		Mc388	330
Traveller Una	6x9cm	plate	H&S	1927	Ross Combinable			N.S. Perfect		Mc389	2900
Tropical Una 6x9	6x9cm	plate	H&S	1910	Ross Convertible		5"	Optimo		Mc389	1100
Tropical Una 3¼x4¼"	3¼x4¼"	plate	H&S	1910	Aldis Anastigmat			B&L Automat		Mc389	520
Tropical Una 4¼x6½"	4¼x6½"	plate	H&S	1910	Aldis Anastigmat		8.25"	B&L Automat		Mc389	1100
Tropical Una Deluxe	6x9cm	plate	H&S	1910	Ross Convertible		5"	B&L Automat			1300
Tropical Una Deluxe	3¼x4¼"	plate	H&S	1910	Ross Convertible			B&L Automat			1300
Tropical Una Deluxe	4¼x6½"	plate	H&S	1910	Ross Convertible			B&L Automat			1300
Una 6x9	6x9cm	plate	H&S	1904	Goerz Doppel An.	6.8	6"	N.S. Perfect	2-100	Mc389	330
Una 3¼x4¼"	3¼x4¼"	plate	H&S	1904	Goerz Doppel An.	6.8		N.S. Perfect	2-100	Mc389	510
Una 4¼x6½"	4¼x6½"	plate	H&S	1904	Goerz Doppel An.	6.8	8.25"	N.S. Perfect	2-100	Mc389	360
Una 5x7"	5x7"	plate	H&S	1904	Goerz Doppel An.	6.8		N.S. Perfect	2-100	Mc389	330
Una Cameo	3¼x4¼"	plate	H&S	1904	Aldis Anastigmat			N.S. Perfect	2-100		150
Una Deluxe 6x9	6x9cm	plate	H&S	1908	Zeiss		3.25"	N.S. Perfect	2-100		900
Una Deluxe 3¼x4¼"	3¼x4¼"	plate	H&S	1908	Zeiss			N.S. Perfect	2-100		900
Una Deluxe 5x7"	5x7"	plate	H&S	1908	Zeiss			N.S. Perfect	2-100		900
...SIRIO - Florence, Italy											
Elettra I	24x36mm	35mm	35VF	1950	Fixed Semitelar	8	50mm		25-200		190
Elettra II	24x36mm	35mm	35VF	1950	Scupltor	5.6	40mm		25-200	Mc389	180
...SIVA											
Siva 6x9	6x9cm	120	VtFoldRo	1930	Boyer Topaz	6.3		Gitzo	25-100,T,B	Mc389	60
Siva 6x9	6x9cm	120	VtFoldRo	1930	Hermagis Anastigmat			Siva	25-100,T,B	Mc389	60
Siva 6.5x11	6.5x11cm	116	VtFoldRo	1930	Boyer Topaz	6.3		Edo	25-100,T,B		60
...S.J.C. & CO. - England											
Camelot	8x10.5cm	plate	Field	1900							220
...SKAIFE (Thomas Skaife) - London, England											
Pistolgraph 28mm	28mm dia.	WetPl	WetPlate	1858	Dallmeyer Petzval	2.2	40mm	Double-flap			17000
Pistolgraph 40mm	40mm dia.	WetPl	WetPlate	1858	Dallmeyer Petzval	2.2	40mm	Double-flap		A814	12000
...SKYFLEX											
Skyflex	6x6cm	120	TLR	1955	Tri-Lasar	3.5	80mm		B,1-300	Mc389	120
...SKYVIEW CAMERA CO. - Cleveland, OH											
Skyview Aerial Mod. D	3¼x4¼"	124	Aerial	1939	Goerz Dogmar	4.5		Ilex Acme			120
Skyview Aerial Mod. K	2¼x3¼"	Sheet	Aerial	1939	Woll. Aerialstigma	4.5	5"				120
...SMEDLEY & CO. - Blackburn, England											
Up-to-Date	10x12"	plate	Field	1901	Rapid Rectilinear						380

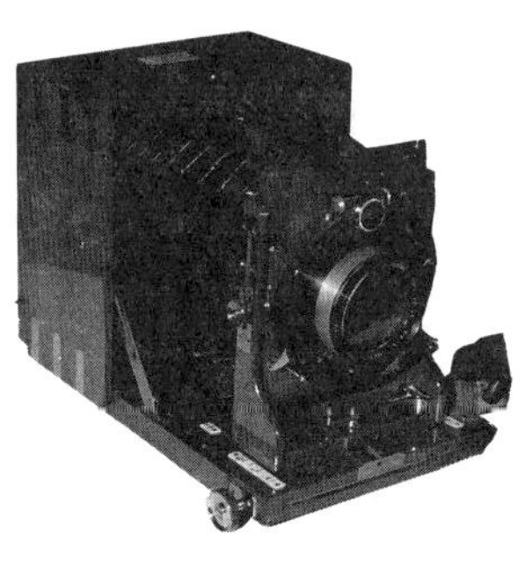

Sinclair Tropical Una

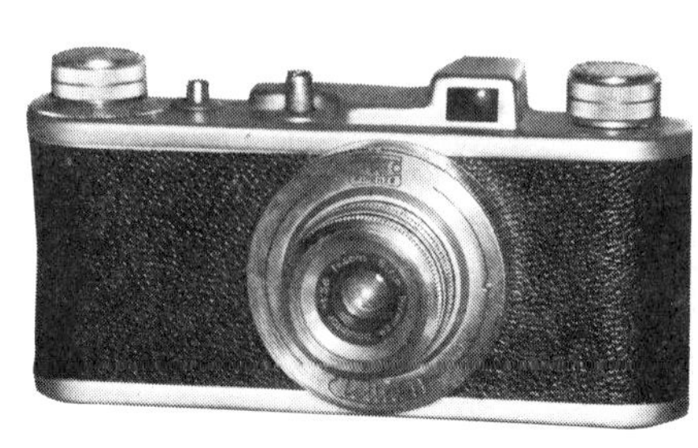

Sirio Elettra II

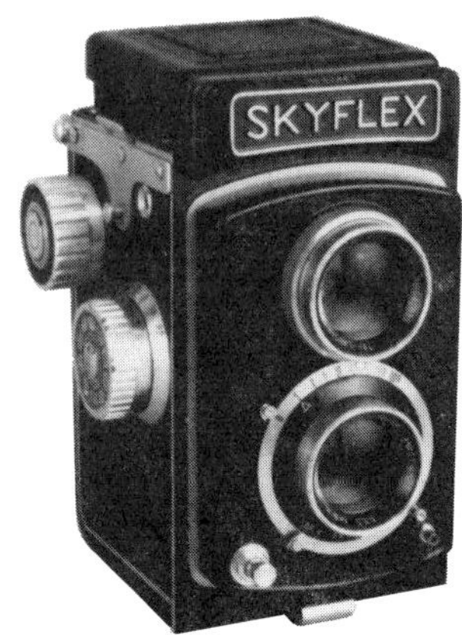

Skyflex

MODEL	FORMAT	FILM	TYPE	Year	LENS	Apert	FL	SHUTTER	SPEEDS	ILLUS	U.S.$
...SMITH - Gosport, England											
Detective camera	3¼x4¼"	plate	MagBox					guillotine			600
...SMITH (James H. Smith) - Chicago, IL											
Multiplying Camera	4¾x6½"	plate	Multiply	1870	Portrait			pneumatic			800
...SÖNNECKEN & CO. - Munich											
Field camera	5x7"	plate	Field		Univ.Rap.Aplanat						130
Folding camera	6x9cm	plate	VtFoldPl		Steinheil Unofocal	5.4	105mm				50
...SOHO LTD. - London											
Soho Altrex	6x9cm	120	VtFoldRo	1932	Kershaw Anast.			7-speed		Mc390	30
Soho Cadet	6x9cm	120	BakFoldRo	1930	Meniscus			2-speed		Mc390	60
Soho Mod. B	6x9cm	120	StrutRo		Fixed focus				I,T	Mc390	30
Soho Myna Mod. SK12	6x9cm	120	VtFoldRo								30
Soho Pilot	6x9cm	120	BakFoldRo	1933	Fixed focus				I,T	Mc390	30
Soho Precision	2½x3½"	plate	H&S								330
Soho Reflex 6x9	6x9cm	120	LgSLR	1933	Cooke Anastigmat			focal plane		A1600	390
Soho Reflex 3¼x4¼"	3¼x4¼"	plate	LgSLR	1933	Tessar	4.5		focal plane			160
Soho Reflex Tropical	3¼x4¼"	plate	LgSLR	1933	Tessar	4.5		focal plane			1600
Soho Vest Pocket	4x6.5cm	127	StrutRo	1930	Single Achromatic			3-speed		Mc390	40
Stereo Soho Reflex	2¼x5"	plate	SterRefl	1933	Dagor	6.8		focal plane		A2694	700
Stereo Soho Reflex	3½x5½"	plate	SterRefl	1933	Dagor	6.8	125mm	focal plane		A1816	700
...SOLIGOR											
AF-25	24x36mm	35mm	35AF	1993	Soligor	3.8	35mm	programmed			40
AF-26	24x36mm	35mm	35AF	1994	Soligor	4.5	35mm		1/125		40
AF-27	24x36mm	35mm	35AF	1994	Soligor	4.5	35mm		1/125		50
AF-27 Date	24x36mm	35mm	35AF	1994	Soligor	4.5	35mm		1/125		70
AF-30 Mini	24x36mm	35mm	35AF	1994	Soligor	4.5	28mm	automatic			50
AF-30 Mini Date	24x36mm	35mm	35AF	1994	Soligor	4.5	28mm	automatic			70
AF-35 LCD	24x36mm	35mm	35AF	1994	Soligor	4.5	30mm	automatic			70
AF-35 LCD Date	24x36mm	35mm	35AF	1994	Soligor	4.5	30mm	programmed			90
AF-40 Mini	24x36mm	35mm	35AF	1993	Soligor	3.5	35mm	programmed			70
AF-40 Mini Date	24x36mm	35mm	35AF	1993	Soligor	3.5	35mm	programmed			70
AF-70 Zoom	24x36mm	35mm	35AF	1992	Soligor	3.8	35-70				110
Flash Click	24x36mm	35mm	35VF	1994	Soligor						10
Presto	24x36mm	35mm	35AF	1987	Soligor	3.8	35mm	automatic	30-250		60
Quick Click	24x36mm	35mm	35VF	1994	Soligor	11	35mm				30
Reflex	6x6cm	120	TLR	1952	Soligor	3.5	80mm	Rector		Mc390	100
Reflex II	6x6cm	120	TLR	1952	Soligor	3.5	80mm	Rector		Mc390	100
SC-1	24x36mm	35mm	35SLR	1982	Soligor	2	50mm	focal plane	1-1000		140
SC-4	24x36mm	35mm	35SLR	1992	Soligor	4.5	34mm				10
SC-12 Motor	24x36mm	35mm	35VF	1994	Soligor	4.5	35mm				30
Semi-Auto	6x6cm	120	TLR	1952	Soligor	3.5	80mm	Rector			90
Soligor 35	24x36mm	35mm	35SLR	1955	Soligor	3.5	50mm	Leaf	1-200,B		100

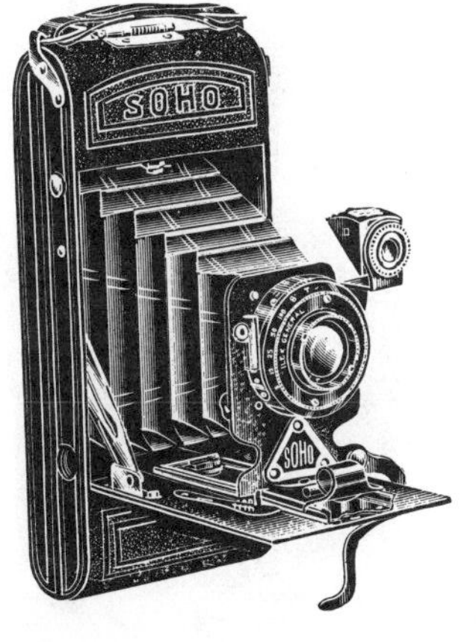

Soho Altrex

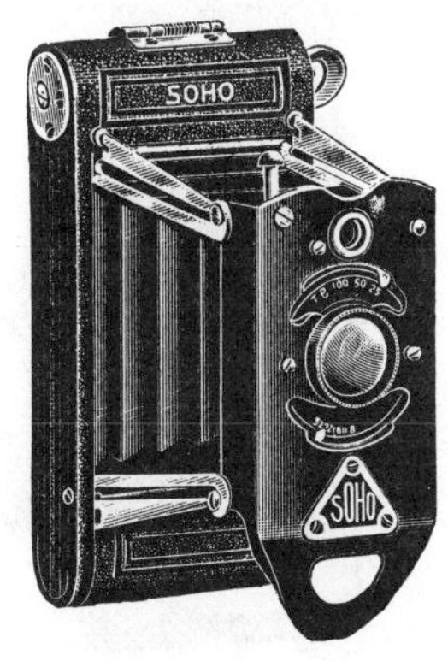

Soho Vest Pocket

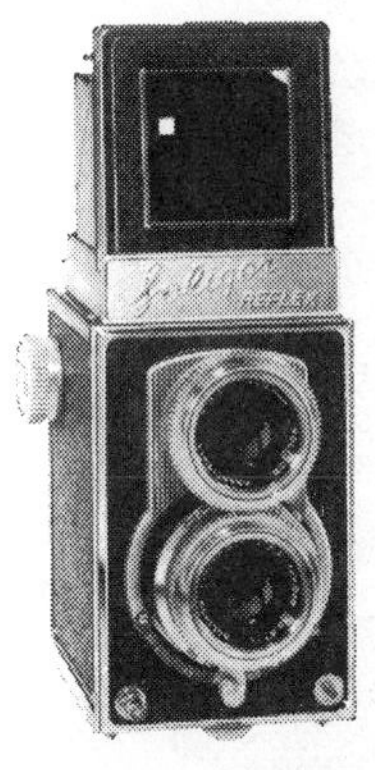

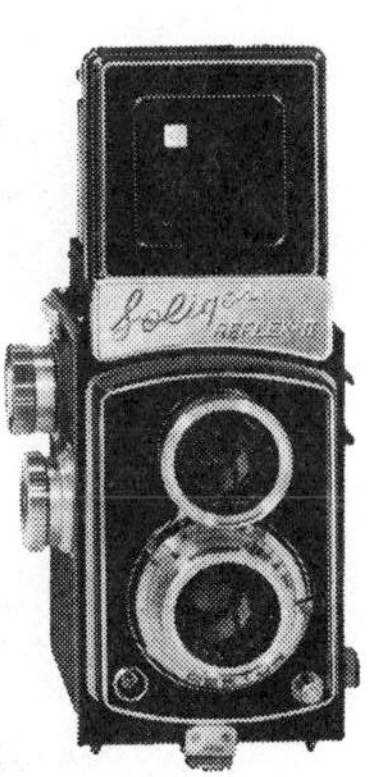

Soligor Reflex

MODEL	FORMAT	FILM	TYPE	Year	LENS	Apert	FL	SHUTTER	SPEEDS	ILLUS	U.S.$
Soligor 45	24x36mm	35mm	35VF	1955	Soligor	4.5	40mm		25-100		90
Soligor 66	6x6cm	120	MedSLR	1957	Soligor	3.5	80mm	focal plane	25-500,T,B		120
SR-300 MD body	24x36mm	35mm	35SLR	1993	body only	---	---	focal plane	4-1/1000		100
SR-300 MD + 35-70	24x36mm	35mm	35SLR	1993	Soligor	3.5-4.5	35-70	focal plane	4-1/1000		160
TM	24x36mm	35mm	35SLR	1988	Soligor	2.8	50mm				120
...SOMMER (Bernard Sommer) - Dresden, Germany											
Sommer Mod.I R.I.	6.5x9cm	plate	StrutPl	1927	Anticomar	2.9	100mm	focal plane	-1/1000	HK171	170
...SONORA INDUSTRIAL S.A. - Manaus, Brasil											
Love	13x17mm	16mm	Dispose	1975		11	28mm			Mc391	10
...SPARTUS CORP. - Chicago, Ill.											
Cinex	3x4cm	127	BakeliteRoll							Mc391	10
Spartacord	2¼x2¼"	120	TLR-Box	1953							20
Spartaflex	2¼x2¼"	120	TLR-Box	1950	achromatic	7.7	100mm	rotary	1/60,T		20
Spartus 4 folding	2¼x3¼"	120	StrutRo		Meniscus	11		rotary	I,B	Mc391	30
Spartus 35	24x36mm	35mm	35VF	1947	achromatic	7.7	50mm	rotary	1/60,T	Mc391	20
Spartus 35F	24x36mm	35mm	35VF	1947	achromatic	7.7	50mm	rotary	1/60,T	Mc391	30
Spartus 116 Box	2¼x4¼"	116	RollBox		Meniscus				I,T		10
Spartus 116/616 Box	2¼x4¼"	616	RollBox		Meniscus				I,T		10
Spartus 120 Box	2¼x3¼"	120	RollBox		Meniscus				I,T		10
Spartus 620 Box	2¼x3¼"	620	RollBox		Meniscus				I,T		10
Spartus Full-Vue	2¼x2¼"	120	TLR-Box	1948	Meniscus	16	100mm	rotary	1/60,T	Mc391	10
Spartus Junior Mod.	4x6.5cm	127	StrutRo		achromatic						20
Spartus Press Flash	2¼x3¼"	120	BakeliteBox	1939	Meniscus	16	120mm	rotary	1/60,T	Mc391	30
Spartus Six Twenty	2¼x2¼"	620	TLR	1956	Meniscus						30
Spartus Super R-I	2¼x2¼"	620	TLR-Box		Meniscus					Mc391	10
Spartus Vanguard	4x4cm	127	PlasticBox	1962	Meniscus						10
Spartus Vest Pocket	4x6.5cm	127	StrutRo			16	78mm	rotary	1/50,T	Mc391	20
...SPEICH (Cesare Speich) - Genoa, Italy											
Stereo Speich	10x12mm	35mm	StRefl	1953	Rodenstock	2.8	20mm		1-250	A2700	1500
...SPENCER CO. - Chicago, IL											
Flex-Master	3x4cm	127	Minicam								20
Full-Vue	6x6cm	120	TLR-Box	1940							10
Majestic	3x4cm	127	Minicam							Mc392	10
...SPERLING (Hans Sperling) - Berlin											
Field camera 9x12	9x12cm	plate	Tailboard	1955	various			various		A1377	310
Field camera 13x18	13x18cm	plate	Tailboard	1955	various			various			160
Field camera 18x24	18x24cm	plate	Tailboard	1955	various			various			270
...SPICER BROS. - London, England											
Studio camera	6½x8½"	plate	Studio	1888							250
...SPIROTECHNIQUE - Levallois-Perret, France											
Aquamatic	28x28mm	126	Special	1977					1/50, 100	A3451	120
Aquasport	28x28mm	126	Special	1977					1/50, 100		130

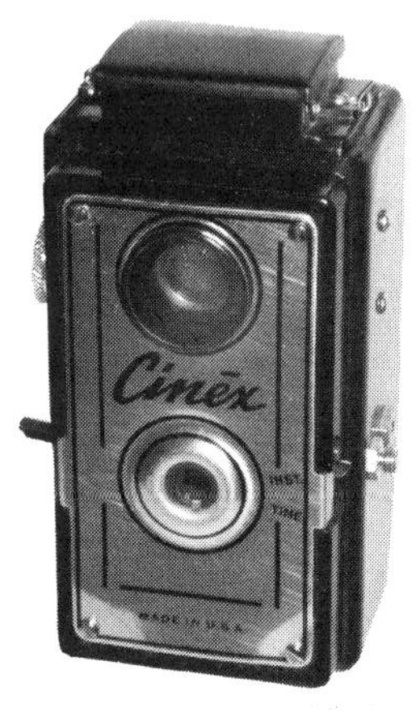

Spartus Cinex

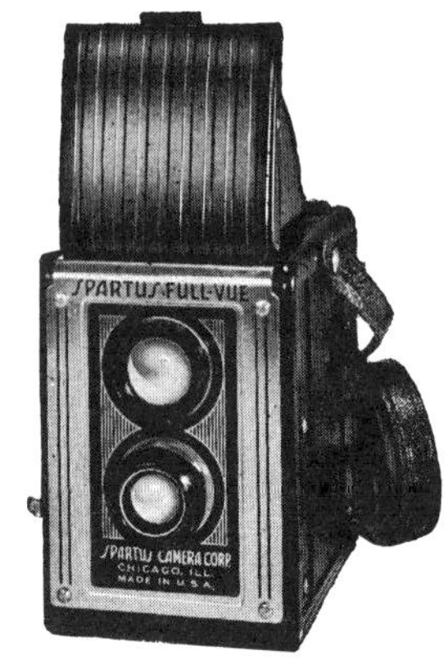

Spartus Full-Vue

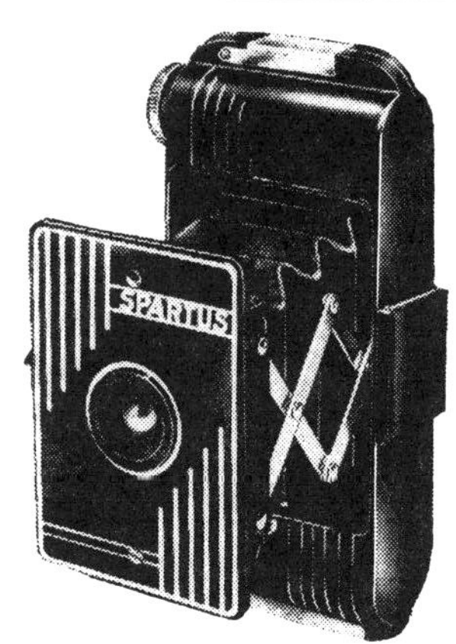

Spartus Vest Pocket

MODEL	FORMAT	FILM	TYPE	Year	LENS	Apert	FL	SHUTTER	SPEEDS	ILLUS	U.S.$
Calypso Mod. 1	24x36mm	35mm	35UW	1960	various			guillotine	30-1000	F1578	220
Calypso Mod. 2	24x36mm	35mm	35UW	1961	various			guillotine	15-500	F1579	220
...SPITZER (Otto Spitzer) - Berlin											
Espi 4.5x6	4.5x6cm	plate	StrutPl		Isconar	6.8	90mm	Pronto			130
Espi 9x12	9x12cm	plate	VtFoldPl	1908	Special Aplanat	11		Singlo		Mc392	120
Espi 10x15	10x15cm	plate	VtFoldPl	1910	Dagor	6.8	180mm	Compound	1/2-250		240
Espi 13x18	13x18cm	plate	VtFoldPl	1910	Dagor	6.8	180mm	Compound	1/2-250		120
Espirette	6.5x9cm	plate	StrutPl	1918	Tessar	6.3	120mm	Compur			80
Matador	13x18cm	plate	FoldPl	1910	Dagor	6.8	180mm	Compound	1/2-250		230
Oceana	10x15cm	plate	FoldPl	1910	Special Aplanat	11					60
Photola	4.5x6cm	plate	PlateBox	1910	Achromat						100
Princess	6.5x9cm	plate	StrutPl	1918	Tessar	6.3	120mm	Compur			50
Sixtograph	9x12cm	plate	Multiply	1902	Dagor	6.8				A3234	210
Victoria	9x12cm	plate	MagBox	1902	Dagor	6.8					50
...S.P.O. (Société de Photographie et d'Optique) - Carpentras, France											
Folding camera	6x9cm	120	VtFoldRo		Anastig. Sphinx	6.3	105mm			Mc392	20
...STAEBLE (Dr. Franz Staeble) - Munich											
Stereo Field camera	9x18cm	plate	SterTail	1910	Aplanat					A1762	270
Tricolor-Camera	9x12cm	plate	3-Color	1935	Colorplas	6.3	19.5cm	Compur	1-200	A3422	360
Unoplast	9x12cm	plate	FoldPl	1910	Polyplast	6	135mm				140
...STANDARD CAMERAS LTD. - Birmingham											
Conway Colour Filter	6x9cm	120	RollBox	1953	Meniscus	14			I		20
Conway Deluxe	6x9cm	120	RollBox								30
Conway Standard	6x9cm	120	RollBox		Meniscus				I	Mc393	20
Kenilworth Mod. II	6x6cm	120	RollBox						I		20
Robin Hood	45x107	Sheet	SterBox	1930	Meniscus	18	80mm		I		180
Standard Camera No. 2	6x9cm	120	RollBox						I,T	Mc393	30
...STANDARD PROJECTOR & EQUIPMENT CO.											
Gatling f1.7	18x24mm	35mm	35Half	1963	Color Rikenon	1.7	35mm			Mc393	120
...STAR MFG. CO. - Brooklyn, NY											
Star View	8x10"	plate	Field	1930	Century						300
...STARFLEX											
Starflex	6x6cm	120	TLR	1955	Tri-Lausar	3.5	8cm		1-300	Mc393	100
...STEGEMANN (A. Stegemann) - Berlin											
Detective camera	9x12cm	plate	MagBox	1900	Goerz					A1316	390
Hand-Camera 6.5x9	6.5x9cm	plate	StrutPl	1905	Tessar	4.5	120mm	focal plane			560
Hand-Camera 9x12	9x12cm	plate	StrutPl	1900	Tessar	4.5		focal plane		A293	560
Hand-Camera 13x18	13x18cm	plate	StrutPl	1895	Carl Zeiss Anast.	7.7	195mm	focal plane			1000
Präzisions-Kamera	9x12cm	plate	Tailboard	1905	various			various			480
Reflex 9x9	9x9cm	plate	LgSLR	1900	Tessar	4.5		focal plane		A1594	210
Reflex 9x12	9x12cm	plate	LgSLR	1900	Tessar	4.5		focal plane		A3139	210
Stereo camera	9x12cm	plate	StFoldPl	1900	Murer					A2674	480

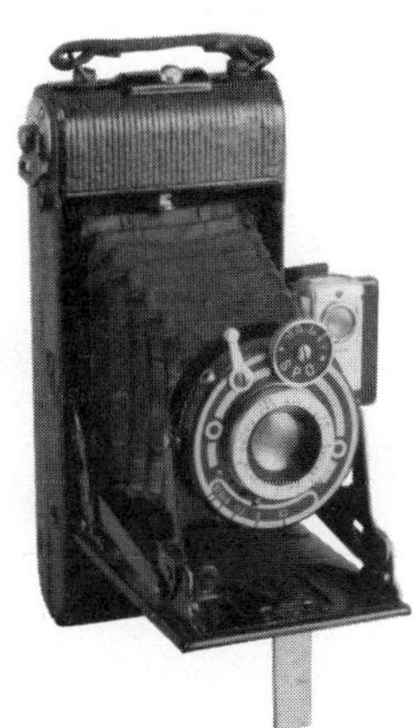

S.P.O. Folding Camera

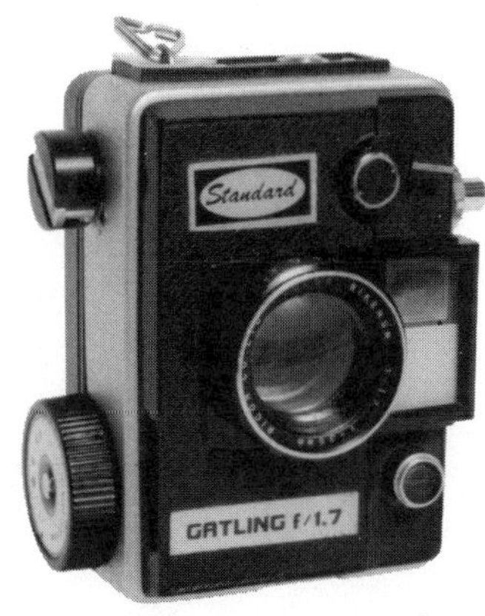

Gatling f1.7

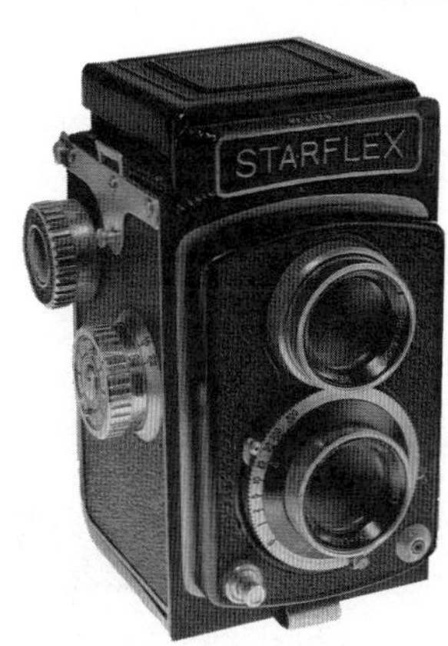

Starflex

MODEL	FORMAT	FILM	TYPE	Year	LENS	Apert	FL	SHUTTER	SPEEDS	ILLUS	U.S.$
Stereo-Hand-Camera	9x18cm	plate	SterStrut	1905	Tessar	4.5		focal plane			700
Strut camera	9x12cm	plate	StrutPl	1900	Goerz					A1418	180
Studio camera 9x12	9x12cm	plate	Monorail	1930	various			various		A135	630
Studio camera 18x24	18x24cm	plate	Studio	1910	various			various			290
Tailboard camera 13x18	13x18cm	plate	Tailboard	1910	**Goerz**						310
Tailboard camera 18x24	18x24cm	plate	Tailboard	1910	Goerz						260
Three-color camera		plate	3-Color	1915	Goerz Dagor					A2033	270
Tropical camera	9x12cm	plate	VtFoldPl	1925	Meyer			focal plane			520
View camera	13x18cm	plate	Field		various			various			290
...STEINECK KAMERAWERK - Tutzing											
Steineck ABC Wristwatch			Submin	1949	Steinheil	2.5	12.5mm	simple		Mc393	800
...STEINER OPTIK - Bayreuth, Germany											
Hunter 35	24x36mm	35mm	35VF	1950	Steiner	3.5	45mm		25-100		40
Ideal Color	24x36mm	35mm	35VF	1950	Steiner	3.5	45mm		25-100		40
Primo	24x36mm	35mm	35VF	1950	Steiner	3.5	45mm		25-100		40
Steinette	24x36mm	35mm	35VF	1950	Steiner	3.5	45mm		25-100	Mc393	40
...STEINHEIL (Optischen Werke C.A. Steinheil Söhne GmbH) - Munich											
Casca I	24x36mm	35mm	35VF	1948	Culminar	2.8	50mm	focal plane	25-1000	A1092	230
Casca II	24x36mm	35mm	35RF	1948	Orthostigmat	4.5	35mm	focal plane	B,½-1000	A1093	310
Casca II	24x36mm	35mm	35RF	1948		2	50mm	focal plane	B,½-1000	Mc393	310
Daguerreotype 7.5x10	7.5x10mm	Dag	Dag	1840	Steinheil					A1290	1000
Daguerreotype 8x11	8x11mm	Dag	Dag	1840	Steinheil					A3259	1000
Detective camera 9x12	9x12cm	plate	MagBox	1895	Steinheil			rotary		Mc393	680
Detective camera 9x12	9x12cm	plate	MagBox	1895	Periskop			rotary		A60	680
Detective camera 10x15	10x15cm	plate	MagBox	1895	Steinheil			rotary			660
Detective camera 10x15	10x15cm	plate	MagBox	1895	Periskop			guillotine			660
Detective camera 13x18	13x18cm	plate	MagBox	1895	Goerz			guillotine			700
Detective camera 13x18	13x18cm	plate	MagBox	1895	Steinheil			guillotine			700
Folding plate camera	4.5x6cm	plate	VtFoldPl	1930	Triplar	4.5	75mm	Ibsor			100
Folding plate camera	9x12cm	plate	VtFoldPl	1930	Triplar	4.5	135mm	Ibsor			40
Kleinfilm Kamera	3x4cm	127	StrutRo	1930	Cassar	2.9	50mm	Compur	1-300		100
Multo Nettel	9x14cm	plate	StFoldPl	1910	Cassar	2.9	5cm	focal plane		Mc394	560
Stereo Detective	8.5x17cm	plate	SterMagBox	1893	Steinheil Anast.			rotary		A689	1200
Tropical camera	9x12cm	plate	VtFoldPl								650
...STELLARFLEX											
Stellarflex	4x4cm	127	TLR-Box								20
...STEREO CORPORATION - Milwaukee, Wisc.											
Contura	24x24mm	35mm	35Ster	1955	Volar	2.7	35mm			Mc394	1300
...STEREOCRAFTERS - Milwaukee, Wisc.											
Videon	24x24mm	35mm	35Ster	1950	Stereon Anast.	3.5	35mm				140
Videon II	24x24mm	35mm	35Ster	1953	Stereon Anast.	3.5	35mm			Mc394	140
Videon Challenger	24x24mm	35mm	35Ster	1950	Stereon Anast.	3.5	35mm				140

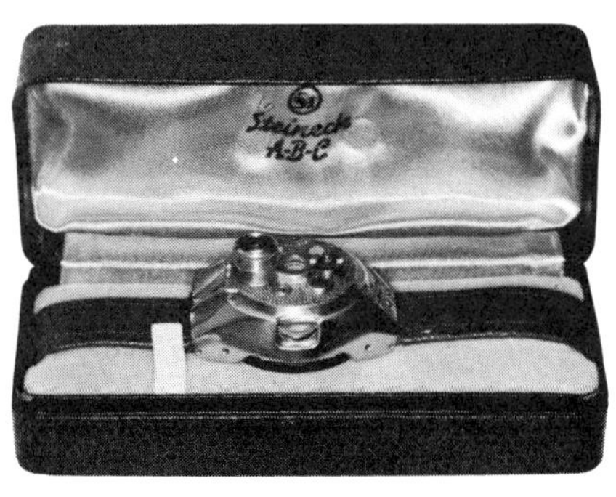

Steineck ABC Wristwatch

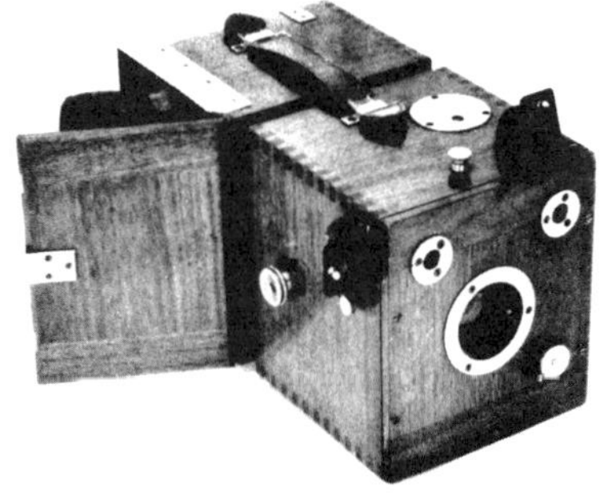

Steinheil Detective camera

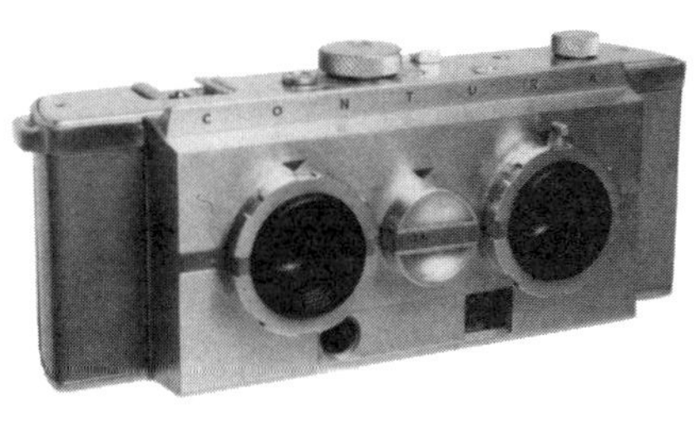

Stereo Corp. Contura

MODEL	FORMAT	FILM	TYPE	Year	LENS	Apert	FL	SHUTTER	SPEEDS	ILLUS	U.S.$
...STERLING CAMERA CORP. - Sterling, Illinois											
2-A Sterling	2½x4¼"	116	RollBox							Mc394	30
Buddie 2A	2½x4¼"	116	RollBox							Mc394	30
...STEWARD (J.H. Steward) - England											
Magazine camera 3¼x4¼"	3¼x4¼"	plate	MagBox	1890							190
Magazine camera 4x5"	4x5"	plate	MagBox	1890							190
...STIEHL (Max Stiehl) - Munich											
Spezial 4x5"	4x5"	plate	WideAng	1920	Steinheil						310
Spezial 13x18	13x18cm	plate	WideAng	1920	Steinheil					A163	310
...STIRN (C.P. Stirn, Stirn & Lyon) (Rudolph Stirn, Berlin) - N.Y.											
America Detective	2 7/8x4"	Roll	DetectivBox	1886	Periscop			rotary			3300
Concealed Vest No. 1	1¾" dia.	plate	Disguised	1886	Aplanetic					Mc394	1300
Concealed Vest No. 1	4x4cm	plate	Disguised	1888	Aplanetic					Mc394	1200
Concealed Vest No. 2	2½" dia.	plate	Disguised	1888	Aplanetic					A1870	1400
Detective Magazine 6x8	6x8cm	plate	MagBox	1891	Aplanetic			guillotine		Mc394	900
Detective Magazine 6x8	6x8cm	plate	MagBox	1893	Aplanetic			rotary			900
Detective Magazine 9x12	9x12cm	plate	MagBox	1891	Aplanetic			guillotine			800
Detective Magazine 9x12	9x12cm	plate	MagBox	1893	Aplanetic			rotary			800
Stereo Detective	9x12cm	plate	SterBox	1893	Aplanetic			rotary			1800
Stereo Detective	9x12cm	plate	SterBox	1893	Periscop			rotary			1800
...S.T.M. - Birmingham, England											
Itakit	3¼x3¼"	plate	MagBox	1890							560
...STOCK (John Stock & Co.) - New York, NY											
Stereo Wet plate	5x8"	WetPl	StWetPl	1860							1600
...STÖCKIG (Hugo Stöckig) - Dresden											
Union Camera 9x12	9x12cm	plate	VtFoldPl	1907	Detective Aplanat	8		Union			200
Union Camera 13x18	13x18cm	plate	VtFoldPl	1907	Union Aplanat	6.8		Union			190
Union Zwei-Verschluss	9x12cm	plate	VtFoldPl	1911	Aristostigmat	6.8	120mm	focal plane	2500		270
Union Zwei-Verschluss	10x15cm	plate	VtFoldPl	1911	Aristostigmat	6.8	135mm	focal plane	2500	A236	270
...SÜDDEUTSCHES CAMERAWERK KÖRNER & MAYER - Sontheim & Heilbronn, Germany											
Cewes-Film-Klapp-Camera	9x12cm	124	StrutPl	1903	Nettel Extra Rap. Aplan.			Unicum		A1422	180
Cewes-Film-Klapp-Camera	10x12.5	123	StrutPl	1903	Aristostigmat			Unicum			180
Cewes-Platten-Klapp	9x12cm	plate	StrutPl	1903	Extra Rap. Aplan.	7.5		B&L Unicum		A1422	360
Deckrullo 9x12	9x12cm	plate		1908	Dogmar	4.5	150mm	focal plane	1/2-2800		140
Deckrullo 10x15	10x15cm	plate		1908	Tessar	4.5	165mm	focal plane	1/2-2800		200
Deckrullo 13x18	13x18cm	plate		1908	Tessar	4.5	18cm	focal plane	1-2800		180
Nettel-Klapp-Camera	9x12m	plate	StrutPl	1903	Aristostigmat	5.5	120mm	focal plane	1-1500	A1420	200
Stereo-Klapp-Camera	9x18cm	plate	SterStrut	1905				focal plane	1-1500		190
...SUGAYA KOKI, SUGAYA OPTICAL CO., LTD. - Japan											
Hope (Sugaya Mod. II)	14x14mm	17.5m	Submin	1950				"Sugaya Model II"		Mc395	140
Myracle	14x14mm	17.5m	Submin	1950	Hope Anastigmat	4.5			25-100		80
Myracle, Mod. II	14x14mm	17.5m	Submin	1950	Hope Anastigmat	4.5			25-100	Mc395	100

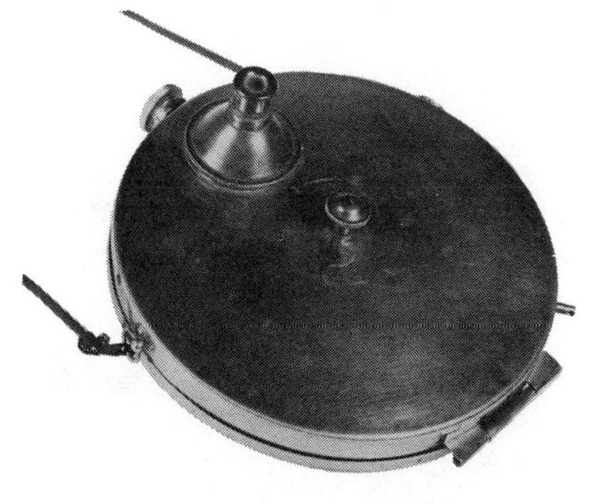

Stirn Concealed Vest No. 1

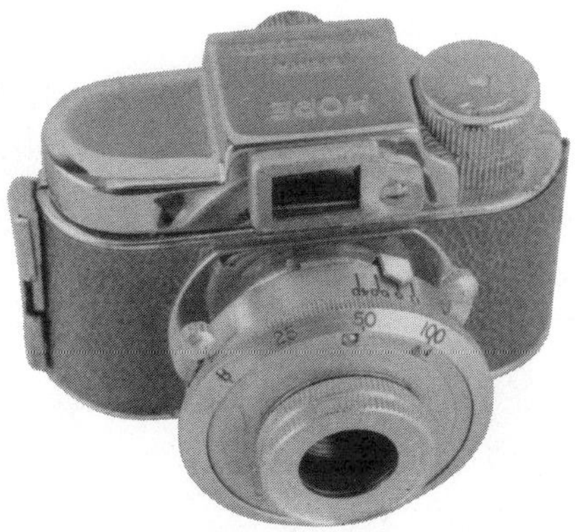

Hope (Sugaya Mod. II)

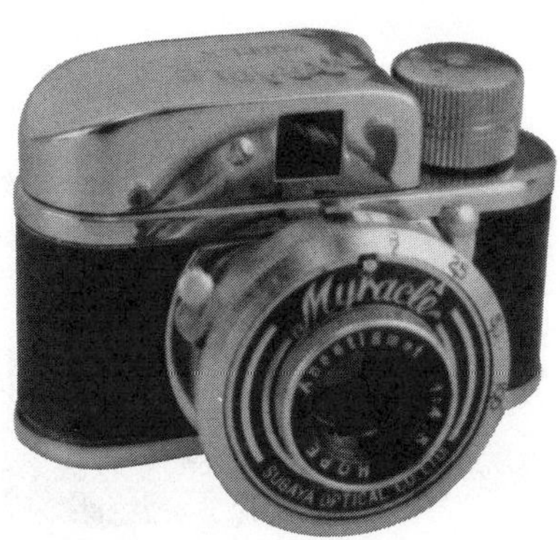

Sugaya Myracle, Mod. II

MODEL	FORMAT	FILM	TYPE	Year	LENS	Apert	FL	SHUTTER	SPEEDS	ILLUS	U.S.$
Rubix 16	10x14mm	16mm	Submin	1950	Hope	3.5	25mm		25-100	Mc395	210
Rubix 16	10x14mm	16mm	Submin	1950	Hope	2.8	25mm		25-150	Mc395	210
...SUMIDA OPTICAL WORKS - Japan											
Proud Chrome Six III	6x6/4.5x6	120	HzFoldRo	1951	Congo	3.5	75mm	Proud Sync.	1-200, B		120
Proud Mod. 50	4.5x6cm	120	HzFoldRo	1950	Proud Anastigmat	3.5	75mm	N.K.S.	1-200,B	Mc396	90
...SUMNER (J. Chase) - Foxcroft, Maine											
Stereo rollfilm box camera	3½x6"	101	SterBox	1905	Rapid Rectilinear						490
...SUNART PHOTO CO. - Rochester, N.Y.											
Sunart Junior 3½x3½"	3½x3½"	plate	PlateBox	1896	achromatic				I,T	Mc396	60
Sunart Junior 4x5"	4x5"	plate	PlateBox	1896	achromatic				I,T	Mc396	60
Sunart Vidi No. 1 4x5"	4x5"	plate	H&S	1898	B&L Rapid Rect.			Unicum			120
Sunart Vidi No. 1 5x7"	5x7"	plate	H&S	1898	B&L Rapid Rect.			Unicum			140
Sunart Vidi No. 2 4x5"	4x5"	plate	H&S	1898	B&L Rapid Rect.			Unicum			120
Sunart Vidi No. 2 5x7"	5x7"	plate	H&S	1898	B&L Rapid Rect.			Unicum			130
...SUNBEAM CAMERA CO.											
Sunbeam Minicam	3x4cm	127	Minicam								10
Sunbeam Six Twenty	6x6cm	620	TLR-Box								30
...SUNNY - Japan											
Sunny	24x24mm	35mm	35VF		Optart	10	35mm		I	Mc396	90
Sunny Twin	24x24mm	35mm	35VF		Crystal	4.5	40mm		I		120
...SURUGA SEIKI CO.											
Mihama Six IIIA	6x6cm	120	HzFoldRo	1953	Kepler Anastigmat	3.5		NKS		Mc396	80
Mihama Six IIIA (2-format)	6x6/4.5x6	120	HzFoldRo	1953	Mihama			NKS		Mc396	90
...SUTER (E. Suter) - Basel, Switzerland											
Detective Magazine	9x12cm	plate	MagBox	1893	Suter	8		rotary		Mc396	630
Detective Magazine	9x12cm	plate	MagBox	1890	Periskop			guillotine		Mc396	700
Folding plate camera	9x12cm	plate	VtFoldPl	1913	Suter Anastigmat	6.8	135mm				120
Folding plate camera	10x15cm	plate	VtFoldPl	1913	Suter Anastigmat	6.8	160mm				130
Magazine camera	9x12cm	plate	MagBox	1893	Suter Anastigmat			rotary		A81	350
Muro	4.5x6cm	plate	StrutPl	1915	Suter Anastigmat			focal plane			240
Non-Plus-Ultra	9x12cm	plate	MagBox	1890	Achromat						520
Stereo Detective	9x12cm	plate	SterBox	1895	Achromat					HK448	1300
Stereo Detective Magazine	9x18cm	plate	SterMagBox	1893	Rectilinear	10	90mm	rotary		A2661	1200
Stereo Magazine	9x18cm	plate	SterMagBox	1895	Achromat			Spezial		A2659	400
Stereo Muro	9x18cm	plate	SterStrut	1890	Suter	5	85mm	focal plane	30-1000		360
...SUZUKI OPTICAL CO. - Japan											
Camera-Lite	6x6mm	8mm	Disguised	1950		8	17mm		1/50	Mc397	500
Camera-Lite-B	6x6mm	8mm	Disguised	1950		8	17mm		1/50		490
Echo 8	6x6mm	8mm	Disguised	1951	Echor	3.5	15mm		1/50,B	Mc397	500
Europco-8	6x6mm	8mm	Disguised	1951	Echor	3.5	15mm			Mc397	510
Press Van 6x6/24x36	6x6/24x36	120	StrutRo	1953	Takumar	3.5	75mm	Seikosha-Rap.	1-500,B		430
Press Van 6x6/4.5x6	6x6/4.5x6	120	StrutRo	1953	Takumar	3.5	75mm	Seikosha-Rap.	1-500,B		430

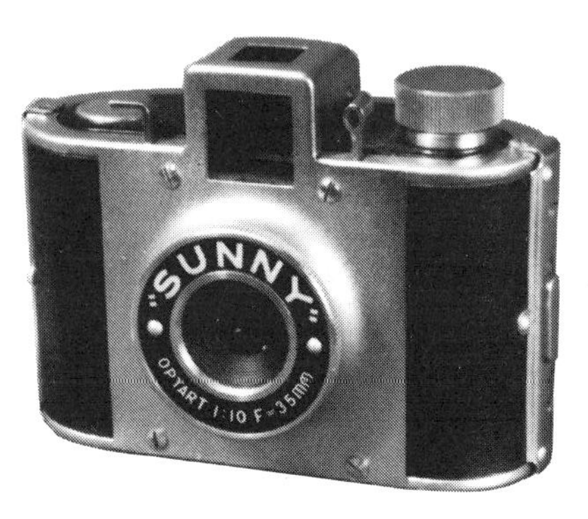

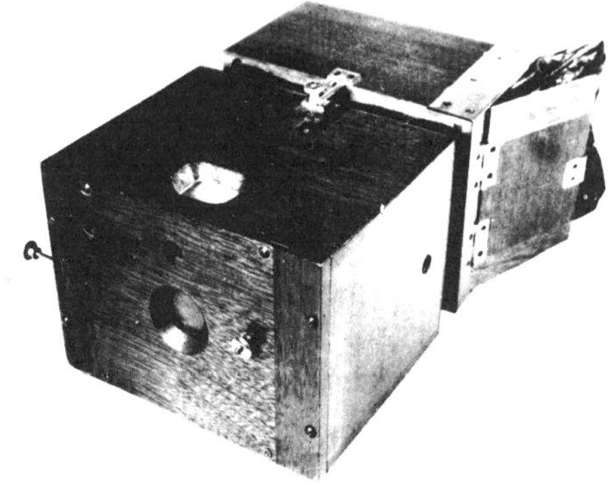

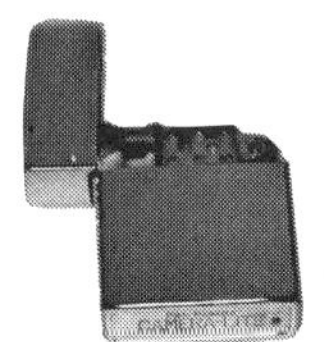

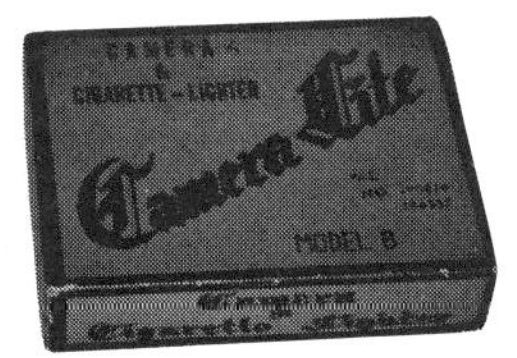

Sunny | **Suter Detective Magazine** | **Suzuki Camera-Lite**

MODEL	FORMAT	FILM	TYPE	Year	LENS	Apert	FL	SHUTTER	SPEEDS	ILLUS	U.S.$
...SVENSSON (Hugo Svensson & Co.) - Göteborg											
Hasselblad Svea 9x12	9x12cm	plate	DetectivBox	1905	Brass barrel			sector			200
Hasselblad Svea 10x15	10x15cm	plate	DetectivBox	1905	Brass barrel			sector		A1320	230
Hasselblad Svea 12x16.5	12x16.5	plate	DetectivBox	1898	Anastigmat	9	196mm	sector			310
Runa	3x4cm	127	RollBox	1935	Duplar	11					40
Stella	8x12cm	plate	StrutPl	1910	Meniscus			guillotine		A1432	290
...SWINDEN and EARP - England											
Magazine camera		plate	MagBox	1887	Clement & Gilmer			roller-blind			80
...TACHIBANA TRADING CO. - Japan											
Beby Pilot	3x4cm	127	BakFoldRo	1940	Pirot Anastigmat	4.5	50mm	"Pilot,O"		Mc397	120
...TACHIHARA - Japan											
Field-Stand 45	4x5"	plate	Field	1987	various				1-500		680
Field-Stand 69	6x9cm	plate	Field	1987	various				1-500		680
Field-Stand 810	8x10"	plate	Field	1987	various				1-500		800
...TAHBES - Holland											
Populair	6x6cm	120	TelescRo	1955		7.7	75mm			Mc397	50
Synchro	6x6cm	120	TelescRo	1955		7.7	75mm			A3118	80
Synchrona	6x6cm	120	TelescRo	1955		7.7	75mm			A3119	60
Synchrona	6x6cm	120	TelescRo	1955		7.7	75mm			A3122	60
...TAISEI KOKI - Japan											
Super Welmy	24x36mm	35mm	35RF	1956	Taikor	2.8	45mm		B,5-300		30
Super Westomat 2-window	24x36mm	35mm	35RF	1956	Terionon	3.5	45mm		B,5-300		30
Super Westomat 3-window	24x36mm	35mm	35RF	1956	Terionon	3.5	45mm		B,25-200	Mc397	30
Welmy Six	6x6cm	120	HzFoldRo	1951	Terionar	4.5	75mm	Nakiro	1-200	Mc397	50
Welmy Six E	6x6cm	120	HzFoldRo	1951	Terionar	3.5	75mm	Nakiro	1-300	Mc397	50
Welmy 35	24x36mm	35mm	35Fold	1954	Terionar	2.8	50mm	Welmy	25-150,B		30
Welmy M-3	24x36mm	35mm	35RF	1956	Terionar	3.5	45mm	Welmy	5-300		50
Welmy Wide	24x36mm	35mm	35VF	1958	Taikor	3.5	35mm		25-200,B		50
Westomat	24x36mm	35mm	35RF	1957	Terionon	3.5	45mm		1/25-200		30
...TAIYODO KOKI (T.K.K.) - Japan											
Beauty	14x14mm	Roll	Submin	1949	Fixed focus	4.5	20mm		B,25-100	Mc398	170
Beauty 35 Super	24x36mm	35mm	35RF	1956	Canter	2.8	45mm	Copal-Sync. MX	B,1-500	Mc398	40
Beauty 35 Super II	24x36mm	35mm	35RF	1958	Canter	2	45mm	Copal-SV	1-500,B		40
Beauty Canter	24x36mm	35mm	35RF	1957	Canter	2.8	45mm	Copal-MXV	1-500,B	Mc398	50
Beauty Super L	24x36mm	35mm	35RF	1958	Canter-S	1.9	45mm		1-500,B	Mc398	50
Beautycord	6x6cm	120	TLR	1955	Beauty	3.5	80mm	Beauty FB	10-200		60
Beautycord S	6x6cm	120	TLR	1955	Tri-Lausar	3.5	80mm	TKK	10-200		90
Beautyflex	6x6cm	120	TLR	1950	Doimer Anast.	3.5	80mm		1-200		60
Beautyflex II	6x6cm	120	TLR	1950	Doimer Anast.	3.5	80mm	NFG	1-200		60
Beautyflex III	6x6cm	120	TLR	1950	Doimer	3.5	80mm		1-200,B		70
Epochs	14x14mm	17.5	Submin	1948	Talent	3.5	20mm	TKK	25,50,B	Mc398	190
Meteor	14x14mm	17.5	Submin	1949	Vestkam	4.5	25mm	TKK	25,50,B		190

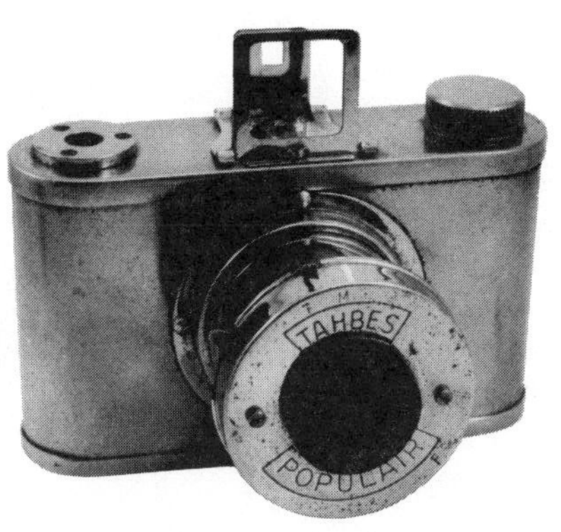

Tahbes Populair

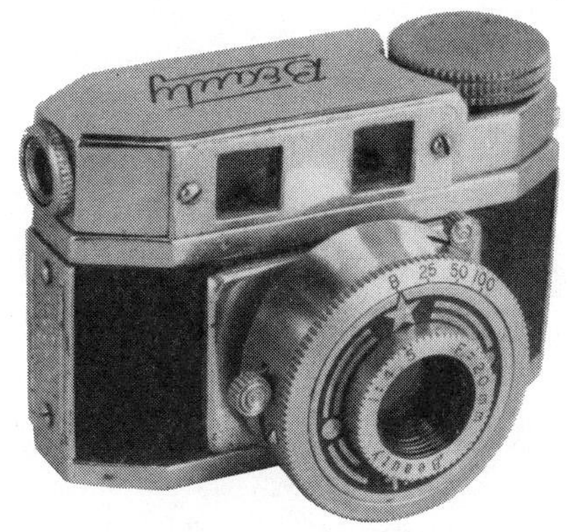

Taiyodo Beauty

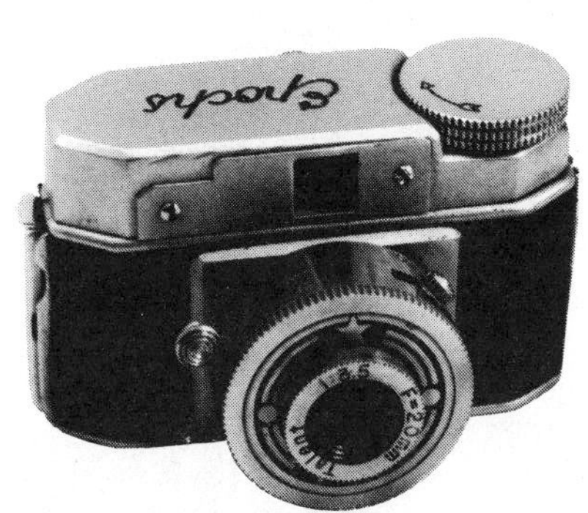

Taiyodo Epochs

MODEL	FORMAT	FILM	TYPE	Year	LENS	Apert	FL	SHUTTER	SPEEDS	ILLUS	U.S.$
Reflex Beauty	6x6cm	120	MedSLR	1954	Canter	3.5	75mm	focal plane	-1/500		210
Vestkam	14x14mm		Submin	1949	Vestkam	3.5	20mm	TKK	25,50,B		140
...TAIYOKOKI CO., LTD. - Japan											
Viscawide-16	10x46mm	16mm	Panoramic	1961	Lausar	3.5	25mm		60-300		240
...TAKAHASHI OPTICAL WORKS											
Arsen	4x4cm	127	TelescRo	1938	Grimmel Anast.	4.5	50mm	Arsen	5-250		90
...TAKAMINE OPTICAL WORKS, TAKANE OPTICAL CO. - Japan											
Mine Six IIF	6x6cm	120	HzFoldRo	1955	Deep-C Anast.	3.5	7.5cm	Rectus	1-300	A1504	140
Mine Six Super 66	6x6/4.5x6	120	HzFoldRo	1957	Takumar	3.5	75mm	Copal MXL	1-500		120
Sisley Mod. 1	6x6/4.5x6	120	HzFoldRo	1950	Deep-C	3.5	75mm	NKS-SC	1-200		80
Sisley 2A	6x6/4.5x6	120	HzFoldRo	1955	Deep-C Anast.	3.5	75mm	Copal	1-300	Mc398	120
...TALBOT (Romain Talbot) - Berlin											
Errtee (folding plate)	9x12cm	plate	VtFoldPl	1930	Laack Pololyt	4.5	135mm	Compur	1-200		50
Errtee (folding rollfilm)	5x8cm	120	VtFoldRo		Poloyt Anastigmat	6.3	90mm	Vero			50
Errtee (folding rollfilm)	6x9cm	120	VtFoldRo		Anast. Talbotar	4.5	105mm	Vario	25-100		60
Errtee button tintype	25mm dia.	Ferro	Button	1912	Laack	4.5	60mm	simple		Mc399	1000
Essemm	9x12cm	plate	VtFoldPl	1904	Rapid Rectilinear	8		Unicum			100
...TALBOT (Walter Talbot) - Berlin											
Invisible Camera			Disguised	1915	Anastigmat	3.5			1/125	Mc399	10000
...TALBOT & EAMER CO. - London, England											
Talmer	8x10.5cm	plate	MagBox	1890	achromatic					Mc399	580
...TANAKA KOGAKU (TANAKA OPTICAL CO., LTD) - Japan											
Tanack IIC	24x36mm	35mm	35RF	1953	Tanar	3.5	50mm	focal plane	20-500		370
Tanack IIIF	24x36mm	35mm	35RF	1954	Tanar	2.8	50mm	focal plane	1-500,B,T		330
Tanack IIIS	24x36mm	35mm	35RF	1954	Tanar	2.8	50mm	focal plane	1-500,B,T		330
Tanack IIISa	24x36mm	35mm	35RF	1955	Tanar	3.5	50mm	focal plane	1-500,B,T		370
Tanack IV-S	24x36mm	35mm	35RF	1955	Tanar	2	50mm	focal plane	1-500,B,T	Mc399	330
Tanack SD	24x36mm	35mm	35RF	1957	Tanar	1.5	5cm	focal plane	1-1000,B,T	Mc399	540
Tanack V3	24x36mm	35mm	35RF	1958	Tanar	1.9	5cm	focal plane	1-500,B,T		370
Tanack VP	24x36mm	35mm	35RF	1959	Tanar	1.8	5cm	focal plane	1-500,B,T		330
...TARGET - Paris											
New Folding Stereo	9x18cm	plate	SterFoldPl							Mc399	460
...TARON CO. LTD. - Japan											
Chic	18x24mm	35mm	35Half	1961	Taronar	2.8	30mm	Taron-LX			70
Fodor 35	24x36mm	35mm	35RF	1955	Tomioka Lausar	2.8	45mm	NKS-MX	1-300,B		40
Taron 35	24x36mm	35mm	35RF	1955	Lausar	2.8	45mm	NKS-MX	1-300,B		40
Taron Eye	24x36mm	35mm	35RF	1960	Taronar	1.8	45mm	NKS-MX	1-500	A2139	60
Taron Super LM	24x36mm	35mm	35RF		Taronar	1.9	45mm				50
Taron VL	24x36mm	35mm	35RF		Taronar	1.8	45mm	NKS-MX	1-300,B		30
...TASCO											
Bino/Cam 7800	13x17mm	110	Special	1977	Tele-Tasco	5.6	112mm		1/125	Mc400	190
Bino/Cam 8000	13x17mm	110	Special	1980	Tele-Tasco	5.6	100mm		125, 250	A3282	190

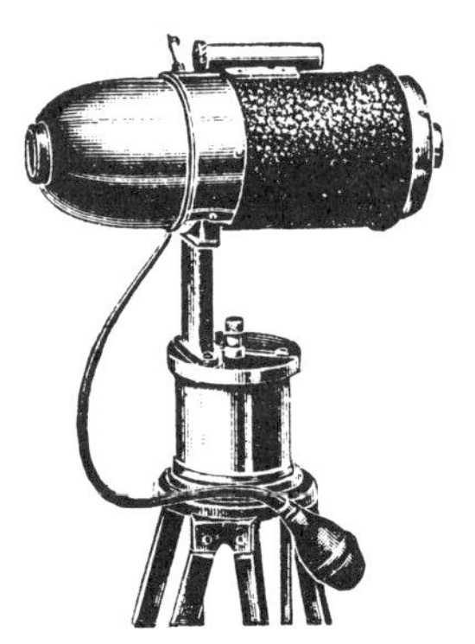

Errtee Button Tintype

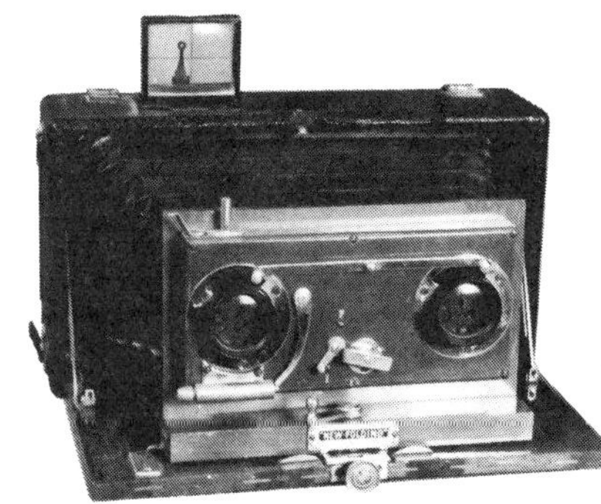

Target New Folding Stereo

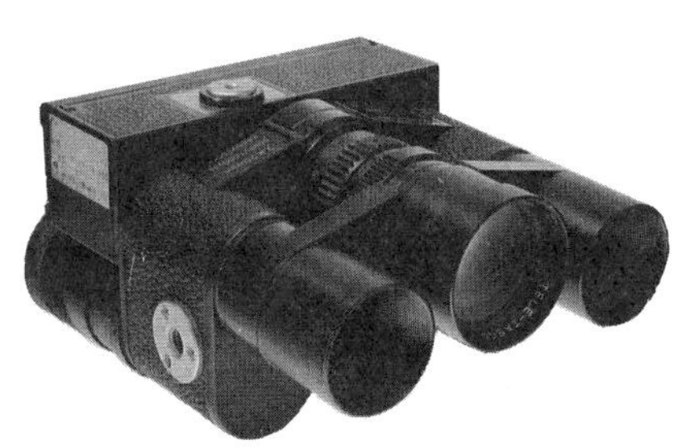

Tasco Bino/Cam 7800

MODEL	FORMAT	FILM	TYPE	Year	LENS	Apert	FL	SHUTTER	SPEEDS	ILLUS	U.S.$
...TAUBER - Wiesbaden											
Brünhilde	9x12cm	plate	MagBox	1899	Achromat						70
Elsa	9x12cm	plate	MagBox	1900	Achromat						70
Elsa II	9x12cm	plate	VtFoldPl	1915	Extra Rap. Aplan.	8	135mm				80
Field camera	13x18cm	plate	Field	1900	Brass barrel						220
Fritz	9x12cm	plate	Field	1900	Meniscus						170
Lady Detective	6.5x9.5cm	plate	MagBox	1899	Meniscus						50
Lilli	6.5x9cm	plate	MagBox	1901	Meniscus						60
Tailboard camera	13x18cm	plate	Tailboard	1898	Busch					A2941	220
Tauber	9x12cm	plate	VtFoldPl	1920	Rapid Aplanat	8	135mm				40
...TAYLOR (A & G Taylor) - England											
View camera	4¼x6½"	plate	Tailboard	1890	Clement & Gilmer						320
...TAYLOR (J. Taylor) - Sheffield, England											
Tailboard camera	6½x8½"	plate	Tailboard		Brassbound Vogel						290
...TEDDY CAMERA CO. - Newark, NJ											
Teddy Mod. A	2x3½"	Ferro	Ferrotype	1924	Meniscus						580
...TELLA CAMERA CO. LTD. - London, England											
No. 3 Magazine		pack	MagBox	1899	Taylor Hobson	6.5		pneumatic			350
...THEM-STEYR (A. Them-Steyr)											
Photo-Sport	24x30mm	35mm	RigidRo	1925	Dialytar	4.5	45mm	Compur	1-300		370
...THOMAS (W. Thomas) - London											
Wet plate camera	4¼x6½"	WetPl	WetPlate	1870	Brass barrel	11					1300
Sliding-box wet plate	4¼x6½"	WetPl	WetPlate	1860	Ross						2200
...THOMPSON (W.J. Thompson Co.) - NY											
Street Camera		plate	Street								160
...THORNTON-PICKARD MFG. CO. - Altrincham, England											
Aerial Camera, Type C	4x5"	plate	Aerial	1915	Ross Xpres	4.5	10 1/4"	focal plane			4000
Amber 3¼x4¼"	3¼x4¼"	plate	Field	1899	Amber R.R.	8	5.5"				280
Amber 4x5"	4x5"	plate	Field	1899	Amber R.R.	8	5.5"				280
Amber 5x7"	5x7"	plate	Field	1899	Amber R.R.	8	11"				280
Amber 6½x8½"	6½x8½"	plate	Field	1899	Amber R.R.	8	11"				290
College 9x12	9x12cm	plate	Field	1912	T-P Rectoplant			roller-blind			350
College 4x5"	4x5"	plate	Field	1912	T-P Rectoplant			roller-blind			350
College 5x7"	5x7"	plate	Field	1912	T-P Rectoplant			roller-blind			350
College 18x24	18x24cm	plate	Field	1912	T-P Rectoplant			roller-blind			350
Duplex Ruby Reflex	6.5x9cm	plate	LgSLR	1920	Aldis Anastigmat	4.5		focal plane		Mc400	230
Duplex Ruby Reflex	9x12cm	plate	LgSLR	1920	Aldis Anastigmat	4.5		focal plane		Mc400	230
Duplex Ruby Reflex Trop.	6.5x9cm	plate	LgSLR	1923	Cooke Anastigmat	6.3		focal plane	1000	Mc400	3000
Duplex Ruby Reflex Trop.	3¼x4¼"	plate	LgSLR	1923	Cooke Anastigmat	6.3		focal plane	1000	Mc400	3000
F.P. Imperial Two-Shutter	5x7"	plate	Field	1909	Beck Symmetrical			focal plane	1000	Mc400	610
Folding plate camera	4¼x6½"	plate	VtFoldPl	1900	Zeiss Unar	5	210mm	focal plane	15-80		230
Folding plate camera	5x7"	plate	VtFoldPl	1900	Zeiss Unar	5	210mm	focal plane	15-80		230

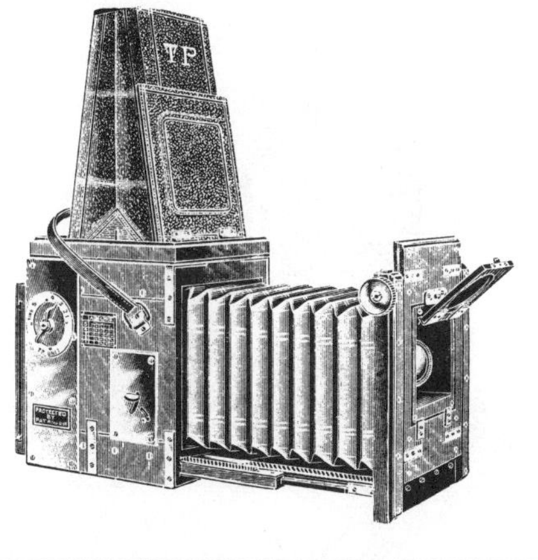
Duplex Ruby Reflex

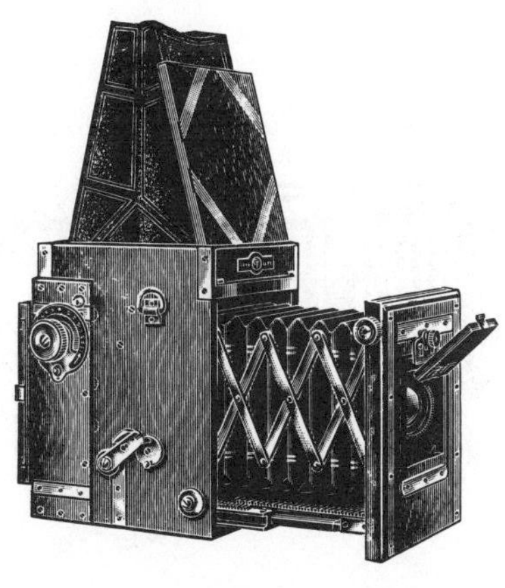
Duplex Ruby Reflex Trop.

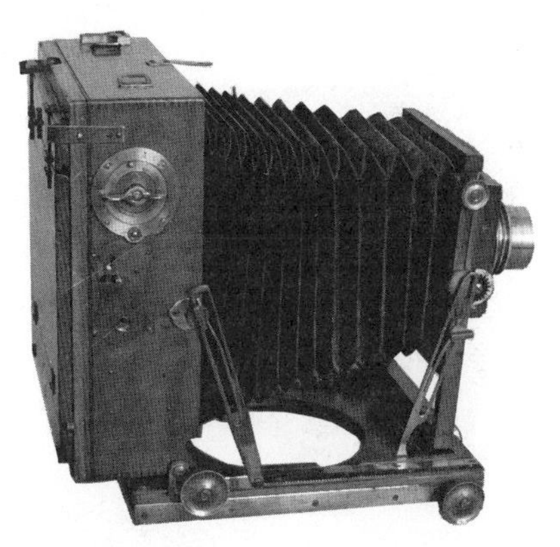
F.P. Imperial Two-Shutter

MODEL	FORMAT	FILM	TYPE	Year	LENS	Apert	FL	SHUTTER	SPEEDS	ILLUS	U.S.$
Folding Ruby	3¼x4¼"	plate	VtFoldPl	1920	Cooke Anastigmat	6.5					220
Horizontal Reflex 3¼x4¼"	3¼x4¼"	plate	LgSLR	1923	Cooke Anastigmat	4.5	5"	focal plane			230
Horizontal Reflex 4x5"	4x5"	plate	LgSLR	1923	Cooke Anastigmat	4.5	5.5"	focal plane			140
Imperial Perfecta 4¼x6½"	4¼x6½"	plate	Field	1913	Zeiss Tessar	4.5		Thornton-Pickard			370
Imperial Perfecta 5x7"	5x7"	plate	Field	1913	Beck Symmetrical			Thornton-Pickard			310
Imperial Perfecta 5x7"	5x7"	plate	Field	1913	Zeiss Protar	6.3		Thornton-Pickard			310
Imperial Perfecta 6½x8½"	6½x8½"	plate	Field	1913	Beck Symmetrical			Thornton-Pickard			370
Imperial Perfecta 7x9½"	7x9½"	plate	Field	1913	Zeiss Protar	6.3		Thornton-Pickard			310
Imperial Perfecta 7x9½"	7x9½"	plate	Field	1913	Zeiss Tessar	4.5		Thornton-Pickard			310
Imperial Pocket	3¼x4¼"	plate	VtFoldPl	1916	achromatic			Everset		Mc401	70
Imperial Rollfilm	2½x3½"	120	StrutRo	1916	achromatic				I,T	A1450	100
Imperial Stereo	9x18cm	plate	StFoldPl	1910							410
Imperial Triple Extension	3¼x4¼"	plate	Field	1904	Beck Symmetrical			roller-blind		Mc401	340
Imperial Triple Extension	3¼x4¼"	plate	Field	1904	Rectoplanat			roller-blind			340
Imperial Triple Extension	4¼x6½"	plate	Field	1904	Beck Symmetrical			roller-blind			440
Imperial Triple Extension	5x7"	plate	Field	1904	Rectoplanat			roller-blind			270
Junior Special Ruby Reflex	6x9cm	plate	LgSLR	1928	Dallmeyer Anast.	4.5		focal plane	10-1000,T	Mc401	180
Junior Special Ruby Reflex	3¼x4¼"	plate	LgSLR	1928	Dallmeyer Anast.	4.5	130mm	focal plane	10-1000,T	Mc401	180
Junior Special Ruby Reflex	9x12cm	plate	LgSLR	1928	Dallmeyer Anast.	4.5	130mm	focal plane	10-1000,T	Mc401	160
Limit	4.5x6cm	Ro+Pl	TelescPl	1912	Cooke	6.3	55mm	focal plane	15-100,T	Mc401	1100
Mark III Hythe Camera	4.5x6cm	120	Military	1915		8	300mm	Central		Mc401	1000
Minim	1¾x2¼"	plate	StrutPl	1913	Cooke Anastigmat	3.5		focal plane	15-1000		190
Nimrod Automan 3¼x4¼"	3¼x4¼"	plate	H&S	1904	Aldis Anastigmat	6		B&L Automat			260
Nimrod Automan 4x5"	4x5"	plate	H&S	1904	Aldis Anastigmat	6		T-P Panoptic			260
Puck	2¼x3¼"	120	RollBox	1932	achromatic				I,T	A2867	60
Puck (colors)	2¼x3¼"	120	RollBox	1932	achromatic				I,T		130
Puck Special	4x5"	plate	PlateBox								80
Royal Ruby 4¼x6½"	4¼x6½"	plate	Field	1904	Rapid Rectilinear			Thornton-Pickard		Mc401	410
Royal Ruby 5x7"	5x7"	plate	Field	1904	Ross Convertible			Thornton-Pickard			460
Royal Ruby Stereo	4¼x6½"	plate	SterField	1904	Rapid Rectilinear			Thornton-Pickard			1000
Royal Ruby Stereo	4¼x6½"	plate	SterField	1904	Ross Convertible			Thornton-Pickard			1000
Ruby 3¼x4¼"	3¼x4¼"	plate	Field	1899	Ruby Rap. Rectil.			Thornton-Pickard		Mc401	340
Ruby 4x5"	4x5"	plate	Field	1899	Ruby Rap. Rectil.			Thornton-Pickard			370
Ruby 5x7"	5x7"	plate	Field	1899	Ruby Rap. Rectil.			Thornton-Pickard			370
Ruby 6½x8½"	6½x8½"	plate	Field	1899	Ruby Rap. Rectil.			Thornton-Pickard			350
Ruby Deluxe Reflex	6.5x9cm	plate	LgSLR	1912	Cooke Anastigmat	2.5		focal plane	10-1000	Mc401	260
Ruby Deluxe Reflex	6.5x9cm	plate	LgSLR	1912	Cooke Anastigmat	2		focal plane	10-1000		390
Ruby Deluxe Reflex	3¼x4¼"	plate	LgSLR	1912	Ross Xpres	4.5		focal plane	10-1000		270
Ruby Deluxe Reflex	4x5"	plate	LgSLR	1912	Ross Xpres	4.5		focal plane	10-1000		270
Ruby Deluxe Reflex	5x7"	plate	LgSLR	1912	Cooke Anastigmat	2.5		focal plane	10-1000		270
Ruby Deluxe Reflex Tropic	4x5"	plate	LgSLR	1912	Cooke Anastigmat	2.5		focal plane	10-1000		320
Ruby Deluxe Reflex Tropic	5x7"	plate	LgSLR	1912	Cooke Anastigmat	2.5		focal plane	10-1000		270

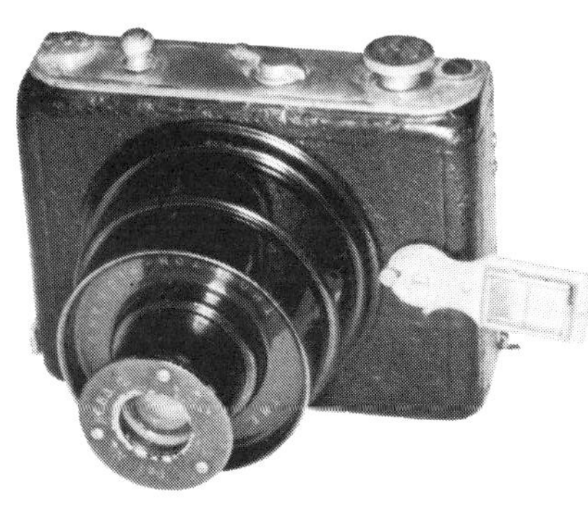

Thornton Limit

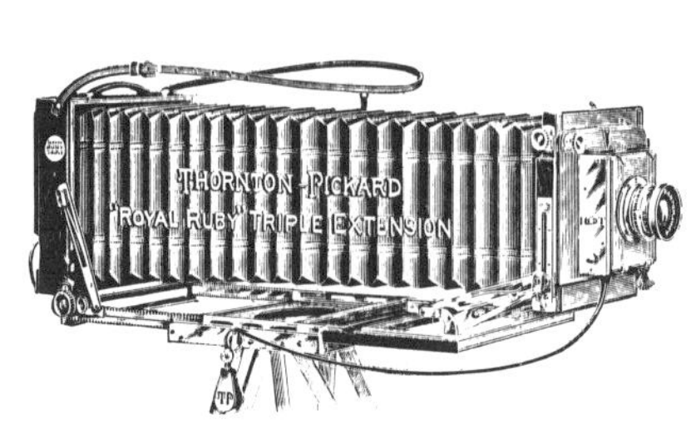

Royal Ruby

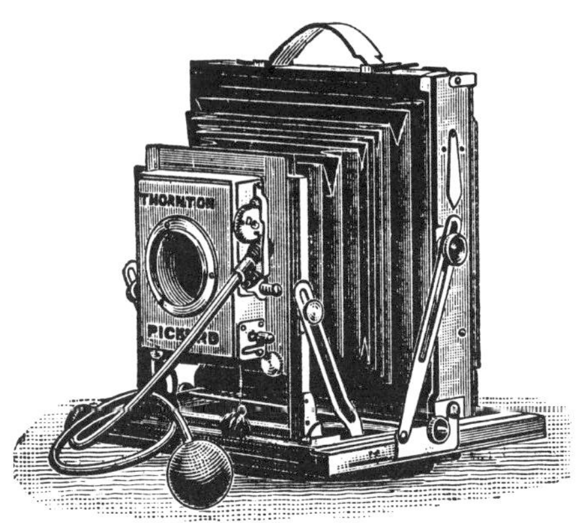

Ruby

MODEL	FORMAT	FILM	TYPE	Year	LENS	Apert	FL	SHUTTER	SPEEDS	ILLUS	U.S.$
Ruby Reflex	4x5"	plate	LgSLR	1928	Ross Homocentric	6.3	6"	focal plane		Mc401	250
Ruby Speed	1¾x2¼"	plate	RigidPl	1925	T.-H. Cooke Anast	2	3"	focal plane	10-1000		3200
Rubyette No. 1	6.5x9cm	Ro+Pl	LgSLR	1934	Dallmeyer Anast.	8		focal plane	10-1000	A1615	220
Rubyette No. 1	6.5x9cm	Ro+Pl	LgSLR	1934	Dallmeyer Anast.	4.5		focal plane	10-1000		220
Rubyette No. 2	6.5x9cm	Ro+Pl	LgSLR	1934	Dallmeyer Anast.	8		focal plane	10-1000		220
Rubyette No. 3	6.5x9cm	Ro+Pl	LgSLR	1934	Dallmeyer Anast.	4.5		focal plane	10-1000		220
Rubyette No. 3	6.5x9cm	Ro+Pl	LgSLR	1934	Dallmeyer Anast.	2.9		focal plane	10-1000		220
Snappa	4.5x6cm	plate	TelescPl	1913	Achromatic					Mc402	510
Special Ruby 9x12	9x12cm	plate	Field	1905	Goerz Doppel An.	2.5		Thornton-Pickard			410
Special Ruby 4x5"	4x5"	plate	Field	1905	Goerz Doppel An.	2.5		Thornton-Pickard			310
Special Ruby 4¼x6½"	4¼x6½"	plate	Field	1905	Goerz Doppel An.	2.5	210mm	Thornton-Pickard			440
Special Ruby Reflex	2¼x3¼"	plate	LgSLR	1923	Cooke Anastigmat	4.5		focal plane		Mc402	160
Special Ruby Reflex	3¼x4¼"	plate	LgSLR	1923	Cooke Anastigmat	4.5		focal plane		Mc402	150
Stereo Puck 6x8.5	6x8.5cm	120	SterBox	1925	Meniscus			simple		Mc402	140
Stereo Puck 4¼x6½"	4¼x6½"	plate	SterBox	1925				Spezial		Mc402	160
Tribune	3¼x4¼"	plate	Field	1913	achromatic				I,T		200
Victo	4¼x6½"	plate	Field	1905	Dallmeyer						160
Victory Reflex	2¼x3¼"	plate	LgSLR	1925	Dallmeyer						180
Victory Reflex	2¼x3¼"	plate	LgSLR	1925	Cooke						180
Weenie	4¼x6½"	plate	VtFoldPl	1913	Single Achromatic			T-P Everset T,B,I			50
...THORPE (J. Thorpe) - NY											
Four-tube camera	5x7"	WetPl	WetPlate	1862							1500
...THOWE CAMERAWERK - Freital & Berlin											
Field camera	9x12cm	plate	Field		Primoplan	3.5	135mm				180
Folding plate camera	9x12cm	plate	VtFoldPl	1910	Doxanar	6	135mm		25-100		50
Thowe Mod. II	6x9cm	120	VtFoldPl	1930	Polynar						50
Thowette	3x4cm	127	TelescRo	1932	Xenar	3.5	50mm	Rim-Compur	1-300	HK244	240
Tropical plate camera	6.5x9cm	plate	VtFoldPl	1930	Triotar						270
Tropical plate camera	9x12cm	plate	VtFoldPl	1921	Dialytar						330
...THURY & AMEY - Switzerland											
Stereo camera	9x18cm	plate	StFoldPl	1890	Protar	9	120mm	guillotine			220
...(unknown)											
Tiezonette	4.5x6cm	plate	StrutPl	1932	Xenar	3.5	45mm	Compur			180
...TIRANTI (Cesare Tiranti) - Rome											
Summa Report	6x9cm	plate	TwinLens	1954	Xenar	4.5	105mm	Sync-Compur		Mc402	5500
Summa Report	6x9cm	plate	TwinLens	1954	Angulon	6.8	65mm	Sync-Compur		Mc402	5500
...TIRANTY - Paris											
Aristograph	6x13cm	plate	StJumelle	1960	Transpar	4.5		St. Compur	B,1-300	F1178	460
Aristograph	6x13cm	plate	StJumelle	1960	Tessar	4.5		St. Compur	B,1-300	F1178	470
Coronet	6x9cm	120	VtFoldRo	1960	Meniscus					A3044	60
ST 280	24x36mm	35mm	35RF	1960	Angenieux	2.8	45mm	Atos 2	B,1-300	Mc402	30
Stereo Pocket	45x107	plate	StJumelle		Transpar	4.5	54mm	Jack	25-100,B,T	F1401	200

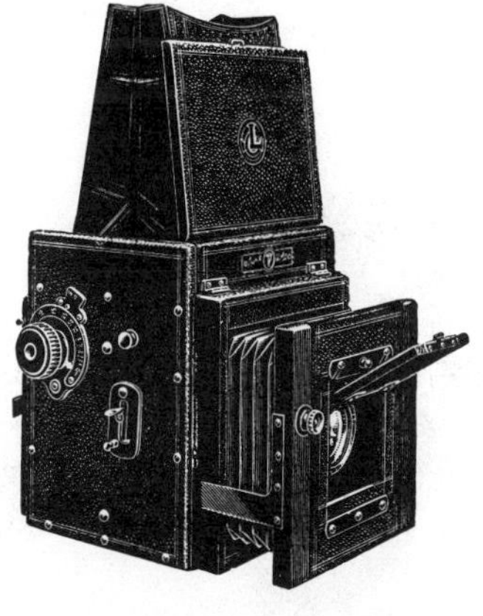

Special Ruby Reflex

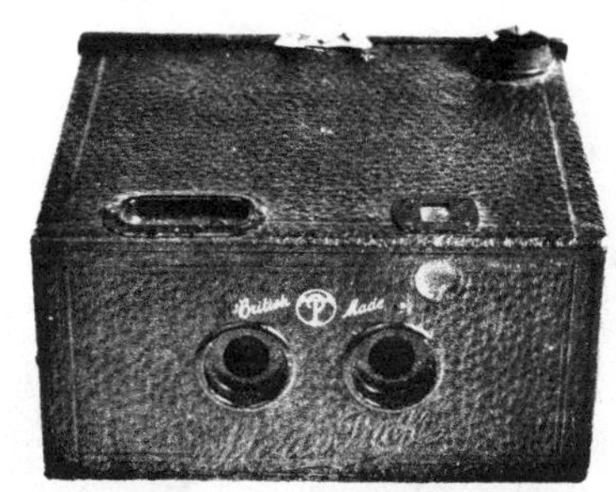

Stereo Puck

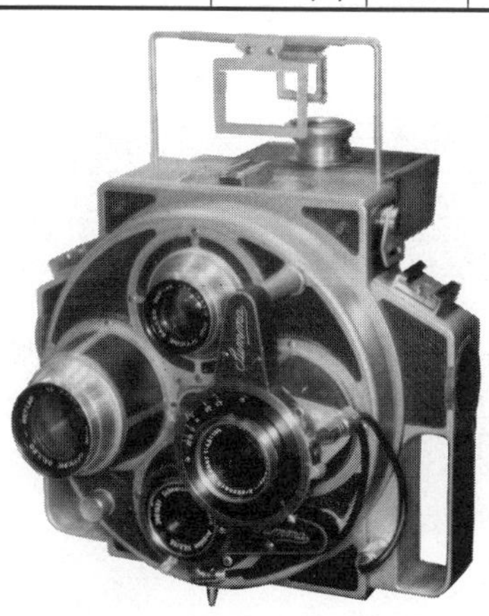

Summa Report

MODEL	FORMAT	FILM	TYPE	Year	LENS	Apert	FL	SHUTTER	SPEEDS	ILLUS	U.S.$
...TISCHLER (Anton Tischler) - Munich, Germany											
Colibri	4x4cm	plate	PlateBox	1893							3400
Monachia	3.5x4cm	plate	PlateBox	1890							520
...TISDELL & WHITTELSEY (pre-1893), TISDELL CAMERA & MFG. CO. (post-1893) - New York											
T&W Detective	3¼x4¼"	plate	DetectivBox	1888	achromatic						1200
T&W Detective (wood)	3¼x4¼"	plate	DetectivBox	1888	achromatic					Mc403	3300
Tisdell Hand	4x5"	plate	DetectivBox	1893	achromatic					Mc403	1100
...TOAKOKI SEISAKUSHO - Japan											
Gelto III	3x4cm	127	TelescRo	1948	Grimmel	4.5	50mm		T,B,5-250		120
Gelto D III	3x4cm	127	TelescRo	1938	Grimmel	4.5	50mm		T,B,5-250	Mc403	120
Gelto D III	3x4cm	127	TelescRo	1950	Grimmel	3.5	50mm		T,B,5-250		120
...TOHOKOKEN CAMERA CO.											
Camel Mod. II	24x36mm	35mm	35VF	1953	Camel	3.5	50mm	Nippol	1-200		70
...TOKIWA SEIKI CO. - Japan											
Bioflex	6x6cm	120	HzFoldRo	1951	First Anastigmat	3.5	8cm		B,10-200		70
First Six I	6x6/4.5x6	120	HzFoldRo	1952	Tri-Lauser Anast.	3.5	80mm				70
First Six III	6x6/4.5x6	120	HzFoldRo	1952	Tri-Lauser Anast.	3.5	80mm				70
First Six V	6x6/4.5x6	120	HzFoldRo	1952	Tri-Lauser Anast.	3.5	80mm				70
Firstflex	6x6cm	120	TLR	1951	First Anastigmat	3.5	80mm		1/200		70
Firstflex	6x6cm	120	TLR	1951	First Anastigmat	3.5	80mm	MSK	1-400,B		70
Firstflex 35 (1955)	24x36mm	35mm	35SLR	1955		3.5	50mm		25-150,B		160
Firstflex 35 (1958)	24x36mm	35mm	35SLR	1958	Auto Tokinon	2.8	45mm				70
Kenflex	6x6cm	120	TLR	1951	First Anastigmat	3.5	80mm		B,10-200		60
Kwikflex	6x6cm	120	TLR	1950	Tri-Lauser Anast.	3.5	80mm	Rectus			80
Kwikflex Automatic	6x6cm	120	TLR	1958	Tri-Lauser Anast.	3.5	80mm	Rectus			60
Lafayette 35	24x36mm	35mm	35SLR	1955	Soligor Anast.	3.5	50mm		B,25-100		130
Windsorflex	24x36mm	35mm	35SLR	1955	First	3.5	50mm		25-150		130
...TOKO PHOTO CO. - Japan											
Cyclops	10x14mm	16mm	Special	1950		4.5	35mm		25-100	Mc403	550
Teleca	10x14mm	16mm	Special	1950		4.5			25-100	Mc403	700
...TOKYO CAMERA WORKS - Japan											
Secrette	4.5x6cm	plate	Disguised	1924	achromatic		50mm		I,T		1700
Secrette Special	4.5x6cm	plate	Disguised	1923	Testar	4.5	50mm		I,T		2040
...TOKYO KOGAKU - Japan											
Laurelflex	6x6cm	120	TLR	1951	Toko	3.5	75mm	Konan Rap.S	1-500,B		70
Laurelflex	6x6cm	120	TLR	1951	Simlar	3.5	75mm	Seikosha-Rap.	1-500,B		70
Minion	4x5cm	127	HzFoldRo	1938	Toko	3.5	60mm	Seikosh.Licht	25-100,B,T	Mc403	120
Minion 35 A	24x32mm	35mm	35VF	1948	Toko	3.5	40mm	Seikosha-Rap.	1-500,B		130
Minion 35 B	24x32mm	35mm	35VF	1948	Toko	3.5	40mm	Seikosha-Rap.	1-500,B		130
Minion 35 C	24x36mm	35mm	35VF	1948	Toko	3.5	40mm	Seikosha-Rap.	1-500,B	Mc403	130
Primo Jr.	4x4cm	127	TLR	1958	Topcor	2.8	60mm	Seikosha	1-500,B		110
Primo Jr. II	4x4cm	127	TLR	1958	Topcor	2.8	60mm	Seikosha	1-500,B		110

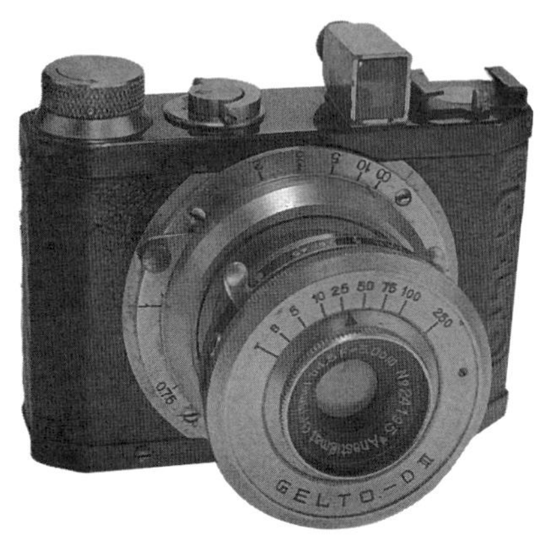

Gelto D III

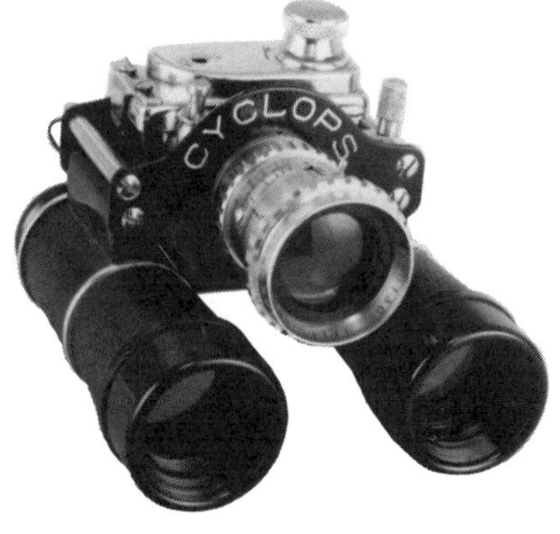

Toko Cyclops

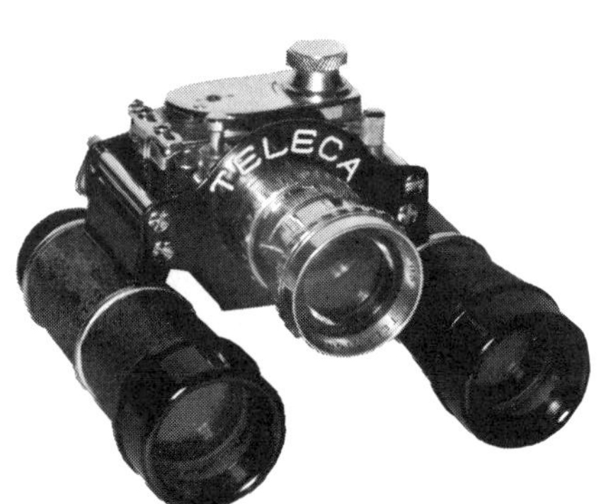

Toko Teleca

MODEL	FORMAT	FILM	TYPE	Year	LENS	Apert	FL	SHUTTER	SPEEDS	ILLUS	U.S.$
Primoflex	6x6cm	120	TLR	1950	Toko	3.5	75mm	Rectus			90
Primoflex Automat	6x6cm	120	TLR	1956	Topcor	3.5	75mm	Seikosha-MX			100
Sawyers Mark IV	4x4cm	127	TLR	1950	Topcor	2.6					130
Topcoflex	6x6cm	120	TLR	1950	Toko	3.5	75mm	Rectus			80
Topcoflex Automat	6x6cm	120	TLR	1950	Topcor	3.5	75mm	Seikosha-MX		Mc404	80
Topcon 35-L	24x36mm	35mm	35RF	1958	Topcor	2	45mm	Seiko. MXL	1-550	Mc404	60
Topcon Auto 100	24x36mm	35mm	35SLR	1965	UV Topcor	2	53mm		1/8-500		70
Topcon B	24x36mm	35mm	35SLR	1959	Auto-Topcor	1.8	58mm	focal plane	1-1000,B		110
Topcon C	24x36mm	35mm	35SLR	1960	Auto-Topcor	1.8	58mm	focal plane	1-1000,B		100
Topcon D-1	24x36mm	35mm	35SLR	1965	Auto-Topcor	1.8	58mm	focal plane	1-1000,B		80
Topcon R	24x36mm	35mm	35SLR	1958	Auto-Topcor	1.8	58mm	focal plane	1-1000,B		170
Topcon RE 2	24x36mm	35mm	35SLR	1965	Auto-Topcor	1.8	58mm	focal plane	1-1000,B		140
Topcon RE Super	24x36mm	35mm	35SLR	1963	Topcor	1.4	58mm	focal plane	1-1000,B		220
Topcon Super D	24x36mm	35mm	35SLR	1963	RE-Auto Topcor	1.8	58mm	focal plane	1-1000,B		240
Topcon Super DM	24x36mm	35mm	35SLR	1973	GN Topcor	1.4	50mm	focal plane	1-1000,B	A3199	260
Topcon Uni	24x36mm	35mm	35SLR	1965	UV Topcor	2	53mm	focal plane	1/8-500	Mc404	70
...TOKYO KOKEN CO. - Tokyo											
Dolca 35 (Mod. I)	24x36mm	35mm	35VF	1953	Komeil	3.5	50mm	Nipol	B, 1-200	Mc404	70
...TOKYO KOKI CO. - Japan											
Rubina Sixteen Mod. II	10x14mm	16mm	Submin	1951	Ruby	3.5	25mm		25-100,B	Mc404	180
...TOKYO SEIKI CO. LTD.											
Doris	4.5x6cm	120	HzFoldRo	1952	Perfa Anastigmat	3.5	75mm	NKS	B,10-200		50
...TOP CAMERA WORKS											
Top	18x18mm	Roll	Submin	1948	Fixed focus				B,I	A1941	200
...TOPPER											
Secret Sam Attache Case	3x4cm	127	Disguised	1965	Meniscus						160
Secret Sam Spy Dictionary	3x4cm	127	Disguised	1966	Meniscus						160
Topper	3x4cm	127	PlasticBox	1962	Meniscus					A3072	20
...TOSEI OPTICAL - Japan											
Frank Six	6x6cm	120	HzFoldRo	1951	Anastigmat	3.5	75mm	T.K.S.	B,1-200		100
Frank Six Mod. IV	6x6cm	120	HzFoldRo	1953	Tri-Lausar	3.5	80mm	T.K.S.		Mc404	70
Frank Six Mod. IV	6x6cm	120	HzFoldRo	1953	Tosei Anastigmat	3.5	80mm	T.K.S.		Mc404	70
...TOUGODO OPTICAL - Japan											
Baby-Max	14x14mm	16mm	Submin	1951	Fixed focus			single speed		Mc405	40
Buena 35-S	24x36mm	35mm	35VF	1957	Buena	3.5	45mm		B,25-300		50
Click	14x14mm	16mm	Submin	1951							30
Colly	14x14mm	16mm	Submin	1951	Meniscus	11					30
Hit	14x14mm	16mm	Submin	1950						Mc405	30
Hobiflex Mod. III	6x6cm	120	TLR	1952	Hobi Anastigmat	3.5	80mm		1-200,B		60
Hobix	28x28mm	Bolta	RigidRo	1951	Meniscus	8	40mm	Complete	25,50,100	Mc405	60
Hobix Junior	28x28mm	Bolta	RigidRo	1955	Fixed focus				B,I		40
Kino-44	4x4cm	127	TLR	1959	Kinokkor	3.5	60mm	Citizen MSV	1-500		120

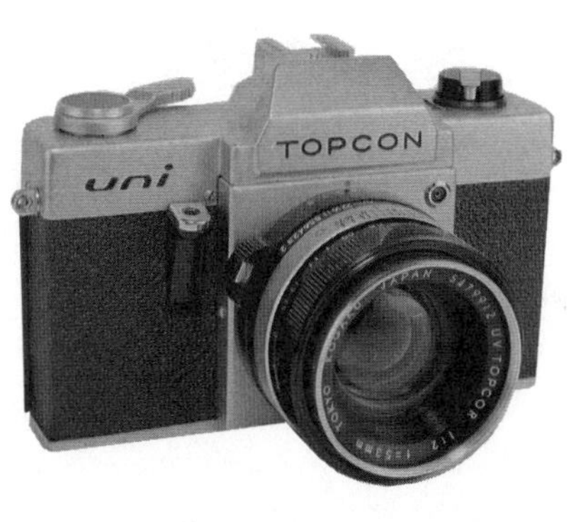

Topcon Uni

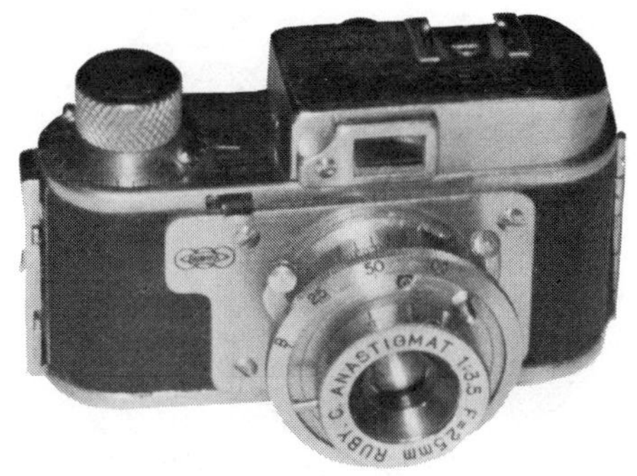

Rubina Sixteen Mod. II

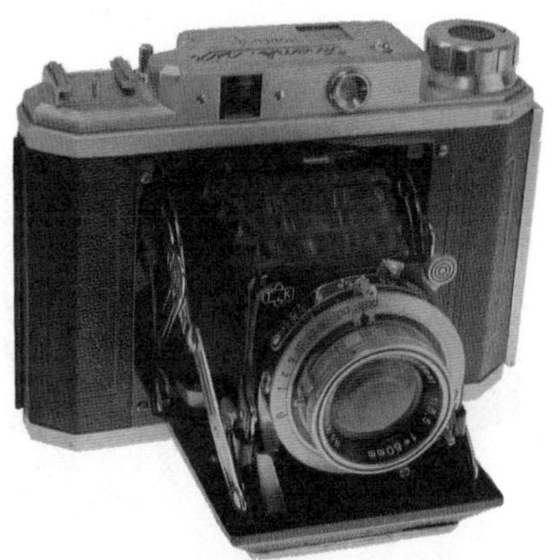

Frank Six Mod. IV

MODEL	FORMAT	FILM	TYPE	Year	LENS	Apert	FL	SHUTTER	SPEEDS	ILLUS	U.S.$
Leader	23x24mm	35mm	35Ster	1955	Anastigmat	4.5	45mm		1/25-100		350
Meikai	3x4cm	35mm	35TLR	1937	Meikai	3.5	50mm				460
Meikai	3x4cm	35mm	35TLR	1937	Anastigmat	4.5	50mm				460
Meikai EL	24x36mm	35mm	35VF	1963	Fixed focus			simple			10
Meiritto No. 3	28x40mm	Roll	TLR	1940	Fixed focus	6.3			25100		220
Meisupi	3x4cm	Roll	TLR	1937	Meikai Anastigmat	4.5	50mm		25-101	Mc405	540
Meisupi II	3x4cm	Roll	TLR	1937	Meikai Anastigmat	6.3	50mm		25-102	Mc405	540
Meisupi IV	3x4cm	Roll	TLR	1937	Meikai Anastigmat	5.6	50mm		25-103		540
Meisupii Half	18x24mm	35mm	35Half	1959						Mc405	30
Meisuppi Ia	24x36mm	35mm	RigidRo	1950	fixed focus	8	50mm				30
Metraflex II	6x6cm	120	TLR		Metar Anastigmat	80mm					80
Stereo Hit	3x4cm	127	Stereo	1955	S-Owla	4.5	35mm	synch	B,I	A2715	140
Tougo Camera	3x4cm	127	Yen	1930	Fixed focus				I		30
Toyoca 16	14x14mm	16mm	Submin	1955						Mc406	150
Toyoca 35	24x36mm	35mm	35RF	1957	Owla	3.5	45mm	Leaf	B,1-300	Mc406	60
Toyoca 44	4x4cm	127	TLR	1950	Hacor						80
Toyoca Ace	14x14mm	16mm	Submin	1965				Toyoca Ace			70
Toyocaflex	6x6cm	120	TLR	1954	Tritar	3.5	8cm	Synchro NKS	25-300		80
Toyocaflex	6x6cm	120	TLR	1954	Tri-Lausar	3.5	80mm	Synchro NKS	1-200		80
Toyocaflex IB	6x6cm	120	TLR	1954	Tritar	3.5	80mm	Synchro NKS	25-300		80
Toyocaflex IB	6x6cm	120	TLR	1954	Tri-Lausar	3.5	80mm	Synchro NKS	25-300		80
Toyocaflex 35	24x36mm	35mm	35TLR	1955	Owla Anastigmat	3.5	45mm	NSK	1-300,B	Mc406	900
...TOYO KOGAKU (TOKO) - Japan											
Mighty	14x14mm	Roll	Submin	1947	Meniscus				I	Mc406	100
Mighty, gift box	14x14mm	Roll	Submin	1948	Meniscus						260
Peacock III	3x4cm	127	RigidRo	1939	Peacock	6.3	50mm	Peacock	1/10-100		50
Tone	14x14mm	Roll	Submin	1948		3.5	25mm				180
...TRAMBOUZE - Paris											
Tailboard camera	13x18cm	plate	Tailboard			8				Mc406	270
...TROTTER (John Trotter) - Glasgow											
Field camera 4¼x6½"	4¼x6½"	plate	Field								270
Field camera 6½x8½"	6½x8½"	plate	Field								310
...TRUSITE CAMERA CO.											
Girl Scout Official Camera	3x4cm	127	Minicam		Meniscus					Mc407	40
Trusite Minicam	3x4cm	127	Minicam	1947	Meniscus					Mc407	10
...T.S.C. - Japan											
Tacker	14x14mm	16mm	Submin			4.5	26mm		25-100		180
...TUCHT (Carl Tucht) - Dusseldorf											
Focal plane camera	13x18cm	plate	FoldPl	1900	Busch Rapid Apl.	7		focal plane			260
...TUDOR PHOTOGRAPHIC GROUP LTD. - London											
Tudormatic 300	13x17mm	110	110VF	1978	Meniscus	11	30mm				10
Tudormatic 301	13x17mm	110	110VF	1980	Meniscus	11	30mm			A3367	20

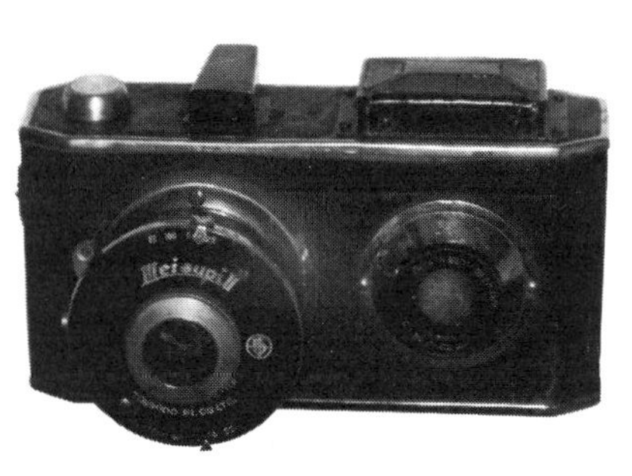

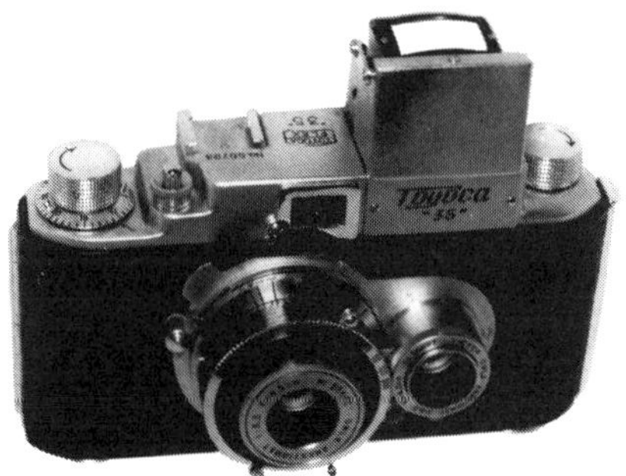

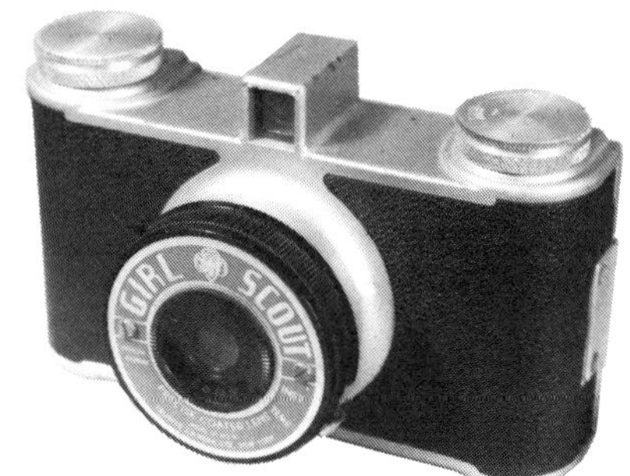

Meisupi | **Toyocaflex 35** | **Trusite Girl Scout Official Cam.**

MODEL	FORMAT	FILM	TYPE	Year	LENS	Apert	FL	SHUTTER	SPEEDS	ILLUS	U.S.$
Tudormatic 302 Electrofl.	13x17mm	110	110VF	1980	Achromat	8	27mm			A3368	50
Tudormatic 303 Autowind	13x17mm	110	110VF	1980	Achromat	8	22mm			A3369	50
...TURILLON (Louis Turillon) - Paris											
Photo-Ticket No. 2	4x5cm	120	Jumelle	1905	Petzval-type	4.5	95mm	focal plane		F1107	1300
Photo-Ticket No. 3	4.5x6cm	120	Jumelle	1905	Petzval-type	4.5	95mm	focal plane		Mc407	1300
...TURRET CAMERA CO. - Brooklyn, N.Y.											
Panoramic camera	4x10"	plate	Panoramic	1905						Mc407	1200
...TYLAR (William T. Tylar) - Birmingham, England											
Detective camera	9x12cm	plate	DetectivBox	1895	Achromat			guillotine			460
Gnu Stereo	3¼x4¼"	plate	StMagBox	1900	Achromat						520
Pocket Titbit	6x9cm	plate	StrutPl	1890	Achromat						350
Tit-bit	6x9cm	plate	PlateBox	1895	Achromat					Mc407	400
...TYNAR CORP. - Los Angeles, CA											
Tynar	10x14mm	16mm	Submin	1950	Tynar Anastigmat	6.3	45mm	guillotine	I	Mc407	50
...UCA (Uca Werkstätten für Feinmechanik & Optik) - Flensburg, Germany											
Elcaflex	24x36mm	35mm	35SLR	1950	Elolux	1.9	50mm	focal plane	1-1000		550
Ucanett	24x24mm	35mm	35VF	1952	Ucapan	2.5	40mm	Prontor-S		HK582	170
Unaflex	24x36mm	35mm	35SLR	1950	Elolux	1.9	50mm	focal plane	1-1000	Mc407	600
...ULCA CAMERA CORP. - Pittsburgh, PA											
Ulca 20x20	20x20mm	Roll	Submin	1935	Meniscus			simple		A3304	50
Ulca 24x24	24x24mm	Roll	Submin	1935	Meniscus			simple		Mc407	70
...UNDERWOOD (E. & T. Underwood) - Birmingham, England											
Club 3¼x4¼"	3¼x4¼"	plate	Field	1896	Underwood	11		Thornton-Pickard			290
Club 4¼x6½"	4¼x6½"	plate	Field	1896	Underwood	11		Thornton-Pickard			300
Convention 3¼x4¼"	3¼x4¼"	plate	Field	1896	Underwood	11		Thornton-Pickard			290
Convention 4¼x6½"	4¼x6½"	plate	Field	1896	Underwood	11		Thornton-Pickard			300
Exhibition 3¼x4¼"	3¼x4¼"	plate	Field	1896	Underwood	11		Thornton-Pickard			290
Exhibition 4¼x6½"	4¼x6½"	plate	Field	1896	Underwood	11		Thornton-Pickard			300
Field camera 3¼x4¼"	3¼x4¼"	plate	Field	1896	Underwood	11		Thornton-Pickard			250
Field camera 4¼x6½"	4¼x6½"	plate	Field	1896	Underwood	11		Thornton-Pickard		Mc408	310
Instanto 3¼x4¼"	3¼x4¼"	plate	Tailboard	1896	Underwood						370
Instanto 4¼x6½"	4¼x6½"	plate	Tailboard	1896	Underwood						370
Instanto 6½x8½"	6½x8½"	plate	Tailboard	1896	Underwood						290
Instanto 8x10"	8x10"	plate	Tailboard	1896	Underwood						260
Stereograph	4¼x6½"	plate	SterTail	1896							480
Umbra	4¼x6½"	plate	Field								220
...UNGER & HOFFMAN - Dresden											
Verax 4.5x6	4.5x6cm	plate	VtFoldPl	1924	Steinheil	3.5		Compound		A230	100
Verax 4.5x6	4.5x6cm	plate	VtFoldPl	1924	Steinheil	4.5		Compound			100
Verax 6.5x9	6.5x9cm	plate	VtFoldPl	1924	Steinheil	3.5		Compound			100
Verax 9x12	9x12cm	plate	VtFoldPl	1924	Xenar	4.5	135mm	Compound			100
Verax Favorit	6.5x9cm	plate	VtFoldPl	1924	Aplanat	8	120mm	Compound			40

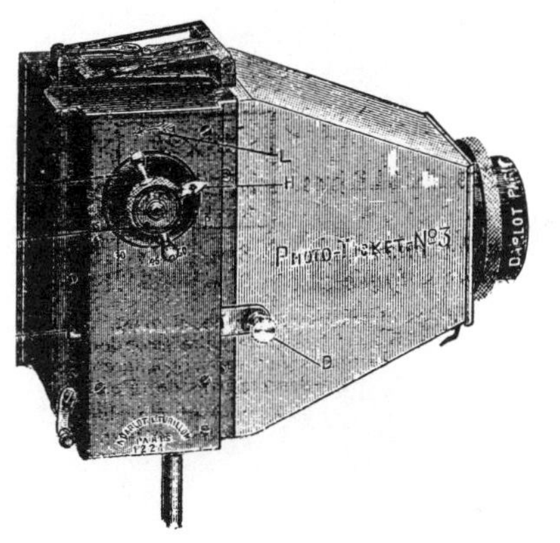

Photo-Ticket No. 3

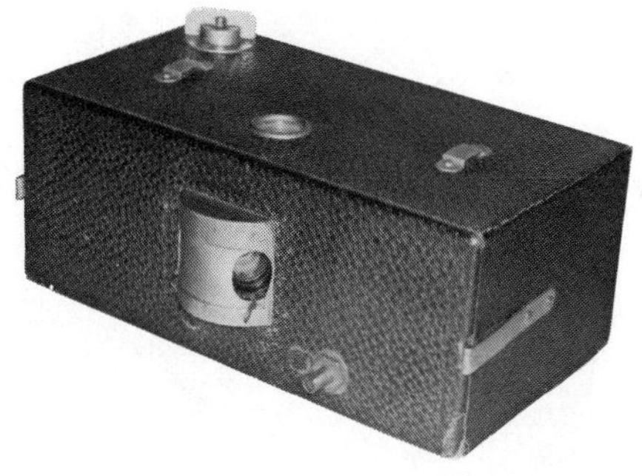

Turret Panoramic camera

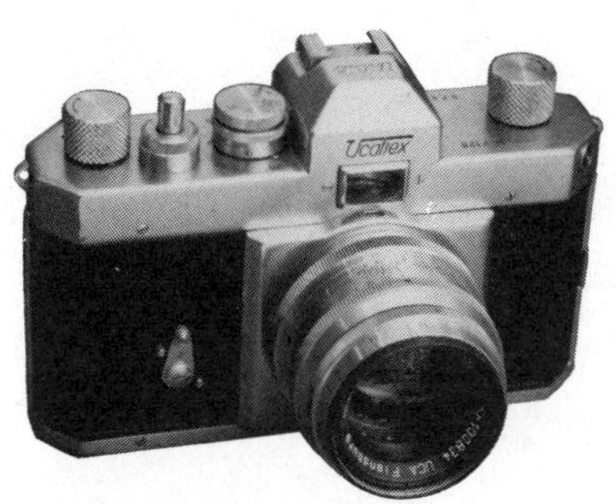

Unaflex

MODEL	FORMAT	FILM	TYPE	Year	LENS	Apert	FL	SHUTTER	SPEEDS	ILLUS	U.S.$
Verax Gloria	4.5x6cm	plate	VtFoldPl	1924	Dogmar	4.5	75mm	Compur	1-300		360
Verax Superb	6x9cm	120	VtFoldRo	1930							30
Verax Tropical	9x12cm	plate	VtFoldPl	1910	Verax	6.3	105mm	Compound			390
...UNIBOX - Sweden											
Unibox	6x6cm	120	TLR-Box	1950	Meniscus				M,T	Mc408	80
...UNIMARK PHOTO INC.											
Unimatic 606	24x36mm	35mm	35VF	1961	Lordonar	2.8	50mm	Prontor-Matic	30-500	Mc408	30
Unimatic 707	24x36mm	35mm	35RF	1961	Lordonar	2.8	50mm	Prontor-Matic	30-500		30
...UNION OPTICAL CO. - Japan											
Union C-II	4.5x6cm	120	VtFoldRo	1953	Coonor Anast.	3.5	7.5cm	Copal	B,1-300	Mc408	70
...UNITED CAMERA CO. - Chicago											
Ucet	6.5x11cm	116	RollBox								20
...UNITED OPTICAL INSTRUMENTS - England											
Merlin	20x20mm	Roll	Submin	1936						Mc408	120
...UNITED STATES CAM-O CORP.											
Cam-O	4x6.5cm	70mm	Special		Wollensak Raptar	4.5	117mm	Alphax			80
...UNITED STATES CAMERA CORP. - Chicago											
Auto Fifty	6x6cm	120	TLR		Biokor	3.5	80mm	Synchro MX	1-300,B	Mc408	50
Auto Forty	6x6cm	120	TLR		Tritar Anast.	3.5	8cm	Sync	B,25-300	Mc408	60
Automatic	6x6cm	620	TLR	1960	Fixed focus					Mc409	60
Reflex	6x6cm	120	TLR-Box	1960							10
Reflex II	6x6cm	120	TLR-Box	1960						A3170	10
Rollex 20	6x9cm	120	VtFoldRo	1950	Achromat						20
USC 35	24x36mm	35mm	35VF		Steinheil Cassar	2.8	45mm	Vario	25-200		30
Vagabond 120 Eveready	2¼x3¼"	120	MetalBox	1951						Mc409	10
...UNIVERSAL CAMERA CORP. - NYC											
Buccaneer	24x36mm	35mm	35RF	1945	Tricor	3.5	50mm	Chronomatic	10-300	Mc409	30
Corsair I	24x36mm	35mm	35VF	1938	Univex	4.5	50mm	Rimset	25-200	Mc409	30
Corsair II	24x36mm	35mm	35VF	1939	Univex	4.5	50mm	Rimset	25-200		30
Duovex	1⅛x1⅝"	Roll	Stereo	1934						Mc409	290
G.E. Toppers Club	1⅛x1⅝"	Roll	StrutRo	1936	achromatic					Mc411	240
Hollywood	1⅛x1⅝"	Roll	StrutRo	1936	achromatic					Mc411	240
Iris	1⅛x1⅝"	Roll	TelescRo	1938	Vitar	7.9	50mm	Ilex	I,B,T	Mc410	30
Iris Deluxe	1⅛x1⅝"	Roll	TelescRo	1938	Vitar	7.9	50mm	Ilex	I,B,T		30
Mercury (Mod. CC)	18x24mm	35mm	RigidRo	1938	Wollensak Tricor	3.5		focal plane	20-1000	Mc410	40
Mercury (Mod. CC-1500)	18x24mm	35mm	RigidRo	1939	Hexar	2			1/1500		170
Mercury II (Mod. CX)	18x24mm	35mm	35Half	1945	Universal Tricor	3.5		rotary	20-1000	Mc410	50
Mercury II (Mod. CX)	18x24mm	35mm	35Half	1945	Hexar	2		rotary	20-1000	A1074	100
Meteor	2¼x2¼"	620	TelescRo	1949	Achromat	11			1/50	Mc410	10
Minute 16	10x14mm	16mm	Submin	1949	Meniscus	6.3		guillotine		Mc410	40
Norton-Univex	1¼x1½"	Roll	MiniatRo	1935						Mc410	30
Official Girl Scout model	1⅛x1⅝"	Roll	StrutRo	1936	achromatic					Mc409	240

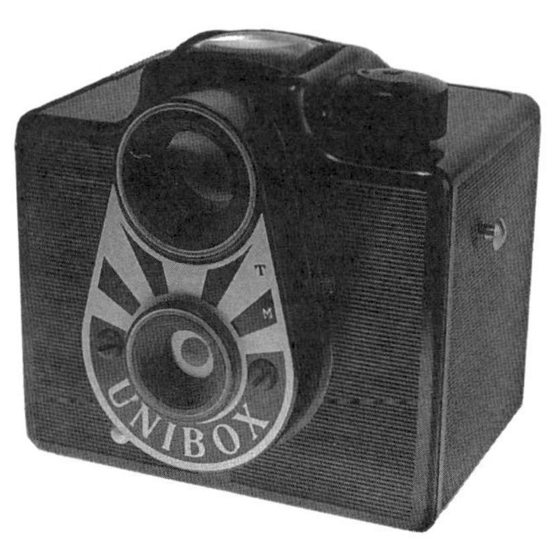

Unibox

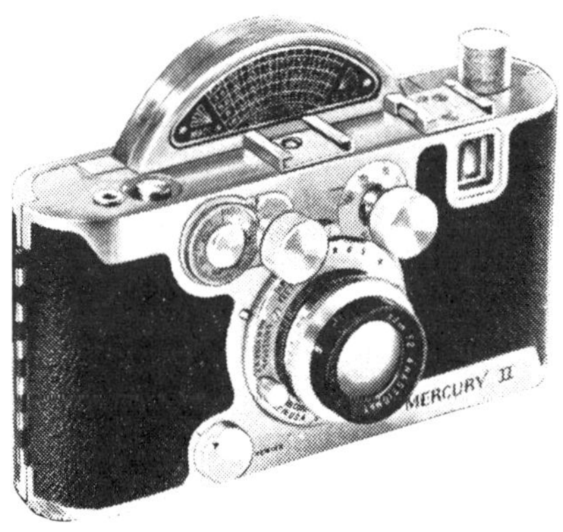

Mercury II (Mod. CX)

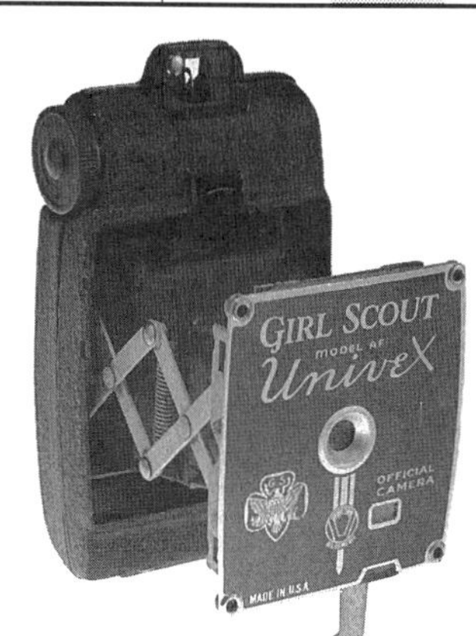

Universal Official Girl Scout

MODEL	FORMAT	FILM	TYPE	Year	LENS	Apert	FL	SHUTTER	SPEEDS	ILLUS	U.S.$
Roamer I	2¼x3¼"	620	VtFoldRo	1948	Doublet	11	100mm		1/50	Mc410	20
Roamer II	2¼x3¼"	620	VtFoldRo	1948	Universal Anast.	4.5	100mm		200		10
Roamer 63	2¼x3¼"	620	VtFoldRo	1948	Universal Anast.	6.3	100mm		200		20
Stere-All	24x24mm	35mm	35Ster	1954	Tricor	3.5	35mm		1/50	A1830	110
Twinflex	1¼x1½"	Roll	TLR-Box	1939	Meniscus			simple		Mc410	50
Uniflash	1⅛x1⅝"	Roll	RigidRo	1940	Vitar	16	60mm		1/40,B	Mc411	30
Uniflex, Mod. I	2¼x2¼"	620/1	TLR	1948	Universal	5.6	75mm		25-200	A646	30
Uniflex, Mod. II	2¼x2¼"	620/1	TLR	1948	Universal	4.5	75mm		10-200	Mc411	30
Univex, Mod. A	1⅛x1⅝"	Roll	MiniatRo	1933	Meniscus					Mc411	30
Mod.A Century of Progress	1⅛x1⅝"	Roll	MiniatRo	1933	Meniscus						100
Univex AF (black)	1⅛x1⅝"	Roll	StrutRo	1935	achromatic						30
Univex AF (colors)	1⅛x1⅝"	Roll	StrutRo	1935	achromatic						30
Univex AF (Special models)	1⅛x1⅝"	Roll	StrutRo	1936	achromatic					Mc411	240
Univex AF-2	1⅛x1⅝"	Roll	StrutRo	1936	achromatic					A1497	30
Univex AF-3	1⅛x1⅝"	Roll	StrutRo	1936	Duo Achromatic						30
Univex AF-4	1⅛x1⅝"	Roll	StrutRo	1938	Duo Achromatic						30
Univex AF-5	1⅛x1⅝"	Roll	StrutRo	1938	Achromar	16	60mm			Mc411	30
Vitar	24x36mm	35mm	35VF	1951	Tricor	3.5	50mm	Chronomatic	25-200		30
Zenith	1⅛x1⅝"	Roll	RigidRo	1939	Univex	4.5	50mm		25-200	Mc411	130
...UNIVERSAL RADIO MFG. CO.											
Cameradio	3x4cm	127	Disguised	1940							150
...UNIVEX (Casa Univex Empresa Enrique Wiese) - Barcelona, Spain											
Univex Supra	6x8cm	120	BakeliteRoll	1948	Meniscus				P&I	Mc411	40
...UTILITY MFG. CO. - New York & Chicago											
Carlton Reflex	6x6cm	120	TLR-Box	1934							20
Falcon	4x6.5cm	127	VtFoldRo	1930						Mc412	20
Falcon Junior (black)	4x6.5cm	127	StrutRo	1948	Achromat	11	75mm			A3039	20
Falcon Junior (colors)	4x6.5cm	127	StrutRo	1948	Achromat	11	75mm				30
Falcon Junior 16 (black)	3x4cm	127	CardBox	1934					1/25	Mc412	30
Falcon Junior 16 (colors)	3x4cm	127	CardBox	1934					1/25		30
Falcon Midget 16 (black)	3x4cm	127	CardBox	1935						Mc412	30
Falcon Midget 16 (colors)	3x4cm	127	CardBox	1935							70
Falcon Minette	3x4cm	127	Minicam	1935							10
Falcon Miniature	3x4cm	127	Minicam	1938	Minivar		50mm			Mc412	10
Falcon Minicam Senior	3x4cm	127	Minicam	1939	Minivar		50mm	leaf			20
Falcon Mod. F	3x4cm	127	RigidRo	1938	Woll. Velostigmat	4.5	50mm	Deltax		Mc412	30
Falcon Mod. FE	3x4cm	127	RigidRo	1938	Woll. Velostigmat	4.5	50mm	Deltax			30
Falcon Mod. Four	2¼x3¼"	120	VtFoldRo	1939					I,T		20
Falcon Mod. G	3x4cm	127	RigidRo	1938	Woll. Velostigmat	3.5	50mm	Alphax	25-200		30
Falcon Mod. GE	3x4cm	127	RigidRo	1938	Woll. Velostigmat	3.5	50mm	Alphax	25-200		30
Falcon Mod. V-16 (black)	3x4cm	127	StrutRo	1938	Meniscus	11	75mm			Mc412	30
Falcon Mod. V-16 (colors)	3x4cm	127	StrutRo	1938	Meniscus	11	75mm				50

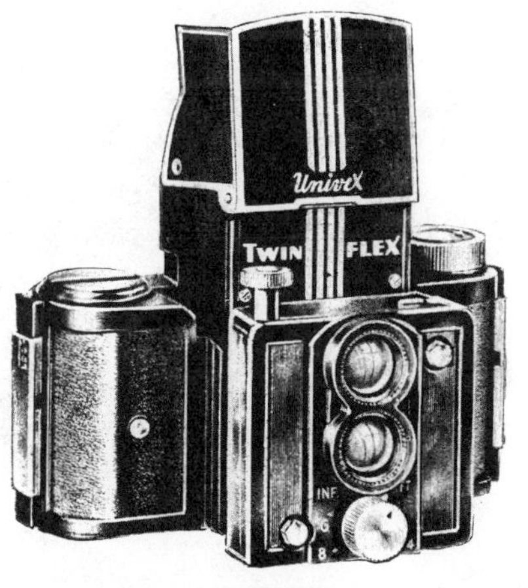

Universal Twinflex

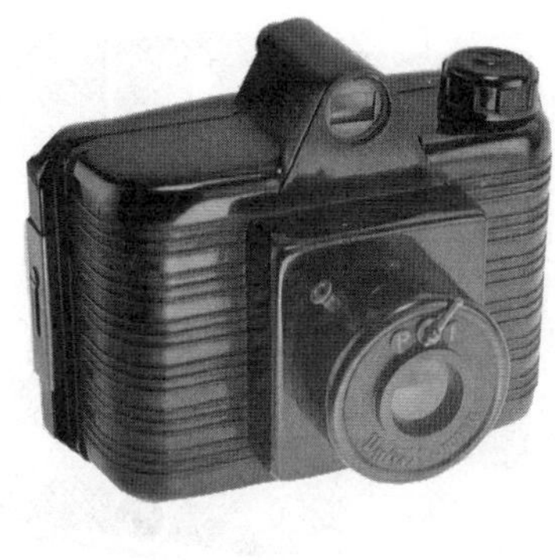

Univex Supra

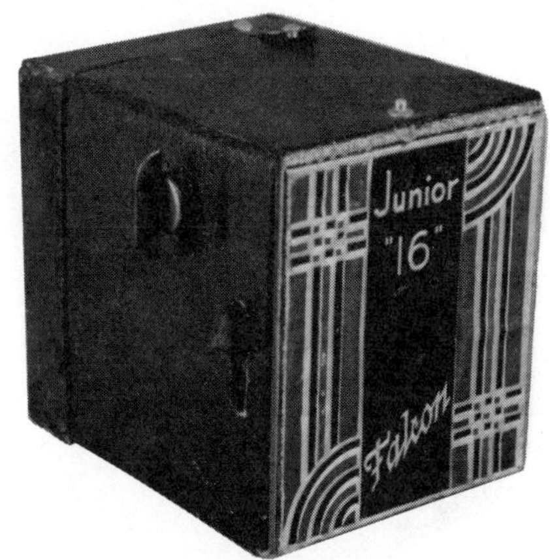

Falcon Junior 16

MODEL	FORMAT	FILM	TYPE	Year	LENS	Apert	FL	SHUTTER	SPEEDS	ILLUS	U.S.$
Falcon Press Flash	6x9cm	120	BakeliteBox	1939	Faltar					Mc412	10
Falcon Special	3x4cm	127	BakeliteRoll	1939	Woll. Velostigmat	4.5	50mm	Alphax Jr.	25-200	Mc412	30
Falcon-Abbey Electricamer	3x4cm	127	BakeliteBox	1940	Meniscus	11	4.5"		40-100		30
Falcon-Flex	3x4cm	127	TLR-Box	1939							20
Falcon-Flex	6x6cm	120	TLR-Box	1939	Meniscus	11			1/30	Mc413	20
Girl Scout Falcon	3x4cm	127	Minicam							Mc413	40
...UYEDA CAMERA - Japan											
Vero Four	4x4cm	127	TelescRo	1938	Verona Anast.	3.5	60mm	Rapid Vero	T,B,1-500		160
...VAN NECK - London, England											
Press camera 9x12	9x12cm	plate	StrutPl		Ross Xpres	4.5					120
Press camera 4x5"	4x5"	plate	StrutPl		Ross Xpres	4.5					120
...VARIMEX - Poland											
Alfa	24x36mm	35mm	35VF	1961	Euktar	4.5	45mm	Sync shutter	30-125	A2159	120
Alfa 2	24x36mm	35mm	35VF	1963	Emitar	4.5	45mm		30-125		130
...VARSITY CAMERA CORP.											
Varsity Mod. V	1 3/8x1 3/8"	Roll	BakeliteRoll							Mc413	70
...VASCONCELLOS (D.F. Vasconcellos) - Sao Paulo, Brasil											
Kapsa	6x9/4x6	620/1	PlasticBox	1950	Vascromat		110mm		I,T	Mc413	30
...VEGA S.A. - Geneva, Switzerland											
Telephot Vega 9x12	9x12cm	plate	Special	1902	Achromat			focal plane		A90	3400
Telephot Vega 13x18	13x18cm	plate	Special	1902	Achromat			focal plane		A90	3400
Telephot Vega 18x24	18x24cm	plate	Special	1902	Achromat			focal plane		A90	3400
Vega 6.5x9	6.5x9cm	plate	Special	1900	Aplanat			guillotine		Mc413	800
Vega 9x12	9x12cm	plate	Special	1900	Aplanat			guillotine		Mc413	900
Vega 9x12	9x12cm	pack	Special	1900	Aplanat			guillotine		Mc413	800
...VENA - Amsterdam, Netherlands											
Sport-Box	6x9cm	120	RollBox	1949	Meniscus	11	105mm			A2903	50
Vena-Box	6x9cm	120	RollBox	1950	Meniscus	9					50
Venaret	6x6cm	120	RigidRo	1949	Doublet	7.7	75mm	simple	24,50	Mc413	40
Venaret (green)	6x6cm	120	RigidRo	1949	Doublet	7.7	75mm				20
Venaret (sync)	6x6cm	120	RigidRo	1949	Doublet	7.7	75mm	simple	24,50	A3121	40
Venaret Junior	6x6cm	120	RigidRo	1949	Doublet	7.7	75mm				10
...VICAM PHOTO APPLIANCE CORP. - Philadelphia, PA											
Vicamphoto	24x36mm	35mm	Special		Fixed focus					Mc413	90
...VIDMAR CAMERA CO. - New York, NY											
Vidax	6x9cm	620	FoldPress	1948	Ektar	4.5				Mc414	510
...VINTEN (W. Vinten, Ltd.) - London											
Aerial camera	55x55mm	70mm	Aerial	1942	Anastigmat	2	4"	focal plane		A2022	220
...VIVE CAMERA CO. - Chicago											
Folding B.B.	4x5"	plate	H&S		Achromat				I,B		70
Souvenir Camera	6x6.5cm	plate	CardBox	1895	Achromat				I,B	Mc414	90
Tourist Magazine No. 3	3¼x4¼"	plate	MagBox		Achromat				I,B		310

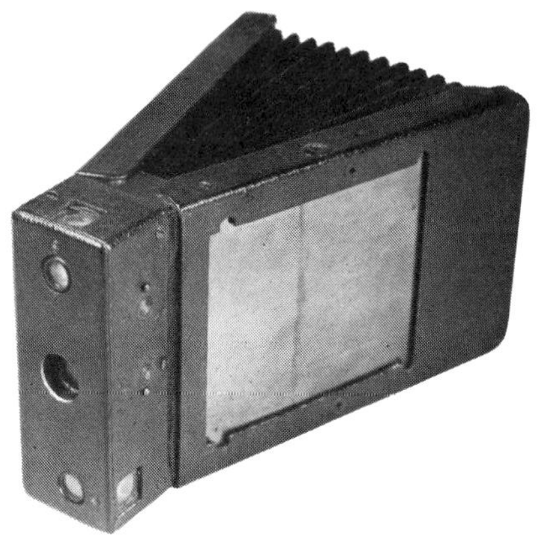

Vega

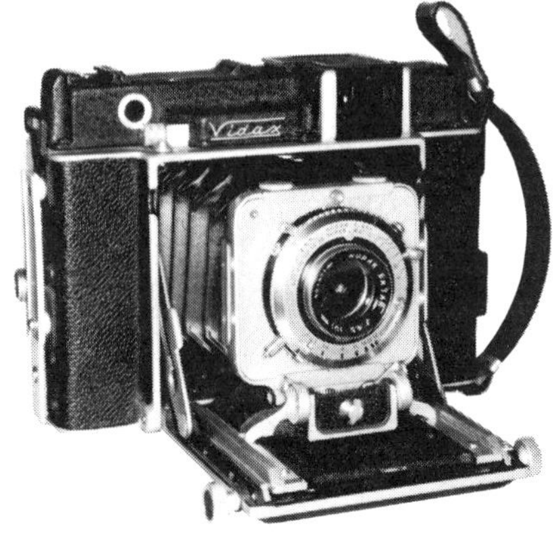

Vidax

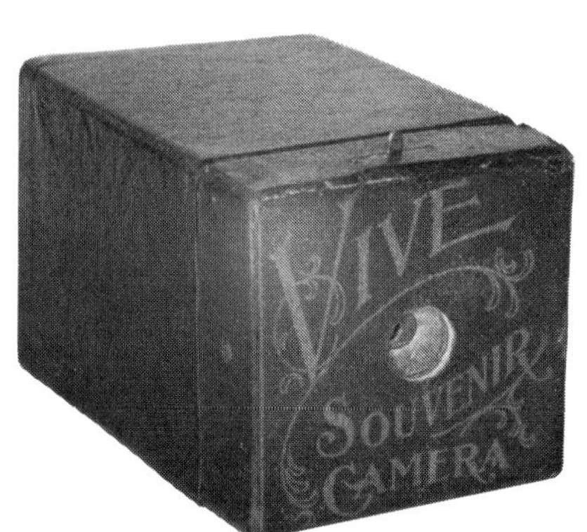

Vive Souvenir Camera

MODEL	FORMAT	FILM	TYPE	Year	LENS	Apert	FL	SHUTTER	SPEEDS	ILLUS	U.S.$
Twin Lens Vive	3½x6"	plate	SterBox	1899	Achromat				I,B		420
Vive M.P.C. 4¼x4¼"	4¼x4¼"	plate	MagBox	1900	Achromat				I,B	Mc414	80
Vive M.P.C. 4x5"	4x5"	plate	MagBox	1900	Achromat				I,B	Mc414	100
Vive No. 1	4¼x4¼"	plate	DetectivBox	1897	Achromat				I,B	Mc414	110
Vive No. 2	4¼x4¼"	plate	DetectivBox	1897	Achromat				I,B		110
Vive No. 4	4x5"	plate	DetectivBox	1897	Achromat				I,B	Mc414	100
...VIVITAR - Japan											
AF255	24x36mm	35mm	35AF	1994	Vivitar		28mm		1/125		30
AF300	24x36mm	35mm	35AF	1994	Vivitar	4.5	30mm		40-250		60
AF400	24x36mm	35mm	35AF	1994	Vivitar	4.5	30mm		40-250		70
PS:135	24x36mm	35mm	35AF	1989	Vivitar	3.8	34mm		1/200		40
Tec 35	24x36mm	35mm	35VF	1983	Vivitar	2.8	35mm	electronic	2-500		60
V3000	24x36mm	35mm	35SLR	1994	Vivitar				1-2000		150
V3000S	24x36mm	35mm	35SLR	1994	Vivitar	1.7	50mm		1-2000		120
XV-1	24x36mm	35mm	35SLR	1979	Vivitar	2	50mm	focal plane	1-1000		120
...(unknown)											
Voigt	2¼x2¼"	120	HzFoldRo	1947	Wirgin Anastigmat	4.5	75mm	Gitzo	25-125		40
Voigt Junior Mod. 1	2¼x2¼"	120	BakFoldRo	1947						Mc414	30
...VOIGTLÄNDER & SOHN - Braunschweig											
Alpin 9x12	9x12cm	plate	HzFoldPl	1907	Voigtl. Collinear	6.8	120mm	Compur	1-200	Mc415	240
Alpin 9x12	9x12cm	plate	HzFoldPl	1907	Heliar	4.5	135mm	Compur	1-200	A209	240
Alpin 10x15	10x15cm	plate	HzFoldPl	1907	Heliar	4.5	180mm	Compound			290
Alpin Stereo-Panoram 6x13	6x13cm	plate	StFoldPl	1914	Unofocal	4.5	75mm	Compound			380
Alpin Stereo-Pan. 10x15	10x15cm	plate	StFoldPl	1914	Kollinear	6.8	105mm	Compound		HK479	480
Alpin Stereo-Pan. 10x15	10x15cm	plate	StFoldPl	1914	Kollinear	6.3	105mm	Compur		HK503	480
Avus (horizontal)	9x12cm	plate	HzFoldPl	1919	Avus	6.8	135mm	Ibso		A208	110
Avus 6.5x9	6.5x9cm	plate	VtFoldPl	1927	Skopar	4.5	105mm	Compur	1-250	Mc415	60
Avus 6.5x9	6.5x9cm	plate	VtFoldPl	1927	Skopar	4.5	105mm	Ibsor		A219	60
Avus 9x12	9x12cm	plate	VtFoldPl	1919	Skopar	4.5	135mm	Ibsor		A218	70
Avus 10x15	10x15cm	plate	VtFoldPl	1919	Avus Anastigmat	6.8	165mm	Ibso			130
Beatrix	6x9cm	120	VtFoldRo	1925	Dynar	6.8	105mm	Compur	1-250		70
Bergheil 4.5x6	4.5x6cm	plate	VtFoldPl	1914	Radiar	6.8	75mm	Compur	1-300	A222	230
Bergheil 6.5x9	6.5x9cm	plate	VtFoldPl	1930	Heliar	4.5	105mm	Compur	1-200	A215	140
Bergheil 9x12	9x12cm	plate	VtFoldPl	1925	Heliar	3.5	135mm	Compur	1-200	Mc415	130
Bergheil 9x12	9x12cm	plate	VtFoldPl	1925	Kollinear	6.8	135mm	Compound		A214	130
Bergheil 10x15	10x15cm	plate	VtFoldPl	1924	Heliar	4.5	165mm	Compur	1-200	A216	140
Bergheil Deluxe (brown)	4.5x6cm	plate	VtFoldPl	1923	Kollinear	6.3	75mm	Compur	1-300	Mc415	900
Bergheil Deluxe (green)	6.5x9cm	plate	VtFoldPl	1933	Heliar	3.5	105mm	Compur	1-200	A217	310
Bergheil Deluxe (green)	9x12cm	plate	VtFoldPl	1933	Heliar	4.5	105mm	Compur	1-200		280
Bessa	6x9cm	120	VtFoldRo	1931	Voigtar	7.7	105mm	Singlo		Mc415	50
Bessa	6x9cm	120	VtFoldRo	1931	Voigtar	6.3	105mm	Prontor		A486	50
Bessa	6x9cm	120	VtFoldRo	1931	Voigtar	4.5	105mm	Compur		HK281	70

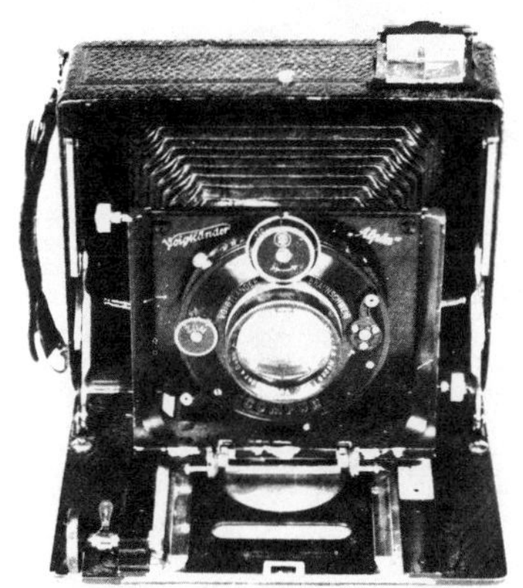

Alpin

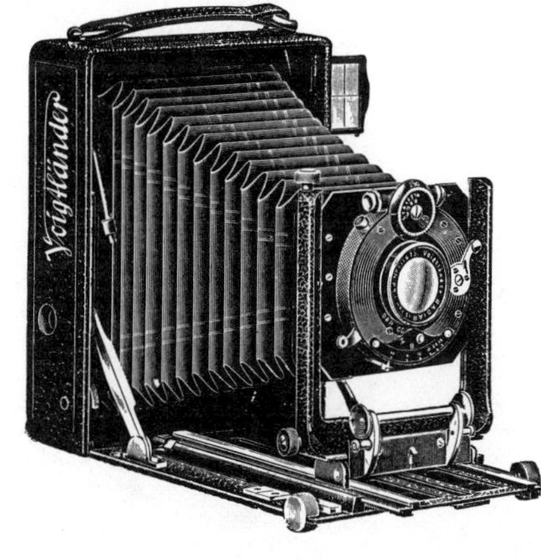

Bergheil

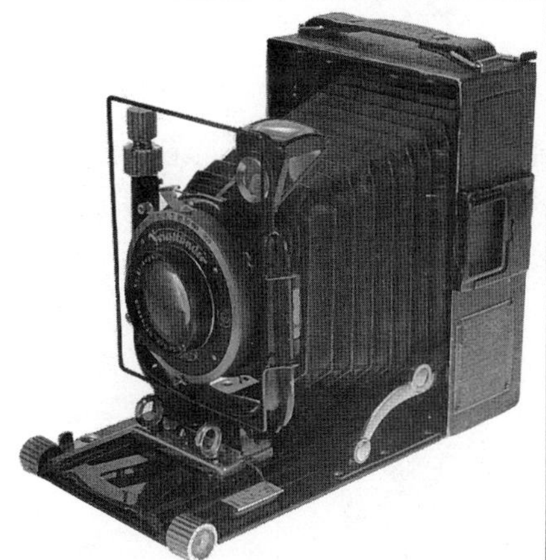

Bergheil Deluxe

MODEL	FORMAT	FILM	TYPE	Year	LENS	Apert	FL	SHUTTER	SPEEDS	ILLUS	U.S.$
Bessa (dual-format)	6x9cm	120	VtFoldRo	1931	Heliar	4.5	105mm	Compur	1-250	A487	50
Bessa I	6x9cm	120	VtFoldRo	1950	Skopar	3.5	105mm	Prontor-S	1-250	Mc416	100
Bessa I (dual-format)	6x9/4.5x6	120	VtFoldRo	1950	Skopar	3.5	105mm	Prontor-S	1-250	A490	80
Bessa II	6x9cm	120	VtFoldRo	1950	Apo-Lanthar	4.5	105mm	Sync-Compur	1-500	HK303	1700
Bessa II	6x9cm	120	VtFoldRo	1950	Heliar	3.5	105mm	Compur-Rap.	1-400	A489	480
Bessa II	6x9cm	120	VtFoldRo	1950	Skopar	3.5	105mm	Sync-Compur	1-500	HK301	340
Bessa II (snake skin)	6x9cm	120	VtFoldRo	1950	Heliar	3.5	105mm	Compur-Rap.	1-400		570
Bessa 46 "Baby Bessa"	4.5x6cm	120	FoldRo	1939	Voigtar	3.5	75mm	Compur	1-300	Mc416	120
Bessa 66 "Baby Bessa"	6x6cm	120	VtFoldRo	1930	Skopar	3.5	75mm	Prontor II		Mc416	50
Bessa 66 "Baby Bessa"	6x6cm	120	VtFoldRo	1930	Vaskar	4.5	75mm	Prontor	1-300	A520	50
Bessa 66 "Baby Bessa"	6x6cm	120	VtFoldRo	1930	Voigtar	4.5	75mm	Compur	1-400		50
Bessa 66 "Baby Bessa"	6x6cm	120	VtFoldRo	1930	Heliar	3.5	75mm	Compur-Rap.	1-400	A521	70
Bessa RF	6x9cm	120	VtFoldRo	1936	Heomar	3.5	105mm	Compur-Rap.	1-400	Mc416	150
Bessa RF	6x9cm	120	VtFoldRo	1936	Skopar	3.5	105mm	Compur-Rap.	1-400		190
Bessa RF	6x9cm	120	VtFoldRo	1936	Voigtar	7.7	105mm	Pronto		A488	140
Bessamatic	24x36mm	35mm	35SLR	1959	Zoomar	2.8	36-82	Sync-Compur		A1138	500
Bessamatic	24x36mm	35mm	35SLR	1959	Skopar	2.8	50mm	Sync-Compur		Mc416	140
Bessamatic CS	24x36mm	35mm	35SLR	1967	Color-Skopar	2.8	50mm	Sync.Comp.X			170
Bessamatic Deluxe	24x36mm	35mm	35SLR	1963	Septon	2	50mm	Sync-Compur		Mc416	150
Bessamatic II	24x36mm	35mm	35SLR	1963	Septon	2	50mm	Sync-Compur			140
Bessamatic M	24x36mm	35mm	35SLR	1964	Color Lanthar	2.18	50mm	Sync-Compur	1-500	A1670	120
Bessy AK	28x28mm	126	126vf	1965	Color Lanthar	2.8	38mm	Prontor-Matic		A2119	10
Bessy AS	28x28mm	126	126vf	1965	Color Lanthar	2.8	38mm	Prontor-Matic			20
Bessy K	28x28mm	126	126vf	1965	Voigtar	8	44mm	Prontor	30-200		10
Bessy S	28x28mm	126	126vf	1966	Voigtar	8	44mm	Prontor	30-200		20
Bijou	4.5x6cm	plate	MedSLR	1908	Heliar		100mm			Mc416	700
Box	6x9cm	120	MetalBox	1950	Meniscus	11		3-speed shutter		A1357	50
Brillant	6x6cm	120	TLR	1933	Voigtar	7.7	75mm	Compur-Rap.	1-400	A668	60
Brillant	6x6cm	120	TLR	1933	Voigtar	9	75mm	Compur-Rap.	1-400	Mc416	50
Brillant	6x6cm	120	TLR	1933	Skopar	4.5	75mm	Compur	1-300	A669	60
Brillant	6x6cm	120	TLR	1933	Voigtar	6.3	75mm	Embezet	25-100	A671	50
Brillant	6x6cm	120	TLR	1933	Vaskar	4.5	75mm	Prontor II		HK422	50
Brillant	6x6cm	120	TLR	1933	Voigtar	4.5	75mm	Compur	1-300		60
Brillant V6	6x6cm	120	TLR	1933	Skopar	4.5	75mm	Compur-Rap.	1-400	HK409	50
Brillant V6	6x6cm	120	TLR	1933	Voigtar	7.7	75mm	Singlo		HK409	50
Daguerreotype "cannon"	8cm dia.	Dag	Dag	1840		3.7					39000
Daguerr. "cannon" replica	8cm dia.	Dag	Dag	1840						Mc417	2300
Dynamatic	24x36mm	35mm	35VF	1961	Color-Skopar	2.8	50mm	Prontormat-SV	30-300	Mc417	70
Dynamatic II	24x36mm	35mm	35VF	1961	Lanthar	2.8	50mm	Prontormat-SV		Mc417	70
Field camera "A" 10x15	10x15cm	plate	Tailboard	1914	various			various			310
Field camera "A" 13x18	13x18cm	plate	Tailboard	1914	various			various		A134	310
Field camera "A" 18x24	18x24cm	plate	Tailboard	1914	various			various			310

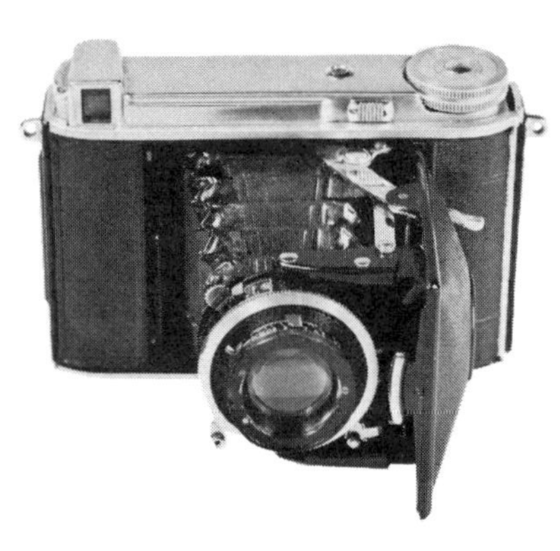

Bessa 46 "Baby Bessa"

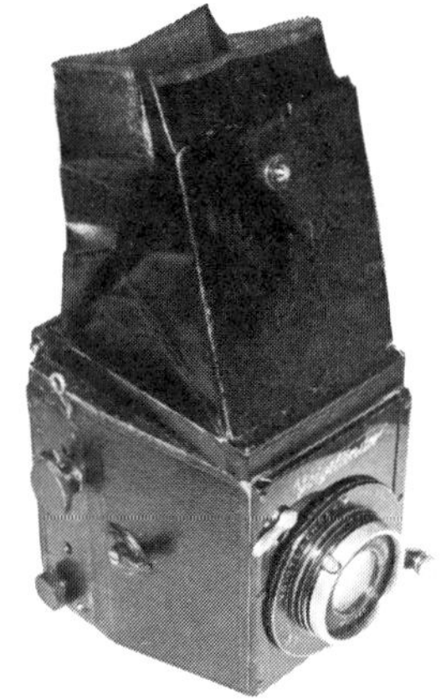

Bijou

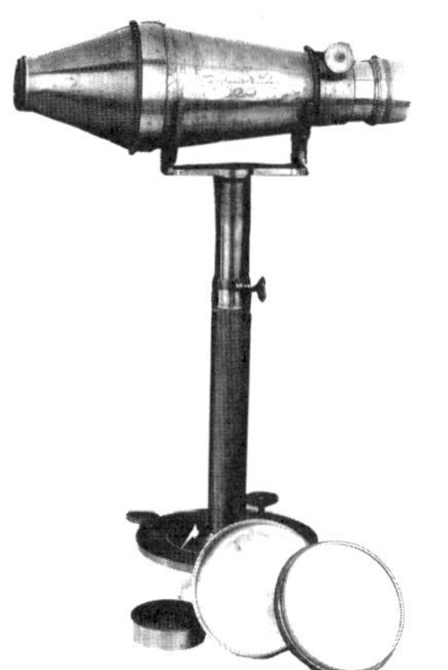

Daguerr. "cannon" replica

MODEL	FORMAT	FILM	TYPE	Year	LENS	Apert	FL	SHUTTER	SPEEDS	ILLUS	U.S.$
Field camera "A" 24x30	24x30cm	plate	Tailboard	1914	various			various			340
Field camera "A" 30x40	30x40cm	plate	Tailboard	1914	various			various			340
Field camera "B" 13x18	13x18cm	plate	Tailboard	1914	various			various		A1371	290
Field camera "B" 18x24	18x24cm	plate	Tailboard	1914	various			various			290
Field camera "B" 24x30	24x30cm	plate	Tailboard	1914	various			various			310
Field camera "B" 30x40	30x40cm	plate	Tailboard	1914	various			various			310
Field camera "B" Luxus	9x12cm	plate	Tailboard	1914	various			various			330
Field camera "B" Luxus	13x18cm	plate	Tailboard	1914	various			various			330
Field camera "B" Luxus	18x24cm	plate	Tailboard	1914	various			various			330
Field camera "B" Luxus	24x30cm	plate	Tailboard	1914	various			various			340
Field camera "B" Luxus	30x40cm	plate	Tailboard	1914	various			various			340
Field camera "C"	13x18cm	plate	Tailboard	1914	various			various			360
Filmkamera 8x10.5	8x10.5cm	124	VtFoldRo	1905	Kollinear	6.8	120mm	Koilos			180
Filmkamera 9x14	9x14cm	122	VtFoldRo	1905	Kollinear	6.8	120mm	Koilos			130
Filmkamera 10x13	10x13cm	123	VtFoldRo	1905	Kollinear	6.8	120mm	Automat			120
Folding rollfilm 5x8	5x8cm	124	VtFoldRo	1927	Heliar	4.5	83mm	Compur	1-300		60
Folding rollfilm 6x9	6x9cm	120	VtFoldRo	1927	Skopar	4.5	105mm	Compur	1-300		50
Folding rollfilm 6.5x11	6.5x11cm	116	VtFoldRo	1927	Skopar	4.5	105mm	Compur	1-300		50
Heliar	9x12cm	plate	HzFoldPl	1909	Heliar	4.5	180mm	focal plane	20-1000	A213	460
Heliar	9x12cm	plate	HzFoldPl	1909	Heliar	4.5	180mm	focal plane	1-1000	A212	460
Heliar Reflex 6.5x9	6.5x9cm	plate	LgSLR	1909	Heliar	4.5	120mm	focal plane	20-1000		260
Heliar Reflex 9x12	9x12cm	plate	LgSLR	1909	Heliar	4.5	180mm	focal plane	20-1000	Mc417	260
Heliar Reflex 12x16.5	12x16.5	plate	LgSLR	1909	Heliar	4.5	240mm	focal plane	20-1000		260
Inos (I)	6x9/4.5x6	120	VtFoldRo	1931	Heliar	4.5	105mm	Compur	1-250	Mc417	120
Inos (I)	6x9/4.5x6	120	VtFoldRo	1931	Skopar	4.5	105mm	Embezet	25-100	A494	100
Inos II 6x9/4.5x6	6x9/4.5x6	120	VtFoldRo	1933	Skopar	4.5	105mm	Compur	1-250	Mc417	100
Inos II 6.5x11/5.5x6.5	6.5x11cm	116	VtFoldRo	1933	Skopar	4.8	118mm	Compur	1-250	A1471	110
Jubilar	6x9cm	120	VtFoldRo	1931	Voigtar	9	105mm	Embezet	25-100	A497	30
Klappkamera	9x12cm	Ro+Pl	VtFoldPl	1903	Collinear	5.4	140mm	focal plane		A372	50
Metall-Klappkamera 9x12	9x12cm	plate	StrutPl	1905	Heliar	4.5	150mm	focal plane			330
Metall-Klappkamera 13x18	13x18cm	plate	StrutPl	1905	Kollinear	5.4	200mm	focal plane			450
Metallkamera +VF	9x14cm	plate	StFoldPl	1908	Dynar	6	120mm	focal plane			1000
Metallkamera f. Ster//Pan	9x14cm	plate	StFoldPl	1908	Kollinear	5.4	120mm	focal plane			580
Nirvana	6x9cm	120	VtFoldRo	1925	Avus Anastigmat	6.8	105mm	Ibso			370
Perkeo (folding VF)	3x4cm	127	FoldRo	1930	Skopar	4.5	55mm	Embezet	25-100		280
Perkeo (rigid VF)	3x4cm	127	FoldRo	1930	Skopar	3.5	55mm	Compur	1-300	A493	290
Perkeo (rigid VF)	3x4cm	127	FoldRo	1930	Skopar	4.5	55mm	Embezet	25-100	HK245	290
Perkeo E	6x6cm	120	FoldRo	1954	Color-Skopar	3.5	75mm	Prontor-SVS		A523	170
Perkeo I	6x6cm	120	FoldRo	1952	Vaskar	4.5	75mm	Prontor		Mc417	90
Perkeo I	6x6cm	120	FoldRo	1952	Color Skopar	3.5	75mm	Prontor		A522	90
Perkeo II	6x6cm	120	FoldRo	1952	Color Skopar	3.5	75mm	Sync-Compur		HK306	100
Prominent (120)	6x9/4.5x6	120	VtFoldRo	1932	Heliar	4.5	105mm	Compur	1-250	Mc417	1000

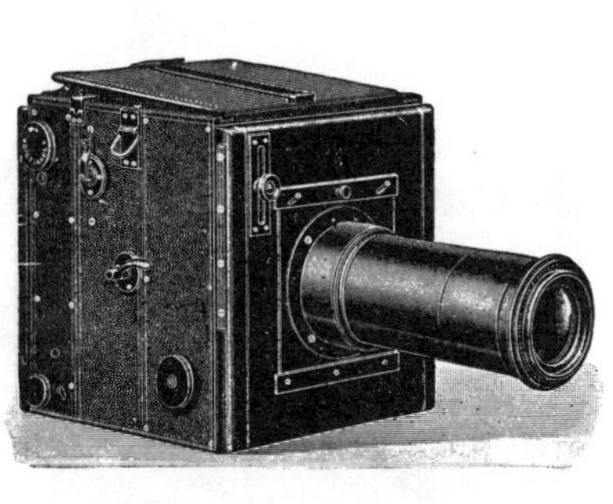

Heliar Reflex

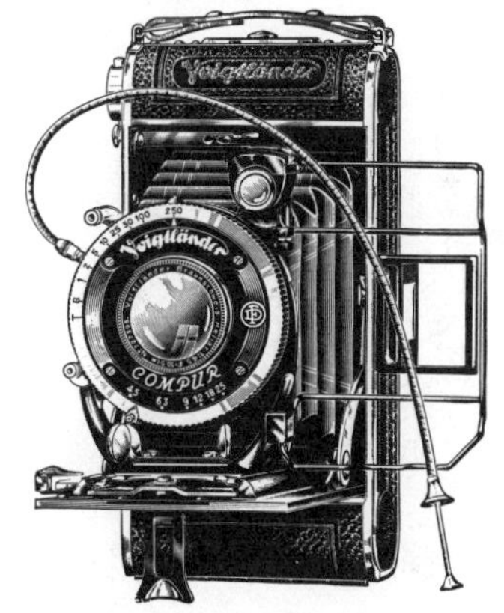

Inos (I)

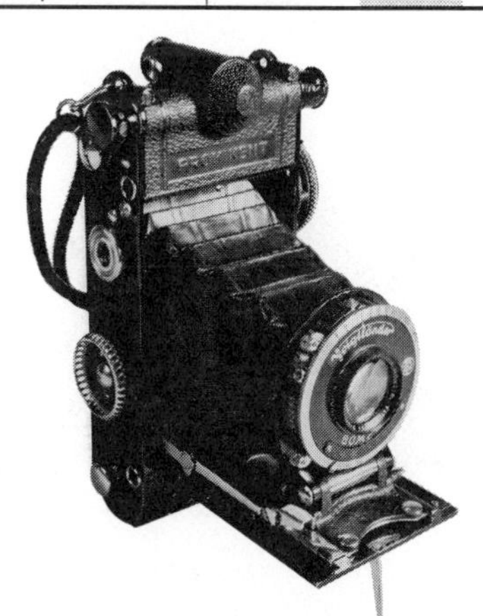

Prominent (120)

MODEL	FORMAT	FILM	TYPE	Year	LENS	Apert	FL	SHUTTER	SPEEDS	ILLUS	U.S.$
Prominent (35mm)	24x36mm	35mm	35RF	1952	Color Skopar	3.5		Compur-Rap.		A1134	200
Prominent (35mm)	24x36mm	35mm	35RF	1952	Nokton	1.5		Sync-Compur		Mc417	320
Prominent II	24x36mm	35mm	35RF	1958	Ultron	2	50mm	Compur-Rap.		A1136	440
Reflex 4.5x6	4.5x6cm	plate	MedSLR	1924	Heliar	3.5	85mm	Compur	1-250	A1614	270
Reflex 10x15	10x15cm	plate	LgSLR	1914	Heliar	4.5	210mm	focal plane	1-1000	A560	240
Scherenkamera	9x12cm	plate	StrutPl	1903	Heliar	4.5	180mm	focal plane	1-1000	A3012	140
Stereflektoskop 45x107	45x107	plate	SterRefl	1913	Heliar	4.5	65mm	sector	250	Mc418	390
Stereflektoskop 45x107	45x107	plate	SterRefl	1913	Heliar	4.5	65mm	St. Compur	1-250	Mc418	380
Stereflektoskop 6x13	6x13cm	plate	SterRefl	1913	Heliar	4.5	75mm	St. Compur	1-250	Mc418	420
Stereo Reflex	45x107	plate	SterRefl	1905	Heliar	4.5	85mm	focal plane		A1815	270
Stereophotoskop	45x107	plate	StJumelle	1907	Heliar	4.5	60mm	Sector		Mc418	390
Stereophotoskop	45x107	plate	StJumelle	1907	Dynar	5.5	55mm	Stereo-Compur		HK514	390
Superb	6x6cm	120	TLR	1933	Heliar	3.5	75mm	Compur		Mc418	330
Superb	6x6cm	120	TLR	1934	Skopar	3.5	75mm	Compur		HK410	260
Telestativ-Kamera	13x18cm	plate	Studio	1908	various			various			290
Ultramatic	24x36mm	35mm	35SLR	1963	Septon	2	50mm	Compur	1-500	A1139	210
Ultramatic CS	24x36mm	35mm	35SLR	1965	Color Skopar	2.8	50mm	Compur			190
V35 F	24x36mm	35mm	35VF	1979	Voigtar	2.8	38mm		60-250	A2175	40
Vag 6.5x9	6.5x9cm	plate	VtFoldPl	1920	Voigtar	6.3	105mm	Ibsor		Mc418	120
Vag 6.5x9	6.5x9cm	plate	VtFoldPl	1920	Skopar	4.5	105mm	Embezet		HK173	120
Vag 9x12	9x12cm	plate	VtFoldPl	1920	Voigtar	6.3	135mm	Ibsor		A220	120
VF 101	24x36mm	35mm	35VF	1976	Color Skopar	2.8	40mm	electronic	4-500	A2121	50
VF 102	24x36mm	35mm	35VF	1977	Color Skopar	2.8	40mm	electronic	4-500		60
VF 135	24x36mm	35mm	35VF	1976	Color Skoparex	2.3	40mm	electronic	4-500	A2120	50
Vida	9x12cm	plate	LgSLR	1911	Heliar	4.5	180mm	focal plane	1/12-1000	HK322	510
Virtus	4.5x6cm	120	VtFoldRo	1935	Heliar	3.5	75mm	Compur	1-250	Mc418	330
Virtus	4.5x6cm	120	VtFoldRo	1935	Skopar	4.5	75mm	Compur	1-250	HK253	340
Vitessa Type 1	24x36mm	35mm	35Fold	1950	Ultron	2	50mm	Compur-Rap.		Mc418	140
Vitessa Type 2	24x36mm	35mm	35Fold	1950	Ultron	2	50mm	Sync-Compur		A1137	140
Vitessa Type 3	24x36mm	35mm	35Fold	1951	Color Skopar	2.8	50mm	Sync-Compur	1-500	HK589	220
Vitessa Type 3	24x36mm	35mm	35Fold	1951	Ultron	2	50mm	Sync-Compur	1-500	HK583	160
Vitessa 126 CS	28x28mm	126	126VF	1968	Voigtar	4.8	44mm	Prontor	1-200		20
Vitessa 126 Electronic	28x28mm	126	126VF	1969	Novar	6.3	40mm	Prontor	1-300		20
Vitessa 126 S	28x28mm	126	126VF	1969	Lanthar	2.8	38mm	Prontor	1-500		20
Vitessa 500 AE	24x36mm	35mm	35VF	1968	Color Lanthar	2.8	42mm	Prontor	1-500		50
Vitessa 500 L	24x36mm	35mm	35VF	1968	Color Lanthar	2.8	42mm	Prontor	1-500		30
Vitessa 500 S	24x36mm	35mm	35VF	1968	Color Lanthar	2.8	42mm	Prontor	1-500	A2118	30
Vitessa 500 SE	24x36mm	35mm	35VF	1968	Color Lanthar	2.8	42mm	Prontor	1-500		30
Vitessa 1000 SR	24x36mm	35mm	35RF	1969	Color Lanthar	2.8	42mm	Prontor	1-1000		70
Vitessa L	24x36mm	35mm	35Fold	1954	Ultron	2	50mm	Sync-Compur	1-500	Mc418	170
Vitessa T	24x36mm	35mm	35RF	1957	Color Skopar	2.8	50mm	Sync-Compur	1-500	Mc418	240
Vitessa T	24x36mm	35mm	35RF	1957	Color Lanthar	2.8	42mm	Sync-Compur	1-500		110

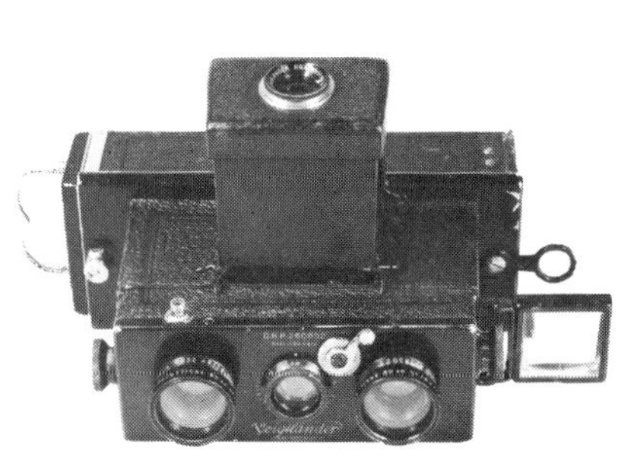

Stereflektoskop

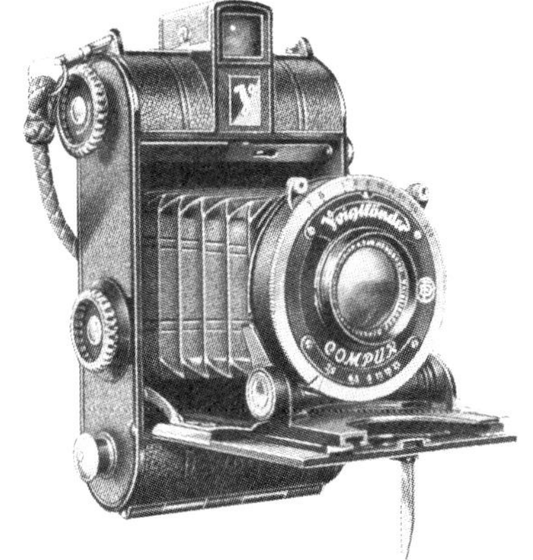

Virtus

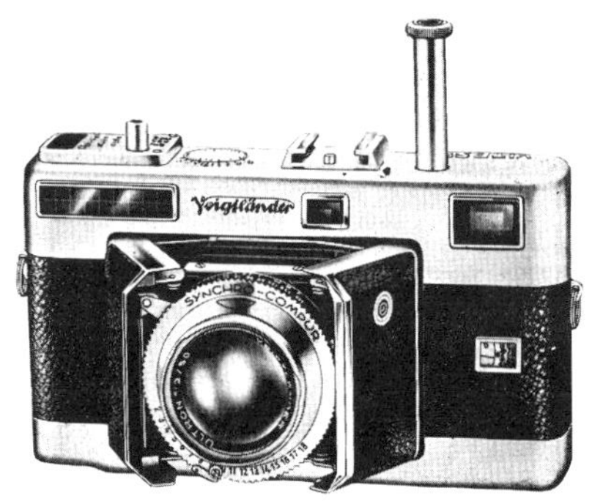

Vitessa L

MODEL	FORMAT	FILM	TYPE	Year	LENS	Apert	FL	SHUTTER	SPEEDS	ILLUS	U.S.$
Vito (folding)	24x36mm	35mm	35Fold	1980	Voigtar	5.6	40mm				60
Vito II	24x36mm	35mm	35Fold	1950	Color Skopar	3.5	50mm	Prontor		Mc418	50
Vito IIa	24x36mm	35mm	35Fold	1955	Color-Skopar	3.5	50mm	Prontor		Mc419	90
Vito III	24x36mm	35mm	35Fold	1950	Ultron	2	50mm	Sync-Compur	1-500	A1034	360
Vito 1939	24x36mm	35mm	35Fold	1939	Skopar	3.5	50mm	Compur	1-300	A1032	100
Vito 1949	24x36mm	35mm	35Fold	1949	Color-Skopar	3.5	50mm	Compur	1-300		70
Vito AF	24x36mm	35mm	35AF	1984	Zoom	3.9-7.1	35-70	programmed			90
Vito Automatic	24x36mm	35mm	35VF	1962	Lanthar	2.8	50mm	Prontor Lux		Mc419	50
Vito Automatic I	24x36mm	35mm	35VF	1962	Lanthar	2.8	50mm	Prontor-matic	125		40
Vito Automatic II	24x36mm	35mm	35VF	1962	Lanthar	2.8	50mm	Prontor-matic	500	Mc419	50
Vito B Type 1	24x36mm	35mm	35VF	1954	Color Skopar	3.5	50mm	Pronto		Mc419	50
Vito B Type 2	24x36mm	35mm	35VF	1957	Color Skopar	2.8	50mm	Prontor-SVS			60
Vito BL Type 1	24x36mm	35mm	35VF	1956	Color-Skopar	2.8	50mm	Prontor-SVS			70
Vito BL Type 2	24x36mm	35mm	35VF	1957	Color-Skopar	3.5	50mm	Prontor-SVS		Mc419	60
Vito BR	24x36mm	35mm	35RF	1958	Color-Skopar	2.8	50mm	Prontor SLK-V	1-300,B		60
Vito C	24x36mm	35mm	35VF	1961	Lanthar	2.8	50mm	Prontor		A1141	30
Vito-C (folding)	24x36mm	35mm	35Fold	1981	Color Skopar	2.8	38mm	programmed	1-500	A3497	100
Vito C-AF	24x36mm	35mm	35AF	1986		3.5	35mm	programmed			130
Vito CD	24x36mm	35mm	35VF	1961	Lanthar	2.8	50mm	Prontor		A1140	30
Vito CL	24x36mm	35mm	35VF	1962	Lanthar	2.8	50mm	Prontor			40
Vito CLR	24x36mm	35mm	35RF	1962	Lanthar	2.8	50mm	Prontor		A1142	40
Vito CS	24x36mm	35mm	35VF	1967	Color Lanthar	2.8	50mm	Prontor	1-500		40
Vito-CS (folding)	24x36mm	35mm	35Fold	1983	Color Skopar	2.8	38mm	programmed			110
Vito CSR	24x36mm	35mm	35RF	1967	Color Lanthar	2.8	50mm	Prontor	1-500		50
Vito Disc	8x10mm	Disc	Disc	1983		2.8	12.5mm			A3382	50
Vitoflex E (VSL-3E Proto.)	24x36mm	35mm	35SLR	1962	Color Ultron	1.8	50mm	focal plane	16-2000		800
Vitomatic I	24x36mm	35mm	35VF	1958	Color-Skopar	2.8	50mm	Prontor SLK-V	1-300,B		60
Vitomatic Ia	24x36mm	35mm	35VF	1960	Color-Skopar	2.8	50mm	Prontor SLK-V	1-500,B	A1143	60
Vitomatic Ib	24x36mm	35mm	35VF	1965	Color-Skopar	2.8	50mm	Prontor SLK-V	1-300,B		70
Vitomatic I CS	24x36mm	35mm	35VF	1967	Color-Skopar	2.8	50mm	Prontor SLK-V	1-500,B		70
Vitomatic II	24x36mm	35mm	35RF	1958	Color-Skopar	2.8	50mm	Prontor SLK-V	1-300,B	Mc419	90
Vitomatic IIa	24x36mm	35mm	35RF	1959	Color-Skopar	2.8	50mm	Pr.500 SLK-V	1-500,B	A1146	100
Vitomatic IIa	24x36mm	35mm	35RF	1959	Ultron	2	50mm	Pr.500 SLK-V	1-500,B	A1146	80
Vitomatic IIb	24x36mm	35mm	35RF	1965	Color-Skopar	2.8	50mm	Prontor SLK-V	1-500,B		90
Vitomatic II CS	24x36mm	35mm	35RF	1967	Color-Skopar	2.8	50mm	Prontor SLK-V	1-500,B		90
Vitomatic IIIb	24x36mm	35mm	35RF	1965	Ultron	2	50mm	Prontor SLK-V	1-500,B		160
Vitomatic III CS	24x36mm	35mm	35RF	1967	Ultron	2	50mm	Prontor SLK-V	1-500,B		190
Vitoret	24x36mm	35mm	35VF	1963	Vaskar	2.8	50mm	Prontor	30-125		20
Vitoret	24x36mm	35mm	35VF	1966	Color-Lanthar	2.8	50mm	Prontor	1-125		20
Vitoret 110	13x17mm	110	110VF	1978	Lanthar	5.6	24mm		60125	A1985	30
Vitoret 110 EL	13x17mm	110	110VF	1978	Lanthar	5.6	24mm	electronic	4-300		50
Vitoret D	24x36mm	35mm	35VF	1963	Color-Lanthar	2.8	50mm	Prontor	1-125		30

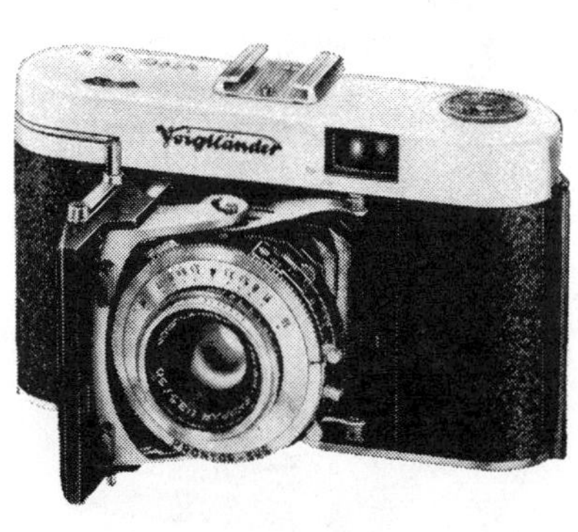

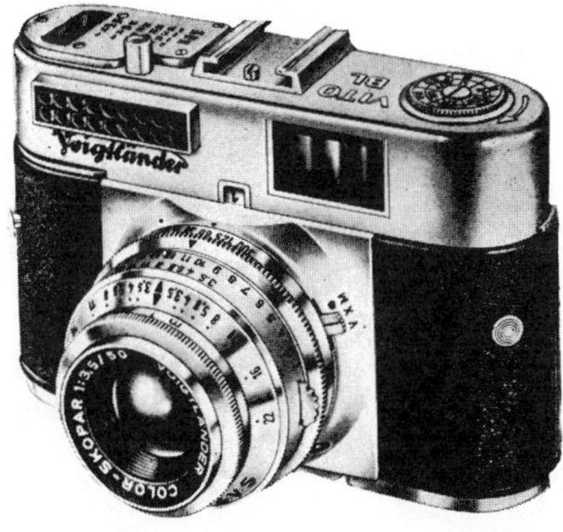

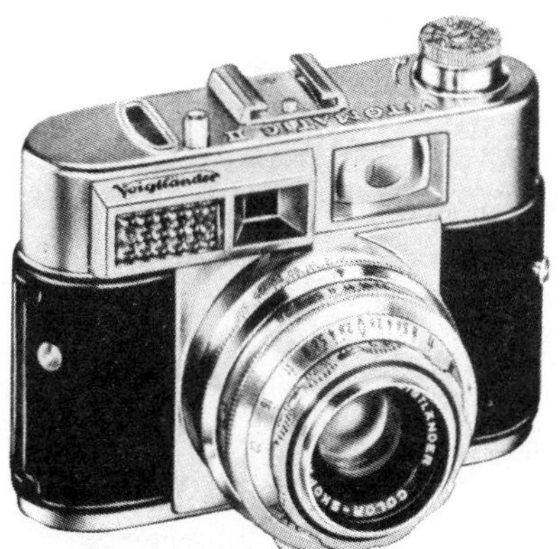

Vito IIa **Vito BL Type 2** **Vitomatic II**

MODEL	FORMAT	FILM	TYPE	Year	LENS	Apert	FL	SHUTTER	SPEEDS	ILLUS	U.S.$
Vitoret D	24x36mm	35mm	35VF	1966	Color-Lanthar	2.8	50mm	Prontor	1-125		20
Vitoret D Rapid	24x36mm	35mm	RigidRo	1964	Color-Lanthar	2.8	40mm	Prontor	1-125		30
Vitoret DR	24x36mm	35mm	35RF	1964	Color-Lanthar	2.8	50mm	Prontor	1-300		40
Vitoret DR	24x36mm	35mm	35RF	1966	Color-Lanthar	2.8	50mm	Prontor	1-125		30
Vitoret F	24x36mm	35mm	35VF	1964	Color-Lanthar	2.8	50mm	Prontor	1-125		30
Vitoret L	24x36mm	35mm	35VF	1964	Color-Lanthar	2.8	50mm	Prontor	1-125		30
Vitoret LR	24x36mm	35mm	35RF	1966	Color-Lanthar	2.8	50mm	Prontor	1-300		40
Vitrona	24x36mm	35mm	35VF	1964	Lanthar	2.8	50mm	Prontor	1-250	Mc419	70
VSL 1 (black)	24x36mm	35mm	35SLR	1976	Ultron	1.8	50mm	focal plane	½-1000		120
VSL 1 (chrome)	24x36mm	35mm	35SLR	1974	Ultron	1.8	50mm	focal plane	½-1000	A1694	110
VSL 2	24x36mm	35mm	35SLR	1974	Ultron	1.8	50mm	focal plane	½-1000	A1695	120
VSL 2 Automatic	24x36mm	35mm	35SLR	1976	Color Ultron	1.8	50mm	focal plane	4-1000		120
VSL 2 CX	24x36mm	35mm	35SLR	1976	Color Ultron	1.8	50mm	focal plane	½-1000		160
VSL 3	24x36mm	35mm	35SLR	1976	Ultron	1.8	50mm	focal plane	2-2000	A1696	120
VSL 3-E (black)	24x36mm	35mm	35SLR	1976	Color Ultron	1.8	50mm	focal plane	16-1000		170
VSL 3-E (chrome)	24x36mm	35mm	35SLR	1976	Color Ultron	1.8	50mm	focal plane	16-1000		130
...VOJTA (Joseph Vojta) - Praque											
Field camera	18x24cm	plate	Field	1905	Rod. Bistigmat						320
Magazine camera	6.5x9cm	plate	MagBox	1900					M,Z		370
...VOKAR CORPORTATION - Dexter, Michigan											
Vokar Mod. A	6x6cm	120	BakFoldRo	1940	Vokar Anastigmat	6.3	75mm		25-100	Mc419	30
Vokar Mod. B	6x6cm	120	BakFoldRo	1940	Ilex Anastigmat	6.3	75mm		25-100	Mc419	30
Vokar I	24x36mm	35mm	35RF	1946	Vokar Anastigmat	2.8	50mm	Leaf	1-300	Mc419	70
...VOOMP - Leningrad											
Pioneer	24x36mm	35mm	35VF	1935		3.5	50mm	focal plane	500		500
...VORMBRUCK CAMERABAU (W. & P. Fertsch) - Germany											
Feca (35mm)	24x36mm	35mm	35VF	1955	Meritar	3.5	50mm	Junior	25-100	Mc195	100
Feca (plate) 6x9	6x9cm	plate	VtFoldPl		Tessar	4.5					60
Feca (plate) 9x12	9x12cm	plate	VtFoldPl		Xenar	4.5					60
...VOSS (W. Voss) - Ulm, Germany											
Diax	24x36mm	35mm	35RF	1948	Xenar	2.8	45mm	Compur-Rap.	1-500	A2091	70
Diax I	24x36mm	35mm	35RF	1950	Cassar	2.8	45mm	Prontor	1-200	A1100	70
Diax Ia	24x36mm	35mm	35RF	1948	Xenon	2	45mm	Sync-Compur	1-500	HK581	60
Diax Ib	24x36mm	35mm	35RF	1948	Xenon	2	45mm	Sync-Compur	1-500	HK593	90
Diax II	24x36mm	35mm	35RF	1950	Xenon	2	45mm	Compur-Rap.	1-500	Mc420	120
Diax IIa	24x36mm	35mm	35RF	1951	Xenar	2.8	50mm	Sync-Compur	1-500	A1103	140
Diax IIb	24x36mm	35mm	35RF	1951	Xenar	2.8	50mm	Sync-Compur		A1104	120
Diaxette	24x36mm	35mm	35VF	1953	Steinheil Cassar	2.8	45mm	Prontor	25-200	A1101	90
...VREDEBORCH - Germany											
Adina	6x9cm	120	RollBox	1950							30
Alka Box	6x9cm	120	MetalBox	1953	Meniscus			simple	25,50,B	Mc420	20
Bunny	6x6cm	120	RigidRo	1950	Meniscus			simple	25,50,B	Mc420	20

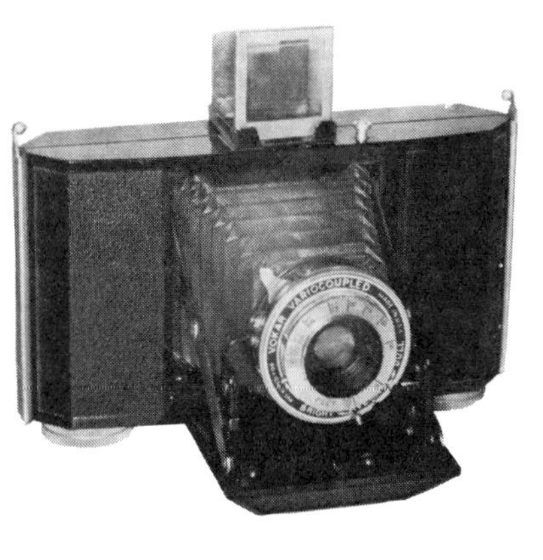

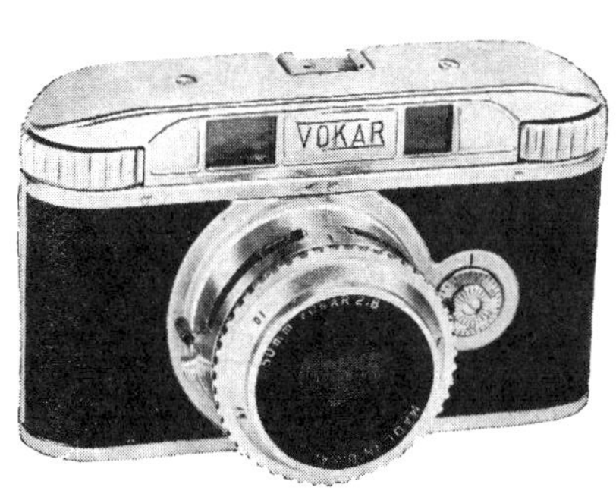

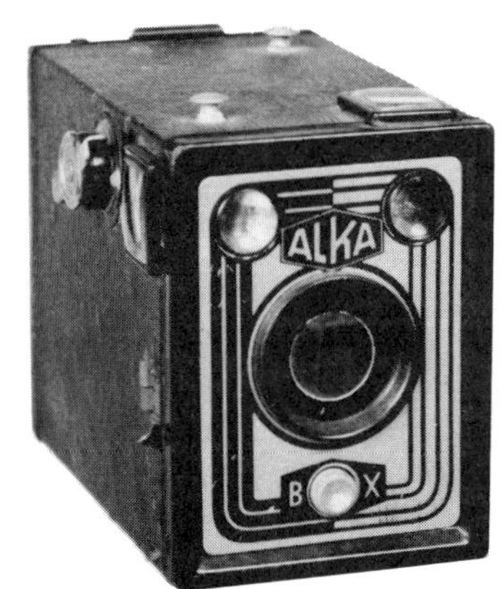

Vokar Mod. A **Vokar I** **Alka Box**

MODEL	FORMAT	FILM	TYPE	Year	LENS	Apert	FL	SHUTTER	SPEEDS	ILLUS	U.S.$
Ecla Box	6x9cm	120	MetalBox	1950	Meniscus			simple	25,50,B		30
Evans Box	6x9cm	120	MetalBox	1950	Meniscus			simple	25,50,B	Mc420	20
Felica (black)	6x6cm	120	RigidRo	1954	Meniscus			simple	25,50,B	Mc420	10
Felica (grey)	6x6cm	120	RigidRo	1954	Meniscus			simple	25,50,B		10
Felica Duo	6x6cm	120	RigidRo	1950	Meniscus			simple	25,50,B		10
Felicetta	24x36mm	35mm	35VF	1965	Nordinar	3.5	45mm	Spezial	30-125		10
Felicetta BL35	24x36mm	35mm	35VF	1965	Nordinar	3.5	45mm	Spezial	30-125		20
Felicette (Vredeborch)	24x36mm	35mm	35VF	1960	Nordinar	3.5	45mm	Vredeborch	30-125		20
Felicette-L (Vredeborch)	24x36mm	35mm	35VF	1960	Nordinar	3.5	45mm	Vredeborch	30-125		20
Felita (black)	4.5x6cm	120	RigidRo	1954	Meniscus			simple	25,50,B	A539	10
Felita (grey)	4.5x6cm	120	RigidRo	1954	Meniscus			simple	25,50,B		10
Fodor Box Syncrona	6x9cm	120	MetalBox	1950	Meniscus				M,B,T		30
Haaga Syncrona Box	6x9cm	120	MetalBox	1955	Meniscus				M,B,T		20
Ideal	6x9cm	120	RollBox	1950	Meniscus				M,B,T		20
Junior	6x6cm	120	RigidRo	1954	Meniscus				M,B,T		10
Kera Jr.	6x6cm	120	RigidRo	1958	Lux Spezial					Mc420	10
Klimax	6x6cm	120	RigidRo	1950	Meniscus					Mc420	10
Kruxo Favorit	6x9cm	120	RollBox	1950	Meniscus						50
Manex	6x9cm	120	RollBox	1950	Meniscus						30
N-Box	6x9cm	120	MetalBox	1950	Meniscus						30
Nordetta 3-D	42x55mm	127	SterStrut	1951		4.5	75mm	guillotine		A783	150
Nordina I	6x6cm	120	TelescRo	1953	Steinar	4.5	75mm	Vario			30
Nordina II	6x6cm	120	TelescRo	1953	Steinar	3.5	75mm	Vario			30
Nordina III	6x6cm	120	TelescRo	1953	Steinar	2.9	75mm	Pronto	25-200		30
Nordina 28C	28x28mm	126	126VF	1966	Nordinar	2.8	38mm		30-125		10
Optomax Syncrona	6x9cm	120	MetalBox	1952	Meniscus				M,T	A108	30
Regia	6x9cm	120	MetalBox	1952	Meniscus				M,T	A2881	20
Reporter Junior II	6x6cm	120	RigidRo	1950	Meniscus			simple	25,50,B	A3100	30
Slomexa	6x9cm	120	MetalBox	1950	Meniscus	11				Mc421	30
Stafetta-duo	6x6cm	120	RigidRo	1950	Meniscus					Mc421	30
Standard	6x9cm	120	RollBox	1950	Meniscus						20
Super-Felita	6x6cm	120	RigidRo	1958	Lux Spezial	8				Mc420	10
Texar Box	6x9cm	120	MetalBox	1950	Meniscus					Mc421	30
Union-Box	6x6cm	120	RollBox	1950	Meniscus				M,Z		20
Vrede Box (black)	6x9cm	120	MetalBox	1953	Meniscus				T,B	A2878	30
Vrede Box (colors)	6x9cm	120	MetalBox	1953	Meniscus				T,B	A2878	80
Vrede Box - Paloma	6x9cm	120	MetalBox	1953	Meniscus				T,B	HK115	20
Vrede Box - Paloma S	6x9cm	120	MetalBox	1953	Meniscus				M,B	HK115	20
Vrede Box - Synchrona	6x9cm	120	MetalBox	1953	Meniscus				T,B		20
...VRSOFOT - Prague, Czechoslovakia											
Epifoka 4.5x6	4.5x6cm	120	Aerial	1947	Tessar	3.5	50mm	Compur	1-300		290
Epifoka 6x9	6x9cm	120	Aerial	1947	Dagor	6.8	75mm	Prontor II	1-150		220

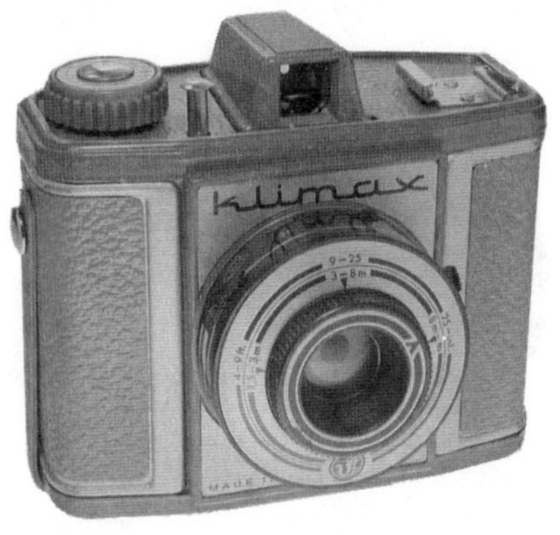

Vredeborch Klimax

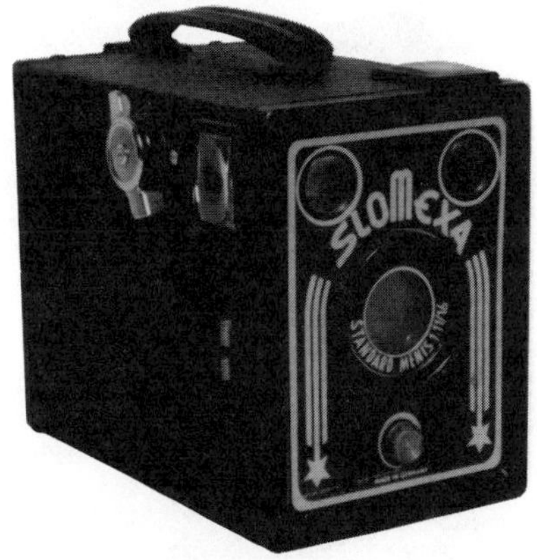

Slomexa

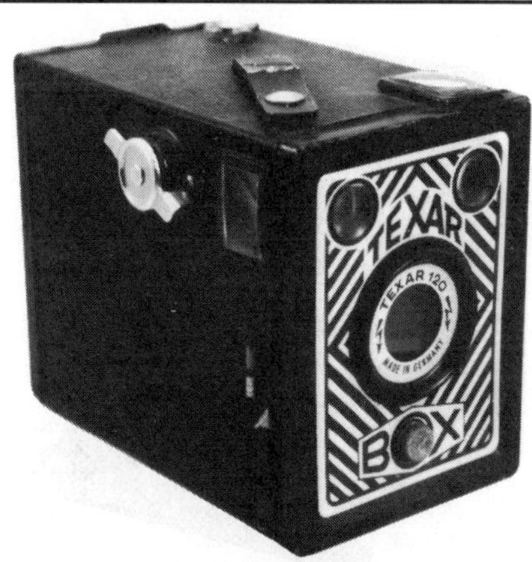

Texar Box

MODEL	FORMAT	FILM	TYPE	Year	LENS	Apert	FL	SHUTTER	SPEEDS	ILLUS	U.S.$
...WACHTL (Bernard Wachtl) - Vienna											
Stock Apparat	40mm dia.	plate	Disguised	1890							8000
...WAITE (J. Waite) - Cheltenham, England											
Wet plate Stereo	4x7½"	WetPl	StWetPl	1855	Derogy						5300
...WALDES & CO. - Dresden											
Foto-Fips	4x4cm	plate	StrutPl	1925	Meniscus						620
...WALDORF CAMERA CO.											
Waldorf Minicam	3x4cm	127	Minicam	1937	Meniscus					Mc421	10
...WALLACE HEATON LTD. - London											
Zodel 6.5x9	6.5x9cm	plate	VtFoldPl	1926	Zodellar	4.5	120mm	Compur		Mc421	70
Zodel 9x12	9x12cm	plate	VtFoldPl	1926	Zodellar	4.8	135mm	Gammax		Mc421	70
...WALZ CO. - Japan											
Walz Automat	4x4cm	127	TLR	1959	Zunow	2.8	60mm	Copal	1-500,B		290
Walz Envoy 35	24x36mm	35mm	35RF	1959	Kominar	1.9	48mm	Copal SLV	1-500,B		40
Walz-wide	24x36mm	35mm	35VF	1958	Walzer	2.8	35mm	Copal	1-300,B	Mc421	60
Walzflex	6x6cm	120	TLR	1955	Kominar	3.5	75mm	Copal		Mc422	130
Walzflex IIIA	6x6cm	120	TLR	1955	Kominar	3.5	75mm	Copal		Mc422	70
...WANAUS (Josef Wanaus & Co.) - Vienna											
Universal Stereo	10x20cm	plate	StFoldPl	1900	Zeiss	6.3	105mm				1600
View camera 9x12	9x12cm	plate	Field	1900	various						120
View camera 13x18	13x18cm	plate	Field	1900	Gustav-Rapp Universal Aplanat						270
...WARWICK - Birmingham, England											
Warwick No. 2	6x9cm	120	RollBox							Mc422	20
...WATSON (W. Watson & Sons) - London											
Acme 4¼x6½"	4¼x6½"	plate	Field	1890	Holostigmat			Koilos		Mc422	380
Acme 6½x8½"	6½x8½"	plate	Field	1890	Holostigmat			Koilos		Mc422	380
Acme 8x10"	8x10"	plate	Field	1890	Holostigmat			Koilos		Mc422	380
Alpha 3¼x4¼"	3¼x4¼"	plate	H&S	1892	Rapid Rectilinear				I,T	Mc422	570
Alpha 4x5"	4x5"	plate	H&S	1892	Rapid Rectilinear				I,T	Mc422	570
Argus Reflex	3¼x4¼"	plate	LgSLR	1907	Holostigmat		6"	focal plane	1/5-1000		180
Detective Camera	3¼x4¼"	plate	DetectivBox	1886	Rapid Rectilinear			guillotine		Mc422	680
Field camera 4¼x6½"	4¼x6½"	plate	Tailboard	1885	Brass Watson	8		Thornton-Pickard		Mc422	350
Field camera 6½x8½"	6½x8½"	plate	Tailboard	1885	Brass Watson	8		Thornton-Pickard		Mc422	340
Field camera 8x10"	8x10"	plate	Tailboard	1885	Brass Watson	8		Thornton-Pickard		Mc422	340
Folding plate camera	10x15cm	plate	H&S	1900	Rapid Rectilinear					A155	180
Gear	3¼x4¼"	plate	DetectivBox	1901	Rapid Rectilinear				15-75		50
Repeater	3¼x4¼"	plate	MagBox	1900	achromatic				I,T		90
Stereoscopic Binocular	45x107	plate	Disguised	1901	Krauss Tessar					Mc422	1400
Tailboard camera	3¼x4¼"	plate	Tailboard	1899	Rapid Rectilinear			Thornton-Pickard	T,I		530
Tropical Alpha	4x5"	plate	H&S	1892	B&L			Unicum			700
Twin Lens Camera	3¼x4¼"	plate	LgTLR	1899	Rapid Rectilinear			Thornton-Pickard	T,I		520
Vanneck	3¼x4¼"	plate	LgSLR	1890	Rapid Rectilinear				T,I		570

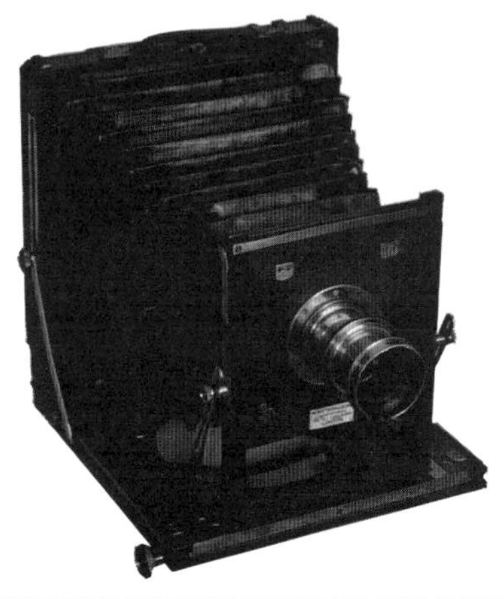

Watson Acme

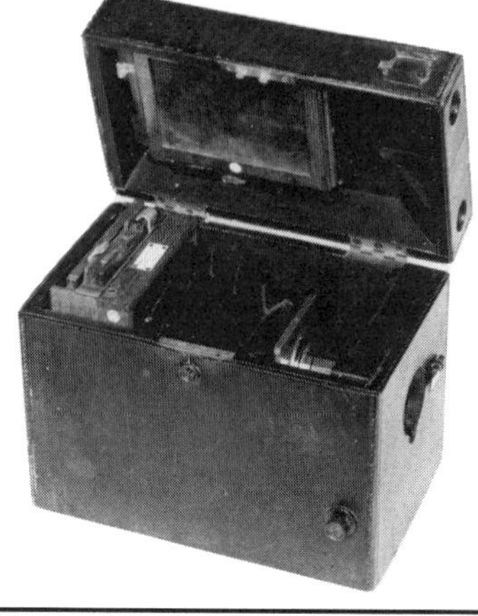

Watson Detective Camera

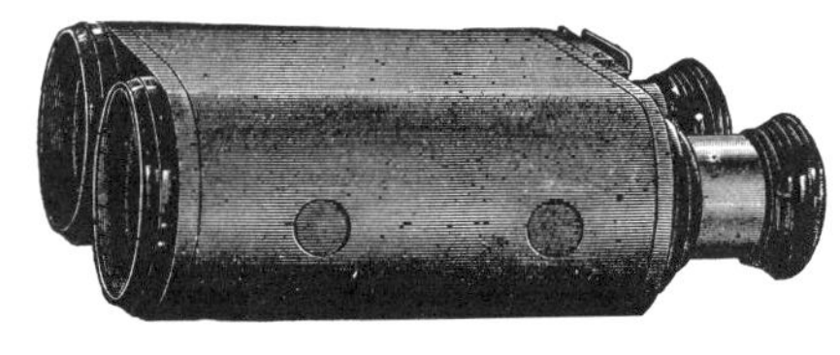

Watson Stereoscopic Binocular

MODEL	FORMAT	FILM	TYPE	Year	LENS	Apert	FL	SHUTTER	SPEEDS	ILLUS	U.S.$
View 10x13	10x13cm	plate	Tailboard	1890	various			various			330
View 13x18	13x18cm	plate	Tailboard	1890	various			various			330
Vril	3¼x4¼"	plate	StrutPl	1910	Holostigmat	6.5	4 1/2"	focal plane	1-2800		290
...WAUCKOSIN - Frankfurt, Germany											
Waranette 3x4	3x4cm	127	StrutRo	1930	Vidar	4.5	50mm	Vario		HK272	100
Waranette 5x8	5x8cm	124	FoldRo	1930	Polluxar	6.3	85mm	Vero	25-100	HK272	50
Waranette 6x9	6x9cm	120	FoldRo	1930	Primo Anastigmat	7.7	105mm	Vario		HK272	50
...WEBSTER INDUSTRIES INC. - Webster, NY											
Winpro 35	24x36mm	35mm	35VF	1947	Crystar	8	40mm	rotary	50,B	Mc423	20
...WEDEMEYER (Eric Wedemeyer) - N.Y.											
Viking Camera	4x6.5cm	127	VtFoldRo	1930	Meniscus					Mc423	30
...WEFO - Dresden											
Meister Korelle	6x6cm	120	MedSLR	1950	Primotar	3.5	85mm				580
Meister Korelle	6x6cm	120	MedSLR	1950	Tessar	3.5	90mm				580
...WELTA KAMERA-WERKE (Waurich & Weber) - Freital, Germany											
Belmira	24x36mm	35mm	35RF	1960	Tessar	2.8	50mm			Mc423	50
Diana	9x12cm	plate	FoldPl	1926	Pololyt	4.5	135mm	Ibsor			40
Dubla 9x12	9x12cm	plate	FoldPl	1930	Eurynar	4.5	135mm				160
Dubla 10x15	10x15cm	plate	FoldPl	1930	Xenar	4.5	165mm			HK192	200
Garant	6x9cm	120	VtFoldRo	1937	Trinar	3.5	105mm	Compur-Rapid	1/400	Mc423	50
Garant (dual-format)	6x9/4.5x6	120	VtFoldRo	1937	Trinar	3.5	105mm	Compur	1/250	Mc423	50
Gucki 3x4	3x4cm	127	StrutRo	1932	Schneider Xenar	2.9	50mm	Compur		HK256	90
Gucki 4x6.5	4x6.5cm	127	StrutRo	1932	Radionar	3.5	50mm	Compur		A409	90
Peerflekta (I)	6x6cm	120	TLR	1956	Pololyt	3.5	75mm	Prontor	1-300		50
Peerflekta II	6x6cm	120	TLR	1956	Pololyt	3.5	75mm	Prontor	1-300	A1714	60
Peerflekta III	6x6cm	120	TLR	1956	Pololyt	3.5	75mm	Prontor	1-300		50
Peerflekta IV	6x6cm	120	TLR	1956	Pololyt	3.5	75mm	Prontor	1-300		50
Peerflekta V	6x6cm	120	TLR	1956	Pololyt	3.5	75mm	Prontor	1-300		60
Penti (beige)	18x24mm	35mm	35Half	1959	Trioplan	3.5	30mm	Pronto	25-125	Mc349	50
Penti (green)	18x24mm	35mm	35Half	1959	Trioplan	3.5	30mm	Pronto	25-125	A1089	50
Penti (red)	18x24mm	35mm	35Half	1959	Trioplan	3.5	30mm	Pronto	25-125		50
Penti I (blue)	18x24mm	35mm	35Half	1961	Domiplan	3.5	30mm	Pronto	25-125		50
Penti I (gold)	18x24mm	35mm	35Half	1961	Domiplan	3.5	30mm	Pronto	25-125	A2103	50
Penti I (silver)	18x24mm	35mm	35Half	1961	Domiplan	3.5	30mm	Pronto	25-125		50
Penti II (blue)	18x24mm	35mm	35Half	1961	Domiplan	3.5	30mm	Pronto	25-125		50
Penti II (gold)	18x24mm	35mm	35Half	1961	Domiplan	3.5	30mm	Pronto	25-125		50
Penti II (silver)	18x24mm	35mm	35Half	1961	Domiplan	3.5	30mm	Pronto	25-125		50
Perfekta	6x6cm	120	StrutTLR	1934	Xenar	3.8	75mm	Compur	1-300	Mc423	210
Perfekta V	6x6cm	120	StrutTLR	1934	Trioplan	3.5	80mm	Compur	1-300	HK392	160
Perle 4.5x6	4.5x6cm	120	VtFoldRo	1934	Tessar	2.9	75mm	Compur			50
Perle 5x8	5x8cm	124	VtFoldRo	1932	Xenar	4.5	90mm	Compur			70
Perle 6x6	6x6cm	120	VtFoldRo	1934	Xenar	3.8	105mm	Compur		Mc423	70

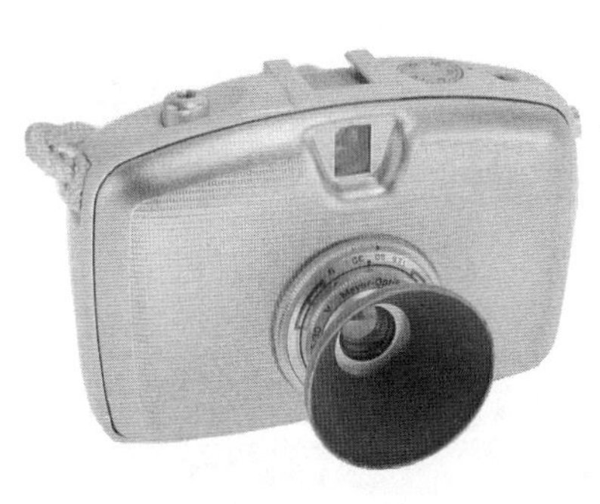

Welta Penti

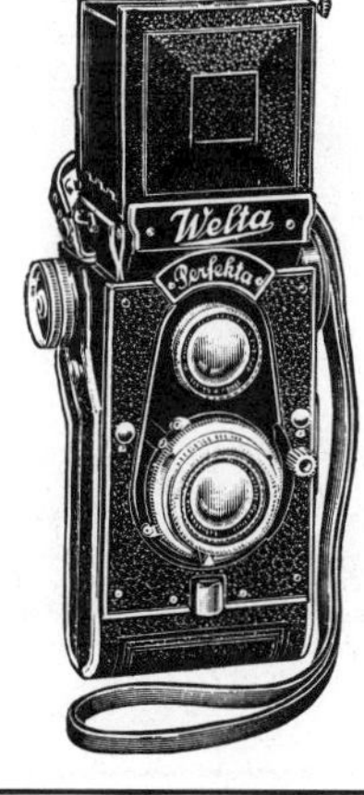

Perfekta

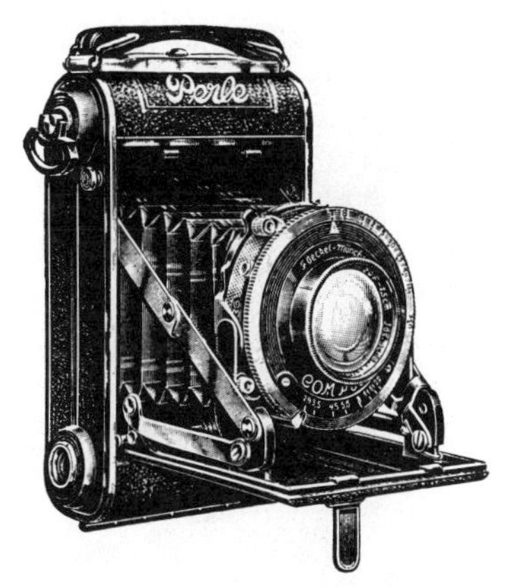

Perle

MODEL	FORMAT	FILM	TYPE	Year	LENS	Apert	FL	SHUTTER	SPEEDS	ILLUS	U.S.$
Perle 6x6	6x6cm	120	VtFoldRo	1934	Trioplan	3.5	105mm	Compur		A473	70
Perle 6x9	6x9cm	120	VtFoldRo	1932	Weltar	6.3	105mm	Ibsor			50
Perle 6.5x11	6.5x11cm	116	VtFoldRo	1932	Tessar	2.9	12cm	Compur		Mc424	50
Perle Luxus 4.5x6	4.5x6cm	120	VtFoldRo	1934	Xenar	3.8	75mm	Compur			90
Perle Luxus 5x8	5x8cm	127	VtFoldRo	1932	Weltar	6.3	90mm	Compur		Mc423	70
Radial	6x9cm	120	VtFoldRo	1930	Xenar	4.5	105mm	Compur	1-300		50
Rak	9x12cm	plate	VtFoldPl	1930	Poloyt	3.5		Compur	1-300		50
Reflecta	6x6cm	120	TLR	1930	Brillantar	3.5	75mm			Mc424	40
Reflecta	6x6cm	120	TLR	1930	Brillantar	4.5	75mm			Mc424	40
Reflekta	6x6cm	120	TLR	1939	Brillantar	3.5	75mm		25-100		70
Reflekta II	6x6cm	120	TLR	1950	Meritar	3.5	75mm	Junior		Mc424	40
Reflekta II	6x6cm	120	TLR	1950	Trioplan	3.5	75mm	Vebur		A1713	40
Reflekta III	6x6cm	120	TLR	1955	Row Poloyt	3.5	70mm	Prontor-SV	1-300		40
Sica	6x9cm	120	BakeliteBox	1950	Achromat	7.7	105mm				370
Solida	6x9cm	120	VtFoldRo	1933	Schn. Radionar	4.5	105mm	Compur	1-250,T,B	A432	90
Special Mod. M	9x12cm	plate	VtFoldPl	1930	Trinar	4.5	135mm				50
Superfekta	6x9cm	120	StrutTLR	1932	Tessar	3.8	105mm	Compur		Mc424	400
Superfekta	6x9cm	120	StrutTLR	1932	Trioplan	3.8	105mm	Compur		HK391	400
Symbol	6x9cm	120	VtFoldRo	1937	Weltar	6.3	105mm	Vario		Mc424	30
Symbol (dual-format)	6x9/4.5x6	120	VtFoldRo	1937	Weltar	6.3	105mm	Prontor			30
Trio	6x9cm	120	VtFoldRo	1936	Tessar	4.5	105mm	Compur		Mc424	30
Walta	6x9cm	120	VtFoldRo	1932	Weltar	9	105mm	Singlo		HK246	30
Watson 9x12	9x12cm	plate	VtFoldPl	1930	Xenar	3.5	150mm				50
Watson 10x15	10x15cm	plate	VtFoldPl	1930	Xenar	3.5	165mm				50
Watson 35	24x36mm	35mm	35VF	1940	Cassar	2.9	5cm	Compur			60
Welta 35	24x36mm	35mm	35VF	1936	Trioplan	2.9	50mm	Rim-Compur			40
Welta 6x6	6x6cm	120	VtFoldRo	1932	Tessar	2.8	75mm	Compur			40
Welta 6x9	6x9cm	plate	VtFoldPl	1932	Orion Rionar	4.5	105mm	Ibsor	1-125		50
Welta 9x12	9x12cm	plate	VtFoldPl	1933	Rod. Eurynar	3.5	135mm	Compur			60
Welta 10x15	10x15cm	plate	VtFoldPl	1933	Trinar	3.8	150mm	Compur			50
Weltaflex	6x6cm	120	TLR	1955	Ludwig Meritar	3.5	75mm	Prontor	1-300	A1712	50
Weltax	6x6cm	120	VtFoldRo	1939	Xenar	2.8	75mm	Compur		Mc424	50
Weltax	6x6cm	120	VtFoldRo	1939	Trioplan	3.5	75mm	Junior		A472	50
Weltax II	6x6cm	120	VtFoldRo	1939	Meritar	3.5	75mm	Tempor			40
Welti	24x36mm	35mm	35VF	1935	Tessar	2.8	50mm	Compur		Mc424	50
Welti	24x36mm	35mm	35VF	1935	Xenar	3.5	50mm	Cludor		A2051	50
Welti Ic	24x36mm	35mm	35VF	1935	Tessar	2.8	50mm	Vebur		A1028	50
Welti II	24x36mm	35mm	35VF	1935	Tessar	2.8	50mm	Vebur		HK563	50
Weltini	24x36mm	35mm	35RF	1937	Xenon	2	50mm	Compur		A1026	60
Weltini + Compur-Rapid	24x36mm	35mm	35RF	1937	Elmar	3.5	50mm	Compur-Rapid		Mc425	210
Weltini II	24x36mm	35mm	35RF	1937	Tessar	2.8	50mm	Compur		HK548	60
Weltini II + Compur-Rapid	24x36mm	35mm	35RF	1937	Elmar	3.5	50mm	Compur-Rapid		Mc425	220

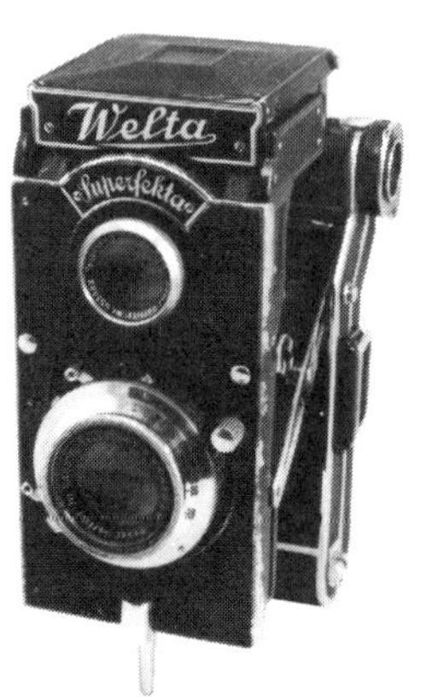

Superfekta

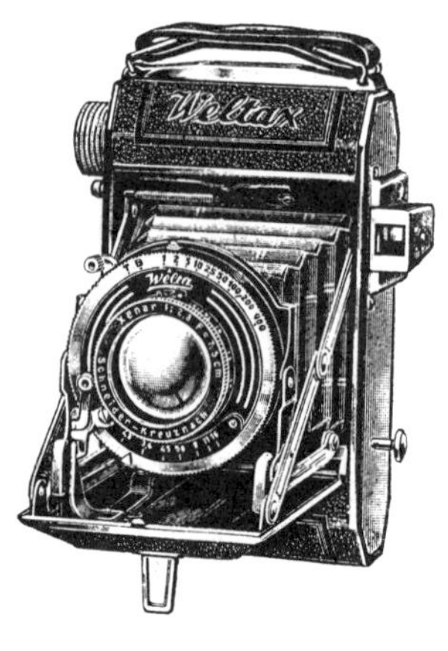

Weltax

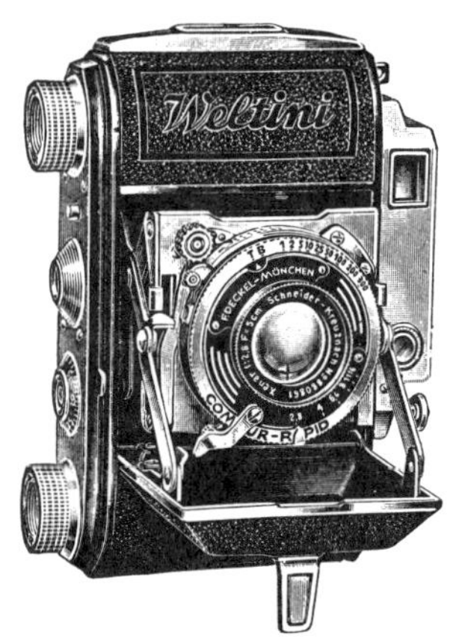

Weltini + Compur-Rapid

MODEL	FORMAT	FILM	TYPE	Year	LENS	Apert	FL	SHUTTER	SPEEDS	ILLUS	U.S.$
Weltix	24x36mm	35mm	35VF	1939	Steinheil Cassar	2.9	50mm	Compur		A1027	60
Weltur 4.5x6 (black)	4.5x6cm	120	VtFoldRo	1936	Trioplan	2.9	50mm	Compur	1-300	A471	160
Weltur 4.5x6 (chrome)	4.5x6cm	120	VtFoldRo	1936	Trioplan	2.9	50mm	Compur	1-300	Mc425	110
Weltur 4.5x6 (chrome)	4.5x6cm	120	VtFoldRo	1936	Xenar	2.8	50mm	Compur	1-300	A471	110
Weltur 6x6	6x6cm	120	VtFoldRo	1936	Tessar	2.8	75mm	Compur-Rapid	1-400		100
Weltur 6x6 (dual-format)	6x6/4.5x6	120	VtFoldRo	1936	Tessar	2.8	75mm	Compur	1-300		100
Weltur 6x9 (dual-format)	6x9/4.5x6	120	VtFoldRo	1936	Cassar	2.9	105mm	Compur	1-300		100
...WENK (Gebr. Wenk) - Nürnberg, Germany											
Wenka	24x36mm	35mm	35RF	1951	Xenar	2.8	50mm	focal plane	1-500	Mc425	500
Wenka II	24x36mm	35mm	35RF	1952	Xenar	2.8	50mm	focal plane	1-500		560
...WERNER - Vienna											
Field camera 13x18	13x18cm	plate	Field	1900	various			various			510
Field camera 18x24	18x24cm	plate	Field	1900	various			various			800
...WESTERN CAMERA MFG. CO. - Chicago											
Cyclone Jr.	3½x3½"	plate	PlateBox	1899	achromatic			Automatic	I,T		40
Cyclone Sr.	4x5"	plate	PlateBox	1899	achromatic			Automatic	I,T		100
Magazine Cyclone No. 2	3¼x4¼"	plate	MagBox	1899	achromatic			Automatic	I,T	Mc425	50
Magazine Cyclone No. 3	4x5"	plate	MagBox	1899	achromatic			Automatic	I,T		50
Magazine Cyclone No. 4	3¼x4¼"	plate	MagBox	1899	achromatic			Automatic	I,T	Mc425	50
Magazine Cyclone No. 5	4x5"	plate	MagBox	1899	achromatic			Automatic	I,T		50
Pocket Zar	2x2"	plate	PlateBox	1897						Mc425	70
...WESTFÄLISCHER KAMERA & APPARATEBAU											
Navax	24x36mm	35mm	35VF	1950	Röschein Pointar	2.8	45mm	focal plane	5-1000	Mc425	540
Navax II	24x36mm	35mm	35VF	1953	Röschein Pointar	2.8	45mm	focal plane	5-1000		680
...(unknown)											
Weston WX-7	24x36mm	35mm	35VF	1985	Weston	3.5	50mm				10
...WHITE (David White Co.) - Milwaukee, Wisc.											
Realist 35	24x36mm	35mm	35VF	1955	Cassar	2.8	50mm	Vero	1-300	Mc426	30
Realist 35 B	24x36mm	35mm	35VF	1955	Cassar	2.9	50mm	Vero	1-300		30
Realist 45 (Mod. 1045)	23x24mm	35mm	35Ster	1953	Cassar	3.5	35mm	Vero	25-200		150
Stereo Realist Mod. 1041	22x24mm	35mm	35Ster	1950	Realist	3.5	35mm		1-150	A2709	180
Stereo Realist Mod. 1042	22x24mm	35mm	35Ster	1950	Realist	2.8	35mm		1-200	Mc426	350
Stereo Realist Custom	22x24mm	35mm	35Ster	1960	"Rare Earth"	2.8	35mm		1-200,T,B	Mc426	500
Stereo Realist Macro	22x24mm	35mm	35Ster	1971	Realist	3.5	35mm		1-125	A2710	1500
...WHITEHOUSE PRODUCTS - Brooklyn, NY											
Beacon	3x4cm	127	PlasticBox	1947	Whitar		46mm		1/50,T	A1542	10
Beacon II	3x4cm	127	PlasticBox	1947	Whitar	11	49mm		1/50,T	A3127	10
Beacon 225	6x6cm	620	PlasticBox	1950	Whitar	12	70mm		1/50,T	A3090	30
Beacon Reflex		Roll	TLR-Box								10
...WHITTAKER (Wm. R. Whittaker Co., Ltd.) - Los Angeles, Calif.											
Micro 16	10x14mm	16mm	Submin	1950	Meniscus				I	Mc426	60
Pixie	10x14mm	16mm	Submin	1950	Microtar	6.3	25mm	sector		A1924	60

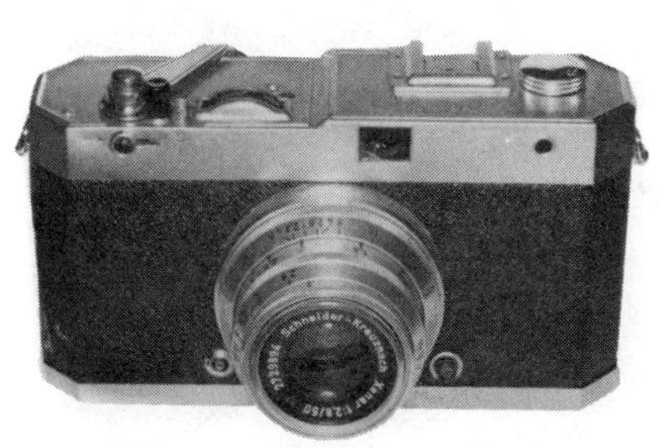

Wenka

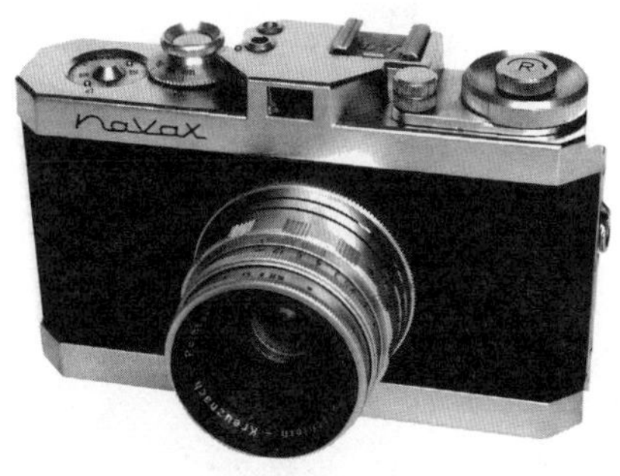

Navax

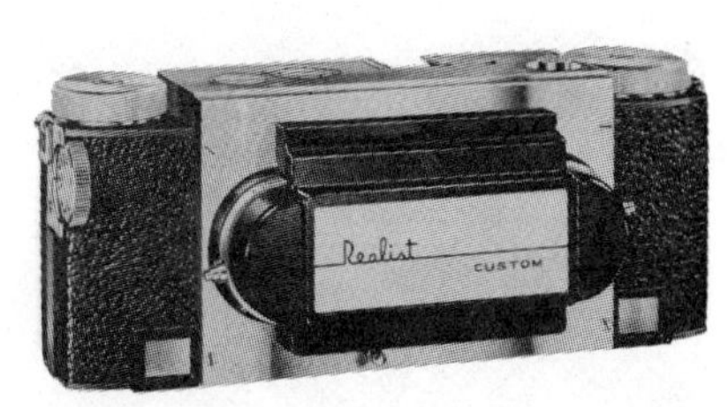

Stereo Realist Custom

MODEL	FORMAT	FILM	TYPE	Year	LENS	Apert	FL	SHUTTER	SPEEDS	ILLUS	U.S.$
Pixie (with flash)	10x14mm	16mm	Submin	1950	Microtar	6.3	25mm	sector		A1925	70
Pixie Custom	10x14mm	16mm	Submin	1950	Microtar	6.3		sector			250
...WIDMAYER (Rudolph Widmayer) - Leipzig											
Paris	18x24cm	35mm	Field		Dallmeyer						270
...WIDMER (Robert Widmer) - Germany											
Cowi	32x40mm	828	MiniatRo							Mc427	50
...WILCA KAMERABAU - West Germany											
Wilca Automatic	10x19mm	16mm	Submin	1963	Wilcalux Filtra	2	16mm	Sync.Prontor		Mc427	800
...WILKIN WELSH CO. - Syracuse, NY USA											
Folding plate camera	4x5"	plate	FoldPl	1900				Rauber & W.			140
...WILLIAMSON MANUFACTURING CO. LTD. - London, England											
Pistol Aircraft camera	6x9cm	plate	Aerial	1930	Ross Xpres	4.5	5"		50-200	Mc427	290
Revolver Aircraft camera	6x6cm	120	Aerial	1940	Ross Xpres	4.5				A3442	270
...WINDSOR CAMERA CO. - Japan											
Windsor 35	24x36mm	35mm	35RF	1953	Color Sygmar	3.5	50mm		1-200	Mc427	30
Windsor 35	24x36mm	35mm	35RF	1953	Color Sygmar	3.5	50mm		1-300,B	Mc427	30
Windsor Stereo	23x24mm	35mm	35Ster	1954	Windsor	4.5	35mm	Windsor	25,50		160
...WING (Simon Wing) - Charlestown, MA											
Multiple-lens camera		WetPl	MultiLens	1870	4-lens			Wing Pat.			2400
Multiple-lens camera		plate	MultiLens	1870	9-lens			Wing Pat.			3600
Multiplying View Camera	5x7"	plate	Multiply	1900						A1856	570
Multiplying Wet Plate View	5x7"	WetPl	Multiply	1862						Mc427	7000
New Gem	5x7"	plate	Multiply	1901						Mc427	900
...WINTER (Chr. Fr.) & SOHN - Leipzig, Germany											
Field camera 10x15	10x15cm	plate	Field	1900	Brassbound						200
Field camera 13x18	13x18cm	plate	Field	1900	Brassbound						200
...WIRGIN (Gebr. Wirgin) - Wiesbaden, Germany											
Alka 16	12x17mm	16mm	Submin	1960	Travegar	2.8	25mm				70
Astraflex 1000	24x36mm	35mm	35SLR	1958	Primoplan	1.9	50mm	focal plane	1-1000		50
Astraflex 1000 LM	24x36mm	35mm	35SLR	1959	Primoplan	1.9	50mm	focal plane	1-1000		60
Auta	6x9cm	120	FoldRo	1936	Gewir	4.5	105mm	Prontor	25-150		40
Baky (black)	4.5x6cm	120	BakFoldRo	1935	Xenar	2.9	75mm	Compur			130
Baky (brown)	4.5x6cm	120	BakFoldRo	1935	Cassar	2.9	75mm	Prontor II			130
Edina	24x36mm	35mm	35VF	1954	Edinar	2.8	45mm	Vario	25-200	Mc428	40
Edinex	24x36mm	35mm	Telesc35	1930	Radionar	4.5	50mm	Compur-Rapid		Mc428	50
Edinex	24x36mm	35mm	Telesc35	1930	Cassar	2.8	50mm	Prontor-S		HK567	50
Edinex	24x36mm	35mm	Telesc35	1930	Xenon	2	50mm	Compur-Rapid		HK546	70
Edinex III	24x36mm	35mm	Telesc35	1939	Heligon	2	50mm	Compur-Rapid		HK564	70
Edinex 120	6x9/4.5x6	120	FoldRo	1953	Cassar	6.3	105mm	Vario	1-300		40
Edixa	24x36mm	35mm	35VF	1955	Cassar	3.5	40mm	Vario	1-300	Mc428	40
Edixa	24x36mm	35mm	35VF	1955	Cassar	3.5	40mm	Vero	1-200	A1115	40
Edixa 16	12x17mm	16mm	Submin	1960	Xenar	2.8	25mm	Synchro	30-150		70

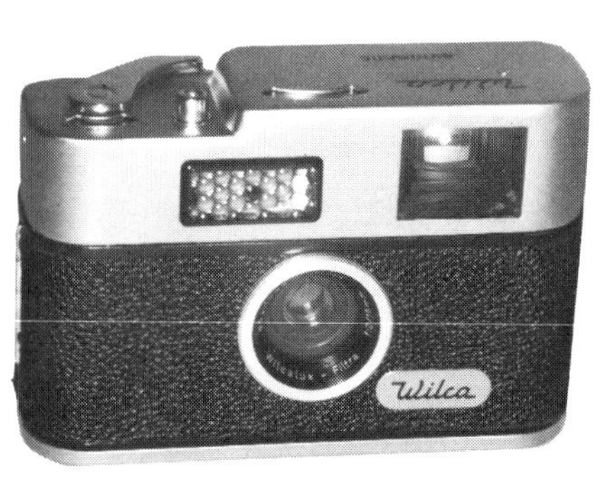

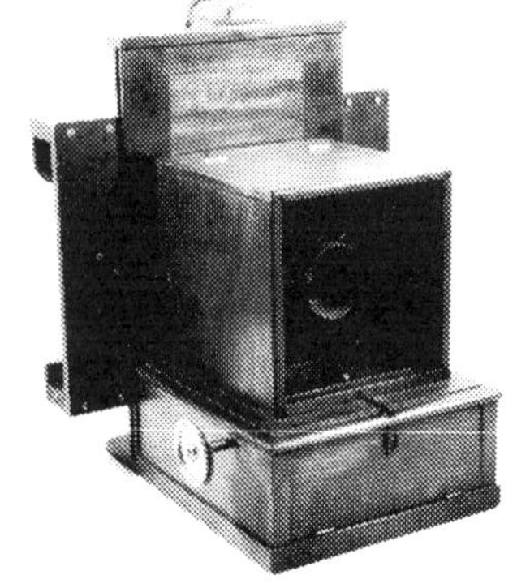

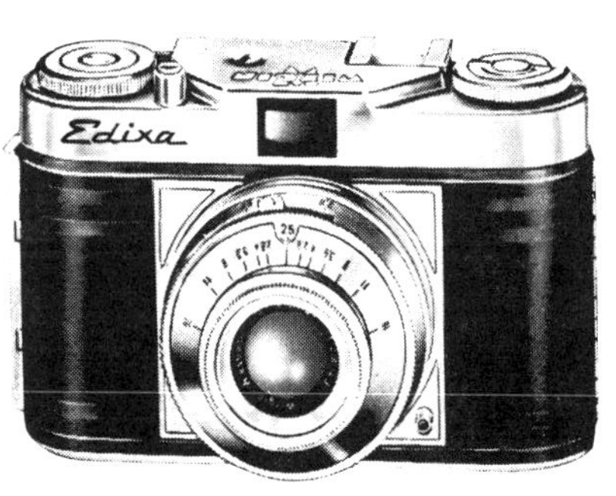

Wilca Automatic **Wing Multiplying Wet Plate View** **Wirgin Edixa**

MODEL	FORMAT	FILM	TYPE	Year	LENS	Apert	FL	SHUTTER	SPEEDS	ILLUS	U.S.$
Edixa 16M	12x17mm	16mm	Submin	1967	Xenar	2.8	25mm	Synchro	30-150		70
Edixa 16MB	12x17mm	16mm	Submin	1967	Xenar	2.8	25mm	Synchro	30-150		140
Edixa 16S	12x17mm	16mm	Submin	1960	Xenar	2.8	25mm	Synchro	30-150	A925	70
Edixa 16U	12x17mm	16mm	Submin	1960	Xenar	2.8	25mm	Synchro	30-150		60
Edixa 66B	6x6cm	120	TLR	1962	Spezial	8	80mm		1/30		80
Edixa 66T	6x6cm	120	TLR	1965	Spezial	8	70mm		1/30		80
Edixa 125	24x36mm	35mm	35SLR	1965	Color-Isconar	2.8	45mm	Prontor	25-125		50
Edixa 125 L	24x36mm	35mm	35SLR	1965	Color-Isconar	2.8	45mm	Prontor	25-125		50
Edixa 500	24x36mm	35mm	35SLR	1963	Auto Cassaron	2.8	50mm	focal plane	30-500		50
Edixa 750	24x36mm	35mm	35SLR	1965	Isconar	2.8	50mm	focal plane	30-1000		80
Edixa electronica	24x36mm	35mm	35SLR	1962	Culminar	2.8	50mm	Compur sync	1-500	Mc428	270
Edixa electronica	24x36mm	35mm	35SLR	1962	Xenar	2.8	50mm	Compur sync	1-500	A627	270
Edixa electronica TL	24x36mm	35mm	35SLR	1962	Edixa-Xenon	1.7	55mm	focal plane	16-1000	A628	220
Edixa II	24x36mm	35mm	35RF	1956	Isconar	2.8	43mm	Prontor-SVS		A116	40
Edixa II-L	24x36mm	35mm	35RF	1956	Westanar	2.8	45mm	Prontor-S			50
Edixa Kadett	24x36mm	35mm	35SLR	1963	Auto Cassaron	2.8	50mm	focal plane	30-500		70
Edixa Prismaflex	24x36mm	35mm	35SLR	1965	Steinheil	2.8	50mm	focal plane	30-500		90
Edixa Prismaflex CdS	24x36mm	35mm	35SLR	1966	Steinheil	2.8	50mm	focal plane	30-500		100
Edixa Prismaflex LTL	24x36mm	35mm	35SLR	1968	Steinheil	2.8	50mm	focal plane	30-1000		100
Edixa Prismaflex TTL	24x36mm	35mm	35SLR	1966	Steinheil	2.8	50mm	focal plane	4-1000		100
Edixa Prismat (black)	24x36mm	35mm	35SLR	1965	Iscotar	2.8	50mm	focal plane	1-1000		100
Edixa Prismat (chrome)	24x36mm	35mm	35SLR	1965	Iscotar	2.8	50mm	focal plane	1-1000		90
Edixa Prismat CdS	24x36mm	35mm	35SLR	1966	Iscotar	2.8	50mm	focal plane	1-1000		90
Edixa Prismat LTL	24x36mm	35mm	35SLR	1968	Auto Cassaron	2.8	50mm	focal plane	1-1000		80
Edixa Prismat TTL	24x36mm	35mm	35SLR	1967	Xenon	1.9	50mm	focal plane	1-1000		100
Edixa Reflex	24x36mm	35mm	35SLR	1955	Iscotar	2.8	50mm	focal plane	1-1000	A625	70
Edixa Reflex 6x6	6x6cm	120	TLR	1957	Cassar	2.8	80mm		1-300		70
Edixa Reflex A	24x36mm	35mm	35SLR	1955	Cassar	2.8	50mm	focal plane	1-1000		70
Edixa Reflex B	24x36mm	35mm	35SLR	1958	Travenar	2.8	50mm	focal plane	1-1000,B	Mc428	70
Edixa Reflex Ba	24x36mm	35mm	35SLR	1958	Xenon	1.9	50mm	focal plane	1-1000,B		80
Edixa Reflex C	24x36mm	35mm	35SLR	1958	Westanar	2.8	50mm	focal plane	1-1000		80
Edixa Reflex D	24x36mm	35mm	35SLR	1958	Travenar	2.8	50mm	focal plane	9-1000		80
Edixa Reflex S-V	24x36mm	35mm	35SLR	1962	Xenon	1.9	50mm	focal plane			100
Edixa Rex B	24x36mm	35mm	35SLR	1966	Xenar	2.8	50mm	focal plane	1-1000,B		110
Edixa Rex CdS	24x36mm	35mm	35SLR	1966	Xenar	2.8	50mm	focal plane	1-1000,B		110
Edixa Rex D	24x36mm	35mm	35SLR	1966	Xenon	1.9	50mm	focal plane	9-1000		130
Edixa Rex TTL	24x36mm	35mm	35SLR	1966	Xenon	1.9	50mm	focal plane	1-1000,B		110
Edixa Standard	24x36mm	35mm	35SLR	1959	Iscolar	2.8	50mm	focal plane	2-500		70
Edixa Standard-V	24x36mm	35mm	35SLR	1962	Iscolor	2.8	50mm	focal plane	2-500		100
Edixa Stereo	22x24mm	35mm	35Ster	1955	Cassar	3.5	35mm	Vario		Mc428	170
Edixa Stereo IA	22x24mm	35mm	35Ster	1957	Cassar	3.5	35mm	Vario			170
Edixa Stereo II	22x24mm	35mm	35Ster	1957	Cassar	3.5	35mm	Pronto	1-200	A2714	130

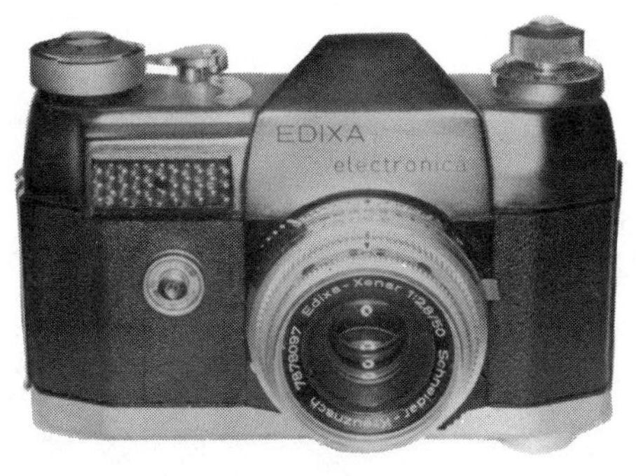

Edixa electronica

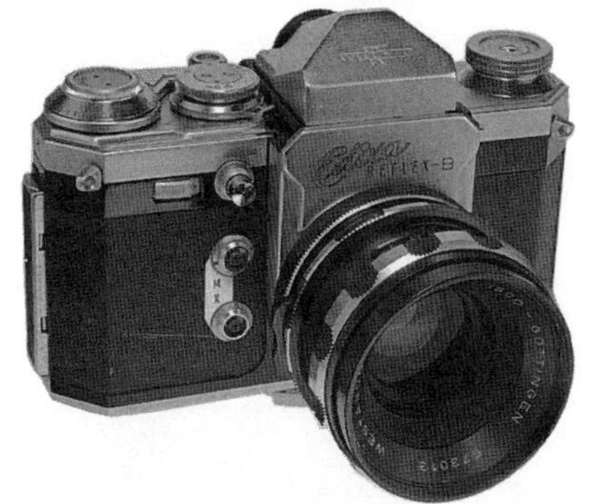

Edixa Reflex B

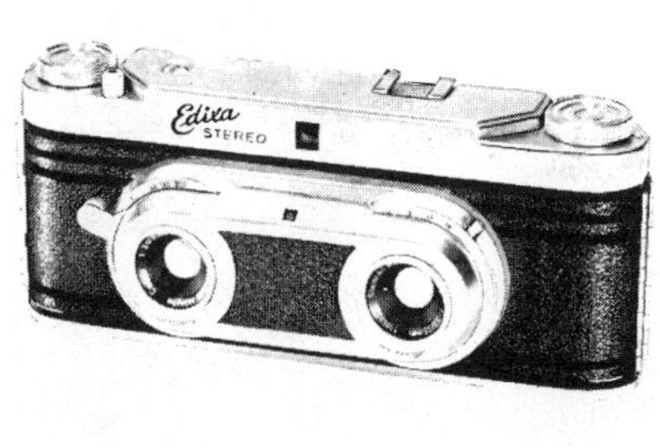

Edixa Stereo

MODEL	FORMAT	FILM	TYPE	Year	LENS	Apert	FL	SHUTTER	SPEEDS	ILLUS	U.S.$
Edixa Stereo II	22x24mm	35mm	35Ster	1957	Cassar	3.5	35mm	Prontor-SVS	1-200	HK528	130
Edixa Stereo IIa	22x24mm	35mm	35Ster	1957	Cassar	3.5	35mm	Prontor-SVS	1-200		130
Edixa Stereo III	22x24mm	35mm	35Ster	1957	Cassar	3.5	35mm	Prontor-SVS			200
Edixa Stereo IIIa	22x24mm	35mm	35Ster	1957	Cassar	3.5	35mm	Prontor-SVS		A791	170
Edixa-Lux	24x36mm	35mm	35VF	1962	Isconar	2.8	50mm	focal plane			30
Edixa-Mat B	24x36mm	35mm	35SLR	1961	Steinheil	1.9	50mm	focal plane	1-1000,B		90
Edixa-Mat B	24x36mm	35mm	35SLR	1961	Xenar	2.8	50mm	focal plane	1-1000,B		100
Edixa-Mat BL	24x36mm	35mm	35SLR	1961	S-Travelon	1.8	50mm	focal plane	1-1000,B		90
Edixa-Mat C	24x36mm	35mm	35SLR	1961	Xenon	1.9	50mm	focal plane	1-1000,B		100
Edixa-Mat CdS	24x36mm	35mm	35SLR	1967	Edixagon	2	50mm	focal plane	1/4-1000		70
Edixa-Mat CL	24x36mm	35mm	35SLR	1961	Xenar	2.8	50mm	focal plane	1-1000,B		100
Edixa-Mat D	24x36mm	35mm	35SLR	1961	Xenar	2.8	50mm	focal plane	9-1000	A626	100
Edixa-Mat DL	24x36mm	35mm	35SLR	1961	S-Travelon	1.8	50mm	focal plane	9-1000	A626	100
Edixa-mat Kadett	24x36mm	35mm	35SLR	1965	Auto Cassaron	2.8	50mm	focal plane	30-500		80
Edixa-Mat Reflex	24x36mm	35mm	35SLR	1960	Travenar	2.8	50mm	focal plane	1-1000,B		70
Edixa-Mat Reflex D	24x36mm	35mm	35SLR	1960	Xenon	1.9	50mm	focal plane	1-1000		70
Edixaflex	24x36mm	35mm	35SLR	1958	Xenar	2.8	50mm	focal plane	25-1000		70
Edixet 125 L	24x36mm	35mm	35VF	1963	Isconar	2.8	50mm	Prontor			30
Franka 16	12x17mm	16mm	Submin	1962	Travenar	2.8	25mm	Synchro	30-150		130
Gewir	6.5x9cm	plate	FoldPl	1936	Zecanar	3.8	105mm	Compur S			80
Gewirette 3x4	3x4cm	127	TelescRo	1937	Gewironar	4.5	50mm	Prontor II	1-175	Mc428	120
Gewirette 3x4	3x4cm	127	TelescRo	1937	Xenar	2.9	50mm	Prontor II	1-175	HK274	120
Gewirette 4.5x6	4.5x6cm	120	TelescRo	1936	Reporter Anast.	4.5	50mm	Prontor II	1-175		140
Klein-Edinex	3x4cm	127	TelescRo	1938	Xenar	2.8	50mm	Prontor	25-125	A1534	120
Reporter 3x4	3x4cm	127	TelescRo	1930	Fixanar	2.9	50mm	Compur	1-300		160
Reporter 4.5x6	4.5x6cm	120	TelescRo	1930	Fixanar	2.9	50mm	Compur	1-300		180
Twin Lens Reflex	6x9cm	120	TLR	1940	Anastigmat Triolar	4.5	75mm	Stelo	25-100	Mc428	70
Wirgin Deluxe	6x6cm	120	BakFoldRo							Mc429	30
Wirgin folding rollfilm	6x9cm	120	FoldRo	1950	Gewironar	6.3	105mm	Pronto	25-250	A431	30
Wirgin Stereo	22x24mm	35mm	35Ster	1954	Steinheil Cassar	3.5	35mm	Vario	25-200	Mc429	150
Wirgin TLR	6x6cm	120	TLR	1950	Trinar	2.9	75mm				70
Wirginex (Baky)	4.5x6cm	120	BakFoldRo	1935	Cassar	2.9		Compur-Rapid		Mc429	140
...WITT (Iloca Werk, Wilhelm Witt) - Hamburg, Germany											
Iloca I	24x36mm	35mm	35VF	1950	Ilitar	3.5	45mm	Pronto II			40
Iloca Ia	24x36mm	35mm	35VF	1950	Ilitar	2.9	45mm	Prontor		Mc429	40
Iloca II	24x36mm	35mm	35RF	1950	Ilitar	3.5	45mm	Prontor			40
Iloca IIa	24x36mm	35mm	35RF	1950	Ilitar	3.5	45mm	Prontor		Mc429	40
Iloca III	24x36mm	35mm	35RF	1950	Ilitar	3.5	45mm	Prontor			30
Iloca Automatic	24x36mm	35mm	35RF	1950	Cassarit	2.8	50mm	Sync-Compur	1-500		50
Iloca Electric	24x36mm	35mm	35El-Mot	1959	Heligon	1.9	50mm	Sync-Compur	1-500		230
Iloca Quick	24x36mm	35mm	35VF	1952	Ilitar	2.8	45mm	Prontor			30
Iloca Quick A	24x36mm	35mm	35VF	1954	Ilitar	3.5	45mm	Vario	25-200,B		30

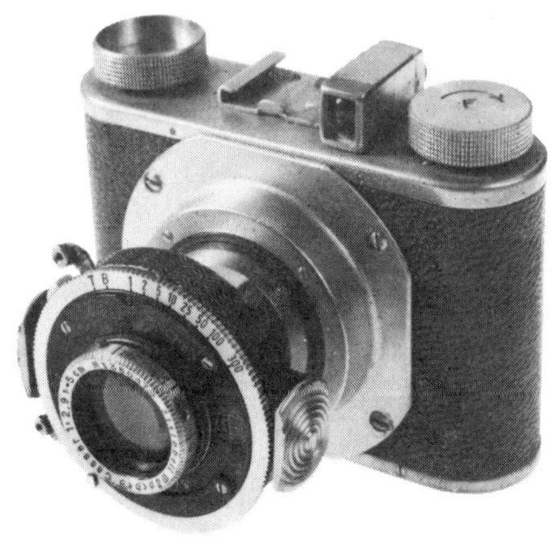

Gewirette

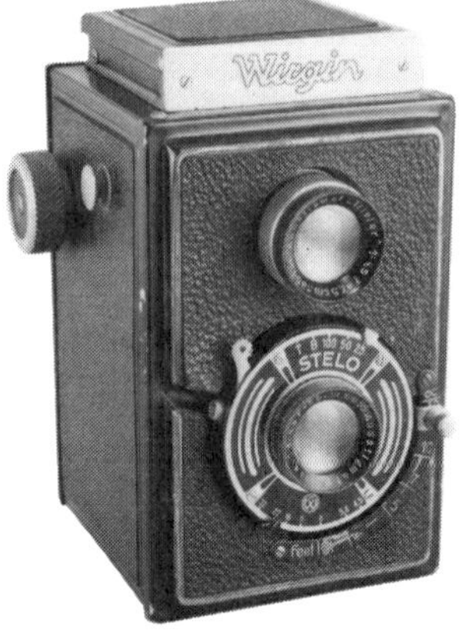

Twin Lens Reflex

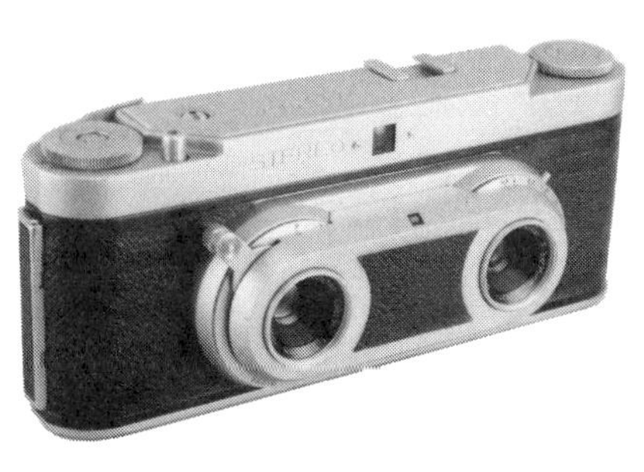

Wirgin Stereo

MODEL	FORMAT	FILM	TYPE	Year	LENS	Apert	FL	SHUTTER	SPEEDS	ILLUS	U.S.$
Iloca Quick B	24x36mm	35mm	35VF	1954	Ilitar	2.9	45mm	Prontor-SV	1-300		30
Iloca Quick R	24x36mm	35mm	35VF	1954	Cassar	2.8	45mm	Vero	25-200,B		30
Iloca Quick S	24x36mm	35mm	35VF	1954	Ilitar	3.5	45mm	Prontor-SV	1-300		30
Iloca Rapid	24x36mm	35mm	35RF	1950	Ilitar	2.8	50mm	Prontor-SV	1-300		40
Iloca Rapid I	24x36mm	35mm	35RF	1950	Cassar	2.8	50mm	Compur-Rapid	1-500		40
Iloca Rapid IL	24x36mm	35mm	35RF	1950	Ilitar	2.8	50mm	Compur-Rapid	1-500		30
Iloca Rapid IIL	24x36mm	35mm	35RF	1950	Cassar	2.8	50mm	Gauthier			50
Iloca Rapid A1	24x36mm	35mm	35RF	1950	Cassar	2.8	50mm	Vero	25-200,B		30
Iloca Rapid B	24x36mm	35mm	35RF	1950	Ilitar Super	2.8	50mm	Prontor-SV	1-300		50
Iloca Reporter	24x36mm	35mm	35VF	1951	Reporter Anast.	3.5	45mm	Prontor-S			40
Iloca Stereo (original)	24x30mm	35mm	35Ster	1950	Ilitar	3.5	45mm	Prontor-S	1-300	Mc429	240
Iloca Stereo, Mod. I	24x30mm	35mm	35Ster	1950	Ilitar	3.5	45mm	Prontor-S	1-300	Mc429	220
Iloca Stereo, Mod. II	23x24mm	35mm	35Ster	1950	Ilitar	3.5	35mm	Prontor-S	1-300	Mc429	220
Iloca Stereo, Mod. IIa	23x24mm	35mm	35Ster	1950	Ilitar	3.5	35mm	Prontor-S	1-300	Mc429	220
Iloca Stereo Rapid	23x24mm	35mm	35Ster	1955	Cassarit	2.8	35mm	Prontor-SVS	1-300		340
Photrix Quick B	24x36mm	35mm	35VF	1950	Cassar	2.8	50mm	Prontor-SVS	1-300		30
Photrix Stereo	22x25mm	35mm	35Ster	1950	Ilitar	3.5	35mm	Prontor-S	1-300		120
...WITTMAN (R. Wittman) - Dresden, Germany											
Tailboard camera 1880	13x18cm	plate	Tailboard	1880	Aplanat			various			350
Tailboard camera 1890	13x18cm	plate	Tailboard	1890	Aplanat			various		A2934	310
...WITTNAUER											
Wittnette Auto. Electric Eye	6x6cm	120	TLR-Box	1959	Meniscus					Mc429	40
Wittnette Reflex	6x6cm	120	TLR-Box	1959	Meniscus					Mc430	30
...WÖHLER (Dr. Wöhler) - St Ingbert, Saarland											
Favor	24x36mm	35mm	35VF	1949	Docar	2.8	45mm	Prontor-S		Mc430	160
Favor	24x36mm	35mm	35VF	1949	Citar	3.5	45mm	Prontor-SVS		F567	160
...WOLLENSAK OPTICAL CO.											
Wollensak Stereo Mod. 10	23x24mm	35mm	35Ster	1955	Amaton	2.7	35mm	Rapax	1-300	Mc430	210
...WOOD (E.G. Wood) - London											
Wet plate sliding box	14x14cm	WetPl	WetPlate	1850	Petzval					A2792	900
Wet plate sliding box	4¼x6½"	WetPl	WetPlate	1850	Petzval						1300
...WRATTEN & WAINWRIGHT - London, England											
Tailboard camera 5x8"	5x8"	plate	Tailboard	1890	Rap. Symmetrical					Mc430	380
Tailboard camera 8x10"	8x10"	plate	Tailboard	1890	Rap. Symmetrical					Mc430	340
Tailboard camera 10x12"	10x12"	plate	Tailboard	1890	Rap. Symmetrical					Mc430	330
Tailboard camera 13x18"	13x18"	plate	Tailboard	1890	Rap. Symmetrical					Mc430	340
...WRAY OPTICAL WORKS - London											
Peckham Wray	4x5"	Sheet	LgSLR	1955	Wray Lustrar	4.8	135mm	FP/Compur	1-500		230
Stereo Graphic	24x24mm	35mm	35Ster	1950	Wray	4	35mm		I	Mc430	160
Wrayflex I	24x32mm	35mm	35SLR	1950	Wray	2	50mm	focal plane	½-1000	Mc430	160
Wrayflex Ia	24x36mm	35mm	35SLR	1950	Wray	2	50mm	focal plane	½-1000	Mc430	140
Wrayflex II	24x36mm	35mm	35SLR	1950	Wray	2.8	50mm	focal plane	½-1000	Mc430	250

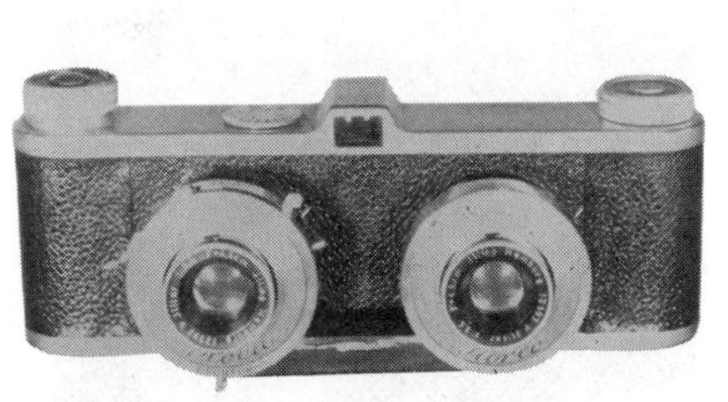

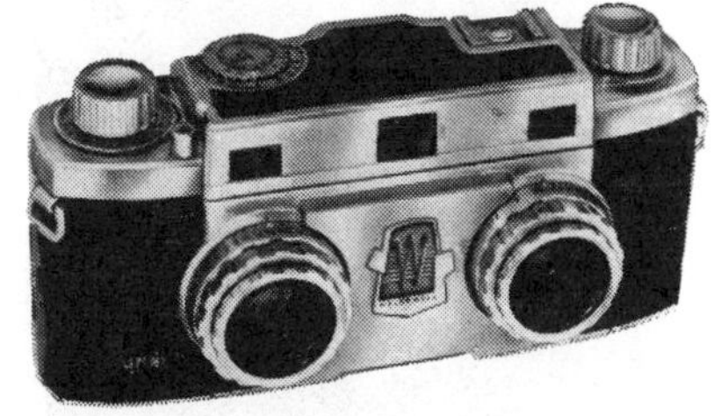

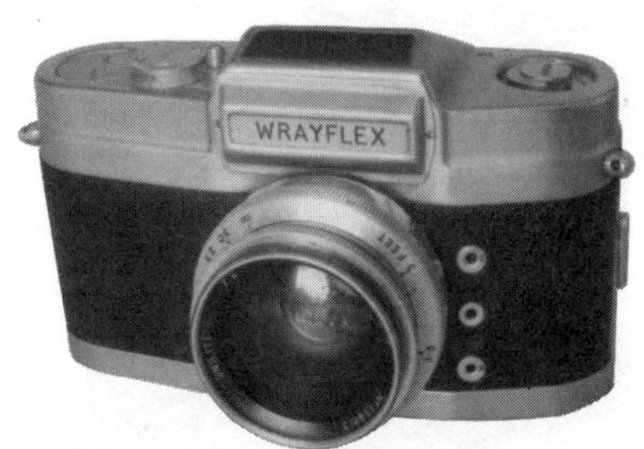

Iloca Stereo (original) **Wollensak Stereo Mod. 10** **Wrayflex Ia**

MODEL	FORMAT	FILM	TYPE	Year	LENS	Apert	FL	SHUTTER	SPEEDS	ILLUS	U.S.$
...WÜNSCHE (Emil Wünsche) - Reick b/Dresden											
Afpi (metal shutter) 9x12	9x12cm	plate	Fold Pl	1904							220
Afpi (square) 9x12	9x12cm	plate	Fold Pl	1904	Imagonal	6	135mm	Compound	1-250		120
Afpi (square) 10x13	10x13cm	plate	Fold Pl	1904	Extra Rap. Aplan.	8	150mm	Automat	1-100		120
Afpi (square) 13x18	13x18cm	plate	Fold Pl	1908	Symmar	4.8	180mm	Compound	1-250	HK132	120
Afpi (vertical) 9x12	9x12cm	plate	VtFoldPl	1904	Extra Rap. Aplan.	8	150mm	Automat	1-100		110
Afpi (vertical) 10x13	10x13cm	plate	VtFoldPl	1904	Extra Rap. Aplan.	8	150mm	Automat	1-100		110
Afpi Stereo	10x15cm	plate	StFoldPl	1907	Symmar			Stereo Automat			480
Bosco	9x9cm	Roll	RollBox	1902	Aplanat	12			M,Z		170
Bosco II Reflex	9x9cm	Roll	LgSLR	1902	Mars Anastigmat	6.8	135mm				210
Bosco III 9x9	9x9cm	Roll	RollBox	1902	Extra Rap. Aplan.	8			M,Z	A71	170
Bosco III 10x13	10x13cm	Roll	RollBox	1902	Mars Anastigmat	6.8			M,Z		220
Detective Magazine	9x12cm	plate	MagBox	1889						A52	500
Elite	9x18cm	plate	SterMagBox	1900	Periscope				M,Z	A727	460
Elite	9x18cm	plate	SterMagBox	1900	Doppel Anast.				M,Z	A1811	460
Eureka	18x24cm	plate	Tailboard	1908	Extra Rap. Rectil.						320
Excelsior 9x12	9x12cm	plate	Tailboard	1900	Rapid Aplanat	8	150mm				220
Excelsior 13x18	13x18cm	plate	Tailboard	1900	Rapid Aplanat	8	220mm				580
Excelsior 13x18	13x18cm	plate	Tailboard	1900	Ernon	4.5	220mm				580
Excelsior 30x40	30x40cm	plate	Tailboard	1900	Rapid Aplanat	8	550mm				700
Excelsior Stereo	13x18cm	plate	SterTail	1900	Mars Anastigmat	6.8		St. roller-blind			900
Favorit (stereo) 8x14	8x14cm	plate	StFoldPl	1908	Baldour	8	150mm	Compur			190
Favorit (stereo) 9x18	9x18cm	plate	StFoldPl	1900	Busch Rapid Apl.	8		St. roller-blind			330
Field camera 3¼x4¼"	3¼x4¼"	plate	Field	1900	Wünsche Rectilin.	8					220
Field camera 5x7"	5x7"	plate	Field	1900	Wünsche Rectilin.	8					210
Field camera 10x15"	10x15"	plate	Field	1900	Wünsche Rectilin.	8					220
Field camera 18x24cm	18x24cm	plate	Field	1900	Wünsche Rectilin.	8					260
Folding plate camera	9x12cm	plate	VtFoldPl	1908	Anastigmat	5.5	120mm	Univers	25-100	A183	70
Folding plate camera	13x18cm	plate	VtFoldPl	1908	Doppel Anast.	4.6	210mm	Compound	1-200	A1393	100
Fulgar Film-camera	6x9cm	120	VtFoldRo	1903	meniscus				M,Z		350
Furror	9x12cm	plate	Tailboard	1902	Achromat			rotary		A2945	450
Julia	8x8cm	Roll	FoldRo	1899	Achromat				M,Z		160
Juwel	9x12cm	plate	MagBox	1895	Achromat	12			M,Z		110
Knox	9x12cm	plate	FoldPl	1906	Achromat				M,Z		470
Kobold	9x12cm	plate	MagBox	1904	Achromat				M,Z	HK64	50
Kolibri	6x6cm	120	HzFoldRo	1904	meniscus				M,Z	HK201	170
Legion	9x12cm	plate	MagBox	1905	Aplanat	12			M,Z	HK65	90
Lilli	6x9cm	120	PlateBox	1903							140
Lola	9x12cm	plate	StrutPl	1905	Anastigmat	6.8	120mm		M,Z		420
Lola Stereo	9x18cm	plate	SterStrut	1905	Anastigmat	7.7	90mm		M,Z		510
Mars 99	9x12cm	plate	PlateBox	1895	Aplanat	12	150mm	rotary		A70	350
Mars Detektiv (leather)	3¼x4¼"	plate	MagBox	1895	Aplanat	8	130mm	rotary			340

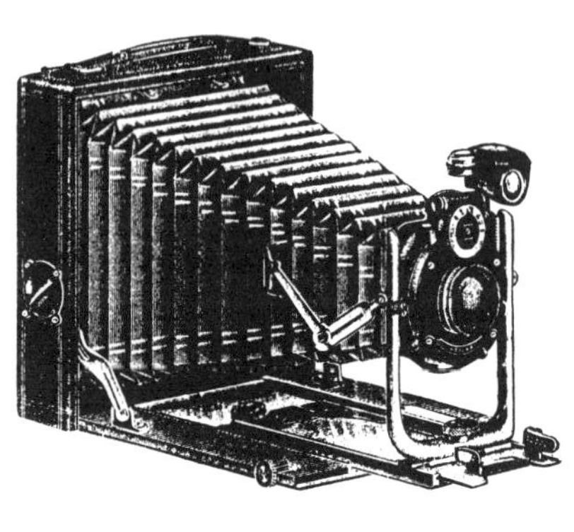

Afpi (square)

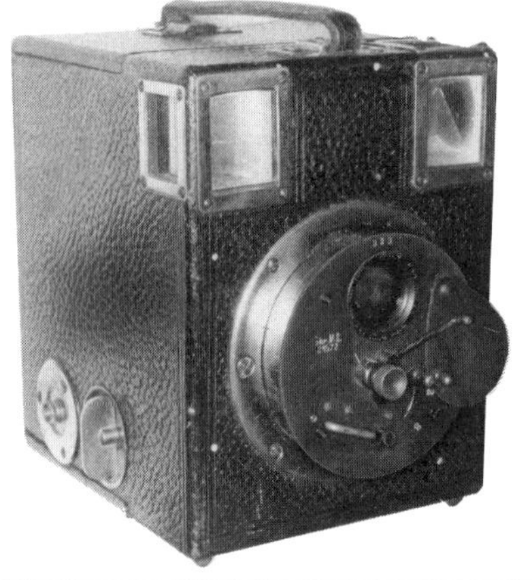

Bosco III

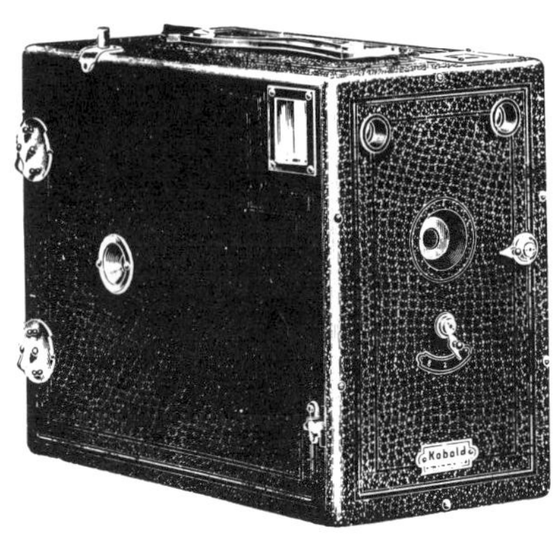

Kobold

MODEL	FORMAT	FILM	TYPE	Year	LENS	Apert	FL	SHUTTER	SPEEDS	ILLUS	U.S.$
Mars Detektiv (wood)	6.5x9cm	plate	MagBox	1893	Aplanat			rotary			470
Mars Detektiv (wood)	8x10cm	plate	MagBox	1900	Achromat			rotary		A69	390
Mars Detektiv (wood)	3¼x4¼"	plate	MagBox	1893	Aplanat	8	130mm	rotary		A1302	580
Mars Detektiv (wood)	4¼x6½"	plate	MagBox	1893	Aplanat			rotary		HK39	700
Mars Detectiv-Stereoskop	8.5x17cm	plate	SterMagBox	1897	Aplanat			rotary			1200
Meteor	13x18cm	plate	Tailboard	1895	various			various			220
Minimal	9x12cm	plate	VtFoldPl	1906	Rapid Aplanat	8	150mm	Presto	1-100		100
Nero 1a	6.5x9cm	plate	MagBox	1900							90
Nixe 6x9	6x9cm	120	VtFoldRo	1900	Mars Anastigmat	6.8	105mm	Auto	I,B,T	A1451	70
Nixe 8x10.5	8x10.5cm	124	VtFoldRo	1900	Aplanat			Univers	25-100		100
Nixe 8x10.5	8x10.5cm	124	VtFoldRo	1900	Imagonal	6		Compound	1-250		100
Nixe-Minimal	8x10.5cm	plate	VtFoldPl	1906	Anastigmat	6		Koilos	1-300	A374	100
Nova	9x12cm	plate	MagBox	1907	Extra Rap. Aplan.	8			M,Z	HK68	120
Nymphe	6x9cm	120	StrutRo	1904	Anastigmat	6.8			M,Z		140
Nymphe III	9x9cm	Roll	StrutRo	1904	Aplanat				M,Z	A1443	140
Postage stamp camera	24x30mm	plate	MultiLens	1907	Achromat					A3228	2300
Reicka 8x11	8x11cm	plate	VtFoldPl	1906	Rapid Rectilinear			Koilos	1-300		80
Reicka 9x12	9x12cm	plate	VtFoldPl	1906	Rod. Heligonal	5.4	120mm	Koilos	1-300		70
Reicka 13x18	13x18cm	plate	VtFoldPl	1906	Goerz Dagor	6.8	180mm	Koilos	1-300		180
Reicka Stereo	10x15cm	plate	StFoldPl	1908	Goerz Dagor	6.8		Stereo Koilos	1-300		160
Spiegel-Reflex-Camera	9x12cm	plate	LgSLR	1907	Goerz Celor	4.6	135mm				220
Sport	8.5x17cm	plate	SterBox	1895	Antiplanat			Stereo sector		A1808	1400
Stereo camera	13x18cm	plate	SterField	1900	Velostigmat	6.8	200mm	Automatic	25-100	A2672	330
Transvaal	13x18cm	plate	Tailboard	1900	various			various			140
Tropica	9x12cm	plate	FoldPl	1908	Goerz Celor	4.6	135mm				460
Victoria	9x12cm	plate	MagBox	1900	Achromat				M,Z		70
Victrix	9x12cm	plate	StrutPl	1906	Tessar	6.3	135mm	focal plane		HK134	180
Victrix	9x12cm	plate	StrutPl	1906	Mars Anastigmat	6.8	135mm	focal plane		HK134	150
Victrix Stereo	6x13cm	plate	SterStrut	1906	Extra Rap. Aplan.	8		focal plane		HK471	560
...WZFO - Warsaw, Poland											
Druh	6x6cm	120	BakeliteRoll	1950	Bilar	8	65mm		B,M	Mc431	20
Fenix I	24x36mm	35mm	35VF	1960	Euktar		50mm				20
Fenix II	24x36mm	35mm	35RF	1962	Euktar		50mm				70
Noco-Flex	6x6cm	120	TLR	1970						Mc431	70
Start	6x6cm	120	TLR	1956	Euktar	4.5	75mm		B,10-200	Mc431	30
...XIBEI OPTICAL INSTRUMENT FACTORY - China											
Huashan DF-S	24x36mm	35mm	35SLR	1980	Jing Tou	2.8	40mm			Mc431	50
...YALE CAMERA CO.											
Yale Camera	5x5cm	plate	PlateBox	1910							110
...YAMAMOTO CAMERA CO.											
Kinka Hand Camera	6.5x9cm	plate	VtFoldPl	1933	Maro Anast.	6.3	105mm	Maro	25-150		110
Semi Kinka	4.5x6cm	120	VtFoldRo	1938	Ceronar Anast.	4.5	75mm	Felix	25-150		100

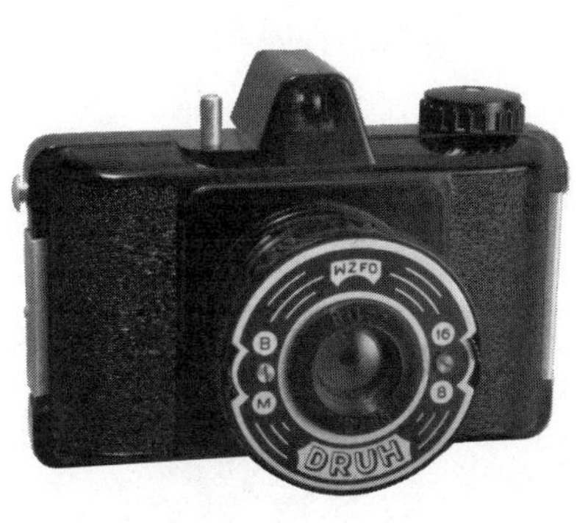

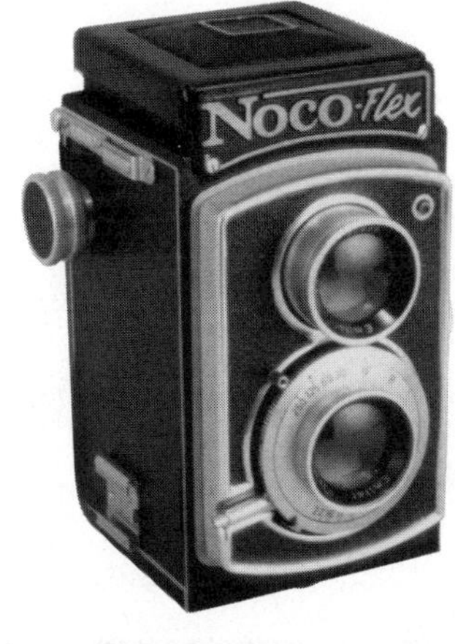

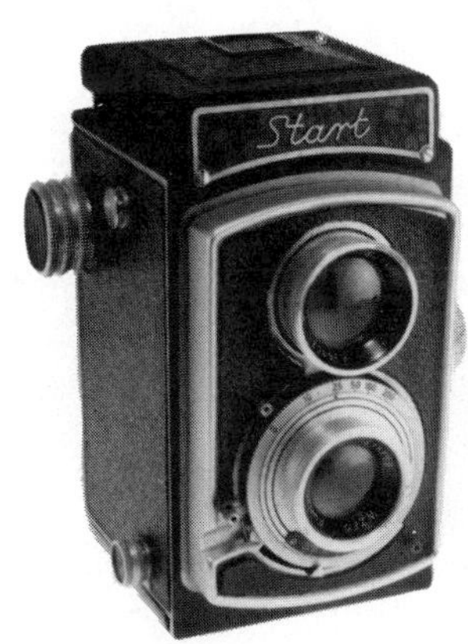

WZFO Druh **WZFO Noco-Flex** **WZFO Start**

MODEL	FORMAT	FILM	TYPE	Year	LENS	Apert	FL	SHUTTER	SPEEDS	ILLUS	U.S.$
...YAMATO KOKI KOGYO CO. LTD., YAMATO CAMERA INDUSTRY CO. LTD. - Tokyo											
Alpina M35	24x36mm	35mm	35RF	1957	Luminor	2.8	45mm	Synchro	10-300		40
Atlas 35	24x36mm	35mm	35VF	1959	Color Luna	3.5	45mm	Synchro	B,25-300	Mc432	50
Atlas Deluxe	24x36mm	35mm	35VF		Luna	2.8	45mm				50
Barclay	24x36mm	35mm	35VF		Luminor Anast.	3.5	45mm			Mc432	40
Bonny Six	6x6cm	120	FoldRo		Bonny Anast.	4.5	75mm				50
Hilka	24x36mm	35mm	35VF		Luminor Anast.	3.5	45mm	Synchro	B,25-300	Mc432	40
Konair Ruby	24x36mm	35mm	35RF	1955	Konair	3.5	45mm	Synchro	10-300	Mc432	30
Lycon M3	24x36mm	35mm	35RF	1957	Lycon Anastigmat	2.8	45mm	Leaf	B,10-300	Mc432	90
Mini Electro 35 Automatic	24x36mm	35mm	35VF		Luminor	3.5	40mm			Mc432	50
Minon 35	24x24mm	Bolta	35VF	1949	Eira Anastigmat	3.5	40mm		25-100		500
Minox Six II	6x6cm	120	FoldRo	1950	Minon Anastigmat	3.5	75mm	TSK	1-200,B		90
Pal Jr.	24x36mm	35mm	35VF	1960	Yamanon	3.5	45mm			Mc432	40
Pal M4	24x36mm	35mm	35RF		Luminor	2.8	45mm	Synchro	10-300		60
Palmat Automatic	24x36mm	35mm	35VF		Luminor		40mm			Mc432	50
Pax (I)	24x36mm	35mm	35RF	1952	Magino	4.5	40mm	Silver-C	25-200	Mc432	70
Pax Golden View	24x36mm	35mm	35RF		Luminor Anast.	3.5	45mm	Synchro	10-300		300
Pax M2	24x36mm	35mm	35RF	1956	Luminor	3.5	45mm	Synchro	10-300	Mc432	60
Pax M3	24x36mm	35mm	35RF	1957	Lycon	2.8	45mm	Synchro	10-300		50
Pax M4	24x36mm	35mm	35RF	1958	Luminor	2.8	45mm	Synchro	10-300		70
Pax Ruby	24x36mm	35mm	35RF	1958	Color Luna	3.5	45mm	Synchro	10-300		50
Pax Sunscope	24x36mm	35mm	35RF	1958	Color Luna	3.5	45mm	Synchro	10-300		40
Rex Kaysons	24x36mm	35mm	35RF			3.5	45mm	Compur	1-300	Mc433	50
Ricsor	24x36mm	35mm	35RF		Colour Luna	2.8	45mm	Synchro	10-300	Mc433	50
Rippa	24x36mm	35mm	35VF	1950	Color-Luna	3.5	45mm		25-300	Mc433	40
Rippaflex	6x6cm	120	TLR	1950	Tri-Lausar	3.5	80mm	Rectus			80
Simflex 35	24x36mm	35mm	35VF	1962	Luminor Anast.	3.5	45mm	Leaf	B,25-300	Mc433	50
Skymaster	24x36mm	35mm	35RF		Luminor Anast.	2.8	45mm	Synchro	10-300	Mc433	50
Starlite	24x36mm	35mm	35VF	1960	Luminar	3.5	45mm		25-300,B	Mc433	30
Tac Deluxe	24x36mm	35mm	35VF		Luminar	3.5	45mm	Synchro	10-300		50
...YASHICA - Japan											
Yashica 12	6x6cm	120	TLR	1967	Yashinon	3.5	80mm		1-500		80
Yashica 24	6x6cm	220	TLR	1966	Yashinon	3.5	80mm		1-500		120
Yashica 35	24x36mm	35mm	35VF	1959	Yashinon	2.8	50mm				50
Yashica 35 EE	24x36mm	35mm	35VF	1962	Yashinon	1.9	45mm	Copal-SVA	1-500		90
Yashica 35 J	24x36mm	35mm	35RF	1960	Yashinon	2.8	45mm		25-300		70
Yashica 35 ME	24x36mm	35mm	35VF	1974							50
Yashica 35 ME-S	24x36mm	35mm	35VF	1976		2.8			650		50
Yashica 35 MF	24x36mm	35mm	35VF	1977	Yashica	2.8	38mm	programmed	60-250		50
Yashica 35 YL	24x36mm	35mm	35RF	1960							50
Yashica 44 (black)	4x4cm	127	TLR	1958	Yashikor	3.5	60mm	Copal-SV	1-500,B	Mc433	100
Yashica 44 (brown)	4x4cm	127	TLR	1958	Yashikor	3.5	60mm	Copal-SV	1-500,B	Mc433	80

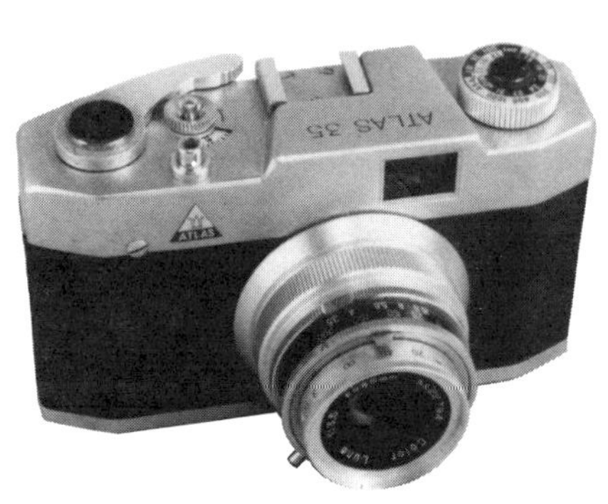

Yamato Atlas 35

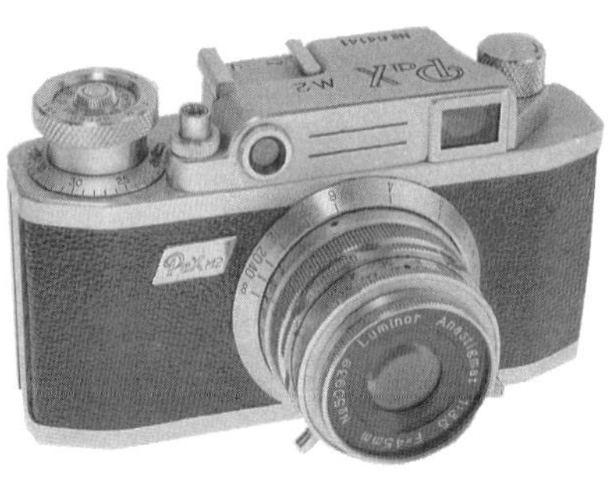

Yamato Pax M2

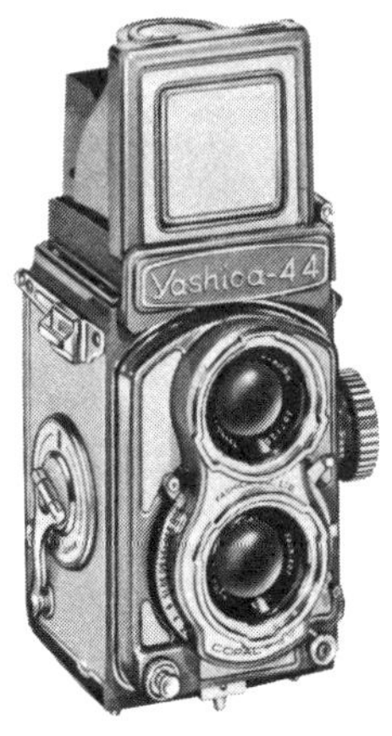

Yashica 44

MODEL	FORMAT	FILM	TYPE	Year	LENS	Apert	FL	SHUTTER	SPEEDS	ILLUS	U.S.$
Yashica 44 (grey)	4x4cm	127	TLR	1958	Yashikor	3.5	60mm	Copal-SV	1-500,B		100
Yashica 44 (lavender)	4x4cm	127	TLR	1958	Yashikor	3.5	60mm	Copal-SV	1-500,B		120
Yashica 44A (black)	4x4cm	127	TLR	1959	Yashikor	3.5	60mm	Copal	25-300,B	Mc433	70
Yashica 44A (blue)	4x4cm	127	TLR	1959	Yashikor	3.5	60mm	Copal	25-300,B		70
Yashica 44A (grey)	4x4cm	127	TLR	1959	Yashikor	3.5	60mm	Copal	25-300,B		100
Yashica 44A (rose)	4x4cm	127	TLR	1959	Yashikor	3.5	60mm	Copal	25-300,B		100
Yashica 44LM (black)	4x4cm	127	TLR	1959	Yashinon	3.5	60mm	Copal-SV	1-500,B	Mc433	70
Yashica 44LM (brown)	4x4cm	127	TLR	1959	Yashinon	3.5	60mm	Copal-SV	1-500,B		70
Yashica 44LM (grey)	4x4cm	127	TLR	1959	Yashinon	3.5	60mm	Copal-SV	1-500,B	A1737	100
Yashica 72E	18x24mm	35mm	35Half	1962	Yashinon	2.8	28mm	Copal-X	8-250		80
107 Multi Program body	24x36mm	35mm	35SLR	1989	body only	---	---	focal plane	16-2000		120
107 Multi Program+50/1.9	24x36mm	35mm	35SLR	1989	Yashica ML	1.9	50mm	focal plane	16-2000		160
108 Multi Program body	24x36mm	35mm	35SLR	1990	body only	---	---	focal plane	16-2000		150
108 Multi Program+35-70	24x36mm	35mm	35SLR	1990	Yashica MC	3.5-4.5	35-70	focal plane	16-2000		200
Yashica 200 AF body	24x36mm	35mm	35AFSLR	1987	body only	---	---	focal plane	8-2000		180
Yashica 200 AF + 50/1.8	24x36mm	35mm	35AFSLR	1987	AF	1.8	50mm	focal plane	8-2000		270
Yashica 230 AF body	24x36mm	35mm	35AFSLR	1987	body only	---	---	focal plane	16-2000		160
Yashica 230 AF + 28-85	24x36mm	35mm	35AFSLR	1987	AF Zoom	3.5-4.5	28-85	focal plane	16-2000		280
Yash. 230 AF Super body	24x36mm	35mm	35AFSLR	1992	body only	---	---	focal plane	8-2000		160
Y. 230 AF Super + 28-70	24x36mm	35mm	35AFSLR	1992	AF Zoom	3.5-4.5	28-70	focal plane	8-2000		270
Yashica 300 AF body	24x36mm	35mm	35AFSLR	1994	body only	---	---	focal plane	8-2000		210
Yashica 300 AF + 28-70	24x36mm	35mm	35AFSLR	1994	AF Zoom	3.5-4.5	28-70	focal plane	8-2000		370
Yashica 635	6x6/24x36	120	TLR	1958	Yashikor	3.5	80mm	Copal-MXV	1-500,B		110
Yashica 635 (35mm kit)	6x6/24x36	120	TLR	1958	Yashikor	3.5	80mm	Copal-MXV	1-500,B		200
Yashica A (black)	6x6cm	120	TLR	1959	Yashikor	3.5	80mm	Copal	25-300	Mc433	50
Yashica A (grey)	6x6cm	120	TLR	1959	Yashikor	3.5	80mm	Copal	25-300		80
Yashica A III	6x6cm	120	TLR	1959	Yashinon	3.5	80mm				70
Yashica AF-J	24x36mm	35mm	35AF	1988		3.5	32mm	programmed			70
Yashica AF-J databack	24x36mm	35mm	35AF	1990		3.5	32mm	programmed			70
Yashica AF-J2	24x36mm	35mm	35AF	1990		3.5	32mm	programmed			50
Yashica AF-J2 databack	24x36mm	35mm	35AF	1990		3.5	32mm	programmed			60
Yashica AF-J3	24x36mm	35mm	35AF	1993	Yashica	3.9	33mm	programmed			60
Yashica AF-J3 databack	24x36mm	35mm	35AF	1993	Yashica	3.9	33mm	programmed			70
Yashica AFM-II	24x36mm	35mm	35AF	1986		3.5	35mm	programmed	30-700		50
Yashica Atoron	8x11mm	9.5mm	Submin	1965	Yashinon	2.8	18mm		45-250,B	Mc434	50
Yashica Atoron Electro	8x11mm	9.5mm	Submin	1970	Yashinon DX	2.8	18mm	Automatic	8-350	Mc434	50
Yashica Auto	6x6cm	120	TLR	1959	Yashinon	3.5	80mm	Copal-MXV	1-500		70
Yashica Auto Focus	24x36mm	35mm	35AF	1983	Yashica	2.8	38mm	programmed	60-360		100
Yashica Auto Focus Motor	24x36mm	35mm	35AF	1983	Yashica	2.8	38mm	programmed	8-500		100
Auto Focus Motor II	24x36mm	35mm	35AF	1987		3.5	35mm	programmed	30-700		90
Auto Focus Motor IID	24x36mm	35mm	35AF	1987		3.5	35mm	programmed	30-700		110
Auto Focus Motor-D	24x36mm	35mm	35AF	1983	Yashica	2.8	38mm	programmed	8-500		120

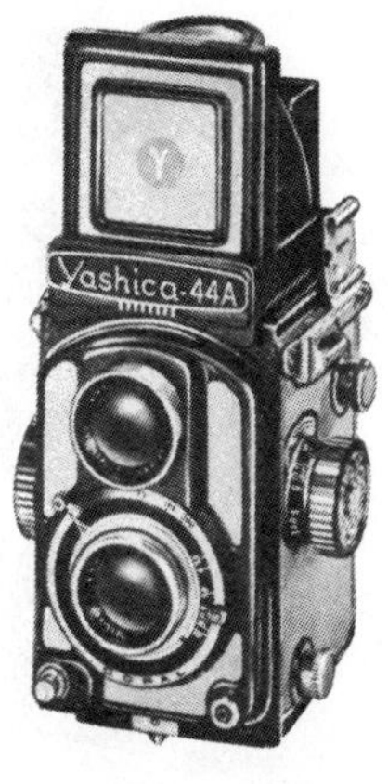

Yashica 44A

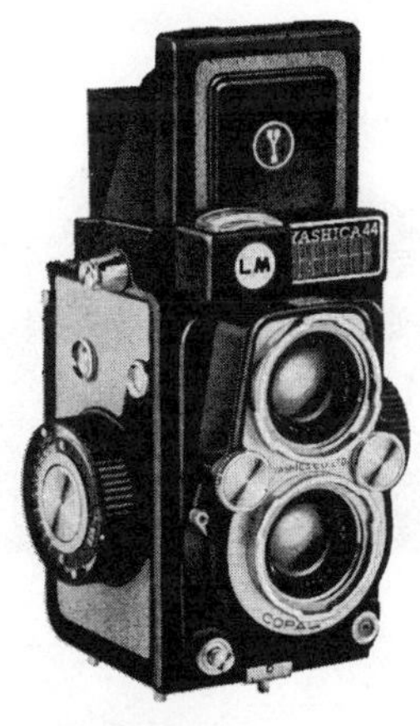

Yashica 44LM

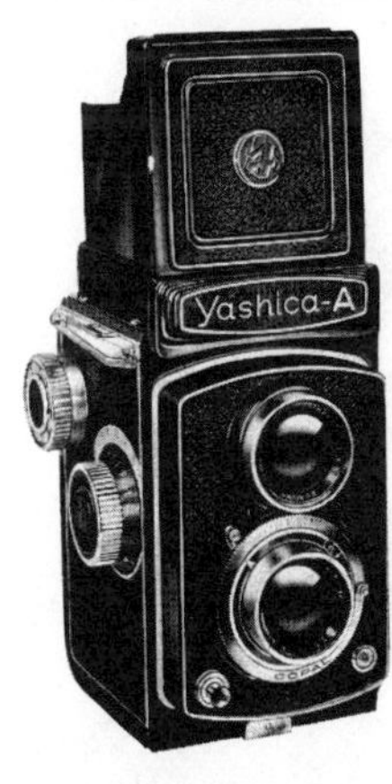

Yashica A

MODEL	FORMAT	FILM	TYPE	Year	LENS	Apert	FL	SHUTTER	SPEEDS	ILLUS	U.S.$
Yashica Auto Focus S	24x36mm	35mm	35AF	1983	Yashica	2.8	38mm	programmed	60-360		80
Yashica AW Mini	24x36mm	35mm	35AW-AF	1991		3.5	32mm	programmed	120-600		60
Yashica C	6x6cm	120	TLR	1958	Yashikor	3.5	80mm	Copal MX	1-300	Mc434	70
Contax 137 MA Qz body	24x36mm	35mm	35SLR	1983	body only	---	---	focal plane	11-1000		240
---137 MA Quartz + 50/1.4	24x36mm	35mm	35SLR	1983	Planar T*	1.4	50mm	focal plane	11-1000		310
Contax 137 MD Qz body	24x36mm	35mm	35SLR	1979	body only	---	---	focal plane	11-1000		210
---137 MD Quartz + 50/1.4	24x36mm	35mm	35SLR	1979	Planar T*	1.4	50mm	focal plane	11-1000	A1691	310
Contax 139 Quartz body	24x36mm	35mm	35SLR	1978	body only	---	---	focal plane	11-1000		170
Contax 139 Quartz + 50/1.7	24x36mm	35mm	35SLR	1978	Planar T*	1.7	50mm	focal plane	11-1000		280
Contax 159 MM body	24x36mm	35mm	35SLR	1985	body only	---	---	focal plane	60-4000		260
Contax 159 MM + 50/1.4	24x36mm	35mm	35SLR	1985	Carl Zeiss T*	1.4	50mm	focal plane	60-4000	A3210	330
Contax 167 MT body	24x36mm	35mm	35SLR	1987	body only	---	---	focal plane	16-4000		370
Contax 167 MT + 50/1.4	24x36mm	35mm	35SLR	1987	Carl Zeiss T*	1.4	50mm	focal plane	16-4000		640
Contax G1 body	24x36mm	35mm	35AF	1994	body only	---	---	focal plane	16-2000		1200
Contax G1 + 45/2	24x36mm	35mm	35AF	1994	Planar T*	2	45mm	focal plane	16-2000		1400
Contax Preview	24x36mm	Pola	Instant	1982		1.4	50mm	focal plane	1-1000	A3389	250
Contax RTS body	24x36mm	35mm	35SLR	1975	body only	---	---	focal plane	4-2000		310
Contax RTS + 50/1.4	24x36mm	35mm	35SLR	1975	Planar	1.4	50mm	focal plane	4-2000	A1690	360
Contax RTS (Gold)	24x36mm	35mm	35SLR	1980	Planar	1.4	50mm	focal plane	4-2000		2300
Contax RTS II body	24x36mm	35mm	35SLR	1982	body only	---	---	focal plane	16-2000		510
Contax RTS II + 50/1.4	24x36mm	35mm	35SLR	1982	Planar	1.4	50mm	focal plane	16-2000		630
Contax RTS II Quartz body	24x36mm	35mm	35SLR	1983	body only	---	---	focal plane	16-2000		500
---RTS II Quartz + 50/1.4	24x36mm	35mm	35SLR	1983	Carl Zeiss T*	1.4	50mm	focal plane	16-2000		540
Contax RTS III body	24x36mm	35mm	35SLR	1991	body only	---	---	focal plane	32-8000		1500
Contax RTS III + 50/1.4	24x36mm	35mm	35SLR	1991	Carl Zeiss T*	1.4	50mm	focal plane	32-8000		1900
Contax RX body	24x36mm	35mm	35SLR	1994	body only	---	---	focal plane	16-4000		1000
Contax RX + 50/1.4	24x36mm	35mm	35SLR	1994	Carl Zeiss T*	1.4	50mm	focal plane	16-4000		1400
Contax S2 body	24x36mm	35mm	35SLR	1993	body only	---	---	focal plane	1-4000		800
Contax S2 + 50/1.4	24x36mm	35mm	35SLR	1993	Planar T*	1.4	50mm	focal plane	1-4000		1000
Contax S2b body	24x36mm	35mm	35SLR	1993	body only	---	---	focal plane	1-4000		900
Contax S2b + 50/1.4	24x36mm	35mm	35SLR	1993	Carl Zeiss T*	1.4	50mm	focal plane	1-4000		900
Contax ST body	24x36mm	35mm	35SLR	1993	body only	---	---	focal plane	16-6000		1000
Contax ST + 50/1.4	24x36mm	35mm	35SLR	1993	Planar T*	1.4	50mm	focal plane	16-6000		1100
Contax T (black)	24x36mm	35mm	35RF	1985	Sonnar T*	2.8	38mm	programmed	8-500		670
Contax T (chrome)	24x36mm	35mm	35RF	1985	Sonnar T*	2.8	38mm	programmed	8-500	A3498	650
Contax T2 (black)	24x36mm	35mm	35AF	1992	Sonnar T*	2.8	38mm	programmed	1-500		800
Contax T2 (gold)	24x36mm	35mm	35AF	1992	Sonnar T*	2.8	38mm	programmed	1-500		1400
Contax T2 (silver)	24x36mm	35mm	35AF	1991	Sonnar T*	2.8	38mm	programmed	1-500		700
Contax T2 Data (black)	24x36mm	35mm	35AF	1991	Sonnar T*	2.8	38mm	programmed	1-500		900
Contax T2 Data (silver)	24x36mm	35mm	35AF	1991	Sonnar T*	2.8	38mm	programmed	1-500		900
Contax T VS	24x36mm	35mm	35AF	1994	Vario Sonnar T*	3.5-6.5	28-56	programmed	16-700		1200
Yashica D	6x6cm	120	TLR	1958	Yashikor	3.5	80mm	Copal MXV	500	Mc434	100

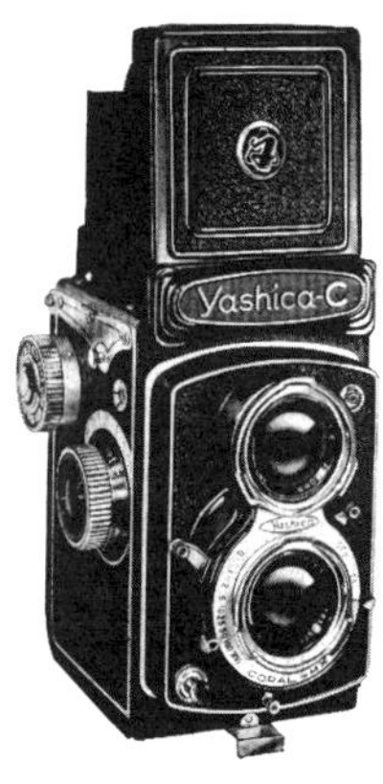

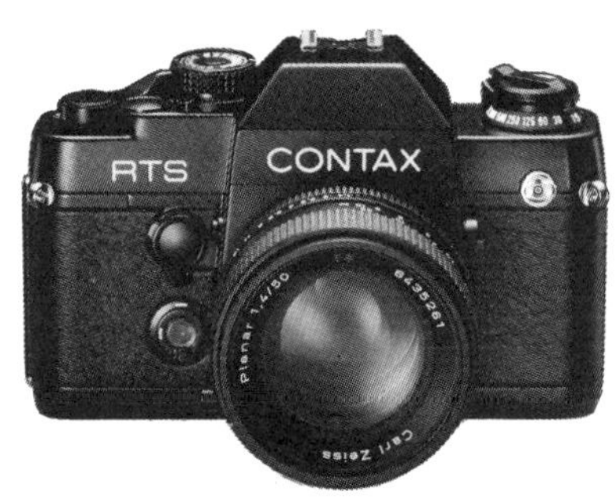

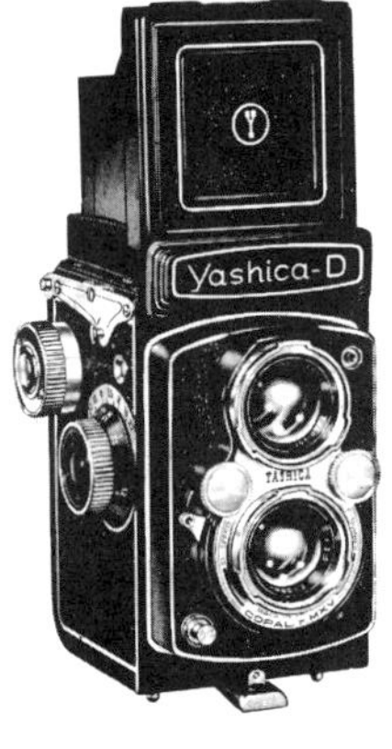

Yashica C | **Yashica Contax RTS II Quartz** | **Yashica D**

MODEL	FORMAT	FILM	TYPE	Year	LENS	Apert	FL	SHUTTER	SPEEDS	ILLUS	U.S.$
Yashica Dental-Eye II	24x36mm	35mm	35SLR	1991	Macro	4	100mm	focal plane	16-2000		900
Yashica DF-10	24x36mm	35mm	35BiFocal	1988		5.6/8.5	35/55		1/60, 125		60
Yashica DF-10-S	24x36mm	35mm	35BiFocal	1988		5.6/8.5	35/55		1/60, 125		50
Yashica DF-100 AF	24x36mm	35mm	35AF-BiF	1990		5.6/8.5	35/55		1/60, 125		60
Yashica DF-100 AF databac	24x36mm	35mm	35AF-BiF	1990		5.6/8.5	35/55		1/60, 125		70
Diary	24x36mm	35mm	35VF	1978	Yashica	2.8	38mm	programmed	60-360		80
Yashica E	6x6cm	120	TLR	1964	Yashinon	3.5	80mm	Yashica	1/60		90
Yashica E-Flash	6x6cm	120	TLR	1962	Yashinon	3.5	80mm	Yashica	1/60		100
Yashica EE	24x36mm	35mm	35VF	1962	Yashinon	1.9	45mm	Copal-SVA	1-500, MX		50
Electro 35 (original)	24x36mm	35mm	35RF	1966	Yashinon-GX	1.7	45mm	Copal	30-500		50
Electro 35 AF-mini	24x36mm	35mm	35AF	1990		4.5	34mm	programmed	2-1/360		70
Elec. 35 AF-mini databack	24x36mm	35mm	35AF	1990		4.5	34mm	programmed	2-1/360		80
Electro 35 CC	24x36mm	35mm	35RF	1971	Yashinon	1.8	35mm	Auto	8-250		50
Electro 35 FC	24x36mm	35mm	35RF	1974	Yashinon	2.8	40mm	focal plane	4-1000		40
Electro 35 G	24x36mm	35mm	35RF	1970	Yashinon	1.7	45mm				50
Electro 35 GL	24x36mm	35mm	35RF	1975	Yashinon	1.7	40mm	Auto	4-500		50
Electro 35 GS	24x36mm	35mm	35RF	1969	Yashinon	1.7	45mm	Auto	30-500		50
Electro 35 GSN	24x36mm	35mm	35RF	1983	Yashinon	1.7	45mm	Auto	30-500	Mc434	60
Electro 35 GT	24x36mm	35mm	35RF	1970	Yashinon	1.7	45mm	Copal	30-500		100
Electro 35 GTN	24x36mm	35mm	35RF	1983	Yashinon	1.7	45mm	Copal	30-500		80
Electro 35 GTS	24x36mm	35mm	35RF	1970							140
Electro 35 GX	24x36mm	35mm	35RF	1978	Yashinon	1.7	45mm				80
Electro 35 MC	24x36mm	35mm	35RF	1973	Yashinon	2.8	40mm	Auto	30-500		50
Electro AX	24x36mm	35mm	35SLR	1973	Auto Yashinon	1.4	50mm	focal plane	8-1000		70
Electro Half (black)	18x24mm	35mm	35Half	1966	Yashinon	1.7			2-1/500		70
Electro Half (chrome)	18x24mm	35mm	35Half	1966	Yashinon	1.7			2-1/500		70
Electro M5	24x36mm	35mm	35VF	1966	Yashinon	2.8	45mm		8-1000		50
Electro Professional	24x36mm	35mm	35RF	1969	Yashinon	1.7	45mm	Copal	30-500		50
Electro X	24x36mm	35mm	35SLR	1960	Yashinon			focal plane			60
FR body	24x36mm	35mm	35SLR	1976	body only	---	---	focal plane	1-1000		100
FR + 50/1.7	24x36mm	35mm	35SLR	1976	Auto Yashinon	1.7	50mm	focal plane	1-1000		100
FR I body	24x36mm	35mm	35SLR	1978	body only	---	---	focal plane	4-1000		100
FR I + 50/1.7	24x36mm	35mm	35SLR	1978	Auto Yashinon	1.7	50mm	focal plane	4-1000		120
FR II body	24x36mm	35mm	35SLR	1978	body only	---	---	focal plane	4-1000		100
FR II + 50/1.9	24x36mm	35mm	35SLR	1978	Auto Yashinon	1.9	50mm	focal plane	4-1000		120
FX-1 body	24x36mm	35mm	35SLR	1975	body only	---	---	focal plane	2-1000		80
FX-1 + 50/1.4	24x36mm	35mm	35SLR	1975	Auto Yashinon	1.4	50mm	focal plane	2-1000		100
FX-2 body	24x36mm	35mm	35SLR	1976	body only	---	---	focal plane	1-1000		80
FX-2 + 50/1.9	24x36mm	35mm	35SLR	1976	Auto Yashinon	1.9	50mm	focal plane	1-1000		100
FX-3 body	24x36mm	35mm	35SLR	1983	body only	---	---	focal plane	1-1000		80
FX-3 + 50/2	24x36mm	35mm	35SLR	1983	Yashica ML	2	50mm	focal plane	1-1000		120
FX-3 Super body	24x36mm	35mm	35SLR	1985	body only	---	---	focal plane	1-1000		80

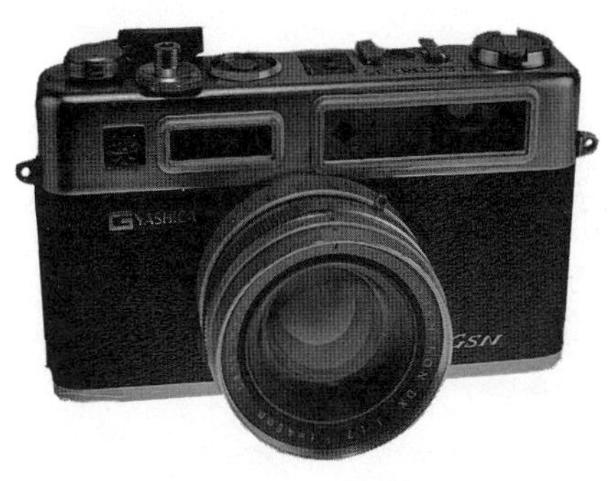

Yashica Electro 35 GSN

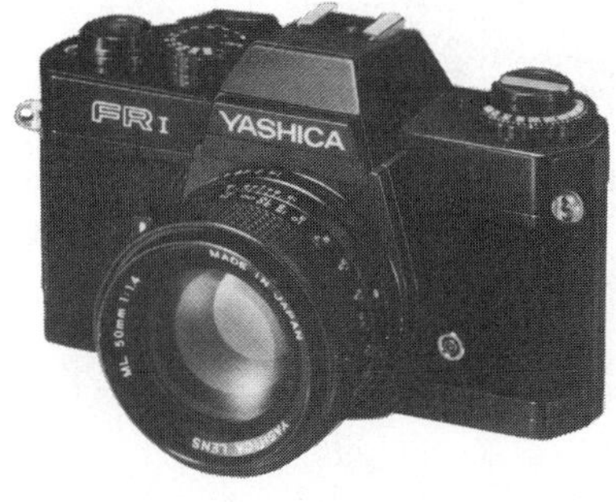

Yashica FR I

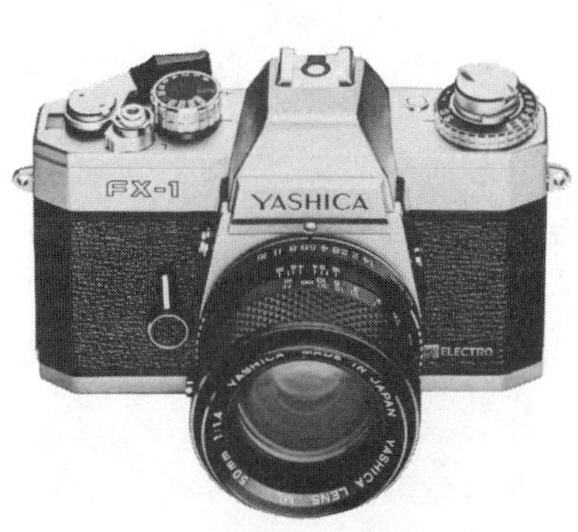

Yashica FX-1

MODEL	FORMAT	FILM	TYPE	Year	LENS	Apert	FL	SHUTTER	SPEEDS	ILLUS	U.S.$
FX-3 Super + 50/2	24x36mm	35mm	35SLR	1985	Carl Zeiss T*	2	50mm	focal plane	1-1000		110
FX-3 Super 2000 body	24x36mm	35mm	35SLR	1987	body only	---	---	focal plane	1-2000		120
FX-3 Super 2000 + 50/1.9	24x36mm	35mm	35SLR	1987	Yashica ML	1.9	50mm	focal plane	1-2000		130
FX-7 body	24x36mm	35mm	35SLR	1983	body only	---	---	focal plane	1-1000		70
FX-7 + 50/2	24x36mm	35mm	35SLR	1983	Yashica ML	2	50mm	focal plane	1-1000		110
FX-7 Super body	24x36mm	35mm	35SLR	1985	body only	---	---	focal plane	1-1000		90
FX-7 Super + 50/2	24x36mm	35mm	35SLR	1985	Carl Zeiss T*	2	50mm	focal plane	1-1000		100
FX-70 body	24x36mm	35mm	35SLR	1982	body only	---	---	focal plane	11-1000		100
FX-70 + 50/1.4	24x36mm	35mm	35SLR	1982	Yashica ML	1.4	50mm	focal plane	11-1000		140
FX-103 Program body	24x36mm	35mm	35SLR	1986	body only	---	---	focal plane	16-1000		110
FX-103 Program + 50/1.9	24x36mm	35mm	35SLR	1986	Yashica ML	1.9	50mm	focal plane	16-1000		130
FX-A body	24x36mm	35mm	35SLR	1982	body only	---	---	focal plane	11-1000		130
FX-A + 50/1.7	24x36mm	35mm	35SLR	1982	Planar	1.7	50mm	focal plane	11-1000		140
FX-D Quartz (black) body	24x36mm	35mm	35SLR	1983	body only	---	---	focal plane	11-1000	A3211	100
FX-D Qrtz (black) + 50/1.4	24x36mm	35mm	35SLR	1983	Yashica ML	1.4	50mm	focal plane	11-1000		140
FX-D Qrtz (chrome) body	24x36mm	35mm	35SLR	1983	body only	---	---	focal plane	11-1000		110
FX-D Q. (chrome) + 50/1.4	24x36mm	35mm	35SLR	1983	Yashica ML	1.4	50mm	focal plane	11-1000		160
Yashica Half 1.4	18x24mm	35mm	35Half	1966	Yashinon	1.4	32mm	programmed	15-500		60
Yashica Half 1.7	18x24mm	35mm	35Half	1965	Yashinon	1.7	32mm	programmed	30-800		50
Yashica Half 17 EE Rapid	18x24mm	Rapid	35Half	1965	Yashinon	1.7	32mm	programmed	30-800		50
Yashica Half 17 Rapid	18x24mm	Rapid	35Half	1965	Yashinon	1.7	32mm	programmed	30-800	A2147	40
IC 5000E	24x36mm	35mm	35VF	1968	Yashinon	1.8	45mm				20
J-3	24x36mm	35mm	35SLR	1963	Auto Yashinon	2	50mm	focal plane	2-500		70
J-4	24x36mm	35mm	35SLR	1963	Auto Yashinon	2	50mm	focal plane	2-500		60
J-5	24x36mm	35mm	35SLR	1964	Auto Yashinon	1.8	55mm	focal plane	2-1000	Mc434	70
J-7	24x36mm	35mm	35SLR	1966	Auto Yashinon	1.7	50mm	focal plane	2-1000		70
J-mini	24x36mm	35mm	35VF	1991		3.5	32mm		1/60, 125		50
J-mini databack	24x36mm	35mm	35VF	1991		3.5	32mm		1/60, 125		60
J-mini Super	24x36mm	35mm	35VF	1994	Yashica	3.5	32mm	programmed	60-200		70
J-mini Super Data	24x36mm	35mm	35VF	1994	Yashica	3.5	32mm	programmed	60-200		70
J-P	24x36mm	35mm	35SLR	1964	Yashinon	2	50mm	focal plane	2-500		50
L AF	24x36mm	35mm	35AF	1987		3.5	32mm	programmed	30-450		90
L AF-D	24x36mm	35mm	35AF	1987		3.5	32mm	programmed	30-450		100
Yashica LM	6x6cm	120	TLR	1957	Yashikor	3.5	80mm	Synchro	1-300		70
Lynx 14	24x36mm	35mm	35RF	1965	Yashinon	1.4	45mm	focal plane	1-1000		70
Lynx 14 E	24x36mm	35mm	35RF	1969	Yashinon	1.4	45mm	focal plane	1-500		80
Lynx 1000	24x36mm	35mm	35RF	1960	Yashinon	1.8	45mm	focal plane	1-1000		50
Lynx 5000	24x36mm	35mm	35RF	1968	Yashinon	1.8	45mm	focal plane	1-1000		50
Lynx 5000 E	24x36mm	35mm	35RF	1968	Yashinon	1.8	45mm	focal plane	1-1000		50
ME-1	24x36mm	35mm	35VF	1983	Yashica	2.8	38mm	programmed	60-360		30
ME-1 Data	24x36mm	35mm	35VF	1978	Yashica	2.8	38mm	programmed	60-360		40
MF-1	24x36mm	35mm	35VF	1983	Yashica	2.8	38mm	programmed	60-360		30

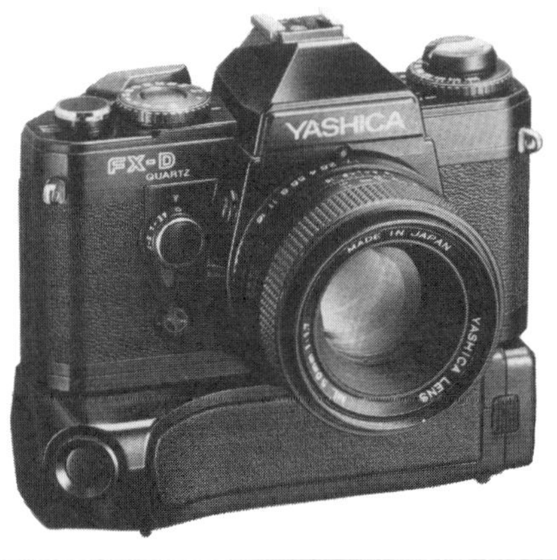

Yashica FX-D Quartz

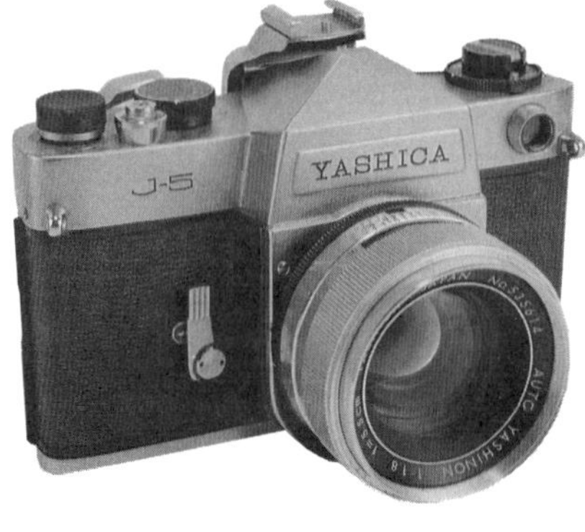

Yashica J-5

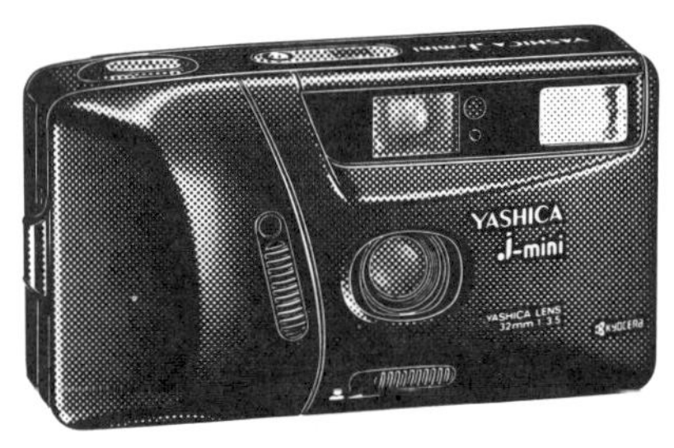

Yashica J-mini

MODEL	FORMAT	FILM	TYPE	Year	LENS	Apert	FL	SHUTTER	SPEEDS	ILLUS	U.S.$
MF-2	24x36mm	35mm	35VF	1983		4	38mm		1/125		50
MF-2 Super	24x36mm	35mm	35VF	1987	Yashica	3.8	38mm		1/125		50
MF-3	24x36mm	35mm	35VF	1987	Yashica	3.5	38mm		1/125		40
MF-3 Super	24x36mm	35mm	35VF	1989	Yashica	3.5	38mm		1/125		40
MG-1	24x36mm	35mm	35RF	1983	Yashinon	2.8	45mm	electronic	2-1/500		50
MG-2	24x36mm	35mm	35VF	1991		4.3	34mm		1/125		30
MG-3	24x36mm	35mm	35VF	1994		4.5	34mm		1/125		30
Microtec Zoom	24x36mm	35mm	35AFZ	1993		3.6-6	28-50	programmed	2-1/330		140
Microtec Zoom 70	24x36mm	35mm	35AFZ	1994		4.5-8.3	35-70	programmed	2-1/300		170
Microtec Zoom 90	24x36mm	35mm	35AFZ	1994	Yashica	4-9	38-90	programmed	2-1/500		210
Mimy	18x24mm	35mm	35Half	1964	Yashinon	2.8	2.8cm	Auto			40
Mimy S	18x24mm	35mm	35Half	1964	Yashinon	2.8	2.8cm				40
Minimatic C	24x36mm	35mm	35VF	1963	Yashinon	2.8	45mm		30-500		40
Minister	24x36mm	35mm	35RF	1960	Yashinon	2.8	4.5cm	Copal SLV	1-500		20
Minister II	24x36mm	35mm	35RF	1962	Yashinon	2.8	4.5cm	Copal SLV	1-500		30
Minister III	24x36mm	35mm	35RF	1968	Yashinon	2.8	45mm		1-500		30
Minister D	24x36mm	35mm	35RF	1963	Yashinon	2.8	4.5cm	Copal SLV	1-500		30
Minitec AF	24x36mm	35mm	35AF	1993	Yashica	3.5	32mm	programmed			70
Minitec AF Data	24x36mm	35mm	35AF	1993	Yashica	3.5	32mm	programmed			100
Minitec Super	24x36mm	35mm	35AF	1993	Yashica	3.5	33mm	programmed	1-700		90
Minitec Super Data	24x36mm	35mm	35AF	1993	Yashica	3.5	33mm	programmed	1-700		100
Motor-J (black)	24x36mm	35mm	35VF	1990	Yashica	3.5	32mm		1/125		50
Motor-J (blue)	24x36mm	35mm	35VF	1990	Yashica	3.5	32mm		1/125		50
Motor-J databack	24x36mm	35mm	35VF	1990	Yashica	3.5	32mm		1/125		70
Partner	24x36mm	35mm	35Fold	1985	Yashica	4.5	38mm		1/125		30
Partner AF	24x36mm	35mm	35AF	1985		3.5	35mm	programmed			70
Partner AF-D	24x36mm	35mm	35AF	1985		3.5	35mm	programmed			70
Patio	24x36mm	35mm	35VF	1993	Yashica	4.5	35mm		1/125		60
Penta J	24x36mm	35mm	35SLR	1962	Auto Yashinon	2	50mm	focal plane	2-500		50
Pentamatic	24x36mm	35mm	35SLR	1960	Auto Yashinon	1.8	55mm	focal plane	1-1000,B		70
Pentamatic II	24x36mm	35mm	35SLR	1961	Auto Yashinon	1.7	58mm	focal plane	1-1000,B		50
Pentamatic S	24x36mm	35mm	35SLR	1962	Auto Yashinon	1.8	55mm	focal plane	1-1000,B		50
Yashica Rapide	18x24mm	35mm	35Half	1961	Yashinon	2.8	28mm	Copal	1-500	Mc435	70
Revue mini-star	8x11mm		Submin	1965	Yashinon	2.8	18mm			A926	50
Rookie	6x6cm	120	TLR	1956	Yashimar	3.5	80mm	Copal	25-300	Mc435	70
Samurai X3.0	18x24mm	35mm	35SLR	1989		3.5-4.3	25-75	programmed	2-1/500		180
Samurai X4.0	18x24mm	35mm	35SLR	1989		3.8-4.8	25-100	programmed	3-1/300		230
Samurai Z	18x24mm	35mm	35SLR	1989		4-5.6	25-75	programmed	4-1/500		190
Samurai Z-2 (purple)	18x24mm	35mm	35SLR	1989		4-5.6	25-75	programmed	4-1/500		140
Samurai Z-2 L (red)	18x24mm	35mm	35SLR	1989		4-5.6	25-75	programmed	4-1/500		140
Samurai Z-L	18x24mm	35mm	35SLR	1989		4-5.6	25-75	programmed	4-1/500		190
Sensation Plus	24x36mm	35mm	35VF	1994		4.3	31mm	programmed	100-650		100

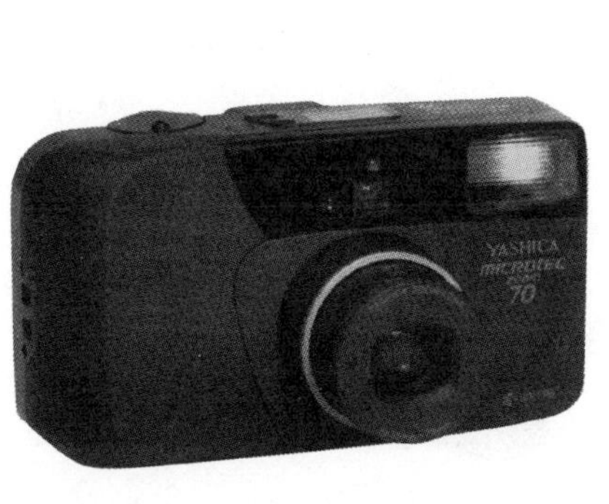

Yashica Microtec Zoom 70

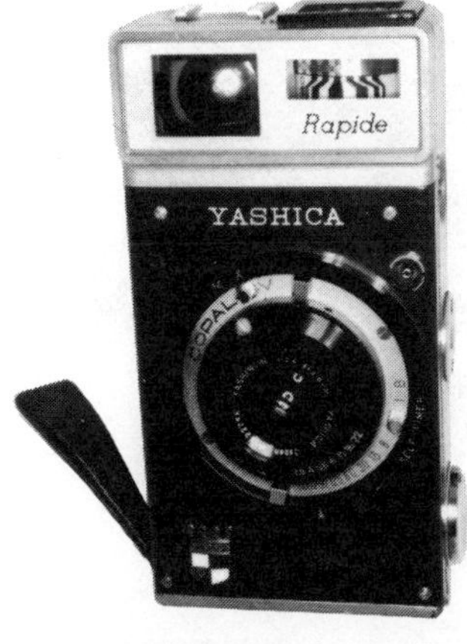

Yashica Rapide

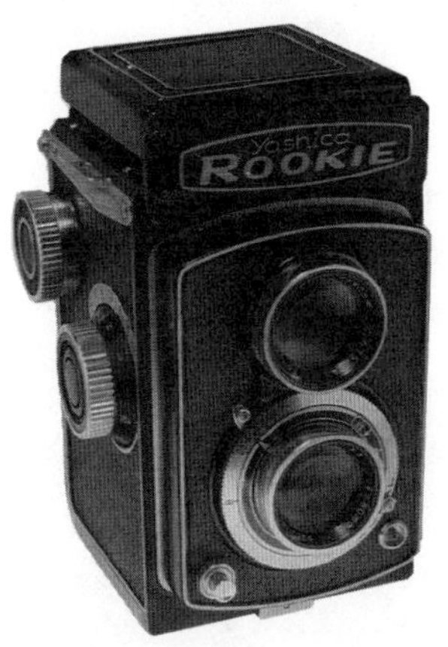

Yashica Rookie

MODEL	FORMAT	FILM	TYPE	Year	LENS	Apert	FL	SHUTTER	SPEEDS	ILLUS	U.S.$
Sequelle	18x24mm	35mm	35Half	1962	Yashinon	2.8	28mm	Seikosha-L	30-250,B	Mc435	100
T AF	24x36mm	35mm	35AF	1985	Tessar T*	3.5	35mm	programmed	30-700		80
T AF-D	24x36mm	35mm	35AF	1985	Tessar T*	3.5	35mm	programmed	30-700		100
T AF-DX	24x36mm	35mm	35AF	1986	Tessar T*	3.5	35mm	programmed	8-500		70
T2 AF	24x36mm	35mm	35AF	1986	Tessar T*	3.5	35mm	programmed	8-500		110
T2-D AF	24x36mm	35mm	35AF	1987	Tessar T*	3.5	35mm	programmed	30-450		150
T3 AF	24x36mm	35mm	35AF	1988	Tessar T*	2.8	35mm	programmed	1-630		120
T3 Super	24x36mm	35mm	35AW-AF	1991	Tessar T*	2.8	35mm	programmed	1-630		50
T3 Super-D	24x36mm	35mm	35AW-AF	1991	Tessar T*	2.8	35mm	programmed	1-630		70
T3-D AF	24x36mm	35mm	35AF	1989	Tessar T*	2.8	35mm	programmed	1-630		90
T4	24x36mm	35mm	35AF	1993	Tessar T*	3.5	35mm	programmed	1-700		130
T4 Data (black)	24x36mm	35mm	35AF	1993	Tessar T*	3.5	35mm	programmed	1-700		140
T4 Data (green)	24x36mm	35mm	35AF	1993	Tessar T*	3.5	35mm	programmed	1-700		140
TL	24x36mm	35mm	35SLR	1968	Auto Yashinon	2	50mm	focal plane	2-500		80
TL-E	24x36mm	35mm	35SLR	1970	Auto Yashinon	1.4	50mm	focal plane	2-1000		70
TL-Electro	24x36mm	35mm	35SLR	1972	Auto Yashinon	2	50mm	focal plane	1-1000		90
TL-Electro X	24x36mm	35mm	35SLR	1969	Auto Yashinon	1.4	50mm	focal plane	2-1000		90
TL-Electro X ITS	24x36mm	35mm	35SLR	1970	Auto Yashinon	1.4	50mm	focal plane	2-1000		70
TL-Super	24x36mm	35mm	35SLR	1967	Auto Yashinon	1.4	50mm	focal plane	1-1000		80
Twintec	24x36mm	35mm	35AF-BiF	1993	Yashica	4/6.2	33/53	programmed	50-500		50
Y 16	10x14mm	16mm	Submin	1959	Yashinon	2.8	25mm		25-200	Mc435	50
Y 16 (aqua)	10x14mm	16mm	Submin	1959	Yashinon	3.5	25mm		25-200		50
Y 16 (blue)	10x14mm	16mm	Submin	1959	Yashinon	3.5	25mm		25-200		50
Y 16 (grey)	10x14mm	16mm	Submin	1959	Yashinon	3.5	25mm		25-200		50
Y 16 (maroon)	10x14mm	16mm	Submin	1959	Yashinon	3.5	25mm		25-200		50
Y 16 (tangerine)	10x14mm	16mm	Submin	1959	Yashinon	3.5	25mm		25-200		50
Y 16 EE	10x14mm	16mm	Submin	1964	Yashinon	2.8	25mm	programmed	1-250		50
Yashica-Flex A (new)	6x6cm	120	TLR	1957	Yashikor	3.5	80mm	Copal	25-300		50
Yashica-Flex A-2	6x6cm	120	TLR	1956	Yashimar	3.5	80mm		1-400		70
Yashica-Flex A-II	6x6cm	120	TLR	1954	Yashimar	3.5	80mm	Copal	10-200		50
Yashica-Flex A-III	6x6cm	120	TLR	1959	Yashikor	3.5	80mm	Copal	25-300		70
Yashica-Flex AS-1	6x6cm	120	TLR	1957	Yashikor	3.5	80mm		1-400		60
Yashica-Flex B (Yashima)	6x6cm	120	TLR	1957	Yashikor	3.5	80mm	Copal	1-500		70
Yashica-Flex S	6x6cm	120	TLR	1956	Yashinon	3.5	80mm	Copal	1-300	HK439	70
Yashica-Mat	6x6cm	120	TLR	1957	Yashinon	3.5	80mm	Copal-MXV	1-500,B		130
Yashica-Mat 124	6x6cm	120	TLR	1968	Yashinon	3.5	80mm	Copal-SV	1-500		210
Yashica-Mat 124G	6x6cm	120	TLR	1983	Yashinon	3.5	80mm	Copal-SV	1-500		230
Yashica-Mat EM	6x6cm	120	TLR	1965	Yashinon	3.5	80mm	Copal-MXV	1-500,B		90
Yashica-Mat LM	6x6cm	120	TLR	1960	Yashinon	3.5	80mm	Copal-MXV	1-500,B	Mc435	90
Yashimaflex	6x6cm	120	TLR	1953	Tri-Lausar	3.5	80mm	NKS-TB	B,1-200		180
YE	24x36mm	35mm	35RF	1959	Yashikor	2.8	50mm	focal plane	2-500	Mc435	350
YF	24x36mm	35mm	35RF	1959	Yashinor	1.8	50mm	focal plane	1-1000,B	A3485	390

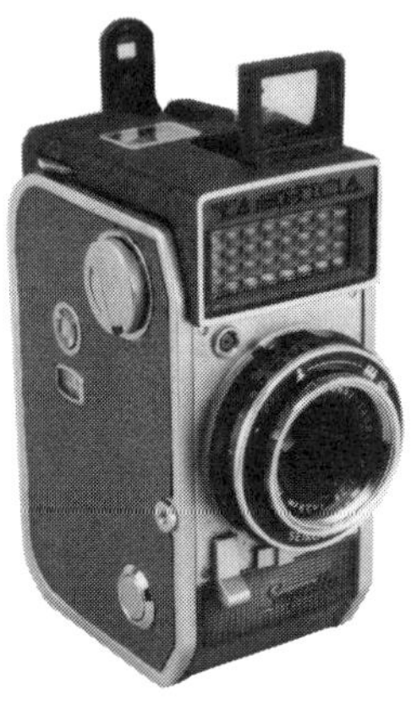

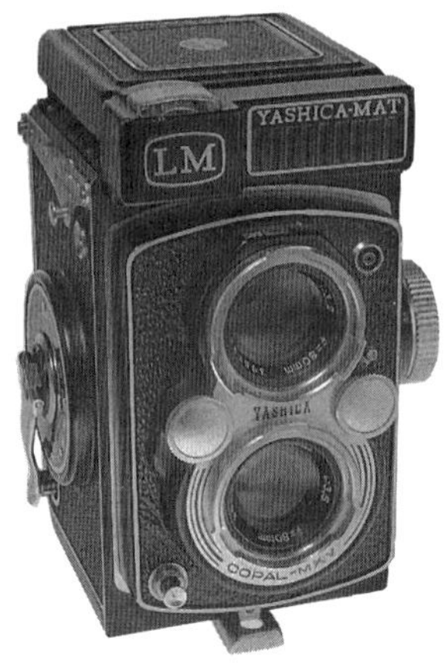

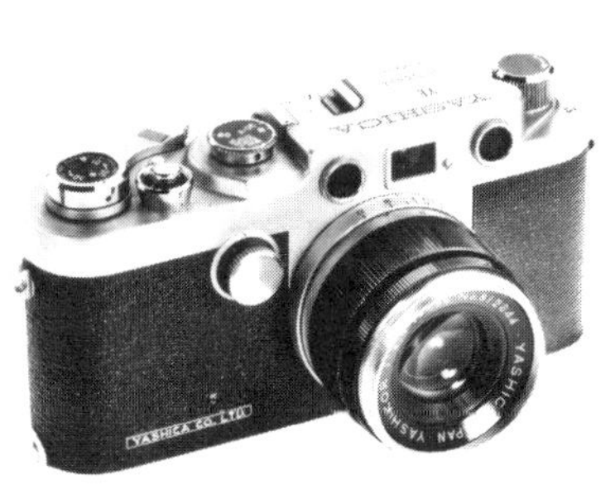

Yashica Sequelle | **Yashica-Mat LM** | **Yashica YE**

MODEL	FORMAT	FILM	TYPE	Year	LENS	Apert	FL	SHUTTER	SPEEDS	ILLUS	U.S.$
YK	24x36mm	35mm	35RF	1959	Yashinon	2.8	45mm		25-300		50
Zoom Image 70	24x36mm	35mm	35AFZ	1994		3.5-6.7	35-70	programmed			110
Zoom Image 70 Data	24x36mm	35mm	35AFZ	1994		3.5-6.7	35-70	programmed			120
Zoomtec	24x36mm	35mm	35AFZ	1990	Yashica	3.8-7.6	38-80	programmed	5-250		170
Zoomtec 60	24x36mm	35mm	35AFZ	1991	Yashica	4.5-6.7	38-60	programmed	35-180		110
Zoomtec 70	24x36mm	35mm	35AFZ	1993	Yashica	3.5-6.7	35-70	programmed	5-250		130
Zoomtec 70 Data	24x36mm	35mm	35AFZ	1993	Yashica	3.5-6.7	35-70	programmed	5-250		140
Zoomtec 80	24x36mm	35mm	35AFZ	1990	Yashica	3.8-7.6	38-80	programmed	5-250		120
Zoomtec 90	24x36mm	35mm	35AFZ	1993	Yashica	3.5-7.8	38-90	programmed	2-1/300		160
Zoomtec 90 Super	24x36mm	35mm	35AFZ	1994	Yashica	3.5-7.8	38-90	programmed	2-1/300		160
Zoomtec 90 Super Data	24x36mm	35mm	35AFZ	1994	Yashica	3.5-7.8	38-90	programmed	2-1/300		170
Zoomtec 105	24x36mm	35mm	35AFZ	1993	Yashica	3.5-8	35-105	programmed	2-1000		230
Zoomtec 105 D	24x36mm	35mm	35AFZ	1993	Yashica	3.5-8	35-105	programmed	2-1000		220
Zoomtec mini	24x36mm	35mm	35AFZ	1993	Yashica	3.5-8	35-105	programmed			180
Zoomtec mini Data	24x36mm	35mm	35AFZ	1993	Yashica	3.5-8	35-105	programmed			190
...YASHINA SEIKI CO. LTD. - Japan											
Pigeonflex	6x6cm	120	TLR	1953	Tri-Lausar	3.5	80mm	NKS	1-200,B		70
...(unknown)											
Yunon YN 500	24x36mm	35mm	35VF	1984		6	50mm		I		10
...ZEH (Zeh-Camera-Fabrik, Paul Zeh) - Dresden											
Bettax 6x6	6x6cm	120	VtFoldRo	1936	Radionar	4.5	105mm	Compur			50
Bettax 6x9	6x9cm	120	VtFoldRo	1936	Radionar	4.5	105mm	Compur		A1467	50
Colorprint	3x4cm	127	VtFoldRo	1930	Colorprint Anast.	4.5	50mm	Vario		Mc435	100
Goldi 3x4	3x4cm	127	VtFoldRo	1930	Zecanar	2.9	5cm	Compur		Mc436	90
Goldi 3x4	3x4cm	127	VtFoldRo	1930	Zecanar	4.5	5cm	Vario		HK247	90
Goldi 4x6	4x6cm	127	VtFoldRo	1935	Xenar	3.8	7cm	Prontor		HK248	50
Goldi 4x6	4x6cm	127	VtFoldRo	1935	Xenar	3.8	7cm	Compur		Mc436	50
Ralikona	3x4cm	127	VtFoldRo	1930	Zecanar	2.9	5cm	Compur			90
Rhacofix	3x4cm	127	VtFoldRo	1930	Zecanar	4.5	5cm	Prontor			90
Sport	6.5x9cm	plate	VtFoldRo	1933	Zecanar Anast.	6.3	105mm	Prontor	25-100		50
Zeca 6x9	6x9cm	Sheet	FoldSht	1940	Steinheil	6.8		Vario	25-100		50
Zeca 9x12	9x12cm	Sheet	FoldSht	1937	Radionar	6.3				Mc436	50
Zeca-Flex	6x6cm	120	StrutTLR	1937	Xenar	3.5	75mm	Compur		A1707	1100
Zeca-Flex	6x6cm	120	StrutTLR	1937	Zeiss Tessar	3.5	75mm	Compur-Rapid		Mc436	1100
...ZEISS (Carl Zeiss Jena) - Jena, Germany											
HK 1a	14x17cm	plate	Aerial	1918	Tessar		250mm				370
Magnar-Kamera	9x12cm	plate	Special	1906	Magnar	10	800mm			Mc436	2300
Minimum Palmos 6.5x9	6.5x9cm	plate	StrutPl	1905	Tessar	6.3		focal plane	1/15-1000	Mc436	180
Minimum Palmos 6.5x9	6.5x9cm	plate	StrutPl	1905	Tessar	4.5		focal plane	1/15-1000		180
Minimum Palmos 3¼x4¼"	3¼x4¼"	plate	StrutPl	1905	Tessar	6.3		focal plane	1/15-1000		180
Minimum Palmos 3¼x4¼"	3¼x4¼"	plate	StrutPl	1905	Tessar	4.5		focal plane	1/15-1000		180
Minimum Palmos 9x12	9x12cm	plate	StrutPl	1905	Tessar	6.3		focal plane	1/15-1000	Mc436	180

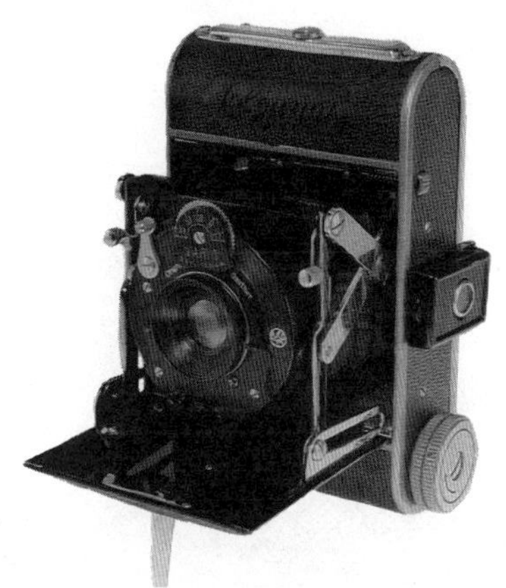

Zeh Colorprint

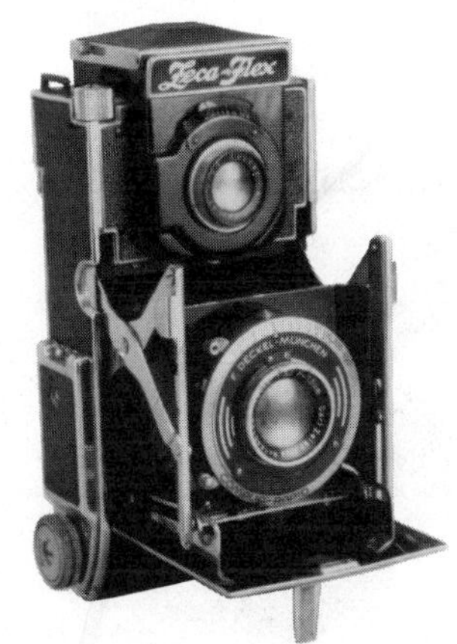

Zeh Zeca-Flex

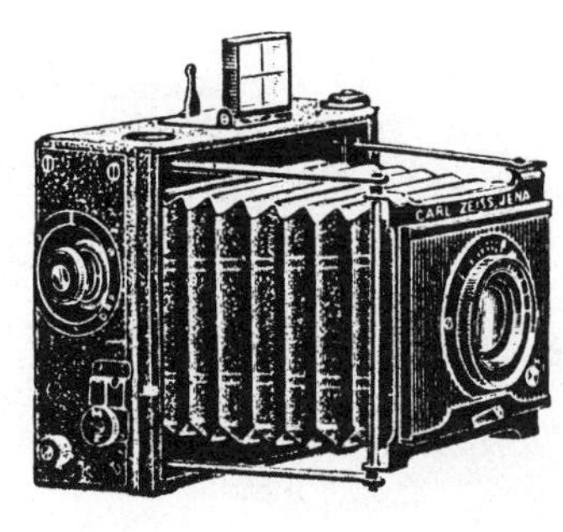

Zeiss Minimum Palmos

MODEL	FORMAT	FILM	TYPE	Year	LENS	Apert	FL	SHUTTER	SPEEDS	ILLUS	U.S.$
Minimum Palmos 9x12	9x12cm	plate	StrutPl	1905	Tessar	4.5		focal plane	1/15-1000		180
Minimum Palmos Stereo	9x18cm	plate	SterStrut	1907	Tessar	6.3	84mm	focal plane	10-1000	Mc436	490
Stereo Palmos	9x12cm	plate	StFoldPl	1905	Zeiss Tessar	6.3	84mm	focal plane	25-1000	Mc436	500
Universal Palmos 9x12	9x12cm	plate	FoldPl	1904	Tessar	6.3	150mm	Compound			330
Universal Palmos 12x16.5	12x16.5	plate	FoldPl	1904	Double-Protar	7	143mm	Compound			330
...ZEISS IKON A.G.											
Adoro	6.5x9cm	plate	VtFoldPl	1927	Tessar	4.5	105mm	Compur			390
Baby Deckrullo (12)	4.5x6cm	plate	StrutPl	1926	Zeiss Tessar	2.7	80mm	focal plane	-1/1200		350
Baby Deckrullo (870)	4.5x6cm	plate	StrutPl	1926	Zeiss Tessar	4.5	75mm	focal plane	-1/1200		350
Baby-Box Tengor 54/18	3x4cm	127	RollBox	1931	Frontar	11	50mm			Mc437	60
Baby-Box Tengor 54/18	3x4cm	127	RollBox	1934	Frontar	11	50mm			Mc437	50
Baby-Box Tengor 54/18(E)	3x4cm	127	RollBox	1931	Novar	6.3				Mc437	70
Baldur Box (51)	4.5x6cm	120	RollBox	1934	Frontar	11	90mm		1/30,T	Mc437	60
Baldur Box 51/2	6x9cm	120	RollBox	1934	Goerz Frontar	11	115mm		1/30,T	A104	50
Bebe (342)	4.5x6cm	plate	StrutPl	1928	Triotar	3.5	75mm	Dial-Compur			270
Bebe (342)	4.5x6cm	plate	StrutPl	1930	Tessar	3.5	75mm	Rim-Compur			380
Bebe (342/3)	6.5x9cm	plate	StrutPl	1928	Tessar	4.5	105mm			A316	290
Bob (510)	4.5x6cm	120	VtFoldRo	1934	Nettar			Gauthier	25-75,B,T		60
Bob (510/2)	6x9cm	120	VtFoldRo	1934	Nettar			Gauthier	25-75,B,T		50
Bob IV	6x9cm	120	VtFoldRo	1927	Anastigmat	6.8	105mm	Cronos A			50
Bob V 4x6.5	4x6.5cm	127	VtFoldRo	1927	Ernar	6.3	75mm	Cronos B			50
Bob V 6x6	6x6cm	120	VtFoldRo	1927	Ernar	6.3	75mm	Cronos B			50
Bob V 6x9	6x9cm	120	VtFoldRo	1927	Ernar	6.3	120mm	Cronos B			50
Bob V 6.5x11	6.5x11cm	116	VtFoldRo	1927	Ernar	6.3	120mm	Cronos B			50
Bob V 7.25x12.5	7.25x12.5	130	VtFoldRo	1927	Ernar	6.3	135mm	Cronos B			60
Bobette I (549)	22x31mm	Roll	StrutRo	1929	Ernoplast	4.5	50mm	Bob			240
Bobette I (549)	22x31mm	Roll	StrutRo	1929	Erid	8	40mm	Bob			240
Bobette II (548)	22x31mm	Roll	VtFoldRo	1929	Ernostar	2	42mm	Bob	½-100		630
Bobette II (548)	22x31mm	Roll	VtFoldRo	1929	Ernon	3.5	50mm	Bob	½-100		630
Box Tengor 54	4.5x6cm	120	RollBox	1934	Goerz Frontar	11	75mm		I		70
Box Tengor 54/2	6x9cm	120	RollBox	1926	Frontar	11			I,T		50
Box Tengor 54/2	6x9cm	120	RollBox	1928	Frontar	11			I,T	Mc438	40
Box Tengor 54/2	6x9cm	120	RollBox	1934	Frontar	11			I,T	Mc438	30
Box Tengor 54/2	6x9cm	120	RollBox	1938	Frontar	11			I,T	A105	30
Box Tengor 54/2	6x9cm	120	RollBox	1939	Frontar	11			I,T	A106	60
Box Tengor 54/14	5x7.5cm	127	RollBox	1926	Frontar	11			I,T	A102	160
Box Tengor 54/14	5x7.5cm	127	RollBox	1928	Frontar	11			I,T	A102	120
Box Tengor 54/15	6.5x11cm	116	RollBox	1926	Goerz Frontar	11			I,T	Mc438	70
Box Tengor 54/15	6.5x11cm	116	RollBox	1928	Goerz Frontar	11			I,T		70
Box Tengor 54/15	6.5x11cm	116	RollBox	1933	Goerz Frontar	11			I,T		70
Box Tengor 56/2	6x9cm	120	RollBox	1948	Frontar	9				Mc438	40
Citoskop 671/1	45x107	plate	SterRefl	1928	Sucher Triplett	4.5	65mm	St. Compur		A769	370

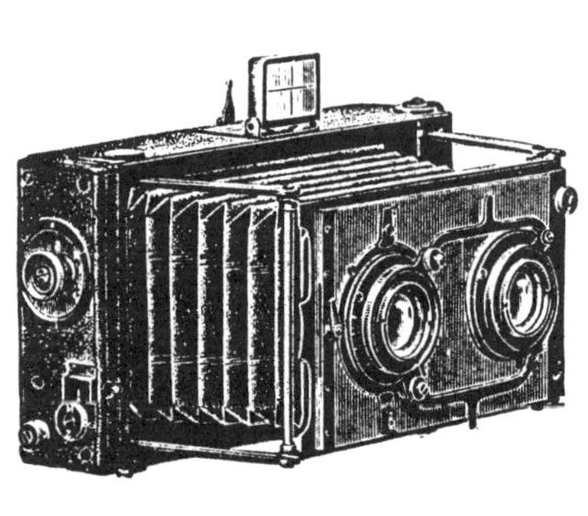

Minimum Palmos Stereo

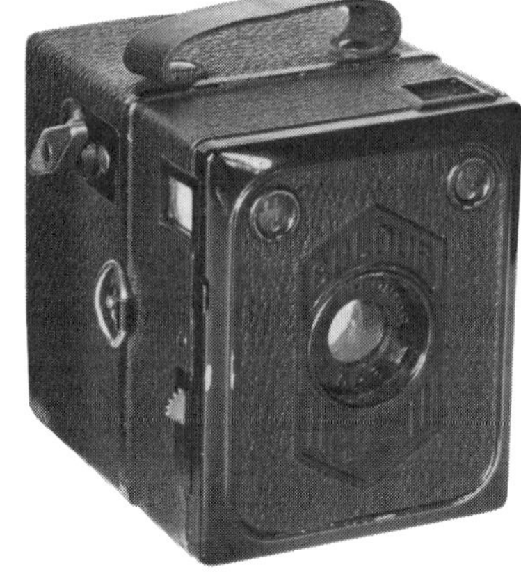

Baldur Box (51)

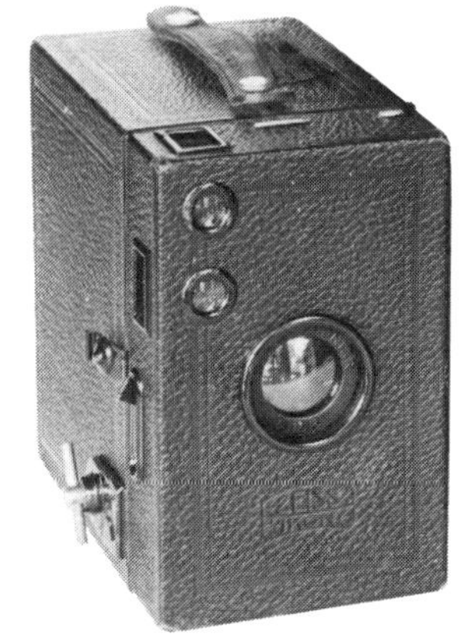

Box Tengor 54/15

MODEL	FORMAT	FILM	TYPE	Year	LENS	Apert	FL	SHUTTER	SPEEDS	ILLUS	U.S.$
Cocarette 207/14	5x7.5cm	127	VtFoldRo	1926	Tessar	4.5	90mm	Compur		Mc438	80
Cocarette 209/2	6x9cm	120	VtFoldRo	1926	Nettar	6.3	105mm	Derval			50
Cocarette 210	6x9cm	120	VtFoldRo	1926	Frontar	9	105mm				50
Cocarette 220	5x7.5cm	127	VtFoldRo	1926	Novar	6.3	130mm	Derval			50
Cocarette 514	8x10.5cm	124	VtFoldRo	1926	Dominar	6.3	125mm	Klio			50
Cocarette 514/2	6x9cm	120	VtFoldRo	1926	Dominar	4.5	105mm	Derval			60
Cocarette 514/14	5x7.5cm	127	VtFoldRo	1926	Novar	6.3	90mm	Derval			50
Cocarette 517	6x9cm	120	VtFoldRo	1926	Teronar	5.4	105mm	Derval			50
Cocarette 518	6.5x11cm	116	VtFoldRo	1926	Trianastigmat	6.8	105mm	Derval			70
Cocarette 519/2	6x9cm	120	VtFoldRo	1926	Tessar	4.5	105mm	Dialset Compur			70
Cocarette 519/14	5x7.5cm	127	VtFoldRo	1926	Novar	4.5	90mm	Dialset Compur			50
Cocarette Luxus 521/2	6x9cm	120	VtFoldRo	1928	Tessar	4.5	105mm	Dialset Compur		Mc438	230
Cocarette Luxus 521/15	6.5x11cm	116	VtFoldRo	1928	Dominar	4.5		Dialset Compur			150
Cocarette Luxus 522/17	8x10.5cm	124	VtFoldRo	1928	Tessar	4.5	125mm	Dialset Compur			220
Colora (10.0641)	24x36mm	35mm	35VF	1963	Novica	2.8	50mm	Prontor	125		40
Colora F (10.0641)	24x36mm	35mm	35VF	1964	Novica	2.8	50mm	Prontor	125		30
Contaflex (860/24)	24x36mm	35mm	35TLR	1935	Sonnar	1.5	80mm	focal plane	2-1000	Mc439	1000
Contaflex I (861/24)	24x36mm	35mm	35SLR	1953	Tessar	2.8	45mm	Sync-Compur		A1662	110
Contaflex II (862/24)	24x36mm	35mm	35SLR	1954	Tessar	2.8	45mm	Sync-Compur		A1663	120
Contaflex III (863/24)	24x36mm	35mm	35SLR	1957	Tessar	2.8	45mm	Sync-Compur			120
Contaflex IV (864/24)	24x36mm	35mm	35SLR	1957	Tessar	2.8	45mm	Sync-Compur			120
Contaflex 126 (10.1102)	28x28mm	126	126SLR	1970	Tessar	2.8	45mm	focal plane		A1665	150
Contaflex 126 (10.1102)	28x28mm	126	126SLR	1970	Color Pantar	2.8	45mm	focal plane		Mc439	150
Contaflex Alpha (10.1241)	24x36mm	35mm	35SLR	1958	Pantar	2.8	45mm	Sync-Compur			100
Contaflex Beta (10.1251)	24x36mm	35mm	35SLR	1958	Pantar	2.8	45mm	Sync-Compur			120
Contaflex Prima (10.1291)	24x36mm	35mm	35SLR	1959	Pantar	2.8	45mm	Sync-Compur		A1664	120
Contaflex Rapid (10.1261)	24x36mm	35mm	35SLR	1959	Tessar	2.8	50mm	Sync-Compur			100
Contaflex S Autom. (black)	24x36mm	35mm	35SLR	1970	Tessar	2.8	50mm	Sync-Compur			240
Contaflex S Autom. (chr.)	24x36mm	35mm	35SLR	1970	Tessar	2.8	50mm	Sync-Compur			200
Contaflex Super (10.1262)	24x36mm	35mm	35SLR	1959	Tessar	2.8	50mm	Sync-Compur		Mc439	120
Contaflex Super (New)	24x36mm	35mm	35SLR	1962	Tessar	2.8	50mm	Sync-Compur			160
Contafl. Super B (10.1272)	24x36mm	35mm	35SLR	1963	Tessar	2.8	50mm	Sync-Compur		Mc439	140
Contaflex Super BC "BW"	24x36mm	35mm	35SLR	1965	Tessar	2.8	50mm	Sync-Compur			240
Contafl. Super BC (10.1273)	24x36mm	35mm	35SLR	1967	Tessar	2.8	50mm	Sync-Compur			150
Contarex EE "Bullseye"	24x36mm	35mm	35SLR	1959	Planar	2	50mm	focal plane		Mc440	500
Contarex Electron.(10.2800)	24x36mm	35mm	35SLR	1970	Planar	2	50mm	focal plane		A634	1400
Contarex Microscope Cam.	24x36mm	35mm	SciMed	1971				focal plane			410
Contarex Profess. (10.2700)	24x36mm	35mm	35SLR	1967	Planar	2	50mm	focal plane		A633	1100
Contarex Special (10.2500)	24x36mm	35mm	35SLR	1960	Tessar	2.8	50mm	focal plane		A632	800
Contarex Super (10.2600)	24x36mm	35mm	35SLR	1968	Planar	2	50mm	focal plane			900
Contarex Super electronic	24x36mm	35mm	35SLR	1970	Planar	2	50mm	focal plane		A634	1400
Contax I (540/24)(1931)	24x36mm	35mm	35RF	1931	Sonnar	2	50mm	focal plane		A994	590

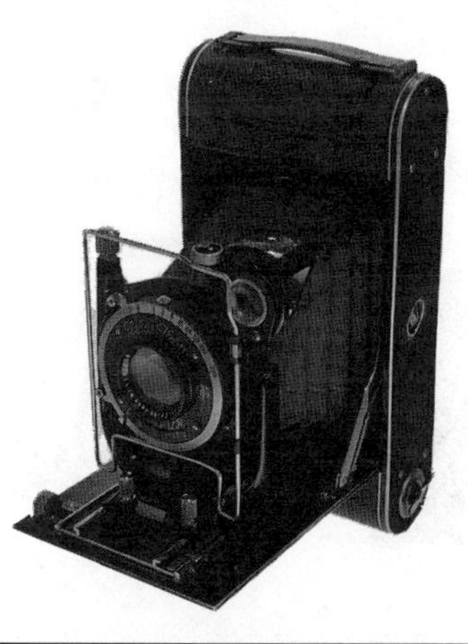

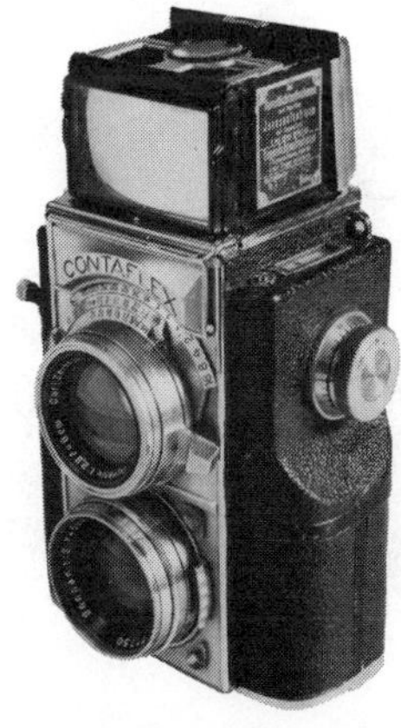

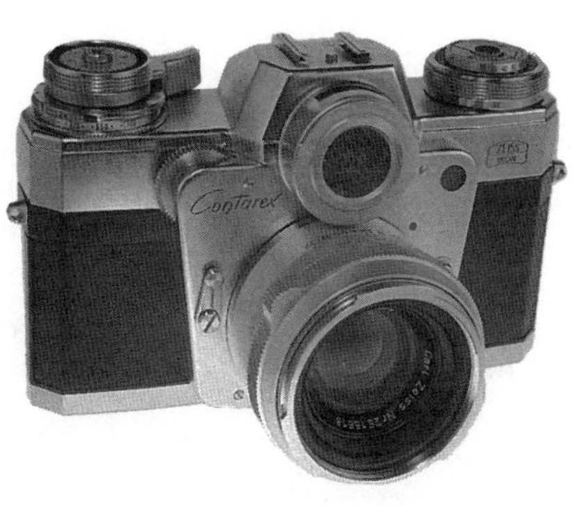

Cocarette Luxus 521/2 | **Contaflex (860/24)** | **Contarex EE "Bullseye"**

MODEL	FORMAT	FILM	TYPE	Year	LENS	Apert	FL	SHUTTER	SPEEDS	ILLUS	U.S.$
Contax I (540/24)(1934)	24x36mm	35mm	35RF	1934	Tessar	3.5	50mm	focal plane		Mc440	430
Contax II (543/24)	24x36mm	35mm	35RF	1936	Sonnar	1.5	50mm	focal plane		A995	280
Contax II (543/24)	24x36mm	35mm	35RF	1936	Tessar	2.8	50mm	focal plane		Mc441	280
Contax II(a) (563/24)(1950)	24x36mm	35mm	35RF	1950	Sonnar	2	50mm	focal plane		A997	370
Contax II(a) (563/24)(1954)	24x36mm	35mm	35RF	1954	Tessar	2.8	50mm	focal plane		A997	350
Contax III (544/24)	24x36mm	35mm	35RF	1936	Sonnar	2	50mm	focal plane		Mc441	350
Contax III (544/24)	24x36mm	35mm	35RF	1936	Tessar	3.5	50mm	focal plane		A996	350
Contax IIIa	24x36mm	35mm	35RF	1950	Opton Sonnar	2	50mm	focal plane		A998	380
Contessa 35 (533/24)(1950)	24x36mm	35mm	35Fold	1950	Tessar	2.8	45mm	Compur-Rapid		Mc441	170
Contessa 35 (533/24)(1953)	24x36mm	35mm	35Fold	1953	Tessar	2.8	45mm	Sync-Compur		A1030	170
Contessa 35 (533/24)(1960)	24x36mm	35mm	35RF	1960	Tessar	2.8	50mm	Pronto	30-250	A1162	70
Contessa LBE (20.0639)	24x36mm	35mm	35RF	1965	Tessar	2.8	50mm	Prontor 500LK			70
Contessa LK (10.0637)	24x36mm	35mm	35VF	1963	Tessar	2.8	50mm	Prontor 500LK			70
Contessa LKE (10.0638)	24x36mm	35mm	35RF	1963	Tessar	2.8	50mm	Prontor 500LK			70
Contessa S-310 (10.0351)	24x36mm	35mm	35VF	1971	Tessar	2.8	40mm	Prontor 500S	8-1/500	A2112	140
Contessa S-312 (10.0354)	24x36mm	35mm	35RF	1971	Tessar	2.8	40mm	Prontor 500S	8-1/500		180
Contessamat	24x36mm	35mm	35VF	1964	Color Pantar	2.8	45mm	Prontormatic	30-125		50
Contessamat SBE (10.0652)	24x36mm	35mm	35RF	1963	Tessar	2.8	50mm	P-matic 500SL		Mc442	60
Contessamat SE (10.0654)	24x36mm	35mm	35RF	1963	Color Pantar	2.8	45mm	Prontormatic 500	30-500	Mc442	50
Contessamat STE	24x36mm	35mm	35RF	1965	Tessar	2.8	50mm	P-matic 500SL	1-500		50
Contessamatic	24x36mm	35mm	35VF	1960	Tessar	2.8	50mm	Prontor SLK		Mc442	50
Contessamatic E (10.0645)	24x36mm	35mm	35RF	1960	Tessar	2.8	50mm	Pr. SLK Spezial	1-500,MX		50
Contina (10.0626)	24x36mm	35mm	35VF	1962	Color Pantar	2.8	45mm	Pronto	-1/250		50
Contina I (522/24)	24x36mm	35mm	35Fold	1952	Novar	3.5	45mm	Prontor-SV		A1031	50
Contina Ia (526/24)	24x36mm	35mm	35VF	1956	Pantar	2.8	45mm			Mc442	40
Contina Ic (10.0603)	24x36mm	35mm	35VF	1958	Pantar	2.8	45mm	Prontor-SVS	1-300		50
Contina II (524/24)	24x36mm	35mm	35Fold	1952	Novar	3.5	45mm	Prontor-SV	1-500		100
Contina IIa (527/24)	24x36mm	35mm	35VF	1956	Novar	3.5	45mm				50
Contina IIa (527/24)	24x36mm	35mm	35VF	1956	Novicar	2.8		Prontor-SVS	1-300,MX	Mc442	50
Contina IIc (527/24)	24x36mm	35mm	35VF	1956	Pantar	2.8	45mm	Prontor-SVS	1-300,MX		50
Contina III (529/24)	24x36mm	35mm	35VF	1955	Pantar	2.8	45mm	Prontor-SVS			50
Contina III Microscope	24x36mm	35mm	SciMed	1955				Ibsor B	1-125, X		160
Contina IIIa (529/24)	24x36mm	35mm	35VF	1955	Pantar	2.8	45mm				50
Contina L (10.0605)	24x36mm	35mm	35VF	1964	Color Pantar	2.8	45mm	Prontor 250	30-250		50
Contina LK (10.0637)	24x36mm	35mm	35VF	1963	Color Pantar	2.8	45mm	Prontor 250			80
Contina LKE	24x36mm	35mm	35VF	1963	Color Pantar	2.8	45mm	Prontor 250			50
Continamatic II	24x36mm	35mm	35VF	1963	Color Pantar	2.8	45mm	Prontor			50
Continamatic IIC	24x36mm	35mm	35VF	1963	Color Pantar	2.8	45mm	Prontor			50
Continamatic III	24x36mm	35mm	35VF	1963	Color Pantar	2.8	45mm	Prontor			50
Continette (10.0625)	24x36mm	35mm	35VF	1960	Lucinar	2.8	45mm	Pronto	30-250		50
Deckrullo (36)	6.5x9cm	plate	StrutPl	1926	Zeiss Tessar	4.5	120mm	focal plane	1-2800		170
Deckrullo (90)	9x12cm	plate	StrutPl	1926	Triotar	3.5	150mm	focal plane	1-2800		160

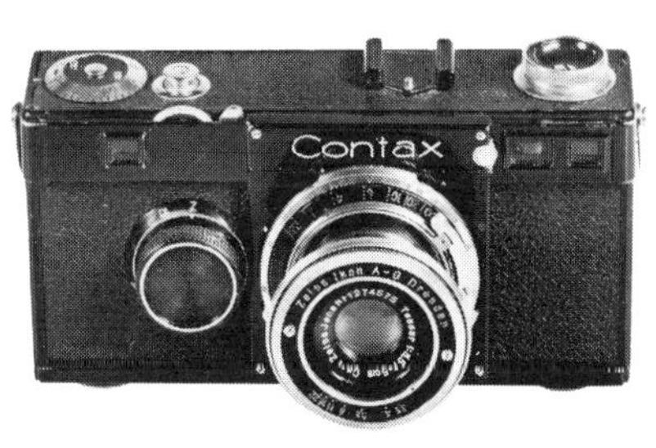

Zeiss Contax I (540/24)

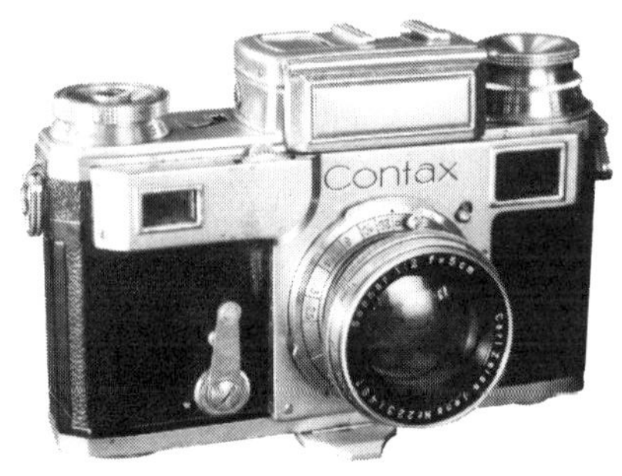

Contax III (544/24)

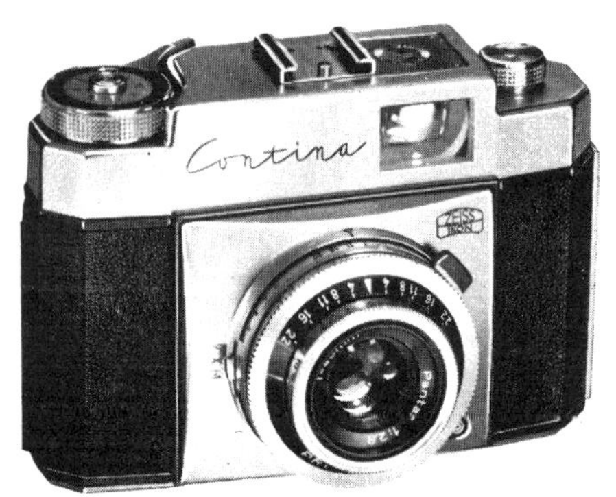

Contina Ia (526/24)

MODEL	FORMAT	FILM	TYPE	Year	LENS	Apert	FL	SHUTTER	SPEEDS	ILLUS	U.S.$
Deckrullo (120)	10x15cm	plate	StrutPl	1926	Zeiss Tessar	4.5	180mm	focal plane	1-2800		150
Deckrullo (165)	13x18cm	plate	StrutPl	1926	Triotar	3.5	210mm	focal plane	1-2800		150
Deckrullo Nettel (36)	6.5x9cm	plate	StrutPl	1926	Triotar	3.5	120mm	focal plane	1-2800		170
Deckrullo Nettel (90)	9x12cm	plate	StrutPl	1926	Zeiss Tessar	2.7	165mm	focal plane	1-2800		160
Deckrullo Nettel (120)	10x15cm	plate	StrutPl	1926	Triotar	3.5	180mm	focal plane	1-2800		150
Deckrullo Nettel (165)	13x18cm	plate	StrutPl	1926	Zeiss Tessar	4.5	210mm	focal plane	1-2800		150
Deckrullo Nettel Tropical	6.5x9cm	plate	StrutPl	1926	Zeiss Tessar	2.7	120mm	focal plane	1-2800		650
Deckrullo Nettel Tropical	9x12cm	plate	StrutPl	1926	Triotar	3.5	150mm	focal plane	1-2800		650
Deckrullo Nettel Tropical	10x15cm	plate	StrutPl	1926	Zeiss Tessar	4.5	180mm	focal plane	1-2800		650
Deckrullo Nettel Tropical	13x18cm	plate	StrutPl	1926	Triotar	3.5	210mm	focal plane	1-2800		650
Deckrullo Tropical 6.5x9	6.5x9cm	plate	StrutPl	1926	Zeiss Tessar	4.5	120mm	focal plane	1-2800		650
Deckrullo Tropical 9x12	9x12cm	plate	StrutPl	1926	Triotar	3.5	150mm	focal plane	1-2800		650
Deckrullo Tropical 10x15	10x15cm	plate	StrutPl	1926	Zeiss Tessar	4.5	180mm	focal plane	1-2800		650
Deckrullo Tropical 13x18	13x18cm	plate	StrutPl	1926	Triotar	3.5	210mm	focal plane	1-2800		650
Donata (68/1)	9x12cm	plate	VtFoldPl	1927	Preminar	4.5	135mm	Ibsor			50
Donata (227/3)	6.5x9cm	plate	VtFoldPl	1927	Preminar	4.5	105mm	Compur			70
Donata (227/7)	9x12cm	plate	VtFoldPl	1927	Dominar	4.5	135mm	Compur		A269	60
Duchessa (5)	4.5x6cm	plate	StrutPl	1926	Tessar	4.5	75mm	Compur			240
Duchessa (302)	4.5x6cm	plate	StrutPl	1926	Tessar	4.5	75mm	Compur		HK180	240
Duroll	9x12cm	plate	VtFoldPl	1926	Dominar	4.5	135mm	Compur			70
Elegante	13x18cm	plate	Tailboard	1927	various			various		A1375	440
Erabox 4.5x6	4.5x6cm	120	RollBox	1934	Frontar	11					60
Erabox 6x9	6x9cm	120	RollBox	1934	Frontar	11				Mc443	30
Ergo (301)	4.5x6cm	plate	Disguised	1927	Tessar	4.5	55mm		25-100	Mc443	1200
Ermanox (858)	4.5x6cm	plate	RigidPl	1927	Ernostar	1.8	85mm	focal plane	20-1200	HK340	1700
Ermanox (858/3)	6.5x9cm	plate	StrutPl	1927	Ernostar	1.8	125mm	focal plane	1-1000	HK182	1500
Ermanox (858/7)	9x12cm	plate	StrutPl	1927	Ernostar	1.8	165mm	focal plane	1-1000		2900
Ermanox (858/9)	10x15cm	plate	StrutPl	1927	Ernostar	1.8		focal plane	1-1000		3200
Ermanox (858/11)	13x18cm	plate	StrutPl	1927	Ernostar	1.8		focal plane	1-1000		3200
Ermanox Reflex	4.5x6cm	plate	MedSLR	1927	Ernostar	1.8	105mm	focal plane	20-1200		2000
Erni (27)	6.5x9cm	plate	PlateBox	1927		12.5				HK76	200
Erni (27/3)	4.5x6cm	plate	PlateBox	1927		12.5				HK76	290
Ernoflex I 4.5x6	4.5x6cm	plate	FoldSLR	1926	Ernon	3.5	75mm	focal plane	1-1000	A574	660
Ernoflex I 6.5x9	6.5x9cm	plate	FoldSLR	1926	Ernon	3.5	135mm	focal plane	1-1000		460
Ernoflex I 9x12	9x12cm	plate	FoldSLR	1926	Tessar	4.5	165mm	focal plane	1-1000		460
Ernoflex II	9x12cm	plate	FoldSLR	1926	Ernon	3.5	180mm	focal plane	1-1000		670
Favorit (265)	9x12cm	plate	VtFoldPl	1927	Protar	6.3	135mm	Compur			190
Favorit (265/7)	9x12cm	plate	VtFoldPl	1927	Tessar	4.5	135mm	Compur			190
Favorit (265/9)	10x15cm	plate	VtFoldPl	1927	Dominar	4.5	165mm	Compur			200
Favorit (265/11)	13x18cm	plate	VtFoldPl	1927	Dominar	4.5	180mm	Compur			260
Favorit Tropical (266/1)	9x12cm	plate	VtFoldPl	1927	Dominar	4.5	135mm	Compur			640
Favorit Tropical (266/7)	9x12cm	plate	VtFoldPl	1927	Tessar	4.5	135mm	Compur			640

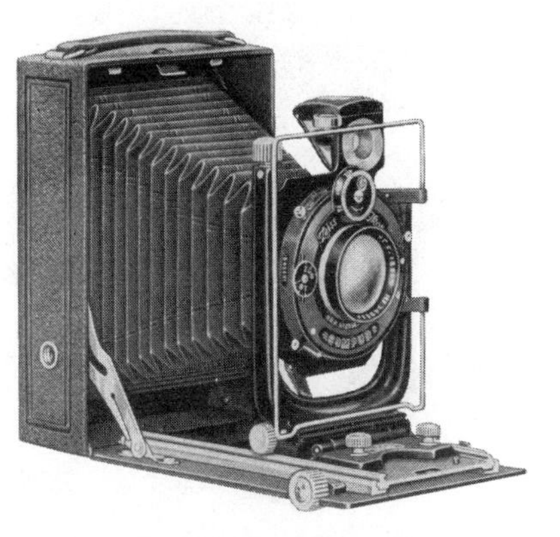

Donata (227/7)

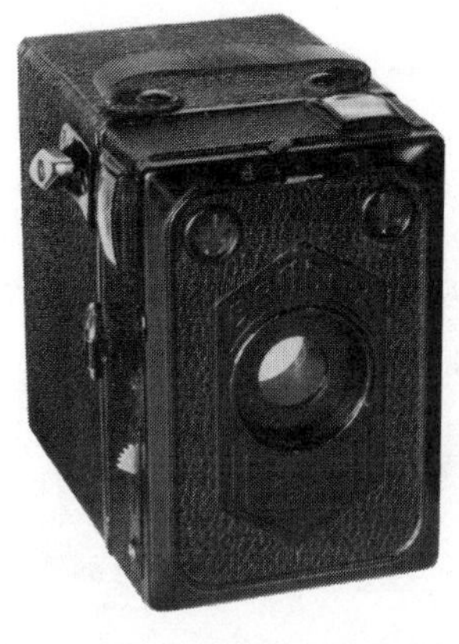

Erabox

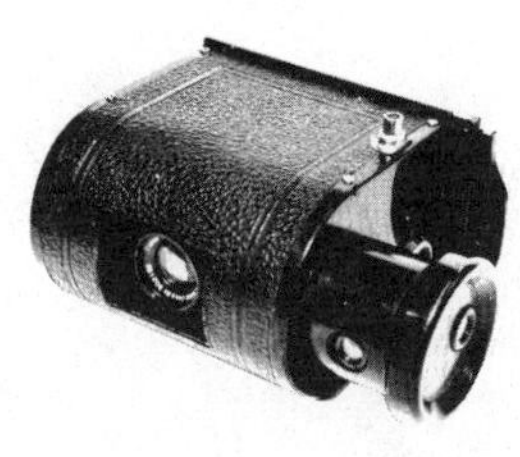

Ergo (301)

MODEL	FORMAT	FILM	TYPE	Year	LENS	Apert	FL	SHUTTER	SPEEDS	ILLUS	U.S.$
Favorit Tropical (266/9)	10x15cm	plate	VtFoldPl	1927	Dominar	4.5	165mm	Compur			640
Halloh (505/1)	8x10.5cm	124	VtFoldRo	1927	Hekla	6.8	135mm	Dial-Compur			90
Hochtourist 5x7"	5x7"	plate	Tailboard	1927	various			various			180
Hochtourist 8x10"	8x10"	plate	Tailboard	1927	various			various			180
Hochtourist 10x12"	10x12"	plate	Tailboard	1927	various			various			200
Hologon	24x36mm	35mm	WideAng	1968	Hologon	8	15mm	focal plane	1-500	A1176	5300
Icarette 496/1	6x6cm	120	HzFoldRo	1927	Novar	6.3	75mm	Automat			100
Icarette 498/1	6x9cm	120	VtFoldRo	1927	Novar	6.3	105mm	Automat			70
Icarette 500/1	6x9cm	120	VtFoldRo	1927	Tessar	4.5	105mm	Compur		A410	70
Icarette 500/12	4x6.5cm	127	VtFoldRo	1927	Tessar	4.5	75mm	Compur			80
Icarette 509/17	8x10.5cm	124	VtFoldRo	1927	Tessar	4.5	120mm	Compur		Mc443	70
Icarette 512/15	6.5x11cm	116	VtFoldRo	1927	Novar	6.3	125mm	Derval			70
Icarette 551/2	6x9cm	120	VtFoldRo	1927	Dominar	4.5	105mm	Compur			70
Icarex 35 (10.2200)	24x36mm	35mm	35SLR	1967	Color Pantar	2.8	50mm	Cloth FP	½-1000		130
Icarex 35 (black)	24x36mm	35mm	35SLR	1967	Tessar	2.8	50mm	Cloth FP	½-1000		130
Icarex 35 CS	24x36mm	35mm	35SLR	1967	Ultron	1.8	50mm	Cloth FP	½-1000		130
Icarex 35 CS (black)	24x36mm	35mm	35SLR	1967	Tessar	2.8	50mm	Cloth FP	½-1000		130
Icarex 35 CS TM	24x36mm	35mm	35SLR	1967	Ultron	1.8	50mm	Cloth FP	½-1000		130
Icarex 35 TM	24x36mm	35mm	35SLR	1967	Ultron	2.8	50mm	Cloth FP	½-1000		160
Icarex 35S BM (10.3300)	24x36mm	35mm	35SLR	1970	Ultron	1.8	50mm	Cloth FP	½-1000	A1667	160
Icarex 35S TM (10.3600)	24x36mm	35mm	35SLR	1970	Ultron	1.8	50mm	Cloth FP	½-1000	Mc443	160
Ideal (250/3)	6.5x9cm	plate	VtFoldPl	1927	Tessar	4.5	105mm	Compur		A265	80
Ideal (250/7)	9x12cm	plate	VtFoldPl	1927	Double Protar	6.3	130mm	Compur			100
Ideal (250/9)	10x15cm	plate	VtFoldPl	1927	Tessar	4.5	165mm	Compur		Mc443	120
Ideal (250/11)	13x18cm	plate	VtFoldPl	1927	Double Protar	7	185mm	Compur			120
Ikoflex (850/16)	6x6cm	120/6	TLR	1934	Novar	6.3	80mm	Derval		Mc444	150
Ikoflex (850/16) Comp.Rap.	6x6cm	120/6	TLR	1934	Novar	4.5	80mm	Compur-Rapid		A3157	200
Ikoflex I (850/16)	6x6cm	120/6	TLR	1939	Tessar	3.5	75mm	Compur	-1/250	HK393	130
Ikoflex I (850/16)	6x6cm	120/6	TLR	1939	Novar	3.5	75mm	Klio	-1/250	A663	130
Ikoflex Ia (854/16)	6x6cm	120/6	TLR	1952	Opton Tessar	3.5	75mm	Prontor-SV	-1/300	A666	140
Ikoflex Ia (854/16)	6x6cm	120/6	TLR	1952	Novar	3.5	75mm	Prontor-SV	-1/300		130
Ikoflex Ib (856/16)	6x6cm	120/6	TLR	1957	Novar	3.5	75mm	Prontor-SVS	-1/300		120
Ikoflex Ic (886/16)	6x6cm	120/6	TLR	1956	Tessar	3.5	75mm	Prontor-SVS	-1/300	Mc444	160
Ikoflex Ic (886/16)	6x6cm	120/6	TLR	1956	Novar	3.5	75mm	Prontor-SVS	-1/300	HK438	160
Ikoflex II (851/16)	6x6cm	120/6	TLR	1936	Tessar	3.5	75mm	Compur-Rapid	1-500	Mc444	110
Ikoflex II (851/16)	6x6cm	120/6	TLR	1936	Triotar	3.8	75mm	Compur	1-300	A664	110
Ikoflex II/III (852/16)	6x6cm	120/6	TLR	1938	Tessar	3.5	75mm	Compur-Rapid	1-500	HK405	170
Ikoflex II/III (852/16)	6x6cm	120/6	TLR	1938	Triotar	3.5	75mm	Compur	1-300	HK418	170
Ikoflex IIa (855/16, early)	6x6cm	120/6	TLR	1950	Tessar	3.5	75mm	Compur-Rapid		HK424	130
Ikoflex IIa (855/16, later)	6x6cm	120/6	TLR	1953	Tessar	3.5	75mm	Sync-Compur		A665	130
Ikoflex III (853/16)	6x6cm	120/6	TLR	1939	Tessar	2.8	80mm	Compur-Rapid	1-1/500	Mc444	210
Ikoflex III (853/16)	6x6cm	120/6	TLR	1939	Tessar	3.5	80mm	Compur-Rapid	1-1/400	HK414	210

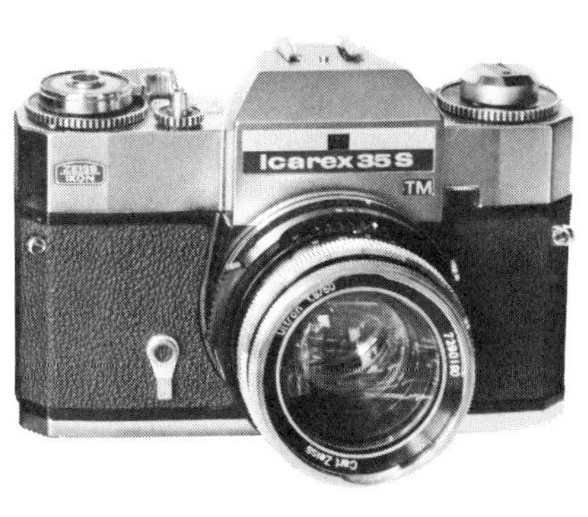

Icarex 35S TM (10.3600)

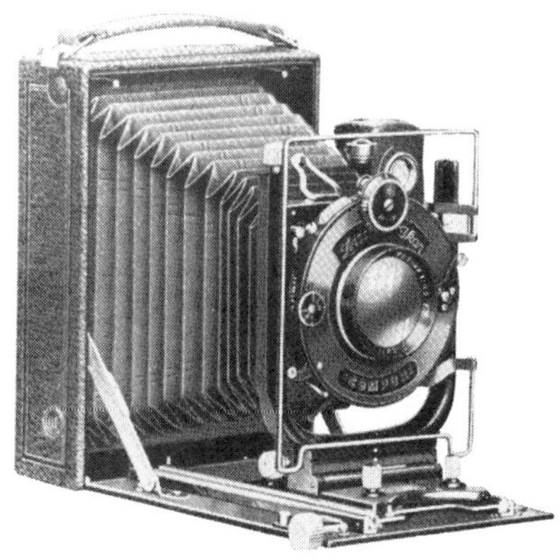

Zeiss Ideal (250/9)

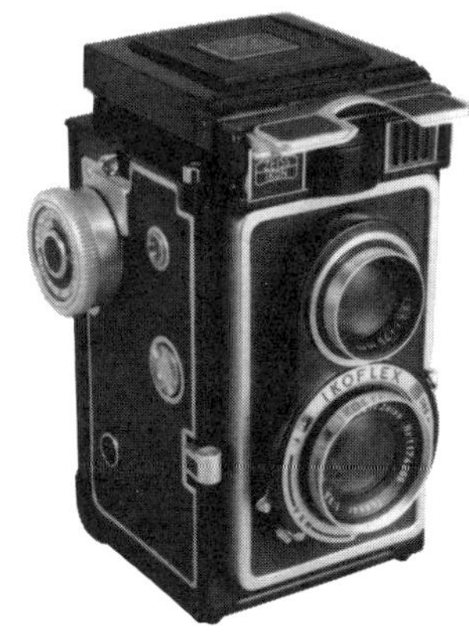

Ikoflex Ic (886/16)

MODEL	FORMAT	FILM	TYPE	Year	LENS	Apert	FL	SHUTTER	SPEEDS	ILLUS	U.S.$
Ikoflex Favorit (887/16)	6x6cm	120/6	TLR	1957	Tessar	3.5	75mm	S.Comp.MXV MX	-1/500	Mc444	390
Ikomat (520/15)	6.5x11cm	116	VtFoldRo	1931	Novar	6.3	120mm	Derval			80
Ikomat (520/18)	3x4cm	127	VtFoldRo	1936	Novar	6.3	50mm	Derval			60
Ikomat (521/2)	6x9cm	120	VtFoldRo	1947	Tessar	3.5	105mm	Compur			100
Ikomatic A (10.0552)	28x28mm	126	126VF	1964	Color Citar	6.3	45mm		1/30, 90	A1975	30
Ikomatic CF	28x28mm	126	126VF	1964	Frontar	8	42mm			A1976	30
Ikomatic F (10.0551)	28x28mm	126	126VF	1964	Frontar	8	42mm		1/30, 90		30
Ikomatic F (10.0551)	28x28mm	126	126VF	1964	Bilotar	8	42mm		1/30, 90		30
Ikonette (504/12)	4x6.5cm	127	VtFoldRo	1929	Frontar	9	80mm		M,Z	A422	50
Ikonette (504/18)	3x4cm	127	VtFoldRo	1930	Frontar	9	50mm		M,Z		70
Ikonette 35 (500/24)	24x36mm	35mm	35VF	1958	Novar	3.5	45mm	Pronto	1-250	A3473	50
Ikonta (520/14)	5x7.5cm	Roll	VtFoldRo	1931	Tessar	4.5	80mm	Compur			60
Ikonta (520/18) + Novar	3x4cm	127	VtFoldRo	1932	Novar	4.5	50mm	Derval		A499	120
Ikonta (520/18) + Tessar	3x4cm	127	VtFoldRo	1936	Tessar	3.5	50mm	Compur		HK227	330
Ikonta 35 (522/24)	24x36mm	35mm	35Fold	1949	Novar	3.5	45mm	Compur-Rapid	1-500	A1029	60
Ikonta 35 (522/24)	24x36mm	35mm	35Fold	1949	Xenar	2.8	45mm	Compur-Rapid	1-500		70
Ikonta 35 (524/24)	24x36mm	35mm	35Fold	1952	Novar	3.5	45mm	Prontor-SV	1-300		280
Ikonta A (520)	4.5x6cm	120	VtFoldRo	1933	Novar	6.3	75mm	Derval		A500	50
Ikonta A (520) CompurRap.	4.5x6cm	120	VtFoldRo	1933	Tessar	3.5	75mm	Compur-Rapid	1-500	A503	70
Ikonta A (521)	4.5x6cm	120	VtFoldRo	1940	Novar	3.5	75mm	Prontor			50
Ikonta B (520/16)	6x6cm	120	VtFoldRo	1937	Tessar	3.5	75mm	Compur-Rapid		A525	120
Ikonta B (521/16)	6x6cm	120	VtFoldRo	1948	Novar	3.5	75mm	Compur		Mc445	80
Ikonta B (523/16)	6x6cm	120	VtFoldRo	1954	Opton Tessar	3.5	75mm	Sync-Compur			200
Ikonta B (523/16)	6x6cm	120	VtFoldRo	1954	Novar	4.5	75mm	Prontor-SV		Mc445	200
Ikonta B (524/16)	6x6cm	120	VtFoldRo	1954	Novar	4.5	75mm	Prontor-SV			160
Ikonta C (520/2)	6x9cm	120	VtFoldRo	1930	Novar	4.5	105mm	Telma		A421	80
Ikonta C (521/2)	6x9cm	120	VtFoldRo	1947	Tessar	3.5	105mm	Compur		A426	140
Ikonta C (523/2)	6x9cm	120	VtFoldRo	1950	Tessar	3.5	105mm	Compur		A428	120
Ikonta C (523/2)	6x9cm	120	VtFoldRo	1950	Novar	4.5	105mm	Compur			120
Ikonta C (524/2)	6x9cm	120	VtFoldRo	1954	Tessar	3.5	105mm	Compur			220
Ikonta D (520/15)	6.5x11cm	116/6	VtFoldRo	1931	Tessar	4.5	120mm	Compur			140
Jena Contax (II)	24x36mm	35mm	35RF	1947	Tessar	3.5	50mm	focal plane			800
Juwel (275/7)	9x12cm	plate	FoldPl	1927	Protar					A264	490
Juwel (275/11)	13x18cm	plate	FoldPl	1927	Tessar	4.5	210mm	Compound		Mc445	550
Juwel Tropical	9x12cm	plate	FoldPl	1929	Tessar	6.3				A1403	540
Künstler-Klappreflex	6.5x9cm	plate	FoldSLR	1927	Tessar	2.7	120mm	focal plane	1-750		190
Künstler-Klappreflex	9x12cm	plate	FoldSLR	1927	Triotar	3.5	150mm	focal plane	1-1000		190
Künstler-Klappreflex	10x15cm	plate	FoldSLR	1927	Tessar	4.5	180mm	focal plane	1-1000		220
Künstler-Reflex	9x12cm	plate	LgSLR	1927	Triotar	3.5	210mm	focal plane	1-1000		190
Kolibri (523/18) (Biotar 2.0)	3x4cm	127	TelescRo	1930	Biotar	2	50mm	Rim-Compur	1-300	HK230	900
Kolibri (523/18) (Tessar 2.8)	3x4cm	127	TelescRo	1930	Tessar	2.8	50mm	Rim-Compur	1-300	HK230	310
Kolibri (523/18) (Tessar 3.5)	3x4cm	127	TelescRo	1930	Tessar	3.5	50mm	Rim-Compur	1-300	A883	200

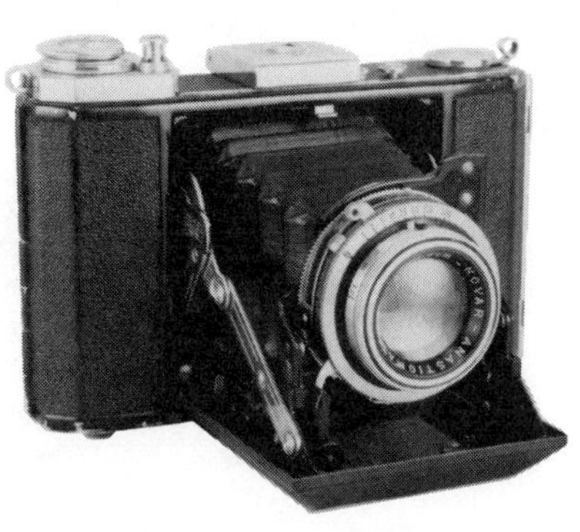

Ikonta B (521/16)

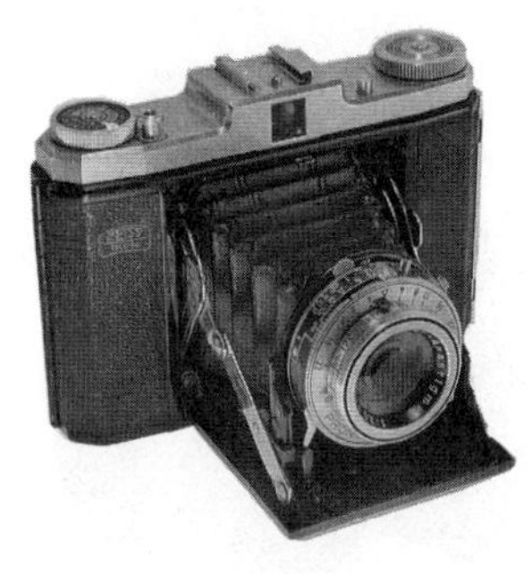

Ikonta B (523/16)

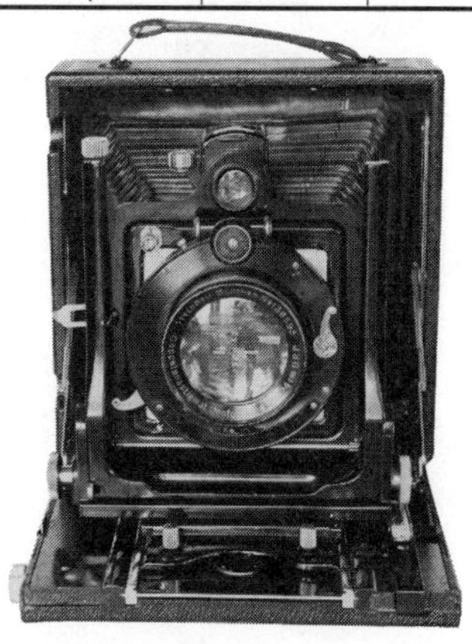

Juwel (275/11)

MODEL	FORMAT	FILM	TYPE	Year	LENS	Apert	FL	SHUTTER	SPEEDS	ILLUS	U.S.$
Kolibri (523/18) (Novar 3.5)	3x4cm	127	TelescRo	1930	Novar	3.5	50mm	Telma		A884	180
Kolibri (523/18) (Novar 4.5)	3x4cm	127	TelescRo	1930	Novar	4.5	50mm	Telma		Mc445	150
Kolibri (523/18) Microscope	3x4cm	127	SciMed	1930	none		50mm	none			290
Kosmopolit (818/11)	5x7"	plate	Field	1927	various			various			290
Kosmopolit (819)	7x9½"	plate	Field	1927	various			various			290
Liliput (361)	4.5x6cm	plate	StrutPl	1927		12.5			M,Z		140
Liliput (370)	6.5x9cm	plate	StrutPl	1927		12.5			M,Z		140
Lloyd (510/17)	8x10.5cm	124	VtFoldRo	1926	Tessar	4.5	120mm	Compur			50
Lloyd (510/17)	8x10.5cm	124	VtFoldRo	1926	Tessar	4.5	135mm	Compur			50
Luftbild (Aerial) 13x18cm	13x18cm	plate	Aerial	1930	Tessar	3.5	250mm	focal plane	750		480
Maximar (207/9)	10x15cm	plate	VtFoldPl	1927	Tessar	4.5	165mm	Compur			90
Maximar A (207/3)	6.5x9cm	plate	VtFoldPl	1927	Tessar	4.5	105mm	Compur			70
Maximar A (207/3) (green)	6.5x9cm	plate	VtFoldPl	1927	Preminar	4.5	105mm	Compur			220
Maximar B (207/7)	9x12cm	plate	VtFoldPl	1927	Novar	6.3	135mm	Klio		Mc445	80
Mess-Ikonta (524/16)	6x6cm	120	VtFoldRo	1954	Novar	4.5	75mm	Prontor-SV			160
Mess-Ikonta (524/24)	24x36mm	35mm	35Fold	1952	Novar	3.5	45mm	Prontor-SV	1-300		280
Micro	24x36mm	35mm	SciMed	1960				focal plane		A1179	390
Miroflex A (859/3)	6.5x9cm	plate	FoldSLR	1927	Tessar	2.7	145mm	focal plane	3-2000		400
Miroflex B (859/7)	9x12cm	plate	FoldSLR	1927	Tessar	3.5	165mm	focal plane	3-2000	Mc445	290
Nettar (510)	4.5x6cm	120	VtFoldRo	1937	Novar	4.5	75mm	Telma	25-100		40
Nettar (510/2)	6x9cm	120	VtFoldRo	1937	Novar	4.5	105mm	Telma	25-100		40
Nettar (515)	4.5x6cm	120	VtFoldRo	1937	Tessar	4.5	75mm	Compur			50
Nettar (515/2)	6x9cm	120	VtFoldRo	1937	Tessar	4.5	105mm	Compur			50
Nettar (515/2)	6x9cm	120	VtFoldRo	1937	Nettar	4.5	105mm	Compur		Mc446	40
Nettar (515/16)	6x6cm	120	HzFoldRo	1937	Novar	4.5	75mm	Telma	25-100	A524	40
Nettar (516/16)	6x6cm	120	HzFoldRo	1937	Nettar	4.5	75mm	Telma	25-100		40
Nettar (517/2)	6x9cm	120	VtFoldRo	1949	Novar	4.5	105mm	Pronto		A427	40
Nettar (517/16)	6x6cm	120	HzFoldRo	1937	Novar	4.5	75mm	Vario	25-200		50
Nettar (517/16)	6x6cm	120	HzFoldRo	1937	Nettar	4.5	75mm	Telma	25-100		50
Nettar IIb (518/16)	6x6cm	120	VtFoldRo	1949	Novar	4.5	75mm	Pronto			50
Nettar IIc (518/2)	6x9cm	120	VtFoldRo	1949	Novar	4.5	105mm	Pronto			40
Nettar S	6x9cm	120	VtFoldRo	1937	Nettar	6.3	105mm	Nettar-S	25-250	A423	40
Nettax (513/16)	6x6cm	120	HzFoldRo	1955	Novar	4.5	75mm	Pronto		A532	120
Nettax (538/24)(2.8)	24x36mm	35mm	35RF	1936	Tessar	2.8	50mm	focal plane	-1/1000	Mc446	800
Nettax (538/24)(3.5)	24x36mm	35mm	35RF	1936	Tessar	3.5	50mm	focal plane	-1/1000	HK545	800
Nettel (870)	4.5x6cm	plate	StrutPl	1929	Tessar	4.5	75mm	focal plane	1-1200	A318	100
Nettel (870)	4.5x6cm	plate	StrutPl	1929	Tessar	2.7	75mm	focal plane	1-1200	HK196	100
Nettel (870/3)	6.5x9cm	plate	StrutPl	1929	Tessar	2.7	120mm	focal plane	1-1200		100
Nettel (870/7)	9x12cm	plate	StrutPl	1929	Tessar	4.5	150mm	focal plane	1-2000	A314	90
Nettel (870/9)	10x15cm	plate	StrutPl	1929	Tessar	3.5	180mm	focal plane	1-2000		120
Nettel (870/11)	5x7"	plate	StrutPl	1929	Tessar	4.5	210mm	focal plane	1-2000		120
Nettel, Tropen (871/3)	6.5x9cm	plate	StrutPl	1929	Tessar	4.5	120mm	focal plane	1-1200	Mc446	700

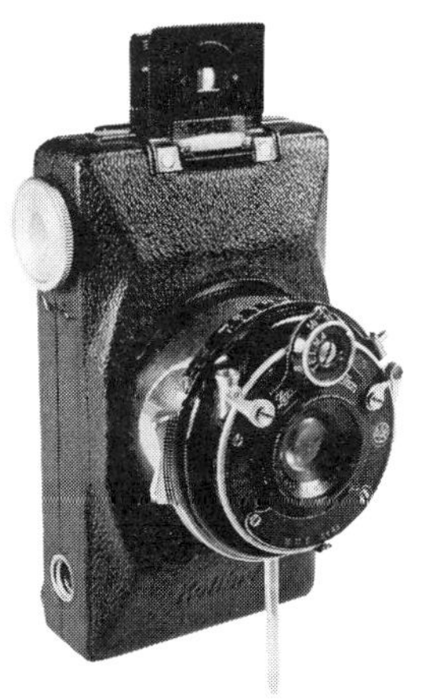

Kolibri (523/18)

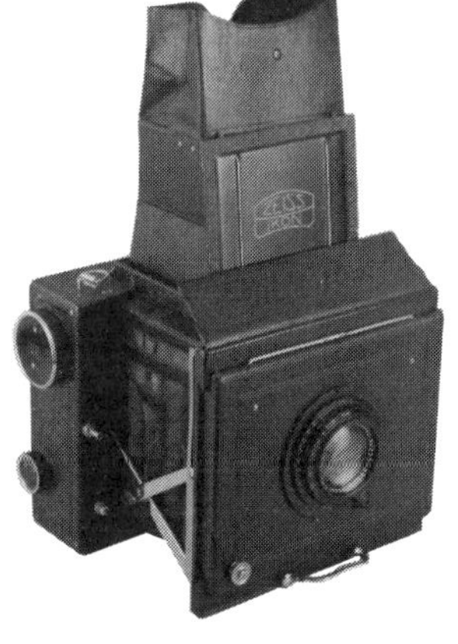

Miroflex B (859/7)

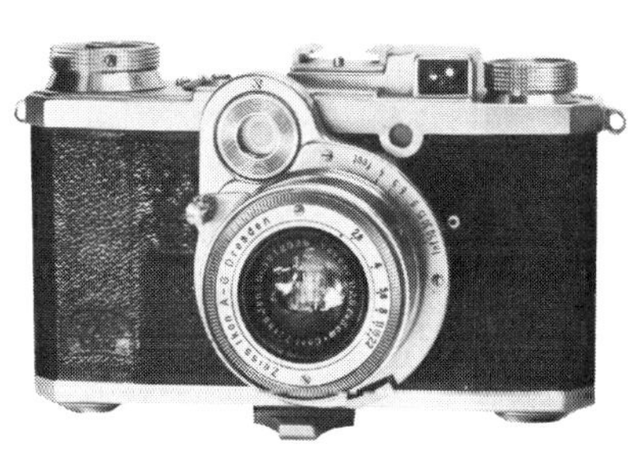

Nettax (538/24)

MODEL	FORMAT	FILM	TYPE	Year	LENS	Apert	FL	SHUTTER	SPEEDS	ILLUS	U.S.$
Nettel, Tropen (871/7)	9x12cm	plate	StrutPl	1929	Tessar	4.5	150mm	focal plane	1-2000	A1423	700
Nettel, Tropen (871/9)	10x15cm	plate	StrutPl	1929	Tessar	3.5	180mm	focal plane	1-2000	HK197	700
Nettel, Tropen (871/11)	5x7"	plate	StrutPl	1929	Tessar	4.5	210mm	focal plane	1-2000		700
Nixe (551/16)	8x14cm	122	VtFoldRo	1927	Double Protar	7	145mm	Compur			100
Nixe (551/17)	8x10.5cm	124	VtFoldRo	1927	Dominar	4.5	135mm	Compur		Mc446	100
Onito (126/3)	6.5x9cm	plate	VtFoldPl	1927	Novar	6.3	105mm			Mc446	90
Onito (126/7)	9x12cm	plate	VtFoldPl	1927	Novar	6.3	135mm				70
Orix (308)	10x15cm	plate	VtFoldPl	1928	Tessar	4.5	150mm			Mc446	100
Palmos-O	4.5x6cm	plate	StrutPl	1927	Tessar	2.7	80mm	focal plane	20-1000		550
Perfekt (834/11)	5x7"	plate	Field	1927	various			various			210
Perfekt (835)	5x7"	plate	Field	1927	various			various			150
Perfekt (835/11)	5x7"	plate	Field	1927	various			various			210
Perfekt (836)	18x24cm	plate	Field	1927	various			various			210
Perfekt (837)	18x24cm	plate	Field	1927	various			various			210
Piccolette (545/12)	4x6.5cm	127	StrutRo	1927	Achromat	11	75mm	Acro			100
Piccolette-Luxus (546/12)	4x6.5cm	127	StrutRo	1927	Dominar	4.5	75mm	Dial-Compur		A1493	330
Piccolette-Luxus (546/12)	4x6.5cm	127	StrutRo	1927	Tessar	4.5	75mm	Dial-Compur		HK215	330
Plaskop 602/1	45x107	plate	StJumelle	1927	Achromat	12	60mm			HK518	140
Plaskop 603/1	45x107	plate	StJumelle	1927	Novar	6.8	60mm			HK518	200
Plaskop 603/4	6x13cm	plate	StJumelle	1927	Novar	6.8	60mm			HK518	240
Polyskop (609/1)	45x107	plate	StJumelle	1927	Tessar	4.5	60mm	St. Compur			270
Polyskop (609/4)	6x13cm	plate	StJumelle	1927	Tessar	4.5	75mm	St. Compur			270
Raupp	13x18cm	plate	Studio	1925	various			various			240
Simplex (112/7)	9x12cm	plate	VtFoldPl	1928	Novar	6.3	135mm	Derval			50
Simplex (511/2)	6x9cm	120	VtFoldRo	1928	Nettar	6.3	150mm	Derval		Mc446	70
Simplex-Ernoflex (853)	4.5x6cm	plate	LgSLR	1927	Ernoplast	4.5	75mm	focal plane	20-1000	HK343	800
Simplex-Ernoflex (853/3)	6.5x9cm	plate	LgSLR	1927	Ernon	3.5	105mm	focal plane	20-1000	HK343	290
Simplex-Ernoflex (853/7)	9x12cm	plate	LgSLR	1927	Tessar	4.5	135mm	focal plane	20-1000	HK343	290
Sirene (135/3)	6.5x9cm	plate	VtFoldPl	1927	Dominar	4.5	135mm	Compur			60
Sirene (135/5)	8x10.5cm	plate	VtFoldPl	1930	Dominar	4.5	135mm	Compur			60
Sirene (135/7)	9x12cm	plate	VtFoldPl	1927	Dominar	4.5	135mm	Compur			60
SL-706 (10.3700)	24x36mm	35mm	35SLR	1972	Ultron	1.8	50mm	focal plane			260
SL-706 (10.3700)	24x36mm	35mm	35SLR	1971	Ultron	1.8	50mm	focal plane			220
Sonnet (303)	4.5x6cm	plate	StrutPl	1927	Tessar	4.5	75mm	Compur		HK184	530
Sonnet (303/3)	6.5x9cm	plate	StrutPl	1927	Novar	6.3	105mm	Compur		HK184	530
Stereax	6x13cm	plate	SterStrut	1926	Tessar	4.5	90mm	focal plane	1/20-1200		1000
Stereo Ideal (650)	9x18cm	Sheet	StFoldPl	1927	Tessar	4.5	120mm	Compur			350
Stereo Ideal (651)	6x13cm	plate	StFoldPl	1927	Tessar	4.5	90mm	Compound			250
Stereo Nettel (613/4)	6x13cm	plate	SterStrut	1927	Tessar	4.5	75mm	focal plane		HK521	370
Stereo Nettel (613/9)	10x15cm	plate	SterStrut	1927	Tessar	4.5	165mm	focal plane		HK521	330
Stereo Nettel, Trop. (614/4)	6x13cm	plate	SterStrut	1927	Tessar	4.5	75mm	focal plane			900
Stereo Nettel, Trop. (614/9)	10x15cm	plate	SterStrut	1927	Tessar	4.5	165mm	focal plane			900

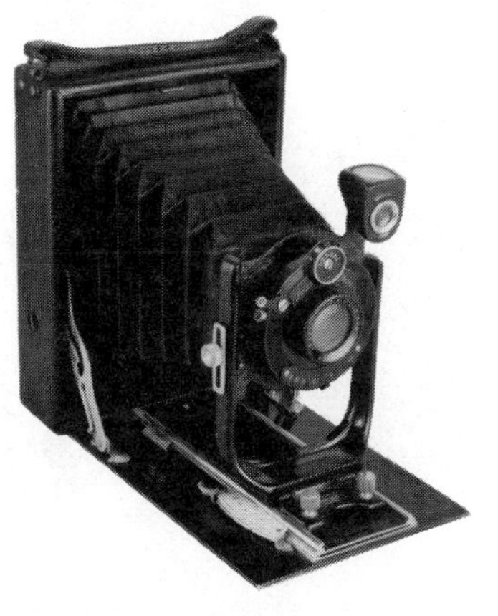

Onito (126/3)

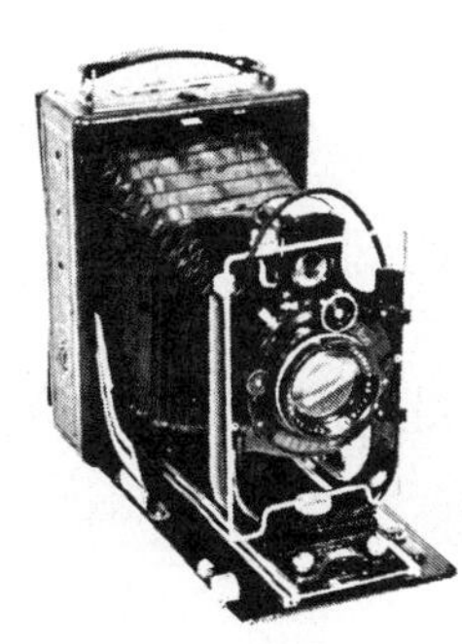

Orix (308)

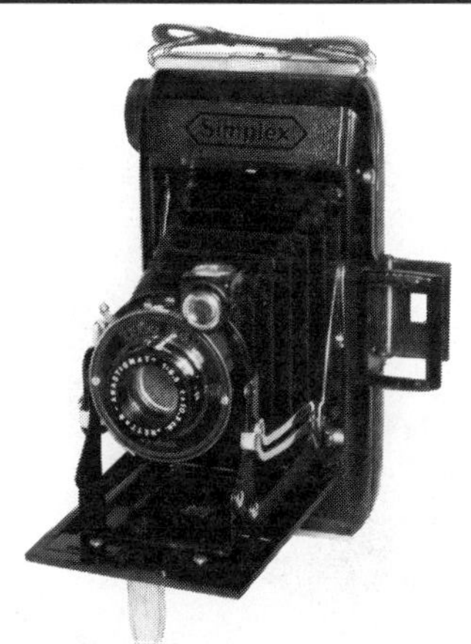

Simplex (511/2)

MODEL	FORMAT	FILM	TYPE	Year	LENS	Apert	FL	SHUTTER	SPEEDS	ILLUS	U.S.$
Stereo-Ernoflex (621/1)	45x107	plate	SterRefl	1927	Ernon	3.5	75mm	focal plane	1/20-1000	HK520	1200
Ster.-Simplex-Erno. (615/1)	45x107	plate	SterRefl	1927	Tessar	4.5	80mm	focal plane			700
Stereoco (612/1)	45x107	plate	StJumelle	1927	Tessar	6.3	55mm	Dial-Compur			370
Stereolette-Cupido (611)	45x107	plate	StFoldPl	1927	Dominar	4.5	65mm	Compur			230
Suevia	6.5x9cm	plate	VtFoldPl	1926	C-N Periskop	11	105mm	Derval	25-100		110
Super Ikomat B (530/16)	6x6cm	120	HzFoldRo	1935	Tessar	2.8	80mm	Compur-Rapid	1-400		160
Super Ikonta A (530)	4.5x6cm	120	VtFoldRo	1934	Tessar	3.5	70mm	Compur	1-300	Mc447	180
Super Ikonta A (531)	4.5x6cm	120	VtFoldRo	1937	Tessar	3.5	75mm	Compur-Rapid	1-500	Mc447	210
Super Ikonta A (531)	4.5x6cm	120	VtFoldRo	1948	Xenar	3.5	75mm	Compur-Rapid	1-500	HK289	210
Super Ikonta A (531) X	4.5x6cm	120	VtFoldRo	1950	Tessar	3.5	75mm	CompurRapX	1-500	HK289	260
Super Ikonta A (531) MX	4.5x6cm	120	VtFoldRo	1953	Tessar	3.5	75mm	CompurRapMX		HK289	700
Super Ikonta A (531) MX	4.5x6cm	120	VtFoldRo	1953	Tessar	3.5	75mm	Sync-Compur		HK289	700
Super Ikonta B (530/16)	6x6cm	120	HzFoldRo	1935	Tessar	2.8	80mm	Compur-Rapid	-1/400	Mc447	330
Super Ikonta B (532/16)	6x6cm	120	HzFoldRo	1937	Tessar	2.8	80mm	Compur-Rapid		Mc447	180
Super Ikonta B (532/16) MX	6x6cm	120	HzFoldRo	1951	Tessar	2.8	80mm	Sync-Compur		A527	390
Super Ikonta BX (533/16)	6x6cm	120	HzFoldRo	1937	Tessar	2.8	80mm	Compur-Rapid	-1/400	Mc448	210
Super Ik. BX (533/16) MX	6x6cm	120	HzFoldRo	1952	Tessar	2.8	80mm	S.Comp.MX	1-500	Mc448	370
Super Ik. BX (533/16) MX	6x6cm	120	HzFoldRo	1952	Opton Tessar	2.8	80mm	S.Comp.MX	1-500	HK299	370
Super Ikonta C (530/2)	6x9cm	120	VtFoldRo	1934	Triotar	4.5	120mm	Klio		HK269	160
Super Ikonta C (530/2)	6x9cm	120	VtFoldRo	1934	Tessar	3.8	105mm	Compur-Rapid	1-400	Mc448	200
Super Ikonta C (531/2)	6x9cm	120	VtFoldRo	1950	Tessar	3.5	105mm	Compur-Rapid	1-400	Mc448	270
S. Ik. C (531/2) (dual-format	6x9cm	120	VtFoldRo	1938	Tessar	4.5	105mm	Compur-Rapid	1-400	A430	230
S. Ik. C (531/2) (dual-format	6x9cm	120	VtFoldRo	1938	Tessar	3.5	105mm	Compur	1-250	Mc448	230
Super Ikonta C (531/2) MX	6x9cm	120	VtFoldRo	1950	Opton Tessar	3.5	106mm	S.Comp.MX		HK275	650
Super Ikonta D (530/15)	6.5x11cm	116	VtFoldRo	1934	Tessar	4.5	120mm	Compur	1-250	Mc448	240
Super Ikonta D (530/15)	6.5x11cm	116	VtFoldRo	1936	Tessar	4.5	120mm	Compur-Rapid	1-400		240
Super Ikonta III (531/16)	6x6cm	120	HzFoldRo	1954	Novar	3.5	75mm	S.Comp.MX	1-500	Mc448	290
Super Ik. III (531/16) Tessar	6x6cm	120	HzFoldRo	1954	Opton Tessar	3.5	80mm	S.Comp.MX	1-500	A1511	310
Super Ikonta IV (534/16)	6x6cm	120	HzFoldRo	1956	Tessar	3.5	75mm	S.Comp.MX	1-500	Mc448	390
Super Nettel (536/24)	24x36mm	35mm	35Fold	1934	Tessar	3.5	50mm	focal plane	5-1000	Mc448	330
Super Nettel (536/24)	24x36mm	35mm	35Fold	1935	Triotar	3.5	50mm	focal plane	5-1000	Mc448	330
Super Nettel II (537/24)	24x36mm	35mm	35Fold	1936	Tessar	2.8	50mm	focal plane		Mc449	700
Symbolica	24x36mm	35mm	35VF	1959	Tessar	2.8	45mm	Prontormat		A2115	70
Symbolica (II)	24x36mm	35mm	35VF	1959	Tessar	2.8	50mm	Prontormat			50
Taxo (122/3)	6.5x9cm	plate	VtFoldPl	1927	Dominar	4.5	105mm	Derval			70
Taxo (122/7)	9x12cm	plate	VtFoldPl	1927	Novar	6.3	135mm	Klio		A267	60
Taxo (126/3)	6.5x9cm	plate	VtFoldPl	1927	Frontar	9	105mm	Derval			70
Taxo (126/7)	9x12cm	plate	VtFoldPl	1927	Dominar	4.5	135mm	Derval		Mc449	70
Tenax 4.5x6	4.5x6cm	plate	StrutPl	1927	Dagor	6.8	75mm	Compound	1-250		140
Tenax 6.5x9	6.5x9cm	plate	StrutPl	1927	Dogmar	6.3	100mm	Compound	1-250		150
Tenax 45x107	45x107	plate	SterStrut	1927	Dagor	6.8	60mm	Compound	1-250	HK566	160
Tenax Automatic (10.0651)	24x36mm	35mm	35VF	1960	Tessar	2.8	50mm	Prontormat		Mc449	40

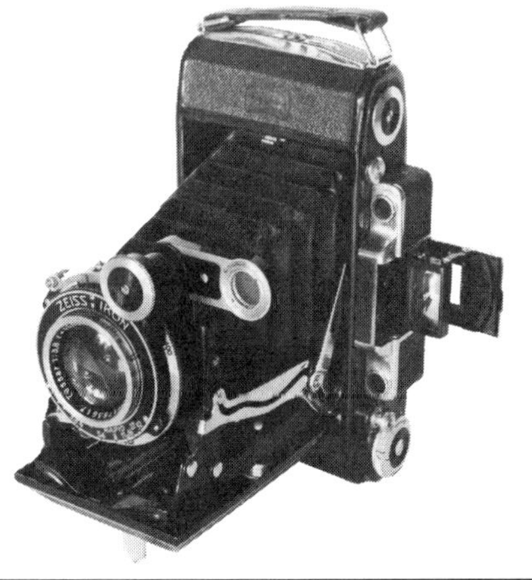

Super Ikonta C (531/2)

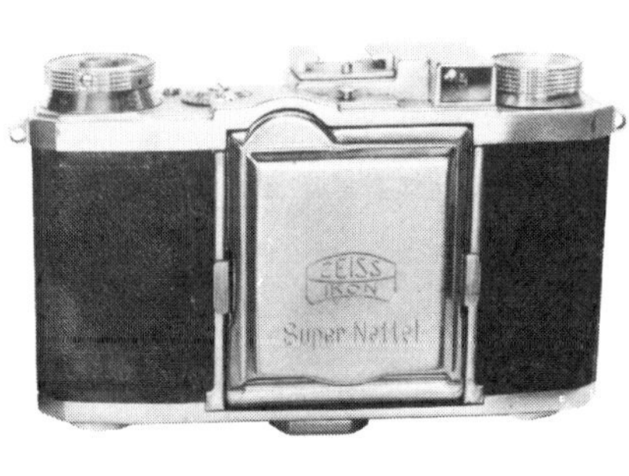

Super Nettel II (537/24)

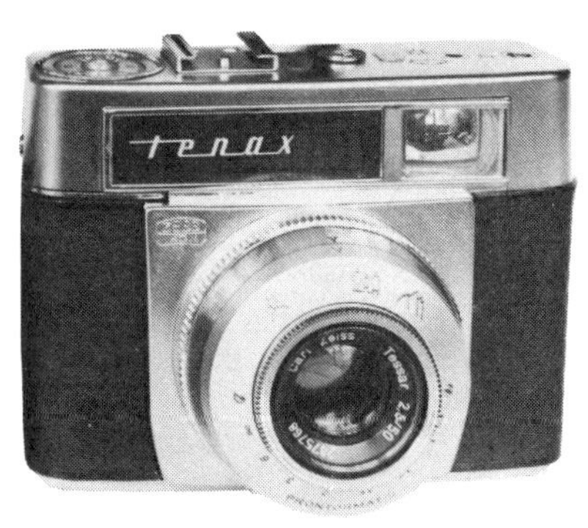

Tenax Automatic (10.0651)

MODEL	FORMAT	FILM	TYPE	Year	LENS	Apert	FL	SHUTTER	SPEEDS	ILLUS	U.S.$
Tenax I (570/27)	24x24mm	35mm	35VF	1930	Novar	3.5	35mm	Compur		Mc449	70
Tenax I (East Germany)	24x24mm	35mm	35VF	1948	Tessar	3.5	37.5mm			Mc449	70
Tenax II (580/27)	24x24mm	35mm	35RF	1937	Tessar	2.8	40mm	Compur	1-400	Mc449	320
Tengoflex (85/16)	6x6cm	120	TLR-Box	1941	Frontar	11				A1710	430
Tessco (76/1)	9x12cm	plate	VtFoldPl	1927	Tessar	4.5	135mm	Compur			90
Toska (400)	13x18cm	plate	HzFoldPl	1927	Litonar	6.8	180mm	Chronos B			240
Trona (210/3)	6.5x9cm	plate	VtFoldPl	1927	Dominar	4.5	105mm	Klio			80
Trona (210/5)	8.5x11cm	plate	VtFoldPl	1927	Tessar	4.5	135mm	Compur			80
Trona (210/7)	9x12cm	plate	VtFoldPl	1927	Tessar	4.5	135mm	Compur			70
Trona (212/7)	9x12cm	plate	VtFoldPl	1928	Tessar	4.5	135mm	Compur		Mc449	70
Trona (214/3)	6.5x9cm	plate	VtFoldPl	1931	Tessar	3.5	105mm	Compur		A270	110
Trona (214/7)	9x12cm	plate	VtFoldPl	1929	Tessar	3.5	135mm	Compur			100
Tropen Adoro (230/3)	6.5x9cm	plate	VtFoldPl	1927	Tessar	4.5	105mm	Compur		Mc449	660
Tropen Adoro (230/7)	9x12cm	plate	VtFoldPl	1927	Tessar	4.5	135mm	Compur			660
Tropen Adoro (230/9)	10x15cm	plate	VtFoldPl	1927	Tessar	4.5	165mm	Compur		A271	660
Tropica (285/7)	9x12cm	plate	FoldPl	1927	Dominar	4.5	135mm	Compur			1100
Tropica (285/9)	10x15cm	plate	FoldPl	1927	Dominar	4.5	165mm	Compur		Mc450	1100
Tropica (285/11)	5x7"	plate	FoldPl	1927	Dominar	4.5	180mm	Compur			1100
Tudor 6.5x9	6.5x9cm	plate	LgSLR	1927	Tessar	4.5	150mm	focal plane		A1593	270
Tudor 9x9	9x9cm	plate	LgSLR	1927	Triotar	3.5	150mm	focal plane			270
Tudor 9x12	9x12cm	plate	LgSLR	1927	Tessar	4.5	150mm	focal plane			270
Tudor 10x15	10x15cm	plate	LgSLR	1927	Triotar	3.5	180mm	focal plane			270
Unette (550)	22x31mm	Roll	RollBox	1927	Tessar	4.5	40mm	focal plane			290
Unitak	8x10.5cm	124	VtFoldRo	1927	Nettar	6.3	130mm	Derval			120
Victrix (101)	4.5x6cm	plate	VtFoldPl	1927	Novar	6.3	75mm	Compur		Mc450	120
Volta (135/3)	6.5x9cm	plate	VtFoldPl	1927	Dominar	4.5	105mm	Compur			60
Volta (135/7)	9x12cm	plate	VtFoldPl	1927	Tessar	4.5	135mm	Compur			60
Volta (146/3)	6.5x9cm	plate	VtFoldPl	1927	Tessar	4.5	105mm	Compur			60
Volta (146/7)	9x12cm	plate	VtFoldPl	1927	Dominar	4.5	135mm	Klio		A268	50
...ZENITH CAMERA CORP.											
Comet	4x6cm	127	RigidRo	1947		11			I,T	Mc450	20
Comet Flash	4x6cm	127	RigidRo	1948		11			I,T	Mc450	20
Sharpshooter	6x9cm	120	MetalBox	1948	Meniscus				1/40,B		10
Vu-Flash "120"	6x9cm	120	MetalBox		Meniscus						10
...ZENZA - Tokyo											
Bronica C (black)	6x6cm	120	MedSLR	1964	Nikkor	2.8	75mm	focal plane	1-500		290
Bronica C (chrome)	6x6cm	120	MedSLR	1964	Nikkor	2.8	75mm	focal plane	1-500		290
Bronica C2	6x6cm	220	MedSLR	1965	Nikkor	2.8	75mm	focal plane	1-500		290
Bronica D (Deluxe)	6x6cm	220	MedSLR	1958	Nikkor	2.8	75mm	focal plane	1-1250		320
Bronica EC	6x6cm	220	MedSLR	1972	Nikkor	2.8	75mm	focal plane	4-1000		390
Bronica EC-TL	6x6cm	220	MedSLR	1975	Nikkor	2.8	75mm	focal plane	4-1000		520
Bronica EC-TL II	6x6cm	220	MedSLR	1978	Nikkor	2.8	75mm	focal plane			460

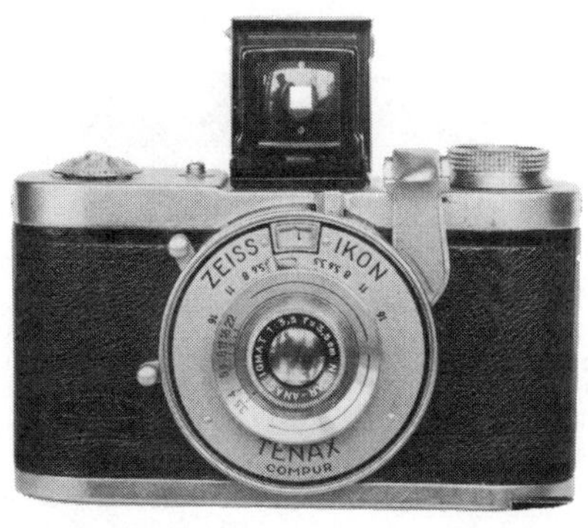

Tenax I (570/27)

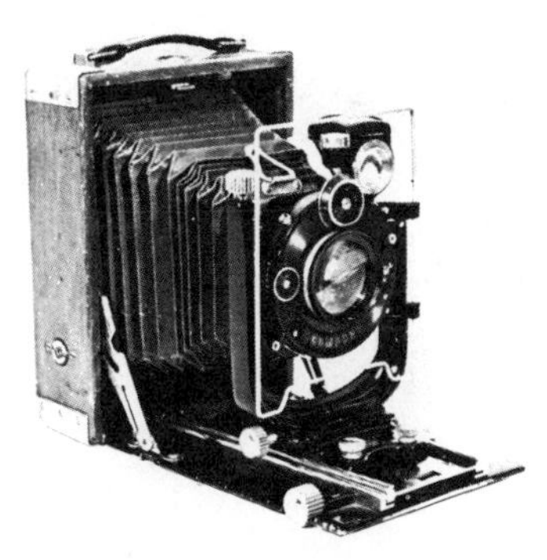

Tropen Adoro (230/3)

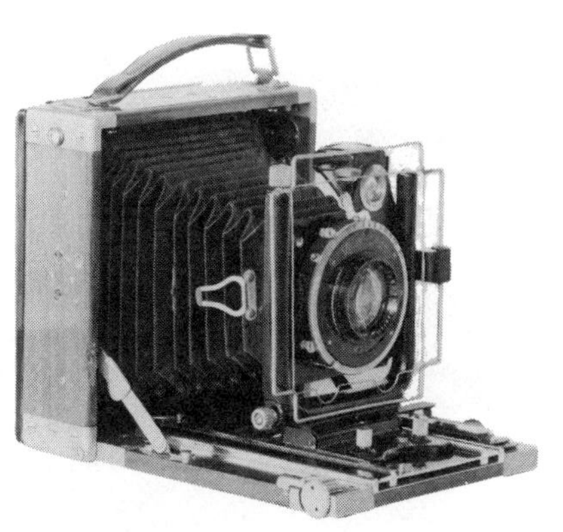

Tropica (285/9)

MODEL	FORMAT	FILM	TYPE	Year	LENS	Apert	FL	SHUTTER	SPEEDS	ILLUS	U.S.$
Bronica ETR body	4.5x6cm	220	MedSLR	1975	body only	---	---	electronic	8-1/500		240
Bronica ETR + 75/2.8	4.5x6cm	220	MedSLR	1975	Zenzanon	2.8	75mm	electronic	8-1/500		610
Bronica ETRS body	4.5x6cm	220	MedSLR	1978	body only	---	---	electronic	8-1/500		340
Bronica ETRS + 75/2.8	4.5x6cm	220	MedSLR	1978	Zenzanon	2.8	75mm	electronic	8-1/500		700
Bronica ETRSi body	4.5x6cm	220	MedSLR	1987	body only	---	---	electronic	8-1/500		620
Bronica ETRSi + 75/2.8	4.5x6cm	220	MedSLR	1987	Zenzanon	2.8	75mm	electronic	8-1/500		1100
Bronica GS-1 body	6x7cm	220	MedSLR	1983	body only	---	---	electronic	16-1/500		900
Bronica GS-1 + 100/3.5	6x7cm	220	MedSLR	1983	Zenzanon	3.5	100mm	electronic	16-1/500		1700
Bronica S	6x6cm	220	MedSLR	1961	Nikkor	2.8	75mm	focal plane	1-1000	Mc450	290
Bronica S2 (black)	6x6cm	220	MedSLR	1965	Nikkor	2.8	75mm	focal plane	1-1000		310
Bronica S2 (chrome)	6x6cm	220	MedSLR	1965	Nikkor	2.8	75mm	focal plane	1-1000		310
Bronica S2A	6x6cm	220	MedSLR	1970	Nikkor	2.8	75mm	focal plane	1-1000		480
Bronica SQ body	6x6cm	220	MedSLR	1980	body only	---	---	electronic	8-1/500		450
Bronica SQ + 80/2.8	6x6cm	220	MedSLR	1980	Zenzanon	2.8	80mm	electronic	8-1/500		900
Bronica SQ-A body	6x6cm	220	MedSLR	1982	body only	---	---	electronic	8-1/500		480
Bronica SQ-A + 80/2.8	6x6cm	220	MedSLR	1982	Zenzanon	2.8	80mm	electronic	8-1/500		1100
Bronica SQ-Ai body	6x6cm	220	MedSLR	1991	body only	---	---	electronic	16-1/500		900
Bronica SQ-Ai + 80/2.8	6x6cm	220	MedSLR	1991	Zenzanon	2.8	80mm	electronic	16-1/500		1700
Bronica SQ-AM body	6x6cm	220	MedSLR	1982	body only	---	---	electronic	8-1/500		700
Bronica SQ-AM + 80/2.8	6x6cm	220	MedSLR	1982	Zenzanon	2.8	80mm	electronic	8-1/500		1500
...ZIMMERMAN - Zirndorf b/Nürnberg											
Gezi II	4x4cm	127	BakeliteRoll	1950	Achromat	9	6cm			Mc211	50
...ZION (Ed. Zion) - Paris											
Pocket Z	6.5x9cm	plate	StrutPl	1920	Rex Luxia	4.5	105mm	Compur		Mc452	120
Pocket Z	6.5x9cm	plate	StrutPl	1920	Boyer Sapphir	4.5	105mm	Compur		Mc452	120
Pocket Z, stereo	6x13cm	plate	SterStrut	1928	Zion Anastigmat	6.3	75mm	Gitzo stereo		F1402	220
Simili Jumelle (black)	6.5x9cm	plate	Jumelle	1893	Zion Anastigmat			guillotine		A840	200
Simili Jumelle (brown)	6.5x9cm	plate	Jumelle	1893	Zion Anastigmat			guillotine		A840	210
Simili Jumelle 9x12	9x12cm	plate	Jumelle	1893	Zion Anastigmat	8	150mm	guillotine		A832	200
Simili Jumelle Stereo	9x18cm	plate	StJumelle	1893	Zion Anastigmat			guillotine			190
Zionscope	45x107	plate	StJumelle	1900				guillotine		Mc452	410
...ZUIHO OPTICAL CO. - Japan											
Honor	24x36mm	35mm	35RF	1956	Konishiroku Hexar	3.5	50mm	focal plane	1-500		580
Honor	24x36mm	35mm	35RF	1956	Honor	1.9	50mm	focal plane	1-1000		560
...ZUIHO SOKURYO KIKI K.K. (Zuiho Optical & Measuring Instruments Co. Ltd.) - Tokyo											
Nice	10x14mm	16mm	Submin	1946	Anastigmat	3.5	25mm			Mc452	1700
...ZULAUF (G. Zulauf) - Zurich											
Bebe	4.5x6cm	plate	StrutPl	1911							220
Polyscop	45x107	plate	StJumelle	1910	Goerz				2-250	HK482	270
...ZUNOW OPTICAL INDUSTRY											
Zunow	24x36mm	35mm	35SLR	1958	Zunow	1.8	50mm				3500
Zunow	24x36mm	35mm	35SLR	1958	Zunow	1.2	58mm				3500

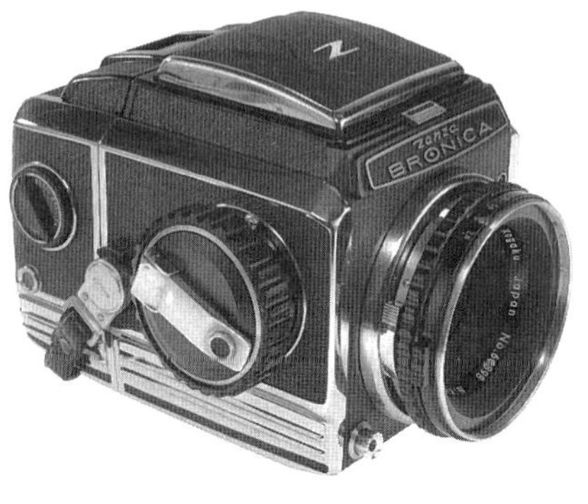

Bronica S

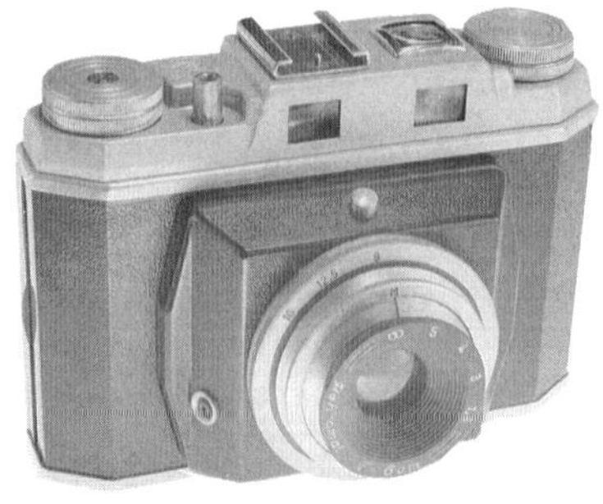

Zimmerman Gezi II

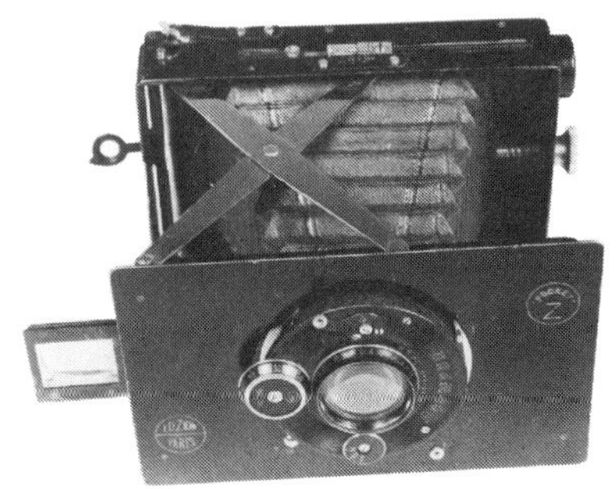

Zion Pocket Z

Nikon Data Guide
by Paul Common 276x214mm 66 B/W illustrations
SB.13896 .... £16.95

Nikon Fascination
by Peter Braczko. History, Technique and Myths from 1917 to Today. 215x240mm 12 Col. 400 B/W Written in German.
HB. 12035 .... £49.95

Nikon Lenses
by 'Moose' Peterson 13660 £10.95

Nikon Pocket Book
by Peter Braczko. English Edition with Price Guide 13668 ...... £25.95

Nikon Price Guide
by Peter Braczko Pocket-size paperback. Written in German 14849 .... £6.95

Nikon System Handbook
'Moose' Peterson 278x216mm 15 Col. 30 B/W illustrations
SB. 13897 .... £16.95

Nikon Rangefinder Camera
Robert Rotoloni. Illustrated History from the end of the war to the very last rangefinder model,with lenses and accessories. 217x155mm 302 B/W HB. 1038 .... £17.95

Plaubel Cameras and Lenses
Udo Afalter 297x210 More than 90 photographs, illustrations, tables and related adverts.
SB. 19318 .... £15.95

Rectaflex

Rectaflex
by Patrice-Hervé Pont. 245x167mm 65 B/W Line Drawings. Written in French with short English translation. SB. 12052 .... £19.95

Rollei

Collector's Guide to Rollei Cameras
Arthur Evans. Helps identify every model and variant.216x148mm 125 B/W HB. 1005 .... £17.95

Rollei 1920-1993
by Udo Afalter. 298x211mm 262 B/W illustrations. Written in German. SB. 12021 .... £47.00

Rollei from Heidoscop to Rolleiflex 6008
303x214mm 3 Col. 490 B/W
HB. 12020 .... £58.95

Rollei TLR Collectors Guide
by Ian Parker. Comprehensive guide to Rollei and Rolleicord models, including special editions, 72 Col. 7 B/W
SB. 10100 .... £16.95

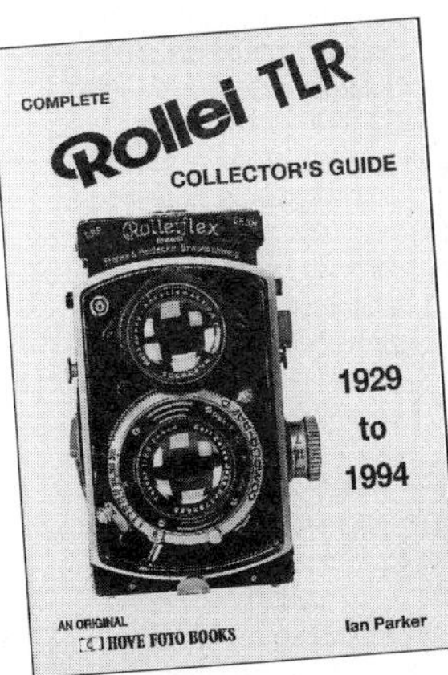

Rollei TLR - Complete Users Manual
Ian Parker 210x148mm - 20 Col. 160 B/W illustrations
SB. 13425 .... £16.95

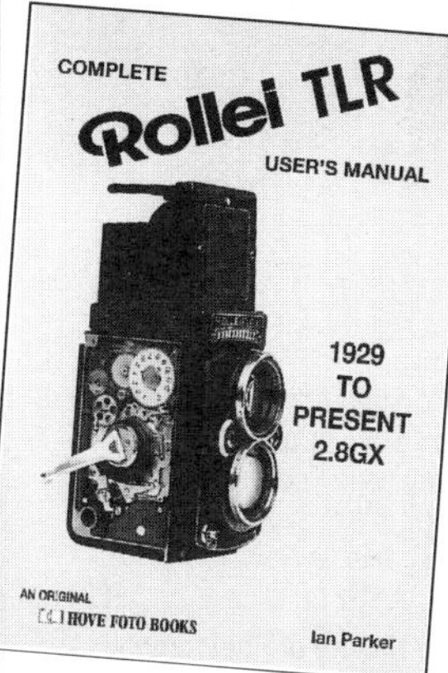

Rollei TLR - The History
by Ian Parker, 250x170mm 80 B/W German Text
HB.13047 .... £19.95
English 1813 .... £14.95

Rolleiflex and Rolleicord 1928-1993
by Udo Afalter. 290x210mm 26 col. 231 B/W illustrations. Written in German.
HB. 12022 .... £45.50

Rolleiflex Guide
Focal Press Reprint 212x140mm over 100 line drawings. Guide to the twin lens cameras SB.15112 .... £10.95

Twenty-five Years of the Rollei 35
by Udo Afalter. 210x150mm 30 Col. 107 B/W illustrations. Written in German.
HB.12023 .... £35.45

Thornton Pickard Story
296x206mm 49 B/W
SB. 4001 .... £6.00

Voigtlander

Voigtlander
Reprint of a leaflet from 1926. 64 pages 90 B/W illustrations. In German. SB. 12039 .... £14.45

Voigtlander 1945-1991
by Udo Afalter HB 13664 ... £46.50

Zeiss Ikon

Zeiss Compendium
East and West 1940-1972 Charles Barringer 255x195mm Almost 400 illustrations in B/W HB. 22982 .... £29.95

On the Track of Contax 1932 -1945
by Hans-Jürgen Kuc. 260x218mm 1 Col. 387 B/W illustrations. Written in German.
HB. 12033 .... £49.95

The Collector's Checklist of Contax and Zeiss Classic Miniature Cameras
by Dr. Neill Wright and Ivor Matanle. 300x213mm 56 pages of text only.
SB. 12030 .... £27.95

The Contax S Camera Family
by Peter Dechert. 280x215mm 28 B/W illustrations. Written in English. SB. 12029 .... £18.95

Zeiss Contax Repair Manual
by Peter Tooke. Models II & III Step-by-Step guide to repairing Contax cameras.211x148mm
SB. 9878 .... £15.00

Zeiss Ikon 1926-1993
by Udo Afalter. 297x210mm over 300 B/W illustrations Written in German. SB. 12019 .... £39.95

Zeiss Ikon Cameras 1926-39
by D.B. Tubbs. The story of the birth of Zeiss Ikon, the resulting array of cameras in the Zeiss catalogue, followed by rationalisation and development of new cameras, especially the Contax and other 35mm cameras up to 1939. The last part lists Zeiss Ikon cameras from 1926. 217x154mm 303 B/W HB. 6011 .... £17.95

Collectors' guides

Abring - From Daguerre to Today
Illustrated guide in three volumes - each £19.95
Set of 3 1791-92-93 .... £55.95

Collecting & Using Classic Cameras
by Ivor Matanle. For the collector who also enjoys using older cameras 259x198mm 317 B/W SB. 6369 .... £14.95

Collector's Guide to Japanese Cameras 1845-1984
340 pages, 215x310mm 19 Col. and 2221 B&W illustrations Written in English and Japanese HB 20542 .... £119.00

Cameras from Belgium and Holland
120 pages, covering 19th and 20th Century, 148 B/W illustrations. Written in English and Dutch 298x206mm
SB.12031 .... £13.50

Collectors Guide to Kuribayashi-Petri
222x142mm 173 B/W
HB. 1007 .... £22.95

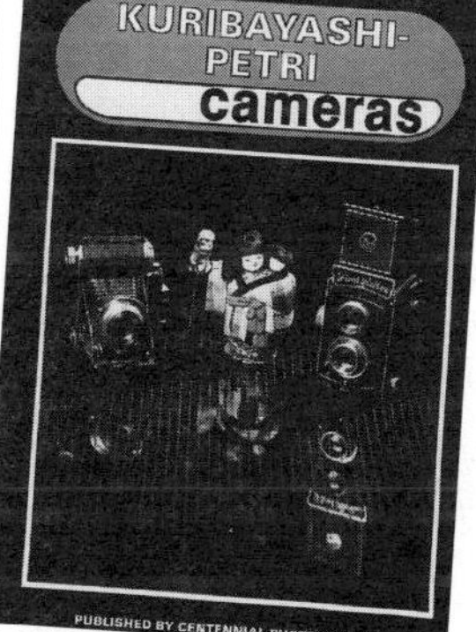

French Camera Catalogue
by Patrice-Hervé Pont. 250x170mm 48 pages covering 200 cameras with 140 B/W. In French. SB. 12051 .... £19.95

Geheim Disguised Cameras
by Eaton S. Lothrop Jnr and Michel Auer. 280x270mm 8 Col. 277 B/W Written in German.
HB.12044 .... £49.95

German Cameras 1900-1945
by Willi Kerkmann. 297x211mm 375 pages, 1,700 cameras from 141 manufacturers fully illustrated. In German. SB. 12026 .... £49.95

German Cameras 1945 -1986
by Willi Kerkmann. 297x211mm 1570 B/W 360 pages Cameras from 120 manufacturers. Written in German. SB. 12025 .... £49.95

Illustrated History of Colour Photography
by Jack H. Coote 303x240mm 125 Col. 55 B/W
HB. 5931 .... £29.95

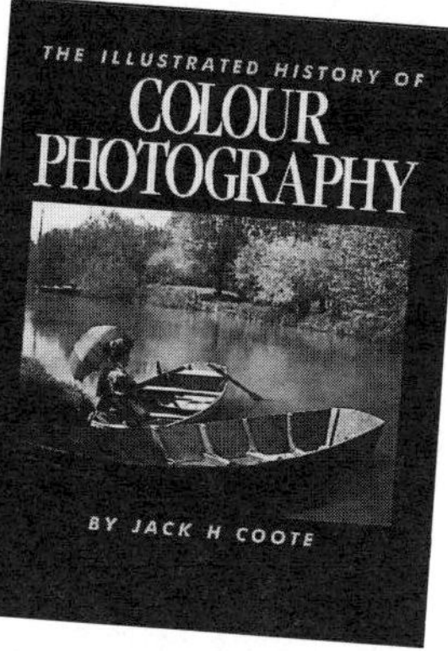

Michel Auer Collectors Guide
240x226mm HB. 1013 (Price Guide SB. 235x110mm) 2856 B/W £49.95

150 Classic Cameras from 1839 to the Present
by P.H. van Hasbroeck
HB 7459 .... £39.95

Photography: 12 Legendary Cameras
by Patrice-Hervé Pont. 240x345mm 12 pages with 12 B/W illustrations. In French. SB. 13042 .... £12.99

Register of 35mm Single Lens Reflex Cameras
by Rudolph Lea 210x148mm 489 B/W SB. 11781 .... £24.95

Review of Graflex
by Richard P. Paine. Information on models, years, technical details and features of every model made.254x205mm 74 B/W illustrations SB. 15114 .... £12.95

Russian and Soviet Cameras1840-1991
Historical and technical details of from the early days to the present
HB 13665 .... £9.95

Spy Camera
by Michael Pritchard and Douglas St. Denny. Comprehensive guide to a century of spy, detective and subminiature cameras. 298x225mm 16 Col. 192 B/W HB. 7667 .... £39.95

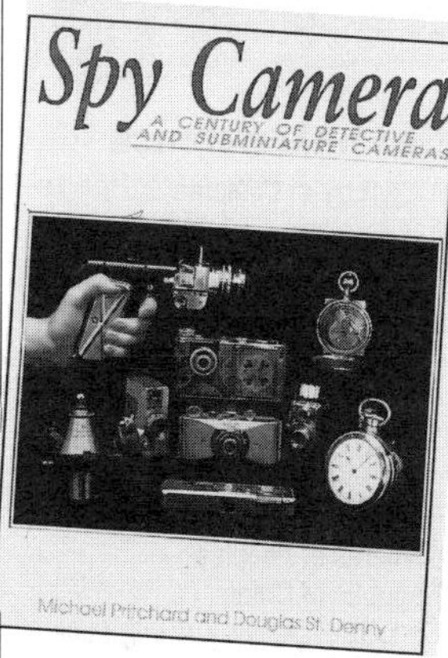

The Japanese Camera
by John Baird. History of the start of the industry that became the photo and optical giant of the world, covering virtually every major Japanese manufacturer. 274x210mm 80 B/W illustrations. SB. 12045 .... £36.95

Classic Collection Photo Books

Books on Nikon, Rollei, Voigtlander, Zeiss Ikon, spy, subminiature and detective cameras

ORDER NOW FOR IMMEDIATE DESPATCH

TURN 4 PAGES ON FOR THE FASTEST WAY TO PLACE YOUR ORDERS
ALL PRICES IN UK£

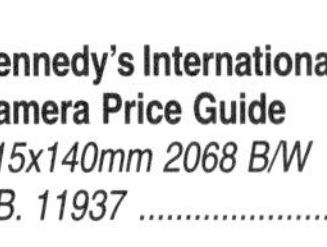

Classic Collection Photo Books

Collectors' reference books, classic camera guides, price guides, optical toys, magic lanterns

ORDER NOW FOR IMMEDIATE DESPATCH

PRIORITY ORDER LINES:
PHONE (UK) + 171-831 6000
FAX (UK) + 171-831 5424
4 Galen Place, London WC1A 2JR, England

Turn 3 pages on for Order Form

ALL PRICES IN UK£

Thirty Fotofiches
8-page B/W illustrated leaflets. 250x170mm Written in French - each leaflet £3.95
1. Eljy - *12054*
2. Semflex - *12055*
3. SEM S.A. - *12056*
4. Contax I - *12057*
5. Cyclope & Alsaflex - *12058*
6. Le Dubroni - *12059*
7. Le Werra - *12060*
8. Le Minox 8x11 - *12061*
9. Le Bolsey - *12062*
10. Le Periflex - *12063*
11. Nikkormat - *12064*
12. Photosphére - *12065*
13. Agfa Karat - *12066*
14. Le Pascal - *12067*
15. Lynx - *12068*
16. Nadar Detective Express - *12069*
17. Kodak, French 6x9 - *12070*
18. Argus C3 - *12071*
19. Contaflex, post war - *12072*
20. Rollei 35 - *12073*
21 Foca Universal - *12074*
22. Contax D - *12075*
23. Kodak Retinettes - *12076*
24. Angenieux for Leica - *12077*
25. French submin - *12078*
26. Telka - *12079*
27. Praktina - *12080*
28. Flexaret (Meopta) - *12081*
29. Nikon F - *12082*
30. Photax - *12083*

Univex Story
by Cynthia Repinski. A detailed examination of the company, the cameras, the people and the business that was Univex from the 1930s to the 1960s. 223x143mm 169 B/W HB. 1006 .... £22.95

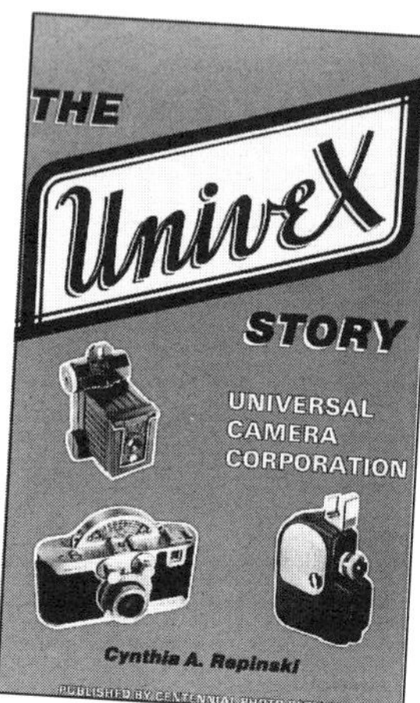

General reference

A Century of Cameras
Eaton Lothrop 215x280mm 178 B/W illustrations SB. 21865 .... £19.95

A History of the Photographic Lens
Rudolf Kingslake 235x155mm - Approx. 80 B/W photos and 140 line drawings 18202 .... £31.00

Cameras of Peoples' Republic of China
Douglas St Denny The only book to cover this fascinating subject in such detail. 245x180mm 131 B/W illustrations HB. 13618 .... £19.95

Christies Spy/Submin/Detective Auction Catalogue
266x210mm 254 B/W illustrations SB. 1081 .... £19.95

The First-Time Collector's Guide to Classic Cameras -
Kate Rouse 287x290mm - Over 100 classic collectable cameras illustrated and described in colour HB. 13675 .... £7.99

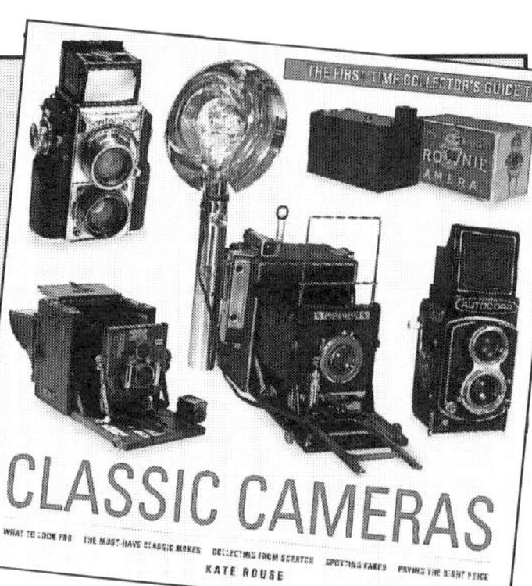

Directory of London Photographers
1841-1908 by Michael Pritchard 251x178mm HB. 15485 .... £14.95

Guide to French Cameras
Francesch 280x277mm - 35 Col. photos, 1770 B/W photos and drawings. French and English text HB. 19271 .... £59.95

Hausamann & Co Photo Catalogue 1927
Reprint 220x160mm. 750 B/W Illustrations Written in German. HB. 12042 .... £59.95

History of 35mm Cameras
Roger Hicks HB 17865 .... £12.95

Lutton's List
210x135mm 114 B/W SB. 1512 .... £15.00

Mirror Reflex Cameras from Dresden 1896-1990
Richard Hum 300x235mm Over 400 B/W photos, tables and related ads. HB. 17813 .... £44.95

Photo Ads
Photographic advertising 1845-1915 210x148mm158 B/W SB. 6368 .... £6.95

Photographic and Cinematographic Periodicals 1840-1940
270x192mm SB.3191 .... £34.95

Photographic Inter-Lens Shutters
Guide to cleaning and repairing 15117 .... £10.95

The Microscopic Photographs of J.B. Dancer
by Brian Bracegirdle and James B. McCormick. 322x242mm. Nearly 500 monochrome illustrations. HB. 12024 .... £65.00

Union Cases: A Collector's Guide
312x273mm 773 B/W illustrations HB. 1004 .... £54.95

When Photography Was Still An Adventure
By Uwe Scheid. 192 Col. and B/W illustrations. 175x120mm Printed in German. SB. 13044 .... £14.95

Optical Toys & Magic Lanterns

Dates and Sources
by Franz Paul Liesegang. A pre-cinema history 16780 .... £19.95

Emile Reynaud and the Animated Image
by Dominique Auzel. 275x245mm 120 pages with over 75 Col. illustrations and over 70 B/W . Written in French. HB. 12047 .... £42.95

Magic Images
Hand-Painted and Photographic Lantern Slides 293x215mm 138 Col. 134 B/W 8052 .... £19.95

The Authentic Guide to Russian and Soviet Cameras
Jean Loup Princelle 297x210mm - Over 570 cameras and lenses illustrated. in B/W. SB. 22961 .... £24.95

The History of Photography
Alma Davenport 280x215mm 8 Col. 130 B/W illustrations SB. 13829 .... £25.00

The Key Numbers
English and French Text 2nd Improved Edition 210x100 - Gathers more than 30 important manufacturer's serial numbers and production years. SB. 13658 .... £12.95

The Lantern Image
Iconography of the Magic Lantern 1420-1880 230x232mm 20 Col. 258 B/W SB. 8053 .... £19.95

The Magic Lantern Journal
Vol 5 16781 .... £15.00

The Magic Lantern
(Reprint) Vol 5 No.59 Apr 1894 16786 .... £7.49
(Reprint) Vol 5 No.67 Dec 1894 16785 .... £7.49
(Reprint) Vol 6 No.71 Apr 1895 16784 .... £7.49
(Reprint) Vol 7 No.80 Jan 1896 16787 .... £7.49
The Ten-Year Book Magic Lantern Vol 4 16782 .... £19.95

Optical Toys
by Georg Füsslin. 255x215mm 120 pages with 52 Col. and 65 B/W illustrations. Written in German. HB. 12050 .... £38.50

Price guides

Hove International Blue Book '94-'95
Giving camera value and rarity. 210x135mm. 700 B/W SB. 13333 .... £17.95

Kennedy's International Camera Price Guide
215x140mm 2068 B/W SB. 11937 .... £19.95

McKeown's Price Guide to Cameras 1995/1996
Recognised as the leading authority on classic cameras and their prices. Now with over 9,000 cameras listed and priced, and with more than 3,000 illustrations.
Softbound. 14633 .... £39.95
Hardbound. 14634 .... £47.95

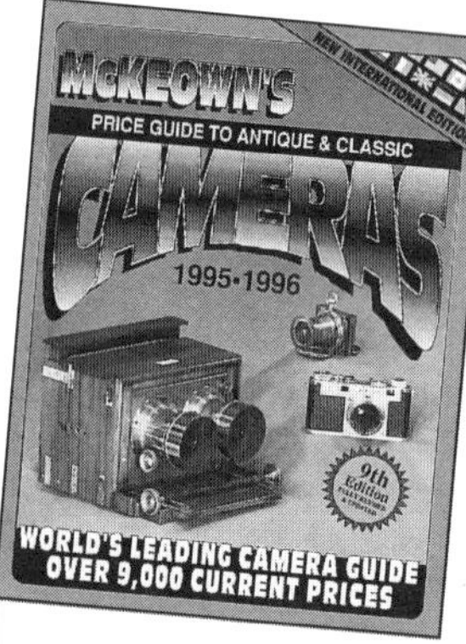

Classic Collector Catalogues
Back issues of the regularly published catalogue of Classic Collection, featuring articles on classic cameras plus lists of cameras, lenses and accessories that have been for sale at Classic Collection. Useful for checking current prices.
No: 2 - 7702 .... £3.00
No: 3 - 7703 .... £3.00
No: 4 - 7704 .... £3.00
No: 6 - 7706 .... £3.00
No: 8 - 7708 .... £3.00
No: 9 - 7709 .... £4.00
No:10 - 7710 .... £4.00
No: 12 - 7712 .... £4.00

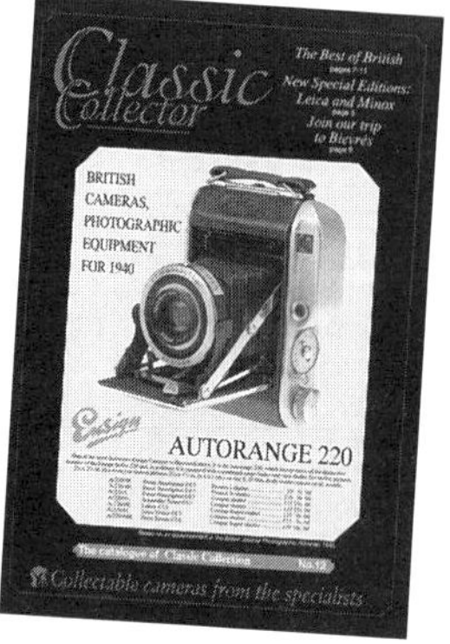

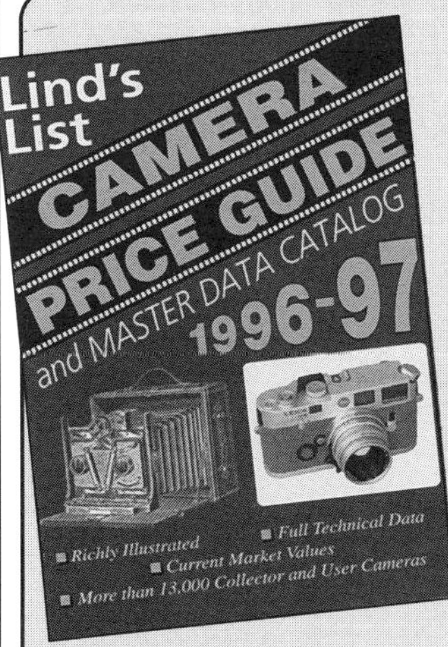

Lind's List
by Barbara Lind
Compiled by the Assistant Editor of McKeown's Price Guide to Antique and Classic Cameras, this is the most complete guide to classic and usable cameras available today and contains many cameras not covered in any other guide. Illustrated throughout, the book covers not just collectable cameras, but many thousands of modern classics too. 215x295mm, 350 pages, more than 13,000 cameras. Comes complete with Pocket Price Guide SB 28888 .... £29.95

STOP PRESS

New titles at

Classic Collection Photo Books

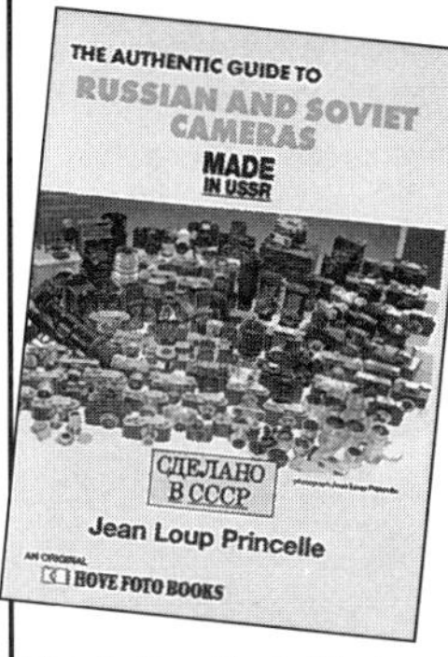

The Authentic Guide to Russian & Soviet Cameras
by Jean Loup Princelle
Information on production and prototype models to come out of the USSR, including many cameras which never reached the West. More than 400 illustrations
HB 22961..........................£24.95

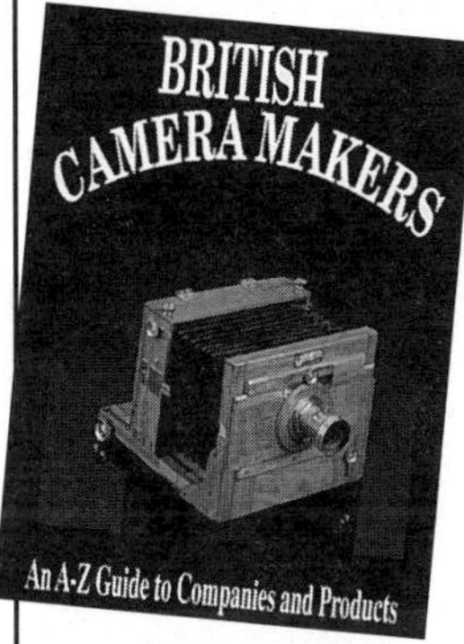

British Camera Makers
by Mike D Dunn & Norman E Channing. Dates, addresses, activities and amalgamations, with each manufacturer's product range, detailing around 1,400 cameras. 197x210mm, 160 pages.
HB 28889..........................£29.95

Cameras of The People's Republic of China
by Douglas St. Denny. The only guide to Chinese cameras, and manufacture, past and present.
HB 26239..........................£9.95

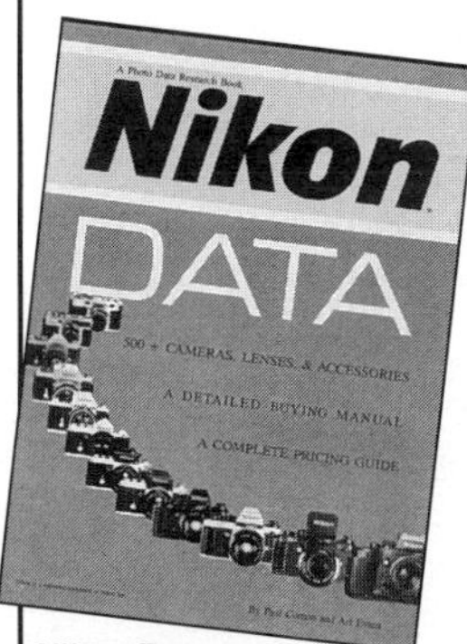

Nikon Data
by Paul Comon & Art Evans. Buying manual and complete pricing guide SB 13896....£10.95

PHOTO TECHNIQUE

Advanced Black & White Photography
Michael Langford 276x215mm 5 Col. 107 B/W illustrations SB. 13707 .... £11.95

Advanced Photography
Michael Langford. 245x188mm 38 Col. 157 B/W illustrations SB. 13816 .... £25.00

Adventure Travel Photography
Nevada Wier. Backpack, mountain climbing, hike cross-country. This book will help to get those images. 265x214mm 125 Col. SB. 13746 .... £17.95

Adventures in Close-up Photography
Ericksenn/Sincebaugh. 280x210mm 118 Col. 8 B/W illustrations SB. 13740 .... £16.95

Advertising Photography
305x230mm 79 Col. 21 B/W illustrations. SB. 13753 .... £14.95

Aerial Photography
Harvey Lloyd professional techniques and Commercial Application. What to shoot, how to shoot and how to sell. 280x210mm 107 Co. SB. 13802 .... £16.95

Amphoto Black & White Data Guide
George Schaub 215x138mm 132 B/W illustrations. SB. 13770 .... £14.95

Art of Autofocus Photography
M Levey. 280x210mm 122 Col. 1 B/W illustration. SB. 13742 .... £16.95

Art of Photographic Lighting
Michael Busselle 285x215mm 117 Co 29 B/W illustrations HB. 13908 .... £17.99

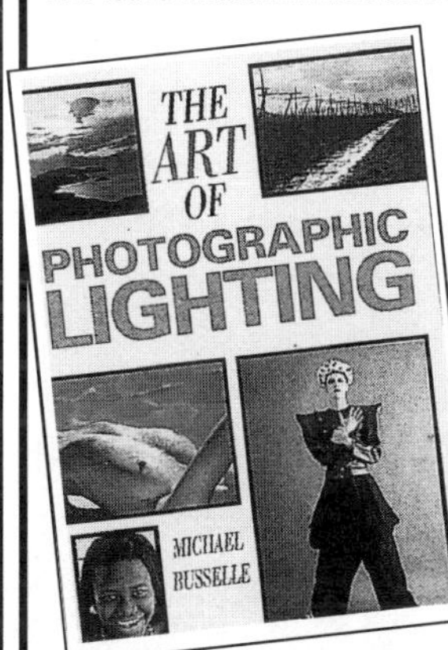

Available Light Photography
Lou Jacobs Jr. How to shoot without flash in all kinds of light. 280x210mm SB. 13808 ..... £16.95

Basic Photography
Michael Langford. 245x188mm 36 Col. 200 B/W illustrations SB.13820 .... £18.95

Best Places to Photograph North American Wildlife
Mark Warner 228x152mm 85 Col. 11 B/W illustrations SB. 13784 .... £14.95

Beyond Basic Photography
Henry Horenstein 216x213mm 90 B/W illustrations. SB. 13857 .... £9.95

Black & White Photography A Basic Manual
Henry Horenstein. How to get good results from the beginners standpoint. 235 x205mm 128 B/W illustrations SB. 13858 .... £12.99

Boudoir Photography
Mario Venticinque. How to make every woman look like her dream 280x210mm 93 Col. 3 B/W illustrations SB. 13743 .... £16.95

Boudoir Studio
Becker-Wortham and Wortham SB 13744 .... £16.95

Capturing the Landscape with your Camera
P Caulfield 280x210mm 123 Col. illustrations SB. 13745 .... £16.95

Cokin Filter System
Heiner Henninges 210x148mm 54 Col. 19 B/W illustrations SB. 13894 .... £10.95

Complete Guide to Wildlife Photography
Joe McDonald 267x215mm 126 Col. 6 B/W illustrations SB. 13795 .... £16.95

Create Dynamic Photographs with Visual Impact
J Zuckerman 275x215 110 Col. illustrations SB. 13613 .... £16.95

Designing a Photograph
Bill Smith 280x210mm 105 Col. 23 B/W illustrations SB. 13748 .... £14.95

Expressionist Landscape
Yuan Li 305x230mm 133 Col. illustrations SB. 13750 .... £16.95

Fashion Photography
L Khornak 280x210mm 114 Col. illustrations SB. 13800 .... £16.95

Flora Photographica
William A Ewing 306x254mm 48 Col. 148 B/W illustrations HB.13941 .... £24.95

High Contrast
J Seeley 280x215mm 167 B/W SB.13828 .... £30.00

Hot Shots - How to Photograph Beauty that Sells
J B O'Rourke 260x215 118 Col. 1 B/W illustration SB.13761 .... £17.95

How to be a Successful Amateur Photographer
Lancaster 160x105mm 90 pages with linedrawings SB. 15993 .... £9.00

How to Photograph the Human Figure
Robert & Sheila Hurth 276x216mm 89 Coll. 4 B/W illustrations SB. 13899 .... £16.95

How to Photograph Women Beautifully
J. Barry O'Rourke 280x210mm 129 Col. 5 B/W illustrations SB. 13754 .... £16.95

How to Photograph Works of Art
Sheldan Collins 267x215mm 26 Col. 75 B/W illustrations SB. 13796 .... £19.95

How to take Great Nature and Wild Life Photographs
Michael Freeman 277x217mm 159 Col.170 B/W. SB. 13614 .... £14.95

Illusion - The Art and Craft of Special Effects for Still Photographers
Fil Hunter and Paul Fuqua. Provides hard-to-find tips and techniques for creating physical in-camera, optical and laboratory effects. HB. 13831 .... £35.00

Illustration Photography
Jack Reznicki 285x217mm 93 Col. B/W illustrations HB. 13755 .... £16.95

Industrial Photography
Jack Neubart 280x210mm 100 Col. SB. 13799 .... £16.95

John Hedgecoe's Introductory Photography Course
Basic, vital camera skills, providing a wealth of creative photo ideas SB 13867 .... £12.99

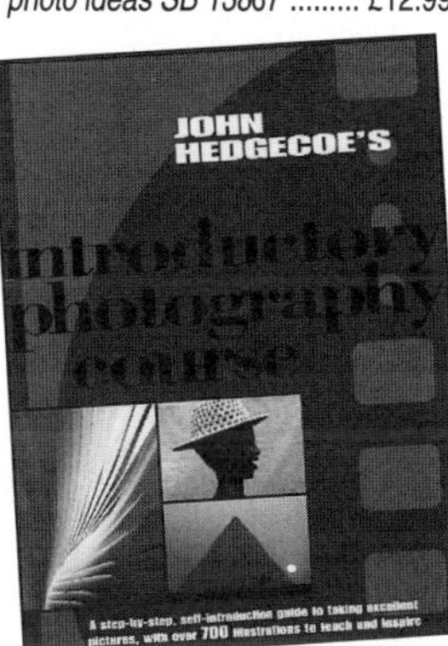

John Shaw's Close-ups in Nature
280x210mm 132 Col. SB. 13773 .... £16.95

Landscape Photography
275x215mm 84 Col.18 B/W Drawings SB. 13692 .... £10.95

Landscape Photography
The Art and Technique of 8 Modern Masters 302x230mm 114 Col. 8 B/W illustrations SB. 13757 .... £16.95

Learning to see Creatively
B Peterson 280x210mm 135 Col. SB. 13758 .... £16.95

Leica Reflex Photography
Brian Bower 286x216mm 72 Col.36 B/W illustrations SB. 13910 .... £14.99

Lens, Light, Landscape
Brian Bower HB 13914 .... £17.99

Lenses for 35mm Photography
278x215mm 146 Col. 4 B/W illustrations SB. 13712 .... £9.95

Low Light & Night Photography
Roger Hicks Advice on the latest equipment and techniques. 13912 .... £10.99

Classic Collection Photo Books

Easy to understand guides by today's top authors, helping you to make the most of your camera and to take better pictures

ORDER NOW FOR IMMEDIATE DESPATCH

TURN 2 PAGES ON FOR THE FASTEST WAY TO PLACE YOUR ORDERS
ALL PRICES IN UK£

Classic Collection
Photo Books

Techniques for amateurs and professionals looking at lighting, exposure, filters, glamour, wildlife, landscapes, portraits... and more

Manual of Photography
245x188mm 248 B/W illustrations 13837 .... £25.00

Medium Format Photography
Leif Ericksenn A User's Guide to Equipment and Applications - especially good read if you are moving up from 35mm. 280x210mm 83 Col. 31 B/W illustrations SB. 13810......... £16.95

Medium Format Photography
Erikson 21866 HB. £16.95

Michael Langford's 35mm Handbook
210x140mm 87 Col. 114 B/W illustrations SB. 13862........... £9.99

Nature Photographer
John Shaw Complete Guide to Pro-Field Techniques 280x210mm 132 Col. SB. 13759 .... £16.95

Panoramic Photography
Joseph Meehan. Covering equipment to composition, film, exposure etc. 210x280mm 86 Col. 39 B/W illustrations SB. 13805 .... £16.95

People in Focus
B Peterson 280x210mm 101 Col. SB. 13771 .... £17.95

Photographer's Guide to Exposure
Jack Neubart 280x210mm 107 Col. 22 B/W illustrations SB. 13762 .... £16.95

Photographic Assignments on Location
Adrian Taylor 280x210mm 256 Col. 3 B/W illustrations SB. 13765 .... £14.95

Photographic Composition
T Gill/M Scanlon 280x210mm 50 Col. 58 B/W illustrations SB.13804 .... £16.95

Photographing Buildings Inside and Out
Norman McGrath explains virtually everything there is to know about the way great architectural photographs are made. 288x218mm 118 Col. 13 B/W illustrations SB. 13840....... £19.95

Photographing People for Advertising
Nancy Brown. 280x210mm 143 Col. 3 B/W illustrations SB. 13767 .... £16.95

Photographing People for Stock
Nancy Brown.267x215mm 125 Col. SB. 13764 .... £17.95

Photographing Still Life
Seith Joel 280x210mm 63 Col. 11 B/W illustrations SB. 13801 .... £16.95

Photographing the Patterns of Nature
278x210mm 127 Col. SB. 13807 .... £16.95

Photographing Wildlife
P Caulfield 280x210mm 101 Col. SB. 13768 .... £16.95

Photography Art and Technique
Alfred A Blaker 235x210mm 24 Col. 330 B/W illustrations SB. 13841 .... £28.50

Photography for the Art Market
K Marx. 280x210mm 71 Col. 56 B/W illustrations SB. 13769 .... £16.95

Photography for Graphic Designers
Joseph Meehan 230x178mm 59 Col. 37 B/W illustrations SB. 13787 .... £16.95

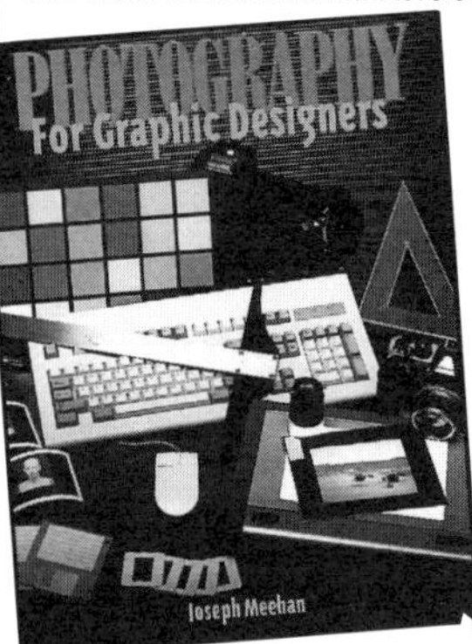

Photomontage
189x125 67 B/W illustrations SB.13934 .... £4.95

Pocket Guide to Practical Photography
John Hedgecoe 195x93mm 47 Col.67 B/W illustrations HB. 13864 .... £5.95

Point & Shoot Great Pictures with Automatic Cameras
Lou Jacobs, Jr 280x210mm 128 Col. SB. 13774 .... £17.95

Posing Techniques for Artist and Models
by Cheyenne 280x208mm 33 Col. 104 B/W illustrations SB. 13772 .... £16.95

Pro Techniques of Studio Photography
Jerry Fruchtman 275x215mm 100 Col. SB. 13616 .... £16.95

Retouching your Photographs
Jan Way Miller 280x210mm 111 Col. 20 B/W illustrations SB. 13777 .... £16.95

Satterwhite on Colour & Design
Joy & Al Satterwhite 13779 .... £16.95

Secrets of Studio Still Life Photography
Gary Perweiler 280x210mm 111 Col.111 B/W illustrations SB. 13780 .... £16.95

Shoot!
Everything you wanted to know about 35mm Photography 280x210mm 240 Col.40 B/W illustrations SB 13766.......... £22.95

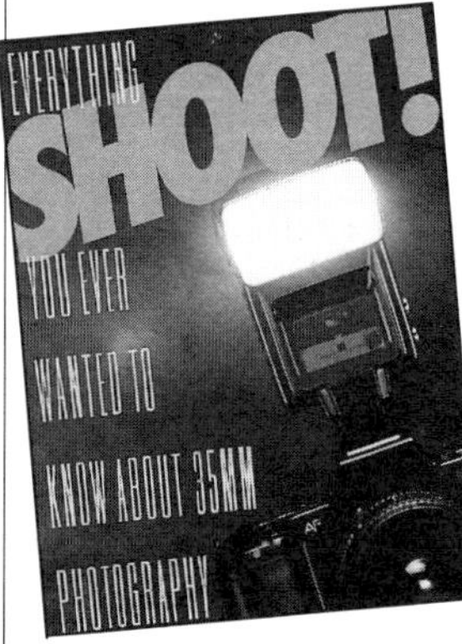

Starting Photography
Michael Langford. For absolute beginners to using cameras and processing facilities. 233x155mm 29 Col. 115 B/W illustrations SB.13844 .... £12.95

Successful Black & White Photography
Roger Hicks 287x215mm 143 B/W illustrations HB.13906 .... £16.99

Successful Fine Art Photography
Harold Davis 279x217mm 19 Col. 22 B/W illustrations SB. 13904 .... £16.95

Technique of Photographic Lighting
Norman Kerr 215x215mm 16 Col. 78 B/W illustrations SB. 13760 .... £12.95

The Art of Black & White Photography
J Garrett 257x262mm 3 Col. 143 B/W illustrations SB. 13870 .... £12.99

The Art of Seeing
275x215mm 150 Col. 17 B/W SB. 13708 .... £9.95

The Art of Special Effects
Martin Sage 280x210mm 100 Col. SB. 13803 .... £16.95

The Complete 35mm Source Book
Michael Busselle. Covers Autofocus, Compacts, SLRs and Accessories. 256x259mm 165 Col. 61 B/W illustrations SB. 13868 .... £12.95

The Complete Photographer
Ron Spillman 255x183mm 90 Col. 47 B/W illustrations SB. 13891 .... £12.95

The Essential Image
Lisl Dennis 280x210mm 136 Col. SB. 13798 .... £14.95

The Lens Book
Roger Hicks & Frances Schultz 248x204mm 62 Col. 70 B/W Photos/Drawings HB. 13655 .... £15.99

The Manual of Interior Photography
Michael Harris 247x188mm 27 Col. 38 B/W illustrations SB.13836 .... £19.95

The Nude in Black & White
L Khornak 267x215mm 123 B/W illustrations. 13783 .... £17.95

The Photographers Guide to Using Light
Schwartz/Stoppee 13763 .... £16.95

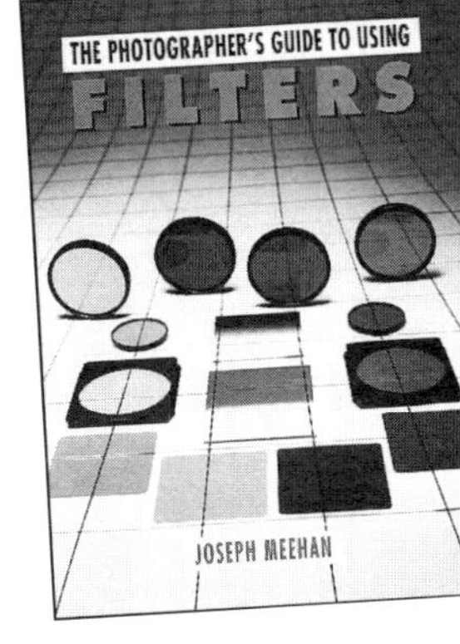

The Photographers Guide to Using Filters
Joseph Meehan 280x210mm 112 Col. 22 B/W illustrations SB. 13749 .... £16.95

The Photographers Handbook
Revised John Hedgecoe 13863 .... £18.99

The Right Picture
Ken Heyman/John Durniak 287x217mm 43 Col. 85 B/W illustrations HB. 13778 .... £14.95

The RSPB Guide to Bird & Nature Photography
Laurie Campbell 279x216mm 110 Col. 4 B/W illustrations SB. 13911 .... £11.99

The Traveling Photographer
Ann & Carl Purcell 280x210mm 125 Col SB. 13785 .... £16.95

The Workbook of Nudes and Glamour
John Hedgecoe 220x120mm 92 Col 67 B/W illustrations SB. 13873 .... £7.99

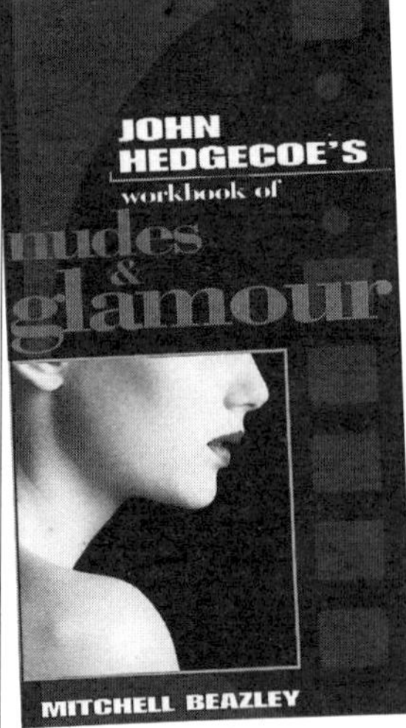

The Workbook of Photo Techniques
John Hedgecoe 220x120mm. Compact guide to creative photography, packed with expert ways to take successful and imaginative pictures. SB. 13872 .... £7.99

Understanding Exposure
Bryan Peterson 278x207mm 113 Col. SB. 13806 .... £16.95

Underwater Photography
Charles Seaborn 280x210mm 130 Col.SB. 13786 .... £16.95

Using Filters
279x215mm 208 Col. 42 B/W illustrations SB. 13713......... £11.95

Using the View Camera
Revised. Simmonds. A Creative Guide to large format photography, new photos, precise directions and a high visual approach. 280x210mm 29 B/W Col. 80 B/W illustrations SB. 13751 .... £17.95

Using your Autofocus 35mm Camera
279x216mm 203 Col. 20 B/W illustrations SB.13714........... £9.95

Using your Autofocus SLR System
Peter Lester SB 13886 .... £7.95

Using your Compact Camera
John Wade SB 13884 .... £7.95

Wildlife Photography
Guilfoyle/Rayfield 305x230mm 110 Col. 15 B/W illustrations SB. 13791 .... £16.95

Women - A Secret Portfolio
Limited Edition Philip Porcella 273x360mm 57 Col. 27 B/W illustrations HB. 13905 .... £19.95

ORDER NOW FOR IMMEDIATE DESPATCH

PRIORITY ORDER LINES:
PHONE (UK) + 171-831 6000
FAX (UK) + 171-831 5424
4 Galen Place, London WC1A 2JR, England

Turn to next page for Order Form

ALL PRICES IN UK£

Freelance Photography

Books to help you sell your pictures

Careers in Photography
Art Evans 276x214mm 84 B/W illustrations SB. 13898 .... £16.95

Commercial Photography
John Tinsley 13876 .... £22.50

Freelancing for Magazines
by John Morrison. How to get your work into print and produce saleable pictures. 223x155mm 33 B/W illustrations HB. 13878 .... £12.95

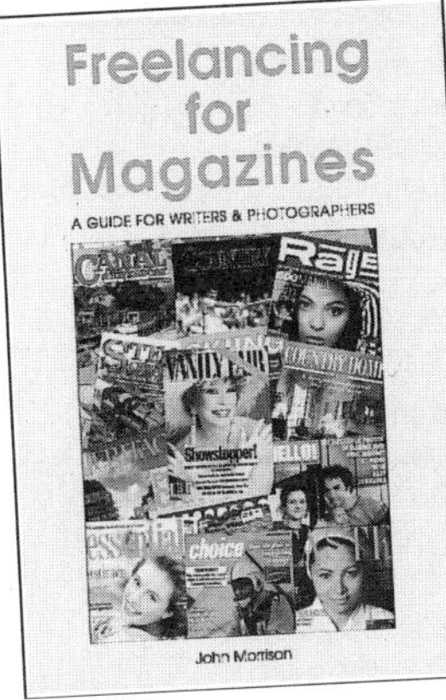

Freelance Photographer's Britain
Kevin MacDonnell 244x178mm 13 Col. 61 B/W illustrations HB. 13881 .... £10.95

Freelance Travel Photography
by Helene Rogers. This book will not only prove essential reading for all travel photographers, but will be equally fascinating for the armchair traveller who simply likes to be immersed in new landscapes and cultures. 275x200mm 14 Col. 83 B/W illustrations HB. 13882 .... £14.95

Freelancing in Europe
Barry Winbolt 245x180mm SB. 18126 .... £16.95

Getting to the Top in Photography
Peter Gambaccini 283x217 16 Col. 37 B/W illustrations HB. 13752 .... £12.95

Photographers Publishing Handbook
Harold Davis 278x216mm 21 B/W illustrations SB. 13901 .... £10.95

Photographic Assignments - Expert Approach
287x215mm 103 Col. 35 B/W illustrations HB. 13907 .... £17.99

Photojournalism
by Ken Kobre, Second Edition. A Professional approach. 276mmx219mm SB. 13842 .... £29.95

Professional Techniques for the Wedding Photographer
Schaub 280x210mm 107 Col. 13 B/W SB. 13775 .... £16.95

Profitable Model Photography
A Ketchum 13903 .... £14.95

Photo Libraries and Agencies
by David Askham. Comprehensive overview of the whole picture library and agency scene 240x175mm HB. 13880 .... £14.95

Promoting Yourself as a Photographer
Frederic W Rosen 228x152mm 16 Col. 14 B/W illustrations SB. 13776 .... £13.95

Selling Stock Photography
Lou Jacobs Jr 229x152mm SB. 13794 .... £12.95

Shooting for Stock
George Schaub 280x210mm 90 Col. 8 B/W illustrations SB. 13781 .... £16.95

The Photographer and the Law
by Don Cassell. Guide through the legal minefields surrounding photography. Written for the layman 223x155mm HB. 13879 .... £9.95

The BFP Book of Freelance Photography
Edited by John Wade Everything you need to know about getting started and improving your chances as a freelance photographer in one complete package. 275x200 HB 13877 .... £15.95

The Freelance Photographer's Market Handbook
Detailed information on hundreds of markets where you can sell your pictures (and articles) for cash. 216x150mm SB. 13874 .... £10.95

What to Photograph in 1995/6
by The Bureau of Freelance Photographers. A comprehensive guide to all the most photogenic events of the year 215x138mm 29 B/W illustrations SB. 18125 ... £9.95

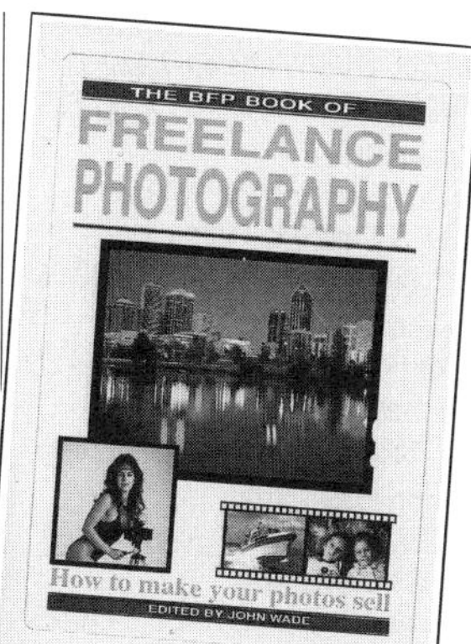

Video

A-Z of Camcorders & Videos
210x110mm 102 B/W illustrations SB. 13915 .... £10.95

Canon Camcorder Handbook
190x125mm 75 B/W illustrations SB. 13917 .... £10.95

Hedgecoe on Video
290x190mm 203 Col. 10 B/W illustrations SB. 13869 .... £9.99

How to Videotape Weddings
276x217mm 70 Col. 35 B/W illustrations SB. 13920 .... £12.95

JVC Camcorder Handbook
190x125mm 70 B/W illustrations SB. 13918 .... £10.95

Lighting for Action Videos and Films
280x210mm 80 Col. 46 B/W illustrations SB. 13793 .... £16.95

Lights! Camera! Advertising!
280x210mm 107 Col. 10 B/W illustrations SB. 13809 .... £16.95

Panasonic Camcorder Handbook
190x125mm 74 B/W illustrations SB. 13919 .... £10.95

Sony Camcorder Handbook
190x125mm 72 B/W illustrations SB. 13916 .... £10.95

Using your Camcorder
280x210mm 72 Col. 28 B/W illustrations SB. 13789 .... £16.95

ORDER FORM

Fill out your details as shown below, complete the reverse of this form and send your orders to: Classic Collection Photo Books, 4 Galen Place, London WC1A 2JR, UK, or fax your order on (UK) + 171-831 5424. You can also order books from us, using the Internet on: **http://www.demon.co.uk/classicscr/camera.html**
E-MAIL: CLASSIC COLLECTION@LEICA.DEMON.CO.UK

Bronica Systems ◀ ***Book title*** — ***Order number*** — ***Price***
ETR-si, SQ-Ai, GS-1 190x125mm 13 Col. 51 B/W Photos/Drawings SB. 13647 — £10.95

13647	Bronica Systems	10.95
Order number	*Book title*	*Price*

Order No.	Books	Price

* Post and packing: £3 per order in the UK. Overseas at cost.

TOTAL	
POST AND PACKING *	
TOTAL AMOUNT	

Don't forget to fill in the other side of the order form

Classic Collection Photo Books

Modern Camera Guides

Guides to help you make the most of your new camera

Prices correct at time of going to press and subject to change without notice. 1.4.96. E.&O.E.

Bronica Systems
ETR-si, SQ-Ai, GS-1 190x125mm 13 Col. 51 B/W Photos/Drawings SB. 13647 .... £10.95

Canon EOS 1
190x125mm 16 Col. 86 B/W Photos/Drawings SB. 13624 .... £10.95

Canon EOS 5/A2E/A2
190x125mm 20 Col. 50 B/W Photos/Drawings SB. 13626 .... £10.95

Canon EOS 10/10S
190x125mm 16 Col. 52 B/W Photos/Drawings SB. 13623 .... £10.95

Canon EOS 100/Elan
190x125mm SB. 13620 ...... £10.95

Canon EOS 500/Rebel XS/X
90x125mm SB. 13619 .... £10.95

Canon EOS 600/630
190x125mm 114 B/W Photos/ Drawings SB. 13625 .... £10.95

Canon EOS 1000/1000FN/Rebel
190x125mm 22 Col. 79 B/W Photos/Drawings SB. 13621 .... £10.95

Canon EOS System
Pro Guide Inc EOS 5 216x150mm 35 Col. 85 B/W Photos/Drawings HB. 13648 .... £14.95

Canon Modern Classics
F-1, FTB, EF, AE-1, AE-1P 190x125mm 132 B/W Photos/Drawings SB. 13651 .... *£10.95*

Canon T/60
190x125mm 17 Col. 75 B/W Photos/Drawings SB. 13622 .... £10.95

Canon T/90
190x125mm 78 B/W Photos/ Drawings SB. 13627 .... £10.95

Hasselblad System Pro Guide
216x148mm 36 Col. 82 B/W Photos/Drawings HB. 13649 .... £14.95

Mamiya System Guide
216x148mm 34 Col. 73 B/W Photos/Drawings HB.13650 .... £15.95

Minolta 7000
2nd Edition 190x122mm 16 Col. 58 B/W Photos/Drawings SB. 13629 .... £10.95

Minolta 8000i
190x125mm 16 Col. 89 B/W Photos/Drawings SB. 13633 .... £10.95

Minolta Dynax/Maxxum 3xi/SPxi
190x125mm 16 Col. 59 B/W Minolta Dynax/Maxxum 7xi 190x125mm 16 Col. 87 B/W Photos/Drawings SB. 13635 .... £10.95

Minolta Dynax/Maxxum 5xi
190x125mm 6 Col. 91 B/W Photos/Drawings SB. 13637 .... £10.95

Minolta Dynax/Maxxum 9xi
190x125mm 16 Col. 91 B/W Photos/Drawings SB. 13630 .... £10.95

Minolta Dynax/Maxxum 3000i/5000i
190x125mm 14 Col. 69 B/W Photos/Drawings SB. 13632 .... £10.95

Minolta Dynax/Maxxum 7000i
190x125mm 106 B/W Photos/ Drawings SB. 13631 .... £10.95

Minolta X300s/X700
190x125mm 16 Col. 53 B/W Photos/Drawings SB. 13634 .... £10.95

Nikon F-2 Modern Classics
190x125mm 80 B/W Photos/ Drawings SB. 13653 .... £10.95

Nikon F4/F3
Inc: F4s/F4e 190x125mm 14 Col.122 B/W SB. 13641 ..... £10.95

Nikon F50/N50
190x125mm SB. 13638 ..... £10.95

Nikon F90/N90
190x125mm 16 Col. 47 B/W Photos/Drawings SB. 13639 .... £10.95

Nikon F4/F3
Inc: F4s/F4e 190x125mm 14 Col. 122 B/W photos and drawings SB 13641 .... £10.95

Nikon F601 AF&M/N6006
190x125mm 14 Col. 46 B/W Photos/Drawings SB. 13642 .... £10.95

Nikon F801s/N8008
190x125mm 14 Col. 54 B/W Photos/Drawings SB. 13640 .... £10.95

Nikon Modern Classics
F2, EL, FM FE2, FT2, FA 190x125mm 104 B/W SB. 13652 .... £10.95

Nikon SB-24
With SB-25 supplement 190x125mm 14 Col. 46 B/W Photos/Drawings SB. 13643 .... £10.95

Nikon SB-25 Systems
190x125mm 20 Col. 60 B/W Photos/Drawings SB. 13644 .... £10.95

Olympus Modern Classics
OM1 OM2 Spot OM3 OM4 OM10 OM40 190x125 157 B/W illustrations SB.12014 .... £10.95

Olympus IS 1000/2000/3000
190x125mm 20 Col. 42 B/W Photos/Drawings SB. 13628 .... £10.95

Pentax K1000/P30n
190x125mm 16 Col. 85 B/W Photos/Drawings SB. 13646 .... £10.95

Pentax Modern Classics
ES11, Spotmatic F, K2, KC/KM, ME/MX, M 190x125mm 120 B/W Photos/Drawings SB. 13654 .... £10.95

Pentax SF-7
190x125mm 16 Col. 59 B/W Photos/Drawings SB. 13645 .... £10.95

ORDER FORM

Please send me the books listed on the previous page.
I enclose my cheque or international money order for UK£__________

Alternatively, please debit my credit card:

POST AND PACKING:
Please tick your preference
- ☐ UK ordinary post (£3 all items)
- ☐ UK Datapost 24-hour £10
- ☐ UK Datapost 48-hour £5

Overseas charged at cost:
- ☐ Courier (2-3 days)
- ☐ Airmail (7-14 days)
- ☐ Economy Airmail (2-3 weeks)
- ☐ Surface (4-6 weeks)

☐ American Express ☐ Visa ☐ Access
☐ Mastercard ☐ Eurocard ☐ JCB

Card No. ☐☐☐☐☐☐☐☐☐☐☐☐☐☐☐☐

Expiry date: / /

Signed ______________________ Date __________

NAME ______________________

ADDRESS ______________________

____

____

____

__________ POST CODE __________

COUNTRY ______________________

TEL: __________ FAX: __________

Send your order to: Classic Collection Photo Books
4 Galen Place, London WC1A 2JR, England

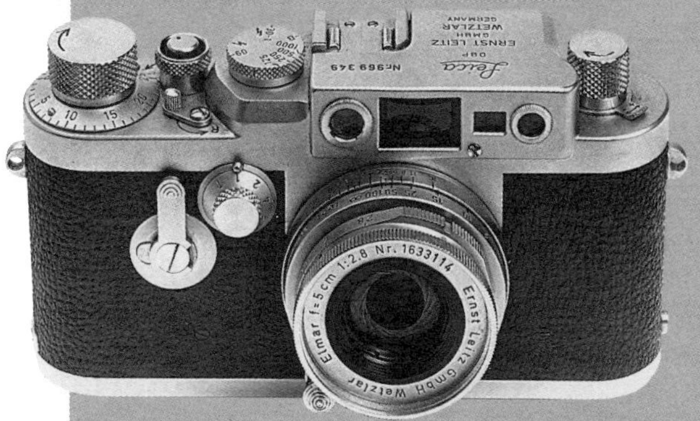

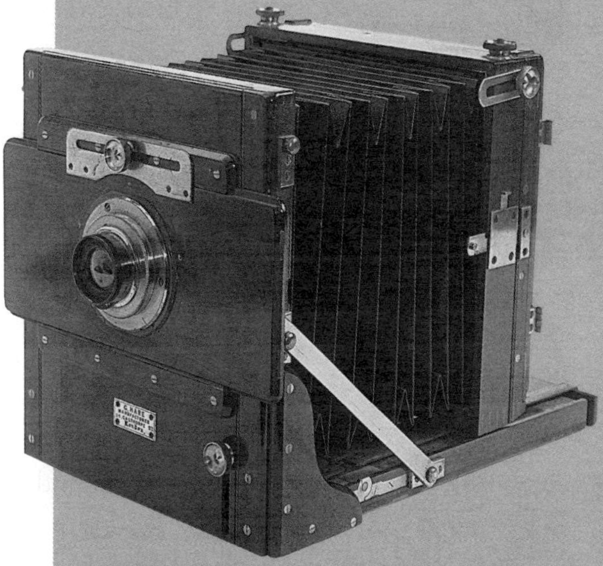

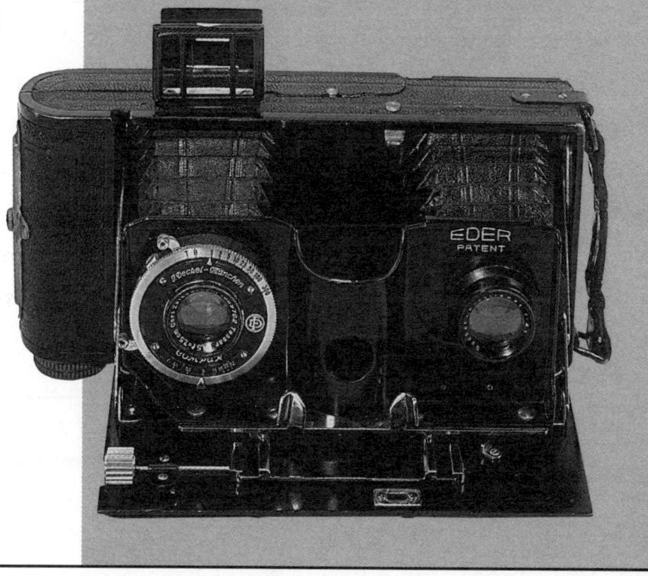